# CRICKETERS'
# WHO'S WHO
# 1996

# THE CRICKETERS' WHO'S WHO 1996

Introduction by
NIGEL BRIERS

Statistics by
RICHARD LOCKWOOD

Portraits photographed or researched by
BILL SMITH

*Queen Anne Press*

QUEEN ANNE PRESS
a division of Lennard Associates Limited
Mackerye End, Harpenden, Herts AL5 5DR

Published in association with
The Cricketers' Who's Who Limited

First published in Great Britain 1996

© The Cricketers' Who's Who Limited

British Library Cataloguing in Publication is available

ISBN 1 85291 568 4

Typeset in Times and Univers Condensed
Editors: Kirsty Ennever and Chris Hawkes
Cover design by Paul Cooper

Printed and bound by
Butler and Tanner Limited, Frome and London

**PICTURE ACKNOWLEDGEMENTS**

Cover photographs by Allsport feature the leading players
from the 1995 Whyte and Mackay rankings (*see page 682*)
(*from top to bottom*) Dominic Cork, Nasser Hussain,
Mark Ramprakash and Angus Fraser
(*background photograph*) Graeme Hick

# CONTENTS

# THE QUIZ

Throughout this book there are 100 quiz questions

The answers can be found on page 688

# INTRODUCTION

Edward Heath was the British Prime Minister and Richard Nixon was President of the United States. The year was 1971, and I made my debut for Leicestershire against a Cambridge University side, which included Majid Khan (Pakistan), Phil Edmonds and Mike Selvey (both Middlesex and England). It really does not seem that long ago, but it was before my team-mates Ben Smith and Darren Maddy were even born and Paul Nixon was only one year old. What's more Cambridge won!

When opening the 1972 Wisden which dealt with that 1971 season, I was suddenly hit by the headline 'It happened 25 years ago'. It engendered a feeling of nostalgia to think that I had made my debut so long ago, even though the article in question was about that irreplaceable maestro, Denis Compton, and his unbelievable season of 1947.

Of course some things have changed during my time in cricket. Harold Macmillan's immortal words 'they've never had it so good' could quite easily be applied to the younger players of today, although they probably would not agree! Wages are certainly better now. They should have improved in 25 years – the pay had been too low for too long – but now the pay structure is becoming more realistic thanks to the increased role of the Professional Cricketers' Association. I can't remember anyone at Leicester having a sponsored car in those days either, and two bats for the price of one was very common: the free one never seemed that good! Although I played in the 1st XI against Cambridge I never got given a sweater and you had to be in the 1st XI squad regularly to have a chance of getting a track-suit top. The apprenticeship seemed harder in those days and it felt as though you really had to work hard and achieve lots of success before any 'luxuries' came your way. That way you tended to appreciate your position in the team all the more, whether 1st XI or 2nd XI. Obviously it has to be

7

remembered that my memories are based on the views of a teenager and you always view things differently as a youngster. I don't want to fall into the old player syndrome of 'in my day', but where would the modern game be without sponsorship? If a club works hard to provide all its players with cars, clothes and other perks, so be it! Commercialism now plays a far more important role in our game. Society has changed, as have outlook and expectations. Yet could it be argued that if everything comes too easily or too quickly, then we are not so mentally prepared for when things go wrong?

Although he never played in that game at Cambridge in 1971, Ray Illingworth was the captain of Leicestershire: professional, astute, shrewd and the best captain I ever played under. How well I remember the first televised Sunday League game I played against Worcestershire at New Road. The opposing team fielded a side that included Basil D'Oliveira and that great New Zealand Test player, Glenn Turner. Although I scored a good 80, Leicestershire dropped a lot of catches that eventually cost us the game off the penultimate ball. Yours truly dropped two important ones – ecstasy and despondency within a couple of hours. I dropped Glenn Turner at cover and later Phil Neale on the cover boundary off, of all people, the bowling of Ray Illingworth. Not only did I drop the catch but the ball hit me on the side of the jaw and went for six! Illy stamped his feet, and although I looked for sympathy because my jaw hurt, he sent me off the field! I travelled to the game with Illy in the morning – he did not take me home! I had to cadge a lift with Jack Birkenshaw. I learned my cricket in a very hard school and it gave you a mental toughness, which is something that English cricketers have been criticised for lacking in recent years.

Bobby Simpson, the Australian coach, became the Leicestershire Cricket Manager in 1990 and helped to foster this sort of toughness in his players. He believed that English cricketers were too easily pleased with mediocre performances and even helped me in this area, despite the fact that I was already 35 years old. He gave me a hard time after I was out for 102 on a flat pitch at Chelmsford against Essex, and enquired if I liked getting big scores. I replied that I got 201 not out once. 'Huh,' he replied, 'never mind that, what about getting 300s like I used to.' He commented on how so many players thought they had done well when they got to a century and how the majority got out between 100 and 115. That was as true then as it was 25 years ago.

One aspect of the game which has definitely changed is that there are fewer 'characters' in the game nowadays. The game was played hard and there was a lot of 'chat' and gamesmanship back then, yet there also seem to have been far more comic moments. You soon became tougher or you wilted under pressure. Ken Higgs (Lancashire, Leicestershire and England) was as quiet a man off the field as you could possibly meet. However, on it and when bowling he could be very fierce, and some of the expletives he came out with were soon added to my grammar school vocabulary – he would have been reported constantly these days and Sadiq Mohammed (Gloucestershire and Pakistan) and John Shepherd (Kent and West Indies) could probably have used the Race Discrimination Act on him – but it all seemed part of the game. There are characters around in the game now but they are far more subdued due to the greater emphasis on cutting out 'talk' on the field. It is ironic that some of today's umpires were among those who gave me quite an earful when I was younger.

Was the game simpler in those days? It certainly seemed so, especially judging by the amount of rules and regulations the umpires carry around with them nowadays. We now have a different points system in the County Championship and important measures relating to pitches have been introduced. In the '70s and early '80s pitches seemed so much better to bat on: certainly Grace Road! For quite a long time now there has been much debate over what sort of pitches our domestic game should be played on and whether they are helping to provide the right breeding for Test cricketers. Are we complicating our game or is it that today there is just a much keener eye for detail and perfection?

There has also been much debate regarding the use of overseas players. In my earlier days, a club was allowed two on its staff. I remember playing against Hampshire in a Gillette Cup game when they had Gordon Greenidge and Barry Richards opening the batting and

Andy Roberts opening the bowling: Greenidge, of course, was not classified as an 'overseas' player. From experience I believe that having one overseas player in the team is good for the English game. They bring a new perspective to the dressing room, improve standards of play, bring in the crowds and give English players the chance to pit their skills against some of the best players in the world on a regular basis. Yet it seems to me that the day is not that far away when they will no longer grace our county grounds.

Our game has moved forward in the last 25 years and I believe it is in a much better state than a lot of people think. I may have picked out some things that were different then but it is still a great game, and it continues to progress. If more notice is taken of the players' views in this book, particularly those of the county captains, then this game can move dramatically forward into the 21st century. What will the game be like 25 years on? I look forward to reading the views of one of the players in *The Cricketers' Who's Who* 2020.

Nigel Briers
Leicestershire CCC

# THE PLAYERS

# Editor's Notes

The cricketers listed in this volume include all those who played for a first-class county at least once last season, in any form of cricket, and all those registered (at the time of going to press) to play for the 18 first-class counties in 1996, even those who have yet to make a first-team appearance. All statistics are complete to the end of the last English season. Figures about 1000 runs and 50 wickets in a season refer to matches in England only. All first-class figures include figures for Test matches which are also extracted and listed separately. One-day 100s and one-day five wickets in an innings are for the English domestic competitions and all one-day Internationals, home and abroad. Career records include 'rebel' tours to South Africa.

The following abbreviations apply: * means not out; All First – all first-class matches; 1-day Int – one-day Internationals; Sunday – Sunday League; NatWest – NatWest Trophy; B&H – Benson & Hedges Cup. The figures for batting and bowling averages refer to the full first-class English list for 1995, followed in brackets by the 1994 figures. Inclusion in the batting averages depends on a minimum of six completed innings, and an average of at least 10 runs; a bowler has to have taken at least 10 wickets. The same qualification has been used for compiling the bowlers' strike rate.

Readers will notice occasional differences in the way the same kind of information is presented. This is because it is has been decided to follow the way in which the cricketers themselves have provided the relevant information.

Each year in *The Cricketers' Who's Who,* in addition to those cricketers who are playing during the current season, we also include the biographical and career details of those who played in the previous season but retired at the end of it. The purpose of this is to have, on the record, the full and final cricketing achievements of every player when his career has ended.

A book of this complexity and detail has to be prepared several months in advance of the cricket season, and occasionally there are recent changes in a player's circumstances which cannot be included in time. Many examples of facts and statistics which can quickly become outdated in the period between the actual compilation of the book and its publication, months later, will spring to the reader's mind, and I ask him or her to make the necessary commonsense allowance and adjustments.

Richard Lockwood, March 1996

# ADAMS, C. J.        Derbyshire

**Name:** Christopher John Adams
**Role:** Right-hand bat, right-arm medium bowler, slip fielder
**Born:** 6 May 1970, Whitwell, Derbyshire
**Height:** 6ft **Weight:** 13st 7lbs
**Nickname:** Grizzly
**County debut:** 1988
**County cap:** 1992
**1000 runs in season:** 2
**1st-Class 50s:** 28
**1st-Class 100s:** 13
**1st-Class 200s:** 1
**1st-Class catches:** 121
**One-Day 100s:** 4
**Place in batting averages:** 65th av. 40.59 (1994 105th av. 33.41)
**Strike rate:** (career 85.33)
**Parents:** John and Eluned (Lyn)

**Wife and date of marriage:** Samantha Claire, 26 September 1992
**Children:** Georgia Louise, 4 October 1993
**Family links with cricket:** Brother David played 2nd XI cricket for Derbyshire and Gloucestershire. Father played for Yorkshire Schools and uncle played for Essex 2nd XI
**Education:** Tapton House School; Chesterfield Boys Grammar School; Repton School
**Qualifications:** 6 O-levels, NCA coaching awards
**Overseas tours:** Repton School to Barbados 1987; England NCA North to N Ireland 1987
**Overseas teams played for:** Takapuna, New Zealand 1987-88; Te Puke, New Zealand 1989-90; Primrose, Cape Town, South Africa 1991-92
**Cricketers particularly admired:** Ian Botham, Geoff Palmer, Adrian Kuiper
**Other sports followed:** Football, golf, rally driving and Formula 1
**Relaxations:** Mountain biking, golf and squash. 'My daughter, Georgia, is very interesting but definitely not relaxing.'
**Extras:** Beat Richard Hutton's 25-year-old record for most runs scored in a season at Repton. Represented English Schools U15 and U19, MCC Schools U19 and, in 1989, England YC. Took two catches as 12th man for England v India at Old Trafford in 1990. Holds county records for the fastest century by a Derbyshire batsman (57 mins) and the highest score in the Sunday League (141*). Whittingdale Young Player Award 1992
**Opinions on cricket:** 'I love it.'
**Best batting:** 216 Derbyshire v Kent, Maidstone 1995
**Best bowling:** 4-29 Derbyshire v Lancashire, Derby 1991

## 1995 Season

|  | M | Inns | NO | Runs | HS | Avge | 100s | 50s | Ct | St | O | M | Runs | Wkts | Avge | Best | 5wI | 10wM |
|---|---|---|---|---|---|---|---|---|---|---|---|---|---|---|---|---|---|---|
| Test |  |  |  |  |  |  |  |  |  |  |  |  |  |  |  |  |  |  |
| All First | 15 | 27 | 0 | 1096 | 216 | 40.59 | 3 | 5 | 17 | - | 15 | 3 | 47 | 0 | - |  | - | - |
| 1-day Int |  |  |  |  |  |  |  |  |  |  |  |  |  |  |  |  |  |  |
| NatWest | 3 | 3 | 1 | 141 | 109 * | 70.50 | 1 | - | 1 | - |  |  |  |  |  |  |  |  |
| B & H | 3 | 3 | 0 | 111 | 94 | 37.00 | - | 1 | - | - |  |  |  |  |  |  |  |  |
| Sunday | 15 | 15 | 1 | 387 | 79 | 27.64 | - | 3 | 8 | - |  |  |  |  |  |  |  |  |

## Career Performances

|  | M | Inns | NO | Runs | HS | Avge | 100s | 50s | Ct | St | Balls | Runs | Wkts | Avge | Best | 5wl | 10wM |
|---|---|---|---|---|---|---|---|---|---|---|---|---|---|---|---|---|---|
| Test |  |  |  |  |  |  |  |  |  |  |  |  |  |  |  |  |  |
| All First | 120 | 192 | 16 | 5922 | 216 | 33.64 | 13 | 28 | 121 | - | 1536 | 1028 | 18 | 57.11 | 4-29 | - | - |
| 1-day Int |  |  |  |  |  |  |  |  |  |  |  |  |  |  |  |  |  |
| NatWest | 12 | 11 | 2 | 464 | 109 * | 51.55 | 2 | 2 | 7 | - | 18 | 15 | 1 | 15.00 | 1-15 | - |  |
| B & H | 22 | 20 | 3 | 404 | 94 | 23.76 | - | 3 | 8 | - | 24 | 21 | 0 | - | - | - | - |
| Sunday | 95 | 89 | 16 | 2695 | 141 * | 36.91 | 2 | 20 | 49 | - | 178 | 181 | 2 | 90.50 | 2-15 | - |  |

# AFFORD, J. A.         Nottinghamshire

**Name:** John Andrew Afford
**Role:** Slow left-arm 'high' bowler,
right-hand bat and 'hopeless fielder'
**Born:** 12 May 1964, Crowland, Peterborough
**Height:** 6ft 2in **Weight:** 'A fleshy 14st'
**Nickname:** Aff, Des
**County debut:** 1984
**County cap:** 1990
**50 wickets in a season:** 4
**1st-Class 5 w. in innings:** 14
**1st-Class 10 w. in match:** 2
**1st-Class catches:** 50
**Place in bowling averages:** 104th av. 47.18
(1994 92nd av. 34.40)
**Strike rate:** 89.95 (career 72.97)
**Parents:** Jill
**Wife and date of marriage:** Lynn,
1 October 1988
**Children:** Lily Meagan, 1 June 1991;
Daisy Tallulah, 12 October 1993
**Family links with cricket:** Cousin Nicholas plays in the Pearl Assurance 25-over mid-week interdepartmentals

**Education:** Spalding Grammar School; Stamford College for Further Education
**Qualifications:** 5 O-levels, NCA coaching certificate
**Off-season:** Coaching on the Bridge scheme and studying Human and Educational Studies at Nottingham Trent University
**Overseas tours:** England A to Kenya and Zimbabwe 1989-90; Nottinghamshire to Cape Town 1992-93
**Overseas teams played for:** Upper Hutt, Taita and Petone, all in Wellington, New Zealand between 1984 and 1991
**Cricketers particularly admired:** John Childs
**Other sports followed:** Watch Notts County and the 'Tricky Trees' although my first love is the Posh. 'Dodgy left back in the Notts CCC football team – still unbeaten'
**Injuries:** Poorly toe and a bit of a sore back – toe played me up all year
**Relaxations:** Going to the football. Bit of fishing and a keen conkerer!
**Extras:** Hat-trick against Leics 2nd XI in 1989, also took 100 wickets in that season, 47 in 2nd XI and 53 in 1st XI. 'I think I beat Chris Cairns for player of the month once!'
**Opinions on cricket:** 'It was bloody hot last year!'
**Best batting:** 22* Nottinghamshire v Leicestershire, Trent Bridge 1989
**Best bowling:** 6-68 Nottinghamshire v Sussex, Trent Bridge 1992

### 1995 Season

| | M | Inns | NO | Runs | HS | Avge | 100s | 50s | Ct | St | O | M | Runs | Wkts | Avge | Best | 5wI | 10wM |
|---|---|---|---|---|---|---|---|---|---|---|---|---|---|---|---|---|---|---|
| Test | | | | | | | | | | | | | | | | | | |
| All First | 7 | 9 | 3 | 57 | 15 * | 9.50 | - | - | 3 | - | 314.5 | 69 | 991 | 21 | 47.19 | 4-58 | - | - |
| 1-day Int | | | | | | | | | | | | | | | | | | |
| NatWest | | | | | | | | | | | | | | | | | | |
| B & H | 6 | 0 | 0 | 0 | 0 | - | - | - | 1 | - | 63 | 5 | 236 | 4 | 59.00 | 2-44 | - | |
| Sunday | | | | | | | | | | | | | | | | | | |

### Career Performances

| | M | Inns | NO | Runs | HS | Avge | 100s | 50s | Ct | St | Balls | Runs | Wkts | Avge | Best | 5wI | 10wM |
|---|---|---|---|---|---|---|---|---|---|---|---|---|---|---|---|---|---|
| Test | | | | | | | | | | | | | | | | | |
| All First | 151 | 142 | 58 | 351 | 22 * | 4.17 | - | - | 50 | - | 30211 | 13926 | 414 | 33.63 | 6-68 | 14 | 2 |
| 1-day Int | | | | | | | | | | | | | | | | | |
| NatWest | 7 | 4 | 3 | 3 | 2 * | 3.00 | - | - | - | - | 486 | 218 | 6 | 36.33 | 3-32 | - | |
| B & H | 21 | 1 | 1 | 1 | 1 * | - | - | - | 3 | - | 1336 | 870 | 21 | 41.42 | 4-38 | - | |
| Sunday | 19 | 5 | 3 | 1 | 1 | 0.50 | - | - | 7 | - | 690 | 576 | 15 | 38.40 | 3-33 | - | |

1. Which was the first international side to play a first-class fixture in Soweto and in which year?

# AFZAAL, U.                    Nottinghamshire

**Name:** Usman Afzaal
**Role:** Left-hand bat, slow left-arm bowler
**Born:** 9 June 1977, Rawalpindi, Pakistan
**Height:** 6ft **Weight:** 11st 7lbs
**Nickname:** Gulfraz
**County debut:** 1995
**1st-Class catches:** 3
**Place in batting averages:** 264th av. 13.40
**Strike rate:** (career 218.40)
**Parents:** Mohammed and Firdous
**Marital status:** Single
**Family links with cricket:** Brother played
for Nottinghamshire U9
**Education:** Manvers Pierrepont School
**Qualifications:** NCA coaching certificate
**Off-season:** Playing for England U19
**Overseas tours:** England U19 to West Indies
1994-95, to Zimbabwe 1995-96

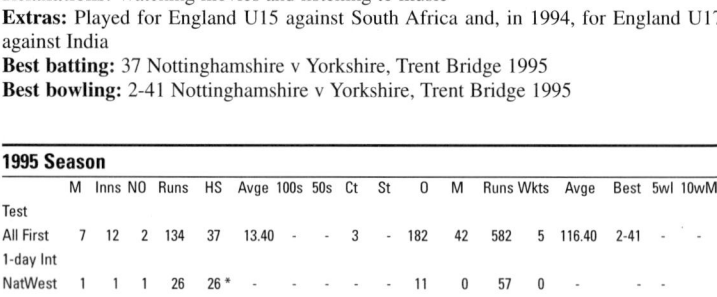

**Cricketers particularly admired:**
Paul Johnson, Phil Tufnell, Mick Newell
**Other sports followed:** 'Cricket and cricket'
**Relaxations:** Watching movies and listening to music
**Extras:** Played for England U15 against South Africa and, in 1994, for England U17
against India
**Best batting:** 37 Nottinghamshire v Yorkshire, Trent Bridge 1995
**Best bowling:** 2-41 Nottinghamshire v Yorkshire, Trent Bridge 1995

## 1995 Season

|  | M | Inns | NO | Runs | HS | Avge | 100s | 50s | Ct | St | O | M | Runs | Wkts | Avge | Best | 5wI | 10wM |
|---|---|---|---|---|---|---|---|---|---|---|---|---|---|---|---|---|---|---|
| Test |  |  |  |  |  |  |  |  |  |  |  |  |  |  |  |  |  |  |
| All First | 7 | 12 | 2 | 134 | 37 | 13.40 | - | - | 3 | - | 182 | 42 | 582 | 5 | 116.40 | 2-41 | - | - |
| 1-day Int |  |  |  |  |  |  |  |  |  |  |  |  |  |  |  |  |  |  |
| NatWest | 1 | 1 | 1 | 26 | 26 * | - | - | - | - | - | 11 | 0 | 57 | 0 | - |  | - | - |
| B & H |  |  |  |  |  |  |  |  |  |  |  |  |  |  |  |  |  |  |  |
| Sunday | 6 | 2 | 1 | 2 | 2 | 2.00 | - | - | 3 | - | 34 | 1 | 165 | 8 | 20.62 | 2-25 | - |  |

## Career Performances

| | M | Inns | NO | Runs | HS | Avge | 100s | 50s | Ct | St | Balls | Runs | Wkts | Avge | Best | 5wI | 10wM |
|---|---|------|----|----|----|------|------|-----|----|----|-------|------|------|------|------|-----|------|
| Test | | | | | | | | | | | | | | | | | |
| All First | 7 | 12 | 2 | 134 | 37 | 13.40 | - | - | 3 | - | 1092 | 582 | 5 | 116.40 | 2-41 | - | - |
| 1-day Int | | | | | | | | | | | | | | | | | |
| NatWest | 1 | 1 | 1 | 26 | 26 * | - | - | - | - | - | 66 | 57 | 0 | - | | - | - |
| B & H | | | | | | | | | | | | | | | | | |
| Sunday | 6 | 2 | 1 | 2 | 2 | 2.00 | - | - | 3 | - | 204 | 165 | 8 | 20.62 | 2-25 | - | |

# ALDRED, P.                    Derbyshire

**Name:** Paul Aldred
**Role:** Right-hand bat, right-arm
medium bowler
**Born:** 4 February 1969, Chellaston, Derby
**Height:** 5ft 10in **Weight:** 12st
**Nickname:** Aldo
**County debut:** 1995
**1st-Class catches:** 4
**Place in bowling averages:** 28th av. 25.00
**Strike rate:** 43.33 (career 43.33)
**Parents:** Harry and Lynette
**Marital status:** Single
**Family links with cricket:** None other than
father who played local cricket
**Education:** Chellaston Primary School; Lady
Manners, Bakenall, Derbyshire
**Qualifications:** 'None worth worrying
about!'

**Career outside cricket:** Building trade – self-employed
**Off-season:** Coaching for Derbyshire CCC or playing in South Africa
**Cricketers particularly admired:** Ian Botham, Daryll Cullinan, Viv Richards
**Other sports played:** Golf and rugby, also played hockey for Derbyshire in 1985
**Other sports followed:** Rugby, golf
**Relaxations:** Playing sports, a beer with friends in the local pub, long distance running
with Karl Krikken
**Extras:** 'Had the great opportunity to play against New Zealand with the England NCA
team in 1994 which was a great day.' Represented Derbyshire U18 and U21 hockey team
at the age of 15
**Opinions on cricket:** 'I think a lot of injuries picked up are due to the amount of cricket
played in England. You just don't have time to recover to full fitness. I think the cricket
schedule could be lightened a little, at first-class level at least.'

**Best batting:** 33 Derbyshire v Warwickshire, Edgbaston 1995
**Best bowling:** 3-47 Derbyshire v Young Australia, Chesterfield 1995

## 1995 Season

|  | M | Inns | NO | Runs | HS | Avge | 100s | 50s | Ct | St | O | M | Runs | Wkts | Avge | Best | 5wI | 10wM |
|---|---|---|---|---|---|---|---|---|---|---|---|---|---|---|---|---|---|---|
| Test |  |  |  |  |  |  |  |  |  |  |  |  |  |  |  |  |  |  |
| All First | 7 | 12 | 0 | 97 | 33 | 8.08 | - | - | 4 | - | 108.2 | 23 | 375 | 15 | 25.00 | 3-47 | - | - |
| 1-day Int |  |  |  |  |  |  |  |  |  |  |  |  |  |  |  |  |  |  |
| NatWest |  |  |  |  |  |  |  |  |  |  |  |  |  |  |  |  |  |  |  |
| B & H |  |  |  |  |  |  |  |  |  |  |  |  |  |  |  |  |  |  |  |
| Sunday | 8 | 3 | 2 | 18 | 11 * | 18.00 | - | - | 1 | - | 39.5 | 1 | 237 | 8 | 29.62 | 3-28 | - |  |

## Career Performances

|  | M | Inns | NO | Runs | HS | Avge | 100s | 50s | Ct | St | Balls | Runs | Wkts | Avge | Best | 5wI | 10wM |
|---|---|---|---|---|---|---|---|---|---|---|---|---|---|---|---|---|---|
| Test |  |  |  |  |  |  |  |  |  |  |  |  |  |  |  |  |  |
| All First | 7 | 12 | 0 | 97 | 33 | 8.08 | - | - | 4 | - | 650 | 375 | 15 | 25.00 | 3-47 | - | - |
| 1-day Int |  |  |  |  |  |  |  |  |  |  |  |  |  |  |  |  |  |
| NatWest |  |  |  |  |  |  |  |  |  |  |  |  |  |  |  |  |  |
| B & H |  |  |  |  |  |  |  |  |  |  |  |  |  |  |  |  |  |
| Sunday | 8 | 3 | 2 | 18 | 11 * | 18.00 | - | - | 1 | - | 239 | 237 | 8 | 29.62 | 3-28 | - |  |

# ALLEYNE, M. W. Gloucestershire

**Name:** Mark Wayne Alleyne
**Role:** Right-hand bat, right-arm medium bowler, cover fielder, occasional wicket-keeper
**Born:** 23 May 1968, Tottenham
**Height:** 5ft 11in **Weight:** 13st 7lbs
**Nickname:** Boo-Boo
**County debut:** 1986
**County cap:** 1990
**1000 runs in a season:** 4
**1st-Class 50s:** 43
**1st-Class 100s:** 11
**1st-Class 200s:** 1
**1st-Class 5 w. in innings:** 1
**1st-Class catches:** 140
**1st-Class stumpings:** 2
**One-Day 100s:** 2
**One-Day 5 w. in innings:** 3

**Place in batting averages:** 106th av. 33.56 (1993 107th av. 32.88)
**Place in bowling averages:** 126th av. 42.34 (1993 37th av. 26.90)
**Strike rate:** 87.27 (career 64.69)
**Parents:** Euclid Clevis and Hyacinth Cordeilla
**Marital status:** Single
**Family links with cricket:** Brother played for Gloucestershire 2nd XI and Middlesex YCs. Father played club cricket in Barbados and England
**Education:** Harrison College, Barbados; Cardinal Pole School, E London
**Qualifications:** 6 O-levels, NCA Senior Coaching Award, volleyball coaching certificate
**Overseas tours:** England YC to Sri Lanka 1986-87 and Australia 1987-88
**Cricketers particularly admired:** Gordon Greenidge, Viv Richards
**Other sports followed:** Football, volleyball, athletics
**Relaxations:** Watching films and sport; listening to music
**Extras:** Youngest player to score a century for Gloucestershire. In 1990 also became the youngest to score a double hundred for the county. Graduate of Haringey Cricket College. Cricket Select Sunday League Player of the Year 1992. Highest Sunday League score for Gloucestershire
**Best batting:** 256 Gloucestershire v Northamptonshire, Northampton 1990
**Best bowling:** 5-78 Gloucestershire v Kent, Cheltenham 1994

## 1995 Season

| | M | Inns | NO | Runs | HS | Avge | 100s | 50s | Ct | St | O | M | Runs | Wkts | Avge | Best | 5wI | 10wM |
|---|---|---|---|---|---|---|---|---|---|---|---|---|---|---|---|---|---|---|
| Test | | | | | | | | | | | | | | | | | | |
| All First | 19 | 32 | 2 | 1007 | 141 | 33.56 | 1 | 7 | 9 | - | 421.5 | 125 | 1228 | 29 | 42.34 | 3-59 | - | - |
| 1-day Int | | | | | | | | | | | | | | | | | | |
| NatWest | 3 | 3 | 0 | 91 | 43 | 30.33 | - | - | - | - | 30 | 4 | 96 | 3 | 32.00 | 2-35 | - | |
| B & H | 6 | 6 | 0 | 132 | 42 | 22.00 | - | - | 3 | - | 50 | 6 | 179 | 7 | 25.57 | 2-30 | - | |
| Sunday | 15 | 15 | 3 | 352 | 70 | 29.33 | - | 3 | 5 | - | 92.1 | 5 | 475 | 14 | 33.92 | 5-28 | 1 | |

## Career Performances

| | M | Inns | NO | Runs | HS | Avge | 100s | 50s | Ct | St | Balls | Runs | Wkts | Avge | Best | 5wI | 10wM |
|---|---|---|---|---|---|---|---|---|---|---|---|---|---|---|---|---|---|
| Test | | | | | | | | | | | | | | | | | |
| All First | 182 | 299 | 30 | 8293 | 256 | 30.82 | 11 | 43 | 140 | 2 | 10222 | 5543 | 158 | 35.08 | 5-78 | 1 | - |
| 1-day Int | | | | | | | | | | | | | | | | | |
| NatWest | 23 | 19 | 4 | 356 | 73 | 23.73 | - | 1 | 9 | - | 788 | 514 | 17 | 30.23 | 5-30 | 1 | |
| B & H | 33 | 27 | 4 | 411 | 42 | 17.86 | - | - | 10 | - | 1261 | 881 | 29 | 30.37 | 5-27 | 1 | |
| Sunday | 145 | 130 | 32 | 3106 | 134 * | 31.69 | 2 | 13 | 52 | - | 4401 | 3723 | 120 | 31.02 | 5-28 | 1 | |

# ALTREE, D. A.        Warwickshire

**Name:** Darren Anthony Altree
**Role:** Right-hand bat, left-arm fast bowler
**Born:** 30 September 1974, Rugby
**Height:** 5ft 11in
**Weight:** 12st
**Nickname:** Bobby, Bobster, Dazzler
**County debut:** No first-team appearance
**Parents:** Tony and Margaret
**Marital status:** Single
**Education:** Ashlawn School, Rugby
**Overseas tours:** Warwickshire U19 to Cape Town 1992-93
**Overseas teams played for:** Avendale, Cape Town 1994-95
**Cricketers particularly admired:**
Dennis Lillee, Dennis Amiss, Jeff Thomson
**Injuries:** Hamstring, out for four weeks
**Relaxations:** Watching television

# AMBROSE, C. E. L.      Northamptonshire

**Name:** Curtly Elconn Lynwall Ambrose
**Role:** Left-hand bat, right-arm fast bowler, 'like the gully area'
**Born:** 21 September 1963, Antigua
**Height:** 6ft 7in  **Weight:** 14st
**Nickname:** Ambie
**County debut:** 1989
**County cap:** 1990
**Test debut:** 1987-88
**Tests:** 59
**One-day internationals:** 114
**50 wickets in a season:** 7
**1st-Class 50s:** 4
**1st-Class 5 w. innings:** 34
**1st-Class 10 w. in match:** 7
**1st-Class catches:** 60
**One-day 5 w. in innings:** 4

**Place in batting averages:** 169th av. 24.60 (1994 214th av. 18.35)
**Place in bowling averages:** 70th av. 29.76 (1994 2nd av. 14.45)
**Strike rate:** 62.92 (career 51.65)
**Parents:** Jasper (deceased) and Hillie
**Wife and date of marriage:** Bridgette, 6 September 1991
**Children:** Tanya, May 1990
**Family links with cricket:** Brother used to play club cricket and had trials for Antigua. Cousin Rolston Otto plays for Antigua and Leeward Islands
**Education:** Swetes Primary School; All Saints Secondary School
**Qualifications:** 3 O-levels, 3 A-levels, qualified carpenter
**Off-season:** Playing for West Indies
**Overseas tours:** West Indies to England 1988, to Australia 1988-89, to India for Nehru Cup 1989-90, to Pakistan 1990-91, to England 1991, to Pakistan 1991-92, to Australia for Benson & Hedges World Series and World Cup 1991-92, to Australia and South Africa 1992-93, to Sharjah, India (Hero Cup) and Sri Lanka 1993-94, to New Zealand 1994-95, to England 1995, to Australia 1995-96, to India and Pakistan (World Cup) 1995-96
**Overseas teams played for:** Leeward Islands
**Cricketers particularly admired:** David Gower, Richard Hadlee, Robin Smith and all West Indian Test cricketers
**Other sports followed:** NBA (American) basketball and tennis
**Relaxations:** Going to the movies, relaxing on the beach, listening to and playing music (bass guitar)
**Extras:** A basketball player who only began playing cricket seriously at the age of 17. Took a wicket with his first ball on Championship debut for Northamptonshire against Glamorgan in 1989. Played in two Nat West finals in three years with Northants. Figures of 8 for 45 are the best in Tests for West Indies v England. One of *Wisden's* Five Cricketers of the Year 1992
**Best batting:** 78 Northamptonshire v Somerset, Taunton 1994
**Best bowling:** 8-45 West Indies v England, Bridgetown 1989-90

## 1995 Season

|  | M | Inns | NO | Runs | HS | Avge | 100s | 50s | Ct | St | O | M | Runs | Wkts | Avge | Best | 5wI | 10wM |
|---|---|---|---|---|---|---|---|---|---|---|---|---|---|---|---|---|---|---|
| Test | 5 | 7 | 4 | 77 | 23 * | 25.66 | - | - | 2 | - | 185.1 | 43 | 506 | 21 | 24.09 | 5-96 | 1 | - |
| All First | 10 | 13 | 7 | 147 | 27 * | 24.50 | - | - | 8 | - | 262.1 | 70 | 744 | 25 | 29.76 | 5-96 | 1 | - |
| 1-day Int | 3 | 2 | 0 | 11 | 10 | 5.50 | - | - | - | - | 29 | 3 | 125 | 0 | - | - | - | - |
| NatWest |  |  |  |  |  |  |  |  |  |  |  |  |  |  |  |  |  |  |
| B & H |  |  |  |  |  |  |  |  |  |  |  |  |  |  |  |  |  |  |  |
| Sunday |  |  |  |  |  |  |  |  |  |  |  |  |  |  |  |  |  |  |  |

## Career Performances

|          | M   | Inns | NO | Runs | HS   | Avge  | 100s | 50s | Ct | St | Balls | Runs  | Wkts | Avge  | Best | 5wI | 10wM |
|----------|-----|------|----|------|------|-------|------|-----|----|----|-------|-------|------|-------|------|-----|------|
| Test     | 59  | 84   | 18 | 815  | 53   | 12.34 | -    | 1   | 13 | -  | 13869 | 5493  | 258  | 21.29 | 8-45 | 13  | 3    |
| All First| 173 | 219  | 53 | 2506 | 78   | 15.09 | -    | 4   | 60 | -  | 35852 | 14393 | 694  | 20.73 | 8-45 | 34  | 7    |
| 1-day Int| 114 | 58   | 25 | 391  | 26 * | 11.84 | -    | -   | 31 | -  | 6095  | 3570  | 154  | 23.18 | 5-17 | 4   |      |
| NatWest  | 19  | 7    | 1  | 89   | 48   | 14.83 | -    | -   | 6  | -  | 1265  | 474   | 29   | 16.34 | 4-7  | -   |      |
| B & H    | 10  | 7    | 4  | 71   | 17 * | 23.66 | -    | -   | 5  | -  | 619   | 302   | 20   | 15.10 | 4-31 | -   |      |
| Sunday   | 45  | 23   | 8  | 201  | 37   | 13.40 | -    | -   | 8  | -  | 1979  | 1211  | 41   | 29.53 | 4-20 | -   |      |

# ANDREW, S. J. W. Essex

**Name:** Stephen Jon Walter Andrew
**Role:** Right-hand bat, right-arm
fast-medium bowler
**Born:** 27 January 1966, London
**Height:** 6ft 3in **Weight:** 15st
**Nickname:** Rip
**County debut:** 1984 (Hampshire),
1990 (Essex)
**1st-Class 5 w. in innings:** 7
**1st-Class catches:** 24
**One-Day 5 w. in innings:** 1
**Strike rate:** (career 60.02)
**Parents:** Jon Trevor and Victoria Julia Maud
**Marital status:** Single
**Education:** Hordle House Prep School;
Milton Abbey, Portchester School for Boys
**Qualifications:** 3 O-levels
**Overseas tours:** England YC to West Indies
1984-85

**Overseas teams played for:** Pirates, Durban 1983-84; SAP, Durban 1984-86; Manly, Sydney 1987-88; Pinetown, Durban 1988-89; Taita, Wellington 1990-91; Parnell, Auckland, 1991-92, Primrose, Cape Town 1993-94
**Cricketers particularly admired:** Dennis Lillee ('god')
**Other sports followed:** Golf, rugby
**Injuries:** Neck for one month and achilles for three weeks
**Relaxations:** Music, socialising, films and books
**Opinions on cricket:** 'The seams should go back to the way they were originally to give those bowlers with the ability more chance of swinging and seaming the ball on the generally flat pitches that we play on.'
**Best batting:** 35 Essex v Northamptonshire, Chelmsford 1990
**Best bowling:** 7-47 Essex v Lancashire, Old Trafford 1993

**1995 Season**

| | M | Inns | NO | Runs | HS | Avge | 100s | 50s | Ct | St | O | M | Runs | Wkts | Avge | Best | 5wI | 10wM |
|---|---|---|---|---|---|---|---|---|---|---|---|---|---|---|---|---|---|---|
| Test | | | | | | | | | | | | | | | | | | |
| All First | 2 | 4 | 0 | 7 | 4 | 1.75 | - | - | - | - | 38 | 9 | 107 | 1 | 107.00 | 1-24 | - | - |
| 1-day Int | | | | | | | | | | | | | | | | | | |
| NatWest | | | | | | | | | | | | | | | | | | |
| B & H | | | | | | | | | | | | | | | | | | |
| Sunday | 7 | 2 | 0 | 12 | 7 | 6.00 | - | - | - | - | 45 | 2 | 203 | 9 | 22.55 | 4-40 | - | |

**Career Performances**

| | M | Inns | NO | Runs | HS | Avge | 100s | 50s | Ct | St | Balls | Runs | Wkts | Avge | Best | 5wI | 10wM |
|---|---|---|---|---|---|---|---|---|---|---|---|---|---|---|---|---|---|
| Test | | | | | | | | | | | | | | | | | |
| All First | 119 | 95 | 36 | 411 | 35 | 6.96 | - | - | 24 | - | 17887 | 9815 | 298 | 32.93 | 7-47 | 7 | - |
| 1-day Int | | | | | | | | | | | | | | | | | |
| NatWest | 8 | 2 | 2 | 1 | 1* | - | - | - | 2 | - | 426 | 256 | 9 | 28.44 | 2-34 | - | |
| B & H | 11 | 3 | 3 | 5 | 4* | - | - | - | 1 | - | 654 | 363 | 20 | 18.15 | 5-24 | 1 | |
| Sunday | 47 | 13 | 4 | 68 | 14 | 7.55 | - | - | 2 | - | 1860 | 1565 | 40 | 39.12 | 4-40 | - | |

# ANTHONY, H. A. G.     Glamorgan

**Name:** Hamish Aubrey Gervaise Anthony
**Role:** Right-hand bat, right-arm fast bowler
**Born:** 16 January 1972, Hurlings Village, Antigua
**Height:** 6ft 2in **Weight:** 13st
**Nickname:** Hammo
**County debut:** 1990
**Ist-Class 50s:** 6
**1st-Class 5 w. innings:** 3
**1st-Class catches:** 22
**Place in batting averages:** 224th av. 18.04
**Place in bowling averages:** 84th av. 31.86
**Strike rate:** 54.25 (career 51.10)
**Marital status:** Single
**Family links with cricket:** Brother plays for Antigua
**Career outside cricket:** Customs official
**Off-season:** Hong Kong Sixes, Sharjah Cup, Shell/Sandals 1-days, Red Stripe
**Overseas tours:** West Indies to England 1990, to Canada 1990, to Sharjah 1992, to England 1993, to Australia 1994, to Canada 1994, to Hong Kong 1995, to Sharjah 1995

**Overseas teams played for:** Antigua, Leeward Islands
**Cricketers particularly admired:** Viv Richards, Kapil Dev
**Other sports followed:** Tennis and football
**Relaxations:** Listening to reggae, relaxing in general
**Extras:** Best figures in Red Stripe Final against Barbados in 1995 (7 for 15) beating Malcolm Marshall's long-standing record. Signed for 1995 as a replacement for Ottis Gibson
**Opinions on cricket:** 'The English season is far too long.'
**Best batting:** 91 Glamorgan v Surrey, The Oval 1995
**Best bowling:** 6-22 Leeward Islands v Windward Islands, Castries 1992-93

## 1995 Season

|  | M | Inns | NO | Runs | HS | Avge | 100s | 50s | Ct | St | O | M | Runs | Wkts | Avge | Best | 5wI | 10wM |
|---|---|---|---|---|---|---|---|---|---|---|---|---|---|---|---|---|---|---|
| Test |  |  |  |  |  |  |  |  |  |  |  |  |  |  |  |  |  |  |
| All First | 14 | 25 | 1 | 433 | 91 | 18.04 | - | 2 | 6 | - | 397.5 | 70 | 1402 | 44 | 31.86 | 6-77 | 2 | - |
| 1-day Int |  |  |  |  |  |  |  |  |  |  |  |  |  |  |  |  |  |  |
| NatWest | 4 | 2 | 0 | 12 | 8 | 6.00 | - | - | 1 | - | 32.5 | 6 | 111 | 5 | 22.20 | 4-25 | - |  |
| B & H | 1 | 1 | 0 | 2 | 2 | 2.00 | - | - | - | - | 11 | 1 | 40 | 3 | 13.33 | 3-40 | - |  |
| Sunday | 11 | 8 | 2 | 22 | 7 | 3.66 | - | - | - | - | 75 | 1 | 404 | 11 | 36.72 | 3-40 | - |  |

## Career Performances

|  | M | Inns | NO | Runs | HS | Avge | 100s | 50s | Ct | St | Balls | Runs | Wkts | Avge | Best | 5wI | 10wM |
|---|---|---|---|---|---|---|---|---|---|---|---|---|---|---|---|---|---|
| Test |  |  |  |  |  |  |  |  |  |  |  |  |  |  |  |  |  |
| All First | 60 | 86 | 7 | 1373 | 91 | 17.37 | - | 6 | 22 | - | 9250 | 5211 | 181 | 28.79 | 6-22 | 5 | - |
| 1-day Int |  |  |  |  |  |  |  |  |  |  |  |  |  |  |  |  |  |
| NatWest | 4 | 2 | 0 | 12 | 8 | 6.00 | - | - | 1 | - | 197 | 111 | 5 | 22.20 | 4-25 | - |  |
| B & H | 1 | 1 | 0 | 2 | 2 | 2.00 | - | - | - | - | 66 | 40 | 3 | 13.33 | 3-40 | - |  |
| Sunday | 11 | 8 | 2 | 22 | 7 | 3.66 | - | - | - | - | 450 | 404 | 11 | 36.72 | 3-40 | - |  |

# ARCHER, G. F.                          Nottinghamshire

**Name:** Graeme Francis Archer
**Role:** Right-hand bat, right-arm 'very medium'
**Born:** 26 September 1970, Carlisle, Cumbria
**Height:** 6ft 1in **Weight:** 13st 7lbs
**Nickname:** Bunka
**County debut:** 1992
**County cap:** 1995
**1000 runs in season:** 1
**1st-Class 50s:** 13
**1st-Class 100s:** 6

**1st-Class catches:** 44
**Place in batting averages:** 68th av. 40.37 (1994 103rd av. 33.76)
**Strike rate:** (career 85.50)
**Parents:** Christopher William and Jean Elizabeth
**Marital status:** Single
**Family links with cricket:** Father played for Carlisle in N Lancashire League; brother Neil plays in the S Cheshire Alliance League
**Education:** King Edward VI High School; Stafford College
**Qualifications:** 3 O-levels, City & Guilds and BTEC National Diploma in Leisure Management, NCA Senior Coaching Award
**Career outside cricket:** 'Not decided'
**Off-season:** Playing in Christchurch, New Zealand
**Overseas teams played for:** Hutt Districts, New Zealand 1991-92; Hutt Valley representative side 1991-92, Old Collegians, Christchurch 1994-96
**Cricketers particularly admired:** Graeme Hick, Ian Botham, Derek Randall, Chris Cairns and Jimmy Adams
**Other sports followed:** Badminton, football (Carlisle United) and squash
**Injuries:** Fractured jaw but no time off
**Relaxations:** Music and concerts, 'the odd round of golf', photography, spending time with friends
**Extras:** Scored 200* in a 15 (8-ball) over match for Walsall U18s. Awarded the A.A.Thompson Fielding Prize by The Cricket Society in 1990. Made 2nd XI debut for Notts in 1987 aged 15. Played for Staffordshire in 1990-91. Rapid Cricketline Player of the Month April/May 1994. Awarded county cap in September 1995
**Opinions on cricket:** 'I feel that the over rates are far too high. It is very hard, especially for fast bowlers, to rush through their overs. If we expect 100 per cent we should give them a little more time. Also tea should be 30 minutes long.'
**Best batting:** 168 Nottinghamshire v Glamorgan, Worksop 1994
**Best bowling:** 3-50 Nottinghamshire v Durham, Chester-le-Street 1995

## 1995 Season

|  | M | Inns | NO | Runs | HS | Avge | 100s | 50s | Ct | St | O | M | Runs | Wkts | Avge | Best | 5wI | 10wM |
|---|---|---|---|---|---|---|---|---|---|---|---|---|---|---|---|---|---|---|
| Test |  |  |  |  |  |  |  |  |  |  |  |  |  |  |  |  |  |  |
| All First | 17 | 32 | 3 | 1171 | 158 | 40.37 | 3 | 4 | 16 | - | 79 | 11 | 261 | 6 | 43.50 | 3-50 | - | - |
| 1-day Int |  |  |  |  |  |  |  |  |  |  |  |  |  |  |  |  |  |  |
| NatWest | 2 | 1 | 0 | 15 | 15 | 15.00 | - | - | 1 | - |  |  |  |  |  |  |  |  |
| B & H | 4 | 3 | 0 | 125 | 74 | 41.66 | - | 1 | - | - | 6 | 0 | 44 | 0 | - |  | - | - |
| Sunday | 16 | 15 | 2 | 213 | 53 | 16.38 | - | 1 | 9 | - | 23 | 0 | 127 | 6 | 21.16 | 2-16 | - |  |

## Career Performances

| | M | Inns | NO | Runs | HS | Avge | 100s | 50s | Ct | St | Balls | Runs | Wkts | Avge | Best | 5wI | 10wM |
|---|---|---|---|---|---|---|---|---|---|---|---|---|---|---|---|---|---|
| Test | | | | | | | | | | | | | | | | | |
| All First | 46 | 80 | 8 | 2732 | 168 | 37.94 | 6 | 13 | 44 | - | 513 | 333 | 6 | 55.50 | 3-50 | - | - |
| 1-day Int | | | | · | | | | | | | | | | | | | |
| NatWest | 3 | 2 | 0 | 54 | 39 | 27.00 | - | - | 1 | - | | | | | | | |
| B & H | 5 | 4 | 0 | 134 | 74 | 33.50 | - | 1 | - | - | 36 | 44 | 0 | - | | - | - |
| Sunday | 32 | 28 | 3 | 382 | 53 | 15.28 | - | 1 | 12 | - | 138 | 127 | 6 | 21.16 | 2-16 | - | |

# ASIF DIN, M.                    Warwickshire

**Name:** Mohamed Asif Din
**Role:** Right-hand bat, leg-spin bowler
**Born:** 21 September 1960, Kampala, Uganda
**Height:** 5ft 9in **Weight:** 10st 7lbs
**Nickname:** Gunga 'and many others'
**County debut:** 1981
**County cap:** 1987
**Benefit:** 1994
**1000 runs in a season:** 2
**1st-Class 50s:** 42
**1st-Class 100s:** 9
**1st-Class 200s:** 1
**1st-Class 5 w. in innings:** 2
**1st-Class catches:** 114
**One-Day 100s:** 7
**One-Day 5 w. in innings:** 1
**Strike rate:** (career 83.20)
**Parents:** Jamiz and Mumtaz

**Wife and date of marriage:** Ahmerin, 27 September 1987
**Children:** Zahra, 18 October 1990; Sarah, 14 December 1991
**Family links with cricket:** Brothers Khalid and Abid play in Birmingham League
**Education:** Ladywood Comprehensive School, Birmingham
**Qualifications:** CSEs and O-levels and qualified coach
**Off-season:** Playing indoor cricket for Stumps
**Overseas tours:** Warwickshire to Zimbabwe April 1994
**Cricketers particularly admired:** Zaheer Abbas, Majid Khan
**Injuries:** Left shoulder, missed last month of season
**Other sports followed:** American football, basketball
**Relaxations:** Fishing and shooting
**Extras:** Man of the Match in NatWest final 1993, Man of the Match in NatWest semi-final 1989. Retired from county cricket at the end of 1995

**Best batting:** 217 Warwickshire v Mashonaland XI, Harare 1993-94
**Best bowling:** 5-61 Warwickshire v Boland, Brackenfell 1992-93

## 1995 Season

| | M | Inns | NO | Runs | HS | Avge | 100s | 50s | Ct | St | O | M | Runs | Wkts | Avge | Best | 5wl | 10wM |
|---|---|---|---|---|---|---|---|---|---|---|---|---|---|---|---|---|---|---|
| Test | | | | | | | | | | | | | | | | | | |
| All First | | | | | | | | | | | | | | | | | | |
| 1-day Int | | | | | | | | | | | | | | | | | | |
| NatWest | | | | | | | | | | | | | | | | | | |
| B & H | | | | | | | | | | | | | | | | | | |
| Sunday | 2 | 1 | 0 | 4 | 4 | 4.00 | - | - | 1 | - | | | | | | | | |

## Career Performances

| | M | Inns | NO | Runs | HS | Avge | 100s | 50s | Ct | St | Balls | Runs | Wkts | Avge | Best | 5wl | 10wM |
|---|---|---|---|---|---|---|---|---|---|---|---|---|---|---|---|---|---|
| Test | | | | | | | | | | | | | | | | | |
| All First | 210 | 341 | 45 | 9058 | 217 | 30.60 | 9 | 42 | 114 | - | 6573 | 4393 | 79 | 55.60 | 5-61 | 2 | - |
| 1-day Int | | | | | | | | | | | | | | | | | |
| NatWest | 30 | 27 | 7 | 806 | 104 | 40.30 | 1 | 3 | 6 | - | 169 | 99 | 7 | 14.14 | 5-40 | 1 | |
| B & H | 43 | 40 | 5 | 1211 | 137 | 34.60 | 2 | 5 | 5 | - | 126 | 102 | 1 | 102.00 | 1-26 | - | |
| Sunday | 171 | 155 | 27 | 3792 | 132 * | 29.62 | 4 | 16 | 32 | - | 230 | 261 | 4 | 65.25 | 1-11 | - | |

# ATHERTON, M. A. Lancashire

**Name:** Michael Andrew Atherton
**Role:** Right-hand bat, leg-break bowler,
county vice-captain
**Born:** 23 March 1968, Manchester
**Height:** 6ft **Weight:** 12st 7lbs
**Nickname:** Athers, Dread
**County debut:** 1987
**County cap:** 1989
**Test debut:** 1989
**Tests:** 51
**One-Day Internationals:** 25
**1000 runs in a season:** 7
**1st-Class 50s:** 64
**1st-Class 100s:** 38
**1st-Class 5 w. in innings:** 3
**1st-Class catches:** 167
**One-Day 100s:** 8
**Place in batting averages:** 51st av. 44.10

(1994 87th av. 35.96)
**Strike rate:** (career 83.20)
**Parents:** Alan and Wendy
**Marital status:** Single
**Family links with cricket:** Father and brother both play league cricket
**Education:** Briscoe Lane Primary; Manchester GS; Downing College, Cambridge
**Qualifications:** 10 O-levels, 3 A-levels; BA (Hons) (Cantab)
**Off-season:** England tour to South Africa
**Overseas tours:** England YC to Sri Lanka 1986-87, to Australia 1987-88; England A to Zimbabwe 1989-90; England to Australia and New Zealand 1990-91, to India and Sri Lanka 1992-93, to West Indies 1993-94, to Australia 1994-95, to South Africa 1995-96, to India and Pakistan (World Cup) 1995-96
**Cricketers particularly admired:** Graham Gooch
**Other sports followed:** Golf, squash, football
**Relaxations:** 'Decent novels (Heller, Kundera, etc.), good movies, food and wine, travelling, most sports, music'
**Extras:** In 1987 was first player to score 1000 runs in his debut season since Paul Parker in 1976. Youngest Lancastrian to score a Test century (151 v NZ at Trent Bridge in 1990); second Lancastrian to score a Test century at Old Trafford (138 v India in 1990). First captained England U19 aged 16. Selected for England tour to New Zealand and also England A tour to Bermuda and West Indies in 1991-92 but ruled out of both through injury. Appointed England captain in 1993. Cornhill England Player of the Year 1994. Voted England's Player of the Series against the West Indies. Hit 185 not out in the second Test against South Africa in Johannesburg in 1995-96 series. The innings lasted 645 minutes and was the fourth longest by an Englishman in Test matches
**Best batting:** 199 Lancashire v Durham, Gateshead Fell 1992
**Best bowling:** 6-78 Lancashire v Nottinghamshire, Trent Bridge 1990

## 1995 Season

| | M | Inns | NO | Runs | HS | Avge | 100s | 50s | Ct | St | O | M | Runs | Wkts | Avge | Best | 5wI | 10wM |
|---|---|---|---|---|---|---|---|---|---|---|---|---|---|---|---|---|---|---|
| Test | 6 | 12 | 0 | 488 | 113 | 40.66 | 1 | 2 | 3 | - | | | | | | | | |
| All First | 18 | 31 | 1 | 1323 | 155 * | 44.10 | 4 | 6 | 14 | - | 1 | 0 | 1 | 0 | - | - | - | - |
| 1-day Int | 3 | 3 | 0 | 227 | 127 | 75.66 | 1 | 1 | 4 | - | | | | | | | | |
| NatWest | 3 | 3 | 0 | 92 | 70 | 30.66 | - | 1 | 1 | - | | | | | | | | |
| B & H | 8 | 7 | 1 | 347 | 114 | 57.83 | 1 | 2 | 4 | - | | | | | | | | |
| Sunday | 9 | 8 | 0 | 245 | 103 | 30.62 | 1 | - | 3 | - | | | | | | | | |

2. Which player, formerly captain of the Australia U19 side, made his Test debut for England in 1995?

## Career Performances

|        | M   | Inns | NO | Runs  | HS    | Avge  | 100s | 50s | Ct  | St | Balls | Runs | Wkts | Avge   | Best | 5wI | 10wM |
|--------|-----|------|----|-------|-------|-------|------|-----|-----|----|-------|------|------|--------|------|-----|------|
| Test   | 51  | 96   | 1  | 3812  | 151   | 40.12 | 8    | 25  | 37  | -  | 366   | 282  | 1    | 282.00 | 1-60 | -   | -    |
| All First | 198 | 343 | 32 | 13722 | 199   | 44.12 | 38   | 64  | 167 | -  | 8903  | 4691 | 107  | 43.84  | 6-78 | 3   | -    |
| 1-day Int | 25 | 25  | 2  | 1068  | 127   | 46.43 | 1    | 8   | 10  | -  |       |      |      |        |      |     |      |
| NatWest | 15  | 15   | 2  | 535   | 109 * | 41.15 | 1    | 3   | 6   | -  | 188   | 154  | 6    | 25.66  | 2-15 | -   |      |
| B & H  | 42  | 41   | 3  | 1525  | 114   | 40.13 | 2    | 11  | 19  | -  | 252   | 228  | 7    | 32.57  | 4-42 | -   |      |
| Sunday | 65  | 63   | 3  | 2035  | 111   | 33.91 | 4    | 9   | 22  | -  | 216   | 248  | 7    | 35.42  | 3-33 | -   |      |

# ATHEY, C. W. J.                              Sussex

**Name:** Charles William Jeffrey Athey
**Role:** Right-hand bat, occasional right-arm
medium bowler, occasional wicket-keeper
**Born:** 27 September 1957, Middlesbrough
**Height:** 5ft 10in **Weight:** 12st 7lbs
**Nickname:** Bumper, Wingnut, Ath
**County debut:** 1976 (Yorkshire),
1984 (Gloucestershire), 1993 (Sussex)
**County cap:** 1980 (Yorkshire),
1985 (Gloucestershire), 1993 (Sussex)
**Benefit:** 1990
**Test debut:** 1980
**Tests:** 23
**One-Day Internationals:** 31
**1000 runs in a season:** 12
**1st-Class 50s:** 116
**1st-Class 100s:** 51
**1st-Class catches:** 405
**1st-Class stumpings:** 2
**One-Day 100s:** 11
**One-Day 5 w. in innings:** 1

**Place in batting averages:** 89th av. 35.73 (1994 122nd av. 30.96)
**Strike rate:** (career 99.93)
**Parents:** Peter and Maree
**Wife and date of marriage:** Janet Linda, 9 October 1982
**Family links with cricket:** 'Father played league cricket in North Yorkshire and South
Durham League for 29 years, 25 of them with Middlesbrough, and has been President
of Middlesbrough CC since 1975. Brother-in-law Colin Cook played for Middlesex,
other brother-in-law (Martin) plays in Thames Valley League. Father-in-law deeply
involved in Middlesex Youth cricket'
**Education:** Linthorpe Junior; Stainsby Secondary School; Acklam Hall High School

**Qualifications:** 4 O-levels, some CSEs, NCA coaching certificate
**Off-season:** Working for Sussex CCC in marketing department and coaching
**Overseas tours:** England YC to West Indies 1975-76; England to West Indies 1980-81, to Australia 1986-87, to Pakistan, Australia and New Zealand 1987-88; England B to Sri Lanka 1985-86; unofficial English XI to South Africa 1989-90; MCC to Bahrain 1994-95; BSI World Cup, India 1994-95
**Cricketers particularly admired:** 'Too many to mention, but those with enthusiasm for the game.'
**Other sports followed:** Most sports, especially football (Middlesbrough FC)
**Injuries:** Shingles, missed one month
**Relaxations:** Gardening, sport and military history
**Extras:** Played for Teesside County Schools U16 at age 12. Played for Yorkshire Colts 1974. Played football for Middlesbrough Schools U16 and Junior XI. Offered but declined apprenticeship terms with Middlesbrough FC. Captain of Gloucestershire in 1989. Suspension for playing in South Africa in 1990 was remitted in 1992. 'Scored four hundreds in four innings for Gloucestershire CCC.'
**Opinions on cricket:** 'Must play county cricket on better wickets.'
**Best batting:** 184 England B v Sri Lanka XI, Galle 1985-86
**Best bowling:** 3-3 Gloucestershire v Hampshire, Bristol 1985

## 1995 Season

| | M | Inns | NO | Runs | HS | Avge | 100s | 50s | Ct | St | O | M | Runs | Wkts | Avge | Best | 5wI | 10wM |
|---|---|---|---|---|---|---|---|---|---|---|---|---|---|---|---|---|---|---|
| Test | | | | | | | | | | | | | | | | | | |
| All First | 15 | 27 | 1 | 929 | 163 * | 35.73 | 2 | 5 | 6 | - | 7 | 1 | 35 | 0 | - | - | - | - |
| 1-day Int | | | | | | | | | | | | | | | | | | |
| NatWest | 1 | 1 | 0 | 20 | 20 | 20.00 | - | - | - | - | 2 | 0 | 12 | 0 | - | | - | - |
| B & H | 4 | 4 | 0 | 295 | 118 | 73.75 | 1 | 1 | - | 1 | | | | | | | | |
| Sunday | 11 | 10 | 2 | 279 | 61 * | 34.87 | - | 2 | 2 | - | | | | | | | | |

## Career Performances

| | M | Inns | NO | Runs | HS | Avge | 100s | 50s | Ct | St | Balls | Runs | Wkts | Avge | Best | 5wI | 10wM |
|---|---|---|---|---|---|---|---|---|---|---|---|---|---|---|---|---|---|
| Test | 23 | 41 | 1 | 919 | 123 | 22.97 | 1 | 4 | 13 | - | | | | | | | |
| All First | 437 | 730 | 69 | 23680 | 184 | 35.82 | 51 | 116 | 405 | 2 | 4768 | 2652 | 48 | 55.25 | 3-3 | - | - |
| 1-day Int | 31 | 30 | 3 | 848 | 142 * | 31.40 | 2 | 4 | 16 | - | 6 | 10 | 0 | - | - | - | |
| NatWest | 46 | 45 | 8 | 1636 | 115 | 44.21 | 2 | 12 | 21 | - | 199 | 168 | 1 | 168.00 | 1-18 | - | |
| B & H | 75 | 71 | 11 | 2332 | 118 | 38.86 | 1 | 18 | 33 | 1 | 478 | 364 | 16 | 22.75 | 4-48 | - | |
| Sunday | 257 | 246 | 22 | 7214 | 121 * | 32.20 | 6 | 46 | 97 | - | 913 | 857 | 30 | 28.56 | 5-35 | 1 | |

# ATKINS, C. S.                    Northamptonshire

**Name:** Craig Stuart Atkins
**Role**: Left-hand bat, slow left-arm bowler
**Born:** 29 May 1966, Melbourne, Australia
**Height:** 6ft 2in **Weight:** 13st
**Nickname:** Greencard
**County debut:** 1995
**Parents:** Gordon and Heather
**Wife and date of marriage:** Sandra, 31
March 1989
**Children:** Three step-children – Lori, Hayley
and Becky
**Education:** Swan Hill Technical School
**Qualifications:** Fifth form pass, qualified
motor vehicle technician and Levelone
cricket coach
**Off-season:** Spend time with my wife.
Training for the 1996 season and playing
rugby league for my home team, Dalton
**Overseas teams played for:** Hawthorn East, Melbourne 1986-87
**Cricketers particularly admired:** Dennis Lillee, Michael Atherton, Michael Slater,
Anil Kumble and Mal Loye
**Other sports followed:** Australian Rules and rugby league
**Injuries:** Lower back, missed two weeks
**Relaxations:** Spending time with my wife and playing rugby
**Extras:** 'Played as a professional for Lancaster in the Northern League for four years.'
**Opinions on cricket:** 'Too much cricket is played, and there are not enough days off so
that you can work on your skills, especially fielding.'
**Best batting:** 8* Northamptonshire v Surrey, Northampton 1995
**Best bowling:** 1-46 Northamptonshire v Surrey, Northampton 1995

## 1995 Season

|          | M | Inns | NO | Runs | HS | Avge | 100s | 50s | Ct | St | O | M | Runs | Wkts | Avge | Best | 5wI | 10wM |
|----------|---|------|----|------|-----|------|------|-----|----|----|-----|---|------|------|-------|------|-----|------|
| Test     |   |      |    |      |     |      |      |     |    |    |     |   |      |      |       |      |     |      |
| All First | 1 | 2   | 1  | 13   | 8 * | 13.00 | -    | -   | -  | -  | 11  | 4 | 46   | 1    | 46.00 | 1-46 | -   | -    |
| 1-day Int |   |      |    |      |     |      |      |     |    |    |     |   |      |      |       |      |     |      |
| NatWest  |   |      |    |      |     |      |      |     |    |    |     |   |      |      |       |      |     |      |
| B & H    |   |      |    |      |     |      |      |     |    |    |     |   |      |      |       |      |     |      |
| Sunday   | 1 | 0    | 0  | 0    | 0   | -    | -    | -   | -  | -  | 4.2 | 0 | 38   | 0    | -     |      | -   | -    |

**Career Performances**

| | M | Inns | NO | Runs | HS | Avge | 100s | 50s | Ct | St | Balls | Runs | Wkts | Avge | Best | 5wI | 10wM |
|---|---|---|---|---|---|---|---|---|---|---|---|---|---|---|---|---|---|
| Test | | | | | | | | | | | | | | | | | |
| All First | 1 | 2 | 1 | 13 | 8 * | 13.00 | - | - | - | - | 66 | 46 | 1 | 46.00 | 1-46 | - | - |
| 1-day Int | | | | | | | | | | | | | | | | | |
| NatWest | | | | | | | | | | | | | | | | | |
| B & H | | | | | | | | | | | | | | | | | |
| Sunday | 1 | 0 | 0 | 0 | 0 | - | - | - | - | - | 26 | 38 | 0 | - | | - | - |

# AUSTIN, I. D.                              Lancashire

**Name:** Ian David Austin
**Role:** Left-hand bat, right-arm medium bowler
**Born:** 30 May 1966, Haslingden, Lancs
**Height:** 5ft 10in **Weight:** 14st 7lbs
**Nickname:** Oscar, Bully
**County debut:** 1986
**County cap:** 1990
**1st-Class 100s:** 2
**1st-Class 50s:** 7
**1st-Class 5 w. in innings:** 4
**1st-Class 10 w. in match:** 1
**1st-Class catches:** 15
**One-Day 5 w. in innings:** 1
**Place in batting averages:** 180th av. 22.88
(1994 156th av. 25.73)
**Place in bowling averages:** 33rd av. 25.40
(1994 5th av. 20.06)
**Strike rate:** 62.34 (career 68.19)
**Parents:** Jack and Ursula
**Wife and date of marriage:** Alexandra, 27 February 1993
**Family links with cricket:** Father opened batting for Haslingden CC
**Education:** Haslingden High School
**Qualifications:** 4 O-levels, NCA coaching certificate
**Career outside cricket:** 'Trying to qualify as a wine taster'
**Off-season:** Working for local bed firm
**Overseas tours:** NAYC to Bermuda 1985; Lancashire to Jamaica 1986-87, 1987-88, to Zimbabwe 1988-89, to Tasmania and Western Australia 1989-90, 1990-91
**Overseas teams played for:** Maroochydore, Queensland 1987-88, 1991-92; Randwick, Sydney 1990-91
**Cricketers particularly admired:** Ian Botham, Hartley Alleyne

**Other sports followed:** Football (Burnley), golf
**Relaxations:** Golf, and listening to music
**Extras:** Holds amateur Lancashire League record for highest individual score (147*).
Broke Lancashire CCC record for most wickets in the Sunday League in 1991. Scored
quickest first-class century in 1991 off authentic bowling (64 balls)
**Best batting:** 115* Lancashire v Derbyshire, Blackpool 1992
**Best bowling:** 5-23 Lancashire v Middlesex, Old Trafford 1994

## 1995 Season

| | M | Inns | NO | Runs | HS | Avge | 100s | 50s | Ct | St | O | M | Runs | Wkts | Avge | Best | 5wI | 10wM |
|---|---|---|---|---|---|---|---|---|---|---|---|---|---|---|---|---|---|---|
| Test | | | | | | | | | | | | | | | | | | |
| All First | 13 | 22 | 4 | 412 | 80 * | 22.88 | - | 1 | 3 | - | 363.4 | 111 | 889 | 35 | 25.40 | 4-50 | - | - |
| 1-day Int | | | | | | | | | | | | | | | | | | |
| NatWest | 3 | 2 | 2 | 22 | 15 * | - | - | - | - | - | 35.2 | 5 | 106 | 6 | 17.66 | 3-32 | - | |
| B & H | 8 | 4 | 2 | 42 | 16 * | 21.00 | - | - | 3 | - | 78 | 17 | 274 | 13 | 21.07 | 4-8 | - | |
| Sunday | 15 | 11 | 8 | 137 | 36 * | 45.66 | - | - | 5 | - | 108.3 | 6 | 462 | 18 | 25.66 | 3-30 | - | |

## Career Performances

| | M | Inns | NO | Runs | HS | Avge | 100s | 50s | Ct | St | Balls | Runs | Wkts | Avge | Best | 5wI | 10wM |
|---|---|---|---|---|---|---|---|---|---|---|---|---|---|---|---|---|---|
| Test | | | | | | | | | | | | | | | | | |
| All First | 77 | 107 | 22 | 2078 | 115 * | 24.44 | 2 | 7 | 15 | - | 10025 | 4603 | 147 | 31.31 | 5-23 | 4 | 1 |
| 1-day Int | | | | | | | | | | | | | | | | | |
| NatWest | 16 | 10 | 7 | 183 | 57 | 61.00 | - | 1 | 1 | - | 1069 | 684 | 18 | 38.00 | 3-32 | - | |
| B & H | 37 | 21 | 8 | 327 | 80 | 25.15 | - | 2 | 8 | - | 2181 | 1429 | 40 | 35.72 | 4-8 | - | |
| Sunday | 125 | 74 | 31 | 830 | 48 | 19.30 | - | - | 26 | - | 5108 | 3951 | 138 | 28.63 | 5-56 | | |

3. Which former Australian Test player will captain Derbyshire in
1996 and for which other county has he previously played?

# AVERIS, J. M. M.                    Gloucestershire

**Name:** James Max Michael Averis
**Role:** Right-hand bat, right-arm
medium bowler
**Born:** 28 May 1974, Bristol
**Height:** 5ft 11in **Weight:** 12st 7lb
**Nickname:** Fish
**County debut:** 1994 (one-day)
**Parents:** Michael and Carol
**Marital status:** Single
**Family links with cricket:** Grandfather
played club cricket for Gloucester Gypsies
**Education:** Bristol Cathedral School,
Portsmouth University
**Qualifications:** 10 GCSEs, 3 A-levels
**Career outside cricket:** Studying Geography
at Portsmouth University
**Overseas tours:** Bristol Schools to Australia
1990-91
**Other sports followed:** Rugby and football
**Extras:** Played for Gloucestershire from U16 to U19 and ESCA U19. On Bristol RFC
U21 tour to South Africa in Spring 1995

---

## 1995 (did not make any first-class or one-day appearances)

## Career Performances

|           | M | Inns | NO | Runs | HS | Avge | 100s | 50s | Ct | St | Balls | Runs | Wkts | Avge | Best | 5wI | 10wM |
|-----------|---|------|----|------|----|------|------|-----|----|----|-------|------|------|------|------|-----|------|
| Test      |   |      |    |      |    |      |      |     |    |    |       |      |      |      |      |     |      |
| All First |   |      |    |      |    |      |      |     |    |    |       |      |      |      |      |     |      |
| 1-day Int |   |      |    |      |    |      |      |     |    |    |       |      |      |      |      |     |      |
| NatWest   |   |      |    |      |    |      |      |     |    |    |       |      |      |      |      |     |      |
| B & H     |   |      |    |      |    |      |      |     |    |    |       |      |      |      |      |     |      |
| Sunday    | 1 | 1    | 1  | 2    | 2* | -    | -    | -   | 1  | -  | 36    | 44   | 0    | -    | -    |     | -    |

---

4. Which county cricketer was voted one of Britain's most eligible
bachelors in a survey for Company magazine in 1995?

# AYMES, A. N.                    Hampshire

**Name:** Adrian Nigel Aymes
**Role:** Right-hand bat, wicket-keeper
**Born:** 4 June 1964, Southampton
**Height:** 6ft **Weight:** 13st
**Nickname:** Aymser, Adi
**County debut:** 1987
**County cap:** 1991
**1st-Class 50s:** 20
**1st-Class 100s:** 1
**1st-Class catches:** 244
**1st-Class stumpings:** 21
**Place in batting averages:** 128th av. 30.00
(1994 173rd av. 24.03)
**Parents:** Michael and Barbara
**Wife and date of marriage:** Marie, 12
November 1992
**Children:** Lucie, 9 November 1994
**Family links with cricket:** 'Father once
walked into a Holt and Haskell Sports Shop'
**Education:** Shirley Middle; Bellemoor Secondary; Hill College
**Qualifications:** 4 O-levels, 1 A-level, NCA coaching award
**Career outside cricket:**
Selling cricket equipment
**Off-season:** 'Coaching, relaxing and working out in my gym.'
**Overseas tours:** Hampshire CCC to Isle of Wight 1992, to Portutgal 1993, to Guernsey
1994
**Cricketers particularly admired:** Gordon Greenidge, Malcolm Marshall and wicket-
keepers past and present
**Other sports followed:** Boxing and non-sport martial arts
**Injuries:** Cracked thumb, no time off
**Relaxations:** Watching videos, exercising
**Extras:** Half century on debut v Surrey; equalled club record of 6 catches in an innings
and 10 in a match. Hampshire Exiles Young Player of the Year 1990.
**Opinions on cricket:** 'Great game.'
**Best batting:** 107* Hampshire v Sussex, Portsmouth 1993
**Best bowling:** 1-75 Hampshire v Sussex, Southampton 1992

## 1995 Season

|  | M | Inns | NO | Runs | HS | Avge | 100s | 50s | Ct | St | O | M | Runs | Wkts | Avge | Best | 5wI | 10wM |
|---|---|---|---|---|---|---|---|---|---|---|---|---|---|---|---|---|---|---|
| Test |  |  |  |  |  |  |  |  |  |  |  |  |  |  |  |  |  |  |
| All First | 20 | 33 | 9 | 720 | 62 * | 30.00 | - | 5 | 53 | 3 |  |  |  |  |  |  |  |  |
| 1-day Int |  |  |  |  |  |  |  |  |  |  |  |  |  |  |  |  |  |  |
| NatWest | 1 | 1 | 0 | 18 | 18 | 18.00 | - | - | 2 | - |  |  |  |  |  |  |  |  |
| B & H | 5 | 4 | 1 | 47 | 29 | 15.66 | - | - | 6 | - |  |  |  |  |  |  |  |  |
| Sunday | 16 | 13 | 6 | 221 | 41 | 31.57 | - | - | 23 | 3 |  |  |  |  |  |  |  |  |

## Career Performances

|  | M | Inns | NO | Runs | HS | Avge | 100s | 50s | Ct | St | Balls | Runs | Wkts | Avge | Best | 5wI | 10wM |
|---|---|---|---|---|---|---|---|---|---|---|---|---|---|---|---|---|---|
| Test |  |  |  |  |  |  |  |  |  |  |  |  |  |  |  |  |  |
| All First | 108 | 157 | 40 | 3528 | 107 * | 30.15 | 1 | 20 | 244 | 21 | 42 | 75 | 1 | 75.00 | 1-75 | - | - |
| 1-day Int |  |  |  |  |  |  |  |  |  |  |  |  |  |  |  |  |  |
| NatWest | 10 | 3 | 0 | 54 | 34 | 18.00 | - | - | 12 | 2 |  |  |  |  |  |  |  |
| B & H | 22 | 10 | 4 | 98 | 29 | 16.33 | - | - | 20 | 7 |  |  |  |  |  |  |  |
| Sunday | 77 | 52 | 26 | 872 | 54 | 33.53 | - | 1 | 77 | 15 |  |  |  |  |  |  |  |

# AYRES, D. W.     Essex

**Name:** Duncan Wallace Ayres
**Role:** Right-hand bat, right-arm medium bowler
**Born:** 8 October 1976, Basildon
**Height:** 5ft 11in **Weight:** 13st
**Nickname:** Pam, 'Duncan Dares'
**County debut:** No first-team appearance
**Parents:** Andrew and Betty
**Marital status:** Single
**Family links with cricket:** Father played club cricket
**Education:** Falmouth Comprehensive; Millfield School
**Qualifications**: Coaching Award
**Career outside cricket:** Car sales
**Off-season:** Coaching and playing in Sydney
**Overseas tours:** West of England U11 to Holland 1988; West of England U15 to West Indies 1990-91, 1991-92
**Overseas teams played for:** Sutherland District, Sydney, Australia 1993-94, 1995-96
**Cricketers particularly admired:** Eldine Baptiste, Allan Donald, Neil Foster
**Other sports followed:** Football (Manchester United), rugby league (Sutherland Sharks)

**Injuries:** Double stress fracture in back, 'out for the winter.'
**Relaxations:** 'Round of golf, listening to music, spending time with my girlfriend, Michelle'
**Extras:** Has played soccer for Wimbledon and minor county cricket for Cornwall
**Opinions on cricket:** 'Lunch is too short.'

# BAILEY, R. J.                                    Northamptonshire

**Name:** Robert John Bailey
**Role:** Right-hand bat, off-spin bowler, county captain
**Born:** 28 October 1963, Biddulph, Stoke-on-Trent
**Height:** 6ft 3in **Weight:** 14st 7lbs
**Nickname:** Biff, Nose Bag
**County debut:** 1982
**County cap:** 1985
**Benefit:** 1993
**Test debut:** 1988
**Tests:** 4
**One-Day Internationals:** 4
**1000 runs in a season:** 12
**1st-Class 50s:** 91
**1st-Class 100s:** 38
**1st-Class 200s:** 4
**1st-Class 5 w. in innings:** 2
**1st-Class catches:** 214
**One-Day 100s:** 7
**Place in batting averages:** 76th av. 38.44 (1994 42nd av. 43.35)
**Place in bowling averages:** (1994 143rd av. 51.63)
**Strike rate:** (career 80.19)
**Parents:** Marie, father deceased
**Wife and date of marriage:** Rachel, 11 April 1987
**Children:** Harry John, 7 March 1991; Alexandra Joy, 13 November 1993
**Family links with cricket:** Father played in North Staffordshire League for 30 years for Knypersley and Minor Counties cricket for Staffordshire as wicket-keeper. Brother Simon now plays for Knypersley in the North Staffs/South Cheshire League
**Education:** Biddulph High School
**Qualifications:** 6 CSEs, 1 O-level, NCA advanced cricket coach
**Off-season:** 'Working for John Liddington wholesale drinks suppliers'
**Overseas tours:** England to Sharjah 1984-85 and 1986-87, to West Indies 1989-90; Northants to Durban 1991-92, to Cape Town 1992-93, to Zimbabwe 1994-95; Singapore

Sixes October 1994

**Overseas teams played for:** Rhodes University, South Africa 1982-83; Uitenhage, Melbourne 1983-84, 1984-85; Fitzroy, Melbourne, 1985-86; Gosnells, Perth 1987-88

**Cricketers particularly admired:** Dennis Lillee, David Steele and any other player who still performs well after many years in the game, i.e. Allan Lamb, Graham Gooch and Mike Gatting

**Other sports followed:** Football (Stoke City)

**Relaxations:** Walking and drinking at the local village pub

**Extras:** Played for Young England v Young Australia 1983. Selected for cancelled tour of India 1988-89. Youngest Northamptonshire player to score 10,000 runs. Won three consecutive Man of the Match Awards in the Nat West Trophy in 1995. Takes over the Northamptonshire captaincy for the 1996 season

**Best batting:** 224* Northamptonshire v Glamorgan, Swansea 1986

**Best bowling:** 5-54 Northamptonshire v Nottinghamshire, Northampton 1993

### 1995 Season

|          | M  | Inns | NO | Runs | HS   | Avge  | 100s | 50s | Ct | St | O     | M  | Runs | Wkts | Avge  | Best | 5wI | 10wM |
|----------|----|------|----|------|------|-------|------|-----|----|----|-------|----|------|------|-------|------|-----|------|
| Test     |    |      |    |      |      |       |      |     |    |    |       |    |      |      |       |      |     |      |
| All First| 18 | 30   | 3  | 1038 | 157  | 38.44 | 4    | 2   | 21 | -  | 114.3 | 21 | 403  | 8    | 50.37 | 4-66 | -   | -    |
| 1-day Int|    |      |    |      |      |       |      |     |    |    |       |    |      |      |       |      |     |      |
| NatWest  | 5  | 5    | 1  | 262  | 93 * | 65.50 | -    | 2   | 3  | -  | 26    | 2  | 91   | 3    | 30.33 | 2-42 | -   |      |
| B & H    | 4  | 4    | 1  | 164  | 93 * | 54.66 | -    | 2   | 2  | -  | 15    | 2  | 50   | 1    | 50.00 | 1-29 | -   |      |
| Sunday   | 16 | 13   | 3  | 340  | 61 * | 34.00 | -    | 3   | 2  | -  | 47    | 0  | 290  | 11   | 26.36 | 3-28 | -   |      |

### Career Performances

|          | M   | Inns | NO | Runs  | HS    | Avge  | 100s | 50s | Ct  | St | Balls | Runs | Wkts | Avge  | Best | 5wI | 10wM |
|----------|-----|------|----|-------|-------|-------|------|-----|-----|----|-------|------|------|-------|------|-----|------|
| Test     | 4   | 8    | 0  | 119   | 43    | 14.87 | -    | -   | -   | -  |       |      |      |       |      |     |      |
| All First| 288 | 485  | 73 | 17299 | 224 * | 41.98 | 38   | 91  | 214 | -  | 7458  | 4033 | 93   | 43.36 | 5-54 | 2   | -    |
| 1-day Int| 4   | 4    | 2  | 137   | 43 *  | 68.50 | -    | -   | 1   | -  | 36    | 25   | 0    | -     | -    | -   |      |
| NatWest  | 42  | 42   | 11 | 1502  | 145   | 48.45 | 1    | 10  | 12  | -  | 558   | 327  | 13   | 25.15 | 3-47 | -   |      |
| B & H    | 51  | 48   | 5  | 1831  | 134   | 42.58 | 2    | 14  | 12  | -  | 294   | 180  | 2    | 90.00 | 1-22 | -   |      |
| Sunday   | 183 | 172  | 25 | 5298  | 125 * | 36.04 | 4    | 33  | 42  | -  | 1090  | 1021 | 34   | 30.02 | 3-23 | -   |      |

# BAILEY, T. M. B.                    Northamptonshire

**Name:** Tobin Michael Barnaby Bailey
**Role:** Right-hand bat, wicket-keeper
**Born:** 28 August 1976, Kettering
**Height:** 5ft 10in  **Weight:** 12st 7lbs
**Nickname:** Bill, Mad Dog
**County debut:** No first-team appearance

**Parents:** Terry and Penny
**Marital status:** Single
**Family links with cricket:** 'Step Dad watches a lot'
**Education:** Bedford School; Loughborough University
**Qualifications:** 3 A-levels
**Off-season:** Studying at Loughborough University
**Overseas tours:** Bedford to South Africa 1994
**Cricketers particularly admired:** Jack Russell, Mike Atherton
**Other sports followed:** Hockey, rugby (Bedford Town) and football (Leicester City)
**Relaxations:** Spending time with friends
**Extras:** Bedfordshire Young Player of the Year. Northants County League Young Player of the Year. Holmwoods Schools Cricketer of the Year. Played for England

Schools U19 and was a reserve for the England U19 tour to Zimbabwe
**Opinions on cricket:** 'BBC and ITV should put more games on television. Lunch and tea should be five minutes longer.'

# BAINBRIDGE, P.        Durham

**Name:** Philip Bainbridge
**Role:** Right-hand bat, right-arm medium bowler
**Born:** 16 April 1958, Stoke-on-Trent
**Height:** 5ft 10in **Weight:** 12st 7lbs
**Nickname:** Bains, Robbo, Red
**County debut:** 1977 (Gloucestershire), 1992 (Durham)
**County cap:** 1981
**Benefit:** 1989
**1000 runs in a season:** 9
**1st-Class 50s:** 89
**1st-Class 100s:** 24
**1st-Class 5 w. in innings:** 10
**1st-Class catches:** 139
**One-Day 100s:** 1
**One-Day 5 w. in innings:** 1

**Place in batting averages:** 188th 22.00 (1993 61st av. 38.33)
**Place in bowling averages:** 147th av. 77.28 (1993 33rd av. 25.52)
**Strike rate:** (career 73.11)
**Parents:** Leonard George and Lilian Rose
**Wife and date of marriage:** Barbara, 22 September 1979
**Children:** Neil, 11 January 1984; Laura, 15 January 1985
**Family links with cricket:** Cousin, Stephen Wilkinson, played for Somerset
**Education:** Hanley High School; Stoke-on-Trent Sixth Form College; Borough Road College of Education
**Qualifications:** 9 O-levels, 2 A-levels, BEd
**Career outside cricket:** Runs own corporate hospitality company and sports tour operators – Rhodes Leisure, Bristol. Specialises in sports tours to South Africa
**Overseas tours:** British Colleges to West Indies 1978; English Counties XI to Zimbabwe 1984-85; plus other tours to West Indies, Sri Lanka, Holland, South Africa, Pakistan and Zimbabwe
**Overseas teams played for:** Alberton, Johannesburg 1980-81, 1982-83
**Cricketers particularly admired:** Mike Procter
**Other sports followed:** Rugby union, soccer, golf, American football, boxing
**Extras:** Played for four 2nd XIs in 1976 – Gloucestershire, Derbyshire, Northamptonshire and Warwickshire. Played for Young England v Australia 1977. Scored first century for Stoke-on-Trent aged 14. One of *Wisden*'s Five Cricketers of the Year 1985. Joined Durham for their first season in first-class cricket after 14 seasons with Gloucestershire. Played for Leyland CC as professional in 1991 – they won the Northern League. Player of the Year for Durham 1993. Appointed captain of Durham for 1994 season but handed over captaincy to Mike Roseberry for 1995 season
**Opinions on cricket:** 'I think the four-day format has worked very well.'
**Best batting:** 169 Gloucestershire v Yorkshire, Cheltenham 1988
**Best bowling:** 8-53 Gloucestershire v Somerset, Bristol 1986

## 1995 Season

| | M | Inns | NO | Runs | HS | Avge | 100s | 50s | Ct | St | O | M | Runs | Wkts | Avge | Best | 5wI | 10wM |
|---|---|---|---|---|---|---|---|---|---|---|---|---|---|---|---|---|---|---|
| Test | | | | | | | | | | | | | | | | | | |
| All First | 2 | 3 | 0 | 4 | 4 | 1.33 | - | - | 1 | - | 15 | 2 | 55 | 1 | 55.00 | 1-5 | - | - |
| 1-day Int | | | | | | | | | | | | | | | | | | |
| NatWest | 2 | 2 | 1 | 20 | 10 * | 20.00 | - | - | - | - | 17 | 1 | 56 | 0 | - | | - | - |
| B & H | | | | | | | | | | | | | | | | | | |
| Sunday | 6 | 5 | 2 | 62 | 31 * | 20.66 | - | - | 2 | - | 26 | 0 | 158 | 3 | 52.66 | 3-56 | - | |

---

5. Who was the first coloured player to play Test cricket for Zimbabwe?
When did he play and against whom?

## Career Performances

|        | M   | Inns | NO | Runs  | HS    | Avge  | 100s | 50s | Ct  | St | Balls | Runs  | Wkts | Avge  | Best | 5wI | 10wM |
|--------|-----|------|----|-------|-------|-------|------|-----|-----|----|-------|-------|------|-------|------|-----|------|
| Test   |     |      |    |       |       |       |      |     |     |    |       |       |      |       |      |     |      |
| All First | 313 | 520 | 72 | 15090 | 169 | 33.68 | 24 | 89 | 139 | - | 25005 | 12712 | 342 | 37.16 | 8-53 | 10 | - |
| 1-day Int |    |      |    |       |       |       |      |     |     |    |       |       |      |       |      |     |      |
| NatWest | 33 | 29  | 5  | 857   | 89  | 35.70 | -  | 8  | 5   | -  | 1891  | 1093  | 32   | 34.15 | 3-49 | -   |      |
| B & H  | 53  | 49   | 9  | 1104  | 96  | 27.60 | -  | 6  | 17  | -  | 2524  | 1539  | 47   | 32.74 | 4-38 | -   |      |
| Sunday | 206 | 179 | 31 | 3336  | 106 * | 22.54 | 1 | 13 | 48 | - | 7357 | 6188 | 206 | 30.03 | 5-22 | 1 | |

# BAIRSTOW, A. D.        Derbyshire

**Name:** Andrew David Bairstow
**Role:** Left-hand bat, wicket-keeper
**Born:** 16 June 1975, Dewsbury
**Height:** 5ft 10in **Weight:** 13st
**County debut:** 1995
**1st-Class catches:** 7
**1st-Class stumpings:** 1
**Parents:** David Leslie
**Marital status:** Single
**Family links with cricket:** Father David
played for Yorkshire and England
**Education:** Woodhouse Grove, Leeds
**Qualifications:** 7 GCSEs, 2 A-levels
**Off-season:** Playing in South Africa
**Overseas teams played for:**
Northern Natal 1995-96
**Other sports followed:**
Rugby union and golf
**Extras:** Captained England Schools U19 and MCC Schools U19. Released by
Derbyshire at the end of the 1995 season
**Best batting:** 26 Derbyshire v Young Australia, Chesterfield 1995

## 1995 Season

|        | M | Inns | NO | Runs | HS | Avge  | 100s | 50s | Ct | St | O | M | Runs | Wkts | Avge | Best | 5wI | 10wM |
|--------|---|------|----|------|----|-------|------|-----|----|----|---|---|------|------|------|------|-----|------|
| Test   |   |      |    |      |    |       |      |     |    |    |   |   |      |      |      |      |     |      |
| All First | 3 | 6  | 0  | 73   | 26 | 12.16 | -  | -  | 7  | 1  |   |   |      |      |      |      |     |      |
| 1-day Int |   |    |    |      |    |       |      |     |    |    |   |   |      |      |      |      |     |      |
| NatWest |   |      |    |      |    |       |      |     |    |    |   |   |      |      |      |      |     |      |
| B & H  |   |      |    |      |    |       |      |     |    |    |   |   |      |      |      |      |     |      |
| Sunday | 1 | 1  | 0  | 0    | 0  | 0.00  | -  | -  | 3  | -  |   |   |      |      |      |      |     |      |

## Career Performances

|         | M | Inns | NO | Runs | HS | Avge  | 100s | 50s | Ct | St | Balls | Runs | Wkts | Avge | Best | 5wI | 10wM |
|---------|---|------|----|------|----|-------|------|-----|----|----|-------|------|------|------|------|-----|------|
| Test    |   |      |    |      |    |       |      |     |    |    |       |      |      |      |      |     |      |
| All First | 3 | 6 | 0 | 73 | 26 | 12.16 | - | - | 7 | 1 |       |      |      |      |      |     |      |
| 1-day Int |   |      |    |      |    |       |      |     |    |    |       |      |      |      |      |     |      |
| NatWest |   |      |    |      |    |       |      |     |    |    |       |      |      |      |      |     |      |
| B & H   |   |      |    |      |    |       |      |     |    |    |       |      |      |      |      |     |      |
| Sunday  | 1 | 1 | 0 | 0 | 0 | 0.00 | - | - | 3 | - |       |      |      |      |      |     |      |

# BALL, M. C. J. Gloucestershire

**Name:** Martyn Charles John Ball
**Role:** Right-hand bat, off-spin bowler, slip fielder
**Born:** 26 April 1970, Bristol
**Height:** 5ft 9in **Weight:** 12st 4lbs
**Nickname:** Benny, Barfo
**County debut:** 1988
**1st-Class 50s:** 3
**1st-Class 5 w. in innings:** 7
**1st-Class 10 w. in match:** 1
**1st-Class catches:** 83
**Place in batting averages:** 192nd av. 21.94 (1994 211th av. 18.72)
**Place in bowling averages:** 99th av. 35.26 (1994 135th av. 45.47)
**Strike rate:** 82.47 (career 72.40)
**Parents:** Kenneth Charles and Pamela Wendy
**Wife and date of marriage:** Mona, 28 September 1991

**Children:** Kristina, 9 May 1990; Alexandra, 2 August 1993
**Education:** King Edmund Secondary School, Yate; Bath College of Further Education
**Qualifications:** 6 O-levels, 2 AO-levels
**Off-season:** 'Working for father's security fencing company. Playing football for AFC Horton and getting ready for the 1996 season'
**Overseas tours:** Gloucestershire to Namibia 1991, to Kenya 1992, Sri Lanka 1993
**Overseas teams played for:** North Melbourne, Australia 1988-89; Old Hararians, Zimbabwe 1990-91
**Cricketers most admired:** Ian Botham, John Emburey, Vic Marks
**Other sports followed:** All sports except show-jumping
**Relaxations:** 'Listening to music, watching sport and celebrating a victory for AFC Horton.'

**Extras:** Played for Young England against New Zealand in 1989. Produced best bowling figures in a match for the Britannic County Championship 1993 season – 14-169 against Somerset

**Opinions on cricket:** 'Things seem to be moving in the right direction, but I believe that if a club allows a player to run out of contract then he should be a free agent like in any other profession and not be restricted by regulations like those of contested registration.'

**Best batting:** 71 Gloucestershire v Nottinghamshire, Bristol 1993

**Best bowling:** 8-46 Gloucestershire v Somerset, Taunton 1993

## 1995 Season

|          | M  | Inns | NO | Runs | HS | Avge  | 100s | 50s | Ct | St | O     | M   | Runs | Wkts | Avge  | Best | 5wI | 10wM |
|----------|----|------|----|------|----|-------|------|-----|----|----|-------|-----|------|------|-------|------|-----|------|
| Test     |    |      |    |      |    |       |      |     |    |    |       |     |      |      |       |      |     |      |
| All First | 18 | 28  | 9  | 417  | 48 | 21.94 | -    | -   | 16 | -  | 577.2 | 144 | 1481 | 42   | 35.26 | 5-49 | 2   | -    |
| 1-day Int |    |     |    |      |    |       |      |     |    |    |       |     |      |      |       |      |     |      |
| NatWest  | 3  | 1    | 0  | 12   | 12 | 12.00 | -    | -   | 1  | -  | 35    | 3   | 124  | 4    | 31.00 | 2-40 | -   |      |
| B & H    | 6  | 5    | 0  | 31   | 12 | 6.20  | -    | -   | 2  | -  | 58    | 7   | 163  | 8    | 20.37 | 3-26 | -   |      |
| Sunday   | 14 | 9    | 2  | 84   | 20 | 12.00 | -    | -   | 3  | -  | 78    | 3   | 424  | 10   | 42.40 | 2-37 | -   |      |

## Career Performances

|          | M  | Inns | NO | Runs | HS   | Avge  | 100s | 50s | Ct | St | Balls | Runs | Wkts | Avge  | Best | 5wI | 10wM |
|----------|----|------|----|------|------|-------|------|-----|----|----|-------|------|------|-------|------|-----|------|
| Test     |    |      |    |      |      |       |      |     |    |    |       |      |      |       |      |     |      |
| All First | 72 | 110 | 21 | 1408 | 71   | 15.82 | -    | 3   | 83 | -  | 11078 | 5427 | 153  | 35.47 | 8-46 | 7   | 1    |
| 1-day Int |    |     |    |      |      |       |      |     |    |    |       |      |      |       |      |     |      |
| NatWest  | 6  | 2    | 1  | 28   | 16 * | 28.00 | -    | -   | 2  | -  | 330   | 199  | 8    | 24.87 | 3-42 | -   |      |
| B & H    | 15 | 9    | 1  | 76   | 20 * | 9.50  | -    | -   | 6  | -  | 786   | 470  | 13   | 36.15 | 3-26 | -   |      |
| Sunday   | 54 | 35   | 13 | 250  | 28 * | 11.36 | -    | -   | 14 | -  | 1718  | 1474 | 30   | 49.13 | 3-24 | -   |      |

6. Name the three New Zealand Test players who were suspended following allegations of smoking marijuana in 1994?

# BANTON, C.      Nottinghamshire

**Name:** Colin Banton
**Role:** Right-hand bat
**Born:** 15 September 1969, Fishhoek,
Cape Town, South Africa
**Height:** 5ft 9in   **Weight:** 12st
**Nickname:** Bants
**County debut:** 1995
**1st-Class 50s:** 2
**1st-Class catches:** 4
**Place in batting averages:** 140th av. 29.20
**Parents:** Frank and Loralie Patricia
**Wife and date of marriage:**
Jayne, 24 June 1995
**Education:** Fishhoek High School
**Qualifications:** Matriculation
**Career outside cricket:** Accountant
**Off-season:** Working for Capespan
International plc as accountant

**Overseas teams played for:**
Fishhoek, Cape Town; Western Province Defence Force
**Cricketers particularly admired:** Peter Kirsten, Ken McEwan
**Other sports followed:** Football (Liverpool FC)
**Injuries:** Missed one and a half months with a broken left arm
**Relaxations:** Eating, cinema, going out
**Extras:** Plays hockey for Slough in the National League and played hockey for Western
Province in South Africa. Released by Nottinghamshire at the end of the 1995 season
**Opinions on cricket:** 'Make the season longer – from March until September.'
**Best batting:** 80* Nottinghamshire v Cambridge University, Fenner's 1995

## 1995 Season

|  | M | Inns | NO | Runs | HS | Avge | 100s | 50s | Ct | St | O | M | Runs | Wkts | Avge | Best | 5wI | 10wM |
|---|---|---|---|---|---|---|---|---|---|---|---|---|---|---|---|---|---|---|
| Test |  |  |  |  |  |  |  |  |  |  |  |  |  |  |  |  |  |  |
| All First | 7 | 14 | 4 | 292 | 80 * | 29.20 | - | 2 | 4 | - | 8 | 1 | 37 | 0 | - | - | - | - |
| 1-day Int |  |  |  |  |  |  |  |  |  |  |  |  |  |  |  |  |  |  |
| NatWest |  |  |  |  |  |  |  |  |  |  |  |  |  |  |  |  |  |  |  |
| B & H | 1 | 1 | 0 | 40 | 40 | 40.00 | - | - | - | - |  |  |  |  |  |  |  |  |
| Sunday | 1 | 1 | 0 | 1 | 1 | 1.00 | - | - | - | - |  |  |  |  |  |  |  |  |

## Career Performances

|  | M | Inns | NO | Runs | HS | Avge | 100s | 50s | Ct | St | Balls | Runs | Wkts | Avge | Best | 5wI | 10wM |
|---|---|---|---|---|---|---|---|---|---|---|---|---|---|---|---|---|---|
| Test |  |  |  |  |  |  |  |  |  |  |  |  |  |  |  |  |  |
| All First | 7 | 14 | 4 | 292 | 80 * | 29.20 | - | 2 | 4 | - | 48 | 37 | 0 | - | - | - | - |
| 1-day Int |  |  |  |  |  |  |  |  |  |  |  |  |  |  |  |  |  |
| NatWest |  |  |  |  |  |  |  |  |  |  |  |  |  |  |  |  |  |  |
| B & H | 1 | 1 | 0 | 40 | 40 | 40.00 | - | - | - | - |  |  |  |  |  |  |  |
| Sunday | 1 | 1 | 0 | 1 | 1 | 1.00 | - | - | - | - |  |  |  |  |  |  |  |

# BARNETT, K. J. Derbyshire

**Name:** Kim John Barnett
**Role:** Right-hand bat, leg-break bowler
**Born:** 17 July 1960, Stoke-on-Trent
**Height:** 6ft **Weight:** 13st
**Nickname:** Skippo, Barn
**County debut:** 1979
**County cap:** 1982
**Benefit:** 1993 (£37,056)
**Test debut:** 1988
**Tests:** 4
**One-Day Internationals:** 1
**1000 runs in a season:** 12
**1st-Class 50s:** 117
**1st-Class 100s:** 46
**1st-Class 200s:** 2
**1st-Class 5 w. in innings:** 3
**1st-Class catches:** 234
**One-Day 100s:** 10
**One-Day 5 w. in innings:** 1

**Place in batting averages:** 46th av. 44.67 (1994 65th av. 38.50)
**Place in bowling averages:** 119th av. 39.68 (1994 1st av. 13.30
**Strike rate:** 81.87 (career 74.91)
**Parents:** Derek and Doreen
**Wife:** Janet
**Children:** Michael Nicholas, 24 April 1990
**Education:** Leek High School, Staffs
**Qualifications:** 7 O-levels
**Career outside cricket:** Bank clerk
**Overseas tours:** English Schools to India 1977-78; England YC to Australia 1978-79; England B to Sri Lanka 1985-86 (vice-captain); unofficial English XI to South Africa 1989-90

**Overseas teams played for:** Boland 1980-81, 1982-83
**Cricketers particularly admired:** Eddie Barlow
**Other sports followed:** Football, golf, horse racing
**Relaxations:** Golf
**Extras:** Played for Northamptonshire 2nd XI when aged 15, Staffordshire and Warwickshire 2nd XI. Became youngest captain of a first-class county when appointed in 1983. One of *Wisden*'s Five Cricketers of the Year 1989. Banned from Test cricket after joining tour to South Africa, suspension remitted in 1992. Relinquished captaincy at the end of the 1995 season
**Opinions on cricket:** 'There are still too many people, both inside and outside the game, complaining about pitches. If we are to have a balanced game, players have got to be able to perform in all conditions and back their skills when conditions are not in their favour. Perhaps then we will have a harder game.'
**Best batting:** 239* Derbyshire v Leicestershire, Leicester 1988
**Best bowling:** 6-28 Derbyshire v Glamorgan, Chesterfield 1991

### 1995 Season

|  | M | Inns | NO | Runs | HS | Avge | 100s | 50s | Ct | St | O | M | Runs | Wkts | Avge | Best | 5wI | 10wM |
|---|---|---|---|---|---|---|---|---|---|---|---|---|---|---|---|---|---|---|
| Test |  |  |  |  |  |  |  |  |  |  |  |  |  |  |  |  |  |  |
| All First | 17 | 31 | 3 | 1251 | 169 | 44.67 | 2 | 7 | 5 | - | 218.2 | 42 | 635 | 16 | 39.68 | 3-51 | - | - |
| 1-day Int |  |  |  |  |  |  |  |  |  |  |  |  |  |  |  |  |  |  |
| NatWest | 3 | 2 | 0 | 70 | 53 | 35.00 | - | 1 | 1 | - | 32 | 3 | 127 | 5 | 25.40 | 3-40 | - |  |
| B & H | 3 | 3 | 1 | 98 | 58 * | 49.00 | - | 1 | 2 | - | 6 | 2 | 21 | 0 | - | - | - |  |
| Sunday | 16 | 15 | 3 | 313 | 53 * | 26.08 | - | 2 | 2 | - | 22 | 0 | 92 | 2 | 46.00 | 2-32 | - |  |

### Career Performances

|  | M | Inns | NO | Runs | HS | Avge | 100s | 50s | Ct | St | Balls | Runs | Wkts | Avge | Best | 5wI | 10wM |
|---|---|---|---|---|---|---|---|---|---|---|---|---|---|---|---|---|---|
| Test | 4 | 7 | 0 | 207 | 80 | 29.57 | - | 2 | 1 | - | 36 | 32 | 0 | - | - | - | - |
| All First | 381 | 612 | 57 | 21816 | 239 * | 39.30 | 46 | 117 | 234 | - | 12586 | 6210 | 168 | 36.96 | 6-28 | 3 | - |
| 1-day Int | 1 | 1 | 0 | 84 | 84 | 84.00 | - | 1 | - | - |  |  |  |  |  |  |  |
| NatWest | 33 | 32 | 3 | 1046 | 113 * | 36.06 | 1 | 8 | 14 | - | 418 | 264 | 16 | 16.50 | 6-24 | 1 |  |
| B & H | 71 | 62 | 4 | 2173 | 115 | 37.46 | 3 | 16 | 29 | - | 342 | 219 | 6 | 36.50 | 1-10 | - |  |
| Sunday | 239 | 228 | 37 | 6443 | 131 * | 33.73 | 6 | 33 | 82 | - | 893 | 779 | 23 | 33.86 | 3-39 | - |  |

# BARTLE, S.        Leicestershire

**Name:** Steven Bartle
**Role:** Left-hand bat, right-arm medium bowler
**Born:** 5 September 1971, Shipley, Yorkshire
**Height:** 6ft 4in **Weight:** 15st
**Nickname:** Barts

**County debut:** 1995
**1st-Class catches:** 1
**Parents:** John and Judith
**Marital status:** Single
**Family links with cricket:** Father played for Windhill in the Bradford League
**Education:** Wood End Middle School; Beckfoot GS; Windhill College of Education; Calderdale College
**Qualifications:** 7 GCSEs, coaching qualifications
**Overseas tours:** England U19 to New Zealand 1990-91
**Overseas teams played for:** Mossman, Sydney 1993-94
**Cricketers particularly admired:** David Gower, Curtly Ambrose, Robin Smith
**Other sports followed:** Football, tennis, golf, snooker, squash, badminton
**Relaxations:** Astronomy and weight-lifting
**Extras:** Was on the Yorkshire staff in 1993, joined Leicestershire for 1995 season. Released at the end of the 1995 season
**Best batting:** 32 Leicestershire v Oxford University, The Parks 1995

## 1995 Season

| | M | Inns | NO | Runs | HS | Avge | 100s | 50s | Ct | St | O | M | Runs | Wkts | Avge | Best | 5wI | 10wM |
|---|---|---|---|---|---|---|---|---|---|---|---|---|---|---|---|---|---|---|
| Test | | | | | | | | | | | | | | | | | | |
| All First | 1 | 1 | 0 | 32 | 32 | 32.00 | - | - | 1 | - | 2 | 0 | 42 | 0 | - | - | - | - |
| 1-day Int | | | | | | | | | | | | | | | | | | |
| NatWest | | | | | | | | | | | | | | | | | | |
| B & H | | | | | | | | | | | | | | | | | | |
| Sunday | | | | | | | | | | | | | | | | | | |

## Career Performances

| | M | Inns | NO | Runs | HS | Avge | 100s | 50s | Ct | St | Balls | Runs | Wkts | Avge | Best | 5wI | 10wM |
|---|---|---|---|---|---|---|---|---|---|---|---|---|---|---|---|---|---|
| Test | | | | | | | | | | | | | | | | | | |
| All First | 1 | 1 | 0 | 32 | 32 | 32.00 | - | - | 1 | - | 12 | 42 | 0 | - | - | - | - |
| 1-day Int | | | | | | | | | | | | | | | | | | |
| NatWest | | | | | | | | | | | | | | | | | | |
| B & H | | | | | | | | | | | | | | | | | | |
| Sunday | | | | | | | | | | | | | | | | | | |

# BARWICK, S. R. Glamorgan

**Name:** Stephen Royston Barwick
**Role:** Right-hand bat, right-arm
medium bowler
**Born:** 6 September 1960, Neath
**Height:** 6ft 2in **Weight:** 13st
**Nickname:** Bas
**County debut:** 1981
**County cap:** 1987
**Benefit:** 1995
**50 wickets in a season:** 2
**1st-Class 5 w. in innings:** 10
**1st-Class 10 w. in match:** 1
**1st-Class catches:** 44
**One-Day 5 w. in innings:** 5
**Place in bowling averages:** 144th av. 48.64
(1994 76th av. 31.41)
**Strike rate:** 100.14 (career 79.12)

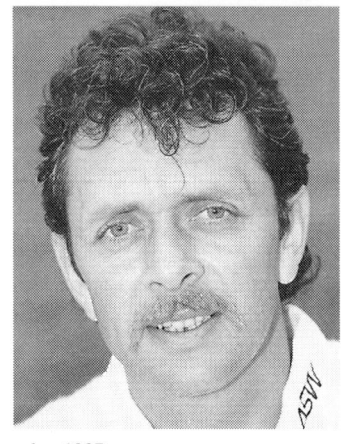

**Parents:** Margaret and Roy
**Wife and date of marriage:** Margaret, 12 December 1987
**Children:** Michael Warren, 25 September 1990; Katheryn Elizabeth, 17 February 1993;
Jessica Margaret, 30 July 1994
**Family links with cricket:** 'My Uncle David played for Glamorgan 2nd XI'
**Education:** Cwrt Sart Comprehensive; Dwr-y-Felin Comprehensive
**Qualifications:** 'Commerce, human biology, mathematics, English'
**Career outside cricket:** Ex-steelworker
**Off-season:** Working on benefit for 1995
**Overseas teams played for:** Benoni, South Africa
**Cricketers particularly admired:** Ian Botham, Richard Hadlee
**Other sports followed:** Football and rugby
**Relaxations:** 'Sea fishing and the odd pint or two'
**Best batting:** 30 Glamorgan v Hampshire, Bournemouth 1988
**Best bowling:** 8-42 Glamorgan v Worcestershire, Worcester 1983

## 1995 Season

| | M | Inns | NO | Runs | HS | Avge | 100s | 50s | Ct | St | O | M | Runs | Wkts | Avge | Best | 5wI | 10wM |
|---|---|---|---|---|---|---|---|---|---|---|---|---|---|---|---|---|---|---|
| Test | | | | | | | | | | | | | | | | | | |
| All First | 7 | 6 | 2 | 19 | 14 | 4.75 | - | - | 1 | - | 233.4 | 58 | 681 | 14 | 48.64 | 4-116 | - | - |
| 1-day Int | | | | | | | | | | | | | | | | | | |
| NatWest | 3 | 2 | 1 | 1 | 1 * | 1.00 | - | - | - | - | 29.1 | 8 | 87 | 2 | 43.50 | 2-15 | - | |
| B & H | 4 | 2 | 2 | 10 | 10 * | - | - | - | - | - | 42 | 1 | 167 | 3 | 55.66 | 2-36 | - | |
| Sunday | 14 | 3 | 2 | 11 | 9 | 11.00 | - | - | 1 | - | 99.4 | 4 | 451 | 30 | 15.03 | 6-49 | 2 | |

## Career Performances

|  | M | Inns | NO | Runs | HS | Avge | 100s | 50s | Ct | St | Balls | Runs | Wkts | Avge | Best | 5wI | 10wM |
|---|---|---|---|---|---|---|---|---|---|---|---|---|---|---|---|---|---|
| Test |  |  |  |  |  |  |  |  |  |  |  |  |  |  |  |  |  |
| All First | 205 | 196 | 73 | 839 | 30 | 6.82 | - | - | 44 | - | 35686 | 15785 | 451 | 35.00 | 8-42 | 10 | 1 |
| 1-day Int |  |  |  |  |  |  |  |  |  |  |  |  |  |  |  |  |  |
| NatWest | 29 | 12 | 6 | 23 | 6 | 3.83 | - | - | 4 | - | 1669 | 885 | 41 | 21.58 | 5-26 | 1 |  |
| B & H | 47 | 26 | 14 | 97 | 18 | 8.08 | - | - | 9 | - | 2629 | 1636 | 57 | 28.70 | 4-11 | - |  |
| Sunday | 166 | 52 | 30 | 221 | 48 * | 10.04 | - | - | 23 | - | 6609 | 4948 | 186 | 26.60 | 6-28 | 4 |  |

# BASE, S. J. Derbyshire

**Name:** Simon John Base
**Role:** Right-hand bat, right-arm
fast-medium bowler
**Born:** 2 January 1960, Maidstone
**Height:** 6ft 3in **Weight:** 14st 7lbs
**Nickname:** Basey, Moose Man
**County debut:** 1986 (Glamorgan),
1988 (Derbyshire)
**County cap:** 1990
**50 wickets in a season:** 1
**1st-Class 50s:** 2
**1st-Class 5 w. in innings:** 16
**1st-Class 10 w. in match:** 1
**1st-Class catches:** 60
**Strike rate:** (career 54.10)
**Parents:** Christine and Peter (deceased)
**Wife and date of marriage:** Louise Ann,
23 September 1989
**Children:** Christopher Peter Elliott, 15 December 1991
**Family links with cricket:** Grandfather played, 'brother-in-law pretends he can!'
**Education:** Fishhoek Primary School; Fishhoek High School, Cape Town, South
Africa
**Qualifications:** High School, School Certificate Matriculation, refrigeration and air
conditioning technician
**Career outside cricket:** Hall-Thermotank in South Africa as a technician, GSPK
Electronics, Rhodes Fabrics
**Overseas tours:** England XI to Holland 1989
**Overseas teams played for:** Western Province B 1982-83; Boland 1986-89; Border
1989-94 (all South Africa)
**Cricketers particularly admired:** Graham Gooch, Graeme Pollock, Mike Procter,
Richard Hadlee, Malcolm Marshall

**Other sports followed:** Most other sports
**Relaxations:** Spending time with family, swimming, windsurfing, 'braaing'
**Extras:** Suspended from first-class cricket for ten weeks during 1988 season for a supposed breach of contract, joining Derbyshire when he was still said to be contracted to Glamorgan. The TCCB fined Derbyshire £2000. Retired from county cricket at end of 1993 season to play as a non-overseas player for Border, South Africa
**Best batting:** 58 Derbyshire v Yorkshire, Chesterfield 1990
**Best bowling:** 7-60 Derbyshire v Yorkshire, Chesterfield 1989

## 1995 Season

|          | M | Inns | NO | Runs | HS | Avge | 100s | 50s | Ct | St | O | M | Runs | Wkts | Avge | Best | 5wI | 10wM |
|----------|---|------|----|------|----|------|------|-----|----|----|---|---|------|------|------|------|-----|------|
| Test     |   |      |    |      |    |      |      |     |    |    |   |   |      |      |      |      |     |      |
| All First | 1 | 2    | 1  | 17   | 10 | 17.00 | -    | -   | -  | -  | 17 | 2 | 99   | 1    | 99.00 | 1-99 | --  |      |
| 1-day Int |   |      |    |      |    |      |      |     |    |    |   |   |      |      |      |      |     |      |
| NatWest  |   |      |    |      |    |      |      |     |    |    |   |   |      |      |      |      |     |      |
| B & H    |   |      |    |      |    |      |      |     |    |    |   |   |      |      |      |      |     |      |
| Sunday   | 2 | 1    | 1  | 5    | 5 *| -    | -    | -   | -  | -  | 8 | 0 | 55   | 2    | 27.50 | 2-55 | -   |      |

## Career Performances

|          | M   | Inns | NO | Runs | HS  | Avge | 100s | 50s | Ct | St | Balls | Runs  | Wkts | Avge  | Best | 5wI | 10wM |
|----------|-----|------|----|------|-----|------|------|-----|----|----|-------|-------|------|-------|------|-----|------|
| Test     |     |      |    |      |     |      |      |     |    |    |       |       |      |       |      |     |      |
| All First | 132 | 169  | 35 | 1525 | 58  | 11.38 | -    | 2   | 60 | -  | 20939 | 11258 | 387  | 29.09 | 7-60 | 16  | 1    |
| 1-day Int |     |      |    |      |     |      |      |     |    |    |       |       |      |       |      |     |      |
| NatWest  | 3   | 2    | 0  | 6    | 4   | 3.00 | -    | -   | 1  | -  | 156   | 124   | 3    | 41.33 | 2-49 | -   |      |
| B & H    | 15  | 9    | 3  | 53   | 15 *| 8.83 | -    | -   | -  | -  | 870   | 629   | 15   | 41.93 | 3-33 | -   |      |
| Sunday   | 89  | 36   | 9  | 184  | 31  | 6.81 | -    | -   | 24 | -  | 3783  | 2765  | 112  | 24.68 | 4-14 | -   |      |

# BATES, J. J. Sussex

**Name:** Justin J. Bates
**Role:** Right-hand bat, off-spin bowler
**Born:** 9 April 1976, Farnborough, Hants
**Height:** 6ft **Weight:** 12st 7lbs
**County debut:** No first-team appearance
**Parents:** Barry and Sandra
**Marital status:** Single
**Family links with cricket:** Father played cricket for Staplefield and Crawley; brother plays for Three Bridges and used to play for Sussex Young Cricketers; Alan Igglesden (Kent and England) is second cousin
**Education:** St Mark's Primary School; Warden Park Secondary School; Hurstpierpoint College

**Qualifications:** 8 GCSEs, 3 A-levels, NCA coaching award
**Career outside cricket:** Freelance computer graphic designer
**Off-season:** Coaching
**Overseas tours:** Sussex YC to India 1990-91, to Barbados 1992-93, to Sri Lanka 1994-95
**Cricketers particularly admired:** Carl Hooper, Brian Lara, Eddie Hemmings
**Injuries:** Fracture of middle finger, out for one week
**Other sports followed:** Golf and rugby
**Relaxations:** Watching television, Caroline and ju-jitsu
**Opinions on cricket:** 'More second XI cricket should be played on county grounds.'

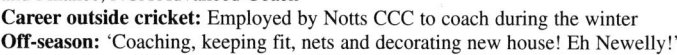

# BATES, R. T.  Nottinghamshire

**Name:** Richard Terry Bates
**Role:** Right-hand bat, off-spin bowler, slip fielder
**Born:** 17 June 1972, Stamford, Lincs
**Height:** 6ft 1in **Weight:** 13st 7lbs
**Nickname:** Blast, Batesy, Beaver
**County debut:** 1993
**1st-Class 5 w. innings:** 1
**1st-Class catches:** 4
**Place in bowling averages:** 108th av. 36.70
**Strike rate:** 69.10 (career 91.72)
**Parents:** Terry and Sue
**Marital status:** Engaged to Suzanne
**Family links with cricket:** Father is NCA Development and Administration Manager
**Education:** Bourne Grammar School; Stamford College for Further Education
**Qualifications:** 8 GCSEs, BTEC in Business and Finance, NCA Advanced Coach
**Career outside cricket:** Employed by Notts CCC to coach during the winter
**Off-season:** 'Coaching, keeping fit, nets and decorating new house! Eh Newelly!'
**Overseas tours:** Lincolnshire Colts (U19) to Australia 1989-90
**Overseas teams played for:** Redwood, New Zealand 1991-92

**Cricketers particularly admired:** Ian Botham, Derek Randall, Viv Richards, Paul Johnson, James Hindson
**Other sports followed:** Football
**Injuries:** Shoulder operation in January 1995. Unable to bowl for two-thirds of season
**Relaxations:** Socialising, films, Chinese and Indian food
**Opinions on cricket:** 'Better prospects for winter employment, i.e. coaching jobs, training and netting.'
**Best batting:** 33* Nottinghamshire v Oxford University, The Parks 1993
**Best bowling:** 5-88 Nottinghamshire v Durham, Chester-le-Street 1995

## 1995 Season

|          | M | Inns | NO | Runs | HS | Avge | 100s | 50s | Ct | St | O | M | Runs | Wkts | Avge | Best | 5wI | 10wM |
|----------|---|------|----|------|----|------|------|-----|----|----|---|---|------|------|------|------|-----|------|
| Test     |   |      |    |      |    |      |      |     |    |    |   |   |      |      |      |      |     |      |
| All First | 4 | 7 | 0 | 50 | 11 | 7.14 | - | - | 1 | - | 115.1 | 32 | 369 | 10 | 36.90 | 5-88 | 1- | |
| 1-day Int |   |      |    |      |    |      |      |     |    |    |   |   |      |      |      |      |     |      |
| NatWest   |   |      |    |      |    |      |      |     |    |    |   |   |      |      |      |      |     |      |
| B & H     |   |      |    |      |    |      |      |     |    |    |   |   |      |      |      |      |     |      |
| Sunday    |   |      |    |      |    |      |      |     |    |    |   |   |      |      |      |      |     |      |

## Career Performances

|          | M | Inns | NO | Runs | HS | Avge | 100s | 50s | Ct | St | Balls | Runs | Wkts | Avge | Best | 5wI | 10wM |
|----------|---|------|----|------|----|------|------|-----|----|----|-------|------|------|------|------|-----|------|
| Test     |   |      |    |      |    |      |      |     |    |    |       |      |      |      |      |     |      |
| All First | 11 | 16 | 4 | 135 | 33 * | 11.25 | - | - | 4 | - | 1651 | 794 | 18 | 44.11 | 5-88 | 1 | - |
| 1-day Int |   |      |    |      |    |      |      |     |    |    |       |      |      |      |      |     |      |
| NatWest   |   |      |    |      |    |      |      |     |    |    |       |      |      |      |      |     |      |
| B & H     |   |      |    |      |    |      |      |     |    |    |       |      |      |      |      |     |      |
| Sunday    | 9 | 4 | 1 | 18 | 16 | 6.00 | - | - | 2 | - | 365 | 333 | 10 | 33.30 | 3-43 | - | |

# BATTY, G. J.                                          Yorkshire

**Name:** Gareth Jon Batty
**Role:** Right-hand bat, right-arm off-spin bowler
**Born:** 13 October 1977
**Height:** 5ft 11in **Weight:** 11st 4lbs
**Nickname:** Batts, Ginner
**County debut:** No first-team appearance
**Parents:** David and Rosemary
**Family links with cricket:** Father a coach at Yorkshire Academy, brother Jeremy plays for Somerset
**Education:** Parkside Middle School; Bingley Grammar School
**Qualifications:** 9 GCSEs, BTEC National Diploma, NCA Coaching Award

**Career outside cricket:** Undecided
**Off-season:** Going to Zimbabwe with England U19
**Overseas tours:** England U15 to South Africa. England U19 to Zimbabwe 1995-96
**Cricketers particularly admired:** John Emburey, Viv Richards, Robin Smith
**Other sports followed:** Rugby league (Leeds), golf, football
**Relaxations:** Listening to music and socialising with friends
**Extras:** *Daily Telegraph* Under 15 Bowler of the Year 1993
**Opinions on cricket:** 'There is possibly too much one-day cricket played at times, so when we play longer games it can be played a little bit like a one-day season.'

---

# BATTY, J. D.                    Somerset

**Name:** Jeremy David Batty
**Role:** Right-hand bat, off-spin bowler
**Born:** 15 May 1971, Bradford
**Height:** 6ft 1in **Weight:** Variable
**Nickname:** Nora, Chip, Batts
**County debut:** 1989 (Yorkshire), 1995 (Somerset)
**1st-Class 50s:** 2
**1st-Class 5 w. in innings:** 3
**1st-Class catches:** 28
**Strike rate:** (career 72.95)
**Parents:** David and Rosemary
**Marital status:** Engaged to Liz
**Family links with cricket:** Father coach at Yorkshire Academy and played in Bradford League. Brother is on Yorkshire playing staff
**Education:** Parkside Middle School; Bingley Grammar School; Horsforth College
**Qualifications:** 5 O-levels, BTEC Diploma in Leisure Studies, coaching certificate
**Off-season:** 'Working on my house and in my parents' sports shop'
**Overseas tours:** England YC to Australia 1989-90; Yorkshire CCC to Barbados 1990, to Cape Town 1992-93, to Leeward Islands 1993-94; Sheffield Cricket Lovers to Spain

1991, to Majorca 1992

**Overseas teams played for:** Sunrise 1989-90, Country Districts 1990-91 (both Zimbabwe); M.O.B., Pietermaritzburg, South Africa 1992-93; Wellington, Cape Town 1993-94; Techs, Cape Town 1994-95

**Cricketers particularly admired:** John Emburey, Phil Tufnell, Dean Jones, Peter Robinson

**Other sports followed:** Rugby league, football and hockey

**Injuries:** Tendonitis in wrist, sprained thumb but 'bit the bullet'

**Relaxations:** Movies, eating out and 'listening to Peter Robinson'

**Extras:** Took five wickets on first-class debut v Lancashire in 1989. Yorkshire Young Player of the Year 1991. Whittingdale Bowler of the Month, June 1991. Moved to Somerset for the 1995 season

**Opinions on cricket:** 'Inspection at 1p.m. after overnight rain. Why change our set-up, it's good as it is.'

**Best batting:** 51 Yorkshire v Sri Lanka, Headingley 1991

**Best bowling:** 6-48 Yorkshire v Nottinghamshire, Worksop 1991

### 1995 Season

| | M | Inns | NO | Runs | HS | Avge | 100s | 50s | Ct | St | O | M | Runs | Wkts | Avge | Best | 5wl | 10wM |
|---|---|---|---|---|---|---|---|---|---|---|---|---|---|---|---|---|---|---|
| Test | | | | | | | | | | | | | | | | | | |
| All First | 4 | 6 | 1 | 125 | 45 * | 25.00 | - | - | 3 | - | 111.4 | 13 | 583 | 7 | 83.28 | 4-70 | - | - |
| 1-day Int | | | | | | | | | | | | | | | | | | |
| NatWest | | | | | | | | | | | | | | | | | | |
| B & H | 4 | 2 | 2 | 19 | 19 * | - | - | - | 1 | - | 33 | 6 | 111 | 5 | 22.20 | 2-13 | - | |
| Sunday | 2 | 1 | 0 | 3 | 3 | 3.00 | - | - | - | - | 13 | 2 | 70 | 0 | - | - | - | |

### Career Performances

| | M | Inns | NO | Runs | HS | Avge | 100s | 50s | Ct | St | Balls | Runs | Wkts | Avge | Best | 5wl | 10wM |
|---|---|---|---|---|---|---|---|---|---|---|---|---|---|---|---|---|---|
| Test | | | | | | | | | | | | | | | | | |
| All First | 68 | 73 | 21 | 828 | 51 | 15.92 | - | 2 | 28 | - | 10725 | 5869 | 147 | 39.92 | 6-48 | 3 | - |
| 1-day Int | | | | | | | | | | | | | | | | | |
| NatWest | 3 | 2 | 0 | 7 | 4 | 3.50 | - | - | 1 | - | 126 | 97 | 1 | 97.00 | 1-17 | - | |
| B & H | 8 | 3 | 3 | 21 | 19 * | - | - | - | 2 | - | 372 | 220 | 6 | 36.66 | 2-13 | - | |
| Sunday | 33 | 14 | 6 | 44 | 13 * | 5.50 | - | - | 16 | - | 1470 | 1161 | 40 | 29.02 | 4-33 | - | |

7. Which Australian scored a century on his Test debut against England in 1994-95, and then went on to score another one in his second Test match?

# BELL, M. A. V.                    Warwickshire

**Name:** Michael Anthony Vincent Bell
**Role:** Right-hand bat, left-arm
fast-medium bowler
**Born:** 19 December 1967, Birmingham
**Height:** 6ft 2in **Weight:** 13st 2lbs
**Nickname:** Belly, Nelly, Breezer
**County debut:** 1992
**1st-Class 5 w. in innings:** 3
**1st-Class catches:** 7
**One-Day 5 w. in innings:** 2
**Strike rate:** (career 55.10)
**Parents:** Vincent and Adelheid
**Marital status:** Single
**Family links with cricket:** Father played
cricket mainly for Mitchells & Butler in the
Birmingham League. An uncle played a few
games for Jamaica
**Education:** Bishop Milner Comprehensive;

Dudley Technical College
**Qualifications:** 5 O-levels, City and Guilds in Recreation and Leisure Parts 1 & 2
**Career outside cricket:** Casino croupier, worked with the PE staff at Earls High
School
and also worked in the corporate hospitality department at EMP plc for two years
**Overseas tours:** BWIA to Barbados and Trinidad & Tobago 1989; John Morris's
Madcap CC to Australia 1992
**Overseas teams played for:** Swanbourne, Perth 1986-87; Norwood, Melbourne 1989-
90; Phoenix, Perth 1992-93; Sunshine Heights 1993-94
**Cricketers particularly admired:** Dennis Lillee, Viv Richards, Michael Holding,
Imran Khan, Wasim Akram, Shane Warne
**Other sports followed:** Any sport played by the best in that particular field
**Injuries:** Lower back problem, out for most of the season
**Relaxations:** 'Golf (although I'm no Calvin Peete), good movies and going to a hot
country before winter sets in.'
**Opinions on cricket:** 'When are the batsmen going to be prevented from taking the
initiative over the bowlers and get limited to, for instance, one extra-cover drive – on the
up – per over ... and when will a cow jump over the moon!'
**Best batting**: 22* Warwickshire v Gloucestershire, Edgbaston 1993
**Best bowling**: 7-48 Warwickshire v Gloucestershire, Edgbaston 1993

## 1995 Season

| | M | Inns | NO | Runs | HS | Avge | 100s | 50s | Ct | St | O | M | Runs | Wkts | Avge | Best | 5wI | 10wM |
|---|---|---|---|---|---|---|---|---|---|---|---|---|---|---|---|---|---|---|
| Test | | | | | | | | | | | | | | | | | | |
| All First | 3 | 1 | 1 | 0 | 0 * | - | - | - | - | 2 | - | 80 | 25 | 265 | 7 | 37.85 | 2-59 | - | - |
| 1-day Int | | | | | | | | | | | | | | | | | | |
| NatWest | 1 | 0 | 0 | 0 | 0 | - | - | - | - | - | - | 8.5 | 1 | 41 | 2 | 20.50 | 2-41 | - |
| B & H | 1 | 0 | 0 | 0 | 0 | - | - | - | - | - | - | | | | | | | |
| Sunday | 7 | 1 | 1 | 8 | 8 * | - | - | - | - | 1 | - | 47 | 1 | 206 | 10 | 20.60 | 3-25 | - |

## Career Performances

| | M | Inns | NO | Runs | HS | Avge | 100s | 50s | Ct | St | Balls | Runs | Wkts | Avge | Best | 5wI | 10wM |
|---|---|---|---|---|---|---|---|---|---|---|---|---|---|---|---|---|---|
| Test | | | | | | | | | | | | | | | | | |
| All First | 17 | 21 | 10 | 79 | 22 * | 7.18 | - | - | 7 | - | 2535 | 1333 | 46 | 28.97 | 7-48 | 3 | - |
| 1-day Int | | | | | | | | | | | | | | | | | |
| NatWest | 1 | 0 | 0 | 0 | 0 | - | - | - | - | - | 53 | 41 | 2 | 20.50 | 2-41 | - |
| B & H | 2 | 0 | 0 | 0 | 0 | - | - | - | 1 | - | 66 | 34 | 2 | 17.00 | 2-34 | - |
| Sunday | 13 | 5 | 2 | 27 | 8 * | 9.00 | - | - | 1 | - | 570 | 411 | 22 | 18.68 | 5-19 | 2 | |

# BENJAMIN, J. E. Surrey

**Name:** Joseph Emmanuel Benjamin
**Role:** Right-hand bat, right-arm
fast-medium bowler
**Born:** 2 February 1961, Christchurch,
St Kitts, West Indies
**Height:** 6ft 2in **Weight:** 12st 7lbs
**Nickname:** Boggy, Moon Man
**County debut:** 1988 (Warwickshire),
1992 (Surrey)
**County cap:** 1993 (Surrey)
**Test debut:** 1994
**Tests:** 1
**One-day Internationals:** 2
**50 wickets in a season:** 3
**1st-Class 5 w. in innings:** 16
**1st-Class 10 w. in match:** 1
**1st-Class catches:** 22
**Place in batting averages:** 269th av. 12.42
**Place in bowling averages:** 30th av. 25.01
(1994 7th av. 20.72)
**Strike rate:** 47.62 (career 57.37)
**Parents:** Henry and Judith

**Marital status:** Single
**Education:** Cayon High School, St Kitts; Mount Pleasant, Highgate, Birmingham
**Qualifications:** 4 O-levels
**Career outside cricket:** Landscape gardener, store manager
**Overseas teams played for:** Prahran, Melbourne 1992-93
**Overseas tours:** England to Australia 1994-95
**Cricketers particularly admired:** Imran Khan, Viv Richards, Malcolm Marshall
**Other sports followed:** Rugby, squash, football
**Relaxations:** Music, going to the cinema, reading
**Extras:** Released by Warwickshire at the end of the 1991 season and signed up by Surrey for 1992. Enjoyed his best batting and bowling performances of 1992 on the same day at Guildford. Surrey Player of the Year in 1993
**Opinions on cricket:** 'The four-day game has been very beneficial to county cricket. It helps batters and bowlers to achieve individual milestones and gives players more time to recover after the game.'
**Best batting:** 49 Surrey v Essex, The Oval 1995
**Best bowling:** 6-19 Surrey v Nottinghamshire, The Oval 1993

## 1995 Season

|  | M | Inns | NO | Runs | HS | Avge | 100s | 50s | Ct | St | O | M | Runs | Wkts | Avge | Best | 5wl | 10wM |
|---|---|---|---|---|---|---|---|---|---|---|---|---|---|---|---|---|---|---|
| Test |  |  |  |  |  |  |  |  |  |  |  |  |  |  |  |  |  |  |
| All First | 12 | 18 | 4 | 174 | 49 | 12.42 | - | - | 1 | - | 420.4 | 85 | 1326 | 53 | 25.01 | 5-37 | 3 |  |
| 1-day Int |  |  |  |  |  |  |  |  |  |  |  |  |  |  |  |  |  |  |
| NatWest | 2 | 1 | 0 | 7 | 7 | 7.00 | - | - | - | - | 24 | 7 | 67 | 6 | 11.16 | 4-20 | - |  |
| B & H | 3 | 0 | 0 | 0 | 0 | - | - | - | 1 | - | 31 | 6 | 97 | 4 | 24.25 | 4-27 | - |  |
| Sunday | 8 | 4 | 1 | 19 | 13 | 6.33 | - | - | - | - | 64 | 2 | 328 | 9 | 36.44 | 3-51 | - |  |

## Career Performances

|  | M | Inns | NO | Runs | HS | Avge | 100s | 50s | Ct | St | Balls | Runs | Wkts | Avge | Best | 5wl | 10wM |
|---|---|---|---|---|---|---|---|---|---|---|---|---|---|---|---|---|---|
| Test | 1 | 1 | 0 | 0 | 0 | 0.00 | - | - | - | - | 168 | 80 | 4 | 20.00 | 4-42 | - | - |
| All First | 92 | 105 | 28 | 802 | 49 | 10.41 | - | - | 22 | - | 17902 | 8908 | 312 | 28.55 | 6-19 | 16 | 1 |
| 1-day Int | 2 | 1 | 0 | 0 | 0 | 0.00 | - | - | - | - | 72 | 47 | 1 | 47.00 | 1-22 | - |  |
| NatWest | 14 | 7 | 3 | 60 | 25 | 15.00 | - | - | 2 | - | 837 | 493 | 15 | 32.86 | 4-20 | - |  |
| B & H | 17 | 3 | 2 | 24 | 20 | 24.00 | - | - | 6 | - | 1050 | 658 | 20 | 32.90 | 4-27 | - |  |
| Sunday | 66 | 30 | 13 | 172 | 24 | 10.11 | - | - | 12 | - | 2967 | 2252 | 65 | 34.64 | 4-44 | - |  |

8. Who topped England's first-class batting averages in South Africa in 1995-96?

# BENJAMIN, W. K. M.                    Hampshire

**Name:** Winston Keithroy Matthew Benjamin
**Role:** Right-hand bat, right-arm fast bowler
**Born:** 31 December 1964, St John's, Antigua
**Height:** 6ft 3in
**County debut:** 1986 (Leicestershire),
1994 (Hampshire)
**County cap:** 1989 (Leicestershire)
**Test debut:** 1987-88
**Tests:** 21
**One-Day Internationals:** 84
**50 wickets in a season:** 1
**1st-Class 50s:** 21
**1st-Class 100s:** 1
**1st-Class 5 w. in innings:** 23
**1st-Class 10 w. in match:** 2
**1st-Class catches:** 92
**One-Day 5 w. in innings:** 4
**Strike rate:** (career 56.29)
**Education:** All Saints School, Antigua
**Overseas teams played for:** Leeward Islands 1985-95
**Overseas tours:** West Indies to Australia 1986-87, to Pakistan 1986-87, to India 1987-88, to Sharjah 1988, to England 1988, to Australia 1988-89, to Sharjah 1991, to Australia and New Zealand 1992-93, to Sharjah, India (Hero Cup) and Sri Lanka 1993-94, to England 1995
**Extras:** Signed for Hampshire in 1994 after seven years at Leicestershire. During net practice in 1994 he smashed a ball through the rear window of a Hampshire committee member's Porsche!
**Best batting:** 101* Leicestershire v Derbyshire, Leicester 1992
**Best bowling:** 7-54 Leicestershire v Australia, Leicester 1992

## 1995 Season

|         | M | Inns | NO | Runs | HS | Avge | 100s | 50s | Ct | St | O | M | Runs | Wkts | Avge | Best | 5wI | 10wM |
|---------|---|------|----|------|----|------|------|-----|----|----|----|----|------|------|------|------|-----|------|
| Test    |   |      |    |      |    |      |      |     |    |    |    |    |      |      |      |      |     |      |
| All First | 3 | 2 | 0 | 11 | 7 | 5.50 | - | - | 1 | - | 33 | 10 | 73 | 1 | 73.00 | 1-10 | - | - |
| 1-day Int | 3 | 2 | 0 | 23 | 17 | 11.50 | - | - | - | - | 28.4 | 1 | 138 | 4 | 34.50 | 2-61 | - |   |
| NatWest |   |      |    |      |    |      |      |     |    |    |    |    |      |      |      |      |     |      |
| B & H   |   |      |    |      |    |      |      |     |    |    |    |    |      |      |      |      |     |      |
| Sunday  |   |      |    |      |    |      |      |     |    |    |    |    |      |      |      |      |     |      |

## Career Performances

| | M | Inns | NO | Runs | HS | Avge | 100s | 50s | Ct | St | Balls | Runs | Wkts | Avge | Best | 5wI | 10wM |
|---|---|---|---|---|---|---|---|---|---|---|---|---|---|---|---|---|---|
| Test | 21 | 26 | 1 | 470 | 85 | 18.80 | - | 2 | 12 | - | 3694 | 1648 | 61 | 27.01 | 4-46 | - | - |
| All First | 169 | 209 | 36 | 3845 | 101 * | 22.22 | 1 | 21 | 92 | - | 26460 | 12157 | 470 | 25.86 | 7-54 | 23 | 2 |
| 1-day Int | 84 | 52 | 12 | 298 | 31 | 7.45 | - | - | 16 | - | 4394 | 3067 | 97 | 31.61 | 5-22 | 1 | |
| NatWest | 16 | 12 | 2 | 76 | 24 * | 7.60 | - | - | 4 | - | 1011 | 528 | 22 | 24.00 | 5-32 | 1 | |
| B & H | 19 | 13 | 3 | 188 | 45 | 18.80 | - | - | 3 | - | 1115 | 645 | 31 | 20.80 | 5-17 | 2 | |
| Sunday | 58 | 42 | 8 | 385 | 55 | 11.32 | - | 1 | 9 | - | 2532 | 1753 | 66 | 26.56 | 4-19 | - | |

# BENSON, M. R.                  Kent

**Name:** Mark Richard Benson
**Role:** Left-hand bat, off-spin bowler,
county captain
**Born:** 6 July 1958, Shoreham, Sussex
**Height:** 5ft 10in **Weight:** 12st 7lbs
**Nickname:** Benny, Beefy
**County debut:** 1980
**County cap:** 1981
**Benefit:** 1991 (£174,619)
**Test debut:** 1986
**Tests:** 1
**One-Day Internationals:** 1
**1000 runs in a season:** 11
**1st-Class 50s:** 99
**1st-Class 100s:** 48
**1st-Class 200s:** 1
**1st-Class catches:** 140
**One-Day 100s:** 5
**Place in batting averages:** 108th av. 33.42
(1994 144th av. 27.29)
**Parents:** Frank and Judy
**Wife and date of marriage:** Sarah, 20 September 1986
**Children:** Laurence Mark Edward, 16 October 1987; Edward 23 June 1990
**Family links with cricket:** Father played for Ghana; sister Tina is marketing manager
for Kent CCC
**Education:** Sutton Valence School
**Qualifications:** O and A-levels and 1 S-level, qualified tennis coach
**Cricketers particularly admired:**
Malcolm Marshall, Jimmy Cook, Chris Tavaré
**Other sports followed:** Golf, football (Charlton FC)
**Injuries:** Broken finger, out for six weeks

**Extras:** Scored 1000 runs in first full season. Record for most runs in career and season at Sutton Valence School. Appointed Kent captain at end of 1990 season. Captained England in two one-day matches against Holland in 1993
**Best batting:** 257 Kent v Hampshire, Southampton 1991
**Best bowling:** 2-55 Kent v Surrey, Dartford 1986

## 1995 Season

|           | M  | Inns | NO | Runs | HS  | Avge  | 100s | 50s | Ct | St | O | M | Runs | Wkts | Avge | Best | 5wI | 10wM |
|-----------|----|------|----|------|-----|-------|------|-----|----|----|---|---|------|------|------|------|-----|------|
| Test      |    |      |    |      |     |       |      |     |    |    |   |   |      |      |      |      |     |      |
| All First | 13 | 21   | 0  | 702  | 192 | 33.42 | 2    | 1   | 4  | -  |   |   |      |      |      |      |     |      |
| 1-day Int |    |      |    |      |     |       |      |     |    |    |   |   |      |      |      |      |     |      |
| NatWest   |    |      |    |      |     |       |      |     |    |    |   |   |      |      |      |      |     |      |
| B & H     | 6  | 6    | 1  | 401  | 119 | 80.20 | 1    | 3   | 3  | -  |   |   |      |      |      |      |     |      |
| Sunday    | 9  | 9    | 0  | 255  | 92  | 28.33 | -    | 2   | 2  | -  |   |   |      |      |      |      |     |      |

## Career Performances

|           | M   | Inns | NO | Runs  | HS    | Avge  | 100s | 50s | Ct  | St | Balls | Runs | Wkts | Avge  | Best | 5wI | 10wM |
|-----------|-----|------|----|-------|-------|-------|------|-----|-----|----|-------|------|------|-------|------|-----|------|
| Test      | 1   | 2    | 0  | 51    | 30    | 25.50 | -    | -   | -   | -  |       |      |      |       |      |     |      |
| All First | 292 | 491  | 34 | 18387 | 257   | 40.23 | 48   | 99  | 140 | -  | 467   | 493  | 5    | 98.60 | 2-55 | -   | -    |
| 1-day Int | 1   | 1    | 0  | 24    | 24    | 24.00 | -    | -   | -   | -  |       |      |      |       |      |     |      |
| NatWest   | 35  | 35   | 1  | 1136  | 113 * | 33.41 | 1    | 8   | 11  | -  |       |      |      |       |      |     |      |
| B & H     | 65  | 64   | 7  | 2450  | 119   | 42.98 | 4    | 17  | 12  | -  |       |      |      |       |      |     |      |
| Sunday    | 164 | 154  | 2  | 4214  | 97    | 27.72 | -    | 28  | 45  | -  |       |      |      |       |      |     |      |

# BETTS, M. M.                                    Durham

**Name:** Melvyn Morris Betts
**Role:** Right-hand bat, right-arm medium-fast bowler
**Born:** 26 March 1975, Durham
**Height:** 5ft 11in **Weight:** 12st 2lbs
**Nickname:** Betsy, Alpha
**County debut:** 1993
**1st-Class catches:** 2
**Place in bowling averages:** 145th av. 50.17
**Strike rate:** 68.76 (career 66.94)
**Parents:** Melvyn and Shirley
**Marital status:** Engaged
**Family links with cricket:** Father and uncle played for local club, Sacriston
**Education:** Fyndoune Comprehensive
**Qualifications:** 9 GCSEs, plus qualifications in engineering and sports and recreational studies

**Overseas tours:** England U19 to Sri Lanka 1993-94

**Other sports followed:** Football (Newcastle United FC)

**Injuries:** Achilles, missed six weeks

**Relaxations:** Football

**Extras:** Played for England U19 in home series against India in 1994

**Opinions on cricket:** 'I think that it is getting harder for bowlers due to the reduction in the seam on the cricket ball and now the one-bouncer-per-over rule.'

**Best batting:** 14 Durham v Yorkshire, Harrogate 1995

**Best bowling:** 3-35 Durham v Hampshire, Stockton 1995

## 1995 Season

| | M | Inns | NO | Runs | HS | Avge | 100s | 50s | Ct | St | O | M | Runs | Wkts | Avge | Best | 5wI | 10wM |
|---|---|---|---|---|---|---|---|---|---|---|---|---|---|---|---|---|---|---|
| Test | | | | | | | | | | | | | | | | | | |
| All First | 9 | 15 | 5 | 55 | 14 | 5.50 | - | - | 2 | - | 194.5 | 31 | 853 | 17 | 50.17 | 3-35 | - | - |
| 1-day Int | | | | | | | | | | | | | | | | | | |
| NatWest | 1 | 1 | 0 | 9 | 9 | 9.00 | - | - | - | - | 12 | 0 | 47 | 1 | 47.00 | 1-47 | - | |
| B & H | | | | | | | | | | | | | | | | | | |
| Sunday | 9 | 4 | 4 | 33 | 14 * | - | - | - | 1 | - | 64.1 | 2 | 302 | 11 | 27.45 | 3-39 | - | |

## Career Performances

| | M | Inns | NO | Runs | HS | Avge | 100s | 50s | Ct | St | Balls | Runs | Wkts | Avge | Best | 5wI | 10wM |
|---|---|---|---|---|---|---|---|---|---|---|---|---|---|---|---|---|---|
| Test | | | | | | | | | | | | | | | | | |
| All First | 10 | 17 | 6 | 59 | 14 | 5.36 | - | - | 2 | - | 1205 | 872 | 18 | 48.44 | 3-35 | - | - |
| 1-day Int | | | | | | | | | | | | | | | | | |
| NatWest | 1 | 1 | 0 | 9 | 9 | 9.00 | - | - | - | - | 72 | 47 | 1 | 47.00 | 1-47 | - | |
| B & H | | | | | | | | | | | | | | | | | |
| Sunday | 9 | 4 | 4 | 33 | 14 * | - | - | - | 1 | - | 385 | 302 | 11 | 27.45 | 3-39 | - | |

---

9. Who was top of England's Test match bowling averages in South Africa in 1995-96?

---

# BEVAN, M. G. — Yorkshire

**Name:** Michael Gwyl Bevan
**Role:** Left-hand bat, slow left-arm bowler, county vice-captain
**Born:** 8 May 1970, Canberra, Australia
**County debut:** 1995
**Test debut:** 1994-95
**Tests:** 6
**One-day Internationals:** 15
**1000 runs in season:** 1
**1st-Class 50s:** 32
**1st-Class 100s:** 22
**1st-Class 200s:** 1
**1st-Class catches:** 52
**Place in batting averages:** 13th av. 55.10
**Strike rate:** (career 131.81)
**Marital status:** Single
**Education:** Australian Cricket Academy
**Off-season:** Playing for New South Wales and Australia

**Overseas teams played for:** South Australia 1989-90, New South Wales 1990-95
**Overseas tours:** Australia to Sharjah 1994, to Pakistan 1994-95, to India and Pakistan (World Cup) 1995-96
**Extras:** In 1990-91 he became the first player to score a century in five successive Sheffield Shield matches. Made 82 on his Test debut against Pakistan in Karachi, 1994-95. Played for Rawtenstall in the Lancashire League in 1993 and 1994. Appointed Yorkshire's vice-captain for 1996
**Best batting:** 203* New South Wales v Western Australia, Sydney 1993-94
**Best bowling:** 3-6 New South Wales v Wellington, North Sydney 1990-91

## 1995 Season

|  | M | Inns | NO | Runs | HS | Avge | 100s | 50s | Ct | St | O | M | Runs | Wkts | Avge | Best | 5wI | 10wM |
|---|---|---|---|---|---|---|---|---|---|---|---|---|---|---|---|---|---|---|
| Test |  |  |  |  |  |  |  |  |  |  |  |  |  |  |  |  |  |  |
| All First | 20 | 34 | 5 | 1598 | 153 * | 55.10 | 6 | 7 | 18 | - | 99 | 24 | 351 | 6 | 58.50 | 3-55 | - | - |
| 1-day Int |  |  |  |  |  |  |  |  |  |  |  |  |  |  |  |  |  |  |
| NatWest | 4 | 4 | 2 | 166 | 91 * | 83.00 | - | 2 | - | - | 9 | 0 | 42 | 1 | 42.00 | 1-14 | - |  |
| B & H | 4 | 3 | 1 | 147 | 83 * | 73.50 | - | 2 | 1 | - |  |  |  |  |  |  |  |  |
| Sunday | 17 | 16 | 3 | 704 | 103 * | 54.15 | 2 | 5 | 5 | - | 43.1 | 0 | 234 | 12 | 19.50 | 3-21 | - |  |

## Career Performances

|          | M  | Inns | NO | Runs | HS    | Avge  | 100s | 50s | Ct | St | Balls | Runs | Wkts | Avge  | Best | 5wI | 10wM |
|----------|----|------|----|------|-------|-------|------|-----|----|----|-------|------|------|-------|------|-----|------|
| Test     | 6  | 10   | 0  | 324  | 91    | 32.40 | -    | 3   | 5  | -  | 90    | 67   | 1    | 67.00 | 1-21 | -   | -    |
| All First| 88 | 150  | 23 | 6486 | 203 * | 51.07 | 22   | 32  | 52 | -  | 2109  | 1198 | 16   | 74.87 | 3-6  | -   | -    |
| 1-day Int| 15 | 13   | 5  | 432  | 53 *  | 54.00 | -    | 1   | 6  | -  | 12    | 17   | 0    | -     |      | -   |      |
| NatWest  | 4  | 4    | 2  | 166  | 91 *  | 83.00 | -    | 2   | -  | -  | 54    | 42   | 1    | 42.00 | 1-14 | -   |      |
| B & H    | 4  | 3    | 1  | 147  | 83 *  | 73.50 | -    | 2   | 1  | -  |       |      |      |       |      |     |      |
| Sunday   | 17 | 16   | 3  | 704  | 103 * | 54.15 | 2    | 5   | 5  | -  | 259   | 234  | 12   | 19.50 | 3-21 | -   |      |

# BICKNELL, D. J. Surrey

**Name:** Darren John Bicknell
**Role:** Left-hand opening bat, slow left-arm
**Born:** 24 June 1967, Guildford
**Height:** 6ft 4in **Weight:** 14st
**Nickname:** Denzil
**County debut:** 1987
**County cap:** 1990
**1000 runs in a season:** 6
**1st-Class 50s:** 55
**1st-Class 100s:** 26
**1st-Class 200s:** 2
**1st-Class catches:** 65
**One-Day 100s:** 7
**Place in batting averages:**
71st av. 39.88 (1994 15th av. 52.07)
**Strike rate:** (career 69.00)
**Parents:** Vic and Valerie
**Wife and date of marriage:** Rebecca,
26 September 1992
**Children:** Lauren Elizabeth, 21 October 1993
**Family links with cricket:** 'Brother Martin plays a bit (I mean only a bit)'
**Education:** Robert Haining County Secondary; Guildford County College of
Technology
**Qualifications:** 8 O-levels, 2 A-levels, senior coaching award
**Career outside cricket:** Marketing executive
**Off-season:** 'Working for Courage Ltd.'
**Overseas tours:** Surrey to Sharjah 1988, 1989, to Dubai 1990, to Perth 1995; England
A to Zimbabwe and Kenya 1989-90, to Pakistan 1990-91, to Bermuda and West Indies
1991-92
**Overseas teams played for:** Coburg, Melbourne 1986-87
**Cricketers particularly admired:** Mark Taylor, Michael Atherton, Michael Slater

**Other sports followed:** Football ('follow West Ham United'), golf

**Relaxations:** Golf, decorating my new home and spending time with my family

**Extras:** Shared county record third-wicket stand of 413 with David Ward v Kent at Canterbury in 1990 – both made career bests. Surrey batsman of the year four times. Hit the fastest hundred of the year in 1990

**Opinions on cricket:** 'Sunday League should not be played during championship games.'

**Best batting:** 235* Surrey v Nottinghamshire, Trent Bridge 1994

**Best bowling:** 3-88 Surrey v Kent, Canterbury 1995

## 1995 Season

|  | M | Inns | NO | Runs | HS | Avge | 100s | 50s | Ct | St | O | M | Runs | Wkts | Avge | Best | 5wI | 10wM |
|---|---|---|---|---|---|---|---|---|---|---|---|---|---|---|---|---|---|---|
| Test |  |  |  |  |  |  |  |  |  |  |  |  |  |  |  |  |  |  |
| All First | 15 | 28 | 3 | 997 | 228 * | 39.88 | 2 | 4 | 5 | - | 24.3 | 5 | 96 | 3 | 32.00 | 3-88 | - | - |
| 1-day Int |  |  |  |  |  |  |  |  |  |  |  |  |  |  |  |  |  |  |
| NatWest | 2 | 2 | 1 | 129 | 77 | 129.00 | - | 2 | - | - |  |  |  |  |  |  |  |  |
| B & H | 4 | 4 | 1 | 105 | 81 * | 35.00 | - | 1 | 2 | - |  |  |  |  |  |  |  |  |
| Sunday | 13 | 13 | 1 | 545 | 102 * | 45.41 | 1 | 4 | 4 | - | 6 | 0 | 39 | 2 | 19.50 | 1-11 | - |  |

## Career Performances

|  | M | Inns | NO | Runs | HS | Avge | 100s | 50s | Ct | St | Balls | Runs | Wkts | Avge | Best | 5wI | 10wM |
|---|---|---|---|---|---|---|---|---|---|---|---|---|---|---|---|---|---|
| Test |  |  |  |  |  |  |  |  |  |  |  |  |  |  |  |  |  |
| All First | 174 | 306 | 31 | 11133 | 235 * | 40.48 | 26 | 55 | 65 | - | 414 | 383 | 6 | 63.83 | 3-88 | - | - |
| 1-day Int |  |  |  |  |  |  |  |  |  |  |  |  |  |  |  |  |  |
| NatWest | 18 | 18 | 4 | 725 | 135 * | 51.78 | 1 | 5 | 1 | - |  |  |  |  |  |  |  |
| B & H | 28 | 28 | 2 | 1133 | 119 | 43.57 | 2 | 9 | 8 | - |  |  |  |  |  |  |  |
| Sunday | 80 | 77 | 9 | 2556 | 125 | 37.58 | 4 | 15 | 17 | - | 36 | 39 | 2 | 19.50 | 1-11 | - |  |

# BICKNELL, M. P.                    Surrey

**Name:** Martin Paul Bicknell

**Role:** Right-hand bat, right-arm fast-medium bowler

**Born:** 14 January 1969, Guildford

**Height:** 6ft 4in **Weight:** 14st 7lbs

**Nickname:** Bickers

**County debut:** 1986

**County cap:** 1989

**Test debut:** 1993

**Tests:** 2

**One-Day Internationals:** 7

**50 wickets in a season:** 5
**1st-Class 50s:** 7
**1st-Class 5 w. in innings:** 23
**1st-Class 10 w. in match:** 2
**1st-Class catches:** 53
**Place in batting averages:** 172nd av. 23.66
(1994 235th av. 15.55)
**Place in bowling averages:**
26th av. 23.85 (88th av. 33.68)
**Strike rate:** 41.70 (career 55.12)
**Parents:** Vic and Valerie
**Wife and date of marriage:**
Loraine, 29 September 1995
**Children:** Eleanor, 31 March 1995
**Family links with cricket:** 'Brother plays,
but with no luck'
**Education:** Robert Haining County
Secondary

**Qualifications:** 2 O-levels, NCA coach
**Career outside cricket:** Amateur golfer
**Off-season:** Playing golf and training
**Overseas tours:** England YC to Sri Lanka 1986-87, to Australia 1987-88; England A
to Zimbabwe and Kenya 1989-90, to Bermuda and West Indies 1991-92, to South
Africa 1993-94; England to Australia 1990-91
**Cricketers particularly admired:** Ian Botham
**Other sports followed:** 'Leeds United and golf'
**Injuries:** Hamstring, out for six weeks. Calf strain, missed one week
**Relaxations:** Playing golf and spending time with the family
**Extras:** Youngest player to play for Surrey since David Smith. His figures of 9 for 45
were the best for the county for 30 years. One of four players on stand-by as reserves for
England's World Cup squad 1991-92. Supporters' Player of the Year 1993. Had to return
home early from England A tour to South Africa through injury
**Opinions on cricket:** 'Stop knocking our players! New ball at 85 overs.'
**Best batting:** 88 Surrey v Hampshire, Southampton 1992
**Best bowling:** 9-45 Surrey v Cambridge University, Fenner's 1988

---

## 1995 Season

| | M | Inns | NO | Runs | HS | Avge | 100s | 50s | Ct | St | O | M | Runs | Wkts | Avge | Best | 5wI | 10wM |
|---|---|---|---|---|---|---|---|---|---|---|---|---|---|---|---|---|---|---|
| Test | | | | | | | | | | | | | | | | | | |
| All First | 9 | 12 | 3 | 213 | 61 | 23.66 | - | 1 | 1 | - | 285 | 65 | 978 | 41 | 23.85 | 5-61 | 3 | - |
| 1-day Int | | | | | | | | | | | | | | | | | | |
| NatWest | | | | | | | | | | | | | | | | | | |
| B & H | 3 | 1 | 0 | 43 | 43 | 43.00 | - | - | - | - | 29 | 5 | 103 | 3 | 34.33 | 1-14 | - | |
| Sunday | 11 | 7 | 2 | 86 | 25 | 17.20 | - | - | - | - | 74 | 1 | 349 | 8 | 43.62 | 3-43 | - | |

## Career Performances

| | M | Inns | NO | Runs | HS | Avge | 100s | 50s | Ct | St | Balls | Runs | Wkts | Avge | Best | 5wl | 10wM |
|---|---|---|---|---|---|---|---|---|---|---|---|---|---|---|---|---|---|
| Test | 2 | 4 | 0 | 26 | 14 | 6.50 | - | - | - | - | 522 | 263 | 4 | 65.75 | 3-99 | - | - |
| All First | 150 | 177 | 48 | 2341 | 88 | 18.14 | - | 7 | 53 | - | 28666 | 13598 | 520 | 26.15 | 9-45 | 23 | 2 |
| 1-day Int | 7 | 6 | 2 | 96 | 31 * | 24.00 | - | - | 2 | - | 413 | 347 | 13 | 26.69 | 3-55 | - | |
| NatWest | 23 | 12 | 5 | 102 | 66 * | 14.57 | - | 1 | 10 | - | 1455 | 816 | 31 | 26.32 | 4-35 | - | |
| B & H | 31 | 18 | 3 | 160 | 43 | 10.66 | - | - | 8 | - | 1866 | 1178 | 48 | 24.54 | 4-49 | - | |
| Sunday | 107 | 45 | 20 | 331 | 25 | 13.24 | - | - | 26 | - | 4627 | 3276 | 126 | 26.00 | 5-12 | 1 | |

# BIRBECK, S. D. Durham

**Name:** Shaun David Birbeck
**Role:** Left-hand bat, right-arm
medium bowler
**Born:** 26 July 1972, Sunderland
**Height:** 5ft 11in **Weight:** 14st
**Nickname:** Birbs
**County debut:** 1994
**1st-Class 50s:** 1
**1st-Class catches:** 2
**Strike rate:** (career 71.00)
**Parents:** James and Joyce
**Marital status:** Single
**Family links with cricket:**
Brother Tony played Minor Counties
cricket for Durham
**Education:** Hetton Comprehensive
**Qualifications:** GCSEs
**Off-season:** 'Working in some boring
factory or going to Australia'

**Overseas teams played for:** Scarborough, Perth, Western Australia 1992-94
**Cricketers particularly admired:** Jimmy Adams, Jimmy Daley, Stuart Hutton, Justin
Langer, Barrie Welch, David Ligertwood, Lee Welch, Darren Blenkiron
**Other sports followed:** Football (Sunderland), golf, tennis, ice hockey (Durham
Wasps)
**Relaxations:** Reading and listening to music
**Extras:** Once ran in the Great North Run. First person to get a hat-trick in Rapid
Cricketline Championship for Durham
**Opinions on cricket:** 'Cricket is a great game so why change it?'
**Best batting:** 75* Durham v Derbyshire, Chester-le-Street 1995
**Best bowling:** 3-119 Durham v Surrey, The Oval 1995

## 1995 Season

| | M | Inns | NO | Runs | HS | Avge | 100s | 50s | Ct | St | O | M | Runs | Wkts | Avge | Best | 5wl | 10wM |
|---|---|---|---|---|---|---|---|---|---|---|---|---|---|---|---|---|---|---|
| Test | | | | | | | | | | | | | | | | | | |
| All First | 4 | 6 | 2 | 106 | 75 * | 26.50 | - | 1 | 1 | - | 64 | 8 | 271 | 4 | 67.75 | 3-119 | - | - |
| 1-day Int | | | | | | | | | | | | | | | | | | |
| NatWest | 1 | 0 | 0 | 0 | 0 | - | - | - | - | - | 8 | 0 | 27 | 2 | 13.50 | 2-27 | - | |
| B & H | 2 | 1 | 0 | 1 | 1 | 1.00 | - | - | 1 | - | 11 | 0 | 64 | 3 | 21.33 | 3-64 | - | |
| Sunday | 5 | 4 | 0 | 48 | 23 | 12.00 | - | - | - | - | 25 | 2 | 109 | 3 | 36.33 | 1-14 | | |

## Career Performances

| | M | Inns | NO | Runs | HS | Avge | 100s | 50s | Ct | St | Balls | Runs | Wkts | Avge | Best | 5wl | 10wM |
|---|---|---|---|---|---|---|---|---|---|---|---|---|---|---|---|---|---|
| Test | | | | | | | | | | | | | | | | | |
| All First | 5 | 7 | 2 | 112 | 75 * | 22.40 | - | 1 | 2 | - | 426 | 284 | 6 | 47.33 | 3-119 | - | - |
| 1-day Int | | | | | | | | | | | | | | | | | |
| NatWest | 1 | 0 | 0 | 0 | 0 | - | - | - | - | - | 48 | 27 | 2 | 13.50 | 2-27 | - | |
| B & H | 2 | 1 | 0 | 1 | 1 | 1.00 | - | - | 1 | - | 66 | 64 | 3 | 21.33 | 3-64 | - | |
| Sunday | 10 | 6 | 0 | 57 | 23 | 9.50 | - | - | 1 | - | 306 | 275 | 4 | 68.75 | 1-14 | - | |

# BLAKEY, R. J.                                    Yorkshire

**Name:** Richard John Blakey
**Role:** Right-hand bat, wicket-keeper
**Born:** 15 January 1967, Huddersfield
**Height:** 5ft 10in **Weight:** 11st 4lbs
**Nickname:** Dick
**County debut:** 1985
**County cap:** 1987
**Test debut:** 1992-93
**Tests:** 2
**One-Day Internationals:** 3
**1000 runs in a season:** 4
**1st-Class 50s:** 56
**1st-Class 100s:** 9
**1st-Class 200s:** 2
**1st-Class catches:** 420
**1st-Class stumpings:** 38
**One-Day 100s:** 3
**Place in batting averages:** 231st av. 17.30
(1994 32nd av. 45.77)
**Parents:** Brian and Pauline
**Wife and date of marriage:** Michelle, 28 September 1991
**Children:** Harrison Brad, 22 September 1993

**Family links with cricket:** Father played local cricket
**Education:** Woodhouse Primary; Rastrick Grammar School
**Qualifications:** 4 O-levels, Senior NCA Coach
**Career outside cricket:** Started own leisure company
**Overseas tours:** England YC to West Indies 1984-85; Yorkshire to Barbados 1986-87, to Cape Town 1990-91; England A to Zimbabwe and Kenya 1989-90, to Pakistan 1990-91; England to India and Sri Lanka 1992-93
**Overseas teams played for:** Waverley, Sydney 1985-87; Mt Waverley, Sydney 1987-88; Bionics, Zimbabwe 1989-90
**Cricketers particularly admired:** Martyn Moxon, Dermot Reeve, Ian Botham, Alan Knott
**Other sports followed:** All
**Relaxations:** All sports, particularly golf and squash, eating out, drawing, photography
**Extras:** Established himself in Huddersfield League. Made record 2nd XI score – 273* v Northamptonshire 1986. Yorkshire's Young Player of the Year 1989. Made Test debut in second Test against India at Madras, February 1993. He was awarded a citation by the International Committee for Fair Play. He was the only cricketer among the 25 winners worldwide
**Opinions on cricket:** 'Four-day game is much more enjoyable and the best team wins. National anthem should be played before the start of every international, like football.'
**Best batting:** 221 England A v Zimbabwe, Bulawayo 1989-90
**Best bowling:** 1-68 Yorkshire v Nottinghamshire, Sheffield 1986

## 1995 Season

|            | M  | Inns | NO | Runs | HS   | Avge  | 100s | 50s | Ct | St | O | M | Runs | Wkts | Avge | Best | 5wI | 10wM |
|------------|----|------|----|------|------|-------|------|-----|----|----|---|---|------|------|------|------|-----|------|
| Test       |    |      |    |      |      |       |      |     |    |    |   |   |      |      |      |      |     |      |
| All First  | 20 | 29   | 6  | 398  | 77 * | 17.30 | -    | 1   | 59 | 4  |   |   |      |      |      |      |     |      |
| 1-day Int  |    |      |    |      |      |       |      |     |    |    |   |   |      |      |      |      |     |      |
| NatWest    | 3  | 2    | 0  | 40   | 39   | 20.00 | -    | -   | 4  | 1  |   |   |      |      |      |      |     |      |
| B & H      | 4  | 3    | 1  | 38   | 19 * | 19.00 | -    | -   | 4  | 1  |   |   |      |      |      |      |     |      |
| Sunday     | 17 | 11   | 3  | 276  | 61   | 34.50 | -    | 2   | 15 | 3  |   |   |      |      |      |      |     |      |

## Career Performances

|            | M   | Inns | NO | Runs | HS    | Avge  | 100s | 50s | Ct  | St | Balls | Runs | Wkts | Avge  | Best | 5wI | 10wM |
|------------|-----|------|----|------|-------|-------|------|-----|-----|----|-------|------|------|-------|------|-----|------|
| Test       | 2   | 4    | 0  | 7    | 6     | 1.75  | -    | -   | 2   | -  |       |      |      |       |      |     |      |
| All First  | 219 | 356  | 53 | 9805 | 221   | 32.35 | 9    | 56  | 420 | 38 | 63    | 68   | 1    | 68.00 | 1-68 | -   | -    |
| 1-day Int  | 3   | 2    | 0  | 25   | 25    | 12.50 | -    | -   | 2   | 1  |       |      |      |       |      |     |      |
| NatWest    | 20  | 15   | 2  | 316  | 75    | 24.30 | -    | 2   | 24  | 2  |       |      |      |       |      |     |      |
| B & H      | 34  | 30   | 4  | 733  | 79    | 28.19 | -    | 5   | 30  | 1  |       |      |      |       |      |     |      |
| Sunday     | 117 | 107  | 19 | 3531 | 130 * | 40.12 | 3    | 22  | 90  | 16 |       |      |      |       |      |     |      |

# BLANCHETT, I. N.

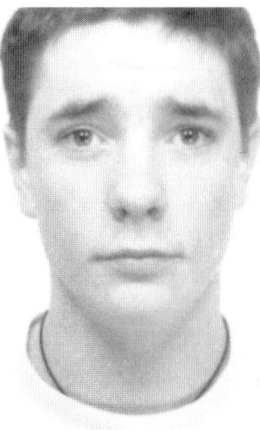

**Name:** Ian Neale Blanchett
**Role:** Right-hand bat, right-arm
fast-medium bowler
**Born:** 2 February 1975, Melbourne, Australia
**Height:** 6ft 4in  **Weight:** 14st 7lbs
**Nickname:** Blanchy, Noisy, Ozzy, Terry
('from Viz!')
**County debut:** No first-team appearance
**Parents:** Edward Arthur Blanchett and Susan
Anne Billons
**Marital status:** Single
**Family links with cricket:** 'Uncle played for
Surrey U19. None other that I know of'
**Education:** Feltwell Primary, Norfolk;
Methwold High School, Norfolk; Downham
Market High School; Luton University
**Qualifications:** 8 GCSEs, 2 A-levels, 'in
process of completing a Health
Science/Leisure degree
**Off-season:** 'Continuing my degree at Luton University'
**Cricketers particularly admired:** Richard Hadlee, Ian Botham, Allan Donald,
Graeme Hick
**Other sports followed:** Football (Norwich City), rugby (Bath and England), snooker,
tennis, American football (San Fransisco 49ers)
**Injuries:** Snapped ligaments in right hand, out for ten weeks
**Relaxations:** 'Spending time with friends socialising over a few drinks. Listening to
my favourite tunes. Chilling out on my Grandfather's boat in Marbella, Spain. Deep-
sea diving'
**Extras:** Voted Player of the Year four times successively by his club in Norfolk.
Awarded a special achievement prize in the 1994 NAYC Cambridge Festival
**Opinions on cricket:** 'There could be more invovlement of former Test cricketers in the
coaching, development and selection of the national teams. I also feel that the Sunday
League games should not be played in between Championship games, as the adverse
situation sometimes affects both contests.'

---

10. Which two Pakistan bowlers have taken over 250 Test wickets?

---

# BLENKIRON, D. A.  Durham

**Name:** Darren Andrew Blenkiron
**Role:** Left-hand bat, right-arm
medium bowler
**Born:** 4 February 1974, Solihull
**Height:** 5ft 10in **Weight:** 12st 7lbs
**Nickname:** Blue Dog, Pit Bull
**County debut:** 1991 (one-day),
1994 (first-class)
**1st-Class 50s:** 2
**1st-Class 100s:** 1
**1st-Class catches:** 3
**Place in batting averages:** 146th av. 27.87
**Parents:** William and Margaret
**Marital status:** Single
**Family links with cricket:**
Father played for Warwickshire and MCC
**Education:** Bishop Barrington
Comprehensive School

**Qualifications:** 4 O-Levels
**Off-season:** Playing in South Africa
**Overseas tours:** England U19 to Pakistan 1991-92; Durham CCC to South Africa 1995
**Overseas teams played for:** Alberton, South Africa 1993-95
**Cricketers particularly admired:** Graeme Hick, Phil Bainbridge,
Paul Romaines, my father
**Other sports followed:** Football (Liverpool FC)
**Injuries:** Neck
**Relaxations:** Music, socialising
**Opinions on cricket:** 'Over rate should be reduced, lunches and tea should be extended.'
**Best batting:** 145 Durham v Glamorgan, Swansea 1995
**Best bowling:** 1-10 Durham v Essex, Chelmsford 1995

## 1995 Season

|        | M | Inns | NO | Runs | HS | Avge | 100s | 50s | Ct | St | O | M | Runs | Wkts | Avge | Best | 5wI | 10wM |
|--------|---|------|----|------|----|------|------|-----|----|----|---|---|------|------|------|------|-----|------|
| Test   |   |      |    |      |    |      |      |     |    |    |   |   |      |      |      |      |     |      |
| All First | 9 | 17 | 1 | 446 | 145 | 27.87 | 1 | 2 | 3 | - | 16 | 1 | 64 | 1 | 64.00 | 1-10 | - | - |
| 1-day Int |   |      |    |      |    |      |      |     |    |    |   |   |      |      |      |      |     |      |
| NatWest | 2 | 2 | 1 | 38 | 29 | 38.00 | - | - | 1 | - | 3 | 0 | 14 | 0 | - |  | - | - |
| B & H  |   |      |    |      |    |      |      |     |    |    |   |   |      |      |      |      |     |      |
| Sunday | 9 | 8 | 1 | 131 | 56 | 18.71 | - | 1 | 2 | - | 17 | 0 | 111 | 1 | 111.00 | 1-25 | - | |

## Career Performances

| | M | Inns | NO | Runs | HS | Avge | 100s | 50s | Ct | St | Balls | Runs | Wkts | Avge | Best | 5wl | 10wM |
|---|---|---|---|---|---|---|---|---|---|---|---|---|---|---|---|---|---|
| Test | | | | | | | | | | | | | | | | | |
| All First | 10 | 17 | 1 | 446 | 145 | 27.87 | 1 | 2 | 3 | - | 96 | 64 | 1 | 64.00 | 1-10 | - | - |
| 1-day Int | | | | | | | | | | | | | | | | | |
| NatWest | 3 | 3 | 1 | 94 | 56 | 47.00 | - | 1 | 1 | - | 18 | 14 | 0 | - | | - | - |
| B & H | | | | | | | | | | | | | | | | | |
| Sunday | 11 | 9 | 2 | 170 | 56 | 24.28 | - | 1 | 2 | - | 120 | 136 | 1 | 136.00 | 1-25 | - | |

# BODEN, D. J. P. Gloucestershire

**Name:** David Jonathan Peter Boden
**Role:** Right-hand bat, right-arm fast bowler
**Born:** 26 November 1970, Eccleshall, Staffs
**Height:** 6ft 3in **Weight:** 14st 7lbs
**Nickname:** Bodie, Horse, Congo
**County debut:** 1989 (Middlesex),
1992 (Essex), 1995 (Gloucestershire)
**1st-Class catches:** 2
**Strike rate:** (career 55.92)
**Parents:** Peter and Mary
**Marital status:** Single
**Family links with cricket:** 'Dad is an avid
follower of the game and ferried me
everywhere when I was younger'
**Education:** Stone Alleynes High School;
Stafford College of Further Education
**Qualifications:** 3 CSEs, 6 O-levels, BTEC
National Diploma in Business
Studies, NCA coaching certificate, Senior NCA Coach
**Off-season:** Visiting Australia, playing for Waverley CC, Sydney
**Overseas teams played for:** Waverley, Sydney 1990-95
**Cricketers particularly admired:** Ian Botham, Don Topley
**Other sports followed:** Tiddlywinks, rugby, golf, football (Manchester United FC)
**Injuries:** Ligament muscles in back, missed six weeks
**Relaxations:** Playing golf, listening to music, watching *Pulp Fiction*, relaxing on beach
**Extras:** Staffordshire Wellington Boot Throwing Champion. Signed by Gloucestershire
for 1995 season after spells with both Middlesex and Essex
**Best batting:** 5 Essex v Cambridge University, Fenner's 1992. 5 Essex v Middlesex,
Colchester 1993
**Best bowling:** 4-11 Middlesex v Oxford University, The Parks 1989

## 1995 Season

| | M | Inns | NO | Runs | HS | Avge | 100s | 50s | Ct | St | O | M | Runs | Wkts | Avge | Best | 5wI | 10wM |
|---|---|---|---|---|---|---|---|---|---|---|---|---|---|---|---|---|---|---|
| Test | | | | | | | | | | | | | | | | | | |
| All First | 2 | 1 | 0 | 2 | 2 | 2.00 | - | - | 2 | - | 59.4 | 10 | 187 | 7 | 26.71 | 3-38 | - | - |
| 1-day Int | | | | | | | | | | | | | | | | | | |
| NatWest | 1 | 0 | 0 | 0 | 0 | - | - | - | - | - | 12 | 2 | 26 | 6 | 4.33 | 6-26 | 1 | |
| B & H | | | | | | | | | | | | | | | | | | |
| Sunday | 3 | 3 | 0 | 6 | 5 | 2.00 | - | - | - | - | 18.1 | 3 | 103 | 3 | 34.33 | 3-34 | - | |

## Career Performances

| | M | Inns | NO | Runs | HS | Avge | 100s | 50s | Ct | St | Balls | Runs | Wkts | Avge | Best | 5wI | 10wM |
|---|---|---|---|---|---|---|---|---|---|---|---|---|---|---|---|---|---|
| Test | | | | | | | | | | | | | | | | | |
| All First | 6 | 4 | 0 | 12 | 5 | 3.00 | - | - | 4 | - | 783 | 471 | 14 | 33.64 | 4-11 | - | - |
| 1-day Int | | | | | | | | | | | | | | | | | |
| NatWest | 1 | 0 | 0 | 0 | 0 | - | - | - | - | - | 72 | 26 | 6 | 4.33 | 6-26 | 1 | |
| B & H | | | | | | | | | | | | | | | | | |
| Sunday | 7 | 5 | 0 | 10 | 5 | 2.00 | - | - | 2 | - | 313 | 265 | 7 | 37.85 | 3-34 | - | |

# BOILING, J.                         Durham

**Name:** James Boiling
**Role:** Right-hand bat, right-arm off-spin
bowler, 'wicket-keeper in benefit matches'
**Born:** 8 April 1968, New Delhi
**Height:** 6ft 2in **Weight:** 13st 2lbs
**Nickname:** The Train Spotter
('courtesy of Darren Blenkiron')
**County debut:** 1988 (Surrey),
1995 (Durham)
**1st-Class 50s:** 1
**1st-Class 5 w. in innings:** 4
**1st-Class 10 w. in match:** 1
**1st-Class catches:** 49
**One-Day 5 w. in innings:** 1
**Place in batting averages:** 267th av. 12.48
**Place in bowling averages:** 150th av. 63.03
**Strike rate:** 133.11 (career 101.91)
**Parents:** Graham and Geraldine
**Wife and date of marriage:**
Rachel, 7 October 1995
**Family links with cricket:** 'On family holidays we would all play for hours on the beach. Mother had a useful arm ball when the tide came in'

**Education:** Rutlish School, Merton; Durham University (College of St Hild and Bede)
**Qualifications:** 10 O-levels, 3 A-levels, BA (Hons) in History, NCA Senior Coaching Award. Currently studying Fabric and Textile Design at night school
**Career outside cricket:** 'Cricket is my life'
**Off-season:** 'Enjoying the fresh air of the North East.'
**Overseas tours:** Surrey Schools to Australia 1985-86; England YC to Australia (Youth World Cup) 1987-88; England A to Australia 1992-93
**Overseas teams played for:** Bionics, Harare 1991-92; St Augustine, Cape Town 1992-93
**Cricketers particularly admired:** Mick Kersey
**Other sports followed:** Football (Epsom and Ewell FC), snooker ('I am a big fan of Neal Foulds')
**Injuries:** Fatigue
**Relaxations:** 'Anything that takes my mind off cricket. At the moment I am learning to play bridge and my wife and I enjoy many pleasant evenings around the card table.'
**Extras:** Believed to be the only player to win a Gold Award against his own county, returning 8-3-9-3 analysis for Combined Universities against Surrey in 1989. Late call-up for England A tour to Australia when Ian Salisbury stayed in India. Moved to Durham for 1995 season
**Opinions on cricket:** 'The Andrew Symonds affair reflected badly upon all those involved, apart from the player. The ICC must act quickly to clarify dual nationality rulings, otherwise we could see county cricketers born abroad going to play for the country of their birth e.g. Adrian Dale playing for South Africa, myself for India and Jonathan Longley representing the USA. On the domestic front, it is good to see the Cricketers' Association so positively involved in improving the lot of their members. Congratulations to Warwickshire for maintaining the standards they set last season and providing an example for all teams to aspire to.'
**Best batting:** 69 Durham v West Indies, Chester-le-Street 1995
**Best bowling:** 6-84 Surrey v Gloucestershire, Bristol 1992

## 1995 Season

|            | M  | Inns | NO | Runs | HS   | Avge  | 100s | 50s | Ct | St | O    | M   | Runs | Wkts | Avge  | Best | 5wI | 10wM |
|------------|----|------|----|------|------|-------|------|-----|----|----|------|-----|------|------|-------|------|-----|------|
| Test       |    |      |    |      |      |       |      |     |    |    |      |     |      |      |       |      |     |      |
| All First  | 18 | 32   | 7  | 312  | 69   | 12.48 | -    | 1   | 11 | -  | 599  | 149 | 1702 | 27   | 63.03 | 5-73 | 2   | -    |
| 1-day Int  |    |      |    |      |      |       |      |     |    |    |      |     |      |      |       |      |     |      |
| NatWest    | 1  | 0    | 0  | 0    | 0    | -     | -    | -   | -  | -  | 9.4  | 5   | 22   | 4    | 5.50  | 4-22 | -   |      |
| B & H      | 5  | 4    | 2  | 8    | 5 *  | 4.00  | -    | -   | -  | -  | 32   | 1   | 156  | 2    | 78.00 | 1-6  | -   |      |
| Sunday     | 14 | 7    | 4  | 62   | 21 * | 20.66 | -    | -   | 12 | -  | 72   | 3   | 333  | 6    | 55.50 | 2-22 | -   |      |

> 11. Which county has awarded associate membership to both
> Tony Blair and Bryan Robson?

## Career Performances

|  | M | Inns | NO | Runs | HS | Avge | 100s | 50s | Ct | St | Balls | Runs | Wkts | Avge | Best | 5wI | 10wM |
|---|---|---|---|---|---|---|---|---|---|---|---|---|---|---|---|---|---|
| Test |  |  |  |  |  |  |  |  |  |  |  |  |  |  |  |  |  |
| All First | 63 | 88 | 30 | 747 | 69 | 12.87 | - | 1 | 49 | - | 11211 | 5126 | 110 | 46.60 | 6-84 | 4 | 1 |
| 1-day Int |  |  |  |  |  |  |  |  |  |  |  |  |  |  |  |  |  |
| NatWest | 13 | 5 | 1 | 60 | 24 | 15.00 | - | - | 6 | - | 808 | 411 | 13 | 31.61 | 4-22 | - |  |
| B & H | 30 | 19 | 12 | 66 | 9 * | 9.42 | - | - | 12 | - | 1624 | 1139 | 24 | 47.45 | 3-9 | - |  |
| Sunday | 71 | 31 | 15 | 189 | 23 * | 11.81 | - | - | 30 | - | 2866 | 2213 | 72 | 30.73 | 5-24 | 1 |  |

# BOON, T. J. Leicestershire

**Name:** Timothy James Boon
**Role:** Right-hand bat, right-arm medium
bowler
**Born:** 1 November 1961, Doncaster
**Height:** 6ft  **Weight:** 12st 7lbs
**Nickname:** Boony, Ted
**County debut:** 1980
**County cap:** 1986
**1000 runs in a season:** 7
**1st-Class 50s:** 68
**1st-Class 100s:** 14
**1st-Class catches:** 124
**One-Day 100s:** 3
**Place in batting averages:** 254th av. 14.75
(1994 176th av. 23.30)
**Parents:** Jeffrey and Elizabeth
**Marital status:** Single
**Family links with cricket:** Father played
club cricket

**Education:** Mill Lane Primary; Edlington Comprehensive;
three months at Doncaster Art School; Peter Van School of Business
**Qualifications:** 6 O-levels, 1 A-level, advanced coach
**Career outside cricket:** Selling, owning a fitness studio, renovating property
**Overseas tours:** England YC to West Indies 1980-81; Leicestershire to Zimbabwe
1980-81
**Overseas teams played for:** Old Hararians, Zimbabwe 1980;
Pirates, Pinetown, Natal 1990-91
**Cricketers particularly admired:** 'All those who have made it into international
cricket, all those who have given me assistance (such as Chris Balderstone, Ken Higgs,
Bob Simpson, Jackie Birkenshaw and many more)'
**Other sports followed:** Leicester Tigers (rugby union) and Leicester City FC

**Relaxations:** Keeping fit at the University, following local sport, 'producing zany ideas'
**Extras:** Captain England YC v West Indies 1980 and v India 1981; missed 1985 season due to broken leg sustained in a car crash in South Africa the previous winter. Released at the end of the 1995 season
**Opinions on cricket:** 'More direction should be given to young cricketers off-season by providing assistance with winter/future employment.'
**Best batting:** 144 Leicestershire v Gloucestershire, Leicester 1984
**Best bowling:** 3-40 Leicestershire v Yorkshire, Leicester 1986

## 1995 Season

| | M | Inns | NO | Runs | HS | Avge | 100s | 50s | Ct | St | O | M | Runs | Wkts | Avge | Best | 5wI | 10wM |
|---|---|---|---|---|---|---|---|---|---|---|---|---|---|---|---|---|---|---|
| Test | | | | | | | | | | | | | | | | | | |
| All First | 6 | 12 | 0 | 177 | 38 | 14.75 | - | - | 5 | - | | | | | | | | |
| 1-day Int | | | | | | | | | | | | | | | | | | |
| NatWest | | | | | | | | | | | | | | | | | | |
| B & H | 1 | 1 | 0 | 54 | 54 | 54.00 | - | 1 | - | - | | | | | | | | |
| Sunday | | | | | | | | | | | | | | | | | | |

## Career Performances

| | M | Inns | NO | Runs | HS | Avge | 100s | 50s | Ct | St | Balls | Runs | Wkts | Avge | Best | 5wI | 10wM |
|---|---|---|---|---|---|---|---|---|---|---|---|---|---|---|---|---|---|
| Test | | | | | | | | | | | | | | | | | |
| All First | 248 | 419 | 42 | 11821 | 144 | 31.35 | 14 | 68 | 124 | - | 667 | 563 | 11 | 51.18 | 3-40 | - | - |
| 1-day Int | | | | | | | | | | | | | | | | | |
| NatWest | 19 | 17 | 4 | 498 | 117 | 38.30 | 1 | 2 | 8 | - | 6 | 2 | 0 | - | - | - |
| B & H | 34 | 31 | 7 | 866 | 103 | 36.08 | 1 | 6 | 9 | - | | | | | | |
| Sunday | 115 | 102 | 11 | 2175 | 135 * | 23.90 | 1 | 9 | 25 | - | 42 | 55 | 1 | 55.00 | 1-23 | - |

12. Which Australian-born player captained a first-class
county in 1995 at the age of 24?

# BOSWELL, S. A. J.          Northamptonshire

**Name:** Scott Antony John Boswell
**Role:** Right-hand bat, right-hand
fast-medium bowler
**Born:** 11 September 1974, York
**Height:** 6ft 5in **Weight:** 14st
**Nickname:** Joey
**County debut:** 1995 (one-day)
**Parents:** Tony and Judy
**Marital status:** Single
**Education:** Pocklington School;
Wolverhampton University
**Qualifications:** 9 GCSEs, 3 A-levels
**Off-season:** Studying Sports Studies and PE
at Wolverhampton University
**Overseas teams played for:** Hutt Valley,
New Zealand 1994-95
**Cricketers particularly admired:**
Nick Cook, Dennis Lillee, Richard Hadlee
**Other sports followed:**
Football (York City), rugby union
**Relaxations:** Watching most sports, sleeping and 'going out with friends, family and girlfriend'
**Opinions on cricket:** 'Overseas players should be allowed in the county championship because they are essential for younger players, like myself, to learn from and to play with and against. Also for the crowds to be able to watch top international players perform.'

## 1995 Season

|        | M | Inns | NO | Runs | HS | Avge | 100s | 50s | Ct | St | O  | M | Runs | Wkts | Avge  | Best | 5wI | 10wM |
|--------|---|------|----|------|----|------|------|-----|----|----|----|---|------|------|-------|------|-----|------|
| Test   |   |      |    |      |    |      |      |     |    |    |    |   |      |      |       |      |     |      |
| All First |   |   |    |      |    |      |      |     |    |    |    |   |      |      |       |      |     |      |
| 1-day Int |   |   |    |      |    |      |      |     |    |    |    |   |      |      |       |      |     |      |
| NatWest |   |     |    |      |    |      |      |     |    |    |    |   |      |      |       |      |     |      |
| B & H  | 1 | 0    | 0  | 0    | 0  | -    | -    | -   | -  | -  | 5  | 2 | 6    | 1    | 6.00  | 1-6  | -   |      |
| Sunday | 4 | 1    | 0  | 2    | 2  | 2.00 | -    | -   | -  | -  | 23 | 1 | 104  | 3    | 34.66 | 1-20 | -   |      |

13. Who will replace Hugh Morris as Glamorgan's captain for 1996?

## Career Performances

| | M | Inns | NO | Runs | HS | Avge | 100s | 50s | Ct | St | Balls | Runs | Wkts | Avge | Best | 5wI | 10wM |
|---|---|---|---|---|---|---|---|---|---|---|---|---|---|---|---|---|---|
| Test | | | | | | | | | | | | | | | | | |
| All First | | | | | | | | | | | | | | | | | |
| 1-day Int | | | | | | | | | | | | | | | | | |
| NatWest | | | | | | | | | | | | | | | | | |
| B & H | 1 | 0 | 0 | 0 | 0 | - | - | - | - | - | 30 | 6 | 1 | 6.00 | 1-6 | - | |
| Sunday | 4 | 1 | 0 | 2 | 2 | 2.00 | - | - | - | - | 138 | 104 | 3 | 34.66 | 1-20 | - | |

# BOTHAM, L. J. Hampshire

**Name:** Liam James Botham
**Role:** Right-hand bat, right-arm fast bowler
**Born:** 26 August 1977, Doncaster
**Height:** 6ft 1in **Weight:** 13st 7lbs
**Nickname:** Limo
**County debut:** No first-team appearance
**Parents:** Ian and Kathryn
**Marital status:** Single
**Family links with cricket:** 'Father played!'
**Education:** Cundall Manor Prep School;
Rossall School
**Qualifications:** 6 GCSEs and 2 A-levels
**Off-season:** Singapore sixes competition,
'rugby or cricket abroad'
**Overseas tours:** Rossall School to Australia
1994-95
**Cricketers particularly admired:**
Malcolm Marshall, Viv Richards
**Others sports followed:** Rugby
**Relaxations:** Fishing, golf, rugby

**Extras:** Played for England U17 v India U17 in 1994. Plays rugby for Lancashire U18.
Appeared on *Beadle's About*, as the victim of a practical joke set up by his father
**Opinions on cricket:** 'Have not been in the game long enough.'

**Name:** James Noel Bruce Bovill
**Role:** Right-hand bat, right-arm
fast-medium bowler
**Born:** 2 June 1971, High Wycombe
**Height:** 6ft **Weight:** 12st 8lbs
**Nickname:** Jimma, Ned, Chopsy
**County debut:** 1993
**1st-Class 5 w. in innings:** 3
**1st-Class 10 w match:** 1
**1st-Class catches:** 2
**Place in bowling averages:** 50th av. 27.13
(1994 60th av. 30.07)
**Strike rate:** 50.30 (career 49.93)
**Parents:** Mike and Anne
**Marital status:** Single
**Family links with cricket:** Father played for
Dorset 1957-60 and captained Basingstoke
for seven years
**Education:** Sandroyd Preparatory School;
Charterhouse; Durham University
**Qualifications:** 8 O-levels, 3 A-levels, BA (Hons) in Combined Social Sciences
**Career outide cricket**: 'In the process of looking'
**Off-season:** Playing and coaching in Durban, South Africa
**Overseas tours:** Hampshire Maniacs to Guernsey and Jersey 1989; Bucks to Zimbabwe
1991-92; Durham University to South Africa 1992-93, MCC to Far East and India 1995-96
**Overseas teams played for:** Western Province CC, South Africa 1989-90, Tigers
Parow, South Africa 1994-95
**Cricketers particularly admired:** Cardigan Connor, Gregor Macmillan, Clive Smith,
Reg Peacock
**Other sports followed:** Rugby, football (Notts Forest)
**Injuries:** Stress fracture of lower back, missed July to end of season
**Relaxations:** 'Discussing "Havanic ritual" with J. Snape', sailing, skiing, current affairs
and photography
**Extras:** Member of the Durham University team that won the indoor six-a-side club
championship at Lord's, March 1993. Organised University tour to South Africa 1992-
93. Played for Buckinghamshire 1990-92 and for Combined Universities in the B&H
Cup in 1992. Holds school U14 javelin record
**Opinions on cricket:** 'The whole system of benefit years for individuals is hopelessly
out of date and needs reviewing.'
**Best batting:** 31 Hampshire v Worcestershire, Southampton 1995
**Best bowling:** 6-29 Hampshire v Durham, Stockton 1995

**1995 Season**

| | M | Inns | NO | Runs | HS | Avge | 100s | 50s | Ct | St | O | M | Runs | Wkts | Avge | Best | 5wI | 10wM |
|---|---|---|---|---|---|---|---|---|---|---|---|---|---|---|---|---|---|---|
| Test | | | | | | | | | | | | | | | | | | |
| All First | 8 | 10 | 5 | 90 | 31 | 18.00 | - | - | 1 | - | 251.3 | 62 | 814 | 30 | 27.13 | 6-29 | 2 | 1 |
| 1-day Int | | | | | | | | | | | | | | | | | | |
| NatWest | | | | | | | | | | | | | | | | | | |
| B & H | 2 | 0 | 0 | 0 | 0 | - | - | - | - | - | 16.1 | 1 | 87 | 1 | 87.00 | 1-37 | - | |
| Sunday | 2 | 1 | 0 | 0 | 0 | 0.00 | - | - | 1 | - | 11 | 0 | 66 | 1 | 66.00 | 1-36 | - | |

**Career Performances**

| | M | Inns | NO | Runs | HS | Avge | 100s | 50s | Ct | St | Balls | Runs | Wkts | Avge | Best | 5wI | 10wM |
|---|---|---|---|---|---|---|---|---|---|---|---|---|---|---|---|---|---|
| Test | | | | | | | | | | | | | | | | | |
| All First | 15 | 21 | 12 | 128 | 31 | 14.22 | - | - | 2 | - | 2347 | 1283 | 47 | 27.29 | 6-29 | 3 | 1 |
| 1-day Int | | | | | | | | | | | | | | | | | |
| NatWest | | | | | | | | | | | | | | | | | |
| B & H | 7 | 1 | 1 | 14 | 14* | - | - | - | 1 | - | 373 | 249 | 5 | 49.80 | 2-21 | - | |
| Sunday | 8 | 4 | 1 | 8 | 7* | 2.66 | - | - | 1 | - | 333 | 278 | 6 | 46.33 | 3-40 | - | |

# BOWEN, M. N.      Nottinghamshire

**Name:** Mark Nicholas Bowen
**Role:** Right-hand bat, right-arm medium bowler
**Born:** 6 December 1967, Redcar
**Height:** 6ft 1in **Weight:** 13st
**Nickname:** Jim
**County debut:** 1991-92
**1st-Class catches:** 3
**Strike rate:** (career 65.80)
**Parents:** Keith
**Marital status:** Single
**Family links with cricket:** 'Father has always played and still has great interest in the game'
**Education:** Sacred Heart Secondary School, Redcar; St Mary's Sixth Form College, Middlesbrough; Teesside Polytechnic
**Qualifications:** 8 O-levels, 3 A-levels, BSc (Hons) in Chemical Engineering
**Career outside cricket:** Commissioning engineer for British Nuclear Fuels
**Overseas tours:** Northamptonshire to Durban 1992, to Cape Town 1993; Christians in Sport to Zimbabwe 1994-95

**Cricketers particularly admired:** Richard Hadlee, Dennis Lillee, Ian Botham, Viv Richards

**Other sports followed:** Football (Middlesbrough FC) and most other sports

Injuries: Neck and arm, missed eight weeks in total

**Relaxations:** Keeping fit, playing golf, and a good pint

**Extras:** Made debut for Northants first team in Natal on 1991-92 tour to South Africa before playing in the 2nd XI. Released by Northamptonshire at the end of the 1995 season and has joined Nottinghamshire for 1996

**Opinions on cricket:** 'Four-day game is a good contest, it allowstime for the game to develop and tests the full strength of a side. The surfaces still need to be produced for a balnced contest. Four-day games would allow greater rest between fixtures with time to allow players to work on technical apects of their game.'

**Best batting:** 23* Northamptonshire v Durham, Northampton 1993

**Best bowling:** 4-124 Northamptonshire v Kent, Canterbury 1993

### 1995 Season

| | M | Inns | NO | Runs | HS | Avge | 100s | 50s | Ct | St | O | M | Runs | Wkts | Avge | Best | 5wI | 10wM |
|---|---|---|---|---|---|---|---|---|---|---|---|---|---|---|---|---|---|---|
| Test | | | | | | | | | | | | | | | | | | |
| All First | | | | | | | | | | | | | | | | | | |
| 1-day Int | | | | | | | | | | | | | | | | | | |
| NatWest | | | | | | | | | | | | | | | | | | |
| B & H | | | | | | | | | | | | | | | | | | |
| Sunday | 5 | 3 | 1 | 14 | 7 * | 7.00 | - | - | 2 | - | 32 | 1 | 148 | 6 | 24.66 | 2-11 | - | |

### Career Performances

| | M | Inns | NO | Runs | HS | Avge | 100s | 50s | Ct | St | Balls | Runs | Wkts | Avge | Best | 5wI | 10wM |
|---|---|---|---|---|---|---|---|---|---|---|---|---|---|---|---|---|---|
| Test | | | | | | | | | | | | | | | | | |
| All First | 13 | 14 | 4 | 116 | 23 * | 11.60 | - | - | 3 | - | 1974 | 1196 | 30 | 39.86 | 4-124 | - | - |
| 1-day Int | | | | | | | | | | | | | | | | | |
| NatWest | | | | | | | | | | | | | | | | | |
| B & H | 1 | 1 | 0 | 0 | 0 | 0.00 | - | - | - | - | 60 | 39 | 1 | 39.00 | 1-39 | - | |
| Sunday | 21 | 11 | 5 | 93 | 27 * | 15.50 | - | - | 2 | - | 804 | 648 | 17 | 38.11 | 3-35 | | |

-

# BOWLER, P. D.                    Somerset

**Name:** Peter Duncan Bowler

**Role:** Right-hand opening bat, occasional off-spin bowler, wicket-keeper, county vice-captain

**Born:** 30 July 1963, Plymouth

**Height:** 6ft 1in **Weight:** 13st

**Nickname:** Croc

**County debut:** 1986 (Leicestershire), 1988 (Derbyshire), 1995 (Somerset)

**County cap:** 1989 (Derbyshire),
1995 (Somerset)
**1000 runs in a season:** 7
**1st-Class 50s:** 63
**1st-Class 100s:** 26
**1st-Class 200s:** 2
**1st-Class catches:** 115
**1st-Class stumpings:** 1
**One-Day 100s:** 5
**Place in batting averages:** 18th av. 53.96
(1994 174th av. 23.73)
**Strike rate:** (career 119.38)
**Parents:** Peter and Etta
**Wife and date of marriage:** Joanne,
10 October 1992
**Children:** Peter Robert, 21 September 1993
**Education:** Daramalan College, Canberra,
Australia
**Qualifications:** Australian Year 12 certificate
**Career outside cricket:** Has worked for BBC Radio as a sports journalist on occasions
**Cricketers particularly admired:** Gus Valence, Rob Jeffery
**Other sports followed:** Rugby union, football
**Relaxations:** Spending time with the family, reading, gardening, decorating
**Extras:** First Leicestershire player to score a first-class century on debut (100* v Hampshire 1986). Moved to Derbyshire at end of 1987 season and scored a hundred on his debut v Cambridge University in 1988. First batsman to 2000 runs in 1992, finishing equal leading run-scorer (2044) with Mike Roseberry of Middlesex. Derbyshire Player of the Year 1992. Signed a five-year contract with Somerset starting in 1995
**Best batting:** 241* Derbyshire v Hampshire, Portsmouth 1992
**Best bowling:** 3-41 Derbyshire v Leicestershire, Leicester 1991

## 1995 Season

|  | M | Inns | NO | Runs | HS | Avge | 100s | 50s | Ct | St | O | M | Runs | Wkts | Avge | Best | 5wI | 10wM |
|---|---|---|---|---|---|---|---|---|---|---|---|---|---|---|---|---|---|---|
| Test |  |  |  |  |  |  |  |  |  |  |  |  |  |  |  |  |  |  |
| All First | 19 | 33 | 3 | 1619 | 196 | 53.96 | 6 | 5 | 9 | - | 16.2 | 3 | 68 | 1 | 68.00 | 1-13 | - | - |
| 1-day Int |  |  |  |  |  |  |  |  |  |  |  |  |  |  |  |  |  |  |
| NatWest | 1 | 1 | 0 | 8 | 8 | 8.00 | - | - | - | - |  |  |  |  |  |  |  |  |
| B & H | 6 | 6 | 0 | 169 | 54 | 28.16 | - | 3 | 2 | - | 4 | 0 | 29 | 0 | - |  | - | - |
| Sunday | 14 | 14 | 0 | 349 | 76 | 24.92 | - | 3 | 5 | - |  |  |  |  |  |  |  |  |

## Career Performances

|       | M | Inns | NO | Runs | HS | Avge | 100s | 50s | Ct | St | Balls | Runs | Wkts | Avge | Best | 5wl | 10wM |
|-------|---|------|----|------|----|------|------|-----|----|----|-------|------|------|------|------|-----|------|
| Test |   |      |    |      |    |      |      |     |    |    |       |      |      |      |      |     |      |
| All First | 177 | 308 | 28 | 11544 | 241 * | 41.22 | 26 | 63 | 115 | 1 | 2507 | 1579 | 21 | 75.19 | 3-41 | - | - |
| 1-day Int |   |      |    |      |    |      |      |     |    |    |       |      |      |      |      |     |      |
| NatWest | 13 | 13 | 0 | 294 | 111 | 22.61 | 1 | 1 | 6 | - | 36 | 26 | 0 | - | - | - | - |
| B & H | 36 | 35 | 1 | 1131 | 109 | 33.26 | 2 | 10 | 18 | 1 | 270 | 154 | 4 | 38.50 | 1-15 | - |  |
| Sunday | 129 | 125 | 14 | 3850 | 138 * | 34.68 | 2 | 31 | 52 | 1 | 242 | 237 | 7 | 33.85 | 3-31 | - |  |

# BRIERS, N. E. Leicestershire

**Name:** Nigel Edwin Briers
**Role:** Right-hand opening bat, right-arm medium bowler
**Born:** 15 January 1955, Leicester
**Height:** 6ft **Weight:** 13st
**Nickname:** Kudu
**County debut:** 1971
**County cap:** 1981
**Benefit:** 1990
**1000 runs in a season:** 11
**1st-Class 50s:** 95
**1st-Class 100s:** 31
**1st-Class 200s:** 1
**1st-Class catches:** 152
**One-Day 100s:** 6
**Place in batting averages:**
59th av. 41.84 (1994 69th av. 38.00)
**Strike rate:** (career 63.96)
**Parents:** Leonard Arthur Roger and Eveline
**Wife and date of marriage:** Suzanne Mary Tudor, 3 September 1977
**Children:** Michael Edward Tudor, 25 March 1983; Andrew James Tudor, 30 June 1986
**Family links with cricket:** Father was captain and wicket-keeper of Narborough and Littlethorpe in the South Leicestershire League for 15 years and mother was scorer. Father was also captain of South Leicestershire Representative XI and played for the Royal Marines in the same team as Trevor Bailey. Cousin, Norman Briers, played once for Leicestershire in 1967
**Education:** Lutterworth Grammar School; Borough Road College of Education
**Qualifications:** Qualified teacher (Cert Ed), BEd (Hons), MCC advanced cricket coach
**Career outside cricket:** Teaching PE and History at Ludgrove School
**Off-season:** Teaching PE and History at Ludgrove School
**Overseas tours:** Derrick Robbins tour to South America 1978-79; MCC to the Far East

1980-81; Leicestershire to Zimbabwe, Holland, Jersey and Guernsey; MCC to the Virgin and Leeward Islands 1991-92

**Cricketers particularly admired:** Ray Illingworth, Richard Hadlee, Geoff Boycott, Barry Richards, Viv Richards

**Other sports followed:** Rugby (Leicester Tigers) and football (Leicester City)

**Injuries:** Broken knuckle, missed three weeks

**Extras:** Youngest player ever to appear for Leicestershire (aged 16 years 104 days). Shares county record with Roger Tolchard for highest fifth wicket stand of 233 v Somerset, 1979. Appointed county captain in 1990. Captained MCC on 1991-92 tour of the Virgin and Leeward Islands. Wombwell Cricket Lovers' Society Captain of the Year 1992. One of *Wisden*'s Five Cricketers of the Year 1993. 1995 was his 25th season in the game. He now becomes the longest-serving county player still in the game

**Best batting:** 201* Leicestershire v Warwickshire, Edgbaston 1983

**Best bowling:** 4-29 Leicestershire v Derbyshire, Leicester 1985

## 1995 Season

|          | M  | Inns | NO | Runs | HS    | Avge  | 100s | 50s | Ct | St | O | M | Runs | Wkts | Avge | Best | 5wI | 10wM |
|----------|----|------|----|------|-------|-------|------|-----|----|----|---|---|------|------|------|------|-----|------|
| Test     |    |      |    |      |       |       |      |     |    |    |   |   |      |      |      |      |     |      |
| All First | 15 | 27  | 2  | 1046 | 175 * | 41.84 | 3    | 3   | 1  | -  |   |   |      |      |      |      |     |      |
| 1-day Int |    |      |    |      |       |       |      |     |    |    |   |   |      |      |      |      |     |      |
| NatWest  | 2  | 2    | 0  | 23   | 15    | 11.50 | -    | -   | -  | -  |   |   |      |      |      |      |     |      |
| B & H    | 4  | 4    | 0  | 46   | 28    | 11.50 | -    | -   | -  | -  |   |   |      |      |      |      |     |      |
| Sunday   | 13 | 13   | 1  | 446  | 108 * | 37.16 | 1    | 2   | 3  | -  |   |   |      |      |      |      |     |      |

## Career Performances

|          | M   | Inns | NO | Runs  | HS    | Avge  | 100s | 50s | Ct  | St | Balls | Runs | Wkts | Avge  | Best | 5wI | 10wM |
|----------|-----|------|----|-------|-------|-------|------|-----|-----|----|-------|------|------|-------|------|-----|------|
| Test     |     |      |    |       |       |       |      |     |     |    |       |      |      |       |      |     |      |
| All First | 381 | 628 | 61 | 18726 | 201 * | 33.02 | 31   | 95  | 152 | -  | 2047  | 988  | 32   | 30.87 | 4-29 | -   | -    |
| 1-day Int |     |      |    |       |       |       |      |     |     |    |       |      |      |       |      |     |      |
| NatWest  | 39  | 39   | 2  | 737   | 88    | 19.91 | -    | 2   | 9   | -  | 84    | 75   | 6    | 12.50 | 2-6  | -   |      |
| B & H    | 63  | 58   | 5  | 1317  | 102   | 24.84 | 1    | 7   | 20  | -  | 330   | 266  | 3    | 88.66 | 1-26 | -   |      |
| Sunday   | 231 | 227  | 25 | 6096  | 119 * | 30.17 | 5    | 31  | 63  | -  | 482   | 384  | 10   | 38.40 | 3-29 | -   |      |

14. Who will replace Mark Nicholas as Hampshire's captain for 1996?

# BRIMSON, M. T. Leicestershire

**Name:** Matthew Thomas Brimson
**Role:** Right-hand bat, slow left-arm bowler
**Born:** 1 December 1970, Plumstead, London
**Height:** 6ft **Weight:** 11st 6lbs
**Nickname:** Brimmo, Doogie, Ginger Cat
**County debut:** 1993
**1st-Class catches:** 1
**Place in bowling averages:** 35th av. 25.83
**Strike rate:** 55.00 (career 79.31)
**Parents:** David and Jennifer
**Wife and date of marriage:**
Lyn, 29 December 1993
**Family links with cricket:** Brother plays
club cricket with Beckenham
**Education:** St Joseph's Preparatory School,
Blackheath; Chislehurst and Sidcup
Grammar School, Sidcup; Durham University
**Qualifications:** 8 O-levels, 3 A-levels, BA
(Hons) degree in Geography
**Off-season:** Working for Nat West bank
**Overseas tours:** Kent Schools U17 to Singapore and New Zealand 1987-88; Leicestershire to South Africa 1994 and 1995
**Cricketers particularly admired:** Ian Botham, Hansie Cronje, Colin Bridge, all members of Leics CCC 2nd XI who won Bain Hogg Trophy 1995
**Other sports followed:** Golf, tennis and football (Charlton Athletic)
**Relaxations:** 'Reading, relaxing with Lyn, walking, working out Adrian Pierson's theories, working out Gregor Macmillan'
**Extras:** Was on the Kent staff in 1991, Rapidline 2nd XI Player of the Month, July 1995
**Opinions on cricket:** 'Counties should do more to find players winter employment.'
**Best batting:** 25 Leicestershire v Surrey, Leicester 1995
**Best bowling:** 2-11 Leicestershire v Gloucestershire, Leicester 1995

## 1995 Season

|          | M | Inns | NO | Runs | HS | Avge | 100s | 50s | Ct | St | O | M | Runs | Wkts | Avge | Best | 5wI | 10wM |
|----------|---|------|----|------|----|------|------|-----|----|----|---|---|------|------|------|------|-----|------|
| Test     |   |      |    |      |    |      |      |     |    |    |   |   |      |      |      |      |     |      |
| All First | 7 | 5 | 3 | 40 | 25 | 20.00 | - | - | 1 | - | 110 | 24 | 310 | 12 | 25.83 | 2-11 | - | - |
| 1-day Int |   |      |    |      |    |      |      |     |    |    |   |   |      |      |      |      |     |      |
| NatWest  |   |      |    |      |    |      |      |     |    |    |   |   |      |      |      |      |     |      |
| B & H    |   |      |    |      |    |      |      |     |    |    |   |   |      |      |      |      |     |      |
| Sunday   |   |      |    |      |    |      |      |     |    |    |   |   |      |      |      |      |     |      |

## Career Performances

| | M | Inns | NO | Runs | HS | Avge | 100s | 50s | Ct | St | Balls | Runs | Wkts | Avge | Best | 5wI | 10wM |
|---|---|---|---|---|---|---|---|---|---|---|---|---|---|---|---|---|---|
| Test | | | | | | | | | | | | | | | | | |
| All First | 14 | 15 | 6 | 85 | 25 | 9.44 | - | - | 1 | - | 1507 | 723 | 19 | 38.05 | 2-11 | - | - |
| 1-day Int | | | | | | | | | | | | | | | | | |
| NatWest | | | | | | | | | | | | | | | | | |
| B & H | | | | | | | | | | | | | | | | | |
| Sunday | 1 | 0 | 0 | 0 | 0 | - | - | - | - | - | 60 | 28 | 1 | 28.00 | 1-28 | - | |

# BRINKLEY, J. E. Worcestershire

**Name:** James Edward Brinkley
**Role:** Right-hand bat, right-arm fast-medium bowler
**Born:** 13 March 1974, Helensburgh, Scotland
**Height:** 6ft 3in **Weight:** 14st
**Nickname:** JB
**County debut:** 1993-94
**1st-Class catches:** 5
**1st-Class 5 w. in innings:** 2
**Strike rate:** (career 65.55)
**Parents:** Tom and Sharon
**Marital status:** Single
**Family links with cricket:** Father played service cricket in the Royal Navy, mother coaches junior teams in Western Australia
**Education:** Marist College, Canberra; Trinity College, Perth
**Qualifications:** West Australian Tertiary Entrance Examinations
**Career outside cricket:** Sales, PR
**Off-season:** Playing and coaching overseas
**Overseas teams played for:** Scarborough, Perth 1990-93; Western Australian U19 1993; Matabeleland, Zimbabwe 1994-95
**Cricketers particularly admired:** Michael Holding, Viv Richards, Ian Botham, David Gower
**Other sports followed:** Rugby union and golf
**Injuries:** Glandular fever ('missed from early May to mid-July'), ligament in right knee ('missed from late July to late August')
**Relaxations:** Golf, fitness training, music, reading, cricket
**Extras:** Taken a hat-trick in both the 2nd XI Championship and the Bain Clarkson

Trophy, against Surrey and Somerset respectively. Coached Zimbabwe Under 19 in South African provincial Coca Cola Cup in 1994

**Opinions on cricket:** 'Wickets need to offer something to both bowler and batsman. Too many are biased one way or the other. Counties are to be congratulated on their improvements to salaries and pension arrangements for the coming season.'

**Best batting:** 29 Matebeleland v Mashonaland Under-24, Harare 1994-95

**Best bowling:** 6-35 Matebeleland v Mashonaland Country Districts, Harare South 1994-95

### 1995 Season

|  | M | Inns | NO | Runs | HS | Avge | 100s | 50s | Ct | St | O | M | Runs | Wkts | Avge | Best | 5wI | 10wM |
|---|---|---|---|---|---|---|---|---|---|---|---|---|---|---|---|---|---|---|
| Test |  |  |  |  |  |  |  |  |  |  |  |  |  |  |  |  |  |  |
| All First | 1 | 1 | 1 | 5 | 5 * | - | - | - | - | - | 26 | 5 | 99 | 1 | 99.00 | 1-50 | - | - |
| 1-day Int |  |  |  |  |  |  |  |  |  |  |  |  |  |  |  |  |  |  |
| NatWest |  |  |  |  |  |  |  |  |  |  |  |  |  |  |  |  |  |  |  |
| B & H |  |  |  |  |  |  |  |  |  |  |  |  |  |  |  |  |  |  |  |  |
| Sunday | 1 | 0 | 0 | 0 | 0 | - | - | - | - | - | 8 | 0 | 24 | 0 | - | - | - |  |

### Career Performances

|  | M | Inns | NO | Runs | HS | Avge | 100s | 50s | Ct | St | Balls | Runs | Wkts | Avge | Best | 5wI | 10wM |
|---|---|---|---|---|---|---|---|---|---|---|---|---|---|---|---|---|---|
| Test |  |  |  |  |  |  |  |  |  |  |  |  |  |  |  |  |  |
| All First | 14 | 16 | 4 | 89 | 29 | 7.41 | - | - | 5 | - | 2229 | 1115 | 34 | 32.79 | 6-35 | 2 | - |
| 1-day Int |  |  |  |  |  |  |  |  |  |  |  |  |  |  |  |  |  |
| NatWest |  |  |  |  |  |  |  |  |  |  |  |  |  |  |  |  |  |
| B & H |  |  |  |  |  |  |  |  |  |  |  |  |  |  |  |  |  |  |
| Sunday | 1 | 0 | 0 | 0 | 0 | - | - | - | - | - | 48 | 24 | 0 | - | - | - | - |

# BROADHURST, M.  Nottinghamshire

**Name:** Mark Broadhurst
**Role:** Right-hand bat, right-arm fast-medium bowler
**Born:** 20 June 1974, Barnsley
**Height:** 6ft **Weight:** 12st
**Nickname:** Broady, Stanley, Gibby
**County debut:** 1991 (Yorkshire)
**Parents:** Robert and Pamela
**Marital status:** Single
**Family links with cricket:** Father played local league
**Education:** Worsborough Common Junior School; Kingstone Comprehensive
**Qualifications:** 8 GCSEs, City and Guilds qualification in Leisure and Recreation
**Off-season:** 'Playing golf, football and clubbing'
**Overseas tours:** England U19 to New Zealand 1990-91, to India 1992-93;

NCA YC to Canada 1991; Yorkshire to South Africa 1993

**Cricketers particularly admired:** Dennis Lillee, Michael Holding, Malcolm Marshall, Bobby Chapman

**Other sports followed:** Football (Liverpool FC and Barnsley FC), golf, athletics, snooker

**Injuries:** Muscular defect in right leg, out for ten weeks

**Relaxations:** Reading, music, nightclubs

**Extras:** Selected for England U19 squad aged 16. Made first-class debut for Yorks at age 16, becoming the third youngest in Yorkshire history. Contributor to Wombwell Cricket Society's *Twelfth Man* magazine. Played for England U19 v Australia 1991. Selected for England U19 tour to Pakistan 1991-92 but forced to drop out through back injury. Signed by Nottinghamshire for 1995 season

**Opinions on cricket:** 'I think that the game today is heading in ther right direction and there are great opportunities, but it is still too much of a batsman's game.'

**Best batting:** 1 Yorkshire v Sri Lanka, Headingley 1991

**Best bowling:** 3-61 Yorkshire v Oxford University, The Parks 1991

---

**1995 (did not make any first-class or one-day appearances)**

---

**Career Performances**

| | M | Inns | NO | Runs | HS | Avge | 100s | 50s | Ct | St | Balls | Runs | Wkts | Avge | Best | 5wI | 10wM |
|---|---|---|---|---|---|---|---|---|---|---|---|---|---|---|---|---|---|
| Test | | | | | | | | | | | | | | | | | |
| All First | 5 | 3 | 0 | 7 | 6 | 2.33 | - | - | - | - | 415 | 231 | 7 | 33.00 | 3-61 | - | - |
| 1-day Int | | | | | | | | | | | | | | | | | |
| NatWest | | | | | | | | | | | | | | | | | |
| B & H | | | | | | | | | | | | | | | | | |
| Sunday | 1 | 0 | 0 | 0 | 0 | - | - | - | - | - | 48 | 27 | 0 | - | | - | - |

---

15. Who will replace Nigel Briers as Leicestershire's captain for 1996?

# BROWN, A. D.                                     Surrey

**Name:** Alistair Duncan Brown
**Role:** Right-hand bat, occasional
leg-break bowler, occasional wicket-keeper
**Born:** 11 February 1970, Beckenham
**Height:** 5ft 10in **Weight:** 12st
**Nickname:** Lordy
**County debut:** 1992
**1000 runs in a season:** 3
**1st-Class 50s:** 16
**1st-Class 100s:** 11
**1st-Class catches:** 60
**One-Day 100s:** 6
**Place in batting averages:** 57th av. 42.16
(1994 25th av. 47.68)
**Parents:** Robert and Ann
**Marital status:** Single
**Family links with cricket:**

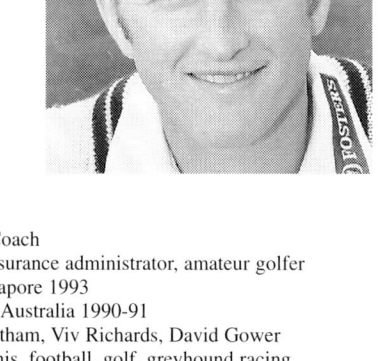

Father played for Surrey Young Amateurs
**Education:** Cumnor House School;
Caterham School
**Qualifications:** 5 O-levels, NCA Senior Coach
**Career outside cricket:** Cricket coach, insurance administrator, amateur golfer
**Overseas tours:** England 6-a-side to Singapore 1993
**Overseas teams played for:** North Perth, Australia 1990-91
**Cricketers particularly admired:** Ian Botham, Viv Richards, David Gower
**Other sports followed:** Horse racing, tennis, football, golf, greyhound racing
**Relaxations:** Tennis and golf
**Extras:** Scored three of the eight fastest centuries of the 1992 season (71, 78 & 79 balls)
**Opinions on cricket:** 'Four-day cricket has proved very successful. 40 overs is right for
Sundays with coloured clothing and white balls.'
**Best batting:** 187 Surrey v Gloucestershire, The Oval 1995

### 1995 Season

|          | M  | Inns | NO | Runs | HS  | Avge  | 100s | 50s | Ct | St | O | M | Runs | Wkts | Avge | Best | 5wI | 10wM |
|----------|----|------|----|------|-----|-------|------|-----|----|----|---|---|------|------|------|------|-----|------|
| Test     |    |      |    |      |     |       |      |     |    |    |   |   |      |      |      |      |     |      |
| All First| 16 | 29   | 4  | 1054 | 187 | 42.16 | 3    | 3   | 20 | -  |   |   |      |      |      |      |     |      |
| 1-day Int|    |      |    |      |     |       |      |     |    |    |   |   |      |      |      |      |     |      |
| NatWest  | 2  | 1    | 0  | 24   | 24  | 24.00 | -    | -   | -  | -  |   |   |      |      |      |      |     |      |
| B & H    | 4  | 4    | 1  | 118  | 82  | 39.33 | -    | 1   | 1  | -  |   |   |      |      |      |      |     |      |
| Sunday   | 16 | 16   | 0  | 462  | 100 | 28.87 | 1    | 1   | 7  | -  |   |   |      |      |      |      |     |      |

## Career Performances

|        | M  | Inns | NO | Runs | HS   | Avge  | 100s | 50s | Ct | St | Balls | Runs | Wkts | Avge | Best | 5wI | 10wM |
|--------|----|------|----|------|------|-------|------|-----|----|----|-------|------|------|------|------|-----|------|
| Test   |    |      |    |      |      |       |      |     |    |    |       |      |      |      |      |     |      |
| All First | 63 | 103 | 10 | 4225 | 187  | 45.43 | 11   | 16  | 60 | -  | 192   | 131  | 0    | -    | -    | -   | -    |
| 1-day Int |   |      |    |      |      |       |      |     |    |    |       |      |      |      |      |     |      |
| NatWest | 9 | 6   | 1  | 156  | 52   | 31.20 | -    | 1   | 2  | -  |       |      |      |      |      |     |      |
| B & H  | 17 | 17   | 5  | 417  | 82   | 34.75 | -    | 1   | 3  | -  |       |      |      |      |      |     |      |
| Sunday | 78 | 74   | 2  | 2390 | 142 * | 33.19 | 6    | 10  | 22 | -  |       |      |      |      |      |     |      |

# BROWN, C. Lancashire

**Name:** Christopher Brown
**Role:** Right-hand bat, off-spin bowler
**Born:** 16 August 1974, Oldham
**Height:** 6ft 2in **Weight:** 12st
**Nickname:** Browney, Browneye, Tnuc,
Stick, Scooby, Shaggy
**County debut:** No first-team appearance
**Parents:** Paul and Anne
**Marital status:** Engaged to Gail
**Family links with cricket:** Uncle played for
Middletown in the Central Lancashire League
**Education:** Failsworth High School;
Tameside College of Technology
**Qualifications:** 5 GCSEs, City and Guilds
qualification in Recreation and Leisure
**Off-season:** 'Resting and coaching'
**Overseas teams played for:** Cape Town,
South Africa 1992-95
**Cricketers particularly admired:**
Phil Tufnell, Tim May, Greg Matthews, Steve O'Shaughnessy, Peter Such, Peter Seal
**Other sports followed:** Football (Manchester United), horse racing
**Relaxations:** 'Listening to good music, following Man United, drinking good beer,
socialising, and listening to P. Seal's views on dodging nets.'
**Extras:** Equalled Gary Yates's 32 wickets in a season in 1993 with Lancashire Cricket
Federation. Represented Lancashire Schools U19 1991-92, Lancashire Cricket
Federation 1992-93, Lancashire Cricket Federation Player of the Year 1992, 1993.
Member of the Lancashire Cricket Federation side which won the NAYC
Cambridge/Oxford Festival 1993. Played for NAYC 1993 and Werneth CC in Central
Lancashire League.
**Opinions on cricket:** 'League cricket across the country should be extended from 40 or
50-over "slogs" to two-day cricket. This would produce better players as in South Africa

and abroad. Far too much cricket is being played on the county circuit – results in average performances – quality not quantity.'

# BROWN, D. R. Warwickshire

**Name:** Douglas Robert Brown
**Role:** Right-hand bat, right-arm
fast-medium bowler
**Born:** 29 October 1969, Stirling
**Height:** 6ft 2in **Weight:** 13st 7lbs
**Nickname:** J.D.,. Hoots
**County debut:** 1992
**County Cap:** 1995
**1st-Class 50s:** 5
**1st-Class catches:** 9
**Place in batting averages:** 143rd av. 28.11
**Place in bowling averages:** 51st av. 27.32
**Strike rate:** 50.54 (career 50.40)
**Parents:** Alastair and Janette
**Wife and date of marriage:**
Brenda, 2 October 1993
**Family links with cricket:**
Both grandfathers played club cricket
**Education:** Alloa Academy;West London
Institute of Higher Education (Borough Road College)
**Qualifications:** 9 O-Grades, 5 Higher Grades; BEd (Hons) Physical Education; qualified coach football, cricket, basketball, trampolining and rugby league
**Career outside cricket:** PE teacher
**Off-season:** Playing in Wellington, New Zealand
**Overseas tours:** Scotland XI to Pakistan 1988-89
**Overseas teams played for:** Primrose, Cape Town 1992-93; Uredenburg Salohana, Cape Town 1994
**Cricketers particularly admired:** Richard Hadlee and all the Warwickshire players
**Other sports followed:** Football, indoor cricket, golf, rugby union
**Injuries:** Ankle injury kept him out of cricket for 18 months
**Relaxations:** Listening to music, golf
**Extras:** Played football at Hampden Park for Scotland U18. Played first-class and B & H cricket for Scotland in 1989, and played again for Scotland against Ireland in 1992
**Opinions on cricket:** 'Still a great game!'
**Best batting**: 85 Warwickshire v Essex, Ilford 1995
**Best bowling**: 4-24 Warwickshire v Yorkshire, Edgbaston 1995

## 1995 Season

| | M | Inns | NO | Runs | HS | Avge | 100s | 50s | Ct | St | O | M | Runs | Wkts | Avge | Best | 5wI | 10wM |
|---|---|---|---|---|---|---|---|---|---|---|---|---|---|---|---|---|---|---|
| Test | | | | | | | | | | | | | | | | | | |
| All First | 15 | 20 | 2 | 506 | 85 | 28.11 | - | 4 | 7 | - | 311.4 | 71 | 1011 | 37 | 27.32 | 4-24 | - | - |
| 1-day Int | | | | | | | | | | | | | | | | | | |
| NatWest | 4 | 4 | 1 | 101 | 58 | 33.66 | - | 1 | - | - | 21 | 2 | 104 | 3 | 34.66 | 2-35 | - | |
| B & H | 2 | 0 | 0 | 0 | 0 | - | - | - | - | - | 11 | 2 | 43 | 3 | 14.33 | 3-43 | - | |
| Sunday | 17 | 16 | 3 | 212 | 78 * | 16.30 | - | 1 | 2 | - | 77 | 2 | 355 | 10 | 35.50 | 2-41 | - | |

## Career Performances

| | M | Inns | NO | Runs | HS | Avge | 100s | 50s | Ct | St | Balls | Runs | Wkts | Avge | Best | 5wI | 10wM |
|---|---|---|---|---|---|---|---|---|---|---|---|---|---|---|---|---|---|
| Test | | | | | | | | | | | | | | | | | |
| All First | 22 | 31 | 6 | 711 | 85 | 28.44 | - | 5 | 9 | - | 2621 | 1394 | 52 | 26.80 | 4-24 | - | - |
| 1-day Int | | | | | | | | | | | | | | | | | |
| NatWest | 4 | 4 | 1 | 101 | 58 | 33.66 | - | 1 | - | - | 126 | 104 | 3 | 34.66 | 2-35 | - | |
| B & H | 5 | 3 | 0 | 57 | 24 | 19.00 | - | - | 1 | - | 249 | 183 | 6 | 30.50 | 3-43 | - | |
| Sunday | 25 | 20 | 4 | 241 | 78 * | 15.06 | - | 1 | 2 | - | 762 | 545 | 16 | 34.06 | 3-21 | - | |

# BROWN, J. F.                    Northamptonshire

**Name:** Jason F. Brown
**Role:** Right-hand bat, off-spin bowler
**Born:** 10 October 1974, Stoke-on-Trent
**Height:** 6ft 1in  **Weight:** 12st
**Nickname:** Macey, Brown Fish
**County debut:** No first-team appearance
**Parents:** Peter and Cynthia
**Marital status:** Engaged to Samantha
**Education:** St Margaret Ward RC School
**Qualifications:** 9 O-levels
**Off-season:** 'Winter nets and keeping fit'
**Overseas tours:** Kidsgrove League U18 to Australia 1991
**Cricketers particularly admired:**
 John Emburey
**Other sports followed:** Football, golf, snooker
**Relaxations:** Watching videos and listening to music. Playing and watching all sports, socialising
**Extras:** Represented Staffordshire at all junior levels and Staffordshire's Minor Counties. 'Once took 10 for 16 in a Kidsgrove League game against Haslington Under 18 playing for Sandyford Under 18.' Played for Staffordshire in the 1995 Nat West competition

## 1995 Season

| | M | Inns | NO | Runs | HS | Avge | 100s | 50s | Ct | St | O | M | Runs | Wkts | Avge | Best | 5wI | 10wM |
|---|---|---|---|---|---|---|---|---|---|---|---|---|---|---|---|---|---|---|
| Test | | | | | | | | | | | | | | | | | | |
| All First | | | | | | | | | | | | | | | | | | |
| 1-day Int | | | | | | | | | | | | | | | | | | |
| NatWest | 1 | 0 | 0 | 0 | 0 | - | - | - | - | - | 12 | 1 | 72 | 1 | 72.00 | 1-72 | - | |
| B & H | | | | | | | | | | | | | | | | | | |
| Sunday | | | | | | | | | | | | | | | | | | |

## Career Performances

| | M | Inns | NO | Runs | HS | Avge | 100s | 50s | Ct | St | Balls | Runs | Wkts | Avge | Best | 5wI | 10wM |
|---|---|---|---|---|---|---|---|---|---|---|---|---|---|---|---|---|---|
| Test | | | | | | | | | | | | | | | | | |
| All First | | | | | | | | | | | | | | | | | |
| 1-day Int | | | | | | | | | | | | | | | | | |
| NatWest | 1 | 0 | 0 | 0 | 0 | - | - | - | - | - | 72 | 72 | 1 | 72.00 | 1-72 | - | |
| B & H | | | | | | | | | | | | | | | | | |
| Sunday | | | | | | | | | | | | | | | | | |

# BROWN, K. R.      Middlesex

**Name:** Keith Robert Brown
**Role:** Right-hand bat, wicket-keeper
**Born:** 18 March 1963, Edmonton
**Height:** 5ft 11in **Weight:** 13st 7lbs
**Nickname:** Browny, Scarface, Stally
**County debut:** 1984
**County cap:** 1990
**1000 runs in a season:** 2
**1st-Class 50s:** 44
**1st-Class 100s:** 12
**1st-Class 200s:** 1
**1st-Class catches:** 318
**1st-Class stumpings:** 24
**One-Day 100s:** 2
**Place in batting averages:**
56th av. 42.17 (1994 55th av. 39.93)
**Parents:** Kenneth William and Margaret Sonia
**Wife and date of marriage:**
Marie, 3 November 1984
**Children:** Zachary, 24 February 1987; Rosanna, 18 December 1989;
Alex, 29 December 1992
**Family links with cricket:** Brother Gary was on Middlesex staff for three years and

then played for Durham. Father is a qualified umpire
**Education:** Chace Comprehensive School, Enfield
**Qualifications:** French O-level; NCA Senior Coaching Award; qualified plasterer
**Career outside cricket:** Plasterer, PE instructor, coach
**Off-season:** Playing and coaching in Nelson, New Zealand
**Overseas tours:** NCA Youth tour to Denmark; Middlesex pre-season tours to La Manga 1985, 1986 and Portugal 1991, 1992, 1993
**Overseas teams played for:** Sydney University, Australia 1988-89; Motueka Cricket Association, Nelson, New Zealand 1991-92
**Cricketers particularly admired:** Clive Radley and Derek Randall
**Other sports followed:** Most sports apart from motor racing
**Injuries:** Fractured fingers, missed one Sunday League game
**Relaxations:** 'Long country walks with family and pet greyhound, finishing with a couple of pints in local.'
**Extras:** Had promising boxing career but gave it up in order to concentrate on cricket. Picked to play rugby for Essex
**Opinions on cricket:** '110 overs in a day is too many.'
**Best batting:** 200* Middlesex v Nottinghamshire, Lord's 1990
**Best bowling:** 2-7 Middlesex v Gloucestershire, Bristol 1987

## 1995 Season

|  | M | Inns | NO | Runs | HS | Avge | 100s | 50s | Ct | St | O | M | Runs | Wkts | Avge | Best | 5wI | 10wM |
|---|---|---|---|---|---|---|---|---|---|---|---|---|---|---|---|---|---|---|
| Test |  |  |  |  |  |  |  |  |  |  |  |  |  |  |  |  |  |  |
| All First | 19 | 27 | 4 | 970 | 147 * | 42.17 | 1 | 7 | 45 | 6 | 15 | 0 | 114 | 1 | 114.00 | 1-114 | - | - |
| 1-day Int |  |  |  |  |  |  |  |  |  |  |  |  |  |  |  |  |  |  |
| NatWest | 3 | 3 | 0 | 53 | 34 | 17.66 | - | - | 3 | 4 |  |  |  |  |  |  |  |  |
| B & H | 6 | 5 | 1 | 123 | 75 | 30.75 | - | 1 | 10 | - |  |  |  |  |  |  |  |  |
| Sunday | 15 | 14 | 3 | 279 | 54 * | 25.36 | - | 1 | 16 | 4 |  |  |  |  |  |  |  |  |

## Career Performances

|  | M | Inns | NO | Runs | HS | Avge | 100s | 50s | Ct | St | Balls | Runs | Wkts | Avge | Best | 5wI | 10wM |
|---|---|---|---|---|---|---|---|---|---|---|---|---|---|---|---|---|---|
| Test |  |  |  |  |  |  |  |  |  |  |  |  |  |  |  |  |  |
| All First | 193 | 288 | 55 | 8393 | 200 * | 36.02 | 12 | 44 | 318 | 24 | 321 | 276 | 6 | 46.00 | 2-7 | - | - |
| 1-day Int |  |  |  |  |  |  |  |  |  |  |  |  |  |  |  |  |  |
| NatWest | 19 | 16 | 3 | 412 | 103 * | 31.69 | 1 | - | 13 | 5 | 6 | 8 | 0 | - | - | - | - |
| B & H | 30 | 27 | 5 | 553 | 75 | 25.13 | - | 2 | 21 | 5 | 6 | 0 | 0 | - | - | - | - |
| Sunday | 133 | 111 | 33 | 2351 | 102 | 30.14 | 1 | 9 | 78 | 21 | 28 | 29 | 0 | - | - | - | - |

# BROWN, S. J. E.        Durham

**Name:** Simon John Emmerson Brown
**Role:** Right-hand bat, left-arm medium pace bowler, gully fielder
**Born:** 29 June 1969, Cleadon Village, Sunderland
**Height:** 6ft 3in **Weight:** 13st
**Nickname:** Chubby
**County debut:** 1987 (Northamptonshire), 1992 (Durham)
**50 wickets in a season:** 3
**1st-Class 50s:** 1
**1st-Class 5 w. in innings:** 16
**1st-Class 10 w. match:** 1
**1st-Class catches:** 29
**Place in batting averages:** 273rd av. 11.58 (1994 219th av. 17.86)
**Place in bowling averages:** 92nd av. 34.22 (1994 47th av. 28.10)

**Strike rate:** 62.05 (career 56.66)
**Parents:** Ernest and Doreen
**Wife and date of marriage:** Sarah, 3 October 1992
**Education:** Boldon Comprehensive, Tyne & Wear; South Tyneside College
**Qualifications:** 6 O-levels, qualified electrician
**Career outside cricket:** Electrician
**Overseas tours:** England YC to Sri Lanka 1986-87, to Australia for Youth World Cup 1987-88; MCC to Bahrain 1994-95
**Overseas teams played for:** Marist, Christchurch, New Zealand
**Cricketers particularly admired:** John Lever, Dennis Lillee
**Other sports followed:** Basketball and golf
**Injuries:** Damaged tendon in foot, missed one week
**Relaxations:** Playing basketball and golf
**Extras:** Offered basketball scholarship in America. Durham supporters' Player of the Year 1992. Durham Player of the Year 1994
**Best batting:** 69 Durham v Leicestershire, Durham University 1994
**Best bowling:** 7-70 Durham v Australians, Durham University 1993

16. Who will replace Martyn Moxon as Yorkshire's captain for 1996?

## 1995 Season

| | M | Inns | NO | Runs | HS | Avge | 100s | 50s | Ct | St | O | M | Runs | Wkts | Avge | Best | 5wI | 10wM |
|---|---|---|---|---|---|---|---|---|---|---|---|---|---|---|---|---|---|---|
| Test | | | | | | | | | | | | | | | | | | |
| All First | 18 | 30 | 6 | 278 | 36 | 11.58 | - | - | 6 | - | 589.3 | 117 | 1951 | 57 | 34.22 | 6-69 | 4 | 1 |
| 1-day Int | | | | | | | | | | | | | | | | | | |
| NatWest | 2 | 1 | 1 | 1 | 1 * | - | - | - | - | - | 21 | 2 | 86 | 5 | 17.20 | 3-64 | - | |
| B & H | 3 | 3 | 0 | 22 | 12 | 7.33 | - | - | - | - | 30.5 | 6 | 108 | 7 | 15.42 | 3-39 | - | |
| Sunday | 11 | 8 | 3 | 27 | 7 | 5.40 | - | - | 5 | - | 76.5 | 4 | 321 | 17 | 18.88 | 4-20 | - | |

## Career Performances

| | M | Inns | NO | Runs | HS | Avge | 100s | 50s | Ct | St | Balls | Runs | Wkts | Avge | Best | 5wI | 10wM |
|---|---|---|---|---|---|---|---|---|---|---|---|---|---|---|---|---|---|
| Test | | | | | | | | | | | | | | | | | |
| All First | 88 | 117 | 40 | 965 | 69 | 12.53 | - | 1 | 29 | - | 14847 | 8707 | 262 | 33.23 | 7-70 | 16 | 1 |
| 1-day Int | | | | | | | | | | | | | | | | | |
| NatWest | 7 | 4 | 3 | 11 | 7 * | 11.00 | - | - | - | - | 466 | 340 | 13 | 26.15 | 5-22 | 1 | |
| B & H | 10 | 5 | 2 | 28 | 12 | 9.33 | - | - | - | - | 561 | 349 | 13 | 26.84 | 3-39 | - | |
| Sunday | 50 | 18 | 7 | 51 | 7 | 4.63 | - | - | 11 | - | 2166 | 1799 | 55 | 32.70 | 4-20 | - | |

# BURNS, M. Warwickshire

**Name:** Michael Burns
**Role:** Right-hand bat, right-arm medium bowler, wicket-keeper
**Born:** 6 February 1969, Barrow-in-Furness
**Height:** 6ft **Weight:** 13st
**Nickname:** George, Red Hot
**County debut:** 1991
**1st-Class 50s:** 1
**1st-Class catches:** 25
**1st-Class stumpings:** 3
**Parents:** Robert and Linda, stepfather Stan
**Wife and date of marriage:** Carolyn, 9 October 1994
**Family links with cricket:** 'Grandfather was a great back-garden bowler'
**Education:** Walney Comprehensive; Barrow College of Further Education
**Qualifications:** 'Few CSEs, couple of GCEs', qualified fitter at VSEL in Barrow, coaching award
**Career outside cricket:** 'Signing autographs for DHSS'
**Off-season:** 'Small shoulder operation, training, hopefully cricket abroad when fit'

**Overseas teams played for:** Gill College, South Africa 1991-92; Motueka, Nelson, New Zealand 1992-93; Alex CC, Harare
**Cricketers particularly admired:**
Dermot Reeve, Allan Donald, Roger Twose
**Other sports followed:** Rugby league ('had trials for Barrow RLFC and Carlisle RLFC') and golf
**Injuries:** Shoulder
**Relaxations:** 'Eating Indians, socialising with friends. One or two pints with Pop Welch'
**Extras:** Played for Cumberland 1989-90. Had a trial with Glamorgan, went to La Manga with Lancashire junior side 1984. Player of the Tournament at Benson and Hedges Thailand International Cricket Sixes in 1989
**Opinions on cricket:** 'More should be done to help players in the winter and to help players find work after cricket.'
**Best batting:** 78 Warwickshire v Cambridge University, Fenner's 1992

## 1995 Season

|  | M | Inns | NO | Runs | HS | Avge | 100s | 50s | Ct | St | O | M | Runs | Wkts | Avge | Best | 5wI | 10wM |
|---|---|---|---|---|---|---|---|---|---|---|---|---|---|---|---|---|---|---|
| Test |  |  |  |  |  |  |  |  |  |  |  |  |  |  |  |  |  |  |
| All First | 3 | 5 | 0 | 78 | 35 | 15.60 | - | - | 9 | 1 |  |  |  |  |  |  |  |  |
| 1-day Int |  |  |  |  |  |  |  |  |  |  |  |  |  |  |  |  |  |  |
| NatWest |  |  |  |  |  |  |  |  |  |  |  |  |  |  |  |  |  |  |
| B & H | 4 | 2 | 0 | 12 | 12 | 6.00 | - | - | 2 | 1 |  |  |  |  |  |  |  |  |
| Sunday | 2 | 2 | 0 | 8 | 7 | 4.00 | - | - | 1 | - |  |  |  |  |  |  |  |  |

## Career Performances

|  | M | Inns | NO | Runs | HS | Avge | 100s | 50s | Ct | St | Balls | Runs | Wkts | Avge | Best | 5wI | 10wM |
|---|---|---|---|---|---|---|---|---|---|---|---|---|---|---|---|---|---|
| Test |  |  |  |  |  |  |  |  |  |  |  |  |  |  |  |  |  |
| All First | 12 | 19 | 1 | 295 | 78 | 16.38 | - | 1 | 25 | 3 | 42 | 8 | 0 | - | - | - | - |
| 1-day Int |  |  |  |  |  |  |  |  |  |  |  |  |  |  |  |  |  |
| NatWest |  |  |  |  |  |  |  |  |  |  |  |  |  |  |  |  |  |
| B & H | 8 | 6 | 0 | 55 | 22 | 9.16 | - | - | 6 | 2 |  |  |  |  |  |  |  |
| Sunday | 19 | 16 | 2 | 158 | 37 | 11.28 | - | - | 20 | 7 |  |  |  |  |  |  |  |

# BUTCHER, G. P.                               Glamorgan

**Name:** Gary Paul Butcher
**Role:** Right-hand opening bat, right-arm medium bowler
**Born:** 11 March 1975, Clapham, South London
**Height:** 5ft 9in **Weight:** 11st
**Nickname:** Butch, Bouché, The Meatseller
**County debut:** 1994

**1st-Class catches:** 2
**Parents:** Alan and Elaine
**Marital status:** Single
**Family links with cricket:** Father Alan
played for Surrey, Glamorgan and England
and is now with Essex; brother Mark plays
for Surrey and uncle Ian played for
Gloucestershire and Leicestershire
**Education:** Cumnor House; Trinity School;
Riddlesdown Comprehensive;
Heath Clark College
**Qualifications:** 4 GCSEs, BTEC 1st Diploma
in Leisure Studies
**Career outside cricket:** Salesman
**Overseas tours:** England U18 to Denmark
1993; England U19 to Sri Lanka 1993-94
**Cricketers particularly admired:**
David Gower, Viv Richards, Brian Lara,
Curtly Ambrose, Nick Moss
**Other sports followed:** Football, gymnastics, chess
**Relaxations:** 'Music, the slide, the economy and the odd night or two in Bridgend'
**Extras:** Won ASW Player of the Month, May 1993
**Opinions on cricket:** 'All 2nd XI games should be played at county grounds, with two
qualified umpires.'
**Best batting:** 41 Glamorgan v Leicestershire, Cardiff 1994
**Best bowling:** 2-36 Glamorgan v Oxford University, The Parks 1994

## 1995 Season

|          | M | Inns | NO | Runs | HS | Avge | 100s | 50s | Ct | St | O | M | Runs | Wkts | Avge | Best | 5wl | 10wM |
|----------|---|------|----|------|----|------|------|-----|----|----|---|---|------|------|------|------|-----|------|
| Test     |   |      |    |      |    |      |      |     |    |    |   |   |      |      |      |      |     |      |
| All First | 1 | 2 | 2 | 7 | 4* | - | - | - | - | - | 16 | 5 | 45 | 0 | - | - | - | - |
| 1-day Int |   |      |    |      |    |      |      |     |    |    |   |   |      |      |      |      |     |      |
| NatWest  |   |      |    |      |    |      |      |     |    |    |   |   |      |      |      |      |     |      |
| B & H    | 3 | 1 | 0 | 0 | 0 | 0.00 | - | - | - | - | 2 | 0 | 12 | 0 | - | - | - |   |
| Sunday   |   |      |    |      |    |      |      |     |    |    |   |   |      |      |      |      |     |      |

## Career Performances

|          | M | Inns | NO | Runs | HS | Avge | 100s | 50s | Ct | St | Balls | Runs | Wkts | Avge | Best | 5wl | 10wM |
|----------|---|------|----|------|----|------|------|-----|----|----|-------|------|------|------|------|-----|------|
| Test     |   |      |    |      |    |      |      |     |    |    |       |      |      |      |      |     |      |
| All First | 5 | 7 | 2 | 64 | 41 | 12.80 | - | - | 2 | - | 372 | 239 | 2 | 119.50 | 2-36 | - | - |
| 1-day Int |   |      |    |      |    |      |      |     |    |    |       |      |      |      |      |     |      |
| NatWest  |   |      |    |      |    |      |      |     |    |    |       |      |      |      |      |     |      |
| B & H    | 3 | 1 | 0 | 0 | 0 | 0.00 | - | - | - | - | 12 | 12 | 0 | - | - | - |   |
| Sunday   | 3 | 0 | 0 | 0 | 0 | - | - | - | - | - | 60 | 66 | 2 | 33.00 | 2-8 | - |   |

# BUTCHER, M. A.  Surrey

**Name:** Mark Alan Butcher
**Role:** Left-hand bat, right-arm medium bowler
**Born:** 23 August 1972, Croydon
**Height:** 5ft 11in **Weight:** 12st 7lbs
**Nickname:** Butch, Baz
**County debut:** 1991
**1000 runs in a season:** 1
**1st-Class 50s:** 14
**1st-Class 100s:** 3
**1st-Class catches:** 40
**Place in batting averages:** 82nd av. 36.66
(1994 86th av. 36.05)
**Place in bowling averages:** 127th av. 42.50
(1994 125th av. 41.87)
**Strike rate:** 64.04 (career 68.83)
**Parents:** Alan and Elaine
**Marital status:** Engaged to Judy
**Family links with cricket:** Father Alan played
for Glamorgan, Surrey and England and is now with Essex; brother Gary plays for
Glamorgan; uncle Ian played for Gloucestershire and Leicestershire
**Education:** Cumnor House School; Trinity School; Archbishop Tenison's, Croydon
**Qualifications:** 5 O-levels, senior coaching award
**Career outside cricket:** Singer, guitar player, female impersonator
**Off-season:** 'Open to suggestions'
**Overseas tours:** England YC to New Zealand 1990-91; Surrey to Dubai 1990 and
1993, to Perth 1995
**Overseas teams played for:** South Melbourne, Australia 1993-94; North Perth 1994-95
**Cricketers particularly admired:** Carl Rackemann, Mark and Steve Waugh,
Ian Botham, David Gower, Michael Holding, Jason Ratcliffe for his driving skills
('behind the wheel')
**Other sports followed:** Football, tennis, rhythmic gymnastics
**Relaxations:** 'Books, collecting CDs and records, playing guitar and singing in my
band with my brother Gary, Peter James and Jo Fulman'
**Extras:** Played his first game for Surrey against his father's Glamorgan in the Refuge
Assurance League at The Oval, the first-ever match of any sort between first-class
counties in which a father and son have been in opposition
**Opinions on cricket:** 'Since introducing four-day cricket, the aim of those involved in
producing the directives for pitches and the pitches themselves seems to be to have the
game finish as soon as possible. The standard of first-class pitches is extremely poor and
if they are not improved, neither will the standard of the players. Surely a hard-fought
draw over four days is more beneficial to producing Test cricketers than a game which

is over in two days. Secondly, why in England are first-class games played over 110 overs? Nowhere else in the world do cricketers play so many games let alone over so many overs. Fewer overs would produce a better quality of cricket throughout the day.'

**Best batting:** 167 Surrey v Durham, The Oval 1995
**Best bowling:** 4-31 Surrey v Worcestershire, The Oval 1994

## 1995 Season

|          | M  | Inns | NO | Runs | HS   | Avge   | 100s | 50s | Ct | St | O     | M  | Runs | Wkts | Avge  | Best | 5wI | 10wM |
|----------|----|------|----|------|------|--------|------|-----|----|----|-------|----|------|------|-------|------|-----|------|
| Test     |    |      |    |      |      |        |      |     |    |    |       |    |      |      |       |      |     |      |
| All First | 18 | 34   | 1  | 1210 | 167  | 36.66  | 2    | 10  | 15 | -  | 234.5 | 37 | 935  | 22   | 42.50 | 4-72 | -   | -    |
| 1-day Int |    |      |    |      |      |        |      |     |    |    |       |    |      |      |       |      |     |      |
| NatWest  | 2  | 2    | 1  | 105  | 79 * | 105.00 | -    | 1   | 1  | -  | 12    | 2  | 34   | 1    | 34.00 | 1-5  | -   |      |
| B & H    | 1  | 1    | 0  | 5    | 5    | 5.00   | -    | -   | -  | -  |       |    |      |      |       |      |     |      |
| Sunday   | 14 | 10   | 2  | 108  | 29   | 13.50  | -    | -   | 1  | -  | 62.3  | 1  | 455  | 8    | 56.87 | 2-35 | -   |      |

## Career Performances

|          | M  | Inns | NO | Runs | HS   | Avge  | 100s | 50s | Ct | St | Balls | Runs | Wkts | Avge  | Best | 5wI | 10wM |
|----------|----|------|----|------|------|-------|------|-----|----|----|-------|------|------|-------|------|-----|------|
| Test     |    |      |    |      |      |       |      |     |    |    |       |      |      |       |      |     |      |
| All First | 38 | 66   | 7  | 2093 | 167  | 35.47 | 3    | 14  | 40 | -  | 3717  | 2156 | 54   | 39.92 | 4-31 | -   | -    |
| 1-day Int |    |      |    |      |      |       |      |     |    |    |       |      |      |       |      |     |      |
| NatWest  | 4  | 4    | 2  | 124  | 79 * | 62.00 | -    | 1   | 3  | -  | 216   | 127  | 3    | 42.33 | 2-57 | -   |      |
| B & H    | 6  | 4    | 0  | 15   | 5    | 3.75  | -    | -   | 1  | -  | 271   | 217  | 6    | 36.16 | 3-37 | -   |      |
| Sunday   | 36 | 24   | 10 | 309  | 48 * | 22.07 | -    | -   | 8  | -  | 1329  | 1270 | 27   | 47.03 | 3-23 | -   |      |

# BYAS, D.                                      Yorkshire

**Name:** David Byas
**Role:** Left-hand bat, right-arm medium bowler, county captain
**Born:** 26 August 1963, Middledale, Kilham
**Height:** 6ft 4in **Weight:** 15st
**Nickname:** Bingo, Gadgett, Giles
**County debut:** 1986
**County cap:** 1991
**1000 runs in a season**: 4
**1st-Class 50s:** 50
**1st-Class 100s:** 15
**1st-Class 200s:** 1
**1st-Class catches:** 188
**One-Day 100s:** 2
**Place in batting averages:** 9th av. 56.26 (1994 74th av. 37.05)
**Strike rate:** (career 91.00)

**Parents:** Richard and Anne
**Wife and date of marriage:**
Rachael Elizabeth, 27 October 1990
**Children:** Olivia Rachael, 16 December 1991; Georgia Elizabeth, 30 December 1993
**Family links with cricket:** Father played in local league
**Education:** Scarborough College
**Qualifications:** 1 O-level (Engineering)
**Career outside cricket:** Partner in family farming business
**Off-season:** Working on farm
**Overseas teams played for:** Papatoetoe, Auckland 1988
**Cricketers particularly admired:** David Gower, Viv Richards, Ian Botham
**Other sports followed:** Hockey, motor racing, rugby union
**Relaxations:** 'Looking after my two active daughters. Dining out with my wife. Gardening.'
**Extras:** Became youngest captain (aged 21) of Scarborough CC in 1985. Broke John Hampshire's Sunday League record with 702 runs in 1994, which had stood since 1976. Runner-up in the Sunday League averages 1994. Played hockey for England Under 21. Awarded the captaincy of Yorkshire for 1996
**Opinions on cricket:** 'Too much one-day cricket. Definitely should not have a Sunday League game in the middle of a four-day game.'
**Best batting:** 213 Yorkshire v Worcestershire, Scarborough 1995
**Best bowling:** 3-55 Yorkshire v Derbyshire, Chesterfield 1990

## 1995 Season

| | M | Inns | NO | Runs | HS | Avge | 100s | 50s | Ct | St | O | M | Runs | Wkts | Avge | Best | 5wI | 10wM |
|---|---|---|---|---|---|---|---|---|---|---|---|---|---|---|---|---|---|---|
| Test | | | | | | | | | | | | | | | | | | |
| All First | 20 | 37 | 3 | 1913 | 213 | 56.26 | 4 | 10 | 42 | - | 6 | 1 | 37 | 0 | - | - | - | - |
| 1-day Int | | | | | | | | | | | | | | | | | | |
| NatWest | 4 | 4 | 0 | 104 | 50 | 26.00 | - | 1 | 1 | - | | | | | | | | |
| B & H | 4 | 3 | 0 | 111 | 47 | 37.00 | - | - | 1 | - | | | | | | | | |
| Sunday | 17 | 16 | 1 | 399 | 78 | 26.60 | - | 3 | 6 | - | | | | | | | | |

## Career Performances

| | M | Inns | NO | Runs | HS | Avge | 100s | 50s | Ct | St | Balls | Runs | Wkts | Avge | Best | 5wI | 10wM |
|---|---|---|---|---|---|---|---|---|---|---|---|---|---|---|---|---|---|
| Test | | | | | | | | | | | | | | | | | |
| All First | 159 | 269 | 25 | 8799 | 213 | 36.06 | 15 | 50 | 188 | - | 1092 | 719 | 12 | 59.91 | 3-55 | - | - |
| 1-day Int | | | | | | | | | | | | | | | | | |
| NatWest | 16 | 14 | 1 | 418 | 71 | 32.15 | - | 4 | 8 | - | 18 | 23 | 1 | 23.00 | 1-23 | - | |
| B & H | 24 | 21 | 1 | 524 | 92 | 26.20 | - | 2 | 5 | - | 283 | 155 | 5 | 31.00 | 2-38 | - | |
| Sunday | 123 | 119 | 18 | 3004 | 106 * | 29.74 | 2 | 15 | 30 | - | 529 | 463 | 19 | 24.36 | 3-19 | - | |

# CADDICK, A. R. Somerset

**Name:** Andrew Richard Caddick
**Role:** Right-hand bat, right-arm
fast-medium bowler
**Born:** 21 November 1968, Christchurch,
New Zealand
**Height:** 6ft 6in **Weight:** 15st 7lbs
**Nickname:** Kiwi, Doi, Shack, Bean
('Quite a few')
**County debut:** 1991
**County cap:** 1992
**Test debut:** 1993
**Tests:** 8
**One-Day Internationals:** 5
**50 wickets in a season:** 3
**1st-Class 50s:** 4
**1st-Class 5 w. in innings:** 14
**1st-Class 10 w. in match:** 5
**1st-Class catches:** 22
**One-Day 5 w. in innings:** 2
**Place in batting averages:**
103rd av. 33.85 (1994 250th av. 13.68)
**Place in bowling averages:** 34th av. 25.54 (1994 12th av. 23.25)
**Strike rate:** 45.79 (50.21)
**Parents:** Christopher and Audrey
**Wife and date of marriage:** Sarah, 27 January 1995
**Education:** Papanui High School, Christchurch, New Zealand
**Qualifications:** Qualified plasterer and tiler
**Career outside cricket:** Plasterer and tiler
**Off-season:** 'Working anywhere'
**Overseas tours:** New Zealand YC to Australia (Youth World Cup) 1987-88, to
England 1988; England A to Australia 1992-93; England to West Indies 1993-94
**Cricketers particularly admired:**
Dennis Lillee, Richard Hadlee, Robin Smith, Jimmy Cook
**Other sports followed:** 'Mostly all'
**Injuries:** Shin problems after operations restricted season to only six games
**Relaxations:** Music, videos, golf, most sports
**Extras:** Rapid Cricketline Player of the Year 1991
**Opinions on cricket:** 'For a bowler it's a very hard game.'
**Best batting:** 92 Somerset v Worcestershire, Worcester 1995
**Best bowling:** 9-32 Somerset v Lancashire, Taunton 1993

## 1995 Season

| | M | Inns | NO | Runs | HS | Avge | 100s | 50s | Ct | St | O | M | Runs | Wkts | Avge | Best | 5wI | 10wM |
|---|---|---|---|---|---|---|---|---|---|---|---|---|---|---|---|---|---|---|
| Test | | | | | | | | | | | | | | | | | | |
| All First | 6 | 7 | 0 | 237 | 92 | 33.85 | - | 2 | 1 | - | 183.1 | 34 | 613 | 24 | 25.54 | 8-69 | 1 | 1 |
| 1-day Int | | | | | | | | | | | | | | | | | | |
| NatWest | | | | | | | | | | | | | | | | | | |
| B & H | 2 | 2 | 1 | 38 | 28 | 38.00 | - | - | - | - | 19 | 2 | 69 | 2 | 34.50 | 1-27 | - | |
| Sunday | 5 | 2 | 2 | 23 | 22 * | - | - | - | - | - | 28 | 0 | 127 | 5 | 25.40 | 3-41 | - | |

## Career Performances

| | M | Inns | NO | Runs | HS | Avge | 100s | 50s | Ct | St | Balls | Runs | Wkts | Avge | Best | 5wI | 10wM |
|---|---|---|---|---|---|---|---|---|---|---|---|---|---|---|---|---|---|
| Test | 8 | 14 | 2 | 170 | 29 * | 14.16 | - | | 4 | - | 1940 | 1033 | 23 | 44.91 | 6-65 | 2 | - |
| All First | 64 | 81 | 13 | 1156 | 92 | 17.00 | - | 4 | 22 | - | 12253 | 6535 | 244 | 26.78 | 9-32 | 14 | 5 |
| 1-day Int | 5 | 3 | 3 | 23 | 20 * | - | - | - | 1 | - | 318 | 258 | 6 | 43.00 | 3-39 | - | |
| NatWest | 9 | 5 | 1 | 12 | 8 | 3.00 | - | - | 2 | - | 533 | 282 | 18 | 15.66 | 6-30 | 2 | |
| B & H | 9 | 8 | 5 | 60 | 28 | 20.00 | - | - | 2 | - | 558 | 331 | 9 | 36.77 | 2-20 | - | |
| Sunday | 33 | 13 | 5 | 111 | 36 * | 13.87 | - | - | 1 | - | 1362 | 1048 | 36 | 29.11 | 4-18 | - | |

# CAIRNS, C. L.        Nottinghamshire

**Name:** Christopher Lance Cairns
**Role:** Right-hand bat, right-arm
fast-medium bowler
**Born:** 13 June 1970, Picton, New Zealand
**Height:** 6ft 2in **Weight:** 14st
**Nickname:** Sheep
**County debut:** 1988
**County cap:** 1993
**Test debut:** 1990-91
**Tests:** 10
**One-Day Internationals:** 29
**1000 runs in a season:** 1
**50 wickets in a season:** 3
**1st-Class 50s:** 33
**1st-Class 100s:** 5
**1st-Class 5 w. in innings:** 13
**1st-Class 10 w. in match:** 3
**1st-Class catches:** 47
**One-day 100s:** 2
**One-Day 5 w. in innings:** 1
**Place in batting averages:** 67th av. 40.37
**Place in bowling averages:** 8th av. 19.90

**Strike rate:** 43.36 (career 53.66)
**Parents:** Lance and Sue
**Family links with cricket:** Father played for New Zealand, uncle played first-class cricket in New Zealand
**Education:** Christchurch Boys' High School, New Zealand
**Qualifications:** 5th and 6th form certificates
**Marital status:** Single
**Off-season:** Playing for New Zealand
**Overseas tours:** New Zealand YC to Australia (Youth World Cup) 1987-88; New Zealand to Australia 1989-90, 1993-94, to India 1995-96, to India and Pakistan (World Cup) 1995-96
**Overseas teams played for:** Northern Districts 1988-89; Canterbury 1990-95
**Cricketers particularly admired:** Mick Newell, Richard Hadlee, Dennis Lillee
**Other sports followed:** Most sports
**Extras:** Hit the fastest first-class hundred of the 1995 season (in 65 balls versus Cambridge University)
**Opinions on cricket:** 'Great game.'
**Best batting:** 115 Nottinghamshire v Middlesex, Lord's 1995
**Best bowling:** 8-47 Nottinghamshire v Sussex, Arundel 1995

## 1995 Season

| | M | Inns | NO | Runs | HS | Avge | 100s | 50s | Ct | St | O | M | Runs | Wkts | Avge | Best | 5wI | 10wM |
|---|---|---|---|---|---|---|---|---|---|---|---|---|---|---|---|---|---|---|
| Test | | | | | | | | | | | | | | | | | | |
| All First | 17 | 30 | 1 | 1171 | 115 | 40.37 | 2 | 7 | 7 | - | 375.5 | 89 | 1035 | 52 | 19.90 | 8-47 | 3 | 1 |
| 1-day Int | | | | | | | | | | | | | | | | | | |
| NatWest | 2 | 2 | 1 | 75 | 48 * | 75.00 | - | - | 1 | - | 24 | 2 | 80 | 4 | 20.00 | 2-39 | - | |
| B & H | 6 | 4 | 0 | 73 | 46 | 18.25 | - | - | 2 | - | 46.5 | 1 | 186 | 10 | 18.60 | 4-47 | - | |
| Sunday | 15 | 14 | 1 | 615 | 101 | 47.30 | 1 | 4 | 6 | - | 82.2 | 4 | 451 | 20 | 22.55 | 3-34 | - | |

## Career Performances

| | M | Inns | NO | Runs | HS | Avge | 100s | 50s | Ct | St | Balls | Runs | Wkts | Avge | Best | 5wI | 10wM |
|---|---|---|---|---|---|---|---|---|---|---|---|---|---|---|---|---|---|
| Test | 10 | 17 | 0 | 349 | 78 | 20.52 | - | 2 | 6 | - | 1995 | 1207 | 28 | 43.10 | 6-52 | 2 | - |
| All First | 107 | 158 | 17 | 4813 | 115 | 34.13 | 5 | 33 | 47 | - | 17494 | 9228 | 326 | 28.30 | 8-47 | 13 | 3 |
| 1-day Int | 29 | 26 | 4 | 586 | 72 | 26.63 | - | 2 | 12 | - | 1151 | 892 | 27 | 33.03 | 4-55 | - | |
| NatWest | 6 | 6 | 1 | 301 | 77 | 60.20 | - | 3 | 2 | - | 410 | 203 | 13 | 15.61 | 4-18 | - | |
| B & H | 11 | 7 | 0 | 91 | 46 | 13.00 | - | - | 3 | - | 557 | 404 | 15 | 26.93 | 4-47 | - | |
| Sunday | 45 | 38 | 4 | 1241 | 126 * | 36.50 | 2 | 7 | 17 | - | 1830 | 1449 | 61 | 23.75 | 6-52 | 1 | |

# CAMPBELL, C. L.         Durham

**Name:** Colin Lockey Campbell
**Role:** Right-hand bat, right-arm
fast-medium bowler
**Born:** 11 August 1977, Newcastle
**Height:** 6ft 5in  **Weight:** 13st 10lbs
**Nickname:** Scunner
**County debut:** No first-team appearance
**Parents:** Paul and Jacqueline
**Marital status:** Single
**Education:** Winlayton West Lane Primary
School; Blaydon Comprehensive
**Qualifications:** 9 GCSEs, 2 A-levels
**Off-season:** Touring Zimbabwe with
England U19
**Overseas tours:** Durham to South Africa
1995; England U19 to Zimbabwe 1995-96
**Cricketers particularly admired:**
Graeme Hick, Allan Donald
**Other sports followed:** Golf and football
**Injuries:** Calf muscle, out for two months
**Relaxations:** Playing golf and watching football
**Extras:** Top of the bowling averages for Blaydon 1st XI for three years and Blaydon
U18s for two years. Had match figures of nine for 86 on his debut for Durham 2nd XI

17. Which three Indian Test players played county cricket in
1995 and for which counties did they play?

104

# CAMPBELL, S. L.                    Durham

**Name:** Sherwin Legay Campbell
**Role:** Right-hand opening bat
**Born:** 1 November 1970, Bridgetown,
Barbados
**Height:** 5ft 4in
**County debut:** No first-team appearance
**Test debut:** 1994-95
**Tests:** 9
**One-day Internationals:** 9
**1000 runs in a season:** 1
**1st-Class 50s:** 13
**1st-Class 100s:** 7
**1st-Class catches:** 39
**One-day 50s:** 1
**Place in batting averages:** 35th av. 47.11
**Education:** Ellerslie Secondary School,
Barbados

**Overseas tours:** West Indies to New Zealand
1994-95, to England 1995, to Australia 1995-96, to India and Pakistan (World Cup) 1995-96
**Extras:** Was the leading run-scorer in first-class games for West Indies on their 1995
tour to England
**Best batting:** 172 West Indies v Hampshire, Southampton 1995

## 1995 Season

|           | M  | Inns | NO | Runs | HS  | Avge  | 100s | 50s | Ct | St | O | M | Runs | Wkts | Avge | Best | 5wI | 10wM |
|-----------|----|------|----|------|-----|-------|------|-----|----|----|---|---|------|------|------|------|-----|------|
| Test      | 6  | 10   | 0  | 454  | 93  | 45.40 | -    | 4   | 9  | -  |   |   |      |      |      |      |     |      |
| All First | 16 | 26   | 0  | 1225 | 172 | 47.11 | 3    | 6   | 15 | -  |   |   |      |      |      |      |     |      |
| 1-day Int | 2  | 2    | 0  | 100  | 80  | 50.00 | -    | 1   | -  | -  |   |   |      |      |      |      |     |      |
| NatWest   |    |      |    |      |     |       |      |     |    |    |   |   |      |      |      |      |     |      |
| B & H     |    |      |    |      |     |       |      |     |    |    |   |   |      |      |      |      |     |      |
| Sunday    |    |      |    |      |     |       |      |     |    |    |   |   |      |      |      |      |     |      |

## Career Performances

|           | M  | Inns | NO | Runs | HS  | Avge  | 100s | 50s | Ct | St | Balls | Runs | Wkts | Avge | Best | 5wI | 10wM |
|-----------|----|------|----|------|-----|-------|------|-----|----|----|-------|------|------|------|------|-----|------|
| Test      | 9  | 14   | 0  | 599  | 93  | 42.78 | -    | 6   | 11 | -  |       |      |      |      |      |     |      |
| All First | 37 | 60   | 2  | 2309 | 172 | 39.81 | 7    | 13  | 39 | -  | 12    | 3    | 0    | -    | -    | -   | -    |
| 1-day Int | 9  | 9    | 0  | 192  | 80  | 21.33 | -    | 1   | 2  | -  |       |      |      |      |      |     |      |
| NatWest   |    |      |    |      |     |       |      |     |    |    |       |      |      |      |      |     |      |
| B & H     |    |      |    |      |     |       |      |     |    |    |       |      |      |      |      |     |      |
| Sunday    |    |      |    |      |     |       |      |     |    |    |       |      |      |      |      |     |      |

# CAPEL, D. J.      Northamptonshire

**Name:** David John Capel
**Role:** Right-hand bat, right-arm medium
bowler, all-rounder, slip fielder
**Born:** 6 February 1963, Northampton
**Height:** 5ft 11in **Weight:** 12st 10lbs
**Nickname:** Capes, Fiery
**County debut:** 1981
**County cap:** 1986
**Benefit:** 1994
**Test debut:** 1987
**Tests:** 15
**One-Day Internationals:** 23
**1000 runs in a season:** 3
**50 wickets in a season:** 4
**1st-Class 50s:** 67
**1st-Class 100s:** 15
**1st-Class 5 w. in innings:** 14
**1st-Class catches:** 142
**One-Day 100s:** 3
**Place in batting averages:** 90th av. 35.61
**Place in bowling averages:** 25th av. 23.64
**Strike rate:** 42.15 (career 60.37)
**Parents:** John and Janet
**Wife and date of marriage:** Debbie, 21 September 1985
**Children:** Jenny, 21 October 1987; Jordan, 18 May 1993
**Family links with cricket:** Father and brother Andrew both captained
their local league sides
**Education:** Roade Primary School; Roade Comprehensive School
**Qualifications:** 3 O-levels, 4 CSEs, NCA advanced coaching certificate
**Off-season:** 'Trying to find work in England – no easy task'
**Overseas tours:** England to Sharjah 1986-87, to Pakistan 1987-88, to New Zealand
and Australia 1987-88, to India (Nehru Cup) 1989-90, to West Indies 1989-90;
England A to Australia 1992-93
**Overseas teams played for:** Eastern Province, South Africa 1985-87; Petersham-
Marrickville, Sydney 1991-92
**Other sports followed:** 'Golf, local rugby and soccer teams'
**Relaxations:** 'Family, gardening, golf, walking, cycling, coarse fishing, most music'
**Extras:** Only second Northampton-born man to play for England. Two centuries in a
match against Sussex 1989. All-Rounder of the Year 'Wetherall Award' 1989. Broke
Northants records for fourth wicket in Sunday League with K.M. Curran and for fifth
wicket in NatWest Trophy with A.J. Lamb. Record Northants CCC benefit of £192,000

**Opinions on cricket:** 'I fail to believe that it is necessary to have three one-day competitions. Surely it could be arranged to have one knock-out competition and one league competition of 50 overs per side and scrap 40-over cricket. The league format should be two divisions and have play-offs for a final.'

**Best batting:** 175 Northmptonshire v Leicestershire, Northampton 1995
**Best bowling:** 7-44 Northamptonshire v Warwickshire, Edgbaston 1995

## 1995 Season

| | M | Inns | NO | Runs | HS | Avge | 100s | 50s | Ct | St | O | M | Runs | Wkts | Avge | Best | 5wI | 10wM |
|---|---|---|---|---|---|---|---|---|---|---|---|---|---|---|---|---|---|---|
| Test | | | | | | | | | | | | | | | | | | |
| All First | 19 | 29 | 3 | 926 | 175 | 35.61 | 3 | 3 | 13 | - | 358.2 | 70 | 1206 | 51 | 23.64 | 7-44 | 2 | - |
| 1-day Int | | | | | | | | | | | | | | | | | | |
| NatWest | 5 | 4 | 0 | 32 | 12 | 8.00 | - | - | 1 | - | 44.5 | 1 | 199 | 3 | 66.33 | 2-43 | - | |
| B & H | 3 | 3 | 0 | 29 | 23 | 9.66 | - | - | - | - | 22 | 1 | 76 | 1 | 76.00 | 1-21 | - | |
| Sunday | 14 | 12 | 3 | 264 | 57 * | 29.33 | - | 1 | 7 | - | 62 | 2 | 367 | 4 | 91.75 | 2-55 | - | |

## Career Performances

| | M | Inns | NO | Runs | HS | Avge | 100s | 50s | Ct | St | Balls | Runs | Wkts | Avge | Best | 5wI | 10wM |
|---|---|---|---|---|---|---|---|---|---|---|---|---|---|---|---|---|---|
| Test | 15 | 25 | 1 | 374 | 98 | 15.58 | - | 2 | 6 | - | 2000 | 1064 | 21 | 50.66 | 3-88 | - | - |
| All First | 291 | 440 | 64 | 11248 | 175 | 29.91 | 15 | 67 | 142 | - | 30669 | 16146 | 508 | 31.78 | 7-44 | 14 | - |
| 1-day Int | 23 | 19 | 2 | 327 | 50 * | 19.23 | - | 1 | 6 | - | 1038 | 805 | 17 | 47.35 | 3-38 | - | |
| NatWest | 37 | 32 | 8 | 877 | 101 | 36.54 | 1 | 4 | 9 | - | 1614 | 1059 | 30 | 35.30 | 3-21 | - | |
| B & H | 49 | 43 | 5 | 745 | 97 | 19.60 | - | 1 | 9 | - | 2242 | 1408 | 51 | 27.60 | 4-29 | - | |
| Sunday | 162 | 148 | 32 | 3460 | 121 | 29.82 | 2 | 14 | 39 | - | 4747 | 3827 | 112 | 34.16 | 4-30 | - | |

18. Who captained the England U19 side against South Africa U19 in 1995?

**Name:** John Donald Carr
**Role:** Right-hand bat, right-arm medium bowler, county vice-captain
**Born:** 15 June 1963, St John's Wood
**Height:** 6ft **Weight:** 12st
**Nickname:** Carsy, Gold
**County debut:** 1983
**County cap:** 1987
**1000 runs in a season:** 4
**1st-Class 50s:** 46
**1st-Class 100s:** 24
**1st-Class 200s:** 1
**1st-Class 5 w. in innings:** 3
**1st-Class catches:** 232
**One-day 100s:** 1
**Place in batting averages:** 32nd 47.73 (1994 1st av. 90.70)
**Strike rate:** (career 98.33)
**Parents:** Donald and Stella
**Wife and date of marriage:** Vicky, 5 May 1990
**Children:** Holly, 14 December 1992; Elinor, 6 August 1994
**Family links with cricket:** Father played for Derbyshire and England and is now secretary of the TCCB. Uncle, Major Douglas Carr, was secretary of Derbyshire CCC
**Education:** The Hall, Hampstead; Repton School; Worcester College, Oxford
**Qualifications:** Degree in Philosophy, Politics and Economics; senior coaching certificate
**Career outside cricket:** One year with Barclays Bank
**Off-season:** 'Close to home, working if possible!'
**Overseas tours:** Oxbridge to Australia and Hong Kong 1985-86; Troubadours to Argentina and Brazil 1990; MCC to Bahrain 1994-95
**Overseas teams played for:** Sydney University 1985-86; Weston Creek, Canberra 1987-88; Argentina Colts XI 1989-90
**Cricketers particularly admired:** Allan Border, Curtly Ambrose
**Relaxations:** Watching and playing a variety of sports – Eton fives, real tennis, golf, squash, football – good food and the cinema
**Extras:** Retired from first-class cricket at the end of 1990 season and played for Hertfordshire in 1991. Returned to full-time cricket in 1992. Holds the record for the most consecutive runs scored at Lord's without being dismissed (539 runs)
**Opinions on cricket:** 'I feel very strongly that there is a place for overseas players in county cricket. One per county is ideal. English players must be able to learn from playing with and against the world's top players. Overseas players greatly add to the

entertainment value of county cricket. I am amazed by proposals to get rid of them.'
**Best batting:** 261* Middlesex v Gloucestershire, Lord's 1994
**Best bowling:** 6-61 Middlesex v Gloucestershire, Lord's 1985

## 1995 Season

| | M | Inns | NO | Runs | HS | Avge | 100s | 50s | Ct | St | O | M | Runs | Wkts | Avge | Best | 5wl | 10wM |
|---|---|---|---|---|---|---|---|---|---|---|---|---|---|---|---|---|---|---|
| Test | | | | | | | | | | | | | | | | | | |
| All First | 20 | 29 | 6 | 1098 | 129 | 47.73 | 4 | 3 | 39 | - | | | | | | | | |
| 1-day Int | | | | | | | | | | | | | | | | | | |
| NatWest | 3 | 3 | 1 | 94 | 62 | 47.00 | - | 1 | 2 | - | | | | | | | | |
| B & H | 6 | 6 | 0 | 151 | 47 | 25.16 | - | - | 3 | - | | | | | | | | |
| Sunday | 16 | 16 | 0 | 149 | 27 | 9.31 | - | - | 6 | - | | | | | | | | |

## Career Performances

| | M | Inns | NO | Runs | HS | Avge | 100s | 50s | Ct | St | Balls | Runs | Wkts | Avge | Best | 5wl | 10wM |
|---|---|---|---|---|---|---|---|---|---|---|---|---|---|---|---|---|---|
| Test | | | | | | | | | | | | | | | | | |
| All First | 195 | 303 | 50 | 10111 | 261 * | 39.96 | 24 | 46 | 232 | - | 6687 | 2939 | 68 | 43.22 | 6-61 | 3 | - |
| 1-day Int | | | | | | | | | | | | | | | | | |
| NatWest | 20 | 19 | 1 | 457 | 83 | 25.38 | - | 2 | 6 | - | 204 | 93 | 4 | 23.25 | 2-19 | - |
| B & H | 34 | 33 | 1 | 921 | 70 | 28.78 | - | 5 | 19 | - | 752 | 466 | 12 | 38.83 | 3-22 | - |
| Sunday | 117 | 107 | 21 | 2393 | 104 * | 27.82 | 1 | 10 | 51 | - | 1038 | 815 | 28 | 29.10 | 4-21 | - |

# CASSAR, M. E.                    Derbyshire

**Name:** Matthew Edward Cassar
**Role:** Right-hand bat, right-arm
fast-medium bowler
**Born:** 16 October 1972, Sydney, Australia
**Height:** 6ft  **Weight:** 13st
**Nickname:** Charchie, Oz
**County debut:** 1994
**1st-Class 50s:** 1
**1st-Class catches:** 2
**Strike rate:** (career 41.12)
**Parents:** Edward and Joan
**Marital status:** Engaged to Jane
**Education:** Punchbowl Primary School,
Sydney; Sir Joseph Banks High School,
Sydney
**Qualifications:** School certificate and NCA
Coaching Certificate
**Off-season:** 'Training for next season's pre-

season bleep test at Derby! First English Christmas. Playing in Australia after Christmas and working on the sun tan lying on the beach'

**Overseas teams played for:** Petersham/Marrickville, Sydney 1988-95

**Cricketers particularly admired:** Steve Waugh, Allan Border, Ian Botham, Dennis Lillee, Malcolm Marshall, Viv Richards, David Capel, 'but most of all my fiancée, Jane Smit (England women's wicket-keeper)'

**Other sports followed:** Football, golf, racquet ball

**Injuries:** Four broken ribs 'thanks to Matt Hayden running straight over the top of me like a steam train', missed six weeks

**Relaxations:** Playing social sports, listening to music, watching television, sleeping 'and spending as much time as possible with Jane'

**Extras:** Played for New South Wales Colts

**Opinions on cricket:** 'I feel that overseas players are a vital part of county cricket. As well as attracting many more spectators, they can only benefit the game. English players can only improve by playing with and against overseas players. One per team is ideal. I also think that if your overseas player is injured at any time during the season you should be able to have a replacement overseas player for the games they miss. Second team games should be four-day games as well. It is the only true test of a player's ability and gives everyone a chance to develop their game. Three-day cricket is almost always contrived in some way, which I totally disagree with. 100 overs per day is plenty.'

**Best batting:** 66 Derbyshire v New Zealanders, Derby 1994

**Best bowling:** 4-54 Derbyshire v Oxford University, The Parks 1995

## 1995 Season

| | M | Inns | NO | Runs | HS | Avge | 100s | 50s | Ct | St | O | M | Runs | Wkts | Avge | Best | 5wI | 10wM |
|---|---|---|---|---|---|---|---|---|---|---|---|---|---|---|---|---|---|---|
| Test | | | | | | | | | | | | | | | | | | |
| All First | 2 | 3 | 0 | 68 | 32 | 22.66 | - | - | 2 | - | 30.3 | 9 | 91 | 5 | 18.20 | 4-54 | - | - |
| 1-day Int | | | | | | | | | | | | | | | | | | |
| NatWest | | | | | | | | | | | | | | | | | | |
| B & H | | | | | | | | | | | | | | | | | | |
| Sunday | | | | | | | | | | | | | | | | | | |

## Career Performances

| | M | Inns | NO | Runs | HS | Avge | 100s | 50s | Ct | St | Balls | Runs | Wkts | Avge | Best | 5wI | 10wM |
|---|---|---|---|---|---|---|---|---|---|---|---|---|---|---|---|---|---|
| Test | | | | | | | | | | | | | | | | | |
| All First | 3 | 4 | 0 | 134 | 66 | 33.50 | - | 1 | 2 | - | 329 | 185 | 8 | 23.12 | 4-54 | - | - |
| 1-day Int | | | | | | | | | | | | | | | | | |
| NatWest | | | | | | | | | | | | | | | | | |
| B & H | | | | | | | | | | | | | | | | | |
| Sunday | | | | | | | | | | | | | | | | | |

# CAWDRON, M. J.                      Gloucestershire

**Name:** Michael John Cawdron
**Role:** Left-hand bat, right-arm medium bowler
**Born:** 7 October 1974, Luton
**Height:** 6ft 3in **Weight:** 12st 7lbs
**Nickname:** Muscles
**County debut:** 1995 (one-day)
**Parents:** William and Mandy
**Marital status:** Single
**Family links with cricket:** Father and brother played local village cricket
**Education:** Cheltenham College
**Qualifications:** 10 GCSEs, 3 A-Levels, NCA Coaching Award
**Career outside cricket:** 'Vocationally challenged'
**Off-season:** Tour to South Africa with Gloucestershire Gypsies
**Overseas tours:** West of England U14 to Holland; Cheltenham College to Zimbabwe 1992; Gloucestershire YC to Sri Lanka 1993-94; Gloucestershire Gypsies to Zimbabwe 1994-95
**Cricketers particularly admired:** David Gower, Richard Hadlee, Reg Williams 'for his disco antics'
**Other sports followed:** Rugby, hockey, racquets, clay-pigeon shooting, golf
**Relaxations:** Cinema, videos, eating and going out with friends
**Extras:** Winner of the *Daily Telegraph* Regional Bowling Award 1993. Captain of MCC Schools and ESCA U19, 1993. 'Made 50 off 32 balls on Sunday League debut against Essex at my old school' (Cheltenham College)
**Opinions on cricket:** 'Twelve-month contracts would be of great benefit to those players who do not wish to winter abroad, as work opportunities are not secure, as other employers are not eager to take on people on such a temporary basis.'

## 1995 Season

| | M | Inns | NO | Runs | HS | Avge | 100s | 50s | Ct | St | O | M | Runs | Wkts | Avge | Best | 5wl | 10wM |
|---|---|---|---|---|---|---|---|---|---|---|---|---|---|---|---|---|---|---|
| Test | | | | | | | | | | | | | | | | | | |
| All First | | | | | | | | | | | | | | | | | | |
| 1-day Int | | | | | | | | | | | | | | | | | | |
| NatWest | | | | | | | | | | | | | | | | | | |
| B & H | | | | | | | | | | | | | | | | | | |
| Sunday | 5 | 3 | 0 | 58 | 50 | 19.33 | - | 1 | 1 | - | 35 | 3 | 134 | 1 | 134.00 | 1-23 | - | |

## Career Performances

| | M | Inns | NO | Runs | HS | Avge | 100s | 50s | Ct | St | Balls | Runs | Wkts | Avge | Best | 5wl | 10wM |
|---|---|---|---|---|---|---|---|---|---|---|---|---|---|---|---|---|---|
| Test | | | | | | | | | | | | | | | | | |
| All First | | | | | | | | | | | | | | | | | |
| 1-day Int | | | | | | | | | | | | | | | | | |
| NatWest | | | | | | | | | | | | | | | | | |
| B & H | | | | | | | | | | | | | | | | | |
| Sunday | 5 | 3 | 0 | 58 | 50 | 19.33 | - | 1 | 1 | - | 210 | 134 | 1 | 134.00 | 1-23 | - | |

# CHAPMAN, C. A. *Yorkshire*

**Name:** Colin Anthony Chapman
**Role:** Right-hand bat, wicket-keeper
**Born:** 8 June 1971, Bradford
**Height:** 5ft 8in **Weight:** 11st 7lbs
**Nickname:** Chappy
**County debut:** 1990
**1st-Class catches:** 5
**1st-Class stumpings:** 2
**Parents:** Mick and Joyce
**Marital status:** 'Live with Mandy'
**Education:** Nabwood Middle; Beckfoot
Grammar; Bradford & Ilkley Community
College
**Qualifications:** 5 O-levels, BTEC Diploma
in Graphic Design, senior coaching certificate
**Off-season:** 'Chilling out'
**Overseas teams played for:** Waitamata,
Auckland 1989-91

**Overseas tours:** Yorkshire CCC to South
Africa 1993 and South Africa 1995
**Cricketers particularly admired:** Phil Carrick, Alan Knott
**Other sports followed:** Anything
**Injuries:** Epileptic fit and dislocated finger, missed five weeks
**Relaxations:** 'A few beers or a meal out'
**Extras:** Swallowed his tongue in a swimming pool during a pre-season tour of South
Africa with Yorkshire, but was rescued by a bystander
**Opinions on cricket:** 'Far too much play with all the one-day matches. Nine month
contracts for all the pre-season training and practise.'
**Best batting:** 20 Yorkshire v Middlesex, Uxbridge 1990

## 1995 Season

| | M | Inns | NO | Runs | HS | Avge | 100s | 50s | Ct | St | O | M | Runs | Wkts | Avge | Best | 5wI | 10wM |
|---|---|---|---|---|---|---|---|---|---|---|---|---|---|---|---|---|---|---|
| Test | | | | | | | | | | | | | | | | | | |
| All First | | | | | | | | | | | | | | | | | | |
| 1-day Int | | | | | | | | | | | | | | | | | | |
| NatWest | 1 | 0 | 0 | 0 | 0 | - | - | - | 1 | - | | | | | | | | |
| B & H | | | | | | | | | | | | | | | | | | |
| Sunday | | | | | | | | | | | | | | | | | | |

## Career Performances

| | M | Inns | NO | Runs | HS | Avge | 100s | 50s | Ct | St | Balls | Runs | Wkts | Avge | Best | 5wI | 10wM |
|---|---|---|---|---|---|---|---|---|---|---|---|---|---|---|---|---|---|
| Test | | | | | | | | | | | | | | | | | |
| All First | 4 | 7 | 1 | 72 | 20 | 12.00 | - | - | 5 | 2 | | | | | | | |
| 1-day Int | | | | | | | | | | | | | | | | | |
| NatWest | 1 | 0 | 0 | 0 | 0 | - | - | - | 1 | - | | | | | | | |
| B & H | | | | | | | | | | | | | | | | | |
| Sunday | 7 | 6 | 3 | 89 | 36 * | 29.66 | - | - | 2 | - | | | | | | | |

# CHAPMAN, R. J.      Nottinghamshire

**Name:** Robert James Chapman
**Role:** Right-hand bat, right-arm
fast-medium bowler
**Born:** 28 July 1972, Nottingham
**Height:** 6ft 1in **Weight:** 13st 7lbs
**Nickname:** Berty, Battling Berty, Bobby
Chapper Flapper, Charfish
**County debut:** 1992
**1st-Class catches:** 2
**Place in bowling averages:** 152nd av. 70.63
**Strike rate:** 97.81 (career 85.05)
**Parents:** Robert Dennis and Hazel Janice
**Marital status:** Single
**Family links with cricket:** Father plays club
cricket for CC, 'sister has a good arm'
**Education:** South Wilford School;
Farnborough School, Clifton, Nottingham;
South Nottingham College
**Qualifications:** 7 O-levels, 2 A-levels
**Off-season:** Playing club cricket in Geelong, Victoria, Australia with Matt Dowman
**Overseas teams played for**: South Barwon, Geelong, Australia 1995-96
**Cricketers particularly admired:** Allan Donald, Chris Cairns, Andy Pick,

Alec Cottingham (Clifton CC)

**Other sports followed:** Football (Nottingham Forest, Sheffield United)

**Injuries:** Shin sores, missed four weeks

**Relaxations:** Nirvana, Pearl Jam, Oasis, U2, Radiohead, The Cure and Pulp. Going to the cinema and concerts

**Extras:** 'Father (Sammy) played for Nottingham Forest, Notts County and Shrewsbury Town. Brother-in-law Phil Starbuck plays for Huddersfield Town

**Opinions on cricket:** 'There are plenty of talented players in the country coming through, watch out you Aussies and you Windies (sorry Chris, and of course you Kiwis).'

**Best batting:** 25 Nottinghamshire v Lancashire, Trent Bridge 1994

**Best bowling:** 3-119 Nottinghamshire v Surrey, Guildford 1995

## 1995 Season

|          | M | Inns | NO | Runs | HS | Avge | 100s | 50s | Ct | St | O     | M  | Runs | Wkts | Avge  | Best  | 5wI | 10wM |
|----------|---|------|----|------|-----|------|------|-----|----|----|-------|----|------|------|-------|-------|-----|------|
| Test     |   |      |    |      |     |      |      |     |    |    |       |    |      |      |       |       |     |      |
| All First | 8 | 11   | 3  | 78   | 22  | 9.75 | -    | -   | 1  | -  | 179.2 | 23 | 777  | 11   | 70.63 | 3-119 | -   | -    |
| 1-day Int |   |      |    |      |     |      |      |     |    |    |       |    |      |      |       |       |     |      |
| NatWest  | 1 | 0    | 0  | 0    | 0   | -    | -    | -   | -  | -  | 12    | 1  | 40   | 0    | -     |       | -   | -    |
| B & H    |   |      |    |      |     |      |      |     |    |    |       |    |      |      |       |       |     |      |
| Sunday   | 6 | 1    | 1  | 4    | 4 * | -    | -    | -   | -  | -  | 32    | 0  | 212  | 4    | 53.00 | 2-36  | -   |      |

## Career Performances

|          | M  | Inns | NO | Runs | HS  | Avge | 100s | 50s | Ct | St | Balls | Runs | Wkts | Avge  | Best  | 5wI | 10wM |
|----------|----|------|----|------|-----|------|------|-----|----|----|-------|------|------|-------|-------|-----|------|
| Test     |    |      |    |      |     |      |      |     |    |    |       |      |      |       |       |     |      |
| All First | 12 | 15   | 3  | 114  | 25  | 9.50 | -    | -   | 2  | -  | 1446  | 1041 | 17   | 61.23 | 3-119 | -   | -    |
| 1-day Int |    |      |    |      |     |      |      |     |    |    |       |      |      |       |       |     |      |
| NatWest  | 1  | 0    | 0  | 0    | 0   | -    | -    | -   | -  | -  | 72    | 40   | 0    | -     |       | -   | -    |
| B & H    |    |      |    |      |     |      |      |     |    |    |       |      |      |       |       |     |      |
| Sunday   | 11 | 3    | 2  | 6    | 4 * | 6.00 | -    | -   | -  | -  | 369   | 368  | 7    | 52.57 | 2-36  | -   |      |

# CHAPPLE, G.                                    Lancashire

**Name:** Glen Chapple
**Role:** Right-hand bat, right-arm
medium bowler
**Born:** 23 January 1974, Skipton, Yorkshire
**Height:** 6ft 2in **Weight:** 12st 7lbs
**Nickname:** Chappy, Boris, Boomor, Cheeky
**County debut:** 1992
**50 wickets in a season:** 1
**1st-Class 50s:** 1
**1st-Class 100s:** 1
**1st-Class 5 w. in innings:** 6
**1st-Class catches:** 18
**Place in batting averages:** 210th av. 19.46
(1994 242nd av. 15.00)
**Place in bowling averages:** 91st av. 34.13
(1994 35th av. 26.80)
**Strike rate:** 63.36 (career 56.55)
**Parents:** Eileen and Michael
**Marital status:** Single
**Family links with cricket:** Father played in Lancashire League for Nelson and was a
professional for Darwen and Earby
**Education:** West Craven High School; Nelson and Colne College
**Qualifications:** 8 GCSEs, 2 A-Levels in Geography and Economics
**Overseas tours:** England U18 to Canada 1991; England U19 to New Zealand 1990-
91,to Pakistan 1991-92, to India 1992-93; England A to India 1994-95
**Cricketers particularly admired:** Dennis Lillee, Robin Smith
**Other sports followed:** Football (Liverpool), golf
**Relaxations:** 'Watching films, cinema, music, socialising'
**Extras:** Hit fastest century (21 minutes) against Glamorgan at Old Trafford 1993
**Best batting:** 109* Lancashire v Glamorgan, Old Trafford 1993
**Best bowling:** 6-48 Lancashire v Durham, Stockton 1994

## 1995 Season

|          | M  | Inns | NO | Runs | HS | Avge  | 100s | 50s | Ct | St | O     | M  | Runs | Wkts | Avge  | Best | 5wl | 10wM |
|----------|----|------|----|------|----|-------|------|-----|----|----|-------|----|------|------|-------|------|-----|------|
| Test     |    |      |    |      |    |       |      |     |    |    |       |    |      |      |       |      |     |      |
| All First | 15 | 21  | 6  | 292  | 58 | 19.46 | -    | 1   | 6  | -  | 380.1 | 81 | 1229 | 36   | 34.13 | 4-44 | -   | -    |
| 1-day Int |    |      |    |      |    |       |      |     |    |    |       |    |      |      |       |      |     |      |
| NatWest  | 2  | 1    | 0  | 0    | 0  | 0.00  | -    | -   | -  | -  | 23.3  | 1  | 116  | 2    | 58.00 | 1-47 | -   |      |
| B & H    | 6  | 0    | 0  | 0    | 0  | -     | -    | -   | 2  | -  | 54    | 3  | 275  | 3    | 91.66 | 2-55 | -   |      |
| Sunday   | 13 | 3    | 1  | 14   | 8  | 7.00  | -    | -   | 1  | -  | 87.2  | 2  | 400  | 15   | 26.66 | 3-36 | -   |      |

## Career Performances

|        | M  | Inns | NO | Runs | HS   | Avge  | 100s | 50s | Ct | St | Balls | Runs | Wkts | Avge  | Best | 5wI | 10wM |
|--------|----|------|----|------|------|-------|------|-----|----|----|-------|------|------|-------|------|-----|------|
| Test   |    |      |    |      |      |       |      |     |    |    |       |      |      |       |      |     |      |
| All First | 44 | 63 | 26 | 777 | 109 * | 21.00 | 1 | 1 | 18 | - | 7183 | 3675 | 127 | 28.93 | 6-48 | 6 | - |
| 1-day Int |    |      |    |      |      |       |      |     |    |    |       |      |      |       |      |     |      |
| NatWest | 3 | 1 | 0 | 0 | 0 | 0.00 | - | - | - | - | 213 | 151 | 3 | 50.33 | 1-35 | - | |
| B & H | 7 | 0 | 0 | 0 | 0 | - | - | - | 2 | - | 390 | 305 | 5 | 61.00 | 2-30 | - | |
| Sunday | 30 | 7 | 4 | 30 | 9 * | 10.00 | - | - | 3 | - | 1104 | 813 | 27 | 30.11 | 3-29 | - | |

# CHILDS, J. H. Essex

**Name:** John Henry Childs
**Role:** Left-hand bat, slow left-arm bowler
**Born:** 15 August 1951, Plymouth
**Height:** 6ft  **Weight:** 12st 6lbs
**Nickname:** Charlie
**County debut:** 1975 (Glos), 1985 (Essex)
**County cap:** 1977 (Glos), 1986 (Essex)
**Benefit:** 1994
**Testimonial:** 1985
**Test debut:** 1988
**Tests:** 2
**50 wickets in a season:** 9
**1st-Class 5 w. in innings:** 52
**1st-Class 10 w. in match:** 8
**1st-Class catches:** 115
**Place in bowling averages:** 36th av. 25.83
(1994 81st av. 32.15)
**Strike rate:** 59.85 (career 68.71)
**Parents:** Sydney and Barbara (both deceased)
**Wife and date of marriage:** Jane Anne, 11 November 1978
**Children:** Lee Robert, 28 November 1980; Scott Alexander, 21 August 1984
**Education:** Audley Park Secondary Modern, Torquay
**Qualifications:** Advanced cricket coac
**Off-season:** 'Meeting my family (!) and improving my golf'
**Cricketers particularly admired:** Gary Sobers, Mike Procter
**Other sports followed:** Football (Tottenham Hotspur)
**Injuries:** 'Old age'
**Relaxations:** 'Watching rugby, decorating at home, walking on moors and beaches, enjoying my family'
**Extras:** Played for Devon 1973-74. Released by Gloucestershire at end of 1984 and joined Essex. One of *Wisden*'s Five Cricketers of the Year 1986. Selected for England's

cancelled tour to India 1988-89. Essex Player of the Year 1992. 1,000 first-class wickets
**Best batting:** 43 Essex v Hampshire, Chelmsford 1992
**Best bowling:** 9-56 Gloucestershire v Somerset, Bristol 1981

## 1995 Season

|          | M  | Inns | NO | Runs | HS | Avge | 100s | 50s | Ct | St | O     | M   | Runs | Wkts | Avge  | Best | 5wI | 10wM |
|----------|----|------|----|------|----|------|------|-----|----|----|-------|-----|------|------|-------|------|-----|------|
| Test     |    |      |    |      |    |      |      |     |    |    |       |     |      |      |       |      |     |      |
| All First | 17 | 28   | 11 | 113  | 18 | 6.64 | -    | -   | 6  | -  | 678.2 | 183 | 1757 | 68   | 25.83 | 6-36 | 2   |      |
| 1-day Int |    |      |    |      |    |      |      |     |    |    |       |     |      |      |       |      |     |      |
| NatWest  | 1  | 0    | 0  | 0    | 0  | -    | -    | -   | -  | -  | 12    | 3   | 26   | 1    | 26.00 | 1-26 | -   |      |
| B & H    |    |      |    |      |    |      |      |     |    |    |       |     |      |      |       |      |     |      |
| Sunday   |    |      |    |      |    |      |      |     |    |    |       |     |      |      |       |      |     |      |

## Career Performances

|          | M   | Inns | NO  | Runs | HS   | Avge  | 100s | 50s | Ct  | St | Balls | Runs  | Wkts | Avge  | Best | 5wI | 10wM |
|----------|-----|------|-----|------|------|-------|------|-----|-----|----|-------|-------|------|-------|------|-----|------|
| Test     | 2   | 4    | 4   | 2    | 2 *  |       | -    | -   | 1   | -  | 516   | 183   | 3    | 61.00 | 1-13 | -   | -    |
| All First | 375 | 354  | 170 | 1689 | 43   | 9.17  | -    | -   | 115 | -  | 69333 | 29835 | 1009 | 29.56 | 9-56 | 52  | 8    |
| 1-day Int |     |      |     |      |      |       |      |     |     |    |       |       |      |       |      |     |      |
| NatWest  | 11  | 5    | 4   | 35   | 14 * | 35.00 | -    | -   | -   | -  | 718   | 404   | 11   | 36.72 | 2-15 | -   |      |
| B & H    | 23  | 7    | 5   | 25   | 10   | 12.50 | -    | -   | 6   | -  | 1272  | 688   | 21   | 32.76 | 3-36 | -   |      |
| Sunday   | 84  | 32   | 18  | 117  | 16 * | 8.35  | -    | -   | 16  | -  | 3283  | 2494  | 64   | 38.96 | 4-15 | -   |      |

# CHURCH, M. J. — Worcestershire

**Name:** Matthew John Church
**Role:** Right-hand bat, right-arm medium bowler
**Born:** 26 July 1972, Guildford
**Height:** 6ft 2in **Weight:** 13st
**Nickname:** Money, Churchy, Loose Unit, Maddy, Larse
**County debut:** 1994
**1st-Class catches:** 4
**Place in batting averages:** 244th av. 15.75
**Parents:** Anthony and Annette
**Marital status:** Single
**Education:** St George's College, Weybridge; Guildford Technical College; Stuart Cricket Academy
**Qualifications:** 4 GCSEs, 1 A-level ('Thanks Mr Dav and Les')
**Off-season:** Relaxing, netting, training,

working and 'enjoying myself'
**Overseas tours:** Surrey Young Cricketers to Australia 1989-90; St George's College to Zimbabwe 1990-91
**Overseas teams played for:** Harmony, Orange Free State 1991-92; North Shore, Geelong 1992-93; Adelaide University 1994-95
**Cricketers particularly admired:** Ian Glover, Graham Thorpe, Robin Smith, Tim Edwards and Karl Thomas
**Other sports followed:** All sports
**Injuries:** Fractured rib, missed three weeks
**Extras:** Former MCC Young Cricketer, signed by Worcestershire at the beginning of the 1994 season. Sold scorecards at the 1993 Benson & Hedges Cup final and was 12th Man for Worcestershire at the NatWest final the following year. Fielded for England as substitute in 1995 Lord's Test against South Africa. Played for Surrey from U12 to U19.
**Best batting:** 38 Worcestershire v Yorkshire, Worcester 1994

## 1995 Season

|          | M | Inns | NO | Runs | HS | Avge  | 100s | 50s | Ct | St | O | M | Runs | Wkts | Avge | Best | 5wI | 10wM |
|----------|---|------|----|------|----|-------|------|-----|----|----|---|---|------|------|------|------|-----|------|
| Test     |   |      |    |      |    |       |      |     |    |    |   |   |      |      |      |      |     |      |
| All First | 5 | 9 | 1 | 126 | 35 | 15.75 | - | - | 3 | - |   |   |      |      |      |      |     |      |
| 1-day Int |   |      |    |      |    |       |      |     |    |    |   |   |      |      |      |      |     |      |
| NatWest  |   |      |    |      |    |       |      |     |    |    |   |   |      |      |      |      |     |      |
| B & H    | 1 | 0 | 0 | 0 | 0 | - | - | - | - | - |   |   |      |      |      |      |     |      |
| Sunday   | 6 | 5 | 0 | 25 | 17 | 5.00 | - | - | 4 | - |   |   |      |      |      |      |     |      |

## Career Performances

|          | M | Inns | NO | Runs | HS | Avge  | 100s | 50s | Ct | St | Balls | Runs | Wkts | Avge | Best | 5wI | 10wM |
|----------|---|------|----|------|----|-------|------|-----|----|----|-------|------|------|------|------|-----|------|
| Test     |   |      |    |      |    |       |      |     |    |    |       |      |      |      |      |     |      |
| All First | 8 | 14 | 1 | 191 | 38 | 14.69 | - | - | 4 | - | 6 | 4 | 0 | - | - | - | - |
| 1-day Int |   |      |    |      |    |       |      |     |    |    |       |      |      |      |      |     |      |
| NatWest  |   |      |    |      |    |       |      |     |    |    |       |      |      |      |      |     |      |
| B & H    | 1 | 0 | 0 | 0 | 0 | - | - | - | - | - |       |      |      |      |      |     |      |
| Sunday   | 11 | 9 | 0 | 62 | 18 | 6.88 | - | - | 7 | - |       |      |      |      |      |     |      |

# CLARKE, V. P.      Leicestershire

**Name:** Vincent Paul Clarke
**Role:** Right-hand bat, leg-break bowler
**Born:** 11 November 1971, Liverpool
**Height:** 6ft 3in **Weight:** 15st 10lbs
**County debut:** 1994 (Somerset),
1995 (Leicestershire)
**1st-Class catches:** 1
**Parents:** Vinnie and Sandra
**Marital status:** Single
**Family links with cricket:** Father played
representative schoolboy cricket
**Education:** Craigie Primary School; Sacred
Heart College, Sorrento; Perth College,
Western Australia
**Qualifications:** Diploma in Social Training
**Overseas teams played for:** Wanneroo
District, Perth 1990-94
**Cricketers particularly admired:**

Shane Warne, Ian Botham
**Other sports followed:** Windsurfing, Aussie Rules football, most sports
**Relaxations:** Playing the guitar, golf, watching sport
**Extras:** Brought up in Australia but has English birth qualification. Was in Western
Australian Development Squads from U14 to U19. Represented Western Australia at
indoor cricket in 1991. Played for Bridgwater and Somerset 2nd XI in 1993. Released
by Somerset at end of 1994 season. Joined Leicestershire at the start of the 1995 season
**Best batting:** 38 Somerset v Gloucestershire, Bristol 1994
**Best bowling:** 3-72 Leicestershire v Worcestershire, Worcester 1995

## 1995 Season

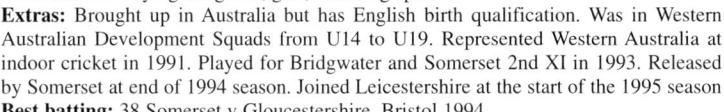

|  | M | Inns | NO | Runs | HS | Avge | 100s | 50s | Ct | St | O | M | Runs | Wkts | Avge | Best | 5wI | 10wM |
|---|---|---|---|---|---|---|---|---|---|---|---|---|---|---|---|---|---|---|
| Test | | | | | | | | | | | | | | | | | | |
| All First | 4 | 7 | 1 | 55 | 29 | 9.16 | - | - | 1 | - | 73.3 | 10 | 284 | 5 | 56.80 | 3-72 | - | - |
| 1-day Int | | | | | | | | | | | | | | | | | | |
| NatWest | | | | | | | | | | | | | | | | | | |
| B & H | | | | | | | | | | | | | | | | | | |
| Sunday | 2 | 2 | 0 | 6 | 5 | 3.00 | - | - | - | - | | | | | | | | |

| | M | Inns | NO | Runs | HS | Avge | 100s | 50s | Ct | St | Balls | Runs | Wkts | Avge | Best | 5wI | 10wM |
|---|---|---|---|---|---|---|---|---|---|---|---|---|---|---|---|---|---|
| Test | | | | | | | | | | | | | | | | | |
| All First | 6 | 11 | 1 | 101 | 38 | 10.10 | - | - | 1 | - | 579 | 389 | 6 | 64.83 | 3-72 | - | - |
| 1-day Int | | | | | | | | | | | | | | | | | |
| NatWest | | | | | | | | | | | | | | | | | |
| B & H | 1 | 1 | 0 | 22 | 22 | 22.00 | - | - | - | - | | | | | | | |
| Sunday | 8 | 8 | 0 | 58 | 26 | 7.25 | - | - | 2 | - | 104 | 100 | 2 | 50.00 | 1-15 | - | |

# COLLINGWOOD, P. D.                    Durham

**Name:** Paul Davis Collingwood
**Role:** Right-hand bat, right-arm
medium bowler
**Born:** 26 May 1976, Shotley Bridge,
Tyneside
**Height:** 5ft 11in  **Weight:** 11st 4lbs
**Nickname:** Colly, Shep
**County debut:** 1995 (one-day)
**Parents:** David and Janet
**Marital status:** Single
**Family links with cricket:** Father and
brother play in the Tyneside Senior League
for Shotley Bridge CC
**Education:** Benfieldside Junior School;
Blackfyne Comprehensive School;
Derwentside College
**Qualifications:** 9 GCSEs and 2 A-levels
**Off-season:** Working and relaxing
**Cricketers particularly admired:**
Dermot Reeve, Graham Thorpe and Ian Botham
**Other sports followed:** Football (Sunderland AFC) and table tennis
**Relaxations:** 'I enjoy watching most sports programmes and listening to music. Also
going to Sunderland matches home and away'
**Opinions on cricket:** 'I believe there is far too much cricket played during the season.
Surely if there was less first-class cricket played the standard would improve overall.'

19. Who was South Africa's leading run-scorer in the
Test series against England in 1995-96?

## 1995 Season

| | M | Inns | NO | Runs | HS | Avge | 100s | 50s | Ct | St | O | M | Runs | Wkts | Avge | Best | 5wI | 10wM |
|---|---|---|---|---|---|---|---|---|---|---|---|---|---|---|---|---|---|---|
| Test | | | | | | | | | | | | | | | | | | |
| All First | | | | | | | | | | | | | | | | | | |
| 1-day Int | | | | | | | | | | | | | | | | | | |
| NatWest | | | | | | | | | | | | | | | | | | |
| B & H | | | | | | | | | | | | | | | | | | |
| Sunday | 2 | 2 | 1 | 37 | 33 * | 37.00 | - | - | - | - | 11 | 0 | 53 | 0 | - | | - | - |

## Career Performances

| | M | Inns | NO | Runs | HS | Avge | 100s | 50s | Ct | St | Balls | Runs | Wkts | Avge | Best | 5wl | 10wM |
|---|---|---|---|---|---|---|---|---|---|---|---|---|---|---|---|---|---|
| Test | | | | | | | | | | | | | | | | | |
| All First | | | | | | | | | | | | | | | | | |
| 1-day Int | | | | | | | | | | | | | | | | | |
| NatWest | | | | | | | | | | | | | | | | | |
| B & H | | | | | | | | | | | | | | | | | |
| Sunday | 2 | 2 | 1 | 37 | 33 * | 37.00 | - | - | - | - | 66 | 53 | 0 | - | | - | - |

# CONNOR, C. A. Hampshire

**Name:** Cardigan Adolphus Connor
**Role:** Right-hand bat, right-arm
fast-medium bowler
**Born:** 24 March 1961, The Valley, Anguilla
**Height:** 5ft 10in **Weight:** 12st 4lbs
**Nickname:** Cardi
**County debut:** 1984
**County cap:** 1988
**50 wickets in a season:** 5
**1st-Class 50s:** 2
**1st-Class 5 w. in innings:** 15
**1st-Class 10 w. in match:** 4
**1st-Class catches:** 61
**Place in batting averages:** 240th av. 16.00
(1994 259th av. 11.31)
**Place in bowling averages:** 89th av. 34.10
(1994 20th av. 24.50)
**Strike rate:** 58.35 (career 62.14)
**Parents:** Ethleen
**Wife and date of marriage:** Jacqui, 18 March 1995
**Education:** The Valley Secondary School, Anguilla; Langley College
**Qualifications:** Engineer

121

**Career outside cricket:** Keep-fit instructor and masseur
**Off-season:** Coaching the schoolchildren on Anguilla
**Overseas teams played for:** Merewether DCC, Newcastle, Australia 1983-92; Valley Secondary School, Anguilla 1992-96
**Cricketers particularly admired:** Malcolm Marshall, Viv Richards, Kevan James
**Other sports followed:** Football (Arsenal), tennis, golf ('poorly'), American football ('Raiders')
**Relaxations:** Keeping fit and watching sport on television
**Extras:** Played for Buckinghamshire in Minor Counties before joining Hampshire. First Anguillan-born player to appear in the County Championship
**Best batting:** 59 Hampshire v Surrey, The Oval 1993
**Best bowling:** 7-31 Hampshire v Gloucestershire, Portsmouth 1989

## 1995 Season

|          | M  | Inns | NO | Runs | HS | Avge  | 100s | 50s | Ct | St | O     | M   | Runs | Wkts | Avge  | Best | 5wI | 10wM |
|----------|----|------|----|------|-----|-------|------|-----|----|----|-------|-----|------|------|-------|------|-----|------|
| Test     |    |      |    |      |     |       |      |     |    |    |       |     |      |      |       |      |     |      |
| All First| 17 | 27   | 6  | 336  | 33  | 16.00 | -    | -   | 7  | -  | 554.2 | 115 | 1944 | 57   | 34.10 | 6-44 | 3   | 1    |
| 1-day Int|    |      |    |      |     |       |      |     |    |    |       |     |      |      |       |      |     |      |
| NatWest  | 1  | 1    | 1  | 1    | 1 * | -     | -    | -   | -  | -  | 12    | 4   | 41   | 4    | 10.25 | 4-41 | -   |      |
| B & H    | 5  | 2    | 1  | 13   | 11  | 13.00 | -    | -   | 1  | -  | 44.1  | 10  | 136  | 3    | 45.33 | 3-36 | -   |      |
| Sunday   | 12 | 5    | 1  | 18   | 8   | 4.50  | -    | -   | 1  | -  | 90    | 4   | 463  | 16   | 28.93 | 2-23 | -   |      |

## Career Performances

|          | M   | Inns | NO | Runs | HS | Avge  | 100s | 50s | Ct | St | Balls | Runs  | Wkts | Avge  | Best | 5wI | 10wM |
|----------|-----|------|----|------|-----|-------|------|-----|----|----|-------|-------|------|-------|------|-----|------|
| Test     |     |      |    |      |     |       |      |     |    |    |       |       |      |       |      |     |      |
| All First| 202 | 189  | 48 | 1640 | 59  | 11.63 | -    | 2   | 61 | -  | 34178 | 17837 | 550  | 32.43 | 7-31 | 15  | 4    |
| 1-day Int|     |      |    |      |     |       |      |     |    |    |       |       |      |       |      |     |      |
| NatWest  | 29  | 6    | 3  | 34   | 13  | 11.33 | -    | -   | 8  | -  | 1882  | 1130  | 59   | 19.15 | 4-11 | -   |      |
| B & H    | 50  | 11   | 5  | 32   | 11  | 5.33  | -    | -   | 10 | -  | 2851  | 1831  | 73   | 25.08 | 4-19 | -   |      |
| Sunday   | 171 | 49   | 15 | 224  | 25  | 6.58  | -    | -   | 31 | -  | 7554  | 5576  | 212  | 26.30 | 4-11 | -   |      |

# COOK, N. G. B.                  Northamptonshire

**Name:** Nicholas Grant Billson Cook
**Role:** Right-hand bat, slow left-arm bowler
**Born:** 17 June 1956, Leicester
**Height:** 6ft  **Weight:** 13st 10lbs
**Nickname:** Beast, Strop
**County debut:** 1978 (Leicestershire), 1986 (Northamptonshire)
**County cap:** 1982 (Leicestershire), 1986 (Northamptonshire)
**Benefit:** 1995
**Test debut:** 1983

**Tests:** 15
**One-Day Internationals:** 3
**50 wickets in a season:** 8
**1st-Class 50s:** 4
**1st-Class 5 w. in innings:** 31
**1st-Class 10 w. in match:** 4
**1st-Class catches:** 197
**Place in bowling averages:** (127th av. 42.05)
**Strike rate:** (career 73.34)
**Parents:** Peter and Cynthia
**Wife and date of marriage:** Shân, 20
September 1991
**Family links with cricket:** Father played
club cricket
**Education:** Stokes Croft Junior; Lutterworth
High; Lutterworth Upper
**Qualifications:** 7 O-levels, 1 A-level,
advanced cricket coach

**Off-season:** 'Finishing off the benefit year
and then having a good long holiday'
**Oversaes tours:** England to New Zealand and Pakistan 1983-84, to Pakistan 1987-88,
to India (Nehru Trophy) 1989-90; English Counties to Zimbabwe 1984-85; England B
to Sri Lanka 1985-86; MCC to Bahrain 1994-95
**Cricketers particularly admired:** John Emburey, Phil Carrick
**Other sports followed:** Soccer (especially Leicester City), rugby, horse racing
**Relaxations:** Crosswords, reading ('especially Wilbur Smith'), good comedy
programmes, good food
**Extras:** In 1975 played for England Schools and for Young England v Young West
Indies. Left Leicestershire to join Northamptonshire in 1986. Has been appointed
Second XI captain for 1996
**Opinions on cricket:** 'Still of the opinion that groundsman should be employed by the
TCCB – with the object of making the best cricket pitch, i.e. pace, bounce and turn by
the third day. Sunday League should again have good wickets and limited over run-ups,
therefore plenty of runs will be scored.'
**Best batting:** 75 Leicetsreshire v Somerset, Taunton 1980
**Best bowling:** 7-34 Leicestershire v Essex, Chelmsford 1982

> 20. Which two Pakistan Test players quit the tour of southern
> Africa in acrimonious circumstances in March 1995?

### Career Performances

|  | M | Inns | NO | Runs | HS | Avge | 100s | 50s | Ct | St | Balls | Runs | Wkts | Avge | Best | 5wl | 10wM |
|---|---|---|---|---|---|---|---|---|---|---|---|---|---|---|---|---|---|
| Test | 15 | 25 | 1 | 179 | 31 | 8.52 | - | - | 5 | - | 4172 | 1689 | 52 | 32.48 | 6-65 | 4 |  |
| All First | 356 | 365 | 96 | 3137 | 75 | 11.66 | - | 4 | 197 | - | 64469 | 25507 | 879 | 29.01 | 7-34 | 31 | 4 |
| 1-day Int | 3 | 0 | 0 | 0 | 0 | - | - | - | 2 | - | 144 | 95 | 5 | 19.00 | 2-18 | - |  |
| NatWest | 28 | 9 | 2 | 44 | 13 | 6.28 | - | - | 8 | - | 1817 | 1046 | 28 | 37.35 | 4-24 | - |  |
| B & H | 36 | 16 | 6 | 129 | 23 | 12.90 | - | - | 12 | - | 1849 | 1121 | 22 | 50.95 | 3-35 | - |  |
| Sunday | 141 | 57 | 26 | 284 | 21 * | 9.16 | - | - | 48 | - | 5479 | 4039 | 132 | 30.59 | 4-22 | - |  |

# COOPER, K. E. Gloucestershire

**Name:** Kevin Edwin Cooper
**Role:** Left-hand bat, right-arm, fast-medium bowler
**Born:** 27 December 1957, Sutton-in-Ashfield
**Height:** 6ft 1in **Weight:** 13st 2lbs
**Nickname:** Henry
**County debut:** 1976 (Nottinghamshire), 1993 (Gloucestershire)
**County cap:** 1980 (Nottinghamshire), 1995 (Gloucestershire)
**Benefit:** 1990
**50 wickets in a season:** 8
**1st-Class 50s:** 1
**1st-Class 5 w. in innings:** 26
**1st-Class 10 w. in match:** 1
**1st-Class catches:** 93
**Place in bowling averages:** 4th av. 17.53 (1994 50th av. 28.81)
**Strike rate:** 47.53 (career 60.66)
**Parents:** Gerald Edwin and Margaret
**Wife and date of marriage:** Linda Carol, 14 February 1981
**Children:** Kelly Louise, 8 April 1982; Tara Amy, 22 November 1984
**Family links with cricket:** Father played local cricket
**Education:** Hucknall National Secondary School, Nottingham
**Qualifications:** Senior coach
**Career outside cricket:** Sales rep. for Golden Needles
**Overseas tours:** Derrick Robins U23 to Australasia, 1979-80; Gloucestershire to Sri Lanka, 1993; MCC to Bahrain 1994-95
**Overseas teams played for:** Nedlands CC, Perth, Australia 1978-79

**Cricketers particularly admired:** John Snow
**Other sports followed:** Golf, football (Manchester United)
**Relaxations:** Golf
**Extras:** In 1974 took 10-6 in one innings for Hucknall Ramblers against Sutton College in the Mansfield and District League. First bowler to 50 first-class wickets in 1988 season. Took 101 first-class wickets in 1988. Released by Notts at end of 1992 season
**Best batting:** 52 Gloucestershire v Lancashire, Cheltenham 1993
**Best bowling:** 8-44 Nottinghamshire v Middlesex, Lord's 1984

## 1995 Season

|  | M | Inns | NO | Runs | HS | Avge | 100s | 50s | Ct | St | O | M | Runs | Wkts | Avge | Best | 5wl | 10wM |
|---|---|---|---|---|---|---|---|---|---|---|---|---|---|---|---|---|---|---|
| Test |  |  |  |  |  |  |  |  |  |  |  |  |  |  |  |  |  |  |
| All First | 4 | 5 | 1 | 36 | 32 | 9.00 | - | - | 1 | - | 103 | 32 | 228 | 13 | 17.53 | 4-34 | - | - |
| 1-day Int |  |  |  |  |  |  |  |  |  |  |  |  |  |  |  |  |  |  |
| NatWest | 2 | 1 | 0 | 5 | 5 | 5.00 | - | - | 1 | - | 17 | 5 | 32 | 4 | 8.00 | 3-15 | - |  |
| B & H | 6 | 4 | 3 | 25 | 16 * | 25.00 | - | - | 1 | - | 57 | 7 | 158 | 4 | 39.50 | 2-41 | - |  |
| Sunday | 2 | 0 | 0 | 0 | 0 | - | - | - | - | - | 12 | 1 | 66 | 1 | 66.00 | 1-35 | - |  |

## Career Performances

|  | M | Inns | NO | Runs | HS | Avge | 100s | 50s | Ct | St | Balls | Runs | Wkts | Avge | Best | 5wl | 10wM |
|---|---|---|---|---|---|---|---|---|---|---|---|---|---|---|---|---|---|
| Test |  |  |  |  |  |  |  |  |  |  |  |  |  |  |  |  |  |
| All First | 304 | 329 | 83 | 2479 | 52 | 10.07 | - | 1 | 93 | - | 49258 | 21928 | 812 | 27.00 | 8-44 | 26 | 1 |
| 1-day Int |  |  |  |  |  |  |  |  |  |  |  |  |  |  |  |  |  |
| NatWest | 27 | 9 | 1 | 50 | 11 | 6.25 | - | - | 7 | - | 1814 | 814 | 41 | 19.85 | 4-49 | - |  |
| B & H | 71 | 27 | 17 | 143 | 25 * | 14.30 | - | - | 13 | - | 4141 | 2232 | 77 | 28.98 | 4-9 | - |  |
| Sunday | 167 | 60 | 21 | 248 | 31 | 6.35 | - | - | 28 | - | 6994 | 5170 | 141 | 36.66 | 4-25 | - |  |

21. Which West Indian bowler claimed his 300th Test wicket during the 1995 series against England?

# CORK, D. G.          Derbyshire

**Name:** Dominic Gerald Cork
**Role:** Right-hand bat, right-arm, fast-medium bowler
**Born:** 7 August 1971, Newcastle-under-Lyme, Staffordshire
**Height:** 6ft 3in **Weight:** 13st
**Nickname:** Corky, Golden, Daz Ultra
**County debut:** 1990
**County cap:** 1993
**Test debut:** 1995
**Tests:** 5
**One-Day Internationals:** 8
**50 wickets in a season:** 2
**1st-Class 50s:** 15
**1st-Class 100s:** 1
**1st-Class 5 w. in innings:** 9
**1st-Class 10 w. in match:** 2
**1st-Class catches:** 65
**Place in batting averages:** 195th av. 21.81 (1994 172nd av. 24.14)
**Place in bowling averages:** 9th av. 20.00 (1994 58th av. 30.05)
**Strike rate:** 39.12 (career 51.36)
**Parents:** Gerald and Mary
**Wife and date of marriage:** Jane, 2 October 1993
**Children:** Gregory Theodore Gerald, 29 September 1994
**Family links with cricket:** 'We played local league cricket together. My two brothers and myself in the same side'
**Education:** St Joseph's College, Stoke-on-Trent
**Qualifications:** History O-Level, leisure and recreation, qualified coach
**Off-season:** Touring South Africa with England
**Overseas tours:** England YCs to Australia 1989-90; England A to Bermuda and West Indies 1991-92, to Australia 1992-93, to South Africa 1993-94, to India 1994-95; England to South Africa 1995-96, to India and Pakistan (World Cup) 1995-96
**Overseas teams played for:** East Shirley, Christchurch, New Zealand 1990-91
**Cricketers particularly admired:** Ian Botham, Kim Barnett, Richard Hadlee and Malcolm Marshall
**Other sports followed:** Horse racing, football (Stoke), tennis and golf
**Injuries:** Knee problems, missed two months
**Relaxations:** 'Relaxing on holiday with my family.'
**Extras:** First played cricket for Betley CC in the North Staffs & South Cheshire League. In 1990 he took a wicket in his first over in first-class cricket v New Zealand at Derby

and scored a century as nightwatchman for England U19 v Pakistan at Taunton. Played Minor Counties cricket for Staffordshire in 1989 and 1990. Selected for England A in 1991 – his first full season of first-class cricket. The Cricket Association Young Player of 1991. Took eight wickets for 53 runs on 20th birthday. Achieved first-class hat-trick against Kent, 1994. Took seven wickets for 43 runs on Test debut against West Indies at Lord's. Achieved hat-trick against the West Indies at Old Trafford in the fourth Test. Won two Man of the Match awards in three Test matches. Voted Player of the Year by the Professional Cricketers' Association for 1995. Finished at the top of the Whyte and Mackay ratings for bowling in 1995

**Opinions on cricket:** 'Too much cricket played and not enough time off. More quality, less quantity.'

**Best batting:** 104 Derbyshire v Gloucestershire, Cheltenham 1993
**Best bowling:** 9-43 Derbyshire v Northamptonshire, Derby 1995

## 1995 Season

| | M | Inns | NO | Runs | HS | Avge | 100s | 50s | Ct | St | O | M | Runs | Wkts | Avge | Best | 5wI | 10wM |
|---|---|---|---|---|---|---|---|---|---|---|---|---|---|---|---|---|---|---|
| Test | 5 | 8 | 1 | 197 | 56 * | 28.14 | - | 1 | 1 | - | 184.2 | 30 | 661 | 26 | 25.42 | 7-43 | 1 | - |
| All First | 18 | 31 | 4 | 589 | 84 * | 21.81 | - | 3 | 8 | - | 586.5 | 111 | 1800 | 90 | 20.00 | 9-43 | 4 | 1 |
| 1-day Int | 3 | 2 | 0 | 14 | 14 | 7.00 | - | - | 1 | - | 31 | 2 | 131 | 6 | 21.83 | 3-27 | - | |
| NatWest | 3 | 1 | 0 | 21 | 21 | 21.00 | - | - | - | - | 26 | 0 | 119 | 5 | 23.80 | 4-50 | - | |
| B & H | 3 | 2 | 0 | 38 | 26 | 19.00 | - | - | 1 | - | 33 | 0 | 142 | 3 | 47.33 | 2-43 | - | |
| Sunday | 13 | 13 | 2 | 232 | 57 | 21.09 | - | 1 | 4 | - | 84 | 2 | 392 | 15 | 26.13 | 3-38 | - | |

## Career Performances

| | M | Inns | NO | Runs | HS | Avge | 100s | 50s | Ct | St | Balls | Runs | Wkts | Avge | Best | 5wI | 10wM |
|---|---|---|---|---|---|---|---|---|---|---|---|---|---|---|---|---|---|
| Test | 5 | 8 | 1 | 197 | 56 * | 28.14 | - | 1 | 1 | - | 1106 | 661 | 26 | 25.42 | 7-43 | 1 | - |
| All First | 101 | 149 | 19 | 2938 | 104 | 22.60 | 1 | 15 | 65 | - | 16333 | 8052 | 318 | 25.32 | 9-43 | 9 | 2 |
| 1-day Int | 8 | 3 | 0 | 25 | 14 | 8.33 | - | - | 1 | - | 504 | 344 | 11 | 31.27 | 3-27 | - | |
| NatWest | 9 | 7 | 0 | 154 | 62 | 22.00 | - | 1 | - | - | 545 | 313 | 25 | 12.52 | 5-18 | 2 | |
| B & H | 14 | 10 | 4 | 237 | 92 * | 39.50 | - | 2 | 6 | - | 878 | 589 | 14 | 42.07 | 4-26 | - | |
| Sunday | 57 | 45 | 4 | 726 | 66 | 17.70 | - | 2 | 21 | - | 2388 | 1956 | 63 | 31.04 | 4-44 | - | |

# COSKER, D. A.         Glamorgan

**Name:** Dean Andrew Cosker
**Role:** Slow left-arm bowler
**Born:** 7 January 1978, Weymouth, Dorset
**Height:** 5ft 11in   **Weight:** 11st 5lbs
**County debut:** No first-team appearance
**Parents:** Desmond and Carol
**Marital status:** Single
**Education:** Preston Primary School, Yeovil;
Ravenswood Prep School, Devon;
Millfield School
**Qualifications:** 10 GCSEs,
Class 3 soccer referee
**Off-season:** Indoor nets
**Overseas tours:** West of England U15 to
West Indies 1993-94; Millfield School
to Sri Lanka 1994-95; England U17 to
Holland 1995
**Cricketers particularly admired:** Mark
Ramprakash and Phil Tufnell
**Other sports followed:** Soccer (Millfield School 1st XI captain, Somerset U19)
**Relaxations:** Music
**Extras:** *Daily Telegraph* Regional Bowling Award, England U15 and U17. Played for
U19 TCCB Development of Excellence XI against South Africa U19 in 1995
**Opinions on cricket:** 'Too much cricket is being played generally. Professional
players, especially Test players, are often playing a very high standard of cricket all
year round and it is not only a physical drain but a mental one as well. But at the
moment there is no resolution of this.'

# COTTAM, A. C.         Derbyshire

**Name:** Andrew Colin Cottam
**Role:** Right-hand bat, slow-left arm bowler
**Born:** 14 July 1973, Northampton
**Height:** 6ft 2in   **Weight:** 11st
**Nickname:** Worm, Cotts, Doggers
**County debut:** 1995
**1st-Class catches:** 1
**Strike rate:** (career 117.40)
**Parents:** Bob and Jackie

**Marital status:** Single

**Family links with cricket:** Father played for Hampshire, Northants and England and is now coach at Somerset. Brothers Michael and David played for Devon.

**Education:** Seaton Primary School; Axminster Secondary School

**Qualifications:** Qualified cricket coach

**Overseas tours:** England U18 to Canada 1991; England U19 to Pakistan 1991-92

**Other sports followed:** Football (Tottenham Hotspur)

**Relaxations:** Listening to music, 'especially Bob Marley', or watching TV

**Opinions on cricket:** 'Play on uncovered wickets.'

**Best batting:** 36 Derbyshire v Oxford University, The Parks 1995

**Best bowling:** 2-5 Derbyshire v Oxford University, The Parks 1995

## 1995 Season

| | M | Inns | NO | Runs | HS | Avge | 100s | 50s | Ct | St | O | M | Runs | Wkts | Avge | Best | 5wI | 10wM |
|---|---|---|---|---|---|---|---|---|---|---|---|---|---|---|---|---|---|---|
| Test | | | | | | | | | | | | | | | | | | |
| All First | 5 | 6 | 0 | 95 | 36 | 15.83 | - | - | - | - | 79.3 | 16 | 291 | 4 | 72.75 | 2-5 | - | - |
| 1-day Int | | | | | | | | | | | | | | | | | | |
| NatWest | | | | | | | | | | | | | | | | | | |
| B & H | | | | | | | | | | | | | | | | | | |
| Sunday | | | | | | | | | | | | | | | | | | |

## Career Performances

| | M | Inns | NO | Runs | HS | Avge | 100s | 50s | Ct | St | Balls | Runs | Wkts | Avge | Best | 5wI | 10wM |
|---|---|---|---|---|---|---|---|---|---|---|---|---|---|---|---|---|---|
| Test | | | | | | | | | | | | | | | | | |
| All First | 11 | 14 | 1 | 138 | 36 | 10.61 | - | - | 1 | - | 1174 | 571 | 10 | 57.10 | 2-5 | - | - |
| 1-day Int | | | | | | | | | | | | | | | | | |
| NatWest | 1 | 1 | 0 | 2 | 2 | 2.00 | - | - | 1 | - | 72 | 45 | 1 | 45.00 | 1-45 | - |
| B & H | 1 | 0 | 0 | 0 | 0 | - | - | - | - | - | 42 | 34 | 0 | - | - | - |
| Sunday | 1 | 0 | 0 | 0 | 0 | - | - | - | - | - | 36 | 24 | 0 | - | - | - |

# COTTEY, P. A.                              Glamorgan

**Name:** Phillip Anthony Cottey
**Role:** Right-hand bat
**Born:** 2 June 1966, Swansea
**Height:** 5ft 5in **Weight:** 11st
**Nickname:** Cotts, Baba
**County debut:** 1986
**County cap:** 1992
**1000 runs in season:** 5
**1st-Class 50s:** 42
**1st-Class 100s:** 15
**1st-Class catches:** 89
**Place in batting averages:** 31st av. 48.83
(1994 17th av. 51.59)
**Strike rate:** (career 97.22)
**Parents:** Bernard John and Ruth
**Wife and date of marriage:**
Gail, 5 October 1992
**Children:** Lowri, 16 October 1993
**Family links with cricket:**

Father played for Swansea
**Education:** Bishopston Comprehensive School, Swansea
**Qualifications:** 9 O-levels
**Overseas tours:** Glamorgan to La Manga, Barbados, Trinidad, Zimbabwe and Cape Town 1987-92
**Overseas teams played for:** Penrith, Sydney 1986-88; Benoni, Johannesburg 1989-90; Eastern Transvaal 1991-92
**Cricketers particularly admired:** John Steele, Alan Jones, Paul Johnson
**Other sports followed:** All sports, especially football
**Relaxations:** 'Watching films, training, lager tasting and spending time with new family.'
**Extras:** Left school at 16 to play for Swansea City FC for three years as a professional. Three Welsh Youth caps (one as captain)
**Opinions on cricket:** 'Four-day cricket should be played on better wickets, but wickets must be allowed to have some sideways movement (be it seam or spin). However the pitches must be of even bounce and pace.'
**Best batting:** 191 Glamorgan v Somerset, Swansea 1994
**Best bowling:** 2-42 Eastern Transvaal v Western Transvaal, Potchefstroom 1991-92

## 1995 Season

| | M | Inns | NO | Runs | HS | Avge | 100s | 50s | Ct | St | O | M | Runs | Wkts | Avge | Best | 5wI | 10wM |
|---|---|---|---|---|---|---|---|---|---|---|---|---|---|---|---|---|---|---|
| Test | | | | | | | | | | | | | | | | | | |
| All First | 19 | 33 | 3 | 1465 | 130 | 48.83 | 5 | 7 | 14 | - | 32.1 | 2 | 109 | 1 | 109.00 | 1-29 | - | - |
| 1-day Int | | | | | | | | | | | | | | | | | | |
| NatWest | 4 | 3 | 1 | 85 | 61 * | 42.50 | - | 1 | - | - | 11 | 0 | 29 | 1 | 29.00 | 1-11 | - | |
| B & H | 5 | 5 | 2 | 119 | 38 * | 39.66 | - | - | 1 | - | | | | | | | | |
| Sunday | 15 | 11 | 1 | 287 | 56 | 28.70 | - | 2 | 7 | - | 15 | 0 | 91 | 2 | 45.50 | 1-8 | - | |

## Career Performances

| | M | Inns | NO | Runs | HS | Avge | 100s | 50s | Ct | St | Balls | Runs | Wkts | Avge | Best | 5wI | 10wM |
|---|---|---|---|---|---|---|---|---|---|---|---|---|---|---|---|---|---|
| Test | | | | | | | | | | | | | | | | | |
| All First | 146 | 238 | 36 | 7524 | 191 | 37.24 | 15 | 42 | 89 | - | 875 | 641 | 9 | 71.22 | 2-42 | - | - |
| 1-day Int | | | | | | | | | | | | | | | | | |
| NatWest | 18 | 17 | 5 | 330 | 61 * | 27.50 | - | 2 | 3 | - | 102 | 59 | 2 | 29.50 | 1-11 | - | |
| B & H | 19 | 19 | 3 | 362 | 68 | 22.62 | - | 1 | 5 | - | 6 | 1 | 0 | - | - | - | |
| Sunday | 88 | 70 | 14 | 1387 | 92 * | 24.76 | - | 8 | 30 | - | 198 | 185 | 5 | 37.00 | 2-30 | - | |

# COUSINS, D. M.      Essex

**Name:** Darren Mark Cousins
**Role:** Right-hand bat, right-arm fast-medium bowler, outfielder
**Born:** 24 September 1971, Cambridge
**Height:** 6ft 1in **Weight:** 13st
**Nickname:** Mad Dog, Cuz, Cuzza, Cuzzi, Skuz
**County debut:** 1993
**1st-Class 5 w. in innings:** 1
**1st-Class catches:** 5
**Place in batting averages:** 280th av. 10.08
**Place in bowling averages:** 148th av. 53.33 (1994 30th av. 25.92)
**Strike rate:** 88.00 (career 72.69)
**Parents:** Dennis Charles and Deanna Maureen (deceased)
**Marital status:** Single
**Family links with cricket:**
Father opened the bowling and was capped for Cambridgeshire
**Education:** Milton Primary School; Impington Village College
**Qualifications:** 7 GCSEs; NCA coaching award
**Career outside cricket:** PE teaching

131

**Off-season:** 'Training and working on my bowling up until Christmas and then going abroad for the remaining three months to train and coach'

**Overseas teams played for:** Gold Coast Dolphins, Queensland 1994-95

**Cricketers particularly admired:** 'Too many to mention.'

**Other sports followed:** Football (Liverpool, Cambridge United), 'I follow all sports apart from anything to do with horses, cars or motorbikes, but have no particular favourite teams'

**Relaxations:** 'Listening to many kinds of music from soul to Indie, playing sport, watching television and socialising with mates'

**Extras:** Represented Cambridgeshire at football and swimming and every level at cricket. Played for a Bull Development Squad against Australia in 1991, taking four wickets in each innings. Played 2nd XI cricket for Northants and Worcs. Holds the record for both number of wickets in any single Colts festival (21) and number of wickets taken in the Hilda Overy Festival overall (74). Awarded 2nd XI cap and Essex Young Player of the Year, 1994. Essex Cricket Society 2nd XI Player of the Year, 1994. Leading Essex wicket-taker in Sunday League and top of the bowling averages in 1994

**Opinions on cricket:** 'I think that all second-class matches should be played on first-class grounds with first-class balls. They should also be played by the rules of first-class cricket e.g no overtime when it has rained. The over-rate is too high.'

**Best batting:** 18* Essex v Durham, Chelmsford 1995

**Best bowling:** 6-35 Essex v Cambridge University, Fenner's 1994

## 1995 Season

|          | M  | Inns | NO | Runs | HS   | Avge  | 100s | 50s | Ct | St | O    | M  | Runs | Wkts | Avge   | Best | 5wI | 10wM |
|----------|----|------|----|------|------|-------|------|-----|----|----|------|----|------|------|--------|------|-----|------|
| Test     |    |      |    |      |      |       |      |     |    |    |      |    |      |      |        |      |     |      |
| All First | 9 | 16   | 4  | 121  | 18 * | 10.08 | -    | -   | 3  | -  | 176  | 23 | 640  | 12   | 53.33  | 3-73 | -   | -    |
| 1-day Int |   |      |    |      |      |       |      |     |    |    |      |    |      |      |        |      |     |      |
| NatWest  | 1  | 1    | 0  | 0    | 0    | 0.00  | -    | -   | -  | -  | 12   | 1  | 60   | 0    | -      |      | -   | -    |
| B & H    | 4  | 1    | 1  | 12   | 12 * | -     | -    | -   | 1  | -  | 25.1 | 1  | 130  | 1    | 130.00 | 1-46 | -   |      |
| Sunday   | 16 | 4    | 3  | 7    | 4 *  | 7.00  | -    | -   | 1  | -  | 112  | 7  | 506  | 18   | 28.11  | 3-20 | -   |      |

## Career Performances

|          | M  | Inns | NO | Runs | HS   | Avge | 100s | 50s | Ct | St | Balls | Runs | Wkts | Avge   | Best | 5wI | 10wM |
|----------|----|------|----|------|------|------|------|-----|----|----|-------|------|------|--------|------|-----|------|
| Test     |    |      |    |      |      |      |      |     |    |    |       |      |      |        |      |     |      |
| All First | 14 | 23  | 5  | 145  | 18 * | 8.05 | -    | -   | 5  | -  | 1890  | 1086 | 26   | 41.76  | 6-35 | 1   | -    |
| 1-day Int |   |      |    |      |      |      |      |     |    |    |       |      |      |        |      |     |      |
| NatWest  | 3  | 2    | 1  | 1    | 1 *  | 1.00 | -    | -   | -  | -  | 132   | 117  | 1    | 117.00 | 1-33 | -   |      |
| B & H    | 4  | 1    | 1  | 12   | 12 * | -    | -    | -   | 1  | -  | 151   | 130  | 1    | 130.00 | 1-46 | -   |      |
| Sunday   | 28 | 10   | 4  | 17   | 6    | 2.83 | -    | -   | 2  | -  | 1155  | 888  | 37   | 24.00  | 3-18 | -   |      |

# COWAN, A. P.                                    Essex

**Name:** Ashley Preston Cowan
**Role:** Right-hand bat,
right-hand fast-medium bowler
**Born:** 7 May 1975, Hitchin, Hertfordshire
**Height:** 6ft 4in **Weight:** 14st 2lbs
**Nickname:** Victor
**County debut:** 1995
**1st-Class catches:** 1
**Parents:** Jeff and Pam
**Marital status:** Single
**Family links with cricket:** 'My father
played for the local village team'
**Education:** Kingshott Prep; Framlingham
College
**Qualifications:** 5 GCSEs, 1 A-level;
vocational business course
**Career outside cricket:** Family business
**Off-season:** Playing cricket abroad or
working in the family business
**Cricketers particularly admired:** Ian Botham
**Other sports followed:** Rugby, hockey, golf, football (Newcastle United)
**Relaxations:** Playing golf, pool, listening to music and socialising
**Extras:** Played rugby and hockey for East of England U18. The youngest person to play
for Cambridgeshire
**Opinions on cricket:** 'Due to the amount of cricket played, injury counts around the
circuit are increasing.'
**Best batting:** 22 Essex v Yorkshire, Chelmsford 1995
**Best bowling:** 1-53 Essex v Yorkshire, Chelmsford 1995

## 1995 Season

|           | M | Inns | NO | Runs | HS | Avge | 100s | 50s | Ct | St | O | M | Runs | Wkts | Avge | Best | 5wI | 10wM |
|-----------|---|------|----|----|----|------|------|-----|----|----|----|----|------|------|------|------|-----|------|
| Test      |   |      |    |      |    |      |      |     |    |    |    |    |      |      |      |      |     |      |
| All First | 2 | 4    | 1  | 47   | 22 | 15.66| -    | -   | 1  | -  | 24 | 2  | 113  | 1    | 113.00| 1-53 | -   | -    |
| 1-day Int |   |      |    |      |    |      |      |     |    |    |    |    |      |      |      |      |     |      |
| NatWest   |   |      |    |      |    |      |      |     |    |    |    |    |      |      |      |      |     |      |
| B & H     |   |      |    |      |    |      |      |     |    |    |    |    |      |      |      |      |     |      |
| Sunday    | 1 | 1    | 1  | 0    | 0* | -    | -    | -   | -  | -  | 4  | 0  | 20   | 0    | -    |      | -   | -    |

## Career Performances

| | M | Inns | NO | Runs | HS | Avge | 100s | 50s | Ct | St | Balls | Runs | Wkts | Avge | Best | 5wI | 10wM |
|---|---|---|---|---|---|---|---|---|---|---|---|---|---|---|---|---|---|
| Test | | | | | | | | | | | | | | | | | |
| All First | 2 | 4 | 1 | 47 | 22 | 15.66 | - | - | 1 | - | 144 | 113 | 1 | 113.00 | 1-53 | - | - |
| 1-day Int | | | | | | | | | | | | | | | | | |
| NatWest | | | | | | | | | | | | | | | | | |
| B & H | | | | | | | | | | | | | | | | | |
| Sunday | 1 | 1 | 1 | 0 | 0* | - | - | - | - | - | 24 | 20 | 0 | - | | - | - |

# COWDREY, G. R. Kent

**Name:** Graham Robert Cowdrey
**Role:** Right-hand bat, right-arm medium bowler, cover fielder
**Born:** 27 June 1964, Farnborough, Kent
**Height:** 5ft 11in **Weight:** 13st 9lbs
**Nickname:** Van, Mervyn
**County debut:** 1984
**County cap:** 1988
**1000 runs in season:** 3
**1st-Class 50s:** 42
**1st-Class 100s:** 15
**1st-Class catches:** 85
**One-Day 100s:** 3
**Place in batting averages:** 49th av. 44.28
(1994 119th av. 31.33)
**Strike rate:** (career 100.63)
**Parents:** Michael Colin and Penelope Susan
**Wife and date of marriage:**
Maxine, 20 February 1993

**Family links with cricket:** Father (M.C.) and brother (C.S.) played for, and captained, Kent and England
**Education:** Wellesley House, Broadstairs; Tonbridge School; Durham University
**Qualifications:** 8 O-levels, 3 A-levels, qualified glazier
**Off-season:** 'Working for my wife'
**Overseas tours:** Christians in Sport to India 1985-86, 1989-90; MCC to West Indies 1991-92
**Overseas teams played for:** Avendale, Cape Town 1983-84; Mossman, Sydney 1985-86; Randwick, Sydney 1986-87
**Cricketers particularly admired:** Aravinda De Silva and Julian Wilson
**Other sports followed:** Horse racing (Giles Bravery), American football (Miami Dolphins), football (Arsenal), rugby (West Hartlepool)

**Relaxations:** 'Horse racing – watching wife winning races! Reading – Brian Moore and Jonathan Smith. Music – Van Morrison, Bob Dylan and Paul Brady.'

**Extras:** Played for England YC. Made 1000 runs for Kent 2nd XI first season on staff, and broke 2nd XI record with 1300 runs in 26 innings in 1985. Plays in contact lenses. Holds Kent record partnership for any wicket with Aravinda De Silva, 382 runs against Derbyshire 1995

**Opinions on cricket:** 'I hope that the TCCB do not tinker with the county system. A two division set-up would be a disaster. Am convinced that the England selectors do not know that Kent are a first-class county. How Kent had no representatives on the tours 1995-96 is a real mystery – Ward, Headley, Patel, Ealham – ever heard of them?'

**Best batting:** 147 Kent v Gloucestershire, Bristol 1992

**Best bowling:** 1-5 Kent v Warwickshire, Edgbaston 1988

## 1995 Season

|           | M  | Inns | NO | Runs | HS    | Avge  | 100s | 50s | Ct | St | O | M | Runs | Wkts | Avge | Best | 5wI | 10wM |
|-----------|----|------|----|------|-------|-------|------|-----|----|----|---|---|------|------|------|------|-----|------|
| Test      |    |      |    |      |       |       |      |     |    |    |   |   |      |      |      |      |     |      |
| All First | 13 | 22   | 1  | 930  | 137   | 44.28 | 2    | 6   | 8  | -  | 3 | 0 | 46   | 0    | -    |      | -   | -    |
| 1-day Int |    |      |    |      |       |       |      |     |    |    |   |   |      |      |      |      |     |      |
| NatWest   | 2  | 2    | 0  | 84   | 65    | 42.00 | -    | 1   | 1  | -  | 2 | 0 | 21   | 0    | -    |      | -   | -    |
| B & H     | 7  | 5    | 0  | 90   | 28    | 18.00 | -    | -   | 3  | -  |   |   |      |      |      |      |     |      |
| Sunday    | 15 | 14   | 3  | 593  | 105 * | 53.90 | 2    | 2   | 7  | -  | 1 | 0 | 7    | 0    | -    |      | -   |      |

## Career Performances

|           | M   | Inns | NO | Runs | HS    | Avge  | 100s | 50s | Ct | St | Balls | Runs | Wkts | Avge  | Best | 5wI | 10wM |
|-----------|-----|------|----|------|-------|-------|------|-----|----|----|-------|------|------|-------|------|-----|------|
| Test      |     |      |    |      |       |       |      |     |    |    |       |      |      |       |      |     |      |
| All First | 159 | 252  | 29 | 7887 | 147   | 35.36 | 15   | 42  | 85 | -  | 1107  | 799  | 11   | 72.63 | 1-5  | -   | -    |
| 1-day Int |     |      |    |      |       |       |      |     |    |    |       |      |      |       |      |     |      |
| NatWest   | 21  | 18   | 4  | 372  | 65    | 26.57 | -    | 1   | 3  | -  | 297   | 151  | 8    | 18.87 | 2-4  | -   |      |
| B & H     | 42  | 37   | 3  | 797  | 70 *  | 23.44 | -    | 5   | 14 | -  | 154   | 94   | 2    | 47.00 | 1-8  | -   |      |
| Sunday    | 136 | 120  | 20 | 2815 | 105 * | 28.15 | 3    | 11  | 48 | -  | 606   | 465  | 21   | 22.14 | 4-15 | -   |      |

22. Which England bowler took his 100th Test wicket in the series against West Indies in 1995?

# COX, D. M. Durham

**Name:** David Matthew Cox
**Role:** Left-hand bat, slow left-arm bowler
**Born:** 2 March 1972, Southall, Middlesex
**Height:** 5ft 11in **Weight:** 13st
**Nickname:** Coxy
**County debut:** 1994
**1st-Class catches:** 1
**Place in bowling averages:** 112th av. 38.36
**Strike rate:** 70.81 (career 102.33)
**Parents:** Charles and Georgina
**Wife and date of marriage:**
Hazel Jennifer, 1 October 1994
**Family links with cricket:**
Father played for Old Actonians
**Education:** Greenford High School
**Qualifications:** 5 GCSEs, cricket coaching
certificate, part-qualified plasterer
**Career outside cricket:** Plasterer
**Off-season:** Keeping fit and looking for work
**Cricketers particularly admired:** Clive Radley, Wayne Larkins
**Other sports followed:** Snooker, darts, football (QPR)
**Relaxations:** Going horse racing
**Extras:** First Durham player to get over 50 2nd XI Championship wickets in a season
(1995)
**Best batting:** 26* Durham v South Africans, Chester-le-Street 1994
**Best bowling:** 4-141 Durham v Glamorgan, Swansea 1995

---

### 1995 Season

| | M | Inns | NO | Runs | HS | Avge | 100s | 50s | Ct | St | O | M | Runs | Wkts | Avge | Best | 5wI | 10wM |
|---|---|---|---|---|---|---|---|---|---|---|---|---|---|---|---|---|---|---|
| Test | | | | | | | | | | | | | | | | | | |
| All First | 3 | 5 | 0 | 23 | 17 | 4.60 | - | - | - | - | 129.5 | 28 | 422 | 11 | 38.36 | 4-141 | - | - |
| 1-day Int | | | | | | | | | | | | | | | | | | |
| NatWest | | | | | | | | | | | | | | | | | | |
| B & H | | | | | | | | | | | | | | | | | | |
| Sunday | | | | | | | | | | | | | | | | | | |

## Career Performances

| | M | Inns | NO | Runs | HS | Avge | 100s | 50s | Ct | St | Balls | Runs | Wkts | Avge | Best | 5wI | 10wM |
|---|---|---|---|---|---|---|---|---|---|---|---|---|---|---|---|---|---|
| Test | | | | | | | | | | | | | | | | | |
| All First | 6 | 9 | 1 | 55 | 26 * | 6.87 | - | - | 1 | - | 1228 | 767 | 12 | 63.91 | 4-141 | - | - |
| 1-day Int | | | | | | | | | | | | | | | | | |
| NatWest | | | | | | | | | | | | | | | | | |
| B & H | | | | | | | | | | | | | | | | | |
| Sunday | 3 | 0 | 0 | 0 | 0 | - | - | - | - | - | 120 | 89 | 1 | 89.00 | 1-25 | - | |

# CRAWLEY, J. P.                     Lancashire

**Name:** John Paul Crawley
**Role:** Right-hand bat, occasional
wicket-keeper
**Born:** 21 September 1971, Malden, Essex
**Height:** 6ft 2in **Weight:** 13st 2lbs
**Nickname:** Creeps, Jonty, JC
**County debut:** 1990
**Test debut:** 1994
**Tests:** 9
**One-day Internationals:** 3
**1000 runs in a season:** 4
**1st-Class 50s:** 48
**1st-Class 100s:** 14
**1st-Class 200s:** 3
**1st-Class catches:** 89
**One-day 100s:** 1
**Place in batting averages:** 33rd av. 47.48
(1994 19th av. 50.64)

**Parents:** Frank and Jean
**Marital status:** Single
**Family links with cricket:** Father played in Manchester Association; brother Mark played for Lancashire before moving to Nottinghamshire; other brother Peter plays for Warrington CC and has played for Scottish Universities and Cambridge University; uncle was excellent fast bowler; godfather umpires in Manchester Association
**Education:** Manchester Grammar School; Trinity College, Cambridge
**Qualifications:** 10 O-levels, 2 AO-Levels, 3 A-levels, 2 S-levels, BA in History
**Off-season:** England tour to South Africa
**Overseas tours:** England YC to Australia 1989-90, to New Zealand 1990-91; England A to South Africa 1993-94; England to Australia 1994-95, to South Africa 1995-96
**Overseas teams played for:** Midland Guildford, Perth 1990
**Cricketers particularly admired:** Michael Atherton, Neil Fairbrother, Graham

Gooch, Alec Stewart, David Gower, Allan Donald, Ian Salisbury

**Other sports followed:** Football (Manchester United), golf

**Relaxations:** Music, foreign languages (French and Russian), dining out, golf, soccer and squash

**Extras:** Captained England YC (U19) to New Zealand 1990-91 and played for England YC in three home series v New Zealand 1989, Pakistan 1990 and Australia (as captain) 1991. Made his maiden first-class century for Cambridge University on the same day that brother Mark made his for Notts. First to score 1000 runs in U19 Tests. Scored 286 for England A against Eastern Province at Port Elizabeth in 1994, the highest score by an Englishman on an England or England A tour for almost 30 years. Finished top of the first-class batting averages on England's tour to South Africa in 1995-96 with 336 runs at 67.20, but had to fly home after suffering a hamstring injury whilst fielding in the third Test at Durban

**Opinions on cricket:** 'I think it's good that the four-day schedule has been introduced, and that the Sunday League has been commercialised.'

**Best batting:** 286 England A v Eastern Province, Port Elizabeth 1993-94

**Best bowling:** 1-90 Lancashire v Sussex, Hove 1992

## 1995 Season

|           | M  | Inns | NO | Runs | HS  | Avge  | 100s | 50s | Ct | St | O | M | Runs | Wkts | Avge | Best | 5wI | 10wM |
|-----------|----|------|----|------|-----|-------|------|-----|----|----|---|---|------|------|------|------|-----|------|
| Test      | 3  | 6    | 1  | 100  | 50  | 20.00 | -    | 1   | 4  | -  |   |   |      |      |      |      |     |      |
| All First | 18 | 31   | 2  | 1377 | 182 | 47.48 | 3    | 10  | 21 | -  |   |   |      |      |      |      |     |      |
| 1-day Int |    |      |    |      |     |       |      |     |    |    |   |   |      |      |      |      |     |      |
| NatWest   | 3  | 3    | 0  | 66   | 31  | 22.00 | -    | -   | 1  | -  |   |   |      |      |      |      |     |      |
| B & H     | 8  | 7    | 1  | 385  | 114 | 64.16 | 1    | 2   | 2  | -  |   |   |      |      |      |      |     |      |
| Sunday    | 14 | 13   | 0  | 362  | 75  | 27.84 | -    | 3   | 5  | -  |   |   |      |      |      |      |     |      |

## Career Performances

|           | M   | Inns | NO | Runs | HS  | Avge  | 100s | 50s | Ct | St | Balls | Runs | Wkts | Avge   | Best | 5wI | 10wM |
|-----------|-----|------|----|------|-----|-------|------|-----|----|----|-------|------|------|--------|------|-----|------|
| Test      | 9   | 16   | 1  | 330  | 72  | 22.00 | -    | 3   | 9  | -  |       |      |      |        |      |     |      |
| All First | 107 | 179  | 17 | 7890 | 286 | 48.70 | 14   | 48  | 89 | -  | 78    | 108  | 1    | 108.00 | 1-90 | -   | -    |
| 1-day Int | 3   | 3    | 0  | 34   | 18  | 11.33 | -    | -   | -  | -  |       |      |      |        |      |     |      |
| NatWest   | 5   | 5    | 0  | 97   | 31  | 19.40 | -    | -   | 2  | -  |       |      |      |        |      |     |      |
| B & H     | 19  | 18   | 1  | 710  | 114 | 41.76 | 1    | 4   | 5  | -  |       |      |      |        |      |     |      |
| Sunday    | 37  | 35   | 1  | 915  | 91  | 26.91 | -    | 7   | 11 | -  |       |      |      |        |      |     |      |

# CROFT, R. D. B.       Glamorgan

**Name:** Robert Damien Bale Croft
**Role:** Right-hand bat, off-spinner
**Born:** 25 May 1970, Swansea
**Height:** 5ft 11in **Weight:** 11st 5lbs
**Nickname:** Crofty
**County debut:** 1989
**County cap:** 1992
**50 wickets in a season:** 3
**1st-Class 50s:** 14
**1st-Class 100s:** 2
**1st-Class 5 w. in innings:** 14
**1st-Class 10 w. in match:** 2
**1st-Class catches:** 59
**Place in batting averages:** 184th av. 22.37
(1994 152nd av. 26.08)
**Place in bowling averages:** 95th av. 34.60
(1994 144th av. 52.82)
**Strike rate:** 74.73 (career 82.23)
**Parents:** Malcolm and Susan
**Family links with cricket:** Father and grandfather played local cricket
**Education:** St John Lloyd Catholic School; Neath Trinity College; West Glamorgan
Institute of Higher Education
**Qualifications:** 6 O-levels; OND Business Studies; HND Business Studies; NCA
senior coaching certificate
**Career outside cricket:** Personnel management ('not as yet!')
**Overseas tours:** England A to Bermuda and West Indies 1991-92, to South Africa
1993-94
**Cricketers particularly admired:** Alan Jones, Tom Cartwright, Don Shepherd,
John Steele, John Emburey
**Other sports followed:** Rugby, soccer
**Relaxations:** Shooting, fishing, driving, music, golf
**Extras:** Captained England South to victory in International Youth Tournament 1989
and was voted Player of the Tournament. Glamorgan Young Player of the Year 1992
**Opinions on cricket:** 'Enjoyment is of the utmost importance.'
**Best batting:** 143 Glamorgan v Somerset, Taunton 1995
**Best bowling:** 8-66 Glamorgan v Warwickshire, Swansea 1992

---

23. Who won the 1995 Hong Kong Sixes competition, and
whom did they defeat in the final?

---

**1995 Season**

| | M | Inns | NO | Runs | HS | Avge | 100s | 50s | Ct | St | O | M | Runs | Wkts | Avge | Best | 5wI | 10wM |
|---|---|---|---|---|---|---|---|---|---|---|---|---|---|---|---|---|---|---|
| Test | | | | | | | | | | | | | | | | | | |
| All First | 20 | 36 | 4 | 716 | 143 | 22.37 | 1 | 1 | 8 | - | 847 | 209 | 2353 | 68 | 34.60 | 6-104 | 4 | 1 |
| 1-day Int | | | | | | | | | | | | | | | | | | |
| NatWest | 4 | 2 | 2 | 39 | 23 * | - | - | - | 1 | - | 43 | 5 | 143 | 3 | 47.66 | 2-53 | - | |
| B & H | 5 | 3 | 1 | 100 | 50 * | 50.00 | - | 1 | 1 | - | 50 | 4 | 171 | 5 | 34.20 | 3-33 | - | |
| Sunday | 16 | 11 | 6 | 196 | 66 * | 39.20 | - | 1 | 6 | - | 115 | 5 | 516 | 20 | 25.80 | 3-28 | - | |

**Career Performances**

| | M | Inns | NO | Runs | HS | Avge | 100s | 50s | Ct | St | Balls | Runs | Wkts | Avge | Best | 5wI | 10wM |
|---|---|---|---|---|---|---|---|---|---|---|---|---|---|---|---|---|---|
| Test | | | | | | | | | | | | | | | | | |
| All First | 138 | 201 | 41 | 4090 | 143 | 25.56 | 2 | 14 | 59 | - | 27468 | 13250 | 330 | 40.15 | 8-66 | 14 | 2 |
| 1-day Int | | | | | | | | | | | | | | | | | |
| NatWest | 17 | 13 | 5 | 197 | 50 | 24.62 | - | 1 | 3 | - | 976 | 561 | 15 | 37.40 | 3-30 | - | |
| B & H | 13 | 11 | 6 | 214 | 50 * | 42.80 | - | 1 | 6 | - | 756 | 430 | 14 | 30.71 | 3-28 | - | |
| Sunday | 78 | 55 | 19 | 623 | 66 * | 17.30 | - | 1 | 20 | - | 3094 | 2331 | 71 | 32.83 | 6-20 | 1 | |

# CRONJE, W. J.      Leicestershire

**Name:** Wessel Johannes Cronje
**Role:** Right-hand bat, right-arm
medium bowler
**Born:** 25 September 1969, Bloemfontein,
South Africa
**Nickname:** Hansie, Sampras
**County debut:** 1995
**Test debut:** 1992-93
**Tests:** 21
**One-day Internationals:** 68
**1st-Class 50s:** 30
**1st-Class 100s:** 20
**1st-Class 200s:** 2
**1st-Class catches:** 70
**One-Day 100s:** 3
**One-day 5 w. innings:** 1
**Place in batting averages:** 25th av. 50.44
(1994 91st av. 34.78)
**Place in bowling averages:** 134th av. 45.86
(1994 61st av. 30.38)
**Strike rate:** 102.53 (career 100.82)
**Parents:** Ewie and San-Marie

**Family links with cricket:** Father former Orange Free State captain and now President of the Orange Free State Cricket Union. Brother (Frans) played first-class cricket for Border, Orange Free State and Griquas. He scored two hundreds in the same match in 1993-94

**Qualifications:** B. Comm 1991

**Education:** Grey College, Bloemfontein; University of Orange Free State

**Overseas tours:** South Africa to India 1991-92, to Australia 1991-92, to West Indies 1991-92, to Sri Lanka 1993-94, to Australia 1993-94, to England 1994, to New Zealand 1994-95, to Zimbabwe 1995-96, to India and Pakistan (World Cup) 1995-96

**Overseas teams played for:** South African Universities; Orange Free State

**Cricketers particularly admired:** Allan Donald, Franklyn Stephenson, Kepler Wessels, Steve Waugh

**Extras:** Became captain of Orange Free State at age 21. Scored a century for South African Universities against Mike Gatting's England XI in 1989-90. Succeeded Kepler Wessels as captain of South Africa after the England tour in 1994

**Opinions on cricket:** 'Four-day cricket should be 100 overs in a day. More specific training.'

**Best batting:** 251 Orange Free State v Australia, Bloemfontein 1993-94

**Best bowling:** 4-47 South Africans v Kent, Canterbury 1994

## 1995 Season

| | M | Inns | NO | Runs | HS | Avge | 100s | 50s | Ct | St | O | M | Runs | Wkts | Avge | Best | 5wI | 10wM |
|---|---|---|---|---|---|---|---|---|---|---|---|---|---|---|---|---|---|---|
| Test | | | | | | | | | | | | | | | | | | |
| All First | 16 | 28 | 1 | 1362 | 213 | 50.44 | 4 | 7 | 13 | - | 256.2 | 82 | 688 | 15 | 45.86 | 3-42 | - | - |
| 1-day Int | | | | | | | | | | | | | | | | | | |
| NatWest | | | | | | | | | | | | | | | | | | |
| B & H | 5 | 5 | 0 | 228 | 158 | 45.60 | 1 | - | 2 | - | 44 | 2 | 165 | 5 | 33.00 | 2-26 | - | |
| Sunday | 13 | 13 | 3 | 357 | 93 * | 35.70 | - | 2 | 4 | - | 98 | 3 | 466 | 11 | 42.36 | 3-37 | - | |

## Career Performances

| | M | Inns | NO | Runs | HS | Avge | 100s | 50s | Ct | St | Balls | Runs | Wkts | Avge | Best | 5wI | 10wM |
|---|---|---|---|---|---|---|---|---|---|---|---|---|---|---|---|---|---|
| Test | 21 | 38 | 4 | 1342 | 135 | 39.47 | 5 | 3 | 9 | - | 1537 | 493 | 8 | 61.62 | 2-17 | - | - |
| All First | 101 | 180 | 16 | 6931 | 251 | 42.26 | 20 | 30 | 70 | - | 5142 | 2146 | 51 | 42.07 | 4-47 | - | - |
| 1-day Int | 68 | 65 | 11 | 1975 | 112 | 36.57 | 2 | 10 | 24 | - | 2295 | 1601 | 45 | 35.57 | 5-32 | 1 | |
| NatWest | | | | | | | | | | | | | | | | | |
| B & H | 5 | 5 | 0 | 228 | 158 | 45.60 | 1 | - | 2 | - | 264 | 165 | 5 | 33.00 | 2-26 | - | |
| Sunday | 13 | 13 | 3 | 357 | 93 * | 35.70 | - | 2 | 4 | - | 588 | 466 | 11 | 42.36 | 3-37 | - | |

# CROWE, C. D. Leicestershire

**Name:** Carl Daniel Crowe
**Role:** Right-hand bat, off-spin bowler
**Born:** 25 November 1975, Leicester
**Height:** 6ft  **Weight:** 12st 6lbs
**Nickname:** Strutter, Sheryl
**County debut:** 1995
**1st-Class catches:** 1
**Parents:** Edward and Jeannette
**Marital status:** Single
**Family links with cricket:** Younger brother
has played for Leicestershire U15, U16 and
U17 and County Colts. Dad manager of
Hinckley Town U15s
**Education:** Lutterworth Grammar School
**Qualifications:** 11 GCSEs, 2 A-levels, NCA
Senior Coach
**Off-season:** Coaching and getting fit.
'Hopefully going to South Africa in January'
**Overseas tours:** Leicestershire U19 to South
Africa 1993-94

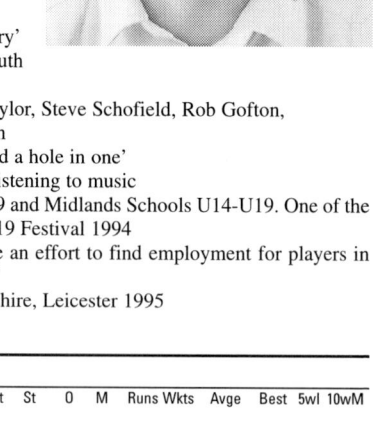

**Cricketers particularly admired:** Les Taylor, Steve Schofield, Rob Gofton,
Darren Maddy, Vince Wells, Phil Robinson
**Other sports followed:** Try all sports, 'had a hole in one'
**Relaxations:** Sleeping, going to cinema, listening to music
**Extras:** Played for Leicestershire U12-U19 and Midlands Schools U14-U19. One of the
Cricketers of the Festival at Cambridge U19 Festival 1994
**Opinions on cricket:** 'Clubs should make an effort to find employment for players in
the winter i.e. nine or 12 month contracts.'
**Best batting:** 9 Leicestershire v Warwickshire, Leicester 1995

---

## 1995 Season

| | M | Inns | NO | Runs | HS | Avge | 100s | 50s | Ct | St | O | M | Runs | Wkts | Avge | Best | 5wI | 10wM |
|---|---|---|---|---|---|---|---|---|---|---|---|---|---|---|---|---|---|---|
| Test | | | | | | | | | | | | | | | | | | |
| All First | 1 | 2 | 0 | 10 | 9 | 5.00 | - | - | 1 | - | 3 | 2 | 4 | 0 | - | - | - | - |
| 1-day Int | | | | | | | | | | | | | | | | | | |
| NatWest | | | | | | | | | | | | | | | | | | |
| B & H | | | | | | | | | | | | | | | | | | |
| Sunday | | | | | | | | | | | | | | | | | | |

## Career Performances

|  | M | Inns | NO | Runs | HS | Avge | 100s | 50s | Ct | St | Balls | Runs | Wkts | Avge | Best | 5wI | 10wM |
|---|---|---|---|---|---|---|---|---|---|---|---|---|---|---|---|---|---|
| Test | | | | | | | | | | | | | | | | | |
| All First | 1 | 2 | 0 | 10 | 9 | 5.00 | - | - | 1 | - | 18 | 4 | 0 | - | | - | - | - |
| 1-day Int | | | | | | | | | | | | | | | | | |
| NatWest | | | | | | | | | | | | | | | | | |
| B & H | | | | | | | | | | | | | | | | | |
| Sunday | | | | | | | | | | | | | | | | | |

# CULLINAN, D. J.                     Derbyshire

**Name:** Daryll John Cullinan
**Role:** Right-hand bat, off-spin bowler
**Born:** 4 March 1967, East London,
South Africa
**County debut:** 1995
**Test debut:** 1992-93
**Tests:** 13
**One-day Internationals:** 38
**1000 runs in a season:** 1
**1st-Class 50s:** 39
**1st-Class 100s:** 17
**1st-Class 300s:** 1
**1st-Class catches:** 106
**One-day 100s:** 2
**Place in batting averages:** 43rd av. 45.59
(1994 62nd av. 38.90)
**Family links with cricket:** Brother Ralph
has played for Border and Orange Free State
**Education:** Queens College, Queenstown; Stellenbosch University
**Overseas tours:** South Africa to Australia 1991-92, to Sri Lanka 1993-94, to Australia
1993-94, to England 1994, to New Zealand 1994-95, to Zimbabwe 1995-96, to India
and Pakistan (World Cup) 1995-96
**Overseas teams played for:** South African Universities; Border; Western Province
**Extras:** In 1983-84 became the youngest player to score a first-class century in South
Africa. Holds record for the highest first-class score in South African cricket
**Best batting:** 337* Transvaal v Northern Transvaal, Johannesburg 1993-94
**Best bowling:** 2-27 Border v Natal B, East London 1983-84

## 1995 Season

| | M | Inns | NO | Runs | HS | Avge | 100s | 50s | Ct | St | O | M | Runs | Wkts | Avge | Best | 5wI | 10wM |
|---|---|---|---|---|---|---|---|---|---|---|---|---|---|---|---|---|---|---|
| Test | | | | | | | | | | | | | | | | | | |
| All First | 14 | 26 | 4 | 1003 | 161 | 45.59 | 5 | 1 | 8 | - | | | | | | | | |
| 1-day Int | | | | | | | | | | | | | | | | | | |
| NatWest | 3 | 3 | 2 | 148 | 119 * | 148.00 | 1 | - | 2 | - | | | | | | | | |
| B & H | 3 | 3 | 2 | 106 | 101 * | 106.00 | 1 | - | 1 | - | | | | | | | | |
| Sunday | 12 | 11 | 3 | 365 | 76 * | 45.62 | - | 3 | 4 | - | | | | | | | | |

## Career Performances

| | M | Inns | NO | Runs | HS | Avge | 100s | 50s | Ct | St | Balls | Runs | Wkts | Avge | Best | 5wI | 10wM |
|---|---|---|---|---|---|---|---|---|---|---|---|---|---|---|---|---|---|
| Test | 13 | 24 | 2 | 777 | 102 | 35.31 | 1 | 5 | 8 | - | | | | | | | |
| All First | 120 | 214 | 32 | 7404 | 337 * | 40.68 | 17 | 39 | 106 | - | 138 | 70 | 3 | 23.33 | 2-27 | - | - |
| 1-day Int | 38 | 37 | 3 | 860 | 70 * | 25.29 | - | 5 | 13 | - | | | | | | | |
| NatWest | 3 | 3 | 2 | 148 | 119 * | 148.00 | 1 | - | 2 | - | | | | | | | |
| B & H | 3 | 3 | 2 | 106 | 101 * | 106.00 | 1 | - | 1 | - | | | | | | | |
| Sunday | 12 | 11 | 3 | 365 | 76 * | 45.62 | - | 3 | 4 | - | | | | | | | |

# CUNLIFFE, R. J. — Gloucestershire

**Name:** Robert John Cunliffe
**Role:** Right-hand bat, cover fielder, occasional wicket-keeper
**Born:** 8 November 1973, Oxford
**Height:** 5ft 11in **Weight:** 12st 9lbs
**Nickname:** 'Too rude to mention'
**County debut:** 1993 (one-day), 1994 (first-class)
**1st-Class 100s:** 2
**1st-Class 50s:** 2
**1st-Class catches:** 10
**Parents:** Barry and Janet
**Marital status:** Single
**Family links with cricket:** 'Dad played in his younger days for his wife's village team and was groundsman for nine years at Banbury Twenty CC'
**Education:** Banbury School and Banbury Technical College
**Qualifications:** 'Not too many'
**Off-season:** Doing as little as possible and relaxing. Training

**Overseas tours:** England U19 to India 1992-93
**Cricketers particularly admired:** Robin Smith
**Other sports followed:** Football, squash ('not the best'), 'can't watch any sport'
**Injuries:** Back problems, missed two months and broken thumb, missed five weeks
**Relaxations:** Training and socialising with mates
**Extras:** Played in England U19 home series against West Indies in 1993
**Opinions on cricket:** 'Maybe the 2nd XI games should be four days to get used to first-class cricket.'
**Best batting:** 190* Gloucestershire v Oxford University, The Parks 1995

## 1995 Season

|         | M | Inns | NO | Runs | HS | Avge | 100s | 50s | Ct | St | O | M | Runs | Wkts | Avge | Best | 5wI | 10wM |
|---------|---|------|----|------|-----|------|------|-----|----|----|---|---|------|------|------|------|-----|------|
| Test    |   |      |    |      |     |      |      |     |    |    |   |   |      |      |      |      |     |      |
| All First | 7 | 8  | 3  | 412  | 190 * | 82.40 | 1 | 2 | 5 | - |   |   |      |      |      |      |     |      |
| 1-day Int |   |      |    |      |     |      |      |     |    |    |   |   |      |      |      |      |     |      |
| NatWest | 2 | 2   | 0  | 40   | 40  | 20.00 | - | - | 1 | - |   |   |      |      |      |      |     |      |
| B & H   |   |      |    |      |     |      |      |     |    |    |   |   |      |      |      |      |     |      |
| Sunday  | 1 | 1   | 0  | 10   | 10  | 10.00 | - | - | - | - |   |   |      |      |      |      |     |      |

## Career Performances

|         | M | Inns | NO | Runs | HS | Avge | 100s | 50s | Ct | St | Balls | Runs | Wkts | Avge | Best | 5wI | 10wM |
|---------|---|------|----|------|-----|------|------|-----|----|----|-------|------|------|------|------|-----|------|
| Test    |   |      |    |      |     |      |      |     |    |    |       |      |      |      |      |     |      |
| All First | 14 | 21 | 4  | 766  | 190 * | 45.05 | 2 | 2 | 10 | - |     |      |      |      |      |     |      |
| 1-day Int |   |      |    |      |     |      |      |     |    |    |       |      |      |      |      |     |      |
| NatWest | 2 | 2   | 0  | 40   | 40  | 20.00 | - | - | 1 | - |       |      |      |      |      |     |      |
| B & H   |   |      |    |      |     |      |      |     |    |    |       |      |      |      |      |     |      |
| Sunday  | 2 | 2   | 0  | 32   | 22  | 16.00 | - | - | - | - |       |      |      |      |      |     |      |

24. Who was named Player of the Tournament at the 1995 Hong Kong Sixes?

# CURRAN, K. M.　　　　Northamptonshire

**Name:** Kevin Malcolm Curran
**Role:** Right-hand bat, right-arm
fast-medium bowler
**Born:** 7 September 1959, Rusape, Rhodesia
**Height:** 6ft 2in **Weight:** 14st
**Nickname:** KC
**County debut:** 1985 (Glos),
1991 (Northamptonshire)
**County cap:** 1985 (Glos),
1992 (Northamptonshire)
**One-Day Internationals:** 11
**1000 runs in a season:** 5
**50 wickets in a season:** 5
**1st-Class 50s:** 62
**1st-Class 100s:** 21
**1st-Class 5 w. in innings:** 15
**1st-Class 10 w. in match:** 4
**1st-Class catches:** 157

**One-day 100s:** 1
**One-Day 5 w. in innings:** 1
**Place in batting averages:** 88th av. 35.95 (1994 23rd av 48.65)
**Place in bowling averages:** 85th av. 32.48 (1994 137th av 47.19)
**Strike rate:** 57.91 (career 51.56)
**Parents:** Kevin and Sylvia
**Wife and date of marriage:** Sarah, 5 June 1993
**Children:** Thomas, 12 March 1995
**Family links with cricket:** Father played for Rhodesia 1947-54. Cousin Patrick
Curran played for Rhodesia 1975
**Education:** Marandellas High School, Zimbabwe
**Qualifications:** 6 O-levels, 2 M-levels
**Career outside cricket:** Tobacco buyer/farmer
**Overseas tours:** Zimbabwe to Sri Lanka 1982 and 1984, to England 1982 and for
World Cup 1983, to Pakistan and India for World Cup 1987
**Overseas teams played for:** Zimbabwe and Natal 1988-92, Boland 1994-95
**Other sports followed:** Rugby union
**Relaxations:** 'Game fishing, especially along the North Natal coast, the Mozambique
coast, and Magaruque Island'
**Extras:** First player to take a Sunday League hat-trick, and score 50 in the same match,
Gloucestershire v Warwickshire, Edgbaston 1989. Released by Gloucestershire at end of
1990  after he had completed the season's double of 1000 runs and 50 wickets. Chose to
join Northamptonshire for the 1991 season after he had been approached by several counties.

**Best batting:** 144* Gloucestershire v Sussex, Bristol 1990
**Best bowling:** 7-47 Northamptonshire v Yorkshire, Harrogate 1993

## 1995 Season

|          | M  | Inns | NO | Runs | HS    | Avge  | 100s | 50s | Ct | St | O     | M  | Runs | Wkts | Avge  | Best | 5wI | 10wM |
|----------|----|------|----|------|-------|-------|------|-----|----|----|-------|----|------|------|-------|------|-----|------|
| Test     |    |      |    |      |       |       |      |     |    |    |       |    |      |      |       |      |     |      |
| All First| 17 | 27   | 3  | 863  | 117   | 35.95 | 1    | 4   | 22 | -  | 357.1 | 84 | 1202 | 37   | 32.48 | 4-78 | -   | -    |
| 1-day Int|    |      |    |      |       |       |      |     |    |    |       |    |      |      |       |      |     |      |
| NatWest  | 5  | 5    | 1  | 113  | 30    | 28.25 | -    | -   | 4  | -  | 46    | 8  | 144  | 4    | 36.00 | 2-44 | -   |      |
| B & H    | 4  | 4    | 0  | 127  | 53    | 31.75 | -    | 2   | 1  | -  | 26    | 3  | 121  | 4    | 30.25 | 4-38 | -   |      |
| Sunday   | 14 | 13   | 1  | 424  | 119 * | 35.33 | 1    | 2   | 1  | -  | 75    | 1  | 400  | 11   | 36.36 | 3-49 | -   |      |

## Career Performances

|          | M   | Inns | NO | Runs  | HS    | Avge  | 100s | 50s | Ct  | St | Balls | Runs  | Wkts | Avge  | Best | 5wI | 10wM |
|----------|-----|------|----|-------|-------|-------|------|-----|-----|----|-------|-------|------|-------|------|-----|------|
| Test     |     |      |    |       |       |       |      |     |     |    |       |       |      |       |      |     |      |
| All First| 267 | 413  | 67 | 12448 | 144 * | 35.97 | 21   | 62  | 157 | -  | 28415 | 14878 | 551  | 27.00 | 7-47 | 15  | 4    |
| 1-day Int| 11  | 11   | 0  | 287   | 73    | 26.09 | -    | 2   | 1   | -  | 506   | 398   | 9    | 44.22 | 3-65 | -   |      |
| NatWest  | 37  | 32   | 7  | 753   | 78 *  | 30.12 | -    | 3   | 11  | -  | 1931  | 1092  | 36   | 30.33 | 4-34 | -   |      |
| B & H    | 40  | 35   | 6  | 763   | 57    | 26.31 | -    | 5   | 7   | -  | 1914  | 1303  | 48   | 27.14 | 4-38 | -   |      |
| Sunday   | 156 | 147  | 31 | 3673  | 119 * | 31.66 | 1    | 20  | 30  | -  | 5001  | 4020  | 145  | 27.72 | 5-15 | 1   |      |

# CURTIS, T. S. Worcestershire

**Name:** Timothy Stephen Curtis
**Role:** Right-hand bat, leg-spin bowler
**Born:** 15 January 1960, Chislehurst, Kent
**Height:** 5ft 11in **Weight:** 12st 5lbs
**Nickname:** TC, Duracell, Professor
**County debut:** 1979
**County cap:** 1984
**Benefit:** 1994 (£129,501)
**Test debut:** 1988
**Tests:** 5
**1000 runs in a season:** 11
**1st-Class 50s:** 97
**1st-Class 100s:** 37
**1st-Class 200s:** 2
**1st-Class catches:** 170
**One-Day 100s:** 6
**Place in batting averages:** 64th av. 40.70
(1994 123rd av. 30.96)
**Strike rate:** (career 94.00)

**Parents:** Bruce and Betty
**Wife and date of marriage:** Philippa, 21 September 1985
**Children:** Jennifer May, 9 February 1991; Andrew Stephen Neild, 17 February 1993
**Family links with cricket:** Father played good club cricket in Bristol and Stafford
**Education:** Royal Grammar School, Worcester; Durham University; Cambridge University
**Qualifications:** 12 O-levels, 4 A-levels, BA (Hons) in English, PCGE in English and Games
**Off-season:** Teaching at RGS, Worcester
**Overseas tours:** NCA U19 tour of Canada 1979
**Other sports followed:** Rugby, tennis, squash, golf
**Injuries:** Split finger, missed one Sunday game
**Extras:** Captained Durham University to UAU Championship in 1981. Chairman of the Professional Cricketers' Association. Appointed county captain in 1992. Worcestershire supporters' Player of the Year 1992. A century against Durham in 1993 meant that he had scored a century against every other first-class county. Raised £129,501 from his benefit in 1994. Relinquished the captaincy during the 1995 season
**Opinions on cricket:** 'Things are moving in the right direction, but quality of pitches is still dubious.'
**Best batting:** 248 Worcestershire v Somerset, Taunton 1991
**Best bowling:** 2-17 Worcestershire v Oxford University, The Parks 1991

## 1995 Season

| | M | Inns | NO | Runs | HS | Avge | 100s | 50s | Ct | St | O | M | Runs | Wkts | Avge | Best | 5wI | 10wM |
|---|---|---|---|---|---|---|---|---|---|---|---|---|---|---|---|---|---|---|
| Test | | | | | | | | | | | | | | | | | | |
| All First | 20 | 35 | 5 | 1221 | 169 * | 40.70 | 2 | 5 | 8 | - | 3 | 1 | 8 | 0 | - | - | - | - |
| 1-day Int | | | | | | | | | | | | | | | | | | |
| NatWest | 2 | 2 | 1 | 110 | 106 * | 110.00 | 1 | - | - | - | 2 | 0 | 16 | 0 | - | - | - | |
| B & H | 6 | 6 | 1 | 183 | 54 * | 36.60 | - | 2 | 1 | - | | | | | | | | |
| Sunday | 16 | 16 | 3 | 480 | 82 * | 36.92 | - | 5 | 4 | - | | | | | | | | |

## Career Performances

| | M | Inns | NO | Runs | HS | Avge | 100s | 50s | Ct | St | Balls | Runs | Wkts | Avge | Best | 5wI | 10wM |
|---|---|---|---|---|---|---|---|---|---|---|---|---|---|---|---|---|---|
| Test | 5 | 9 | 0 | ·140 | 41 | 15.55 | - | - | 3 | - | 18 | 7 | 0 | - | - | - | - |
| All First | 307 | 525 | 64 | 19131 | 248 | 41.49 | 37 | 97 | 170 | - | 1034 | 730 | 11 | 66.36 | 2-17 | - | - |
| 1-day Int | | | | | | | | | | | | | | | | | |
| NatWest | 38 | 37 | 5 | 1665 | 136 * | 52.03 | 4 | 10 | 11 | - | 36 | 31 | 2 | 15.50 | 1-6 | - | |
| B & H | 58 | 58 | 5 | 1698 | 97 | 32.03 | - | 15 | 12 | - | 2 | 4 | 0 | - | - | - | |
| Sunday | 180 | 174 | 27 | 6031 | 124 | 41.02 | 2 | 52 | 54 | - | | | | | | | |

# DAKIN, J. M.                    Leicestershire

**Name:** Jonathan Michael Dakin
**Role:** Left-hand bat, right-arm
medium-fast bowler,
**Born:** 28 February 1973, Hitchin, Herts
**Height:** 6ft 5in **Weight:** 14st 4lb
**Nickname:** J.D., F.C., Half-bat, The Sweep
**County debut:** 1993
**1st-Class 100s:** 1
**1st-Class 50s:** 2
**1st-Class catches:** 6
**Place in batting averages:** 135th av. 29.63
**Strike rate:** (career 78.54)
**Parents:** Fred John and Gloria May
**Marital status:** Single
**Family links with cricket:** Brother plays
club cricket for Wanderers 1st XI in
South Africa
**Education:** King Edward VII School,
Johannesburg, South Africa
**Qualifications:** Matriculation
**Off-season:** Playing cricket for Kaponga in New Zealand
**Overseas tours:** Rutland Tourists to Jersey 1992
**Overseas teams played for:** Wanderers, South Africa, 1986-92; Alberts, South Africa
1993
**Cricketers particularly admired:** Vince 'Clarke Kent' Wells, 'Roasting' Darren
Maddy, Gordon 'F.M.' Parsons
**Other sports followed:** Most sports, especially rugby (Tigers)
**Relaxations:** Watching television, movies, listening to music, following sport and
playing golf
**Extras:** 'Only man to lose to David Millns in a two-mile race ... ever.'
**Opinions on cricket:** 'Second-team games should be played on first-class wickets over
four days to allow for natural results. Two white balls should be used on Sundays to
even up the contest between bat and ball.'
**Best batting:** 101* Leicestershire v Nottinghamshire, Leicester 1995
**Best bowling:** 4-45 Leicestershire v Cambridge University, Fenner's 1993

25. Who was the captain of Sri Lanka in the World Series in Australia in 1995-96?

## 1995 Season

| | M | Inns | NO | Runs | HS | Avge | 100s | 50s | Ct | St | O | M | Runs | Wkts | Avge | Best | 5wI | 10wM |
|---|---|---|---|---|---|---|---|---|---|---|---|---|---|---|---|---|---|---|
| Test | | | | | | | | | | | | | | | | | | |
| All First | 8 | 13 | 2 | 326 | 101 * | 29.63 | 1 | 2 | 6 | - | 99 | 15 | 370 | 6 | 61.66 | 2-20 | - | - |
| 1-day Int | | | | | | | | | | | | | | | | | | |
| NatWest | 2 | 2 | 0 | 31 | 26 | 15.50 | - | - | - | - | 12 | 3 | 37 | 0 | - | | - | - |
| B & H | 1 | 1 | 0 | 8 | 8 | 8.00 | - | - | - | - | 2 | 0 | 27 | 0 | - | | - | - |
| Sunday | 11 | 11 | 3 | 157 | 45 | 19.62 | - | - | 2 | - | 43.2 | 0 | 255 | 10 | 25.50 | 3-23 | - | |

## Career Performances

| | M | Inns | NO | Runs | HS | Avge | 100s | 50s | Ct | St | Balls | Runs | Wkts | Avge | Best | 5wI | 10wM |
|---|---|---|---|---|---|---|---|---|---|---|---|---|---|---|---|---|---|
| Test | | | | | | | | | | | | | | | | | |
| All First | 11 | 17 | 2 | 360 | 101 * | 24.00 | 1 | 2 | 6 | - | 864 | 490 | 11 | 44.54 | 4-45 | - | - |
| 1-day Int | | | | | | | | | | | | | | | | | |
| NatWest | 2 | 2 | 0 | 31 | 26 | 15.50 | - | - | - | - | 72 | 37 | 0 | - | | - | - |
| B & H | 1 | 1 | 0 | 8 | 8 | 8.00 | - | - | - | - | 12 | 27 | 0 | - | | - | - |
| Sunday | 33 | 29 | 4 | 331 | 45 | 13.24 | - | - | 8 | - | 855 | 828 | 26 | 31.84 | 3-23 | - | |

# DALE, A. Glamorgan

**Name:** Adrian Dale
**Role:** Right-hand bat, right-arm medium bowler
**Born:** 24 October 1968, Germiston, South Africa
**Height:** 5ft 11in **Weight:** 11st 10lbs
**Nickname:** Arthur
**County debut:** 1989
**County cap:** 1992
**1000 runs in a season:** 2
**1st-Class 50s:** 25
**1st-Class 100s:** 11
**1st-Class 200s:** 1
**1st-Class 5 w. in innings:** 1
**1st-Class catches:** 46
**One-day 100s:** 1
**One-Day 5 w. in innings:** 1
**Place in batting averages:**
136th av. 29.61 (1994 161st av. 25.39)
**Strike rate:** (career 71.65)
**Parents:** John and Maureen
**Marital status:** Single

**Family links with cricket:** Father played for Glamorgan 2nd XI and Chepstow CC
**Education:** Pembroke Primary; Chepstow Comprehensive; Swansea University
**Qualifications:** 9 O-levels, 3 A-levels, BA (Hons) in Economics
**Off-season:** 'Touring Europe and America with my girlfriend Ruth.' Playing for three months in Auckland, New Zealand
**Overseas tours:** Welsh Schools U16 to Australia 1986-87; Combined Universities to Barbados 1988-89; Glamorgan to Trinidad 1989-90, to Zimbabwe 1990-91, to Trinidad 1991-92, to Cape Town 1992-93; England A to South Africa 1993-94
**Overseas teams played for:** Bionics, Zimbabwe 1990-91; Cornwall, New Zealand 1991-93
**Cricketers particularly admired:** Ian Botham, Michael Holding, Mike Gatting
**Other sports followed:** Football (Arsenal), athletics, US basketball, rugby league (Auckland Warriors and Wales), rugby union (Wales), ice hockey (Cardiff Devils)
**Injuries:** Broken thumb, out for three weeks
**Relaxations:** Eating out, following other sports, travelling
**Extras:** Played in successful Combined Universities sides of 1989 and 1990. Only batsman to score two half-centuries against the West Indies tourists in the same match in 1991. Took a wicket with his first delivery at Lord's. Recorded Glamorgan's best one-day bowling figures, 6-22 against Durham 1993. Recorded Glamorgan's highest ever partnership, 425, with Viv Richards against Middlesex, 1993
**Opinions on cricket:** 'Too much cricket. Too much quantity leads to less quality.'
**Best batting:** 214* Glamorgan v Middlesex, Cardiff 1993
**Best bowling:** 6-18 Glamorgan v Warwickshire, Cardiff 1993

## 1995 Season

|           | M  | Inns | NO | Runs | HS   | Avge  | 100s | 50s | Ct | St | O     | M  | Runs | Wkts | Avge  | Best | 5wI | 10wM |
|-----------|----|------|----|------|------|-------|------|-----|----|----|-------|----|------|------|-------|------|-----|------|
| Test      |    |      |    |      |      |       |      |     |    |    |       |    |      |      |       |      |     |      |
| All First | 12 | 23   | 2  | 622  | 133  | 29.61 | 2    | 2   | 7  | -  | 144.5 | 28 | 472  | 9    | 52.44 | 2-38 | -   | -    |
| 1-day Int |    |      |    |      |      |       |      |     |    |    |       |    |      |      |       |      |     |      |
| NatWest   | 3  | 3    | 1  | 37   | 30   | 18.50 | -    | -   | 1  | -  | 19    | 1  | 62   | 2    | 31.00 | 2-28 | -   |      |
| B & H     | 5  | 5    | 2  | 108  | 37 * | 36.00 | -    | -   | 3  | -  | 33    | 2  | 131  | 6    | 21.83 | 3-42 | -   |      |
| Sunday    | 12 | 9    | 1  | 212  | 48   | 26.50 | -    | -   | 3  | -  | 69.2  | 3  | 421  | 9    | 46.77 | 2-30 | -   |      |

## Career Performances

|           | M   | Inns | NO | Runs | HS    | Avge  | 100s | 50s | Ct | St | Balls | Runs | Wkts | Avge  | Best | 5wI | 10wM |
|-----------|-----|------|----|------|-------|-------|------|-----|----|----|-------|------|------|-------|------|-----|------|
| Test      |     |      |    |      |       |       |      |     |    |    |       |      |      |       |      |     |      |
| All First | 111 | 186  | 18 | 5551 | 214 * | 33.04 | 11   | 25  | 46 | -  | 8599  | 4616 | 120  | 38.46 | 6-18 | 1   | -    |
| 1-day Int |     |      |    |      |       |       |      |     |    |    |       |      |      |       |      |     |      |
| NatWest   | 19  | 17   | 2  | 403  | 110   | 26.86 | 1    | 1   | 5  | -  | 898   | 596  | 19   | 31.36 | 3-54 | -   |      |
| B & H     | 20  | 19   | 3  | 380  | 53    | 23.75 | -    | 1   | 6  | -  | 840   | 582  | 21   | 27.71 | 3-24 | -   |      |
| Sunday    | 87  | 72   | 9  | 1650 | 67 *  | 26.19 | -    | 9   | 24 | -  | 2770  | 2514 | 77   | 32.64 | 6-22 | 1   |      |

# DALEY, J. A.                                    Durham

**Name:** James Arthur Daley
**Role:** Right-hand bat
**Born:** 24 September 1973, Sunderland
**Height:** 5ft 11in **Weight:** 12st
**Nickname:** Bebs, Jonty
**County debut:** 1992
**1st-Class 50s:** 12
**1st-Class 100s:** 1
**1st-Class catches:** 17
**Place in batting averages:**
53rd av. 43.50 (1994 112th av. 32.06)
**Parents:** William and Christine
**Marital status:** Single
**Family links with cricket:**
Brother played representative
cricket for Durham
**Education:** Hetton Comprehensive
**Qualifications:** 5 GCSEs
**Career outside cricket:** Travel agent
**Overseas tours:** Durham to Zimbabwe, 1991-92; England U19 to India 1992-93;
England XI to Holland 1993
**Cricketers particularly admired:** David Graveney, Wayne Larkins, Jimmy Adams
**Other sports followed:** Most sports
**Relaxations:** Socialising, listening to all types of music
**Extras:** Scored three centuries in 1991 for MCC Young Cricketers at Lord's. Northern
Electric Foundation for Sport award winner 1992
**Best batting:** 159* Durham v Hampshire, Portsmouth 1994

## 1995 Season

|          | M | Inns | NO | Runs | HS | Avge | 100s | 50s | Ct | St | O | M | Runs | Wkts | Avge | Best | 5wI | 10wM |
|----------|---|------|----|------|-----|-------|------|-----|----|----|---|---|------|------|------|------|-----|------|
| Test     |   |      |    |      |     |       |      |     |    |    |   |   |      |      |      |      |     |      |
| All First| 7 | 12   | 2  | 435  | 55  | 43.50 | -    | 4   | 5  | -  |   |   |      |      |      |      |     |      |
| 1-day Int|   |      |    |      |     |       |      |     |    |    |   |   |      |      |      |      |     |      |
| NatWest  |   |      |    |      |     |       |      |     |    |    |   |   |      |      |      |      |     |      |
| B & H    | 2 | 1    | 0  | 17   | 17  | 17.00 | -    | -   | -  | -  |   |   |      |      |      |      |     |      |
| Sunday   | 6 | 6    | 2  | 129  | 53* | 32.25 | -    | 1   | 1  | -  |   |   |      |      |      |      |     |      |

## Career Performances

|        | M  | Inns | NO | Runs | HS    | Avge  | 100s | 50s | Ct | St | Balls | Runs | Wkts | Avge | Best | 5wI | 10wM |
|--------|----|------|----|------|-------|-------|------|-----|----|----|-------|------|------|------|------|-----|------|
| Test   |    |      |    |      |       |       |      |     |    |    |       |      |      |      |      |     |      |
| All First | 32 | 56 | 5 | 1701 | 159 * | 33.35 | 1 | 12 | 17 | - | 12 | 9 | 0 | - | - | - | - |
| 1-day Int |  |      |    |      |       |       |      |     |    |    |       |      |      |      |      |     |      |
| NatWest |   |      |    |      |       |       |      |     |    |    |       |      |      |      |      |     |      |
| B & H  | 2  | 1    | 0  | 17   | 17    | 17.00 | -    | -   | -  | -  |       |      |      |      |      |     |      |
| Sunday | 15 | 13   | 4  | 357  | 98 *  | 39.66 | -    | 3   | 3  | -  |       |      |      |      |      |     |      |

---

# DALTON, A. J. Glamorgan

**Name:** Alistair John Dalton
**Role:** Right-hand bat, right-arm bowler
**Born:** 27 April 1973, Bridgend
**Height:** 5ft 8in **Weight:** 11st
**Nickname:** Ali, Dalts, A.J., Dolly
**County debut:** 1994
**1st-Class 50s:** 1
**1st-Class catches:** 9
**Place in batting averages:** 186th av. 22.33
(1994 175th av. 23.50)
**Parents:** John and Christine
**Marital status:** Single
**Family links with cricket:** Father captained
Bridgend Town 1st XI for ten years; brother
Simon now plays for the same 1st XI and
used to play for Welsh Schools
**Education:** Brynteg Comprehensive School;
Millfield School; New College, Cardiff
**Qualifications:** 8 GCSEs, 3 A-levels, NCA Coach
**Career outside cricket:** Working for family business
**Off-season:** Working for father's business DMA. Ltd. 'Following Bridgend RFC and
perfecting the "Mike Rayer"'
**Overseas tours:** Millfield School to Jamaica 1990; Glamorgan Schools to
Singapore/Malaysia 1992; Cardiff Eagles to Cape Town 1994; Glamorgan to Portugal 1994
**Overseas teams played for:** Paramatta, Sydney 1992-93; Crusaders, Durban 1994-95
**Cricketers particularly admired:** Tony Cottey, Mark Waugh, Courtney Walsh, Jamie
Bishop, Ollie Slipper, 'my brother Simon', Bobby Shafto
**Other sports followed:** Rugby (played scrum-half for Millfield 1st XV and follows
Bridgend RFC)
**Relaxations:** All sports especially rugby, good films, Chinese food, travelling, 'a few
pints with the boys'

**Extras:** ASW Player of the Month, July 1994.  ASW Young Player of the Year, 1994.
Glamorgan 2nd XI Player of the Year. ASW Young Player for May and June 1995
**Best batting:** 51* Glamorgan v South Africans, Pontypridd, 1994

### 1995 Season

|  | M | Inns | NO | Runs | HS | Avge | 100s | 50s | Ct | St | O | M | Runs | Wkts | Avge | Best | 5wI | 10wM |
|---|---|---|---|---|---|---|---|---|---|---|---|---|---|---|---|---|---|---|
| Test | | | | | | | | | | | | | | | | | | |
| All First | 5 | 10 | 1 | 201 | 46 | 22.33 | - | - | 4 | - | | | | | | | | |
| 1-day Int | | | | | | | | | | | | | | | | | | |
| NatWest | | | | | | | | | | | | | | | | | | |
| B & H | | | | | | | | | | | | | | | | | | |
| Sunday | | | | | | | | | | | | | | | | | | |

### Career Performances

|  | M | Inns | NO | Runs | HS | Avge | 100s | 50s | Ct | St | Balls | Runs | Wkts | Avge | Best | 5wI | 10wM |
|---|---|---|---|---|---|---|---|---|---|---|---|---|---|---|---|---|---|
| Test | | | | | | | | | | | | | | | | | |
| All First | 11 | 20 | 3 | 389 | 51 * | 22.88 | - | 1 | 9 | - | | | | | | | |
| 1-day Int | | | | | | | | | | | | | | | | | |
| NatWest | | | | | | | | | | | | | | | | | |
| B & H | | | | | | | | | | | | | | | | | |
| Sunday | | | | | | | | | | | | | | | | | |

# DAVIES, A. P.                    Glamorgan

**Name:** Andrew Philip Davies
**Role:** Left-hand bat, right-arm
medium-fast bowler
**Born:** 7 November 1976, Neath
**Height:** 6ft **Weight:** 12st 7lbs
**County debut:** 1995
**Parents:** Philip and Anne
**Marital status:** Single
**Family links with cricket:** Father and
brother play local cricket. Mother tea lady
for 20 years
**Education:** Dwr-y-felin Comprehensive
School; Christ College, Brecon
**Qualifications:** 6 GCSEs, 1 A-level
**Off-season:** Playing in New Zealand
**Overseas tours:** Wales to Barbados
**Overseas teams played for:** Whangarei,
New Zealand 1995-96

**Cricketers particularly admired:** Graeme Hick
**Other sports followed:** Football (Tottenham Hotspur, Swansea City)
**Relaxations:** Pop music, reading sports pages, buying clothes
**Extras:** Trials at Birmingham City FC. Rugby trials for Wales U17. Welsh U19 Player of the Year 1995

## 1995 Season

| | M | Inns | NO | Runs | HS | Avge | 100s | 50s | Ct | St | O | M | Runs | Wkts | Avge | Best | 5wI | 10wM |
|---|---|---|---|---|---|---|---|---|---|---|---|---|---|---|---|---|---|---|
| Test | | | | | | | | | | | | | | | | | | |
| All First | 1 | 0 | 0 | 0 | 0 | - | - | - | - | - | 3 | 0 | 17 | 0 | - | - | - | - |
| 1-day Int | | | | | | | | | | | | | | | | | | |
| NatWest | | | | | | | | | | | | | | | | | | |
| B & H | | | | | | | | | | | | | | | | | | |
| Sunday | | | | | | | | | | | | | | | | | | |

## Career Performances

| | M | Inns | NO | Runs | HS | Avge | 100s | 50s | Ct | St | Balls | Runs | Wkts | Avge | Best | 5wI | 10wM |
|---|---|---|---|---|---|---|---|---|---|---|---|---|---|---|---|---|---|
| Test | | | | | | | | | | | | | | | | | |
| All First | 1 | 0 | 0 | 0 | 0 | - | - | - | - | - | 18 | 17 | 0 | - | - | - | - |
| 1-day Int | | | | | | | | | | | | | | | | | |
| NatWest | | | | | | | | | | | | | | | | | |
| B & H | | | | | | | | | | | | | | | | | |
| Sunday | | | | | | | | | | | | | | | | | |

26. Which England cricketer achieved the notable feat of 1,000 Test runs in a calendar year in 1994?

# DAVIES, M.                                    Gloucestershire

**Name:** Mark Davies
**Role:** Right-hand bat, slow left-arm bowler
**Born:** 18 April 1969, Neath
**Height:** 5ft 8in **Weight:** 11st 6lb
**Nickname:** Sparky, Freddie, 'many other anti-Welsh names'
**County debut:** 1990 (Glamorgan), 1992 (Gloucestershire)
**50 wickets in a season:** 1
**1st-Class 50s:** 1
**1st-Class 5 w. in innings:** 3
**1st-Class 10 w. in match:** 1
**1st-Class catches:** 19
**Strike rate:** (career 72.70)
**Parents:** Peter Holbrook and Dorothy
**Wife and date of marriage:**
Carol Elizabeth, 16 October 1993
**Family links with cricket:**
Brother plays league cricket in Wales
**Education:** Cwrt Sart Comprehensive; Neath Tertiary College
**Qualifications:** 6 O-levels; BTEC ONC in Science; NCA advanced coach; qualified lifeguard
**Overseas tours:** Fred Rumsey's XI to Barbados 1989; Gloucestershire to Sri Lanka 1992-93
**Overseas teams played for:** Newcastle City, New South Wales 1990-91; Villagers, Pretoria 1992-93
**Cricketers particularly admired:** Courtney Walsh, Tom Cartwright, John Steele
**Other sports followed:** Rugby union and league, boxing, athletics
**Relaxations:** 'Reading, good food and real ale, writing, listening to T.H.C. Hancock's opinions on everything from football to fudge-making.'
**Extras:** On the MCC groundstaff in 1987. Glamorgan 2nd XI Player of the Year 1991. Released by Glamorgan at the end of 1991. Gloucestershire Young Player of the Year 1993.
**Best batting:** 54 Gloucestershire v Nottinghamshire, Trent Bridge 1994
**Best bowling:** 5-57 Gloucestershire v Northamptonshire, Northampton 1993

## 1995 Season

|         | M | Inns | NO | Runs | HS | Avge | 100s | 50s | Ct | St | O | M | Runs | Wkts | Avge | Best | 5wI | 10wM |
|---------|---|------|----|------|----|------|------|-----|----|----|-------|----|------|------|-------|------|-----|------|
| Test    |   |      |    |      |    |      |      |     |    |    |       |    |      |      |       |      |     |      |
| All First | 6 | 7 | 4 | 77 | 22 | 25.66 | - | - | - | - | 107.2 | 28 | 288 | 6 | 48.00 | 4-86 | - | - |
| 1-day Int |   |      |    |      |    |      |      |     |    |    |       |    |      |      |       |      |     |      |
| NatWest |   |      |    |      |    |      |      |     |    |    |       |    |      |      |       |      |     |      |
| B & H   |   |      |    |      |    |      |      |     |    |    |       |    |      |      |       |      |     |      |
| Sunday  | 1 | 0 | 0 | 0 | 0 | - | - | - | - | - | 8 | 0 | 35 | 0 | - | - | - | - |

## Career Performances

| | M | Inns | NO | Runs | HS | Avge | 100s | 50s | Ct | St | Balls | Runs | Wkts | Avge | Best | 5wl | 10wM |
|---|---|---|---|---|---|---|---|---|---|---|---|---|---|---|---|---|---|
| Test | | | | | | | | | | | | | | | | | |
| All First | 45 | 64 | 22 | 632 | 54 | 15.04 | - | 1 | 19 | - | 7997 | 3878 | 110 | 35.25 | 5-57 | 3 | 1 |
| 1-day Int | | | | | | | | | | | | | | | | | |
| NatWest | | | | | | | | | | | | | | | | | |
| B & H | | | | | | | | | | | | | | | | | |
| Sunday | 17 | 8 | 2 | 66 | 14 | 11.00 | - | - | 2 | - | 506 | 440 | 12 | 36.66 | 2-23 | - | |

# DAVIS, R. P. Gloucestershire

**Name:** Richard Peter Davis
**Role:** Right-hand bat, slow left-arm bowler
**Born:** 18 March 1966, Westbrook, Margate
**Height:** 6ft 4in **Weight:** 14st 4lbs
**Nickname:** Dicky and 'plenty more'
**County debut:** 1986 (Kent), 1994
(Warwickshire)
**County cap:** 1990 (Kent), 1994
(Warwickshire)

**50 wickets in season:** 2
**1st-Class 50s:** 4
**1st-Class 5 w. in innings:** 16
**1st-Class 10 w. in match:** 2
**1st-Class catches:** 128
**One-day 5 w. in innings:** 1
**Place in batting averages:**
265th av. 13.16 (1994 212nd av. 18.71)
**Place in bowling averages:**
114th av. 38.40 (1994 80th av. 31.80)
**Strike rate:** 86.66 (career 74.28)
**Parents:** Brian and Silvia
**Wife and date of marriage:** Samantha Jane, 3 March 1990
**Family links with cricket:** Father played club cricket and is an NCA coach; father-in-law Colin Tomlin helped with England's fitness training for tours from 1990–93; brother-in-law Raj Sharma played for Derbyshire
**Education:** King Ethelbert's School, Birchington; Thanet Technical College, Broadstairs
**Qualifications:** CSEs; NCA coaching certificate
**Off-season:** Coaching and keeping fit
**Overseas tours:** Kent Schools U17 to Canada 1983; Kent to Zimbabwe 1992-93; Warwickshire to Zimbabwe 1993-94, to Cape Town, South Africa 1994-95

**Other sports followed:** Football (Derby County), rugby, squash, golf, badminton
**Relaxations:** 'Cinema, eating out with my wife, Sam, television and reading'
**Extras:** Moved to Warwickshire at the end of the 1993 season after nine years at Kent. Released by Warwickshire at the end of the 1995 season. Has joined Gloucestershire for the 1996 season
**Opinions on cricket:** 'I think the structure of English cricket should be left as it is. The only improvement should be to the "four-day wicket"'
**Best batting:** 67 Kent v Hampshire, Southampton 1989
**Best bowling:** 7-64 Kent v Durham, Gateshead Fell 1992

### 1995 Season

| | M | Inns | NO | Runs | HS | Avge | 100s | 50s | Ct | St | O | M | Runs | Wkts | Avge | Best | 5wI | 10wM |
|---|---|---|---|---|---|---|---|---|---|---|---|---|---|---|---|---|---|---|
| Test | | | | | | | | | | | | | | | | | | |
| All First | 6 | 8 | 2 | 79 | 30 | 13.16 | - | - | 5 | - | 216.4 | 58 | 576 | 15 | 38.40 | 5-118 | 1 | - |
| 1-day Int | | | | | | | | | | | | | | | | | | |
| NatWest | | | | | | | | | | | | | | | | | | |
| B & H | 2 | 0 | 0 | 0 | 0 | - | - | - | 1 | - | 7 | 0 | 30 | 0 | - | | - | |
| Sunday | 2 | 2 | 2 | 5 | 3 * | - | - | - | - | - | 16 | 0 | 64 | 2 | 32.00 | 2-30 | - | |

### Career Performances

| | M | Inns | NO | Runs | HS | Avge | 100s | 50s | Ct | St | Balls | Runs | Wkts | Avge | Best | 5wI | 10wM |
|---|---|---|---|---|---|---|---|---|---|---|---|---|---|---|---|---|---|
| Test | | | | | | | | | | | | | | | | | |
| All First | 145 | 174 | 44 | 2009 | 67 | 15.45 | - | 4 | 128 | - | 27666 | 12883 | 374 | 34.44 | 7-64 | 16 | 2 |
| 1-day Int | | | | | | | | | | | | | | | | | |
| NatWest | 13 | 6 | 1 | 46 | 22 | 9.20 | - | - | 10 | - | 729 | 392 | 15 | 26.13 | 3-19 | - | |
| B & H | 18 | 8 | 4 | 45 | 18 * | 11.25 | - | - | 7 | - | 979 | 634 | 10 | 63.40 | 2-33 | - | |
| Sunday | 85 | 40 | 16 | 229 | 40 * | 9.54 | - | - | 27 | - | 3224 | 2450 | 90 | 27.22 | 5-52 | 1 | |

# DAWOOD, I.                                    Worcestershire

**Name:** Ismail Dawood
**Role:** Right-hand bat, wicket-keeper
**Born:** 23 July 1976, Dewsbury
**Height:** 5ft 8in **Weight:** 11st
**Nickname:** Hectic
**County debut:** 1994 (Northamptonshire)
**Parents:** Saleem and Rashida
**Marital status:** Single
**Family links with cricket:** Grandfather and father played local league cricket
**Education:** Batley Grammar School
**Qualifications:** 8 GCSEs, NCA coaching award

**Overseas teams played for:** Hutt Districts, New Zealand 1986-88
**Cricketers particularly admired:** Graham Gooch, Carl Hooper, Allan Donald
**Off-season:** Playing overseas
**Overseas tours:** England U19 to Sri Lanka 1993-94, to West Indies 1994-95
**Overseas teams played for:** Grafton, Auckland 1992-93
**Cricketers particularly admired:**
Mohammed Azharuddin, Allan Border, Ian Healy 'and many others'
**Other sports followed:** Local soccer team
**Relaxations:** 'Spending time with family and friends. Eating curries with Michael Foster'
**Extras:** Left Northamptonshire at the end of 1995 season and has joined Worcestershire for 1996
**Opinions on cricket:** 'The game should be played in good spirit and enjoyed at all levels from junior to Test cricket.'
**Best batting:** 2* Northamptonshire v Somerset, Taunton 1994

## 1995 Season (did not make any first-class or one-day appearance)

## Career Performances

|  | M | Inns | NO | Runs | HS | Avge | 100s | 50s | Ct | St | Balls | Runs | Wkts | Avge | Best | 5wl | 10wM |
|---|---|---|---|---|---|---|---|---|---|---|---|---|---|---|---|---|---|
| Test | | | | | | | | | | | | | | | | | |
| All First | 1 | 1 | 1 | 2 | 2* | - | - | - | - | - | | | | | | | |
| 1-day Int | | | | | | | | | | | | | | | | | |
| NatWest | | | | | | | | | | | | | | | | | |
| B & H | | | | | | | | | | | | | | | | | |
| Sunday | 1 | 1 | 0 | 2 | 2 | 2.00 | - | - | - | - | | | | | | | |

# DAWSON, R. I.        Gloucestershire

**Name:** Robert Ian Dawson
**Role:** Right-hand bat, right-arm
medium bowler
**Born:** 29 March 1970, Exmouth, Devon
**Height:** 5ft 11in   **Weight:** 12st
**Nickname:** Daws
**County debut:** 1991 (one-day),
1992 (first-class)
**1000 runs in a season:** 1
**1st-Class 50s:** 11
**1st-Class 100s:** 2
**1st-Class catches:** 24
**Place in batting averages:**
173rd av. 23.66 (1994 46th av. 42.76)
**Parents:** Barry and Shirley
**Marital status:** Single
**Family links with cricket:** Father and
brother both played club cricket
**Education:** Millfield School;
Newcastle Polytechnic

**Qualifications:** 8 O-levels, 3 A-levels
**Overseas teams played for:** Amanzimtoti, South Africa, 1993-94
**Cricketers particularly admired:** Ian Botham, David Gower, Viv Richards
**Other sports followed:** Football mainly and most other sports
**Relaxations:** 'Watching most sports and going down the pub for a pint'
**Extras:** Played in NatWest for Devon (from 1988), before joining Gloucestershire
**Best batting:** 127* Gloucestershire v Cambridge University, Bristol 1994
**Best bowling:** 2-38 Gloucestershire v Derbyshire, Chesterfield 1994

## 1995 Season

|           | M  | Inns | NO | Runs | HS  | Avge  | 100s | 50s | Ct | St | O   | M | Runs | Wkts | Avge  | Best | 5wI | 10wM |
|-----------|----|------|----|------|-----|-------|------|-----|----|----|-----|---|------|------|-------|------|-----|------|
| Test      |    |      |    |      |     |       |      |     |    |    |     |   |      |      |       |      |     |      |
| All First | 9  | 16   | 1  | 355  | 101 | 23.66 | 1    | 3   | 3  | -  | 15  | 6 | 28   | 0    | -     |      | -   | -    |
| 1-day Int |    |      |    |      |     |       |      |     |    |    |     |   |      |      |       |      |     |      |
| NatWest   |    |      |    |      |     |       |      |     |    |    |     |   |      |      |       |      |     |      |
| B & H     | 6  | 6    | 0  | 147  | 38  | 24.50 | -    | -   | 1  | -  | 3   | 0 | 12   | 0    | -     |      | -   | -    |
| Sunday    | 13 | 12   | 2  | 136  | 45  | 13.60 | -    | -   | 2  | -  | 5.2 | 0 | 51   | 1    | 51.00 | 1-19 | -   |      |

## Career Performances

|  | M | Inns | NO | Runs | HS | Avge | 100s | 50s | Ct | St | Balls | Runs | Wkts | Avge | Best | 5wI | 10wM |
|---|---|---|---|---|---|---|---|---|---|---|---|---|---|---|---|---|---|
| Test |  |  |  |  |  |  |  |  |  |  |  |  |  |  |  |  |  |
| All First | 40 | 71 | 6 | 1905 | 127 * | 29.30 | 2 | 11 | 24 | - | 276 | 103 | 2 | 51.50 | 2-38 | - | - |
| 1-day Int |  |  |  |  |  |  |  |  |  |  |  |  |  |  |  |  |  |
| NatWest | 4 | 3 | 0 | 73 | 60 | 24.33 | - | 1 | - | - | 24 | 37 | 1 | 37.00 | 1-37 | - |  |
| B & H | 6 | 6 | 0 | 147 | 38 | 24.50 | - | - | 1 | - | 18 | 12 | 0 | - | - | - |  |
| Sunday | 46 | 40 | 4 | 564 | 45 | 15.66 | - | - | 11 | - | 80 | 87 | 1 | 87.00 | 1-19 | - |  |

# DEFREITAS, P. A. J. Derbyshire

**Name:** Phillip Anthony Jason DeFreitas
**Role:** Right-hand bat, right-arm fast bowler
**Born:** 18 February 1966, Scotts Head, Dominica
**Height:** 6ft **Weight:** 13st 7lbs
**Nickname:** Daffy, Lunchy
**County debut:** 1985 (Leics), 1989 (Lancs), 1994 (Derbys)
**County cap:** 1986 (Leics), 1989 (Lancs), 1994 (Derbys)
**Test debut:** 1986-87
**Tests:** 44
**One-Day Internationals:** 93
**50 wickets in a season:** 8
**1st-Class 50s:** 33
**1st-Class 100s:** 6
**1st-Class 5 w. in innings:** 38
**1st-Class 10 w. in match:** 3
**1st-Class catches:** 78
**One-Day 5 w. in innings:** 5
**Place in batting averages:** 200th av. 20.60 (1994 139th av. 28.68)
**Place in bowling averages:** 64th av. 29.18 (1994 22nd av. 24.93)
**Strike rate:** 59.11 (career 57.93)
**Parents:** Sybil and Martin
**Wife and date of marriage:** Nicola, 10 December 1990
**Children:** Alexandra Elizabeth Jane, 5 August 1991
**Family links with cricket:** Father played in Windward Islands. All six brothers play
**Education:** Willesden High School
**Qualifications:** 2 O-levels
**Overseas tours:** England YC to West Indies 1984-85; England to Australia 1986-87, to Pakistan, Australia and New Zealand 1987-88, to India and West Indies 1989-90, to

Australia 1990-91, to New Zealand 1991-92, to India and Sri Lanka 1992-93, to Australia 1994-95, to South Africa 1995-96, to India and Pakistan (World Cup) 1995-96
**Overseas teams played for:** Port Adelaide, South Australia 1985; Mossman, Sydney 1988; Boland, South Africa 1993-94, 1995-96
**Cricketers particularly admired:** Ian Botham, Graham Gooch, Geoff Boycott, Mike Gatting
**Other sports followed:** Football (Manchester City) and rugby league (Warrington)
**Relaxations:** 'Golf, gardening, visiting stately homes, spending spare time with wife and daughter Alexandra'
**Extras:** Left Leicestershire and joined Lancashire at end of 1988 season. Originally agreed to join unofficial English tour of South Africa 1989-90, but withdrew under pressure. Man of the Match in 1990 NatWest Trophy final. One of *Wisden*'s Five Cricketers of the Year 1992. Man of the Tournament in the Hong Kong Sixes 1993. Left Lancashire at the end of the 1993 season. Player of the Series against New Zealand 1994. He was called up to the England one-day squad in South Africa after spending the winter with Boland and went on to play in the World Cup
**Best batting:** 113 Leicestershire v Nottinghamshire, Worksop 1988
**Best bowling:** 7-21 Lancashire v Middlesex, Lord's 1989

## 1995 Season

|  | M | Inns | NO | Runs | HS | Avge | 100s | 50s | Ct | St | O | M | Runs | Wkts | Avge | Best | 5wI | 10wM |
|---|---|---|---|---|---|---|---|---|---|---|---|---|---|---|---|---|---|---|
| Test | 1 | 2 | 0 | 24 | 23 | 12.00 | - | - | - | - | 27 | 3 | 115 | 2 | 57.50 | 2-82 | - | - |
| All First | 16 | 26 | 3 | 474 | 94 * | 20.60 | - | 2 | 10 | - | 591.1 | 128 | 1751 | 60 | 29.18 | 6-35 | 2- |  |
| 1-day Int | 2 | 1 | 0 | 15 | 15 | 15.00 | - | - | 1 | - | 20.4 | 1 | 117 | 1 | 117.00 | 1-73 |  |  |
| NatWest | 3 | 1 | 0 | 4 | 4 | 4.00 | - | - | 2 | - | 36 | 9 | 79 | 7 | 11.28 | 5-28 | 1 |  |
| B & H | 3 | 2 | 0 | 37 | 37 | 18.50 | - | - | 3 | - | 31.1 | 4 | 74 | 4 | 18.50 | 2-22 | - |  |
| Sunday | 12 | 10 | 0 | 167 | 28 | 16.70 | - | - | 5 | - | 91.1 | 7 | 349 | 11 | 31.72 | 2-15 | - |  |

## Career Performances

|  | M | Inns | NO | Runs | HS | Avge | 100s | 50s | Ct | St | Balls | Runs | Wkts | Avge | Best | 5wI | 10wM |
|---|---|---|---|---|---|---|---|---|---|---|---|---|---|---|---|---|---|
| Test | 44 | 68 | 5 | 934 | 88 | 14.82 | - | 4 | 14 | - | 9838 | 4700 | 140 | 33.57 | 7-70 | 4 | - |
| All First | 235 | 330 | 34 | 6490 | 113 | 21.92 | 6 | 33 | 78 | - | 44665 | 21765 | 771 | 28.22 | 7-21 | 38 | 3 |
| 1-day Int | 93 | 60 | 23 | 566 | 49 * | 15.29 | - | - | 26 | - | 5213 | 3401 | 105 | 32.39 | 4-35 | - |  |
| NatWest | 26 | 18 | 3 | 233 | 69 | 15.53 | - | 1 | 4 | - | 1613 | 778 | 42 | 18.52 | 5-13 | 4 |  |
| B & H | 45 | 29 | 6 | 481 | 75 * | 20.91 | - | 2 | 13 | - | 2671 | 1461 | 71 | 20.57 | 5-16 | 1 |  |
| Sunday | 128 | 91 | 17 | 1210 | 49 * | 16.35 | - | - | 21 | - | 5286 | 3863 | 153 | 25.24 | 5-26 | 1 |  |

# DE LA PEÑA, J. M.  Surrey

**Name:** Jason Michael de la Peña
**Role:** Right-hand bat,
right-arm fast-medium bowler
**Born:** 16 September 1972, Middlesex
**Height:** 6ft 6in **Weight:** 14st 7lb
**Nickname:** Greasy Wop, Gin, Flying
Spaniard
**County debut:** 1991 (Gloucestershire),
1994 (Surrey – one-day), 1995 (Surrey –
first-class)
**Strike rate:** (career 47.53)
**Parents:** Michael and Jacqueline, Mikki and
Loy
**Marital status:** Single
**Education:** Lambrook Prep School, Ascot;
Stowe School; Bournside Sixth Form
College, Cheltenham
**Qualifications:** 8 GCSEs, 3 A-Levels

**Off-season:** Playing in Pretoria, Northern Transvaal
**Overseas tours:** England U19 to Pakistan
1991-92; Gloucestershire to Namibia 1990, Kenya 1991, Sri Lanka 1992-93
**Overseas teams played for:** North Hobart, Tasmania, Australia 1991-93; Mossman,
Sydney 1994-95
**Cricketers particularly admired:** David 'Syd' Lawrence, Dennis Lillee, Graham
Dilley, Michael Holding, Allan Donald and Richard Hadlee
**Other sports followed:** Golf, tennis, surfing, windsurfing, rugby union
**Injuries:** Torn ankle ligaments, out for two weeks
**Relaxations:** The cinema, music, girlfriend
**Extras:** England U19 against Young Australia. Selected for England U19 tour to
Pakistan 1991-92, but had to pull out two hours before leaving owing to severe illness
and underwent an operation one day later. Joined Surrey from Gloucestershire in 1994
**Opinions on cricket:** 'It is still a batsman's game.'
**Best batting:** 7* Gloucestershire v Yorkshire, Sheffield 1993
**Best bowling:** 4-77 Gloucestershire v Australians, Bristol 1993

27. Who were *Wisden's* five Cricketers of the Year for 1994-5?

## 1995 Season

| | M | Inns | NO | Runs | HS | Avge | 100s | 50s | Ct | St | O | M | Runs | Wkts | Avge | Best | 5wI | 10wM |
|---|---|---|---|---|---|---|---|---|---|---|---|---|---|---|---|---|---|---|
| Test | | | | | | | | | | | | | | | | | | |
| All First | 2 | 3 | 3 | 2 | 2 * | - | - | - | - | - | 44 | 8 | 208 | 6 | 34.66 | 3-53 | - | - |
| 1-day Int | | | | | | | | | | | | | | | | | | |
| NatWest | | | | | | | | | | | | | | | | | | |
| B & H | | | | | | | | | | | | | | | | | | |
| Sunday | 1 | 1 | 1 | 2 | 2 * | - | - | - | - | - | 4 | 0 | 27 | 0 | - | | - | - |

## Career Performances

| | M | Inns | NO | Runs | HS | Avge | 100s | 50s | Ct | St | Balls | Runs | Wkts | Avge | Best | 5wI | 10wM |
|---|---|---|---|---|---|---|---|---|---|---|---|---|---|---|---|---|---|
| Test | | | | | | | | | | | | | | | | | |
| All First | 6 | 7 | 5 | 10 | 7 * | 5.00 | - | - | - | - | 618 | 502 | 13 | 38.61 | 4-77 | - | - |
| 1-day Int | | | | | | | | | | | | | | | | | |
| NatWest | | | | | | | | | | | | | | | | | |
| B & H | | | | | | | | | | | | | | | | | |
| Sunday | 2 | 2 | 2 | 2 | 2 * | - | - | - | - | - | 42 | 61 | 0 | - | | - | - |

# DERBYSHIRE, N. A.                    Essex

**Name:** Nicholas Alexander Derbyshire
**Role:** Right-hand bat, right-arm
fast-medium bowler
**Born:** 11 September 1970, Ramsbottom
**Height:** 6ft **Weight:** 13st
**Nickname:** Derbs, Nifty, Trent
**County debut:** 1994 (Lancashire),
1995 (Essex)
**Parents:** Desmond and Pauline
**Marital status:** Single
**Family links with cricket:** None
**Education:** Ampleforth College;
University of London
**Qualifications:** 4 A-levels, BA (Hons)
**Career outside cricket:** None
**Off-season:** Playing for Manly,
Sydney, Australia
**Overseas tours:**
Lancashire to Johannesburg 1991-92
**Overseas teams played for:** DHS Old Boys, South Africa 1992-93;
Manly, Sydney 1994-96

**Cricketers particularly admired:** Dennis Lillee, Michael Holding
**Other sports followed:** Rugby, skiing
**Relaxations:** 'Chicago Rock Cafe, Chelmsford. Travelling globally'
**Extras:** Moved from Lancashire to join Essex for 1995 season
**Opinions on cricket:** 'Too much cricket – other countries such as South Africa or Australia play far less and, therefore, are totally ready to play – no niggles, aches and pains or tiredness. There is no sense of monotony for them, whereas in our game it is a perpetual problem, leading to mediocrity on the field.'
**Best batting:** 17 Essex v Durham, Chelmsford 1995
**Best bowling:** 1-18 Essex v Cambridge University, Fenner's 1994

## 1995 Season

|          | M | Inns | NO | Runs | HS | Avge | 100s | 50s | Ct | St | O | M | Runs | Wkts | Avge | Best | 5wl | 10wM |
|----------|---|------|----|------|----|------|------|-----|----|----|---|---|------|------|------|------|-----|------|
| Test     |   |      |    |      |    |      |      |     |    |    |   |   |      |      |      |      |     |      |
| All First | 2 | 4 | 1 | 47 | 17 | 15.66 | - | - | - | - | 21 | 5 | 48 | 2 | 24.00 | 1-18 | - | - |
| 1-day Int |   |      |    |      |    |      |      |     |    |    |   |   |      |      |      |      |     |      |
| NatWest  |   |      |    |      |    |      |      |     |    |    |   |   |      |      |      |      |     |      |
| B & H    | 1 | 0 | 0 | 0 | 0 | - | - | - | - | - |   |   |      |      |      |      |     |      |
| Sunday   |   |      |    |      |    |      |      |     |    |    |   |   |      |      |      |      |     |      |

## Career Performances

|          | M | Inns | NO | Runs | HS | Avge | 100s | 50s | Ct | St | Balls | Runs | Wkts | Avge | Best | 5wl | 10wM |
|----------|---|------|----|------|----|------|------|-----|----|----|-------|------|------|------|------|-----|------|
| Test     |   |      |    |      |    |      |      |     |    |    |       |      |      |      |      |     |      |
| All First | 4 | 5 | 1 | 52 | 17 | 13.00 | - | - | - | - | 390 | 216 | 4 | 54.00 | 1-18 | - | - |
| 1-day Int |   |      |    |      |    |      |      |     |    |    |       |      |      |      |      |     |      |
| NatWest  |   |      |    |      |    |      |      |     |    |    |       |      |      |      |      |     |      |
| B & H    | 1 | 0 | 0 | 0 | 0 | - | - | - | - | - |       |      |      |      |      |     |      |
| Sunday   |   |      |    |      |    |      |      |     |    |    |       |      |      |      |      |     |      |

# DE SILVA, P. A.                            Kent

**Name:** Pinaduwage Aravinda de Silva
**Role:** Right-hand bat, off-spin bowler
**Born:** 17 October 1965, Colombo, Sri Lanka
**Height:** 5ft 4in
**County debut:** 1995
**Test debut:** 1984
**Tests:** 48
**One-Day Internationals:** 156
**1st-Class 50s:** 48
**1st-Class 100s:** 27
**1st-Class 200s:** 4
**1st-Class 5 w. in innings:** 3
**1st-Class catches:** 77
**1st-Class 5 w. innings:** 3
**One-Day 100s:** 6
**Place in batting averages:** 4th av. 59.36
**Strike rate:** (career 83.12)
**Education:** D.S. Senanayaka College
**Qualifications:** 4 GCEs, qualified cricket
coach and umpire
**Career outside cricket:** Self-employed
**Off-season:** Touring Australia, South Africa and West Indies with Sri Lanka, and World
Cup
**Overseas tours:** Sri Lanka to England 1984, 1988, 1991, to Pakistan 1984-85, to India
1986-87, 1990-91, 1993-94, to Australia 1987-88, 1988-89, 1995-96, to New Zealand
1990-91, 1994-95, to Zimbabwe 1994-95, to India and Pakistan (World Cup) 1986-87,
1995-96, to Australia and New Zealand (World Cup) 1991-92
**Overseas teams played for:** Nondescripts, Colombo
**Cricketers particularly admired:** Viv Richards, Richard Hadlee
**Other sports followed:** Tennis and rugby
**Injuries:** Neck and index finger, missed one preliminary game in Australia
**Relaxations:** Cars, music and racing
**Extras:** Made his Test debut in Sri Lanka's first appearance at Lord's in 1984 and
captained Sri Lanka on their 1991 tour to England. Became the first Sri Lankan Test
cricketer to play county cricket in England. Awarded the Man of the Match Award for
his century in the Benson and Hedges Cup final in 1995
**Opinions on cricket:** 'There is too much sledging and intimidation which is
unbecoming of good sportsmanship. Teams are humiliated through no fault of their own
and as a result good relations between countries are disrupted. Spectators expect players
to be robots and perform well all the time. They are excellent when things are going well
but too quick to condemn and accuse in times of failure.'

**Best batting:** 267 Sri Lanka v New Zealand, Wellington 1990-91
**Best bowling:** 5-31 Nondescripts v Rio, Colombo 1992-93

## 1995 Season

|         | M  | Inns | NO | Runs | HS  | Avge  | 100s | 50s | Ct | St | O   | M  | Runs | Wkts | Avge   | Best | 5wI | 10wM |
|---------|----|------|----|------|-----|-------|------|-----|----|----|-----|----|------|------|--------|------|-----|------|
| Test    |    |      |    |      |     |       |      |     |    |    |     |    |      |      |        |      |     |      |
| All First | 16 | 30 | 0 | 1781 | 255 | 59.36 | 7 | 7 | 3 | - | 215 | 36 | 641 | 5 | 128.20 | 1-5 | - | - |
| 1-day Int |    |      |    |      |     |       |      |     |    |    |     |    |      |      |        |      |     |      |
| NatWest | 2  | 2    | 0  | 46   | 24  | 23.00 | -    | -   | 1  | -  | 24  | 0  | 90   | 3    | 30.00  | 2-45 | -   |      |
| B & H   | 7  | 6    | 1  | 203  | 112 | 40.60 | 1    | -   | 3  | -  | 38  | 1  | 128  | 4    | 32.00  | 2-12 | -   |      |
| Sunday  | 15 | 15   | 2  | 473  | 124 | 36.38 | 2    | -   | 3  | -  | 57  | 1  | 297  | 8    | 37.12  | 4-28 | -   |      |

## Career Performances

|         | M   | Inns | NO | Runs | HS   | Avge  | 100s | 50s | Ct | St | Balls | Runs | Wkts | Avge  | Best | 5wI | 10wM |
|---------|-----|------|----|------|------|-------|------|-----|----|----|-------|------|------|-------|------|-----|------|
| Test    | 48  | 83   | 4  | 2965 | 267  | 37.53 | 7    | 13  | 22 | -  | 786   | 424  | 11   | 38.54 | 3-39 | -   | -    |
| All First | 145 | 223 | 21 | 9882 | 267  | 48.92 | 27   | 48  | 77 | -  | 4738  | 2139 | 57   | 37.52 | 5-31 | 3   | -    |
| 1-day Int | 156 | 152 | 14 | 4389 | 107 * | 31.80 | 3 | 32 | 43 | - | 1928 | 1612 | 35 | 46.05 | 3-58 | - |      |
| NatWest | 2   | 2    | 0  | 46   | 24   | 23.00 | -    | -   | 1  | -  | 144   | 90   | 3    | 30.00 | 2-45 | -   |      |
| B & H   | 7   | 6    | 1  | 203  | 112  | 40.60 | 1    | -   | 3  | -  | 228   | 128  | 4    | 32.00 | 2-12 | -   |      |
| Sunday  | 15  | 15   | 2  | 473  | 124  | 36.38 | 2    | -   | 3  | -  | 342   | 297  | 8    | 37.12 | 4-28 | -   |      |

# DESSAUR, W. A.     Derbyshire

**Name:** Wayne Anthony Dessaur
**Role:** Right-hand bat, off-spin bowler
**Born:** 4 February 1971, Nottingham
**Height:** 6ft **Weight:** 12st
**Nickname:** Bed
**County debut:** 1992 (Notts), 1995 (Derbys)
**1st-Class 50s:** 4
**1st-Class 100s:** 3
**1st-Class catches:** 6
**Place in batting averages:** 101st av. 34.14
(1994 204th av. 19.25)
**Parents:** Pat and Tony
**Marital status:** Engaged
**Family links with cricket:** Father and
brother play local league cricket, father is
coach of county U15 side
**Education:** Loughborough Grammar School
**Qualifications:** 6 O-levels, 2 A-levels,
qualified coach

**Off-season:** Playing in Australia
**Overseas teams played for:** Grange, Adelaide 1991-96
**Cricketers particularly admired:** Tim Robinson, Derek Randall, Martin Crowe
**Other sports followed:** Football
**Relaxations:** Sleeping, reading, listening to music, 'receiving mail from Mick Newell'
**Extras:** Scored century in second first-class match. Nottinghamshire Young Player of the Year 1993. Released by Nottinghamshire at end of 1994 season. Signed for Derbyshire at the beginning of 1995 season and released at the end of the season
**Best batting:** 148 Nottinghamshire v Cambridge University, Trent Bridge 1992
**Best bowling:** 1-8 Derbyshire v Young Australia, Chesterfield 1995

## 1995 Season

|          | M  | Inns | NO | Runs | HS   | Avge  | 100s | 50s | Ct | St | O | M | Runs | Wkts | Avge  | Best | 5wI | 10wM |
|----------|----|------|----|------|------|-------|------|-----|----|----|---|---|------|------|-------|------|-----|------|
| Test     |    |      |    |      |      |       |      |     |    |    |   |   |      |      |       |      |     |      |
| All First | 8  | 16   | 2  | 478  | 119 *| 34.14 | 1    | 2   | 1  | -  | 7 | 1 | 24   | 1    | 24.00 | 1-8  | -   | -    |
| 1-day Int |    |      |    |      |      |       |      |     |    |    |   |   |      |      |       |      |     |      |
| NatWest  | 2  | 1    | 0  | 85   | 85   | 85.00 | -    | 1   | -  | -  |   |   |      |      |       |      |     |      |
| B & H    |    |      |    |      |      |       |      |     |    |    |   |   |      |      |       |      |     |      |
| Sunday   | 2  | 2    | 0  | 23   | 18   | 11.50 | -    | -   | -  | -  |   |   |      |      |       |      |     |      |

## Career Performances

|          | M  | Inns | NO | Runs | HS  | Avge  | 100s | 50s | Ct | St | Balls | Runs | Wkts | Avge   | Best | 5wI | 10wM |
|----------|----|------|----|------|-----|-------|------|-----|----|----|-------|------|------|--------|------|-----|------|
| Test     |    |      |    |      |     |       |      |     |    |    |       |      |      |        |      |     |      |
| All First | 22 | 38   | 3  | 1121 | 148 | 32.02 | 3    | 4   | 6  | -  | 144   | 118  | 1    | 118.00 | 1-8  | -   | -    |
| 1-day Int |    |      |    |      |     |       |      |     |    |    |       |      |      |        |      |     |      |
| NatWest  | 2  | 1    | 0  | 85   | 85  | 85.00 | -    | 1   | -  | -  |       |      |      |        |      |     |      |
| B & H    |    |      |    |      |     |       |      |     |    |    |       |      |      |        |      |     |      |
| Sunday   | 4  | 4    | 1  | 39   | 18  | 13.00 | -    | -   | -  | -  |       |      |      |        |      |     |      |

# DIBDEN, R.R.                    Hampshire

**Name:** Richard Rockley Dibden
**Role:** Right-hand bat, right-arm off-spin bowler
**Born:** 29 January 1975, Southampton
**Height:** 6ft **Weight:** 11st 7lbs
**County debut:** 1995
**Nickname:** Dibbers, Rocky
**Parents:** Keith and Nancy
**Marital status:** Single
**Family links with cricket:** 'Dad played competitive club cricket'
**Education:** Mountbatten School, Romsey; Loughborough University
**Qualifications:** 10 GCSEs, 4 A-levels, degree ('hopefully 2:1'), NCA coaching award

**Career outside cricket:** Student
**Off-season:** 'University for now. Tours to Australia and South Africa later'
**Overseas teams played for:** Techs, South Africa 1994
**Cricketers particularly admired:** David Gower ('for his natural ability'), Raj Maru ('for his enthusiasm'), Malcolm Marshall ('for his ability and positive attitude') and Andy Long ('for his sheer pace and aggression')
**Other sports followed:** Football (Southampton FC –'European Champions in the year 2000!')
**Relaxations:** 'Pint of Guinness at the end of a long, hard day in the field'
**Extras:** *Daily Telegraph* Under-15 Bowling Award winner
**Opinions on cricket:** 'Extend lunch break to one hour and reduce number of overs to 100 per day (minimum).'
**Best bowling:** 2-36 Hampshire v Yorkshire, Scarborough 1995

## 1995 Season

|           | M | Inns | NO | Runs | HS | Avge | 100s | 50s | Ct | St | O | M | Runs | Wkts | Avge | Best | 5wI | 10wM |
|-----------|---|------|----|------|----|------|------|-----|----|----|----|----|----|----|------|------|-----|------|
| Test      |   |      |    |      |    |      |      |     |    |    |    |    |    |    |      |      |     |      |
| All First | 4 | 7    | 2  | 0    | 0* | 0.00 | -    | -   | -  | -  | 103.1 | 20 | 428 | 6 | 71.33 | 2-36 | -   | -    |
| 1-day Int |   |      |    |      |    |      |      |     |    |    |    |    |    |    |      |      |     |      |
| NatWest   |   |      |    |      |    |      |      |     |    |    |    |    |    |    |      |      |     |      |
| B & H     |   |      |    |      |    |      |      |     |    |    |    |    |    |    |      |      |     |      |
| Sunday    |   |      |    |      |    |      |      |     |    |    |    |    |    |    |      |      |     |      |

## Career Performances

|           | M | Inns | NO | Runs | HS | Avge | 100s | 50s | Ct | St | Balls | Runs | Wkts | Avge | Best | 5wI | 10wM |
|-----------|---|------|----|------|----|------|------|-----|----|----|-------|------|------|------|------|-----|------|
| Test      |   |      |    |      |    |      |      |     |    |    |       |      |      |      |      |     |      |
| All First | 4 | 7    | 2  | 0    | 0* | 0.00 | -    | -   | -  | -  | 619   | 428  | 6    | 71.33 | 2-36 | -   | -    |
| 1-day Int |   |      |    |      |    |      |      |     |    |    |       |      |      |      |      |     |      |
| NatWest   |   |      |    |      |    |      |      |     |    |    |       |      |      |      |      |     |      |
| B & H     |   |      |    |      |    |      |      |     |    |    |       |      |      |      |      |     |      |
| Sunday    |   |      |    |      |    |      |      |     |    |    |       |      |      |      |      |     |      |

# DIMOND, M.                                    Somerset

**Name:** Matthew Dimond
**Role:** Right-hand bat, right-arm fast bowler
**Born:** 24 September 1975, Taunton
**Height:** 6ft 2in **Weight:** 12st
**Nickname:** Dougie, Dominic, Shearer
**County debut:** 1994
**1st-Class catches:** 4
**Parents:** Roger and Gillian
**Marital status:** Single
**Education:** Castle School, Taunton; Richard
Huish College, Taunton
**Qualifications:** 8 GCSEs, 1 A-level
**Off-season:** Working for Shell as a General
Assistant
**Overseas tours:** West of England U15 to
Trinidad and Tobago, 1991-92; Somerset
Youth to Holland, 1992; England U19 to
West Indies 1994-95
**Cricketers particularly admired:**
Allan Donald, Dominic Cork
**Other sports followed:** Football (Yeovil Town), golf, American football
**Relaxations:** Listening to music, playing golf, 'spending time with my girlfriend,
Rachel, and having nights out with my college mates (MS, PH, AW)'
**Extras:** Man of the Match for West of England U15 v Trinidad and Tobago, with a score
of 56
**Opinions on cricket:** 'Cricket is becoming more and more fitness orientated due to the
amount that is played through the season. So players have got to be fitter and more agile
for the modern game.'
**Best batting:** 26 Somerset v Derbyshire, Derby 1995
**Best bowling:** 4-73 Somerset v Yorkshire, Bradford 1994

## 1995 Season

|          | M | Inns | NO | Runs | HS | Avge | 100s | 50s | Ct | St | O | M | Runs | Wkts | Avge | Best | 5wI | 10wM |
|----------|---|------|----|------|----|------|------|-----|----|----|---|---|------|------|------|------|-----|------|
| Test     |   |      |    |      |    |      |      |     |    |    |   |   |      |      |      |      |     |      |
| All First | 1 | 2 | 0 | 33 | 26 | 16.50 | - | - | - | - | 14 | 2 | 70 | 1 | 70.00 | 1-16 | - | - |
| 1-day Int |   |      |    |      |    |      |      |     |    |    |   |   |      |      |      |      |     |      |
| NatWest  |   |      |    |      |    |      |      |     |    |    |   |   |      |      |      |      |     |      |
| B & H    |   |      |    |      |    |      |      |     |    |    |   |   |      |      |      |      |     |      |
| Sunday   |   |      |    |      |    |      |      |     |    |    |   |   |      |      |      |      |     |      |

## Career Performances

|  | M | Inns | NO | Runs | HS | Avge | 100s | 50s | Ct | St | Balls | Runs | Wkts | Avge | Best | 5wI | 10wM |
|---|---|---|---|---|---|---|---|---|---|---|---|---|---|---|---|---|---|
| Test |  |  |  |  |  |  |  |  |  |  |  |  |  |  |  |  |  |
| All First | 4 | 4 | 1 | 67 | 26 | 22.33 | - | - | 4 | - | 417 | 286 | 6 | 47.66 | 4-73 | - | - |
| 1-day Int |  |  |  |  |  |  |  |  |  |  |  |  |  |  |  |  |  |
| NatWest |  |  |  |  |  |  |  |  |  |  |  |  |  |  |  |  |  |  |
| B & H |  |  |  |  |  |  |  |  |  |  |  |  |  |  |  |  |  |  |
| Sunday | 3 | 0 | 0 | 0 | 0 | - | - | - | - | - | 60 | 76 | 0 | - |  | - | - |

# DITTA, A. I. Leicestershire

**Name:** Adil Iqbal Ditta
**Role:** Right-hand bat, right-arm
fast-medium bowler
**Born:** 10 October 1974, Middlesbrough
**Height:** 5ft 10in **Weight:** 11st
**County debut:** 1994 (one-day)
**Parents:** Ali and Naseem
**Marital status:** Single
**Education:** Boynton Comprehensive School;
Acklam College, Middlesbrough
**Qualifications:** 8 GCSEs
**Overseas teams played for:** CBC Old Boys,
Orange Free State 1994-95
**Cricketers particularly admired:** Hansie
Cronje, Sachin Tendulkar, Allan Donald
**Other sports followed:** Football
(Middlesbrough), snooker, golf
**Relaxations:** Spending time with friends and
family

**Extras:** Played for Yorkshire Cricket Association from U16 to U19, North of England U14 and U15 and for England U15. Played for England U17 against Zimbabwe and U19 against India

28. Which player lost seven teeth after being hit in the mouth during his side's Championship match against Essex?

**Career Performances**

| | M | Inns | NO | Runs | HS | Avge | 100s | 50s | Ct | St | Balls | Runs | Wkts | Avge | Best | 5wI | 10wM |
|---|---|---|---|---|---|---|---|---|---|---|---|---|---|---|---|---|---|
| Test | | | | | | | | | | | | | | | | | |
| All First | | | | | | | | | | | | | | | | | |
| 1-day Int | | | | | | | | | | | | | | | | | |
| NatWest | | | | | | | | | | | | | | | | | |
| B & H | | | | | | | | | | | | | | | | | |
| Sunday | 1 | 1 | 1 | 1 | 1* | - | - | - | - | - | | - | | | | | |

# D'OLIVEIRA, D. B. Worcestershire

**Name:** Damian Basil D'Oliveira
**Role:** Right-hand bat, off-spin bowler, slip or boundary fielder
**Born:** 19 October 1960, Cape Town, South Africa
**Height:** 'half an inch taller than Steve Rhodes' **Weight:** 11st 10lbs
**Nickname:** Dolly
**County debut:** 1982
**County cap:** 1985
**Benefit:** 1993 (£153,030 in joint benefit with Martin Weston)
**1000 runs in a season:** 4
**1st-Class 50s:** 46
**1st-Class 100s:** 10
**1st-Class 200s:** 1
**1st-Class catches:** 205
**One-Day 100s:** 1
**Place in batting averages:** (1993 186th av. 21.37)
**Strike rate:** (career 81.61)
**Parents:** Basil and Naomi
**Wife and date of marriage:** Tracey Michele, 26 September 1983
**Children:** Marcus Damian, 27 April 1986; Dominic James, 29 April 1988; Brett Louis, 28 February 1992
**Family links with cricket:** Father played for Worcestershire and England
**Education:** St George's RC Primary School; Blessed Edward Oldcorne Secondary School
**Qualifications:** 3 O-levels, 5 CSEs, advanced coach
**Overseas tours:** English Counties to Zimbabwe 1984-85

**Overseas teams played for:** West Perth, Australia 1980-81; East Christchurch, Shirley 1982-83, 1983-84
**Cricketers particularly admired:** Greg Chappell, Viv Richards, Dennis Lillee, Malcolm Marshall, Richard Hadlee
**Other sports followed:** 'Most sport, but not horse racing, also follow Manchester City because father supports United'
**Relaxations:** Watching films, television, eating out, and playing with the kids
**Extras:** Captains the Second XI and is Worcestershire's official coach
**Best batting:** 237 Worcestershire v Oxford University, The Parks 1991
**Best bowling:** 4-67 Worcestershire v Oxford University, Worcester 1994

## 1995 Season

|          | M | Inns | NO | Runs | HS | Avge | 100s | 50s | Ct | St | O | M | Runs | Wkts | Avge | Best | 5wI | 10wM |
|----------|---|------|----|------|-----|------|------|-----|----|----|------|----|------|------|-------|------|-----|------|
| Test     |   |      |    |      |     |      |      |     |    |    |      |    |      |      |       |      |     |      |
| All First | 2 | 4   | 0  | 59   | 25  | 14.75 | -   | -   | 2  | -  | 113.5 | 15 | 369 | 5    | 73.80 | 3-88 | --  |      |
| 1-day Int |   |      |    |      |     |      |      |     |    |    |      |    |      |      |       |      |     |      |
| NatWest  |   |      |    |      |     |      |      |     |    |    |      |    |      |      |       |      |     |      |
| B & H    |   |      |    |      |     |      |      |     |    |    |      |    |      |      |       |      |     |      |
| Sunday   | 1 | 0    | 0  | 0    | 0   | -    | -    | -   | -  | -  | 8    | 0  | 45  | 3    | 15.00 | 3-45 | -   |      |

## Career Performances

|          | M | Inns | NO | Runs | HS | Avge | 100s | 50s | Ct | St | Balls | Runs | Wkts | Avge | Best | 5wI | 10wM |
|----------|----|------|----|------|-----|-------|------|-----|-----|----|-------|------|------|-------|------|-----|------|
| Test     |    |      |    |      |     |       |      |     |     |    |       |      |      |       |      |     |      |
| All First | 234 | 366 | 22 | 9504 | 237 | 27.62 | 10  | 46  | 205 | -  | 4489 | 2479 | 55  | 45.07 | 4-67 | -   | -    |
| 1-day Int |    |      |    |      |     |       |      |     |     |    |       |      |      |       |      |     |      |
| NatWest  | 27 | 26   | 4  | 588  | 99  | 26.72 | -   | 3   | 3   | -  | 264  | 155  | 8   | 19.37 | 2-17 | -   |      |
| B & H    | 51 | 46   | 4  | 818  | 66  | 19.47 | -   | 4   | 20  | -  | 234  | 150  | 5   | 30.00 | 3-12 | -   |      |
| Sunday   | 175 | 154 | 17 | 3210 | 103 | 23.43 | 1   | 11  | 44  | -  | 360  | 323  | 11  | 29.36 | 3-23 | -   |      |

# DONALD, A. A. Warwickshire

**Name:** Allan Anthony Donald
**Role:** Right-hand bat, right-arm fast bowler
**Born:** 20 October 1966, Bloemfontein, South Africa
**Height:** 6ft 3in **Weight:** 14st
**County debut:** 1987
**County cap:** 1989
**Test debut:** 1991-92
**Tests:** 19
**One-Day Internationals:** 50
**50 wickets in a season:** 4
**1st-Class 5 w. in innings:** 43
**1st-Class 10 w. in match:** 6
**1st-Class catches:** 84
**One-Day 5 w. in innings:** 6
**Place in batting averages:** 229th av. 16.07
**Place in bowling averages:** 1st av. 16.07
(1994 68th av. 31.00)

**Strike rate:** 36.10 (career 48.33)
**Parents:** Stuart and Francine
**Wife and date of marriage:** Tina, 21 September 1991
**Family links with cricket:** Father and uncle played club cricket
**Education:** Grey College High School; Technical High School, Bloemfontein
**Qualifications:** Matriculation
**Off-season:** Playing cricket for South Africa
**Overseas tours:** South Africa to India 1991-92, to Australia and New Zealand (World Cup) 1991-92, to West Indies 1991-92, to Sri Lanka 1992-93, to Australia 1992-93, to England 1994, to New Zealand 1994-95, to Zimbabwe 1995-95, to India and Pakistan (World Cup) 1995-96
**Overseas teams played for:** Orange Free State, South Africa 1985-96
**Cricketers particularly admired:** Richard Hadlee, Malcolm Marshall, Gladstone Small, Andy Lloyd, Eddie Barlow
**Other sports followed:** Rugby, golf, tennis
**Relaxations:** 'Listening to music, having a barbecue, playing golf and having a few beers with my friends'
**Extras:** Played for South African XI v Australian XI in 1986-87 and v English XI in 1989-90. Retained by Warwickshire for 1991 season ahead of Tom Moody. Toured with South Africa on first-ever visit to India and to West Indies in 1991-92. One of *Wisden's* Five Cricketers of the Year 1992. Accepted the appointment of fitness coach for Warwickshire for the 1996 season. Took his 100th Test wicket against England in Johannesburg 1995-96. Voted Man of the Series against England finishing with 19

wickets at an average of 26.15
**Best batting:** 46* Orange Free State v Western Province, Cape Town 1990-91
**Best bowling:** 8-37 Orange Free State v Transvaal, Johannesburg 1986-87

## 1995 Season

| | M | Inns | NO | Runs | HS | Avge | 100s | 50s | Ct | St | O | M | Runs | Wkts | Avge | Best | 5wI | 10wM |
|---|---|---|---|---|---|---|---|---|---|---|---|---|---|---|---|---|---|---|
| Test | | | | | | | | | | | | | | | | | | |
| All First | 15 | 16 | 5 | 194 | 44 | 17.63 | - | - | 7 | - | 535.3 | 134 | 1431 | 89 | 16.07 | 6-56 | 6 | 1 |
| 1-day Int | | | | | | | | | | | | | | | | | | |
| NatWest | 5 | 0 | 0 | 0 | 0 | - | - | - | 2 | - | 57.5 | 8 | 215 | 11 | 19.54 | 5-41 | 1 | |
| B & H | 3 | 2 | 0 | 2 | 2 | 1.00 | - | - | - | - | 31 | 2 | 131 | 3 | 43.66 | 2-39 | - | |
| Sunday | 11 | 3 | 3 | 14 | 5 * | - | - | - | 2 | - | 84.4 | 5 | 311 | 19 | 16.36 | 6-15 | 1 | |

## Career Performances

| | M | Inns | NO | Runs | HS | Avge | 100s | 50s | Ct | St | Balls | Runs | Wkts | Avge | Best | 5wI | 10wM |
|---|---|---|---|---|---|---|---|---|---|---|---|---|---|---|---|---|---|
| Test | 19 | 25 | 14 | 132 | 27 | 12.00 | - | - | 5 | - | 4437 | 2226 | 84 | 26.50 | 7-84 | 4 | 1 |
| All First | 212 | 240 | 95 | 1744 | 46 * | 12.02 | - | - | 84 | - | 38285 | 18433 | 792 | 23.27 | 8-37 | 43 | 6 |
| 1-day Int | 50 | 17 | 9 | 29 | 7 * | 3.62 | - | - | 5 | - | 2660 | 1764 | 67 | 26.32 | 5-29 | 1 | |
| NatWest | 24 | 7 | 4 | 28 | 14 * | 9.33 | - | - | 3 | - | 1516 | 800 | 58 | 13.79 | 5-12 | 4 | |
| B & H | 20 | 11 | 5 | 59 | 23 * | 9.83 | - | - | 3 | - | 1201 | 837 | 30 | 27.90 | 4-28 | - | |
| Sunday | 57 | 22 | 10 | 134 | 18 * | 11.16 | - | - | 12 | - | 2594 | 1738 | 72 | 24.13 | 6-15 | 1 | |

# DOWMAN, M. P.       Nottinghamshire

**Name:** Matthew Peter Dowman
**Role:** Left-hand bat, right-arm
medium bowler
**Born:** 10 May 1974, Grantham, Lincs
**Height:** 5ft 10in **Weight:** 11st
**Nickname:** Doomer, Dowers, Boz
**County debut:** 1993 (one-day),
1994 (first-class)
**1st-Class 50s:** 2
**1st-Class 100s:** 2
**1st-Class catches:** 7
**Place in batting averages:** 99th av. 34.25
**Parents:** Clive Stuart and Jackie Anne
**Marital status:** Single
**Family links with cricket:** Dad played for
Grantham Town. Three brothers also play for
Grantham, two of them representing
Lincolnshire Schools and Lincolnshire U19

**Education:** St Hugh's Comprehensive; Grantham College
**Qualifications:** Senior coach
**Off-season:** Playing in Geelong, Melbourne
**Overseas tours:** England U19 to India 1992-93; Lincolnshire U16 to Zimbabwe 1988-89; Nottinghamshire to Cape Town 1992-93; also to Guernsey for Tim Robinson's benefit 1992
**Cricketers particularly admired:** Robin Smith, Mike Gatting, Malcolm Marshall, Jimmy Adams, Andy Afford 'for his wit'
**Other sports followed:** Most sports, 'follow Notts Forest and County and Lincoln City'
**Relaxations:** Watching films, playing golf, listening to music
**Extras:** Played for England U19 in home series against West Indies in 1993, scoring 267 in second 'Test'. Played in winning Midlands team at ESCA Festival 1989. Most runs in a season for Lincolnshire Schools and holds record for most runs in Lincolnshire Schools career
**Opinions on cricket:** 'More 2nd XI fixtures should be played on county grounds.'
**Best batting:** 107 Nottinghamshire v Oxford University, The Parks 1995

## 1995 Season

|          | M | Inns | NO | Runs | HS  | Avge  | 100s | 50s | Ct | St | O | M | Runs | Wkts | Avge | Best | 5wI | 10wM |
|----------|---|------|----|------|-----|-------|------|-----|----|----|---|---|------|------|------|------|-----|------|
| Test     |   |      |    |      |     |       |      |     |    |    |   |   |      |      |      |      |     |      |
| All First | 9 | 18   | 2  | 548  | 107 | 34.25 | 2    | 2   | 7  | -  | 5 | 0 | 30   | 0    | -    | -    | -   | -    |
| 1-day Int |   |      |    |      |     |       |      |     |    |    |   |   |      |      |      |      |     |      |
| NatWest  |   |      |    |      |     |       |      |     |    |    |   |   |      |      |      |      |     |      |
| B & H    | 4 | 2    | 1  | 6    | 6   | 6.00  | -    | -   | 2  | -  |   |   |      |      |      |      |     |      |
| Sunday   | 4 | 4    | 0  | 37   | 22  | 9.25  | -    | -   | 2  | -  |   |   |      |      |      |      |     |      |

## Career Performances

|          | M  | Inns | NO | Runs | HS   | Avge  | 100s | 50s | Ct | St | Balls | Runs | Wkts | Avge  | Best | 5wI | 10wM |
|----------|----|------|----|------|------|-------|------|-----|----|----|-------|------|------|-------|------|-----|------|
| Test     |    |      |    |      |      |       |      |     |    |    |       |      |      |       |      |     |      |
| All First | 12 | 23   | 2  | 659  | 107  | 31.38 | 2    | 2   | 7  | -  | 102   | 75   | 0    | -     | -    | -   | -    |
| 1-day Int |    |      |    |      |      |       |      |     |    |    |       |      |      |       |      |     |      |
| NatWest  |    |      |    |      |      |       |      |     |    |    |       |      |      |       |      |     |      |
| B & H    | 4  | 2    | 1  | 6    | 6    | 6.00  | -    | -   | 2  | -  |       |      |      |       |      |     |      |
| Sunday   | 13 | 13   | 1  | 162  | 52 * | 13.50 | -    | 1   | 3  | -  | 102   | 98   | 2    | 49.00 | 1-33 | -   |      |

# DRAKES, V. C.        Sussex

**Name:** Vasbert Conneil Drakes
**Role:** Right-hand bat, right-arm fast-medium
**Born:** 5 August 1969, St James, Barbados
**Height:** 6ft 2in
**One-day Internationals:** 5

**1st-Class 50s:** 1
**1st-Class 100s:** 2
**1st-Class catches:** 6
**1st-Class 5 w. innings**: 3
**Place in batting averages:**
255th av. 14.75
**Place in bowling averages:**
29th av. 25.00
**Education:** St Lucy Secondary and College
School, Barbados
**Off-season:** Playing for Barbados in
the Red Stripe Cup
**Overseas teams played for:**
Barbados 1991-95
**Overseas tours:** West Indies to England 1995
**Extras:** Was called up to the West Indies
squad as a replacement for Winston Benjamin
on the 1995 tour to England. Played for West
Indies in one-day international series against
Australia in 1994-95
**Best batting:** 180* Barbados v Leeward Islands, Anguilla 1994-95
**Best bowling:** 7-47 Barbados v Guyana, Bridgetown 1994-95

## 1995 Season

| | M | Inns | NO | Runs | HS | Avge | 100s | 50s | Ct | St | O | M | Runs | Wkts | Avge | Best | 5wI | 10wM |
|---|---|---|---|---|---|---|---|---|---|---|---|---|---|---|---|---|---|---|
| Test | | | | | | | | | | | | | | | | | | |
| All First | 6 | 9 | 1 | 118 | 48 * | 14.75 | - | - | 2 | - | 106 | 17 | 400 | 16 | 25.00 | 5-20 | 1 | - |
| 1-day Int | | | | | | | | | | | | | | | | | | |
| NatWest | | | | | | | | | | | | | | | | | | |
| B & H | | | | | | | | | | | | | | | | | | |
| Sunday | | | | | | | | | | | | | | | | | | |

## Career Performances

| | M | Inns | NO | Runs | HS | Avge | 100s | 50s | Ct | St | Balls | Runs | Wkts | Avge | Best | 5wI | 10wM |
|---|---|---|---|---|---|---|---|---|---|---|---|---|---|---|---|---|---|
| Test | | | | | | | | | | | | | | | | | |
| All First | 26 | 38 | 8 | 880 | 180 * | 29.33 | 2 | 1 | 6 | - | 3845 | 2250 | 85 | 26.47 | 7-47 | 3 | - |
| 1-day Int | 5 | 2 | 0 | 25 | 16 | 12.50 | - | - | 1 | - | 239 | 204 | 3 | 68.00 | 1-36 | - | |
| NatWest | | | | | | | | | | | | | | | | | |
| B & H | | | | | | | | | | | | | | | | | |
| Sunday | | | | | | | | | | | | | | | | | |

# DUTCH, K. P.                                    Middlesex

**Name:** Keith Peter Dutch
**Role:** Right-hand bat, off-spin bowler
**Born:** 21 March 1973, Harrow, Middlesex
**Height:** 5ft 10in **Weight:** 11st 6lbs
**Nickname:** Dutchy, Kitten, Crutch, Double
**County debut:** 1993
**1st-Class catches:** 4
**Parents:** Alan and Ann
**Marital status:** 'Very single'
**Family links with cricket:**
Father is a qualified youth cricket
coach at Bessborough CC
**Education:** Nower Hill High School, Pinner;
Weald College, Harrow
**Qualifications:** 4 GCSEs and 1 A-level
**Off-season:** 'Relaxing and working part-time
and at my game'
**Overseas teams played for:**
Worcester United, South Africa 1992-93;
Geelong City, Australia, 1994
**Cricketers particularly admired:** Mark Ramprakash
**Other sports followed:** Most sports, especially football (Arsenal and Old Actonians FC)
**Relaxations:** 'In car entertainment, music and football'
**Extras:** On MCC groundstaff for one year before becoming a contracted player. Rapid
Cricketline 2nd XI Player of the Year 1993
**Opinions on cricket:** 'All 2nd XI Championship games should be allowed to be played
on county grounds with good wickets and one-day games should be spread around club
grounds if needed.'

## 1995 Season

|          | M | Inns | NO | Runs | HS  | Avge  | 100s | 50s | Ct | St | O  | M | Runs | Wkts | Avge | Best | 5wI | 10wM |
|----------|---|------|----|------|-----|-------|------|-----|----|----|----|---|------|------|------|------|-----|------|
| Test     |   |      |    |      |     |       |      |     |    |    |    |   |      |      |      |      |     |      |
| All First | 1 | 0   | 0  | 0    | 0   | -     | -    | -   | 2  | -  | 14 | 7 | 24   | 0    | -    | -    | -   | -    |
| 1-day Int |   |      |    |      |     |       |      |     |    |    |    |   |      |      |      |      |     |      |
| NatWest  |   |      |    |      |     |       |      |     |    |    |    |   |      |      |      |      |     |      |
| B & H    |   |      |    |      |     |       |      |     |    |    |    |   |      |      |      |      |     |      |
| Sunday   | 3 | 2    | 1  | 33   | 21* | 33.00 | -    | -   | 1  | -  | 12 | 0 | 57   | 0    | -    | -    | -   |      |

## Career Performances

|        | M | Inns | NO | Runs | HS | Avge | 100s | 50s | Ct | St | Balls | Runs | Wkts | Avge | Best | 5wl | 10wM |
|--------|---|------|----|------|----|------|------|-----|----|----|-------|------|------|------|------|-----|------|
| Test   |   |      |    |      |    |      |      |     |    |    |       |      |      |      |      |     |      |
| All First | 2 | 0 | 0 | 0 | 0 | - | - | - | 4 | - | 114 | 42 | 0 | - | - | - | - |
| 1-day Int |   |      |    |      |    |      |      |     |    |    |       |      |      |      |      |     |      |
| NatWest |   |      |    |      |    |      |      |     |    |    |       |      |      |      |      |     |      |
| B & H  |   |      |    |      |    |      |      |     |    |    |       |      |      |      |      |     |      |
| Sunday | 3 | 2 | 1 | 33 | 21 * | 33.00 | - | - | 1 | - | 72 | 57 | 0 | - | - | - |      |

# EALHAM, M. A. Kent

**Name:** Mark Alan Ealham
**Role:** Right-hand bat, right-arm medium bowler
**Born:** 27 August 1969, Willesborough, Kent
**Height:** 5ft 10in **Weight:** 13st 9lbs
**Nickname:** Ealy, Skate
**County debut:** 1989
**County cap:** 1992
**1st-Class 50s:** 20
**1st-Class 100s:** 1
**1st-Class 5 w. in innings:** 5
**1st-Class catches:** 25
**One-Day 5 w. in innings:** 1
**One-Day 100s:** 1
**Place in batting averages:** 134th av. 29.70 (1994 146th av. 26.58)
**Place in bowling averages:** 113th av. 38.36 (1994 48th av. 28.22)

**Strike rate:** 59.03 (career 58.59)
**Parents:** Alan and Sue
**Marital status:** Engaged to Kirsty Stennett
**Family links with cricket:** Father played county cricket for Kent
**Education:** Stour Valley Secondary School
**Qualifications:** 9 CSEs
**Off-season:** Cricket coaching at home
**Overseas teams played for:** South Perth, Australia 1992-93; University, Perth, Australia 1993-94
**Cricketers particularly admired:** Ian Botham, Viv Richards, Robin Smith, Paul Blackmore and Albert 'for his F and G'
**Other sports followed:** Golf, snooker and most other sports
**Injuries:** Groin strain, missed six weeks

**Relaxations:** Playing golf and snooker, watching films
**Best batting:** 121 Kent v Nottinghamshire, Trent Bridge 1995
**Best bowling:** 7-53 Kent v Hampshire, Canterbury 1994

## 1995 Season

| | M | Inns | NO | Runs | HS | Avge | 100s | 50s | Ct | St | O | M | Runs | Wkts | Avge | Best | 5wI | 10wM |
|---|---|---|---|---|---|---|---|---|---|---|---|---|---|---|---|---|---|---|
| Test | | | | | | | | | | | | | | | | | | |
| All First | 18 | 31 | 1 | 891 | 121 | 29.70 | 1 | 4 | 7 | - | 384.2 | 95 | 1151 | 30 | 38.36 | 3-37 | - | - |
| 1-day Int | | | | | | | | | | | | | | | | | | |
| NatWest | 2 | 2 | 0 | 23 | 18 | 11.50 | - | - | 1 | - | 14 | 2 | 46 | 2 | 23.00 | 2-17 | - | |
| B & H | 6 | 5 | 0 | 105 | 52 | 21.00 | - | 1 | 1 | - | 59.5 | 6 | 210 | 10 | 21.00 | 3-55 | - | |
| Sunday | 15 | 13 | 3 | 369 | 112 | 36.90 | 1 | 1 | 1 | - | 100.3 | 7 | 443 | 17 | 26.05 | 4-21 | - | |

## Career Performances

| | M | Inns | NO | Runs | HS | Avge | 100s | 50s | Ct | St | Balls | Runs | Wkts | Avge | Best | 5wI | 10wM |
|---|---|---|---|---|---|---|---|---|---|---|---|---|---|---|---|---|---|
| Test | | | | | | | | | | | | | | | | | |
| All First | 71 | 114 | 14 | 2879 | 121 | 28.79 | 1 | 20 | 25 | - | 9162 | 4701 | 147 | 31.97 | 7-53 | 5 | - |
| 1-day Int | | | | | | | | | | | | | | | | | |
| NatWest | 11 | 11 | 4 | 191 | 58 * | 27.28 | - | 1 | 3 | - | 575 | 296 | 12 | 24.66 | 4-10 | - | |
| B & H | 20 | 17 | 4 | 222 | 52 | 17.07 | - | 1 | 9 | - | 1097 | 675 | 29 | 23.27 | 4-29 | - | |
| Sunday | 82 | 64 | 20 | 1031 | 112 | 23.43 | 1 | 1 | 20 | - | 3217 | 2444 | 81 | 30.17 | 6-53 | 1 | |

# ECCLESTONE, S. C.     Somerset

**Name:** Simon Charles Ecclestone
**Role:** Left-hand bat, right-arm
fast-medium bowler
**Born:** 16 July 1971, Great Dunmow, Essex
**Height:** 6ft 3in **Weight:** 14st 7lbs
**Nickname:** Major
**County debut:** 1994
**1st-Class 50s:** 4
**1st-Class catches:** 4
**Place in batting averages:** 34th av. 47.20
(1994 185th av. 22.26)
**Place in bowling averages:** 96th av. 34.81
(1994 111th av. 37.50)
**Strike rate:** 57.27 (career 73.36)
**Parents:** Jonathan and Pippa
**Marital status:** Single
**Family links with cricket:** Brother Giles
played for Essex and Cambridgeshire

**Education:** Bryanston School; Durham University; Keble College, Oxford
**Qualifications:** 9 O-levels, 3 A-levels, BA (Hons) Social Sciences, Dip Soc (Oxon)
**Off-season:** Playing for Umfalozi and Zululand, South Africa
**Overseas tours:** Bryanston to West Indies 1989; Durham University to South Africa 1992-93
**Cricketers particularly admired:** David Gower
**Other sports followed:** Rugby and all other sports
**Injuries:** Knee injury and broken thumb, out for six weeks
**Relaxations:** 'Continuous cycle of cooking it, eating it, drinking it and getting rid of the evidence'
**Extras:** Played for Essex from U11 to U19/2nd XI and for ESCA U19 v New Zealand 1989; captained Durham University, played for Cambridgeshire, Blue for Oxford University 1994, '"brother of" first *Daily Telegraph* Fantasy League winner'
**Opinions on cricket:** 'One hand one bounce rule should be implemented in one-day games as well as last-man stand. Would like to see the introduction of cheerleaders and topless barmaids at all county grounds.'
**Best batting:** 81 Somerset v Northamptonshire, Northampton 1995
**Best bowling:** 4-66 Oxford University v Surrey, The Oval 1994

## 1995 Season

|           | M | Inns | NO | Runs | HS  | Avge  | 100s | 50s | Ct | St | O   | M  | Runs | Wkts | Avge  | Best | 5wl | 10wM |
|-----------|---|------|----|------|-----|-------|------|-----|----|----|-----|----|------|------|-------|------|-----|------|
| Test      |   |      |    |      |     |       |      |     |    |    |     |    |      |      |       |      |     |      |
| All First | 7 | 12   | 2  | 472  | 81  | 47.20 | -    | 3   | 1  | -  | 105 | 20 | 383  | 11   | 34.81 | 2-31 | -   | -    |
| 1-day Int |   |      |    |      |     |       |      |     |    |    |     |    |      |      |       |      |     |      |
| NatWest   | 1 | 1    | 0  | 0    | 0   | 0.00  | -    | -   | -  | -  | 8   | 0  | 31   | 0    | -     |      | -   | -    |
| B & H     | 4 | 4    | 1  | 65   | 30  | 21.66 | -    | -   | 2  | -  | 23  | 1  | 108  | 3    | 36.00 | 2-44 | -   |      |
| Sunday    | 9 | 9    | 2  | 196  | 45 *| 28.00 | -    | -   | 2  | -  | 45  | 2  | 306  | 6    | 51.00 | 2-21 | -   |      |

## Career Performances

|           | M  | Inns | NO | Runs | HS | Avge  | 100s | 50s | Ct | St | Balls | Runs | Wkts | Avge  | Best | 5wl | 10wM |
|-----------|----|------|----|------|----|-------|------|-----|----|----|-------|------|------|-------|------|-----|------|
| Test      |    |      |    |      |    |       |      |     |    |    |       |      |      |       |      |     |      |
| All First | 20 | 31   | 6  | 806  | 81 | 32.24 | -    | 4   | 4  | -  | 2421  | 1208 | 33   | 36.60 | 4-66 | -   | -    |
| 1-day Int |    |      |    |      |    |       |      |     |    |    |       |      |      |       |      |     |      |
| NatWest   | 2  | 2    | 0  | 1    | 1  | 0.50  | -    | -   | -  | -  | 66    | 53   | 0    | -     |      | -   | -    |
| B & H     | 5  | 4    | 1  | 65   | 30 | 21.66 | -    | -   | 2  | -  | 162   | 124  | 3    | 41.33 | 2-44 | -   |      |
| Sunday    | 17 | 17   | 3  | 414  | 66 | 29.57 | -    | 1   | 2  | -  | 542   | 544  | 17   | 32.00 | 4-31 | -   |      |

# EDWARDS, A. D. — Sussex

**Name:** Alexander David Edwards
**Role:** Right-hand bat, right-arm fast-medium bowler
**Born:** 2 August 1975, Cuckfield, Sussex
**Height:** 6ft **Weight:** 12st 9lbs
**Nickname:** Al, Steady, Eddy
**County debut:** 1994 (one-day), 1995 (first-class)
**1st-Class catches:** 2
**Parents:** Richard John and Angela Janet
**Marital status:** Single
**Family links with cricket:** 'Parents drove me everywhere to play or practise cricket and have been absolutely wonderful'
**Education:** Felbridge Primary; Imberhorne Comprehensive; Loughborough University
**Qualifications:** 10 GCSEs, 4 A-levels
**Career outside cricket:** Studying at Loughborough
**Off-season:** Studying for BSc in Physical Education and Sports Science
**Overseas tours:** Sussex U18 to India 1990-91; England U18 to South Africa 1992-93, to Denmark 1993
**Cricketers particularly admired:** Dennis Lillee, Michael Holding, Viv Richards, Stan Berry and Pat Cale 'for their tremendous support, belief and encouragement'
**Other sports followed:** All sports except show jumping
**Relaxations:** Reading sports psychology, training, playing snooker, swimming, listening to a variety of music and watching sport on television
**Extras:** Lord's Taverners U15 Young Cricketer of the Year 1991 and a *Cricketer* magazine Young Cricketer of the Month in the same year. Played for England U19 against India U19 in 1994
**Opinions on cricket:** 'Second XI cricket should mirror the first-class game, e.g. same grounds, practice facilities and duration of matches in the championship (four days). This would help young players to make the transition from 2nd XI to first-class cricket. Young players should be given ample opportunity to prove themselves in first-class cricket. They shouldn't be afraid of initial failure.'
**Best batting:** 22 Sussex v Young Australia, Hove 1995
**Best bowling:** 3-83 Sussex v Young Australia, Hove 1995

## 1995 Season

| | M | Inns | NO | Runs | HS | Avge | 100s | 50s | Ct | St | O | M | Runs | Wkts | Avge | Best | 5wl | 10wM |
|---|---|---|---|---|---|---|---|---|---|---|---|---|---|---|---|---|---|---|
| Test | | | | | | | | | | | | | | | | | | |
| All First | 2 | 3 | 0 | 38 | 22 | 12.66 | - | - | 2 | - | 47 | 4 | 246 | 3 | 82.00 | 3-83 | - | - |
| 1-day Int | | | | | | | | | | | | | | | | | | |
| NatWest | | | | | | | | | | | | | | | | | | |
| B & H | 5 | 4 | 1 | 21 | 7 * | 7.00 | - | - | 5 | - | 54 | 6 | 232 | 5 | 46.40 | 2-51 | - | |
| Sunday | | | | | | | | | | | | | | | | | | |

## Career Performances

| | M | Inns | NO | Runs | HS | Avge | 100s | 50s | Ct | St | Balls | Runs | Wkts | Avge | Best | 5wl | 10wM |
|---|---|---|---|---|---|---|---|---|---|---|---|---|---|---|---|---|---|
| Test | | | | | | | | | | | | | | | | | |
| All First | 2 | 3 | 0 | 38 | 22 | 12.66 | - | - | 2 | - | 282 | 246 | 3 | 82.00 | 3-83 | - | - |
| 1-day Int | | | | | | | | | | | | | | | | | |
| NatWest | | | | | | | | | | | | | | | | | |
| B & H | 5 | 4 | 1 | 21 | 7 * | 7.00 | - | - | 5 | - | 324 | 232 | 5 | 46.40 | 2-51 | - | - |
| Sunday | 1 | 0 | 0 | 0 | 0 | - | - | - | - | - | 30 | 24 | 0 | - | - | - | |

# EDWARDS, G. J. M.     Glamorgan

**Name:** Gareth John Maldwyn Edwards
**Role:** Right-hand bat, off-spin bowler
**Born:** 13 November 1976, St Asaph, Wales
**Height:** 6ft 3in  **Weight:** 11st 4lbs
**Nickname:** Crazy Legs
**County debut:** No first-team appearance
**Parents:** Roger and Manon
**Marital status:** Single
**Family links with cricket:** Father played
for Ruthin CC for over 20 years
**Education:** Ysgol Brynhyfryd, Ruthin, North
Wales; University College, London
**Qualifications:** 12 GCSEs, 3 A-levels;
currently studying as an undergraduate
**Off-season:** England U19 tour to Zimbabwe
**Overseas tours:**
England U19 to Zimbabwe 1995-96
**Cricketers particularly admired:**
Russell Pewrkyn Jones, Eldine Baptiste
**Other sports followed:** Rugby, football (Clydesbank FC), tennis, golf
**Relaxations:** Music and walking
**Extras:** North Wales Young Cricketer of the Year 1993, Denbighshire Young Cricketer
of the Year 1993

# ELLIS, S. W. K.  Worcestershire

**Name:** Scott William Kenneth Ellis
**Role:** Right-hand bat, right-arm
fast-medium bowler
**Born:** 3 October 1975, Newcastle-u-Lyme
**Height:** 6ft 3in **Weight:** 14st
**County debut:** No first-team appearance
**1st-Class catches:** 1
**1st-Class 5 w. innings:** 1
**Parents:** Tony and Valerie Anne
**Marital status:** Single
**Education:** Shrewsbury School; Warwick
University
**Qualifications:** 9 GCSEs, 3 A-levels
**Off-season:** Studying ancient history and
philosophy at university
**Overseas tours:**
England U19 to West Indies 1994-95
**Cricketers particularly admired:** Curtly
Ambrose, Desmond Haynes, Robin Smith
**Other sports followed:** Football
**Relaxations:** Listening to music, reading
**Extras:** Played for England U18 against India U19 in 1994. Made first-class debut for
Combined Universities against West Indies in 1995
**Best bowling:** 5-59 Combined Universities v West Indies, The Parks 1995

## 1995 Season

|           | M | Inns | NO | Runs | HS | Avge | 100s | 50s | Ct | St | O  | M | Runs | Wkts | Avge  | Best | 5wI | 10wM |
|-----------|---|------|----|------|----|------|------|-----|----|----|----|---|------|------|-------|------|-----|------|
| Test      |   |      |    |      |    |      |      |     |    |    |    |   |      |      |       |      |     |      |
| All First | 1 | 1    | 0  | 0    | 0  | 0.00 | -    | -   | 1  | -  | 35 | 3 | 146  | 5    | 29.20 | 5-59 | 1   | -    |
| 1-day Int |   |      |    |      |    |      |      |     |    |    |    |   |      |      |       |      |     |      |
| NatWest   |   |      |    |      |    |      |      |     |    |    |    |   |      |      |       |      |     |      |
| B & H     |   |      |    |      |    |      |      |     |    |    |    |   |      |      |       |      |     |      |
| Sunday    |   |      |    |      |    |      |      |     |    |    |    |   |      |      |       |      |     |      |

## Career Performances

|           | M | Inns | NO | Runs | HS | Avge | 100s | 50s | Ct | St | Balls | Runs | Wkts | Avge  | Best | 5wI | 10wM |
|-----------|---|------|----|------|----|------|------|-----|----|----|-------|------|------|-------|------|-----|------|
| Test      |   |      |    |      |    |      |      |     |    |    |       |      |      |       |      |     |      |
| All First | 1 | 1    | 0  | 0    | 0  | 0.00 | -    | -   | 1  | -  | 210   | 146  | 5    | 29.20 | 5-59 | 1   | -    |
| 1-day Int |   |      |    |      |    |      |      |     |    |    |       |      |      |       |      |     |      |
| NatWest   |   |      |    |      |    |      |      |     |    |    |       |      |      |       |      |     |      |
| B & H     |   |      |    |      |    |      |      |     |    |    |       |      |      |       |      |     |      |
| Sunday    |   |      |    |      |    |      |      |     |    |    |       |      |      |       |      |     |      |

# ELWORTHY, S.        Lancashire

**Name:** Steven Elworthy
**Role:** Right-hand bat, right-arm
fast-medium bowler
**Born:** 23 February 1965, Zimbabwe
**Height:** 6ft 4in  **Weight:** 13st 9lbs
**County debut:** No first-team appearance
**1st-Class 50s:** 3
**1st-Class catches:** 18
**!st-Class 5 w. in innings:** 8
**1st-Class 10 w. in innings:** 1
**Education:** Wits University, South Africa
**Qualifications:** O and M-levels,TED
Matriculation, degree in Electrical
Engineering, National Higher Diploma
**Off-season:** Playing for Northern Transvaal
**Overseas teams played for:** Northern
Transvaal 1988-1996
**Extras:** Represented Zimbabwe at cricket,
tennis, swimming, rugby, football at junior

level before leaving to complete his education in South Africa. Represented Transvaal in
1987, but in 1988 started two years of national service and moved to Northern Transvaal
whom he has represented since 1988, and was voted Player of the Year for 1993-94 and
1994-95. He played for Bishop Auckland in the North Yorkshire/South Durham league
in 1989 and for Rishton in the Lancashire league in 1991. He has also represented South
Africa 'A'
**Best batting:** 75 Northern Transvaal v Eastern Province, Port Elizabeth 1994-95
**Best bowling:** 7-65 Northern Transvaal v Natal, Durban 1994-95

---

## 1995 Season (did not make any first-class or one-day appearance)

## Career Performances

| | M | Inns | NO | Runs | HS | Avge | 100s | 50s | Ct | St | Balls | Runs | Wkts | Avge | Best | 5wI | 10wM |
|---|---|---|---|---|---|---|---|---|---|---|---|---|---|---|---|---|---|
| Test | | | | | | | | | | | | | | | | | |
| All First | 51 | 84 | 16 | 1379 | 75 | 26.27 | - | 3 | 18 | - | 9613 | 5238 | 183 | 28.62 | 7-65 | 8 | 1 |
| 1-day Int | | | | | | | | | | | | | | | | | |
| NatWest | | | | | | | | | | | | | | | | | |
| B & H | | | | | | | | | | | | | | | | | |
| Sunday | | | | | | | | | | | | | | | | | |

# EMBUREY, J. E.        Northamptonshire

**Name:** John Ernest Emburey
**Role:** Right-hand bat, off-spin bowler
**Born:** 20 August 1952, Peckham
**Height:** 6ft 2in **Weight:** 14st
**Nickname:** Embers, Ern
**County debut:** 1973
**County cap:** 1977
**Benefit:** 1986
**Testimonial:** 1995
**Test debut:** 1978
**Tests:** 64
**One-Day Internationals:** 61
**50 wickets in a season:** 17
**1st-Class 50s:** 54
**1st-Class 100s:** 7
**1st-Class 5 w. in innings:** 72
**1st-Class 10 w. in match:** 12
**1st-Class catches:** 452
**One-Day 5 w. in innings:** 3

**Place in batting averages:** 205th av. 20.36 (1994 245th av. 14.50)
**Place in bowling averages:** 23rd av. 22.98 (1994 28th av. 25.66)
**Strike rate:** 57.45 (career 69.66)
**Parents:** John (deceased) and Rose
**Wife and date of marriage:** Susie, 20 September 1980
**Children:** Clare, 1 March 1983; Chloë, 31 October 1985
**Education:** Peckham Manor Secondary School
**Qualifications:** O-levels, advanced cricket coaching certificate
**Overseas tours:** England to Australia 1978-79, to Australia and India 1979-80, to West Indies 1980-81, to India and Sri Lanka 1981-82, to West Indies 1985-86, to Australia 1986-87, to Pakistan, Australia and New Zealand 1987-88, to India 1992-93; unofficial English XI to South Africa 1981-82 and 1989-90
**Overseas teams played for:** Prahran, Melbourne 1977-78; St Kilda, Melbourne 1984-85; Western Province 1982-84
**Cricketers particularly admired:** Ken Barrington, Alan Knott
**Other sports followed:** Golf
**Relaxations:** Reading, golf
**Extras:** Played for Surrey YC 1969-70. Phil Edmonds of Middlesex and England was the best man at his wedding. Middlesex vice-captain 1983-93. One of *Wisden*'s Five Cricketers of the Year 1983. Captain of England v West Indies for two Tests in 1988. Banned from Test cricket for three years for touring South Africa in 1981-82, and for five more for touring in 1989-90, suspension remitted in 1992. Published autobiography

*Emburey* in 1988. In the match against Somerset at Lord's in 1992 he became only the 9th player to take 1,000 wickets for Middlesex. Middlesex Player of the Year 1993. Manager of the England A tour to Pakistan 1995-96. Left Middlesex at the end of the 1995 season to join Northamptonshire as the club's Chief Coach

**Opinions on cricket:** 'Young players seem very uptight. They should relax and enjoy the game. The less pressure you put yourself under, the easier it will become. Good players don't become bad players, bad players can become good players. They just have to work a little harder.'

**Best batting:** 133 Middlesex v Essex, Chelmsford 1983
**Best bowling:** 8-40 Middlesex v Hampshire, Lord's 1993

## 1995 Season

|  | M | Inns | NO | Runs | HS | Avge | 100s | 50s | Ct | St | O | M | Runs | Wkts | Avge | Best | 5wI | 10wM |
|---|---|---|---|---|---|---|---|---|---|---|---|---|---|---|---|---|---|---|
| Test | 1 | 1 | 0 | 8 | 8 | 8.00 | - | - | 1 | - | 30 | 7 | 82 | 0 | - | - | - | - |
| All First | 17 | 20 | 1 | 387 | 87 | 20.36 | - | 1 | 18 | - | 708.4 | 198 | 1701 | 74 | 22.98 | 7-82 | 5 | 2 |
| 1-day Int |  |  |  |  |  |  |  |  |  |  |  |  |  |  |  |  |  |  |
| NatWest | 3 | 2 | 0 | 15 | 9 | 7.50 | - | - | 2 | - | 33.2 | 4 | 90 | 6 | 15.00 | 3-18 | - |  |
| B & H | 6 | 3 | 2 | 3 | 3 * | 3.00 | - | - | - | - | 58 | 7 | 197 | 5 | 39.40 | 2-23 | - |  |
| Sunday | 7 | 5 | 1 | 40 | 14 * | 10.00 | - | - | 1 | - | 43 | 1 | 223 | 5 | 44.60 | 2-15 | - |  |

## Career Performances

|  | M | Inns | NO | Runs | HS | Avge | 100s | 50s | Ct | St | Balls | Runs | Wkts | Avge | Best | 5wI | 10wM |
|---|---|---|---|---|---|---|---|---|---|---|---|---|---|---|---|---|---|
| Test | 64 | 96 | 20 | 1713 | 75 | 22.53 | - | 10 | 34 | - | 15391 | 5646 | 147 | 38.40 | 7-78 | 6 | - |
| All First | 499 | 628 | 126 | 11782 | 133 | 23.47 | 7 | 54 | 452 | - | 109863 | 40657 | 1577 | 25.78 | 8-40 | 72 | 12 |
| 1-day Int | 61 | 45 | 10 | 501 | 34 | 14.31 | - | - | 19 | - | 3425 | 2346 | 76 | 30.86 | 4-37 | - |  |
| NatWest | 57 | 36 | 11 | 473 | 36 * | 18.92 | - | - | 21 | - | 3815 | 1772 | 64 | 27.68 | 3-11 | - |  |
| B & H | 81 | 56 | 16 | 629 | 50 | 15.72 | - | 1 | 39 | - | 4349 | 2276 | 84 | 27.09 | 5-37 | 1 |  |
| Sunday | 250 | 166 | 57 | 1853 | 50 | 17.00 | - | 1 | 77 | - | 10703 | 7846 | 338 | 23.21 | 5-23 | 2 |  |

# EVANS, A. W.                    Glamorgan

**Name:** Alun Wyn Evans
**Role:** Right-hand bat, right-arm medium bowler
**Height:** 5ft 8in  **Weight:** 12st
**Born:** 20 August 1975, Glanamen, Dyfed
**County debut:** No first-team appearance
**Parents:** Gareth and Lynfa
**Marital status:** Single
**Family links with cricket:** Father formerly with Ammanford CC, now Treasurer with Dinas CC. Brother (Huw) wicket-keeper and batsman with Ammanford CC
**Education:** Fishguard County High School; Neath Tertiary College

**Qualifications:** 11 GCSEs, B. Tech National Diploma in Sports Science
**Off-season:** Playing in New Zealand
**Overseas tours:** Welsh Schools U17 to Australia 1992-93
**Cricketers particularly admired:**
Brian Lara
**Other sports followed:**
Rugby (Cardiff RFC), football (Tottenham Hotspur FC), golf and tennis
**Injuries:** Broken toe, out for two weeks
**Relaxations:** Music, videos, reading sports magazines
**Extras:** Welsh Schools Player of the Year 1994, MCC Young Cricketer 1995

# EVANS, K. P.                    Nottinghamshire

**Name:** Kevin Paul Evans
**Role:** Right-hand bat, right-arm medium  bowler
**Born:** 10 September 1963, Calverton, Nottingham
**Height:** 6ft 2in **Weight:** 13st
**Nickname:** Ghost, Texas
**County debut:** 1984
**County cap:** 1990
**1st-Class 50s:** 17
**1st-Class 100s:** 3
**1st-Class 5 w. in innings:** 4

**1st-Class catches:** 99
**One-day 5 w. innings:** 2
**Place in batting averages:** 174th av. 23.63
(1994 126th av. 30.23)
**Place in bowling averages:** 125th av. 42.14
(1994 57th av. 30.02)
**Strike rate:** 102.05 (career 68.84)
**Parents:** Eric and Eileen
**Wife and date of marriage:**
Sandra, 19 March 1988
**Family links with cricket:** Brother Russell
played for Nottinghamshire and still plays for
Minor Counties and Lincolnshire. Father
played local cricket
**Education:** William Lee Primary; Colonel
Frank Seely Comprehensive, Calverton
**Qualifications:** 10 O-levels, 3 A-levels,
qualified coach
**Off-season:** Working locally
**Cricketers particularly admired:**
Richard Hadlee
**Other sports followed:** Football (Leeds United), tennis, squash
**Injuries:** Operation on Achilles tendon, out for ten weeks
**Relaxations**: Listening to music, reading, DIY, gardening
**Extras:** With brother, Russell, first brothers to bat together for Nottinghamshire in first-class cricket for 50 years. Kept wicket for the first time in the Championship match against Essex at Colchester in 1992. Second Notts cricketer to bowl Sunday League hat-trick v Glamorgan at Trent Bridge, Mark Saxelby was the other
**Opinions on cricket:** 'Four-day format is very good. Also Sunday cricket is back to its best (40 overs).'
**Best batting:** 104 Nottinghamshire v Surrey, Trent Bridge 1992, 104 Nottinghamshire v Sussex, Trent Bridge 1994
**Best bowling:** 6-67 Nottinghamshire v Yorkshire, Trent Bridge 1993

---

### 1995 Season

|          | M | Inns | NO | Runs | HS   | Avge  | 100s | 50s | Ct | St | O     | M  | Runs | Wkts | Avge  | Best | 5wI | 10wM |
|----------|---|------|----|------|------|-------|------|-----|----|----|-------|----|------|------|-------|------|-----|------|
| Test     |   |      |    |      |      |       |      |     |    |    |       |    |      |      |       |      |     |      |
| All First | 7 | 13   | 2  | 260  | 78 * | 23.63 | -    | 2   | 9  | -  | 238.1 | 60 | 590  | 14   | 42.14 | 3-66 | -   | -    |
| 1-day Int |   |      |    |      |      |       |      |     |    |    |       |    |      |      |       |      |     |      |
| NatWest  | 1 | 1    | 0  | 14   | 14   | 14.00 | -    | -   | 1  | -  | 12    | 1  | 64   | 1    | 64.00 | 1-64 | -   |      |
| B & H    | 6 | 4    | 1  | 69   | 47   | 23.00 | -    | -   | -  | -  | 57.2  | 9  | 227  | 14   | 16.21 | 4-19 | -   |      |
| Sunday   | 5 | 5    | 2  | 62   | 26 * | 20.66 | -    | -   | 1  | -  | 31.2  | 2  | 163  | 4    | 40.75 | 2-26 | -   |      |

## Career Performances

|  | M | Inns | NO | Runs | HS | Avge | 100s | 50s | Ct | St | Balls | Runs | Wkts | Avge | Best | 5wI | 10wM |
|---|---|---|---|---|---|---|---|---|---|---|---|---|---|---|---|---|---|
| Test |  |  |  |  |  |  |  |  |  |  |  |  |  |  |  |  |  |
| All First | 122 | 171 | 40 | 3379 | 104 | 25.79 | 3 | 17 | 99 | - | 17830 | 8798 | 259 | 33.96 | 6-67 | 4 | - |
| 1-day Int |  |  |  |  |  |  |  |  |  |  |  |  |  |  |  |  |  |
| NatWest | 18 | 13 | 2 | 105 | 21 | 9.54 | - | - | 6 | - | 1090 | 589 | 24 | 24.54 | 6-10 | 1 |  |
| B & H | 27 | 18 | 5 | 215 | 47 | 16.53 | - | - | 8 | - | 1514 | 1037 | 39 | 26.58 | 4-19 | - |  |
| Sunday | 107 | 67 | 28 | 688 | 30 | 17.64 | - | - | 17 | - | 4335 | 3758 | 114 | 32.96 | 5-29 | 1 |  |

# EVANS, M. R. Middlesex

**Name:** Matthew Robert Evans
**Role:** Right-hand bat, right-arm
medium-fast bowler
**Born:** 27 November 1974, Gravesend, Kent
**Height:** 6ft 3in  **Weight:** 13st
**Nickname:** Shenley
**County debut:** No first-team appearance
**Parents:** Tony and Penny
**Marital status:** Single
**Family links with cricket:** Father plays club
cricket in the Hertfordshire league and is a
playing member of the MCC
**Education:** Aldwickbury School, Harpenden;
Bedford School; Loughborough University
**Qualifications:** 10 GCSEs, 3 A-levels, 2nd
year BSc student, NCA senior cricket coach
**Off-season:** Studying and training
**Cricketers particularly admired:**
Sir Richard Hadlee
**Other sports followed:** Rugby and golf
**Relaxations**: Cinema, theatre, socialising with friends, eating out
**Extras:** Played rugby for East Midlands U18 and county hockey U18. Completed a hat-trick against Durham University in the UAU semi-final. As captain of Bedford School received the Henry Grierson trophy from Brian Johnston. Played for Hertfordshire U19 for three years, two as captain. Played Minor Counties cricket for Hertfordshire from 1994-95
**Opinions on cricket:** 'Young players in club cricket must be given more opportunity to play longer, more competitive games.'

# FAIRBROTHER, N. H. Lancashire

**Name:** Neil Harvey Fairbrother
**Role:** Left-hand bat, left-arm medium bowler
**Born:** 9 September 1963, Warrington, Cheshire
**Height:** 5ft 8in **Weight:** 11st 4lbs
**Nickname:** Harvey
**County debut:** 1982
**County cap:** 1985
**Benefit:** 1995
**Test debut:** 1987
**Tests:** 10
**One-Day Internationals:** 46
**1000 runs in a season:** 9
**1st-Class 50s:** 81
**1st-Class 100s:** 33
**1st-Class 200s:** 2
**1st-Class 300s:** 1
**1st-Class catches:** 191
**One-Day 100s:** 6
**Place in batting averages:** 125th av. 30.10 (1994 20th av. 50.10)
**Parents:** Les and Barbara
**Wife and date of marriage:** Audrey, 23 September 1988
**Children:** Rachael Elizabeth, 4 April 1991; Sam, 3 April 1994
**Family links with cricket:** Father and two uncles played local league cricket
**Education:** St Margaret's Church of England School, Oxford; Lymn Grammar School
**Qualifications:** 5 O-levels
**Overseas tours:** England to Sharjah 1986-87, to India and Pakistan (World Cup) 1987 and 1995-96, Australia and New Zealand 1987-88; England A to Pakistan 1990-91; England to New Zealand 1991-92, to India 1992-93, to Australia 1994-95, to South Africa 1995-96
**Cricketers particularly admired:** Clive Lloyd, Allan Border, David Gower
**Other sports followed:** Football, rugby union, rugby league
**Relaxations:** Music and playing sport
**Extras:** 'I was named after the Australian cricketer Neil Harvey, who was my mum's favourite cricketer.' Played for England YC v Australia 1983. His innings of 366 in 1990 was the third highest score ever made in the County Championship, the second highest first-class score by a Lancashire batsman and the best at The Oval. Appointed Lancashire captain for 1992 but resigned in 1993. Called up to join England tour party as a replacement in Australia 1994-95 but was immediately injured in a collision with Steven Rhodes while fielding and forced to return home. Played in the one-day series between England and South Africa and represented England in the World Cup
**Opinions on cricket:** 'There is too much cricket. The game has to be made more entertaining.'

**Best batting:** 366 Lancashire v Surrey, The Oval 1990
**Best bowling:** 2-91 Lancashire v Nottinghamshire, Old Trafford 1987

## 1995 Season

|  | M | Inns | NO | Runs | HS | Avge | 100s | 50s | Ct | St | O | M | Runs | Wkts | Avge | Best | 5wl | 10wM |
|---|---|---|---|---|---|---|---|---|---|---|---|---|---|---|---|---|---|---|
| Test |  |  |  |  |  |  |  |  |  |  |  |  |  |  |  |  |  |  |
| All First | 14 | 23 | 3 | 602 | 132 | 30.10 | 2 | 1 | 17 | - | 1.5 | 1 | 14 | 0 | - | - | - | - |
| 1-day Int | 2 | 2 | 1 | 73 | 61 * | 73.00 | - | 1 | - | - |  |  |  |  |  |  |  |  |
| NatWest | 2 | 2 | 1 | 80 | 46 | 80.00 | - | - | 2 | - |  |  |  |  |  |  |  |  |
| B & H | 8 | 6 | 1 | 228 | 60 * | 45.60 | - | 1 | 6 | - | 3 | 0 | 17 | 1 | 17.00 | 1-17 | - |  |
| Sunday | 14 | 13 | 4 | 412 | 99 * | 45.77 | - | 3 | 5 | - | 6 | 0 | 33 | 1 | 33.00 | 1-33 | - |  |

## Career Performances

|  | M | Inns | NO | Runs | HS | Avge | 100s | 50s | Ct | St | Balls | Runs | Wkts | Avge | Best | 5wl | 10wM |
|---|---|---|---|---|---|---|---|---|---|---|---|---|---|---|---|---|---|
| Test | 10 | 15 | 1 | 219 | 83 | 15.64 | - | 1 | 4 | - | 12 | 9 | 0 | - | - | - | - |
| All First | 275 | 439 | 66 | 15227 | 366 | 40.82 | 33 | 81 | 191 | - | 673 | 440 | 5 | 88.00 | 2-91 | - | - |
| 1-day Int | 46 | 44 | 10 | 1341 | 113 | 39.44 | 1 | 10 | 19 | - | 6 | 9 | 0 | - | - | - |  |
| NatWest | 29 | 28 | 5 | 1151 | 93 * | 50.04 | - | 9 | 12 | - | 18 | 16 | 0 | - | - | - |  |
| B & H | 56 | 53 | 16 | 1865 | 116 * | 50.40 | 1 | 13 | 28 | - | 54 | 67 | 1 | 67.00 | 1-17 | - |  |
| Sunday | 170 | 157 | 36 | 4598 | 116 * | 38.00 | 4 | 27 | 49 | - | 48 | 48 | 1 | 48.00 | 1-33 | - |  |

# FARBRACE, P.           Middlesex

**Name:** Paul Farbrace
**Role:** Right-hand bat, wicket-keeper
**Born:** 7 July 1967, Ash, nr Canterbury
**Height:** 5ft 10in **Weight:** 'Variable'
**Nickname:** Farby
**County debut:** 1987 (Kent),
1990 (Middlesex)
**1st-Class 50s:** 4
**1st-Class catches:** 89
**1st-Class stumpings:** 12
**Parents:** David and Betty
**Wife and date of marriage:** Elizabeth Jane, 27 July 1985
**Children:** Jemma Elizabeth, 30 March 1985; Eleanor Kate, 3 September 1988
**Family links with cricket:** Father played village cricket; two brothers play, Ian in South Wales and Colin plays for Ash
**Education:** Ash CE Primary School; Geoffrey Chaucer School, Canterbury
**Qualifications:** O-levels, NCA senior/advanced/staff coach
**Career outside cricket:** PE teacher, previously customs officer, BBC radio reporter (Kent), postman and farm labourer

**Off-season:** Teaching at Hampton School
**Overseas tours:** Kent Schools to Canada
1983; Middlesex to Portugal 1991, 1992
**Cricketers particularly admired:** Derek
Underwood, Alan Knott, Jon Cook 'sadly a
Yorkshireman though'
**Other sports followed:** All sports except
those with horses
**Injuries:** Knee, 'wicket-keepers play through
injuries unlike bowlers'
**Relaxations:** 'Reading, spending time with
my wife and children, plus Henry the dog.'
**Extras:** Played County Schools football, had
England Schools U18 trial, attracted attention
from Notts County and Coventry City.
Captained Kent v Essex in a five-a-side cricket
game in Dartford Tunnel in February 1989 to
raise money for Children in Need. Has bowled

only once in first-class cricket and took the wicket of Graham Gooch at Lord's.
Middlesex Uncapped Player of the Year 1993. Middlesex Young Player of the Year 1993
('aged 27'). Chairman of Ash CC, club captain of Mote CC (Maidstone). Retired from
county cricket at the end of the 1995 season
**Opinions on cricket:** 'If the cricket authorities think that scrapping 2nd XI competition
and cutting back playing staffs are the solutions to better 1st XI and Test cricket they are
wrong. The 2nd XI competition needs improving because good players will not emerge
from what is becoming glorified club cricket. Sadly club and minor counties cricket is
also in rapid decline. County clubs need to spend money on youngsters from about 14
or 15 years old and not think that they will turn up and play for counties and consider it
to be an honour – they won't. The idea of one academy just won't work either, the clubs
won't send their best players to be coached by someone else!'
**Best batting:** 79 Middlesex v Cambridge University, Fenner's 1990
**Best bowling:** 1-64 Middlesex v Essex, Lord's 1991

## 1995 Season

| | M | Inns | NO | Runs | HS | Avge | 100s | 50s | Ct | St | O | M | Runs | Wkts | Avge | Best | 5wI | 10wM |
|---|---|---|---|---|---|---|---|---|---|---|---|---|---|---|---|---|---|---|
| Test | | | | | | | | | | | | | | | | | | |
| All First | 2 | 2 | 0 | 17 | 16 | 8.50 | - | - | 3 | - | 1 | 1 | 0 | 0 | - | - | - | - |
| 1-day Int | | | | | | | | | | | | | | | | | | |
| NatWest | | | | | | | | | | | | | | | | | | |
| B & H | | | | | | | | | | | | | | | | | | |
| Sunday | 4 | 4 | 1 | 46 | 26 | 15.33 | - | - | - | - | | | | | | | | |

| | M | Inns | NO | Runs | HS | Avge | 100s | 50s | Ct | St | Balls | Runs | Wkts | Avge | Best | 5wI | 10wM |
|---|---|---|---|---|---|---|---|---|---|---|---|---|---|---|---|---|---|
| Test | | | | | | | | | | | | | | | | | |
| All First | 40 | 50 | 11 | 711 | 79 | 18.23 | - | 4 | 89 | 12 | 31 | 64 | 1 | 64.00 | 1-64 | - | - |
| 1-day Int | | | | | | | | | | | | | | | | | |
| NatWest | 6 | 4 | 1 | 41 | 17 | 13.66 | - | - | 8 | 1 | | | | | | | |
| B & H | | | | | | | | | | | | | | | | | |
| Sunday | 22 | 16 | 5 | 119 | 26 * | 10.81 | - | - | 11 | 10 | | | | | | | |

# FAY, R. A.                   Middlesex

**Name:** Richard Anthony Fay
**Role:** Right-hand bat, right-arm medium-fast bowler
**Born:** 14 May 1974, Kilburn, London
**Height:** 6ft 4in **Weight:** 14st 7lbs
**Nickname:** Ginga, Red, Bestey
**County debut:** 1995
**Parents:** James Peter and Margaret Christine
**Marital status:** 'girlfriend named Julie'
**Family links with cricket:** Father played Combined Services. Great uncle was Maurice Tait
**Education:** Kilburn Park; Brondesbury and Kilburn, Queen's Park Community School; City of Westminster College
**Qualifications:** 4 GCSEs, BTEC in Business Studies, BTEC in Design and Realisation
**Off-season:** 'Working with my brother and trying to stay fit'
**Cricketers particularly admired:** Angus Fraser, Simon Marcus, Darren Wyrill, Matt Church, Clive Radley, Chris Sketchley, Ian Kidd
**Other sports followed:** Football (Chelsea and 'play for Brondesbury CC'), badminton, pool and table tennis
**Injuries:** Twisted ankle, out for four days
**Relaxations:** Going to the pub and having a quiet drink with my mates. Spending time with my girlfriend
**Extras:** Best league performance of nine wickets for 45 runs against Wembley CC. MCC YC 1992-95
**Opinions on cricket:** 'I don't think that the day should be 110 overs. I think that it should be 90 or 100 overs at the most so that lunch and tea intervals could be made longer'
**Best batting:** 1* Middlesex v Yorkshire, Headingley 1995

## 1995 Season

| | M | Inns | NO | Runs | HS | Avge | 100s | 50s | Ct | St | O | M | Runs | Wkts | Avge | Best | 5wI | 10wM |
|---|---|---|---|---|---|---|---|---|---|---|---|---|---|---|---|---|---|---|
| Test | | | | | | | | | | | | | | | | | | |
| All First | 1 | 1 | 1 | 1 | 1 * | - | - | - | - | - | 3 | 0 | 25 | 0 | - | - | - | - |
| 1-day Int | | | | | | | | | | | | | | | | | | |
| NatWest | | | | | | | | | | | | | | | | | | |
| B & H | | | | | | | | | | | | | | | | | | |
| Sunday | 6 | 4 | 2 | 34 | 12 * | 17.00 | - | - | - | - | 37 | 0 | 155 | 3 | 51.66 | 2-32 | - | |

## Career Performances

| | M | Inns | NO | Runs | HS | Avge | 100s | 50s | Ct | St | Balls | Runs | Wkts | Avge | Best | 5wI | 10wM |
|---|---|---|---|---|---|---|---|---|---|---|---|---|---|---|---|---|---|
| Test | | | | | | | | | | | | | | | | | |
| All First | 1 | 1 | 1 | 1 | 1 * | - | - | - | - | - | 18 | 25 | 0 | - | - | - | - |
| 1-day Int | | | | | | | | | | | | | | | | | |
| NatWest | | | | | | | | | | | | | | | | | |
| B & H | | | | | | | | | | | | | | | | | |
| Sunday | 6 | 4 | 2 | 34 | 12 * | 17.00 | - | - | - | - | 222 | 155 | 3 | 51.66 | 2-32 | - | |

# FELTHAM, M. A.　　　　　Middlesex

**Name:** Mark Andrew Feltham
**Role:** Right-hand bat, right-arm
medium bowler
**Born:** 26 June 1963, London
**Height:** 6ft 2in **Weight:** 13st 10lbs
**Nickname:** Felts, Felpsy, Boff or Douglas
**County debut:** 1983 (Surrey),
1993 (Middlesex)
**County cap:** 1990 (Surrey),
1995 (Middlesex)
**50 wickets in a season:** 1
**1st-Class 50s:** 9
**1st-Class 100s:** 1
**1st-Class 5 w. in innings:** 8
**1st-Class catches:** 67
**One-Day 5 w. in innings:** 3
**Place in batting averages:**
277th av. 10.45 (1994 225th av. 17.06)
**Place in bowling averages:**
48th av. 27.00 (1994 86th av. 33.52)
**Strike rate:** 56.50 (career 61.51)
**Parents:** Leonard William and Patricia Louise

**Wife and date of marriage:** Debra Elizabeth, 22 September 1990

**Children:** Zoë Elizabeth, 23 June 1992; Harrison Leonard Walter, 20 August 1995

**Family links with cricket:** 'Mum responsible for fund-raising to build new development at Foster's Oval. Brother plays cricket in Middlesex League'

**Education:** Roehampton Church School; Tiffin Boys' School

**Qualifications:** 7 O-levels; advanced cricket coach

**Career outside cricket:** PR, marketing and media

**Off-season:** Coaching in London primary schools. Playing indoor cricket and working for a media/advertising agency

**Overseas teams played for:** Glenwood Old Boys, Durban, South Africa 1983-84, 1986-87

**Cricketers particularly admired:** Ian Botham, Gordon Greenidge, Waqar Younis and Sylvester Clarke

**Other sports followed:** Football, American football and most others

**Injuries:** Ankle, missed last two games

**Relaxations:** 'Music, particularly Luther Vandross, Woody Allen films and listening to Keith Brown and John Emburey talk chess.'

**Extras:** 'I write a weekly column in *Wandsworth Borough News*. Dismissed both Clive Rice and Richard Hadlee in their last innings in county cricket.' Released by Surrey at the end of 1992 season and signed by Middlesex for 1993. Writes monthly column in *Cricket World* magazine.

**Opinions on cricket:** 'Sunday League games should not be played in the middle of four-day games.'

**Best batting:** 101 Surrey v Middlesex, The Oval 1990

**Best bowling:** 6-41 Middlesex v West Indies, Lord's 1995

## 1995 Season

|  | M | Inns | NO | Runs | HS | Avge | 100s | 50s | Ct | St | O | M | Runs | Wkts | Avge | Best | 5wI | 10wM |
|---|---|---|---|---|---|---|---|---|---|---|---|---|---|---|---|---|---|---|
| Test |  |  |  |  |  |  |  |  |  |  |  |  |  |  |  |  |  |  |
| All First | 14 | 15 | 4 | 115 | 25 | 10.45 | - | - | 8 | - | 273.1 | 72 | 783 | 29 | 27.00 | 6-41 | 1 | - |
| 1-day Int |  |  |  |  |  |  |  |  |  |  |  |  |  |  |  |  |  |  |
| NatWest | 3 | 3 | 0 | 67 | 37 | 22.33 | - | - | 1 | - | 18.5 | 4 | 55 | 3 | 18.33 | 2-24 | - |  |
| B & H | 6 | 3 | 1 | 52 | 37 | 26.00 | - | - | 1 | - | 40 | 4 | 161 | 4 | 40.25 | 2-42 | - |  |
| Sunday | 12 | 8 | 1 | 102 | 33 * | 14.57 | - | - | 5 | - | 57.5 | 1 | 278 | 13 | 21.38 | 5-51 | 1 |  |

## Career Performances

|  | M | Inns | NO | Runs | HS | Avge | 100s | 50s | Ct | St | Balls | Runs | Wkts | Avge | Best | 5wI | 10wM |
|---|---|---|---|---|---|---|---|---|---|---|---|---|---|---|---|---|---|
| Test |  |  |  |  |  |  |  |  |  |  |  |  |  |  |  |  |  |
| All First | 157 | 192 | 47 | 3185 | 101 | 21.96 | 1 | 9 | 67 | - | 23623 | 12094 | 384 | 31.49 | 6-41 | 8 | - |
| 1-day Int |  |  |  |  |  |  |  |  |  |  |  |  |  |  |  |  |  |
| NatWest | 19 | 14 | 4 | 168 | 37 | 16.80 | - | - | 3 | - | 1060 | 749 | 19 | 39.42 | 2-23 | - |  |
| B & H | 38 | 24 | 5 | 259 | 37 | 13.63 | - | - | 11 | - | 2067 | 1354 | 57 | 23.75 | 5-28 | 2 |  |
| Sunday | 128 | 87 | 24 | 1113 | 75 | 17.66 | - | 3 | 33 | - | 4937 | 4173 | 118 | 35.36 | 5-51 | 1 |  |

# FIELD-BUSS, M. G.          Nottinghamshire

**Name:** Michael Gwyn Field-Buss
**Role:** Right-hand bat, off-spin bowler
**Born:** 23 September 1964, Malta
**Height:** 5ft 10in **Weight:** 11st
**Nickname:** Mouse
**County debut:** 1987 (Essex),
1989 (Nottinghamshire)
**1st-Class 5 w. in innings:** 1
**1st-Class catches:** 13
**Strike rate:** (career 88.42)
**Parents:** Gwyn and Monica
**Marital status:** Engaged to Paula
**Family links with cricket:** Father played
local cricket with Ilford RAFA
**Education:** Wanstead High School
**Qualifications:** Qualified coach
**Overseas teams played for:**
Werribee, Melbourne 1987-88
**Cricketers particularly admired:** 'Bill Morris (coach at Ilford Cricket School) during
my early years, Ray East and David Acfield at Essex, Eddie Hemmings at Notts'
**Other sports followed:** 'Watching Leyton Orient (although I support Arsenal). Keen
on most other sports'
**Relaxations:** 'Spending as much time as possible with my fiancée, Paula, and my
family, listening to music, playing with new kittens (Sam and Cassey)'
**Opinions on cricket:** 'More 2nd XI games should be played on first-class grounds.'
**Best batting:** 34* Essex v Middlesex, Lord's 1987
**Best bowling:** 6-42 Nottinghamshire v Kent, Trent Bridge 1993

---

## 1995 Season

| | M | Inns | NO | Runs | HS | Avge | 100s | 50s | Ct | St | O | M | Runs | Wkts | Avge | Best | 5wI | 10wM |
|---|---|---|---|---|---|---|---|---|---|---|---|---|---|---|---|---|---|---|
| Test | | | | | | | | | | | | | | | | | | |
| All First | 2 | 2 | 0 | 4 | 2 | 2.00 | - | - | 1 | - | 57 | 14 | 172 | 1 | 172.00 | 1-28 | - | - |
| 1-day Int | | | | | | | | | | | | | | | | | | |
| NatWest | | | | | | | | | | | | | | | | | | |
| B & H | | | | | | | | | | | | | | | | | | |
| Sunday | | | | | | | | | | | | | | | | | | |

## Career Performances

|  | M | Inns | NO | Runs | HS | Avge | 100s | 50s | Ct | St | Balls | Runs | Wkts | Avge | Best | 5wI | 10wM |
|---|---|---|---|---|---|---|---|---|---|---|---|---|---|---|---|---|---|
| Test |  |  |  |  |  |  |  |  |  |  |  |  |  |  |  |  |  |
| All First | 38 | 43 | 14 | 311 | 34 * | 10.72 | - | - | 13 | - | 5571 | 2464 | 63 | 39.11 | 6-42 | 1 | - |
| 1-day Int |  |  |  |  |  |  |  |  |  |  |  |  |  |  |  |  |  |
| NatWest | 5 | 3 | 2 | 10 | 5 * | 10.00 | - | - | 1 | - | 294 | 191 | 7 | 27.28 | 4-62 | - |  |
| B & H | 1 | 0 | 0 | 0 | 0 | - | - | - | - | - | 66 | 21 | 0 | - | - | - | - |
| Sunday | 33 | 16 | 6 | 46 | 10 * | 4.60 | - | - | 6 | - | 1398 | 1178 | 31 | 38.00 | 3-25 | - |  |

# FISHER, I. Yorkshire

**Name:** Ian Douglas Fisher
**Role:** Left-hand bat, slow left-arm bowler
**Born:** 31 March 1976, Bradford
**Height:** 5ft 11in **Weight:** 14st 2lbs
**Nickname:** Fish, Burger
**County debut:** No first-team appearance
**Parents:** Geoff and Linda
**Marital status:** Single
**Family links with cricket:** Father played
club cricket for Denholme and sister played
junior cricket
**Education:** Parkside Middle School;
Beckfoot Grammar School
**Qualifications:** 8 GCSEs, City and Guilds
Sports and Leisure course, NCA coaching
award, Sports Leaders Award
**Overseas teams played for:** Somerset West,
South Africa 1994-95
**Cricketers particularly admired:** Shane Warne, Phil Tufnell, Graham Thorpe, Allan
Donald
**Other sports followed:** Football (Leeds United), rugby league (Leeds), golf
**Relaxations**: Socialising, watching television, listening to music
**Extras:** Played England U17 and Yorkshire Schools U15, U16 and Yorkshire U19
**Opinions on cricket:** 'Players should have the option of signing a 12-month contract
instead of only six months.'

---

29. Who won the 1995 Asia Cup in Sharjah?

---

# FLEMING, M. V. Kent

**Name:** Matthew Valentine Fleming
**Role:** Right-hand bat, right-arm
medium bowler
**Born:** 12 December 1964, Macclesfield (by
mistake - one month early!)
**Height:** 6ft **Weight:** 12st 4lbs
**Nickname:** Jazzer, Bloodnut
**County debut:** 1988
**County cap:** 1990
**1st-Class 50s:** 29
**1st-Class 100s:** 6
**1st-Class catches:** 46
**Place in batting averages:** 130th av. 29.80
(1994 136th av. 28.92)
**Strike rate:** (career 91.25)
**Parents:** Valentine and Elizabeth
**Wife and date of marriage:**
Caroline, 23 September 1989
**Children:** Hannah, 9 October 1992; Victoria, 16 June 1994
**Family links with cricket:** Great-grandfather C.F. Leslie played for England in 1880s;
father played for Eton 2nd XI; mother opened the bowling for Heathfield School
**Education:** St Aubyns School, Rottingdean; Eton College
**Qualifications:** 8 O-levels, 3 A-levels, commissioned Royal Green Jackets in 1985
**Career outside cricket:** 'Unemployable'
**Overseas tours:** 'Never selected for anything'
**Overseas teams played for:** Avendale, Cape Town 1983-84
**Cricketers particularly admired:**
Graham Cowdrey, Wayne Larkins and 'all who hit hard and enjoy'
**Other sports followed:** Football (Arsenal), American football (San Francisco 49ers),
golf, squash, rugby
**Injuries:** 'None except pride'
**Relaxations:** 'Blood sports'
**Extras:** Ex-army officer in the Royal Green Jackets. First two scoring shots in
Championship cricket were sixes. Vice-chairman of the Professional Cricketers'
Association. Out twice before lunch batting at number three for Kent against West Indies
in 1995
**Opinions on cricket:** 'Too many Chiefs and the Indians can't comprehend most of the
smoke signals.'
**Best batting:** 116 Kent v West Indies, Canterbury 1991
**Best bowling:** 4-31 Kent v Gloucestershire, Tunbridge Wells 1993

## 1995 Season

| | M | Inns | NO | Runs | HS | Avge | 100s | 50s | Ct | St | O | M | Runs | Wkts | Avge | Best | 5wI | 10wM |
|---|---|---|---|---|---|---|---|---|---|---|---|---|---|---|---|---|---|---|
| Test | | | | | | | | | | | | | | | | | | |
| All First | 10 | 16 | 1 | 447 | 100 | 29.80 | 1 | 2 | 2 | - | 127 | 19 | 436 | 6 | 72.66 | 3-93 | - | - |
| 1-day Int | | | | | | | | | | | | | | | | | | |
| NatWest | 2 | 2 | 0 | 47 | 35 | 23.50 | - | - | - | - | 19 | 0 | 87 | 1 | 87.00 | 1-44 | - | |
| B & H | 7 | 5 | 1 | 76 | 44 * | 19.00 | - | - | 2 | - | 61.4 | 1 | 268 | 13 | 20.61 | 3-18 | - | |
| Sunday | 16 | 16 | 1 | 305 | 70 | 20.33 | - | 2 | 4 | - | 88 | 3 | 496 | 15 | 33.06 | 2-14 | - | |

## Career Performances

| | M | Inns | NO | Runs | HS | Avge | 100s | 50s | Ct | St | Balls | Runs | Wkts | Avge | Best | 5wI | 10wM |
|---|---|---|---|---|---|---|---|---|---|---|---|---|---|---|---|---|---|
| Test | | | | | | | | | | | | | | | | | |
| All First | 113 | 183 | 21 | 5044 | 116 | 31.13 | 6 | 29 | 46 | - | 10768 | 5097 | 118 | 43.19 | 4-31 | - | - |
| 1-day Int | | | | | | | | | | | | | | | | | |
| NatWest | 15 | 15 | 1 | 278 | 53 | 19.85 | - | 1 | 9 | - | 585 | 382 | 17 | 22.47 | 3-28 | - | |
| B & H | 28 | 25 | 2 | 552 | 69 | 24.00 | - | 3 | 7 | - | 1390 | 958 | 36 | 26.61 | 3-18 | - | |
| Sunday | 106 | 98 | 12 | 2018 | 79 | 23.46 | - | 9 | 33 | - | 3910 | 3387 | 119 | 28.46 | 4-36 | - | |

# FLINT, D. P. J.     Hampshire

**Name:** Darren Peter John Flint
**Role:** Right-hand bat, slow left-arm bowler
**Born:** 14 June 1970, Basingstoke
**Height:** 6ft   **Weight:** 14st
**County debut:** 1993
**1st-Class 5 w. in innings:** 1
**1st-Class catches:** 8
**Strike rate:** (career 82.00)
**Parents:** Peter and Linda
**Marital status:** Engaged
**Education:** Cranbourne Comprehensive;
Queen Mary's College, Basingstoke
**Qualifications:**
5 O-levels, NCA senior coach
**Overseas tours:** Hampshire to Isle of Wight
1990, 1991, 1992, 1993
**Cricketers particularly admired:**
Derek Underwood, John Emburey,
Malcolm Marshall, Sean 'The Pedigree' Morris and Rupert 'Mature' Cox
**Other sports followed:** Rugby, shooting, fishing
**Relaxations:** Enjoying good food and drink, especially sampling real ales
**Extras:** Thames Valley League Bowler of the Year 1989. Rapid Cricketline Player of

the Month August/September 1991.  Took 5 wickets in an innings on his first-class debut
**Best batting:** 17* Hampshire v Worcestershire, Southampton 1995
**Best bowling:** 5-32 Hampshire v Gloucestershire, Bristol 1993

## 1995 Season

| | M | Inns | NO | Runs | HS | Avge | 100s | 50s | Ct | St | O | M | Runs | Wkts | Avge | Best | 5wI | 10wM |
|---|---|---|---|---|---|---|---|---|---|---|---|---|---|---|---|---|---|---|
| Test | | | | | | | | | | | | | | | | | | |
| All First | 2 | 1 | 1 | 17 | 17 * | - | - | - | - | - | 50 | 16 | 123 | 2 | 61.50 | 2-52 | - | - |
| 1-day Int | | | | | | | | | | | | | | | | | | |
| NatWest | | | | | | | | | | | | | | | | | | |
| B & H | | | | | | | | | | | | | | | | | | |
| Sunday | | | | | | | | | | | | | | | | | | |

## Career Performances

| | M | Inns | NO | Runs | HS | Avge | 100s | 50s | Ct | St | Balls | Runs | Wkts | Avge | Best | 5wI | 10wM |
|---|---|---|---|---|---|---|---|---|---|---|---|---|---|---|---|---|---|
| Test | | | | | | | | | | | | | | | | | |
| All First | 15 | 16 | 7 | 72 | 17 * | 8.00 | - | - | 8 | - | 2924 | 1318 | 34 | 38.76 | 5-32 | 1 | - |
| 1-day Int | | | | | | | | | | | | | | | | | |
| NatWest | | | | | | | | | | | | | | | | | |
| B & H | | | | | | | | | | | | | | | | | |
| Sunday | | | | | | | | | | | | | | | | | |

# FLINTOFF, A.                                    Lancashire

**Name:** Andrew Flintoff
**Role:** Right-hand bat, right-arm
medium bowler
**Born:** 6 December 1977, Preston
**Height:** 6ft 4in  **Weight:** 13st 10lb
**County debut:** 1995
**1st-Class catches:** 2
**Parents:** Colin and Susan
**Family links with cricket:**
Brother Chris and father both play local
league cricket
**Education:** Greenlands County Primary;
Ribbleton Hall High School
**Qualifications:** 9 GCSEs
**Off-season:** Touring Zimbabwe
**Overseas tours:** England Schools U15 to
South Africa 1993; England U19 to West
Indies 1994-95, to Zimbabwe 1995-96

**Cricketers particularly admired:** Jason Gallian, John Crawley, Stephen Titchard, Warren Hegg
**Other sports followed:** Football (Preston North End and Liverpool FC)
**Injuries:** Bad back, 'did not bowl for two months'
**Relaxations:** Listening to music and sleeping
**Extras:** Won a *Daily Telegraph* regional award for batting. Represented England U14 to U19 and played for U17 against India in 1994
**Opinions on cricket:** 'Cricket should be promoted more in state schools.'
**Best batting:** 7 Lancashire v Middlesex, Portsmouth 1995

### 1995 Season

|  | M | Inns | NO | Runs | HS | Avge | 100s | 50s | Ct | St | O | M | Runs | Wkts | Avge | Best | 5wl | 10wM |
|---|---|---|---|---|---|---|---|---|---|---|---|---|---|---|---|---|---|---|
| Test |  |  |  |  |  |  |  |  |  |  |  |  |  |  |  |  |  |  |
| All First | 1 | 2 | 0 | 7 | 7 | 3.50 | - | - | 2 | - | 11 | 0 | 39 | 0 | - |  | - | - |
| 1-day Int |  |  |  |  |  |  |  |  |  |  |  |  |  |  |  |  |  |  |
| NatWest |  |  |  |  |  |  |  |  |  |  |  |  |  |  |  |  |  |  |
| B & H | 1 | 0 | 0 | 0 | 0 | - | - | - | - | - | 6 | 2 | 10 | 1 | 10.00 | 1-10 | - |  |
| Sunday | 2 | 2 | 0 | 34 | 22 | 17.00 | - | - | - | - |  |  |  |  |  |  |  |  |

### Career Performances

|  | M | Inns | NO | Runs | HS | Avge | 100s | 50s | Ct | St | Balls | Runs | Wkts | Avge | Best | 5wl | 10wM |
|---|---|---|---|---|---|---|---|---|---|---|---|---|---|---|---|---|---|
| Test |  |  |  |  |  |  |  |  |  |  |  |  |  |  |  |  |  |
| All First | 1 | 2 | 0 | 7 | 7 | 3.50 | - | - | 2 | - | 66 | 39 | 0 | - |  | - | - |
| 1-day Int |  |  |  |  |  |  |  |  |  |  |  |  |  |  |  |  |  |
| NatWest |  |  |  |  |  |  |  |  |  |  |  |  |  |  |  |  |  |
| B & H | 1 | 0 | 0 | 0 | 0 | - | - | - | - | - | 36 | 10 | 1 | 10.00 | 1-10 | - |  |
| Sunday | 2 | 2 | 0 | 34 | 22 | 17.00 | - | - | - | - |  |  |  |  |  |  |  |

# FOLLETT, D.                             Middlesex

**Name:** David Follett
**Role:** Right-hand bowler, right-arm fast bowler
**Born:** 14 October 1968, Hanley, Stoke-on-Trent
**Height:** 6ft 2in **Weight:** 12st
**Nickname:** Foll
**County debut:** 1995
**1st-Class catches:** 1
**Parents:** Gordon and Sandra
**Marital status:** Single
**Family links with cricket:** Father played club cricket for Burslem
**Education:** Moorland Road High School, Burslem, Stoke-on-Trent
**Qualifications:** Engineer

**Career outside cricket:** Engineer
**Overseas teams played for:** Queenbeyan, New South Wales, Australia, 1994-95
**Cricketers particularly admired:** Imran Khan, Ian Botham
**Other sports followed:** Football, motor racing
**Relaxations:** Keeping fit, music
**Extras:** Played for Staffordshire in the Minor Counties before joining Middlesex
**Best batting:** 4* Middlesex v Warwickshire, Edgbaston 1995
**Best bowling:** 1-61 Middlesex v Warwickshire, Edgbaston 1995

## 1995 Season

| | M | Inns | NO | Runs | HS | Avge | 100s | 50s | Ct | St | O | M | Runs | Wkts | Avge | Best | 5wI | 10wM |
|---|---|---|---|---|---|---|---|---|---|---|---|---|---|---|---|---|---|---|
| Test | | | | | | | | | | | | | | | | | | |
| All First | 1 | 2 | 1 | 5 | 4 * | 5.00 | - | - | 1 | - | 30 | 6 | 95 | 1 | 95.00 | 1-61 | - | - |
| 1-day Int | | | | | | | | | | | | | | | | | | |
| NatWest | | | | | | | | | | | | | | | | | | |
| B & H | 3 | 1 | 0 | 4 | 4 | 4.00 | - | - | - | - | 24 | 1 | 100 | 4 | 25.00 | 2-44 | - | |
| Sunday | 1 | 0 | 0 | 0 | 0 | - | - | - | 1 | - | 7 | 1 | 27 | 2 | 13.50 | 2-27 | - | |

## Career Performances

| | M | Inns | NO | Runs | HS | Avge | 100s | 50s | Ct | St | Balls | Runs | Wkts | Avge | Best | 5wI | 10wM |
|---|---|---|---|---|---|---|---|---|---|---|---|---|---|---|---|---|---|
| Test | | | | | | | | | | | | | | | | | |
| All First | 1 | 2 | 1 | 5 | 4 * | 5.00 | - | - | 1 | - | 180 | 95 | 1 | 95.00 | 1-61 | - | - |
| 1-day Int | | | | | | | | | | | | | | | | | |
| NatWest | | | | | | | | | | | | | | | | | |
| B & H | 3 | 1 | 0 | 4 | 4 | 4.00 | - | - | - | - | 144 | 100 | 4 | 25.00 | 2-44 | - | |
| Sunday | 1 | 0 | 0 | 0 | 0 | - | - | - | 1 | - | 42 | 27 | 2 | 13.50 | 2-27 | - | |

# FORDHAM, A.       Northamptonshire

**Name:** Alan Fordham
**Role:** Right-hand bat, occasional
right-arm medium bowler, county vice-captain
**Born:** 9 November 1964, Bedford
**Height:** 6ft 1in **Weight:** 13st
**Nickname:** Forders
**County debut:** 1986
**County cap:** 1990
**1000 runs in a season:** 5
**1st-Class 50s:** 46
**1st-Class 100s:** 24
**1st-Class 200s:** 1
**1st-Class catches:** 99
**One-Day 100s:** 6
**Place in batting averages:** 84th av. 36.60
(1994 36th av. 44.42)
**Parents:** Clifford and Ruth
**Marital status:** Single
**Family links with cricket:** Brother John played school and college cricket
**Education:** Bedford Modern School; Durham University
**Qualifications:** 9 O-levels, 3 A-levels, BSc (Hons) Chemistry, NCA senior coaching award
**Career outside cricket:** 'Still groping in the dark'
**Off-season:** Coaching and playing in Bangladesh and South Africa
**Overseas tours:** Bedford Modern to Barbados 1983; Gentlemen of Leicestershire to Jersey and Guernsey 1987; International Ambassadors XI/Christians in Sport to India 1989-90, to Zimbabwe 1994-95; MCC to Leeward Islands 1991-92, to Bangladesh 1995-96; Northamptonshire to Natal 1991-92; Singapore Sixes 1995
**Overseas teams played for:** Richmond, Melbourne 1983-84; Camberwell, Melbourne 1987-88; Curtin University, Perth, Western Australia 1988; Nirman Schools XI, Dhaka, Bangladesh 1989-90; Montrose, Cape Town, South Africa 1992-93
**Cricketers particularly admired:** Allan Lamb, Bob Willis, Mike Brearley
**Other sports followed:** Rugby union (Bedford RFC) and football (Aston Villa)
**Injuries:** Appendicitis, missed five weeks
**Relaxations:** Television, music, travel
**Extras:** Has appeared for Bedfordshire in Minor Counties Championship. Played for Combined Universities in B&H Cup 1987. Shared county third-wicket record stand of 393 with Allan Lamb v Yorkshire at Headingley in 1990. Only white man to have played league cricket in Bangladesh. Treasurer of the Professional Cricketers' Association
**Opinions on cricket:** 'Pitch quality remains a huge concern. The health of county cricket depends on the surfaces we play on to a great extent, so if pitches are sub-standard then English and ultimately England cricket will under-achieve, I'm sure no-one wants that.'

**Best batting:** 206* Northamptonshire v Yorkshire, Headingley 1990
**Best bowling:** 1-0 Northamptonshire v West Indies, Northampton 1995

## 1995 Season

|          | M  | Inns | NO | Runs | HS  | Avge  | 100s | 50s | Ct | St | O | M | Runs | Wkts | Avge  | Best | 5wl | 10wM |
|----------|----|------|----|------|-----|-------|------|-----|----|----|---|---|------|------|-------|------|-----|------|
| Test     |    |      |    |      |     |       |      |     |    |    |   |   |      |      |       |      |     |      |
| All First | 16 | 29   | 1  | 1025 | 130 | 36.60 | 4    | 4   | 14 | -  | 7 | 1 | 51   | 1    | 51.00 | 1-0  | -   | -    |
| 1-day Int |    |      |    |      |     |       |      |     |    |    |   |   |      |      |       |      |     |      |
| NatWest  | 5  | 5    | 0  | 310  | 132 | 62.00 | 1    | 1   | -  | -  |   |   |      |      |       |      |     |      |
| B & H    | 3  | 3    | 0  | 128  | 108 | 42.66 | 1    | -   | 1  | -  |   |   |      |      |       |      |     |      |
| Sunday   | 14 | 13   | 0  | 336  | 57  | 25.84 | -    | 2   | 4  | -  |   |   |      |      |       |      |     |      |

## Career Performances

|          | M   | Inns | NO | Runs | HS    | Avge  | 100s | 50s | Ct | St | Balls | Runs | Wkts | Avge  | Best | 5wl | 10wM |
|----------|-----|------|----|------|-------|-------|------|-----|----|----|-------|------|------|-------|------|-----|------|
| Test     |     |      |    |      |       |       |      |     |    |    |       |      |      |       |      |     |      |
| All First | 148 | 262  | 19 | 9764 | 206 * | 40.18 | 24   | 46  | 99 | -  | 404   | 289  | 4    | 72.25 | 1-0  | -   | -    |
| 1-day Int |     |      |    |      |       |       |      |     |    |    |       |      |      |       |      |     |      |
| NatWest  | 23  | 23   | 1  | 1131 | 132 * | 51.40 | 3    | 6   | 3  | -  | 21    | 6    | 1    | 6.00  | 1-3  | -   |      |
| B & H    | 22  | 21   | 1  | 703  | 108   | 35.15 | 2    | 4   | 4  | -  |       |      |      |       |      |     |      |
| Sunday   | 101 | 95   | 1  | 2546 | 111   | 27.08 | 1    | 17  | 25 | -  | 6     | 10   | 0    | -     | -    | -   |      |

# FRANCIS, S. R. G. Hampshire

**Name:** Simon Richard George Francis
**Role:** Right-hand bat, right-arm medium-fast bowler
**Born:** 15 August 1978, Bromley
**Height:** 6ft 2in **Weight:** 13st
**Nickname:** Drakie, Geoffrey
**Parents:** Daniel and Linda
**Marital status:** Single
**Family links with cricket:** Father and grandfather both played club cricket
**Education:** Yardley Court, Tonbridge; King Edward VI, Southampton
**Qualifications:** 9 GCSEs, 1 AO-level
**Off-season:** 'Studying at school and university and playing golf and hockey, plus winter training'
**Overseas tours:** England U17 to Holland for International Youth Tournament
**Cricketers particularly admired:** Jonty Rhodes (fielding), Malcolm Marshall and

Dominic Cork (bowling), Robin Smith and Graham Thorpe (batting)
**Other sports followed:** Football (Arsenal) and rugby league (Wigan)
**Injuries:** Inflamed Achilles tendon, out for two weeks
**Relaxations:** Listening to swing, soul and dance music. Watching television and films.
Nightlife – pubs and clubs
**Extras:** *Daily Telegraph* West Region Bowling Award U15
**Opinions on cricket:** 'Selectors should be younger and should have left the game at a
high standard within the last seven or eight years (i.e. younger than 50 and not relying
on experience from many years ago). Not enough coverage of youth sport in the country.
How are we supposed to develop into a great sporting nation when youth sport gets little
recognition by media. Create more determination in the England side like that of Mr
Cork and Mr Atherton.'

# FRASER, A. R. C. Middlesex

**Name:** Angus Robert Charles Fraser
**Role:** Right-hand bat, right-arm medium-fast
bowler, outfielder 'specialist'
**Born:** 8 August 1965, Billinge, Lancashire
**Height:** 6ft 6in **Weight:** 'Just under 16st'
**Nickname:** Gus, Soup
**County debut:** 1984
**County cap:** 1988
**Test debut:** 1989
**Tests:** 29
**One-Day Internationals:** 33
**50 wickets in a season:** 6
**1st-Class 50s:** 1
**1st-Class 5 w. in innings:** 22
**1st-Class 10 w. in match:** 2
**1st-Class catches:** 34
**Place in bowling averages:** 63rd av. 29.14
(1994 36th av. 26.86)

**Strike rate:** 63.44 (career 61.93)
**Parents:** Don and Irene
**Marital status:** Engaged to Denise
**Children**: Alexander Charles Mitchell Fraser and Bethan Louise
**Family links with cricket:** Brother Alastair played for Middlesex and Essex. Parents are
keen followers
**Education:** Gayton High School, Harrow; Orange Senior High School, Edgware
**Qualifications:** 7 O-levels, qualified cricket coach
**Career outside cricket:** Worked for Whittingdale 1991-93 whilst injured
**Off-season:** Touring South Africa with England

**Overseas tours:** Thames Valley Gentlemen to Barbados 1985; Middlesex to La Manga 1985 and 1986, to Portugal 1991-93; England to India (Nehru Cup) 1989-90, to West Indies 1989-90, to Australia 1990-91, to West Indies 1993-94, to Australia 1994-95, to South Africa 1995-96

**Overseas teams played for:** Plimmerton, Wellington 1985-86 and 1987-88; Western Suburbs, Sydney 1988-89 and 1994-95

**Cricketers particularly admired:** Richard Hadlee, Allan Border, Graham Gooch, Curtly Ambrose and Mark Feltham 'for talking a truly great game'

**Other sports followed:** 'Follow Liverpool FC keenly. Enjoy watching rugby internationals at my local rugby club, Harrow'

**Injuries:** 'Severe earache listening to Jason Pooley all summer. His rise in noise level seemed to coincide with a good season'

**Relaxations:** Watching Liverpool FC, rugby internationals and Harrow RFC, spending time with my family and 'watching Paul Weekes scratching around on a shirt-front and Richard Johnson and Dion Nash playing short-pitched bowling'

**Extras:** Middlesex Player of the Year 1988 and 1989. Took a hat-trick in the Benson and Hedges Cup in 1989. Selected for England tour to New Zealand 1991-92 but ruled out by injury. Originally left out of England tour party to Australia 1994-95 but called up when Martin McCague was injured. Took his 100th Test wicket against West Indies in 1995. Finished 2nd in the Whyte and Mackay bowling ratings for 1995

**Opinions on cricket:** 'Why is a wicket that doesn't give a bowler any help at all and is easy to bat on a good wicket? Middlesex's seamers would like to thank the rest of the side for making us feel so valuable and not totally reliant on spin. Not!'

**Best batting:** 92 Middlesex v Surrey, The Oval 1990
**Best bowling:** 8-75 England v West Indies, Bridgetown, 1994

## 1995 Season

|  | M | Inns | NO | Runs | HS | Avge | 100s | 50s | Ct | St | O | M | Runs | Wkts | Avge | Best | 5wI | 10wM |
|---|---|---|---|---|---|---|---|---|---|---|---|---|---|---|---|---|---|---|
| Test | 5 | 8 | 4 | 22 | 10 * | 5.50 | - | - | 1 | - | 187.5 | 52 | 563 | 16 | 35.18 | 5-66 | 1 | - |
| All First | 17 | 21 | 8 | 95 | 20 | 7.30 | - | - | 2 | - | 592.1 | 156 | 1632 | 56 | 29.14 | 5-56 | 2 | - |
| 1-day Int | 2 | 1 | 1 | 4 | 4 * | - | - | - | - | - | 21 | 5 | 63 | 3 | 21.00 | 3-34 | - |  |
| NatWest | 3 | 2 | 2 | 8 | 6 * | - | - | - | 1 | - | 27 | 6 | 77 | 3 | 25.66 | 2-2 | - |  |
| B & H | 6 | 2 | 0 | 2 | 1 | 1.00 | - | - | 2 | - | 56.2 | 6 | 198 | 13 | 15.23 | 4-49 | - |  |
| Sunday | 12 | 7 | 5 | 34 | 12 * | 17.00 | - | - | 1 | - | 80.4 | 10 | 267 | 19 | 14.05 | 5-32 | 1 |  |

## Career Performances

|  | M | Inns | NO | Runs | HS | Avge | 100s | 50s | Ct | St | Balls | Runs | Wkts | Avge | Best | 5wI | 10wM |
|---|---|---|---|---|---|---|---|---|---|---|---|---|---|---|---|---|---|
| Test | 29 | 42 | 8 | 255 | 29 | 7.50 | - | - | 7 | - | 7571 | 3322 | 115 | 28.88 | 8-75 | 8 | - |
| All First | 178 | 200 | 49 | 1657 | 92 | 10.97 | - | 1 | 34 | - | 34437 | 14782 | 556 | 26.58 | 8-75 | 22 | 2 |
| 1-day Int | 33 | 14 | 6 | 80 | 38 * | 10.00 | - | - | 1 | - | 1876 | 1132 | 38 | 29.78 | 4-22 | - |  |
| NatWest | 23 | 7 | 6 | 38 | 19 | 38.00 | - | - | 3 | - | 1539 | 777 | 36 | 21.58 | 4-34 | - |  |
| B & H | 30 | 14 | 6 | 42 | 13 * | 5.25 | - | - | 7 | - | 1815 | 1050 | 41 | 25.60 | 4-49 | - |  |
| Sunday | 115 | 42 | 20 | 247 | 30 * | 11.22 | - | - | 17 | - | 4988 | 3278 | 117 | 28.01 | 5-32 | 1 |  |

# FRENCH, B. N.    Nottinghamshire

**Name:** Bruce Nicholas French
**Role:** Right-hand bat, wicket-keeper
**Born:** 13 August 1959, Warsop, Notts
**Height:** 5ft 8in **Weight:** 10st
**Nickname:** Frog
**County debut:** 1976
**County cap:** 1980
**Benefit:** 1991
**Test debut:** 1986
**Tests:** 16
**One-Day Internationals:** 13
**1st-Class 50s:** 25
**1st-Class 100s:** 2
**1st-Class catches:** 817
**1st-Class stumpings:** 100
**Parents:** Maurice and Betty
**Wife and date of marriage:**
Ellen Rose, 9 March 1978

**Children:** Charles Daniel, 31 August 1978; Catherine Ellen, 28 December 1980
**Family links with cricket:** Brothers, Neil, David, Charlie, Joe, play for Welbeck and father is treasurer. Neil also plays for Lincolnshire
**Education:** Meden School, Warsop
**Qualifications:** O-level and CSE
**Overseas tours:** England to India and Sri Lanka 1984-85, to West Indies 1985-86, to Australia 1986-87, to India and Pakistan (World Cup), Australia and New Zealand 1987-88; unofficial England XI to South Africa 1989-90
**Cricketers particularly admired:** Bob Taylor
**Other sports followed:** Rock climbing, fell walking and all aspects of mountaineering
**Injuries:** Missed most of 1988 season following operations in May on index finger of left hand, and in 1989 broke the same finger again, missing end of season. Previously, French was bitten by a dog whilst jogging in the Caribbean in 1985-86; had to be carried off the field with a cut head and concussion after being struck by a short-pitched delivery from Richard Hadlee at Lord's in 1986; contracted a chest infection after being hit in the chest by a ball in Australia in 1986-87; in Pakistan in 1987-88, he needed stitches in a cut eye and on the way to hospital a car struck his legs
**Relaxations:** Reading, pipe smoking and drinking Theakston's Ale
**Extras:** Youngest player to play for Nottinghamshire, aged 16 years 10 months. Equalled Nottinghamshire record for dismissals in match with 10 (7ct, 3st), and in innings with 6 catches; also set new county record in 1984 for dismissals in a season with 87 (75ct, 12st). Banned from Test cricket for touring South Africa in 1989-90, suspension remitted in 1992. Made his maiden first-class century in 1990 in 15th season of county cricket. Retired from county cricket at the end of the 1995 season

**Best batting:** 123 Nottinghamshire v Durham, Chester-le-Street 1993
**Best bowling:** 1-37 Nottinghamshire v Derbyshire, Derby 1991

## 1995 Season

| | M | Inns | NO | Runs | HS | Avge | 100s | 50s | Ct | St | O | M | Runs | Wkts | Avge | Best | 5wI | 10wM |
|---|---|---|---|---|---|---|---|---|---|---|---|---|---|---|---|---|---|---|
| Test | | | | | | | | | | | | | | | | | | |
| All First | 2 | 3 | 1 | 19 | 16 | 9.50 | - | - | 3 | - | | | | | | | | |
| 1-day Int | | | | | | | | | | | | | | | | | | |
| NatWest | | | | | | | | | | | | | | | | | | |
| B & H | 4 | 1 | 0 | 9 | 9 | 9.00 | - | - | 6 | 1 | | | | | | | | |
| Sunday | 1 | 0 | 0 | 0 | 0 | - | - | - | - | - | | | | | | | | |

## Career Performances

| | M | Inns | NO | Runs | HS | Avge | 100s | 50s | Ct | St | Balls | Runs | Wkts | Avge | Best | 5wI | 10wM |
|---|---|---|---|---|---|---|---|---|---|---|---|---|---|---|---|---|---|
| Test | 16 | 21 | 4 | 308 | 59 | 18.11 | - | 1 | 38 | 1 | | | | | | | |
| All First | 360 | 471 | 92 | 7160 | 123 | 18.89 | 2 | 25 | 817 | 100 | 90 | 70 | 1 | 70.00 | 1-37 | - | - |
| 1-day Int | 13 | 8 | 3 | 34 | 9 * | 6.80 | - | - | 13 | 3 | | | | | | | |
| NatWest | 32 | 27 | 6 | 368 | 49 | 17.52 | - | - | 47 | 4 | | | | | | | |
| B & H | 65 | 43 | 12 | 425 | 48 * | 13.70 | - | - | 68 | 12 | | | | | | | |
| Sunday | 178 | 111 | 38 | 1103 | 37 | 15.10 | - | - | 141 | 17 | | | | | | | |

# FROST, A.      Warwickshire

**Name:** Anthony Frost
**Role:** Right-hand bat, wicket-keeper
**Born:** 17 November 1975, Stoke-on-Trent
**Height:** 5ft 10in **Weight:** 10st 6lbs
**County debut:** No first-team apppearance
**Parents:** Ivan and Christine
**Marital status:** Single
**Family links with cricket:** Father played for Staffordshire
**Education:** James Brinkley High School; Stoke-on-Trent College
**Qualifications:** 5 GCSEs
**Off-season:** Training
**Overseas tours:** Kidsgrove U18 to Australia 1990-91
**Cricketers particularly admired:** Alan Knott, Viv Richards, Gary Sobers
**Other sports followed:** Football, golf
**Relaxations:** Listening to music, watching films, reading aircraft magazines

209

**Extras:** Has represented Staffordshire at all levels from U11 to U19. Won Texaco U16 competition with Staffordshire in 1992. Played for Development of Excellence XI U17 v South Africa and U18 v West Indies and U19 v India

**Opinions on cricket:** 'What a great game but I think that the amount of overs in a day should be reduced. '

---

# FULTON, D. P. Kent

**Name:** David Paul Fulton
**Role:** Right-hand bat, slow left-arm bowler
**Born:** 15 November 1971, Lewisham
**Height:** 6ft 2in **Weight:** 12st
**Nickname:** Rave, Pheasant
**County debut:** 1992
**1st-Class 50s:** 7
**1st-Class 100s:** 2
**1st-Class catches:** 42
**Place in batting averages:** 107th av.33.46
(1994 145th av. 27.06)
**Parents:** John and Ann
**Marital status:** Single
**Family links with cricket:** Father plays for
Otford village side
**Education:** Otford County Primary; The
Judd School, Tonbridge; Kent University
**Qualifications:** 10 GCSEs, 3 A-levels, BA
(Hons) Politics and International Relations
**Off-season:** Playing in Australia
**Overseas tours:** Kent Schools U17 to Singapore and New Zealand 1986-87
**Overseas teams played for:** Avendale, Cape Town 1993-94; Victoria, Cape Town 1994-95
**Cricketers particularly admired:** Gordon Greenidge, Graham Gooch, Carl Hooper,
Aravinda De Silva, Ian Bishop
**Other sports followed:** Rugby (Harlequins) and football (Nottingham Forest)
**Injuries:** Broken fibula, out for six weeks
**Relaxations:** 'Spending time with my girlfriend, Jannine. Clubbing. Golf and
snooker. Interested in current political issues such as Europe, Bosnia etc'
**Extras:** 'Was the last man to catch the great Viv Richards in a first-class match. Opened
the batting and the bowling against South Africa in their first county game'
**Opinions on cricket:** 'Pitches are still too inconsistent around the counties and from
week to week depending on who's the opposition. Counties tend to throw games away
that can't be won rather than battling to the death. Maybe points should be considered
for a draw e.g. 3 which would take the emphasis from winning but might encourage not losing.'
**Best batting:** 116 Kent v Cambridge University, Folkestone 1995

## 1995 Season

| | M | Inns | NO | Runs | HS | Avge | 100s | 50s | Ct | St | O | M | Runs | Wkts | Avge | Best | 5wI | 10wM |
|---|---|---|---|---|---|---|---|---|---|---|---|---|---|---|---|---|---|---|
| Test | | | | | | | | | | | | | | | | | | |
| All First | 8 | 16 | 1 | 502 | 116 | 33.46 | 1 | 4 | 12 | - | | | | | | | | |
| 1-day Int | | | | | | | | | | | | | | | | | | |
| NatWest | 2 | 2 | 0 | 23 | 19 | 11.50 | - | - | - | - | 1 | 0 | 9 | 0 | - | | - | - |
| B & H | 1 | 1 | 0 | 25 | 25 | 25.00 | - | - | 1 | - | | | | | | | | |
| Sunday | 4 | 4 | 0 | 24 | 11 | 6.00 | - | - | 1 | - | | | | | | | | |

## Career Performances

| | M | Inns | NO | Runs | HS | Avge | 100s | 50s | Ct | St | Balls | Runs | Wkts | Avge | Best | 5wI | 10wM |
|---|---|---|---|---|---|---|---|---|---|---|---|---|---|---|---|---|---|
| Test | | | | | | | | | | | | | | | | | |
| All First | 26 | 47 | 2 | 1300 | 116 | 28.88 | 2 | 7 | 42 | - | 1 | 0 | 0 | - | - | - | - |
| 1-day Int | | | | | | | | | | | | | | | | | |
| NatWest | 3 | 3 | 0 | 41 | 19 | 13.66 | - | - | - | - | 6 | 9 | 0 | - | - | - | |
| B & H | 1 | 1 | 0 | 25 | 25 | 25.00 | - | - | 1 | - | | | | | | | |
| Sunday | 7 | 7 | 0 | 59 | 29 | 8.42 | - | - | 3 | - | | | | | | | |

# GALLIAN, J. E. R.            Lancashire

**Name:** Jason Edward Riche Gallian
**Role:** Right-hand bat, right-arm
medium bowler
**Born:** 25 June 1971, Manly, NSW, Australia
**Height:** 6ft **Weight:** 13st
**Nickname:** Gally
**County debut:** 1990
**County cap:** 1994
**Test debut:** 1995
**Tests:** 2
**1000 runs in a season:** 1
**1st-Class 50s:** 18
**1st-Class 100s:** 7
**1st-Class catches:** 35
**One-Day 100s:** 3
**Place in batting averages:** 80th av. 37.40
(1994 39th av. 43.70)
**Place in bowling averages:** 87th av.33.31
(1994 105th av. 36.80)
**Strike rate:** 48.68 (career 70.80)
**Parents:** Ray and Marilyn
**Marital status:** Single

**Family links with cricket:** Father played for Stockport
**Education:** The Pittwater House Schools, Australia; Oxford University
**Qualifications:** Higher School Certificate, Diploma in Social Studies
(Keble College, Oxford)
**Off-season:** Touring Pakistan with England A
**Overseas tours:** Australia U20 to West Indies 1989-90; England A to India 1994-95, to Pakistan 1995-96, England to South Africa 1995-95
**Overseas teams played for:** NSW and Australia U19 1988-89; NSW Colts and NSW 2nd XI 1990-91; Australia U20 and U21 1991-92; Manly 1993-94
**Cricketers particularly admired:** Desmond Haynes, Mike Gatting
**Other sports followed:** Rugby league and union, football
**Injuries:** Fractured thumb, missed four weeks; twisted ankle, missed three weeks
**Relaxations:** Listening to music, playing golf
**Extras:** Played for Oxford University in 1992 and for Combined Universities in the B&H Cup. Captained Oxford University 1993. Was called up to the England squad in South Africa as a replacement for the injured John Crawley and played in the fourth Test at Port Elizabeth
**Best batting:** 171 Lancashire v Surrey, Old Trafford 1994
**Best bowling:** 4-29 Oxford University v Lancashire, The Parks 1992

## 1995 Season

| | M | Inns | NO | Runs | HS | Avge | 100s | 50s | Ct | St | O | M | Runs | Wkts | Avge | Best | 5wI | 10wM |
|---|---|---|---|---|---|---|---|---|---|---|---|---|---|---|---|---|---|---|
| Test | 2 | 4 | 0 | 32 | 25 | 8.00 | - | - | 1 | - | 12 | 1 | 56 | 0 | - | - | - | - |
| All First | 18 | 33 | 3 | 1122 | 158 | 37.40 | 2 | 4 | 18 | - | 129.5 | 17 | 533 | 16 | 33.31 | 3-14 | - | |
| 1-day Int | | | | | | | | | | | | | | | | | | |
| NatWest | 2 | 2 | 1 | 108 | 101 * | 108.00 | 1 | - | - | - | 3 | 0 | 19 | 0 | - | - | - | |
| B & H | 8 | 7 | 1 | 335 | 134 | 55.83 | 2 | - | 1 | - | 21.5 | 3 | 107 | 6 | 17.83 | 5-15 | 1 | |
| Sunday | 14 | 13 | 1 | 385 | 62 | 32.08 | - | 3 | 5 | - | 25.5 | 1 | 150 | 8 | 18.75 | 2-11 | - | |

## Career Performances

| | M | Inns | NO | Runs | HS | Avge | 100s | 50s | Ct | St | Balls | Runs | Wkts | Avge | Best | 5wI | 10wM |
|---|---|---|---|---|---|---|---|---|---|---|---|---|---|---|---|---|---|
| Test | 2 | 4 | 0 | 32 | 25 | 8.00 | - | - | 1 | - | 72 | 56 | 0 | - | - | - | - |
| All First | 56 | 98 | 7 | 3510 | 171 | 38.57 | 7 | 18 | 35 | - | 3965 | 2240 | 56 | 40.00 | 4-29 | - | - |
| 1-day Int | | | | | | | | | | | | | | | | | |
| NatWest | 3 | 3 | 1 | 109 | 101 * | 54.50 | 1 | - | - | - | 54 | 40 | 0 | - | - | - | |
| B & H | 14 | 13 | 1 | 497 | 134 | 41.41 | 2 | 2 | 1 | - | 323 | 262 | 8 | 32.75 | 5-15 | 1 | |
| Sunday | 23 | 22 | 3 | 645 | 84 | 33.94 | - | 5 | 6 | - | 351 | 322 | 17 | 18.94 | 2-10 | - | |

# GARAWAY, M.        Hampshire

**Name:** Mark Garaway
**Role:** Right-hand bat, wicket-keeper
**Born:** 20 July 1973, Swindon, Wilts
**Height:** 5ft 7in **Weight:** 11st 8lbs
**Nickname:** Garas, Wolf, Hair, Val de Lobo
**County debut:** No first-team appearance
**Parents:** Michael and Valerie Anne
**Marital status:** 'Very single'
**Family links with cricket:** 'Grandfather kept wicket for 40 years for Glamorgan. Father regularly outscores and outclasses me at club level for Ventnor 1st XI. Sister captains Ventnor U14'

**Education:** Carhampton Primary, Somerset; Ventnor Middle and Sandown High School, Isle of Wight, 'Ventnor CC, the Astoria (Hermanus, SA)'
**Qualifications:** 10 O-levels, 3 A-levels, NCA cricket coach
**Overseas tours:** Isle of Wight U14 and U17 to Jersey and Guernsey 1988-91; Ventnor to Winchester 1994; Hampshire to Val de Lobo 1994
**Overseas teams played for:** Worcester, Boland, South Africa 1991-93; Hermanus, South Africa 1993; 'Ventnor, Isle of Wight 1982-94'
**Cricketers particularly admired:** Ian Botham, Robin Smith, Rupert Cox, Jeff Hose, Adam Hose and Mark Brumer (Hermanus CC)
**Other sports followed:** Rugby, football, hockey and any sport on television
**Injuries:** Groin injury, missed one day
**Relaxations:** 'Music, socialising over a "quiet beer" at the local nitespot and watching Ventnor Youth 93 in Division 3 of the Sunday Football League.'
**Extras:** Represented England at U15, U17 and U19 level. Played for Isle of Wight at U16, U17, U21 and senior level in the same season. Spent two years (1991 and 1992) as MCC Young Professional. Hampshire Schools Wicketkeepers Award 1988. Andrew Swallow Memorial Cup 1987. Wight Waters Sports Award 1989-91

# GARNHAM, M. A.                    Essex

**Name:** Michael Anthony Garnham
**Role:** Right-hand bat, wicket-keeper
**Born:** 20 August 1960, Johannesburg
**Height:** 5ft 11in **Weight:** 12st
**Nickname:** Bones, Fred
**County debut:** 1979 (Gloucestershire),
1980 (Leicestershire), 1989 (Essex)
**County cap:** 1989 (Essex)
**1st-Class 50s:** 33
**1st-Class 100s:** 5
**1st-Class catches:** 429
**1st-Class stumpings:** 41
**One-Day 100s:** 1
**Parents:** Pauline Anne and Robert Arthur
**Wife and date of marriage:** Lorraine,
15 September 1984
**Children:** Laura Clare, 3 November 1988;
Eleanor Louise, 22 October 1990

**Family links with cricket:** Father was a club cricketer in Essex. He lost the sight of an eye keeping wicket
**Education:** Camberwell Grammar, Melbourne, Australia; Scotch College, Perth, Australia; Park School, Barnstaple, North Devon; North Devon College; University of East Anglia (for one year)
**Qualifications:** 10 O-levels, 2 A-levels
**Overseas tours:** English Schools to India 1977-78; England YC to Australia 1978-79
**Cricketers particularly admired:** Bob Taylor
**Other sports followed:** Squash
**Injuries:** Dislocated finger and 18-20 stitches in an eye injury but missed no cricket
**Relaxations:** Carpentry – furniture making, building and DIY
**Extras:** Moved to England in 1975 after living in South Africa for four years and in Australia for ten years. Played for Devon in 1976 and 1977 before joining Gloucestershire. Signed for Leicestershire in 1980 and was banned by the registration committee from competitive first-team cricket for a month for breach of registration regulations. Retired at end of 1985, but returned for one one-day and one three-day game in 1988 following injury to Phil Whitticase. Signed for Essex in 1989, having been playing for Cambridgeshire. 'Having run a business making 'keeping gloves, I wear gloves I have made myself.' Retired from first-class cricket at the end of the 1995 season
**Best batting:** 123 Essex v Leicestershire, Leicester 1991

| | M | Inns | NO | Runs | HS | Avge | 100s | 50s | Ct | St | O | M | Runs | Wkts | Avge | Best | 5wI | 10wM |
|---|---|---|---|---|---|---|---|---|---|---|---|---|---|---|---|---|---|---|
| Test | | | | | | | | | | | | | | | | | | |
| All First | 1 | 2 | 0 | 48 | 41 | 24.00 | - | - | 1 | - | | | | | | | | |
| 1-day Int | | | | | | | | | | | | | | | | | | |
| NatWest | | | | | | | | | | | | | | | | | | |
| B & H | 2 | 2 | 0 | 25 | 24 | 12.50 | - | - | - | - | | | | | | | | |
| Sunday | 1 | 1 | 0 | 0 | 0 | 0.00 | - | - | - | - | | | | | | | | |

**Career Performances**

| | M | Inns | NO | Runs | HS | Avge | 100s | 50s | Ct | St | Balls | | Runs | Wkts | Avge | Best | 5wI | 10wM |
|---|---|---|---|---|---|---|---|---|---|---|---|---|---|---|---|---|---|---|
| Test | | | | | | | | | | | | | | | | | | |
| All First | 207 | 282 | 55 | 6240 | 123 | 27.48 | 5 | 33 | 429 | 41 | 24 | | 39 | 0 | - | | - | - | - |
| 1-day Int | | | | | | | | | | | | | | | | | | |
| NatWest | 27 | 22 | 7 | 393 | 110 | 26.20 | 1 | 1 | 20 | 6 | | | | | | | | |
| B & H | 59 | 42 | 16 | 561 | 55 | 21.57 | - | 1 | 53 | 7 | | | | | | | | |
| Sunday | 164 | 123 | 28 | 1555 | 79 * | 16.36 | - | 1 | 140 | 23 | | | | | | | | |

# GATTING, M. W. Middlesex

**Name:** Michael William Gatting
**Role:** Right-hand bat, right-arm medium bowler, slip fielder
**Born:** 6 June 1957, Kingsbury, Middlesex
**Height:** 5ft 10in **Weight:** 15st
**Nickname:** Gatt, Jabba
**County debut:** 1975
**County cap:** 1977
**Benefit:** 1988 (£205,000)
**Test debut:** 1977-78
**Tests:** 79
**One-Day Internationals:** 92
**1000 runs in a season:** 17
**1st-Class 50s:** 162
**1st-Class 100s:** 89
**1st-Class 200s:** 9
**1st-Class 5 w. in innings:** 2
**1st-Class catches:** 441
**One-Day 100s:** 12
**Place in batting averages:** 16th av. 54.23 (1994 3rd av. 69.62)
**Strike rate:** (career 63.87)
**Parents:** Bill and Vera

**Wife and date of marriage:** Elaine, September 1980
**Children:** Andrew, 21 January 1983; James, 11 July 1986
**Family links with cricket:** Father used to play club cricket. Brother Steve played for Middlesex 2nd XI
**Education:** Wykeham Primary School; John Kelly Boys' High School
**Qualifications:** 4 O-levels
**Overseas tours:** England to New Zealand and Pakistan 1977-78, to West Indies 1980-81, to India and Sri Lanka 1981-82, to New Zealand and Pakistan 1983-84, to India 1984-85, to West Indies 1985-86, to Australia 1986-87, to India and Pakistan (World Cup), Australia and New Zealand 1987-88; unofficial English XI to South Africa 1989-90; England to India and Sri Lanka 1992-93, to Australia 1994-95
**Cricketers particularly admired:** Gary Sobers, Len Hutton
**Other sports followed:** Football, golf, tennis, swimming, indoor cricket, rugby
**Injuries:** Groin/thigh, out for 12 days
**Relaxations:** Golf, swimming, reading, music
**Extras:** Awarded OBE in Queen's Birthday Honours 1987 for services to cricket. Captain of Middlesex since 1983. Captain of England from 1986 to 1988. Published autobiography *Leading From the Front* in 1988. Won a bronze medal for ballroom dancing at the Neasden Ritz. Played football for Edgware Town as a teenager. Started as a goalkeeper, but also played centre-half for Middlesex Schools. Was recommended to West Ham, had a trial with QPR and offered an apprenticeship by Watford. His brother Steve has had a successful football career with Arsenal and Brighton. Mike started his cricket career as wicket-keeper for his school team. He toured West Indies with England Young Cricketers in 1976 and 'to my immense pleasure (and to most other people's total disbelief) I was given the job of opening the bowling in the "Test" matches.' One of *Wisden*'s Five Cricketers of the Year 1983. His finest achievement was as captain of England on victorious tour of Australia, 1986-87, when they won the Ashes, the Perth Challenge Cup and World Series Cup. Was relieved of England captaincy after the First Test against West Indies in 1988. Captain of unofficial English team in South Africa in 1989-90 and was banned from Test cricket for five years; suspension remitted in 1992. Captained Middlesex to Championship title in 1990 and 1993. Retired from Test cricket after the final Test of the 1994-95 series against Australia
**Opinions on cricket:** 'Four-day cricket has been an eye-opener.'
**Best batting:** 258 Middlesex v Somerset, Bath 1984
**Best bowling:** 5-34 Middlesex v Glamorgan, Swansea 1982

## 1995 Season

|  | M | Inns | NO | Runs | HS | Avge | 100s | 50s | Ct | St | O | M | Runs | Wkts | Avge | Best | 5wI | 10wM |
|---|---|---|---|---|---|---|---|---|---|---|---|---|---|---|---|---|---|---|
| Test |  |  |  |  |  |  |  |  |  |  |  |  |  |  |  |  |  |  |
| All First | 16 | 22 | 1 | 1139 | 148 | 54.23 | 5 | 3 | 13 | - | 5 | 0 | 31 | 0 | - | - | - | - |
| 1-day Int |  |  |  |  |  |  |  |  |  |  |  |  |  |  |  |  |  |  |  |
| NatWest | 2 | 2 | 0 | 42 | 40 | 21.00 | - | - | - | - |  |  |  |  |  |  |  |  |
| B & H | 6 | 6 | 1 | 198 | 93 * | 39.60 | - | 1 | - | - |  |  |  |  |  |  |  |  |
| Sunday | 10 | 9 | 0 | 298 | 68 | 33.11 | - | 3 | 4 | - | 9.4 | 0 | 53 | 4 | 13.25 | 4-44 | - |  |

## Career Performances

|          | M   | Inns | NO  | Runs  | HS    | Avge  | 100s | 50s | Ct  | St  | Balls | Runs | Wkts | Avge  | Best | 5wl | 10wM |
|----------|-----|------|-----|-------|-------|-------|------|-----|-----|-----|-------|------|------|-------|------|-----|------|
| Test     | 79  | 138  | 14  | 4409  | 207   | 35.55 | 10   | 21  | 59  | -   | 752   | 317  | 4    | 79.25 | 1-14 | -   | -    |
| All First| 499 | 778  | 118 | 33456 | 258   | 50.69 | 89   | 162 | 441 | -   | 9965  | 4623 | 156  | 29.63 | 5-34 | 2   | -    |
| 1-day Int| 92  | 88   | 17  | 2095  | 115 * | 29.50 | 1    | 9   | 22  | -   | 392   | 336  | 10   | 33.60 | 3-32 | -   |      |
| NatWest  | 59  | 57   | 13  | 2006  | 132 * | 45.59 | 2    | 14  | 24  | -   | 1004  | 643  | 19   | 33.84 | 2-14 | -   |      |
| B & H    | 87  | 81   | 18  | 2776  | 143 * | 44.06 | 3    | 18  | 24  | -   | 1382  | 940  | 41   | 22.92 | 4-49 | -   |      |
| Sunday   | 245 | 219  | 28  | 6132  | 124 * | 32.10 | 6    | 37  | 82  | -   | 3196  | 2730 | 90   | 30.33 | 4-30 | -   |      |

# GIBSON, O. D.          Glamorgan

**Name:** Ottis Delroy Gibson
**Role:** Right-hand bat, right-arm fast bowler
**Born:** 16 March 1969, St James, Barbados
**Height:** 6ft 2in **Weight:** 13st 3lb
**County debut:** 1994
**Test debut:** 1995
**Tests:** 1
**One-day Internationals:** 1
**50 wickets in a season:** 1
**1st-Class 50s:** 10
**1st-Class 100s:** 1
**1st-Class 5 w. in innings:** 8
**1st-Class 10 w. in match:** 2
**1st-Class catches:** 22
**Place in batting averages:** 149th av. 27.54
(1994 148th av. 26.29)
**Place in bowling averages:** 80th av. 31.36
(1994 101st av. 36.15)
**Strike rate:** 46.96 (career 50.56)
**Marital status:** Single
**Education:** St Silas Primary; Ellerslie Secondary
**Qualifications:** 3 O-levels
**Overseas tours:** West Indies to England 1995, to Australia 1995-96, to India and
Pakistan (World Cup) 1995-96
**Overseas teams played for:** Fremantle, Perth 1989-90; Spartan, Barbados and
Barbados 1991-94 ; Border, South Africa 1992-95
**Cricketers particularly admired:** Malcolm Marshall, Ian Botham, Viv Richards,
Brian Lara.
**Other sports followed:** All sports
**Extras:** Played for Farnworth in the Bolton League 1992 and 1993. South African Player
of the Year 1992-93. Has played for West Indies A. Reported to have hit a straight six 150
yards over the pavilion at Buffalo Park, East London (South Africa) and into a car park

**Best batting:** 101* West Indies v Somerset, Taunton 1995
**Best bowling:** 7-78 Barbados v Trinidad, Port of Spain 1991-92

## 1995 Season

| | M | Inns | NO | Runs | HS | Avge | 100s | 50s | Ct | St | O | M | Runs | Wkts | Avge | Best | 5wI | 10wM |
|---|---|---|---|---|---|---|---|---|---|---|---|---|---|---|---|---|---|---|
| Test | 1 | 2 | 0 | 43 | 29 | 21.50 | - | - | - | - | 34 | 3 | 132 | 2 | 66.00 | 2-81 | - | - |
| All First | 11 | 13 | 2 | 303 | 101 * | 27.54 | 1 | - | 5 | - | 242.4 | 36 | 966 | 31 | 31.16 | 4-32 | - | - |
| 1-day Int | 1 | 1 | 0 | 7 | 7 | 7.00 | - | - | - | - | 11 | 0 | 51 | 3 | 17.00 | 3-51 | - | |
| NatWest | | | | | | | | | | | | | | | | | | |
| B & H | | | | | | | | | | | | | | | | | | |
| Sunday | | | | | | | | | | | | | | | | | | |

## Career Performances

| | M | Inns | NO | Runs | HS | Avge | 100s | 50s | Ct | St | Balls | Runs | Wkts | Avge | Best | 5wI | 10wM |
|---|---|---|---|---|---|---|---|---|---|---|---|---|---|---|---|---|---|
| Test | 1 | 2 | 0 | 43 | 29 | 21.50 | - | - | - | - | 204 | 132 | 2 | 66.00 | 2-81 | - | - |
| All First | 63 | 89 | 13 | 1659 | 101 * | 21.82 | 1 | 10 | 22 | - | 11024 | 6423 | 218 | 29.46 | 7-78 | 8 | 2 |
| 1-day Int | 1 | 1 | 0 | 7 | 7 | 7.00 | - | - | - | - | 66 | 51 | 3 | 17.00 | 3-51 | - | |
| NatWest | 3 | 3 | 0 | 68 | 44 | 22.66 | - | - | 1 | - | 162 | 116 | 5 | 23.20 | 3-34 | - | |
| B & H | 1 | 1 | 0 | 37 | 37 | 37.00 | - | - | - | - | 52 | 50 | 2 | 25.00 | 2-50 | - | |
| Sunday | 17 | 15 | 7 | 206 | 33 | 25.75 | - | - | 4 | - | 557 | 446 | 12 | 37.16 | 2-35 | - | |

# GIDDINS, E. S. H.  Sussex

**Name:** Edward Simon Hunter Giddins
**Role:** Right-hand bat, right-arm
medium-fast bowler
**Born:** 20 July 1971, Eastbourne
**Height:** 6ft 4in **Weight:** 13st 7lb
**Nickname:** Geezer
**County debut:** 1991
**County cap:** 1994
**50 wickets in a season:** 2
**1st-Class 5 w. in innings:** 10
**1st-Class 10 w. in match:** 1
**1st-Class catches:** 12
**Place in bowling averages:** 67th av. 29.47
(1994 19th av. 24.38)
**Strike rate:** 53.44 (career 54.93)
**Parents:** Simon and Pauline
**Marital status:** Single
**Family links with cricket:** Great-
grandmother played cricket for England Ladies.

'Family members George and Misty have a fantastic eye for the ball'
**Education:** St Bede's Prep School; Eastbourne College
**Qualifications:** 'Various O and A-levels, national coaching certificate, recorder (grade 2), shorthand and typing 100/60.'
**Career outside cricket:** 'PR for executive search companies'
**Off-season:** England A tour to Pakistan
**Overseas tours:** Eastbourne College cricket/drama/debating tour to New Zealand 1988; England A to Pakistan 1995-96
**Overseas teams played for:** Discovery Bay Hotel, Barbados 1991; Bondi Surf, Sydney 1991-92; Bayswater Morley, Perth 1992
**Cricketers particularly admired:** Eddie Hemmings
**Other sports followed:** Brighton & Hove Albion, football; 'the sport in Browns Bar, Shoreditch'
**Relaxations:** *Neighbours*, *Home and Away*, Guinness
**Extras:** Took four wickets for no runs in ten balls against Derbyshire at Eastbourne in 1992. Sussex U23 Player of the Year 1992 and 1994. Nominated as one of England's three most eligible bachelors in *Company* magazine, March 1995
**Best batting:** 34 Sussex v Essex, Hove 1995
**Best bowling:** 6-73 Sussex v Somerset, Bath 1995

## 1995 Season

|            | M  | Inns | NO | Runs | HS  | Avge | 100s | 50s | Ct | St | O     | M   | Runs | Wkts | Avge  | Best | 5wI | 10wM |
|------------|----|------|----|------|-----|------|------|-----|----|----|-------|-----|------|------|-------|------|-----|------|
| Test       |    |      |    |      |     |      |      |     |    |    |       |     |      |      |       |      |     |      |
| All First  | 18 | 27   | 12 | 137  | 34  | 9.13 | -    | -   | 3  | -  | 605.4 | 110 | 2004 | 68   | 29.47 | 6-73 | 4   | 1    |
| 1-day Int  |    |      |    |      |     |      |      |     |    |    |       |     |      |      |       |      |     |      |
| NatWest    | 2  | 0    | 0  | 0    | 0   | -    | -    | -   | -  | -  | 21.5  | 1   | 90   | 1    | 90.00 | 1-49 | -   |      |
| B & H      | 4  | 1    | 1  | 0    | 0 * | -    | -    | -   | 1  | -  | 40    | 5   | 137  | 6    | 22.83 | 3-28 | -   |      |
| Sunday     | 16 | 7    | 2  | 2    | 1 * | 0.40 | -    | -   | -  | -  | 100.1 | 5   | 548  | 16   | 34.25 | 2-1  | -   |      |

## Career Performances

|            | M  | Inns | NO | Runs | HS  | Avge  | 100s | 50s | Ct | St | Balls | Runs | Wkts | Avge  | Best | 5wI | 10wM |
|------------|----|------|----|------|-----|-------|------|-----|----|----|-------|------|------|-------|------|-----|------|
| Test       |    |      |    |      |     |       |      |     |    |    |       |      |      |       |      |     |      |
| All First  | 63 | 77   | 31 | 261  | 34  | 5.67  | -    | -   | 12 | -  | 10437 | 6000 | 190  | 31.57 | 6-73 | 10  | 1    |
| 1-day Int  |    |      |    |      |     |       |      |     |    |    |       |      |      |       |      |     |      |
| NatWest    | 8  | 2    | 1  | 13   | 13  | 13.00 | -    | -   | -  | -  | 551   | 335  | 7    | 47.85 | 2-21 | -   |      |
| B & H      | 9  | 2    | 1  | 0    | 0 * | 0.00  | -    | -   | 2  | -  | 526   | 346  | 10   | 34.60 | 3-28 | -   |      |
| Sunday     | 56 | 25   | 10 | 22   | 9 * | 1.46  | -    | -   | 8  | -  | 2346  | 1987 | 66   | 30.10 | 4-23 | -   |      |

# GIE, N. A.        Nottinghamshire

**Name:** Noel Addison Gie
**Role:** Right-hand bat, right-arm medium bowler
**Born:** 12 April 1977, Pretoria, South Africa
**Height:** 6ft   **Weight:** 12st 8lbs
**County debut:** 1995
**Place in batting averages:** 238th av. 16.33
**Parents:** Clive and Lindy
**Marital status:** Single
**Family links with cricket:** Father played first-class cricket in South Africa for Western Province, Northern Transvaal and Natal
**Education:** Fornwood School, Nottingham; Trent College, Nottingham; Nottingham Trent University
**Qualificatons:** Studying for degree in Business Studies from October 1996, NCA coaching award

**Off-season:**
Touring Zimbabwe with England U19
**Overseas tours:** Trent College to Australia 1993-94; England U19 to Zimbabwe 1995-96
**Overseas teams played for:** Berea Rovers, Durban, South Africa 1995
**Cricketers particularly admired:** Robin Smith
**Other sports followed:** Squash, tennis, rugby league
**Relaxations:** Reading and cycling
**Extras:** Scored 3,153 runs for the Ist XI during his time at Trent College
**Opinions on cricket:** 'Counties need to be more competitive i.e. fewer in "top league" and fewer players on full-time staff.'
**Best batting:** 34 Nottinghamshire v Glamorgan, Cardiff 1995

## 1995 Season

|           | M | Inns | NO | Runs | HS | Avge  | 100s | 50s | Ct | St | O | M | Runs | Wkts | Avge | Best | 5wI | 10wM |
|-----------|---|------|----|------|----|-------|------|-----|----|----|---|---|------|------|------|------|-----|------|
| Test      |   |      |    |      |    |       |      |     |    |    |   |   |      |      |      |      |     |      |
| All First | 3 | 6    | 0  | 98   | 34 | 16.33 | -    | -   | -  | -  |   |   |      |      |      |      |     |      |
| 1-day Int |   |      |    |      |    |       |      |     |    |    |   |   |      |      |      |      |     |      |
| NatWest   |   |      |    |      |    |       |      |     |    |    |   |   |      |      |      |      |     |      |
| B & H     |   |      |    |      |    |       |      |     |    |    |   |   |      |      |      |      |     |      |
| Sunday    |   |      |    |      |    |       |      |     |    |    |   |   |      |      |      |      |     |      |

## Career Performances

| | M | Inns | NO | Runs | HS | Avge | 100s | 50s | Ct | St | Balls | Runs | Wkts | Avge | Best | 5wI | 10wM |
|---|---|---|---|---|---|---|---|---|---|---|---|---|---|---|---|---|---|
| Test | | | | | | | | | | | | | | | | | |
| All First | 3 | 6 | 0 | 98 | 34 | 16.33 | - | - | - | - | | | | | | | |
| 1-day Int | | | | | | | | | | | | | | | | | |
| NatWest | | | | | | | | | | | | | | | | | |
| B & H | | | | | | | | | | | | | | | | | |
| Sunday | | | | | | | | | | | | | | | | | |

# GILES, A. F.                    Warwickshire

**Name:** Ashley Fraser Giles
**Role:** Right-hand bat, slow left-arm bowler
**Born:** 19 March 1973, Chertsey, Surrey
**Height:** 6ft 4in **Weight:** 14st
**Nickname:** Splash, Skinny, Sumo
**County debut:** 1993
**1st-Class 5 w. innings:** 1
**Place in bowling averages:** 17th av. 22.12
**Strike rate:** 55.06 (career 59.47)
**Parents:** Michael and Paula
**Marital status:** 'Long-term girlfriend
Melanie'
**Family links with cricket:** Father, brother
and brother-in-law play and played a good
standard of club cricket
**Education:** George Abbot County Secondary,
Guildford
**Qualifications:** 9 GCSEs, 2 A-levels, NCA
coaching award
**Off-season:** Coaching and playing in Cape Town, South Africa
**Overseas tours:** Surrey U19 to Barbados 1990-91
**Overseas teams played for:** Vredenburg/Saldanha, South Africa 1992-94;
Warwickshire CCC to Cape Town 1993
**Cricketers particularly admired:** Ian Botham, Allan Donald, Dermot Reeve, 'my
girlfriend, Melanie'
**Other sports followed:** Football (QPR), golf, basketball
**Relaxations:** Golf, spending evenings in with Melanie, films
**Extras:** Surrey Young Cricketer Player of the Year 1991, MCC School of Merit most
improved player
**Opinions on cricket:** 'Great game. Four-day cricket sorts out the good sides from the
poor sides which is great for competitive cricket.'

**Best batting:** 32 Warwickshire v Hampshire, Southampton 1995
**Best bowling:** 5-23 Warwickshire v Worcestershire, Edgbaston 1995

## 1995 Season

|          | M | Inns | NO | Runs | HS | Avge | 100s | 50s | Ct | St | O | M | Runs | Wkts | Avge | Best | 5wI | 10wM |
|----------|---|------|----|------|----|------|------|-----|----|----|---|---|------|------|------|------|-----|------|
| Test     |   |      |    |      |    |      |      |     |    |    |   |   |      |      |      |      |     |      |
| All First | 6 | 5 | 0 | 84 | 32 | 16.80 | - | - | - | - | 146.5 | 46 | 354 | 16 | 22.12 | 5-23 | 1 | - |
| 1-day Int |   |      |    |      |    |      |      |     |    |    |   |   |      |      |      |      |     |      |
| NatWest  | 2 | 1 | 1 | 21 | 21 * | - | - | - | - | - | 15 | 3 | 39 | 3 | 13.00 | 3-14 | - |   |
| B & H    |   |      |    |      |    |      |      |     |    |    |   |   |      |      |      |      |     |      |
| Sunday   | 3 | 0 | 0 | 0 | 0 | - | - | - | 2 | - |   |   |      |      |      |      |     |      |

## Career Performances

|          | M | Inns | NO | Runs | HS | Avge | 100s | 50s | Ct | St | Balls | Runs | Wkts | Avge | Best | 5wI | 10wM |
|----------|---|------|----|------|----|------|------|-----|----|----|-------|------|------|------|------|-----|------|
| Test     |   |      |    |      |    |      |      |     |    |    |       |      |      |      |      |     |      |
| All First | 8 | 9 | 1 | 137 | 32 | 17.12 | - | - | - | - | 1130 | 482 | 19 | 25.36 | 5-23 | 1 | - |
| 1-day Int |   |      |    |      |    |      |      |     |    |    |       |      |      |      |      |     |      |
| NatWest  | 2 | 1 | 1 | 21 | 21 * | - | - | - | - | - | 90 | 39 | 3 | 13.00 | 3-14 | - |   |
| B & H    |   |      |    |      |    |      |      |     |    |    |       |      |      |      |      |     |      |
| Sunday   | 3 | 0 | 0 | 0 | 0 | - | - | - | 2 | - |       |      |      |      |      |     |      |

# GOOCH, G. A.        Essex

**Name:** Graham Alan Gooch
**Role:** Right-hand bat, right-arm medium bowler
**Born:** 23 July 1953, Leytonstone
**Height:** 6ft **Weight:** 13st
**Nickname:** Zap, Goochie
**County debut:** 1973
**County cap:** 1975
**Benefit:** 1985 (£153,906)
**Testimonial:** 1995
**Test debut:** 1975
**Tests:** 118
**One-Day Internationals:** 125
**1000 runs in a season:** 19
**1st-Class 100s:** 120
**1st-Class 200s:** 11
**1st-Class 5 w. in innings:** 3
**1st-Class catches:** 525
**One-Day 100s:** 40

**One-day 5 w. innings:** 1
**Place in batting averages:** 24th av. 50.27 (1994 4th av. 64.70)
**Strike rate:** (career 76.42)
**Parents:** Alfred and Rose
**Wife and date of marriage:** Brenda, 23 October 1976
**Children:** Hannah; Megan and Sally (twins)
**Family links with cricket:** Father played local cricket for East Ham Corinthians. Second cousin, Graham Saville, played for Essex CCC and is now England U19 team manager
**Education:** Cannhall School and Norlington Junior High School, Leytonstone; Redbridge Technical College
**Qualifications:** 6 CSEs; four-year apprenticeship in tool-making
**Overseas tours:** England YC to West Indies 1971-72; England to Australia 1978-79, to Australia and India 1979-80, to West Indies 1980-81, to India and Sri Lanka 1981-82, to World Cup and Pakistan 1987-88, to India and West Indies 1989-90, to Australia 1990-91, to New Zealand 1991-92, to Australia (World Cup) 1991-92, to India 1992-93, to Australia 1994-95; unofficial English XI to South Africa 1981-82
**Overseas teams played for:** Western Province, South Africa 1982-84
**Cricketers particularly admired:** Bob Taylor, a model sportsman; Mike Procter for his enthusiasm; Barry Richards for his ability
**Other sports followed:** Squash, soccer, golf. Has trained with West Ham United FC
**Relaxations:** 'Relaxing at home'
**Extras:** One of *Wisden*'s Five Cricketers of the Year 1979. Captained English rebel team in South Africa in 1982 and was banned from Test cricket for three years. Hit a hole in one at Tollygunge Golf Club during England's tour in India, 1981-82. Appointed Essex captain 1986, but resigned captaincy at end of 1987, being reappointed in 1989 following retirement of Keith Fletcher. Captain of England for last two Tests of 1988 season against West Indies and Sri Lanka in 1988 and chosen to captain England on the cancelled tour of India in 1988-89. Reappointed captain for the tour to India and West Indies in 1989-90, and led England to their first Test victory over West Indies for 16 years. His 333 in the Lord's Test v India was the third highest score ever by an England batsman in a Test match, and by hitting 123 in the second innings he created a record Test aggregate of 456 runs and became the first man to hit a triple century and a century in the same first-class match. His aggregate for the season (2746 runs at 101.70 ) was the best since 1961 and he was only the fourth batsman to finish an English season with an average better than 100. When he first joined Essex, he was a wicket-keeper and batted at No 11 in his first match. He went on a Young England tour to the West Indies as second wicket-keeper to Andy Stovold of Gloucestershire. Autobiography *Out of the Wilderness* published in 1988; *Test of Fire,* an account of the West Indies tour, published in 1990; *Captaincy* published in 1992. Scored his 100th century in 1993. Resigned as England captain after Australia had retained the Ashes in 1993. Became the 15th player to pass 40,000 runs in first-class cricket. Resigned as Essex captain at end of 1994 season. Retired from Test cricket after final Test of 1994-95 series against Australia. *Graham Gooch: My Autobiography* written with Frank Keating was published in 1995

**Best batting:** 333 England v India, Lord's 1990
**Best bowling:** 7-14 Essex v Worcestershire, Ilford 1982

## 1995 Season

|  | M | Inns | NO | Runs | HS | Avge | 100s | 50s | Ct | St | O | M | Runs | Wkts | Avge | Best | 5wI | 10wM |
|---|---|---|---|---|---|---|---|---|---|---|---|---|---|---|---|---|---|---|
| Test |  |  |  |  |  |  |  |  |  |  |  |  |  |  |  |  |  |  |
| All First | 18 | 34 | 1 | 1669 | 165 | 50.57 | 7 | 6 | 12 | - | 29.4 | 4 | 112 | 6 | 18.66 | 2-15 | - | - |
| 1-day Int |  |  |  |  |  |  |  |  |  |  |  |  |  |  |  |  |  |  |
| NatWest | 2 | 2 | 0 | 34 | 17 | 17.00 | - | - | 1 | - | 2.4 | 0 | 8 | 5 | 1.60 | 5-8 | 1 |  |
| B & H | 5 | 5 | 2 | 327 | 117 * | 109.00 | 2 | 1 | 1 | - | 21.3 | 1 | 77 | 0 | - |  | - | - |
| Sunday | 17 | 17 | 2 | 453 | 65 | 30.20 | - | 5 | 5 | - | 17 | 0 | 101 | 4 | 25.25 | 2-27 | - |  |

## Career Performances

|  | M | Inns | NO | Runs | HS | Avge | 100s | 50s | Ct | St | Balls | Runs | Wkts | Avge | Best | 5wI | 10wM |
|---|---|---|---|---|---|---|---|---|---|---|---|---|---|---|---|---|---|
| Test | 118 | 215 | 6 | 8900 | 333 | 42.58 | 20 | 46 | 103 | - | 2655 | 1069 | 23 | 46.47 | 3-39 | - | - |
| All First | 553 | 941 | 73 | 42528 | 333 | 48.99 | 120 | 209 | 525 | - | 18647 | 8397 | 244 | 34.41 | 7-14 | 3 | - |
| 1-day Int | 125 | 122 | 6 | 4290 | 142 | 36.98 | 8 | 23 | 45 | - | 2066 | 1516 | 36 | 42.11 | 3-19 | - |  |
| NatWest | 52 | 51 | 4 | 2417 | 144 | 51.42 | 6 | 15 | 25 | - | 1655 | 855 | 33 | 25.90 | 5-8 | 1 |  |
| B & H | 106 | 105 | 13 | 4934 | 198 * | 53.63 | 14 | 30 | 63 | - | 3770 | 2195 | 69 | 31.81 | 3-24 | - |  |
| Sunday | 266 | 261 | 23 | 8359 | 176 | 35.12 | 12 | 57 | 96 | - | 2576 | 4244 | 143 | 29.67 | 4-33 | - |  |

# GOODCHILD, D. J. Middlesex

**Name:** David John Goodchild
**Role:** Right-hand bat, right-arm
medium bowler
**Born:** 17 September 1976, Harrow
**Height:** 6ft 3in **Weight:** 14st 7lbs
**County debut:** No first-team appearance
**Nickname:** Golden, G, Goody
**Parents:** John and Brenda
**Marital status:** Single
**Family links with cricket:**
Father played club cricket
**Education:** Vaughan First and Middle
School; Whitmore High School; Weald
College; North London University
**Qualifications:** 9 GCSEs, 3 A-levels and
NCA coaching award
**Off-season:** At university
**Cricketers particularly admired:**
Graham Gooch, Mike Gatting

**Other sports followed:** Football (Arsenal), basketball, badminton, fishing
**Injuries:** Broken finger, out for one week
**Relaxations:** Fishing, socialising, going to the cinema, bowling alley with friends, golf
**Extras:** Awarded junior county cap when only 12, the youngest ever. Holds the record for the U11 top score and most runs in a season (153 and 563). Awarded young cricketer cap when 17
**Opinions on cricket:** 'I am pleased to find young players given the opportunity to play first-class matches – it looks good for English cricket in the future.'

---

# GOODWIN, G. J. A. Essex

**Name:** Giles Jeremy Anthony Goodwin
**Role:** Right-hand bat, left-arm bowler
**Born:** 16 September 1976, Isle of Sheppey
**Height:** 6ft 3in **Weight:** 13st
**Nickname:** Jazza
**County debut:** No first-team appearance
**Parents:** Keith and Susan
**Marital status:** Single
**Education:** Felsted School; UMIST
**Qualifications:** 10 GCSEs, 3 A-levels
**Off-season:** School tour to Australia and travelling
**Cricketers particularly admired:** Phil Tufnell
**Other sports followed**: Rugby (Leicester RFC)
**Relaxations:** Playing golf, travelling, socialising

**Extras:** Five seasons in Felsted 1st XI. Played England Schools U19, HMC Schools U19 and NCA XI
**Opinions on cricket:** 'A better set-up for youngsters i.e. too many representative sides.'

# GOUGH, D. Yorkshire

**Name:** Darren Gough
**Role:** Right-hand bat, right-arm fast bowler
**Born:** 18 September 1970, Barnsley
**Height:** 5ft 11in **Weight:** 12st 12lbs
**Nickname:** Dazzler
**County debut:** 1989
**County cap:** 1993
**Test debut:** 1994
**Tests:** 10
**One-Day Internationals:** 10
**50 wickets in a season:** 2
**1st-Class 50s:** 5
**1st-Class 5 w. in innings:** 11
**1st-Class 10 w. in innings:** 2
**1st-Class catches:** 24
**One-day 5 w. innings:** 2
**Place in batting averages:** 219th av. 18.44
(1994 186th av. 22.18)
**Place in bowling averages:** 43rd av. 26.76 (1994 21st av. 24.61)
**Strike rate:** 48.80 (career 54.61)
**Parents:** Trevor and Christine
**Wife and date of marriage:** Anna, 16 October 1993
**Children:** Liam James, 24 November 1994
**Education:** St Helens Junior; Priory Comprehensive; Airedale and Wharfdale College
(part-time)
**Qualifications:** 2 O-levels, 5 CSEs, BTEC Leisure, distinction coaching award 1
**Off-season:** 'Touring South Africa with England and hopefully the World Cup in India
and Pakistan'
**Overseas tours:** England YC to Australia 1989-90; Yorkshire to Barbados 1989-90, to
South Africa 1991-92 and 1992-93; England A to South Africa 1993-94; England to
Australia 1994-95, to South Africa 1995-96, to India and Pakistan (World Cup) 1995-96
**Overseas teams played for:** East Shirley, Christchurch, New Zealand 1991-92
**Cricketers particularly admired:** Ian Botham, Richard Hadlee, Malcolm Marshall and
Martin Crowe
**Other sports followed:** Football (Tottenham Hotspur) and golf
**Injuries:** Fractured foot and stress fracture of the same foot, out for 18 weeks
**Relaxations:** Spending time with wife, son, and dog, watching videos, eating Mexican food
**Extras:** England Cornhill Player of the Year 1994. Yorkshire Sports Personality of the
Year 1994. Took a hat-trick against Kent in 1995. Named Player of the Year by Cornhill
Insurance for 1995 season. He was locked up in prison for a day for charity
**Opinions on cricket:** 'Too many bad ones are starting to write. Read my book for young
cricketers to find out'

**Best batting:** 72 Yorkshire v Northamptonshire, Northampton 1991
**Best bowling:** 7-28 Yorkshire v Lancashire, Headingley 1995

## 1995 Season

| | M | Inns | NO | Runs | HS | Avge | 100s | 50s | Ct | St | O | M | Runs | Wkts | Avge | Best | 5wI | 10wM |
|---|---|---|---|---|---|---|---|---|---|---|---|---|---|---|---|---|---|---|
| Test | 3 | 6 | 0 | 73 | 29 | 12.16 | - | - | 2 | - | 70 | 6 | 255 | 6 | 42.50 | 3-79 | - | |
| All First | 14 | 19 | 1 | 332 | 60 | 18.44 | - | 1 | 6 | - | 414.5 | 89 | 1365 | 51 | 26.76 | 7-28 | 1 | 1 |
| 1-day Int | 3 | 3 | 1 | 19 | 8 * | 9.50 | - | - | 1 | - | 32 | 1 | 123 | 5 | 24.60 | 2-30 | - | |
| NatWest | 4 | 3 | 0 | 65 | 33 | 21.66 | - | - | - | - | 39 | 5 | 130 | 3 | 43.33 | 1-18 | - | |
| B & H | 4 | 2 | 0 | 17 | 14 | 8.50 | - | - | - | - | 39 | 7 | 120 | 5 | 24.00 | 2-21 | - | |
| Sunday | 10 | 7 | 0 | 76 | 30 | 10.85 | - | - | 2 | - | 65.4 | 3 | 292 | 11 | 26.54 | 4-35 | - | |

## Career Performances

| | M | Inns | NO | Runs | HS | Avge | 100s | 50s | Ct | St | Balls | Runs | Wkts | Avge | Best | 5wI | 10wM |
|---|---|---|---|---|---|---|---|---|---|---|---|---|---|---|---|---|---|
| Test | 10 | 16 | 3 | 317 | 65 | 24.38 | - | 2 | 6 | - | 2359 | 1246 | 43 | 28.97 | 6-49 | 1 | - |
| All First | 95 | 125 | 26 | 1674 | 72 | 16.90 | - | 6 | 24 | - | 16383 | 8856 | 300 | 29.52 | 7-28 | 11 | 2 |
| 1-day Int | 10 | 7 | 2 | 78 | 45 | 15.60 | - | - | 2 | - | 556 | 350 | 17 | 20.58 | 5-44 | 1 | |
| NatWest | 14 | 8 | 0 | 91 | 33 | 11.37 | - | - | 1 | - | 880 | 503 | 20 | 25.15 | 3-31 | - | |
| B & H | 12 | 7 | 1 | 37 | 14 | 6.16 | - | - | - | - | 636 | 373 | 14 | 26.64 | 2-21 | - | |
| Sunday | 64 | 39 | 10 | 350 | 72 * | 12.06 | - | 1 | 13 | - | 2733 | 2007 | 71 | 28.26 | 5-13 | 1 | |

# GRAYSON, A. P. Essex

**Name:** Adrian Paul Grayson
**Role:** Right-hand bat, slow left-arm bowler, slip fielder
**Born:** 31 March 1971, Ripon
**Height:** 6ft 2in **Weight:** 12st 2lb
**Nickname:** PG, Laz, Ravi
**County debut:** 1990
**1000 runs in a season:** 1
**1st-Class 50s:** 12
**1st-Class 100s:** 1
**1st-Class catches:** 36
**Place in batting averages:**
222nd av. 18.07 (1994 64th av. 38.74)
**Strike rate:** (career 138.69)
**Parents:** Adrian and Carol
**Wife and date of marriage:** Alison, 30 September 1994
**Family links with cricket:**
'Dad played good league cricket and is also an NCA staff

coach; brother also plays when free from football commitments'

**Education:** Bedale Comprehensive School

**Qualifications:** 8 CSEs, BTEC in Leisure, NCA Senior Coaching Award

**Off-season:** Playing in Wellington, New Zealand

**Overseas tours:** England YC to Australia 1989-90; Yorkshire to Barbados 1989-90, to Cape Town 1991-92, to Cape Town 1992-93, to Leeward Islands 1993-94, to Cape Town 1994-95

**Overseas teams played for:** Petone, Wellington 1991-92 and 1995-96

**Cricketers particularly admired:** Graham Gooch, Martyn Moxon, Darren Gough, Mark Ramprakash

**Other sports followed:** Any sport on television, football (Leeds United and Leicester City 'brother plays for them')

**Relaxations:** Playing golf, eating out

**Extras:** Played for England YC v New Zealand 1989 and Pakistan 1990. Brother plays football for Leicester City. Scored 1000 runs for first time this season (1994). Yorkshire Player of the Year 1994. Released by Yorkshire at end of 1995 but has joined Essex for 1996 season

**Opinions on cricket:** 'Players should be allowed to move to another county during the season as footballers do. More cricket should be played in schools. The reverse sweep should be banned.'

**Best batting:** 100 Yorkshire v Worcestershire, Worcester 1994

**Best bowling:** 2-5 Yorkshire v Cambridge University, Fenner's 1995

## 1995 Season

|          | M  | Inns | NO | Runs | HS   | Avge  | 100s | 50s | Ct | St | O  | M  | Runs | Wkts | Avge  | Best | 5wI | 10wM |
|----------|----|------|----|------|------|-------|------|-----|----|----|----|----|------|------|-------|------|-----|------|
| Test     |    |      |    |      |      |       |      |     |    |    |    |    |      |      |       |      |     |      |
| All First| 9  | 14   | 1  | 235  | 73   | 18.07 | -    | 2   | 4  | -  | 32 | 13 | 80   | 2    | 40.00 | 2-5  | -   | -    |
| 1-day Int|    |      |    |      |      |       |      |     |    |    |    |    |      |      |       |      |     |      |
| NatWest  | 3  | 2    | 0  | 27   | 20   | 13.50 | -    | -   | 2  | -  | 32 | 1  | 160  | 2    | 80.00 | 1-36 | -   |      |
| B & H    | 4  | 2    | 0  | 32   | 18   | 16.00 | -    | -   | 2  | -  | 10 | 0  | 56   | 2    | 28.00 | 2-36 | -   |      |
| Sunday   | 14 | 10   | 2  | 87   | 33 * | 10.87 | -    | -   | 3  | -  | 68 | 2  | 329  | 11   | 29.90 | 2-9  | -   |      |

## Career Performances

|          | M  | Inns | NO | Runs | HS   | Avge  | 100s | 50s | Ct | St | Balls | Runs | Wkts | Avge  | Best | 5wI | 10wM |
|----------|----|------|----|------|------|-------|------|-----|----|----|-------|------|------|-------|------|-----|------|
| Test     |    |      |    |      |      |       |      |     |    |    |       |      |      |       |      |     |      |
| All First| 52 | 80   | 10 | 1958 | 100  | 27.97 | 1    | 12  | 36 | -  | 1803  | 846  | 13   | 65.07 | 2-5  | •   | -    |
| 1-day Int|    |      |    |      |      |       |      |     |    |    |       |      |      |       |      |     |      |
| NatWest  | 7  | 6    | 0  | 91   | 29   | 15.16 | -    | -   | 3  | -  | 306   | 241  | 4    | 60.25 | 1-25 | -   |      |
| B & H    | 9  | 7    | 1  | 117  | 22 * | 19.50 | -    | -   | 2  | -  | 162   | 118  | 3    | 39.33 | 2-36 | -   |      |
| Sunday   | 49 | 35   | 6  | 367  | 55   | 12.65 | -    | 1   | 14 | -  | 1242  | 1051 | 31   | 33.90 | 4-25 | -   |      |

# GREEN, R. J. Lancashire

**Name:** Richard James Green
**Role:** Right-hand bat
**Born:** 13 March 1976, Warrington, Cheshire
**Height:** 6ft **Weight:** 12st 5lbs
**County debut:** 1995
**Parents:** Jim and Christina
**Marital status:** Single
**Family links with cricket:** Grandfather and
father both played
**Education:** Bridgewater County High
School, Warrington; Hartford College
**Qualifications:** 5 GCSEs, BTEC National
Business and Finance
**Off-season:** Coaching and training
**Overseas teams played for:** Pro Waratah,
Newcastle, NSW 1994-95

**Cricketers particularly admired:** David
Gower, Warren Hegg and Lee Marland ('first
Chinese cricketer to play for Lancashire CCC')
**Other sports followed:** Rugby league (Warrington)
**Injuries:** Broken thumb, out for pre-season
**Relaxations:** Driving fast cars and listening to music
**Extras:** Cheshire County League's youngest century-maker. Played for England U17
and England U19. Professional for Elland CC
**Opinions on cricket:** 'Tea break is far too short. Should be three two-hour sessions'
**Best batting:** 1 Lancashire v Surrey, The Oval 1995
**Best bowling:** 2-40 Lancashire v Surrey, The Oval 1995

## 1995 Season

| | M | Inns | NO | Runs | HS | Avge | 100s | 50s | Ct | St | O | M | Runs | Wkts | Avge | Best | 5wI | 10wM |
|---|---|---|---|---|---|---|---|---|---|---|---|---|---|---|---|---|---|---|
| Test | | | | | | | | | | | | | | | | | | |
| All First | 1 | 1 | 0 | 1 | 1 | 1.00 | - | - | - | - | 20 | 2 | 87 | 3 | 29.00 | 2-40 | - | - |
| 1-day Int | | | | | | | | | | | | | | | | | | |
| NatWest | | | | | | | | | | | | | | | | | | |
| B & H | | | | | | | | | | | | | | | | | | |
| Sunday | 2 | 0 | 0 | 0 | 0 | - | - | - | - | - | 13 | 0 | 62 | 3 | 20.66 | 3-38 | - | |

## Career Performances

| | M | Inns | NO | Runs | HS | Avge | 100s | 50s | Ct | St | Balls | Runs | Wkts | Avge | Best | 5wI | 10wM |
|---|---|---|---|---|---|---|---|---|---|---|---|---|---|---|---|---|---|
| Test | | | | | | | | | | | | | | | | | |
| All First | 1 | 1 | 0 | 1 | 1 | 1.00 | - | - | - | - | 120 | 87 | 3 | 29.00 | 2-40 | - | - |
| 1-day Int | | | | | | | | | | | | | | | | | |
| NatWest | | | | | | | | | | | | | | | | | |
| B & H | | | | | | | | | | | | | | | | | |
| Sunday | 2 | 0 | 0 | 0 | 0 | - | - | - | - | - | 78 | 62 | 3 | 20.66 | 3-38 | - | |

# GREENFIELD, K. Sussex

**Name:** Keith Greenfield
**Role:** Right-hand bat, right-arm off-spin bowler
**Born:** 6 December 1968, Brighton
**Height:** 6ft **Weight:** 12st 12lbs
**Nickname:** Grubby, G-Man
**County debut:** 1987
**1st-Class 50s:** 10
**1st-Class 100s:** 5
**1st-Class catches:** 43
**One-Day 100s:** 1
**Place in batting averages:** 151st av. 27.51
**Strike rate:** (career 123.20)
**Parents:** Leslie Ernest and Sheila
**Wife and date of marriage:**
Caroline Susannah, 22 February 1992
**Family links with cricket:** Father keen spectator, father-in-law played club cricket for 20 years and now umpires

**Education:** Coldean First and Middle Schools; Falmer High School
**Qualifications:** 3 O-levels, BTEC National Diploma in Leisure and Management, junior, senior and advanced coaching certificates
**Career outside cricket:** Cricket coach
**Off-season:** Coaching at Hove for Sussex
**Overseas tours:** Sussex U16 to Guernsey 1985; Select XI to Malaga 1993; Sussex to Malaga 1993-94; David Smith Testimonial XI to Malaga 1994; MCC Tour to SE Asia and Far East 1994-95
**Overseas teams played for:** Cornwall, Auckland 1988-90
**Cricketers particularly admired:** Derek Randall, Ian Botham, Chris Tugwell and Malcolm Eldridge (St Peters) and Ray Bierber (Brighton & Hove)
**Other sports followed:** 'All sports interest me', Liverpool FC

**Relaxations:** 'Eating out with friends, music (Dire Straits, UB40), spending time with Caz and decorating new house'

**Extras:** First person taken on Youth Training Scheme to become a professional cricketer at Sussex. Only uncapped player to have captained Sussex at Hove (v Cambridge U), scored century in this game. Captained 2nd XI to Championship title in 1990. Sussex Team Man of the Year 1990, 1993

**Opinions on cricket:** 'Cricket maufacturers should invest more time and money into the design of batting gloves to stop so many breaks. The batting gloves around at the moment are not good enough.'

**Best batting:** 127* Sussex v Cambridge University, Hove 1991

**Best bowling:** 2-40 Sussex v Essex, Hove 1993

## 1995 Season

|  | M | Inns | NO | Runs | HS | Avge | 100s | 50s | Ct | St | O | M | Runs | Wkts | Avge | Best | 5wI | 10wM |
|---|---|---|---|---|---|---|---|---|---|---|---|---|---|---|---|---|---|---|
| Test |  |  |  |  |  |  |  |  |  |  |  |  |  |  |  |  |  |  |
| All First | 19 | 32 | 1 | 853 | 121 | 27.51 | 1 | 5 | 11 | - | 21.1 | 1 | 82 | 0 | - |  | - | -- |
| 1-day Int |  |  |  |  |  |  |  |  |  |  |  |  |  |  |  |  |  |  |
| NatWest | 2 | 2 | 0 | 42 | 40 | 21.00 | - | - | - | - | 2 | 0 | 13 | 0 | - |  | - | - |
| B & H | 4 | 3 | 0 | 43 | 21 | 14.33 | - | - | 1 | - | 29 | 0 | 138 | 0 | - |  | - | - |
| Sunday | 17 | 17 | 0 | 488 | 102 | 28.70 | 1 | 2 | 9 | - | 28.4 | 0 | 146 | 7 | 20.85 | 3-34 | - |  |

## Career Performances

|  | M | Inns | NO | Runs | HS | Avge | 100s | 50s | Ct | St | Balls | Runs | Wkts | Avge | Best | 5wI | 10wM |
|---|---|---|---|---|---|---|---|---|---|---|---|---|---|---|---|---|---|
| Test |  |  |  |  |  |  |  |  |  |  |  |  |  |  |  |  |  |
| All First | 53 | 88 | 11 | 2262 | 127 * | 29.37 | 5 | 10 | 43 | - | 616 | 427 | 5 | 85.40 | 2-40 | - | - |
| 1-day Int |  |  |  |  |  |  |  |  |  |  |  |  |  |  |  |  |  |
| NatWest | 8 | 7 | 2 | 166 | 96 * | 33.20 | - | 1 | 2 | - | 258 | 159 | 3 | 53.00 | 2-35 | - |  |
| B & H | 14 | 13 | 1 | 306 | 62 | 25.50 | - | 2 | 6 | - | 354 | 279 | 1 | 279.00 | 1-35 | - |  |
| Sunday | 80 | 78 | 7 | 1865 | 102 | 26.26 | 1 | 10 | 26 | - | 796 | 797 | 16 | 49.81 | 3-34 | - |  |

# GRIFFITH, F. A. Derbyshire

**Name:** Frank Alexander Griffith
**Role:** Right-hand bat, right-arm medium bowler
**Born:** 15 August 1968, Leyton
**Height:** 6ft **Weight:** 12st
**Nickname:** Sir Learie
**County debut:** 1988
**1st-Class 50s:** 4
**1st-Class catches:** 28
**Place in batting averages:** 156th av. 26.66
**Place in bowling averages:** 104th av. 36.11
**Strike rate:** 67.29 (career 60.38)
**Parents:** Alex and Daisy
**Marital status:** Single
**Education:** William Morris High School, Walthamstow
**Qualifications:** Food and Nutrition and Art O-levels; NCA coaching certificate
**Cricketers particularly admired:** Collis King, Franklyn Stephenson
**Other sports followed:** Table tennis, basketball, football
**Relaxations:** Listening to music
**Extras:** Attended Haringey Cricket College
**Best batting:** 81 Derbyshire v Glamorgan, Chesterfield 1992
**Best bowling:** 4-33 Derbyshire v Leicestershire, Ilkeston 1992

## 1995 Season

|  | M | Inns | NO | Runs | HS | Avge | 100s | 50s | Ct | St | O | M | Runs | Wkts | Avge | Best | 5wI | 10wM |
|---|---|---|---|---|---|---|---|---|---|---|---|---|---|---|---|---|---|---|
| Test |  |  |  |  |  |  |  |  |  |  |  |  |  |  |  |  |  |  |
| All First | 8 | 13 | 4 | 240 | 53 | 26.66 | - | 1 | 10 | - | 190.4 | 42 | 614 | 17 | 36.11 | 4-89 | - | - |
| 1-day Int |  |  |  |  |  |  |  |  |  |  |  |  |  |  |  |  |  |  |
| NatWest | 2 | 0 | 0 | 0 | 0 | - | - | - | 2 | - | 15 | 3 | 58 | 1 | 58.00 | 1-33 | - |  |
| B & H |  |  |  |  |  |  |  |  |  |  |  |  |  |  |  |  |  |  |  |
| Sunday | 10 | 5 | 1 | 23 | 12 | 5.75 | - | - | 3 | - | 60 | 3 | 316 | 12 | 26.33 | 4-56 |  |  |

30. Who was captain of the England Women's team in 1995?

## Career Performances

|       | M  | Inns | NO | Runs | HS  | Avge  | 100s | 50s | Ct | St | Balls | Runs | Wkts | Avge  | Best | 5wI | 10wM |
|-------|----|------|----|------|-----|-------|------|-----|----|----|-------|------|------|-------|------|-----|------|
| Test  |    |      |    |      |     |       |      |     |    |    |       |      |      |       |      |     |      |
| All First | 42 | 63 | 9  | 1087 | 81  | 20.12 | -    | 4   | 28 | -  | 4348  | 2434 | 72   | 33.80 | 4-33 | -   | -    |
| 1-day Int |    |      |    |      |     |       |      |     |    |    |       |      |      |       |      |     |      |
| NatWest | 7 | 4  | 0  | 16   | 8   | 4.00  | -    | -   | 4  | -  | 314   | 190  | 5    | 38.00 | 1-13 | -   |      |
| B & H | 6  | 5    | 1  | 35   | 13* | 8.75  | -    | -   | 3  | -  | 254   | 211  | 7    | 30.14 | 2-48 | -   |      |
| Sunday | 44 | 31  | 5  | 261  | 31  | 10.03 | -    | -   | 8  | -  | 1675  | 1486 | 47   | 31.61 | 4-48 | -   |      |

# GRIFFITHS, S. P. Derbyshire

**Name:** Stephen Paul Griffiths
**Role:** Right-hand bat, wicket-keeper,
**Born:** 31 March 1973, Hereford
**Height:** 5ft 11in **Weight:** 11st 7lbs
**Nickname:** Griff
**County debut:** 1995
**1st-Class catches:** 14
**Parents:** Paul and Lesley
**Marital status:** Single
**Family links with cricket:** 'Father has
played a good
standard of club cricket for years'
**Education:** Bathford Primary School;
Beechen Cliff School, Bath;
Brunel College of Art and Technology
**Qualifications:** 7 GCSEs, basic coaching award
**Career outside cricket:** Studying antique
furniture restoration and conservation
**Off-season:** 'Studying at Brunel College of Art and Technology and keeping fit'
**Overseas tours:** Bath Schools to Zimbabwe and Kenya 1989
**Overseas teams played for:** C.B.C Old Boys, Bloemfontein, South Africa 1992-93
**Cricketers particularly admired:** Jack Russell, Bob Taylor, Alan Knott,
Doug C. Storey, Gregg Brown
**Other sports followed:** Rugby (Bath RFC) and golf
**Injuries:** Sore hands ('hazard of the job'), out for one week
**Relaxations:** 'Music (listening to and collecting blues, jazz, reggae, Irish, Motown),
roaming through flea markets, reading, going to pubs in Bath with friends, spending
time with girlfriend Ceri, eating foreign food and doing up old furniture'
**Extras:** Took six catches on first-class debut against Worcestershire in 1995 (five of
them in the first innings). Played for Somerset 2nd XI before joining Derbyshire.
Member of Bath CC and Buccaneers CC

**Opinions on cricket:** 'It is far too easy for young cricketers to slip through the net. The standard of coaching in many schools is very poor and luck plays a big part in being spotted.'

**Best batting:** 20 Derbyshire v Surrey, Derby 1995

## 1995 Season

| | M | Inns | NO | Runs | HS | Avge | 100s | 50s | Ct | St | O | M | Runs | Wkts | Avge | Best | 5wI | 10wM |
|---|---|---|---|---|---|---|---|---|---|---|---|---|---|---|---|---|---|---|
| Test | | | | | | | | | | | | | | | | | | |
| All First | 5 | 9 | 0 | 75 | 20 | 8.33 | - | - | 14 | - | | | | | | | | |
| 1-day Int | | | | | | | | | | | | | | | | | | |
| NatWest | | | | | | | | | | | | | | | | | | |
| B & H | | | | | | | | | | | | | | | | | | |
| Sunday | | | | | | | | | | | | | | | | | | |

## Career Performances

| | M | Inns | NO | Runs | HS | Avge | 100s | 50s | Ct | St | Balls | Runs | Wkts | Avge | Best | 5wI | 10wM |
|---|---|---|---|---|---|---|---|---|---|---|---|---|---|---|---|---|---|
| Test | | | | | | | | | | | | | | | | | |
| All First | 5 | 9 | 0 | 75 | 20 | 8.33 | - | - | 14 | - | | | | | | | |
| 1-day Int | | | | | | | | | | | | | | | | | |
| NatWest | | | | | | | | | | | | | | | | | |
| B & H | | | | | | | | | | | | | | | | | |
| Sunday | | | | | | | | | | | | | | | | | |

# HABIB, A.                    Leicestershire

**Name:** Aftab Habib
**Role:** Right-hand bat, right-arm bowler
**Born:** 7 February 1972, Reading, Berks
**Height:** 5ft 11in
**County debut:** 1992 (Middlesex), 1995 (Leicestershire)
**1st-Class 100s:** 1
**Parents:** Hussain and Tahira
**Marital status:** Single
**Family links with cricket:** Cousin of Zahid Sadiq (ex-Surrey and Derbyshire)
**Education:** Millfield School; Taunton School
**Qualifications:** 7 GCSEs, NCA coaching certificate
**Career outside cricket:** Salesman for Sewards
**Overseas tours:** England YC to Australia 1989-90, to New Zealand 1990-91

**Overseas teams played for:** Gloobe Wakatu, Nelson, New Zealand, 1992-93
**Cricketers particularly admired:**
Desmond Haynes, Javed Miandad, Dean Jones and Mark Waugh
**Other sports followed:** All sports
**Relaxations:** Music, videos, reading and magazines
**Extras:** 2nd XI Seaxe Player of the Year 1992. Released by Middlesex at end of 1994 season
**Best batting:** 174* Leicestershire v Oxford University, The Parks 1995

## 1995 Season

| | M | Inns | NO | Runs | HS | Avge | 100s | 50s | Ct | St | O | M | Runs | Wkts | Avge | Best | 5wI | 10wM |
|---|---|---|---|---|---|---|---|---|---|---|---|---|---|---|---|---|---|---|
| Test | | | | | | | | | | | | | | | | | | |
| All First | 3 | 5 | 2 | 230 | 174 * | 76.66 | 1 | - | - | - | | | | | | | | |
| 1-day Int | | | | | | | | | | | | | | | | | | |
| NatWest | 1 | 1 | 0 | 3 | 3 | 3.00 | - | - | - | - | | | | | | | | |
| B & H | | | | | | | | | | | | | | | | | | |
| Sunday | 1 | 1 | 0 | 15 | 15 | 15.00 | - | - | - | - | | | | | | | | |

## Career Performances

| | M | Inns | NO | Runs | HS | Avge | 100s | 50s | Ct | St | Balls | Runs | Wkts | Avge | Best | 5wI | 10wM |
|---|---|---|---|---|---|---|---|---|---|---|---|---|---|---|---|---|---|
| Test | | | | | | | | | | | | | | | | | | |
| All First | 4 | 7 | 3 | 249 | 174 * | 62.25 | 1 | - | - | - | | | | | | | | |
| 1-day Int | | | | | | | | | | | | | | | | | | |
| NatWest | 1 | 1 | 0 | 3 | 3 | 3.00 | - | - | - | - | | | | | | | | |
| B & H | | | | | | | | | | | | | | | | | | |
| Sunday | 3 | 3 | 0 | 41 | 15 | 13.66 | - | - | - | - | | | | | | | | |

31. Who are the only players to have completed their Test careers
with a Test batting average of over 60?

# HALL, J. W.                                    Sussex

**Name:** James William Hall
**Role:** Right-hand opening batsman
**Born:** 30 March 1968, Chichester
**Height:** 6ft 3in **Weight:** 14st
**Nickname:** Gus
**County debut:** 1990
**County cap:** 1992
**1000 runs in a season:** 2
**1st-Class 50s:** 27
**1st-Class 100s:** 6
**1st-Class catches:** 41
**Place in batting averages:** 170th av. 24.40
(1994 135th av. 29.22)
**Parents:** Maurice and Marlene (deceased)
**Marital status:** Single
**Family links with cricket:** Father played
club cricket for Chichester Priory Park.
Brother David a very keen supporter
**Education:** Chichester Boys' High School
**Qualifications:** 9 O-levels, level 1 and 2 Coaching Awards
**Career outside cricket:** Coach
**Off-season:** Coaching at the Scots College in Sydney, Australia
**Overseas tours:** Malaga Select XI, Spain, 1993
**Overseas teams played for:** Southern Districts, Perth, Western Australia 1986-87;
Swanbourne, Perth 1988-89; University St Helliers, Auckland 1991-92; Malaga Select
XI, 1993-94
**Cricketers particularly admired:** Peter Moores, Alec Stewart, Allan Green,
Robin Smith and 'all those who have played as professional cricketers'
**Other sports followed:** Football (Brighton & Hove Albion and Carlisle United)
**Injuries:** Broken left hand, out for four weeks
**Relaxations:** Music, socialising, 'exploring the Sydney club scene, Brighton's wide
and varied pubs and the occasional all-nighter with a few beers'
**Extras:** Scored 53 on 1st XI debut v Zimbabwe and scored maiden first-class century in
same week (120* v New Zealand) in 1990, going on to make over 1000 runs in debut
season of first-class cricket. Run out without facing a ball on NatWest debut v
Glamorgan ('thanks Neil'). Whittingdale Young Cricketer of the Month for May 1991.
Scorer of slowest ever Championship 50 v Surrey, The Oval 29 July 1994
**Opinions on cricket:** 'The usual – play too much, paid too little, too many overs in a
day, tea too short, wickets too inconsistent – all in all it's a great game that allows us to
travel all over the world and country. All those lucky enough to have played as
professional cricketers should never take it for granted and always enjoy the good days

as the not so good ones will surely turn up.'
**Best batting:** 140* Sussex v Lancashire, Hove 1992

## 1995 Season

| | M | Inns | NO | Runs | HS | Avge | 100s | 50s | Ct | St | O | M | Runs | Wkts | Avge | Best | 5wl | 10wM |
|---|---|---|---|---|---|---|---|---|---|---|---|---|---|---|---|---|---|---|
| Test | | | | | | | | | | | | | | | | | | |
| All First | 12 | 22 | 0 | 537 | 100 | 24.40 | 1 | 2 | 5 | - | | | | | | | | |
| 1-day Int | | | | | | | | | | | | | | | | | | |
| NatWest | 1 | 1 | 0 | 70 | 70 | 70.00 | - | 1 | - | - | | | | | | | | |
| B & H | 4 | 4 | 0 | 185 | 67 | 46.25 | - | 2 | 1 | - | | | | | | | | |
| Sunday | 6 | 6 | 0 | 128 | 47 | 21.33 | - | - | 2 | - | | | | | | | | |

## Career Performances

| | M | Inns | NO | Runs | HS | Avge | 100s | 50s | Ct | St | Balls | Runs | Wkts | Avge | Best | 5wl | 10wM |
|---|---|---|---|---|---|---|---|---|---|---|---|---|---|---|---|---|---|
| Test | | | | | | | | | | | | | | | | | |
| All First | 90 | 162 | 10 | 4667 | 140 * | 30.70 | 6 | 27 | 41 | - | 12 | 14 | 0 | - | - | - | - |
| 1-day Int | | | | | | | | | | | | | | | | | |
| NatWest | 5 | 5 | 0 | 120 | 70 | 24.00 | - | 1 | - | - | | | | | | | |
| B & H | 13 | 13 | 0 | 524 | 81 | 40.30 | - | 5 | 2 | - | | | | | | | |
| Sunday | 29 | 28 | 0 | 753 | 77 | 26.89 | - | 6 | 8 | - | | | | | | | |

# HALLETT, J. C. Somerset

**Name:** Jeremy Charles Hallett
**Role:** Right-hand bat, right-arm
medium-fast bowler
**Born:** 18 October 1970, Yeovil
**Height:** 6ft 2in **Weight:** 12st
**Nickname:** Chicks, Pikey
**County debut:** 1990
**1st-Class 50s:** 1
**1st-Class 100s:** 1
**1st-Class catches:** 7
**Place in batting averages:** 261st av. 11.28
**Strike rate:** (career 71.35)
**Parents:** Glyn and Rosemarie
**Marital status:** Single
**Family links with cricket:**
'Father has played Somerset League cricket
for years, and sister plays for Sussex Ladies
and English Universities.'

**Education:** Wells Cathedral Junior School; Millfield School; Durham University

**Qualifications:** 10 O-levels, 3 A-levels, degree in economics, management, history
**Overseas tours:** England YC to Australia, 1989-90; Durham University to South Africa 1992-93
**Cricketers particularly admired:** Malcolm Marshall, Viv Richards, Terry Alderman, Richard Hadlee, Martin Crowe, Jimmy Cook
**Other sports followed:** Football (Yeovil Town), golf, Bath RFC, 'all sports really'
**Relaxations:** 'Films, music, playing golf, a good pub, food!'
**Extras:** Cricketer of the Series, England YC in Australia 1989-90. Also played v New Zealand YC 1989 and Pakistan YC 1990. Somerset Young Player of the Year 1990. Played for Combined Universities in B&H Cup 1991,1992 and 1993 and v Australians 1993
**Best batting:** 111* Somerset v Middlesex, Taunton 1995
**Best bowling:** 4-59 Somerset v Kent, Canterbury 1994

### 1995 Season

|           | M  | Inns | NO | Runs | HS    | Avge  | 100s | 50s | Ct | St | O  | M | Runs | Wkts | Avge  | Best | 5wI | 10wM |
|-----------|----|------|----|------|-------|-------|------|-----|----|----|----|---|------|------|-------|------|-----|------|
| Test      |    |      |    |      |       |       |      |     |    |    |    |   |      |      |       |      |     |      |
| All First | 2  | 4    | 1  | 229  | 111 * | 76.33 | 1    | -   | 1  | -  | 14 | 1 | 86   | 2    | 43.00 | 2-22 | -   | -    |
| 1-day Int |    |      |    |      |       |       |      |     |    |    |    |   |      |      |       |      |     |      |
| NatWest   |    |      |    |      |       |       |      |     |    |    |    |   |      |      |       |      |     |      |
| B & H     |    |      |    |      |       |       |      |     |    |    |    |   |      |      |       |      |     |      |
| Sunday    | 2  | 1    | 0  | 2    | 2     | 2.00  | -    | -   | -  | -  | 12 | 2 | 80   | 4    | 20.00 | 3-33 | -   |      |

### Career Performances

|           | M  | Inns | NO | Runs | HS    | Avge  | 100s | 50s | Ct | St | Balls | Runs | Wkts | Avge  | Best | 5wI | 10wM |
|-----------|----|------|----|------|-------|-------|------|-----|----|----|-------|------|------|-------|------|-----|------|
| Test      |    |      |    |      |       |       |      |     |    |    |       |      |      |       |      |     |      |
| All First | 18 | 19   | 4  | 349  | 111 * | 23.26 | 1    | 1   | 7  | -  | 2212  | 1342 | 31   | 43.29 | 4-59 | -   | -    |
| 1-day Int |    |      |    |      |       |       |      |     |    |    |       |      |      |       |      |     |      |
| NatWest   | 1  | 0    | 0  | 0    | 0     | -     | -    | -   | -  | -  | 72    | 31   | 0    | -     | -    | -   |      |
| B & H     | 11 | 5    | 1  | 13   | 5 *   | 3.25  | -    | -   | 1  | -  | 541   | 342  | 7    | 48.85 | 3-36 | -   |      |
| Sunday    | 21 | 9    | 3  | 73   | 26    | 12.16 | -    | -   | 2  | -  | 710   | 678  | 19   | 35.68 | 3-33 | -   |      |

# HAMILTON, G. M.                                        Yorkshire

**Name:** Gavin Mark Hamilton
**Role:** Right-hand bat, right-arm fast bowler
**Born:** 16 September 1974, Broxburn
**Height:** 6ft 1in **Weight:** 12st 7lb
**Nickname:** Hammy, Scotty, Jock
**County debut:** 1994
**1st-Class catches:** 4
**1st-Class 5 w. innings:** 1
**Parents:** Gavin and Wendy

**Marital status:** Single
**Family links with cricket:** Father is a long-term club cricketer for Sidcup and West Lothian. Brother Scotland opening bat
**Education:** Hurstmere School, Sidcup
**Qualifications:** 10 O-levels
**Off-season:** Coaching at Paarl Gymnasium High School and playing for Stellenbosch University in South Africa
**Overseas teams played for:** Municipals, Orange Free State, South Africa; Wellington, Cape Town, South Africa; Stellenbosch University, Boland, South Africa
**Cricketers particularly admired:** Mark Robinson, David Gower
**Other sports followed:** Golf, football (Arsenal YTS)
**Injuries:** Shin splints, missed three weeks, twisted ankle, missed two weeks
**Relaxations:** Listening to music, 'watching and playing a slow game of golf'
**Extras:** Has played first-class cricket for Scotland
**Opinions on cricket:** 'Too much cricket being played. Season should be longer and spaced out more. Over-rate should be cut substantially.'
**Best batting:** 48 Yorkshire v Kent, Maidstone 1994
**Best bowling:** 5-65 Scotland v Ireland, Eglinton 1993

## 1995 Season

|          | M | Inns | NO | Runs | HS | Avge | 100s | 50s | Ct | St | O | M | Runs | Wkts | Avge | Best | 5wI | 10wM |
|----------|---|------|----|------|----|------|------|-----|----|----|----|---|------|------|------|------|-----|------|
| Test     |   |      |    |      |    |      |      |     |    |    |      |    |      |      |      |      |     |      |
| All First | 3 | 4 | 2 | 59 | 29 | 29.50 | - | - | 2 | - | 75.2 | 24 | 224 | 7 | 32.00 | 3-41 | - | - |
| 1-day Int |   |      |    |      |    |      |      |     |    |    |      |    |      |      |      |      |     |      |
| NatWest  |   |      |    |      |    |      |      |     |    |    |      |    |      |      |      |      |     |      |
| B & H    |   |      |    |      |    |      |      |     |  . |    |      |    |      |      |      |      |     |      |
| Sunday   | 8 | 6 | 0 | 5 | 3 | 0.83 | - | - | 2 | - | 48 | 0 | 249 | 11 | 22.63 | 4-27 | - | |

## Career Performances

|          | M | Inns | NO | Runs | HS | Avge | 100s | 50s | Ct | St | Balls | Runs | Wkts | Avge | Best | 5wI | 10wM |
|----------|---|------|----|------|----|------|------|-----|----|----|-------|------|------|------|------|-----|------|
| Test     |   |      |    |      |    |      |      |     |    |    |       |      |      |      |      |     |      |
| All First | 8 | 9 | 2 | 129 | 48 | 18.42 | - | - | 4 | - | 1267 | 688 | 17 | 40.47 | 5-65 | 1 | - |
| 1-day Int |   |      |    |      |    |      |      |     |    |    |       |      |      |      |      |     |      |
| NatWest  | 2 | 1 | 0 | 2 | 2 | 2.00 | - | - | 1 | - | 120 | 86 | 4 | 21.50 | 2-42 | - | |
| B & H    | 2 | 1 | 1 | 8 | 8 * | - | - | - | - | - | 78 | 42 | 0 | - | - | - | |
| Sunday   | 14 | 9 | 2 | 46 | 16 * | 6.57 | - | - | 2 | - | 529 | 491 | 19 | 25.84 | 4-27 | - | |

# HANCOCK, T. H. C.                    Gloucestershire

**Name:** Timothy Harold Coulter Hancock
**Role:** Right-hand bat, occasional right-arm
medium bowler, short-leg or cover fielder
**Born:** 20 April 1972, Reading
**Height:** 5ft 11in **Weight:** 12st 12lb
**Nickname:** Herbie
**County debut:** 1991
**1st-Class 50s:** 15
**1st-Class 100s:** 2
**1st-Class catches:** 37
**Place in batting averages:** 179th av. 22.91
(1994 59th av. 25.55)
**Strike rate:** (career 59.84)
**Parents:** John and Jennifer
**Marital status:** Single
**Family links with cricket:** 'Dad still plays'
**Education:** St Edward's, Oxford;
Henley College
**Qualifications:** 8 GCSEs
**Off-season:** In Durban, South Africa
**Overseas tours:** Gloucestershire to Kenya 1991, to Sri Lanka 1993
**Overseas teams played for:** CBC Old Boys, Bloemfontein 1991-92; Wynnum
Manley, Brisbane 1992-93
**Cricketers particularly admired:** Ian Botham, Viv Richards
**Other sports followed:** Rugby union, golf, hockey
**Relaxations:** Playing golf, watching television, 'having a pint or two with friends'
**Extras:** Played hockey for Oxfordshire U19
**Best batting:** 123 Gloucestershire v Essex, Chelmsford 1994
**Best bowling:** 3-10 Gloucestershire v Glamorgan, Abergavenny 1993

## 1995 Season

|           | M | Inns | NO | Runs | HS   | Avge  | 100s | 50s | Ct | St | O | M | Runs | Wkts | Avge | Best | 5wI | 10wM |
|-----------|---|------|----|------|------|-------|------|-----|----|----|---|---|------|------|------|------|-----|------|
| Test      |   |      |    |      |      |       |      |     |    |    |   |   |      |      |      |      |     |      |
| All First | 8 | 13   | 1  | 275  | 79 * | 22.91 | -    | 1   | 6  | -  | 5 | 1 | 20   | 0    | -    | -    | -   | -    |
| 1-day Int |   |      |    |      |      |       |      |     |    |    |   |   |      |      |      |      |     |      |
| NatWest   |   |      |    |      |      |       |      |     |    |    |   |   |      |      |      |      |     |      |
| B & H     | 4 | 4    | 0  | 77   | 36   | 19.25 | -    | -   | -  | -  |   |   |      |      |      |      |     |      |
| Sunday    | 4 | 4    | 0  | 58   | 32   | 14.50 | -    | -   | 2  | -  |   |   |      |      |      |      |     |      |

## Career Performances

| | M | Inns | NO | Runs | HS | Avge | 100s | 50s | Ct | St | Balls | Runs | Wkts | Avge | Best | 5wI | 10wM |
|---|---|---|---|---|---|---|---|---|---|---|---|---|---|---|---|---|---|
| Test | | | | | | | | | | - | | | | | | | |
| All First | 60 | 107 | 7 | 2452 | 123 | 24.52 | 2 | 15 | 37 | - | 778 | 499 | 13 | 38.38 | 3-10 | - | - |
| 1-day Int | | | | | | | | | | | | | | | | | |
| NatWest | 2 | 2 | 0 | 74 | 45 | 37.00 | - | - | 1 | - | 41 | 39 | 2 | 19.50 | 2-7 | - | |
| B & H | 11 | 9 | 0 | 138 | 36 | 15.33 | - | - | 2 | - | | | | | | | |
| Sunday | 43 | 40 | 1 | 557 | 46 | 14.28 | - | - | 17 | - | 114 | 121 | 3 | 40.33 | 2-31 | - | |

# HARDEN, R. J.        Somerset

**Name:** Richard John Harden
**Role:** Right-hand bat, left-arm medium bowler
**Born:** 16 August 1965, Bridgwater
**Height:** 5ft 11in **Weight:** 13st 7lbs
**Nickname:** Sumo, Curtis
**County debut:** 1985
**County cap:** 1989
**1000 runs in a season:** 6
**1st-Class 50s:** 59
**1st-Class 100s:** 25
**1st-Class catches:** 158
**One-Day 100s:** 4
**Place in batting averages:** 30th av. 49.27
(1994 53rd av. 40.80)
**Parents:** Chris and Anne
**Wife and date of marriage:** Nicki Rae, 25
September 1992

**Family links with cricket:** Grandfather played club cricket for Bridgwater
**Education:** King's College, Taunton
**Qualifications:** 8 O-levels, 2 A-levels, coaching award
**Career outside cricket:** Print broker for Pennine Dataforms
**Off-season:** Working for Pennine Dataforms
**Overseas teams played for:** Central Districts, New Zealand
**Cricketers particularly admired:** Viv Richards, Jimmy Cook
**Other sports followed:** Squash, golf, rugby
**Relaxations:** 'Love my domestic duties (dusting, Hoovering, etc.) rather than golf.
Good food and the odd drink.'
**Best batting:** 187 Somerset v Nottinghamshire, Taunton 1992
**Best bowling:** 2-7 Central Districts v Canterbury, Blenheim 1987-88

## 1995 Season

|  | M | Inns | NO | Runs | HS | Avge | 100s | 50s | Ct | St | O | M | Runs | Wkts | Avge | Best | 5wl | 10wM |
|---|---|---|---|---|---|---|---|---|---|---|---|---|---|---|---|---|---|---|
| Test |  |  |  |  |  |  |  |  |  |  |  |  |  |  |  |  |  |  |
| All First | 19 | 35 | 6 | 1429 | 129 * | 49.27 | 5 | 6 | 13 | - | 1 | 0 | 17 | 0 | - | - | - | - |
| 1-day Int |  |  |  |  |  |  |  |  |  |  |  |  |  |  |  |  |  |  |
| NatWest | 1 | 1 | 0 | 104 | 104 | 104.00 | 1 | - | 1 | - |  |  |  |  |  |  |  |  |
| B & H | 6 | 6 | 1 | 96 | 50 | 19.20 | - | 1 | 3 | - |  |  |  |  |  |  |  |  |
| Sunday | 14 | 14 | 1 | 491 | 100 * | 37.76 | 1 | 3 | 4 | - |  |  |  |  |  |  |  |  |

## Career Performances

|  | M | Inns | NO | Runs | HS | Avge | 100s | 50s | Ct | St | Balls | Runs | Wkts | Avge | Best | 5wl | 10wM |
|---|---|---|---|---|---|---|---|---|---|---|---|---|---|---|---|---|---|
| Test |  |  |  |  |  |  |  |  |  |  |  |  |  |  |  |  |  |
| All First | 210 | 343 | 55 | 11525 | 187 | 40.01 | 25 | 59 | 158 | - | 1406 | 969 | 19 | 51.00 | 2-7 | - | - |
| 1-day Int |  |  |  |  |  |  |  |  |  |  |  |  |  |  |  |  |  |
| NatWest | 19 | 17 | 2 | 699 | 108 * | 46.60 | 3 | 2 | 11 | - | 18 | 23 | 0 | - | - | - | - |
| B & H | 42 | 41 | 4 | 744 | 76 | 20.10 | - | 3 | 11 | - |  |  |  |  |  |  |  |
| Sunday | 141 | 135 | 22 | 3444 | 100 * | 30.47 | 1 | 19 | 41 | - | 1 | 0 | 0 | - | - | - | - |

# HARRIS, A. J. Derbyshire

**Name:** Andrew James Harris
**Role:** Right-hand bat, right-arm fast bowler
**Born:** 26 June 1973, Ashton-under-Lyne
**Height:** 6ft **Weight:** 11st 7lbs
**Nickname:** AJ 'and the odd person
resorts to Rolf'
**County debut:** 1994
**Place in bowling averages:** 32nd av. 25.28
**Strike rate:** 36.78 (career 37.21)
**Parents:** Norman and Joyce
**Marital status:** Single
**Education:** Tintwistle Primary School;
Hadfield Comprehensive School;
Glossopdale Community College
**Qualifications:** 6 GCSEs, 1 A-Level
**Overseas teams played for:** Ginninderra,
West Belconnen, Australia 1992-93
**Cricketers particularly admired:**
'Being a bowler by trade I particularly
admire Kim Barnett, obviously (I have to stay in his good books), Brian Lara – he's
top drawer – and Merv Hughes for his effort and determination'
**Other sports followed:** 'Soccer, as my brother plays for Altrincham, but I support the

True Blues, Man City, and every sport I will view with great determination'
**Relaxations:** 'Playing any sport, golf in particular. As relaxing goes, watching television, playing on my Sega, and how could I forget having quite a few beers, although I have never been to the Pink Coconut'
**Best batting:** 14* Derbyshire v Young Australia, Chesterfield 1995
**Best bowling:** 4-84 Derbyshire v Glamorgan, Derby 1995

## 1995 Season

| | M | Inns | NO | Runs | HS | Avge | 100s | 50s | Ct | St | O | M | Runs | Wkts | Avge | Best | 5wI | 10wM |
|---|---|---|---|---|---|---|---|---|---|---|---|---|---|---|---|---|---|---|
| Test | | | | | | | | | | | | | | | | | | |
| All First | 4 | 6 | 3 | 47 | 14 * | 15.66 | - | - | - | - | 85.5 | 16 | 354 | 14 | 25.28 | 4-84 | - | - |
| 1-day Int | | | | | | | | | | | | | | | | | | |
| NatWest | | | | | | | | | | | | | | | | | | |
| B & H | 1 | 1 | 0 | 5 | 5 | 5.00 | - | - | - | - | 11 | 0 | 54 | 1 | 54.00 | 1-54 | - | |
| Sunday | 10 | 2 | 1 | 3 | 2 | 3.00 | - | - | 3 | - | 60.4 | 2 | 321 | 13 | 24.69 | 3-15 | - | |

## Career Performances

| | M | Inns | NO | Runs | HS | Avge | 100s | 50s | Ct | St | Balls | Runs | Wkts | Avge | Best | 5wI | 10wM |
|---|---|---|---|---|---|---|---|---|---|---|---|---|---|---|---|---|---|
| Test | | | | | | | | | | | | | | | | | |
| All First | 6 | 9 | 3 | 58 | 14 * | 9.66 | - | - | - | - | 707 | 519 | 19 | 27.31 | 4-84 | - | - |
| 1-day Int | | | | | | | | | | | | | | | | | |
| NatWest | | | | | | | | | | | | | | | | | |
| B & H | 1 | 1 | 0 | 5 | 5 | 5.00 | - | - | - | - | 66 | 54 | 1 | 54.00 | 1-54 | - | |
| Sunday | 11 | 2 | 1 | 3 | 2 | 3.00 | - | - | 3 | - | 412 | 370 | 15 | 24.66 | 3-15 | - | |

32. Who were Durham's first opponents at their new
Riverside ground at Chester-le-Street?

# HARRISON, C. P.  Worcestershire

**Name:** Christopher Paul Harrison
**Role:** Right-hand bat, off-spin bowler
**Born:** 23 October 1976, Bury
**Height:** 6ft 2in  **Weight:** 13st 10lbs
**Nickname:** Harry
**County debut:** No first-team appearance
**Parents:** Alistair and Lynda
**Marital status:** Single
**Education:** Lytham St Anne's High School;
Worcester College of Higher Education
**Qualifications:** 7 GCSEs, 3 A-levels, second
level cricket coach
**Off-season:** Studying sports studies and
psychology at Worcester College
**Overseas tours:** Blackpool and Fylde Cricket
Association to Australia 1991, to Honk Kong,
Singapore and Malaysia 1992; George Evans
Foundation for Cricket to South Africa 1994
**Cricketers particularly admired:**
'All who make it to the very top level'
**Other sports followed:** Hockey, golf and football (Blackpool and Manchester City)
**Relaxations:** Listening to music
**Opinions on cricket:** 'The game must be more widespread, to attract young players.'

---

# HARRISON, J. C.  Middlesex

**Name:** Jason Christian Harrison
**Role:** Right-hand bat, off-spin bowler, slip fielder
**Born:** 15 January 1972, Amersham, Bucks
**Height:** 6ft 3in  **Weight:** 13st 10lbs
**Nickname:** Harry
**County debut:** 1994
**1st-Class catches:** 2
**Parents:** Paul and Carry (deceased)
**Marital status:** Single
**Education:** Great Marlow, Bucks, College of Higher Education
**Qualifications:** 6 GCSEs, NCA coaching certificate, City & Guilds apprenticeship in
sheet metal fabrication
**Career outside cricket:** Sheet metal fabricator
**Off-season:** Back operation, touring South Africa with Buckinghamshire and 'working

hard on fitness and technique for 1996 season'

**Overseas tours:** Middlesex to Portugal 1992, 1993, 1994, 1995; Buckinghamshire to South Africa 1995-96

**Overseas teams played for:** Bellville, South Africa 1993-95

**Cricketers particularly admired:** Malcolm Roberts, Mike Roseberry, Keith Brown, Mike Gatting, Jason Pooley

**Other sports followed:** Football (Wycombe Wanderers)

**Injuries:** Disc problems, missed last two months of the season and broken thumb, missed two weeks

**Relaxations:** Listening to music, spending time with friends, gym work

**Extras:** Played for Buckinghamshire 1991 and

1992 and for NCA U19 and NAYC in 1991. Holds the record for the highest score in the Thames Valley League. Offered contract by Leicestershire as well as Middlesex. Was out first ball in first-class cricket

**Opinions on cricket:** 'All 2nd XI to be played on first-class grounds. A second overseas player allowed for second-class cricket only, thus improving standard.'

**Best batting:** 46* Middlesex v Cambridge University, Fenner's 1995

## 1995 Season

|  | M | Inns | NO | Runs | HS | Avge | 100s | 50s | Ct | St | O | M | Runs | Wkts | Avge | Best | 5wI | 10wM |
|---|---|---|---|---|---|---|---|---|---|---|---|---|---|---|---|---|---|---|
| Test |  |  |  |  |  |  |  |  |  |  |  |  |  |  |  |  |  |  |
| All First | 2 | 3 | 1 | 95 | 46 * | 47.50 | - | - | - | - |  |  |  |  |  |  |  |  |
| 1-day Int |  |  |  |  |  |  |  |  |  |  |  |  |  |  |  |  |  |  |
| NatWest |  |  |  |  |  |  |  |  |  |  |  |  |  |  |  |  |  |  |
| B & H |  |  |  |  |  |  |  |  |  |  |  |  |  |  |  |  |  |  |
| Sunday | 3 | 2 | 1 | 15 | 13 * | 15.00 | - | - | - | - | 1 | 0 | 3 | 1 | 3.00 | 1-3 | - |  |

## Career Performances

|  | M | Inns | NO | Runs | HS | Avge | 100s | 50s | Ct | St | Balls | Runs | Wkts | Avge | Best | 5wI | 10wM |
|---|---|---|---|---|---|---|---|---|---|---|---|---|---|---|---|---|---|
| Test |  |  |  |  |  |  |  |  |  |  |  |  |  |  |  |  |  |
| All First | 3 | 5 | 1 | 99 | 46 * | 24.75 | - | - | 2 | - |  |  |  |  |  |  |  |
| 1-day Int |  |  |  |  |  |  |  |  |  |  |  |  |  |  |  |  |  |
| NatWest |  |  |  |  |  |  |  |  |  |  |  |  |  |  |  |  |  |
| B & H |  |  |  |  |  |  |  |  |  |  |  |  |  |  |  |  |  |
| Sunday | 4 | 3 | 1 | 17 | 13 * | 8.50 | - | - | - | - | 6 | 3 | 1 | 3.00 | 1-3 | - |  |

# HARRISON, T. W.       Derbyshire

**Name:** Tom William Harrison
**Role:** Left-hand bat, left-arm
fast-medium bowler
**Born:** 11 December 1971, Peterborough
**Height:** 6ft 2in  **Weight:** 14st 8lbs
**Nickname:** Pie Man, Pies
**County debut:** 1995
**1st-Class 50s:** 1
**1st-Class catches:** 3
**Place in batting averages:** 275th av. 11.33
**Marital status:** Single
**Family links with cricket:**
Father is a club cricketer
**Education:** St Peter's Prep, Rivonia,
Johannesburg; Oundle School;
Manchester University
**Qualifications:** 8 O-levels, 3 A-levels, BA
(Hons) in French and History
**Overseas teams played for:** Claremont Nedlands, Perth, Western Australia 1989-90
**Extras:** Was on the Northamptonshire staff in 1994
**Best batting:** 61* Derbyshire v Surrey, The Oval 1995
**Best bowling:** 4-153 Derbyshire v Essex, Chelmsford 1995

## 1995 Season

|  | M | Inns | NO | Runs | HS | Avge | 100s | 50s | Ct | St | O | M | Runs | Wkts | Avge | Best | 5wI | 10wM |
|---|---|---|---|---|---|---|---|---|---|---|---|---|---|---|---|---|---|---|
| Test |  |  |  |  |  |  |  |  |  |  |  |  |  |  |  |  |  |  |
| All First | 5 | 10 | 1 | 102 | 61 * | 11.33 | - | 1 | 3 | - | 76 | 19 | 282 | 5 | 56.40 | 4-153 | - | - |
| 1-day Int |  |  |  |  |  |  |  |  |  |  |  |  |  |  |  |  |  |  |
| NatWest |  |  |  |  |  |  |  |  |  |  |  |  |  |  |  |  |  |  |  |
| B & H | 1 | 1 | 0 | 25 | 25 | 25.00 | - | - | - | - |  |  |  |  |  |  |  |  |
| Sunday | 6 | 5 | 1 | 40 | 15 | 10.00 | - | - | 3 | - | 4 | 0 | 41 | 0 | - |  | - | - |

## Career Performances

|  | M | Inns | NO | Runs | HS | Avge | 100s | 50s | Ct | St | Balls | Runs | Wkts | Avge | Best | 5wI | 10wM |
|---|---|---|---|---|---|---|---|---|---|---|---|---|---|---|---|---|---|
| Test |  |  |  |  |  |  |  |  |  |  |  |  |  |  |  |  |  |
| All First | 5 | 10 | 1 | 102 | 61 * | 11.33 | - | 1 | 3 | - | 456 | 282 | 5 | 56.40 | 4-153 | - | - |
| 1-day Int |  |  |  |  |  |  |  |  |  |  |  |  |  |  |  |  |  |
| NatWest |  |  |  |  |  |  |  |  |  |  |  |  |  |  |  |  |  |  |
| B & H | 1 | 1 | 0 | 25 | 25 | 25.00 | - | - | - | - |  |  |  |  |  |  |  |
| Sunday | 6 | 5 | 1 | 40 | 15 | 10.00 | - | - | 3 | - | 24 | 41 | 0 | - |  | - | - |

# HART, J. P.  Nottinghamshire

**Name:** Jamie Paul Hart
**Role:** Right-hand bat, right-arm medium bowler
**Born:** 31 December 1975, Blackpool
**Height:** 6ft 2in **Weight:** 13st 8lbs
**Nickname:** Harty
**County debut:** 1995 (one-day)
**Parents:** Paul and Vicky
**Marital status:** Single
**Education:** Grosvenor School, Nottingham; Millfield School
**Qualifications:** 8 GCSEs and 1 A-level
**Career outside cricket:** Sales
**Off-season:** 'Hope to go abroad, possibly South Africa to play and coach'
**Oversaes tours:** Millfield School to Sri Lanka 1993
**Cricketers particularly admired:** Ian Botham, Dermot Reeve

**Other sports followed:** Football (Leeds United)
**Relaxations:** Listening to music and reading
**Extras:** Father played professional football and is now at Leeds United on the coaching staff
**Opinions on cricket:** 'The different standards of second-class pitches compared with first-class pitches and grounds often make the step up harder ie. more often than not one can get more out of a second eleven pitch than a first-class one (as a bowler).'

## 1995 Season

|          | M | Inns | NO | Runs | HS | Avge | 100s | 50s | Ct | St | O | M | Runs | Wkts | Avge | Best | 5wI | 10wM |
|----------|---|------|----|------|----|------|------|-----|----|----|---|---|------|------|------|------|-----|------|
| Test     |   |      |    |      |    |      |      |     |    |    |   |   |      |      |      |      |     |      |
| All First|   |      |    |      |    |      |      |     |    |    |   |   |      |      |      |      |     |      |
| 1-day Int|   |      |    |      |    |      |      |     |    |    |   |   |      |      |      |      |     |      |
| NatWest  |   |      |    |      |    |      |      |     |    |    |   |   |      |      |      |      |     |      |
| B & H    |   |      |    |      |    |      |      |     |    |    |   |   |      |      |      |      |     |      |
| Sunday   | 2 | -    | -  | -    | -  | -    | -    | -   | -  | -  | 12| 1 | 87   | 1    | 87.00| 1-48 | -   |      |

33. Who, in 1995, became the player to score the most runs in successive innings at Lord's without being dismissed?

## Career Performances

|  | M | Inns | NO | Runs | HS | Avge | 100s | 50s | Ct | St | Balls | Runs | Wkts | Avge | Best | 5wI | 10wM |
|---|---|---|---|---|---|---|---|---|---|---|---|---|---|---|---|---|---|
| Test |  |  |  |  |  |  |  |  |  |  |  |  |  |  |  |  |  |
| All First |  |  |  |  |  |  |  |  |  |  |  |  |  |  |  |  |  |  |
| 1-day Int |  |  |  |  |  |  |  |  |  |  |  |  |  |  |  |  |  |  |
| NatWest |  |  |  |  |  |  |  |  |  |  |  |  |  |  |  |  |  |  |
| B & H |  |  |  |  |  |  |  |  |  |  |  |  |  |  |  |  |  |  |
| Sunday | 2 | - | - | - | - | - | - | - | - | - | 72 | 87 | 1 | 87.00 | 1-48 | - |  |

# HARTLEY, P. J. *Yorkshire*

**Name:** Peter John Hartley
**Role:** Right-hand bat, right-arm
medium-fast bowler
**Born:** 18 April 1960, Keighley
**Height:** 6ft **Weight:** 13st 6lbs
**Nickname:** Jack
**County debut:** 1982 (Warwickshire),
1985 (Yorkshire)
**County cap:** 1987 (Yorkshire)
**Benefit:** 1996
**50 wickets in a season:** 5
**1st-Class 50s:** 10
**1st-Class 100s:** 2
**1st-Class 5 w. in innings:** 18
**1st-Class 10 w. match:** 1
**1st-Class catches:** 49
**One-Day 50s:** 2
**One-Day 5 w. in innings:** 4

**Place in batting averages:** 262nd av. 13.47 (1994 224th av. 17.15)
**Place in bowling averages:** 22nd av. 22.97 (1994 46th av. 27.88)
**Strike rate:** 40.66 (career 55.32)
**Parents:** Thomas and Molly
**Wife and date of marriage:** Sharon Louise, 12 March 1988
**Children:** Megan Grace, 25 April 1992; Courtney Piage, 25 July 1995
**Family links with cricket:** Father played local league cricket
**Education:** Hartington/Greenhead Grammar School; Bradford College
**Qualifications:** City & Guilds in textile design and management, senior Coaching Award
**Career outside cricket:** Textiles
**Off-season:** Working on benefit for 1996, golf
**Overseas tours:** Yorkshire pre-season tours to Barbados 1986-87, to South Africa
1991-92, 1992-93

**Overseas teams played for:** Melville, New Zealand 1983-84; Adelaide, Australia 1985-86; Harmony and Orange Free State, South Africa 1988-89
**Cricketers particularly admired:** Malcolm Marshall, Richard Hadlee
**Other sports followed:** Rugby league (Keighley Cougars), football (Chelsea FC)
**Injuries:** Sore achilles, missed two weeks
**Relaxations:** Golf, gardening and walking
**Best batting:** 127* Yorkshire v Lancashire, Old Trafford 1988
**Best bowling:** 9-41 Yorkshire v Derbyshire, Chesterfield 1995

## 1995 Season

|  | M | Inns | NO | Runs | HS | Avge | 100s | 50s | Ct | St | O | M | Runs | Wkts | Avge | Best | 5wI | 10wM |
|---|---|---|---|---|---|---|---|---|---|---|---|---|---|---|---|---|---|---|
| Test | | | | | | | | | | | | | | | | | | |
| All First | 18 | 23 | 4 | 256 | 38 | 13.47 | - | - | 4 | - | 549 | 120 | 1861 | 81 | 22.97 | 9-41 | 4 | 1 |
| 1-day Int | | | | | | | | | | | | | | | | | | |
| NatWest | 4 | 3 | 2 | 23 | 16 | 23.00 | - | - | - | - | 46 | 6 | 156 | 6 | 26.00 | 2-34 | - | |
| B & H | 4 | 2 | 1 | 8 | 8 * | 8.00 | - | - | 1 | - | 35.4 | 9 | 107 | 9 | 11.88 | 4-21 | - | |
| Sunday | 12 | 7 | 2 | 43 | 15 * | 8.60 | - | - | 2 | - | 77.4 | 9 | 327 | 14 | 23.35 | 2-7 | - | |

## Career Performances

|  | M | Inns | NO | Runs | HS | Avge | 100s | 50s | Ct | St | Balls | Runs | Wkts | Avge | Best | 5wI | 10wM |
|---|---|---|---|---|---|---|---|---|---|---|---|---|---|---|---|---|---|
| Test | | | | | | | | | | | | | | | | | |
| All First | 172 | 207 | 49 | 3278 | 127 * | 20.74 | 2 | 10 | 53 | - | 27496 | 15452 | 497 | 31.09 | 9-41 | 18 | 1 |
| 1-day Int | | | | | | | | | | | | | | | | | |
| NatWest | 21 | 14 | 7 | 163 | 52 | 23.28 | - | 1 | - | - | 1331 | 850 | 36 | 23.61 | 5-46 | 1 | |
| B & H | 31 | 18 | 7 | 105 | 29 * | 9.54 | - | - | 9 | - | 1745 | 1100 | 50 | 22.00 | 5-43 | 1 | |
| Sunday | 115 | 79 | 24 | 776 | 51 | 14.10 | - | 1 | 17 | - | 4973 | 3775 | 137 | 27.55 | 5-36 | 2 | |

---

34. Which county did the Minor Counties defeat in a zonal match
of the Benson & Hedges Cup in 1995?

---

# HARVEY, M. E.        Lancashire

**Name:** Mark Edward Harvey
**Role:** Right-hand bat, right-arm
medium bowler
**Born:** 26 June 1974, Burnley, Lancs
**Height:** 5ft 9in **Weight:** 12st 6lbs
**Nickname:** Harv, Vadge, Baz
**County debut:** 1994
**1st-Class catches:** 1
**Parents:** David and Wendy
**Marital status:** Single
**Family links with cricket:** Brother Jonathan
spent four years as MCC young player and
was professional for Greenmount CC in the
Bolton League, 'father, David, is still playing
local club cricket, 50 n.o.'
**Education:** Worsthorne County Primary;
Habergham High School, Burnley;
Loughborough University
**Qualifications:** 8 GCSEs, 3 A-levels
**Off-season:** Studying Physical Education, Sports Science and Recreation Management
at university
**Overseas tours:** England U19 to India 1992-93
**Cricketers particularly admired:** 'David Gower (someone who makes it all look so
easy), Dean Jones (exciting both batting and fielding), Mudassar Nazar (an admired
professional for many years at Burnley), Les "The Whirlwind" Seal'
**Other sports followed:** Football (Manchester United, Burnley and Oxford United)
**Relaxations:** 'I'd love to say that watching Burnley FC was a relaxation, but
unfortunately it's very frustrating', watching and reading about Eric Cantona, 'drinking
at the Crooked Billet, Workthorne with father and brother'
**Extras:** Captained England U17, represented England at U17, U18 and U19 levels,
represented Lancashire from U13 to U19. In an attempt to produce a result in a rain-
affected 2nd XI match v Yorkshire at Todmorden, he bowled an over costing 108 runs
from 18 no-balls, all of which went for four without hitting the bat. 'This allowed both
teams to contrive a game in five rather than 50 minutes. A claim to fame which earns me
never-ending stick at the local pub!' Played for Combined Universities in 1995
**Opinions on cricket:** 'The increasing introduction of top class, ex-Test playing coaches,
and alike, whether foreign or British can only be a good thing, allowing young players
such as myself to benefit from their vast knowledge and experience. Different methods
and approaches can only serve to widen our horizons of the game.'
**Best batting:** 23 Lancashire v Nottinghamshire, Trent Bridge 1994; Combined
Universities v West Indies, The Parks 1995

## 1995 Season

| | M | Inns | NO | Runs | HS | Avge | 100s | 50s | Ct | St | O | M | Runs | Wkts | Avge | Best | 5wI | 10wM |
|---|---|---|---|---|---|---|---|---|---|---|---|---|---|---|---|---|---|---|
| Test | | | | | | | | | | | | | | | | | | |
| All First | 1 | 1 | 0 | 23 | 23 | 23.00 | - | - | - | - | | | | | | | | |
| 1-day Int | | | | | | | | | | | | | | | | | | |
| NatWest | | | | | | | | | | | | | | | | | | |
| B & H | 2 | 2 | 0 | 3 | 3 | 1.50 | - | - | 2 | - | | | | | | | | |
| Sunday | | | | | | | | | | | | | | | | | | |

## Career Performances

| | M | Inns | NO | Runs | HS | Avge | 100s | 50s | Ct | St | Balls | Runs | Wkts | Avge | Best | 5wI | 10wM |
|---|---|---|---|---|---|---|---|---|---|---|---|---|---|---|---|---|---|
| Test | | | | | | | | | | | | | | | | | |
| All First | 3 | 4 | 0 | 67 | 23 | 16.75 | - | - | 1 | - | | | | | | | |
| 1-day Int | | | | | | | | | | | | | | | | | |
| NatWest | | | | | | | | | | | | | | | | | |
| B & H | 2 | 2 | 0 | 3 | 3 | 1.50 | - | - | 2 | - | | | | | | | |
| Sunday | | | | | | | | | | | | | | | | | |

# HAYHURST, A. N.                     Somerset

**Name:** Andrew Neil Hayhurst
**Role:** Right-hand bat, right-arm medium
bowler, county captain
**Born:** 23 November 1962, Davyhulme,
Manchester
**Height:** 6ft **Weight:** 13st 7lbs
**Nickname:** Bully, Sponge
**County debut:** 1985 (Lancashire),
1990 (Somerset)
**County cap:** 1990 (Somerset)
**1000 runs in a season:** 3
**1st-Class 50s:** 38
**1st-Class 100s:** 14
**1st-Class catches:** 51
**One-Day 5 w. in innings:** 1
**Place in batting averages:** 95th av. 34.37
(1994 14th av. 52.08)
**Place in bowling averages:** 146th av. 51.90
**Strike rate:** 83.60 (career 81.07)
**Parents:** William and Margaret
**Wife and date of marriage:** April, 17 February 1990
**Children:** Myles William David, 31 March 1992

**Family links with cricket:** Father played club cricket for Worsley in the Manchester and District Cricket Association, grew up in house lived in by Tyldesley brothers (Lancashire and England)

**Education:** St Mark's Primary School; Worsley Wardley High; Eccles Sixth Form College; Leeds Polytechnic (Carnegie College of PE)

**Qualifications:** 8 O-levels, 4 A-levels, BA (Hons) Human Movement, advanced cricket coach, qualified financial consultant

**Off-season:** Working as financial consultant, coaching and training

**Overseas tours:** Lancashire to Jamaica 1986-87 and 1987-88, to Zimbabwe 1988-89; Somerset to Bahamas 1989-90

**Overseas teams played for:** South Launceston, Tasmania 1987-89

**Cricketers particularly admired:** Clive Lloyd, Malcolm Marshall, Jack Simmons, Dermot Reeve

**Other sports followed:** All sports, especially football and rugby league

**Injuries:** Broken finger and broken thumb, missed one month

**Relaxations:** Animals, gardening, decorating

**Extras:** Made 110* on his first-class debut for Somerset and was appointed captain for the 1994 season

**Opinions on cricket:** 'Still play too much cricket although the four-day game is perfect (unlike pitches). Would like to see two divisions, as long as we kept a tight grip on registering players – but is this realistic? Smaller staffs generate more competition for places, rather than the opposite, as everybody registered is capable of first-class cricket. 2nd XI competition should be regional with more emphasis on new type representative matches (i.e. North v South West etc.).'

**Best batting:** 172* Somerset v Gloucestershire, Bath 1991

**Best bowling:** 4-27 Lancashire v Middlesex, Old Trafford 1987

## 1995 Season

|  | M | Inns | NO | Runs | HS | Avge | 100s | 50s | Ct | St | O | M | Runs | Wkts | Avge | Best | 5wI | 10wM |
|---|---|---|---|---|---|---|---|---|---|---|---|---|---|---|---|---|---|---|
| Test |  |  |  |  |  |  |  |  |  |  |  |  |  |  |  |  |  |  |
| All First | 17 | 29 | 5 | 825 | 107 | 34.37 | 1 | 5 | 3 | - | 139.2 | 21 | 519 | 10 | 51.90 | 2-39 | - | - |
| 1-day Int |  |  |  |  |  |  |  |  |  |  |  |  |  |  |  |  |  |  |
| NatWest |  |  |  |  |  |  |  |  |  |  |  |  |  |  |  |  |  |  |  |
| B & H | 6 | 5 | 2 | 114 | 69 * | 38.00 | - | 1 | - | - | 25.2 | 4 | 94 | 5 | 18.80 | 3-2 | - |  |
| Sunday | 10 | 10 | 3 | 210 | 70 * | 30.00 | - | 2 | 1 | - | 21.3 | 1 | 112 | 3 | 37.33 | 2-17 | - |  |

## Career Performances

|  | M | Inns | NO | Runs | HS | Avge | 100s | 50s | Ct | St | Balls | Runs | Wkts | Avge | Best | 5wI | 10wM |
|---|---|---|---|---|---|---|---|---|---|---|---|---|---|---|---|---|---|
| Test |  |  |  |  |  |  |  |  |  |  |  |  |  |  |  |  |  |
| All First | 155 | 250 | 33 | 7595 | 172 * | 35.00 | 14 | 38 | 51 | - | 8756 | 4870 | 108 | 45.09 | 4-27 | - | - |
| 1-day Int |  |  |  |  |  |  |  |  |  |  |  |  |  |  |  |  |  |
| NatWest | 19 | 18 | 4 | 563 | 91 * | 40.21 | - | 3 | 4 | - | 761 | 502 | 24 | 20.91 | 5-60 | 1 |  |
| B & H | 30 | 27 | 3 | 620 | 95 | 25.83 | - | 5 | 2 | - | 970 | 674 | 27 | 24.96 | 4-50 | - |  |
| Sunday | 112 | 96 | 20 | 2111 | 84 | 27.77 | - | 11 | 16 | - | 2667 | 2372 | 62 | 38.25 | 4-37 | - |  |

# HAYNES, G. R. Worcestershire

**Name:** Gavin Richard Haynes
**Role:** Right-hand bat, right-arm medium bowler
**Born:** 29 September 1969, Stourbridge
**Height:** 5ft 10in **Weight:** 12st
**Nickname:** Splash
**County debut:** 1991
**County cap:** 1994
**1000 runs in a season:** 1
**1st-Class 50s:** 13
**1st-Class 100s:** 3
**1st-Class catches:** 31
**One-day 100s:** 1
**Place in batting averages:** 168th av. 24.56 (1994 101st av. 34.03)
**Place in bowling averages:** 121st av. 40.00
**Strike rate:** 77.71 (career 93.91)
**Parents:** Nicholas and Dorothy
**Marital status:** Single
**Family links with cricket:** Father played club cricket and manages Worcester U14 side. Cousin Peter Haynes played very good club cricket
**Education:** Gigmill Junior School; High Park Comprehensive; King Edward VI College, Stourbridge
**Qualifications:** 5 O-levels, 1 A-level, NCA advanced coaching award
**Off-season:** Coaching in England, resting
**Overseas tours:** Worcestershire to Zimbabwe and South Africa
**Overseas teams played for:** Sunrise Sports Club, Zimbabwe 1989-90
**Cricketers particularly admired:** Ian Botham, Graham Dilley, Graham Gooch, Malcolm Marshall, Viv Richards, Graeme Hick
**Other sports followed:** Football (Aston Villa), golf
**Relaxations:** Playing golf, watching television
**Extras:** Represented England Schools U15. Worcestershire Uncapped Player of the Year 1993
**Opinions on cricket:** 'Play far too much cricket. Over rates are ridiculous. To keep to 18.5 is unrealistic, teams end up at the end of the season bowling spinners to get the over rate up, simply to keep their fines down.'
**Best batting:** 158 Worcestershire v Kent, Worcester 1993
**Best bowling:** 4-33 Worcestershire v Kent, Worcester 1995

## 1995 Season

| | M | Inns | NO | Runs | HS | Avge | 100s | 50s | Ct | St | O | M | Runs | Wkts | Avge | Best | 5wI | 10wM |
|---|---|---|---|---|---|---|---|---|---|---|---|---|---|---|---|---|---|---|
| Test | | | | | | | | | | | | | | | | | | |
| All First | 18 | 30 | 0 | 737 | 78 | 24.56 | - | 4 | 10 | - | 272 | 76 | 840 | 21 | 40.00 | 4-33 | - | - |
| 1-day Int | | | | | | | | | | | | | | | | | | |
| NatWest | 2 | 2 | 1 | 118 | 116 * | 118.00 | 1 | - | 1 | - | 14 | 1 | 43 | 1 | 43.00 | 1-17 | - | |
| B & H | 6 | 5 | 1 | 68 | 27 | 17.00 | - | - | 1 | - | 41.5 | 5 | 144 | 9 | 16.00 | 3-17 | - | |
| Sunday | 17 | 14 | 1 | 229 | 41 | 17.61 | - | - | 7 | - | 100.4 | 8 | 403 | 19 | 21.21 | 4-21 | - | |

## Career Performances

| | M | Inns | NO | Runs | HS | Avge | 100s | 50s | Ct | St | Balls | Runs | Wkts | Avge | Best | 5wI | 10wM |
|---|---|---|---|---|---|---|---|---|---|---|---|---|---|---|---|---|---|
| Test | | | | | | | | | | | | | | | | | |
| All First | 62 | 95 | 6 | 2630 | 158 | 29.55 | 3 | 13 | 31 | - | 3259 | 1643 | 35 | 46.94 | 4-33 | - | - |
| 1-day Int | | | | | | | | | | | | | | | | | |
| NatWest | 8 | 6 | 1 | 277 | 116 * | 55.40 | 1 | 1 | 2 | - | 264 | 186 | 4 | 46.50 | 1-9 | - | |
| B & H | 12 | 10 | 3 | 191 | 65 | 27.28 | - | 1 | 4 | - | 443 | 263 | 12 | 21.91 | 3-17 | - | |
| Sunday | 50 | 40 | 3 | 786 | 83 | 21.24 | - | 2 | 16 | - | 1378 | 920 | 30 | 30.66 | 4-21 | - | |

# HEADLEY, D. W.     Kent

**Name:** Dean Warren Headley
**Role:** Right-hand bat, right-arm medium-fast bowler
**Born:** 27 January 1970, Stourbridge
**Height:** 6ft 5in **Weight:** 13st 7lbs
**Nickname:** Frog
**County debut:** 1991 (Middlesex), 1993 (Kent)
**County cap:** 1993 (Kent)
**1st-Class 50s:** 3
**1st-Class 5 w. in innings:** 9
**1st-Class catches:** 31
**One-Day 5 w. in innings:** 2
**Place in batting averages:** 257th av. 14.05 (1994 228th av. 16.75)
**Place in bowling averages:** 59th av. 29.00 (1994 43rd av. 27.47)
**Strike rate:** 58.75 (career 62.35)
**Parents:** Ronald George Alphonso and Gail
**Marital status:** Single
**Family links with cricket:** Father Ron played for Worcestershire, Jamaica and West Indies and grandfather George played for Jamaica and West Indies

**Education:** Gigmill Junior School; Oldswinford Hospital School; Royal Grammar School, Worcester
**Qualifications:** 7 O-levels
**Career outside cricket:** 'Not established'
**Off-season:** England A tour to Pakistan
**Overseas tours:** RGS Worcester to Zimbabwe 1988; Christians in Sport to India 1989-90; England A to Pakistan 1995-96
**Overseas teams played for:** Melbourne, Jamaica 1991-92; Primrose CC, South Africa 1993-95
**Cricketers particularly admired:** Clive Lloyd, Minal Patel, Ian Botham, Robin Smith, Malcolm Marshall, Carl Hooper
**Other sports followed:** Any sport
**Injuries:** Intercostal muscle, missed three weeks
**Relaxations:** Sleeping, socialising with friends and colleagues
**Extras:** Took five wickets on debut including a wicket with his first ball in Championship cricket. Played for Worcestershire 2nd XI 1988-89. Left Middlesex at the end of 1992 season and signed for Kent. Called up as a replacement for the England A tour to Pakistan
**Opinions on cricket:** 'None. I am a bowler.'
**Best batting:** 91 Middlesex v Leicestershire, Leicester 1992
**Best bowling:** 7-58 Kent v Sussex, Hove 1995

## 1995 Season

|          | M  | Inns | NO | Runs | HS   | Avge  | 100s | 50s | Ct | St | O     | M   | Runs | Wkts | Avge  | Best | 5wI | 10wM |
|----------|----|------|----|------|------|-------|------|-----|----|----|-------|-----|------|------|-------|------|-----|------|
| Test     |    |      |    |      |      |       |      |     |    |    |       |     |      |      |       |      |     |      |
| All First | 14 | 24   | 6  | 253  | 54   | 14.05 | -    | 1   | 7  | -  | 430.5 | 101 | 1276 | 44   | 29.00 | 7-58 | 3   | -    |
| 1-day Int |    |      |    |      |      |       |      |     |    |    |       |     |      |      |       |      |     |      |
| NatWest  | 1  | 1    | 1  | 24   | 24 * | -     | -    | -   | -  | -  | 12    | 0   | 40   | 1    | 40.00 | 1-40 | -   |      |
| B & H    | 6  | 3    | 2  | 16   | 7 *  | 16.00 | -    | -   | 2  | -  | 64    | 9   | 226  | 8    | 28.25 | 3-47 | -   |      |
| Sunday   | 14 | 3    | 1  | 10   | 6 *  | 5.00  | -    | -   | 3  | -  | 107   | 3   | 533  | 24   | 22.20 | 6-42 | 1   |      |

## Career Performances

|          | M  | Inns | NO | Runs | HS   | Avge  | 100s | 50s | Ct | St | Balls | Runs | Wkts | Avge  | Best | 5wI | 10wM |
|----------|----|------|----|------|------|-------|------|-----|----|----|-------|------|------|-------|------|-----|------|
| Test     |    |      |    |      |      |       |      |     |    |    |       |      |      |       |      |     |      |
| All First | 67 | 86   | 22 | 1140 | 91   | 17.81 | -    | 3   | 31 | -  | 11349 | 5999 | 182  | 32.96 | 7-58 | 9   | -    |
| 1-day Int |    |      |    |      |      |       |      |     |    |    |       |      |      |       |      |     |      |
| NatWest  | 9  | 6    | 5  | 50   | 24 * | 50.00 | -    | -   | -  | -  | 553   | 359  | 15   | 23.93 | 5-20 | 1   |      |
| B & H    | 15 | 7    | 2  | 57   | 26   | 11.40 | -    | -   | 4  | -  | 887   | 565  | 17   | 33.23 | 4-19 | -   |      |
| Sunday   | 60 | 16   | 8  | 67   | 10 * | 8.37  | -    | -   | 12 | -  | 2543  | 2044 | 74   | 27.62 | 6-42 | 1   |      |

# HEGG, W. K.                                          Lancashire

**Name:** Warren Kevin Hegg
**Role:** Right-hand bat, wicket-keeper
**Born:** 23 February 1968, Radcliffe,
Lancashire
**Height:** 5ft 9in **Weight:** 12st 4lbs
**Nickname:** Chucky
**County debut:** 1986
**1st-Class 50s:** 22
**1st-Class 100s:** 3
**1st-Class catches:** 432
**1st-Class stumpings:** 56
**Place in batting averages:** 145th av. 27.87
(1994 200th av. 19.92)
**Parents:** Kevin and Glenda
**Wife and date of marriage:**
Joanne, 29 October 1994
**Family links with cricket:** Father and
brother Martin play in local leagues
**Education:** Unsworth High School; Stand College, Whitefield
**Qualifications:** 5 O-levels, 7 CSEs, qualified coach
**Overseas tours:** NCA North U19 to Bermuda 1985; England YC to Sri Lanka 1986-87, to Australia (Youth World Cup) 1987-88; England A to Pakistan and Sri Lanka 1990-91
**Overseas teams played for:** Sheffield, Tasmania 1988-90, 1992-93
**Cricketers particularly admired:** Ian Botham, Alan Knott, Bob Taylor, Gehan Mendis
**Other sports followed:** Football, golf, fishing, Aussie Rules football
**Relaxations:** Listening to music, walking on my own
**Extras:** First player to make county debut from Lytham CC. Youngest player for 30 years to score a century for Lancashire, 130 v Northamptonshire in his fourth first-class game. Eleven victims in match v Derbyshire, equalling world record. Wombwell Cricket Lovers' Society joint Wicket-keeper of the Year 1993
**Best batting:** 130 Lancashire v Northamptonshire, Northampton 1987

## 1995 Season

|           | M  | Inns | NO | Runs | HS   | Avge  | 100s | 50s | Ct | St | O | M | Runs | Wkts | Avge | Best | 5wI | 10wM |
|-----------|----|------|----|------|------|-------|------|-----|----|----|---|---|------|------|------|------|-----|------|
| Test      |    |      |    |      |      |       |      |     |    |    |   |   |      |      |      |      |     |      |
| All First | 18 | 28   | 4  | 669  | 101  | 27.87 | 1    | 2   | 53 | 9  |   |   |      |      |      |      |     |      |
| 1-day Int |    |      |    |      |      |       |      |     |    |    |   |   |      |      |      |      |     |      |
| NatWest   | 3  | 1    | 0  | 7    | 7    | 7.00  | -    | -   | 5  | -  |   |   |      |      |      |      |     |      |
| B & H     | 8  | 2    | 2  | 35   | 31 * | -     | -    | -   | 8  | -  |   |   |      |      |      |      |     |      |
| Sunday    | 16 | 10   | 4  | 123  | 29 * | 20.50 | -    | -   | 21 | 1  |   |   |      |      |      |      |     |      |

## Career Performances

| | M | Inns | NO | Runs | HS | Avge | 100s | 50s | Ct | St | Balls | Runs | Wkts | Avge | Best | 5wI | 10wM |
|---|---|---|---|---|---|---|---|---|---|---|---|---|---|---|---|---|---|
| Test | | | | | | | | | | | | | | | | | |
| All First | 185 | 271 | 51 | 5451 | 130 | 24.77 | 3 | 22 | 432 | 56 | 6 | 7 | 0 | - | - | - | - |
| 1-day Int | | | | | | | | | | | | | | | | | |
| NatWest | 20 | 10 | 1 | 157 | 32 | 17.44 | - | - | 27 | 2 | | | | | | | |
| B & H | 42 | 15 | 7 | 158 | 31 * | 19.75 | - | - | 54 | 2 | | | | | | | |
| Sunday | 128 | 69 | 36 | 733 | 52 | 22.21 | - | 1 | 134 | 14 | | | | | | | |

# HEMMINGS, E. E. Sussex

**Name:** Edward Ernest Hemmings
**Role:** Right-hand bat, off-spin bowler
**Born:** 20 February 1949, Leamington Spa,
Warwickshire
**Height:** 5ft 10in **Weight:** 14st 7lb
**Nickname:** Sideways, Yakka
**County debut:** 1966 (Warwickshire),
1979 (Nottinghamshire), 1993 (Sussex)
**County cap:** 1974 (Warwickshire),
1980 (Nottinghamshire), 1993 (Sussex)
**Benefit:** 1987
**Test debut:** 1982
**Tests:** 16
**One-Day Internationals:** 33
**50 wickets in a season:** 15
**1st-Class 50s:** 27
**1st-Class 100s:** 1
**1st-Class 5 w. in innings:** 70
**1st-Class 10 w. in match:** 15
**1st-Class catches:** 212
**One-Day 5 w. in innings:** 4

**Place in bowling averages:** 66th av. 29.46 (1994 av. 53rd av. 29.06)
**Strike rate:** 71.13 (career 67.12)
**Parents:** Edward and Dorothy Phyllis
**Wife and date of marriage:** Christine Mary, 23 October 1971
**Children:** Thomas Edward, 26 July 1977; James Oliver, 9 September 1979
**Family links with cricket:** Father and father's father played Minor Counties and
league cricket
**Education:** Campion School, Leamington Spa
**Overseas tours:** England to Australia and New Zealand 1982-83, to Pakistan (World Cup),
Australia and New Zealand 1987-88, to India and West Indies 1989-90, to Australia 1990-91

**Other sports followed:** Golf, football, rugby
**Relaxations:** Coaching cricket at all levels and working with off-spin bowlers
**Extras:** Took a hat-trick for Warwickshire in 1977; hit first (and only) century – 127* for Nottinghamshire v Yorkshire at Worksop, July 1982 – after 16 years in first-class game. Released by Notts end of the 1992 season and signed by Sussex. Retired from first-class cricket in 1995
**Best batting:** 127* Nottinghamshire v Yorkshire, Worksop 1982
**Best bowling:** 10-175 International XI v West Indies XI, Kingston 1982-83

### 1995 Season

| | M | Inns | NO | Runs | HS | Avge | 100s | 50s | Ct | St | O | M | Runs | Wkts | Avge | Best | 5wI | 10wM |
|---|---|---|---|---|---|---|---|---|---|---|---|---|---|---|---|---|---|---|
| Test | | | | | | | | | | | | | | | | | | |
| All First | 7 | 12 | 7 | 70 | 18 | 14.00 | - | - | 1 | - | 177.5 | 51 | 442 | 15 | 29.46 | 4-33 | - | - |
| 1-day Int | | | | | | | | | | | | | | | | | | |
| NatWest | 2 | 1 | 1 | 1 | 1* | - | - | - | 1 | - | 24 | 2 | 63 | 0 | - | | - | - |
| B & H | | | | | | | | | | | | | | | | | | |
| Sunday | | | | | | | | | | | | | | | | | | |

### Career Performances

| | M | Inns | NO | Runs | HS | Avge | 100s | 50s | Ct | St | Balls | Runs | Wkts | Avge | Best | 5wI | 10wM |
|---|---|---|---|---|---|---|---|---|---|---|---|---|---|---|---|---|---|
| Test | 16 | 21 | 4 | 383 | 95 | 22.52 | - | 2 | 5 | - | 4437 | 1825 | 43 | 42.44 | 6-58 | 1 | - |
| All First | 518 | 683 | 169 | 9533 | 127* | 18.54 | 1 | 27 | 212 | - | 101688 | 44403 | 1515 | 29.30 | 10-175 | 70 | 15 |
| 1-day Int | 33 | 12 | 6 | 30 | 8* | 5.00 | - | - | 5 | - | 1752 | 1293 | 37 | 34.94 | 4-52 | - | |
| NatWest | 46 | 32 | 12 | 262 | 31* | 13.10 | - | - | 9 | - | 3082 | 1722 | 47 | 36.63 | 3-27 | - | |
| B & H | 92 | 54 | 17 | 505 | 61* | 13.64 | - | 1 | 21 | - | 5533 | 2951 | 83 | 35.55 | 4-47 | - | |
| Sunday | 275 | 170 | 54 | 1606 | 44* | 13.84 | - | - | 86 | - | 10792 | 8274 | 281 | 29.44 | 5-22 | 4 | |

# HEMP, D. L.      Glamorgan

**Name:** David Lloyd Hemp
**Role:** Left-hand bat, right-arm medium bowler
**Born:** 15 November 1970, Bermuda
**Height:** 6ft **Weight:** 12st 7lbs
**Nickname:** Hempy, Soc, Mad Dog
**County debut:** 1991
**1000 runs in a season:** 1
**1st-Class 50s:** 21
**1st-Class 100s:** 5
**1st-Class catches:** 45
**One-day 100s:** 1
**Place in batting averages:** 154th av. 27.25 (1994 48th av. 42.70)
**Parents:** Clive and Elisabeth

**Wife and date of marriage:** Angie, 16 March 1996

**Family links with cricket:** Father plays for Ffynone, brother Tim plays for Swansea and Wales Minor Counties, sister Charlotte played for Parklands Junior School

**Education:** Olchfa Comprehensive School; Millfield School; West Glamorgan Institute of Further Education

**Qualifications:** 5 O-levels, 2 A-levels, NCA Coaching Award

**Career outside cricket:** Working in accountancy firm

**Off-season:** Playing in South Africa

**Overseas tours:** Welsh Schools U19 to Australia 1986-87; Welsh Cricket Association U18 to Barbados 1987; Glamorgan to Trinidad 1990; South Wales Cricket Association to New Zealand and Australia 1991-92; England A to India 1994-95

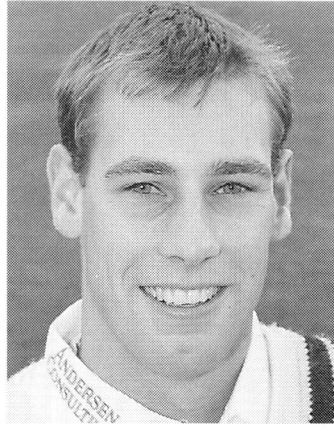

**Overseas teams played for:** Hirsh Crusaders, Durban, South Africa 1992-94, 1995-96

**Cricketers particularly admired:** Viv Richards, David Gower, Keith Arthurton, Mark Waugh

**Other sports followed:** Football

**Relaxations:** Watching football and television, going to movies

**Extras:** Scored 258* for Wales v MCC 1991. In 1990 scored 104* and 101* for Welsh Schools U19 v Scottish Schools U19 and 120 & 102* v Irish Schools U19

**Opinions on cricket:** 'All 2nd XI games should be played on county grounds rather than club grounds as the quality of wickets is usually poorer at clubs, also they do not have such good facilities for covering wickets. If third umpires are going to be used in semi-finals and finals then they should be used in all the previous rounds.'

**Best batting:** 157 Glamorgan v Gloucestershire, Abergavenny 1995

**Best bowling:** 1-9 Glamorgan v Somerset, Taunton 1995

---

## 1995 Season

|           | M  | Inns | NO | Runs | HS  | Avge  | 100s | 50s | Ct | St | O  | M | Runs | Wkts | Avge  | Best | 5wI | 10wM |
|-----------|----|------|----|------|-----|-------|------|-----|----|----|----|---|------|------|-------|------|-----|------|
| Test      |    |      |    |      |     |       |      |     |    |    |    |   |      |      |       |      |     |      |
| All First | 18 | 32   | 0  | 872  | 157 | 27.25 | 1    | 4   | 14 | -  | 22 | 2 | 110  | 3    | 36.66 | 1-9  | -   | -    |
| 1-day Int |    |      |    |      |     |       |      |     |    |    |    |   |      |      |       |      |     |      |
| NatWest   | 4  | 3    | 0  | 143  | 78  | 47.66 | -    | 1   | 1  | -  |    |   |      |      |       |      |     |      |
| B & H     | 5  | 5    | 0  | 202  | 121 | 40.40 | 1    | 1   | 1  | -  |    |   |      |      |       |      |     |      |
| Sunday    | 15 | 11   | 0  | 164  | 74  | 14.90 | -    | 1   | 11 | -  |    |   |      |      |       |      |     |      |

## Career Performances

|         | M  | Inns | NO | Runs | HS  | Avge  | 100s | 50s | Ct | St | Balls | Runs | Wkts | Avge  | Best | 5wI | 10wM |
|---------|----|------|----|------|-----|-------|------|-----|----|----|-------|------|------|-------|------|-----|------|
| Test    |    |      |    |      |     |       |      |     |    |    |       |      |      |       |      |     |      |
| All First | 67 | 118 | 10 | 3458 | 157 | 32.01 | 5    | 21  | 45 | -  | 180   | 151  | 3    | 50.33 | 1-9  | -   | -    |
| 1-day Int |    |      |    |      |     |       |      |     |    |    |       |      |      |       |      |     |      |
| NatWest | 6  | 5    | 0  | 162  | 78  | 32.40 | -    | 1   | 1  | -  |       |      |      |       |      |     |      |
| B & H   | 5  | 5    | 0  | 202  | 121 | 40.40 | 1    | 1   | 1  | -  |       |      |      |       |      |     |      |
| Sunday  | 39 | 29   | 1  | 469  | 74  | 16.75 | -    | 2   | 21 | -  | 2     | 1    | 0    | -     |      | -   | -    |

# HERZBERG, S. Kent

**Name:** Steven Herzberg
**Role:** Right-hand bat, off-spin bowler
**Born:** 25 May 1967, Carshaton, Surrey
**Height:** 6ft 4in **Weight:** 13st
**Nickname:** Hertzy, Cheese, The Burger
**County debut:** 1991 (Worcestershire), 1995 (Kent)
**1st-Class 50s:** 1
**1st-Class 5 w. innings:** 1
**1st-Class catches:** 3
**Strike rate:** (career 79.89)
**Parents:** Louis and Brenda
**Marital status:** Single
**Family links with cricket:** 'Father very keen supporter and administrator. Yonger brother (Daniel) was promising fast bowler until a stress fracture aged 13 (now a windsurfer). Mother a useful all-rounder'

**Education:** Claremont and Hollywood, Western Australia; Hollywood Senior High School , Western Australia; Curtin University, Western Australia
**Qualifications:** Batchelor of Business, level one coaching
**Career outside cricket:** 'Perhaps media or marketing. Still working on it'
**Off-season:** Captaining Subiaco-Floreat in the WACA competition (in Perth, Australia). Trying to improve my golf'
**Overseas teams played for:** University of WA, Perth 1989-93; Western Australia 1991-93; North Hobart, Australia 1993-94; Tasmania 1993-94; University of NSW, Australia 1994-95
**Cricketers particularly admired:** Greg Matthews, Mark Atkinson (Tasmania), Robin Smith, Mike Hussey (Western Australia)
**Other sports followed:** Golf ('I have a hole in one') and tennis
**Injuries:** Stomach muscle tear (abdominis rectus), missed most of season

**Relaxations:** 'Trying to improve my golf. Taking money off Dave Fulton on the golf course. Spending time with my girlfriend. Swimming on North Cottesloe beach (Western Australia)'

**Extras:** Has played first-class cricket for Western Australia and Tasmania as well as Kent

**Opinions on cricket:** 'Doctoring wickets to suit your own attack is very small-minded and achieves very little in the long term. Look at the big picture and play cricket on the best (hardest) wickets you can possibly prepare. Too much one-day cricket in the UK and far too much cricket crammed into a season. Quality rather than quantity. Encourage young spinners to spin hard at all times.'

**Best batting:** 57* Western Australia v New South Wales, Sydney 1992-93

**Best bowling:** 5-33 Kent v Leicestershire, Canterbury 1995

## 1995 Season

|  | M | Inns | NO | Runs | HS | Avge | 100s | 50s | Ct | St | O | M | Runs | Wkts | Avge | Best | 5wI | 10wM |
|---|---|---|---|---|---|---|---|---|---|---|---|---|---|---|---|---|---|---|
| Test |  |  |  |  |  |  |  |  |  |  |  |  |  |  |  |  |  |  |
| All First | 5 | 9 | 2 | 61 | 18 | 8.71 | - | - | 1 | - | 115.4 | 21 | 401 | 9 | 44.55 | 5-33 | 1 | - |
| 1-day Int |  |  |  |  |  |  |  |  |  |  |  |  |  |  |  |  |  |  |
| NatWest |  |  |  |  |  |  |  |  |  |  |  |  |  |  |  |  |  |  |  |
| B & H |  |  |  |  |  |  |  |  |  |  |  |  |  |  |  |  |  |  |  |
| Sunday |  |  |  |  |  |  |  |  |  |  |  |  |  |  |  |  |  |  |  |

## Career Performances

|  | M | Inns | NO | Runs | HS | Avge | 100s | 50s | Ct | St | Balls | Runs | Wkts | Avge | Best | 5wI | 10wM |
|---|---|---|---|---|---|---|---|---|---|---|---|---|---|---|---|---|---|
| Test |  |  |  |  |  |  |  |  |  |  |  |  |  |  |  |  |  |
| All First | 14 | 18 | 5 | 1871 | 57* | 14.38 | - | 1 | 3 | - | 2956 | 1532 | 37 | 41.40 | 5-33 | 1 | - |
| 1-day Int |  |  |  |  |  |  |  |  |  |  |  |  |  |  |  |  |  |
| NatWest |  |  |  |  |  |  |  |  |  |  |  |  |  |  |  |  |  |  |
| B & H |  |  |  |  |  |  |  |  |  |  |  |  |  |  |  |  |  |  |
| Sunday | 1 | 0 | 0 | 0 | 0 | - | - | - | - | - | 30 | 28 | 0 | - | - | - |

**Name:** James Peter Hewitt
**Role:** Left-hand bat, right-arm
medium-fast bowler
**Born:** 26 February 1976, London
**Height:** 6ft 3in **Weight:** 12st 8lbs
**Nickname:** Hewiey
**County debut:** 1995 (one-day)
**Parents:** Mr T.D. Hewitt and
Mrs G.J. Underhay
**Marital status:** Single
**Family links with cricket**: Father played
club cricket and had trials with Surrey.
Grandfather played club cricket and had
trials with Surrey
**Education:** Buckingham School, Hampton;
Teddington School, Middlesex; Richmond
College; Kingston College; City of
Westminster College
**Qualifications:** GCSEs; City and Guilds Part I, II and III in Recreation and Leisure;
GNVQ Leisure and Tourism; coaching awards in cricket intermediate and advanced;
squash, basketball, hockey, gymnastics, badminton, football, volleyball and referee
qualification; Community Sports Leadership Award
**Career outside cricket:** Retail, cricket and coaching
**Off-season:** Studying at Westminster College
**Cricketers particularly admired:** Richard Hadlee, David Gower, Curtly Ambrose,
Dominic Cork, Richard Johnson, Philip Hudson
**Other sports followed:** Athletics ('represented South of England at cross country'),
football ('played for Chelsea Youth'), badminton, volleyball, rugby (Harlequins)
**Relaxations:** Watching and playing a number of sports and sports quiz programmes
**Extras:** 'I was invited back to my old school, Teddington, to present the sports awards
to the pupils – I consider this to be an honour'
**Opinions on cricket:** 'I am pleased to see the injection of youth into the game at Test
level as well as county. I think the young blood together with the more experienced
players can only be good for the game.'

---

35. Which Minor Counties player won a Gold Award in the
Benson & Hedges Cup against his former county in 1995?

## 1995 Season

| | M | Inns | NO | Runs | HS | Avge | 100s | 50s | Ct | St | O | M | Runs | Wkts | Avge | Best | 5wl | 10wM |
|---|---|---|---|---|---|---|---|---|---|---|---|---|---|---|---|---|---|---|
| Test | | | | | | | | | | | | | | | | | | |
| All First | | | | | | | | | | | | | | | | | | |
| 1-day Int | | | | | | | | | | | | | | | | | | |
| NatWest | | | | | | | | | | | | | | | | | | |
| B & H | | | | | | | | | | | | | | | | | | |
| Sunday | 2 | 2 | 1 | 3 | 3 | 3.00 | - | - | 1 | - | 9 | 0 | 53 | 2 | 26.50 | 2-31 | - | |

## Career Performances

| | M | Inns | NO | Runs | HS | Avge | 100s | 50s | Ct | St | Balls | Runs | Wkts | Avge | Best | 5wl | 10wM |
|---|---|---|---|---|---|---|---|---|---|---|---|---|---|---|---|---|---|
| Test | | | | | | | | | | | | | | | | | |
| All First | | | | | | | | | | | | | | | | | |
| 1-day Int | | | | | | | | | | | | | | | | | |
| NatWest | | | | | | | | | | | | | | | | | |
| B & H | | | | | | | | | | | | | | | | | |
| Sunday | 2 | 2 | 1 | 3 | 3 | 3.00 | - | - | 1 | - | 54 | 53 | 2 | 26.50 | 2-31 | - | |

# HEWSON, D. R.        Gloucestershire

**Name:** Dominic Robert Hewson
**Role:** Right-hand bat, right-arm
medium bowler
**Born:** 3 October 1974, Cheltenham
**Height:** 5ft 9in **Weight:** 12st 11lbs
**Nickname:** Condom, Poppadom
**County debut:** No first-team appearance
**Parents:** Robert and Julie
**Marital status:** Single
**Education:** Cheltenham College; University
of West of England
**Qualifications:** 10 GCSEs, 3 A-levels
**Cricketers particularly admired:** David
Gower, Robin Smith
**Other sports followed:** Rugby
**Injuries:** Ankle ligaments and Achilles
tendon, out for 12 weeks
**Relaxations:** Seeing friends
**Extras:** Made debut for Gloucestershire 2nd XI in July 1993
**Opinions on cricket:** 'Lunch and tea breaks not long enough.'

# HIBBERT, A. J. E.                                          Essex

**Name:** Andrew James Edward Hibbert
**Role:** Right-hand bat, right-arm
medium bowler
**Born:** 17 December 1974, Harold Wood,
Essex
**Height:** 6ft **Weight:** 13st 2lbs
**Nickname:** Buns
**County debut:** 1995
**Parents:** Tony (deceased) and Thelma
**Marital status:** Single
**Family links with cricket:** 'Dad played club
cricket and Mum is an avid cricket follower'
**Education:** St Edward's C of E
Comprehensive, Romford
**Qualifications:** 8 GCSEs, NCA Senior
Coaching Award
**Off-season:** Playing for University of
Newcastle in Australia

**Overseas tours:** England U18 to Denmark (International Youth Tournament ) 1993
**Overseas teams played for:** University of Newcastle, New South Wales, Australia
**Cricketers particularly admired:** Carl Hooper, Graham Thorpe, Graham Gooch
**Other sports followed:** Golf, football (Spurs), snooker
**Injuries:** Broken finger, out for five weeks
**Relaxations:** Music
**Extras:** Played for Essex from U14 upwards, *Daily Telegraph* (South) Batting Award
1990
**Best batting:** 24 Essex v Cambridge University, Fenner's 1995

## 1995 Season

|  | M | Inns | NO | Runs | HS | Avge | 100s | 50s | Ct | St | O | M | Runs Wkts | Avge | Best | 5wl | 10wM |
|---|---|---|---|---|---|---|---|---|---|---|---|---|---|---|---|---|---|
| Test |  |  |  |  |  |  |  |  |  |  |  |  |  |  |  |  |  |
| All First | 1 | 2 | 0 | 31 | 24 | 15.50 | - | - | - | - |  |  |  |  |  |  |  |
| 1-day Int |  |  |  |  |  |  |  |  |  |  |  |  |  |  |  |  |  |  |
| NatWest |  |  |  |  |  |  |  |  |  |  |  |  |  |  |  |  |  |  |
| B & H |  |  |  |  |  |  |  |  |  |  |  |  |  |  |  |  |  |  |  |
| Sunday |  |  |  |  |  |  |  |  |  |  |  |  |  |  |  |  |  |  |  |

## Career Performances

|  | M | Inns | NO | Runs | HS | Avge | 100s | 50s | Ct | St | Balls | Runs | Wkts | Avge | Best | 5wl | 10wM |
|---|---|---|---|---|---|---|---|---|---|---|---|---|---|---|---|---|---|
| Test |  |  |  |  |  |  |  |  |  |  |  |  |  |  |  |  |  |
| All First | 1 | 2 | 0 | 31 | 24 | 15.50 | - | - | - | - |  |  |  |  |  |  |  |
| 1-day Int |  |  |  |  |  |  |  |  |  |  |  |  |  |  |  |  |  |
| NatWest |  |  |  |  |  |  |  |  |  |  |  |  |  |  |  |  |  |
| B & H |  |  |  |  |  |  |  |  |  |  |  |  |  |  |  |  |  |
| Sunday |  |  |  |  |  |  |  |  |  |  |  |  |  |  |  |  |  |

# HICK, G. A. Worcestershire

**Name:** Graeme Ashley Hick
**Role:** Right-hand bat, off-spin bowler
**Born:** 23 May 1966, Salisbury, Rhodesia
**Height:** 6ft 3in **Weight:** 14st 7lbs
**Nickname:** Hicky, Ash
**County debut:** 1984
**County cap:** 1986
**Test debut:** 1991
**Tests:** 37
**One-Day Internationals:** 47
**1000 runs in a season:** 11
**1st-Class 50s:** 98
**1st-Class 100s:** 84
**1st-Class 200s:** 9
**1st-Class 400s:** 1
**1st-Class 5 w. in innings:** 5
**1st-Class 10 w. in match:** 1
**1st-Class catches:** 368
**One-Day 100s:** 18
**Place in batting averages:** 28th av. 49.70 (1994 9th av. 54.92)
**Place in bowling averages:** (1994 126th av. 42.00)
**Strike rate:** (career 87.57)
**Parents:** John and Eve
**Wife and date of marriage:** Jackie, 5 October 1991
**Children:** Lauren Amy, 12 September 1992
**Family links with cricket:** Father served on Zimbabwe Cricket Union Board of
Control since 1984 and played representative cricket in Zimbabwe
**Education:** Banket Primary; Prince Edward Boys' High School, Zimbabwe
**Qualifications:** 4 O-levels, NCA coaching award
**Off-season:** Touring South Africa with England
**Overseas tours:** Zimbabwe to England (World Cup) 1983, to Sri Lanka 1983-84, to

England 1985; England to New Zealand and Australia (World Cup) 1991-92, to India and Sri Lanka 1992-93, to West Indies 1993-94, to Australia 1994-95, to South Africa 1995-96, to India and Pakistan (World Cup) 1995-96

**Overseas teams played for:** Old Hararians, Zimbabwe 1982-90; Northern Districts, New Zealand 1987-89; Queensland, Australia 1990-91

**Cricketers particularly admired:** Duncan Fletcher (Zimbabwe captain) for approach and understanding of the game, David Houghton, Basil D'Oliveira

**Other sports followed:** Follows Liverpool FC, golf, tennis, squash, hockey

**Relaxations:** 'Leaning against Steve Rhodes at first-slip'

**Extras:** Made first century aged six for school team; youngest player participating in 1983 Prudential World Cup (aged 17); youngest player to represent Zimbabwe. Scored 1234 runs in Birmingham League and played for Worcestershire 2nd XI in 1984 – hitting six successive centuries. In 1986, at age 20, he became the youngest player to score 2000 runs in an English season. One of *Wisden*'s Five Cricketers of the Year 1986. In 1988 he made 405* v Somerset at Taunton, the highest individual score in England since 1895, and scored 1000 first-class runs by end of May, hitting a record 410 runs in April. In 1990 became youngest batsman ever to make 50 first-class centuries and scored 645 runs without being dismissed – a record for English cricket. Also in 1990 became the fastest to 10,000 runs in county cricket (179 innings). Qualified as an English player in 1991. Scored first Test century v India in Bombay 1992-93 and was England's leading batsman, bowler and fielder. Published *Hick 'n' Dilley Circus* and *A Champion's Diary*. Also played hockey for Zimbabwe. Finished third in the Whyte and Mackay batting ratings in 1995

**Opinions on cricket:** 'What a great game.'

**Best batting:** 405* Worcestershire v Somerset, Taunton 1988

**Best bowling:** 5-18 Worcestershire v Leicestershire, Worcester 1995

## 1995 Season

|          | M  | Inns | NO | Runs | HS    | Avge   | 100s | 50s | Ct | St | O    | M  | Runs | Wkts | Avge  | Best  | 5wl | 10wM |
|----------|----|------|----|------|-------|--------|------|-----|----|----|------|----|------|------|-------|-------|-----|------|
| Test     | 5  | 10   | 2  | 403  | 118*  | 50.37  | 1    | 3   | 5  | -  | 18   | 4  | 64   | 1    | 64.00 | 1-15  | -   | -    |
| All First| 16 | 27   | 3  | 1193 | 152   | 49.70  | 4    | 5   | 22 | -  | 174  | 39 | 526  | 9    | 58.44 | 5-18  | 1   | -    |
| 1-day Int| 3  | 3    | 0  | 98   | 66    | 32.66  | -    | 1   | -  | -  | 3    | 0  | 22   | 0    | -     |       |     |      |
| NatWest  | 2  | 2    | 0  | 112  | 87    | 56.00  | -    | 1   | 2  | -  | 18   | 1  | 65   | 3    | 21.66 | 2-15  | -   |      |
| B & H    | 6  | 5    | 1  | 466  | 127*  | 116.50 | 3    | 1   | 3  | -  | 12   | 0  | 46   | 2    | 23.00 | 2-30  | -   |      |
| Sunday   | 11 | 11   | 4  | 551  | 130   | 78.71  | 2    | 4   | 1  | -  | 28.3 | 1  | 125  | 13   | 9.61  | 4-21  | -   |      |

## Career Performances

|          | M   | Inns | NO | Runs  | HS    | Avge  | 100s | 50s | Ct  | St | Balls | Runs | Wkts | Avge  | Best  | 5wl | 10wM |
|----------|-----|------|----|-------|-------|-------|------|-----|-----|----|-------|------|------|-------|-------|-----|------|
| Test     | 37  | 66   | 4  | 2336  | 178   | 37.67 | 3    | 14  | 55  | -  | 2507  | 1037 | 20   | 51.85 | 4-126 | -   | -    |
| All First| 300 | 492  | 50 | 25194 | 405*  | 57.00 | 84   | 98  | 368 | -  | 16377 | 8015 | 187  | 42.86 | 5-18  | 5   | 1    |
| 1-day Int| 47  | 46   | 6  | 1571  | 105*  | 39.27 | 1    | 13  | 25  | -  | 588   | 482  | 13   | 37.07 | 3-41  | -   |      |
| NatWest  | 31  | 31   | 6  | 1366  | 172*  | 54.64 | 3    | 8   | 17  | -  | 1005  | 598  | 18   | 33.22 | 4-54  | -   |      |
| B & H    | 49  | 48   | 10 | 2294  | 127*  | 60.36 | 7    | 14  | 32  | -  | 522   | 362  | 9    | 40.22 | 3-36  | -   |      |
| Sunday   | 140 | 135  | 25 | 5211  | 130   | 47.37 | 7    | 40  | 30  | -  | 1967  | 1698 | 60   | 28.30 | 4-21  | -   |      |

# HINDSON, J. E. Nottinghamshire

**Name:** James Edward Hindson
**Role:** Right-hand bat, slow left-arm bowler
**Born:** 13 September 1973, Huddersfield, Yorkshire
**Height:** 6ft 1in **Weight:** 11st 8lbs
**Nickname:** Hindmarsh, Nugget
**County debut:** 1992
**50 w. in a season:** 1
**1st-Class 50s:** 1
**1st-Class 5 w. in innings:** 7
**1st-Class 10 w. match:** 2
**1st-Class catches:** 12
**Place in batting averages:** 263rd av. 13.43
**Place in bowling averages:** 90th av. 34.13
**Strike rate:** 63.87 (career 63.76)
**Parents:** Robert and Gloria
**Marital status:** Single
**Family links with cricket:**
'Older brother captain of village side, younger brother also plays'

**Education:** Robert Sherborne Infants School, Rolleston, Staffs; Ernhale Junior School, Arnold; St Peter's Primary School, East Bridgford; Toot Hill Comprehensive School, Bingham
**Qualifications:** 10 GCSEs, 3 A-levels, senior cricket coach
**Off-season:** Playing for Lancaster Park in Christchurch, New Zealand
**Overseas tours:** England U19 to India 1992-93
**Overseas teams played for:** Lancaster Park, Christchurch, New Zealand 1995-96
**Cricketers particularly admired:** Richard Hadlee, Derek Randall, Robin Smith
**Other sports followed:** Ice hockey, football
**Injuries:** Open dislocation of little finger, missed two weeks
**Relaxations:** 'Being led astray by senior players'
**Extras:** Took five wickets on first-class debut (eight in the match) v Cambridge University. Converted from right-arm to left-arm bowler at age six, still throws right-handed and bowled left-arm medium until 15 years old. Received 2nd team cap at end of 1993 season
**Opinions on cricket:** 'Andy Pick's first ball in each spell should not be tried at home.'
**Best batting:** 53* Nottinghamshire v Oxford University, The Parks 1995
**Best bowling:** 5-42 Nottinghamshire v Cambridge University, Trent Bridge 1992

## 1995 Season

| | M | Inns | NO | Runs | HS | Avge | 100s | 50s | Ct | St | O | M | Runs | Wkts | Avge | Best | 5wI | 10wM |
|---|---|---|---|---|---|---|---|---|---|---|---|---|---|---|---|---|---|---|
| Test | | | | | | | | | | | | | | | | | | |
| All First | 17 | 28 | 5 | 309 | 53 * | 13.43 | - | 1 | 10 | - | 692 | 165 | 2219 | 65 | 34.13 | 5-67 | 5 | 2 |
| 1-day Int | | | | | | | | | | | | | | | | | | |
| NatWest | 2 | 1 | 1 | 16 | 16 * | - | - | - | - | - | 20 | 1 | 83 | 2 | 41.50 | 2-57 | - | |
| B & H | 1 | 1 | 1 | 41 | 41 * | - | - | - | - | - | 10 | 0 | 69 | 1 | 69.00 | 1-69 | - | |
| Sunday | 16 | 5 | 2 | 34 | 14 | 11.33 | - | - | 4 | - | 102 | 4 | 527 | 11 | 47.90 | 3-47 | - | |

## Career Performances

| | M | Inns | NO | Runs | HS | Avge | 100s | 50s | Ct | St | Balls | Runs | Wkts | Avge | Best | 5wI | 10wM |
|---|---|---|---|---|---|---|---|---|---|---|---|---|---|---|---|---|---|
| Test | | | | | | | | | | | | | | | | | |
| All First | 24 | 32 | 5 | 330 | 53 * | 12.22 | - | 1 | 12 | - | 5229 | 2751 | 82 | 33.54 | 5-42 | 7 | 2 |
| 1-day Int | | | | | | | | | | | | | | | | | |
| NatWest | 2 | 1 | 1 | 16 | 16 * | - | - | - | - | - | 120 | 83 | 2 | 41.50 | 2-57 | - | |
| B & H | 1 | 1 | 1 | 41 | 41 * | - | - | - | - | - | 60 | 69 | 1 | 69.00 | 1-69 | - | |
| Sunday | 20 | 7 | 3 | 58 | 21 | 14.50 | - | - | 5 | - | 768 | 639 | 16 | 39.93 | 4-19 | - | |

# HODGSON, G. D.     Gloucestershire

**Name:** Geoffrey Dean Hodgson
**Role:** Right-hand bat
**Born:** 22 October 1966, Carlisle
**Height:** 6ft 1in **Weight:** 13st 7lbs
**Nickname:** Deano, Harrable
**County debut:** 1987 (Warwickshire),
1989 (Gloucestershire)
**County cap:** 1992
**1000 runs in a season:** 4
**1st-Class 50s:** 35
**1st-Class 100s:** 9
**1st-Class catches:** 45
**One-Day 100s:** 2
**Place in batting averages:** 123rd av. 30.82
(1994 167th av. 24.46)
**Parents:** John and Dorothy
**Marital status:** Single
**Education:** Nelson Thomlinson
Comprehensive, Wigton;
Loughborough University
**Qualifications:** 11 O-levels, 4 A-levels, BSc (Hons) Human Biological Sciences, NCA
qualified cricket coach, PFA qualified football coach, LTA qualified tennis coach

**Off-season:** Playing and coaching in South Africa
**Overseas tours:** NCA North U19 to Bermuda 1985; Geoff Humpage Benefit Tour to Barbados 1987; Gloucestershire to Namibia 1990, to Kenya 1991, to Sri Lanka 1992-93
**Overseas teams played for:** Southern Districts, Queensland 1988-89; Wests, Brisbane 1990-91; Belgrano, Buenos Aires, Argentina 1991-93
**Cricketers particularly admired:** Dennis Amiss, Ian Botham, Malcolm Marshall, David Gower, Andrew Symonds and other players who make the most of their abilities
**Other sports followed:** Football, international rugby (league & union), golf, tennis, skiing
**Injuries:** Lower back pain and stiffness since late June, out for last four weeks of the season
**Relaxations:** Listening to music ('all types depending on mood'), reading thrillers and autobiographies, watching comedies and thrillers, going to wine bars
**Extras:** Played Minor County cricket for Cumberland 1982-88; played in 2nd XI for Lancashire 1985-87 and Worcestershire 1989, also played for Warwickshire 1987-88; first-class debut for Gloucestershire in 1989. Rapid Cricketline Player of the Month August/September 1989 while on trial with Gloucestershire and voted Gloucestershire Supporters Player of the Year 1990. Two B&H Man of the Match awards. Increased Championship opening record at Bristol (previously 279 with Chris Broad) to 362 with Tony Wright against Nottinghamshire in May 1995
**Best batting:** 166 Gloucestershire v Hampshire, Southampton 1993

## 1995 Season

|          | M | Inns | NO | Runs | HS | Avge | 100s | 50s | Ct | St | O | M | Runs | Wkts | Avge | Best | 5wI | 10wM |
|----------|---|------|----|----- |----|------|------|-----|----|----|---|---|------|------|------|------|-----|------|
| Test     |   |      |    |      |    |      |      |     |    |    |   |   |      |      |      |      |     |      |
| All First| 9 | 17   | 0  | 524  | 148| 30.82| 1    | 2   | 3  | -  |   |   |      |      |      |      |     |      |
| 1-day Int|   |      |    |      |    |      |      |     |    |    |   |   |      |      |      |      |     |      |
| NatWest  | 2 | 2    | 0  | 24   | 16 | 12.00| -    | -   | -  | -  |   |   |      |      |      |      |     |      |
| B & H    | 2 | 2    | 0  | 31   | 31 | 15.50| -    | -   | -  | -  |   |   |      |      |      |      |     |      |
| Sunday   | 3 | 3    | 1  | 44   | 29 | 22.00| -    | -   | 1  | -  |   |   |      |      |      |      |     |      |

## Career Performances

|          | M   | Inns | NO | Runs | HS    | Avge | 100s | 50s | Ct | St | Balls | Runs | Wkts | Avge | Best | 5wI | 10wM |
|----------|-----|------|----|------|-------|------|------|-----|----|----|-------|------|------|------|------|-----|------|
| Test     |     |      |    |      |       |      |      |     |    |    |       |      |      |      |      |     |      |
| All First| 103 | 179  | 10 | 5675 | 166   | 33.57| 9    | 35  | 45 | -  | 24    | 65   | 0    | -    | -    | -   | -    |
| 1-day Int|     |      |    |      |       |      |      |     |    |    |       |      |      |      |      |     |      |
| NatWest  | 12  | 12   | 0  | 324  | 62    | 27.00| -    | 2   | 1  | -  |       |      |      |      |      |     |      |
| B & H    | 11  | 11   | 1  | 317  | 103 * | 31.70| 1    | 2   | 1  | -  |       |      |      |      |      |     |      |
| Sunday   | 44  | 42   | 5  | 925  | 104 * | 25.00| 1    | 2   | 15 | -  |       |      |      |      |      |     |      |

# HODGSON, T.                                      Essex

**Name:** Timothy Philip Hodgson
**Role:** Left-hand bat, off-spin bowler
**Born:** 27 March 1975, Guildford
**Height:** 5ft 10in  **Weight:** 12st
**Nickname:** Wiggy
**County debut:** No first-team appearance
**Parents:** Simon and Vicky
**Marital status:** Single
**Family links with cricket:** 'Jamie (brother)
played for Cambridge University. Great uncle
Neville Knox toured South Africa with
England in 1902
**Education:** Milbourne Lodge, Esher;
Wellington College, Berkshire; Durham
University
**Off-season:** Student at Durham University
**Overseas tours:** Wellington College to South
Africa
**Cricketers particularly admired:** Jason
Sayers

**Other sports followed:** Football (Southampton FC and Woking FC), tennis and golf
**Relaxations:** Spending time with the family, golf and swimming
**Extras:** Highest first wicket partnership in second team (366). Played Surrey U12 to
U19 and several second team games

36. Who captained the Young Australia side that toured England in 1995?

# HOGGARD, M. J.  Yorkshire

**Name:** Matthew James Hoggard
**Role:** Right-hand bat, right-arm fast bowler
**Born:** 31 December 1976, Leeds
**Height:** 6ft 2in  **Weight:** 12st 12lbs
**Nickname:** Mingh the Merciless
**County debut:** No first-team appearance
**Parents:** John and Margaret
**Marital status:** Single
**Education:** Pudsey Grangefield; Pudsey
Grangefield Sixth Form
**Qualifications:** GCSEs and A-levels
**Overseas tours:** England U19 to Zimbabwe
1995-96
**Cricketers particularly admired:**
David Gower and Ian Botham
**Other sports followed:** Rugby league
(Leeds), football, athletics, rugby
**Injuries:** Pulled side, out for three weeks

**Extras:** Joined England U19 tour to Zimbabwe as a replacement

# HOLLIOAKE, A. J.  Surrey

**Name:** Adam John Hollioake
**Role:** Right-hand bat, right-arm
fast-medium bowler, county vice-captain
**Born:** 5 September 1971, Melbourne,
Australia
**Height:** 5ft 11in **Weight:** 13st
**Nickname:** Smokey, Smokin' Joe, Wolf,
Rock, Rambo, Holly, Strong Dance,
Millionaire, Oaky, The Oak, Hokey Cokey,
Abo, Bong
**County debut:** 1992 (one-day),
1993 (first-class)
**County Cap:** 1995
**1000 runs in a season:** 1
**1st-Class 50s:** 13
**1st-Class 100s:** 5
**1st-Class catches:** 28

**Place in batting average:** 83rd av. 36.63 (1994 83rd av. 36.10)
**Place in bowling averages:** 94th av. 34.33 (1994 107th av. 36.84)
**Strike rate:** 65.85 (career 68.90)
**Parents:** John and Daria
**Marital status:** Single
**Family links with cricket:** Brother plays for Surrey
**Education:** St Joseph's College, Sydney; St Patrick's College, Ballarat, Australia; St George's School, Weybridge; Surrey Tutorial College, Guildford
**Qualifications:** 'Some GCSEs and A-levels'
**Overseas tours:** School trip to Zimbabwe; Surrey YC to Australia; England YC to New Zealand 1990-91
**Overseas teams played for:** Fremantle, Western Australia 1990-91; North Shore, Sydney 1992-93; Geelong, Victoria; North Perth, Western Australia
**Cricketers particularly admired:** Alec Stewart, Graham Thorpe, Joey Benjamin
**Other sports followed:** Rugby, boxing, Aussie Rules football, American football
**Relaxations:** 'A fine bottle of wine, a fine piece of art, a fine piece of jewellery, watching Graham Thorpe compile an innings.'
**Extras:** Played rugby for London Counties, Middlesex and South of England as well as having a trial for England U18. Scored a century on first-class debut against Derbyshire. Surrey Young Player of the Year 1993. Fastest ever one-day 50 – in 15 balls v Yorkshire
**Best batting:** 138 Surrey v Leicestershire, The Oval 1994
**Best bowling:** 4-22 Surrey v Yorkshire, The Oval 1995

## 1995 Season

| | M | Inns | NO | Runs | HS | Avge | 100s | 50s | Ct | St | O | M | Runs | Wkts | Avge | Best | 5wI | 10wM |
|---|---|---|---|---|---|---|---|---|---|---|---|---|---|---|---|---|---|---|
| Test | | | | | | | | | | | | | | | | | | |
| All First | 18 | 32 | 2 | 1099 | 117 * | 36.63 | 1 | 8 | 12 | - | 230.3 | 46 | 721 | 21 | 34.33 | 4-22 | - | - |
| 1-day Int | | | | | | | | | | | | | | | | | | |
| NatWest | 2 | 1 | 0 | 5 | 5 | 5.00 | - | - | - | - | 18 | 3 | 75 | 5 | 15.00 | 4-53 | - | |
| B & H | 4 | 2 | 0 | 26 | 23 | 13.00 | - | - | 3 | - | 23 | 0 | 108 | 2 | 54.00 | 2-30 | - | |
| Sunday | 15 | 14 | 4 | 412 | 93 | 41.20 | - | 2 | 4 | - | 77.1 | 0 | 483 | 17 | 28.41 | 4-22 | - | |

## Career Performances

| | M | Inns | NO | Runs | HS | Avge | 100s | 50s | Ct | St | Balls | Runs | Wkts | Avge | Best | 5wI | 10wM |
|---|---|---|---|---|---|---|---|---|---|---|---|---|---|---|---|---|---|
| Test | | | | | | | | | | | | | | | | | |
| All First | 40 | 64 | 5 | 2173 | 138 | 36.83 | 5 | 13 | 28 | - | 3583 | 1984 | 52 | 38.15 | 4-22 | - | - |
| 1-day Int | | | | | | | | | | | | | | | | | |
| NatWest | 6 | 4 | 1 | 121 | 60 | 40.33 | - | 1 | 3 | - | 238 | 191 | 9 | 21.22 | 4-53 | - | |
| B & H | 8 | 5 | 1 | 40 | 23 | 10.00 | - | - | 4 | - | 276 | 231 | 6 | 38.50 | 3-48 | - | |
| Sunday | 43 | 37 | 9 | 927 | 93 | 33.10 | - | 5 | 7 | - | 1624 | 1596 | 50 | 31.92 | 4-22 | - | |

# HOLLIOAKE, B. C. Surrey

**Name:** Ben Caine Hollioake
**Role:** Right-hand bat, right-arm medium-fast bowler
**Born:** 11 November 1977, Melbourne, Australia
**Height:** 6ft 2in **Weight:** 12st 7lbs
**Nickname:** Oaky, The Bandit, Acorn, Citizen
**County debut:** No first-team appearance
**Parents:** John and Daria
**Marital status:** Engaged
**Family links with cricket:** 'Dad played for Victoria, brother for Surrey and sister used to bowl the odd jaffer in the back yard'
**Education:** Edgarley Hall; Millfield School
**Qualifications:** 'A couple of GCSEs and NCA Coaching Award
**Off-season:** In Perth, Australia and with 'The Coat' and 'Bullwinkle' in the cricket development office
**Overseas tours:** Millfield to Zimbabwe 1992; West of England to West Indies 1992
**Overseas teams played for:** Mellville, Perth 1992-95
**Cricketers particularly admired:** 'Lillee 'n' Thompson', Waugh brothers, Allan Border, Graham Thorpe, Alex Tudor, David Gower, Tony Lock
**Other sports followed:** Australian Rules (Melbourne Demons) and rugby league (Widnes and Balmain Tigers)
**Injuries:** Ankle, out for one game
**Relaxations:** 'Watching the box with a few totties'
**Extras:** Played England U14 and U15. Played Western Australia U17 and U19
**Opinions on cricket:** 'None. People should just get on with it and make a few runs and take the odd wicket.'

# HOLLOWAY, P. C. L.    Somerset

**Name:** Piran Christopher Laity Holloway
**Role:** Left-hand bat, wicket-keeper
**Born:** 1 October 1970, Helston, Cornwall
**Height:** 5ft 8in **Weight:** 11st
**Nickname:** Oggy, Leg, Pill, The Doctor
**County debut:** 1988 (Warwickshire),
1994 (Somerset)
**1st-Class 50s:** 9
**1st-Class 100s:** 3
**1st-Class catches:** 35
**1st-Class stumpings:** 1
**Place in batting averages:** 19th av. 53.93
(1994 205th av. 19.00)
**Parents:** Chris and Mary
**Marital status:** 'Engaged to the lovely Nikki'
**Family links with cricket:** 'Mum and Dad
are keen'
**Education:** Nansloe CP School, Helston;
Millfield School; Taunton School;
Loughborough University
**Qualifications:** 'Some O and A-levels at school, not sure how many, and BSc from Loughborough University'
**Off-season:** 'Coaching and playing cricket for Nedlands in Perth as well as surfing down south in Western Australia'
**Overseas tours:** Millfield School to Barbados 1986; England YC to Australia 1989-90; Warwickshire CCC to Cape Town 1992 and 1993; Somerset CCC to Holland 1994
**Overseas teams played for:** North Perth, 1993-94; Nedlands, Perth 1994-96
**Cricketers particularly admired:** 'More I've played the less I've admired anyone'
**Other sports followed:** 'Very keen surfer. Any spare time that I've got I'm on to it, shared a wave with Tom Caroll at Margaret River last year'
**Injuries:** 'Chewed up foot from wiping out on a wave that sucked dry. Couldn't walk for two weeks'
**Relaxations:** Keeping fit, training at the gym, having a few beers with the Loughborough rugby league team on a Wednesday night, reading
**Extras:** Joined Somerset for the 1995 season. Won the Jack Hobbs Trophy in 1990, played Young England for three years, was fourth in the county averages in 1991
**Opinions on cricket:** 'Too many pseudo-intellectuals trying to change the game radically from the top. If they stopped wittering for five minutes and really considered the state of English cricket they would see that it is at grass-roots level that restructure and investment are needed. "Stop taking yourselves so seriously." No-one with any sense would.'
**Best batting:** 129* Somerset v Sussex, Bath 1995

## 1995 Season

| | M | Inns | NO | Runs | HS | Avge | 100s | 50s | Ct | St | O | M | Runs | Wkts | Avge | Best | 5wI | 10wM |
|---|---|---|---|---|---|---|---|---|---|---|---|---|---|---|---|---|---|---|
| Test | | | | | | | | | | | | | | | | | | |
| All First | 12 | 22 | 6 | 863 | 129 * | 53.93 | 2 | 6 | 3 | - | 2 | 1 | 12 | 0 | - | - | - | - |
| 1-day Int | | | | | | | | | | | | | | | | | | |
| NatWest | 1 | 1 | 1 | 50 | 50 * | - | - | 1 | - | - | | | | | | | | |
| B & H | | | | | | | | | | | | | | | | | | |
| Sunday | 10 | 9 | 2 | 145 | 66 | 20.71 | - | 1 | 1 | 1 | | | | | | | | |

## Career Performances

| | M | Inns | NO | Runs | HS | Avge | 100s | 50s | Ct | St | Balls | Runs | Wkts | Avge | Best | 5wI | 10wM |
|---|---|---|---|---|---|---|---|---|---|---|---|---|---|---|---|---|---|
| Test | | | | | | | | | | | | | | | | | |
| All First | 30 | 49 | 13 | 1481 | 129 * | 41.13 | 3 | 9 | 35 | 1 | 12 | 12 | 0 | - | - | - | - |
| 1-day Int | | | | | | | | | | | | | | | | | |
| NatWest | 4 | 3 | 1 | 68 | 50 * | 34.00 | - | 1 | 3 | 1 | | | | | | | |
| B & H | 6 | 6 | 1 | 67 | 27 | 13.40 | - | - | 7 | - | | | | | | | |
| Sunday | 42 | 34 | 8 | 499 | 66 | 19.19 | - | 2 | 24 | 7 | | | | | | | |

# HOOPER, C. L.         Kent

**Name:** Carl Llewellyn Hooper
**Role:** Right-hand bat, off-spin bowler
**Born:** 15 December 1966, Guyana
**Height:** 6ft **Weight:** 13st
**County debut:** 1992
**County cap:** 1992
**Test debut:** 1987-88
**Tests:** 52
**One-Day Internationals:** 133
**1000 runs in a season:** 5
**1st-Class 50s:** 58
**1st-Class 100s:** 30
**1st-Class 200s:** 1
**1st-Class 5 w. in innings:** 10
**1st-Class catches:** 204
**One-Day 100s:** 6
**One-Day 5 w. in innings:** 1
**Place in batting averages:** 39th av. 46.21
(1994 10th av. 54.44)
**Place in bowling averages:** 142nd av. 48.29
(1994 104th av. 36.37)
**Strike rate:** 94.47 (career 80.47)

**Off-season:** Playing for West Indies
**Overseas tours:** West Indies to India and Pakistan 1987-88, to Australia 1988-89, to Pakistan 1990-91, to England 1991, to Pakistan and Australia (World Cup) 1991-92, to Australia and South Africa 1992-93, to Sharjah, India (Hero Cup) and Sri Lanka 1993-94, to India 1994-95, to England 1995
**Overseas teams played for:** Guyana 1984-95
**Extras:** AXA Equity & Law Award 1993. Withdrew from the West Indies squad for tours to Australia and the World Cup through illness
**Best batting:** 236* Kent v Glamorgan, Canterbury 1993
**Best bowling:** 5-33 West Indies v Queensland, Brisbane 1988-89

### 1995 Season

|           | M  | Inns | NO | Runs | HS  | Avge  | 100s | 50s | Ct | St | O     | M  | Runs | Wkts | Avge  | Best | 5wI | 10wM |
|-----------|----|------|----|------|-----|-------|------|-----|----|----|-------|----|------|------|-------|------|-----|------|
| Test      | 5  | 8    | 1  | 310  | 127 | 44.28 | 1    | 1   | 4  | -  | 68    | 22 | 149  | 3    | 49.66 | 2-36 | -   | -    |
| All First | 15 | 25   | 2  | 1063 | 195 | 46.21 | 5    | 2   | 10 | -  | 267.4 | 54 | 821  | 17   | 48.29 | 3-22 | -   | -    |
| 1-day Int | 3  | 3    | 0  | 91   | 40  | 30.33 | -    | -   | 1  | -  | 31    | 0  | 151  | 3    | 50.33 | 1-38 | -   |      |
| NatWest   |    |      |    |      |     |       |      |     |    |    |       |    |      |      |       |      |     |      |
| B & H     |    |      |    |      |     |       |      |     |    |    |       |    |      |      |       |      |     |      |
| Sunday    |    |      |    |      |     |       |      |     |    |    |       |    |      |      |       |      |     |      |

### Career Performances

|           | M   | Inns | NO | Runs  | HS    | Avge  | 100s | 50s | Ct  | St | Balls | Runs  | Wkts | Avge  | Best | 5wI | 10wM |
|-----------|-----|------|----|-------|-------|-------|------|-----|-----|----|-------|-------|------|-------|------|-----|------|
| Test      | 52  | 87   | 7  | 2548  | 178 * | 31.85 | 5    | 12  | 57  | -  | 6066  | 2672  | 51   | 52.39 | 5-40 | 2   | -    |
| All First | 190 | 297  | 30 | 11921 | 236 * | 44.64 | 30   | 58  | 204 | -  | 25268 | 11175 | 314  | 35.58 | 5-33 | 10  | -    |
| 1-day Int | 133 | 118  | 27 | 3071  | 113 * | 33.74 | 2    | 18  | 64  | -  | 5380  | 3922  | 125  | 31.37 | 4-34 | -   |      |
| NatWest   | 9   | 9    | 1  | 395   | 136 * | 49.37 | 1    | 1   | 7   | -  | 507   | 284   | 5    | 56.80 | 2-12 | -   |      |
| B & H     | 6   | 6    | 0  | 177   | 50    | 29.50 | -    | 1   | 3   | -  | 396   | 188   | 9    | 20.88 | 3-28 | -   |      |
| Sunday    | 48  | 46   | 6  | 1903  | 122   | 47.57 | 3    | 15  | 25  | -  | 2203  | 1431  | 47   | 30.44 | 5-41 | 1   |      |

# HUGHES, J. G.      Northamptonshire

**Name:** John Gareth Hughes
**Role:** Right-hand bat, right-arm medium-fast bowler
**Born:** 3 May 1971, Wellingborough
**Height:** 6ft 2in **Weight:** 13st 7lbs
**Nickname:** Yozzer
**1st-Class 5 w. in innings:** 1
**1st-Class catches:** 4
**Place in bowling averages:**
(1994 63rd av. 30.57)
**Strike rate:** (career 76.10)
**Parents:** John and Jennifer

**Marital status:** Engaged to Helen
**Family links with cricket:** 'My grandad, dad and brother all play or have played for Little Harrowden, whilst two of my uncles umpire for the same club'
**Education:** Little Harrowden Primary School; Westfield Boys/Sir Christopher Hatton School, Wellingborough; Sheffield Hallam University
**Qualifications:** 7 O-levels, 2 A-levels, BEd (Hons) in Physical Education
**Career outside cricket:** Physical education teacher
**Off-season:** Supply teaching in various schools around Northampton
**Overseas tours:** Northamptonshire CA U15 to Holland 1986; Northamptonshire to Durban 1991-92, to Cape Town 1992-93, to Zimbabwe 1994-95
**Overseas teams played for:** Mana and Wellington B 1994-95
**Cricketers particularly admired:** Nick Cook, Alan Walker, David Capel, Greg Thomas, Bob Carter, Curtly Ambrose
**Other sports followed:** 'Football especially, but I enjoy most sports'
**Injuries:** 'Torn intercostal (missed eight weeks); back muscle strain (missed two weeks); damaged stomach muscles (missed three weeks). Just managed to fit in a little cricket in between!'
**Relaxations:** Going out for a pint and a meal
**Extras:** Represented both English Schools and England YC at various age groups. Also represented Northamptonshire at football and basketball at schoolboy level. Grandfather played international football for Wales.
**Best batting:** 17 Northamptonshire v Hampshire, Southampton 1994
**Best bowling:** 5-69 Northamptonshire v Hampshire, Southampton 1994

## 1995 Season

| | M | Inns | NO | Runs | HS | Avge | 100s | 50s | Ct | St | O | M | Runs | Wkts | Avge | Best | 5wI | 10wM |
|---|---|---|---|---|---|---|---|---|---|---|---|---|---|---|---|---|---|---|
| Test | | | | | | | | | | | | | | | | | | |
| All First | 5 | 6 | 1 | 32 | 16 | 6.40 | - | - | - | - | 90 | 15 | 320 | 7 | 45.71 | 3-69 | - | - |
| 1-day Int | | | | | | | | | | | | | | | | | | |
| NatWest | | | | | | | | | | | | | | | | | | |
| B & H | 3 | 3 | 0 | 11 | 9 | 3.66 | - | - | 1 | - | 14.5 | 2 | 79 | 2 | 39.50 | 2-47 | - | |
| Sunday | 2 | 2 | 1 | 0 | 0 * | 0.00 | - | - | - | - | 14 | 0 | 71 | 3 | 23.66 | 2-39 | - | |

## Career Performances

| | M | Inns | NO | Runs | HS | Avge | 100s | 50s | Ct | St | Balls | Runs | Wkts | Avge | Best | 5wI | 10wM |
|---|---|---|---|---|---|---|---|---|---|---|---|---|---|---|---|---|---|
| Test | | | | | | | | | | | | | | | | | |
| All First | 16 | 22 | 1 | 101 | 17 | 4.80 | - | - | 4 | - | 2131 | 1260 | 28 | 45.00 | 5-69 | 1 | - |
| 1-day Int | | | | | | | | | | | | | | | | | |
| NatWest | | | | | | | | | | | | | | | | | |
| B & H | 4 | 3 | 0 | 11 | 9 | 3.66 | - | - | 1 | - | 116 | 106 | 2 | 53.00 | 2-47 | - | |
| Sunday | 6 | 5 | 2 | 31 | 21 | 10.33 | - | - | 1 | - | 174 | 127 | 3 | 42.33 | 2-39 | - | |

# HUMPHRIES, S. Sussex

**Name:** Shaun Humphries
**Role:** Right-hand bat, wicket-keeper
**Born:** 11 January 1973, Horsham,
West Sussex
**Height:** 5ft 11in **Weight:** 10st 7lbs
**Nickname:** Stan, Gooner
**County debut:** 1993
**1st-Class catches:** 2
**Parents:** Peter John and Marilyn Christine
**Marital status:** Single
**Education:** The Weald School, Billingshurst;
Kingston College of Further Education
**Qualifications:** 5 GCSEs, BTEC National
Diploma in Leisure Studies
**Off-season:** Watching Arsenal, drinking and
girlfriend Kate
**Overseas tours:** Sussex U13 to Barbados
1987; Sussex U18 to India 1990-91

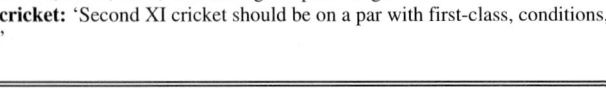

**Overseas teams played for:** Sutherland, Sydney 1994-95
**Cricketers particularly admired:**
Peter Moores, Alec Stewart, Robin Smith, John Berry
**Other sports followed:** Football (Arsenal)
**Relaxations:** Music, raves, Kate, 'marvelling at Spurs' league success'
**Opinions on cricket:** 'Second XI cricket should be on a par with first-class, conditions,
four days etc.'

---

37. Six Lancashire players represented England during the
1995 series against West Indies. Who were they?

**1995 Season (did not make any first-class or one-day appearances)**

## Career Performances

| | M | Inns | NO | Runs | HS | Avge | 100s | 50s | Ct | St | Balls | Runs | Wkts | Avge | Best | 5wI | 10wM |
|---|---|---|---|---|---|---|---|---|---|---|---|---|---|---|---|---|---|
| Test | | | | | | | | | | | | | | | | | |
| All First | 1 | 0 | 0 | 0 | 0 | - | - | - | 2 | - | | | | | | | |
| 1-day Int | | | | | | | | | | | | | | | | | |
| NatWest | | | | | | | | | | | | | | | | | |
| B & H | | | | | | | | | | | | | | | | | |
| Sunday | | | | | | | | | | | | | | | | | |

# HUSSAIN, N.                                    Essex

**Name:** Nasser Hussain
**Role:** Right-hand bat, leg-spin bowler, county vice-captain
**Born:** 28 March 1968, Madras, India
**Height:** 6ft **Weight:** 12st
**Nickname:** Bunny
**County debut:** 1987
**Test debut:** 1989-90
**Tests:** 7
**One-Day Internationals:** 4
**1000 runs in a season:** 3
**1st-Class 50s:** 46
**1st-Class 100s:** 26
**1st-Class catches:** 208
**One-Day 100s:** 2
**Place in batting averages:** 14th av. 54.52
(1994 115th av. 31.79)
**Parents:** Joe and Shireen
**Wife and date of marriage:**
Karen, 24 September 1993

**Family links with cricket:** Father played for Madras in Ranji Trophy 1966-67. Uncle played for Combined Indian Universities. Brother Mel was on Hampshire staff in 1983 and 1984, and has played for England Amateur XI. Brother Abbas played for Essex 2nd XI
**Education:** Forest School, Snaresbrook; Durham University
**Qualifications:** 10 O-levels, 3 A-levels; BSc (Hons) in Geology; NCA cricket coaching award
**Off-season:** England A tour to Pakistan as captain
**Overseas tours:** England YC to Sri Lanka 1986-87, to Australia (Youth World Cup) 1987-88; England to India (Nehru Cup) 1989-90, to West Indies 1989-90 and 1993-94;

England A to Pakistan and Sri Lanka 1990-91, to Bermuda and West Indies 1991-92, to Pakistan 1995-96

**Overseas teams played for:** Madras 1986-87; Petersham, Sydney 1992-93; Adelaide University 1990; Stellenbosch University, South Africa 1994-95

**Cricketers particularly admired:** Graham Gooch, Mark Waugh

**Other sports followed:** Golf, football (Leeds)

**Relaxations:** Watching football, playing golf, listening to music and falling asleep watching old black and white movies

**Extras:** Played for England Schools U15 for two years (one as captain). Youngest player to play for Essex Schools U11 at the age of eight and U15 at the age of 12. At 15, was considered the best young leg-break bowler in the country. Cricket Writers' Club Young Cricketer of the Year, 1989. Holds record for third, fourth and fifth wicket partnerships for Essex (with Mark Waugh, Salim Malik and Mike Garnham). Essex Player of the Year 1993. Appointed Essex's vice-captain for 1996. Captained the England A tour to Pakistan in 1995-96. Finished 2nd in the Whyte and Mackay batting ratings in 1995

**Opinions on cricket:** 'The over-rates for modern cricket are not even close to being possible and should be changed.'

**Best batting:** 197 Essex v Surrey, The Oval 1990

**Best bowling:** 1-38 Essex v Worcestershire, Kidderminster 1992

## 1995 Season

|  | M | Inns | NO | Runs | HS | Avge | 100s | 50s | Ct | St | O | M | Runs | Wkts | Avge | Best | 5wI | 10wM |
|---|---|---|---|---|---|---|---|---|---|---|---|---|---|---|---|---|---|---|
| Test |  |  |  |  |  |  |  |  |  |  |  |  |  |  |  |  |  |  |
| All First | 19 | 35 | 1 | 1854 | 186 | 54.52 | 6 | 10 | 34 | - |  |  |  |  |  |  |  |  |
| 1-day Int |  |  |  |  |  |  |  |  |  |  |  |  |  |  |  |  |  |  |
| NatWest | 2 | 2 | 0 | 52 | 48 | 26.00 | - | - | 3 | - |  |  |  |  |  |  |  |  |
| B & H | 5 | 5 | 1 | 229 | 81 * | 57.25 | - | 2 | 1 | - |  |  |  |  |  |  |  |  |
| Sunday | 17 | 17 | 1 | 634 | 83 | 39.62 | - | 7 | 6 | - |  |  |  |  |  |  |  |  |

## Career Performances

|  | M | Inns | NO | Runs | HS | Avge | 100s | 50s | Ct | St | Balls | Runs | Wkts | Avge | Best | 5wI | 10wM |
|---|---|---|---|---|---|---|---|---|---|---|---|---|---|---|---|---|---|
| Test | 7 | 13 | 2 | 284 | 71 | 25.81 | - | 1 | 3 | - |  |  |  |  |  |  |  |
| All First | 160 | 248 | 32 | 9687 | 197 | 44.84 | 26 | 46 | 208 | - | 276 | 307 | 2 | 153.50 | 1-38 | - | - |
| 1-day Int | 4 | 4 | 1 | 43 | 16 | 14.33 | - | - | 2 | - |  |  |  |  |  |  |  |
| NatWest | 14 | 13 | 1 | 510 | 108 | 42.50 | 1 | 2 | 12 | - |  |  |  |  |  |  |  |
| B & H | 32 | 29 | 5 | 916 | 118 | 38.16 | 1 | 7 | 12 | - |  |  |  |  |  |  |  |
| Sunday | 100 | 90 | 15 | 2243 | 83 | 29.90 | - | 14 | 41 | - |  |  |  |  |  |  |  |

# HUTCHISON, P. M. Yorkshire

**Name:** Paul Michael Hutchison
**Role:** Left-hand bat, left-arm fast bowler
**Born:** 9 June 1977, Leeds
**Height:** 6ft 3in **Weight:** 11st·10lbs
**Nickname:** Hutch, Pooch, Warhair
**County debut:** No first-team appearance
**Parents:** David Hutchison and Rita Laycock
**Marital status:** Single
**Family links with cricket:** 'Grandfather pushed me towards cricket as a five-year old'
**Education:** Pudsey Greenside; Pudsey Crawshaw
**Qualifications:** 4 GCSEs, community sports leader award, qualified cricket coach
**Off-season:**
Working at Yorkshire Cricket School and going to Zimbabwe with England U19
**Overseas tours:** England U19 to Zimbabwe 1995-96

**Cricketers particularly admired:**
David Gower, Darren Gough, Ian Botham, Richard Hadlee
**Other sports followed:** Football (Leeds United) and rugby league (Leeds)
**Relaxations:** Spending time with friends, golf, listening to music
**Extras:** Represented England at U17, U18 and U19 levels. Played for Pudsey St. Lawrence in the Bradford League. Had a place on the Yorkshire Academy and Lord's Taverners
**Opinions on cricket:** 'Far too much cricket crammed into a small season. I think that this destroys quality and increases injury. The game is becoming dull due to easy-paced wickets. Contracts should be nine or 12 months instead of the present six.'

# HUTTON, S.                                    Durham

**Name:** Stewart Hutton
**Role:** Left-hand bat, cover fielder
**Born:** 30 November 1969, Stockton-on-Tees
**Height:** 6ft **Weight:** 12st
**Nickname:** Len
**County debut:** 1992
**1st-Class 50s:** 11
**1st-Class 100s:** 1
**1st-Class catches:** 27
**Place in batting averages:** 141st av. 28.81
(1994 128th av. 30.09)
**Parents:** Leonard and Mavis
**Marital status:** Single
**Education:** De Brus Comprehensive;
Cleveland Technical College
**Qualifications:** 6 O-levels (equivalent),
A-level Economics
**Overseas tours:**
Durham to Zimbabwe 1991-92

**Cricketers particularly admired:** Mike Gatting
**Other sports followed:** Golf, football
**Relaxations:** Playing golf
**Extras:** Scored century for Durham on pre-season tour to Zimbabwe in 1991-92. Appeared as 12th man for England in the 4th Test against West Indies at Old Trafford in 1995
**Best batting:** 101 Durham v Northamptonshire, Hartlepool 1994

## 1995 Season

|           | M  | Inns | NO | Runs | HS  | Avge  | 100s | 50s | Ct | St | O | M | Runs | Wkts | Avge | Best | 5wI | 10wM |
|-----------|----|------|----|------|-----|-------|------|-----|----|----|---|---|------|------|------|------|-----|------|
| Test      |    |      |    |      |     |       |      |     |    |    |   |   |      |      |      |      |     |      |
| All First | 12 | 23   | 1  | 634  | 98  | 28.81 | -    | 4   | 6  | -  | 2 | 0 | 13   | 0    | -    | -    | -   | -    |
| 1-day Int |    |      |    |      |     |       |      |     |    |    |   |   |      |      |      |      |     |      |
| NatWest   | 2  | 2    | 0  | 145  | 125 | 72.50 | 1    | -   | -  | -  |   |   |      |      |      |      |     |      |
| B & H     |    |      |    |      |     |       |      |     |    |    |   |   |      |      |      |      |     |      |
| Sunday    | 11 | 10   | 0  | 156  | 34  | 15.60 | -    | -   | 2  | -  |   |   |      |      |      |      |     |      |

---

38. Two sets of brothers-in law played in the County Championship game between Nottinghamshire and Leicestershire in 1995. Who were they?

## Career Performances

|         | M  | Inns | NO | Runs | HS  | Avge  | 100s | 50s | Ct | St | Balls | Runs | Wkts | Avge | Best | 5wI | 10wM |
|---------|----|------|----|------|-----|-------|------|-----|----|----|-------|------|------|------|------|-----|------|
| Test    |    |      |    |      |     |       |      |     |    |    |       |      |      |      |      |     |      |
| All First | 44 | 79   | 3  | 2171 | 101 | 28.56 | 1    | 11  | 27 | -  | 25    | 18   | 0    | -    | -    | -   | -    |
| 1-day Int |    |      |    |      |     |       |      |     |    |    |       |      |      |      |      |     |      |
| NatWest | 6  | 6    | 1  | 269  | 125 | 53.80 | 1    | 1   | 2  | -  |       |      |      |      |      |     |      |
| B & H   | 1  | 1    | 0  | 8    | 8   | 8.00  | -    | -   | -  | -  |       |      |      |      |      |     |      |
| Sunday  | 36 | 33   | 4  | 662  | 70  | 22.82 | -    | 1   | 9  | -  |       |      |      |      |      |     |      |

# HYAM, B. J. Essex

**Name:** Barry James Hyam
**Role:** Right-hand bat, wicket-keeper
**Born:** 9 September 1975, Romford, Essex
**Height:** 5ft 11in  **Weight:** 12st
**Nickname:** Bazza
**County debut:** 1993
**1st-Class catches:** 2
**Parents:** Peter and Gloria
**Marital status:** Single
**Family links with cricket:** Brother Matthew plays for Harold Wood, brother Richard plays for Gidea Park, 'Matt also has NCA coaching award'
**Education:** Marshalls Park; Havering Sixth Form College
**Qualifications:** 9 GCSEs, 1 A-level, NCA Coaching Award
**Off-season:** Studying at Westminster College and coaching at Essex CCC

**Cricketers particularly admired:** Graham Gooch, Jack Russell
**Other sports followed:** Football, hockey and golf
**Injuries:** Broken left arm, out for six weeks
**Relaxations:** Playing football, hockey and golf
**Extras:** Made first-class debut on his 18th birthday
**Opinions on cricket:** 'Though this season the County Championship has been close and exciting, something needs to be done for those clubs not in the running to keep both players and spectators on their toes.'
**Best batting:** 1 Essex v Glamorgan, Cardiff 1993

**1995 Season (did not make any first-class or one-day appearances)**

**Career Performances**

|  | M | Inns | NO | Runs | HS | Avge | 100s | 50s | Ct | St | Balls | Runs | Wkts | Avge | Best | 5wl | 10wM |
|---|---|---|---|---|---|---|---|---|---|---|---|---|---|---|---|---|---|
| Test |  |  |  |  |  |  |  |  |  |  |  |  |  |  |  |  |  |
| All First | 1 | 2 | 0 | 1 | 1 | 0.50 | - | - | 2 | - |  |  |  |  |  |  |  |
| 1-day Int |  |  |  |  |  |  |  |  |  |  |  |  |  |  |  |  |  |
| NatWest |  |  |  |  |  |  |  |  |  |  |  |  |  |  |  |  |  |
| B & H |  |  |  |  |  |  |  |  |  |  |  |  |  |  |  |  |  |
| Sunday |  |  |  |  |  |  |  |  |  |  |  |  |  |  |  |  |  |

# IGGLESDEN, A. P. — Kent

**Name:** Alan Paul Igglesden
**Role:** Right-hand bat, right-arm fast-medium bowler
**Born:** 8 October 1964, Farnborough, Kent
**Height:** 6ft 6in **Weight:** 15st
**Nickname:** Iggy, Norm, Ivor
**County debut:** 1986
**Test debut:** 1989
**Tests:** 3
**One-Day Internationals:** 4
**50 wickets in a season:** 4
**1st-Class 5 w. in innings:** 23
**1st-Class 10 w. in match:** 4
**1st-Class catches:** 37
**One-Day 5 w. in innings:** 2
**Place in bowling averages:** 45th av. 26.80 (1994 117th av. 38.70)
**Strike rate:** 48.95 (career 52.27)
**Parents:** Alan Trevor and Gillian Catharine
**Wife and date of marriage:** Hilary Moira, 20 January 1990
**Family links with cricket:** Brother Kevin plays for Holmesdale in the Kent League
**Education:** St Mary's Primary School; Hosey School; Churchill Secondary School, Westerham
**Qualifications:** 9 CSEs, coaching certificate
**Overseas tours:** With England A to Zimbabwe and Kenya 1989-90; Fred Rumsey's XI to Barbados 1990; Boland Cricket Union and Kraaifontein 1992-93; England to West Indies 1993-94
**Overseas teams played for:** Avendale, Cape Town 1985-89; Western Province 1987-91; Green Point, Cape Town 1991-92; Boland Cricket Union 1992-93

**Cricketers particularly admired:** Terry Alderman, Dennis Lillee, Carl Hooper, Graeme Hick
**Other sports followed:** 'Very keen Crystal Palace supporter'
**Injuries:** Slipped disc, missed last five weeks of season
**Relaxations:** 'Golf, walking "Lillee", our pet cocker spaniel, with Hilary and drinking'
**Best batting:** 41 Kent v Surrey, Canterbury 1988
**Best bowling:** 7-28 Boland v Griqualand West, Kimberley 1992-93

## 1995 Season

| | M | Inns | NO | Runs | HS | Avge | 100s | 50s | Ct | St | O | M | Runs | Wkts | Avge | Best | 5wI | 10wM |
|---|---|---|---|---|---|---|---|---|---|---|---|---|---|---|---|---|---|---|
| Test | | | | | | | | | | | | | | | | | | |
| All First | 7 | 9 | 4 | 62 | 18 | 12.40 | - | - | 1 | - | 171.2 | 37 | 563 | 21 | 26.80 | 5-92 | 1 | - |
| 1-day Int | | | | | | | | | | | | | | | | | | |
| NatWest | 1 | 0 | 0 | 0 | 0 | - | - | - | - | - | 7 | 0 | 22 | 0 | - | - | - | |
| B & H | 1 | 0 | 0 | 0 | 0 | - | - | - | - | - | 11 | 0 | 45 | 1 | 45.00 | 1-45 | - | |
| Sunday | 11 | 3 | 1 | 16 | 13 | 8.00 | - | - | 3 | - | 76 | 9 | 270 | 10 | 27.00 | 3-11 | - | |

## Career Performances

| | M | Inns | NO | Runs | HS | Avge | 100s | 50s | Ct | St | Balls | Runs | Wkts | Avge | Best | 5wI | 10wM |
|---|---|---|---|---|---|---|---|---|---|---|---|---|---|---|---|---|---|
| Test | 3 | 5 | 3 | 6 | 3 * | 3.00 | - | - | 1 | - | 555 | 329 | 6 | 54.83 | 2-91 | - | - |
| All First | 145 | 158 | 59 | 862 | 41 | 8.70 | - | - | 37 | - | 25247 | 12748 | 483 | 26.39 | 7-28 | 23 | 4 |
| 1-day Int | 4 | 3 | 1 | 20 | 18 | 10.00 | - | - | 1 | - | 168 | 122 | 2 | 61.00 | 2-12 | - | |
| NatWest | 14 | 4 | 3 | 23 | 12 * | 23.00 | - | - | 3 | - | 728 | 375 | 18 | 20.83 | 4-29 | - | |
| B & H | 25 | 10 | 7 | 43 | 26 * | 14.33 | - | - | 5 | - | 1457 | 892 | 35 | 25.48 | 3-24 | - | |
| Sunday | 81 | 27 | 17 | 93 | 13 * | 9.30 | - | - | 19 | - | 3696 | 2437 | 104 | 23.43 | 5-13 | 2 | |

# ILLINGWORTH, R. K. Worcestershire

**Name:** Richard Keith Illingworth
**Role:** Right-hand bat, slow left-arm bowler
**Born:** 23 August 1963, Bradford
**Height:** 6ft **Weight:** 13st
**Nickname:** Lucy, Harry
**County debut:** 1982
**County cap:** 1986
**Test debut:** 1991
**Tests:** 6
**One-Day Internationals:** 18
**50 wickets in a season:** 4
**1st-Class 50s:** 14
**1st-Class 100s:** 3
**1st-Class 5 w. in innings:** 22
**1st-Class 10 w. in match:** 5
**1st-Class catches:** 127
**One-Day 5 w. in innings:** 2
**Place in batting averages:** 241st av. 16.00
(1994 179th av. 23.05)
**Place in bowling averages:** 47th av. 26.93
(1994 64th av. 30.59)
**Strike rate:** 69.86 (career 76.77)
**Parents:** Keith and Margaret
**Wife and date of marriage:** Anne, 20 September 1985
**Children:** Miles, 28 August 1987; Thomas, 20 April 1989
**Family links with cricket:** Father played Bradford League cricket
**Education:** Wrose Brow Middle; Salts Grammar School ('same school as the late Jim Laker')
**Qualifications:** 6 O-levels, senior coaching award
**Off-season:** Touring South Africa with England
**Overseas tours:** England A to Zimbabwe and Kenya 1989-90, to Pakistan and Sri Lanka 1990-91; England to New Zealand and Australia (World Cup) 1991-92, to South Africa 1995-96, to India and Pakistan (World Cup) 1995-96
**Overseas teams played for:** Natal 1988-89
**Cricketers particularly admired:** Ian Botham
**Other sports followed:** Most sports – football, golf and rugby
**Injuries:** Broken right index finger, broken knuckle on left little finger, hernia, missed nine weeks in total
**Relaxations:** 'Golf, playing with my two children, cycling, reading autobiographies, DIY and gardening'
**Extras:** Took 11 for 108 on South African first-class debut for Natal B v Boland 1988.

Scored 120 not out as nightwatchman for Worcestershire v Warwickshire 1988 and 106 for England A v Zimbabwe 1989-90. In 1991, v West Indies, became 11th person in history to take a wicket with first ball in Test cricket. Took a hat-trick in Sunday League v Sussex in 1993, the first Worcestershire player to do this in one-day cricket. Won 1993 Dick Lygon award for contribution to Worcestershire CCC

**Best batting:** 120* Worcestershire v Warwickshire, Worcester 1987
**Best bowling:** 7-50 Worcestershire v Oxford University, The Parks 1985

## 1995 Season

|  | M | Inns | NO | Runs | HS | Avge | 100s | 50s | Ct | St | O | M | Runs | Wkts | Avge | Best | 5wI | 10wM |
|---|---|---|---|---|---|---|---|---|---|---|---|---|---|---|---|---|---|---|
| Test | 4 | 8 | 5 | 69 | 17 * | 23.00 | - | - | 2 | - | 100 | 40 | 215 | 6 | 35.83 | 4-96 | - | - |
| All First | 14 | 19 | 9 | 160 | 23 * | 16.00 | - | - | 5 | - | 524 | 172 | 1212 | 45 | 26.93 | 4-30 | - | - |
| 1-day Int | | | | | | | | | | | | | | | | | | |
| NatWest | 1 | 1 | 0 | 11 | 11 | 11.00 | - | - | - | - | 12 | 2 | 25 | 1 | 25.00 | 1-25 | - | |
| B & H | 6 | 1 | 1 | 4 | 4 * | - | - | - | 2 | - | 59.1 | 7 | 167 | 9 | 18.55 | 4-27 | - | |
| Sunday | 7 | 2 | 2 | 0 | 0 * | - | - | - | 2 | - | 49.5 | 6 | 196 | 8 | 24.50 | 2-3 | - | |

## Career Performances

|  | M | Inns | NO | Runs | HS | Avge | 100s | 50s | Ct | St | Balls | Runs | Wkts | Avge | Best | 5wI | 10wM |
|---|---|---|---|---|---|---|---|---|---|---|---|---|---|---|---|---|---|
| Test | 6 | 12 | 7 | 100 | 17 * | 20.00 | - | - | 3 | - | 940 | 428 | 10 | 42.80 | 4-96 | - | - |
| All First | 297 | 333 | 93 | 5101 | 120 * | 21.25 | 3 | 14 | 127 | - | 52741 | 21045 | 687 | 30.63 | 7-50 | 22 | 5 |
| 1-day Int | 18 | 7 | 2 | 61 | 14 | 12.20 | - | - | 8 | - | 1093 | 760 | 24 | 31.66 | 3-33 | - | |
| NatWest | 31 | 14 | 5 | 108 | 22 | 12.00 | - | - | 10 | - | 1855 | 942 | 26 | 36.23 | 4-20 | - | |
| B & H | 50 | 24 | 14 | 204 | 36 * | 20.40 | - | - | 12 | - | 2560 | 1461 | 48 | 30.43 | 4-27 | - | |
| Sunday | 162 | 74 | 38 | 490 | 31 | 13.61 | - | - | 38 | - | 6188 | 4448 | 189 | 23.53 | 5-24 | 2 | |

# ILOTT, M. C.                                                    Essex

**Name:** Mark Christopher Ilott
**Role:** Left-hand bat (tail end), left-arm
fast-medium bowler
**Born:** 27 August 1970, Watford
**Height:** 6ft 1in **Weight:** 13st
**Nickname:** Ramble, Choock
**County debut:** 1988
**County cap:** 1993
**Test debut:** 1993
**Tests:** 3
**50 wickets in a season:** 3
**1st-Class 50s:** 3
**1st-Class 5 w. in innings:** 17
**1st-Class 10 w. in match:** 3
**1st-Class catches:** 27
**One-Day 5 w. in innings:** 1
**Place in batting averages:** 258th av. 14.00
(1994 221st av. 17.63)
**Place in bowling averages:** 27th av. 24.32 (1994 15th av. 23.57)
**Strike rate:** 44.82 (career 55.74)
**Parents:** John and Glenys
**Wife and date of marriage:** Sandra Jane, 14 October 1994
**Family links with cricket:** Brother keen club and minor counties cricketer, father played club cricket at Watford Town and various others and grandfather played for many years
**Education:** Francis Combe School
**Qualifications:** 6 O-levels, 2 A-levels, 2 AO-levels, coaching qualification, diploma in Fitness and Nutrition
**Career outside cricket:** 'A bit of work for a graphic design company called Centremark of Chelmsford'
**Off-season:** England tour of South Africa and 'hopefully World Cup'
**Overseas tours:** England A to Sri Lanka 1990-91, to Australia 1992-93, to South Africa 1993-94, to India 1994-95; England to South Africa 1995-96
**Overseas teams played for:** East Torrens District, Adelaide 1989-91
**Cricketers particularly admired:** John Lever, Malcolm Marshall, Graham Gooch
**Other sports followed:** 'All sports except horses and rugby league'
**Injuries:** Ilopsoas ('apparently'), missed two weeks
**Relaxations:** Playing the guitar, golf, snooker, listening to music, and 'seeing "The Overtures" play live at Broxbourne'
**Extras:** Youngest player ever to play for Hertfordshire. Missed almost all 1991 season with stress fracture of the back. Injured towards the end of England's tour to South Africa and subsequently left out of the one-day squad
**Opinions on cricket:** 'Not enough rain in 1995.'

**Best batting:** 60 England A v Warwickshire, Edgbaston 1995
**Best bowling:** 9-19 Essex v Northamptonshire, Luton 1995

### 1995 Season

| | M | Inns | NO | Runs | HS | Avge | 100s | 50s | Ct | St | O | M | Runs | Wkts | Avge | Best | 5wI | 10wM |
|---|---|---|---|---|---|---|---|---|---|---|---|---|---|---|---|---|---|---|
| Test | | | | | | | | | | | | | | | | | | |
| All First | 17 | 29 | 4 | 350 | 60 | 14.00 | - | 1 | 4 | - | 582.4 | 126 | 1897 | 78 | 24.32 | 9-19 | 6 | 2 |
| 1-day Int | | | | | | | | | | | | | | | | | | |
| NatWest | 2 | 2 | 1 | 58 | 54 * | 58.00 | - | 1 | - | - | 22 | 5 | 76 | 2 | 38.00 | 1-24 | - | |
| B & H | 5 | 3 | 0 | 34 | 21 | 11.33 | - | - | 1 | - | 44 | 3 | 160 | 3 | 53.33 | 1-22 | - | |
| Sunday | 14 | 12 | 6 | 138 | 56 * | 23.00 | - | 1 | 4 | - | 96.2 | 1 | 442 | 22 | 20.09 | 4-27 | - | |

### Career Performances

| | M | Inns | NO | Runs | HS | Avge | 100s | 50s | Ct | St | Balls | Runs | Wkts | Avge | Best | 5wI | 10wM |
|---|---|---|---|---|---|---|---|---|---|---|---|---|---|---|---|---|---|
| Test | 3 | 5 | 1 | 28 | 15 | 7.00 | - | - | - | - | 774 | 412 | 8 | 51.50 | 3-108 | - | - |
| All First | 100 | 119 | 29 | 1235 | 60 | 13.72 | - | 3 | 27 | - | 19678 | 9969 | 353 | 28.24 | 9-19 | 17 | 3 |
| 1-day Int | | | | | | | | | | | | | | | | | |
| NatWest | 10 | 6 | 3 | 108 | 54 * | 36.00 | - | 1 | 2 | - | 637 | 400 | 12 | 33.33 | 2-23 | - | |
| B & H | 17 | 6 | 1 | 53 | 21 | 10.60 | - | - | 1 | - | 899 | 480 | 23 | 20.86 | 5-21 | 1 | |
| Sunday | 60 | 35 | 12 | 277 | 56 * | 12.04 | - | 1 | 9 | - | 2618 | 1923 | 80 | 24.03 | 4-15 | - | |

# INNES, K. J.          Northamptonshire

**Name:** Kevin John Innes
**Role:** Right-hand bat, right-arm medium bowler
**Born:** 24 September 1975, Wellingborough
**Height:** 5ft 10in **Weight:** 10st 5lbs
**Nickname:** Ernie, Milkman
**County debut:** 1994
**Parents:** Peter and Jane
**Marital status:** Single
**Education:** Boothville Middle School; Weston Favell Upper School, Northampton
**Qualifications:** 6 GCSEs, 4 O-levels
**Off-season:** Working and playing cricket in New Zealand
**Overseas tours:** England U18 to South Africa 1992-93; England U19 to Sri Lanka 1993-94
**Cricketers particularly admired:** Carl Hooper, Viv Richards

**Other sports followed:** Snooker, football, golf
**Relaxations:** Watching and playing most sport, music
**Extras:** Played for England U19 in home series against India in 1994
**Opinions on cricket:** 'It is a shame that employment is not found at the end of the season for a lot more cricketers.'

## 1995 Season

|  | M | Inns | NO | Runs | HS | Avge | 100s | 50s | Ct | St | O | M | Runs | Wkts | Avge | Best | 5wI | 10wM |
|---|---|---|---|---|---|---|---|---|---|---|---|---|---|---|---|---|---|---|
| Test |  |  |  |  |  |  |  |  |  |  |  |  |  |  |  |  |  |  |
| All First |  |  |  |  |  |  |  |  |  |  |  |  |  |  |  |  |  |  |  |
| 1-day Int |  |  |  |  |  |  |  |  |  |  |  |  |  |  |  |  |  |  |  |
| NatWest |  |  |  |  |  |  |  |  |  |  |  |  |  |  |  |  |  |  |  |
| B & H |  |  |  |  |  |  |  |  |  |  |  |  |  |  |  |  |  |  |  |  |
| Sunday | 1 | 0 | 0 | 0 | 0 | - | - | - | - | - | 6 | 0 | 29 | 0 | - |  | - | - |

## Career Performances

|  | M | Inns | NO | Runs | HS | Avge | 100s | 50s | Ct | St | Balls | Runs | Wkts | Avge | Best | 5wI | 10wM |
|---|---|---|---|---|---|---|---|---|---|---|---|---|---|---|---|---|---|
| Test |  |  |  |  |  |  |  |  |  |  |  |  |  |  |  |  |  |
| All First | 1 | 2 | 0 | 0 | 0 | 0.00 | - | - | - | - | 60 | 33 | 0 | - | - | - | - |
| 1-day Int |  |  |  |  |  |  |  |  |  |  |  |  |  |  |  |  |  |
| NatWest |  |  |  |  |  |  |  |  |  |  |  |  |  |  |  |  |  |
| B & H | 1 | 0 | 0 | 0 | 0 | - | - | - | - | - | 36 | 25 | 1 | 25.00 | 1-25 | - |
| Sunday | 6 | 2 | 0 | 8 | 5 | 4.00 | - | - | 2 | - | 192 | 216 | 2 | 108.00 | 1-35 | - |

# IRANI, R.            Essex

**Name:** Ronnie Irani
**Role:** Right-hand bat, right-arm medium bowler
**Born:** 26 October 1971, Leigh, Lancashire
**Height:** 6ft 4in **Weight:** 13st 10lbs
**Nickname:** Reggie, Ledge
**County debut:** 1990 (Lancashire),1994 (Essex)
**County cap:** 1994
**1000 runs in a season:** 1
**1st-Class 50s:** 17
**1st-Class 100s:** 3
**1st-Class catches:** 18
**1st-Class 5 w. innings:** 1
**One-day 100s:** 1
**Place in batting averages:** 85th av. 36.40 (1994 52nd av. 41.93)
**Place in bowling averages:** 133rd av. 45.25 (1994 56th av. 29.78)
**Strike rate:** 80.40 (career 69.98)

**Parents:** Jimmy and Anne
**Marital status:** Single
**Family links with cricket:** 'Father played local league cricket in Bolton for 30 years; mother did teas for many years!'
**Education:** Church Road Primary School; Smithills Comprehensive School
**Qualifications:** 9 GCSEs
**Off-season:** England A tour to Pakistan
**Overseas tours:** England YC to Australia 1989-90; England A to Pakistan 1995-96
**Overseas teams played for:** Technicol Natal, Durban, South Africa 1992-93; Eden-Roskill, Auckland 1993-94
**Cricketers particularly admired:** Mark Waugh, Javed Miandad, Wasim Akram, John Crawley, Graham Gooch
**Other sports followed:** 'Most sports especially football'
**Relaxations:** Sleeping and watching football
**Extras:** Played for England U19 in home series v Australia 1991, scoring a century and three 50s in six innings and being named Bull Man of the Series
**Opinions on cricket:** 'Too much cricket played by English county cricket professionals'
**Best batting:** 119 Essex v Worcestershire, Worcester 1994
**Best bowling:** 5-62 Essex v Kent, Canterbury 1995

## 1995 Season

|  | M | Inns | NO | Runs | HS | Avge | 100s | 50s | Ct | St | O | M | Runs | Wkts | Avge | Best | 5wI | 10wM |
|---|---|---|---|---|---|---|---|---|---|---|---|---|---|---|---|---|---|---|
| Test |  |  |  |  |  |  |  |  |  |  |  |  |  |  |  |  |  |  |
| All First | 18 | 34 | 2 | 1165 | 108 | 36.40 | 1 | 9 | 7 | - | 361.5 | 71 | 1222 | 27 | 45.25 | 5-62 | 1 | - |
| 1-day Int |  |  |  |  |  |  |  |  |  |  |  |  |  |  |  |  |  |  |
| NatWest | 2 | 2 | 0 | 12 | 12 | 6.00 | - | - | - | - | 22 | 1 | 106 | 0 | - |  | - | - |
| B & H | 5 | 4 | 0 | 92 | 40 | 23.00 | - | - | 1 | - | 42 | 5 | 168 | 8 | 21.00 | 3-40 | - |  |
| Sunday | 17 | 17 | 2 | 419 | 101 * | 27.93 | 1 | 2 | 4 | - | 112 | 6 | 543 | 22 | 24.68 | 3-32 | - |  |

## Career Performances

|  | M | Inns | NO | Runs | HS | Avge | 100s | 50s | Ct | St | Balls | Runs | Wkts | Avge | Best | 5wI | 10wM |
|---|---|---|---|---|---|---|---|---|---|---|---|---|---|---|---|---|---|
| Test |  |  |  |  |  |  |  |  |  |  |  |  |  |  |  |  |  |
| All First | 45 | 74 | 9 | 2273 | 119 | 34.96 | 3 | 17 | 18 | - | 4199 | 2354 | 60 | 39.23 | 5-62 | 1 | - |
| 1-day Int |  |  |  |  |  |  |  |  |  |  |  |  |  |  |  |  |  |
| NatWest | 4 | 4 | 0 | 53 | 30 | 13.25 | - | - | - | - | 276 | 227 | 4 | 56.75 | 4-55 | - |  |
| B & H | 7 | 4 | 0 | 92 | 40 | 23.00 | - | - | 1 | - | 336 | 257 | 9 | 28.55 | 3-40 | - |  |
| Sunday | 41 | 37 | 2 | 674 | 101 * | 19.25 | 1 | 2 | 7 | - | 1125 | 864 | 37 | 23.35 | 3-22 | - |  |

# JAMES, K. D.                                     Hampshire

**Name:** Kevan David James
**Role:** Left-hand bat, left-arm medium bowler
**Born:** 18 March 1961, Lambeth, South London
**Height:** 6ft 1/2in **Weight:** 13st 8lbs
**Nickname:** Jambo, Jaimo, Jockey
**County debut:** 1980 (Middlesex), 1985 (Hampshire)
**County cap:** 1989
**1000 runs in a season:** 2
**1st-Class 50s:** 31
**1st-Class 100s:** 8
**1st-Class 5 w. in innings:** 8
**1st-Class catches:** 59
**One-day 5 w. innings:** 1
**Place in batting averages:** 216th av. 18.94 (1994 196th av. 20.85)
**Place in bowling averages:** 134th av. 45.63 (1994 94th av. 34.61)

**Strike rate:** 74.31 (career 65.14)
**Parents:** David (deceased) and Helen
**Wife and date of marriage:** Debbie, October 1987
**Children:** Natalie Ann, 8 October 1992; Naomi, October 1995
**Family links with cricket:** Late father played club cricket in North London; brother Martin plays for Hertfordshire
**Education:** Edmonton County High School
**Qualifications:** 5 O-levels, qualified coach, City and Guilds in Electric Theories
**Off-season:** Working for Southern Electric
**Overseas tours:** England YC to Australia 1978-79, to West Indies 1979-80
**Overseas teams played for:** Wellington, New Zealand 1982-83, 1983-84
**Cricketers particularly admired:** Chris Smith
**Other sports followed:** 'Football but never achieved anything – about the same as cricket'
**Relaxations:** Breeding
**Extras:** Left Middlesex at end of 1984 season and joined Hampshire
**Opinions on cricket:** 'Sick and tired of journalists who slag off professional cricket. If they don't enjoy watching it then they should move over and let others who do enjoy it write about it. We all have a duty to promote county cricket, especially those who earn a living from it and don't even play the game.'
**Best batting:** 162 Hampshire v Glamorgan, Cardiff 1989
**Best bowling:** 6-22 Hampshire v Australia, Southampton 1985

## 1995 Season

| | M | Inns | NO | Runs | HS | Avge | 100s | 50s | Ct | St | O | M | Runs | Wkts | Avge | Best | 5wI | 10wM |
|---|---|---|---|---|---|---|---|---|---|---|---|---|---|---|---|---|---|---|
| Test | | | | | | | | | | | | | | | | | | |
| All First | 12 | 21 | 3 | 341 | 53 | 18.94 | - | 1 | 5 | - | 235.2 | 47 | 867 | 19 | 45.63 | 6-38 | 1 | - |
| 1-day Int | | | | | | | | | | | | | | | | | | |
| NatWest | 1 | 1 | 0 | 9 | 9 | 9.00 | - | - | - | - | 10 | 3 | 21 | 1 | 21.00 | 1-21 | - | |
| B & H | 3 | 2 | 0 | 17 | 15 | 8.50 | - | - | 1 | - | 18 | 3 | 74 | 2 | 37.00 | 1-23 | - | |
| Sunday | 12 | 9 | 4 | 173 | 62 * | 34.60 | - | 1 | 3 | - | 86 | 6 | 393 | 13 | 30.23 | 4-35 | - | |

## Career Performances

| | M | Inns | NO | Runs | HS | Avge | 100s | 50s | Ct | St | Balls | Runs | Wkts | Avge | Best | 5wI | 10wM |
|---|---|---|---|---|---|---|---|---|---|---|---|---|---|---|---|---|---|
| Test | | | | | | | | | | | | | | | | | |
| All First | 182 | 269 | 45 | 6831 | 162 | 30.49 | 8 | 31 | 59 | - | 19542 | 9937 | 300 | 33.12 | 6-22 | 8 | - |
| 1-day Int | | | | | | | | | | | | | | | | | |
| NatWest | 20 | 12 | 2 | 156 | 42 | 15.60 | - | - | 3 | - | 1222 | 772 | 25 | 30.88 | 3-22 | - | |
| B & H | 38 | 26 | 5 | 351 | 45 | 16.71 | - | - | 8 | - | 1873 | 1228 | 30 | 40.93 | 3-31 | - | |
| Sunday | 140 | 95 | 29 | 1413 | 66 | 21.40 | - | 4 | 38 | - | 5629 | 4046 | 128 | 31.60 | 5-42 | 1 | |

# JAMES, S. P.      Glamorgan

**Name:** Stephen Peter James
**Role:** Right-hand opening bat
**Born:** 7 September 1967, Lydney
**Height:** 6ft **Weight:** 12st 5lbs
**Nickname:** Sid, Jamo
**County debut:** 1985
**County cap:** 1992
**1000 runs in a season:** 3
**1st-Class 50s:** 24
**1st-Class 100s:** 17
**1st-Class 200s:** 1
**1st-Class catches:** 101
**One-Day 100s:** 4
**Place in batting averages:** 66th av. 40.44
(1994 67th av. 38.13)
**Parents:** Peter and Margaret
**Marital status:** Single
**Family links with cricket:** Father played for
Gloucestershire 2nd XI. Distant relative of
Dominic Ostler
**Education:** Monmouth School; University College, Swansea; Cambridge University
**Qualifications:** BA (Hons) Wales – Classics; BA (Hons) Cantab – Land Economy

**Off-season:** Playing rugby for Lydney and looking for work
**Overseas tours:** Welsh Schools to Barbados 1984; Monmouth Schools to Sri Lanka 1985; Combined Universities to Barbados 1989; Glamorgan to Trinidad 1989-90, to Zimbabwe 1990-91, Cape Town 1993-94
**Overseas teams played for:** Bionics, Zimbabwe 1990-92; Universals Sports Club, Zimbabwe 1992-95
**Cricketers particularly admired:** Michael Atherton, Graham Burgess
**Other sports followed:** Rugby union ('played for Lydney, Gloucestershire and Cambridge University and was on bench for Varsity Match'), football (West Ham)
**Injuries:** Severed tendon below knee in an accident with a glass door, missed pre-season tour to Zimbabwe
**Relaxations:** Reading, *Telegraph* crosswords, videos, weight training
**Extras:** Scored maiden century in only second first-class game. Broke Matthew Maynard's club record for number of one-day runs in a season in 1995. Also broke Hugh Morris's club record for number of Sunday League runs in a season
**Best batting:** 230* Glamorgan v Leicestershire, Leicester 1995

## 1995 Season

| | M | Inns | NO | Runs | HS | Avge | 100s | 50s | Ct | St | O | M | Runs | Wkts | Avge | Best | 5wI | 10wM |
|---|---|---|---|---|---|---|---|---|---|---|---|---|---|---|---|---|---|---|
| Test | | | | | | | | | | | | | | | | | | |
| All First | 15 | 28 | 3 | 1011 | 230 * | 40.44 | 3 | 2 | 12 | - | | | | | | | | |
| 1-day Int | | | | | | | | | | | | | | | | | | |
| NatWest | 4 | 4 | 1 | 147 | 74 * | 49.00 | - | 2 | 2 | - | | | | | | | | |
| B & H | 5 | 5 | 0 | 301 | 90 | 60.20 | - | 4 | - | - | | | | | | | | |
| Sunday | 16 | 16 | 5 | 815 | 93 * | 74.09 | - | 8 | 5 | - | | | | | | | | |

## Career Performances

| | M | Inns | NO | Runs | HS | Avge | 100s | 50s | Ct | St | Balls | Runs | Wkts | Avge | Best | 5wI | 10wM |
|---|---|---|---|---|---|---|---|---|---|---|---|---|---|---|---|---|---|
| Test | | | | | | | | | | | | | | | | | |
| All First | 128 | 224 | 20 | 6889 | 230 * | 33.76 | 17 | 24 | 101 | - | 2 | 3 | 0 | - | - | - | - |
| 1-day Int | | | | | | | | | | | | | | | | | |
| NatWest | 14 | 14 | 1 | 502 | 123 | 38.61 | 1 | 3 | 2 | - | | | | | | | |
| B & H | 19 | 19 | 0 | 746 | 135 | 39.26 | 1 | 7 | 4 | - | | | | | | | |
| Sunday | 64 | 62 | 6 | 2238 | 107 | 39.96 | 2 | 17 | 16 | - | | | | | | | |

# JARVIS, P. W.                                    Sussex

**Name:** Paul William Jarvis
**Role:** Right-hand bat, right-arm
fast-medium bowler
**Born:** 29 June 1965, Redcar, North Yorkshire
**Height:** 5ft 11in **Weight:** 12st 5lbs
**Nickname:** Jarv, Gnasher
**County debut:** 1981 (Yorkshire), 1994
(Sussex)
**County cap:** 1986 (Yorkshire)
**Test debut:** 1987-88
**Tests:** 9
**One-Day Internationals:** 16
**50 wickets in a season:** 4
**1st-Class 50s:** 6
**1st-Class 5 w. in innings:** 20
**1st-Class 10 w. in match:** 3
**1st-Class catches:** 51
**One-Day 5 w. in innings:** 5
**Place in batting averages:** 239th av. 16.09
(1994 230th av. 16.52)
**Place in bowling averages:** 54th av. 27.65 (1994 96th av. 34.76)
**Strike rate:** 52.76 (career 53.36)
**Parents:** Malcolm and Marjorie
**Wife and date of marriage:** Wendy Jayne, 3 December 1988
**Children:** Alexander Michael, 13 July 1989; Isabella Grace, 21 March 1993
**Family links with cricket:** Father still plays league cricket in Gwent. Brother plays in
Yorkshire (Selby Londesborough)
**Education:** Bydales Comprehensive School, Marske, Cleveland
**Qualifications:** 4 O-levels, advanced coaching awards
**Off-season:** At home
**Overseas tours:** Yorkshire to St Lucia and Barbados 1987, to South Africa 1991;
England to India/Pakistan (World Cup) and Pakistan 1986-87, to Australia and New
Zealand 1987-88, to India and Sri Lanka 1992-93; unofficial English XI to South
Africa 1989-90
**Overseas teams played for:** Mossman Middle Harbour, Sydney 1984-85; Avendale,
Cape Town 1985-86; Manly Warringah, Sydney 1987
**Cricketers particularly admired:** 'Many'
**Other sports followed:** Most sports
**Injuries:** Calf strain and groin strain, missed four weeks
**Relaxations:** DIY, cooking, music, eating and drinking out
**Extras:** Youngest player ever to play for Yorkshire in County Championship (16 years,

2 months, 13 days) and youngest player to take hat-trick in Sunday League (1982) and Championship (1985). Played for England YC v West Indies 1982 and Australia 1983. Banned from Test cricket for joining 1989-90 tour of South Africa, suspension remitted in 1992

**Opinions on cricket:** 'Scrap the Sunday League.'
**Best batting:** 80 Yorkshire v Northamptonshire, Scarborough 1992
**Best bowling:** 7-55 Yorkshire v Surrey, Headingley 1986

### 1995 Season

|  | M | Inns | NO | Runs | HS | Avge | 100s | 50s | Ct | St | O | M | Runs | Wkts | Avge | Best | 5wI | 10wM |
|---|---|---|---|---|---|---|---|---|---|---|---|---|---|---|---|---|---|---|
| Test |  |  |  |  |  |  |  |  |  |  |  |  |  |  |  |  |  |  |
| All First | 9 | 13 | 2 | 177 | 38 | 16.09 | - | - | 8 | - | 228.4 | 45 | 719 | 26 | 27.65 | 5-55 | 1 | - |
| 1-day Int |  |  |  |  |  |  |  |  |  |  |  |  |  |  |  |  |  |  |
| NatWest |  |  |  |  |  |  |  |  |  |  |  |  |  |  |  |  |  |  |  |
| B & H | 2 | 2 | 0 | 10 | 8 | 5.00 | - | - | - | - | 21 | 2 | 105 | 3 | 35.00 | 3-39 | - |  |
| Sunday | 12 | 8 | 4 | 57 | 13 * | 14.25 | - | - | - | - | 68.4 | 3 | 336 | 18 | 18.66 | 6-29 | 1 |  |

### Career Performances

|  | M | Inns | NO | Runs | HS | Avge | 100s | 50s | Ct | St | Balls | Runs | Wkts | Avge | Best | 5wI | 10wM |
|---|---|---|---|---|---|---|---|---|---|---|---|---|---|---|---|---|---|
| Test | 9 | 15 | 2 | 132 | 29 * | 10.15 | - | - | 2 | - | 1912 | 965 | 21 | 45.95 | 4-107 | - | - |
| All First | 132 | 223 | 60 | 2651 | 80 | 16.26 | - | 6 | 51 | - | 30523 | 16103 | 572 | 28.15 | 7-55 | 20 | 3 |
| 1-day Int | 16 | 8 | 2 | 31 | 16 * | 5.16 | - | - | 1 | - | 879 | 672 | 24 | 28.00 | 5-35 | 1 |  |
| NatWest | 17 | 10 | 2 | 87 | 16 | 10.87 | - | - | 3 | - | 1129 | 708 | 19 | 37.26 | 4-41 | - |  |
| B & H | 36 | 17 | 5 | 141 | 42 | 11.75 | - | - | 4 | - | 2072 | 1174 | 58 | 20.24 | 4-34 | - |  |
| Sunday | 118 | 66 | 26 | 451 | 38 * | 11.27 | - | - | 27 | - | 4986 | 3631 | 170 | 21.35 | 6-27 | 4 |  |

# JOHNSON, P.        Nottinghamshire

**Name:** Paul Johnson
**Role:** Right-hand bat, right-arm medium 'occasional' bowler
**Born:** 24 April 1965, Newark
**Height:** 'Below average'  **Weight:** 'Above average'
**Nickname:** Johno, Midget, Gus
**County debut:** 1982
**County cap:** 1986
**Benefit:** 1995
**1000 runs in a season:** 7
**1st-Class 50s:** 83
**1st-Class 100s:** 32
**1st-Class catches:** 166
**1st-Class stumpings:** 1
**One-Day 100s:** 10

**Place in batting averages:** 96th av. 34.34
(1994 43rd av. 43.33)
**Parents:** Donald Edward and Joyce
**Wife's name and date of marriage:** Jackie,
24 December 1993
**Children:** Ruth, 28 September 1994
**Family links with cricket:** Father played
local cricket and is a qualified coach
**Education:** Grove Comprehensive School,
Newark
**Qualifications:** 9 CSEs, NCA advanced
coach
**Overseas tours:** England A to Bermuda and
West Indies 1991-92
**Overseas teams played for:** RAU
Johannesburg, 1985-86; Hutt District,
Wellington, New Zealand 1988-89
**Cricketers particularly admired:** Clive
Rice and Mike Gatting
**Other sports followed:** Watches ice-hockey (Nottingham Panthers), football
(Nottingham Forest and Notts County)
**Injuries:** Irritable bowel syndrome and right knee problem, missed three weeks in all
**Relaxations:** 'Listening to music, crosswords and reading autobiographies'
**Extras:** Played for English Schools in 1980-81 and England YC 1982 and 1983.
Youngest player ever to join the Nottinghamshire staff. Made 235 for Nottinghamshire
2nd XI, July 1982, aged 17. Won Man of the Match award in his first NatWest game
(101* v Staffordshire) in 1985, but missed the final owing to appendicitis. Sunday
morning soccer referee in Nottingham. Takes over the Nottinghamshire captaincy from
Tim Robinson for the 1996 season
**Opinions on cricket:** 'Who would take any notice?'
**Best batting:** 187 Nottinghamshire v Lancashire, Old Trafford 1993
**Best bowling:** 1-9 Nottinghamshire v Oxford University, Trent Bridge 1984

## 1995 Season

| | M | Inns | NO | Runs | HS | Avge | 100s | 50s | Ct | St | O | M | Runs | Wkts | Avge | Best | 5wI | 10wM |
|---|---|---|---|---|---|---|---|---|---|---|---|---|---|---|---|---|---|---|
| Test | | | | | | | | | | | | | | | | | | |
| All First | 17 | 30 | 1 | 996 | 120 * | 34.34 | 1 | 8 | 9 | - | | | | | | | | |
| 1-day Int | | | | | | | | | | | | | | | | | | |
| NatWest | 2 | 2 | 0 | 3 | 3 | 1.50 | - | - | - | - | | | | | | | | |
| B & H | 5 | 4 | 3 | 142 | 70 * | 142.00 | - | 2 | - | - | | | | | | | | |
| Sunday | 15 | 15 | 2 | 617 | 136 * | 47.46 | 2 | 1 | 5 | - | | | | | | | | |

## Career Performances

|  | M | Inns | NO | Runs | HS | Avge | 100s | 50s | Ct | St | Balls | Runs | Wkts | Avge | Best | 5wI | 10wM |
|---|---|---|---|---|---|---|---|---|---|---|---|---|---|---|---|---|---|
| Test |  |  |  |  |  |  |  |  |  |  |  |  |  |  |  |  |  |
| All First | 265 | 439 | 41 | 14732 | 187 | 37.01 | 32 | 83 | 166 | 1 | 478 | 510 | 5 | 102.00 | 1-9 | - | - |
| 1-day Int |  |  |  |  |  |  |  |  |  |  |  |  |  |  |  |  |  |
| NatWest | 28 | 28 | 2 | 763 | 146 | 29.34 | 2 | 1 | 7 | - | 12 | 16 | 0 | - |  | - | - |
| B & H | 46 | 43 | 9 | 1190 | 104 * | 35.00 | 2 | 8 | 14 | - |  |  |  |  |  |  |  |
| Sunday | 174 | 164 | 18 | 4442 | 167 * | 30.42 | 6 | 23 | 59 | - |  |  |  |  |  |  |  |

# JOHNSON, R. L. Middlesex

**Name:** Richard Leonard Johnson
**Role:** Right-hand bat, right-arm fast-medium bowler, outfielder
**Born:** 29 December 1974, Chertsey, Surrey
**Height:** 6ft 2in **Weight:** 13st 6lbs
**Nickname:** Jono, Lenny
**County debut:** 1992
**1st-Class 50s:** 1
**1st-Class 5 w. in innings:** 3
**1st-Class 10 w. in match:** 2
**1st-Class catches:** 16
**Place in batting averages:** 250th av. 14.90 (1994 198th av. 20.50)
**Place in bowling averages:** 10th av. 20.30 (1994 33rd av. 26.47)
**Strike rate:** 45.25 (career 52.25)
**Parents:** Roger and Mary Ann
**Marital status:** Single
**Family links with cricket:** Father and grandfather played club cricket
**Education:** Sunbury Manor School; Spelthorne College
**Qualifications:** 9 GCSEs, A-Level in Physical Education, NCA Senior Coaching Award
**Overseas tours:** England U18 to South Africa 1992-93; England U19 to South Africa 1993-94; England A to India 1994-95
**Cricketers particularly admired:** Ian Botham, Richard Hadlee
**Other sports followed:** Basketball, soccer, snooker and most other sports
**Injuries:** Back strain, missed four weeks
**Relaxations:** Sport and music
**Extras:** Plays for Sunbury CC, has represented Middlesex at all levels since U11. Took 10 for 45 v Derbyshire in July 1994, first person to take 10 wickets in an innings since Ian Thomson (Sussex) in 1964, also most economical figures since Hedley Verity's 10 for 10. Had to pull out of England's 1995-96 tour to South Africa due to a persistent back injury

**Best batting:** 50* Middlesex v Cambridge University, Fenner's 1994
**Best bowling:** 10-45 Middlesex v Derbyshire, Derby 1994

## 1995 Season

|  | M | Inns | NO | Runs | HS | Avge | 100s | 50s | Ct | St | O | M | Runs | Wkts | Avge | Best | 5wI | 10wM |
|---|---|---|---|---|---|---|---|---|---|---|---|---|---|---|---|---|---|---|
| Test |  |  |  |  |  |  |  |  |  |  |  |  |  |  |  |  |  |  |
| All First | 12 | 13 | 2 | 164 | 29 * | 14.90 | - | - | 8 | - | 301.4 | 79 | 812 | 40 | 20.30 | 5-48 | 2 | 1 |
| 1-day Int |  |  |  |  |  |  |  |  |  |  |  |  |  |  |  |  |  |  |
| NatWest | 3 | 3 | 1 | 64 | 33 | 32.00 | - | - | - | - | 26 | 4 | 82 | 6 | 13.66 | 3-33 | - |  |
| B & H | 1 | 1 | 0 | 0 | 0 | 0.00 | - | - | - | - |  |  |  |  |  |  |  |  |
| Sunday | 9 | 6 | 1 | 31 | 18 * | 6.20 | - | - | 1 | - | 52 | 0 | 312 | 5 | 62.40 | 2-54 | - |  |

## Career Performances

|  | M | Inns | NO | Runs | HS | Avge | 100s | 50s | Ct | St | Balls | Runs | Wkts | Avge | Best | 5wI | 10wM |
|---|---|---|---|---|---|---|---|---|---|---|---|---|---|---|---|---|---|
| Test |  |  |  |  |  |  |  |  |  |  |  |  |  |  |  |  |  |
| All First | 27 | 33 | 6 | 442 | 50 * | 16.37 | - | 1 | 16 | - | 4337 | 2110 | 83 | 25.42 | 10-45 | 3 | 2 |
| 1-day Int |  |  |  |  |  |  |  |  |  |  |  |  |  |  |  |  |  |
| NatWest | 6 | 5 | 2 | 81 | 33 | 27.00 | - | - | - | - | 336 | 194 | 7 | 27.71 | 3-33 | - |  |
| B & H | 3 | 2 | 0 | 1 | 1 | 0.50 | - | - | - | - | 120 | 62 | 1 | 62.00 | 1-17 | - |  |
| Sunday | 30 | 17 | 7 | 120 | 18 * | 12.00 | - | - | 3 | - | 1255 | 1137 | 29 | 39.20 | 4-66 | - |  |

# JONES, D. M.  Derbyshire

**Name:** Dean Mervyn Jones
**Role:** Right-hand bat, off-spin bowler, county captain
**Born:** 24 March 1963, Coburg, Melbourne, Australia
**Height:** 6ft 1in  **Weight:** 13st
**Nickname:** Deano
**County debut:** 1992 (Durham)
**Test debut:** 1983-84
**Tests:** 52
**One-day Internationals:** 132
**1st-Class 50s:** 64
**1st-Class 100s:** 43
**1st-Class 200s:** 3
**1st-Class 300s:** 1
**1st-Class catches:** 145
**One-day 100s:** 9
**Strike rate:** (career 122.47)
**Wife and date of marriage:** Jane, 24 April 1986

**Children:** Phoebe, 26 June 1991
**Family links with cricket:** Father was a captain/coach of Carlton, Victoria for 18 years
**Education:** Mt Waverley High School, Victoria
**Qualifications:** High School Certificate
**Off-season:** Playing in Australia
**Overseas tours:** Young Australians to Zimbabwe 1983 and 1985; Australia to West Indies 1984 and 1991, to England 1985 and 1989, to India 1986 and 1987 (World Cup), to Sharjah 1986 and 1990, to Pakistan 1988, to New Zealand 1989, to USA 1990
**Overseas teams played for:** Victoria, Australia
**Other sports followed:** Golf, baseball
**Extras:** Played for Durham in their first season as a first-class county in 1992. Appointed captain of Derbyshire for the 1996 season. He is the highest run-scorer in the history of the Sheffield Shield competition
**Best batting:** 324* Victoria v South Australia, Melbourne 1994-95
**Best bowling:** 1-0 Australia v Indian Under-25 XI 1986-87

## 1995 (did not make any first-class or one-day appearances)

## Career Performances

|          | M   | Inns | NO | Runs  | HS   | Avge  | 100s | 50s | Ct  | St | Balls | Runs | Wkts | Avge  | Best | 5wI | 10wM |
|----------|-----|------|----|-------|------|-------|------|-----|-----|----|-------|------|------|-------|------|-----|------|
| Test     | 52  | 89   | 11 | 3631  | 216  | 46.55 | 11   | 14  | 34  | -  | 198   | 64   | 1    | 64.00 | 1-5  | -   | -    |
| All First| 189 | 315  | 35 | 14805 | 324* | 52.87 | 43   | 64  | 145 | -  | 2082  | 1100 | 17   | 64.70 | 1-0  | -   | -    |
| 1-day Int| 164 | 161  | 25 | 6068  | 145  | 44.61 | 7    | 46  | 54  | -  | 106   | 81   | 3    | 27.00 | 2-34 | -   | -    |
| NatWest  | 2   | 2    | 0  | 71    | 46   | 35.00 | -    | -   | 1   | -  | 12    | 16   | 0    | -     |      | -   | -    |
| B & H    | 4   | 4    | 0  | 25    | 13   | 6.25  | -    | -   | 2   | -  | 42    | 34   | 2    | 17.00 | 2-34 | -   |      |
| Sunday   | 11  | 10   | 2  | 656   | 114  | 82.00 | 2    | 5   | 4   | -  | 37    | 41   | 1    | 41.00 | 1-37 | -   |      |

# JONES, P. S. Glamorgan

**Name:** Philip Steffan Jones
**Role:** Right-hand bat, right-arm fast-medium bowler
**Born:** 9 February 1974, Llanelli
**Height:** 6ft 1in **Weight:** 13st
**Nickname:** Cracker
**County debut:** No first-team appearance
**Parents:** Lyndon and Ann
**Marital status:** Single
**Family links with cricket:** Father played cricket for Welsh Secondary Schools, Glamorgan 2nd XI, Dafen, Hendy
**Education:** Ysgol Gyfun Y Strade (Strade Comp.); Neath Tertiary College
**Qualifications:** Student
**Career outside cricket:** PE teacher
**Cricketers particularly admired:** Michael Holding, Richard Hadlee
**Other sports followed:** Plays rugby

**Relaxations:** Listening to music, art and painting, eating Italian food
**Extras:** Played rugby at U18 and U19 for Wales. Top of the bowling and batting averages for Wales Minor Counties and played for them in the 1994 NatWest Trophy

## 1995 Season (did not make any first-class or one-day appearances)

## Career Performances

|         | M | Inns | NO | Runs | HS | Avge | 100s | 50s | Ct | St | Balls | Runs | Wkts | Avge | Best | 5wI | 10wM |
|---------|---|------|----|------|----|------|------|-----|----|----|-------|------|------|------|------|-----|------|
| Test    |   |      |    |      |    |      |      |     |    |    |       |      |      |      |      |     |      |
| All First |  |      |    |      |    |      |      |     |    |    |       |      |      |      |      |     |      |
| 1-day Int |  |      |    |      |    |      |      |     |    |    |       |      |      |      |      |     |      |
| NatWest | 1 | 1    | 1  | 26   | 26 * | -  | -    | -   | -  | -  | 18    | 30   | 0    | -    |      | -   | -    |
| B & H   |   |      |    |      |    |      |      |     |    |    |       |      |      |      |      |     |      |
| Sunday  |   |      |    |      |    |      |      |     |    |    |       |      |      |      |      |     |      |

# KEECH, M.                                    Hampshire

**Name:** Matthew Keech
**Role:** Right-hand bat, right-arm
medium bowler
**Born:** 21 October 1970, Hampstead
**Height:** 6ft **Weight:** 13st 6lbs
**County debut:** 1991 (Middlesex),
1994 (Hampshire)
**1st-Class 50s:** 3
**1st-Class catches:** 17
**Parents:** Ron and Brenda
**Marital status:** Single
**Education:**
Northumberland Park School, Tottenham
**Qualifications:** 5 O-levels,
NCA coaching certificate
**Overseas tours:**
England YC to Australia 1989-90
**Overseas teams played for:** Mossman,
Sydney 1988-89; Lancaster Park,
Christchurch NZ 1990-91

**Cricketers particularly admired:** Mike Gatting, Richard Hadlee, Paul Downton
**Other sports followed:** Most other sports except horse racing
**Relaxations:** Listening to music, watching videos
**Extras:** Left Middlesex and moved to Hampshire for 1994 season
**Best batting:** 58* Middlesex v Nottinghamshire, Lord's 1991
**Best bowling:** 2-28 Middlesex v Gloucestershire, Bristol 1993

## 1995 Season

|          | M  | Inns | NO | Runs | HS | Avge  | 100s | 50s | Ct | St | O    | M | Runs | Wkts | Avge  | Best | 5wI | 10wM |
|----------|----|------|----|------|----|-------|------|-----|----|----|------|---|------|------|-------|------|-----|------|
| Test     |    |      |    |      |    |       |      |     |    |    |      |   |      |      |       |      |     |      |
| All First | 2  | 4    | 0  | 100  | 41 | 25.00 | -    | -   | 2  | -  | 20.3 | 0 | 98   | 2    | 49.00 | 1-43 | -   | -    |
| 1-day Int |    |      |    |      |    |       |      |     |    |    |      |   |      |      |       |      |     |      |
| NatWest  |    |      |    |      |    |       |      |     |    |    |      |   |      |      |       |      |     |      |
| B & H    |    |      |    |      |    |       |      |     |    |    |      |   |      |      |       |      |     |      |
| Sunday   | 12 | 12   | 0  | 348  | 98 | 29.00 | -    | 2   | 1  | -  | 4    | 0 | 33   | 0    | -     | -    | -   | -    |

39. Which bowler took a hat-trick of LBWs in the county Championship in 1995?

## Career Performances

| | M | Inns | NO | Runs | HS | Avge | 100s | 50s | Ct | St | Balls | Runs | Wkts | Avge | Best | 5wI | 10wM |
|---|---|---|---|---|---|---|---|---|---|---|---|---|---|---|---|---|---|
| Test | | | | | | | | | | | | | | | | | |
| All First | 27 | 47 | 4 | 825 | 58 * | 19.18 | - | 3 | 17 | - | 576 | 286 | 7 | 40.85 | 2-28 | - | - |
| 1-day Int | | | | | | | | | | | | | | | | | |
| NatWest | 2 | 1 | 0 | 3 | 3 | 3.00 | - | - | 2 | - | 60 | 41 | 0 | - | - | - | |
| B & H | 5 | 4 | 0 | 128 | 47 | 32.00 | - | - | 3 | - | 66 | 47 | 1 | 47.00 | 1-37 | - | |
| Sunday | 45 | 40 | 6 | 721 | 98 | 21.20 | - | 2 | 6 | - | 422 | 319 | 6 | 53.16 | 2-22 | - | |

# KEEDY, G. Lancashire

**Name:** Gary Keedy
**Role:** Left-hand bat, slow left-arm bowler
**Born:** 27 November 1974, Wakefield
**Height:** 6ft  **Weight:** 11st 2lbs
**County debut:** 1994 (Yorkshire),
1995 (Lancashire)
**Nickname:** Bod, Keeds
**1st-Class catches:** 2
**Place in bowling averages:** 122nd av. 40.48
**Strike rate:** 81.89 (career 81.89)
**Parents:** Roy and Pat
**Marital status:** Single
**Education:** Garforth Comprehensive
**Qualifications:** 4 GCSEs, junior coaching
award
**Overseas tours:** England U18 to South
Africa 1992-93, to Denmark 1994; England
U19 to Sri Lanka 1993-94

**Cricketers particularly admired:** Shane
Warne, Graham Gooch
**Other sports followed:** Rugby league
**Extras:** Player of the Series for England U19 v West Indies U19 in 1993. Graduate of
the Yorkshire Cricket Academy. Played for England U19 in the home series against India
in 1994. Signed a three-year contract to play for Lancashire from 1995
**Best batting:** 15* Lancashire v Durham, Old Trafford 1995;
                 15* Lancashire v Warwickshire, Old Trafford 1995
**Best bowling:** 4-35 Lancashire v Somerset, Taunton 1995

**1995 Season**

| | M | Inns | NO | Runs | HS | Avge | 100s | 50s | Ct | St | O | M | Runs | Wkts | Avge | Best | 5wI | 10wM |
|---|---|---|---|---|---|---|---|---|---|---|---|---|---|---|---|---|---|---|
| Test | | | | | | | | | | | | | | | | | | |
| All First | 14 | 17 | 12 | 73 | 15 * | 14.60 | - | - | 2 | - | 505 | 128 | 1498 | 37 | 40.48 | 4-35 | - | - |
| 1-day Int | | | | | | | | | | | | | | | | | | |
| NatWest | | | | | | | | | | | | | | | | | | |
| B & H | | | | | | | | | | | | | | | | | | |
| Sunday | 4 | 0 | 0 | 0 | 0 | - | - | - | - | - | 24 | 0 | 128 | 1 | 128.00 | 1-40 | - | |

**Career Performances**

| | M | Inns | NO | Runs | HS | Avge | 100s | 50s | Ct | St | Balls | Runs | Wkts | Avge | Best | 5wI | 10wM |
|---|---|---|---|---|---|---|---|---|---|---|---|---|---|---|---|---|---|
| Test | | | | | | | | | | | | | | | | | |
| All First | 15 | 18 | 12 | 74 | 15 * | 12.33 | - | - | 2 | - | 3030 | 1498 | 37 | 40.48 | 4-35 | - | - |
| 1-day Int | | | | | | | | | | | | | | | | | |
| NatWest | | | | | | | | | | | | | | | | | |
| B & H | | | | | | | | | | | | | | | | | |
| Sunday | 4 | 0 | 0 | 0 | 0 | - | - | - | - | - | 144 | 128 | 1 | 128.00 | 1-40 | - | |

# KELLETT, S. A.                Yorkshire

**Name:** Simon Andrew Kellett
**Role:** Opening bat, occasional right-arm medium bowler
**Born:** 16 October 1967, Mirfield
**Height:** 6ft 1in **Weight:** 12st 7lbs
**Nickname:** Kel, Ginner
**County debut:** 1989
**County cap:** 1992
**1000 runs in a season:** 2
**1st-Class 50s:** 29
**1st-Class 100s:** 2
**1st-Class catches:** 78
**One-Day 100s:** 2
**Place in batting averages:** 181st av. 22.80 (1994 229th av. 16.62)
**Parents:** Brian and Valerie
**Marital status:** Girlfriend, Sarah
**Family links with cricket:**
Father played local league cricket
**Education:** Whitcliffe Mount High School; Huddersfield Technical College
**Qualifications:** 5 CSEs, Sports Management course
**Overseas tours:** Yorkshire U17 to West Indies

**Overseas teams played for:** Upper Hutt, New Zealand 1991-92; Wellington State 1992
**Cricketers particularly admired:** Martyn Moxon, Graham Gooch, Tony Greig
**Other sports followed:** Rugby league (Bradford Northern)
**Relaxations:** Watching Bradford Northern
**Extras:** Captained NAYC against MCC; captained Yorkshire to win U19 County Festival at Cambridge; was out to first ball in first-class cricket. Released by Yorkshire at the end of the 1995 season
**Best batting:** 125* Yorkshire v Derbyshire, Chesterfield 1991

## 1995 Season

|  | M | Inns | NO | Runs | HS | Avge | 100s | 50s | Ct | St | O | M | Runs | Wkts | Avge | Best | 5wI | 10wM |
|---|---|---|---|---|---|---|---|---|---|---|---|---|---|---|---|---|---|---|
| Test |  |  |  |  |  |  |  |  |  |  |  |  |  |  |  |  |  |  |
| All First | 6 | 11 | 1 | 228 | 86 | 22.80 | - | 1 | 5 | - |  |  |  |  |  |  |  |  |
| 1-day Int |  |  |  |  |  |  |  |  |  |  |  |  |  |  |  |  |  |  |
| NatWest | 3 | 3 | 0 | 205 | 107 | 68.33 | 1 | 1 | 3 | - |  |  |  |  |  |  |  |  |
| B & H | 1 | 1 | 0 | 6 | 6 | 6.00 | - | - | - | - |  |  |  |  |  |  |  |  |
| Sunday | 2 | 2 | 0 | 30 | 17 | 15.00 | - | - | 1 | - |  |  |  |  |  |  |  |  |

## Career Performances

|  | M | Inns | NO | Runs | HS | Avge | 100s | 50s | Ct | St | Balls | Runs | Wkts | Avge | Best | 5wI | 10wM |
|---|---|---|---|---|---|---|---|---|---|---|---|---|---|---|---|---|---|
| Test |  |  |  |  |  |  |  |  |  |  |  |  |  |  |  |  |  |
| All First | 87 | 149 | 10 | 4234 | 125 * | 30.46 | 2 | 29 | 78 | - | 30 | 19 | 0 | - | - | - | - |
| 1-day Int |  |  |  |  |  |  |  |  |  |  |  |  |  |  |  |  |  |
| NatWest | 9 | 7 | 0 | 246 | 107 | 35.14 | 1 | 1 | 6 | - |  |  |  |  |  |  |  |
| B & H | 14 | 12 | 1 | 239 | 45 | 21.72 | - | - | - | - |  |  |  |  |  |  |  |
| Sunday | 30 | 30 | 2 | 697 | 118 * | 24.89 | 1 | 3 | 6 | - | 18 | 16 | 0 | - | - | - |  |

# KENDALL, W. S.                    Hampshire

**Name:** William Salwey Kendall
**Role:** Right-hand bat, right-arm
medium bowler
**Born:** 18 December 1973, Wimbledon
**Height:** 5ft 10in **Weight:** 12st 7lb
**Nickname:** Villy, Lemonhead, Lemon
**County debut:** No first-team appearance
**1st-Class 50s:** 3
**1st-Class 100s:** 1
**1st-Class catches:** 13
**Place in batting averages:** 111th av. 32.64
(1994 81st av. 36.14)
**Parents:** Tom and Sue
**Marital status:** Single
**Family links with cricket:** Father played
club cricket with East Horsley, Hampshire
Hogs and MCC. Older brother James played
for Durham University and played for Surrey
Junior team and MCC

**Education:** Bradfield College, Berkshire; Keble College, Oxford University
**Qualifications:** 10 GCSEs, 3 A-levels, 1 AS-level
**Career outside cricket:** Student
**Off-season:** Completing final year at Oxford University
**Overseas tours:** Bradfield College to Barbados, 1991
**Cricketers particularly admired:** Robin Smith, Jonty Rhodes
**Other sports followed:** Hockey for Oxford University and football (offered terms by
Reading) and golf
**Relaxations:** Playing or watching sport, socialising with friends, relaxing at home
**Extras:** Surrey Young Cricketer of the Year 1992. Awarded Gray-Nicolls Trophy for
Schoolboy Cricketer of the Year in memory of Len Newbury 1992. Made first-class
debut for Oxford University in 1994. Played football for Independent Schools 1992.
Offered one-year contract with Reading FC
**Best batting:** 113* Oxford University v Surrey, The Oval 1994
**Best bowling:** 3-37 Oxford University v Derbyshire, The Parks 1995

---

40. Which two cricketers issued writs against *Wisden Cricket Monthly* in 1995?

## 1995 Season

| | M | Inns | NO | Runs | HS | Avge | 100s | 50s | Ct | St | O | M | Runs | Wkts | Avge | Best | 5wI | 10wM |
|---|---|---|---|---|---|---|---|---|---|---|---|---|---|---|---|---|---|---|
| Test | | | | | | | | | | | | | | | | | | |
| All First | 11 | 16 | 2 | 457 | 94 | 32.64 | - | 3 | 5 | - | 81 | 13 | 255 | 8 | 31.87 | 3-37 | - | - |
| 1-day Int | | | | | | | | | | | | | | | | | | |
| NatWest | | | | | | | | | | | | | | | | | | |
| B & H | 3 | 3 | 0 | 54 | 23 | 18.00 | - | - | - | - | | | | | | | | |
| Sunday | | | | | | | | | | | | | | | | | | |

## Career Performances

| | M | Inns | NO | Runs | HS | Avge | 100s | 50s | Ct | St | Balls | Runs | Wkts | Avge | Best | 5wI | 10wM |
|---|---|---|---|---|---|---|---|---|---|---|---|---|---|---|---|---|---|
| Test | | | | | | | | | | | | | | | | | |
| All First | 20 | 26 | 5 | 710 | 113 * | 33.80 | 1 | 3 | 13 | - | 486 | 255 | 8 | 31.87 | 3-37 | - | - |
| 1-day Int | | | | | | | | | | | | | | | | | |
| NatWest | | | | | | | | | | | | | | | | | |
| B & H | 3 | 3 | 0 | 54 | 23 | 18.00 | - | - | - | - | | | | | | | |
| Sunday | | | | | | | | | | | | | | | | | |

# KENDRICK, N. M.      Glamorgan

**Name:** Neil Michael Kendrick
**Role:** Right-hand bat, slow left-arm bowler, gully fielder
**Born:** 11 November 1967, Bromley
**Height:** 5ft 10in **Weight:** 12st 7lbs
**Nickname:** Kendo, Rat, Mers
**County debut:** 1988 (Surrey), 1995 (Glamorgan)
**50 wickets in a season:** 1
**1st-Class 50s:** 4
**1st-Class 5 w. in innings:** 6
**1st-Class 10 w. in match:** 1
**1st-Class catches:** 53
**Place in batting averages:** 234th av. 17.11 (1994 256th av. 12.44)
**Place in bowling averages:** 137th av. 46.48
**Strike rate:** 86.62 (career 78.35)
**Parents:** Michael Hall and Anne Patricia
**Marital status:** Engaged

**Family links with cricket:** Father plays club cricket for Old Wilsonians, and sister has represented Kent Ladies
**Education:** Hayes Primary; Wilson's Grammar School and 'the Surrey dressing-room'

**Qualifications:** 7 O-levels, 1 A-level, senior coaching certificate, qualified fitness instructor
**Career outside cricket:** Sales manager and fitness instructor
**Off-season:** 'Playing football for Old Wilsonians and training'
**Overseas tours:** Surrey U19 to Australia 1985-86; Surrey to Dubai 1988; Glamorgan to Zimbabwe 1995
**Cricketers particularly admired:** Ian Botham, Bishen Bedi and Ed Pillers 'for his flighty leg spin'
**Other sports followed:** Football ('captain of Old Wilsonians and long-time Arsenal supporter'
**Injuries:** External oblique muscle pain, missed three weeks
**Relaxations:** 'Sleeping, acid jazz music, listening to Ed Pillers' views on cricket'
**Extras:** Released by Surrey at the end of the 1994 season
**Opinions on cricket:** 'More sponsorship could be found if the game's marketing people looked beyond insurance companies and photocopier salesmen!'
**Best batting:** 59 Glamorgan v Surrey, The Oval 1995
**Best bowling:** 7-115 Surrey v Nottinghamshire, The Oval 1993

## 1995 Season

|          | M  | Inns | NO | Runs | HS | Avge  | 100s | 50s | Ct | St | O     | M   | Runs | Wkts | Avge  | Best | 5wI | 10wM |
|----------|----|------|----|------|----|-------|------|-----|----|----|-------|-----|------|------|-------|------|-----|------|
| Test     |    |      |    |      |    |       |      |     |    |    |       |     |      |      |       |      |     |      |
| All First | 15 | 21   | 4  | 291  | 59 | 17.11 | -    | 1   | 6  | -  | 389.5 | 102 | 1255 | 27   | 46.48 | 4-70 | -   | -    |
| 1-day Int |    |      |    |      |    |       |      |     |    |    |       |     |      |      |       |      |     |      |
| NatWest  |    |      |    |      |    |       |      |     |    |    |       |     |      |      |       |      |     |      |
| B & H    |    |      |    |      |    |       |      |     |    |    |       |     |      |      |       |      |     |      |
| Sunday   |    |      |    |      |    |       |      |     |    |    |       |     |      |      |       |      |     |      |

## Career Performances

|          | M  | Inns | NO | Runs | HS   | Avge  | 100s | 50s | Ct | St | Balls | Runs | Wkts | Avge  | Best  | 5wI | 10wM |
|----------|----|------|----|------|------|-------|------|-----|----|----|-------|------|------|-------|-------|-----|------|
| Test     |    |      |    |      |      |       |      |     |    |    |       |      |      |       |       |     |      |
| All First | 71 | 95   | 24 | 1171 | 59   | 16.49 | -    | 4   | 53 | -  | 12693 | 6185 | 162  | 38.17 | 7-115 | 6   | 1    |
| 1-day Int |    |      |    |      |      |       |      |     |    |    |       |      |      |       |       |     |      |
| NatWest  | 1  | 0    | 0  | 0    | 0    | -     | -    | -   | -  | -  | 72    | 51   | 1    | 51.00 | 1-51  | -   |      |
| B & H    | 2  | 2    | 1  | 25   | 24   | 25.00 | -    | -   | 1  | -  | 132   | 98   | 3    | 32.66 | 2-47  | -   |      |
| Sunday   | 6  | 4    | 3  | 17   | 13 * | 17.00 | -    | -   | 2  | -  | 237   | 215  | 4    | 53.75 | 2-48  | -   |      |

# KENLOCK, S. G. Surrey

**Name:** Stratford Garfield (Mark) Kenlock
**Role:** Left-hand bat, left-arm medium bowler
**Born:** 16 April 1965, Jamaica
**Height:** 6ft **Weight:** 12st
**Nickname:** Kenny
**County debut:** 1994
**1st-Class catches:** 4
**Strike rate:** (career 93.81)
**Parents:** Vincent and Lynette
**Marital status:** Single
**Children**: Brandon, 13 February 1994
**Family links with cricket:** Brother plays
league cricket
**Education:** Stockwell Manor School;
Vauxhall College
**Career outside cricket:** Engineer
**Off-season:** Coaching children
**Overseas tours:** Surrey to Australia 1995
**Cricketers particularly admired:**
Viv Richards, Michael Holding

**Other sports followed:** Football (Manchester United), American football
**Injuries:** Split webbing on left hand, out for six weeks
**Relaxations:** Listening to music (R&B)
**Extras:** Received 2nd XI cap in 1994 and 2nd XI Bowler of the Year. Won the Gold
Award in the Benson & Hedges Cup for his five for 15 against Ireland in 1995
**Opinions on cricket:** 'Four-day cricket is now proving to be better cricket. Sunday
League cricket should remain 40-over game – coloured clothing is good for the game.'
**Best batting:** 12 Surrey v Northamptonshire, Northampton 1995
**Best bowling:** 3-104 Surrey v Kent, The Oval 1994

## 1995 Season

|          | M  | Inns | NO | Runs | HS | Avge | 100s | 50s | Ct | St | O   | M  | Runs | Wkts | Avge  | Best | 5wl | 10wM |
|----------|----|------|----|------|----|------|------|-----|----|----|-----|----|------|------|-------|------|-----|------|
| Test     |    |      |    |      |    |      |      |     |    |    |     |    |      |      |       |      |     |      |
| All First| 4  | 8    | 2  | 50   | 12 | 8.33 | -    | -   | 3  | -  | 119 | 20 | 440  | 8    | 55.00 | 2-71 | -   | -    |
| 1-day Int|    |      |    |      |    |      |      |     |    |    |     |    |      |      |       |      |     |      |
| NatWest  |    |      |    |      |    |      |      |     |    |    |     |    |      |      |       |      |     |      |
| B & H    | 4  | 0    | 0  | 0    | 0  | -    | -    | -   | -  | -  | 35  | 4  | 171  | 11   | 15.54 | 5-15 | 1   |      |
| Sunday   | 12 | 5    | 1  | 13   | 9  | 3.25 | -    | -   | 3  | -  | 78  | 0  | 455  | 9    | 50.55 | 2-36 | -   |      |

## Career Performances

|  | M | Inns | NO | Runs | HS | Avge | 100s | 50s | Ct | St | Balls | Runs | Wkts | Avge | Best | 5wI | 10wM |
|---|---|------|----|----|----|----|----|----|----|----|------|------|------|------|------|------|------|
| Test |  |  |  |  |  |  |  |  |  |  |  |  |  |  |  |  |  |
| All First | 6 | 8 | 2 | 50 | 12 | 8.33 | - | - | 4 | - | 1032 | 626 | 11 | 56.90 | 3-104 | - | - |
| 1-day Int |  |  |  |  |  |  |  |  |  |  |  |  |  |  |  |  |  |
| NatWest |  |  |  |  |  |  |  |  |  |  |  |  |  |  |  |  |  |  |
| B & H | 4 | 0 | 0 | 0 | 0 | - | - | - | - | - | 210 | 171 | 11 | 15.54 | 5-15 | 1 |  |
| Sunday | 17 | 5 | 1 | 13 | 9 | 3.25 | - | - | 6 | - | 686 | 626 | 19 | 32.94 | 4-30 | - |  |

# KENNIS, G. J. Surrey

**Name:** Gregor John Kennis
**Role:** Right-hand bat, right-arm off-spin bowler
**Born:** 9 March 1974, Yokohama, Japan
**Height:** 6ft 1in **Weight:** 12st
**County debut:** 1994
**1st-Class catches:** 2
**Parents:** Michael and Sally
**Marital status:** Single
**Family links with cricket:** 'Father plays for Lloyds Register of Shipping CC (his company side) and is NCA Senior Coach. Mother made the teas when I was at school.'
**Education:** Tiffin Boys' School; Stewart Cricket Academy; 'Matt Church's room (on the MCC groundstaff)'
**Qualifications:** 9 GCSEs, 1 A-level, NCA senior coach
**Career outside cricket:** 'All I ever wanted to do was to play cricket'
**Overseas tours:** Surrey U19 to Barbados 1991
**Cricketers particularly admired:** Neil Stewart, David Gower, Allan Border, David Boon
**Other sports followed:** Horse racing and football (West Ham)
**Relaxations:** Golf and listening to music
**Extras:** Got hit for the biggest six ever seen at The Oval by David Ward
**Opinions on cricket:** 'I think more should be done to encourage cricket to be played in schools.'
**Best batting:** 29 Surrey v Kent, Canterbury 1995

**1995 Season**

| | M | Inns | NO | Runs | HS | Avge | 100s | 50s | Ct | St | O | M | Runs | Wkts | Avge | Best | 5wI | 10wM |
|---|---|---|---|---|---|---|---|---|---|---|---|---|---|---|---|---|---|---|
| Test | | | | | | | | | | | | | | | | | | |
| All First | 1 | 2 | 0 | 47 | 29 | 23.50 | - | - | - | - | 3 | 3 | 0 | 0 | - | | - | - | - |
| 1-day Int | | | | | | | | | | | | | | | | | | |
| NatWest | | | | | | | | | | | | | | | | | | |
| B & H | | | | | | | | | | | | | | | | | | |
| Sunday | 1 | 1 | 0 | 5 | 5 | 5.00 | - | - | - | - | | | | | | | | |

**Career Performances**

| | M | Inns | NO | Runs | HS | Avge | 100s | 50s | Ct | St | Balls | | Runs | Wkts | Avge | Best | 5wI | 10wM |
|---|---|---|---|---|---|---|---|---|---|---|---|---|---|---|---|---|---|---|
| Test | | | | | | | | | | | | | | | | | | |
| All First | 2 | 4 | 0 | 88 | 29 | 22.00 | - | - | 2 | - | 18 | | 0 | 0 | - | | - | - | - |
| 1-day Int | | | | | | | | | | | | | | | | | | |
| NatWest | | | | | | | | | | | | | | | | | | |
| B & H | | | | | | | | | | | | | | | | | | |
| Sunday | 1 | 1 | 0 | 5 | 5 | 5.00 | - | - | - | - | | | | | | | | |

# KERR, J. I. D. Somerset

**Name:** Jason Ian Douglas Kerr
**Role:** Right-hand bat, right-arm
fast-medium bowler
**Born:** 7 April 1974, Bolton, Lancashire
**Height:** 6ft 3in **Weight:** 12st 6lbs
**Nickname:** Norman, Normski, Stretchy
**County debut:** 1993
**1st-Class 50s:** 1
**1st-Class 5 w. innings:** 1
**1st-Class catches:** 4
**Place in batting averages:** 202nd av. 20.52
**Place in bowling averages:** 123rd av. 40.50
**Strike rate:** 60.03 (career 57.25)
**Parents:** Len and Janet
**Marital status:** Single
**Family links with cricket:** 'Father played for
Tonge CC in the Bolton League and was the
manager'
**Education:** Withins High School;
Bolton Met College

**Qualifications:** 5 GCSEs, BTEC National Diploma in Business Studies, cricket coach
**Off-season:** Relaxing and training

**Overseas tours:** England U19 to India 1992-93
**Overseas teams played for:** Gordon Districts CC, Sydney, Australia 1994-95
**Cricketers particularly admired:** Mushtaq Ahmed, David Gower, Peter Bowler
**Other sports followed:** Bolton 'The Great' Wanderers
**Injuries:** Ripped cartilage on left lower rib, missed four months
**Relaxations:** Playing golf, socialising, squash, television, swimming, sleeping, listening to music, spending time with friends and girlfriend Emma
**Opinions on cricket:** 'Cricketers should have 12-month contracts.'
**Best batting:** 80 Somerset v West Indies, Taunton 1995
**Best bowling:** 5-82 Somerset v West Indies, Taunton 1995

### 1995 Season

|          | M  | Inns | NO | Runs | HS | Avge  | 100s | 50s | Ct | St | O     | M  | Runs | Wkts | Avge  | Best | 5wI | 10wM |
|----------|----|------|----|------|----|-------|------|-----|----|----|-------|----|------|------|-------|------|-----|------|
| Test     |    |      |    |      |    |       |      |     |    |    |       |    |      |      |       |      |     |      |
| All First| 13 | 19   | 2  | 349  | 80 | 20.52 | -    | 1   | 5  | -  | 280.1 | 53 | 1134 | 28   | 40.50 | 5-82 | 1   | -    |
| 1-day Int|    |      |    |      |    |       |      |     |    |    |       |    |      |      |       |      |     |      |
| NatWest  | 1  | 1    | 0  | 3    | 3  | 3.00  | -    | -   | -  | -  | 11    | 0  | 74   | 2    | 37.00 | 2-74 | -   |      |
| B & H    | 1  | 0    | 0  | 0    | 0  | -     | -    | -   | -  | -  | 8     | 0  | 35   | 2    | 17.50 | 2-35 | -   |      |
| Sunday   | 9  | 4    | 0  | 21   | 8  | 5.25  | -    | -   | 1  | -  | 57    | 4  | 335  | 11   | 30.45 | 3-52 | -   |      |

### Career Performances

|          | M  | Inns | NO | Runs | HS | Avge  | 100s | 50s | Ct | St | Balls | Runs | Wkts | Avge  | Best | 5wI | 10wM |
|----------|----|------|----|------|----|-------|------|-----|----|----|-------|------|------|-------|------|-----|------|
| Test     |    |      |    |      |    |       |      |     |    |    |       |      |      |       |      |     |      |
| All First| 21 | 32   | 5  | 421  | 80 | 15.59 | -    | 1   | 9  | -  | 2462  | 1630 | 43   | 37.90 | 5-82 | 1   | -    |
| 1-day Int|    |      |    |      |    |       |      |     |    |    |       |      |      |       |      |     |      |
| NatWest  | 2  | 2    | 0  | 3    | 3  | 1.50  | -    | -   | -  | -  | 66    | 74   | 2    | 37.00 | 2-74 | -   |      |
| B & H    | 1  | 0    | 0  | 0    | 0  | -     | -    | -   | -  | -  | 48    | 35   | 2    | 17.50 | 2-35 | -   |      |
| Sunday   | 23 | 16   | 4  | 87   | 17 | 7.25  | -    | -   | 2  | -  | 938   | 848  | 28   | 30.28 | 3-34 | -   |      |

# KERSEY, G. J.                           Surrey

**Name:** Graham James Kersey
**Role:** Right-hand bat, wicket-keeper
**Born:** 19 May 1971, Greenwich
**Height:** 5ft 8in **Weight;** 10st 7lbs
**Nickname:** Scuz
**County debut:** 1991 (Kent), 1993 (Surrey)
**1st-Class 50s:** 11
**1st-Class catches:** 124
**1st-Class stumpings:** 11
**Place in batting averages:** 137th av. 29.50 (1995 249th av. 14.11)
**Parents:** Don and Beryl

**Marital status:** Single
**Family links with cricket:** Brother Ian played for Kent U19 and UAU 2nd XI
**Education:** Bexley-Erith Technical High School
**Qualifications:** 6 O-levels, 1 A-level, NCA coaching certificate
**Overseas tours:** Kent Schools U17 to Singapore and New Zealand 1987-88
**Overseas teams played for:** Eastern Suburbs District, Brisbane 1989-91; Windhoek College of Education, Namibia 1992-93; Easts, Brisbane 1993-94
**Cricketers particularly admired:** Alan Knott, Jack Russell, David Gower, Steve Waugh, Carl Hooper
**Other sports followed:** Football, rugby
**Relaxations:** 'A pint of Guinness and port with Tony Murphy'
**Best batting:** 83 Surrey v Yorkshire, The Oval 1995

## 1995 Season

| | M | Inns | NO | Runs | HS | Avge | 100s | 50s | Ct | St | O | M | Runs | Wkts | Avge | Best | 5wI | 10wM |
|---|---|---|---|---|---|---|---|---|---|---|---|---|---|---|---|---|---|---|
| Test | | | | | | | | | | | | | | | | | | |
| All First | 15 | 28 | 4 | 708 | 83 | 29.50 | - | 6 | 60 | 5 | | | | | | | | |
| 1-day Int | | | | | | | | | | | | | | | | | | |
| NatWest | 1 | 1 | 0 | 21 | 21 | 21.00 | - | - | - | - | | | | | | | | |
| B & H | | | | | | | | | | | | | | | | | | |
| Sunday | 8 | 6 | 0 | 54 | 24 | 9.00 | - | - | 4 | 1 | | | | | | | | |

## Career Performances

| | M | Inns | NO | Runs | HS | Avge | 100s | 50s | Ct | St | Balls | Runs | Wkts | Avge | Best | 5wI | 10wM |
|---|---|---|---|---|---|---|---|---|---|---|---|---|---|---|---|---|---|
| Test | | | | | | | | | | | | | | | | | | |
| All First | 38 | 62 | 10 | 1176 | 83 | 22.61 | - | 6 | 124 | 11 | | | | | | | | |
| 1-day Int | | | | | | | | | | | | | | | | | | |
| NatWest | 1 | 1 | 0 | 21 | 21 | 21.00 | - | - | - | - | | | | | | | | |
| B & H | | | | | | | | | | | | | | | | | | |
| Sunday | 21 | 13 | 1 | 219 | 50 | 18.25 | - | 1 | 22 | 5 | | | | | | | | |

# KETTLEBOROUGH, R. A. Yorkshire

**Name:** Richard Allan Kettleborough
**Role:** Left-hand bat, right-arm
medium bowler
**Born:** 15 March 1973, Sheffield
**Height:** 5ft 10in **Weight:** 12st
**Nickname:** Kett
**County debut:** 1994
**1st-Class 50s**: 1
**Parents:** Allan and Pat
**Marital status:** Single
**Family links with cricket:** Father played for
Yorkshire 2nd XI and is now coach at
Worksop College
**Education:** Laughton All Saints Junior
School; Worksop College; Airedale and
Wharedale College
**Qualifications:** 5 GCSEs, City & Guilds in
Recreational Management, Senior Coaching
Award
**Career outside cricket:** 'Would like to become a fitness instructor'
**Off-season:** 'Getting fit for next season and going on holiday with friends'
**Overseas tours:** Worksop College to Australia 1988-89; England U18 to Canada 1991;
Yorkshire CCC to South Africa 1995
**Overseas teams played for:** Somerset West, Cape Town 1993-94
**Cricketers particularly admired:** David Gower, Michael Vaughan, Mike Atherton
**Other sports followed:** Football (Sheffield Wednesday FC)
**Relaxations:** 'Going to the pub with friends and buying new clothes'
**Extras:** Won the Lord's Taverners U15 award for the Most Promising Young Cricketer
in 1988. 2nd XI cap at Yorkshire
**Opinions on cricket:** 'Wickets in 2nd XI cricket should be better. 12-month contracts
for everyone.'
**Best batting:** 55 Yorkshire v Essex, Chelmsford 1995

## 1995 Season

| | M | Inns | NO | Runs | HS | Avge | 100s | 50s | Ct | St | O | M | Runs | Wkts | Avge | Best | 5wI | 10wM |
|---|---|---|---|---|---|---|---|---|---|---|---|---|---|---|---|---|---|---|
| Test | | | | | | | | | | | | | | | | | | |
| All First | 1 | 2 | 0 | 59 | 55 | 29.50 | - | 1 | - | - | | | | | | | | |
| 1-day Int | | | | | | | | | | | | | | | | | | |
| NatWest | | | | | | | | | | | | | | | | | | |
| B & H | | | | | | | | | | | | | | | | | | |
| Sunday | 2 | 1 | 0 | 7 | 7 | 7.00 | - | - | - | - | 6 | 0 | 43 | 2 | 21.50 | 2-43 | - | |

314

## Career Performances

| | M | Inns | NO | Runs | HS | Avge | 100s | 50s | Ct | St | Balls | Runs | Wkts | Avge | Best | 5wI | 10wM |
|---|---|---|---|---|---|---|---|---|---|---|---|---|---|---|---|---|---|
| Test | | | | | | | | | | | | | | | | | |
| All First | 2 | 4 | 1 | 108 | 55 | 36.00 | - | 1 | - | - | 36 | 18 | 0 | - | | - | - | - |
| 1-day Int | | | | | | | | | | | | | | | | | |
| NatWest | | | | | | | | | | | | | | | | | |
| B & H | | | | | | | | | | | | | | | | | |
| Sunday | 5 | 3 | 1 | 39 | 28 | 19.50 | - | - | - | - | 66 | 72 | 3 | 24.00 | 2-43 | - | |

# KHAN, A. A. Middlesex

**Name:** Amer Ali Khan
**Role:** Right-hand bat, leg-break bowler
**Born:** 5 November 1969, Lahore,
Pakistan
**Height:** 5ft 9in  **Weight:** 12st
**Nickname:** Aams, Noni, The Chest
**County debut:** 1995
**1st-Class catches:** 1
**Parents:** M. Hanif Khan and Shireen Hanif
**Wife:** Nasara Khan
**Children:** Sarajane Nadia Khan;
Zaryaab Ali Khan
**Family links with cricket:** 'Dad used to
play club cricket'
**Education:** Muslim Model High School,
Lahore, Pakistan; MAO College, Lahore,
Pakistan
**Off-season:** 'I would like to go abroad and
play cricket'

**Overseas teams played for:** 'This winter I am going to Pakistan and I am going to
play for RDCA (Rawalpindi Division Cricket Association) as an overseas player)
**Cricketers particularly admired:** Abdul Qadir, Mike Atherton, Mark Ramprakash,
Shane Warne, Sachin Tendulkar
**Other sports followed:** American football
**Relaxations:** Listening to music and watching films
**Opinions on cricket:** 'I think that we should prepare more turning tracks than flat tracks
and second XI games should be four days and played at county grounds.'

## 1995 Season

| | M | Inns | NO | Runs | HS | Avge | 100s | 50s | Ct | St | O | M | Runs | Wkts | Avge | Best | 5wI | 10wM |
|---|---|------|----|------|----|------|------|-----|----|----|----|---|------|------|------|------|-----|------|
| Test | | | | | | | | | | | | | | | | | | |
| All First | 3 | 0 | 0 | 0 | 0 | - | - | - | 1 | - | 76 | 24 | 142 | 8 | 17.75 | 4-51 | - | - |
| 1-day Int | | | | | | | | | | | | | | | | | | |
| NatWest | | | | | | | | | | | | | | | | | | |
| B & H | | | | | | | | | | | | | | | | | | |
| Sunday | | | | | | | | | | | | | | | | | | |

## Career Performances

| | M | Inns | NO | Runs | HS | Avge | 100s | 50s | Ct | St | Balls | Runs | Wkts | Avge | Best | 5wI | 10wM |
|---|---|------|----|------|----|------|------|-----|----|----|-------|------|------|------|------|-----|------|
| Test | | | | | | | | | | | | | | | | | |
| All First | 3 | 0 | 0 | 0 | 0 | - | - | - | 1 | - | 456 | 142 | 8 | 17.75 | 4-51 | - | - |
| 1-day Int | | | | | | | | | | | | | | | | | |
| NatWest | | | | | | | | | | | | | | | | | |
| B & H | | | | | | | | | | | | | | | | | |
| Sunday | | | | | | | | | | | | | | | | | |

# KHAN, W. G.        Warwickshire

**Name:** Wasim Gulzar Khan
**Role:** Left-hand bat, right-arm
leg-break bowler
**Born:** 26 February 1971, Birmingham
**Height:** 6ft 1in **Weight:** 12st
**Nickname:** Mowgli, Dog and 'many others'
**County debut:** 1992 (one-day),
1995 (first-class)
**1st-Class 50s:** 6
**1st-Class 100s:** 1
**1st-Class catches:** 17
**Place in batting averages:** 27th av. 49.82
**Parents:** Raja Gulzar (deceased)
and Zarina Begum
**Marital status:** Single
**Education:** Small Heath Secondary School,
Birmingham; Josiah Mason Sixth Form
College, Birmingham
**Qualifications:** 6 O-levels, 1 A-level, NCA
Coaching Award
**Off-season:** Playing in Australia after Christmas
**Overseas tours:** Warwicks to Cape Town 1993

**Overseas teams played for:** Western Suburbs, Sydney 1990-91; North Perth, Western Australia 1991-93; Albion, Melbourne 1993-95

**Cricketers particularly admired:** Graham Thorpe 'ability and grit', Andy Moles 'determination and courage', Wasim Akram 'all-round talent', all Warwickshire squad 'belief and will to win'

**Other sports followed:** Football (Leeds United) and 'all sports except horse racing'

**Relaxations:** Listening to music, spending time with family and friends, playing golf, 'listening to Michael Bell's chat-up lines'

**Extras:** Most Promising Young Cricketer 1990. Scored four centuries in a row for Warwickshire U19. Scored 171* v Northants in second trial game for Warwickshire 2nd XI. England Schools U19. Won Oxford/Cambridge U19 Festival 1989,1990

**Opinions on cricket:** 'Too much cricket. 2nd XI wickets should be similar to 1st XI wickets in preparation and standard.'

**Best batting:** 181 Warwickshire v Hampshire, Southampton 1995

## 1995 Season

| | M | Inns | NO | Runs | HS | Avge | 100s | 50s | Ct | St | O | M | Runs | Wkts | Avge | Best | 5wI | 10wM |
|---|---|---|---|---|---|---|---|---|---|---|---|---|---|---|---|---|---|---|
| Test | | | | | | | | | | | | | | | | | | |
| All First | 13 | 23 | 6 | 847 | 181 | 49.82 | 1 | 6 | 17 | - | 7 | 1 | 22 | 0 | - | - | - | - |
| 1-day Int | | | | | | | | | | | | | | | | | | |
| NatWest | | | | | | | | | | | | | | | | | | |
| B & H | | | | | | | | | | | | | | | | | | |
| Sunday | 1 | 1 | 0 | 1 | 1 | 1.00 | - | - | 1 | - | | | | | | | | |

## Career Performances

| | M | Inns | NO | Runs | HS | Avge | 100s | 50s | Ct | St | Balls | Runs | Wkts | Avge | Best | 5wI | 10wM |
|---|---|---|---|---|---|---|---|---|---|---|---|---|---|---|---|---|---|
| Test | | | | | | | | | | | | | | | | | |
| All First | 13 | 23 | 6 | 847 | 181 | 49.82 | 1 | 6 | 17 | - | 42 | 22 | 0 | - | - | - | - |
| 1-day Int | | | | | | | | | | | | | | | | | |
| NatWest | | | | | | | | | | | | | | | | | |
| B & H | | | | | | | | | | | | | | | | | |
| Sunday | 2 | 2 | 0 | 8 | 7 | 4.00 | - | - | 1 | - | | | | | | | |

# KILLEEN, N.                                    Durham

**Name**: Neil Killeen
**Role:** Right-hand bat, right-arm fast-medium
bowler
**Born:** 17 October 1975, Shotley Bridge
**Height:** 6ft 2 in  **Weight:** 14st 12lbs
**Nickname:** Killer
**County debut:** 1995
**1st-Class catches:** 4
**1st-Class 5 w. in innings:** 1
**Place in batting averages:** 260th av. 13.70
**Place in bowling averages:** 132nd av. 45.11
**Strike rate:** 69.00 (career 69.00)
**Parents:** Glen and Thora
**Marital status:** Single
**Education:** Greencroft Comprehensive
School; Derwentside College, University of
Teeside
**Qualifications:** 8 GCSEs, 2 A-levels, cricket
coaching award
**Off-season:** At university doing a sports science degree
**Overseas tours:** Durham CCC to Zimbabwe 1992; England U19 to
West Indies 1994-95
**Cricketers particularly admired:** Ian Botham, Curtly Ambrose
**Other sports followed:** Athletics (English Schools javelin) and football
**Relaxations:** 'Spending time with friends and going out. Listening to music and
watching television'
**Extras:** First Durham bowler to take five wickets in a Sunday League game (5-26
against Northamptonshire in 1995)
**Opinions on cricket:** 'Too many overs in a day in the first-class game.'
**Best batting:** 48 Durham v Somerset, Chester-le-Street 1995
**Best bowling:** 5-118 Durham v Sussex, Hartlepool 1995

## 1995 Season

|           | M | Inns | NO | Runs | HS | Avge | 100s | 50s | Ct | St | O | M | Runs | Wkts | Avge | Best | 5wI | 10wM |
|-----------|---|------|----|----|----|------|------|-----|----|----|------|----|------|------|-------|-------|-----|------|
| Test      |   |      |    |    |    |      |      |     |    |    |      |    |      |      |       |       |     |      |
| All First | 7 | 13   | 3  | 137 | 48 | 13.70 | - | - | 4 | - | 195.3 | 30 | 767 | 17 | 45.11 | 5-118 | 1 | - |
| 1-day Int |   |      |    |    |    |      |      |     |    |    |      |    |      |      |       |       |     |      |
| NatWest   |   |      |    |    |    |      |      |     |    |    |      |    |      |      |       |       |     |      |
| B & H     | 5 | 4    | 1  | 14  | 8  | 4.66 | - | - | 1 | - | 55   | 5 | 234 | 6 | 39.00 | 2-43 | - | |
| Sunday    | 8 | 4    | 1  | 27  | 20 | 9.00 | - | - | 1 | - | 56.4 | 3 | 248 | 12 | 20.66 | 5-26 | 1 | |

## Career Performances

| | M | Inns | NO | Runs | HS | Avge | 100s | 50s | Ct | St | Balls | Runs | Wkts | Avge | Best | 5wI | 10wM |
|---|---|---|---|---|---|---|---|---|---|---|---|---|---|---|---|---|---|
| Test | | | | | | | | | | | | | | | | | |
| All First | 7 | 13 | 3 | 137 | 48 | 13.70 | - | - | 4 | - | 1173 | 767 | 17 | 45.11 | 5-118 | 1 | - |
| 1-day Int | | | | | | | | | | | | | | | | | |
| NatWest | | | | | | | | | | | | | | | | | |
| B & H | 5 | 4 | 1 | 14 | 8 | 4.66 | - | - | 1 | - | 330 | 234 | 6 | 39.00 | 2-43 | - | |
| Sunday | 8 | 4 | 1 | 27 | 20 | 9.00 | - | - | 1 | - | 340 | 248 | 12 | 20.66 | 5-26 | 1 | |

# KIRTLEY, R. J. Sussex

**Name:** Robert James Kirtley
**Role:** Right-hand bat, right-arm
fast-medium bowler
**Born:** 10 January 1975, Eastbourne
**Height:** 6ft **Weight:** 11st 11lbs
**Nickname:** Ambi, Hurtler
**County debut:** 1995
**1st-Class catches:** 2
**Parents:** Bob and Pip
**Marital status:** Single
**Family links with cricket:** Brother played
for Sussex Young cricketers and Eastbourne
**Education:** St Andrews School, Eastbourne;
Clifton College, Bristol
**Qualifications:** 9 GCSEs, 2 A-levels, NCA
coaching first level
**Off-season:** Coaching in Sussex, touring Sri
Lanka with Sussex Youth side
**Overseas tours:** Sussex YC to Barbados 1993
**Cricketers particularly admired:** Curtly Ambrose, Jim Andrew and Darren Gough
**Other sports followed:** Hockey, golf and football (Brighton & Hove Albion)
**Relaxations:** Sleeping
**Opinions on cricket:** 'With hard ground and indoor facilities, the workload of bowlers
should be lessened in order to prolong careers and keep bowlers fresh.'
**Best batting:** 2* Sussex v Glamorgan, Swansea 1995
**Best bowling:** 1-28 Sussex v Glamorgan, Swansea 1995

## 1995 Season

| | M | Inns | NO | Runs | HS | Avge | 100s | 50s | Ct | St | O | M | Runs | Wkts | Avge | Best | 5wI | 10wM |
|---|---|---|---|---|---|---|---|---|---|---|---|---|---|---|---|---|---|---|
| Test | | | | | | | | | | | | | | | | | | |
| All First | 2 | 2 | 2 | 3 | 2* | - | - | - | 2 | - | 38 | 11 | 103 | 2 | 51.50 | 1-28 | - | - |
| 1-day Int | | | | | | | | | | | | | | | | | | |
| NatWest | | | | | | | | | | | | | | | | | | |
| B & H | | | | | | | | | | | | | | | | | | |
| Sunday | 3 | 1 | 0 | 2 | 2 | 2.00 | - | - | - | - | 11 | 0 | 69 | 1 | 69.00 | 1-49 | - | |

## Career Performances

| | M | Inns | NO | Runs | HS | Avge | 100s | 50s | Ct | St | Balls | Runs | Wkts | Avge | Best | 5wI | 10wM |
|---|---|---|---|---|---|---|---|---|---|---|---|---|---|---|---|---|---|
| Test | | | | | | | | | | | | | | | | | |
| All First | 2 | 2 | 2 | 3 | 2* | - | - | - | 2 | - | 228 | 103 | 2 | 51.50 | 1-28 | - | - |
| 1-day Int | | | | | | | | | | | | | | | | | |
| NatWest | | | | | | | | | | | | | | | | | |
| B & H | | | | | | | | | | | | | | | | | |
| Sunday | 3 | 1 | 0 | 2 | 2 | 2.00 | - | - | - | - | 66 | 69 | 1 | 69.00 | 1-49 | - | |

# KNIGHT, N. V. — Warwickshire

**Name:** Nicholas Verity Knight
**Role:** Left-hand bat, right-arm medium-fast bowler, close fielder
**Born:** 28 November 1969, Watford
**Height:** 6ft **Weight:** 13st
**Nickname:** Stitch, Canvas, Fungus
**County debut:** 1991 (Essex), 1995 (Warwickshire)
**County cap:** 1994 (Essex), 1995 (Warwickshire)
**Test debut:** 1995
**Tests:** 2
**1st-Class 50s:** 19
**1st-Class 100s:** 8
**1st-Class catches:** 96
**Place in batting averages:** 29th av. 49.27 (1994 26th av. 47.20)
**Parents:** John and Rosemary
**Marital status:** Single
**Family links with cricket:** Father played for Cambridgeshire, brother plays club cricket for St Giles in Cambridge
**Education:** St John's School, Cambridge; Felsted Prep; Felsted School;

Loughborough University
**Qualifications:** 9 O-levels, 3 A-levels, BSc (Hons) Sociology, coaching qualification
**Off-season:** Touring Pakistan with England A
**Overseas tours:** Felsted School to Australia 1986-87; England A to India 1994-95, to Pakistan 1995-96
**Overseas teams played for:** Northern Districts, Sydney 1991-92; East Torrens, Adelaide 1992-94
**Injuries:** Hit on head twice while fielding, broken finger and bad back, out for six weeks
**Relaxations:** 'Eating good food and painting'
**Extras:** Captained English Schools 1987 and 1988, England YC v New Zealand 1989 and Combined Universities 1991. Played hockey for Essex and Young England. Played rugby for Eastern Counties. Won *Daily Telegraph* award 1988; voted Gray-Nicolls Cricketer of the Year 1988, Cricket Society Cricketer of the Year 1989, Essex Young Player of the Year 1991 and Essex U19 Player of the Year. Left Essex at the end of 1994 season to join Warwickshire
**Opinions on cricket:** 'Tea break not long enough and too many overs in a day.'
**Best batting:** 174 Warwickshire v Kent, Canterbury 1995
**Best bowling:** 1-61 Essex v Middlesex, Uxbridge 1994

## 1995 Season

|  | M | Inns | NO | Runs | HS | Avge | 100s | 50s | Ct | St | O | M | Runs | Wkts | Avge | Best | 5wI | 10wM |
|---|---|---|---|---|---|---|---|---|---|---|---|---|---|---|---|---|---|---|
| Test | 2 | 4 | 0 | 89 | 57 | 22.25 | - | 1 | 5 | - |  |  |  |  |  |  |  |  |
| All First | 13 | 23 | 5 | 887 | 174 | 49.27 | 1 | 7 | 26 | - |  |  |  |  |  |  |  |  |
| 1-day Int |  |  |  |  |  |  |  |  |  |  |  |  |  |  |  |  |  |  |
| NatWest | 5 | 5 | 0 | 238 | 151 | 47.60 | 1 | 1 | 3 | - |  |  |  |  |  |  |  |  |
| B & H | 4 | 4 | 1 | 139 | 91 | 46.33 | - | 1 | - | - |  |  |  |  |  |  |  |  |
| Sunday | 12 | 10 | 1 | 345 | 80 | 38.33 | - | 2 | 5 | - |  |  |  |  |  |  |  |  |

## Career Performances

|  | M | Inns | NO | Runs | HS | Avge | 100s | 50s | Ct | St | Balls | Runs | Wkts | Avge | Best | 5wI | 10wM |
|---|---|---|---|---|---|---|---|---|---|---|---|---|---|---|---|---|---|
| Test | 2 | 4 | 0 | 89 | 57 | 22.25 | - | 1 | 5 | - |  |  |  |  |  |  |  |
| All First | 65 | 109 | 13 | 3669 | 174 | 38.21 | 8 | 19 | 96 | - | 112 | 105 | 1 | 105.00 | 1-61 | - | - |
| 1-day Int |  |  |  |  |  |  |  |  |  |  |  |  |  |  |  |  |  |
| NatWest | 9 | 9 | 1 | 351 | 151 | 43.87 | 1 | 2 | 3 | - |  |  |  |  |  |  |  |
| B & H | 17 | 15 | 3 | 279 | 91 | 23.25 | - | 1 | 7 | - | 6 | 4 | 0 | - | - | - | - |
| Sunday | 57 | 49 | 8 | 1091 | 80 | 26.60 | - | 4 | 24 | - | 84 | 85 | 2 | 42.50 | 1-14 | - |  |

# KNOTT, J.A.

**Name:** James Alan Knott
**Role:** Right-hand bat, leg-spin bowler, wicket-keeper
**Born:** 14 June 1975
**Height:** 5ft 6in **Weight:** 11st 7lbs
**Nickname:** Billy Bunting ('Wolfey to ex-MCC team mates')
**County debut:** 1995
**1st-Class catches:** 1
**Parents:** Alan and Janet
**Marital status:** Single
**Family links with cricket:** 'Dad played a bit'
**Education:** Herne Church of England Primary School; Dane Court Grammar School; City of Westminster College
**Qualifications:** 10 GCSEs, 2 A-levels, 2 GVNQ level 3s, basic basketball and cricket coach
**Off-season:** Playing for Waverley, Sydney, Australia
**Overseas tours:** Canterbury District U15 to Holland
**Overseas teams played for:** Waverley, Sydney, Australia 1993-94
**Cricketers particularly admired:** Graham Gooch, David Boon, Mike Atherton and 'I guess my old man helped me out a bit'
**Other sports followed:** Football (West Ham United)
**Relaxations:** 'Love movies. Love curries. Enjoy a beer now and again'
**Extras:** 'Shortest ever basketball captain at school.' Has never won a trophy through cricket but has won several through football
**Opinions on cricket:** 'Need to get youngsters playing a higher standard of cricket earlier. Need to start producing more players of Test calibre and introduce them early to it.'

## 1995 Season

|  | M | Inns | NO | Runs | HS | Avge | 100s | 50s | Ct | St | O | M | Runs | Wkts | Avge | Best | 5wI | 10wM |
|---|---|---|---|---|---|---|---|---|---|---|---|---|---|---|---|---|---|---|
| Test |  |  |  |  |  |  |  |  |  |  |  |  |  |  |  |  |  |  |
| All First | 1 | 0 | 0 | 0 | 0 | - | - | - | 1 | - |  |  |  |  |  |  |  |  |
| 1-day Int |  |  |  |  |  |  |  |  |  |  |  |  |  |  |  |  |  |  |  |
| NatWest |  |  |  |  |  |  |  |  |  |  |  |  |  |  |  |  |  |  |  |
| B & H |  |  |  |  |  |  |  |  |  |  |  |  |  |  |  |  |  |  |  |  |
| Sunday |  |  |  |  |  |  |  |  |  |  |  |  |  |  |  |  |  |  |  |  |

## Career Performances

| | M | Inns | NO | Runs | HS | Avge | 100s | 50s | Ct | St | Balls | Runs | Wkts | Avge | Best | 5wI | 10wM |
|---|---|---|---|---|---|---|---|---|---|---|---|---|---|---|---|---|---|
| Test | | | | | | | | | | | | | | | | | |
| All First | 1 | 0 | 0 | 0 | 0 | - | - | - | 1 | - | | | | | | | |
| 1-day Int | | | | | | | | | | | | | | | | | |
| NatWest | | | | | | | | | | | | | | | | | |
| B & H | | | | | | | | | | | | | | | | | |
| Sunday | | | | | | | | | | | | | | | | | |

# KRIKKEN, K. M.                    Derbyshire

**Name:** Karl Matthew Krikken
**Role:** Right-hand bat, wicket-keeper
**Born:** 9 April 1969, Bolton
**Height:** 5ft 10in **Weight:** 12st 10lbs
**Nickname:** Krikk
**County debut:** 1987 (one-day), 1989 (first-class)
**County cap:** 1992
**1st-Class 50s:** 9
**1st-Class catches:** 265
**1st-Class stumpings:** 20
**Place in batting averages:** 157th av. 26.18 (1994 162nd av. 25.05)
**Parents:** Brian and Irene
**Marital status:** Single
**Family links with cricket:** Father played for Lancashire and Worcestershire
**Education:** Horwich Parish Church School; Rivington and Blackrod High School and 6th Form College
**Qualifications:** 6 O-levels, 3 A-levels, cricket coaching certificates
**Off-season:** Coaching at Derbyshire schools
**Overseas tours:** Derbyshire to Bermuda 1993, to Torremolinos 1995
**Overseas teams played for:** CBC Old Boys, Kimberley, South Africa 1988-89; Green Island, Dunedin, New Zealand 1990-91; United, Cape Town 1992-93; Rivertonians, Cape Town 1993-94
**Cricketers particularly admired:** Bob Taylor, Bruce French, Jack Russell, John Smedley
**Other sports followed:** Football (Wigan FC, Bolton FC), rugby (Wigan RLFC)
**Injuries:** Chicken pox ('thanks Dev') for three weeks and broken right index finger – out for six weeks ('thanks Daffy')
**Relaxations:** Music, keeping fit, hang-gliding, water skiing, orienteering and abseiling

in the Peak District
**Extras:** Derbyshire Supporters' Player of the Year 1991, Derbyshire Clubman of the Year 1993
**Opinions on cricket:** 'It's the best game in the world.'
**Best batting:** 85* Derbyshire v Glamorgan, Cardiff 1994

## 1995 Season

|  | M | Inns | NO | Runs | HS | Avge | 100s | 50s | Ct | St | O | M | Runs | Wkts | Avge | Best | 5wI | 10wM |
|---|---|---|---|---|---|---|---|---|---|---|---|---|---|---|---|---|---|---|
| Test |  |  |  |  |  |  |  |  |  |  |  |  |  |  |  |  |  |  |
| All First | 11 | 16 | 5 | 288 | 61 | 26.18 | - | 1 | 42 | 1 |  |  |  |  |  |  |  |  |
| 1-day Int |  |  |  |  |  |  |  |  |  |  |  |  |  |  |  |  |  |  |
| NatWest | 3 | 1 | 1 | 7 | 7* | - | - | - | 4 | - |  |  |  |  |  |  |  |  |
| B & H | 2 | 0 | 0 | 0 | 0 | - | - | - | 3 | - |  |  |  |  |  |  |  |  |
| Sunday | 10 | 8 | 6 | 124 | 29 | 62.00 | - | - | 9 | 1 |  |  |  |  |  |  |  |  |

## Career Performances

|  | M | Inns | NO | Runs | HS | Avge | 100s | 50s | Ct | St | Balls | Runs | Wkts | Avge | Best | 5wI | 10wM |
|---|---|---|---|---|---|---|---|---|---|---|---|---|---|---|---|---|---|
| Test |  |  |  |  |  |  |  |  |  |  |  |  |  |  |  |  |  |
| All First | 113 | 165 | 35 | 2617 | 85* | 20.13 | - | 9 | 265 | 20 | 36 | 40 | 0 | - | - | - | - |
| 1-day Int |  |  |  |  |  |  |  |  |  |  |  |  |  |  |  |  |  |
| NatWest | 8 | 5 | 4 | 48 | 18 | 48.00 | - | - | 8 | - |  |  |  |  |  |  |  |
| B & H | 13 | 8 | 3 | 94 | 37* | 18.80 | - | - | 19 | 1 |  |  |  |  |  |  |  |
| Sunday | 63 | 37 | 15 | 439 | 44* | 19.95 | - | - | 75 | 5 |  |  |  |  |  |  |  |

# KUMBLE, A.      Northamptonshire

**Name:** Anil Kumble
**Role:** Right-hand bat, leg-spin bowler
**Born:** 17 December 1969, Bangalore
**Height:** 6ft 1in  **Weight:** 12st 8lbs
**Nickname:** Apple, Kumbles
**County debut:** 1995
**County cap:** 1995
**Test debut:** 1990
**Tests:** 20
**One-Day Internationals:** 66
**100 wickets in a season:** 1
**1st-Class 50s:** 7
**1st-Class 100s:** 3
**1st-Class 5 w. in innings:** 24
**1st-Class 10 w. in match:** 6
**1st-Class catches:** 41

**One-Day 5 w. in innings:** 2
**Strike rate:** 51.40 (career 56.54)
**Parents**: K.N. Krishnaswani and Sarola Swami
**Marital status:** Single
**Education:** Holy Saint English School, Bangalore; National High School, Bangalore; National College and R.V. College of Engineering, Bangalore
**Career outside cricket:** Public relations executive for Titan Industries Ltd. in Bangalore
**Off-season:** 'Playing cricket for my state Karnataka and my country India'
**Overseas tours:** India to England 1990, to Australia 1991-92, to South Africa 1992-93, to Zimbabwe 1992-93, to Sri Lanka 1993-94, to New Zealand 1993-94, to Pakistan and Sri Lanka (World Cup) 1995-96
**Overseas teams played for:** Karnataka, India
**Other sports followed:** Tennis, football
**Relaxations:** Listening to music, watching television
**Extras:** Became the first bowler to take 100 wickets in a season since the introduction of four-day cricket in 1993
**Opinions on cricket:** 'The county itinerary needs looking at. A big final like the Nat West was played on a Saturday after playing continuously for nine days in the County Championship.'
**Best batting:** 154* Karnataka v Kerala, Bijapur 1991-92
**Best bowling:** 8-41 Karnataka v Kerala, Thalassery 1994-95

## 1995 Season

| | M | Inns | NO | Runs | HS | Avge | 100s | 50s | Ct | St | O | M | Runs | Wkts | Avge | Best | 5wI | 10wM |
|---|---|---|---|---|---|---|---|---|---|---|---|---|---|---|---|---|---|---|
| Test | | | | | | | | | | | | | | | | | | |
| All First | 17 | 21 | 5 | 321 | 40 * | 20.06 | - | - | 11 | - | 899.4 | 265 | 2143 | 105 | 20.40 | 7-82 | 8 | 2 |
| 1-day Int | | | | | | | | | | | | | | | | | | |
| NatWest | 5 | 2 | 1 | 8 | 6 * | 8.00 | - | - | 1 | - | 59.3 | 3 | 203 | 11 | 18.45 | 4-50 | - | |
| B & H | 4 | 3 | 0 | 5 | 3 | 1.66 | - | - | 1 | - | 37.4 | 1 | 135 | 3 | 45.00 | 2-40 | - | |
| Sunday | 10 | 3 | 1 | 11 | 8 | 5.50 | - | - | 3 | - | 69 | 2 | 347 | 16 | 21.68 | 3-25 | | |

41. Who was the first player to score 1,000 runs in the 1995 season?

## Career Performances

|         | M  | Inns | NO | Runs | HS   | Avge  | 100s | 50s | Ct | St | Balls | Runs | Wkts | Avge  | Best  | 5wI | 10wM |
|---------|----|------|----|------|------|-------|------|-----|----|----|-------|------|------|-------|-------|-----|------|
| Test    | 20 | 21   | 4  | 249  | 52 * | 14.64 | -    | 1   | 9  | -  | 6567  | 2510 | 99   | 25.35 | 7-59  | 5   | 1    |
| All First | 77 | 96 | 21 | 1964 | 154* | 26.18 | 3    | 7   | 41 |    | 20963 | 8489 | 371  | 22.88 | 8-41  | 24  | 6    |
| 1-day Int | 66 | 28 | 11 | 155  | 24   | 9.11  | -    | -   | 22 | -  | 3613  | 2424 | 81   | 29.92 | 6-12  | 2   |      |
| NatWest | 5  | 2    | 1  | 8    | 6 *  | 8.00  | -    | -   | 1  | -  | 357   | 203  | 11   | 18.45 | 4-50  | -   |      |
| B & H   | 4  | 3    | 0  | 5    | 3    | 1.66  | -    | -   | 1  | -  | 226   | 135  | 3    | 45.00 | 2-40  | -   |      |
| Sunday  | 10 | 3    | 1  | 11   | 8    | 5.50  | -    | -   | 3  | -  | 414   | 347  | 16   | 21.68 | 3-25  | ··  |      |

# LAMB, A. J. Northamptonshire

**Name:** Allan Joseph Lamb
**Role:** Right-hand bat, right-arm medium bowler
**Born:** 20 June 1954, Langebaanweg, Cape Province, South Africa
**Height:** 5ft 8in **Weight:** 12st
**Nickname:** Lambie, Legger, Joe
**County debut:** 1978
**County cap:** 1978
**Benefit:** 1988 (£134,000)
**Test debut:** 1982
**Tests:** 79
**One-Day Internationals:** 122
**1000 runs in a season:** 14
**1st-Class 50s:** 166
**1st-Class 100s:** 89
**1st-Class 200s:** 4
**1st-Class catches:** 371
**One-Day 100s:** 18
**Place in batting averages:** 10th av. 56.22 (1994 44th av. 43.23)
**Parents:** Michael and Joan
**Wife and date of marriage:** Lindsay, 8 December 1979
**Children:** Katie-Ann and Richard Edward Thomas
**Family links with cricket:** Father and brother played in the B section of the Currie Cup
**Education:** Wynberg Boys' High School; Abbotts College
**Qualifications:** Matriculation
**Career outside cricket:** Promotions company
**Overseas tours:** With England to Australia and New Zealand 1982-83, to New Zealand and Pakistan 1983-84, to India and Australia 1984-85, to West Indies 1985-86,

to Australia 1986-87, to India and Pakistan (World Cup) 1987-88, to India and West Indies 1989-90, to Australia 1990-91, to New Zealand 1991-92

**Overseas teams played for:** Western Province 1972-81, 1992-93; Orange Free State 1987-88

**Cricketers particularly admired:** Dennis Lillee, Viv Richards

**Other sports followed:** Tennis, golf, rugby and horse racing

**Relaxations:** Fly-fishing (trout and salmon)

**Extras:** Was primarily a bowler when he first played school cricket in South Africa. Made first-class debut for Western Province in 1972-73. Top of first-class batting averages in 1980, when he was one of *Wisden*'s Five Cricketers of the Year. Qualified to play for England in 1982. Appointed Northamptonshire captain 1989. Captained England in Tests v West Indies in 1989-90 and v Australia in 1990-91 after injuries to Graham Gooch. Hit three centuries in consecutive Tests v West Indies 1984 and, in his first Test as captain, made a century v West Indies at Bridgetown. Northamptonshire Player of the Year 1992. Relinquished county captaincy at the end of the 1995 season

**Opinions on cricket:** 'Get our one-day domestic game in line with overseas, i.e. we should play 50 overs as they do abroad. Our longer competition could be 55 not 60.'

**Best batting:** 294 Orange Free State v Eastern Province, Bloemfontein 1987-88

**Best bowling:** 2-29 Northamptonshire v Lancashire, Lytham 1991

## 1995 Season

| | M | Inns | NO | Runs | HS | Avge | 100s | 50s | Ct | St | O | M | Runs | Wkts | Avge | Best | 5wI | 10wM |
|---|---|---|---|---|---|---|---|---|---|---|---|---|---|---|---|---|---|---|
| Test | | | | | | | | | | | | | | | | | | |
| All First | 16 | 26 | 4 | 1237 | 166 | 56.22 | 3 | 6 | 15 | - | | | | | | | | |
| 1-day Int | | | | | | | | | | | | | | | | | | |
| NatWest | 3 | 3 | 0 | 103 | 63 | 34.33 | - | 1 | 2 | - | | | | | | | | |
| B & H | 3 | 3 | 0 | 79 | 41 | 26.33 | - | - | 1 | - | | | | | | | | |
| Sunday | 2 | 2 | 0 | 82 | 48 | 41.00 | - | - | 1 | - | | | | | | | | |

## Career Performances

| | M | Inns | NO | Runs | HS | Avge | 100s | 50s | Ct | St | Balls | Runs | Wkts | Avge | Best | 5wI | 10wM |
|---|---|---|---|---|---|---|---|---|---|---|---|---|---|---|---|---|---|
| Test | 79 | 139 | 10 | 4656 | 142 | 36.09 | 14 | 18 | 75 | - | 30 | 23 | 1 | 23.00 | 1-6 | - | - |
| All First | 467 | 772 | 108 | 32502 | 294 | 48.94 | 89 | 166 | 371 | - | 305 | 199 | 8 | 24.87 | 2-29 | - | - |
| 1-day Int | 122 | 118 | 16 | 4010 | 118 | 39.31 | 4 | 26 | 31 | - | 6 | 3 | 0 | - | - | - | - |
| NatWest | 53 | 52 | 5 | 1998 | 129 * | 42.51 | 4 | 13 | 16 | - | 8 | 12 | 1 | 12.00 | 1-4 | - | - |
| B & H | 73 | 67 | 11 | 2636 | 126 * | 47.07 | 5 | 17 | 26 | - | 6 | 11 | 1 | 11.00 | 1-11 | - | - |
| Sunday | 188 | 180 | 24 | 5521 | 132 * | 35.39 | 5 | 30 | 50 | - | | | | | | | |

# LAMPITT, S. R.                    Worcestershire

**Name:** Stuart Richard Lampitt
**Role:** Right-hand bat, right-arm
fast-medium bowler
**Born:** 29 July 1966, Wolverhampton
**Height:** 5ft 11in **Weight:** 13st 7lb
**Nickname:** Jed
**County debut:** 1985
**County cap:** 1989
**50 wickets in a season:** 4
**1st-Class 50s:** 13
**1st-Class 100s:** 1
**1st-Class 5 w. in innings:** 10
**1st-Class catches:** 86
**One-Day 5 w. in innings:** 3
**Place in batting averages:** 159th av. 25.68
(1994 131st av. 29.71)
**Place in bowling averages:** 55th av. 27.70
(1994 11th av. 23.18)

**Strike rate:** 53.90 (career 55.31)
**Parents:** Joseph Charles and Muriel Ann
**Marital status:** Single
**Education:** Kingswinford Secondary School; Dudley College of Technology
**Qualifications:** 7 O-levels; Diploma in Business Studies
**Career outside cricket:** 'Coaching and various others'
**Off-season:** 'Hopefully coaching around the Worcester area'
**Overseas tours:** NCA U19 to Bermuda; Worcestershire to Bahamas 1990, to
Zimbabwe 1990-91, to South Africa 1991-92
**Overseas teams played for:** Mangere, Auckland 1986-88; University CC, Perth 1991-93
**Cricketers particularly admired:** All first-class cricketers
**Other sports followed:** Football (Wolves), golf, and most ball sports
**Injuries:** Split finger, out for three weeks
**Relaxations:** 'Playing golf. Play football for Oldbury Utd in West Midlands Premier
League.'
**Extras:** Took five wickets and made 42 for Stourbridge in final of the William Younger
Cup at Lord's in 1986. One of the Whittingdale Young Players of the Year 1990. 'Must
be the only bowler to be hit for six first ball by Adrian Jones and Phil Tufnell (two master
batsmen)'
**Opinions on cricket:** 'Four-day cricket is a winner. Better quality of games, and the
cricket is better. However, I feel there is room for improvement in pitches.'
**Best batting:** 122 Worcestershire v Middlesex, Lord's 1994
**Best bowling:** 5-32 Worcestershire v Kent, Worcester 1989

## 1995 Season

| | M | Inns | NO | Runs | HS | Avge | 100s | 50s | Ct | St | O | M | Runs | Wkts | Avge | Best | 5wI | 10wM |
|---|---|---|---|---|---|---|---|---|---|---|---|---|---|---|---|---|---|---|
| Test | | | | | | | | | | | | | | | | | | |
| All First | 17 | 25 | 6 | 488 | 97 | 25.68 | - | 1 | 11 | - | 494.1 | 124 | 1524 | 55 | 27.70 | 4-34 | - | - |
| 1-day Int | | | | | | | | | | | | | | | | | | |
| NatWest | 1 | 1 | 0 | 29 | 29 | 29.00 | - | - | - | - | 7 | 1 | 36 | 0 | - | | - | - |
| B & H | 5 | 2 | 1 | 14 | 13 | 14.00 | - | - | 2 | - | 47.5 | 9 | 141 | 14 | 10.07 | 4-16 | - | |
| Sunday | 16 | 13 | 6 | 168 | 29 * | 24.00 | - | - | 3 | - | 90.5 | 3 | 382 | 21 | 18.19 | 4-43 | - | |

## Career Performances

| | M | Inns | NO | Runs | HS | Avge | 100s | 50s | Ct | St | Balls | Runs | Wkts | Avge | Best | 5wI | 10wM |
|---|---|---|---|---|---|---|---|---|---|---|---|---|---|---|---|---|---|
| Test | | | | | | | | | | | | | | | | | |
| All First | 141 | 178 | 36 | 3249 | 122 | 22.88 | 1 | 13 | 86 | - | 18862 | 9879 | 341 | 28.97 | 5-32 | 10 | - |
| 1-day Int | | | | | | | | | | | | | | | | | |
| NatWest | 18 | 11 | 3 | 117 | 29 | 14.62 | - | - | 5 | - | 941 | 678 | 27 | 25.11 | 5-22 | 1 | |
| B & H | 27 | 13 | 4 | 141 | 41 | 15.66 | - | - | 9 | - | 1484 | 981 | 50 | 19.62 | 6-26 | 1 | |
| Sunday | 107 | 63 | 24 | 780 | 41 * | 20.00 | - | - | 30 | - | 3626 | 2915 | 113 | 25.79 | 5-67 | 1 | |

# LANEY, J. S.     Hampshire

**Name:** Jason Scott Laney
**Role:** Right-hand bat, right-arm
off-spin bowler
**Born:** 24 April 1973, Winchester
**Height:** 5ft 10in **Weight:** 12st 7lbs
**Nickname:** Chucky, Hurler, Ginga
**County debut:** 1993 (one-day),
1995 (first-class)
**1st-Class 50s:** 2
**1st-Class catches:** 7
**Place in batting averages:** 139th av. 29.37
**Parents:** Geoff and Pam
**Marital status:** Single
**Family links with cricket:** Grandfather
played good club cricket and 'parents carted
me around whilst playing youth cricket'
**Education:** Pewsey Vale Comprehensive; St
John's, Marlborough; Leeds Metropolitan
University
**Qualifications:** 8 GCSEs, 2 A-levels, BA (Hons) in Human Movement Studies
**Off-season:** 'This winter in Zimbabwe playing for "The Rhino" Heath Streak and
sampling copious quantities of Zimbabwean ale'

**Overseas tours:** England U18 to Canada 1991
**Overseas teams played for:** Wakatu, New Zealand 1994-95
**Cricketers particularly admired:** Malcolm Marshall, Rupert Cox and Jim Bovill
**Other sports followed:** Football (Swindon Town and Liverpool FC), golf, rugby league, darts, squash, cards and 'fruit machines'
**Injuries:** Hamstring, out for two weeks during pre-season
**Relaxations:** 'I'm very interested in relaxing all of the time', amateur meteorology ('April to September'), 'having a quiet beer or even a loud beer with friends'
**Extras:** 'Judge Tours' Player of the Month, August 1995
**Opinions on cricket:** 'The usual stuff – lunch and tea breaks too short. Not enough rest time during the season. Outground facilities in 2nd XI matches not great. Also Sunday League shirt design is still fairly droll, perhaps take a look at baseball shirts for design and also the materials used are definitely not conducive to comfort or keeping cool on hot days in July, probably best off using them as pyjamas in December.'
**Best batting:** 73 Hampshire v Somerset, Southampton 1995

## 1995 Season

| | M | Inns | NO | Runs | HS | Avge | 100s | 50s | Ct | St | O | M | Runs | Wkts | Avge | Best | 5wI | 10wM |
|---|---|------|-----|------|-----|------|------|-----|-----|-----|---|---|------|------|------|------|-----|------|
| Test | | | | | | | | | | | | | | | | | | |
| All First | 9 | 17 | 1 | 470 | 73 | 29.37 | - | 2 | 7 | - | | | | | | | | |
| 1-day Int | | | | | | | | | | | | | | | | | | |
| NatWest | | | | | | | | | | | | | | | | | | |
| B & H | | | | | | | | | | | | | | | | | | |
| Sunday | 4 | 4 | 0 | 161 | 53 | 40.25 | - | 1 | - | - | | | | | | | | |

## Career Performances

| | M | Inns | NO | Runs | HS | Avge | 100s | 50s | Ct | St | Balls | Runs | Wkts | Avge | Best | 5wI | 10wM |
|---|---|------|-----|------|-----|------|------|-----|-----|-----|-------|------|------|------|------|-----|------|
| Test | | | | | | | | | | | | | | | | | | |
| All First | 9 | 17 | 1 | 470 | 73 | 29.37 | - | 2 | 7 | - | | | | | | | | |
| 1-day Int | | | | | | | | | | | | | | | | | | |
| NatWest | | | | | | | | | | | | | | | | | | |
| B & H | | | | | | | | | | | | | | | | | | |
| Sunday | 5 | 5 | 0 | 173 | 53 | 34.60 | - | 1 | - | - | | | | | | | | |

# LARKINS, W.                    Durham

**Name:** Wayne Larkins
**Role:** Right-hand bat, right-arm
medium bowler
**Born:** 22 November 1953, Roxton, Beds
**Height:** 5ft 11in **Weight:** 12st
**Nickname:** Ned
**County debut:** 1972 (Northamptonshire),
1992 (Durham)
**County cap:** 1976
**Benefit:** 1986
**Test debut:** 1979-80
**Tests:** 13
**One-Day Internationals:** 25
**1000 runs in a season:** 13
**1st-Class 50s:** 116
**1st-Class 100s:** 59
**1st-Class 200s:** 3
**1st-Class 5 w. in innings:** 1
**1st-Class catches:** 306
**One-Day 100s:** 24
**One-Day 5 w. in innings:** 1
**Place in batting averages:** 114th av. 32.04 (1994 54th av 40.66)
**Parents:** Mavis (father deceased)
**Wife and date of marriage:** Jane Elaine, 22 March 1975
**Children:** Philippa Jane, 30 May 1981
**Family links with cricket:** Father was umpire. Brother, Melvin, played for Bedford
Town for many years
**Education:** Bushmead, Eaton Socon, Huntingdon
**Overseas tours:** England to Australia and India 1979-80, to India and Sri Lanka 1981-
82, to India and West Indies 1989-90, to Australia 1990-91; unofficial English XI to
South Africa 1981-82
**Other sports followed:** Golf, football (was on Notts County's books), squash
**Relaxations:** Gardening
**Extras:** Banned from Test cricket for three years for joining rebel tour of South Africa
in 1982. Recalled to Test team in 1986 but withdrew owing to thumb injury and missed
another Test recall in 1987 because of a football injury. Eventually returned to Test
cricket in the West Indies in 1989-90, nine years after his last appearance. Moved to
Durham at the beginning of the 1992 season. Released at the end of the 1995 season and
hit a century in his last match for Durham. Has joined Minor Counties side Bedfordshire
for the 1996 season
**Best batting :** 252 Northamptonshire v Glamorgan, Cardiff 1983
**Best bowling :** 5-59 Northamptonshire v Worcestershire, Worcester 1984

## 1995 Season

| | M | Inns | NO | Runs | HS | Avge | 100s | 50s | Ct | St | O | M | Runs | Wkts | Avge | Best | 5wI | 10wM |
|---|---|---|---|---|---|---|---|---|---|---|---|---|---|---|---|---|---|---|
| Test | | | | | | | | | | | | | | | | | | |
| All First | 13 | 23 | 0 | 737 | 121 | 32.04 | 2 | 1 | 11 | - | | | | | | | | |
| 1-day Int | | | | | | | | | | | | | | | | | | |
| NatWest | 1 | 1 | 0 | 9 | 9 | 9.00 | - | - | - | - | | | | | | | | |
| B & H | 5 | 5 | 0 | 251 | 123 | 50.20 | 1 | 1 | 3 | - | | | | | | | | |
| Sunday | 10 | 9 | 1 | 121 | 42 | 15.12 | - | - | 5 | - | | | | | | | | |

## Career Performances

| | M | Inns | NO | Runs | HS | Avge | 100s | 50s | Ct | St | Balls | Runs | Wkts | Avge | Best | 5wI | 10wM |
|---|---|---|---|---|---|---|---|---|---|---|---|---|---|---|---|---|---|
| Test | 13 | 25 | 1 | 493 | 64 | 20.54 | - | 3 | 8 | - | | | | | | | |
| All First | 482 | 842 | 54 | 27142 | 252 | 34.44 | 59 | 116 | 306 | - | 3517 | 1915 | 42 | 45.59 | 5-59 | 1 | - |
| 1-day Int | 25 | 24 | 0 | 591 | 124 | 24.62 | 1 | - | 9 | - | 15 | 22 | 0 | - | - | - | - |
| NatWest | 52 | 51 | 3 | 1773 | 121 * | 36.93 | 2 | 12 | 21 | - | 455 | 274 | 4 | 68.50 | 2-38 | - | |
| B & H | 82 | 78 | 4 | 2660 | 132 | 35.94 | 7 | 11 | 21 | - | 675 | 444 | 16 | 27.75 | 4-37 | - | |
| Sunday | 290 | 278 | 18 | 7499 | 172 * | 28.84 | 14 | 36 | 91 | - | 2033 | 1679 | 57 | 29.45 | 5-32 | 1 | |

# LATHWELL, M. N. Somerset

**Name:** Mark Nicholas Lathwell
**Role:** Right-hand bat, right-arm medium and off-break bowler
**Born:** 26 December 1971, Bletchley, Bucks
**Height:** 5ft 8in **Weight:** 11st 6lbs
**Nickname:** Lathers, Rowdy
**County debut:** 1991
**County cap:** 1992
**Test debut:** 1993
**Tests:** 2
**1000 runs in a season:** 3
**1st-Class 50s:** 30
**1st-Class 100s:** 9
**1st-Class 200s:** 1
**1st-Class catches:** 61
**One-Day 100s:** 3
**Place in batting averages:** 118th av. 31.30
(1994 57th av. 39.67)
**Strike rate:** (career 93.54)
**Parents:** Derek Peter and Valerie
**Marital status:** Single
**Family links with cricket:** Brother plays local club cricket; father is a 'retired' club

cricketer and now senior coach

**Education:** Overstone Primary, Wing, Bucks; Southmead Primary, Braunton, North Devon; Braunton Comprehensive

**Qualifications:** 5 GCSEs

**Career outside cricket:** Bank clerk

**Overseas tours:** England A to Australia 1992-93, to South Africa 1993-94

**Cricketers particularly admired:** Ian Botham, Graham Gooch

**Other sports followed:** Snooker, darts

**Relaxations:** Fishing, darts, playing cards, eating, swimming

**Extras:** Spent one season on Lord's groundstaff. Played for England U19 v Australia U19 1991. Young Player of the Year and Somerset Player of the Year 1992. Cricket Writers' Club Young Cricketer of the Year 1993

**Best batting:** 206 Somerset v Surrey, Bath 1994

**Best bowling:** 2-21 Somerset v Sussex, Hove 1994

## 1995 Season

| | M | Inns | NO | Runs | HS | Avge | 100s | 50s | Ct | St | O | M | Runs | Wkts | Avge | Best | 5wI | 10wM |
|---|---|---|---|---|---|---|---|---|---|---|---|---|---|---|---|---|---|---|
| Test | | | | | | | | | | | | | | | | | | |
| All First | 17 | 33 | 0 | 1033 | 111 | 31.30 | 2 | 5 | 9 | - | 25 | 5 | 82 | 2 | 41.00 | 1-15 | - | - |
| 1-day Int | | | | | | | | | | | | | | | | | | |
| NatWest | 1 | 1 | 0 | 15 | 15 | 15.00 | - | - | - | - | | | | | | | | |
| B & H | 6 | 6 | 0 | 145 | 74 | 24.16 | - | 1 | 2 | - | 0.1 | 0 | 1 | 0 | - | | - | - |
| Sunday | 15 | 15 | 0 | 284 | 55 | 18.93 | - | 2 | 3 | - | | | | | | | | |

## Career Performances

| | M | Inns | NO | Runs | HS | Avge | 100s | 50s | Ct | St | Balls | Runs | Wkts | Avge | Best | 5wI | 10wM |
|---|---|---|---|---|---|---|---|---|---|---|---|---|---|---|---|---|---|
| Test | 2 | 4 | 0 | 78 | 33 | 19.50 | - | - | - | - | | | | | | | |
| All First | 84 | 152 | 4 | 5058 | 206 | 34.17 | 9 | 30 | 61 | - | 1026 | 597 | 11 | 54.27 | 2-21 | - | - |
| 1-day Int | | | | | | | | | | | | | | | | | |
| NatWest | 11 | 11 | 0 | 383 | 103 | 34.81 | 1 | 2 | 3 | - | 66 | 23 | 1 | 23.00 | 1-23 | - | - |
| B & H | 11 | 11 | 0 | 440 | 120 | 40.00 | 1 | 3 | 2 | - | 25 | 50 | 0 | - | | - | - |
| Sunday | 60 | 59 | 1 | 1570 | 117 | 27.06 | 1 | 8 | 15 | - | 102 | 85 | 0 | - | | - | - |

# LAW, D. R. C.                                                    Sussex

**Name:** Danny Richard Charles Law
**Role:** Right-hand bat, right-arm fast bowler
**Born:** 15 July 1975, Lambeth, London
**Height:** 6ft 5in **Weight:** 13st 7lbs
**Nickname:** Decas, Desperate
**County debut:** 1993
**1st-Class 100s:** 1
**1st-Class catches:** 6
**Place in batting averages:** 214th av. 19.07
**Strike rate:** (career 72.63)
**Parents:** Richard (deceased) and Claudette
**Marital status:** 'Attached'
**Education:** Wolverton Hall School; Steyning
Grammar School
**Qualifications:** Cricket coach
**Overseas tours:** Sussex Schools U16 to
Jersey 1991; England U18 to South Africa
1992-93, to Denmark 1993; England U19 to
Sri Lanka 1993-94
**Cricketers particularly admired:** Michael Holding, Allan Donald, Courtney Walsh,
Franklyn Stephenson, John North, Chris Tugwell
**Other sports followed:** Most sports
**Relaxations:** Listening to music, spending time at home
**Opinions on cricket:** 'The 2nd XI Championship should be increased from a three-day
game to a four-day game so that younger players are used to playing four-day cricket and
are not thrown in at the deep end if they progress to first-class cricket.'
**Best batting:** 115 Sussex v Young Australia, Hove 1995
**Best bowling:** 2-38 Sussex v Worcestershire, Hove 1993

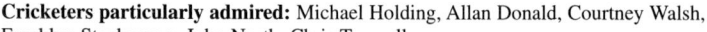

### 1995 Season

|            | M  | Inns | NO | Runs | HS   | Avge  | 100s | 50s | Ct | St | O    | M  | Runs | Wkts | Avge  | Best  | 5wI | 10wM |
|------------|----|------|----|------|------|-------|------|-----|----|----|------|----|------|------|-------|-------|-----|------|
| Test       |    |      |    |      |      |       |      |     |    |    |      |    |      |      |       |       |     |      |
| All First  | 8  | 13   | 0  | 248  | 115  | 19.07 | 1    | -   | 6  | -  | 69.3 | 11 | 303  | 6    | 50.50 | 2-115 | -   | -    |
| 1-day Int  |    |      |    |      |      |       |      |     |    |    |      |    |      |      |       |       |     |      |
| NatWest    | 1  | 0    | 0  | 0    | 0    | -     | -    | -   | -  | -  |      |    |      |      |       |       |     |      |
| B & H      |    |      |    |      |      |       |      |     |    |    |      |    |      |      |       |       |     |      |
| Sunday     | 11 | 8    | 2  | 112  | 41 * | 18.66 | -    | -   | 4  | -  |      |    |      |      |       |       |     |      |

|  | M | Inns | NO | Runs | HS | Avge | 100s | 50s | Ct | St | Balls | Runs | Wkts | Avge | Best | 5wI | 10wM |
|---|---|---|---|---|---|---|---|---|---|---|---|---|---|---|---|---|---|
| Test |  |  |  |  |  |  |  |  |  |  |  |  |  |  |  |  |  |
| All First | 11 | 15 | 0 | 259 | 115 | 17.26 | 1 | - | 6 | - | 799 | 519 | 11 | 47.18 | 2-38 | - | - |
| 1-day Int |  |  |  |  |  |  |  |  |  |  |  |  |  |  |  |  |  |
| NatWest | 1 | 0 | 0 | 0 | 0 | - | - | - | - | - |  |  |  |  |  |  |  |
| B & H |  |  |  |  |  |  |  |  |  |  |  |  |  |  |  |  |  |  |
| Sunday | 11 | 8 | 2 | 112 | 41 * | 18.66 | - | - | 4 | - |  |  |  |  |  |  |  |

# LAWRENCE, J. R. G. Durham

**Name:** James Richard Geoffrey Lawrence
**Role:** Left-arm fast-medium bowler
**Born:** 29 November 1976, Portsmouth
**Height:** 6ft 2in **Weight:** 14st 3lbs
**County debut:** 1995
**Parents:** Richard and Charmian
**Education:** Hurworth Primary; Hurworth
School; Queen Elizabeth Sixth Form College,
Darlington; Durham University (commencing
October 1996)
**Qualificaitons:** 3 A-levels
**Off-season:** Travelling in Australia
**Cricketers particularly admired:** Allan
Donald, Sachin Tendulkar, Jonty Rhodes
**Other sports followed:** Athletics, tennis and
basketball
**Relaxations:** Music and food
**Extras:** Made first-class debut for Durham

against Somerset on 17 August 1995 on the same day that his A-level results were
announced. Played for ESCA U19 against MCC at Lord's on 18 July 1995 and MCC
Schools against NAYC on 19 July 1995. Aslso played for England Schools against
Scotland and Wales
**Opinions on cricket:** 'To revitalise the game and generate income introduce a floodlit
25-over competition. This could be played starting early evening and designed to attract
whole families (in the sytke of US basketball).'
**Best batting:** 7* Durham v Somerset, Chester-le-Street 1995
**Best bowling:** 2-44 Durham v Somerset, Chester-le-Street 1995

## 1995 Season

|          | M | Inns | NO | Runs | HS | Avge | 100s | 50s | Ct | St | O | M | Runs | Wkts | Avge | Best | 5wI | 10wM |
|----------|---|------|----|------|-----|------|------|-----|----|----|----|---|------|------|------|------|-----|------|
| Test     |   |      |    |      |     |      |      |     |    |    |   |   |      |      |      |      |     |      |
| All First | 1 | 2   | 1  | 7    | 7 * | 7.00 | -    | -   | -  | -  | 40 | 8 | 123  | 3    | 41.00 | 2-44 | -   | -    |
| 1-day Int |   |      |    |      |     |      |      |     |    |    |   |   |      |      |      |      |     |      |
| NatWest  |   |      |    |      |     |      |      |     |    |    |   |   |      |      |      |      |     |      |
| B & H    |   |      |    |      |     |      |      |     |    |    |   |   |      |      |      |      |     |      |
| Sunday   |   |      |    |      |     |      |      |     |    |    |   |   |      |      |      |      |     |      |

## Career Performances

|          | M | Inns | NO | Runs | HS | Avge | 100s | 50s | Ct | St | Balls | Runs | Wkts | Avge | Best | 5wI | 10wM |
|----------|---|------|----|------|-----|------|------|-----|----|----|-------|------|------|------|------|-----|------|
| Test     |   |      |    |      |     |      |      |     |    |    |       |      |      |      |      |     |      |
| All First | 1 | 2   | 1  | 7    | 7 * | 7.00 | -    | -   | -  | -  | 240   | 123  | 3    | 41.00 | 2-44 | -   | -    |
| 1-day Int |   |      |    |      |     |      |      |     |    |    |       |      |      |      |      |     |      |
| NatWest  |   |      |    |      |     |      |      |     |    |    |       |      |      |      |      |     |      |
| B & H    |   |      |    |      |     |      |      |     |    |    |       |      |      |      |      |     |      |
| Sunday   |   |      |    |      |     |      |      |     |    |    |       |      |      |      |      |     |      |

# LEATHERDALE, D. A. — Worcestershire

**Name:** David Anthony Leatherdale
**Role:** Right-hand bat, right-arm medium bowler, cover fielder
**Born:** 26 November 1967, Bradford
**Height:** 5ft 10in **Weight:** 11st
**Nickname:** Lugsy, Spock
**County debut:** 1988
**County cap:** 1994
**1st-Class 50s:** 23
**1st-Class 100s:** 5
**1st-Class catches:** 88
**Place in batting averages:** 81st av. 36.67 (1994 34th av. 44.86)
**Strike rate:** (career 93.70)
**Parents:** Paul and Rosalyn
**Wife's name:** Vanessa
**Children:** Callum Edward, 6 July 1990
**Family links with cricket:** Father played local cricket; brother plays for East Bierley in Bradford League; brother-in-law played for England YC in 1979
**Education:** Bolton Royd Primary School; Pudsey Grangefield Secondary School
**Qualifications:** 8 O-levels, 2 A-levels; NCA coaching award (stage 1)

**Career outside cricket:** Marketing executive for Worcestershire CCC
**Overseas tours:** England Indoor to Australia and New Zealand 1994-95
**Overseas teams played for:** Pretoria Police, South Africa 1987-88
**Cricketers particularly admired:** Mark Scott, George Batty, Peter Kippax
**Other sports followed:** Football, American football
**Relaxations:** Golf
**Best batting:** 157 Worcestershire v Somerset, Worcester 1991
**Best bowling:** 2-11 Worcestershire v Cambridge University, Fenner's 1994

## 1995 Season

|  | M | Inns | NO | Runs | HS | Avge | 100s | 50s | Ct | St | O | M | Runs | Wkts | Avge | Best | 5wl | 10wM |
|---|---|---|---|---|---|---|---|---|---|---|---|---|---|---|---|---|---|---|
| Test |  |  |  |  |  |  |  |  |  |  |  |  |  |  |  |  |  |  |
| All First | 18 | 30 | 3 | 993 | 93 | 36.77 | - | 8 | 15 | - | 28 | 3 | 123 | 4 | 30.75 | 2-36 | - | - |
| 1-day Int |  |  |  |  |  |  |  |  |  |  |  |  |  |  |  |  |  |  |
| NatWest | 1 | 1 | 0 | 14 | 14 | 14.00 | - | - | - | - |  |  |  |  |  |  |  |  |
| B & H | 4 | 3 | 1 | 36 | 29 | 18.00 | - | - | - | - |  |  |  |  |  |  |  |  |
| Sunday | 13 | 10 | 1 | 199 | 47 | 22.11 | - | - | 4 | - |  |  |  |  |  |  |  |  |

## Career Performances

|  | M | Inns | NO | Runs | HS | Avge | 100s | 50s | Ct | St | Balls | Runs | Wkts | Avge | Best | 5wl | 10wM |
|---|---|---|---|---|---|---|---|---|---|---|---|---|---|---|---|---|---|
| Test |  |  |  |  |  |  |  |  |  |  |  |  |  |  |  |  |  |
| All First | 96 | 148 | 14 | 4290 | 157 | 32.01 | 5 | 23 | 88 | - | 937 | 521 | 10 | 52.10 | 2-11 | - | - |
| 1-day Int |  |  |  |  |  |  |  |  |  |  |  |  |  |  |  |  |  |
| NatWest | 17 | 14 | 1 | 246 | 43 | 18.92 | - | - | 5 | - | 64 | 45 | 3 | 15.00 | 3-14 | - |  |
| B & H | 15 | 10 | 1 | 117 | 30 | 13.00 | - | - | 2 | - | 42 | 39 | 0 | - | - | - |  |
| Sunday | 82 | 70 | 9 | 972 | 62 * | 15.93 | - | 2 | 41 | - | 129 | 107 | 4 | 26.75 | 2-15 | - |  |

42. Which team won the Cricketer Cup in 1995?

# LEE, S. Somerset

**Name:** Shane Lee
**Role:** Right-hand bat, right-arm
medium bowler
**Height:** 6ft 2in  **Weight:** 85kg
**Born:** 8 August 1973, Wollongong,
New South Wales, Australia
**County debut:** No first team appearance
**1st-Class 100s:** 2
**1st-Class 50s:** 3
**1st-Class catches:** 12
**Strike rate:** (career 100.50)
**Parents:** Robert and Helen
**Marital status:** Single
**Family links with cricket:** Both brothers
Brett and Grant play in New South Wales
**Education:** Balarang Primary School;
Oak Flats Senior High School;
Wollongong University
**Qualifications:** High School Certificate and
currently studying for a degree in psychology
**Off-season:** Playing for New South Wales and going to the World Cup with Australia
**Overseas tours:** Australian Cricket Academy to India and Sri Lanka 1993; Australia
U19 to New Zealand; Australia to India and Pakistan (World Cup) 1995-96
**Overseas teams played for:** New South Wales 1993-96
**Extras:** Made his debut for New South Wales against Western Australia in 1992-93
season. He was offered a full-time scholarship at the Australian Cricket Academy in
1993 but his university studies prevented him from accepting. He attended on a part-time
basis instead. Made his representative debut for Australia in December 1995 in the
World Series match against West Indies. Replaces Mushtaq Ahmed as Somerset's
overseas player for the 1996 season on a one year contract
**Best batting:** 104* New South Wales v Queensland, Sydney 1994-95
**Best bowling:** 3-53 New South Wales v Victoria, Melbourne 1994-95

43. Who was Dominic Cork's first Test victim?

**Career Performances**

|        | M | Inns | NO | Runs | HS | Avge | 100s | 50s | Ct | St | Balls | Runs | Wkts | Avge | Best | 5wl | 10wM |
|--------|---|------|----|------|-----|------|------|-----|----|----|-------|------|------|-------|------|-----|------|
| Test   |   |      |    |      |     |      |      |     |    |    |       |      |      |       |      |     |      |
| All First | 16 | 26 | 4 | 667 | 104 * | 30.31 | 2 | 3 | 12 | - | 1608 | 977 | 16 | 61.06 | 3-53 | - |  |
| 1-day Int |   |      |    |      |     |      |      |     |    |    |       |      |      |       |      |     |      |
| NatWest |   |      |    |      |     |      |      |     |    |    |       |      |      |       |      |     |      |
| B & H  |   |      |    |      |     |      |      |     |    |    |       |      |      |       |      |     |      |
| Sunday |   |      |    |      |     |      |      |     |    |    |       |      |      |       |      |     |      |

# LEFEBVRE, R. P. Glamorgan

**Name:** Roland Philippe Lefebvre
**Role:** Right-hand bat, right-arm medium bowler
**Born:** 7 February 1963, Rotterdam
**Height:** 6ft 1in **Weight:** 12st 6lbs
**Nickname:** Tulip
**County debut:** 1990 (Somerset), 1993 (Glamorgan)
**County cap:** 1991 (Somerset), 1993 (Glamorgan)
**1st-Class 50s:** 3
**1st-Class 100s:** 1
**1st-Class 5 w. in innings:** 3
**1st-Class catches:** 36
**One-Day 5 w. in innings:** 1
**Strike rate:** (career 90.50)
**Parents:** Pierre Joseph Ernest
**Wife's name and date of marriage:**
Sandy, 12 August 1994
**Children:** Kirsty, 9 February 1990; Marc Philippe, 23 March 1995
**Family links with cricket:** Father plays for 'Still Going Strong' CC and brother plays for The Wanderers in Johannesburg
**Education:** Montessori Lyceum, Rotterdam; The Hague Academy of Physiotherapy
**Qualifications:** Qualified physiotherapist
**Career outside cricket:** Physiotherapy
**Off-season:** Coaching, working as physiotherapist, preparing for World Cup
**Overseas tours:** Holland tours to England, Canada, Denmark, New Zealand, Barbados, Zimbabwe, Dubai and South Africa, to New Zealand 1991-92, to South Africa 1992-93, to Kenya (ICC Trophy) 1993-94, to Hong Kong Sixes 1994, to Dubai

1995-96, to India and Pakistan (World Cup) 1995-96; MCC to Leeward Islands 1991-92
**Overseas teams played for:** VOC Rotterdam, Flamingos; East Coast Bays Cricket Club, Auckland 1987-89; Woolston Working Men's Club, Christchurch, New Zealand 1990-91; Canterbury, New Zealand 1990-91; Alma Marist CC, Cape Town 1993-94
**Cricketers particularly admired:** Vivian Richards, Ian Botham
**Other sports followed:** Most other sports
**Injuries:** 'Groin strain for the last three months'
**Relaxations:** Playing the piano, music of various kinds, reading, the countryside, travelling
**Extras:** More than 80 caps for Holland. Played in 1986 and 1990 ICC Trophy competitions – voted Player of Tournament 1990; was a member of the Dutch teams that beat England (captained by Peter Roebuck) in 1989 and West Indies in 1991. First Dutch player to score a first-class century.
**Opinions on cricket:** 'Taking all the money that has recently come into the game into consideration, capped players should be better rewarded for their services. There is too much of a wage gap between certain players. It's very good to see Holland being entered in the NatWest and hopefully it won't take long for them to join the B & H Cup as well.'
**Best batting:** 100 Somerset v Worcestershire, Weston-super-Mare 1991
**Best bowling:** 6-45 Glamorgan v Oxford University, The Parks 1995

## 1995 Season

|          | M  | Inns | NO | Runs | HS   | Avge  | 100s | 50s | Ct | St | O    | M  | Runs | Wkts | Avge  | Best | 5wI | 10wM |
|----------|----|------|----|------|------|-------|------|-----|----|----|------|----|------|------|-------|------|-----|------|
| Test     |    |      |    |      |      |       |      |     |    |    |      |    |      |      |       |      |     |      |
| All First| 3  | 3    | 0  | 55   | 24   | 18.33 | -    | -   | -  | -  | 85.3 | 28 | 179  | 6    | 29.83 | 6-45 | 1   | -    |
| 1-day Int|    |      |    |      |      |       |      |     |    |    |      |    |      |      |       |      |     |      |
| NatWest  | 1  | 0    | 0  | 0    | 0    | -     | -    | -   | -  | -  | 12   | 2  | 32   | 1    | 32.00 | 1-32 | -   |      |
| B & H    | 5  | 3    | 0  | 30   | 16   | 10.00 | -    | -   | 2  | -  | 50.5 | 5  | 183  | 6    | 30.50 | 3-42 | -   |      |
| Sunday   | 10 | 4    | 2  | 23   | 10 * | 11.50 | -    | -   | 7  | -  | 76.3 | 3  | 313  | 16   | 19.56 | 3-29 | -   |      |

## Career Performances

|          | M  | Inns | NO | Runs | HS   | Avge  | 100s | 50s | Ct | St | Balls | Runs | Wkts | Avge  | Best | 5wI | 10wM |
|----------|----|------|----|------|------|-------|------|-----|----|----|-------|------|------|-------|------|-----|------|
| Test     |    |      |    |      |      |       |      |     |    |    |       |      |      |       |      |     |      |
| All First| 77 | 89   | 16 | 1494 | 100  | 20.46 | 1    | 3   | 36 | -  | 13485 | 5399 | 149  | 36.23 | 6-45 | 3   | -    |
| 1-day Int|    |      |    |      |      |       |      |     |    |    |       |      |      |       |      |     |      |
| NatWest  | 13 | 6    | 4  | 65   | 21 * | 32.50 | -    | -   | 8  | -  | 897   | 353  | 26   | 13.57 | 7-15 | 1   |      |
| B & H    | 18 | 13   | 5  | 184  | 37   | 23.00 | -    | -   | 5  | -  | 1051  | 654  | 18   | 36.33 | 3-42 | -   |      |
| Sunday   | 76 | 46   | 15 | 439  | 36 * | 14.16 | -    | -   | 38 | -  | 3348  | 2256 | 97   | 23.25 | 4-23 | -   |      |

# LENHAM, N. J. — Sussex

**Name:** Neil John Lenham
**Role:** Right-hand bat, right-arm medium
bowler
**Born:** 17 December 1965, Worthing
**Height:** 5ft 11in **Weight:** 11st
**Nickname:** Pin
**County debut:** 1984
**County cap:** 1990
**1000 runs in a season:** 3
**1st-Class 50s:** 42
**1st-Class 100s:** 18
**1st-Class 200s:** 1
**1st-Class catches:** 68
**One-day 100s:** 1
**One-Day 5 w. in innings:** 1
**Place in batting averages:** 73rd av. 39.40
(1994 121st av. 31.11)
**Strike rate:** (career 84.61)
**Parents:** Leslie John and Valerie Anne

**Marital status:** Single
**Family links with cricket:** Father played for Sussex and is now one of the NCA's
national coaches
**Education:** Broadwater Manor Prep School; Brighton College
**Qualifications:** 5 O-levels, 2 A-levels, advanced cricket coach
**Off-season:** Coaching in Namibia
**Overseas tours:** England YC to West Indies (as captain) 1985
**Overseas teams played for:** Port Elizabeth, South Africa 1987-88; Brighton,
Tasmania 1989-91; United, Namibia 1994-95
**Cricketers particularly admired:** Ken McEwan, Barry Richards
**Other sports followed:** Golf, horse racing, rugby and fishing
**Injuries:** Broken finger ('shock!'), out for three weeks
**Relaxations:** Fishing, golf, squash
**Extras:** Made debut for England YC in 1983. Broke record for number of runs scored
in season at a public school in 1984 (1534 av. 80.74). Youngest player to appear for
Sussex 2nd XI at 14 years old. Appointed as Eastbourne's first Cricket Development
Officer in 1992
**Opinions on cricket:** 'Four-day cricket should not be disrupted by Sunday League
game. Also improvements should be looked into for raising the quality of pitches.'
**Best batting:** 222* Sussex v Kent, Hove 1992
**Best bowling:** 4-13 Sussex v Durham, Durham University 1993

## 1995 Season

| | M | Inns | NO | Runs | HS | Avge | 100s | 50s | Ct | St | O | M | Runs | Wkts | Avge | Best | 5wI | 10wM |
|---|---|---|---|---|---|---|---|---|---|---|---|---|---|---|---|---|---|---|
| Test | | | | | | | | | | | | | | | | | | |
| All First | 15 | 25 | 3 | 867 | 128 | 39.40 | 2 | 4 | 10 | - | 6 | 0 | 27 | 1 | 27.00 | 1-10 | - | - |
| 1-day Int | | | | | | | | | | | | | | | | | | |
| NatWest | 1 | 1 | 1 | 129 | 129 * | - | | 1 | - | - | - | | | | | | | |
| B & H | 3 | 3 | 2 | 133 | 73 * | 133.00 | - | 1 | 1 | - | | | | | | | | |
| Sunday | 9 | 9 | 1 | 193 | 56 * | 24.12 | - | 1 | 3 | - | | | | | | | | |

## Career Performances

| | M | Inns | NO | Runs | HS | Avge | 100s | 50s | Ct | St | Balls | Runs | Wkts | Avge | Best | 5wI | 10wM |
|---|---|---|---|---|---|---|---|---|---|---|---|---|---|---|---|---|---|
| Test | | | | | | | | | | | | | | | | | |
| All First | 169 | 292 | 26 | 8942 | 222 * | 33.61 | 18 | 42 | 68 | - | 3300 | 1701 | 39 | 43.61 | 4-13 | - | - |
| 1-day Int | | | | | | | | | | | | | | | | | |
| NatWest | 12 | 11 | 3 | 526 | 129 * | 65.75 | 1 | 3 | - | - | 369 | 222 | 9 | 24.66 | 2-12 | - | |
| B & H | 22 | 21 | 6 | 525 | 82 | 35.00 | - | 3 | 3 | - | 258 | 211 | 4 | 52.75 | 1-3 | - | |
| Sunday | 87 | 76 | 16 | 1712 | 86 | 28.53 | - | 11 | 19 | - | 822 | 821 | 27 | 30.40 | 5-28 | 1 | |

# LEWIS, C. C. Surrey

**Name:** Christopher Clairmonte Lewis
**Role:** Right-hand bat, right-arm
fast-medium bowler
**Born:** 14 February 1968, Georgetown,
Guyana
**Height:** 6ft 2in **Weight:** 13st
**Nickname:** Carl
**County debut:** 1987 (Leicestershire), 1992
(Nottinghamshire)
**County cap:** 1990 (Leicestershire), 1992
(Nottinghamshire)
**Test debut:** 1990
**Tests:** 27
**One-Day Internationals:** 48
**50 wickets in a season:** 2
**1st-Class 50s:** 23
**1st-Class 100s:** 7
**1st-Class 200s:** 2
**1st-Class 5 w. in innings:** 15
**1st-Class 10 w. in match:** 3
**1st-Class catches:** 107
**One-Day 5 w. in innings:** 1

**1st-Class 10 w. in match:** 3
**1st-Class catches:** 107
**One-Day 5 w. in innings:** 1
**Place in batting averages:** (1994 5th av. 58.73)
**Place in bowling averages:** (1994 13th av. 23.52)
**Strike rate:** (career 59.52)
**Parents:** Philip and Patricia
**Marital status:** Single
**Education:** Willesden High School
**Qualifications:** 2 O-levels
**Overseas tours:** England YC to Australia (Youth World Cup) 1987; England A to Kenya and Zimbabwe 1989-90; England to West Indies 1989-90, to Australia and New Zealand 1990-91, to New Zealand 1991-92, to India and Sri Lanka 1992-93, to West Indies 1993-94, to Australia 1994-95
**Cricketers particularly admired:** Graham Gooch, Robin Smith
**Other sports followed:** Snooker, football, darts, American football, basketball
**Relaxations:** Music, sleeping
**Extras:** Joined England's tour of West Indies in 1989-90 as a replacement for Ricky Ellcock. Suffers from Raynaud's disease, a problem of blood circulation, and has to spend one night in hospital every two months to have the disease treated. Left Leicestershire at the end of 1991 season and signed for Nottinghamshire. Hit first Test century v India at Madras in 1992-93 tour to India and Sri Lanka. Joined England tour party in Australia following injury to Darren Gough. Suffered a compressed fracture in the ball of his hip joint which prevented him from playing any championship cricket in 1995. Left Nottinghamshire at the end of July and has joined Surrey for the 1996 season
**Best batting:** 247 Nottinghamshire v Durham, Chester-le-Street 1993
**Best bowling:** 6-22 Leicestershire v Oxford University, The Parks 1988

## 1995 Season

|         | M | Inns | NO | Runs | HS | Avge | 100s | 50s | Ct | St | O | M | Runs | Wkts | Avge | Best | 5wI | 10wM |
|---------|---|------|----|----|----|----|----|----|----|----|----|----|----|----|----|----|----|----|
| Test    |   |      |    |      |    |      |      |     |    |    |    |   |      |      |      |      |     |      |
| All First |  |      |    |      |    |      |      |     |    |    |    |   |      |      |      |      |     |      |
| 1-day Int |  |      |    |      |    |      |      |     |    |    |    |   |      |      |      |      |     |      |
| NatWest |   |      |    |      |    |      |      |     |    |    |    |   |      |      |      |      |     |      |
| B & H   | 3 | 2    | 0  | 56   | 48 | 28.00 | -   | -   | 1  | -  | 17 | 3 | 49   | 5    | 9.80 | 3-11 | -   |      |
| Sunday  | 1 | 1    | 0  | 14   | 14 | 14.00 | -   | -   | -  | -  |    |   |      |      |      |      |     |      |

---

44. Which three batsman did Dominic Cork dismiss for his hat-trick in the fourth Test at Old Trafford against West Indies in 1995?

## Career Performances

| | M | Inns | NO | Runs | HS | Avge | 100s | 50s | Ct | St | Balls | Runs | Wkts | Avge | Best | 5wI | 10wM |
|---|---|---|---|---|---|---|---|---|---|---|---|---|---|---|---|---|---|
| Test | 27 | 44 | 2 | 1009 | 117 | 24.02 | 1 | 4 | 23 | - | 5636 | 2870 | 77 | 37.27 | 6-111 | 2 | - |
| All First | 134 | 200 | 25 | 5411 | 247 | 30.92 | 7 | 23 | 106 | - | 23987 | 11799 | 403 | 29.27 | 6-22 | 15 | 3 |
| 1-day Int | 48 | 36 | 11 | 315 | 33 | 12.60 | - | - | 20 | - | 2350 | 1735 | 61 | 28.44 | 4-30 | - | |
| NatWest | 15 | 13 | 0 | 294 | 89 | 22.61 | - | 2 | 9 | - | 810 | 473 | 16 | 29.56 | 3-24 | - | |
| B & H | 23 | 18 | 6 | 320 | 48 * | 26.66 | - | - | 8 | - | 1245 | 833 | 32 | 26.03 | 5-46 | 1 | |
| Sunday | 81 | 70 | 15 | 1427 | 93 * | 25.94 | - | 6 | 21 | - | 3178 | 2353 | 83 | 28.34 | 4-13 | - | |

# LEWIS, J. Gloucestershire

**Name:** Jonathan Lewis
**Role:** Right-hand bat,
right-arm fast-medium bowler
**Born:** 26 August 1975, Aylesbury
**Height:** 6ft 2in **Weight:** 12st 12lbs
**Nickname:** JJ, Pistol
**County debut:** 1995
**Place in bowling averages:** 3rd av. 17.41
**Parents:** John and Jane
**Marital status:** Single
**Education:** Lawn Junior School;
Churchfields Comprehensive School;
Swindon College
**Qualifications:** 9 GCSEs, BTEC in Leisure
and Hospitality
**Off-season:** 'Playing for Richmond City,
Melbourne till January then getting fit till
March'

**Overseas tours:** Bath Schools to New South Wales, Australia 1993
**Overseas teams played for:** Marist, Christchurch, New Zealand 1994-95;
Richmond City, Melbourne 1995-96
**Cricketers particularly admired:** Viv Richards, Richard Hadlee
**Other sports followed:** Golf, tennis and football (Swindon Town)
**Relaxations:** Watching movies
**Extras:** Was on Northamptonshire staff in 1994 but made no first-team appearance
**Opinions on cricket:** 'Not enough opportunity is given to kids at state schools at a junior level. Some counties put too much pressure on lads who are in their first year on the staff.'
**Best batting:** 3 Gloucestershire v Leicestershire, Leicester 1995
**Best bowling**: 4-34 Gloucestershire v Durham, Bristol 1995

## 1995 Season

| | M | Inns | NO | Runs | HS | Avge | 100s | 50s | Ct | St | O | M | Runs | Wkts | Avge | Best | 5wI | 10wM |
|---|---|---|---|---|---|---|---|---|---|---|---|---|---|---|---|---|---|---|
| Test | | | | | | | | | | | | | | | | | | |
| All First | 3 | 3 | 0 | 3 | 3 | 1.00 | - | - | - | - | 67.4 | 12 | 209 | 12 | 17.41 | 4-34 | - | - |
| 1-day Int | | | | | | | | | | | | | | | | | | |
| NatWest | | | | | | | | | | | | | | | | | | |
| B & H | | | | | | | | | | | | | | | | | | |
| Sunday | 3 | 1 | 0 | 5 | 5 | 5.00 | - | - | - | - | 22.3 | 0 | 94 | 4 | 23.50 | 3-27 | - | |

## Career Performances

| | M | Inns | NO | Runs | HS | Avge | 100s | 50s | Ct | St | Balls | Runs | Wkts | Avge | Best | 5wI | 10wM |
|---|---|---|---|---|---|---|---|---|---|---|---|---|---|---|---|---|---|
| Test | | | | | | | | | | | | | | | | | |
| All First | 3 | 3 | 0 | 3 | 3 | 1.00 | - | - | - | - | 406 | 209 | 12 | 17.41 | 4-34 | - | - |
| 1-day Int | | | | | | | | | | | | | | | | | |
| NatWest | | | | | | | | | | | | | | | | | |
| B & H | | | | | | | | | | | | | | | | | |
| Sunday | 3 | 1 | 0 | 5 | 5 | 5.00 | - | - | - | - | 135 | 94 | 4 | 23.50 | 3-27 | - | |

# LEWIS, J. J. B.     Essex

**Name:** Jonathan James Benjamin Lewis
**Role:** Right-hand bat, right-arm slow-medium net bowler
**Born:** 21 May 1970, Middlesex
**Height:** 5ft 9in **Weight:** 11st 7lbs
**Nickname:** Scrubby, Judgey
**County debut:** 1990
**County cap:** 1994
**1st-Class 50s:** 18
**1st-Class 100s:** 4
**1st-Class catches:** 38
**Place in batting averages:** 196th av. 21.35 (1994 137th av. 28.88)
**Parents:** Graham Edward and Regina Mary
**Marital status:** Single
**Family links with cricket:** Father played county schools. Uncle is a life-long Somerset supporter. Sister is right-arm medium-fast bowler for NorTel
**Education:** King Edward VI School, Chelmsford; Roehampton Institute of Higher Education
**Qualifications:** 5 O-levels, 3 A-levels, BSc (Hons) Sports Science, NCA Senior Coach

**Off-season:** Playing and coaching in Natal, South Africa
**Overseas teams played for:** Old Hararians, Zimbabwe 1991-92; Taita District, New Zealand 1992-93; Eshoue and Zululand 1994-95
**Cricketers particularly admired:** John Childs, Graham Gooch, Greg Matthews, Keith Fletcher, Mike Garnham and Richard Pearson
**Other sports followed:** Soccer, rugby, basketball, 'most sports really'
**Relaxations:** 'Pubs with real ale'
**Extras:** Hit century on first-class debut in Essex's final Championship match of the 1990 season
**Opinions on cricket:** 'It will be a poorer game for the loss of Mike Garnham'
**Best batting:** 136* Essex v Nottinghamshire, Trent Bridge 1993

## 1995 Season

| | M | Inns | NO | Runs | HS | Avge | 100s | 50s | Ct | St | O | M | Runs | Wkts | Avge | Best | 5wI | 10wM |
|---|---|---|---|---|---|---|---|---|---|---|---|---|---|---|---|---|---|---|
| Test | | | | | | | | | | | | | | | | | | |
| All First | 7 | 14 | 0 | 299 | 75 | 21.35 | - | 2 | 9 | - | | | | | | | | |
| 1-day Int | | | | | | | | | | | | | | | | | | |
| NatWest | 2 | 2 | 0 | 17 | 16 | 8.50 | - | - | - | - | | | | | | | | |
| B & H | 5 | 5 | 1 | 52 | 19 | 13.00 | - | - | 2 | - | | | | | | | | |
| Sunday | 9 | 8 | 2 | 27 | 18 | 4.50 | - | - | 2 | - | | | | | | | | |

## Career Performances

| | M | Inns | NO | Runs | HS | Avge | 100s | 50s | Ct | St | Balls | Runs | Wkts | Avge | Best | 5wI | 10wM |
|---|---|---|---|---|---|---|---|---|---|---|---|---|---|---|---|---|---|
| Test | | | | | | | | | | | | | | | | | |
| All First | 52 | 90 | 12 | 2721 | 136 * | 34.88 | 4 | 18 | 38 | - | 48 | 32 | 0 | - | - | - | - |
| 1-day Int | | | | | | | | | | | | | | | | | |
| NatWest | 5 | 5 | 1 | 63 | 24 * | 15.75 | - | - | 1 | - | | | | | | | |
| B & H | 5 | 5 | 1 | 52 | 19 | 13.00 | - | - | 2 | - | | | | | | | |
| Sunday | 28 | 22 | 5 | 176 | 23 | 10.35 | - | - | 7 | - | | | | | | | |

# LEWRY, J. D.                                                    Sussex

**Name:** Jason David Lewry
**Role:** Left-hand bat, left-arm fast-medium bowler
**Born:** 2 April 1971, Worthing, West Sussex
**Height:** 6ft 2in **Weight:** 14st 4lb
**County debut:** 1994
**1st-Class 5 w. innings:** 3
**1st-Class catches:** 2
**Place in batting averages:** 281st av. 10.00
**Place in bowling averages:** 42nd av. 26.53
**Strike rate:** 44.70 (career 49.57)

**Parents:** David and Veronica
**Marital status:** Single
**Family links with cricket:** Father coaches
**Education:** Durrington High School, Worthing; Sixth Form College, Worthing
**Qualifications:** 6 O-levels, 3 GCSEs, City & Guilds, NCA Award Course
**Career outside cricket:** Salesman and stores manager for City Electrical Factors Ltd, Chichester branch
**Cricketers particularly admired:** The Sussex staff, David Gower, Wasim Akram, Martin Andrews
**Other sports followed:** Rugby union and league, golf
**Relaxations:** Golf, eating out, going out
**Extras:** Selected in a 15-man England indoor cricket squad for the series against South

Africa in England, alongside Mike Gatting and Asif Din, and for the tour of New Zealand and Australia during 1991-92. The tour was cancelled due to a lack of funds of the UKICF (UK Indoor Cricket Federation)
**Opinions on cricket:** 'Should be an hour for lunch and 30 minutes for tea. 2nd XI cricket should be four-day. More should be done for players during close season, either 12-monthly salary or club could help to find individuals winter employment.'
**Best batting:** 34 Sussex v Kent, Hove 1995
**Best bowling:** 6-43 Sussex v Worcestershire, Eastbourne 1995

## 1995 Season

| | M | Inns | NO | Runs | HS | Avge | 100s | 50s | Ct | St | O | M | Runs | Wkts | Avge | Best | 5wI | 10wM |
|---|---|---|---|---|---|---|---|---|---|---|---|---|---|---|---|---|---|---|
| Test | | | | | | | | | | | | | | | | | | |
| All First | 12 | 19 | 4 | 150 | 34 | 10.00 | - | - | 2 | - | 350.1 | 62 | 1247 | 47 | 26.53 | 6-43 | 3 | - |
| 1-day Int | | | | | | | | | | | | | | | | | | |
| NatWest | 2 | 1 | 1 | 2 | 2 * | - | - | - | - | - | 18 | 1 | 95 | 3 | 31.66 | 3-63 | - | |
| B & H | 3 | 1 | 1 | 14 | 14 * | - | - | - | - | - | 26 | 0 | 152 | 0 | - | - | - | |
| Sunday | 9 | 4 | 1 | 17 | 7 * | 5.66 | - | - | 2 | - | 61.1 | 5 | 290 | 14 | 20.71 | 4-29 | - | |

## Career Performances

| | M | Inns | NO | Runs | HS | Avge | 100s | 50s | Ct | St | Balls | Runs | Wkts | Avge | Best | 5wI | 10wM |
|---|---|---|---|---|---|---|---|---|---|---|---|---|---|---|---|---|---|
| Test | | | | | | | | | | | | | | | | | |
| All First | 16 | 25 | 8 | 164 | 34 | 9.64 | - | - | 2 | - | 2677 | 1562 | 54 | 28.92 | 6-43 | 3 | - |
| 1-day Int | | | | | | | | | | | | | | | | | |
| NatWest | 2 | 1 | 1 | 2 | 2 * | - | - | - | - | - | 108 | 95 | 3 | 31.66 | 3-63 | - | |
| B & H | 3 | 1 | 1 | 14 | 14 * | - | - | - | - | - | 156 | 152 | 0 | - | - | - | |
| Sunday | 14 | 5 | 2 | 18 | 7 * | 6.00 | - | - | 3 | - | 568 | 449 | 18 | 24.94 | 4-29 | - | |

# LIGERTWOOD, D. G. C.                                    Durham

**Name:** David George Coutts Ligertwood
**Role:** Right-hand bat, off-spin bowler,
wicket-keeper
**Born:** 16 May 1969, Oxford
**Height:** 6ft 1in **Weight:** 12st
**Nickname:** Hippy, Woody, Syph
**County debut:** 1992 (Surrey),
1995 (Durham)
**1st-Class catches:** 40
**1st-Class stumpings:** 4
**Place in batting averages:** 242nd av. 15.94
**Parents:** Andrew and Virginia
**Marital status:** Single
**Children:** Charlene, 3 September 1990
**Family links with cricket:** Brother played
for South Australia U17 'and grandmother is
a fanatic'
**Education:** Rose Park Primary School;
Wootton School; Magdalen College School,
Oxford; University of Adelaide
**Qualifications:** BA
**Career outside cricket:** Cricket coach

**Overseas teams played for:** Adelaide University 1987-92
**Extras:** Played for Hertfordshire in 1991 NatWest Trophy. Played for Surrey in 1992.
Appeared as 12th man for England in the 4th Test against West Indies at Old Trafford in
1995
**Best batting:** 40 Durham v Surrey, The Oval 1995

## 1995 Season

| | M | Inns | NO | Runs | HS | Avge | 100s | 50s | Ct | St | O | M | Runs | Wkts | Avge | Best | 5wI | 10wM |
|---|---|---|---|---|---|---|---|---|---|---|---|---|---|---|---|---|---|---|
| Test | | | | | | | | | | | | | | | | | | |
| All First | 12 | 21 | 2 | 303 | 40 | 15.94 | - | - | 33 | 3 | | | | | | | | |
| 1-day Int | | | | | | | | | | | | | | | | | | |
| NatWest | 2 | 1 | 0 | 5 | 5 | 5.00 | - | - | 2 | - | | | | | | | | |
| B & H | 1 | 0 | 0 | 0 | 0 | - | - | - | - | - | | | | | | | | |
| Sunday | 11 | 9 | 3 | 84 | 31 | 14.00 | - | - | 15 | 2 | | | | | | | | |

**Career Performances**

| | M | Inns | NO | Runs | HS | Avge | 100s | 50s | Ct | St | Balls | Runs | Wkts | Avge | Best | 5wI | 10wM |
|---|---|---|---|---|---|---|---|---|---|---|---|---|---|---|---|---|---|
| Test | | | | | | | | | | | | | | | | | |
| All First | 16 | 28 | 2 | 366 | 40 | 14.07 | - | - | 40 | 4 | | | | | | | |
| 1-day Int | | | | | | | | | | | | | | | | | |
| NatWest | 3 | 2 | 1 | 42 | 37 * | 42.00 | - | - | 2 | - | | | | | | | |
| B & H | 1 | 0 | 0 | 0 | 0 | - | - | - | - | - | | | | | | | |
| Sunday | 12 | 9 | 3 | 84 | 31 | 14.00 | - | - | 15 | 3 | | | | | | | |

# LLONG, N. J.                               Kent

**Name:** Nigel James Llong
**Role:** Left-hand bat, off-spin bowler
**Born:** 11 February 1969, Ashford, Kent
**Height:** 6ft **Weight:** 11st 6lb
**Nickname:** Nidge, Lloyd
**County debut:** 1991
**County cap:** 1993
**1st-Class 50s:** 9
**1st-Class 100s:** 4
**1st-Class 5 w. in innings:** 1
**1st-Class catches:** 36
**Place in batting averages:**
105th av. 33.62 (1994 206th av. 19.00)
**Strike rate:** (career 73.65)
**Parents:** Richard and Peggy (deceased)
**Marital status:** Single
**Family links with cricket:** Father and
brother played local club cricket
**Education:** Ashford North Secondary School
**Qualifications:** 6 CSEs, NCA coaching award
**Off-season:** 'Resting and getting married in February 1996'
**Overseas tours:** Kent to Zimbabwe 1992-93
**Overseas teams played for:** Ashburton, Melbourne 1988-90; Green Point, Cape Town
1990-95
**Cricketers particularly admired:** David Gower
**Other sports followed:** American football (Miami Dolphins), golf
**Injuries:** Hamstring strain, out for two weeks
**Relaxations:** Music, cinema, holidays
**Extras:** Kent Supporters Club Young Player of the Year Award 1993
**Opinions on cricket:** 'TCCB should have total control on pitch preparation.
Groundsmen should be employed by the TCCB. Also 12-month contracts.'

**Best batting:** 118 Kent v Surrey, Canterbury 1995
**Best bowling:** 5-63 Kent v Cambridge University, Fenner's 1994

## 1995 Season

|  | M | Inns | NO | Runs | HS | Avge | 100s | 50s | Ct | St | O | M | Runs | Wkts | Avge | Best | 5wI | 10wM |
|---|---|---|---|---|---|---|---|---|---|---|---|---|---|---|---|---|---|---|
| Test |  |  |  |  |  |  |  |  |  |  |  |  |  |  |  |  |  |  |
| All First | 9 | 16 | 0 | 538 | 118 | 33.62 | 2 | 1 | 11 | - | 71.4 | 11 | 273 | 3 | 91.00 | 2-47 | - | - |
| 1-day Int |  |  |  |  |  |  |  |  |  |  |  |  |  |  |  |  |  |  |
| NatWest |  |  |  |  |  |  |  |  |  |  |  |  |  |  |  |  |  |  |
| B & H | 2 | 1 | 0 | 1 | 1 | 1.00 | - | - | - | - | 5 | 0 | 31 | 1 | 31.00 | 1-31 | - |  |
| Sunday | 12 | 10 | 2 | 132 | 51 | 16.50 | - | 1 | 2 | - | 11 | 0 | 74 | 2 | 37.00 | 2-7 | - |  |

## Career Performances

|  | M | Inns | NO | Runs | HS | Avge | 100s | 50s | Ct | St | Balls | Runs | Wkts | Avge | Best | 5wI | 10wM |
|---|---|---|---|---|---|---|---|---|---|---|---|---|---|---|---|---|---|
| Test |  |  |  |  |  |  |  |  |  |  |  |  |  |  |  |  |  |
| All First | 44 | 68 | 8 | 1973 | 118 | 32.88 | 4 | 9 | 36 | - | 1473 | 810 | 20 | 40.50 | 5-63 | 1 | - |
| 1-day Int |  |  |  |  |  |  |  |  |  |  |  |  |  |  |  |  |  |
| NatWest | 3 | 3 | 2 | 41 | 27 * | 41.00 | - | - | 1 | - | 24 | 11 | 1 | 11.00 | 1-11 | - |  |
| B & H | 3 | 2 | 0 | 6 | 5 | 3.00 | - | - | 1 | - | 30 | 31 | 1 | 31.00 | 1-31 | - |  |
| Sunday | 55 | 46 | 15 | 772 | 64 * | 24.90 | - | 3 | 13 | - | 320 | 283 | 13 | 21.76 | 4-24 | - |  |

# LLOYD, G. D.                                    *Lancashire*

**Name:** Graham David Lloyd
**Role:** Right-hand bat, right-arm
medium bowler
**Born:** 1 July 1969, Accrington
**Height:** 5ft 7in **Weight:** 13st
**Nickname:** Bumble
**County debut:** 1988
**County cap:** 1992
**1000 runs in a season:** 2
**1st-Class 50s:** 38
**1st-Class 100s:** 11
**1st-Class catches:** 71
**One-Day 100s:** 1
**Place in batting averages:** 147th av. 27.80
(1994 140th av. 28.50)
**Parents:** David and Susan
**Marital status:** Single
**Family links with cricket:**
Father played for Lancashire and England

**Education:** Hollins County High School, Accrington
**Qualifications:** 3 O-levels, NCA coaching certificate
**Off-season:** 'Working on technique'
**Overseas tours:** England A to Australia 1992-93; Lancashire CCC to Guernsey 1995
**Overseas teams played for:** Maroochydore, Queensland 1988-89 and 1991-95
**Cricketers particularly admired:** Gordon Parsons, David Millns, Nigel Briers
**Other sports followed:** Football (Manchester United)
**Relaxations:** 'Eating out and racing'
**Extras:** His school did not play cricket, so he learnt at Accrington, playing in the same team as his father
**Opinions on cricket:** 'Bring back timeless cricket (i.e. Test and Championship). Everybody wants to see someone win.'
**Best batting:** 132 Lancashire v Kent, Old Trafford 1992
**Best bowling:** 1-57 Lancashire v Yorkshire, Old Trafford 1991

## 1995 Season

|          | M  | Inns | NO | Runs | HS   | Avge  | 100s | 50s | Ct | St | O | M | Runs | Wkts | Avge | Best | 5wl | 10wM |
|----------|----|------|----|------|------|-------|------|-----|----|----|---|---|------|------|------|------|-----|------|
| Test     |    |      |    |      |      |       |      |     |    |    |   |   |      |      |      |      |     |      |
| All First| 14 | 23   | 2  | 584  | 117  | 27.80 | 1    | 3   | 4  | -  |   |   |      |      |      |      |     |      |
| 1-day Int|    |      |    |      |      |       |      |     |    |    |   |   |      |      |      |      |     |      |
| NatWest  | 3  | 2    | 0  | 16   | 16   | 8.00  | -    | -   | -  | -  |   |   |      |      |      |      |     |      |
| B & H    | 8  | 5    | 2  | 196  | 81 * | 65.33 | -    | 2   | 2  | -  | 3 | 0 | 42   | 0    | -    |      | -   | -    |
| Sunday   | 17 | 15   | 5  | 432  | 88 * | 43.20 | -    | 4   | 3  | -  |   |   |      |      |      |      |     |      |

## Career Performances

|          | M   | Inns | NO | Runs | HS    | Avge  | 100s | 50s | Ct | St | Balls | Runs | Wkts | Avge   | Best | 5wl | 10wM |
|----------|-----|------|----|------|-------|-------|------|-----|----|----|-------|------|------|--------|------|-----|------|
| Test     |     |      |    |      |       |       |      |     |    |    |       |      |      |        |      |     |      |
| All First| 113 | 186  | 21 | 5981 | 132   | 36.24 | 11   | 38  | 71 | -  | 151   | 186  | 1    | 186.00 | 1-57 | -   | -    |
| 1-day Int|     |      |    |      |       |       |      |     |    |    |       |      |      |        |      |     |      |
| NatWest  | 9   | 8    | 0  | 142  | 39    | 17.75 | -    | -   | -  | -  |       |      |      |        |      |     |      |
| B & H    | 22  | 18   | 7  | 402  | 81 *  | 36.54 | -    | 2   | 3  | -  | 18    | 42   | 0    | -      |      | -   | -    |
| Sunday   | 95  | 89   | 15 | 2327 | 100 * | 31.44 | 1    | 16  | 20 | -  |       |      |      |        |      |     |      |

45. Who replaced Ken Rutherford as New Zealand captain in 1995?

# LONGLEY, J. I.                                    Durham

**Name:** Jonathan Ian Longley
**Role:** Right-hand bat
**Born:** 12 April 1969, New Brunswick, USA
**Height:** 5ft 8in **Weight:** 11st 10lbs
**County debut:** 1989 (Kent), 1994 (Durham)
**1st-Class 50s:** 8
**1st-Class 100s:** 2
**1st-Class catches:** 18
**Place in batting averages:** 167th av. 24.70
(1994 155th av. 25.82)
**Parents:** Dick and Helen
**Marital status:** Single
**Education:** Tonbridge School; Durham
University
**Qualifications:** 9 O-levels, 3 A-levels, BA
Sociology
**Overseas teams played for:** Prospect
District, Adelaide 1991-92; Green Point,
Cape Town 1992-93

**Cricketers particularly admired:** Robin Smith, Gordon Greenidge, Allan Border
**Other sports followed:** Rugby, golf, squash, tennis
**Relaxations:** 'Love listening to music (Bob Dylan, Van Morrison and the Rolling Stones). Also love old English pubs, Australian beaches and socialising with friends and family'
**Extras:** Member of the Combined Universities team which reached the quarter-finals of the B&H Cup in 1989. Moved from Kent to Durham for 1994 season
**Best batting:** 110 Kent v Cambridge University, Fenner's 1992

## 1995 Season

|           | M | Inns | NO | Runs | HS | Avge  | 100s | 50s | Ct | St | O | M | Runs | Wkts | Avge | Best | 5wl | 10wM |
|-----------|---|------|----|------|----|-------|------|-----|----|----|---|---|------|------|------|------|-----|------|
| Test      |   |      |    |      |    |       |      |     |    |    |   |   |      |      |      |      |     |      |
| All First | 9 | 18   | 1  | 420  | 58 | 24.70 | -    | 2   | 3  | -  | 4 | 0 | 47   | 0    | -    | -    | -   | -    |
| 1-day Int |   |      |    |      |    |       |      |     |    |    |   |   |      |      |      |      |     |      |
| NatWest   |   |      |    |      |    |       |      |     |    |    |   |   |      |      |      |      |     |      |
| B & H     | 4 | 4    | 0  | 62   | 35 | 15.50 | -    | -   | 1  | -  |   |   |      |      |      |      |     |      |
| Sunday    | 9 | 8    | 0  | 203  | 92 | 25.37 | -    | 1   | 1  | -  |   |   |      |      |      |      |     |      |

## Career Performances

| | M | Inns | NO | Runs | HS | Avge | 100s | 50s | Ct | St | Balls | Runs | Wkts | Avge | Best | 5wI | 10wM |
|---|---|---|---|---|---|---|---|---|---|---|---|---|---|---|---|---|---|
| Test | | | | | | | | | | | | | | | | | |
| All First | 33 | 60 | 3 | 1375 | 110 | 24.12 | 2 | 8 | 18 | - | 24 | 47 | 0 | - | - | - | - |
| 1-day Int | | | | | | | | | | | | | | | | | |
| NatWest | 2 | 2 | 0 | 14 | 9 | 7.00 | - | - | - | - | | | | | | | |
| B & H | 21 | 21 | 1 | 381 | 57 | 19.05 | - | 1 | 2 | - | | | | | | | |
| Sunday | 32 | 30 | 3 | 742 | 92 | 27.48 | - | 6 | 5 | - | | | | | | | |

# LOYE, M. B.                    Northamptonshire

**Name:** Malachy Bernard Loye
**Role:** Right-hand bat, off-spin bowler
**Born:** 27 September 1972, Northampton
**Height:** 6ft 2in **Weight:** 13st 7lb
**Nickname:** Mal, Mad Jack, Fruit Bat
**County debut:** 1991
**County cap:** 1994
**1st-Class 50s:** 14
**1st-Class 100s:** 5
**1st-Class catches:** 41
**One-Day 100s:** 1
**Place in batting averages:** 251st av. 14.88
(1994 56th av. 39.73)
**Parents:** Patrick and Anne
**Marital status:** Single
**Family links with cricket:** Father and
brother both play for Cogenhoe CC in
Northampton

**Education:** Moulton Comprehensive School
**Qualifications:** GCSEs and senior coaching certificate
**Overseas tours:** England U18 to Canada 1991; England U19 to Pakistan 1991-92;
England A to South Africa 1993-94
**Overseas teams played for:** Riccarton, New Zealand and Canterbury B 1992-93
**Cricketers particularly admired:** Gordon Greenidge, Wayne Larkins, Curtly
Ambrose
**Other sports followed:** Football, golf, basketball and boxing
**Relaxations:** Watching films, listening to music, and going out with friends
**Extras:** Played for England U19 in the home series against Australia U19 in 1991 and
against Sri Lanka U19 1992. Voted Professional Cricket Association's Young Player of
the Year 1993 and Whittingdale Young Player of the Year 1993
**Best batting:** 153* Northamptonshire v Kent, Canterbury 1993

## 1995 Season

| | M | Inns | NO | Runs | HS | Avge | 100s | 50s | Ct | St | O | M | Runs | Wkts | Avge | Best | 5wl | 10wM |
|---|---|---|---|---|---|---|---|---|---|---|---|---|---|---|---|---|---|---|
| Test | | | | | | | | | | | | | | | | | | |
| All First | 7 | 10 | 1 | 134 | 51 * | 14.88 | - | 1 | 2 | - | | | | | | | | |
| 1-day Int | | | | | | | | | | | | | | | | | | |
| NatWest | 2 | 2 | 1 | 56 | 49 * | 56.00 | - | - | - | - | | | | | | | | |
| B & H | 2 | 2 | 0 | 2 | 2 | 1.00 | - | - | - | - | | | | | | | | |
| Sunday | 13 | 12 | 4 | 332 | 57 * | 41.50 | - | 1 | 3 | - | | | | | | | | |

## Career Performances

| | M | Inns | NO | Runs | HS | Avge | 100s | 50s | Ct | St | Balls | Runs | Wkts | Avge | Best | 5wl | 10wM |
|---|---|---|---|---|---|---|---|---|---|---|---|---|---|---|---|---|---|
| Test | | | | | | | | | | | | | | | | | |
| All First | 60 | 93 | 10 | 2647 | 153 * | 31.89 | 5 | 14 | 41 | - | 1 | 1 | 0 | - | - | - | - |
| 1-day Int | | | | | | | | | | | | | | | | | |
| NatWest | 8 | 8 | 3 | 195 | 65 | 39.00 | - | 1 | 1 | - | | | | | | | |
| B & H | 6 | 6 | 2 | 118 | 68 * | 29.50 | - | 1 | 2 | - | | | | | | | |
| Sunday | 41 | 38 | 5 | 1084 | 122 | 32.84 | 1 | 5 | 9 | - | | | | | | | |

# LUGSDEN, S.      Durham

**Name:** Steven Lugsden
**Role:** Right-hand bat, right-arm fast bowler
**Born:** 10 July 1976, Gateshead
**Height:** 6ft 3in **Weight:** 13st
**County debut:** 1993
**Parents:** William and Nora
**Marital status:** Engaged
**Education:** St Edmund Campion RC School, Wrekenton, Gateshead
**Qualifications:** 7 GCSEs, BTEC Business and Finance
**Overseas tours:** England U19 to West Indies 1994-95
**Cricketers particularly admired:** Curtly Ambrose, Dean Jones, Ian Bishop
**Other sports followed:** Football (Newcastle United)
**Injuries:** Stress fracture of back, out all season
**Relaxations:** Going on holiday
**Extras:** Youngest player (17 years 27 days) to make first-class debut for Durham. Played against India for England U19 in home series 1994

**Opinions on cricket:** 'Too hard for bowlers.'
**Best batting:** 5* Durham v Derbyshire, Durham University 1993
**Best bowling:** 2-43 Durham v Derbyshire, Durham University 1993

## 1995 Season (did not make any first-class or one-day appearances)

## Career Performances

| | M | Inns | NO | Runs | HS | Avge | 100s | 50s | Ct | St | Balls | Runs | Wkts | Avge | Best | 5wI | 10wM |
|---|---|---|---|---|---|---|---|---|---|---|---|---|---|---|---|---|---|
| Test | | | | | | | | | | | | | | | | | |
| All First | 6 | 6 | 3 | 7 | 5* | 2.33 | - | - | - | - | 794 | 497 | 5 | 99.40 | 2-43 | - | - |
| 1-day Int | | | | | | | | | | | | | | | | | |
| NatWest | | | | | | | | | | | | | | | | | |
| B & H | | | | | | | | | | | | | | | | | |
| Sunday | 1 | 0 | 0 | 0 | 0 | - | - | - | - | - | 48 | 55 | 1 | 55.00 | 1-55 | - | |

# LYNCH, M. A.                    Gloucestershire

**Name:** Monte Allan Lynch
**Role:** Right-hand bat, right-arm medium
and off-spin bowler
**Born:** 21 May 1958, Georgetown, Guyana
**Height:** 5ft 9in **Weight:** 13st 3lbs
**Nickname:** Mont
**County debut:** 1977 (Surrey), 1994 (Glos)
**County cap:** 1982 (Surrey), 1995 (Glos)
**Benefit:** 1991 (£107,000)
**One-Day Internationals:** 3
**1000 runs in a season:** 10
**1st-Class 50s:** 80
**1st-Class 100s:** 39
**1st-Class catches:** 348
**One-Day 100s:** 5
**Place in batting averages:** 79th av. 38.00
(1994 58th av. 39.66)
**Strike rate:** (career 84.42)
**Parents:** Lawrence and Doreen Austin
**Marital status:** Single
**Children:** Lours, 31 September 1983; Marissa, 30 July 1989
**Family links with cricket:** 'Father and most of family played at some time or another'
**Education:** Ryden's School, Walton-on-Thames
**Overseas tours:** Unofficial West Indies XI to South Africa 1983-84
**Overseas teams played for:** Guyana 1982-83

**Other sports followed:** Football, table tennis
**Extras:** When he made 141* for Surrey v Glamorgan at Guildford in August 1982, off 78 balls in 88 minutes, one six hit his captain Roger Knight's car. Joined West Indies rebels in South Africa 1983-84, although qualified for England. Appeared in all three One-Day Internationals v West Indies 1988. Moved to Gloucestershire for 1994 season
**Best batting:** 172* Surrey v Kent, The Oval 1989
**Best bowling:** 3-6 Surrey v Glamorgan, Swansea 1981

## 1995 Season

|          | M  | Inns | NO | Runs | HS  | Avge  | 100s | 50s | Ct | St | O   | M | Runs | Wkts | Avge  | Best  | 5wI | 10wM |
|----------|----|------|----|------|-----|-------|------|-----|----|----|-----|---|------|------|-------|-------|-----|------|
| Test     |    |      |    |      |     |       |      |     |    |    |     |   |      |      |       |       |     |      |
| All First| 17 | 29   | 2  | 1026 | 114 | 38.00 | 5    | 2   | 25 | -  | 2   | 0 | 3    | 0    | -     | -     | -   | -    |
| 1-day Int|    |      |    |      |     |       |      |     |    |    |     |   |      |      |       |       |     |      |
| NatWest  | 3  | 3    | 0  | 88   | 58  | 29.33 | -    | 1   | 1  | -  | 3.4 | 0 | 11   | 1    | 11.00 | 1-11  | -   |      |
| B & H    | 6  | 6    | 0  | 76   | 30  | 12.66 | -    | -   | 6  | -  |     |   |      |      |       |       |     |      |
| Sunday   | 14 | 14   | 0  | 320  | 58  | 22.85 | -    | 2   | 5  | -  | 3   | 0 | 23   | 1    | 23.00 | 1-23  | -   |      |

## Career Performances

|          | M   | Inns | NO | Runs  | HS    | Avge  | 100s | 50s | Ct  | St | Balls | Runs | Wkts | Avge  | Best | 5wI | 10wM |
|----------|-----|------|----|-------|-------|-------|------|-----|-----|----|-------|------|------|-------|------|-----|------|
| Test     |     |      |    |       |       |       |      |     |     |    |       |      |      |       |      |     |      |
| All First| 336 | 547  | 62 | 17307 | 172 * | 35.68 | 39   | 80  | 348 | -  | 2195  | 1398 | 26   | 53.76 | 3-6  | -   | -    |
| 1-day Int| 3   | 3    | 0  | 8     | 6     | 2.66  | -    | -   | 1   | -  |       |      |      |       |      |     |      |
| NatWest  | 40  | 35   | 5  | 867   | 129   | 28.90 | 1    | 4   | 19  | -  | 304   | 179  | 7    | 25.57 | 2-28 | -   |      |
| B & H    | 63  | 58   | 3  | 1388  | 112 * | 25.23 | 2    | 7   | 32  | -  | 132   | 121  | 0    | -     | -    | -   |      |
| Sunday   | 223 | 205  | 26 | 4995  | 136   | 27.90 | 2    | 31  | 79  | -  | 167   | 205  | 8    | 25.62 | 2-2  | -   |      |

# MACMILLAN, G. I.　　　　　　　　Leicestershire

**Name:** Gregor Innes Macmillan
**Role:** Right-hand bat, off-spin bowler
**Born:** 7 August 1969, Guildford
**Height:** 6ft 5in  **Weight:** 13st 2lbs
**County debut:** 1994 (one-day), 1995 (first-class)
**1st-Class 50s:** 9
**1st-Class 100s:** 3
**1st-Class catches:** 48
**Place in batting averages:** 91st av. 35.52 (1994 142nd av. 28.21)
**Strike rate:** (career 91.38)
**Parents:** Angus and Evelyn
**Marital status:** Single
**Family links with cricket:** 'Father plays club cricket at Odiham and Greywell and Hampshire Maniacs. Mother takes a mean video. Her mother makes a great tea. Great-

uncle played a match at Kroonstad on Queen Victoria's Jubilee Day'

**Education:** Guildford County School; Charterhouse; Southampton University; Keble College, Oxford University

**Qualifications:** 'A few O- and A-levels', BA (Hons) Philosophy and Politics (Soton), Dip.Soc Admin (Oxon). Currently doing M Litt in Politics at Oxford

**Career outside cricket:** Studying

**Off-season:** 'Playing for Harvinia (Orange Free State) in South African "Champion Clubs" competition in September – then back to Oxford to work on my thesis'

**Overseas teams played for:** Harvinia, Orange Free State 1988-89, 1993-94 'plus the odd game whenever they ask me'

**Cricketers particularly admired:** 'Those like Jim Bovill who put up with me without often complaining. Mickey Carr. Gordon Parsons for being tidy and Richard Montgomerie for being less tidy than I am'

**Other sports followed:** Football (Liverpool FC) and 'Scotland at anything except rugby union and curling'

**Extras:** Captained Southampton University to the UAU final 1991. Played for Surrey from U11 to U19. Captain of Oxford University for 1995 season. Played in Oxford's last two Varsity match victories, plus the winning first one-day match between the two Universities in 1995. Captained both Oxford and Combined Universities ('a good way to stay thin'). Scored a century on his championship debut for Leicestershire

**Opinions on cricket:** 'You'll have to give me time before I become judgmental. That's not something you lightly ask a philosopher to do.'

**Best batting:** 122 Leicestershire v Surrey, Leicester 1995

**Best bowling:** 3-13 Oxford University v Cambridge University, Lord's 1993

## 1995 Season

|  | M | Inns | NO | Runs | HS | Avge | 100s | 50s | Ct | St | O | M | Runs | Wkts | Avge | Best | 5wI | 10wM |
|---|---|---|---|---|---|---|---|---|---|---|---|---|---|---|---|---|---|---|
| Test |  |  |  |  |  |  |  |  |  |  |  |  |  |  |  |  |  |  |
| All First | 17 | 26 | 3 | 817 | 122 | 35.52 | 3 | 3 | 23 | - | 158.3 | 12 | 568 | 7 | 81.14 | 2-108 | - | - |
| 1-day Int |  |  |  |  |  |  |  |  |  |  |  |  |  |  |  |  |  |  |
| NatWest | 1 | 1 | 0 | 9 | 9 | 9.00 | - | - | - | - | 3 | 0 | 13 | 1 | 13.00 | 1-13 | - |  |
| B & H | 5 | 5 | 1 | 214 | 77 | 53.50 | - | 2 | 1 | - | 9.4 | 0 | 63 | 1 | 63.00 | 1-20 | - |  |
| Sunday | 4 | 4 | 0 | 46 | 38 | 11.50 | - | - | - | - |  |  |  |  |  |  |  |  |

## Career Performances

|        | M  | Inns | NO | Runs | HS  | Avge  | 100s | 50s | Ct | St | Balls | Runs | Wkts | Avge  | Best | 5wI | 10wM |
|--------|----|------|----|------|-----|-------|------|-----|----|----|-------|------|------|-------|------|-----|------|
| Test   |    |      |    |      |     |       |      |     |    |    |       |      |      |       |      |     |      |
| All First | 36 | 57 | 7 | 1548 | 122 | 30.96 | 3 | 9 | 48 | - | 1919 | 1103 | 21 | 52.52 | 3-13 | - | - |
| 1-day Int |    |      |    |      |     |       |      |     |    |    |       |      |      |       |      |     |      |
| NatWest | 1 | 1 | 0 | 9 | 9 | 9.00 | - | - | - | - | 18 | 13 | 1 | 13.00 | 1-13 | - | |
| B & H | 8 | 8 | 1 | 252 | 77 | 36.00 | - | 2 | 1 | - | 89 | 81 | 2 | 40.50 | 1-18 | - | |
| Sunday | 8 | 8 | 0 | 159 | 48 | 19.87 | - | - | 1 | - | | | | | | | |

# MADDY, D. L.                    Leicestershire

**Name:** Darren Lee Maddy
**Role:** Right-hand bat, right-arm
medium bowler
**Born:** 23 May 1974, Leicester
**Height:** 5ft 9in **Weight:** 11st
**Nickname:** Dazza, Roasting, Stompie
**County debut:** 1993 (one-day),
1994 (first-class)
**1st-Class 100s:** 1
**1st-Class catches:** 14
**Place in batting averages:** 236th av. 16.50
(1994 252nd av. 13.33)
**Parents:** William Arthur and Hilary Jean
**Marital status:** Single
**Family links with cricket:** Father and
younger brother, Greg, play club cricket
**Education:** Herrick Junior School, Leicester;
Roundhills, Thurmaston; Wreake Valley,
Syston

**Qualifications:** 8 GCSEs
**Off-season:** 'Hopefully playing club cricket in South Africa'
**Overseas teams played for:** Wanderers, Johannesburg 1992-93; Northern Free State,
Orange Free State 1993-95
**Cricketers particularly admired:** Brian Lara, Michael Atherton, Richard Hadlee, Viv
Richards, 'Babe Ruth' Dakin
**Other sports followed:** Rugby union (Leicester Tigers), golf, American football,
baseball, football (Leicester City and Manchester United)
**Relaxations:** Scuba diving, bungee jumping, listening to music
**Extras:** 'Voted having the biggest thighs in Leicester by team-mates.' Set a new 2nd XI
Championship run aggregate record (1498) beating the previous one which had stood
since 1961. Rapid Cricketline 2nd XI Player of the Year 1994

**Opinions on cricket:** '2nd XI cricket should be played on good, first-class wickets. The over-rate fine system is too severe in first-class matches. The third umpire should be used in all one-day domestic competitions'

**Best batting:** 131 Leicestershire v Oxford University, The Parks 1995

## 1995 Season

| | M | Inns | NO | Runs | HS | Avge | 100s | 50s | Ct | St | O | M | Runs | Wkts | Avge | Best | 5wI | 10wM |
|---|---|---|---|---|---|---|---|---|---|---|---|---|---|---|---|---|---|---|
| Test | | | | | | | | | | | | | | | | | | |
| All First | 9 | 17 | 1 | 264 | 131 | 16.50 | 1 | - | 14 | - | 6 | 0 | 41 | 0 | - | | - | - |
| 1-day Int | | | | | | | | | | | | | | | | | | |
| NatWest | 1 | 1 | 0 | 34 | 34 | 34.00 | - | - | - | - | 11 | 1 | 38 | 2 | 19.00 | 2-38 | - |
| B & H | 3 | 3 | 0 | 81 | 50 | 27.00 | - | 1 | 1 | - | | | | | | | |
| Sunday | 15 | 10 | 2 | 197 | 69 | 24.62 | - | 1 | 7 | - | 78 | 3 | 435 | 15 | 29.00 | 3-29 | - |

## Career Performances

| | M | Inns | NO | Runs | HS | Avge | 100s | 50s | Ct | St | Balls | Runs | Wkts | Avge | Best | 5wI | 10wM |
|---|---|---|---|---|---|---|---|---|---|---|---|---|---|---|---|---|---|
| Test | | | | | | | | | | | | | | | | | |
| All First | 12 | 23 | 1 | 344 | 131 | 15.63 | 1 | - | 17 | - | 36 | 41 | 0 | - | | - | - |
| 1-day Int | | | | | | | | | | | | | | | | | |
| NatWest | 1 | 1 | 0 | 34 | 34 | 34.00 | - | - | - | - | 66 | 38 | 2 | 19.00 | 2-38 | - |
| B & H | 3 | 3 | 0 | 81 | 50 | 27.00 | - | 1 | 1 | - | | | | | | |
| Sunday | 27 | 22 | 3 | 413 | 69 | 21.73 | - | 3 | 17 | - | 468 | 435 | 15 | 29.00 | 3-29 | - |

46. Brian Lara's only first class pair came in the 1995 West Indies match against Kent. The same bowler dismissed him in both innings - who was he?

# MALCOLM, D. E.        Derbyshire

**Name:** Devon Eugene Malcolm
**Role:** Right-hand bat, right-arm fast bowler
**Born:** 22 February 1963, Kingston, Jamaica
**Height:** 6ft 2in **Weight:** 15st
**Nickname:** Dude
**County debut:** 1984
**County cap:** 1989
**Benefit:** 1995
**Test debut:** 1989
**Tests:** 34
**One-Day Internationals:** 10
**50 wickets in a season:** 4
**1st-Class 50s:** 1
**1st-Class 5 w. in innings:** 20
**1st-Class 10 w. in innings:** 3
**1st-Class catches:** 30
**One-Day 5 w. in innings:** 1
**Place in bowling averages:** 54th av. 29.20
(1993 79th av. 30.78)

**Strike rate:** 42.61 (career 53.07)
**Parents:** Albert and Brendalee (deceased)
**Wife and date of marriage:** Jennifer, October 1989
**Children:** Erica Cian, 11 June 1991; Natile Jade, 25 June 1993
**Education:** St Elizabeth Technical High School; Richmond College; Derby College of
Higher Education
**Qualifications:** College certificates, O-levels, coaching certificate
**Off-season:** England tour to South Africa
**Overseas tours:** England to West Indies 1989-90, to Australia 1990-91, to India and
Sri Lanka 1992-93, to West Indies 1993-94, to Australia 1994-95, to South Africa
1995-96; England A to Bermuda and West Indies 1991-92
**Overseas teams played for:** Ellerslie, Auckland 1985-87
**Cricketers particularly admired:** Michael Holding, Richard Hadlee, Malcolm
Marshall, Alan Warner, Viv Richards
**Other sports followed:** Football, boxing
**Relaxations:** Music and movies, eating
**Extras:** Played league cricket for Sheffield Works and Sheffield United. Became
eligible to play for England in 1987. Took 10 for 137 v West Indies in Port-of-Spain Test,
1989-90. Struck down with chickenpox early in the England tour to Australia 1994-95.
**Best batting:** 51 Derbyshire v Surrey, Derby 1989
**Best bowling:** 9-57 England v South Africa, The Oval 1994

| | M | Inns | NO | Runs | HS | Avge | 100s | 50s | Ct | St | O | M | Runs | Wkts | Avge | Best | 5wI | 10wM |
|---|---|---|---|---|---|---|---|---|---|---|---|---|---|---|---|---|---|---|
| Test | 2 | 3 | 0 | 15 | 10 | 5.00 | - | - | - | - | 50.3 | 7 | 220 | 5 | 44.00 | 3-160 | - | - |
| All First | 14 | 21 | 4 | 125 | 25 * | 7.35 | - | - | 1 | - | 461.4 | 82 | 1692 | 65 | 26.03 | 6-61 | 3 | 1 |
| 1-day Int | | | | | | | | | | | | | | | | | | |
| NatWest | 3 | 1 | 0 | 8 | 8 | 8.00 | - | - | 1 | - | 29 | 3 | 107 | 3 | 35.66 | 2-53 | - | |
| B & H | 3 | 1 | 0 | 4 | 4 | 4.00 | - | - | 1 | - | 32 | 1 | 154 | 11 | 14.00 | 4-34 | - | |
| Sunday | 9 | 5 | 3 | 11 | 10 * | 5.50 | - | - | 1 | - | 66 | 2 | 317 | 12 | 26.41 | 2-23 | - | |

**Career Performances**

| | M | Inns | NO | Runs | HS | Avge | 100s | 50s | Ct | St | Balls | Runs | Wkts | Avge | Best | 5wI | 10wM |
|---|---|---|---|---|---|---|---|---|---|---|---|---|---|---|---|---|---|
| Test | 34 | 50 | 16 | 223 | 29 | 6.55 | - | - | 5 | - | 7580 | 4246 | 116 | 36.60 | 9-57 | 5 | 2 |
| All First | 190 | 224 | 66 | 1251 | 51 | 7.91 | - | 1 | 30 | - | 33275 | 19438 | 627 | 31.00 | 9-57 | 20 | 3 |
| 1-day Int | 10 | 5 | 2 | 9 | 4 | 3.00 | - | - | 1 | - | 526 | 404 | 16 | 25.25 | 3-40 | - | |
| NatWest | 17 | 10 | 1 | 29 | 10 * | 3.22 | - | - | 1 | - | 1078 | 703 | 23 | 30.56 | 3-29 | - | |
| B & H | 24 | 11 | 2 | 58 | 15 | 6.44 | - | - | 1 | - | 1392 | 971 | 40 | 24.27 | 5-27 | 1 | |
| Sunday | 61 | 23 | 10 | 89 | 18 | 6.84 | - | - | 7 | - | 2731 | 2313 | 85 | 27.21 | 4-21 | - | |

# MALLENDER, N. A.　　　Northamptonshire

**Name:** Neil Alan Mallender
**Role:** Right-hand bat, right-arm
fast-medium bowler
**Born:** 13 August 1961, Kirk Sandall,
Doncaster
**Height:** 6ft  **Weight:** 13st
**Nickname:** Ghostie
**County debut:** 1980 (Northamptonshire),
1987 (Somerset)
**County cap:** 1984 (Northamptonshire),
1987 (Somerset)
**Tests:** 2
**50 wickets in a season:** 6
**1st-Class 50s:** 10
**1st-Class 100s:** 1
**1st-Class 5 w. in innings:** 36
**1st-Class 10 w. in match:** 5
**1st-Class catches:** 110
**One-Day 5 w. in innings:** 3
**Place in batting averages:** 232nd av. 17.28 (1994 129th av. 30.00)
**Place in bowling averages:** 31st av. 25.11 (1994112th av. 37.62)
**Strike rate:** 50.23 (career 56.59)

**Parents:** Ron and Jean

**Wife and date of marriage:** Caroline, 1 October 1984

**Children:** Kirstie Jane, 18 May 1988; Dominic James, 21 September 1991

**Family links with cricket:** Brother Graham used to play good representative cricket before joining the RAF

**Education:** Beverley Grammar School, East Yorkshire

**Qualifications:** 7 O-levels, NCA preliminary coaching course

**Overseas tours:** England YC to West Indies 1979-80

**Overseas teams played for:** Otago, New Zealand 1983-93; Kalkorai, New Zealand 1983-93

**Cricketers particularly admired:** Richard Hadlee, Dennis Lillee, Peter Willey

**Other sports followed:** Golf, rugby league, football

**Relaxations:** Golf

**Extras:** Joined Somerset in 1987. Equalled Somerset first-class record for ninth wicket v Sussex at Hove in 1990 – batting with Chris Tavaré. Called up to join England tour squad in New Zealand 1991-92 as cover for injured fast bowlers. On debut for England v Pakistan in 1992 at Headingley, he achieved a new bowling record for a Test debutant at that ground by taking eight wickets in the game. At school opened both the batting and the bowling. Returned to Northamptonshire for 1995 season

**Opinions on cricket:** 'Still believe that new ball should be available to be taken after 85 overs in first-class cricket.'

**Best batting:** 100* Otago v Central Districts, Palmerston North 1991-92

**Best bowling:** 7-27 Otago v Auckland, Auckland 1984-85

## 1995 Season

|          | M | Inns | NO | Runs | HS | Avge | 100s | 50s | Ct | St | O | M | Runs | Wkts | Avge | Best | 5wl | 10wM |
|----------|---|------|----|------|----|------|------|-----|----|----|---|---|------|------|------|------|-----|------|
| Test     |   |      |    |      |    |      |      |     |    |    |   |   |      |      |      |      |     |      |
| All First | 7 | 10  | 3  | 121  | 49 * | 17.28 | - | - | 3 | - | 142.2 | 32 | 427 | 17 | 25.11 | 4-49 | - | - |
| 1-day Int |   |      |    |      |    |      |      |     |    |    |   |   |      |      |      |      |     |      |
| NatWest  | 1 | 0    | 0  | 0    | 0  | -    | -    | -   | -  | -  | 6 | 1 | 24   | 0    | -    |      | -   | -    |
| B & H    |   |      |    |      |    |      |      |     |    |    |   |   |      |      |      |      |     |      |
| Sunday   | 4 | 0    | 0  | 0    | 0  | -    | -    | -   | -  | -  | 23 | 1 | 75  | 4    | 18.75 | 2-21 | -   |      |

## Career Performances

|          | M | Inns | NO | Runs | HS | Avge | 100s | 50s | Ct | St | Balls | Runs | Wkts | Avge | Best | 5wl | 10wM |
|----------|---|------|----|------|----|------|------|-----|----|----|-------|------|------|------|------|-----|------|
| Test     | 2 | 3    | 0  | 8    | 4  | 2.66 | -    | -   | -  | -  | 449   | 215  | 10   | 21.50 | 5-50 | 1   | -    |
| All First | 342 | 393 | 122 | 4678 | 100 * | 17.26 | 1 | 10 | 110 |  | 52977 | 24517 | 936 | 26.19 | 7-27 | 36 | 5 |
| 1-day Int |   |      |    |      |    |      |      |     |    |    |       |      |      |      |      |     |      |
| NatWest  | 31 | 13  | 6  | 63   | 11 * | 9.00 | -  | -   | 5  | -  | 1892  | 889  | 43   | 20.67 | 7-37 | 1   |      |
| B & H    | 54 | 26  | 10 | 93   | 16 * | 5.81 | -  | -   | 14 | -  | 3033  | 1889 | 64   | 29.51 | 5-53 | 1   |      |
| Sunday   | 178 | 81 | 44 | 557  | 31 * | 15.05 | - | -   | 31 | -  | 7241  | 5315 | 197  | 26.97 | 5-34 | 1   |      |

# MARC, K.                                    Middlesex

**Name:** Kervin Marc
**Role:** Right-hand bat, right-arm fast bowler
**Born:** 9 January 1975, Monrepos, St Lucia
**Height:** 6ft 5in **Weight:** 14st
**Nickname:** Kerv, Swerv
**County debut:** 1994
**Parents:** Linda and Pima
**Marital status:** Single
**Family links with cricket:** Brother Ernest
played for Middlesex U15 and U17 and also
played for London Schools U12–U19: Uncle
Terry plays for Monrepos

**Education:** The London Oratory School;
Central St Martin College of Art and Design
**Qualifications:** 8 GCSEs, 2 A-levels
**Career outside cricket:** Art and design
**Off-season:** Studying Industrial Product
Design at Central St Martin's
**Overseas tours:** Middlesex U16 to Jersey 1991
**Cricketers particularly admired:** Malcolm Marshall, Curtly Ambrose, Desmond
Haynes, Alec Stewart, Nelley, Alf Langley, Carl Menzie and 'everyone at the
Shepherd's Bush CC'
**Injuries:** Palela tendonitis, missed six weeks
**Relaxations:** Music (hip hop, R&B, ragga) and watching any sport on television
**Extras:** Second St Lucian-born player to play first-class cricket in England, Carlos
Remy being the first. Played for MCC Young Cricketers before joining Middlesex
**Opinions on cricket:** 'There should be more careful design of cricket equipment i.e.
gloves, fast-bowling boots. County pitches should not be so one-sided. It seems that
batsmen and groundsmen must have a very good relationship ("It must be love"). Jason
Allan should "eaze back" into the game and shake his dreads.'
**Best batting:** 9 Middlesex v Lancashire, Old Trafford 1994
**Best bowling:** 2-52 Middlesex v Lancashire, Old Trafford 1994

## 1995 Season

|          | M | Inns | NO | Runs | HS | Avge | 100s | 50s | Ct | St | O | M | Runs | Wkts | Avge | Best | 5wI | 10wM |
|----------|---|------|----|------|-----|------|------|-----|----|----|---|---|------|------|------|------|-----|------|
| Test     |   |      |    |      |     |      |      |     |    |    |   |   |      |      |      |      |     |      |
| All First | 1 | 0    | 0  | 0    | 0   | -    | -    | -   | -  | -  | 9 | 0 | 37   | 0    | -    | -    | -   | -    |
| 1-day Int |   |      |    |      |     |      |      |     |    |    |   |   |      |      |      |      |     |      |
| NatWest  |   |      |    |      |     |      |      |     |    |    |   |   |      |      |      |      |     |      |
| B & H    |   |      |    |      |     |      |      |     |    |    |   |   |      |      |      |      |     |      |
| Sunday   |   |      |    |      |     |      |      |     |    |    |   |   |      |      |      |      |     |      |

## Career Performances

|  | M | Inns | NO | Runs | HS | Avge | 100s | 50s | Ct | St | Balls | Runs | Wkts | Avge | Best | 5wI | 10wM |
|---|---|---|---|---|---|---|---|---|---|---|---|---|---|---|---|---|---|
| Test |  |  |  |  |  |  |  |  |  |  |  |  |  |  |  |  |  |
| All First | 2 | 2 | 0 | 17 | 9 | 8.50 | - | - | - | - | 228 | 170 | 3 | 56.66 | 2-52 | - | - |
| 1-day Int |  |  |  |  |  |  |  |  |  |  |  |  |  |  |  |  |  |
| NatWest |  |  |  |  |  |  |  |  |  |  |  |  |  |  |  |  |  |  |
| B & H |  |  |  |  |  |  |  |  |  |  |  |  |  |  |  |  |  |  |
| Sunday |  |  |  |  |  |  |  |  |  |  |  |  |  |  |  |  |  |  |

# MARLAND, L. J. Lancashire

**Name:** Lee John Marland
**Role:** Right-hand bat
**Born:** 21 September 1975, Withington, Manchester
**Nickname:** Marlene, Marlo, Chink
**County debut:** No first-team appearance
**Parents:** Jeff and Liz
**Marital status:** Single
**Family links with cricket:** Father plays for Brooklands and has done so for over twenty years
**Education:** Worthington Primary; Manchester Grammar School; Northumbria University
**Qualifications:** 10 GCSEs, 3 A-levels
**Off-season:** At university
**Cricketers particularly admired:** Graham Gooch, Mike Atherton, Richard Green, Darren Shadford 'the latter for their cricketing brains'
**Other sports followed:** Football (Manchester United) and rugby union (Sale RFC)
**Relaxations:** Eating, sleeping, listening to music
**Extras:** *Daily Telegraph* U15 batting award. Captained England U14 and U15, and North of England U17 and U19.

---

47. Who are the only two brothers to have officiated as umpires in the same first-class match?

# MARSH, S. A.                    Kent

**Name:** Steven Andrew Marsh
**Role:** Right-hand bat, wicket-keeper, county vice-captain
**Born:** 27 January 1961, Westminster
**Height:** 5ft 11in **Weight:** 13st
**Nickname:** Marshy
**County debut:** 1982
**County cap:** 1986
**Benefit:** 1995
**1st-Class 50s:** 43
**1st-Class 100s:** 7
**1st-Class catches:** 529
**1st-Class stumpings:** 42
**Place in batting averages:** 150th av. 27.52
(1994 111th av. 32.28)
**Parents:** Melvyn Graham and Valerie Ann
**Wife and date of marriage:**
Julie, 27 September 1986
**Children:** Hayley Ann, 15 May 1987;

Christian James Robert, 20 November 1990
**Family links with cricket:** Father played local cricket for Lordswood. Father-in-law, Bob Wilson, played for Kent 1954-66
**Education:** Walderslade Secondary School for Boys; Mid-Kent College of Higher and Further Education
**Qualifications:** 6 O-levels, 2 A-levels, OND in Business Studies
**Career outside cricket:** Jazz singer
**Off-season:** 'Running my benefit year'
**Overseas tours:** Fred Rumsey XI to Barbados 1986-87
**Overseas teams played for:** Avendale CC, Cape Town 1985-86
**Cricketers particularly admired:** Robin Smith, Graham Cowdrey, Ian Botham
**Other sports followed:** Golf
**Injuries:** Shoulder and finger, out for two weeks
**Extras:** Appointed Kent vice-captain in 1991. In the match v Middlesex at Lord's in 1991 he held a world record eight catches in an innings and scored 113*. 'Cycling proficiency'
**Opinions on cricket:** 'Generally very tedious, brought on by four-day cricket. Unless of course you watch Kent who will either be bowled out for 150 in a session or score 450 in a day. Now that's what I call cricket. Boredom bores me!'
**Best batting:** 125 Kent v Yorkshire, Canterbury 1992
**Best bowling:** 2-20 Kent v Warwickshire, Edgbaston 1990

| | M | Inns | NO | Runs | HS | Avge | 100s | 50s | Ct | St | O | M | Runs | Wkts | Avge | Best | 5wI | 10wM |
|---|---|---|---|---|---|---|---|---|---|---|---|---|---|---|---|---|---|---|
| Test | | | | | | | | | | | | | | | | | | |
| All First | 16 | 28 | 3 | 688 | 67 * | 27.52 | - | 4 | 32 | 2 | 2 | 1 | 8 | 0 | - | - | - | - |
| 1-day Int | | | | | | | | | | | | | | | | | | |
| NatWest | 1 | 1 | 0 | 55 | 55 | 55.00 | - | 1 | 2 | - | | | | | | | | |
| B & H | 6 | 5 | 1 | 44 | 27 | 11.00 | - | - | 6 | - | | | | | | | | |
| Sunday | 14 | 10 | 4 | 92 | 22 * | 15.33 | - | - | 23 | 1 | | | | | | | | |

**Career Performances**

| | M | Inns | NO | Runs | HS | Avge | 100s | 50s | Ct | St | Balls | Runs | Wkts | Avge | Best | 5wI | 10wM |
|---|---|---|---|---|---|---|---|---|---|---|---|---|---|---|---|---|---|
| Test | | | | | | | | | | | | | | | | | |
| All First | 227 | 328 | 56 | 7697 | 125 | 28.29 | 7 | 43 | 529 | 42 | 166 | 235 | 2 | 117.50 | 2-20 | - | - |
| 1-day Int | | | | | | | | | | | | | | | | | |
| NatWest | 20 | 14 | 3 | 183 | 55 | 16.63 | - | 1 | 29 | 3 | | | | | | | |
| B & H | 45 | 35 | 8 | 424 | 71 | 15.70 | - | 1 | 51 | 2 | | | | | | | |
| Sunday | 149 | 107 | 28 | 1501 | 59 | 19.00 | - | 4 | 153 | 19 | | | | | | | |

# MARTIN, P. J.                    Lancashire

**Name:** Peter James Martin
**Role:** Right-hand bat, right-arm
fast-medium bowler
**Born:** 15 November 1968, Accrington
**Height:** 6ft 5in **Weight:** 15st 4lbs
**Nickname:** Digger, Long John
**County debut:** 1989
**County cap:** 1994
**Test debut:** 1995
**Tests:** 3
**One-day Internationals:** 2
**50 wickets in a season:** 1
**1st-Class 50s:** 4
**1st-Class 100s:** 1
**1st-Class 5 w. in innings:** 3
**1st-Class catches:** 28
**Place in batting averages:** 208th av. 20.00
(1994 232nd av. 15.95)
**Place in bowling averages:** 41st av. 26.34
(1994 55th av. 29.25)
**Strike rate:** 59.97 (career 71.69)
**Parents:** Keith and Catherine Lina

**Marital status:** Single
**Education:** Danum School, Doncaster
**Qualifications:** 6 O-levels, 2 A-levels
**Off-season:** England tour to South Africa
**Overseas tours:** England YC to Australia (Youth World Cup) 1988; 'and various other tours with English Schools and NAYC'; England to South Africa 1995-96, to India and Pakistan (World Cup) 1995-96
**Overseas teams played for:** Southern Districts, Queensland 1988-89; South Launceston, Tasmania 1989-90; South Canberra, ACT 1990-92
**Cricketers particularly admired:** 'Too many to mention'
**Other sports followed:** Football (Manchester United), rugby league (St Helens), golf
**Injuries:** Ankle ligament damage, missed five to six weeks
**Relaxations:** Music, painting, golf, cooking, walking, rugby league
**Extras:** Plays district football and basketball for Doncaster. Played for England A v Sri Lankans 1991. Was originally selected for the England A tour to Pakistan in 1995-96, but was drafted onto the senior tour after the withdrawal of Richard Johnson
**Opinions on cricket:** 'Should only be six-hour days with 100 overs a day.'
**Best batting:** 133 Lancashire v Durham, Gateshead Fell 1992
**Best bowling:** 5-35 Lancashire v Yorkshire, Headingley 1993

## 1995 Season

|          | M  | Inns | NO | Runs | HS  | Avge  | 100s | 50s | Ct | St | O     | M  | Runs | Wkts | Avge  | Best | 5wI | 10wM |
|----------|----|------|----|------|-----|-------|------|-----|----|----|-------|----|------|------|-------|------|-----|------|
| Test     | 3  | 6    | 0  | 52   | 29  | 8.66  | -    | -   | 4  | -  | 84    | 21 | 241  | 5    | 48.20 | 2-65 | -   | -    |
| All First| 13 | 17   | 2  | 300  | 71  | 20.00 | -    | 1   | 7  | -  | 349.5 | 96 | 922  | 35   | 26.34 | 4-51 | -   | -    |
| 1-day Int| 2  | 1    | 1  | 4    | 4 * | -     | -    | -   | -  | -  | 19.2  | 2  | 80   | 6    | 13.33 | 4-44 | -   |      |
| NatWest  | 1  | 0    | 0  | 0    | 0   | -     | -    | -   | -  | -  | 10    | 4  | 25   | 2    | 12.50 | 2-25 | -   |      |
| B & H    | 4  | 0    | 0  | 0    | 0   | -     | -    | -   | -  | -  | 30    | 6  | 104  | 4    | 26.00 | 2-35 | -   |      |
| Sunday   | 11 | 3    | 1  | 3    | 2   | 1.50  | -    | -   | 1  | -  | 74    | 6  | 314  | 12   | 26.16 | 4-29 | -   |      |

## Career Performances

|          | M  | Inns | NO | Runs | HS   | Avge  | 100s | 50s | Ct | St | Balls | Runs | Wkts | Avge  | Best | 5wI | 10wM |
|----------|----|------|----|------|------|-------|------|-----|----|----|-------|------|------|-------|------|-----|------|
| Test     | 3  | 6    | 0  | 52   | 29   | 8.66  | -    | -   | 4  | -  | 504   | 241  | 5    | 48.20 | 2-65 | -   | -    |
| All First| 97 | 111  | 29 | 1723 | 133  | 21.01 | 1    | 4   | 28 | -  | 15989 | 7504 | 223  | 33.65 | 5-35 | 3   | -    |
| 1-day Int| 2  | 1    | 1  | 4    | 4 *  | -     | -    | -   | -  | -  | 116   | 80   | 6    | 13.33 | 4-44 | -   |      |
| NatWest  | 7  | 1    | 0  | 16   | 16   | 16.00 | -    | -   | 1  | -  | 378   | 219  | 10   | 21.90 | 3-63 | -   |      |
| B & H    | 8  | 1    | 1  | 10   | 10 * | -     | -    | -   | 1  | -  | 432   | 249  | 8    | 31.12 | 2-35 | -   |      |
| Sunday   | 51 | 15   | 8  | 79   | 18 * | 11.28 | -    | -   | 8  | -  | 1942  | 1447 | 55   | 26.30 | 5-32 | 1   |      |

# MARTIN-JENKINS, R. S. C.     Sussex

**Name:** Robin Martin-Jenkins
**Role:** Right-hand bat, right-arm
medium-fast bowler
**Born:** 28 October 1975, Guildford
**Height:** 6ft 6in **Weight:** 13st 7lbs
**Nickname:** Tucker, Cérise, Ron
**County debut:** 1995
**1st-Class 50s:** 1
**Parents:** Christopher and Judy
**Marital status:** Single
**Family links with cricket:** Father is *Daily
Telegraph* cricket correspondent
**Education:** Cranleigh Prep. School, Surrey;
Radley College, Oxon; Durham University
**Qualifications:** 10 GCSEs, 3 A-levels, 1 AS-
level, Grade 3 bassoon
**Off-season:** University and Young Cricketers
tour to Sri Lanka
**Overseas tours:** Radley College to Barbados 1992
**Overseas teams played for:** Lima, Peru 1995
**Cricketers particularly admired:** Robin Smith, Angus Fraser, Steve Waugh
**Other sports followed:** Fives, hockey, tennis, skiing, football (Liverpool FC)
**Relaxations:** Watching television ('Pink Panther, James Bond'), listening to music
**Opinions on cricket:** 'Tea should definitely be longer – the time could be added on to
the end of the day's play. This would eradicate the dizzy spell that bowlers like me suffer
from after tea, as the smeggy mix of undigested sandwiches and yoghurt react with one's
body.'
**Best batting:** 50 Sussex v Northamptonshire, Hove 1995

## 1995 Season

| | M | Inns | NO | Runs | HS | Avge | 100s | 50s | Ct | St | O | M | Runs | Wkts | Avge | Best | 5wI | 10wM |
|---|---|---|---|---|---|---|---|---|---|---|---|---|---|---|---|---|---|---|
| Test | | | | | | | | | | | | | | | | | | |
| All First | 2 | 2 | 1 | 50 | 50 | 50.00 | - | 1 | - | - | 3 | 1 | 11 | 0 | - | - | - | - |
| 1-day Int | | | | | | | | | | | | | | | | | | |
| NatWest | | | | | | | | | | | | | | | | | | |
| B & H | | | | | | | | | | | | | | | | | | |
| Sunday | 9 | 5 | 1 | 12 | 10 | 3.00 | - | - | - | - | 53 | 3 | 286 | 5 | 57.20 | 2-41 | | |

**Career Performances**

| | M | Inns | NO | Runs | HS | Avge | 100s | 50s | Ct | St | Balls | Runs | Wkts | Avge | Best | 5wI | 10wM |
|---|---|---|---|---|---|---|---|---|---|---|---|---|---|---|---|---|---|
| Test | | | | | | | | | | | | | | | | | |
| All First | 2 | 2 | 1 | 50 | 50 | 50.00 | - | 1 | - | - | 18 | 11 | 0 | - | - | - | - |
| 1-day Int | | | | | | | | | | | | | | | | | |
| NatWest | | | | | | | | | | | | | | | | | |
| B & H | | | | | | | | | | | | | | | | | |
| Sunday | 9 | 5 | 1 | 12 | 10 | 3.00 | - | - | - | - | 318 | 286 | 5 | 57.20 | 2-41 | - | |

# MARU, R. J. Hampshire

**Name:** Rajesh Jamnadass Maru
**Role:** Right-hand bat, slow left-arm bowler, close fielder
**Born:** 28 October 1962, Nairobi, Kenya
**Height:** 5ft 6in **Weight:** 11st
**Nickname:** Raj
**County debut:** 1980 (Middlesex), 1984 (Hampshire)
**County cap:** 1986 (Hampshire)
**50 wickets in a season:** 4
**1st-Class 50s:** 6
**1st-Class 5 w. in innings:** 15
**1st-Class 10 w. in match:** 1
**1st-Class catches:** 229
**Strike rate:** (career 73.71)
**Parents:** Jamnadass and Prabhavati
**Wife and date of marriage:** Amanda Jane, 21 September 1991
**Children:** Christopher Patrick, 21 January 1993
**Family links with cricket:** Father played in Kenya and in England for North London Polytechnic. Brother Pradip plays for Wembley in the Middlesex League and has played for Middlesex 2nd XI, Middlesex U19 and for Middlesex Colts & Schools
**Education:** Rooks Heath High School, Harrow; Pinner Sixth Form College
**Qualifications:** NCA advanced coach
**Career outside cricket:** Cricket coach
**Off-season:** Coaching for Hampshire CCC
**Overseas tours:** England YC South to Canada 1979; England YC to West Indies 1979-80; Middlesex to Zimbabwe 1980; Hampshire to Barbados 1987,1988,1990; Hampshire to Dubai 1989; Barbican International XI to Dubai 1981; MCC to Leeward Islands 1992, to Far East 1995

**Overseas teams played for:** Marlborough CA, Blenheim, New Zealand 1985-87
**Cricketers particularly admired:** David Gower, Bishen Bedi, Richard Hadlee, Phil Edmonds, John Emburey, Malcolm Marshall, Gordon Greenidge
**Other sports followed:** Football, rugby (Wasps and England), 'would watch any sport'
**Relaxations:** Spending time with wife and son, DIY at home
**Extras:** Played for Middlesex 1980-83; reached 500 first-class wickets in 1995
**Opinions on cricket:** 'Four-day cricket has been good for the game, but the standard of wickets have to change. You have to produce good wickets to make the game last the full four days, or bring back three-day cricket with uncovered pitches.'
**Best batting:** 74 Hampshire v Gloucestershire, Gloucester 1988
**Best bowling:** 8-41 Hampshire v Kent, Southampton 1989

### 1995 Season

|           | M | Inns | NO | Runs | HS | Avge | 100s | 50s | Ct | St | O | M | Runs | Wkts | Avge | Best | 5wI | 10wM |
|-----------|---|------|----|------|----|------|------|-----|----|----|---|---|------|------|------|------|-----|------|
| Test      |   |      |    |      |    |      |      |     |    |    |   |   |      |      |      |      |     |      |
| All First | 2 | 3    | 1  | 8    | 7  | 4.00 | -    | -   | 4  | -  | 105.5 | 47 | 199 | 9 | 22.11 | 3-38 | - | - |
| 1-day Int |   |      |    |      |    |      |      |     |    |    |   |   |      |      |      |      |     |      |
| NatWest   | 1 | 1    | 0  | 1    | 1  | 1.00 | -    | -   | 1  | -  | 10 | 0 | 39 | 1 | 39.00 | 1-39 | - |      |
| B & H     | 1 | 1    | 0  | 0    | 0  | 0.00 | -    | -   | -  | -  | 6  | 0 | 24 | 1 | 24.00 | 1-24 | - |      |
| Sunday    | 8 | 3    | 2  | 16   | 9 * | 16.00 | -   | -   | 1  | -  | 63.3 | 0 | 332 | 7 | 47.42 | 2-31 | - |      |

### Career Performances

|           | M | Inns | NO | Runs | HS | Avge | 100s | 50s | Ct | St | Balls | Runs | Wkts | Avge | Best | 5wI | 10wM |
|-----------|---|------|----|------|----|------|------|-----|----|----|-------|------|------|------|------|-----|------|
| Test      |   |      |    |      |    |      |      |     |    |    |       |      |      |      |      |     |      |
| All First | 212 | 208 | 51 | 2568 | 74 | 16.35 | - | 6 | 229 | - | 37150 | 16477 | 504 | 32.69 | 8-41 | 15 | 1 |
| 1-day Int |   |      |    |      |    |      |      |     |    |    |       |      |      |      |      |     |      |
| NatWest   | 14 | 6 | 2 | 44 | 22 | 11.00 | - | - | 12 | - | 882 | 531 | 13 | 40.84 | 3-30 | - |      |
| B & H     | 11 | 3 | 0 | 13 | 9 | 4.33 | - | - | 5 | - | 531 | 354 | 10 | 35.40 | 3-46 | - |      |
| Sunday    | 57 | 24 | 14 | 151 | 33 * | 15.10 | - | - | 19 | - | 1999 | 1738 | 46 | 37.78 | 3-30 | - |      |

# MASON, T. J.            Leicestershire

**Name:** Timothy James Mason
**Role:** Right-hand bat, right-arm off-spin bowler
**Born:** 12 April 1975, Leicester
**Height:** 5ft 8in **Weight:** 10st 4lbs
**Nickname:** Perry, Biffa, Stone
**County debut:** 1994
**1st-Class catches:** 3
**Parents:** Phil and Anthea
**Marital status:** Single
**Family links with cricket:** Father has played club cricket, is manager and coach of

Leicester U11
**Education:** Brookvale High School, Leicester; Denstone College
**Qualifications:** 9 GCSEs, 3 A-levels
**Off-season:** Coaching in South Africa
**Overseas tours:** Denstone College to South Africa 1993; England U19 to Sri Lanka 1993-94
**Overseas teams played for:** Eastern Freestate, South Africa 1994-95
**Cricketers particularly admired:** Allan Lamb, Malcolm Marshall, Jon Dakin
**Other sports followed:** Rugby union (Leicester Tigers), football (Leicester City)
**Relaxations:** Listening to music, watching most sports, going out with friends and girlfriend
**Extras:** Captained Leicestershire Schools at all age levels. 1992 *Daily Telegraph* U19 Midlands Bowler of the Year; 1993 *Daily*

*Telegraph* U19 National Bowler of the Year; 1993 Gray-Nicolls Outstanding Schoolboy Player of the Year. Dislocated shoulder prevented him from going on England U18 tour to South Africa 1992-93.
**Opinions on cricket:** 'Great game. Has given me opportunities to travel around the world already. Four-day cricket has to be good for the game, as is the introduction of the third umpire.'
**Best batting:** 3 Leicestershire v Essex, Leicester 1994
**Best bowling:** 1-22 Leicestershire v Essex, Leicester 1994

## 1995 Season

|  | M | Inns | NO | Runs | HS | Avge | 100s | 50s | Ct | St | O | M | Runs | Wkts | Avge | Best | 5wI | 10wM |
|---|---|---|---|---|---|---|---|---|---|---|---|---|---|---|---|---|---|---|
| Test |  |  |  |  |  |  |  |  |  |  |  |  |  |  |  |  |  |  |
| All First | 1 | 0 | 0 | 0 | 0 | - | - | - | 1 | - | 25 | 4 | 79 | 0 | - | - | - | - |
| 1-day Int |  |  |  |  |  |  |  |  |  |  |  |  |  |  |  |  |  |  |
| NatWest | 2 | 1 | 0 | 5 | 5 | 5.00 | - | - | 3 | - | 24 | 1 | 72 | 0 | - | - | - |  |
| B & H | 1 | 1 | 1 | 5 | 5 * | - | - | - | - | - | 11 | 2 | 34 | 1 | 34.00 | 1-34 | - |  |
| Sunday | 11 | 3 | 1 | 22 | 17 * | 11.00 | - | - | 1 | - | 69 | 3 | 359 | 6 | 59.83 | 2-41 | - |  |

## Career Performances

|  | M | Inns | NO | Runs | HS | Avge | 100s | 50s | Ct | St | Balls | Runs | Wkts | Avge | Best | 5wI | 10wM |
|---|---|---|---|---|---|---|---|---|---|---|---|---|---|---|---|---|---|
| Test |  |  |  |  |  |  |  |  |  |  |  |  |  |  |  |  |  |
| All First | 2 | 1 | 0 | 3 | 3 | 3.00 | - | - | 3 | - | 192 | 101 | 1 | 101.00 | 1-22 | - | - |
| 1-day Int |  |  |  |  |  |  |  |  |  |  |  |  |  |  |  |  |  |
| NatWest | 2 | 1 | 0 | 5 | 5 | 5.00 | - | - | 3 | - | 144 | 72 | 0 | - | - | - |  |
| B & H | 1 | 1 | 1 | 5 | 5 * | - | - | - | - | - | 66 | 34 | 1 | 34.00 | 1-34 | - |  |
| Sunday | 11 | 3 | 1 | 22 | 17 * | 11.00 | - | - | 1 | - | 414 | 359 | 6 | 59.83 | 2-41 | - |  |

# MAYNARD, M. P.                              Glamorgan

**Name:** Matthew Peter Maynard
**Role:** Right-hand bat, right-arm medium
'declaration' bowler, cover fielder
**Born:** 21 March 1966, Oldham, Lancashire
**Height:** 5ft 11in **Weight:** 12st 12lbs
**Nickname:** Ollie
**County debut:** 1985
**County cap:** 1987
**Test debut:** 1988
**Tests:** 4
**One-Day Internationals:** 5
**1000 runs in a season:** 9
**1st-Class 50s:** 87
**1st-Class 100s:** 34
**1st-Class 200s:** 2
**1st-Class catches:** 230
**1st-Class stumpings:** 5
**One-Day 100s:** 7
**Place in batting averages:** 44th av. 45.42
(1994 84th av. 36.07)
**Parents:** Ken (deceased) and Pat
**Wife and date of marriage:** Susan, 27 September 1986
**Children:** Tom, 25 March 1989; Ceri Lloyd, 5 August 1993
**Family links with cricket:** Father played for many years for Duckinfield. Brother
Charles plays for St Fagans
**Education:** Ysgol David Hughes, Menai Bridge, Anglesey
**Qualifications:** Cricket coach
**Career outside cricket:** Marketing executive
**Off-season:** 'Preparing for my benefit year'
**Overseas tours:** North Wales XI to Barbados 1982; Glamorgan to Barbados 1982, to
South Africa 1993; unofficial England XI to South Africa 1989-90; HKCC (Australia)
to Bangkok and Hong Kong, 1990; England VI to Hong Kong Sixes 1992 and 1994;
England to West Indies 1993-94
**Overseas teams played for:** St Joseph's, Whakatane, New Zealand 1986-88;
Gosnells, Perth, Western Australia 1988-89; Papakura and Northern Districts, New
Zealand 1990-92; Morrinsville College and Northern Districts 1991-92
**Cricketers particularly admired:** Ian Botham, Viv Richards
**Other sports followed:** Golf and squash
**Relaxations:** Spending time with my wife and family and relaxing
**Extras:** Scored century on first-class debut v Yorkshire at Swansea in 1985, when he
became the youngest centurion for Glamorgan, and scored 1000 runs in first full season.

In 1987 scored the fastest ever 50 for Glamorgan (14 mins) v Yorkshire and was youngest player to be awarded Glamorgan cap. Voted Young Cricketer of the Year 1988 by the Cricket Writers' Club. Banned from Test cricket for five years for joining 1989-90 tour of South Africa, ban remitted 1992. Scored 987 runs in July 1991, including a century in each innings v Gloucestershire at Cheltenham. Captained Glamorgan for most of 1992 in Alan Butcher's absence. Second child was born on the morning of the fifth Test against Australia at Edgbaston 1993 – he had a daughter and a duck on the same day. Glamorgan's captain for the 1996 season. Awarded benefit for 1996

**Opinions on cricket:** 'Four-day cricket should start on a Wednesday. It gives more opportunity to sell hospitality. It would also stop having to play a one-day fixture in the middle of a four-day game.'

**Best batting:** 243 Glamorgan v Hampshire, Southampton 1991
**Best bowling:** 3-21 Glamorgan v Oxford University, The Parks 1987

## 1995 Season

|  | M | Inns | NO | Runs | HS | Avge | 100s | 50s | Ct | St | O | M | Runs | Wkts | Avge | Best | 5wI | 10wM |
|---|---|---|---|---|---|---|---|---|---|---|---|---|---|---|---|---|---|---|
| Test |  |  |  |  |  |  |  |  |  |  |  |  |  |  |  |  |  |  |
| All First | 20 | 36 | 1 | 1590 | 164 | 45.42 | 3 | 12 | 23 | - |  |  |  |  |  |  |  |  |
| 1-day Int |  |  |  |  |  |  |  |  |  |  |  |  |  |  |  |  |  |  |
| NatWest | 4 | 3 | 0 | 11 | 11 | 3.66 | - | - | 1 | - |  |  |  |  |  |  |  |  |
| B & H | 5 | 5 | 0 | 170 | 41 | 34.00 | - | - | 2 | - |  |  |  |  |  |  |  |  |
| Sunday | 16 | 14 | 3 | 315 | 69 * | 28.63 | - | 3 | 7 | - |  |  |  |  |  |  |  |  |

## Career Performances

|  | M | Inns | NO | Runs | HS | Avge | 100s | 50s | Ct | St | Balls | Runs | Wkts | Avge | Best | 5wI | 10wM |
|---|---|---|---|---|---|---|---|---|---|---|---|---|---|---|---|---|---|
| Test | 4 | 8 | 0 | 87 | 35 | 10.87 | - | - | 3 | - |  |  |  |  |  |  |  |
| All First | 248 | 410 | 40 | 15520 | 243 | 41.94 | 34 | 87 | 230 | 5 | 816 | 686 | 6 | 114.33 | 3-21 | - | - |
| 1-day Int | 5 | 5 | 1 | 59 | 22 * | 14.75 | - | - | 1 | - |  |  |  |  |  |  |  |
| NatWest | 29 | 28 | 2 | 1211 | 151 * | 46.57 | 2 | 10 | 10 | - |  |  |  |  |  |  |  |
| B & H | 36 | 36 | 3 | 1235 | 115 | 37.42 | 2 | 6 | 10 | - | 24 | 32 | 0 | - | - | - | - |
| Sunday | 149 | 142 | 11 | 3938 | 122 * | 30.06 | 3 | 27 | 50 | - | 16 | 27 | 0 | - | - | - | - |

48. Who won the Women's European Cup final and whom did they defeat?

# McCAGUE, M. J.           Kent

**Name:** Martin John McCague
**Role:** Right-hand bat, right-arm fast bowler
**Born:** 24 May 1969, Larne, Northern Ireland
**Height:** 6ft 5in **Weight:** 17st
**Nickname:** Stinger, Pigsy
**County debut:** 1991
**County cap:** 1992
**Test debut:** 1993
**Tests:** 3
**50 wickets in season:** 3
**1st-Class 50s:** 2
**1st-Class 5 w. in innings:** 17
**1st-Class 10 w. in match:** 2
**1st-Class catches:** 45
**One-Day 5 w. in innings:** 3
**Place in batting averages:** 221st av. 18.10
(1994 189th av. 21.92)
**Place in bowling averages:** 62nd av. 29.14
(1994 4th 19.01)
**Strike rate:** 50.92 (career 51.29)
**Parents:** Mal and Mary
**Marital status:** Single
**Education:** Hedland Senior High School
**Qualifications:** Electrician
**Off-season:** Playing grade cricket in Melbourne, Australia
**Overseas tours:** England A to South Africa 1993-94; England to Australia 1994-95
**Overseas teams played for:** Western Australia 1990-91
**Cricketers particularly admired:** Dennis Lillee, Curtly Ambrose
**Other sports followed:** Football (Crystal Palace and Gillingham)
**Injuries:** Side strain and knee strain, missed total of three weeks
**Relaxations:** Golf and snooker
**Opinions on cricket:** 'Two division championship. Pressure on the teams to perform all year, but who decides which teams start in which divisions?'
**Best batting:** 59 Kent v Nottinghamshire, Trent Bridge 1995
**Best bowling:** 9-86 Kent v Derbyshire, Derby 1994

49. Who won the Man of the Match Award in the
1995 Benson and Hedges Cup final?

## 1995 Season

| | M | Inns | NO | Runs | HS | Avge | 100s | 50s | Ct | St | O | M | Runs | Wkts | Avge | Best | 5wI | 10wM |
|---|---|---|---|---|---|---|---|---|---|---|---|---|---|---|---|---|---|---|
| Test | | | | | | | | | | | | | | | | | | |
| All First | 14 | 25 | 6 | 344 | 59 | 18.10 | - | 1 | 9 | - | 424.2 | 79 | 1457 | 50 | 29.14 | 5-47 | 1 | - |
| 1-day Int | | | | | | | | | | | | | | | | | | |
| NatWest | 2 | 2 | 1 | 34 | 31 * | 34.00 | - | - | 1 | - | 16 | 1 | 76 | 2 | 38.00 | 2-42 | - | |
| B & H | 5 | 3 | 2 | 40 | 24 | 40.00 | - | - | 4 | - | 53 | 2 | 249 | 3 | 83.00 | 1-40 | - | |
| Sunday | 14 | 8 | 3 | 51 | 14 | 10.20 | - | - | 2 | - | 95.3 | 5 | 483 | 21 | 23.00 | 5-40 | 1 | |

## Career Performances

| | M | Inns | NO | Runs | HS | Avge | 100s | 50s | Ct | St | Balls | Runs | Wkts | Avge | Best | 5wI | 10wM |
|---|---|---|---|---|---|---|---|---|---|---|---|---|---|---|---|---|---|
| Test | 3 | 5 | 0 | 21 | 11 | 4.20 | - | - | 1 | - | 593 | 390 | 6 | 65.00 | 4-121 | - | - |
| All First | 77 | 103 | 23 | 1144 | 59 | 14.30 | - | 2 | 45 | - | 13747 | 7347 | 268 | 27.41 | 9-86 | 17 | 2 |
| 1-day Int | | | | | | | | | | | | | | | | | |
| NatWest | 10 | 8 | 4 | 71 | 31 * | 17.75 | - | - | 2 | - | 570 | 380 | 18 | 21.11 | 5-26 | 1 | |
| B & H | 16 | 11 | 5 | 123 | 30 | 20.50 | - | - | 6 | - | 826 | 593 | 25 | 23.72 | 5-43 | 1 | |
| Sunday | 52 | 27 | 12 | 174 | 22 * | 11.60 | - | - | 9 | - | 2140 | 1800 | 86 | 20.93 | 5-40 | 1 | |

# McDONALD, S.　　　　　Warwickshire

**Name:** Stephen McDonald
**Role:** Right-hand bat, off-spin bowler
**Born:** 2 October 1974, Birmingham
**Height:** 5ft 10in **Weight:** 13st
**Nickname:** Mac
**Parents:** Frank McDonald and Patricia Snookes
**Marital status:** Single
**Education:** Uplands Junior School, Smethwick; Bristnall Hall High School, Oldbury; Rowley Regis College, Blackheath
**Qualifications:** 9 GCSEs, 1 A-level, NCA Junior Cricket Coach
**Off-season:** Working and coaching
**Overseas tours:** Warwickshire U19 to South Africa 1992
**Cricketers particularly admired:** David Gower, Brian Lara, Tim May
**Other sports followed:** Football (WBA)
**Injuries:** Bruised hip, out for two weeks
**Relaxations:** Member of fitness club, swimming and reading
**Extras:** NCA England U14, U15. Bull Development U19. Awarded WSCA colours six years running

**Opinions on cricket:** 'Perhaps with most players performing six or seven days per week, I believe that the season may be extended for a month, allowing more time between games for the players to recuperate and recharge. I am pleased to see that wickets are now being prepared to encourage spin.'

---

# McGRATH, A.                                    Yorkshire

**Name:** Anthony McGrath
**Role:** Right-hand bat, off-spin bowler
**Born:** 6 October 1975, Bradford
**Height:** 6ft 1in **Weight:** 13st 2lbs
**Nickname:** Mags, Gripper, Forrest Gump
**County debut:** 1995
**1st-Class 50s:** 1
**1st-Class catches**: 3
**Place in batting averages:** 144th av. 28.00
**Parents:** Terry and Kath
**Marital status:** Single
**Family links with cricket:** Brother Dermot
plays league cricket
**Education:** St Winefrides; St Blaise;
Yorkshire Martyrs Collegiate School
**Qualifications:** 9 GCSEs, BTEC in Leisure
Studies
**Off-season:** England A tour to Pakistan
**Overseas tours:** England U19 to West Indies
1994-95; England A to Pakistan 1995-96

**Cricketers particularly admired:** Graham Thorpe, Robin Smith
**Other sports followed:** Football (Manchester United)
**Injuries:** Gout, missed one game
**Relaxations:** Listening to music, spending time with friends outside cricket, watching sports
**Extras:** Captained Yorkshire Schools U13, U14, U15 and U16; captained English Schools U17. Bradford League Young Cricketer of the Year 1992 and 1993. Played for England U17, and for England U19 in home series against India 1994. Appeared as 12th man for England in the First Test against West Indies at Headingley in 1995. Scored his maiden first-class century on the England A tour to Pakistan
**Opinions on cricket:** 'Too much cricket is played during the season. Players should be given twelve-month contracts.'
**Best batting:** 84 Yorkshire v Somerset, Taunton 1995

## 1995 Season

| | M | Inns | NO | Runs | HS | Avge | 100s | 50s | Ct | St | O | M | Runs | Wkts | Avge | Best | 5wI | 10wM |
|---|---|---|---|---|---|---|---|---|---|---|---|---|---|---|---|---|---|---|
| Test | | | | | | | | | | | | | | | | | | |
| All First | 5 | 10 | 0 | 280 | 84 | 28.00 | - | 1 | 3 | - | | | | | | | | |
| 1-day Int | | | | | | | | | | | | | | | | | | |
| NatWest | | | | | | | | | | | | | | | | | | |
| B & H | 1 | 1 | 0 | 2 | 2 | 2.00 | - | - | - | - | | | | | | | | |
| Sunday | 2 | 1 | 0 | 72 | 72 | 72.00 | - | 1 | 2 | - | | | | | | | | |

## Career Performances

| | M | Inns | NO | Runs | HS | Avge | 100s | 50s | Ct | St | Balls | Runs | Wkts | Avge | Best | 5wI | 10wM |
|---|---|---|---|---|---|---|---|---|---|---|---|---|---|---|---|---|---|
| Test | | | | | | | | | | | | | | | | | |
| All First | 5 | 10 | 0 | 280 | 84 | 28.00 | - | 1 | 3 | - | | | | | | | |
| 1-day Int | | | | | | | | | | | | | | | | | |
| NatWest | | | | | | | | | | | | | | | | | |
| B & H | 1 | 1 | 0 | 2 | 2 | 2.00 | - | - | - | - | | | | | | | |
| Sunday | 2 | 1 | 0 | 72 | 72 | 72.00 | - | 1 | 2 | - | | | | | | | |

# McKEOWN, P. C.                 Lancashire

**Name:** Patrick Christopher McKeown
**Role:** Right-hand bat
**Born:** 1 June 1976, Liverpool
**Height:** 6ft 3in **Weight:** 13st
**Nickname:** Paddy
**County debut:** No first-team appearance
**Parents:** Paddy and Cathy
**Marital status:** Single
**Education:** St Mary's College, Crosby;
Rossall School (Blackpool)
**Qualifications:** 7 GCSEs, 3 A-levels
**Off-season:** Playing grade cricket in Perth
**Overseas tours:** Rossall School to Australia
1994-95
**Overseas teams played for:** Subiaco-Floriat,
Perth, Australia 1995-96
**Cricketers particularly admired:** Graeme
Hick and Neil Fairbrother
**Other sports followed:** Football (Liverpool)
**Relaxations:** 'Playing most sports, especially football and rugby. I enjoy spending
time on the golf course.'
**Extras:** Represented England Schools U19, and U18 versus India. Played for Development

of Excellence U19, National Cricket Association U19, Headmasters' Conference U19
**Opinions on cricket:** 'Tea should be 30 minutes. Players should be on 12-month contracts to give them more security during the winter.'

# METCALFE, A. A.       Nottinghamshire

**Name:** Ashley Anthony Metcalfe
**Role:** Right-hand opening bat,
off-spin bowler
**Born:** 25 December 1963, Horsforth, Leeds
**Height:** 5ft 9½in **Weight:** 11st 7lbs
**County debut:** 1983 (Yorkshire)
**County cap:** 1986 (Yorkshire)
**Benefit:** 1995
**1000 runs in a season:** 6
**1st-Class 50s:** 52
**1st-Class 100s:** 25
**1st-Class 200s:** 1
**1st-Class catches:** 74
**One-Day 100s:** 4
**Parents:** Tony and Ann
**Wife and date of marriage:** Diane,
20 April 1986
**Children:** Zoë, 18 July 1990; Amy, 22
August 1993
**Family links with cricket:** Father played in local league; father-in-law Ray
Illingworth (Yorkshire and England)
**Education:** Ladderbanks Middle School; Bradford Grammar School; University
College, London
**Qualifications:** 9 O-levels, 3 A-levels, NCA coaching certificate
**Career outside cricket:** 'Metcalfe & Sidebottom Associates – sports promotion company'
**Overseas teams played for:** Orange Free State 1988-89
**Cricketers particularly admired:** Barry Richards, Doug Padgett, Don Wilson, Arnie
Sidebottom, Pete Hartley, Paul Jarvis
**Other sports followed:** Most, particularly golf
**Relaxations:** 'Relaxing at home with my family'
**Extras:** Making 122 on first-class debut v Nottinghamshire at Park Avenue in 1983 he
became the youngest Yorkshire player to achieve the feat and recorded the highest debut
score by a Yorkshireman. Reached 2000 runs for the season in the last match of 1990
with 194* and 107 v Nottinghamshire at Trent Bridge. Released by Yorkshire at the end
of the 1995 season and has signed for Nottinghamshire for the 1996 season
**Best batting:** 216* Yorkshire v Middlesex, Headingley 1988
**Best bowling:** 2-18 Yorkshire v Warwickshire, Scarborough 1987

## 1995 Season

| | M | Inns | NO | Runs | HS | Avge | 100s | 50s | Ct | St | O | M | Runs | Wkts | Avge | Best | 5wI | 10wM |
|---|---|---|---|---|---|---|---|---|---|---|---|---|---|---|---|---|---|---|
| Test | | | | | | | | | | | | | | | | | | |
| All First | 4 | 4 | 1 | 200 | 100 | 66.66 | 1 | 1 | 5 | - | 6 | 0 | 46 | 0 | - | - | - | - |
| 1-day Int | | | | | | | | | | | | | | | | | | |
| NatWest | 2 | 2 | 0 | 33 | 33 | 16.50 | - | - | - | - | | | | | | | | |
| B & H | | | | | | | | | | | | | | | | | | |
| Sunday | 9 | 7 | 2 | 131 | 50 | 26.20 | - | 1 | 3 | - | | | | | | | | |

## Career Performances

| | M | Inns | NO | Runs | HS | Avge | 100s | 50s | Ct | St | Balls | Runs | Wkts | Avge | Best | 5wI | 10wM |
|---|---|---|---|---|---|---|---|---|---|---|---|---|---|---|---|---|---|
| Test | | | | | | | | | | | | | | | | | |
| All First | 194 | 333 | 20 | 10892 | 216 * | 34.79 | 25 | 52 | 74 | - | 428 | 362 | 4 | 90.50 | 2-18 | - | - |
| 1-day Int | | | | | | | | | | | | | | | | | |
| NatWest | 20 | 20 | 3 | 714 | 127 * | 42.00 | 1 | 5 | 4 | - | 42 | 44 | 2 | 22.00 | 2-44 | - | |
| B & H | 31 | 31 | 4 | 1277 | 114 | 47.29 | 1 | 8 | 8 | - | | | | | | | |
| Sunday | 140 | 135 | 7 | 3529 | 116 | 27.57 | 2 | 23 | 33 | - | | | | | | | |

# METSON, C. P.  Glamorgan

**Name:** Colin Peter Metson
**Role:** Right-hand bat, wicket-keeper, bowl-out specialist bowler (at one stump)
**Born:** 2 July 1963, Cuffley, Herts
**Height:** 5ft 6in **Weight:** 10st 12lbs
**Nickname:** Meto, Stumpie
**County debut:** 1981 (Middlesex), 1987 (Glamorgan)
**County cap:** 1987 (Glamorgan)
**1st-Class 50s:** 7
**1st-Class catches:** 538
**1st-Class stumpings:** 48
**Place in batting averages:** 223rd av. 18.07 (1994 187th av. 22.11)
**Parents:** Denis Alwyn and Jean Mary
**Wife and date of marriage:** Stephanie Leslie Astrid, 13 October 1991
**Family links with cricket:** Father captained Winchmore Hill
**Education:** Stanborough School, Welwyn Garden City; Enfield Grammar School; Durham University
**Qualifications:** 10 O-levels, 5 A-levels, BA (Hons) Economic History, advanced cricket coach

**Career outside cricket:** Project co-ordinator with Castle Services
**Off-season:** As above, plus the MCC tour to Bangladesh
**Overseas teams played for:** Payneham, Adelaide 1986-88; Rostrevor Old Boys, Adelaide 1987-91
**Cricketers particularly admired:** Bob Taylor, Rod Marsh, Ian Botham, Mike Gatting
**Other sports followed:** Football (Tottenham Hotspur FC), golf, rugby (Saracens RFC) most sports except wrestling
**Relaxations:** Watching sport, videos, good wine, port
**Extras:** Played for England YC v India YC 1981 and was voted Young Wicket-keeper of the Year. In 1984 captained Durham University, losing finalists in UAU competition. Left Middlesex at end of 1986 season. Holds the Glamorgan record for most catches in an innings (7) and match (9). Played 160 consecutive Championship matches for Glamorgan, 1987-94. Wombwell Cricket Lovers' Society Wicket-keeper of the Year 1993. Received Man of the Match Award for the first time in his career in the Nat West quarter-final against Middlesex in 1995, after nine years in the game
**Opinions on cricket:** 'Cricket must find ways to market itself better, and must give the sponsors value for money. The 25-point deduction regarding "unfit" pitches should be more widely used so that the counties will prepare the best possible pitches. Counties should take more interest in the winter and future careers of its players (regarding placements, qualifications, etc). Use of the third umpire in semi-finals as well as the finals. All players should fully support the "new" Professional Cricketers' Association and work together to improve playing standards'
**Best batting:** 96 Middlesex v Gloucestershire, Uxbridge 1984

## 1995 Season

| | M | Inns | NO | Runs | HS | Avge | 100s | 50s | Ct | St | O | M | Runs | Wkts | Avge | Best | 5wI | 10wM |
|---|---|---|---|---|---|---|---|---|---|---|---|---|---|---|---|---|---|---|
| Test | | | | | | | | | | | | | | | | | | |
| All First | 17 | 23 | 9 | 253 | 26 * | 18.07 | - | - | 47 | 7 | | | | | | | | |
| 1-day Int | | | | | | | | | | | | | | | | | | |
| NatWest | 4 | 2 | 0 | 20 | 20 | 10.00 | - | - | 3 | - | | | | | | | | |
| B & H | 5 | 3 | 1 | 32 | 22 | 16.00 | - | - | 7 | - | | | | | | | | |
| Sunday | 16 | 4 | 1 | 7 | 3 | 2.33 | - | - | 20 | 7 | | | | | | | | |

## Career Performances

| | M | Inns | NO | Runs | HS | Avge | 100s | 50s | Ct | St | Balls | Runs | Wkts | Avge | Best | 5wI | 10wM |
|---|---|---|---|---|---|---|---|---|---|---|---|---|---|---|---|---|---|
| Test | | | | | | | | | | | | | | | | | |
| All First | 221 | 288 | 67 | 3990 | 96 | 18.05 | - | 7 | 538 | 48 | 6 | 0 | 0 | - | - | - | - |
| 1-day Int | | | | | | | | | | | | | | | | | |
| NatWest | 27 | 15 | 2 | 89 | 21 | 6.84 | - | - | 26 | 2 | | | | | | | |
| B & H | 32 | 21 | 4 | 185 | 23 | 10.88 | - | - | 21 | 4 | | | | | | | |
| Sunday | 150 | 85 | 42 | 647 | 30 * | 15.04 | - | - | 149 | 46 | | | | | | | |

# MIDDLETON, T. C.                    Hampshire

**Name:** Tony Charles Middleton
**Role:** Right-hand bat, slow left-arm bowler
**Born:** 1 February 1964, Winchester
**Height:** 5ft 10in **Weight:** 11st
**Nickname:** Dogun
**County debut:** 1984
**County cap:** 1990
**1000 runs in a season:** 2
**1st-Class 50s:** 24
**1st-Class 100s:** 13
**1st-Class 200s:** 1
**1st-Class catches:** 79
**Parents:** Peter and Molly
**Wife and date of marriage:** Sherralyn,
23 September 1989
**Family links with cricket:** Brother plays
local club cricket
**Education:** Weeke Infants and Junior
Schools; Montgomery of Alamein

Comprehensive; Peter Symonds Sixth Form College, Winchester
**Qualifications:** 5 O-levels, 1 A-level
**Overseas tours:** Hampshire to Barbados 1989; England A to Australia 1992-93
**Overseas teams played for:** South African Police, Durban 1984-86; Belmont,
Newcastle, NSW, Australia 1987-89
**Cricketers particularly admired:** Barry Richards, Gordon Greenidge, 'I was
particularly helped by Neville Rodgers and Tim Tremlett'
**Other sports followed:** Football, rugby union, badminton, squash
**Relaxations:** Watching sport, gardening, real ale pubs, holidays
**Extras:** Played for English Schools 1982. Scored six consecutive centuries for
Hampshire in May 1990: 104 and 144 v Somerset II; 121 v Yorkshire II; 100 and 124 v
Leicestershire II; 104* for 1st XI v Essex. Scored 78 in NatWest final 1991, on his first
appearance in the competition. Was first batsman to 1000 first-class runs in 1992.
Retired from first-class cricket at the end of the 1995 season to become Hampshire's
Youth Development Officer
**Best batting:** 221 Hampshire v Surrey, Southampton 1992
**Best bowling:** 2-41 Hampshire v Kent, Canterbury 1991

50. Which Australian state side visited England in September 1995?

**1995 Season**

| | M | Inns | NO | Runs | HS | Avge | 100s | 50s | Ct | St | O | M | Runs | Wkts | Avge | Best | 5wI | 10wM |
|---|---|---|---|---|---|---|---|---|---|---|---|---|---|---|---|---|---|---|
| Test | | | | | | | | | | | | | | | | | | |
| All First | 2 | 4 | 0 | 48 | 31 | 12.00 | - | - | 1 | - | | | | | | | | |
| 1-day Int | | | | | | | | | | | | | | | | | | |
| NatWest | | | | | | | | | | | | | | | | | | |
| B & H | | | | | | | | | | | | | | | | | | |
| Sunday | | | | | | | | | | | | | | | | | | |

**Career Performances**

| | M | Inns | NO | Runs | HS | Avge | 100s | 50s | Ct | St | Balls | Runs | Wkts | Avge | Best | 5wI | 10wM |
|---|---|---|---|---|---|---|---|---|---|---|---|---|---|---|---|---|---|
| Test | | | | | | | | | | | | | | | | | |
| All First | 109 | 187 | 16 | 5753 | 221 | 33.64 | 13 | 24 | 79 | - | 236 | 241 | 5 | 48.20 | 2-41 | - | - |
| 1-day Int | | | | | | | | | | | | | | | | | |
| NatWest | 5 | 5 | 0 | 202 | 78 | 40.40 | - | 1 | - | - | | | | | | | |
| B & H | 15 | 15 | 2 | 522 | 91 * | 40.15 | - | 5 | 5 | - | | | | | | | |
| Sunday | 41 | 40 | 4 | 1415 | 98 | 39.30 | - | 14 | 13 | - | | | | | | | |

# MIKE, G. W.                    Nottinghamshire

**Name:** Gregory Wentworth Mike
**Role:** Right-hand bat, right-arm medium-fast bowler
**Born:** 14 July 1966, Nottingham
**Height:** 6ft 1in **Weight:** 14st
**Nickname:** Wenters
**County debut:** 1989
**1st-Class 50s:** 6
**1st-Class 5 w. in innings:** 2
**1st-Class catches:** 11
**Place in batting averages:** 171st av. 23.83
(1994 233rd av. 15.86)
**Place in bowling averages:**
(1994 78th av. 31.60)
**Strike rate:** (career 63.51)
**Parents:** Clinton and Kathleen
**Marital status:** Single
**Family links with cricket:** Father played
**Education:** Claremont Comprehensive; Basford College
**Qualifications:** 5 CSEs, 2 O-levels
**Career outside cricket:** Youth worker
**Overseas tours:** Nottinghamshire to Barbados 1987, 1988, 1991

**Overseas teams played for:** Geelong City, Australia 1990-91; Lancaster Park, New Zealand 1992-93
**Cricketers particularly admired:** Viv Richards, Ian Botham, Richard Hadlee
**Other sports followed:** All sports
**Relaxations:** Listening to music (swing beat, soul and reggae music)
**Opinions on cricket:** 'Great game.'
**Best batting:** 66* Nottinghamshire v Oxford University, The Parks 1995
**Best bowling:** 5-44 Nottinghamshire v Yorkshire, Middlesbrough 1994

## 1995 Season

| | M | Inns | NO | Runs | HS | Avge | 100s | 50s | Ct | St | O | M | Runs | Wkts | Avge | Best | 5wI | 10wM |
|---|---|---|---|---|---|---|---|---|---|---|---|---|---|---|---|---|---|---|
| Test | | | | | | | | | | | | | | | | | | |
| All First | 5 | 9 | 3 | 143 | 66 * | 23.83 | - | 2 | 1 | - | 88.5 | 18 | 294 | 7 | 42.00 | 4-87 | - | - |
| 1-day Int | | | | | | | | | | | | | | | | | | |
| NatWest | | | | | | | | | | | | | | | | | | |
| B & H | 6 | 2 | 0 | 18 | 9 | 9.00 | - | - | 1 | - | 60.3 | 10 | 265 | 5 | 53.00 | 2-73 | - | |
| Sunday | 6 | 3 | 1 | 10 | 9 | 5.00 | - | - | 1 | - | 45 | 2 | 234 | 8 | 29.25 | 2-21 | - | |

## Career Performances

| | M | Inns | NO | Runs | HS | Avge | 100s | 50s | Ct | St | Balls | Runs | Wkts | Avge | Best | 5wI | 10wM |
|---|---|---|---|---|---|---|---|---|---|---|---|---|---|---|---|---|---|
| Test | | | | | | | | | | | | | | | | | |
| All First | 40 | 61 | 11 | 994 | 66 * | 19.88 | - | 6 | 11 | | 5272 | 3108 | 83 | 37.44 | 5-44 | 2 | - |
| 1-day Int | | | | | | | | | | | | | | | | | |
| NatWest | 2 | 2 | 1 | 8 | 5 * | 8.00 | - | - | - | - | 108 | 84 | 1 | 84.00 | 1-71 | - | |
| B & H | 10 | 5 | 2 | 64 | 25 * | 21.33 | - | - | 3 | - | 585 | 430 | 12 | 35.83 | 4-44 | - | |
| Sunday | 54 | 35 | 7 | 301 | 51 * | 10.75 | - | 1 | 11 | - | 2156 | 2001 | 60 | 33.35 | 4-41 | - | |

51. Warwickshire have appeared in the last three NatWest Trophy finals.
Who were their three opponents?

# MILBURN, S. M. Hampshire

**Name:** Stuart Mark Milburn
**Role:** Right-hand bat, right-arm
medium-fast bowler
**Born:** 29 September 1972, Harrogate
**Height:** 6ft 1in **Weight:** 13st
**Nickname:** Miller, Mick
**County debut:** 1992 (Yorkshire)
**Place in bowling averages:** 11th av. 20.40
**Strike rate:** 41.40 (career 59.64)
**Parents:** Ken and Pam
**Wife and date of marriage:** Joanne, 30
September 1995
**Education:** Upper Nidderdale High School,
Pateley Bridge, Harrogate
**Qualifications:** 7 GCSEs, Diploma in
Catering
**Off-season:** Getting married, going on
honeymoon, moving to Hampshire
**Overseas teams played for:** Somerset West,
South Africa 1992-93

**Cricketers particularly admired:** Ian Botham, Richard Hadlee, Malcolm Marshall
**Other sports followed:** Golf, snooker
**Relaxations:** Going to gym, 'staying at home watching a video with a nice cold beer'
**Extras:** '1995 was the first year that I stayed fit all year. No injuries except food poisoning when I played at Edgbaston, where I missed one week through illness'
**Opinions on cricket:** 'I would like to see pitches prepared to keep bowlers interested instead of declaration pitches, although I think that four-day cricket has improved the pitches to force a result instead of a declaration on the last day.'
**Best batting:** 7 Yorkshire v Warwickshire, Edgbaston 1995
**Best bowling:** 4-68 Yorkshire v Northamptonshire, Sheffield 1995

## 1995 Season

|  | M | Inns | NO | Runs | HS | Avge | 100s | 50s | Ct | St | O | M | Runs | Wkts | Avge | Best | 5wI | 10wM |
|---|---|---|---|---|---|---|---|---|---|---|---|---|---|---|---|---|---|---|
| Test |  |  |  |  |  |  |  |  |  |  |  |  |  |  |  |  |  |  |
| All First | 3 | 6 | 1 | 15 | 7 | 3.00 | - | - | - | - | 69 | 15 | 204 | 10 | 20.40 | 4-68 | - | - |
| 1-day Int |  |  |  |  |  |  |  |  |  |  |  |  |  |  |  |  |  |  |
| NatWest |  |  |  |  |  |  |  |  |  |  |  |  |  |  |  |  |  |  |  |
| B & H |  |  |  |  |  |  |  |  |  |  |  |  |  |  |  |  |  |  |  |
| Sunday | 4 | 2 | 1 | 14 | 13 * | 14.00 | - | - | 1 | - | 24 | 1 | 118 | 2 | 59.00 | 2-29 | - |  |

|  | M | Inns | NO | Runs | HS | Avge | 100s | 50s | Ct | St | Balls | Runs | Wkts | Avge | Best | 5wI | 10wM |
|---|---|---|---|---|---|---|---|---|---|---|---|---|---|---|---|---|---|
| Test |  |  |  |  |  |  |  |  |  |  |  |  |  |  |  |  |  |
| All First | 6 | 8 | 2 | 22 | 7 | 3.66 | - | - | - | - | 835 | 431 | 14 | 30.78 | 4-68 | - | - |
| 1-day Int |  |  |  |  |  |  |  |  |  |  |  |  |  |  |  |  |  |
| NatWest |  |  |  |  |  |  |  |  |  |  |  |  |  |  |  |  |  |  |
| B & H |  |  |  |  |  |  |  |  |  |  |  |  |  |  |  |  |  |  |
| Sunday | 4 | 2 | 1 | 14 | 13 * | 14.00 | - | - | 1 | - | 144 | 118 | 2 | 59.00 | 2-29 | - |  |

# MILLNS, D. J. Leicestershire

**Name:** David James Millns
**Role:** Left-hand bat, right-arm fast bowler, slip fielder
**Born:** 27 February 1965, Clipstone, Nottinghamshire
**Height:** 6ft 3in **Weight:** 15st
**Nickname:** Trigger
**County debut:** 1988 (Nottinghamshire), 1990 (Leicestershire)
**County cap:** 1991
**50 wickets in a season:** 3
**1st-Class 50s:** 4
**1st-Class 5 w. in innings:** 17
**1st-Class 10 w. in match:** 2
**1st-Class catches:** 56
**Place in batting averages:** 160th av. 25.58 (1994 199th av. 20.47)
**Place in bowling averages:** 124th av. 41.68 (1994 24th av. 25.01)

**Strike rate:** 64.84 (career 48.97)
**Parents:** Bernard and Brenda
**Wife and date of marriage:** Wanda, 25 September 1993
**Family links with cricket:** Brother Paul plays league cricket in Nottinghamshire. Sister Jennie married Nottinghamshire cricketer Andy Pick. Father played for Notts Over 50s
**Education:** Samuel Barlow Junior; Garibaldi Comprehensive; North Notts College of Further Education; Nottingham Trent Polytechnic
**Career outside cricket:** 'Too busy with cricket career'
**Off-season:** 'Recovering from surgery on left Achilles tendon and watching as much football as possible'
**Overseas tours:** England A to Australia 1992-93; Leicestershire to South Africa 1994 and 1995, to Holland 1994

**Overseas teams played for:** Uitenhage, Port Elizabeth, South Africa 1988-89; Birkenhead, Auckland 1989-91; Tasmania, Australia 1994-95

**Cricketers particularly admired:** Allan Donald

**Other sports followed:** Football (Leicester City), rugby union (Leicester Tigers), basketball, American football

**Injuries:** Torn left Achilles, missed from mid-June to end of season

**Relaxations:** Holidays and reading

**Extras:** Harold Larwood Bowling Award 1984. Asked to be released by Nottinghamshire at the end of 1989 season and joined Leicestershire in 1990. Finished third in national bowling averages in 1990. Britannic Assurance Player of the Month in August 1991 after taking 9-37 v Derbyshire, the best Leicestershire figures since George Geary's 10-18 v Glamorgan in 1929. Players' representative on Cricketers' Association Executive for Leicestershire. Leicestershire Cricketer of the Year 1992. Leicestershire Bowling Award 1990, 1991, 1992 and 1994

**Opinions on cricket:** 'Would like to see a ban on all overseas players in first-class cricket down to club level.'

**Best batting:** 70 Leicestershire v Essex, Chelmsford 1995

**Best bowling:** 9-37 Leicestershire v Derbyshire, Derby 1991

## 1995 Season

|          | M | Inns | NO | Runs | HS | Avge | 100s | 50s | Ct | St | O | M | Runs | Wkts | Avge | Best | 5wI | 10wM |
|----------|---|------|----|----|------|------|------|-----|----|----|------|----|------|------|------|------|-----|------|
| Test     |   |      |    |    |      |      |      |     |    |    |      |    |      |      |      |      |     |      |
| All First | 8 | 14 | 2 | 307 | 70 | 25.58 | - | 2 | 4 | - | 205.2 | 27 | 792 | 19 | 41.68 | 3-47 | - | - |
| 1-day Int |   |      |    |    |      |      |      |     |    |    |      |    |      |      |      |      |     |      |
| NatWest  |   |      |    |    |      |      |      |     |    |    |      |    |      |      |      |      |     |      |
| B & H    | 4 | 2 | 0 | 7 | 6 | 3.50 | - | - | 1 | - | 23 | 3 | 85 | 5 | 17.00 | 4-26 | - |   |
| Sunday   | 1 | 0 | 0 | 0 | 0 | - | - | - | - | - | 4 | 0 | 27 | 0 | - | - | - | - |

## Career Performances

|          | M | Inns | NO | Runs | HS | Avge | 100s | 50s | Ct | St | Balls | Runs | Wkts | Avge | Best | 5wI | 10wM |
|----------|---|------|----|----|------|------|------|-----|----|----|-------|------|------|------|------|-----|------|
| Test     |   |      |    |    |      |      |      |     |    |    |       |      |      |      |      |     |      |
| All First | 106 | 126 | 47 | 1389 | 70 | 17.58 | - | 4 | 56 | - | 16358 | 9574 | 334 | 28.66 | 9-37 | 17 | 2 |
| 1-day Int |   |      |    |    |      |      |      |     |    |    |       |      |      |      |      |     |      |
| NatWest  | 7 | 2 | 2 | 36 | 29 * | - | - | - | 2 | - | 438 | 273 | 11 | 24.81 | 3-22 | - |   |
| B & H    | 14 | 7 | 4 | 37 | 11 * | 12.33 | - | - | 2 | - | 660 | 469 | 20 | 23.45 | 4-26 | - |   |
| Sunday   | 35 | 17 | 8 | 98 | 20 * | 10.88 | - | - | 8 | - | 1320 | 1172 | 25 | 46.88 | 2-11 | - |   |

# MIRZA, P. Worcestershire

**Name:** Parvaz Mirza
**Role:** Right-hand bat, right-arm
fast-medium bowler
**Born:** 17 December 1970, Birmingham
**Height:** 5ft 11in **Weight:** 11st 8lbs
**Nickname:** Parv
**County debut:** 1994
**1st-Class 5 w. innings:** 1
**1st-Class catches:** 6
**Place in bowling averages:** 141st av. 47.21
**Parents:** Mirza Sher Baz (deceased) and
Zarda Bi
**Family links with cricket:** Younger brother,
Maneer, is a talented all-rounder
**Education:** Small Heath School, East
Birmingham College
**Extras:** Died suddenly from natural causes at
his home in Birmingham on 24 September
1995. He had been in perfect health. He had

undergone heart surgery as a baby, but had not suffered from any heart condition
**Best batting:** 40 Worcestershire v Kent, Canterbury 1994
**Best bowling:** 5-110 Worcestershire v Derbyshire, Kidderminster 1995

## 1995 Season

|          | M  | Inns | NO | Runs | HS  | Avge | 100s | 50s | Ct | St | O     | M  | Runs | Wkts | Avge  | Best  | 5wI | 10wM |
|----------|----|------|----|------|-----|------|------|-----|----|----|-------|----|------|------|-------|-------|-----|------|
| Test     |    |      |    |      |     |      |      |     |    |    |       |    |      |      |       |       |     |      |
| All First | 6  | 10   | 2  | 39   | 18* | 4.87 | -    | -   | 5  | -  | 175.1 | 40 | 661  | 14   | 47.21 | 5-110 | 1   | -    |
| 1-day Int |    |      |    |      |     |      |      |     |    |    |       |    |      |      |       |       |     |      |
| NatWest  | 1  | 0    | 0  | 0    | 0   | -    | -    | -   | -  | -  | 11    | 0  | 61   | 1    | 61.00 | 1-61  | -   |      |
| B & H    | 1  | 0    | 0  | 0    | 0   | -    | -    | -   | -  | -  | 9     | 0  | 40   | 0    | -     | - -   | -   |      |
| Sunday   | 13 | 3    | 3  | 2    | 2*  | -    | -    | -   | 2  | -  | 65    | 2  | 337  | 17   | 19.82 | 4-27  | -   |      |

## Career Performances

|          | M  | Inns | NO | Runs | HS  | Avge | 100s | 50s | Ct | St | Balls | Runs | Wkts | Avge  | Best  | 5wI | 10wM |
|----------|----|------|----|------|-----|------|------|-----|----|----|-------|------|------|-------|-------|-----|------|
| Test     |    |      |    |      |     |      |      |     |    |    |       |      |      |       |       |     |      |
| All First | 9  | 15   | 3  | 86   | 40  | 7.16 | -    | -   | 6  | -  | 1421  | 854  | 23   | 37.13 | 5-110 | 1   | -    |
| 1-day Int |    |      |    |      |     |      |      |     |    |    |       |      |      |       |       |     |      |
| NatWest  | 1  | 0    | 0  | 0    | 0   | -    | -    | -   | -  | -  | 66    | 61   | 1    | 61.00 | 1-61  | -   |      |
| B & H    | 1  | 0    | 0  | 0    | 0   | -    | -    | -   | -  | -  | 54    | 40   | 0    | -     | - -   | -   |      |
| Sunday   | 16 | 4    | 3  | 2    | 2*  | 2.00 | -    | -   | 2  | -  | 492   | 419  | 20   | 20.95 | 4-27  | -   |      |

# MOFFAT, S. P.                          Middlesex

**Name:** Scott Park Moffat
**Role:** Right-hand bat, off-spin bowler
**Born:** 1 February 1973, Germiston,
South Africa
**Height:** 6ft **Weight:** 13st 7lbs
**Nickname:** Fraz
**County debut:** No first-team appearance
**Parents:** Duncan and Dagny
**Marital status:** Single
**Family links with cricket:** Father played
league cricket in the Transvaal
**Education:** Bedfordview, South Africa;
Aldenham School, Hertfordshire; Swansea
University
**Qualifications:** 8 GCSEs, 3 A-levels, BSc in
Economics, senior coaching award
**Off-season:** Playing cricket in South Africa
**Overseas tours:** Radlett to India 1995
**Overseas teams played for:** RAU,
Transvaal, South Africa
**Cricketers particularly admired:** Jimmy Cook, Mike Atherton, Graeme Hick, David
Bowen, Andrew Varley
**Other sports followed:** Golf, football (Tottenham Hotspur)
**Injuries:** Wrist ligaments, out for five weeks
**Relaxations:** Socialising, eating out, reading and fishing
**Extras:** Played for Hertfordshire since 1992. Represented NAYC in 1992. Won the
UAU with Swansea University
**Opinions on cricket:** 'Too much cricket is played throughout from first-class to club
cricket and therefore leaves less time to practise and work on faults'

# MOLES, A. J. Warwickshire

**Name:** Andrew James Moles
**Role:** Right-hand opening bat, right-arm medium bowler
**Born:** 12 February 1961, Solihull
**Height:** 5ft 10in **Weight:** 'Above average'
**Nickname:** Moler
**County debut:** 1986
**County cap:** 1987
**1000 runs in a season:** 6
**1st-Class 50s:** 83
**1st-Class 100s:** 26
**1st-Class 200s:** 4
**1st-Class catches:** 129
**One-Day 100s:** 2
**Place in batting averages:** 48th av. 44.37
(1994 18th av. 50.76)
**Strike rate:** (career 84.90)
**Parents:** Stuart Francis and Gillian Margaret
**Wife and date of marriage:**
Jacquie, 17 December 1988
**Children:** Daniel

**Family links with cricket:** Brother plays club cricket
**Education:** Finham Park Comprehensive, Coventry; Henley College of Further Education; Butts College of Further Education
**Qualifications:** 3 O-levels, 4 CSEs, Toolmaker/Standard Room Inspector City & Guilds
**Career outside cricket:** Selling corporate hospitality
**Overseas teams played for:** Griqualand West, South Africa 1986-88
**Cricketers particularly admired:** Dennis Amiss, Fred Gardner, Tom Moody
**Other sports followed:** Football, golf
**Relaxations:** Playing golf and spending time with family
**Best batting:** 230* Griqualand West v Northern Transvaal B, Verwoerdburg 1988-89
**Best bowling:** 3-21 Warwickshire v Oxford University, The Parks 1987

## 1995 Season

|         | M | Inns | NO | Runs | HS  | Avge  | 100s | 50s | Ct | St | O | M | Runs | Wkts | Avge | Best | 5wI | 10wM |
|---------|---|------|----|------|-----|-------|------|-----|----|----|---|---|------|------|------|------|-----|------|
| Test    |   |      |    |      |     |       |      |     |    |    |   |   |      |      |      |      |     |      |
| All First | 9 | 16 | 0  | 710  | 131 | 44.37 | 1    | 6   | 5  | -  | 7 | 0 | 22   | 0    | -    | -    | -   | -    |
| 1-day Int |   |      |    |      |     |       |      |     |    |    |   |   |      |      |      |      |     |      |
| NatWest | 1 | 1    | 0  | 90   | 90  | 90.00 | -    | 1   | -  | -  |   |   |      |      |      |      |     |      |
| B & H   | 5 | 5    | 0  | 237  | 89  | 47.40 | -    | 3   | 1  | -  |   |   |      |      |      |      |     |      |
| Sunday  | 5 | 5    | 0  | 103  | 46  | 20.60 | -    | -   | -  | -  |   |   |      |      |      |      |     |      |

## Career Performances

|        | M   | Inns | NO | Runs  | HS    | Avge  | 100s | 50s | Ct  | St | Balls | Runs | Wkts | Avge  | Best | 5wI | 10wM |
|--------|-----|------|----|-------|-------|-------|------|-----|-----|----|-------|------|------|-------|------|-----|------|
| Test   |     |      |    |       |       |       |      |     |     |    |       |      |      |       |      |     |      |
| All First | 205 | 369 | 37 | 13767 | 230 * | 41.46 | 26 | 83 | 129 | - | 3396 | 1882 | 40 | 47.05 | 3-21 | - | - |
| 1-day Int |   |      |    |       |       |       |      |     |     |    |       |      |      |       |      |     |      |
| NatWest | 29 | 29 | 3 | 962 | 127 | 37.00 | 2 | 5 | 4 | - | 90 | 81 | 0 | - | - | - | - |
| B & H   | 30 | 29 | 0 | 931 | 89 | 32.10 | - | 11 | 8 | - | 300 | 224 | 4 | 56.00 | 1-11 | - | |
| Sunday  | 91 | 86 | 4 | 2139 | 96 * | 26.08 | - | 15 | 25 | - | 446 | 415 | 7 | 59.28 | 2-24 | - | |

# MONTGOMERIE, R. R.     Northamptonshire

**Name:** Richard Robert Montgomerie
**Role:** Right-hand opening bat, right-arm
off-spin bowler
**Born:** 3 July 1971, Rugby
**Height:** 5ft 11in **Weight:** 12st
**Nickname:** Albert, Chesh, Baaaa, Monty
**County debut:** 1991
**County Cap:** 1995
**1000 runs in season:** 1
**1st-Class 50s:** 18
**1st-Class 100s:** 5
**1st-Class catches:** 56
**Place in batting averages:** 153rd av. 27.47
(1994 96th av. 34.25)
**Parents:** Robert and Gillian
**Marital status:** Single
**Family links with cricket:** Father captained
Oxfordshire

**Education:** Rugby School; Worcester
College, Oxford University
**Qualifications:** 12 O-levels, 4 A-levels, BA (Chemistry)
**Career outside cricket:** Chemist
**Off-season:** Playing in Australia
**Overseas tours:** Oxford University to Namibia 1991
**Cricketers particularly admired:** 'Many, particularly Anil Kumble this year'
**Other sports followed:** All sports, particularly hockey, rackets and real tennis, 'I
enjoy watching or reading about any sport without being an avid follower of anyone'
**Injuries:** Broken finger, out for three weeks
**Relaxations:** Any sport, good television, reading and 'occasionally testing my brain'
**Extras:** Scored unbeaten 50 in each innings of 1991 Varsity match and was Oxford
captain in 1994. Oxford rackets Blue 1990. Captain Combined Universities 1994

**Opinions on cricket:** 'Four-day cricket should remain as it is.'
**Best batting:** 192 Northamptonshire v Kent, Canterbury 1995

## 1995 Season

|  | M | Inns | NO | Runs | HS | Avge | 100s | 50s | Ct | St | O | M | Runs | Wkts | Avge | Best | 5wI | 10wM |
|---|---|---|---|---|---|---|---|---|---|---|---|---|---|---|---|---|---|---|
| Test |  |  |  |  |  |  |  |  |  |  |  |  |  |  |  |  |  |  |
| All First | 14 | 24 | 1 | 632 | 192 | 27.47 | 1 | 2 | 27 | - |  |  |  |  |  |  |  |  |
| 1-day Int |  |  |  |  |  |  |  |  |  |  |  |  |  |  |  |  |  |  |
| NatWest | 5 | 5 | 0 | 223 | 109 | 44.60 | 1 | 1 | 1 | - |  |  |  |  |  |  |  |  |
| B & H | 1 | 1 | 0 | 5 | 5 | 5.00 | - | - | - | - |  |  |  |  |  |  |  |  |
| Sunday | 12 | 11 | 0 | 329 | 60 | 29.90 | - | 3 | 6 | - |  |  |  |  |  |  |  |  |

## Career Performances

|  | M | Inns | NO | Runs | HS | Avge | 100s | 50s | Ct | St | Balls | Runs | Wkts | Avge | Best | 5wI | 10wM |
|---|---|---|---|---|---|---|---|---|---|---|---|---|---|---|---|---|---|
| Test |  |  |  |  |  |  |  |  |  |  |  |  |  |  |  |  |  |
| All First | 60 | 102 | 10 | 2993 | 192 | 32.53 | 5 | 18 | 56 | - | 96 | 65 | 0 | - | - | - | - |
| 1-day Int |  |  |  |  |  |  |  |  |  |  |  |  |  |  |  |  |  |
| NatWest | 5 | 5 | 0 | 223 | 109 | 44.60 | 1 | 1 | 1 | - |  |  |  |  |  |  |  |
| B & H | 7 | 7 | 0 | 214 | 75 | 30.57 | - | 2 | - | - | 6 | 0 | 0 | - | - | - |
| Sunday | 17 | 16 | 0 | 465 | 74 | 29.06 | - | 4 | 7 | - |  |  |  |  |  |  |  |

# MOODY, T. M. Worcestershire

**Name:** Thomas Masson Moody
**Role:** Right-hand bat, right-arm medium bowler, county captain
**Born:** 2 October 1965, Adelaide
**Height:** 6ft 7in  **Weight:** 16st
**Nickname:** Moods, Tex
**County debut:** 1990 (Warwickshire), 1991 (Worcestershire)
**County cap:** 1990 (Warwickshire), 1991 (Worcestershire)
**Test debut:** 1989-90
**Tests:** 8
**One-Day Internationals:** 34
**1000 runs in a season:** 4
**1st-Class 50s:** 67
**1st-Class 100s:** 43
**1st-Class 200s:** 3
**1st-Class 5 w. in innings:** 1
**1st-Class 10 w. in match:** 1

**1st-Class catches:** 200
**One-Day 100s:** 10
**Place in batting averages:** 12th av. 55.17 (1994 31st av. 46.40)
**Strike rate:** (career 73.51)
**Parents:** John and Janet
**Wife and date of marriage:** Helen, 3 March 1993
**Children:** Jackson, 5 March 1995
**Family links with cricket:** Father played A Grade cricket in South Australia
**Education:** Guildford Grammar School, Western Australia
**Qualifications:** HSE
**Career outside cricket:** Sports shop owner
**Off-season:** Playing cricket in Australia
**Overseas tours:** Australia to India/Pakistan (World Cup) 1987, to England 1989, to India 1989-90, to Sri Lanka 1992
**Overseas teams played for:** Western Australia 1985-95; Midland Guildford, Perth, Western Australia
**Cricketers particularly admired:** Dennis Lillee, Allan Border, Viv Richards, Rod Marsh
**Other sports followed:** Aussie Rules football (West Coast Eagles), football, golf, tennis
**Injuries:** Back
**Relaxations:** Golf, sleeping and films
**Extras:** Scored 150s in both innings of 1988-89 Sheffield Shield final for Western Australia v Queensland. Hit a century against Warwickshire during Australia's 1989 tour and signed on a one-year contract with them for 1990. Hit centuries in first three first-class matches for Warwickshire, and seven in first eight matches – a unique achievement. Scored the (then) fastest ever first-class century v Glamorgan in 26 minutes – taking advantage of declaration bowling. Reached 1000 first-class runs in first season of county cricket in only 12 innings – another record. Released by Warwickshire at the end of the 1990 season after they had chosen Allan Donald as their one overseas player and was signed by Worcestershire for 1991 when Graeme Hick was no longer considered an overseas player. Not re-signed for 1993 season because he was expected to be touring with the Australian team, although in the event he was not selected. Re-signed for 1994 season. Scored 180* and shared record unbeaten partnership with Tim Curtis in the semi-final of the NatWest Trophy 1994. Appointed Worcestershire's captain for 1996 season after replacing Tim Curtis halfway through the 1995 season
**Opinions on cricket:** 'We need more quality not quantity.'
**Best batting:** 272 Western Australia v Tasmania, Hobart 1994-95
**Best bowling:** 7-43 Western Australia v Victoria, Perth 1990-91

---

52. Which two players share the record for the most centuries in Roses matches and how many have they scored?

---

| | M | Inns | NO | Runs | HS | Avge | 100s | 50s | Ct | St | O | M | Runs | Wkts | Avge | Best | 5wI | 10wM |
|---|---|---|---|---|---|---|---|---|---|---|---|---|---|---|---|---|---|---|
| Test | | | | | | | | | | | | | | | | | | |
| All First | 18 | 31 | 2 | 1600 | 168 | 55.17 | 5 | 7 | 31 | - | 72.1 | 20 | 209 | 5 | 41.80 | 2-23 | - | - |
| 1-day Int | | | | | | | | | | | | | | | | | | |
| NatWest | 2 | 2 | 0 | 37 | 27 | 18.50 | - | - | 2 | - | | | | | | | | |
| B & H | 6 | 5 | 2 | 209 | 75 * | 69.66 | - | 2 | 3 | - | 10 | 4 | 19 | 1 | 19.00 | 1-10 | - | |
| Sunday | 17 | 17 | 2 | 797 | 108 | 53.13 | 2 | 6 | 6 | - | 19 | 0 | 69 | 3 | 23.00 | 3-25 | - | |

**Career Performances**

| | M | Inns | NO | Runs | HS | Avge | 100s | 50s | Ct | St | Balls | Runs | Wkts | Avge | Best | 5wI | 10wM |
|---|---|---|---|---|---|---|---|---|---|---|---|---|---|---|---|---|---|
| Test | 8 | 14 | 0 | 456 | 106 | 32.57 | 2 | 3 | 9 | - | 432 | 147 | 2 | 73.50 | 1-17 | - | - |
| All First | 204 | 339 | 26 | 14647 | 272 | 46.79 | 43 | 67 | 200 | - | 11027 | 4833 | 150 | 32.22 | 7-43 | 1 | 1 |
| 1-day Int | 34 | 32 | 3 | 751 | 89 | 25.89 | - | 7 | 10 | - | 894 | 651 | 16 | 40.68 | 3-56 | - | |
| NatWest | 11 | 11 | 3 | 575 | 180 * | 71.87 | 1 | 3 | 9 | - | 373 | 182 | 8 | 22.75 | 2-33 | - | |
| B & H | 25 | 23 | 6 | 1101 | 110 * | 64.76 | 2 | 9 | 9 | - | 660 | 370 | 13 | 28.46 | 4-59 | - | |
| Sunday | 75 | 73 | 8 | 3013 | 160 | 46.35 | 7 | 23 | 21 | - | 1365 | 911 | 31 | 29.38 | 3-18 | - | |

# MOORES, P.        Sussex

**Name:** Peter Moores
**Role:** Right-hand bat, wicket-keeper
**Born:** 18 December 1962, Macclesfield, Cheshire
**Height:** 6ft **Weight:** 13st
**Nickname:** Billy
**County debut:** 1983 (Worcestershire), 1985 (Sussex)
**County cap:** 1989
**1st-Class 50s:** 28
**1st-Class 100s:** 4
**1st-Class catches:** 413
**1st-Class stumpings:** 42
**Place in batting averages:** 191st av. 22.00 (1994 160th av. 25.53)
**Parents:** Bernard and Winifred
**Wife and date of marriage:** Karen Jane, 28 September 1989
**Children:** Natalie Marie, 4 August 1993
**Family links with cricket:** Brothers, Anthony, Stephen and Robert, all play club cricket
**Education:** King Edward VI School, Macclesfield
**Qualifications:** 7 O-levels, 3 A-levels, advanced cricket coach

**Career outside cricket:** Coach for Sussex in off-season

**Overseas tours:** Christians in Sport to India 1989-90; MCC to Namibia 1990-91, to Leeward Islands 1991-92, to Bahrain 1994-95

**Overseas teams played for:** Orange Free State, South Africa 1988-89

**Cricketers particularly admired:** Bob Taylor, Alan Knott, Clive Lloyd

**Other sports followed:** Football, golf

**Relaxations:** Golf, wine and old films

**Extras:** On MCC groundstaff in 1982 before joining Worcestershire in latter half of 1982 season. Joined Sussex in 1985

**Opinions on cricket:** 'I feel we need to split the Sunday and the four-day game for two reasons: 1. It would prevent injuries in the Sunday game affecting the result in the four-day game. 2. It would benefit players not to have to switch "codes" halfway through a game.'

**Best batting:** 116 Sussex v Somerset, Hove 1989

## 1995 Season

|        | M  | Inns | NO | Runs | HS   | Avge  | 100s | 50s | Ct  | St | O | M | Runs | Wkts | Avge | Best | 5wI | 10wM |
|--------|----|------|----|------|------|-------|------|-----|-----|----|---|---|------|------|------|------|-----|------|
| Test   |    |      |    |      |      |       |      |     |     |    |   |   |      |      |      |      |     |      |
| All First | 19 | 32 | 2 | 660 | 94 | 22.00 | - | 5 | 43 | 2 |   |   |      |      |      |      |     |      |
| 1-day Int |    |      |    |      |      |       |      |     |     |    |   |   |      |      |      |      |     |      |
| NatWest | 2  | 1    | 0  | 8    | 8    | 8.00  | -    | -   | 2   | -  |   |   |      |      |      |      |     |      |
| B & H   | 3  | 2    | 1  | 9    | 6 *  | 9.00  | -    | -   | 1   | -  |   |   |      |      |      |      |     |      |
| Sunday  | 17 | 16   | 8  | 382  | 89 * | 47.75 | -    | 2   | 17  | 4  |   |   |      |      |      |      |     |      |

## Career Performances

|        | M   | Inns | NO | Runs | HS   | Avge  | 100s | 50s | Ct  | St | Balls | Runs | Wkts | Avge | Best | 5wI | 10wM |
|--------|-----|------|----|------|------|-------|------|-----|-----|----|-------|------|------|------|------|-----|------|
| Test   |     |      |    |      |      |       |      |     |     |    |       |      |      |      |      |     |      |
| All First | 192 | 279 | 33 | 5942 | 116 | 24.15 | 4 | 28 | 413 | 42 | 18 | 16 | 0 | - | - | - | - |
| 1-day Int |     |      |    |      |      |       |      |     |     |    |       |      |      |      |      |     |      |
| NatWest | 21  | 14   | 3  | 153  | 26   | 13.90 | -    | -   | 29  | 2  |       |      |      |      |      |     |      |
| B & H   | 25  | 19   | 3  | 241  | 76   | 15.06 | -    | 1   | 20  | 2  |       |      |      |      |      |     |      |
| Sunday  | 138 | 108  | 34 | 1477 | 89 * | 19.95 | -    | 5   | 125 | 21 |       |      |      |      |      |     |      |

# MORRIS, A. C.                                    Yorkshire

**Name:** Alexander Corfield Morris
**Role:** Left-hand bat, right-arm medium
bowler
**Born:** 4 October 1976, Barnsley
**Height:** 6ft 4in **Weight:** 12st 10lbs
**County debut:** 1995
**1st-Class catches:** 1
**Parents:** Chris and Janet
**Marital status:** Single
**Education:** Holgate School, Barnsley;
Barnsley College
**Qualifications:** 4 GCSEs, NCA coaching
**Off-season:** Studying and touring with
England U19 to Zimbabwe
**Overseas tours:** England U19 to West Indies
1994-95 as captain
**Cricketers particularly admired:** Michael
Vaughan, Anthony McGrath, Michael Bevan
**Other sports followed:** Football (Barnsley FC)
**Injuries:** Back, out for one week
**Relaxations:** Listening to music, relaxing with mates
**Extras:** Played for Yorkshire U11-U19. Played for England U15 against Barbados and
in 1994 for both England U17 and U19 against India. Played junior football with both
Barnsley and Rotherham and had trials for Nottingham Forest and Leeds
**Opinions on cricket:** 'Should play more coloured clothing cricket and more one-day
games'
**Best batting:** 1 Yorkshire v Hampshire, Southampton 1995

## 1995 Season

|          | M | Inns | NO | Runs | HS | Avge | 100s | 50s | Ct | St | O | M | Runs | Wkts | Avge | Best | 5wI | 10wM |
|----------|---|------|----|----|-----|------|------|-----|----|----|----|---|------|------|------|------|-----|------|
| Test     |   |      |    |      |    |      |      |     |    |    |    |   |      |      |      |      |     |      |
| All First | 1 | 2 | 1 | 1 | 1 | 1.00 | - | - | 1 | - | 17 | 5 | 62 | 0 | - | - | - | - |
| 1-day Int |   |      |    |      |    |      |      |     |    |    |    |   |      |      |      |      |     |      |
| NatWest  | 1 | 1 | 1 | 1 | 1 * | - | - | - | - | - | 8 | 0 | 43 | 1 | 43.00 | 1-43 | - |      |
| B & H    |   |      |    |      |    |      |      |     |    |    |    |   |      |      |      |      |     |      |
| Sunday   | 4 | 2 | 0 | 7 | 7 | 3.50 | - | - | - | - | 19 | 3 | 72 | 2 | 36.00 | 1-8 |     |      |

## Career Performances

|  | M | Inns | NO | Runs | HS | Avge | 100s | 50s | Ct | St | Balls | Runs | Wkts | Avge | Best | 5wI | 10wM |
|---|---|---|---|---|---|---|---|---|---|---|---|---|---|---|---|---|---|
| Test |  |  |  |  |  |  |  |  |  |  |  |  |  |  |  |  |  |
| All First | 1 | 2 | 1 | 1 | 1 | 1.00 | - | - | 1 | - | 102 | 62 | 0 | - |  | - | - |
| 1-day Int |  |  |  |  |  |  |  |  |  |  |  |  |  |  |  |  |  |
| NatWest | 1 | 1 | 1 | 1 | 1* | - | - | - | - | - | 48 | 43 | 1 | 43.00 | 1-43 | - |  |
| B & H |  |  |  |  |  |  |  |  |  |  |  |  |  |  |  |  |  |  |
| Sunday | 4 | 2 | 0 | 7 | 7 | 3.50 | - | - | - | - | 114 | 72 | 2 | 36.00 | 1-8 | - |  |

# MORRIS, H. Glamorgan

**Name:** Hugh Morris
**Role:** Left-hand bat, right-arm
medium bowler
**Born:** 5 October 1963, Cardiff
**Height:** 5ft 8in **Weight:** 12st 7lbs
**Nickname:** Banners
**County debut:** 1981
**County cap:** 1986
**Benefit:** 1994 (£118,837)
**Test debut:** 1991
**Tests:** 3
**1000 runs in a season:** 8
**1st-Class 50s:** 85
**1st-Class 100s:** 43
**1st-Class catches:** 169
**One-Day 100s:** 11
**Place in batting averages:** 21st av. 52.46
(1994 124th av. 30.51)
**Parents:** Roger and Anne
**Wife:** Debra Jane

**Children:** Bethan Louise; Emily Charlotte
**Family links with cricket:** Father played club cricket. Brother played junior representative
**Education:** Blundells School; South Glamorgan Institute of Higher Education
**Qualifications:** 9 O-levels, 2 A-levels, 1 AO-level, BA (Hons) in Physical Education,
NCA coaching award, senior coaching award
**Career outside cricket:** Journalism and coaching
**Off-season:** After dinner speaking, journalism and coaching
**Overseas tours:** English Public Schoolboys to West Indies 1980-81, to Sri Lanka
1982-83; England A to Pakistan 1990-91 (called up to join England tour party in
Australia), to Bermuda and West Indies 1991-92, to South Africa 1993-94; England to
Australia 1990-91

**Overseas teams played for:** CBC Old Boys, Pretoria 1985-87
**Cricketers particularly admired:** Viv Richards, Ian Botham, David Gower, Brian Lara, Courtney Walsh
**Other sports followed:** Rugby (Aberavon and Cardiff College), golf (handicap 11)
**Injuries:** Back, out for two weeks
**Relaxations:** Spending time at home with family, travelling, eating good food and drinking good wine
**Extras:** Highest schoolboy cricket average in 1979 (89.71), 1981 (184.60) and 1982 (149.20). Captain of English Schools U19 in 1981 and 1982; played for England YC v West Indies 1982, and captain v Australia 1983. Appointed youngest ever Glamorgan captain 1986, but resigned in 1989 to concentrate on batting. In 1990 scored most runs in a season by a Glamorgan player (2276) and hit most centuries (10). After missing selection for the tour of Australia, appointed captain for England A tour of Pakistan in 1990-91; then, after Gooch had required a hand operation and England had lost the first Test to Australia, he flew out to join the senior tour until the England captain recovered. Glamorgan Player of the Year. Captained the England A tour to South Africa 1993-94 and Wombwell Cricket Lovers' Society Captain of the Year 1993. Played first-class rugby for Aberavon 1984-85 and South Glamorgan Institute, scoring over 150 points. Stood down as Glamorgan captain at the end of the 1995 season
**Best batting:** 166* Glamorgan v Nottinghamshire, Cardiff 1995
**Best bowling:** 1-6 Glamorgan v Oxford University, The Parks 1987

## 1995 Season

| | M | Inns | NO | Runs | HS | Avge | 100s | 50s | Ct | St | O | M | Runs | Wkts | Avge | Best | 5wI | 10wM |
|---|---|---|---|---|---|---|---|---|---|---|---|---|---|---|---|---|---|---|
| Test | | | | | | | | | | | | | | | | | | |
| All First | 18 | 33 | 3 | 1574 | 166 * | 52.46 | 6 | 8 | 5 | - | | | | | | | | |
| 1-day Int | | | | | | | | | | | | | | | | | | |
| NatWest | 4 | 4 | 1 | 155 | 105 * | 51.66 | 1 | - | 1 | - | | | | | | | | |
| B & H | 1 | 1 | 0 | 9 | 9 | 9.00 | - | - | - | - | | | | | | | | |
| Sunday | 16 | 15 | 2 | 434 | 100 | 33.38 | 1 | 1 | 7 | - | | | | | | | | |

## Career Performances

| | M | Inns | NO | Runs | HS | Avge | 100s | 50s | Ct | St | Balls | Runs | Wkts | Avge | Best | 5wI | 10wM |
|---|---|---|---|---|---|---|---|---|---|---|---|---|---|---|---|---|---|
| Test | 3 | 6 | 0 | 115 | 44 | 19.16 | - | - | 3 | - | | | | | | | |
| All First | 279 | 482 | 46 | 16780 | 166 * | 38.48 | 43 | 85 | 169 | - | 348 | 380 | 2 | 190.00 | 1-6 | - | - |
| 1-day Int | | | | | | | | | | | | | | | | | |
| NatWest | 31 | 30 | 4 | 1250 | 154 * | 48.07 | 4 | 4 | 10 | - | 12 | 12 | 0 | - | - | - | |
| B & H | 35 | 35 | 2 | 907 | 143 * | 27.48 | 3 | 3 | 13 | - | 18 | 15 | 1 | 15.00 | 1-14 | - | |
| Sunday | 160 | 155 | 17 | 4895 | 127 * | 35.47 | 4 | 33 | 55 | - | | | | | | | |

# MORRIS, J. E.  Durham

**Name:** John Edward Morris
**Role:** Right-hand bat, right-arm
medium bowler
**Born:** 1 April 1964, Crewe
**Height:** 5ft 10in **Weight:** 13st 6lbs
**Nickname:** Animal
**County debut:** 1982 (Derbyshire), 1994
(Durham)
**County cap:** 1986 (Derbyshire)
**Test debut:** 1990
**Tests:** 3
**One-Day Internationals:** 8
**1000 runs in a season:** 10
**1st-Class 50s:** 85
**1st-Class 100s:** 42
**1st-Class 200s:** 2
**1st-Class catches:** 118
**One-Day 100s:** 6
**Place in batting averages:** 77th av. 38.14
(1994 51st av. 42.14)
**Parents:** George (Eddie) and Jean
**Wife and date of marriage:** Sally, 30 September 1990
**Children:** Thomas Edward, 27 June 1991
**Family links with cricket:** Father played for Crewe for many years as an opening
bowler
**Education:** Shavington Comprehensive School; Dane Bank College of Further Education
**Qualifications:** O-levels
**Off-season:** BMW car sales, marketing and coaching for Durham
**Overseas tours:** England to Australia 1990-91; Romany to South Africa 1993: MCC
to Bahrain 1994-95
**Overseas teams played for:** Umbilo, Durban, South Africa 1982-84; Alex Old Boys,
Pietermaritzburg, South Africa 1984-85; Subiaco-Floriat, Western Australia 1986-87;
Griqualand West, South Africa 1988-89, 1993-94; Protea, Johannesburg, South Africa 1993
**Other sports followed:** Golf, football (Derby County and Crewe FC)
**Relaxations:** The golf course and home life
**Extras:** Youngest player to score a Sunday League century. Left Derbyshire at end of
1993 season
**Opinions on cricket:** 110 overs in a day is too many. A more realistic amount would be
100 overs per day
**Best batting:** 229 Derbyshire v Gloucestershire, Cheltenham 1993
**Best bowling:** 1-6 Derbyshire v Cambridge University, Fenner's 1993

## 1995 Season

| | M | Inns | NO | Runs | HS | Avge | 100s | 50s | Ct | St | O | M | Runs | Wkts | Avge | Best | 5wI | 10wM |
|---|---|---|---|---|---|---|---|---|---|---|---|---|---|---|---|---|---|---|
| Test | | | | | | | | | | | | | | | | | | |
| All First | 19 | 35 | 1 | 1297 | 169 | 38.14 | 3 | 6 | 9 | - | | | | | | | | |
| 1-day Int | | | | | | | | | | | | | | | | | | |
| NatWest | 2 | 2 | 0 | 39 | 29 | 19.50 | - | - | 2 | - | | | | | | | | |
| B & H | 4 | 4 | 1 | 120 | 62 | 40.00 | - | 2 | - | - | | | | | | | | |
| Sunday | 14 | 13 | 1 | 342 | 74 | 28.50 | - | 3 | 3 | - | | | | | | | | |

## Career Performances

| | M | Inns | NO | Runs | HS | Avge | 100s | 50s | Ct | St | Balls | Runs | Wkts | Avge | Best | 5wI | 10wM |
|---|---|---|---|---|---|---|---|---|---|---|---|---|---|---|---|---|---|
| Test | 3 | 5 | 2 | 71 | 32 | 23.66 | - | - | 3 | - | | | | | | | |
| All First | 279 | 466 | 29 | 17301 | 229 | 39.59 | 42 | 85 | 118 | - | 986 | 902 | 7 | 128.85 | 1-6 | - | - |
| 1-day Int | 8 | 8 | 1 | 167 | 63 * | 23.85 | - | 1 | 2 | - | | | | | | | |
| NatWest | 24 | 23 | 3 | 604 | 94 * | 30.20 | - | 4 | 8 | - | | | | | | | |
| B & H | 49 | 45 | 6 | 1144 | 123 | 29.33 | 2 | 6 | 9 | - | 24 | 14 | 0 | - | | - | - |
| Sunday | 173 | 164 | 12 | 4000 | 134 | 26.31 | 4 | 19 | 38 | - | 3 | 7 | 0 | - | | - | - |

# MORRIS, R. S. M.  Hampshire

**Name:** Robert Sean Milner Morris
**Role:** Right-hand bat, off-spin bowler, occasional wicket-keeper
**Born:** 10 September 1968, Great Horwood, Buckinghamshire
**Height:** 6ft **Weight:** 12st 7lbs
**Nickname:** Stowers, The Saint
**County debut:** 1992
**1st-Class 50s:** 7
**1st-Class 100s:** 2
**1st-Class catches:** 38
**Place in batting averages:** 204th av. 20.44 (1994 22nd av. 49.00)
**Parents:** Stuart and Sue
**Marital status:** Single
**Family links with cricket:** Great-grandfather played for Worcestershire
**Education:** Swanbourne House School; Stowe School; Durham University 'and Yung's Bar, Bangkok'
**Qualifications:** 8 O-levels, 2 A-levels, BA (Dunelm) Sociology
**Career outside cricket:** 'Beach bumming'

**Off-season:** Golfing in Malaysia, training in Cape Town
**Overseas tours:** Stowe to Australia 1982; Combined Universities to Barbados 1990
**Overseas teams played for:** Midland Guildford, Perth, Western Australia 1987-88; St Albans, Buenos Aires 1991-92; Tigers Parow, Cape Town 1993-94; Western Province, Cape Town 1994-95
**Cricketers particularly admired:** Bill Whyman, Tim Brooke-Taylor, Kevan James
**Other sports followed:** Big game fishing ('SA Blue Marlin record holder'), rugby (Bath RFC)
**Relaxations:** 'Beach life and ornithology'
**Extras:** Captained Durham University hockey and cricket, played hockey for County Durham and the North
**Best batting:** 174 Hampshire v Nottinghamshire, Basingstoke 1994

## 1995 Season

|          | M  | Inns | NO | Runs | HS | Avge  | 100s | 50s | Ct | St | O | M | Runs | Wkts | Avge | Best | 5wI | 10wM |
|----------|----|------|----|------|----|-------|------|-----|----|----|---|---|------|------|------|------|-----|------|
| Test     |    |      |    |      |    |       |      |     |    |    |   |   |      |      |      |      |     |      |
| All First | 10 | 18   | 0  | 368  | 47 | 20.44 | -    | -   | 13 | -  |   |   |      |      |      |      |     |      |
| 1-day Int |    |      |    |      |    |       |      |     |    |    |   |   |      |      |      |      |     |      |
| NatWest  | 1  | 1    | 0  | 23   | 23 | 23.00 | -    | -   | -  | -  |   |   |      |      |      |      |     |      |
| B & H    | 1  | 0    | 0  | 0    | 0  | -     | -    | -   | -  | -  |   |   |      |      |      |      |     |      |
| Sunday   | 13 | 13   | 0  | 422  | 87 | 32.46 | -    | 2   | 3  | -  |   |   |      |      |      |      |     |      |

## Career Performances

|          | M  | Inns | NO | Runs | HS   | Avge  | 100s | 50s | Ct | St | Balls | Runs | Wkts | Avge | Best | 5wI | 10wM |
|----------|----|------|----|------|------|-------|------|-----|----|----|-------|------|------|------|------|-----|------|
| Test     |    |      |    |      |      |       |      |     |    |    |       |      |      |      |      |     |      |
| All First | 32 | 58   | 4  | 1635 | 174  | 30.27 | 2    | 7   | 38 | -  | 4     | 1    | 0    | -    | -    | -   | -    |
| 1-day Int |    |      |    |      |      |       |      |     |    |    |       |      |      |      |      |     |      |
| NatWest  | 3  | 3    | 1  | 86   | 34 * | 43.00 | -    | -   | -  | -  |       |      |      |      |      |     |      |
| B & H    | 1  | 0    | 0  | 0    | 0    | -     | -    | -   | -  | -  |       |      |      |      |      |     |      |
| Sunday   | 18 | 18   | 1  | 481  | 87   | 28.29 | -    | 2   | 5  | -  |       |      |      |      |      |     |      |

# MOXON, M. D. Yorkshire

**Name:** Martyn Douglas Moxon
**Role:** Right-hand bat, right-arm medium bowler
**Born:** 4 May 1960, Barnsley
**Height:** 6ft 1in **Weight:** 14st
**Nickname:** Frog
**County debut:** 1981
**County cap:** 1984
**Benefit:** 1993
**Test debut:** 1986

**Tests:** 10
**One-Day Internationals:** 8
**1000 runs in a season:** 12
**1st-Class 50s:** 106
**1st-Class 100s:** 41
**1st-Class 200s:** 4
**1st-Class catches:** 209
**One-Day 100s:** 6
**One-Day 5 w. in innings:** 1
**Place in batting averages:** 2nd av. 76.33
(1994 7th av. 56.07)
**Strike rate:** (career 94.64)
**Parents:** Audrey and Derek (deceased)
**Wife and date of marriage:** Sue, October
1985
**Children:** Charlotte Louise, 13 March 1990;
Jonathan James, 6 May 1993
**Family links with cricket:** Father and
grandfather played local league cricket
**Education:** Holgate Grammar School, Barnsley
**Qualifications:** 8 O-levels, 3 A-levels, HNC in Business Studies, NCA coaching
award
**Off-season:** Coaching in England
**Overseas tours:** England to India and Australia 1984-85, to Australia and New
Zealand 1987-88; England B to Sri Lanka 1985-86; England A to Bermuda and West
Indies 1991-92, to Australia 1992-93
**Overseas teams played for:** Griqualand West, South Africa 1982-83 and 1983-84
**Cricketers particularly admired:** Viv Richards
**Other sports followed:** Football (supporter of Barnsley FC) and golf
**Injuries:** Broke right thumb twice, out for ten weeks in total
**Relaxations:** Listening to most types of music, having a drink with friends
**Extras:** Captained Yorkshire Schools U15, North of England U15 and Yorkshire Senior
Schools. Played for Wombwell Cricket Lovers' Society U18 side. First Yorkshire player
to make centuries in his first two Championship games in Yorkshire, 116 v Essex at
Headingley (on debut) and 111 v Derbyshire at Sheffield, and scored 153 in his first
innings in a Roses match. Picked for Lord's Test of 1984 v West Indies, but withdrew
through injury and had to wait until 1986 to make Test debut. Appointed Yorkshire
captain in 1990. Appointed captain of England A team to tour Bermuda and West Indies
1991-92, but played no first-class cricket owing to injury. Wombwell Cricket Lovers'
Society Cricketer of the Year 1991. Scored 274* against Worcester which is the highest
individual score for Yorkshire since the war. Stood down as Yorkshire captain at the end
of the 1995 season
**Best batting:** 274* Yorkshire v Worcestershire, Worcester 1994
**Best bowling:** 3-24 Yorkshire v Hampshire, Southampton 1989

## 1995 Season

| | M | Inns | NO | Runs | HS | Avge | 100s | 50s | Ct | St | O | M | Runs | Wkts | Avge | Best | 5wl | 10wM |
|---|---|---|---|---|---|---|---|---|---|---|---|---|---|---|---|---|---|---|
| Test | | | | | | | | | | | | | | | | | | |
| All First | 13 | 23 | 8 | 1145 | 203 * | 76.33 | 3 | 8 | 6 | - | | | | | | | | |
| 1-day Int | | | | | | | | | | | | | | | | | | |
| NatWest | 1 | 1 | 0 | 15 | 15 | 15.00 | - | - | - | - | | | | | | | | |
| B & H | 3 | 3 | 1 | 97 | 66 * | 48.50 | - | 1 | 1 | - | | | | | | | | |
| Sunday | 4 | 4 | 0 | 23 | 8 | 5.75 | - | - | 1 | - | | | | | | | | |

## Career Performances

| | M | Inns | NO | Runs | HS | Avge | 100s | 50s | Ct | St | Balls | Runs | Wkts | Avge | Best | 5wl | 10wM |
|---|---|---|---|---|---|---|---|---|---|---|---|---|---|---|---|---|---|
| Test | 10 | 17 | 1 | 455 | 99 | 28.43 | - | 3 | 10 | - | 48 | 30 | 0 | - | - | - | - |
| All First | 289 | 495 | 44 | 19446 | 274 * | 43.11 | 41 | 106 | 209 | - | 2650 | 1481 | 28 | 52.89 | 3-24 | - | - |
| 1-day Int | 8 | 8 | 0 | 174 | 70 | 21.75 | - | 1 | 5 | - | | | | | | | |
| NatWest | 27 | 27 | 6 | 961 | 107 * | 45.76 | 1 | 8 | 12 | - | 156 | 85 | 5 | 17.00 | 2-19 | - | |
| B & H | 42 | 42 | 6 | 1643 | 141 * | 45.63 | 2 | 12 | 17 | - | 342 | 242 | 9 | 26.88 | 5-31 | 1 | |
| Sunday | 139 | 131 | 8 | 3843 | 129 * | 31.24 | 3 | 23 | 43 | - | 984 | 868 | 21 | 41.33 | 3-29 | - | |

# MULLALLY, A. D. Leicestershire

**Name:** Alan David Mullally
**Role:** Right-hand bat, left-arm fast bowler
**Born:** 12 July 1969, Southend
**Height:** 6ft 5in **Weight:** 14st
**Nickname:** Bob, Bryan, Eric, Spider, 'too many to mention'
**County debut:** 1988 (Hampshire), 1990 (Leicestershire)
**County cap:** 1993
**50 wickets in a season:** 2
**1st-Class 5 w. in innings:** 6
**1st-Class 10 w. in match:** 1
**1st-Class catches:** 23
**Place in bowling averages:** 57th av. 28.81 (1994 115th av. 38.03)
**Strike rate:** 59.35 (career 70.21)
**Parents:** Michael and Ann
**Marital status:** Single
**Family links with cricket:** 'Dad bowls a vicious arm ball on the back patio, two brothers play club cricket in Perth and sister fancied David Gower'
**Education:** Cannington High School and Primary, Perth, Australia; Wembley and Carlisle Technical College

**Qualifications:** 'This and that'
**Career outside cricket:** Musician
**Off-season:** Training hard
**Overseas tours:** Western Australia to India 1990-91; Leicestershire to Jamaica 1992-93
**Overseas teams played for:** Western Australia; Victoria; Australian YC
**Cricketers particularly admired:** Geoff Marsh, Dermot Reeve
**Other sports followed:** Australian rules football, basketball, most sports
**Relaxations:** Music
**Extras:** English-qualified as he was born in Southend, he made his first-class debut for Western Australia in the 1987-88 Sheffield Shield final, and played for Australian YC 1988-89. Played one match for Hampshire in 1988 before joining Leicestershire
**Opinions on cricket:** 'National anthem before each Test match. Forget playing first-class cricket on club grounds .'
**Best batting:** 34 Western Australia v Tasmania, Perth 1989-90
**Best bowling:** 7-72 Leicestershire v Gloucestershire, Leicester 1993

## 1995 Season

|         | M  | Inns | NO | Runs | HS   | Avge | 100s | 50s | Ct | St | O     | M   | Runs | Wkts | Avge  | Best | 5wI | 10wM |
|---------|----|------|----|------|------|------|------|-----|----|----|-------|-----|------|------|-------|------|-----|------|
| Test    |    |      |    |      |      |      |      |     |    |    |       |     |      |      |       |      |     |      |
| All First | 19 | 30 | 6  | 150  | 22   | 6.25 | -    | -   | -  | -  | 583.4 | 172 | 1700 | 59   | 28.81 | 6-50 | 2   | -    |
| 1-day Int |  |      |    |      |      |      |      |     |    |    |       |     |      |      |       |      |     |      |
| NatWest | 2  | 1    | 1  | 10   | 10 * | -    | -    | -   | -  | -  | 19    | 5   | 59   | 2    | 29.50 | 2-27 | -   |      |
| B & H   | 5  | 2    | 0  | 3    | 3    | 1.50 | -    | -   | -  | -  | 42.4  | 4   | 160  | 2    | 80.00 | 2-39 | -   |      |
| Sunday  | 14 | 4    | 1  | 19   | 10 * | 6.33 | -    | -   | 3  | -  | 101.2 | 6   | 486  | 10   | 48.60 | 2-23 | -   |      |

## Career Performances

|         | M   | Inns | NO | Runs | HS   | Avge  | 100s | 50s | Ct | St | Balls | Runs | Wkts | Avge  | Best | 5wI | 10wM |
|---------|-----|------|----|------|------|-------|------|-----|----|----|-------|------|------|-------|------|-----|------|
| Test    |     |      |    |      |      |       |      |     |    |    |       |      |      |       |      |     |      |
| All First | 107 | 124 | 31 | 710  | 34   | 7.63  | -    | -   | 23 | -  | 19169 | 9162 | 273  | 33.56 | 7-72 | 6   | 1    |
| 1-day Int |   |      |    |      |      |       |      |     |    |    |       |      |      |       |      |     |      |
| NatWest | 12  | 6    | 3  | 34   | 19 * | 11.33 | -    | -   | 2  | -  | 726   | 398  | 16   | 24.87 | 2-22 | -   |      |
| B & H   | 21  | 8    | 2  | 21   | 11   | 3.50  | -    | -   | -  | -  | 1150  | 710  | 12   | 59.16 | 2-30 | -   |      |
| Sunday  | 69  | 31   | 14 | 175  | 38   | 10.29 | -    | -   | 15 | -  | 3029  | 2288 | 68   | 33.64 | 3-9  | -   |      |

53. Who won the County 2nd XI Championship in 1995?

# MUNTON, T. A. Warwickshire

**Name:** Timothy Alan Munton
**Role:** Right-hand bat, right-arm fast-medium
bowler, county vice-captain
**Born:** 30 July 1965, Melton Mowbray
**Height:** 6ft 6in **Weight:** 15st 7lbs
**Nickname:** Harry, Captain Sensible
**County debut:** 1985
**County cap:** 1990
**Test debut:** 1991
**Tests:** 2
**50 wickets in a season:** 5
**1st-Class 5 w. in innings:** 25
**1st-Class 10 w. in match:** 6
**1st-Class catches:** 66
**One-Day 5 w. in innings:** 2
**Place in bowling averages:** 7th av. 19.83
(1994 8th av. 21.58)
**Strike rate:** 46.72 (career 59.68)
**Parents:** Alan and Brenda
**Wife and date of marriage:** Helen, 20 September 1986
**Children:** Camilla Dallas, 13 August 1988; Harrison George Samuel, 17 February
1992
**Family links with cricket:** Father played for Buckminster CC
**Education:** Sarson High School; King Edward VII Upper School, Melton Mowbray
**Qualifications:** CSE grade 1, 9 O-levels, 1 A-level,
**Overseas tours:** England A to Pakistan 1990-91, to Bermuda and West Indies 1991-
92, to Pakistan 1995-96
**Overseas teams played for:** Victoria University, Wellington, New Zealand 1985-86;
Witwatersrand University, Johannesburg, South Africa 1986-87
**Cricketers particularly admired:** Richard Hadlee, David Gower
**Other sports followed:** Basketball, soccer, golf
**Relaxations:** 'Playing golf, spending time with my family'
**Extras:** Appeared for Leicestershire 2nd XI 1982-84. Second highest wicket-taker in
1990 with 78. Called into England A squad to tour Bermuda and West Indies 1991-92
when Dermot Reeve replaced the injured Angus Fraser on the senior tour. Was voted
Warwickshire Player of the Season 1990, 1991 and 1994. Missed the first six months of
the 1995 season recovering from a back operation. He was flown out to Pakistan as a
replacement for the injured Mike Smith on the England A tour, and played in the second
'Test' less than a week after his arrival
**Best batting:** 47 Warwickshire v Kent, Edgbaston 1992
**Best bowling:** 8-89 Warwickshire v Middlesex, Edgbaston 1991

## 1995 Season

| | M | Inns | NO | Runs | HS | Avge | 100s | 50s | Ct | St | O | M | Runs | Wkts | Avge | Best | 5wI | 10wM |
|---|---|---|---|---|---|---|---|---|---|---|---|---|---|---|---|---|---|---|
| Test | | | | | | | | | | | | | | | | | | |
| All First | 11 | 10 | 6 | 66 | 19 * | 16.50 | - | - | 3 | - | 373.5 | 111 | 952 | 48 | 19.83 | 5-37 | 3 | 1 |
| 1-day Int | | | | | | | | | | | | | | | | | | |
| NatWest | 4 | 0 | 0 | 0 | 0 | - | - | - | 1 | - | 48 | 13 | 118 | 6 | 19.66 | 2-18 | - | |
| B & H | | | | | | | | | | | | | | | | | | |
| Sunday | 11 | 0 | 0 | 0 | 0 | - | - | - | 7 | - | 82 | 7 | 324 | 14 | 23.14 | 3-45 | - | |

## Career Performances

| | M | Inns | NO | Runs | HS | Avge | 100s | 50s | Ct | St | Balls | Runs | Wkts | Avge | Best | 5wI | 10wM |
|---|---|---|---|---|---|---|---|---|---|---|---|---|---|---|---|---|---|
| Test | 2 | 2 | 1 | 25 | 25 * | 25.00 | - | - | - | - | 405 | 200 | 4 | 50.00 | 2-22 | - | - |
| All First | 191 | 192 | 77 | 1162 | 47 | 10.10 | - | - | 66 | - | 32824 | 14369 | 550 | 26.12 | 8-89 | 25 | 6 |
| 1-day Int | | | | | | | | | | | | | | | | | |
| NatWest | 31 | 9 | 5 | 9 | 5 | 2.25 | - | - | 5 | - | 1912 | 922 | 35 | 26.34 | 3-36 | - | |
| B & H | 27 | 13 | 8 | 52 | 13 | 10.40 | - | - | 6 | - | 1702 | 969 | 33 | 29.36 | 4-35 | - | |
| Sunday | 133 | 33 | 24 | 122 | 15 * | 13.55 | - | - | 27 | - | 5747 | 3710 | 132 | 28.10 | 5-23 | 2 | |

# MUSHTAQ AHMED Somerset

**Name:** Mushtaq Ahmed
**Role:** Right-hand bat, leg-break bowler
**Born:** 28 June 1970, Sahiwal, Pakistan
**Height:** 5ft 4in **Weight:** 13st
**Nickname:** Mushy
**County debut:** 1993
**County cap:** 1993
**Test debut:** 1991-92
**Tests:** 18
**One-Day Internationals:** 82
**50 wickets in a season:** 2
**1st-Class 50s:** 5
**1st-Class 5w. in innings:** 32
**1st-Class 10w. in match:** 8
**1st-Class catches:** 63
**Place in batting averages:** 252nd av. 14.80
(1994 237th av. 15.27)
**Place in bowling averages:** 69th av. 29.69
(1994 34th av. 26.57)
**Strike rate:** 60.12 (career 53.47)
**Marital status:** Married
**Career outside cricket:** Banking

**Off-season:** On tour with Pakistan

**Overseas tours:** Pakistan to Australia 1989-90, to New Zealand and Australia (World Cup) 1991-92, to England 1992, Australia and South Africa 1992-93, to New Zealand 1993-94, 1995-96, to Sri Lanka 1994, to Australia 1995-96, to New Zealand 1995-96, to India and Sri Lanka (World Cup) 1995-96

**Overseas teams played for:** United Bank, Pakistan

**Cricketers particularly admired:** Viv Richards, Waqar Younis

**Other sports followed:** Football (Brazil), hockey

**Relaxations:** Watching videos, eating, spending time with family

**Extras:** Took 6-81 against England for Punjab Chief Minister's XI 1987. Finished second to Wasim Akram as Pakistan's highest wicket-taker in the World Cup 1991-92 with 16 wickets. Received specialist coaching from Intikhab Alam. Named Somerset Player of the Year 1993. Replaced as overseas player by Shane Lee for the 1995 season as he is expected to be named in the Pakistan squad to tour England

**Opinions on cricket:** 'I like the four-day county championship because it gives spin bowlers a good chance to bowl long spells. One-day cricket is exciting to watch and play in. A good cricketer can play all types of cricket successfully. Most of those against that view have never played it.'

**Best batting:** 90 Somerset v Sussex, Taunton 1993

**Best bowling:** 9-93 Multan v Peshawar, Sahiwal 1986-87

## 1995 Season

| | M | Inns | NO | Runs | HS | Avge | 100s | 50s | Ct | St | O | M | Runs | Wkts | Avge | Best | 5wI | 10wM |
|---|---|---|---|---|---|---|---|---|---|---|---|---|---|---|---|---|---|---|
| Test | | | | | | | | | | | | | | | | | | |
| All First | 17 | 23 | 2 | 311 | 62 * | 14.80 | - | 1 | 4 | - | 952 | 286 | 2821 | 95 | 29.69 | 6-38 | 7 | 2 |
| 1-day Int | | | | | | | | | | | | | | | | | | |
| NatWest | 1 | 1 | 0 | 28 | 28 | 28.00 | - | - | - | - | 12 | 1 | 56 | 1 | 56.00 | 1-56 | - | |
| B & H | 6 | 4 | 0 | 36 | 21 | 9.00 | - | - | - | - | 60.4 | 11 | 160 | 10 | 16.00 | 4-29 | - | |
| Sunday | 14 | 12 | 5 | 118 | 23 * | 16.85 | - | - | 1 | - | 99.1 | 7 | 492 | 10 | 49.20 | 3-40 | - | |

## Career Performances

| | M | Inns | NO | Runs | HS | Avge | 100s | 50s | Ct | St | Balls | Runs | Wkts | Avge | Best | 5wI | 10wM |
|---|---|---|---|---|---|---|---|---|---|---|---|---|---|---|---|---|---|
| Test | 18 | 26 | 6 | 163 | 27 | 8.15 | - | - | 5 | - | 3338 | 1605 | 44 | 36.47 | 4-121 | - | - |
| All First | 118 | 138 | 19 | 1809 | 90 | 15.20 | - | 6 | 63 | - | 26470 | 12960 | 495 | 26.18 | 9-93 | 32 | 8 |
| 1-day Int | 82 | 41 | 16 | 203 | 17 * | 8.12 | - | - | 18 | - | 4095 | 3015 | 92 | 32.77 | 3-14 | - | |
| NatWest | 7 | 5 | 1 | 82 | 35 | 20.50 | - | - | 1 | - | 466 | 252 | 9 | 28.00 | 3-26 | - | |
| B & H | 8 | 6 | 0 | 46 | 21 | 7.66 | - | - | - | - | 472 | 243 | 10 | 24.30 | 4-29 | - | |
| Sunday | 34 | 30 | 8 | 236 | 32 | 10.72 | - | - | 2 | - | 1522 | 1080 | 33 | 32.72 | 3-17 | - | |

# NASH, D. C.         Middlesex

**Name:** David Charles Nash
**Role:** Right-hand bat, wicket-keeper
**Born:** 19 January 1978, Chertsey, Surrey
**Height:** 5ft 7in **Weight:** 9st 7lbs
**Nickname:** Nashy
**County debut:** 1995 (one-day)
**Parents:** Dave and Chris
**Marital status:** Single
**Family links with cricket:** Father played club cricket
**Education:** Sunbury Manor; Malvern College, Worcestershire
**Qualifications:** 10 GCSEs
**Overseas tours:** England U15 to South Africa 1993; British Airways Youth Team to West Indies 1993-94; England U19 to Zimbabwe 1995-96
**Cricketers particularly admired:** Colin Metson, Mark Ramprakash, and George Simons 'for his big heart'

**Other sports followed:** Football (Brentford) and most other sports
**Relaxations:** Listening to music, playing golf and going out with friends
**Extras:** A qualified referee. Represented Middlesex at all ages. Played for England U14, U15, U17 and U18. Once took six wickets in six balls when aged 11 – 'when I could bowl!'. *Daily Telegraph* Southern England Batting Award 1993. Seaxe Young Player of the Year 1993
**Opinions on cricket:** 'I would like to see county 2nd XI matches extended to four days so there is more chance of a result. I would also like to see day/night cricket introduced into the English game.'

## 1995 Season

|          | M | Inns | NO | Runs | HS | Avge | 100s | 50s | Ct | St | O | M | Runs | Wkts | Avge | Best | 5wI | 10wM |
|----------|---|------|----|------|----|------|------|-----|----|----|---|---|------|------|------|------|-----|------|
| Test     |   |      |    |      |    |      |      |     |    |    |   |   |      |      |      |      |     |      |
| All First |   |      |    |      |    |      |      |     |    |    |   |   |      |      |      |      |     |      |
| 1-day Int |   |      |    |      |    |      |      |     |    |    |   |   |      |      |      |      |     |      |
| NatWest  |   |      |    |      |    |      |      |     |    |    |   |   |      |      |      |      |     |      |
| B & H    |   |      |    |      |    |      |      |     |    |    |   |   |      |      |      |      |     |      |
| Sunday   | 1 | 0    | 0  | 0    | 0  | -    | -    | -   | -  | 2  | 1 |   |      |      |      |      |     |      |

## Career Performances

|  | M | Inns | NO | Runs | HS | Avge | 100s | 50s | Ct | St | Balls | Runs | Wkts | Avge | Best | 5wI | 10wM |
|---|---|------|-----|------|-----|------|------|-----|-----|-----|-------|------|------|------|------|-----|------|
| Test | | | | | | | | | | | | | | | | | |
| All First | | | | | | | | | | | | | | | | | |
| 1-day Int | | | | | | | | | | | | | | | | | |
| NatWest | | | | | | | | | | | | | | | | | |
| B & H | | | | | | | | | | | | | | | | | |
| Sunday | 1 | 0 | 0 | 0 | 0 | - | - | - | 2 | 1 | | | | | | | |

# NASH, D. J. Middlesex

**Name:** Dion Joseph Nash
**Role:** Right-hand bat, right arm
medium-fast bowler
**Born:** 20 November 1971, Auckland,
New Zealand
**Height:** 6ft 2in **Weight:** 13st 5lbs
**Nickname:** Nashi
**County debut:** 1995
**County cap:** 1995
**Test debut:** 1992
**Tests:** 10
**One-Day Internationals:** 15
**50 w. in a season:** 1
**1st-Class 50s:** 5
**1st-Class 5 w. in innings:** 7
**1st-Class 10 w. in match:** 1
**1st-Class catches:** 29
**Place in batting averages:** 199th av. 20.61
**Place in bowling averages:** 61st av. 29.07
(1994 69th av. 31.00)

**Strike rate:** 53.09 (career 20.61)
**Parents:** Paul and Joan
**Marital status:** Single
**Education:** Pargaville High School; Auckland Grammar School; Otago University
**Qualifications:** School Certificate, 6th Form Certificate, University Bursary Bachelor
of Arts
**Career outside cricket:** 'Yet to pursue one.'
**Off-season:** Playing cricket for and in New Zealand
**Overseas tours:** New Zealand Youth to India 1991-92; New Zealand to Zimbabwe
and Sri Lanka 1992, to England 1994, to South Africa 1994-95, to India 1995-96, to
India and Pakistan (World Cup) 1995-96

**Cricketers particularly admired:** Dennis Lillee, Dean Jones
**Other sports followed:** Rugby, surfing
**Injuries:** Small rib cartilage tear, missed two weeks. Broke finger playing against West Indies in New Zealand 1994-95
**Relaxations:** Reading, music, all sports
**Extras:** Suspended from the New Zealand side for three One-Day Internationals in controversial circumstances along with team-mates Stephen Fleming and Matthew Hart in January 1995. Awarded county cap in August 1995
**Opinions on cricket:** 'More Test cricket should be played as opposed to increasing the number of one-day games.'
**Best batting:** 67 Middlesex v Essex, Chelmsford 1995
**Best bowling:** 6-30 New Zealand Academy XI v Northern Districts, Rotorua 1993-94

## 1995 Season

|  | M | Inns | NO | Runs | HS | Avge | 100s | 50s | Ct | St | O | M | Runs | Wkts | Avge | Best | 5wI | 10wM |
|---|---|---|---|---|---|---|---|---|---|---|---|---|---|---|---|---|---|---|
| Test |  |  |  |  |  |  |  |  |  |  |  |  |  |  |  |  |  |  |
| All First | 19 | 25 | 4 | 433 | 67 | 20.61 | - | 3 | 10 | - | 460.1 | 90 | 1512 | 52 | 29.07 | 5-35 | 2 | - |
| 1-day Int |  |  |  |  |  |  |  |  |  |  |  |  |  |  |  |  |  |  |
| NatWest | 3 | 3 | 0 | 6 | 4 | 2.00 | - | - | 1 | - | 20 | 0 | 93 | 1 | 93.00 | 1-36 | - |  |
| B & H | 6 | 4 | 1 | 97 | 54 | 32.33 | - | 1 | 3 | - | 56 | 7 | 223 | 5 | 44.60 | 2-31 | - |  |
| Sunday | 13 | 8 | 0 | 109 | 35 | 13.62 | - | - | 4 | - | 85 | 4 | 365 | 16 | 22.81 | 3-34 | - |  |

## Career Performances

|  | M | Inns | NO | Runs | HS | Avge | 100s | 50s | Ct | St | Balls | Runs | Wkts | Avge | Best | 5wI | 10wM |
|---|---|---|---|---|---|---|---|---|---|---|---|---|---|---|---|---|---|
| Test | 10 | 16 | 5 | 176 | 56 | 16.00 | - | 1 | 7 | - | 2124 | 1014 | 32 | 31.68 | 6-76 | 2 | 1 |
| All First | 56 | 81 | 17 | 1163 | 67 | 18.17 | - | 5 | 28 | - | 8543 | 4100 | 146 | 28.08 | 6-30 | 7 | 1 |
| 1-day Int | 15 | 11 | 3 | 94 | 40 * | 11.75 | - | - | 4 | - | 654 | 541 | 12 | 45.08 | 3-43 | - |  |
| NatWest | 3 | 3 | 0 | 6 | 4 | 2.00 | - | - | 1 | - | 120 | 93 | 1 | 93.00 | 1-36 | - |  |
| B & H | 6 | 4 | 1 | 97 | 54 | 32.33 | - | 1 | 3 | - | 336 | 223 | 5 | 44.60 | 2-31 | - |  |
| Sunday | 13 | 8 | 0 | 109 | 35 | 13.62 | - | - | 4 | - | 510 | 365 | 16 | 22.81 | 3-34 | - |  |

---

54. Five players who captained their respective counties at some stage during 1995 were born outside Great Britain. Who were they, and which counties did they captain?

# NEWELL, K.

**Name:** Keith Newell
**Role:** Right-hand bat, occasional
medium-pace bowler
**Born:** 25 March 1972, Crawley
**Height:** 6ft **Weight:** 11st 10lbs
**Nickname:** Ede, Wheely
**County debut:** 1993 (one-day),
1995 (first-class)
**1st-Class 50s:** 2
**1st-Class 100s:** 1
**1st-Class catches:** 3
**Place in batting averages:** 138th av. 29.41
**Parents:** Peter Charles and Julie Anne
**Marital status:** Single
**Family links with cricket:** Father played
club cricket. Brother is on the Sussex staff
**Education:** Gossops Green Junior School;
Ifield Community College
**Qualifications:** 'A few token GCSE passes', coaching certificate
**Career outside cricket:** 'Cricket'
**Off-season:** Playing in Zimbabwe
**Overseas teams played for:** Zimbabwe Universals 1989-90; Bulawayo Athletic Club
1991-92, 1995-96; Riverside CC, Wellington 1993-94
**Cricketers particularly admired:** Matthew Church, Ian Botham
**Other sports followed:** Table tennis (National Schools Team Champions U16 and
U19), football, golf and 'would like to try motor racing'
**Relaxations:** Going to the cinema
**Extras:** 'Rather enjoyed scoring a hundred against the West Indies'
**Opinions on cricket:** 'I just think that we play too much cricket. It should somehow be
reduced.'
**Best batting:** 135 Sussex v West Indies, Hove 1995

## 1995 Season

| | M | Inns | NO | Runs | HS | Avge | 100s | 50s | Ct | St | O | M | Runs | Wkts | Avge | Best | 5wI | 10wM |
|---|---|---|---|---|---|---|---|---|---|---|---|---|---|---|---|---|---|---|
| Test | | | | | | | | | | | | | | | | | | |
| All First | 10 | 19 | 2 | 500 | 135 | 29.41 | 1 | 2 | 3 | - | 40 | 8 | 127 | 0 | - | | - | - | - |
| 1-day Int | | | | | | | | | | | | | | | | | | |
| NatWest | 2 | 2 | 0 | 100 | 52 | 50.00 | - | 1 | - | - | | | | | | | | |
| B & H | 1 | 1 | 0 | 35 | 35 | 35.00 | - | - | - | - | | | | | | | | |
| Sunday | 10 | 8 | 1 | 207 | 76 * | 29.57 | - | 1 | 2 | - | 9 | 0 | 58 | 0 | - | | - | |

## Career Performances

| | M | Inns | NO | Runs | HS | Avge | 100s | 50s | Ct | St | Balls | Runs | Wkts | Avge | Best | 5wl | 10wM |
|---|---|---|---|---|---|---|---|---|---|---|---|---|---|---|---|---|---|
| Test | | | | | | | | | | | | | | | | | |
| All First | 10 | 19 | 2 | 500 | 135 | 29.41 | 1 | 2 | 3 | - | 240 | 127 | 0 | - | - | - | - |
| 1-day Int | | | | | | | | | | | | | | | | | |
| NatWest | 2 | 2 | 0 | 100 | 52 | 50.00 | - | 1 | - | - | | | | | | | |
| B & H | 1 | 1 | 0 | 35 | 35 | 35.00 | - | - | - | - | | | | | | | |
| Sunday | 12 | 9 | 1 | 217 | 76 * | 27.12 | - | 1 | 2 | - | 114 | 127 | 0 | - | | - | - |

# NEWELL, M. Sussex

**Name:** Mark Newell
**Role:** Right-hand bat, right-arm fast-medium bowler
**Born:** 19 December 1973, Crawley
**Height:** 6ft 1in **Weight:** 12st
**Nickname:** Little Ede
**County debut:** No first-team appearance
**Parents:** Peter Charles and Julie Anne
**Marital status:** Single
**Family links with cricket:** Brother Keith also on the Sussex staff, father and younger brother Jonathan both play league cricket
**Education:** Hazelwick Comprehensive; City of Westminster College
**Qualifications:** 10 GCSEs, NCA Senior Coaching Award
**Overseas tours:** Sussex U18 to India 1990-91; Sussex U19 to Barbados (as captain) 1993-94
**Overseas teams played for:** Bulawayo Athletic Club, Zimbabwe 1991-92
**Cricketers particularly admired:** Justin Bates, Brian Lara, George Blackmore, Michael Atherton, Adrian Gobin
**Other sports followed:** Table tennis, football (West Ham)
**Relaxations:** Films and the film industry, sleeping
**Extras:** MCC Young Cricketer in 1994. Was on a sponsored scholarship at Arundel Castle which enabled him and two others to work, play and coach all over Sussex for two years. Played Sussex youth cricket since he was nine years old
**Opinions on cricket:** 'Playing situations between 1st XI and 2nd XI cricket (i.e.light, ground conditions, weather) should be the same. I've played some 2nd XI cricket in some atrocious conditions.'

# NEWELL, M.                    Nottinghamshire

**Name:** Michael Newell
**Role:** Right-hand opening bat, leg-break bowler, occasional wicket-keeper
**Born:** 25 February 1965, Blackburn
**Height:** 5ft 10in **Weight:** 11st
**Nickname:** Mugly, Tricky, Animal
**County debut:** 1984
**County cap:** 1987
**1000 runs in a season:** 1
**1st-Class 50s:** 24
**1st-Class 100s:** 6
**1st-Class 200s:** 1
**1st-Class catches:** 93
**1st-Class stumpings:** 1
**One-Day 100s:** 1
**Parents:** Barry and Janet
**Wife and date of marriage:**
Jayne, 23 September 1989

**Children:** Elizabeth Rose, 1 September 1993
**Family links with cricket:** Father chairman of Notts Unity CC and brother, Paul, is the captain
**Education:** West Bridgford Comprehensive
**Qualifications:** 8 O-levels, 3 A-levels. NCA advanced coach
**Cricketers particularly admired:** Mathew Dowman, Dominic Cork, James Hindson
**Other sports followed:** Rugby union, football, darts
**Relaxations:** 'Feet up, slippers on in front of the television. Spending time with my family.'
**Extras:** Captain and coach of Nottinghamshire 2nd XI (The Stiffs)
**Opinions on cricket:** 'There has been a lot of scornful criticism of county cricket and its players from press people who have been too quick to moan. There are a lot of very good players in this country and some excellent young ones. Four-day cricket should lead to a revival in our Test fixtures and should sort out the better players from the average ones.'
**Best batting:** 203* Nottinghamshire v Derbyshire, Derby 1987
**Best bowling:** 2-38 Nottinghamshire v Sri Lankans, Trent Bridge 1988

---

55. Who at the start of the 1996 season will become the longest-serving county player and in which year did he make his first-class debut?

**1995 Season (did not make any first-class or one-day appearances)**

## Career Performances

| | M | Inns | NO | Runs | HS | Avge | 100s | 50s | Ct | St | Balls | Runs | Wkts | Avge | Best | 5wI | 10wM |
|---|---|---|---|---|---|---|---|---|---|---|---|---|---|---|---|---|---|
| Test | | | | | | | | | | | | | | | | | |
| All First | 102 | 178 | 26 | 4636 | 203 * | 30.50 | 6 | 24 | 93 | 1 | 363 | 282 | 7 | 40.28 | 2-38 | - | - |
| 1-day Int | | | | | | | | | | | | | | | | | |
| NatWest | 5 | 5 | 0 | 136 | 60 | 27.20 | - | 1 | 3 | - | 6 | 10 | 0 | - | | - | - |
| B & H | 10 | 10 | 1 | 205 | 39 | 22.77 | - | - | 2 | - | | | | | | | |
| Sunday | 24 | 21 | 4 | 611 | 109 * | 35.94 | 1 | 3 | 8 | - | | | | | | | |

# NEWPORT, P. J. Worcestershire

**Name:** Philip John Newport
**Role:** Right-hand bat, right-arm
fast-medium bowler, outfielder
**Born:** 11 October 1962, High Wycombe
**Height:** 6ft 2in **Weight:** 13st 7lbs
**Nickname:** Schnozz, Newps
**County debut:** 1982
**County cap:** 1986
**Test debut:** 1988
**Tests:** 3
**50 wickets in a season:** 8
**1st-Class 50s:** 19
**1st-Class 5 w. in innings:** 33
**1st-Class 10 w. in match:** 3
**1st-Class catches:** 71
**One-Day 5 w. in innings:** 3
**Place in batting averages:** 155th av. 26.93
(1994 218th av. 18.15)
**Place in bowling averages:** 20th av. 22.47
(1994 72nd av. 31.20)
**Strike rate:** 47.65 (career 52.33)
**Parents:** John and Sheila Diana
**Wife and date of marriage:** Christine Anne, 26 October 1985
**Children:** Nathan Alexander, 10 May 1989
**Family links with cricket:** Brother Stewart is captain of Octopus CC in North London
**Education:** Royal Grammar School, High Wycombe; Portsmouth University
**Qualifications:** 8 O-levels, 3 A-levels, BA (Hons) Geography, coaching qualification
**Overseas tours:** NCA to Denmark 1981; England A to Pakistan 1990-91; England to
Australia 1990-91

**Overseas teams played for:** Vogeltown, New Plymouth, New Zealand 1986; Boland, South Africa 1987-88; Ginnenderra and ACT, Australia 1991; Northern Transvaal, South Africa 1992-93

**Other sports followed:** American football, basketball, golf

**Relaxations:** 'Cinema, spending time with my son (improving his golf swing and cover drive)'

**Extras:** Had trial as schoolboy for Southampton FC. Played cricket for NAYC England Schoolboys 1981 and for Buckinghamshire in Minor Counties Championship in 1981 and 1982. Selected for cancelled England tour to India 1988-89 and selected as a replacement for England's tour to Australia in 1990-91. Winner of Worcestershire's Dick Lygon Award 1992 and voted Worcestershire Player of the Year 1992 and 1993. Finished 3rd in the Whyte and Mackay bowling ratings in 1995

**Opinions on cricket:** 'County staffs will diminish in size as four-day cricket is bound to shrink each club's income.'

**Best batting:** 98 Worcestershire v New Zealanders, Worcester 1990

**Best bowling:** 8-52 Worcestershire v Middlesex, Lord's 1988

## 1995 Season

| | M | Inns | NO | Runs | HS | Avge | 100s | 50s | Ct | St | O | M | Runs | Wkts | Avge | Best | 5wI | 10wM |
|---|---|---|---|---|---|---|---|---|---|---|---|---|---|---|---|---|---|---|
| Test | | | | | | | | | | | | | | | | | | |
| All First | 18 | 23 | 8 | 404 | 50 | 26.93 | - | 1 | 2 | - | 548 | 148 | 1551 | 69 | 22.47 | 5-45 | 4 | - |
| 1-day Int | | | | | | | | | | | | | | | | | | |
| NatWest | 2 | 1 | 1 | 19 | 19 * | - | - | - | - | - | 19 | 3 | 72 | 3 | 24.00 | 2-53 | - | |
| B & H | 6 | 0 | 0 | 0 | 0 | - | - | - | - | - | 62 | 13 | 182 | 9 | 20.22 | 2-9 | - | |
| Sunday | 16 | 5 | 2 | 18 | 15 * | 6.00 | - | - | 2 | - | 106 | 10 | 409 | 17 | 24.05 | 5-32 | 1 | |

## Career Performances

| | M | Inns | NO | Runs | HS | Avge | 100s | 50s | Ct | St | Balls | Runs | Wkts | Avge | Best | 5wI | 10wM |
|---|---|---|---|---|---|---|---|---|---|---|---|---|---|---|---|---|---|
| Test | 3 | 5 | 1 | 110 | 40 * | 27.50 | - | - | 1 | - | 669 | 417 | 10 | 41.70 | 4-87 | - | - |
| All First | 251 | 293 | 87 | 5202 | 98 | 25.25 | - | 19 | 71 | - | 40354 | 20928 | 771 | 27.14 | 8-52 | 33 | 3 |
| 1-day Int | | | | | | | | | | | | | | | | | |
| NatWest | 27 | 13 | 4 | 117 | 25 | 13.00 | - | - | 2 | - | 1437 | 860 | 37 | 23.24 | 4-30 | - | |
| B & H | 46 | 21 | 6 | 149 | 28 | 9.93 | - | - | 9 | - | 2933 | 1475 | 68 | 21.69 | 5-22 | 2 | |
| Sunday | 150 | 67 | 25 | 433 | 26 * | 10.30 | - | - | 32 | - | 5920 | 4197 | 157 | 26.73 | 5-32 | 1 | |

# NICHOLAS, M. C. J.      Hampshire

**Name:** Mark Charles Jefford Nicholas
**Role:** Right-hand bat, 'I think I bowl, but no one else does'
**Born:** 29 September 1957, London
**Height:** 6ft **Weight:** 12st 5lbs
**Nickname:** Skip, Dougie, Cappy
**County debut:** 1978
**County cap:** 1982
**Benefit:** 1991 (£174,260)
**1000 runs in a season:** 10
**1st-Class 50s:** 81
**1st-Class 100s:** 36
**1st-Class 200s:** 1
**1st-Class 5 w. in innings:** 2
**1st-Class catches:** 214
**One-Day 100s:** 1
**Place in batting averages:** 69th av. 40.33
(1994 33rd av. 45.46)

**Strike rate:** (career 81.31)
**Parents:** Anne
**Marital status:** Single
**Family links with cricket:** Grandfather (F.W.H.) played for Essex as batsman and wicket-keeper and toured with MCC. Father played for Navy
**Education:** Fernden Prep School; Bradfield College
**Qualifications:** 9 O-levels, 3 A-levels
**Career outside cricket:** Broadcasting and journalism
**Off-season:** Working as journalist and broadcaster on England tour to South Africa
**Overseas tours:** English Counties XI to Zimbabwe 1984-85; England B to Sri Lanka (captain) 1985-86; England A to Zimbabwe and Kenya (captain) 1989-90
**Cricketers particularly admired:** Barry Richards, John Snow, Mike Brearley
**Other sports followed:** Most – football, golf, fives, squash
**Relaxations:** Theatre, music, golf, going out to dinner
**Extras:** Hampshire captain since 1985 but missed Hampshire's first NatWest final in 1994 after having his knuckle and finger broken a few days earlier by a delivery from Surrey's Waqar Younis in the Championship game between the two NatWest finalists. Retired from first-class cricket at the end of the 1995 season
**Opinions on cricket:** 'Four-day cricket should be played during the week and two, not three, one-day competitions should be played at weekends: 1. A B&H-style 50-over Sunday league with semi-finals and finals; 2. NatWest Trophy .'
**Best batting:** 206* Hampshire v Oxford University, The Parks 1982
**Best bowling:** 6-37 Hampshire v Somerset, Southampton 1989

## 1995 Season

| | M | Inns | NO | Runs | HS | Avge | 100s | 50s | Ct | St | O | M | Runs | Wkts | Avge | Best | 5wI | 10wM |
|---|---|---|---|---|---|---|---|---|---|---|---|---|---|---|---|---|---|---|
| Test | | | | | | | | | | | | | | | | | | |
| All First | 19 | 33 | 3 | 1210 | 147 | 40.33 | 4 | 4 | 5 | - | 7 | 0 | 26 | 0 | - | | - | - |
| 1-day Int | | | | | | | | | | | | | | | | | | |
| NatWest | 1 | 1 | 0 | 0 | 0 | 0.00 | - | - | - | - | | | | | | | | |
| B & H | 5 | 4 | 0 | 15 | 8 | 3.75 | - | - | - | - | 1.3 | 0 | 11 | 0 | - | | - | - |
| Sunday | 11 | 11 | 1 | 264 | 66 | 26.40 | - | 1 | 4 | - | 10 | 0 | 64 | 0 | - | | - | - |

## Career Performances

| | M | Inns | NO | Runs | HS | Avge | 100s | 50s | Ct | St | Balls | Runs | Wkts | Avge | Best | 5wI | 10wM |
|---|---|---|---|---|---|---|---|---|---|---|---|---|---|---|---|---|---|
| Test | | | | | | | | | | | | | | | | | |
| All First | 377 | 620 | 89 | 18262 | 206 * | 34.39 | 36 | 81 | 215 | - | 5855 | 3245 | 72 | 45.06 | 6-37 | 2 | - |
| 1-day Int | | | | | | | | | | | | | | | | | |
| NatWest | 44 | 38 | 6 | 972 | 71 | 30.37 | - | 7 | 14 | - | 521 | 346 | 9 | 38.44 | 2-39 | - | |
| B & H | 68 | 60 | 9 | 1236 | 74 | 24.23 | - | 4 | 19 | - | 1029 | 770 | 24 | 32.08 | 4-34 | - | |
| Sunday | 229 | 208 | 40 | 4738 | 108 | 28.20 | 1 | 27 | 74 | - | 1962 | 1847 | 59 | 31.30 | 4-30 | - | |

# NIXON, P. A.                    Leicestershire

**Name:** Paul Andrew Nixon
**Role:** Left-hand bat, wicket-keeper
**Born:** 21 October 1970, Carlisle
**Height:** 5ft 11in **Weight:** 12st 4lbs
**Nickname:** Nico, Murdock, Nobby
**County debut:** 1989
**1000 runs in a season:** 1
**1st-Class 50s:** 10
**1st-Class 100s:** 5
**1st-Class catches:** 268
**1st-Class stumpings:** 21
**Place in batting averages:** 220th 18.44
(1994 63rd 38.74)
**Parents:** Brian and Sylvia
**Marital status:** Single
**Family links with cricket:** 'Mum makes the teas at Edanhall. Dad still plays local league cricket.'
**Education:** Langwathby Primary; Ullswater High
**Qualifications:** Coaching certificates
**Career outside cricket:** 'Partner in "Time to Relax" stress and relaxation'

**Off-season**: Playing in Cape Town, South Africa with Primrose CC
**Overseas tours:** Cumbria to Denmark 1985; Leicestershire to Holland 1991, to Montego Bay, to Bloemfontein; England A to India 1994-95
**Overseas teams played for:** Melville and North Fremantle, Perth, Western Australia 1989-92; Mitchells Rain, Cape Town 1992; Primrose CC, Cape Town, South Africa 1995-96
**Cricketers particularly admired:** David Gower, Alan Knott, Bob Taylor, Dominic Cork
**Other sports followed:** Football (Carlisle United and Liverrpool FC)
**Injuries:** Broken finger, out for seven weeks
**Relaxations:** 'Time to Relax and Our Jen'
**Extras:** Youngest person to score a century against Yorkshire (at U15). Played for England U15 and played in Minor Counties Championship for Cumberland at 16, MCC Young Pro in 1988. Took eight catches in debut match v Warwickshire at Hinckley in 1989. Played for Carlisle United and 'once got lost in South African township at 3.30am'. Leicester Young Player of the Year two years running. Second Leicester wicket-keeper to score 1000 runs in a season. Voted Cumbrian Sports Personality of the Year 1994-95. Has signed a contract that will keep him at Grace Road until the year 2000
**Opinions on cricket:** 'What a pleasure.'
**Best batting:** 131 Leicestershire v Hampshire, Leicester 1994

## 1995 Season

| | M | Inns | NO | Runs | HS | Avge | 100s | 50s | Ct | St | O | M | Runs | Wkts | Avge | Best | 5wl | 10wM |
|---|---|---|---|---|---|---|---|---|---|---|---|---|---|---|---|---|---|---|
| Test | | | | | | | | | | | | | | | | | | |
| All First | 18 | 30 | 5 | 461 | 79 | 18.44 | - | 2 | 46 | 2 | | | | | | | | |
| 1-day Int | | | | | | | | | | | | | | | | | | |
| NatWest | 2 | 2 | 1 | 36 | 31 * | 36.00 | - | - | 1 | - | | | | | | | | |
| B & H | | | | | | | | | | | | | | | | | | |
| Sunday | 13 | 10 | 1 | 260 | 84 | 28.88 | - | 2 | 10 | 4 | | | | | | | | |

## Career Performances

| | M | Inns | NO | Runs | HS | Avge | 100s | 50s | Ct | St | Balls | Runs | Wkts | Avge | Best | 5wl | 10wM |
|---|---|---|---|---|---|---|---|---|---|---|---|---|---|---|---|---|---|
| Test | | | | | | | | | | | | | | | | | | |
| All First | 104 | 152 | 34 | 3149 | 131 | 26.68 | 5 | 10 | 268 | 21 | | | | | | | | |
| 1-day Int | | | | | | | | | | | | | | | | | | |
| NatWest | 12 | 10 | 3 | 127 | 32 | 18.14 | - | - | 12 | 2 | | | | | | | | |
| B & H | 7 | 6 | 0 | 58 | 27 | 9.66 | - | - | 3 | 1 | | | | | | | | |
| Sunday | 78 | 64 | 10 | 1140 | 84 | 21.11 | - | 6 | 61 | 13 | | | | | | | | |

# NOON, W. M.        Nottinghamshire

**Name:** Wayne Michael Noon
**Role:** Right-hand bat, wicket-keeper
**Born:** 5 February 1971, Grimsby
**Height:** 5ft 9¹/₂in **Weight:** 11st 7lbs
**Nickname:** Noonie
**County debut:** 1988 (one-day),
1989 (first-class) (Northamptonshire),
1994 (Nottinghamshire)
**County cap:** 1995 (Nottinghamshire)
**1st-Class 50s:** 8
**1st-Class catches:** 99
**1st-Class stumpings:** 13
**Place in batting averages:** 131st av. 29.80
(1994 157th av. 25.70)
**Parents:** Trafford and Rosemary
**Marital status:** Single
**Education:** Caistor Grammar School
**Qualifications:** 5 O-levels
**Career outside cricket:** Working for
Kookaburra
**Off-season:** Playing cricket in Christchurch NZ
**Overseas tours:** Lincolnshire U15 to Pakistan 1984; England YC to Australia 1989-90; Rutland tourists to South Africa 1988
**Overseas teams played for:** Burnside West, Christchurch, New Zealand 1989-90 and 1993-96; Rivertonians, Cape Town 1992-93
**Cricketers particularly admired:** Ian Botham, Allan Lamb, Alan Knott
**Other sports followed:** Football (Lincoln City), horse racing
**Injuries:** Thigh, missed two to three weeks
**Relaxations:** A day at the races, wining and dining, 'having a bet'
**Extras:** Played for England YC v New Zealand YC 1989; captain v Australian YC 1989-90 and Pakistan YC 1990. Was the 1000th player to appear in the Sunday League competition. Broke the Northants record for most 2nd XI hundreds in one season in 1993
**Opinions on cricket:** 'We should have a domestic 50 over competition to bring us in line with other countries. Over-rate fines too steep. Overs per hour reduced to 17.5.'
**Best batting:** 75 Nottinghamshire v Northamptonshire, Trent Bridge 1994

---

56. Which West Indian scored the most runs in all first-class
matches during the 1995 tour?

## 1995 Season

| | M | Inns | NO | Runs | HS | Avge | 100s | 50s | Ct | St | O | M | Runs | Wkts | Avge | Best | 5wI | 10wM |
|---|---|---|---|---|---|---|---|---|---|---|---|---|---|---|---|---|---|---|
| Test | | | | | | | | | | | | | | | | | | |
| All First | 17 | 31 | 6 | 745 | 66 | 29.80 | - | 5 | 32 | 5 | | | | | | | | |
| 1-day Int | | | | | | | | | | | | | | | | | | |
| NatWest | 2 | 1 | 0 | 7 | 7 | 7.00 | - | - | - | 1 | | | | | | | | |
| B & H | 2 | 2 | 1 | 40 | 23 | 40.00 | - | - | 1 | - | | | | | | | | |
| Sunday | 15 | 10 | 4 | 154 | 38 | 25.66 | - | - | 12 | 2 | | | | | | | | |

## Career Performances

| | M | Inns | NO | Runs | HS | Avge | 100s | 50s | Ct | St | Balls | Runs | Wkts | Avge | Best | 5wI | 10wM |
|---|---|---|---|---|---|---|---|---|---|---|---|---|---|---|---|---|---|
| Test | | | | | | | | | | | | | | | | | |
| All First | 49 | 81 | 14 | 1549 | 75 | 23.11 | - | 8 | 99 | 13 | | | | | | | |
| 1-day Int | | | | | | | | | | | | | | | | | |
| NatWest | 4 | 2 | 0 | 41 | 34 | 20.50 | - | - | 2 | 2 | | | | | | | |
| B & H | 6 | 4 | 1 | 52 | 23 | 17.33 | - | - | 4 | 1 | | | | | | | |
| Sunday | 45 | 31 | 7 | 305 | 38 | 12.70 | - | - | 31 | 7 | | | | | | | |

# NORTH, J. A. Sussex

**Name:** John Andrew North
**Role:** Right-hand bat, right-arm medium bowler, outfielder
**Born:** 19 November 1970, Slindon
**Height:** 5ft 11in **Weight:** 12st
**Nickname:** Ollie
**County debut:** 1990
**1st-Class 50s:** 3
**1st-Class 100s:** 1
**1st-Class catches:** 4
**Strike rate:** (career 60.02)
**Parents:** John Allan and Margaret Anne
**Marital status:** Single
**Family links with cricket:** Brother Mark played county schoolboy cricket. Father plays club cricket
**Education:** Bishop Luffa Comprehensive School; Slindon College
**Qualifications:** 10 O-levels, 2 A-levels, senior coaching award
**Career outside cricket:** Electrician
**Overseas tours:** Buckingham Cavaliers to Cape Town, South Africa 1989 and 1992; Sussex Martlets to Zimbabwe 1991

**Overseas teams played for:** University St Heliers, Auckland 1989-90
**Cricketers particularly admired:** Mahmoud Nassarian, Daniel Oliver
**Other sports followed:** 'Football and anything without horses.'
**Relaxations:** 'Eating out, watching movies'
**Extras:** Played for English Schools U15 and U17, NAYC and for England YC v Pakistan YC 1990. Released by Sussex at the end of the 1995 season
**Opinions on cricket:** 'Tea intervals should be extended. Young players are important to a county's future and should be treated in accordance.'
**Best batting:** 114 Sussex v Essex, Hove 1993
**Best bowling:** 4-47 Sussex v Sri Lankans, Hove 1991

## 1995 Season

|         | M | Inns | NO | Runs | HS | Avge  | 100s | 50s | Ct | St | O  | M | Runs | Wkts | Avge  | Best | 5wl | 10wM |
|---------|---|------|----|------|----|-------|------|-----|----|----|----|---|------|------|-------|------|-----|------|
| Test    |   |      |    |      |    |       |      |     |    |    |    |   |      |      |       |      |     |      |
| All First |   |      |    |      |    |       |      |     |    |    |    |   |      |      |       |      |     |      |
| 1-day Int |   |      |    |      |    |       |      |     |    |    |    |   |      |      |       |      |     |      |
| NatWest |   |      |    |      |    |       |      |     |    |    |    |   |      |      |       |      |     |      |
| B & H   | 2 | 1    | 0  | 10   | 10 | 10.00 | -    | -   | -  | -  | 7  | 0 | 45   | 0    | -     | -    | -   |      |
| Sunday  | 6 | 6    | 1  | 60   | 32 | 12.00 | -    | -   | 1  | -  | 11 | 1 | 61   | 1    | 61.00 | 1-39 | -   |      |

## Career Performances

|         | M  | Inns | NO | Runs | HS  | Avge  | 100s | 50s | Ct | St | Balls | Runs | Wkts | Avge  | Best | 5wl | 10wM |
|---------|----|------|----|------|-----|-------|------|-----|----|----|-------|------|------|-------|------|-----|------|
| Test    |    |      |    |      |     |       |      |     |    |    |       |      |      |       |      |     |      |
| All First | 23 | 31   | 6  | 513  | 114 | 20.52 | 1    | 3   | 4  | -  | 2641  | 1577 | 44   | 35.84 | 4-47 | -   | -    |
| 1-day Int |    |      |    |      |     |       |      |     |    |    |       |      |      |       |      |     |      |
| NatWest | 2  | 2    | 0  | 31   | 20  | 15.50 | -    | -   | -  | -  | 12    | 17   | 0    | -     | -    | -   | -    |
| B & H   | 9  | 6    | 1  | 74   | 22  | 14.80 | -    | -   | -  | -  | 390   | 345  | 8    | 43.12 | 3-24 | -   |      |
| Sunday  | 35 | 32   | 7  | 329  | 56  | 13.16 | -    | 1   | 9  | -  | 680   | 651  | 19   | 34.26 | 3-29 | -   |      |

# NOWELL, R. W. Surrey

**Name:** Richard William Nowell
**Role:** Left-hand bat, slow left-arm bowler
**Born:** 29 December 1975, Croydon
**Height:** 6ft  **Weight:** 12st 7lbs
**County debut:** 1995
**1st-Class catches:** 5
**Place in bowling averages:** 118th av. 39.50
**Strike rate:** 79.65 (career 79.75)
**Nickname:** Muesli, Nosebleed, Sid Yobbo, Cockforester
**Parents:** Bill and June
**Marital status:** Single

**Family links with cricket:** 'Father played for Surrey club and ground and once ran out Peter May in a benefit match. Mum fancies David Gower'
**Education:** Cumnor House Prep School; Trinity School, Croydon
**Qualifications:** 9 GCSEs, 2 A-levels, coaching certificate
**Career outside cricket:** 'Potential nightclub owner'
**Off-season:** Playing in South Africa
**Overseas tours:** England U18 to South Africa 1992-93
**Overseas teams played for:** Technikon, Natal 1994-95
**Cricketers particularly admired:** Graham Kersey, Tim May, Oliver Slipper
**Other sports followed:** Rugby union and league ('Used to support Arsenal but they have become too exciting to watch lately')
**Relaxations:** Shopping, 'mixing a few tunes on the decks and a pint of Caffrey's with my mates'
**Extras:** Played for Surrey from U11 to U19. Played England U15, U17 and U18. Holds record for highest aggregate of runs in school cricket
**Opinions on cricket:** 'Perhaps the season could be slightly extended to allow for more rest and time to practise. The Sunday League should organise drinking competitions and speakers to liven it up further'
**Best batting:** 27 Surrey v Warwickshire, Edgbaston 1995
**Best bowling:** 4-43 Surrey v Nottinghamshire, Guildford 1995

### 1995 Season

|         | M | Inns | NO | Runs | HS | Avge | 100s | 50s | Ct | St | O | M | Runs | Wkts | Avge | Best | 5wI | 10wM |
|---------|---|------|----|------|-----|------|------|-----|----|----|-----|-----|------|------|-------|------|-----|------|
| Test    |   |      |    |      |     |      |      |     |    |    |     |     |      |      |       |      |     |      |
| All First | 11 | 20 | 2 | 134 | 27 | 7.44 | - | - | 5 | - | 424.5 | 117 | 1264 | 32 | 39.50 | 4-43 | - | - |
| 1-day Int |   |      |    |      |     |      |      |     |    |    |     |     |      |      |       |      |     |      |
| NatWest | 1 | 1 | 1 | 2 | 2 * | - | - | - | 1 | - | 5 | 0 | 35 | 0 | - | - | - |   |
| B & H   | 2 | 1 | 1 | 15 | 15 * | - | - | - | 1 | - | 14 | 1 | 47 | 1 | 47.00 | 1-35 | - |   |
| Sunday  | 2 | 1 | 0 | 0 | 0 | 0.00 | - | - | 1 | - | 8 | 0 | 31 | 0 | - | - | - |   |

57. Who were elected Player of the Year and Young Player of the Year for 1995?

**Career Performances**

| | M | Inns | NO | Runs | HS | Avge | 100s | 50s | Ct | St | Balls | Runs | Wkts | Avge | Best | 5wI | 10wM |
|---|---|---|---|---|---|---|---|---|---|---|---|---|---|---|---|---|---|
| Test | | | | | | | | | | | | | | | | | |
| All First | 11 | 20 | 2 | 134 | 27 | 7.44 | - | - | 5 | - | 2549 | 1264 | 32 | 39.50 | 4-43 | - | - |
| 1-day Int | | | | | | | | | | | | | | | | | |
| NatWest | 1 | 1 | 1 | 2 | 2 * | - | - | - | 1 | - | 30 | 35 | 0 | - | - | - | - |
| B & H | 2 | 1 | 1 | 15 | 15 * | - | - | - | 1 | - | 84 | 47 | 1 | 47.00 | 1-35 | - | |
| Sunday | 2 | 1 | 0 | 0 | 0 | 0.00 | - | - | 1 | - | 48 | 31 | 0 | - | - | - | |

# O'GORMAN, T. J. G. Derbyshire

**Name:** Timothy Joseph Gerard O'Gorman
**Role:** Right-hand bat, off-spin bowler
**Born:** 15 May 1967, Woking
**Height:** 6ft 2in **Weight:** 12st
**County debut:** 1987
**County cap:** 1992
**1000 runs in a season:** 2
**1st-Class 50s:** 22
**1st-Class 100s:** 9
**1st-Class catches:** 69
**Place in batting averages:** 246th av. 15.62
(1994 104th av. 33.53)
**Parents:** Brian and Kathleen
**Marital status:** Single
**Family links with cricket:** Grandfather Joe
O'Gorman played for Surrey
**Education:** St George's College, Weybridge;
St Chad's College, Durham University;
College of Law, Guildford
**Qualifications:** 12 O-levels, 3 A-levels, BA (Hons) Law; Law Society finals
**Career outside cricket:** Solicitor
**Overseas tours:** Troubadours to Argentina 1987, to Brazil 1989; Christians in Sport to
Zimbabwe 1994-95
**Overseas teams played for:** Alexandra, Zimbabwe; Southern Hawkes Bay, New Zealand
**Cricketers particularly admired:** David Gower, Greg Chappell, Richard Hadlee
**Other sports followed:** Tennis, golf, hockey, rugby, football
**Relaxations:** Arts, theatre, music, reading
**Extras:** Surrey Young Cricketer of the Year 1984. Captained Surrey Young Cricketers
for three years. Trials for England schoolboys at hockey
**Best batting:** 148 Derbyshire v Lancashire, Old Trafford 1991
**Best bowling:** 1-7 Derbyshire v Cambridge University, Fenner's 1992

## 1995 Season

| | M | Inns | NO | Runs | HS | Avge | 100s | 50s | Ct | St | O | M | Runs | Wkts | Avge | Best | 5wl | 10wM |
|---|---|---|---|---|---|---|---|---|---|---|---|---|---|---|---|---|---|---|
| Test | | | | | | | | | | | | | | | | | | |
| All First | 5 | 8 | 0 | 125 | 39 | 15.62 | - | - | 3 | - | | | | | | | | |
| 1-day Int | | | | | | | | | | | | | | | | | | |
| NatWest | | | | | | | | | | | | | | | | | | |
| B & H | 3 | 2 | 0 | 17 | 16 | 8.50 | - | - | 2 | - | | | | | | | | |
| Sunday | 6 | 5 | 1 | 89 | 57 | 22.25 | - | 1 | - | - | | | | | | | | |

## Career Performances

| | M | Inns | NO | Runs | HS | Avge | 100s | 50s | Ct | St | Balls | Runs | Wkts | Avge | Best | 5wl | 10wM |
|---|---|---|---|---|---|---|---|---|---|---|---|---|---|---|---|---|---|
| Test | | | | | | | | | | | | | | | | | |
| All First | 106 | 177 | 21 | 4736 | 148 | 30.35 | 9 | 22 | 69 | - | 265 | 215 | 3 | 71.66 | 1-7 | - | - |
| 1-day Int | | | | | | | | | | | | | | | | | |
| NatWest | 7 | 7 | 1 | 164 | 89 | 27.33 | - | 2 | 1 | - | | | | | | | |
| B & H | 25 | 21 | 1 | 404 | 49 | 20.20 | - | - | 6 | - | 6 | 1 | 0 | - | - | - | |
| Sunday | 82 | 76 | 15 | 1534 | 69 | 25.14 | - | 5 | 13 | - | | | | | | | |

# ORMOND, J.                    Leicestershire

**Name:** James Ormond
**Role:** Right-hand bat, right-arm
fast-medium bowler
**Born:** 20 August 1977, Walsgrave, Coventry
**Height:** 6ft 3in  **Weight:** 13st 7lbs
**Nickname:** Horse, Trigger, Jimmy
**County debut:** 1995
**1st-Class catches:** 1
**Parents:** Richard and Margaret
**Marital status:** Single
**Family links with cricket:** Father played
club cricket with Corley
**Education:** St Francis, Bedworth; St Thomas
More, Nuneaton; North Warwickshire
College of Further Education
**Qualifications:** 6 GCSEs
**Off-season:** Touring Zimbabwe with England
U19
**Overseas tours:** England U19 to Zimbabwe
1995-96
**Cricketers particularly admired:** Ian Botham, Richard Hadlee
**Other sports followed:** Football (Coventry City) and rugby

**Injuries:** Side strain, out for six weeks
**Relaxations:** 'Spending time with my girlfriend!'
**Extras:** Played for the Development of Excellence side and England U19 against South Africa U19 in 1995. Was forced to return home after one day of the England U19 tour to Zimbabwe in 1995-96 through injury.
**Opinions on cricket:** 'I have not played long enough to start telling people what I think about the game.'
**Best bowling:** 2-65 Leicestershire v Oxford University, The Parks 1995

### 1995 Season

|  | M | Inns | NO | Runs | HS | Avge | 100s | 50s | Ct | St | O | M | Runs | Wkts | Avge | Best | 5wI | 10wM |
|---|---|---|---|---|---|---|---|---|---|---|---|---|---|---|---|---|---|---|
| Test |  |  |  |  |  |  |  |  |  |  |  |  |  |  |  |  |  |  |
| All First | 1 | 0 | 0 | 0 | 0 | - | - | - | 1 | - | 17 | 6 | 65 | 2 | 32.50 | 2-65 | - | - |
| 1-day Int |  |  |  |  |  |  |  |  |  |  |  |  |  |  |  |  |  |  |
| NatWest |  |  |  |  |  |  |  |  |  |  |  |  |  |  |  |  |  |  |
| B & H |  |  |  |  |  |  |  |  |  |  |  |  |  |  |  |  |  |  |  |
| Sunday | 1 | 0 | 0 | 0 | 0 | - | - | - | - | - | 6 | 0 | 41 | 0 | - |  | - | - |

### Career Performances

|  | M | Inns | NO | Runs | HS | Avge | 100s | 50s | Ct | St | Balls | Runs | Wkts | Avge | Best | 5wI | 10wM |
|---|---|---|---|---|---|---|---|---|---|---|---|---|---|---|---|---|---|
| Test |  |  |  |  |  |  |  |  |  |  |  |  |  |  |  |  |  |
| All First | 1 | 0 | 0 | 0 | 0 | - | - | - | 1 | - | 102 | 65 | 2 | 32.50 | 2-65 | - | - |
| 1-day Int000 |  |  |  |  |  |  |  |  |  |  |  |  |  |  |  |  |  |
| NatWest |  |  |  |  |  |  |  |  |  |  |  |  |  |  |  |  |  |
| B & H |  |  |  |  |  |  |  |  |  |  |  |  |  |  |  |  |  |
| Sunday | 1 | 0 | 0 | 0 | 0 | - | - | - | - | - | 36 | 41 | 0 | - |  | - |  |

# OSTLER, D. P.                    Warwickshire

**Name:** Dominic Piers Ostler
**Role:** Right-hand bat, right-arm medium bowler
**Born:** 15 July 1970, Solihull
**Height:** 6ft 2in **Weight:** 14st
**Nickname:** Ossie, Blondie
**County debut:** 1990
**County cap:** 1991
**1000 runs in a season:** 4
**1st-Class 50s:** 38
**1st-Class 100s:** 9
**1st-Class 200s:** 1
**One-Day 100s:** 1

**Place in batting averages:** 61st av. 40.95 (1994 45th av. 43.00)
**Parents:** Mike and Ann
**Marital status:** Single
**Family links with cricket:** Brother plays for Knowle and Dorridge
**Education:** Princethorpe College; Solihull Technical College
**Qualifications:** 4 O-levels, City and Guilds Recreation Course
**Career outside cricket:** 'Earning vast amounts of money being a businessman'
**Off-season:** England A tour to Pakistan
**Overseas tours:** Gladstone Small's Benefit Tour to Barbados, 1992; England A to Pakistan 1995-96
**Overseas teams played for:** Avendale CC, South Africa 1991-92
**Cricketers particularly admired:** Gladstone Small, Graeme Welch, Jason Radcliffe
**Other sports followed:** Football ('Blues FC'), golf, snooker
**Injuries:** Knee operation (twice), out for ten days
**Relaxations:** 'Spending time with girlfriend Sam and Jack the dog'
**Extras:** Played club cricket for Moseley in the Birmingham League; made his Warwickshire 2nd XI debut in 1989 and was a member of Warwickshire U19 side that won Esso U19 County Festivals in 1988 and 1989. Has collected winner's medals for B&H Cup, Britannic Assurance County Championship, NatWest Trophy and Sunday League
**Best batting:** 208 Warwickshire v Surrey, Edgbaston 1995

## 1995 Season

|  | M | Inns | NO | Runs | HS | Avge | 100s | 50s | Ct | St | O | M | Runs | Wkts | Avge | Best | 5wI | 10wM |
|---|---|---|---|---|---|---|---|---|---|---|---|---|---|---|---|---|---|---|
| Test |  |  |  |  |  |  |  |  |  |  |  |  |  |  |  |  |  |  |
| All First | 18 | 26 | 2 | 983 | 208 | 40.95 | 2 | 6 | 25 | - |  |  |  |  |  |  |  |  |
| 1-day Int |  |  |  |  |  |  |  |  |  |  |  |  |  |  |  |  |  |  |
| NatWest | 5 | 5 | 1 | 171 | 76 | 42.75 | - | 1 | 1 | - |  |  |  |  |  |  |  |  |
| B & H | 5 | 5 | 1 | 279 | 87 | 69.75 | - | 4 | 1 | - |  |  |  |  |  |  |  |  |
| Sunday | 14 | 13 | 1 | 290 | 58 | 24.16 | - | 1 | 4 | - |  |  |  |  |  |  |  |  |

## Career Performances

| | M | Inns | NO | Runs | HS | Avge | 100s | 50s | Ct | St | Balls | Runs | Wkts | Avge | Best | 5wI | 10wM |
|---|---|---|---|---|---|---|---|---|---|---|---|---|---|---|---|---|---|
| Test | | | | | | | | | | | | | | | | | |
| All First | 111 | 186 | 16 | 6271 | 208 | 36.88 | 9 | 38 | 110 | - | 143 | 122 | 0 | - | - | - | - |
| 1-day Int | | | | | | | | | | | | | | | | | |
| NatWest | 24 | 23 | 3 | 620 | 104 | 31.00 | 1 | 3 | 9 | - | 9 | 4 | 1 | 4.00 | 1-4 | - | |
| B & H | 18 | 18 | 2 | 630 | 87 | 39.37 | - | 6 | 7 | - | | | | | | | |
| Sunday | 86 | 79 | 10 | 2084 | 84 * | 30.20 | - | 15 | 23 | - | 6 | 4 | 0 | - | .- | - | |

# OWEN, J. E. Derbyshire

**Name:** John Edward Owen
**Role:** Right-hand bat
**Born:** 7 August 1971, Derby
**Height:** 5ft 10in **Weight:** 11st 8lbs
**County debut:** 1995
**1st-Class 50s:** 2
**Place in batting averages:** 164th av. 25.00
**Parents:** David Horton and Carole
**Marital status:** Single
**Family links with cricket:** Father played in
Derbyshire League for Alvaston, Boulton and
Spondon. Grandfather played for Crewe
**Education:** Spondon School, Derby
**Qualifications:** Qualified green-keeper
**Career outside cricket:** Green-keeper
**Off-season:** Playing in South Africa
**Cricketers particularly admired:**
Ian Botham, Viv Richards
**Other sports followed:** Football (Derby
County), golf, rugby union, rugby league
**Injuries:** Broken hand, 12 stitches in leg wound, 3 stitches in webbing in right hand,
missed eight to nine weeks
**Relaxations:** Listening to music. Socialising with friends. Spending time with girlfriend.
**Opinions on cricket:** 'Too much quantity and not enough quality.'
**Best batting:** 65 Derbyshire v Young Australia, Chesterfield 1995

---

58. Anil Kumble took 100 wickets last season and was the first spin bowler to
do so since three spinners achieved the feat in 1983. Who were they?

---

## 1995 Season

|        | M | Inns | NO | Runs | HS | Avge | 100s | 50s | Ct | St | O | M | Runs | Wkts | Avge | Best | 5wI | 10wM |
|--------|---|------|----|------|-----|------|------|-----|----|----|---|---|------|------|------|------|-----|------|
| Test   |   |      |    |      |     |      |      |     |    |    |   |   |      |      |      |      |     |      |
| All First | 4 | 8 | 0 | 200 | 65 | 25.00 | - | 2 | - | - |   |   |      |      |      |      |     |      |
| 1-day Int |   |      |    |      |     |      |      |     |    |    |   |   |      |      |      |      |     |      |
| NatWest |   |      |    |      |     |      |      |     |    |    |   |   |      |      |      |      |     |      |
| B & H  |   |      |    |      |     |      |      |     |    |    |   |   |      |      |      |      |     |      |
| Sunday | 4 | 4 | 1 | 91 | 45 | 30.33 | - | - | - | - |   |   |      |      |      |      |     |      |

## Career Performances

|        | M | Inns | NO | Runs | HS | Avge | 100s | 50s | Ct | St | Balls | Runs | Wkts | Avge | Best | 5wI | 10wM |
|--------|---|------|----|------|-----|------|------|-----|----|----|-------|------|------|------|------|-----|------|
| Test   |   |      |    |      |     |      |      |     |    |    |       |      |      |      |      |     |      |
| All First | 4 | 8 | 0 | 200 | 65 | 25.00 | - | 2 | - | - |       |      |      |      |      |     |      |
| 1-day Int |   |      |    |      |     |      |      |     |    |    |       |      |      |      |      |     |      |
| NatWest |   |      |    |      |     |      |      |     |    |    |       |      |      |      |      |     |      |
| B & H  |   |      |    |      |     |      |      |     |    |    |       |      |      |      |      |     |      |
| Sunday | 4 | 4 | 1 | 91 | 45 | 30.33 | - | - | - | - |       |      |      |      |      |     |      |

# PARKER, B.     *Yorkshire*

**Name:** Bradley Parker
**Role:** Right-hand bat, right-arm medium bowler, cover point fielder
**Born:** 23 June 1970, Mirfield
**Height:** 5ft 10in **Weight:** 12st 7lbs
**Nickname:** Nesty, Ceefax, Floyd
**County debut:** 1992
**1st-Class 50s:** 4
**1st-Class 100s:** 1
**1st-Class catches:** 10
**Place in batting averages:** 178th av. 23.00 (1994 82nd av. 36.12)
**Parents:** Diane and David
**Marital status:** Single
**Family links with cricket:** Father played club cricket and Lincolnshire U23
**Education:** Bingley Grammar School
**Qualifications:** 'None worth mentioning from school.' Cricket coaching awards
**Career outside cricket:** 'Training, and keeping to my strict diet'
**Overseas teams played for:** Ellerslie, Auckland 1988-90
**Cricketers particularly admired:** Chris Spence, Alec Stewart, Graham Thorpe

**Other sports followed:** Rugby league, boxing
**Relaxations:** Films, eating out, drinking and socialising
**Opinions on cricket:** 'Far too much cricket played in too short a time.'
**Best batting:** 127 Yorkshire v Surrey, Scarborough 1994

## 1995 Season

|  | M | Inns | NO | Runs | HS | Avge | 100s | 50s | Ct | St | O | M | Runs | Wkts | Avge | Best | 5wI | 10wM |
|---|---|---|---|---|---|---|---|---|---|---|---|---|---|---|---|---|---|---|
| Test |  |  |  |  |  |  |  |  |  |  |  |  |  |  |  |  |  |  |
| All First | 4 | 8 | 1 | 161 | 40 | 23.00 | - | - | 3 | - |  |  |  |  |  |  |  |  |
| 1-day Int |  |  |  |  |  |  |  |  |  |  |  |  |  |  |  |  |  |  |
| NatWest | 1 | 0 | 0 | 0 | 0 | - | - | - | - | - |  |  |  |  |  |  |  |  |
| B & H |  |  |  |  |  |  |  |  |  |  |  |  |  |  |  |  |  |  |  |
| Sunday | 11 | 9 | 2 | 118 | 28 | 16.85 | - | - | 3 | - |  |  |  |  |  |  |  |  |

## Career Performances

|  | M | Inns | NO | Runs | HS | Avge | 100s | 50s | Ct | St | Balls | Runs | Wkts | Avge | Best | 5wI | 10wM |
|---|---|---|---|---|---|---|---|---|---|---|---|---|---|---|---|---|---|
| Test |  |  |  |  |  |  |  |  |  |  |  |  |  |  |  |  |  |
| All First | 15 | 28 | 3 | 776 | 127 | 31.04 | 1 | 4 | 10 | - |  |  |  |  |  |  |  |
| 1-day Int |  |  |  |  |  |  |  |  |  |  |  |  |  |  |  |  |  |
| NatWest | 1 | 0 | 0 | 0 | 0 | - | - | - | - | - |  |  |  |  |  |  |  |
| B & H |  |  |  |  |  |  |  |  |  |  |  |  |  |  |  |  |  |  |
| Sunday | 22 | 19 | 3 | 287 | 36 | 17.93 | - | - | 5 | - |  |  |  |  |  |  |  |

# PARKIN, O. T. Glamorgan

**Name:** Owen Thomas Parkin
**Role:** Right-hand bat, right-arm medium-fast bowler
**Born:** 24 August 1972, Coventry
**Height:** 6ft 2in **Weight:** 11st 10lbs
**Nickname:** Parallel, Reverse, Tickets, Cars, Longterm, Disabled
**County debut:** 1994
**Parents:** Vernon Cyrus and Sarah Patricia
**Marital status:** Single
**Family links with cricket:** Younger brother Morgan plays for the county in his age group and took a hat-trick last year
**Education:** Bournemouth Grammar School; Bath University
**Qualifications:** 9 GCSEs, 4 A-levels, 1 S-level, BSc (Hons) in Mathematics
**Off-season:** 'I had an operation on my back in October so will spend the rest of the close season recovering and getting fit for next season'
**Overseas tours:** Dorset Youth to Denmark
**Overseas teams played for:** Kew, Melbourne 1992-93; North Balwyn, Melbourne 1993-94

**Cricketers particularly admired:** Malcolm Marshall, Richard Hadlee
**Other sports followed:** Rugby, football (Nottingham Forest), golf
**Injuries:** Stress-related lower back problems
**Relaxations:** General socialising and listening to 'Green Day'
**Extras:** Played for Dorset in the NatWest Trophy 1992 and 1993. ASW Young Player of the Month July 1994
**Opinions on cricket:** 'I feel that something should be given for a draw in the Championship especially now it is four days. With 16 points for a win, the incentive to win would still be there even if, say three or four points were given for a drawn game.'
**Best batting:** 2* Glamorgan v Middlesex, Lord's 1994
**Best bowling:** 2-45 Glamorgan v Middlesex, Lord's 1994

## 1995 Season (did not make any first-class or one-day appearances)

### Career Performances

|          | M | Inns | NO | Runs | HS | Avge | 100s | 50s | Ct | St | Balls | Runs | Wkts | Avge | Best | 5wI | 10wM |
|----------|---|------|----|------|----|------|------|-----|----|----|-------|------|------|-------|------|-----|------|
| Test     |   |      |    |      |    |      |      |     |    |    |       |      |      |       |      |     |      |
| All First| 2 | 2    | 2  | 2    | 2* | -    | -    | -   | -  | -  | 324   | 170  | 4    | 42.50 | 2-45 | -   | -    |
| 1-day Int|   |      |    |      |    |      |      |     |    |    |       |      |      |       |      |     |      |
| NatWest  | 2 | 1    | 0  | 0    | 0  | 0.00 | -    | -   | -  | -  | 48    | 54   | 0    | -     |      | -   | -    |
| B & H    |   |      |    |      |    |      |      |     |    |    |       |      |      |       |      |     |      |
| Sunday   |   |      |    |      |    |      |      |     |    |    |       |      |      |       |      |     |      |

> 59. What was the highest innings in the County Championship in 1995, who was the batsman and who were the opposition?

# PARSONS, G. J.                    Leicestershire

**Name:** Gordon James Parsons
**Role:** Left-hand bat, right-arm
medium-fast bowler
**Born:** 17 October 1959, Slough
**Height:** 6ft 1in **Weight:** 13st ('April') – 14st
('September')
**Nickname:** Bullhead
**County debut:** 1978 (Leicestershire), 1986
(Warwickshire)
**County cap:** 1984 (Leicestershire), 1987
(Warwickshire)
**Benefit:** 1994
**50 wickets in a season:** 3
**1st-Class 50s:** 26
**1st-Class 5 w. in innings:** 19
**1st-Class 10 w. in match:** 1
**1st-Class catches:** 121
**Place in batting averages:** 211th av. 19.26
(1994 154th av. 25.84)
**Place in bowling averages:** 68th av. 29.62 (1994 42nd av. 27.45)
**Strike rate:** 65.58 (career 60.38)
**Parents:** Dave and Evelyn
**Wife and date of marriage:** Hester Sophia, 8 February 1991
**Children:** Alexandra Suzanna, 5 June 1992
**Family links with cricket:** Brother-in-law, Hansie Cronje, is captain of South Africa
**Education:** Woodside County Secondary School, Slough
**Qualifications:** 6 O-levels
**Career outside cricket:** Coaching Western Transvaal in South Africa
**Overseas tours:** English Schools to India 1977-78; Derrick Robins XI to Australasia
1980; Leicestershire to Zimbabwe 1981, to Jamaica 1993
**Overseas teams played for:** Maharaja's, Sri Lanka 1979,1987; Boland, South Africa
1982-83; Griqualand West, South Africa 1984-85; Orange Free State, South Africa 1986-92
**Cricketers particularly admired:** Vince Wells
**Other sports followed:** Golf, football (Reading FC)
**Injuries:** Broken middle finger
**Relaxations:** 'My wife and daughter'
**Extras:** Played for Leicester 2nd XI from 1976 and for Buckinghamshire in 1977. Left
Leicestershire after 1985 season and joined Warwickshire. Capped by Warwickshire
while in plaster and on crutches. Released at end of 1988 season and returned to his old
county. Justin Benson was best man at his wedding, 'contradiction in terms, though it is!'
**Opinions on cricket:** 'What about a 12th man that can be substituted like football i.e. a

spinner plays instead of a fast bowler on the fourth day. Just a thought!'
**Best batting:** 76 Boland v Western Province B, Cape Town 1984-85
**Best bowling:** 9-72 Boland v Transvaal B, Johannesburg 1984-85

## 1995 Season

| | M | Inns | NO | Runs | HS | Avge | 100s | 50s | Ct | St | O | M | Runs | Wkts | Avge | Best | 5wI | 10wM |
|---|---|---|---|---|---|---|---|---|---|---|---|---|---|---|---|---|---|---|
| Test | | | | | | | | | | | | | | | | | | |
| All First | 18 | 28 | 2 | 501 | 73 | 19.26 | - | 1 | 15 | - | 579.2 | 178 | 1570 | 53 | 29.62 | 4-46 | - | - |
| 1-day Int | | | | | | | | | | | | | | | | | | |
| NatWest | 2 | 2 | 1 | 29 | 25 * | 29.00 | - | - | 1 | - | 24 | 4 | 83 | 2 | 41.50 | 2-46 | - | |
| B & H | 5 | 5 | 3 | 55 | 28 | 27.50 | - | - | - | - | 43.3 | 4 | 185 | 8 | 23.12 | 3-46 | - | |
| Sunday | 14 | 8 | 5 | 65 | 26 * | 21.66 | - | - | 3 | - | 101 | 10 | 419 | 20 | 20.95 | 3-22 | - | |

## Career Performances

| | M | Inns | NO | Runs | HS | Avge | 100s | 50s | Ct | St | Balls | Runs | Wkts | Avge | Best | 5wI | 10wM |
|---|---|---|---|---|---|---|---|---|---|---|---|---|---|---|---|---|---|
| Test | | | | | | | | | | | | | | | | | |
| All First | 312 | 417 | 92 | 6326 | 76 | 19.46 | - | 26 | 121 | - | 45169 | 22325 | 748 | 29.84 | 9-72 | 19 | 1 |
| 1-day Int | | | | | | | | | | | | | | | | | |
| NatWest | 30 | 20 | 6 | 168 | 25 * | 12.00 | - | - | 7 | - | 1676 | 1051 | 23 | 45.69 | 2-11 | - | |
| B & H | 55 | 31 | 14 | 321 | 63 * | 18.88 | - | 1 | 11 | - | 2964 | 1759 | 65 | 27.06 | 4-12 | - | |
| Sunday | 187 | 116 | 47 | 1074 | 38 * | 15.56 | - | - | 27 | - | 7717 | 5671 | 187 | 30.32 | 4-19 | - | |

# PARSONS, K. A.     Somerset

**Name:** Keith Alan Parsons
**Role:** Right-hand bat, right-arm
medium bowler
**Born:** 2 May 1973, Taunton
**Height:** 6ft 1in **Weight:** 13st 7lbs
**Nickname:** Pilot, Pars, Orv
**County debut:** 1992
**1st-Class 50s:** 7
**1st-Class 100s:** 1
**1st-Class catches:** 18
**Place in batting averages:** 117th av. 31.57
**Strike rate:** (career 110.00)
**Parents:** Alan and Lynne
**Marital status:** Single
**Family links with cricket:** Identical twin
brother, Kevin, was on the Somerset staff
1992-94. Father played six seasons for
Somerset 2nd XI and captained National

Civil Service XI
**Education:** Castle School, Taunton; Richard Huish Sixth Form College, Taunton
**Qualifications:** 8 GCSEs, 3 A-levels, NCA coaching award
**Off-season:** Coaching and playing for Taita in Hutt Valley, Wellington, New Zealand
**Overseas tours:** Castle School to Barbados 1989
**Overseas teams played for:** Kapiti Old Boys, New Zealand 1992-93; Harowhenera, New Zealand 1992-93; Taita District, Wellington, New Zealand 1993-96
**Cricketers particularly admired:** Viv Richards, Richard Hadlee, Robin Smith
**Other sports followed:** Rugby union (Bath RFC), football (Nottingham Forest FC), golf
**Relaxations:** 'All sports'
**Extras:** Captained two National Cup winning sides – Taunton St Andrews in National U15 Club Championship and Richard Huish College in National U17 School Championship. Represented English Schools at U15 and U19 level. Somerset Young Player of the Year 1993
**Opinions on cricket:** 'Now that the first-class Championship has been changed to four-day games, in order to improve the Test team and reduce the amount of contrived finishes, shouldn't the next step be to change the 2nd XI competition to a four-day Championship also, to help the younger players, in 2nd XI, become better four-day cricketers?'
**Best batting:** 105 Somerset v Young Australia, Taunton 1995
**Best bowling:** 2-11 Somerset v Derbyshire, Derby 1995

## 1995 Season

|  | M | Inns | NO | Runs | HS | Avge | 100s | 50s | Ct | St | O | M | Runs | Wkts | Avge | Best | 5wI | 10wM |
|---|---|---|---|---|---|---|---|---|---|---|---|---|---|---|---|---|---|---|
| Test |  |  |  |  |  |  |  |  |  |  |  |  |  |  |  |  |  |  |
| All First | 16 | 28 | 2 | 821 | 105 | 31.57 | 1 | 6 | 13 | - | 105 | 16 | 458 | 6 | 76.33 | 2-11 | - | - |
| 1-day Int |  |  |  |  |  |  |  |  |  |  |  |  |  |  |  |  |  |  |
| NatWest | 1 | 1 | 0 | 48 | 48 | 48.00 | - | - | - | - | 8 | 1 | 44 | 0 | - |  | - | - |
| B & H |  |  |  |  |  |  |  |  |  |  |  |  |  |  |  |  |  |  |
| Sunday | 10 | 10 | 1 | 230 | 52 * | 25.55 | - | 1 | 4 | - | 45 | 2 | 196 | 7 | 28.00 | 2-16 | - |  |

## Career Performances

|  | M | Inns | NO | Runs | HS | Avge | 100s | 50s | Ct | St | Balls | Runs | Wkts | Avge | Best | 5wI | 10wM |
|---|---|---|---|---|---|---|---|---|---|---|---|---|---|---|---|---|---|
| Test |  |  |  |  |  |  |  |  |  |  |  |  |  |  |  |  |  |
| All First | 25 | 44 | 4 | 994 | 105 | 24.85 | 1 | 7 | 18 | - | 660 | 493 | 6 | 82.16 | 2-11 | - | - |
| 1-day Int |  |  |  |  |  |  |  |  |  |  |  |  |  |  |  |  |  |
| NatWest | 3 | 3 | 1 | 81 | 48 | 40.50 | - | - | - | - | 120 | 91 | 2 | 45.50 | 2-47 | - |  |
| B & H |  |  |  |  |  |  |  |  |  |  |  |  |  |  |  |  |  |
| Sunday | 18 | 18 | 1 | 331 | 52 * | 19.47 | - | 1 | 5 | - | 324 | 245 | 8 | 30.62 | 2-16 | - |  |

# PATEL, M. M.          Kent

**Name:** Minal Mahesh Patel
**Role:** Right-hand bat, slow left-arm bowler
**Born:** 7 August 1970, Bombay, India
**Height:** 5ft 9in **Weight:** 9st 10lbs
**Nickname:** Geezer, Diamond, Ho-Chi
**County debut:** 1989
**County cap:** 1994
**50 w. in a season:** 2
**1st-Class 50s:** 2
**1st-Class 5 w. in innings:** 13
**1st-Class 10 w. in match:** 6
**1st-Class catches:** 33
**Place in batting averages:** 237th av. 16.34
(1994 266th av. 10.24)
**Place in bowling averages:** 101st av. 35.39
(1994 9th av. 22.86)
**Strike rate:** 71.63 (career 67.54)
**Parents:** Mahesh and Aruna
**Wife and date of marriage:** Karuna,
8 October 1995

**Family links with cricket:** Father played good club cricket in India, Africa and England
**Education:** Dartford GS; Erith College of Technology; Manchester Polytechnic
**Qualifications:** 6 O-levels, 3 A-levels, BA (Hons) in Economics
**Off-season:** 'Honeymoon and rest till Christmas. Possibly work after New Year'
**Overseas tours:** Dartford GS to Barbados 1988; England A to India 1994-95
**Cricketers particularly admired:** Derek Underwood, Kapil Dev, Carl Hooper, Aravinda De Silva
**Other sports followed:** Football (Tottenham Hotspur), American football and basketball
**Injuries:** Double fracture of right cheekbone, missed two games
**Relaxations:** Playing golf, listening to music
**Extras:** Played for English Schools 1988, 1989 and NCA England South 1989. Was voted Kent League Young Player of the Year 1987 while playing for Blackheath. First six overs in NatWest Trophy were all maidens. Whittingdale Young Player of the Year 1994
**Opinions on cricket:** 'Far too much cricket in the domestic season leads to a "going through the motions" attitude if the county is not competing for trophies. The amount of driving could also lead to a serious accident or injury
**Best batting:** 56 Kent v Leicestershire, Canterbury 1995
**Best bowling:** 8-96 Kent v Lancashire, Canterbury 1994

**1995 Season**

| | M | Inns | NO | Runs | HS | Avge | 100s | 50s | Ct | St | O | M | Runs | Wkts | Avge | Best | 5wI | 10wM |
|---|---|---|---|---|---|---|---|---|---|---|---|---|---|---|---|---|---|---|
| Test | | | | | | | | | | | | | | | | | | |
| All First | 18 | 29 | 6 | 376 | 56 | 16.34 | - | 2 | 13 | - | 788 | 194 | 2336 | 66 | 35.39 | 6-74 | 3 | 1 |
| 1-day Int | | | | | | | | | | | | | | | | | | |
| NatWest | 1 | 1 | 0 | 4 | 4 | 4.00 | - | - | - | - | 12 | 1 | 40 | 2 | 20.00 | 2-40 | - | |
| B & H | 4 | 2 | 1 | 1 | 1 | 1.00 | - | - | 1 | - | 40 | 5 | 129 | 2 | 64.50 | 2-29 | - | |
| Sunday | | | | | | | | | | | | | | | | | | |

**Career Performances**

| | M | Inns | NO | Runs | HS | Avge | 100s | 50s | Ct | St | Balls | Runs | Wkts | Avge | Best | 5wI | 10wM |
|---|---|---|---|---|---|---|---|---|---|---|---|---|---|---|---|---|---|
| Test | | | | | | | | | | | | | | | | | |
| All First | 61 | 89 | 20 | 915 | 56 | 13.26 | - | 2 | 33 | - | 14657 | 6552 | 217 | 30.19 | 8-96 | 13 | 6 |
| 1-day Int | | | | | | | | | | | | | | | | | |
| NatWest | 4 | 1 | 0 | 4 | 4 | 4.00 | - | - | 2 | - | 288 | 140 | 5 | 28.00 | 2-29 | - | |
| B & H | 4 | 2 | 1 | 1 | 1 | 1.00 | - | - | 1 | - | 240 | 129 | 2 | 64.50 | 2-29 | - | |
| Sunday | 6 | 2 | 0 | 6 | 5 | 3.00 | - | - | 1 | - | 176 | 191 | 6 | 31.83 | 3-50 | - | |

# PEARSON, R. M.      Surrey

**Name:** Richard Michael Pearson
**Role:** Right-hand bat, right arm
off-spin bowler
**Born:** 27 January 1972, Batley, Yorkshire
**Height:** 6ft 3in **Weight:** 13st 5lbs
**Nickname:** Batley, Pancho
**County debut:** 1992 (Northamptonshire),
1994 (Essex)
**1st-Class 5 w. in innings:** 1
**1st-Class catches:** 11
**Strike rate:** (career 109.76)
**Parents:** Mike and Carol
**Marital status:** Single
**Family links with cricket:** Father played in
Yorkshire League
**Education:** Batley Grammar School; St
John's, Cambridge
**Qualifications:** 2 O-levels, 9 GCSEs, 4 A-
levels, BA Hons in History
**Cricketers particularly admired:** Darren Robinson, Paul Dowson, Mick Kaye, Paul
Marlow
**Other sports followed:** Football (Leeds), rugby league (Batley)

**Relaxations:** Playing football, drinking good beer
**Extras:** Made first-class debut for Cambridge University in 1991 and has played for Combined Universities in the Benson & Hedges Cup since 1991. Football and cricket Blues at Cambridge. Moved to Essex for the 1994 season and has joined Surrey for the 1996 season
**Opinions on cricket:** 'We should be able to play in shorts when it is hot. Second team matches should go back to the end of the week – Monday nights are too quiet.'
**Best batting:** 33* Cambridge University v Surrey, Fenner's 1992
**Best bowling:** 5-108 Cambridge University v Warwickshire, Fenner's 1992

## 1995 Season

|           | M | Inns | NO | Runs | HS | Avge  | 100s | 50s | Ct | St | O  | M  | Runs | Wkts | Avge  | Best | 5wI | 10wM |
|-----------|---|------|----|------|----|-------|------|-----|----|----|----|----|------|------|-------|------|-----|------|
| Test      |   |      |    |      |    |       |      |     |    |    |    |    |      |      |       |      |     |      |
| All First | 2 | 2    | 0  | 27   | 27 | 13.50 | -    | -   | -  | -  | 81 | 13 | 302  | 7    | 43.14 | 3-58 | -   | -    |
| 1-day Int |   |      |    |      |    |       |      |     |    |    |    |    |      |      |       |      |     |      |
| NatWest   |   |      |    |      |    |       |      |     |    |    |    |    |      |      |       |      |     |      |
| B & H     | 2 | 0    | 0  | 0    | 0  | -     | -    | -   | 1  | -  | 22 | 2  | 89   | 3    | 29.66 | 3-46 | -   |      |
| Sunday    | 5 | 2    | 1  | 11   | 7  | 11.00 | -    | -   | 1  | -  | 25 | 0  | 162  | 3    | 54.00 | 2-67 | -   |      |

## Career Performances

|           | M  | Inns | NO | Runs | HS  | Avge  | 100s | 50s | Ct | St | Balls | Runs | Wkts | Avge  | Best  | 5wI | 10wM |
|-----------|----|------|----|------|-----|-------|------|-----|----|----|-------|------|------|-------|-------|-----|------|
| Test      |    |      |    |      |     |       |      |     |    |    |       |      |      |       |       |     |      |
| All First | 36 | 41   | 7  | 332  | 33* | 9.76  | -    | -   | 11 | -  | 7354  | 3917 | 67   | 58.46 | 5-108 | 1   | -    |
| 1-day Int |    |      |    |      |     |       |      |     |    |    |       |      |      |       |       |     |      |
| NatWest   | 1  | 0    | 0  | 0    | 0   | -     | -    | -   | -  | -  | 72    | 47   | 1    | 47.00 | 1-47  | -   |      |
| B & H     | 8  | 2    | 1  | 10   | 8   | 10.00 | -    | -   | 1  | -  | 498   | 324  | 7    | 46.28 | 3-46  | -   |      |
| Sunday    | 15 | 8    | 6  | 34   | 7   | 17.00 | -    | -   | 1  | -  | 494   | 439  | 11   | 39.90 | 3-33  | -   |      |

60. Against whom did Zimbabwe achieve their first Test victory and how many Tests had they played before that match?

# PEIRCE, M. T. E.     Sussex

**Name:** Michael Toby Edward Peirce
**Role:** Left-hand bat, slow left-arm bowler
**Born:** 14 June 1973, Maidenhead
**Height:** 5ft 10in **Weight:** 11st
**Nickname:** Beastie
**County debut:** 1994 (one-day),
1995 (first-class)
**1st-Class 50s:** 1
**1st-Class catches:** 6
**Place in batting averages:** 193rd av. 21.90
**Parents:** Michael Robert and Katherine Ross
**Marital status:** Single
**Education:** Ardingly College; Durham
University
**Qualifications:** 9 GCSEs, 3 A-levels,
1 S-level
**Overseas tours:** Sussex Schools U14 to
Barbados 1987; Sussex Schools U18 to India
1990-91; Ardingly College to India 1988-89
**Overseas teams played for:** Kilbirnie, Wellington, New Zealand 1991-92; Wellington
B, New Zealand 1991-92
**Cricketers particularly admired:** David Smith, David Gower, Phil Edmonds,
'J. Batty Esq'
**Other sports followed:** Most
**Relaxations:** 'Drinks with mates (both of them), music'
**Extras:** Retired from first-class cricket at the end of the 1995 season
**Best batting:** 60 Sussex v Worcestershire, Eastbourne 1995

## 1995 Season

|         | M | Inns | NO | Runs | HS | Avge | 100s | 50s | Ct | St | O | M | Runs | Wkts | Avge | Best | 5wI | 10wM |
|---------|---|------|----|------|-----|-------|------|-----|----|----|---|---|------|------|------|------|-----|------|
| Test    |   |      |    |      |     |       |      |     |    |    |   |   |      |      |      |      |     |      |
| All First | 6 | 10 | 0 | 219 | 60 | 21.90 | - | 1 | 5 | - | 9 | 1 | 30 | 0 | - | - | - | - |
| 1-day Int |   |      |    |      |     |       |      |     |    |    |   |   |      |      |      |      |     |      |
| NatWest |   |      |    |      |     |       |      |     |    |    |   |   |      |      |      |      |     |      |
| B & H   | 5 | 5 | 0 | 134 | 44 | 26.80 | - | - | 1 | - |   |   |      |      |      |      |     |      |
| Sunday  | 1 | 1 | 0 | 7 | 7 | 7.00 | - | - | - | - |   |   |      |      |      |      |     |      |

## Career Performances

|  | M | Inns | NO | Runs | HS | Avge | 100s | 50s | Ct | St | Balls | Runs | Wkts | Avge | Best | 5wI | 10wM |
|---|---|---|---|---|---|---|---|---|---|---|---|---|---|---|---|---|---|
| Test |  |  |  |  |  |  |  |  |  |  |  |  |  |  |  |  |  |
| All First | 7 | 12 | 0 | 243 | 60 | 20.25 | - | 1 | 6 | - | 54 | 30 | 0 | - | - | - | - |
| 1-day Int |  |  |  |  |  |  |  |  |  |  |  |  |  |  |  |  |  |
| NatWest |  |  |  |  |  |  |  |  |  |  |  |  |  |  |  |  |  |  |
| B & H | 5 | 5 | 0 | 134 | 44 | 26.80 | - | - | 1 | - |  |  |  |  |  |  |  |
| Sunday | 2 | 2 | 0 | 13 | 7 | 6.50 | - | - | 2 | - |  |  |  |  |  |  |  |

# PENBERTHY, A. L.     Northamptonshire

**Name:** Anthony Leonard Penberthy
**Role:** Left-hand bat, right-arm medium bowler
**Born:** 1 September 1969, Troon, Cornwall
**Height:** 6ft 1in **Weight:** 12st 7lbs
**Nickname:** Berth, Penbers, Lennie
**County debut:** 1989
**County cap:** 1994
**1st-Class 50s:** 11
**1st-Class 100s:** 1
**1st-Class 5 w. in innings:** 2
**1st-Class catches:** 41
**One-Day 5 w. in innings:** 1
**Place in batting averages:**
(1994 106th av. 32.80)
**Place in bowling averages:**
(1994 110th av. 37.13)
**Strike rate:** (career 65.52)
**Parents:** Gerald and Wendy
**Marital status:** Single
**Family links with cricket:** Father played in local leagues in Cornwall and is now a qualified umpire instructor
**Education:** Troon County Primary; Camborne Comprehensive
**Qualifications:** 3 O-levels, 3 CSEs, coaching certificate
**Off-season:** Working in Northampton
**Overseas tours:** Druids to Zimbabwe 1988; Northants to Durban 1992, to Cape Town 1993, to Zimbabwe 1995
**Cricketers particularly admired:** Ian Botham, David Gower, Dennis Lillee, Viv Richards, Eldine Baptiste
**Other sports followed:** Football (West Ham United), snooker, rugby, golf
**Relaxations:** Listening to music ('especially Luther Vandross'), watching videos and

437

comedy programmes, 'walking my Irish setter'

**Extras:** Had football trials for Plymouth Argyle but came to Northampton for cricket trials instead. Took wicket with first ball in first-class cricket – Mark Taylor caught behind, June 1989. Played for England YC v New Zealand YC 1989

**Opinions on cricket:** 'Back to short run-ups on Sundays. Lunch and tea intervals too short. Over-rate fines are too strict. Good to see that the most important people in the game, the players, are getting a greater financial reward for their efforts. I find it amazing that we still allow players to play in our game who will not commit themselves to playing for England or prefer to go and play for another country.'

**Best batting:** 101* Northamptonshire v Cambridge University, Fenner's 1990
**Best bowling:** 5-37 Northamptonshire v Glamorgan, Swansea 1993

## 1995 Season

|  | M | Inns | NO | Runs | HS | Avge | 100s | 50s | Ct | St | O | M | Runs | Wkts | Avge | Best | 5wI | 10wM |
|---|---|---|---|---|---|---|---|---|---|---|---|---|---|---|---|---|---|---|
| Test | | | | | | | | | | | | | | | | | | |
| All First | 4 | 6 | 1 | 115 | 73 | 23.00 | - | 1 | 1 | - | 52 | 7 | 177 | 4 | 44.25 | 2-6 | - | - |
| 1-day Int | | | | | | | | | | | | | | | | | | |
| NatWest | 5 | 3 | 0 | 9 | 5 | 3.00 | - | - | 2 | - | 37 | 3 | 166 | 5 | 33.20 | 2-42 | - | |
| B & H | 4 | 4 | 0 | 76 | 26 | 19.00 | - | - | 2 | - | 32 | 5 | 111 | 3 | 37.00 | 3-39 | - | |
| Sunday | 14 | 10 | 1 | 106 | 44 | 11.77 | - | - | 2 | - | 93.3 | 4 | 455 | 18 | 25.27 | 4-29 | - | |

## Career Performances

|  | M | Inns | NO | Runs | HS | Avge | 100s | 50s | Ct | St | Balls | Runs | Wkts | Avge | Best | 5wI | 10wM |
|---|---|---|---|---|---|---|---|---|---|---|---|---|---|---|---|---|---|
| Test | | | | | | | | | | | | | | | | | |
| All First | 70 | 103 | 15 | 1876 | 101 * | 21.31 | 1 | 11 | 41 | - | 7273 | 4049 | 111 | 36.47 | 5-37 | 2 | - |
| 1-day Int | | | | | | | | | | | | | | | | | |
| NatWest | 15 | 9 | 1 | 122 | 41 * | 15.25 | - | - | 5 | - | 679 | 460 | 11 | 41.81 | 2-29 | - | |
| B & H | 11 | 9 | 1 | 122 | 26 | 15.25 | - | - | 3 | - | 534 | 354 | 7 | 50.57 | 3-39 | - | |
| Sunday | 66 | 48 | 7 | 601 | 69 * | 14.65 | - | 1 | 14 | - | 2229 | 1979 | 62 | 31.91 | 5-36 | 1 | |

# PENNETT, D. B.                    Nottinghamshire

**Name:** David Barrington Pennett
**Role:** Right-hand bat, right-arm fast-medium bowler
**Born:** 26 October 1969, Leeds
**Height:** 6ft  **Weight:** 12st 7lbs
**Nickname:** Yorkie, Fiery, SJYT
**County debut:** 1992
**1st-Class 50s:** 1
**1st-Class 5 w. in innings:** 1
**1st-Class catches:** 6
**Place in bowling averages:** 154th av. 81.10

**Strike rate:** 124.80 (career 76.92)
**Parents:** Barrie and Valerie
**Marital status:** Engaged
**Education:** Benton Park Grammar School
**Qualifications:** 5 O-levels, ASA teacher's certificate (swimming), coaching certificate, senior coaching certificate
**Career outside cricket:** Modelling, coaching
**Off-season:** Playing in New Zealand
**Overseas tours:** Nottinghamshire to Cape Town, South Africa 1992-93
**Overseas teams played for:** Hamilton Star University, New Zealand 1993-94; Ellerslie, Auckland, New Zealand 1995-96
**Cricketers particularly admired:** Malcolm Marshall, Ian Botham, Viv Richards
**Other sports followed:** Football (Manchester Utd), rugby union (Otley)
**Injuries:** Ten stitches in knee wounds, missed two weeks
**Relaxations:** Buying clothes, playing football, mountaineering
**Extras:** At Yorkshire Cricket Academy in 1990 for two years. Took hat-trick in a Bain Clarkson game for Yorkshire v Nottinghamshire, and one for Nottinghamshire v Herefordshire
**Opinions on cricket:** 'A super league should be set up in the counties amateur league programme, playing over two weekends, bringing more people onto the county scene. We should stop criticising our own system too much and belittling the people presently in it. We are quick to judge and slow to praise both on the county and national scene.'
**Best batting:** 50 Nottinghamshire v Durham, Chester-le-Street 1995
**Best bowling:** 5-36 Nottinghamshire v Durham, Chester-le-Street 1993

## 1995 Season

|         | M  | Inns | NO | Runs | HS | Avge  | 100s | 50s | Ct | St | O     | M  | Runs | Wkts | Avge  | Best  | 5wI | 10wM |
|---------|----|------|----|------|----|-------|------|-----|----|----|-------|----|------|------|-------|-------|-----|------|
| Test    |    |      |    |      |    |       |      |     |    |    |       |    |      |      |       |       |     |      |
| All First | 8  | 12   | 8  | 89   | 50 | 22.25 | -    | 1   | 3  | -  | 208.1 | 35 | 811  | 10   | 81.10 | 3-136 | -   | -    |
| 1-day Int |    |      |    |      |    |       |      |     |    |    |       |    |      |      |       |       |     |      |
| NatWest | 1  | 0    | 0  | 0    | 0  | -     | -    | -   | -  | -  | 12    | 4  | 22   | 1    | 22.00 | 1-22  | -   |      |
| B & H   |    |      |    |      |    |       |      |     |    |    |       |    |      |      |       |       |     |      |
| Sunday  | 11 | 2    | 1  | 2    | 2  | 2.00  | -    | -   | 1  | -  | 74    | 2  | 420  | 15   | 28.00 | 3-27  | -   |      |

## Career Performances

| | M | Inns | NO | Runs | HS | Avge | 100s | 50s | Ct | St | Balls | Runs | Wkts | Avge | Best | 5wI | 10wM |
|---|---|---|---|---|---|---|---|---|---|---|---|---|---|---|---|---|---|
| Test | | | | | | | | | | | | | | | | | |
| All First | 28 | 27 | 11 | 169 | 50 | 10.56 | - | 1 | 6 | - | 4077 | 2321 | 53 | 43.79 | 5-36 | 1 | - |
| 1-day Int | | | | | | | | | | | | | | | | | |
| NatWest | 1 | 0 | 0 | 0 | 0 | - | - | - | - | - | 72 | 22 | 1 | 22.00 | 1-22 | - | |
| B & H | | | | | | | | | | | | | | | | | |
| Sunday | 32 | 7 | 5 | 20 | 12 * | 10.00 | - | - | 5 | - | 1290 | 1097 | 32 | 34.28 | 3-27 | - | |

# PENNEY, T. L. Warwickshire

**Name:** Trevor Lionel Penney
**Role:** Right-hand bat, right-arm
leg-break bowler
**Born:** 12 June 1968, Salisbury, Rhodesia
**Height:** 6ft  **Weight:** 11st
**Nickname:** TP, Lemon Kop
**County debut:** 1992
**County cap:** 1994
**1000 runs in a season:** 1
**1st-Class 50s:** 15
**1st-Class 100s:** 10
**1st-Class catches:** 40
**Place in batting averages:** 26th av. 49.91
(1994 70th av. 38.00)
**Parents:** George and Bets
**Wife and date of marriage:** Deborah Anne,
19 December 1992
**Children:** Samantha Anne, 20 August 1995
**Family links with cricket:** Brother Stephen
played for Zimbabwe U25

**Education:** Blakiston Primary; Prince Edward Boys High School, Zimbabwe
**Qualifications:** 3 O-levels
**Career outside cricket:** Tobacco buyer
**Off-season:** Playing hockey and coaching cricket in Zimbabwe
**Overseas tours:** Zimbabwe to Sri Lanka 1987; ICC Associates to Australia (Youth
World Cup)
**Overseas teams played for:** Old Hararians, Zimbabwe 1983-89 and 1993-94;
Scarborough, Australia 1989-90; Boland, South Africa 1991-92; Avendale, South
Africa 1992-93
**Cricketers particularly admired:** Colin Bland, Ian Botham, Graeme Hick, Allan
Donald

**Other sports followed:** Football (Liverpool FC), American football (San Francisco 49ers), golf and tennis

**Relaxations:** Playing golf and drinking Castle on Lake Kariba. Spending time with family

**Extras:** Captained the ICC Associates team at the Youth World Cup in 1987-88. Played for Zimbabwe against Sri Lanka in 1987. Played hockey for Zimbabwe from 1984-87 and also made the African team who played Asia in 1987. Qualified to play for England in 1992

**Opinions on cricket:** 'The four-day game is fine but there is still too much cricket being played, so maybe two divisions should be considered.'

**Best batting:** 151 Warwickshire v Middlesex, Lord's 1992

**Best bowling:** 3-18 Mashonaland v Mashonaland U24, Harare 1993-94

## 1995 Season

|          | M  | Inns | NO | Runs | HS   | Avge  | 100s | 50s | Ct | St | O | M | Runs | Wkts | Avge | Best | 5wI | 10wM |
|----------|----|------|----|------|------|-------|------|-----|----|----|---|---|------|------|------|------|-----|------|
| Test     |    |      |    |      |      |       |      |     |    |    |   |   |      |      |      |      |     |      |
| All First | 19 | 27   | 3  | 1198 | 144  | 49.91 | 4    | 4   | 9  | -  |   |   |      |      |      |      |     |      |
| 1-day Int |    |      |    |      |      |       |      |     |    |    |   |   |      |      |      |      |     |      |
| NatWest  | 5  | 3    | 1  | 67   | 25   | 33.50 | -    | -   | 3  | -  |   |   |      |      |      |      |     |      |
| B & H    | 4  | 4    | 1  | 30   | 12 * | 10.00 | -    | -   | -  | -  |   |   |      |      |      |      |     |      |
| Sunday   | 16 | 13   | 2  | 176  | 42 * | 16.00 | -    | -   | 7  | -  |   |   |      |      |      |      |     |      |

## Career Performances

|          | M  | Inns | NO | Runs | HS   | Avge  | 100s | 50s | Ct | St | Balls | Runs | Wkts | Avge  | Best | 5wI | 10wM |
|----------|----|------|----|------|------|-------|------|-----|----|----|-------|------|------|-------|------|-----|------|
| Test     |    |      |    |      |      |       |      |     |    |    |       |      |      |       |      |     |      |
| All First | 79 | 122  | 25 | 4189 | 151  | 43.18 | 10   | 15  | 42 | -  | 247   | 183  | 6    | 30.50 | 3-18 | -   | -    |
| 1-day Int |    |      |    |      |      |       |      |     |    |    |       |      |      |       |      |     |      |
| NatWest  | 17 | 15   | 4  | 239  | 65 * | 21.72 | -    | 1   | 11 | -  | 10    | 12   | 1    | 12.00 | 1-8  | -   |      |
| B & H    | 10 | 9    | 2  | 125  | 39   | 17.85 | -    | -   | 5  | 1  |       |      |      |       |      |     |      |
| Sunday   | 58 | 48   | 19 | 902  | 83 * | 31.10 | -    | 3   | 23 | -  | 6     | 2    | 0    | -     | -    | -   |      |

61. Which wicket-keeper was responsible for the most dismissals in first-class cricket in 1995?

# PETERS, S. D.                    Essex

**Name:** Stephen David Peters
**Role:** Right-hand bat
**Born:** 10 December 1976, Harold Wood
**Height:** 5ft 8in **Weight:** 10st
**Nickname:** Rodders, Jordy
**County debut:** No first-team appearance
**Parents:** Brian and Leslie
**Marital status:** Single
**Family links with cricket:** 'Father plays, sister makes teas, mother is a scorer'
**Education:** Upminster Junior School; Coopers Coborn and Company School
**Qualifications:** 9 GCSEs
**Off-season:** Insurance broking
**Cricketers particularly admired:** Graham Gooch, Michael Atherton
**Other sports followed:** Football (West Ham United), rugby, golf
**Injuries**: Broken index finger, out for five weeks
**Relaxations:** Music and television
**Extras:** The Sir John Hobbs Jubilee Memorial Prize 1994, a *Daily Telegraph* regional batting award 1994, represented England at both U14 and U15

# PHILLIPS, B.                    Kent

**Name:** Ben James Phillips
**Role:** Right-hand bat, right-arm fast-medium bowler
**Born:** 30 September 1972
**Height:** 6ft 6in **Weight:** 16st
**Nickname:** Bustle, Bombhead, Jurassic
**County debut:** No first-team appearance
**Parents:** Trevor and Glynnis
**Marital status:** Single
**Family links with cricket:** 'My father has been a keen club cricketer at Hayes since he was at school'
**Education:** St Josephs Primary, Bromley; Langley Park School for Boys, Beckenham; Langley Park Sixth Form
**Qualifications:** 9 GCSEs and 2 A-levels
**Off-season:** Playing and coaching in South Africa

**Overseas teams played for:** University of
Queensland, Australia 1993-94; Cape
Technikon, Cape Town, South Africa 1994-95
**Cricketers particularly admired:** Brian
McMillan, Ian Bishop, Mark Waugh, Carl
Hooper
**Other sports followed:** Basketball (played
for Crystal Palace), football (West Ham
United 'not that it has done them any good'),
golf
**Injuries:** Stress fracture of toes across right
foot, missed three weeks
**Relaxations:** Listening to music, reading
magazines, swimming
**Extras:** Represented England U19 Schools in
1993-94. Holds Langley Park School record
for the fastest half century off 11 balls

# PHILLIPS, N. C. Sussex

**Name:** Nicholas Charles Phillips
**Role:** Right-hand bat, off-spin bowler
**Born:** 10 May 1974, Pembury, Kent
**Height:** 5ft 11in **Weight:** 11st
**County debut:** 1994
**1st-Class 50s:** 3
**Place in batting averages:** 206th av. 20.33
**1st-Class catches:** 1
**Strike rate:** (career 107.92)
**Parents:** Robert and Joan
**Marital status:** Single
**Family links with cricket:** Father
represented Kent Association and the Kent
League while playing for Tunbridge Wells,
and has scored over 100 club centuries
**Education:** Hilden Grange School,
Tonbridge; St Thomas's School, Winchelsea;
William Parker School, Hastings
**Qualifications:** 8 GCSEs, NCA coaching certificate
**Overseas tours:** Sussex U18 to India 1990-91
**Cricketers particularly admired:** Eddie Hemmings, Derek Randall
**Other sports followed:** Hockey, football (West Ham)
**Relaxations:** Playing hockey for South Saxons, music (The Stone Roses), spending time

with friends
**Extras:** Represented England U19 in home series against West Indies U19 1993. Has played hockey for Sussex U14 and U16
**Best batting:** 53 Sussex v Young Australia, Hove 1995
**Best bowling:** 3-39 Sussex v Cambridge University 1995

## 1995 Season

|         | M | Inns | NO | Runs | HS | Avge | 100s | 50s | Ct | St | O | M | Runs | Wkts | Avge | Best | 5wI | 10wM |
|---------|---|------|----|----|------|------|------|-----|----|----|-----|-----|------|------|------|------|-----|------|
| Test      |   |    |   |     |    |       |   |   |   |   |       |    |     |   |       |      |   |   |
| All First | 6 | 10 | 1 | 183 | 53 | 20.33 | - | 3 | 3 | - | 154.5 | 34 | 521 | 8 | 65.12 | 3-78 | - | - |
| 1-day Int |   |    |   |     |    |       |   |   |   |   |       |    |     |   |       |      |   |   |
| NatWest   |   |    |   |     |    |       |   |   |   |   |       |    |     |   |       |      |   |   |
| B & H     |   |    |   |     |    |       |   |   |   |   |       |    |     |   |       |      |   |   |
| Sunday    | 3 | 2  | 0 | 2   | 2  | 1.00  | - | - | 1 | - | 16    | 1  | 69  | 1 | 69.00 | 1-35 | - |   |

## Career Performances

|         | M | Inns | NO | Runs | HS | Avge | 100s | 50s | Ct | St | Balls | Runs | Wkts | Avge | Best | 5wI | 10wM |
|---------|---|------|----|----|------|------|------|-----|----|----|------|------|------|------|------|------|------|
| Test      |   |    |   |     |     |       |   |   |   |   |      |     |    |       |      |   |   |
| All First | 8 | 12 | 2 | 220 | 53  | 22.00 | - | 3 | 4 | - | 1403 | 751 | 13 | 57.76 | 3-39 | - | - |
| 1-day Int |   |    |   |     |     |       |   |   |   |   |      |     |    |       |      |   |   |
| NatWest   |   |    |   |     |     |       |   |   |   |   |      |     |    |       |      |   |   |
| B & H     |   |    |   |     |     |       |   |   |   |   |      |     |    |       |      |   |   |
| Sunday    | 9 | 5  | 2 | 24  | 11* | 8.00  | - | - | 1 | - | 294  | 223 | 5  | 44.60 | 2-19 | - |   |

# PICK, R. A.        Nottinghamshire

**Name:** Robert Andrew Pick
**Role:** Left-hand bat, right-arm fast-medium bowler
**Born:** 19 November 1963, Nottingham
**Height:** 5ft 10in **Weight:** 13st
**Nickname:** Dad
**County debut:** 1983
**County cap:** 1987
**50 wickets in a season:** 4
**1st-Class 50s:** 5
**1st-Class 5 w. in innings:** 16
**1st-Class 10 w. in match:** 3
**1st-Class catches:** 49
**One-Day 5 w. in innings:** 2
**Place in batting averages:** 225th av. 17.95 (1994 240th av. 15.13)
**Place in bowling averages:** 81st av. 31.41 (1994 31st av. 26.16)
**Strike rate:** 57.68 (career 59.26)

**Parents:** Bob and Lillian
**Wife and date of marriage:**
Jennie Ruth, 8 April 1989
**Family links with cricket:** Father, uncles
and cousins all play local cricket; David
Millns (Leicestershire) is brother-in-law
**Education:** Alderman Derbyshire
Comprehensive; High Pavement College
**Qualifications:** 7 O-levels, 1 A-level, senior
cricket coach
**Overseas tours:** England A to Pakistan 1990-
91, to Bermuda and West Indies 1991-92
**Overseas teams played for:** Wellington,
New Zealand 1989-90
**Cricketers particularly admired:** Bob
White, Mike Hendrick, Mike Harris,
Franklyn Stephenson, Wayne Noon
**Other sports followed:** Ice hockey (Nottingham
Panthers), soccer and American football
**Relaxations:** 'Spending time with family, fishing, a good pint and a nice feed'
**Extras:** Played for England YC v Australia YC 1983. Played football for Nottingham
Schoolboys. Took Nottinghamshire's only ever hat-trick in the NatWest against Scotland
this year. Awarded benefit for 1996
**Opinions on cricket:** 'Plenty but no-one who can do anything about them listens.'
**Best batting:** 65* Nottinghamshire v Northamptonshire, Trent Bridge 1994
**Best bowling:** 7-128 Nottinghamshire v Leicestershire, Leicester 1990

## 1995 Season

|  | M | Inns | NO | Runs | HS | Avge | 100s | 50s | Ct | St | O | M | Runs | Wkts | Avge | Best | 5wI | 10wM |
|---|---|---|---|---|---|---|---|---|---|---|---|---|---|---|---|---|---|---|
| Test |  |  |  |  |  |  |  |  |  |  |  |  |  |  |  |  |  |  |
| All First | 17 | 26 | 4 | 395 | 50 * | 17.95 | - | 1 | 9 | - | 490.2 | 105 | 1602 | 51 | 31.41 | 5-82 | 2 | - |
| 1-day Int |  |  |  |  |  |  |  |  |  |  |  |  |  |  |  |  |  |  |
| NatWest | 2 | 0 | 0 | 0 | 0 | - | - | - | - | - | 21 | 1 | 102 | 6 | 17.00 | 5-23 | 1 |  |
| B & H | 6 | 2 | 2 | 31 | 21 * | - | - | - | 1 | - | 53.4 | 6 | 257 | 3 | 85.66 | 1-40 | - |  |
| Sunday | 13 | 5 | 2 | 76 | 58 * | 25.33 | - | 1 | 2 | - | 96 | 4 | 434 | 9 | 48.22 | 2-13 | - |  |

## Career Performances

|  | M | Inns | NO | Runs | HS | Avge | 100s | 50s | Ct | St | Balls | Runs | Wkts | Avge | Best | 5wI | 10wM |
|---|---|---|---|---|---|---|---|---|---|---|---|---|---|---|---|---|---|
| Test |  |  |  |  |  |  |  |  |  |  |  |  |  |  |  |  |  |
| All First | 184 | 195 | 54 | 2161 | 65 * | 15.32 | - | 5 | 49 | - | 28567 | 15606 | 482 | 32.37 | 7-128 | 16 | 3 |
| 1-day Int |  |  |  |  |  |  |  |  |  |  |  |  |  |  |  |  |  |
| NatWest | 27 | 15 | 11 | 120 | 34 * | 30.00 | - | - | 4 | - | 1753 | 1127 | 46 | 24.50 | 5-22 | 2 |  |
| B & H | 40 | 16 | 11 | 107 | 25 * | 21.40 | - | - | 5 | - | 2389 | 1679 | 45 | 37.31 | 4-42 | - |  |
| Sunday | 110 | 39 | 17 | 308 | 58 * | 14.00 | - | 1 | 23 | - | 4815 | 4025 | 116 | 34.69 | 4-32 | - |  |

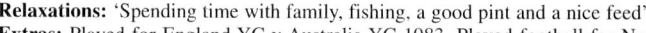

# PIERSON, A. R. K.　　　Leicestershire

**Name:** Adrian Roger Kirshaw Pierson
**Role:** Right-hand bat, right-arm
off-spin bowler
**Born:** 21 July 1963, Enfield, Middlesex
**Height:** 6ft 4in **Weight:** 12st
**Nickname:** Stick, Skirlogue, Bunny, Bun
**County debut:** 1985 (Warwickshire), 1993
(Leicestershire)
**County cap:** 1995 (Leicestershire)
**50 w. in a season:** 1
**1st-Class 50s:** 2
**1st-Class 5 w. in innings:** 10
**1st-Class catches:** 48
**One-day 5 w. innings:** 1
**Place in batting averages:** 227th av. 17.81
(1994 184th av. 22.26)
**Place in bowling averages:** 76th av. 30.65
(1994 91st av. 34.24)
**Strike rate:** 55.40 (career 71.89)
**Parents:** Patrick and Patricia
**Wife and date of marriage:** Helen Majella, 29 September 1990
**Education:** Lochinver House Primary School; Kent College, Canterbury; Hatfield
Polytechnic
**Qualifications:** 8 O-levels, 2 A-levels, senior coaching award
**Career outside cricket:** Production editor for a graphic design company, 'running my
own picture framing business'
**Off-season:** 'Knee operation, cricket event management in Sharjah and MCC tour to
Bangladesh'
**Overseas teams played for:** Walmer, South Africa; Manicaland, Zimbabwe
**Cricketers particularly admired:** John Emburey, Phil Edmonds, Tony Greig, Clive Rice
**Other sports followed:** All sports except horse racing, but especially golf
**Injuries:** Broken finger
**Relaxations:** Golf, driving and squash
**Extras:** On Lord's groundstaff 1984-85 and on Warwickshire staff from 1985-91. First
Championship wicket was Viv Richards
**Opinions on cricket:** 'Four-day cricket matches would last longer if teams had some
sort of incentive to save the match – i.e. a team that loses should not be awarded any first
innings bonus points. I do not believe games in general are finishing earlier because of
poor wickets.'
**Best batting:** 58 Leicestershire v Lancashire, Leicester 1993
**Best bowling:** 8-42 Leicestershire v Warwickshire, Edgbaston 1994

## 1995 Season

| | M | Inns | NO | Runs | HS | Avge | 100s | 50s | Ct | St | O | M | Runs | Wkts | Avge | Best | 5wI | 10wM |
|---|---|---|---|---|---|---|---|---|---|---|---|---|---|---|---|---|---|---|
| Test | | | | | | | | | | | | | | | | | | |
| All First | 20 | 32 | 10 | 392 | 50 | 17.81 | - | 1 | 13 | - | 637.1 | 135 | 2115 | 69 | 30.65 | 5-48 | 2 | - |
| 1-day Int | | | | | | | | | | | | | | | | | | |
| NatWest | 2 | 2 | 1 | 30 | 20 * | 30.00 | - | - | - | - | 21.2 | 3 | 70 | 4 | 17.50 | 3-36 | - | |
| B & H | 4 | 2 | 2 | 19 | 10 * | - | - | - | 1 | - | 22.2 | 1 | 96 | 0 | - | - | - | |
| Sunday | 8 | 4 | 2 | 36 | 21 * | 18.00 | - | - | 7 | - | 37 | 1 | 235 | 11 | 21.36 | 5-36 | 1 | |

## Career Performances

| | M | Inns | NO | Runs | HS | Avge | 100s | 50s | Ct | St | Balls | Runs | Wkts | Avge | Best | 5wI | 10wM |
|---|---|---|---|---|---|---|---|---|---|---|---|---|---|---|---|---|---|
| Test | | | | | | | | | | | | | | | | | |
| All First | 110 | 139 | 50 | 1391 | 58 | 15.62 | - | 2 | 48 | - | 16896 | 8506 | 235 | 36.19 | 8-42 | 10 | - |
| 1-day Int | | | | | | | | | | | | | | | | | |
| NatWest | 10 | 6 | 2 | 33 | 20 * | 8.25 | - | - | 2 | - | 596 | 297 | 9 | 33.00 | 3-20 | - | |
| B & H | 16 | 11 | 7 | 45 | 11 | 11.25 | - | - | 5 | - | 812 | 473 | 12 | 39.41 | 3-34 | - | |
| Sunday | 60 | 32 | 14 | 182 | 29 * | 10.11 | - | - | 28 | - | 2361 | 1895 | 56 | 33.83 | 5-36 | 1 | |

# PIGOTT, A. C. S.　　　Surrey

**Name:** Anthony Charles Shackleton Pigott
**Role:** Right-hand bat, right-arm
fast-medium bowler, slip fielder
**Born:** 4 June 1958, London
**Height:** 6ft 1in **Weight:** 12st 9lbs
**Nickname:** Lester
**County debut:** 1978 (Sussex), 1994 (Surrey)
**County cap:** 1982 (Sussex)
**Benefit:** 1991 (£60,025)
**Test debut:** 1983-84
**Tests:** 1
**50 wickets in a season:** 5
**1st-Class 50s:** 20
**1st-Class 100s:** 1
**1st-Class 5 w. in innings:** 26
**1st-Class 10 w. in match:** 2
**1st-Class catches:** 121
**One-Day 5 w. in innings:** 3
**Place in bowling averages:** 75th av. 30.31
(1994 26th av. 25.41)
**Strike rate:** 57.13 (career 56.61)
**Parents:** Tom and Juliet

**Marital status:** Engaged
**Children:** Elliot Sebastian, 15 March 1983
**Family links with cricket:** Father captained village side, mother played at school 'and claims I got my cricket ability from her'
**Education:** Holmwood House, Kent; Harrow School
**Qualifications:** 5 O-levels, 2 A-levels; junior coaching certificate
**Career outside cricket:** Recently set up sports marketing company
**Off-season:** Starting new business CML – promoting professional sportsmen. Touring South Africa with Surrey Vagrants. Touring Sharjah with England over-35s for The Masters
**Overseas tours:** England to New Zealand 1983-84; MCC to Leeward Islands 1991-92, to West Africa 1993-94; *Cricket World* to Barbados 1993-94
**Overseas teams played for:** Wellington, New Zealand 1982-83 and 1983-84
**Cricketers particularly admired:** Ian Botham, Geoff Arnold, John Snow, Mike Gatting
**Other sports followed:** Squash, soccer, golf, rugby
**Injuries:** Hernia, out for three months
**Extras:** Public schools rackets champion 1975. First three wickets in first-class cricket were a hat-trick. Had operation on back, April 1981, missing most of season, and was told by a specialist he would never play cricket again. Postponed wedding to make Test debut when called into England party on tour of New Zealand 1983-84. Originally going to Somerset for 1984 season, but remained with Sussex. Was diagnosed as a diabetic after he lost 11lbs in two weeks in 1987, but recovered to take 74 wickets in 1988 season. Moved to Surrey at end of 1993 season after 18 years with Sussex
**Best batting:** 104* Sussex v Warwickshire, Edgbaston 1986
**Best bowling:** 7-74 Sussex v Northamptonshire, Eastbourne 1982

## 1995 Season

|  | M | Inns | NO | Runs | HS | Avge | 100s | 50s | Ct | St | O | M | Runs | Wkts | Avge | Best | 5wI | 10wM |
|---|---|---|---|---|---|---|---|---|---|---|---|---|---|---|---|---|---|---|
| Test |  |  |  |  |  |  |  |  |  |  |  |  |  |  |  |  |  |  |
| All First | 6 | 11 | 1 | 76 | 19 | 7.60 | - | - | 1 | - | 209.3 | 50 | 667 | 22 | 30.31 | 6-91 | 2 | 1 |
| 1-day Int |  |  |  |  |  |  |  |  |  |  |  |  |  |  |  |  |  |  |
| NatWest | 2 | 1 | 0 | 3 | 3 | 3.00 | - | - | 2 | - | 22 | 2 | 98 | 0 | - | - | - | - |
| B & H | 4 | 2 | 1 | 13 | 8 | 13.00 | - | - | - | - | 36.1 | 2 | 139 | 5 | 27.80 | 2-52 | - |  |
| Sunday | 7 | 3 | 2 | 35 | 19 * | 35.00 | - | - | 2 | - | 46.4 | 1 | 243 | 10 | 24.30 | 3-31 | - |  |

## Career Performances

|  | M | Inns | NO | Runs | HS | Avge | 100s | 50s | Ct | St | Balls | Runs | Wkts | Avge | Best | 5wI | 10wM |
|---|---|---|---|---|---|---|---|---|---|---|---|---|---|---|---|---|---|
| Test | 1 | 2 | 1 | 12 | 8 * | 12.00 | - | - | - | - | 102 | 75 | 2 | 37.50 | 2-75 | - | - |
| All First | 260 | 317 | 66 | 4841 | 104 * | 19.28 | 1 | 20 | 121 | - | 38047 | 20831 | 672 | 30.99 | 7-74 | 26 | 2 |
| 1-day Int |  |  |  |  |  |  |  |  |  |  |  |  |  |  |  |  |  |
| NatWest | 32 | 17 | 2 | 173 | 53 | 11.53 | - | 1 | 8 | - | 1811 | 1134 | 42 | 27.00 | 3-4 | - |  |
| B & H | 44 | 30 | 10 | 289 | 49 * | 14.45 | - | - | 15 | - | 2428 | 1680 | 57 | 29.47 | 3-29 | - |  |
| Sunday | 182 | 106 | 41 | 1145 | 51 * | 17.61 | - | 1 | 57 | - | 7398 | 6038 | 260 | 23.22 | 5-24 | 3 |  |

# PIKE, V. J.          Gloucestershire

**Name:** Vyvian John Pike
**Role:** Right-hand bat, leg-spin bowler
**Born:** 13 August 1969, Taunton
**Height:** 6ft 1in   **Weight:** 14st 5lbs
**Nickname:** Magnus, Pikey
**County debut:** 1994
**1st-Class 5 w. in innings:** 1
**1st-Class catches:** 5
**Place in bowling averages:** 149th av. 53.81
(1994 51st av. 28.90)
**Strike rate:** 106.63 (career 76.35)
**Parents:** Stephen and Diane
**Wife and date of marriage:** Sharon, 30
September 1995
**Education:** Taunton School, Portsmouth
Polytechnic
**Qualifications:** 8 O-levels, 2 A-levels, BEng
in Civil Engineering
**Career outside cricket:** Bridge engineer
**Off-season:** Working as above
**Cricketers particularly admired:** Courtney Walsh, Viv Richards, Ian Botham
**Other sports followed:** Rugby union and all other sports
**Relaxations:** 'Most sports, music, listening to the world according to Tim Hancock and
the anecdotes of Paul Romaines'
**Best batting:** 27 Gloucestershire v Derbyshire, Chesterfield 1994
**Best bowling:** 6-41 Gloucestershire v Cambridge University, Bristol 1994

## 1995 Season

|  | M | Inns | NO | Runs | HS | Avge | 100s | 50s | Ct | St | O | M | Runs | Wkts | Avge | Best | 5wI | 10wM |
|---|---|---|---|---|---|---|---|---|---|---|---|---|---|---|---|---|---|---|
| Test |  |  |  |  |  |  |  |  |  |  |  |  |  |  |  |  |  |  |
| All First | 5 | 8 | 3 | 42 | 22 | 8.40 | - | - | 3 | - | 195.3 | 39 | 592 | 11 | 53.81 | 3-72 | - | - |
| 1-day Int |  |  |  |  |  |  |  |  |  |  |  |  |  |  |  |  |  |  |
| NatWest |  |  |  |  |  |  |  |  |  |  |  |  |  |  |  |  |  |  |  |
| B & H |  |  |  |  |  |  |  |  |  |  |  |  |  |  |  |  |  |  |  |
| Sunday |  |  |  |  |  |  |  |  |  |  |  |  |  |  |  |  |  |  |  |

> 62. Who scored the most centuries in first-class cricket
> in 1995 and how many did he score?

## Career Performances

|  | M | Inns | NO | Runs | HS | Avge | 100s | 50s | Ct | St | Balls | Runs | Wkts | Avge | Best | 5wI | 10wM |
|---|---|---|---|---|---|---|---|---|---|---|---|---|---|---|---|---|---|
| Test |  |  |  |  |  |  |  |  |  |  |  |  |  |  |  |  |  |
| All First | 14 | 20 | 7 | 156 | 27 | 12.00 | - | - | 5 | - | 2367 | 1170 | 31 | 37.74 | 6-41 | 1 | - |
| 1-day Int |  |  |  |  |  |  |  |  |  |  |  |  |  |  |  |  |  |
| NatWest |  |  |  |  |  |  |  |  |  |  |  |  |  |  |  |  |  |
| B & H |  |  |  |  |  |  |  |  |  |  |  |  |  |  |  |  |  |
| Sunday |  |  |  |  |  |  |  |  |  |  |  |  |  |  |  |  |  |

# PIPER, K. J.                    Warwickshire

**Name:** Keith John Piper
**Role:** Right-hand bat, wicket-keeper
**Born:** 18 December 1969, Leicester
**Height:** 5ft 7in **Weight:** 10st 8lbs
**Nickname:** Tubbsy, Garden Boy
**County debut:** 1989
**County cap:** 1992
**1st-Class 50s:** 8
**1st-Class 100s:** 2
**1st-Class catches:** 307
**1st-Class stumpings:** 17
**Place in batting averages:** 175th av. 23.41
(1994 180th av. 22.70)
**Parents:** John and Charlotte
**Marital status:** Single
**Family links with cricket:** Father plays club
cricket in Leicester
**Education:** Seven Sisters Junior; Somerset
Senior
**Qualifications:** Cricket senior coaching award, basketball coaching award, volleyball
coaching award
**Overseas tours:** Haringey Cricket College to Barbados 1986, to Trinidad 1987, to
Jamaica 1988; Warwickshire to La Manga 1989, to St Lucia 1990; England A to India
1994-95, to Pakistan 1995-96
**Overseas teams played for:** Desmond Haynes's XI, Barbados v Haringey Cricket College
**Cricketers particularly admired:** Jack Russell, Alec Stewart, Dermot Reeve, Colin
Metson
**Other sports followed:** Snooker, football, tennis
**Relaxations:** Music, eating
**Extras:** London Young Cricketer of the Year 1989 and in the last five 1992. Played for
England YC 1989. Was batting partner (116*) to Brian Lara when he reached his 501*

**Best batting:** 116* Warwickshire v Durham, Edgbaston 1994
**Best bowling:** 1-57 Warwickshire v Nottinghamshire, Edgbaston 1992

## 1995 Season

|  | M | Inns | NO | Runs | HS | Avge | 100s | 50s | Ct | St | O | M | Runs | Wkts | Avge | Best | 5wI | 10wM |
|---|---|---|---|---|---|---|---|---|---|---|---|---|---|---|---|---|---|---|
| Test |  |  |  |  |  |  |  |  |  |  |  |  |  |  |  |  |  |  |
| All First | 16 | 19 | 2 | 398 | 99 | 23.41 | - | 2 | 59 | 2 |  |  |  |  |  |  |  |  |
| 1-day Int |  |  |  |  |  |  |  |  |  |  |  |  |  |  |  |  |  |  |
| NatWest | 5 | 1 | 1 | 11 | 11 * | - | - | - | 8 | - |  |  |  |  |  |  |  |  |
| B & H | 1 | 1 | 0 | 6 | 6 | 6.00 | - | - | - | - |  |  |  |  |  |  |  |  |
| Sunday | 15 | 9 | 6 | 73 | 27 * | 24.33 | - | - | 24 | 2 |  |  |  |  |  |  |  |  |

## Career Performances

|  | M | Inns | NO | Runs | HS | Avge | 100s | 50s | Ct | St | Balls | Runs | Wkts | Avge | Best | 5wI | 10wM |
|---|---|---|---|---|---|---|---|---|---|---|---|---|---|---|---|---|---|
| Test |  |  |  |  |  |  |  |  |  |  |  |  |  |  |  |  |  |
| All First | 112 | 151 | 23 | 2553 | 116 * | 19.94 | 2 | 8 | 307 | 17 | 28 | 57 | 1 | 57.00 | 1-57 | - | - |
| 1-day Int |  |  |  |  |  |  |  |  |  |  |  |  |  |  |  |  |  |
| NatWest | 21 | 10 | 5 | 76 | 16 * | 15.20 | - | - | 32 | 2 |  |  |  |  |  |  |  |
| B & H | 8 | 7 | 3 | 42 | 11 * | 10.50 | - | - | 8 | - |  |  |  |  |  |  |  |
| Sunday | 57 | 32 | 17 | 217 | 30 | 14.46 | - | - | 54 | 13 |  |  |  |  |  |  |  |

# POLLARD, P. R.  Nottinghamshire

**Name:** Paul Raymond Pollard
**Role:** Left-hand opening bat, right-arm medium bowler
**Born:** 24 September 1968, Carlton, Nottinghamshire
**Height:** 5ft 11in **Weight:** 12st
**Nickname:** Polly, Sugar Ray
**County debut:** 1987
**County cap:** 1992
**1000 runs in a season:** 3
**1st-Class 50s:** 31
**1st-Class 100s:** 12
**1st-Class catches:** 126
**One-Day 100s:** 4
**Place in batting averages:** 132nd av. 29.76 (1994 127th av. 30.16)
**Parents:** Eric (deceased) and Mary
**Wife's name and date of marriage:** Kate, 14 March 1992

**Education:** Gedling Comprehensive
**Off-season:** Coaching and training at Trent Bridge
**Overseas teams played for:** Southern Districts, Brisbane 1988; North Perth 1990
**Cricketers particularly admired:** David Gower, Derek Randall, Ian Botham, Graham Gooch
**Other sports followed:** Football, golf, ice hockey
**Relaxations:** Watching videos, playing golf and music
**Extras:** Made debut for Nottinghamshire 2nd XI in 1985. Worked in Nottinghamshire CCC office on a Youth Training Scheme. Shared stands of 222 and 282 with Tim Robinson in the same game v Kent 1989. Youngest player to reach 1000 runs for Nottinghamshire
**Opinions on cricket:** 'The one bouncer rule should be abolished.'
**Best batting:** 180 Nottinghamshire v Derbyshire, Trent Bridge 1993
**Best bowling:** 2-79 Nottinghamshire v Gloucestershire, Bristol 1993

## 1995 Season

| | M | Inns | NO | Runs | HS | Avge | 100s | 50s | Ct | St | O | M | Runs | Wkts | Avge | Best | 5wI | 10wM |
|---|---|---|---|---|---|---|---|---|---|---|---|---|---|---|---|---|---|---|
| Test | | | | | | | | | | | | | | | | | | |
| All First | 11 | 19 | 2 | 506 | 120 | 29.76 | 1 | 2 | 13 | - | | | | | | | | |
| 1-day Int | | | | | | | | | | | | | | | | | | |
| NatWest | 2 | 2 | 1 | 179 | 96 | 179.00 | - | 2 | 1 | - | | | | | | | | |
| B & H | 4 | 3 | 0 | 126 | 56 | 42.00 | - | 2 | 1 | - | | | | | | | | |
| Sunday | 10 | 10 | 2 | 577 | 132 * | 72.12 | 1 | 4 | 5 | - | | | | | | | | |

## Career Performances

| | M | Inns | NO | Runs | HS | Avge | 100s | 50s | Ct | St | Balls | Runs | Wkts | Avge | Best | 5wI | 10wM |
|---|---|---|---|---|---|---|---|---|---|---|---|---|---|---|---|---|---|
| Test | | | | | | | | | | | | | | | | | |
| All First | 129 | 225 | 13 | 6930 | 180 | 32.68 | 12 | 31 | 126 | - | 274 | 268 | 4 | 67.00 | 2-79 | - | - |
| 1-day Int | | | | | | | | | | | | | | | | | |
| NatWest | 10 | 10 | 1 | 302 | 96 | 33.55 | - | 2 | 3 | - | 18 | 9 | 0 | - | | - | - |
| B & H | 20 | 19 | 1 | 564 | 104 | 31.33 | 1 | 5 | 8 | - | | | | | | | |
| Sunday | 75 | 68 | 8 | 2153 | 132 * | 35.88 | 3 | 11 | 27 | - | | | | | | | |

# POLLOCK, S. M.                             Warwickshire

**Name:** Shaun Maclean Pollock
**Role:** Right-hand bat, right-arm fast-medium bowler
**Born:** 16 July 1973, Port Elizabeth, South Africa
**Height:** 6ft 3in **Weight:** 13st 5lbs
**Nickname:** Polly
**County debut:** No first-team appearance
**Test debut:** 1995-96

**1st-Class 50s:** 1
**1st-Class catches:** 7
**Strike rate:** (career 57.77)
**Parents:** Peter and Inez
**Marital status:** Single
**Family links with cricket:** Father Peter
played for Eastern Province and South Africa
(1959-71). Uncle Graeme played for Eastern
Province, Transvaal and South Africa (1960-
86). Father is current convenor of selectors
for national teams
**Education:** Northlands Primary School,
Durban, Natal; Northwood, Durban, Natal;
Natal University
**Qualifications:** B Comm
**Career outside cricket:** None at present
**Off-season:** Playing for Natal and South
Africa
**Overseas tours:** South Africa Tertiary Team
to Kenya and Zimbabwe 1994-95; South Africa U24 to Sri Lanka 1995-96; South
Africa to Hong Kong Sixes 1995, to India and Pakistan (World Cup) 1995-96
**Cricketers particularly admired:** Brian Macmillan, Malcolm Marshall and Clive Rice
**Other sports followed:** Golf, hockey, tennis, rugby and soccer
**Relaxations:** Watching sport, spending time with friends and listening to music
**Extras:** Was voted Player of the Series in the South Africa v England one-day series.
Played for Natal Nuffield team and then selected for South Africa Schools in 1991.
Made debut for Natal in all three local competitions against Northern Traansvaal (same
team) at Kingsmead, Durban (same venue)
**Best batting:** 56 Natal v Border, East London 1993-94
**Best bowling:** 4-24 Natal v Orange Free State, Durban 1994-95

## 1995 (no first-team or first-class appearances)

## Career Performances

| | M | Inns | NO | Runs | HS | Avge | 100s | 50s | Ct | St | Balls | Runs | Wkts | Avge | Best | 5wI | 10wM |
|---|---|---|---|---|---|---|---|---|---|---|---|---|---|---|---|---|---|
| Test | | | | | | | | | | | | | | | | | |
| All First | 16 | 22 | 5 | 385 | 56 | 22.64 | - | 1 | 7 | - | 2831 | 1103 | 49 | 22.51 | 4-24 | - | - |
| 1-day Int | | | | | | | | | | | | | | | | | |
| NatWest | | | | | | | | | | | | | | | | | |
| B & H | | | | | | | | | | | | | | | | | |
| Sunday | | | | | | | | | | | | | | | | | |

# POOLEY, J. C.

**Name:** Jason Calvin Pooley
**Role:** Left-hand bat, right-arm slow bowler
**Born:** 8 August 1969, Hammersmith
**Height:** 6ft **Weight:** 12st 7lbs
**County debut:** 1989
**County cap:** 1995
**1000 runs in a season:** 1
**1st-Class 100s:** 5
**1st-Class 50s:** 10
**1st-Class catches:** 37
**One-Day 100s:** 1
**Place in batting averages:** 23rd av. 51.34
**Parents:** Dave and Kath
**Wife and date of marriage:**
Justine, 30 September 1995
**Family links with cricket:** Father and older
brother play club cricket. Younger brother
Gregg has played for Middlesex YC,

Middlesex 2nd XI and Derbyshire 2nd XI
**Education:** Acton High School
**Off-season:** England A tour to Pakistan
**Overseas tours:** England A to Pakistan 1995-96
**Overseas teams played for:** St George's, Sydney 1988-89; Western Suburbs, Sydney
1991-92
**Cricketers particularly admired:** David Gower, Desmond Haynes, Mark
Ramprakash
**Other sports followed:** 'All sports, support Portsmouth FC'
**Relaxations:** 'Eating out with my wife Justine'
**Extras:** Voted Rapid Cricketline 2nd XI Player of the Year in 1989, his first year on the
Middlesex staff. Called up as a late replacement on the England A tour to Pakistan after
the withdrawal of Andrew Symonds
**Opinions on cricket:** 'Too much cricket played. Sunday League should be 30 overs a
side. Angus Fraser will be able to tell you the rest. He seems to know everything you
want to know.'
**Best batting:** 136 Middlesex v Gloucestershire, Bristol 1995

---

63. Two England cricketers, both of whom toured South Africa in 1995-96,
list art as a favourite hobby. Who are they?

## 1995 Season

| | M | Inns | NO | Runs | HS | Avge | 100s | 50s | Ct | St | O | M | Runs | Wkts | Avge | Best | 5wI | 10wM |
|---|---|---|---|---|---|---|---|---|---|---|---|---|---|---|---|---|---|---|
| Test | | | | | | | | | | | | | | | | | | |
| All First | 18 | 30 | 4 | 1335 | 136 | 51.34 | 5 | 6 | 25 | - | 4 | 0 | 15 | 0 | - | - | - | - |
| 1-day Int | | | | | | | | | | | | | | | | | | |
| NatWest | 2 | 2 | 0 | 9 | 8 | 4.50 | - | - | - | - | | | | | | | | |
| B & H | 6 | 6 | 0 | 181 | 47 | 30.16 | - | - | 3 | - | | | | | | | | |
| Sunday | 14 | 14 | 1 | 215 | 51 | 16.53 | - | 1 | 6 | - | | | | | | | | |

## Career Performances

| | M | Inns | NO | Runs | HS | Avge | 100s | 50s | Ct | St | Balls | Runs | Wkts | Avge | Best | 5wI | 10wM |
|---|---|---|---|---|---|---|---|---|---|---|---|---|---|---|---|---|---|
| Test | | | | | | | | | | | | | | | | | |
| All First | 40 | 67 | 6 | 2129 | 136 | 34.90 | 5 | 10 | 37 | - | 36 | 26 | 0 | - | - | - | - |
| 1-day Int | | | | | | | | | | | | | | | | | |
| NatWest | 3 | 3 | 0 | 42 | 33 | 14.00 | - | - | - | - | | | | | | | |
| B & H | 9 | 9 | 0 | 192 | 47 | 21.33 | - | - | 3 | - | | | | | | | |
| Sunday | 29 | 28 | 2 | 633 | 109 | 24.34 | 1 | 4 | 7 | - | | | | | | | |

# POWELL, M. J.     Warwickshire

**Name:** Michael James Powell
**Role:** Right-hand bat, right arm medium bowler
**Born:** 5 April 1975, Bolton
**Height:** 5ft 11in **Weight:** 11st 2lbs
**Nickname:** Powelly, Arthur
**County debut:** No first-team appearance
**Parents:** Terry and Pat
**Marital status:** Single
**Education:** Rivington and Blackrod High School, Horwich; Lawrence Sheriff School, Rugby
**Qualifications:** 6 GCSEs, 2 A-levels
**Career outside cricket:** Part-time PE teacher
**Overseas tours:** England U18 (captain) to South Africa 1992-93, to Denmark (captain) 1993; England U19 to Sri Lanka 1993-94
**Overseas teams played for:** Avendale CC, Cape Town, 1994-95
**Cricketers particularly admired:** Ian Botham, Tim Munton, Roger Twose
**Other sports followed:** Rugby, football
**Relaxations:** Playing golf, snooker and spending time with family, friends,

particularly girlfriend, Sarah

**Opinions on cricket:** 'Second-class cricket should be played in conditions identical to the first-class game, including pitches and length of games.'

# PRABHAKAR, M.        Durham

**Name:** Manoj Prabhakar
**Role:** Right-hand bat, right-arm fast-medium bowler
**Born:** 15 April 1963, Ghaziabad, India
**Height:** 5ft 9in
**County debut:** 1995
**Test debut:** 1984-85
**Tests:** 36
**One-Day Internationals:** 120
**50 w. in a season:** 1
**1st-Class 50s:** 30
**1st-Class 100s:** 18
**1st-Class 200s:** 1
**1st-Class 5 w. in innings:** 10
**1st-Class 10 w. in match:** 1
**1st-Class catches:** 61
**One-Day 100s:** 2
**One-Day 5 w. in innings:** 1
**Strike rate:** 68.13 (career 63.47 )
**Place in batting averages:** 115th av. 32.00
**Place in bowling averages:** 56th av. 28.21
**Off-season:** Playing for India
**Overseas tours:** India to England 1986, to Pakistan 1989-90, New Zealand 1989-90, to England 1990, to Australia and New Zealand (World Cup) 1991-92, to Zimbabwe and South Africa 1992-93, to Sri Lanka and New Zealand 1993-94, to Pakistan and Sri Lanka (World Cup) 1995-96
**Overseas teams played for:** Delhi and Districts, India
**Extras:** Scored maiden Test century against West Indies at Chandigarh in December 1994. Was due to play for Warwickshire in 1994 but was injured and replaced by Brian Lara
**Best batting:** 229* Delhi v Himachal Pradesh, Delhi 1989-90
**Best bowling:** 7-65 Durham v Leicestershire, Leicester 1995

## 1995 Season

| | M | Inns | NO | Runs | HS | Avge | 100s | 50s | Ct | St | O | M | Runs | Wkts | Avge | Best | 5wI | 10wM |
|---|---|---|---|---|---|---|---|---|---|---|---|---|---|---|---|---|---|---|
| Test | | | | | | | | | | - | | | | | | | | |
| All First | 17 | 31 | 3 | 896 | 101 | 32.00 | 1 | 5 | 9 | - | 579.1 | 165 | 1439 | 51 | 28.21 | 7-65 | 1 | - |
| 1-day Int | | | | | | | | | | | | | | | | | | |
| NatWest | 1 | 1 | 0 | 4 | 4 | 4.00 | - | - | 1 | - | 6 | 1 | 23 | 0 | - | - | - | |
| B & H | 5 | 5 | 1 | 148 | 69 | 37.00 | - | 2 | 4 | - | 43 | 3 | 187 | 5 | 37.40 | 2-36 | - | |
| Sunday | 12 | 12 | 0 | 324 | 69 | 27.00 | - | 2 | 2 | - | 87 | 6 | 377 | 17 | 22.17 | 3-30 | - | |

## Career Performances

| | M | Inns | NO | Runs | HS | Avge | 100s | 50s | Ct | St | Balls | Runs | Wkts | Avge | Best | 5wI | 10wM |
|---|---|---|---|---|---|---|---|---|---|---|---|---|---|---|---|---|---|
| Test | 36 | 54 | 8 | 1490 | 120 | 32.39 | 1 | 9 | 19 | - | 7349 | 3533 | 94 | 37.58 | 6-132 | 3 | - |
| All First | 142 | 198 | 33 | 6876 | 229* | 41.67 | 18 | 30 | 61 | - | 22851 | 10612 | 360 | 29.47 | 7-65 | 10 | 1 |
| 1-day Int | 120 | 89 | 19 | 1699 | 106 | 24.27 | 2 | 10 | 25 | - | 5964 | 4190 | 147 | 28.50 | 5-35 | 1 | |
| NatWest | 1 | 1 | 0 | 4 | 4 | 4.00 | - | - | 1 | - | 36 | 23 | 0 | - | - | - | |
| B & H | 5 | 5 | 1 | 148 | 69 | 37.00 | - | 2 | 4 | - | 258 | 187 | 5 | 37.40 | 2-36 | - | |
| Sunday | 12 | 12 | 0 | 324 | 69 | 27.00 | - | 2 | 2 | - | 522 | 377 | 17 | 22.17 | 3-30 | - | |

# PRATT, A.    Durham

**Name:** Andrew Pratt
**Role:** Left-hand bat, wicket-keeper
**Born:** 4 March 1975, Bishop Auckland
**Height:** 6ft **Weight:** 11st 3lbs
**County debut:** No first-team appearance
**Parents:** Gordon and Brenda
**Marital status:** Single
**Family links with cricket:** Brother was with
MCC Young Cricketers for four years.
Younger brother plays for Durham County
Schools and father played in local leagues
**Education:** Parkside Comprehensive School;
Durham New College
**Qualications:** 9 GCSEs, Advanced Diploma
in Information Technology, cricket coaching
certificate
**Off-season:** 'Hopefully go to Australia'
**Cricketers particularly admired:**
Alan Knott, Jack Russell

**Other sports followed:** Golf and football (Middlesborough FC)
**Extras:** Played for Durham County Schools at all levels and for the North of England
U15. Played for MCC Young Cricketers for three years

**Opinions on cricket:** 'I think that the English game is very demanding both physically and mentally. England should take note of Australia and play less matches, especially one-day games. I also think that the better young English players should be given more of a chance to play for their country.'

---

# PREECE, B. Worcestershire

**Name:** Ben Preece
**Height:** 6ft 1in **Weight:** 12st 8lbs
**Nickname:** Nigel Benn, Destroyer
**Parents:** Samuel and Valerie
**Marital status:** Single
**County debut:** No first-team appearance
**Family links with cricket:** Father played for school 1st XI
**Education:** Hourley Grange; Leasoures
**Qualifications:** 4 GCSEs, senior NCA coaching award
**Off-season:** Coaching and playing in Australia
**Cricketers particularly admired:** Steve Perryman, Jason Ratcliffe, Andy Moles
**Other sports followed:** Football (Birmingham City FC)
**Injuries:** Hip, out for two months
**Relaxations:** 'Watching football, going to the gym, hitting the town'
**Extras:** Played for England U15 and was a reserve for the England U19 tour to Zimbabwe
**Opinions on cricket:** 'I feel that too many things are in the batsman'0s favour. The balls used should have bigger seams. Second XI cricket should be played over four days so that players are more equipped to deal with the step up.'

---

# PRESTON, N. W. Kent

**Name:** Nicholas William Preston
**Role:** Right-hand bat, right-arm medium-fast bowler
**Born:** 22 January 1972, Dartford
**Height:** 6ft 1in **Weight:** 11st 5lbs
**Nickname:** North End, Jagback

**County debut:** No first-team appearance
**Parents:** Susan and Geoffrey
**Marital status:** Single
**Family links with cricket:** Grandfather played for Leicestershire. Brother plays for Kent youth teams
**Education:** Gravesend Grammar School; Exeter University
**Qualifications:** BSc (Hons) Biology/Geography
**Overseas teams played for:** Avendale, Cape Town 1993-94; Green Point, Cape Town 1994-95
**Cricketers particularly admired:** Richard Hadlee, Allan Donald, Carl Hooper
**Other sports followed:** Rugby, tennis, football, golf
**Relaxations:** Golf, listening to music, watching movies, spending time with close friends

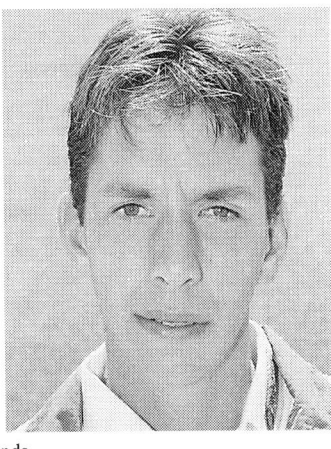

**Extras:** Kent League record of five wickets in five balls for Sevenoaks Vine v Midland Bank, 1994
**Opinions on cricket:** 'All 2nd XI cricket should be played on first-class grounds. Four-day cricket is good, but pitches need to last four days, not two or three. The structure of league cricket needs to be improved, as does the quality of pitches played on.'

64. Which three England players were hospitalised during the course of the Test series against West Indies in 1995?

# PRICHARD, P. J.                    Essex

**Name:** Paul John Prichard
**Role:** Right-hand bat, cover/mid-wicket
fielder, county captain
**Born:** 7 January 1965, Brentwood, Essex
**Height:** 5ft 10in **Weight:** 11st 7lbs
**Nickname:** Pablo
**County debut:** 1984
**County cap:** 1986
**1000 runs in a season:** 7
**1st-Class 50s:** 71
**1st-Class 100s:** 25
**1st-Class 200s:** 2
**1st-Class catches:** 156
**One-Day 100s:** 3
**Place in batting averages:**
104th av. 33.75 (1994 71st av. 37.93)
**Parents:** John and Margaret
**Wife's name and date of marriage:**
Jo-Anne, 24 November 1991
**Children:** Danielle Jade, 23 April 1993; Alexander James, 16 August 1995
**Family links with cricket:** Father played club cricket in Essex
**Education:** Brentwood County High School
**Qualifications:** NCA coaching certificate
**Career outside cricket:** Promotions executive for Ridley's brewery
**Off-season:** As above
**Overseas tours:** England A to Australia 1992-93
**Overseas teams played for:** VOB Cavaliers, Cape Town 1981-82; Sutherland,
Sydney 1984-87; Waverley, Sydney 1987-92
**Cricketers particularly admired:** Malcolm Marshall, Allan Border, David Gower,
Mark Waugh, Greg Matthews
**Other sports followed:** Football (West Ham), golf
**Relaxations:** Sleeping, being with family, watching West Ham
**Extras:** Shared county record second wicket partnership of 403 with Graham Gooch v
Leicestershire in 1990.  Britannic Assurance Cricketer of the Year 1992.  Essex joint
Player of the Year 1993. Appointed Essex captain for 1995. Awarded benefit for 1996
**Best batting:** 245 Essex v Leicestershire, Chelmsford 1990
**Best bowling:** 1-28 Essex v Hampshire, Chelmsford 1991

## 1995 Season

|  | M | Inns | NO | Runs | HS | Avge | 100s | 50s | Ct | St | O | M | Runs | Wkts | Avge | Best | 5wl | 10wM |
|---|---|---|---|---|---|---|---|---|---|---|---|---|---|---|---|---|---|---|
| Test |  |  |  |  |  |  |  |  |  |  |  |  |  |  |  |  |  |  |
| All First | 18 | 33 | 1 | 1080 | 109 | 33.75 | 2 | 5 | 10 | - |  |  |  |  |  |  |  |  |
| 1-day Int |  |  |  |  |  |  |  |  |  |  |  |  |  |  |  |  |  |  |
| NatWest | 2 | 2 | 1 | 116 | 81 | 116.00 | - | 1 | 1 | - |  |  |  |  |  |  |  |  |
| B & H | 5 | 5 | 0 | 167 | 92 | 33.40 | - | 2 | - | - |  |  |  |  |  |  |  |  |
| Sunday | 17 | 17 | 0 | 513 | 81 | 30.17 | - | 4 | 5 | - |  |  |  |  |  |  |  |  |

## Career Performances

|  | M | Inns | NO | Runs | HS | Avge | 100s | 50s | Ct | St | Balls | Runs | Wkts | Avge | Best | 5wl | 10wM |
|---|---|---|---|---|---|---|---|---|---|---|---|---|---|---|---|---|---|
| Test |  |  |  |  |  |  |  |  |  |  |  |  |  |  |  |  |  |
| All First | 244 | 396 | 44 | 12626 | 245 | 35.86 | 25 | 71 | 156 | - | 289 | 497 | 2 | 248.50 | 1-28 | - | - |
| 1-day Int |  |  |  |  |  |  |  |  |  |  |  |  |  |  |  |  |  |
| NatWest | 23 | 22 | 3 | 791 | 94 | 41.63 | - | 6 | 10 | - |  |  |  |  |  |  |  |
| B & H | 46 | 44 | 8 | 1096 | 107 | 30.44 | 1 | 6 | 10 | - |  |  |  |  |  |  |  |
| Sunday | 143 | 125 | 9 | 3019 | 107 | 26.02 | 2 | 15 | 44 | - |  |  |  |  |  |  |  |

# RACKEMANN, C. G.     Surrey

**Name:** Carl Gray Rackemann
**Role:** Right-hand bat, right-arm fast bowler
**Born:** 3 June 1960, Wondai, Australia
**Height:** 6ft 4in **Weight:** 15st 12lbs
**Nickname:** Mocca
**County debut:** 1995
**Test debut:** 1982-83
**Tests:** 12
**One-day Internationals:** 52
**1st-Class 5 w. innings:** 22
**1st-Class 10 w. matches:** 3
**1st-Class catches:** 40
**One-day 5 w. innings:** 1
**Parents:** Robert and Ena
**Marital status:** Single
**Family links with cricket:** Father played
club cricket in Australia
**Education:** Wondai; Kingaroy
**Career outside cricket:** Farmer and
promotional work
**Off-season:** Playing Sheffield Shield for Queensland
**Overseas tours:** Queensland Schoolboys to New Zealand 1977; Vic Lewis tour to

Holland 1981; Australia to West Indies 1984, to India 1984, to West Indies 1985, to England 1989, to New Zealand 1990, to Sharjah 1990, to United States 1990; unofficial Australian tour to South Africa 1985-87

**Overseas teams played for:** Wynnum-Manly, Brisbane 1977-84; Sandgate-Redcliffe 1984-87; Umbilo, Durban, South Africa 1986; Wests, Brisbane 1987-1996

**Cricketers particularly admired:** 'Most opponents'

**Injuries:** Tendon strain in left foot, out for one week

**Relaxations:** 'Resting'

**Best batting:** 33 Queensland v Tasmania, Hobart 1993-94

**Best bowling:** 8-84 Australian XI v South Africa, Johannesburg 1985-86

## 1995 Season

| | M | Inns | NO | Runs | HS | Avge | 100s | 50s | Ct | St | O | M | Runs | Wkts | Avge | Best | 5wI | 10wM |
|---|---|---|---|---|---|---|---|---|---|---|---|---|---|---|---|---|---|---|
| Test | | | | | | | | | | | | | | | | | | |
| All First | 13 | 20 | 12 | 120 | 20 * | 15.00 | - | - | 3 | - | 457 | 114 | 1430 | 48 | 29.79 | 6-60 | 1 | - |
| 1-day Int | | | | | | | | | | | | | | | | | | |
| NatWest | 2 | 1 | 0 | 6 | 6 | 6.00 | - | - | - | - | 20.1 | 2 | 109 | 4 | 27.25 | 3-40 | - | |
| B & H | | | | | | | | | | | | | | | | | | |
| Sunday | 11 | 5 | 3 | 31 | 15 * | 15.50 | - | - | - | - | 79 | 2 | 404 | 8 | 50.50 | 3-36 | - | |

## Career Performances

| | M | Inns | NO | Runs | HS | Avge | 100s | 50s | Ct | St | Balls | Runs | Wkts | Avge | Best | 5wI | 10wM |
|---|---|---|---|---|---|---|---|---|---|---|---|---|---|---|---|---|---|
| Test | 12 | 14 | 4 | 53 | 15 * | 5.30 | - | - | 2 | - | 2719 | 1137 | 39 | 29.15 | 6-86 | 3 | 1 |
| All First | 163 | 184 | 72 | 860 | 33 | 7.67 | - | - | 40 | - | 34455 | 16206 | 608 | 26.65 | 8-84 | 22 | 3 |
| 1-day Int | 52 | 18 | 6 | 34 | 9 * | 2.83 | - | - | 6 | - | 2791 | 1833 | 82 | 22.35 | 5-16 | 1 | |
| NatWest | 2 | 1 | 0 | 6 | 6 | 6.00 | - | - | - | - | 121 | 109 | 4 | 27.25 | 3-40 | - | |
| B & H | | | | | | | | | | | | | | | | | | |
| Sunday | 11 | 5 | 3 | 31 | 15 * | 15.50 | - | - | - | - | 474 | 404 | 8 | 50.50 | 3-36 | - | |

# RADFORD, N. V.                Worcestershire

**Name:** Neal Victor Radford

**Role:** Right-hand bat, right-arm fast-medium bowler, gully fielder

**Born:** 7 June 1957, Luanshya, Zambia

**Height:** 5ft 11in **Weight:** 12st 8lbs

**Nickname:** Radiz, Vic

**County debut:** 1980 (Lancashire), 1985 (Worcestershire)

**County cap:** 1985 (Worcestershire)

**Benefit:** 1995

**Test debut:** 1986

**Tests:** 3

**One-Day Internationals:** 6

**100 wickets in a season:** 2
**50 wickets in a season:** 6
**1st-Class 50s:** 8
**1st-Class 5 w. in innings:** 48
**1st-Class 10 w. in match:** 7
**1st-Class catches:** 130
**One-Day 5 w. in innings:** 3
**Place in batting averages:** 256th av. 14.44
(1994 270th av. 10.06)
**Place in bowling averages:** 102nd av. 35.45
(1994 100th av. 36.10)
**Strike rate:** 60.04 (career 50.95)
**Parents:** Victor Reginald and Edith Joyce
**Wife:** Lynne
**Children:** Luke Anthony, 3 June 1988; Josh
Deckland, 12 February 1990
**Family links with cricket:** Brother Wayne is
pro for Gowerton (SWCA) and plays for
Glamorgan 2nd XI. Also played for Orange
Free State in Currie Cup

**Education:** Athlone Boys High School, Johannesburg
**Qualifications:** Matriculation and university entrance, NCA advanced coach
**Overseas teams played for:** Transvaal 1979-89
**Overseas tours:** England to New Zealand and Australia 1987-88
**Cricketers particularly admired:** Vintcent van der Bijl
**Other sports followed:** All sports
**Relaxations:** Music, television, films, golf
**Extras:** Only bowler to take 100 first-class wickets in 1985 and was first to 100 wickets
in 1987, taking most first-class wickets both years. One of *Wisden*'s Five Cricketers of
the Year 1985. The Cricketers' Association Cricketer of the Year 1985. Retired from
first-class cricket at the end of the 1995 season
**Best batting:** 76* Lancashire v Derbyshire, Blackpool 1981
**Best bowling:** 9-70 Worcestershire v Somerset, Worcestershire 1986

## 1995 Season

|           | M  | Inns | NO | Runs | HS  | Avge  | 100s | 50s | Ct | St | O     | M  | Runs | Wkts | Avge  | Best | 5wI | 10wM |
|-----------|----|------|----|------|-----|-------|------|-----|----|----|-------|----|------|------|-------|------|-----|------|
| Test      |    |      |    |      |     |       |      |     |    |    |       |    |      |      |       |      |     |      |
| All First | 10 | 11   | 2  | 130  | 50  | 14.44 | -    | 1   | -  | -  | 220.1 | 46 | 780  | 22   | 35.45 | 5-45 | 1   | -    |
| 1-day Int |    |      |    |      |     |       |      |     |    |    |       |    |      |      |       |      |     |      |
| NatWest   | 1  | 1    | 0  | 0    | 0   | 0.00  | -    | -   | 1  | -  | 6     | 2  | 10   | 1    | 10.00 | 1-10 | -   |      |
| B & H     | 6  | 1    | 1  | 12   | 12* | -     | -    | -   | 1  | -  | 54    | 7  | 181  | 6    | 30.16 | 3-23 | -   |      |
| Sunday    | 12 | 7    | 3  | 60   | 21  | 15.00 | -    | -   | 3  | -  | 57.5  | 4  | 301  | 13   | 23.15 | 5-57 | 1   |      |

## Career Performances

|         | M   | Inns | NO | Runs | HS   | Avge  | 100s | 50s | Ct  | St | Balls | Runs  | Wkts | Avge   | Best  | 5wl | 10wM |
|---------|-----|------|-----|------|------|-------|------|-----|-----|----|-------|-------|------|--------|-------|-----|------|
| Test    | 3   | 4    | 1   | 21   | 12 * | 7.00  | -    | -   | -   | -  | 678   | 351   | 4    | 87.75  | 2-131 | -   | -    |
| All First | 296 | 298 | 73  | 3537 | 76 * | 15.72 | -    | 8   | 130 | -  | 50652 | 26707 | 994  | 26.86  | 9-70  | 48  | 7    |
| 1-day Int | 6 | 3   | 2   | 0    | 0 *  | 0.00  | -    | -   | 2   | -  | 348   | 230   | 2    | 115.00 | 1-32  | -   |      |
| NatWest | 35  | 19   | 6   | 151  | 37   | 11.61 | -    | -   | 14  | -  | 2010  | 1128  | 49   | 23.02  | 7-19  | 1   |      |
| B & H   | 53  | 29   | 16  | 387  | 40   | 29.76 | -    | -   | 13  | -  | 2903  | 1733  | 74   | 23.41  | 4-25  | -   |      |
| Sunday  | 164 | 100  | 42  | 1141 | 70   | 19.67 | -    | 2   | 39  | -  | 6424  | 4916  | 215  | 22.86  | 5-32  | 2   |      |

# RADFORD, T. A.             Middlesex

**Name:** Toby Alexander Radford
**Role:** Right-hand bat, 'occasional right-arm off-spin bowler'
**Born:** 3 December 1971, Caerphilly, Wales
**Height:** 5ft 10in **Weight:** 10st 4lbs
**Nickname:** Trawlerman, Radders
**County debut:** 1993 (one-day),
1994 (first-class)
**1st-Class 50s:** 2
**1st-Class catches:** 8
**Place in batting averages:** 93rd av. 34.85
**Parents:** Brian and Gillian
**Marital status:** Single
**Family links with cricket:** Dad is a senior
coach

**Education:** Park House School, Newbury; St Bartholomew's School, Newbury; Park House School, Newbury; City University, London
**Qualifications:** 9 O-levels, 3 A-levels, BA (Hons) in Journalism, qualified coach
**Career outside cricket:** Journalism
**Off-season:** Either playing club cricket abroad or doing sports promotion work
**Overseas tours:** England YC to Australia 1989-90, to New Zealand 1990-91
**Cricketers particularly admired:** Desmond Haynes, Allan Donald, Geoff Boycott
**Other sports followed:** Football, snooker, speedway
**Relaxations:** Cinema, pub, snooker, television, crosswords, music ('big U2 fan')
**Extras:** *Daily Telegraph* U15 Batsman of the Year 1987; MCC/Lord's Taverners' Player of the Year at U13, U15 and U19 age-groups. Middlesex Uncapped Player of the Year 1995. Left Middlesex at the end of the 1995 season
**Opinions on cricket:** 'Too many games played and, therefore, not enough time for the players to work on their technique once the season has begun. Would still like to see an

equivalent of the Adelaide Academy. Should be more flexibility for movement of players i.e. use of a transfer system.'

**Best batting:** 69 Middlesex v Essex, Chelmsford 1995
**Best bowling:** 1-0 Middlesex v Oxford University, The Parks 1995

## 1995 Season

|          | M  | Inns | NO | Runs | HS | Avge  | 100s | 50s | Ct | St | O | M | Runs | Wkts | Avge | Best | 5wI | 10wM |
|----------|----|------|----|------|----|-------|------|-----|----|----|---|---|------|------|------|------|-----|------|
| Test     |    |      |    |      |    |       |      |     |    |    |   |   |      |      |      |      |     |      |
| All First| 6  | 11   | 4  | 244  | 69 | 34.85 | -    | 2   | 7  | -  | 1 | 1 | 0    | 1    | 0.00 | 1-0  | -   | -    |
| 1-day Int|    |      |    |      |    |       |      |     |    |    |   |   |      |      |      |      |     |      |
| NatWest  | 1  | 1    | 0  | 82   | 82 | 82.00 | -    | 1   | -  | -  |   |   |      |      |      |      |     |      |
| B & H    |    |      |    |      |    |       |      |     |    |    |   |   |      |      |      |      |     |      |
| Sunday   | 3  | 3    | 1  | 35   | 30 | 17.50 | -    | -   | -  | -  |   |   |      |      |      |      |     |      |

## Career Performances

|          | M  | Inns | NO | Runs | HS | Avge  | 100s | 50s | Ct | St | Balls | Runs | Wkts | Avge | Best | 5wI | 10wM |
|----------|----|------|----|------|----|-------|------|-----|----|----|-------|------|------|------|------|-----|------|
| Test     |    |      |    |      |    |       |      |     |    |    |       |      |      |      |      |     |      |
| All First| 7  | 12   | 4  | 248  | 69 | 31.00 | -    | 2   | 8  | -  | 6     | 0    | 1    | 0.00 | 1-0  | -   | -    |
| 1-day Int|    |      |    |      |    |       |      |     |    |    |       |      |      |      |      |     |      |
| NatWest  | 1  | 1    | 0  | 82   | 82 | 82.00 | -    | 1   | -  | -  |       |      |      |      |      |     |      |
| B & H    |    |      |    |      |    |       |      |     |    |    |       |      |      |      |      |     |      |
| Sunday   | 4  | 4    | 1  | 73   | 38 | 24.33 | -    | -   | -  | -  |       |      |      |      |      |     |      |

65. Who won the Minor Counties Championship in 1995?

# RALPH, J. T. Worcestershire

**Name:** James Trevor Ralph
**Role:** Right-hand bat, leg-break bowler
**Born:** 9 October 1975, Kidderminster
**Height:** 5ft 11in  **Weight:** 12st 4lbs
**Nickname:** Ralphy
**County debut:** No first-team appearance
**Parents:** Alan and Mary
**Marital status:** Single
**Family links with cricket:** Father plays club cricket
**Education:** St John's First and Middle School, Kidderminster; Harry Cheshire High School, Kidderminster
**Qualifications:** 8 GCSEs
**Career outside cricket:** Postman
**Off-season:** Playing club cricket in Australia
**Overseas teams played for:** North Albany, Western Australia 1994-96
**Cricketers particularly admired:** Graeme Hick
**Other sports followed:** Hockey, golf and horse racing
**Relaxations:** Cars
**Extras:** Played for Worcestershire CA and SCA from U11 to U19

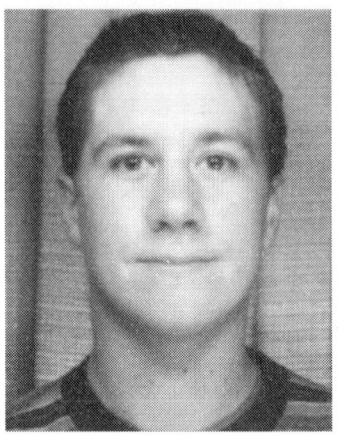

# RAMPRAKASH, M. R. Middlesex

**Name:** Mark Ravindra Ramprakash
**Role:** Right-hand bat, right-arm off-spin bowler
**Born:** 5 September 1969, Bushey, Herts
**Height:** 5ft 10in **Weight:** 12st 4lbs
**Nickname:** Ramps, Bloodaxe
**County debut:** 1987
**County cap:** 1990
**Test debut:** 1991
**Tests:** 17
**One-Day Internationals:** 7
**1000 runs in a season:** 6
**1st-Class 50s:** 56

**1st-Class 100s:** 29
**1st-Class 200s:** 4
**1st-Class catches:** 103
**One-Day 100s:** 6
**One-Day 5 w. in innings:** 1
**Place in batting averages:** 1st av. 77.86
(1994 13th av. 52.95)
**Strike rate:** (career 119.2)
**Parents:** Deonarine and Jennifer
**Date of marriage:** 24 September 1993
**Family links with cricket:** Father played
club cricket in Guyana
**Education:** Gayton High School; Harrow
Weald Sixth Form College
**Qualifications:** 6 O-levels, 2 A-levels
**Career outside cricket:** 'Any ideas
welcome.'
**Off-season:** England to South Africa
**Overseas tours:** England YC to Sri Lanka
1986-87, to Australia (Youth World Cup) 1987-88; England A to Pakistan 1990-91; to
West Indies 1991-92, to India (vice captain) 1994-95; England to New Zealand 1991-
92, to West Indies 1993-94, to Australia 1994-95, to South Africa 1995-96; Lion Cubs
to Barbados 1993
**Overseas teams played for:** Nairobi Jafferys, Kenya 1988; North Melbourne 1989
**Cricketers particularly admired:** 'All the great all-rounders'
**Other sports followed:** Snooker, football
**Relaxations:** 'Being at home with the family, going to movies, eating out'
**Extras:** Did not begin to play cricket until he was nine years old; played for
Bessborough CC at age 13, played for Middlesex 2nd XI aged 16 and made first-team
debut for Middlesex aged 17. Scored 204* in NCA Guernsey Festival Tournament and
in 1987 made 186* on his debut for Stanmore CC. Voted Best U15 Schoolboy of 1985
by Cricket Society, Best Young Cricketer of 1986 and Most Promising Player of the Year
in 1988. Played for England YC v New Zealand YC in 1989. Man of the Match in
Middlesex's NatWest Trophy final win in 1988, on his debut in the competition. While
on tour with England A in India was called up as replacement for Graeme Hick on the
senior tour to Australia 1994-95. Finished top of the Whyte and Mackay batting ratings
in 1995
**Opinions on cricket:** 'To lose overseas players would lower playing standards greatly.
People should think about the positive things that 99% of them bring to county cricket.
Why do the powers-that-be feel that they must constantly tamper with the rules, i.e.
bouncers etc?'
**Best batting:** 235 Middlesex v Yorkshire, Headingley 1995
**Best bowling:** 3-91 Middlesex v Somerset, Taunton 1995

## 1995 Season

|  | M | Inns | NO | Runs | HS | Avge | 100s | 50s | Ct | St | O | M | Runs | Wkts | Avge | Best | 5wI | 10wM |
|---|---|---|---|---|---|---|---|---|---|---|---|---|---|---|---|---|---|---|
| Test | 2 | 4 | 0 | 22 | 18 | 5.50 | - | - | 1 |  |  |  |  |  |  |  |  |  |
| All First | 20 | 32 | 3 | 2258 | 235 | 77.86 | 10 | 7 | 14 | - | 22.2 | 3 | 108 | 4 | 27.00 | 3-91 | - | - |
| 1-day Int | 3 | 3 | 1 | 77 | 32 | 38.50 | - | - | 1 | - |  |  |  |  |  |  |  |  |
| NatWest | 3 | 3 | 0 | 65 | 40 | 21.66 | - | - | 1 | - | 4 | 0 | 24 | 2 | 12.00 | 2-24 | - |  |
| B & H | 6 | 6 | 2 | 214 | 91 * | 53.50 | - | 2 | 1 | - | 6 | 0 | 29 | 0 | - |  | - |  |
| Sunday | 13 | 13 | 3 | 485 | 103 | 48.50 | 1 | 3 | 4 | - | 2.2 | 0 | 20 | 1 | 20.00 | 1-18 | - |  |

## Career Performances

|  | M | Inns | NO | Runs | HS | Avge | 100s | 50s | Ct | St | Balls | Runs | Wkts | Avge | Best | 5wI | 10wM |
|---|---|---|---|---|---|---|---|---|---|---|---|---|---|---|---|---|---|
| Test | 17 | 30 | 1 | 520 | 72 | 17.93 | - | 2 | 12 | - | 241 | 130 | 0 | - |  | - | - |
| All First | 183 | 295 | 41 | 11520 | 235 | 45.35 | 29 | 56 | 103 | - | 1431 | 860 | 12 | 71.66 | 3-91 | - | - |
| 1-day Int | 7 | 7 | 3 | 124 | 32 | 31.00 | - | - | 4 | - |  |  |  |  |  |  |  |
| NatWest | 19 | 18 | 1 | 491 | 104 | 28.88 | 1 | 1 | 6 | - | 198 | 122 | 6 | 20.33 | 2-15 | - |  |
| B & H | 28 | 27 | 7 | 832 | 119 * | 41.60 | 2 | 3 | 8 | - | 36 | 29 | 0 | - |  | - |  |
| Sunday | 104 | 98 | 20 | 3445 | 147 * | 44.16 | 3 | 24 | 32 | - | 209 | 205 | 10 | 20.50 | 5-38 | 1 |  |

# RASHID, U. B. A.     Middlesex

**Name:** Umer Bin Abdul Rashid
**Role:** Left-hand bat, slow left-arm bowler
**Born:** 6 February 1976, Southampton
**Height:** 6ft 3in **Weight:** 12st 7lbs
**Nickname:** Umie, Looney
**County debut:** 1995 (one-day)
**Parents:** Mirza Abdul and Sebea
**Marital status:** Single
**Education:** Southfield Combined First and Middle School; Ealing Green High; Ealing Tertiary College; South Bank University
**Qualifications:** 7 GCSEs, 2 A-levels, 'currently studying for BA (Hons) in Business Studies'
**Off-season:** Studying
**Cricketers particularly admired:** Carl Hooper, Aamir Sohail
**Other sports followed:** Football (Southampton FC)
**Relaxations:** Playing table tennis, relaxing with family and friends
**Extras:** Lord's Taverners' Cricketer of the Year 1994-95. Played England U19 against South Africa in 1995. Played for the Combined Universities side in the Benson and

Hedges Cup

**Opinions on cricket:** 'I think that there should be more emphasis on training techniques, so that cricketers should be able to adapt to any kind of conditions. I think that there should be more world tournament events and not just the World Cup.'

## 1995 Season

| | M | Inns | NO | Runs | HS | Avge | 100s | 50s | Ct | St | O | M | Runs | Wkts | Avge | Best | 5wI | 10wM |
|---|---|---|---|---|---|---|---|---|---|---|---|---|---|---|---|---|---|---|
| Test | | | | | | | | | | | | | | | | | | |
| All First | | | | | | | | | | | | | | | | | | |
| 1-day Int | | | | | | | | | | | | | | | | | | |
| NatWest | | | | | | | | | | | | | | | | | | |
| B & H | 3 | 2 | 1 | 15 | 9 | 15.00 | - | - | - | - | 33 | 0 | 154 | 2 | 77.00 | 1-52 | - | |
| Sunday | 4 | 3 | 0 | 14 | 8 | 4.66 | - | - | - | - | 26 | 2 | 118 | 4 | 29.50 | 2-34 | - | |

## Career Performances

| | M | Inns | NO | Runs | HS | Avge | 100s | 50s | Ct | St | Balls | Runs | Wkts | Avge | Best | 5wI | 10wM |
|---|---|---|---|---|---|---|---|---|---|---|---|---|---|---|---|---|---|
| Test | | | | | | | | | | | | | | | | | |
| All First | | | | | | | | | | | | | | | | | |
| 1-day Int | | | | | | | | | | | | | | | | | |
| NatWest | | | | | | | | | | | | | | | | | |
| B & H | 3 | 2 | 1 | 15 | 9 | 15.00 | - | - | - | - | 198 | 154 | 2 | 77.00 | 1-52 | - | |
| Sunday | 4 | 3 | 0 | 14 | 8 | 4.66 | - | - | - | - | 156 | 118 | 4 | 29.50 | 2-34 | - | |

66. Who, in 1995, became the first Minor Counties player since 1979 to score 1,000 runs in the Minor Counties Championship?

# RATCLIFFE, J. D.                    Surrey

**Name:** Jason David Ratcliffe
**Role:** Right-hand opening bat, right-arm
medium/off-spin bowler, slip fielder
**Born:** 19 June 1969, Solihull
**Height:** 6ft 3in **Weight:** 14st 7lbs
**Nickname:** Ratters
**County debut:** 1988 (Warwickshire),
1995 (Surrey)
**1st-Class 50s:** 26
**1st-Class 100s:** 3
**1st-Class catches:** 50
**One-Day 100s:** 1
**Place in batting averages:** 113th av. 32.35
**Parents:** David and Sheila
**Wife and date of marriage:** Andrea,
7 January 1995
**Family links with cricket:** Father (D.P.
Ratcliffe) played for Warwickshire 1956-62

**Education:** Meadow Green Primary School;
Sharmans Cross Secondary School; Solihull Sixth Form College
**Qualifications:** 6 O-levels; NCA staff coach
**Career outside cricket:** Working for Birmingham City FC marketing team
**Overseas tours:** NCA (South) to Ireland 1988; Warwickshire to South Africa 1991-92
**Overseas teams played for:** West End, Kimberley, South Africa 1987-88; Belmont,
Newcastle, NSW 1990-91; Penrith, Sydney 1992-94
**Cricketers particularly admired:** Geoff Boycott, Jimmy Cook, Allan Donald, Paul
Booth, Andy Moles, Tim Munton, Roger Twose, Gladstone Small, Dominic Ostler
**Other sports followed:** Football, tennis, golf
**Injuries:** Broken thumb, did not miss any cricket
**Relaxations:** Music, reading, eating out
**Extras:** Scored a century against Boland on Warwickshire tour to South Africa 1991-92.
Released by Warwickshire at end of 1994 season and signed for Surrey
**Best batting:** 127* Warwickshire v Cambridge University, Fenner's 1989
**Best bowling:** 1-4 Warwickshire v Mashonaland, Harare 1993-94

---

67. Who were the two captains for the 1995 Varsity Match at Lord's?

## 1995 Season

| | M | Inns | NO | Runs | HS | Avge | 100s | 50s | Ct | St | O | M | Runs | Wkts | Avge | Best | 5wI | 10wM |
|---|---|---|---|---|---|---|---|---|---|---|---|---|---|---|---|---|---|---|
| Test | | | | | | | | | | | | | | | | | | |
| All First | 9 | 17 | 0 | 550 | 75 | 32.35 | - | 5 | 3 | - | | | | | | | | |
| 1-day Int | | | | | | | | | | | | | | | | | | |
| NatWest | 1 | 1 | 0 | 4 | 4 | 4.00 | - | - | - | - | | | | | | | | |
| B & H | 1 | 1 | 0 | 14 | 14 | 14.00 | - | - | - | - | | | | | | | | |
| Sunday | 6 | 6 | 1 | 72 | 31 | 14.40 | - | - | - | - | 13 | 0 | 110 | 1 | 110.00 | 1-15 | - | |

## Career Performances

| | M | Inns | NO | Runs | HS | Avge | 100s | 50s | Ct | St | Balls | Runs | Wkts | Avge | Best | 5wI | 10wM |
|---|---|---|---|---|---|---|---|---|---|---|---|---|---|---|---|---|---|
| Test | | | | | | | | | | | | | | | | | |
| All First | 87 | 161 | 8 | 4413 | 127 * | 28.84 | 3 | 26 | 50 | - | 343 | 235 | 4 | 58.75 | 1-4 | - | - |
| 1-day Int | | | | | | | | | | | | | | | | | |
| NatWest | 9 | 9 | 1 | 337 | 105 | 42.12 | 1 | 2 | 1 | - | 30 | 20 | 0 | - | | - | - |
| B & H | 2 | 2 | 0 | 43 | 29 | 21.50 | - | - | - | - | | | | | | | |
| Sunday | 19 | 18 | 2 | 217 | 37 | 13.56 | - | - | 5 | - | 163 | 179 | 5 | 35.80 | 2-11 | - | |

# RAWNSLEY, M.      Worcestershire

**Name:** Matthew Rawnsley
**Role:** Right-hand bat, slow left-arm bowler
**Born:** 8 June 1976, Birmingham
**Height:** 6ft 4in **Weight:** 13st 7lbs
**County debut:** No first-team appearance
**Parents:** Christopher (deceased) and June
**Marital status:** Single
**Education:** Bourneville School, Birmingham; Shenley Court School, Birmingham
**Qualifications:** 9 GCSEs and 3 A-levels
**Off-season:** Playing in New Zealand
**Overseas teams played for:** Kumeu, Auckland 1995-96
**Other sports followed:** Rugby (plays for Old Griffonians)
**Relaxations:** Listening to music, reading, keeping fit, circuit training

# REEVE, D. A. Warwickshire

**Name:** Dermot Alexander Reeve
**Role:** Right-hand bat, right-arm
medium-fast bowler, county captain
**Born:** 2 April 1963, Hong Kong
**Height:** 6ft **Weight:** 11st 11lbs
**Nickname:** Legend
**County debut:** 1983 (Sussex),
1988 (Warwickshire)
**County cap:** 1986 (Sussex),
1989 (Warwickshire)
**Tests:** 3
**One-Day Internationals:** 25
**1000 runs in a season:** 2
**50 wickets in a season:** 2
**1st-Class 50s:** 52
**1st-Class 100s:** 6
**1st-Class 200s:** 1
**1st-Class 5 w. in innings:** 7
**1st-Class catches:** 193
**One-Day 100s:** 1

**One-Day 5 w. in innings:** 1
**Place in batting averages:** 86th av. 36.22 (1994 255th av. 12.88)
**Place in bowling averages:** 2nd av. 17.39 (1994 66th av. 30.80)
**Strike rate:** 49.26 (career 64.68)
**Parents:** Alexander James and Monica
**Marital status:** Divorced
**Children:** Emily Kaye, 14 September 1988
**Family links with cricket:** Brother Mark still plays club cricket. Dad used to play and mother took over as scorer during the England tour to India and Sri Lanka 1992-93 when Clem Driver was taken ill
**Education:** King George V School, Kowloon, Hong Kong
**Qualifications:** 7 O-levels
**Off-season:** 'Doing some after-dinner speaking and then visiting my daughter in Australia. Lots of sitting on the beach and golf.'
**Overseas tours:** England to New Zealand and Australia (World Cup) 1991-92, to India and Sri Lanka 1992-93, to South Africa 1995-96, to India and Pakistan (World Cup) 1995-96
**Overseas teams played for:** Hong Kong
**Cricketers particularly admired:** 'John Barclay (enthusiasm), Wasim Akram (talent), Tim Munton (commitment), Malcolm Marshall (power with grace), Alec Stewart (timing), Ray Alikhan (guts), Graham Gooch and Mike Gatting (dedication), Allan Donald'

**Other sports followed:** Football (Manchester United)

**Injuries:** Back strain, missed ten days

**Relaxations:** Swimming, golf, eating out, music, movies and popcorn

**Extras:** Formerly on Lord's groundstaff. Represented Hong Kong in ICC Trophy June 1982. Hong Kong Cricketer of the Year 1980-81 and Hong Kong's Cricket Sports Personality of the Year 1981. Twice Western Australian CA Cricketer of the Year. Man of the Match in 1986 NatWest final for Sussex and 1989 final for Warwickshire. Originally selected for England A tour to Bermuda and West Indies 1991-92 but promoted to senior tour to New Zealand when Angus Fraser was ruled out by injury. Appointed Warwickshire captain for 1993 and was voted their Player of the Year 1993 after leading them to victory in the NatWest Trophy. On the Sky Sports commentary team for the England tour of Australia 1994-95. Now holds the record for the number of Man of the Match Awards in the NatWest final with three. During his three years as Warwickshire captain, they have won six trophies. Played for England in the one-day series against South Africa and called up to the England squad for the World Cup in India and Pakistan as a replacement for the injured Craig White. Awarded benefit for 1996

**Opinions on cricket:** '18.5 overs per hour is too many, in Test cricket they only bowl 15 overs per hour. 17 overs per hour would be more realistic for both first-class and Test cricket. Sunday League should be decided on net run-rate if points are level at the end of the season – not just run-rate!'

**Best batting:** 202* Warwickshire v Northamptonshire, Northampton 1990

**Best bowling:** 7-37 Sussex v Lancashire, Lytham 1987

## 1995 Season

|  | M | Inns | NO | Runs | HS | Avge | 100s | 50s | Ct | St | O | M | Runs | Wkts | Avge | Best | 5wI | 10wM |
|---|---|---|---|---|---|---|---|---|---|---|---|---|---|---|---|---|---|---|
| Test |  |  |  |  |  |  |  |  |  |  |  |  |  |  |  |  |  |  |
| All First | 16 | 22 | 4 | 652 | 77 * | 36.22 | - | 5 | 17 | - | 312 | 117 | 661 | 38 | 17.39 | 5-30 | 1 | - |
| 1-day Int |  |  |  |  |  |  |  |  |  |  |  |  |  |  |  |  |  |  |
| NatWest | 5 | 3 | 1 | 69 | 37 * | 34.50 | - | - | 2 | - | 46 | 2 | 168 | 9 | 18.66 | 4-54 | - |  |
| B & H | 4 | 3 | 1 | 48 | 28 * | 24.00 | - | - | 3 | - | 31.3 | 3 | 121 | 5 | 24.20 | 4-37 | - |  |
| Sunday | 15 | 13 | 4 | 230 | 50 | 25.55 | - | 1 | 4 | - | 82.1 | 3 | 355 | 19 | 18.68 | 4-22 | - |  |

## Career Performances

|  | M | Inns | NO | Runs | HS | Avge | 100s | 50s | Ct | St | Balls | Runs | Wkts | Avge | Best | 5wI | 10wM |
|---|---|---|---|---|---|---|---|---|---|---|---|---|---|---|---|---|---|
| Test | 3 | 5 | 0 | 124 | 59 | 24.80 | - | 1 | 1 | - | 149 | 60 | 2 | 30.00 | 1-4 | - | - |
| All First | 236 | 314 | 76 | 8190 | 202 * | 34.41 | 6 | 52 | 193 | - | 28915 | 12037 | 447 | 26.92 | 7-37 | 7 | - |
| 1-day Int | 25 | 17 | 9 | 241 | 33 * | 30.12 | - | - | 11 | - | 969 | 686 | 18 | 38.11 | 3-20 | - |  |
| NatWest | 43 | 33 | 12 | 784 | 81 * | 37.33 | - | 4 | 16 | - | 2452 | 1247 | 49 | 25.44 | 4-20 | - |  |
| B & H | 37 | 31 | 12 | 471 | 80 | 24.78 | - | 1 | 9 | - | 1908 | 1330 | 42 | 31.66 | 4-37 | - |  |
| Sunday | 167 | 123 | 32 | 2342 | 100 | 25.73 | 1 | 9 | 47 | - | 5857 | 4384 | 156 | 28.10 | 5-23 | 1 |  |

# REMY, C. C.                                         Sussex

**Name:** Carlos Charles Remy
**Role:** Right-hand bat, right-arm
fast-medium bowler
**Born:** 24 July 1968, Castries, St Lucia
**Height:** 5ft 10in **Weight:** 11st
**Nickname:** Dredd
**County debut:** 1989
**1st-Class 50s:** 2
**1st-Class catches:** 7
**Strike rate:** (career 86.15)
**Parents:** Mary Annette
**Marital status:** Single
**Family links with cricket:** Stepfather played
club cricket for STC in Morrant League
**Education:** St William of York School,
London
**Qualifications:** 1 O-level, 3 CSEs, NCA
coaching certificate
**Career outside cricket:** 'Doing any job'
**Overseas tours:** Haringey Cricket College to West Indies 1988, 1989
**Overseas teams played for:** Bionics, Harare 1989-90; Parnell, Auckland 1990-91
**Cricketers particularly admired:** Franklyn Stephenson, Robin Smith, Allan Border,
Malcolm Marshall
**Other sports followed:** Football and rugby
**Relaxations:** Listening to music (soul, swing, rap and ragga), dancing
**Extras:** 'Scored my very first hundred for Sussex in my first game for the 2nd XI'
**Best batting:** 60 Sussex v Northamptonshire, Northampton 1994
**Best bowling:** 4-63 Sussex v Cambridge University, Hove 1990

## 1995 Season

|          | M | Inns | NO | Runs | HS | Avge | 100s | 50s | Ct | St | O    | M | Runs | Wkts | Avge | Best | 5wI | 10wM |
|----------|---|------|----|------|----|------|------|-----|----|----|------|---|------|------|------|------|-----|------|
| Test     |   |      |    |      |    |      |      |     |    |    |      |   |      |      |      |      |     |      |
| All First | 1 | 2 | 0 | 5 | 4 | 2.50 | - | - | - | - | 22.3 | 2 | 114 | 0 | - | - | - | - |
| 1-day Int |   |      |    |      |    |      |      |     |    |    |      |   |      |      |      |      |     |      |
| NatWest  |   |      |    |      |    |      |      |     |    |    |      |   |      |      |      |      |     |      |
| B & H    | 2 | 2 | 0 | 10 | 7 | 5.00 | - | - | - | - | 10 | 0 | 37 | 0 | - | - | - |      |
| Sunday   |   |      |    |      |    |      |      |     |    |    |      |   |      |      |      |      |     |      |

## Career Performances

|  | M | Inns | NO | Runs | HS | Avge | 100s | 50s | Ct | St | Balls | Runs | Wkts | Avge | Best | 5wI | 10wM |
|---|---|---|---|---|---|---|---|---|---|---|---|---|---|---|---|---|---|
| Test |  |  |  |  |  |  |  |  |  |  |  |  |  |  |  |  |  |
| All First | 21 | 29 | 3 | 480 | 60 | 18.46 | - | 2 | 7 | - | 1637 | 1051 | 19 | 55.31 | 4-63 | - | - |
| 1-day Int |  |  |  |  |  |  |  |  |  |  |  |  |  |  |  |  |  |
| NatWest | 1 | 1 | 0 | 1 | 1 | 1.00 | - | - | - | - | 60 | 30 | 0 | - | - | - |  |
| B & H | 2 | 2 | 0 | 10 | 7 | 5.00 | - | - | - | - | 60 | 37 | 0 | - | - | - |  |
| Sunday | 28 | 22 | 2 | 151 | 19 | 7.55 | - | - | 7 | - | 994 | 812 | 29 | 28.00 | 4-31 | - |  |

# RENSHAW, S. J.       Hampshire

**Name:** Simon John Renshaw
**Role:** Right-hand bat, right-arm fast bowler
**Born:** 6 March 1974, Bebington, Wirral
**Height:** 6ft 3in  **Weight:** 13st 7lbs
**Nickname:** Spanner
**Parents:** Michael and Barbara
**Marital status:** Single
**Family links with cricket:** Father and
brother play in local league competitions
**Education:** Birkenhead Prep School;
Birkenhead; Leeds University
**Qualifications:** 9 GCSEs, 4 A-levels, BSc in
Microbiology
**Career outside cricket:** 'None yet but
expected to be in microbiology'
**Off-season:** Playing for Mulgrave in
Melbourne
**Overseas teams played for:** Mulgrave,
Melbourne 1995-96
**Cricketers particularly admired:** Ian Botham, Viv Richards
**Other sports followed:** Football (Everton) and snooker
**Injuries:** Groin strain, no time off
**Relaxations:** Music, films and reading
**Extras:** Was captain of the Birkenhead U17 side that won the Barclays Knock-out Cup
in 1991. Captain of Birkenhead 1st XI in 1992. Represented North of England Schools
and MCC Schools. Played for Cheshire in the Minor Counties and for Cheshire U25 in
the Bain Hogg Trophy in 1995. Captain of Cheshire U19 at the Cambridge Festival and
was voted Cheshire Young Player of the Year. Best performance in the Minor Counties
was 7 for 19 against Shropshire. Played for the Combined Universities in the Benson and
Hedges Cup and against West Indies at The Parks. Priestley Cup Final Winner with
Farsley in 1995

**Opinions on cricket:** 'Current County Championship is stagnating. Two divisions with promotion and relegation would increase interest. There should be a greater liaison between minor counties and major ones. There is no structured development plan for any boy who lives outside the major county catchment area, which means that many players of county standard are ignored.'

**Best bowling:** 2-135 Combined Universites v West Indies, The Parks 1995

## 1995 Season

| | M | Inns | NO | Runs | HS | Avge | 100s | 50s | Ct | St | O | M | Runs | Wkts | Avge | Best | 5wI | 10wM |
|---|---|---|---|---|---|---|---|---|---|---|---|---|---|---|---|---|---|---|
| Test | | | | | | | | | | | | | | | | | | |
| All First | 1 | 1 | 0 | 0 | 0 | 0.00 | - | - | - | - | 40 | 5 | 191 | 2 | 95.50 | 2-135 | - | - |
| 1-day Int | | | | | | | | | | | | | | | | | | |
| NatWest | | | | | | | | | | | | | | | | | | |
| B & H | 5 | 2 | 1 | 0 | 0 * | 0.00 | - | - | 1 | - | 49 | 7 | 210 | 5 | 42.00 | 2-34 | - | |
| Sunday | | | | | | | | | | | | | | | | | | |

## Career Performances

| | M | Inns | NO | Runs | HS | Avge | 100s | 50s | Ct | St | Balls | Runs | Wkts | Avge | Best | 5wI | 10wM |
|---|---|---|---|---|---|---|---|---|---|---|---|---|---|---|---|---|---|
| Test | | | | | | | | | | | | | | | | | |
| All First | 1 | 1 | 0 | 0 | 0 | 0.00 | - | - | - | - | 240 | 191 | 2 | 95.50 | 2-135 | - | - |
| 1-day Int | | | | | | | | | | | | | | | | | |
| NatWest | 1 | 1 | 0 | 1 | 1 | 1.00 | - | - | - | - | 42 | 20 | 2 | 10.00 | 2-20 | - | |
| B & H | 5 | 2 | 1 | 0 | 0 * | 0.00 | - | - | 1 | - | 294 | 210 | 5 | 42.00 | 2-34 | - | |
| Sunday | | | | | | | | | | | | | | | | | |

# RHODES, S. J.            Worcestershire

**Name:** Steven John Rhodes
**Role:** Right-hand bat, wicket-keeper, county vice-captain
**Born:** 17 June 1964, Bradford
**Height:** 5ft 8in **Weight:** 12st
**Nickname:** Bumpy
**County debut:** 1981 (Yorkshire), 1985 (Worcestershire)
**County cap:** 1986 (Worcestershire)
**Test debut:** 1994
**Tests:** 11
**One-Day Internationals:** 9
**1000 runs in a season:** 1
**1st-Class 50s:** 45
**1st-Class 100s:** 8
**1st-Class catches:** 734
**1st-Class stumpings:** 96

**Place in batting averages:** 63rd av. 40.72 (1994 8th av. 56.00)

**Parents:** William Ernest and Norma Kathleen

**Wife and date of marriage:** Judy Ann, 6 March 1993

**Children:** Holly Jade, 20 August 1985; George Harry, 26 October 1993; Lily Amber, 3 March 1995

**Family links with cricket:** Father played for Nottinghamshire 1959-64

**Education:** Bradford Moor Junior School; Lapage St Middle; Carlton-Bolling Comprehensive, Bradford

**Qualifications:** 4 O-levels, coaching certificate

**Career outside cricket:** Labourer; trainee sports shop manager

**Off-season:** 'Preparing for my benefit in 1996'

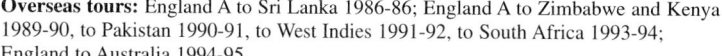

**Overseas tours:** England A to Sri Lanka 1986-86; England A to Zimbabwe and Kenya 1989-90, to Pakistan 1990-91, to West Indies 1991-92, to South Africa 1993-94; England to Australia 1994-95

**Overseas teams played for:** Past Bros, Bundaberg, Queensland; Avis Vogeltown, New Plymouth, New Zealand; Melville, Perth, Australia

**Cricketers particularly admired:** Graeme Hick, Richard Hadlee

**Other sports followed:** Rugby league, horse racing and golf

**Injuries:** 'Niggles'

**Relaxations:** Keeping and breeding tropical fish ('very therapeutic')

**Extras:** Played for England YC v Australia YC in 1983 and holds record for most victims in an innings for England YC. Youngest wicket-keeper to play for Yorkshire. Released by Yorkshire to join Worcestershire at end of 1984 season. Selected for cancelled England tour to India 1988-89 and was one of four players put on stand-by as reserves for 1992 World Cup squad. Writes a weekly cricket column for a Birmingham newspaper. One of the *Wisden* Cricketers of the Year for 1994. Awarded benefit for 1996

**Opinions on cricket:** 'How England Test bowlers can stay fresh in between Test matches is beyond me. They bowl their hearts out in a Test and then go straight into five tough days county cricket. The next day they report to the next Test venue for another gruelling match. No wonder we can't sustain the same high level in the second consecutive bowling day of a Test. Don't ask me how we achieve the perfect answer to the problem. Extending the four-foot rule to six feet would be worth experimenting with, to help spinners on flat pitches.'

**Best batting:** 122* Worcestershire v Young Australia, Worcester 1995

| | M | Inns | NO | Runs | HS | Avge | 100s | 50s | Ct | St | O | M | Runs | Wkts | Avge | Best | 5wI | 10wM |
|---|---|---|---|---|---|---|---|---|---|---|---|---|---|---|---|---|---|---|
| Test | | | | | | | | | | | | | | | | | | |
| All First | 20 | 33 | 8 | 1018 | 122 * | 40.72 | 1 | 7 | 51 | 7 | | | | | | | | |
| 1-day Int | | | | | | | | | | | | | | | | | | |
| NatWest | 2 | 2 | 1 | 9 | 7 | 9.00 | - | - | 4 | 1 | | | | | | | | |
| B & H | 6 | 4 | 1 | 24 | 12 | 8.00 | - | - | 12 | 2 | | | | | | | | |
| Sunday | 17 | 10 | 3 | 75 | 31 * | 10.71 | - | - | 17 | 7 | | | | | | | | |

**Career Performances**

| | M | Inns | NO | Runs | HS | Avge | 100s | 50s | Ct | St | Balls | Runs | Wkts | Avge | Best | 5wI | 10wM |
|---|---|---|---|---|---|---|---|---|---|---|---|---|---|---|---|---|---|
| Test | 11 | 17 | 5 | 294 | 65 * | 24.50 | - | 1 | 46 | 3 | | | | | | | |
| All First | 290 | 396 | 115 | 9246 | 122 * | 32.90 | 8 | 45 | 734 | 96 | 6 | 30 | 0 | - | - | - | - |
| 1-day Int | 9 | 8 | 2 | 107 | 56 | 17.83 | - | 1 | 9 | 2 | | | | | | | |
| NatWest | 35 | 26 | 9 | 372 | 61 | 21.88 · | - | 2 | 43 | 6 | | | | | | | |
| B & H | 53 | 38 | 7 | 469 | 51 * | 15.12 | - | 1 | 76 | 9 | | | | | | | |
| Sunday | 166 | 104 | 24 | 1499 | 48 * | 18.73 | - | - | 172 | 50 | | | | | | | |

# RICHARDSON, A.          Derbyshire

**Name:** Alan Richardson
**Role:** Right-hand bat, right-arm
medium bowler
**Born:** 6 May 1975, Newcastle-under-Lyme
**Height:** 6ft 2in **Weight** 12st 7lbs
**Nickname:** YP, Darren, Shaggy, Ladder,
Steffs, Son of Lovell
**County debut:** 1995
**Parents:** Roy and Sandra
**Marital status:** Single
**Family links with cricket:** Father played
club cricket
**Education:** Alleyne's High School, Stone;
Stafford College of Further Education;
Roehampton Institute
**Qualifications:** 8 GCSEs, 2 A-levels, 2 AS-
levels, Advanced Cricket Coach
**Cricketers particularly admired:** David
Lovell, Greg Pooley, Gary Steer
**Other sports followed:** Football (Stoke City)
**Relaxations:** Any sport, especially golf, badminton and volleyball, listening to music
**Extras:** *The Cricketer*/Slazenger Cricketer of the Month June 1991 and *Cricket World*

award for best bowling performance in Oxford U19 Festival (8-60 v Devon).
**Best batting:** 4 Derbyshire v Oxford University, The Parks 1995
**Best bowling:** 3-27 Derbyshire v Oxford University, The Parks 1995

## 1995 Season

| | M | Inns | NO | Runs | HS | Avge | 100s | 50s | Ct | St | O | M | Runs | Wkts | Avge | Best | 5wI | 10wM |
|---|---|---|---|---|---|---|---|---|---|---|---|---|---|---|---|---|---|---|
| Test | | | | | | | | | | | | | | | | | | |
| All First | 1 | 1 | 0 | 4 | 4 | 4.00 | - | - | - | - | 19 | 3 | 60 | 3 | 20.00 | 3-27 | - | - |
| 1-day Int | | | | | | | | | | | | | | | | | | |
| NatWest | | | | | | | | | | | | | | | | | | |
| B & H | | | | | | | | | | | | | | | | | | |
| Sunday | 1 | 0 | 0 | 0 | 0 | - | - | - | - | - | 6 | 0 | 41 | 0 | - | | - | - |

## Career Performances

| | M | Inns | NO | Runs | HS | Avge | 100s | 50s | Ct | St | Balls | Runs | Wkts | Avge | Best | 5wI | 10wM |
|---|---|---|---|---|---|---|---|---|---|---|---|---|---|---|---|---|---|
| Test | | | | | | | | | | | | | | | | | |
| All First | 1 | 1 | 0 | 4 | 4 | 4.00 | - | - | - | - | 114 | 60 | 3 | 20.00 | 3-27 | - | - |
| 1-day Int | | | | | | | | | | | | | | | | | |
| NatWest | | | | | | | | | | | | | | | | | |
| B & H | | | | | | | | | | | | | | | | | |
| Sunday | 1 | 0 | 0 | 0 | 0 | - | - | - | - | - | 36 | 41 | 0 | - | | - | - |

# RIDGEWAY, P. M.                    Lancashire

**Name:** Paul Matthew Ridgeway
**Role:** Right-hand bat, right-arm
fast-medium bowler
**Born:** 13 February 1977, Airedale, Yorkshire
**Height:** 6ft 4in
**County debut:** No first-team appearance
**Parents:** Peter and Judith
**Marital status:** Single
**Family links with cricket:** Father is first
cousin to Don Wilson (Yorkshire and
England)
**Education:** Settle High School
**Qualifications:** GCSEs, BTEC Business and
Finance
**Cricketers particularly admired:**
Dennis Lillee, Gordon Greenidge
**Other sports followed:** Rugby league
**Relaxations:** Training

# RIPLEY, D.         Northamptonshire

**Name:** David Ripley
**Role:** Right-hand bat, wicket-keeper
**Born:** 13 September 1966, Leeds
**Height:** 5ft 11in **Weight:** 11st 11lbs
**Nickname:** Rips, Spud, Porn Star
**County debut:** 1984
**County cap:** 1987
**1st-Class 50s:** 12
**1st-Class 100s:** 6
**1st-Class catches:** 473
**1st-Class stumpings:** 67
**Place in batting averages:**
(1994 210th av. 18.78)
**Parents:** Arthur and Brenda
**Wife and date of marriage:** Jackie,
24 September 1988
**Children:** Joe David, 11 October 1989;
George William, 5 March 1994

**Education:**
Woodlesford Primary; Royds High, Leeds
**Qualifications:** 5 O-levels, NCA advanced coach
**Career outside cricket:** Coaching
**Off-season:** Coaching at Northants CCC
**Overseas tours:** England YC to West Indies 1984-85; Northants to Durban, South Africa 1991-92, to Cape Town 1992-93, to Zimbabwe 1994-95
**Overseas teams played for:** Marists and Poverty Bay, New Zealand 1985-87
**Cricketers particularly admired:** Alan Knott, Bob Taylor 'and many other keepers', Clive Radley, Ian Botham, Geoff Boycott, Dennis Lillee
**Other sports followed:** Football (Leeds United), rugby league (Castleford), golf
**Injuries:** Broken finger, out for three weeks
**Relaxations:** 'Eating out, and sampling different bitters'
**Extras:** Finished top of wicket-keepers' dismissals list for 1988 and 1992 and was voted Wombwell Cricket Lovers' Society Best Wicket-keeper 1992. Played for England YC v Sri Lanka 1986
**Opinions on cricket:** 'Four-day cricket is working well. I would like to see short run-ups on Sundays as there are too many low-scoring games.'
**Best batting:** 134* Northamptonshire v Yorkshire, Scarborough 1986
**Best bowling:** 2-89 Northamptonshire v Essex, Ilford 1987

| | M | Inns | NO | Runs | HS | Avge | 100s | 50s | Ct | St | O | M | Runs | Wkts | Avge | Best | 5wI | 10wM |
|---|---|---|---|---|---|---|---|---|---|---|---|---|---|---|---|---|---|---|
| Test | | | | | | | | | | | | | | | | | | |
| All First | 6 | 5 | 1 | 90 | 40 | 22.50 | - | - | 7 | 2 | | | | | | | | |
| 1-day Int | | | | | | | | | | | | | | | | | | |
| NatWest | | | | | | | | | | | | | | | | | | |
| B & H | | | | | | | | | | | | | | | | | | |
| Sunday | 3 | 2 | 0 | 10 | 9 | 5.00 | - | - | - | - | | | | | | | | |

**Career Performances**

| | M | Inns | NO | Runs | HS | Avge | 100s | 50s | Ct | St | Balls | Runs | Wkts | Avge | Best | 5wI | 10wM |
|---|---|---|---|---|---|---|---|---|---|---|---|---|---|---|---|---|---|
| Test | | | | | | | | | | | | | | | | | |
| All First | 219 | 283 | 74 | 5029 | 134 * | 24.06 | 6 | 12 | 473 | 67 | 60 | 103 | 2 | 51.50 | 2-89 | - | - |
| 1-day Int | | | | | | | | | | | | | | | | | |
| NatWest | 35 | 20 | 9 | 130 | 27 * | 11.81 | - | - | 36 | 3 | | | | | | | |
| B & H | 37 | 25 | 9 | 305 | 36 * | 19.06 | - | - | 37 | 4 | | | | | | | |
| Sunday | 127 | 79 | 35 | 832 | 52 * | 18.90 | - | 1 | 87 | 13 | | | | | | | |

# ROBERTS, A. R.        Northamptonshire

**Name:** Andrew Richard Roberts
**Role:** Right-hand bat, leg-break bowler
**Born:** 16 April 1971, Kettering
**Height:** 5ft 5in **Weight:** 10st 7lbs
**Nickname:** Reggie
**County debut:** 1989
**1st-Class 50s:** 2
**1st-Class 5 w. in innings:** 1
**1st-Class catches:** 22
**Place in batting averages:** (1994 109th av. 32.62)
**Place in bowling averages:** (1994 142nd av. 51.17)
**Strike rate:** (career 84.18)
**Parents:** David and Shirley
**Marital status:** Engaged to Kirsty
**Family links with cricket:** Father (Dave) played a few games for Northants 2nd XI; brother Tim won the Lord's Taverners U13 award in 1991, played Midlands Schools U14 and England Schoolboys U15
**Education:** Bishop Stopford Comprehensive, Kettering
**Qualifications:** 3 O-levels, 5 CSEs, Carpentry and Joinery City & Guilds

**Career outside cricket:** Carpentry and joinery
**Overseas tours:** Northamptonshire to Durban, South Africa 1991-92, to Cape Town, South Africa 1992-93
**Overseas teams played for:** Woolston Working Men's Club, Christchurch, New Zealand 1989-91; Eastern Suburbs, Wellington 1993-95
**Cricketers particularly admired:** Richard Williams, Wayne Larkins, Dennis Lillee
**Other sports followed:** Rugby (Northampton Saints RFC) and golf
**Injuries:** Shoulder prevented throwing
**Relaxations:** 'Music, sleeping, eating, a good pint of bitter!'
**Extras:** Played for England YC v Pakistan YC 1990. Named the Rapid Cricketline Second XI Championship Player of the Year in 1995
**Opinions on cricket:** 'In favour of uncovered wickets, which would produce better technique and more exciting cricket.'
**Best batting:** 62 Northamptonshire v Nottinghamshire, Trent Bridge 1992
**Best bowling:** 6-72 Northamptonshire v Lancashire, Lytham 1991

## 1995 Season

|          | M | Inns | NO | Runs | HS | Avge | 100s | 50s | Ct | St | O | M | Runs | Wkts | Avge | Best | 5wI | 10wM |
|----------|---|------|----|------|----|------|------|-----|----|----|----|----|------|------|------|------|-----|------|
| Test     |   |      |    |      |    |      |      |     |    |    |    |    |      |      |      |      |     |      |
| All First | 1 | 2 | 0 | 21 | 11 | 10.50 | - | - | - | - | 11 | 2 | 45 | 0 | - | - | - | - |
| 1-day Int |   |      |    |      |    |      |      |     |    |    |    |    |      |      |      |      |     |      |
| NatWest  |   |      |    |      |    |      |      |     |    |    |    |    |      |      |      |      |     |      |
| B & H    |   |      |    |      |    |      |      |     |    |    |    |    |      |      |      |      |     |      |
| Sunday   | 1 | 1 | 0 | 4 | 4 | 4.00 | - | - | - | - | 3.5 | 0 | 33 | 1 | 33.00 | 1-33 | - |   |

## Career Performances

|          | M | Inns | NO | Runs | HS | Avge | 100s | 50s | Ct | St | Balls | Runs | Wkts | Avge | Best | 5wI | 10wM |
|----------|---|------|----|------|----|------|------|-----|----|----|-------|------|------|------|------|-----|------|
| Test     |   |      |    |      |    |      |      |     |    |    |       |      |      |      |      |     |      |
| All First | 55 | 75 | 18 | 1032 | 62 | 18.10 | - | 2 | 22 | - | 8166 | 4302 | 97 | 44.35 | 6-72 | 1 | - |
| 1-day Int |   |      |    |      |    |      |      |     |    |    |       |      |      |      |      |     |      |
| NatWest  | 1 | 0 | 0 | 0 | 0 | - | - | - | 1 | - | 72 | 23 | 1 | 23.00 | 1-23 | - |   |
| B & H    |   |      |    |      |    |      |      |     |    |    |       |      |      |      |      |     |      |
| Sunday   | 11 | 5 | 0 | 42 | 20 | 8.40 | - | - | 4 | - | 263 | 251 | 10 | 25.10 | 3-26 | - |   |

# ROBERTS, D. J.       Northamptonshire

**Name:** David James Roberts
**Role:** Right-hand bat
**Born:** 29 December 1976, Truro, Cornwall
**Height:** 6ft **Weight:** 12st
**Nickname:** Robo
**County debut:** No first-team appearance
**Parents:** Dennis and Pam
**Marital status:** Single
**Family links with cricket:** Cousin, Chris Bullen, played for Surrey. Father played cricket for local club and is also a youth coach. Mother is a keen supporter!
**Education:** Mullion County Primary; Mullion Comprehensive
**Qualifications:** 9 GCSEs, senior cricket coach
**Career outside cricket:** Helping on the family farm
**Off-season:** Touring Zimbabwe with England U19 and working on farm
**Overseas tours:** West of England to Barbados, Trinidad and Tobago 1990-91 and 1991-92 (captain)
**Cricketers particularly admired:** Mal Loye
**Other sports followed:** Football (Manchester United), NBA basketball and all sports
**Relaxations:** Watching television, listening to music, playing football
**Extras:** Played for English Schools since the age of 14, including matches against South Africa in 1992. Represented England U17 against India U17 in 1994
**Opinions on cricket:** 'Tea is too short, should be increased from 10 minutes to 30 minutes. Second team cricket should be played at first-class grounds instead of club grounds.'

68. Who has the highest batting average as captain for England?

# ROBINSON, D. D. J.                    Essex

**Name:** Darren David John Robinson
**Role:** Right-hand opening bat, occasional
right-arm medium bowler
**Born:** 2 March 1973, Braintree, Essex
**Height:** 5ft 11in **Weight:** 14st 4lbs
**Nickname:** Robbo
**County debut:** 1993
**1st-Class 50s:** 2
**1st-Class 100s:** 2
**1st-Class catches:** 28
**Place in batting averages:** 189th av. 22.25
**Parents:** David John and Dorothy May
**Marital status:** Single
**Family links with cricket:** Father plays club
cricket for Halstead
**Education:** Tabor High School, Braintree;
Chelmsford College of Further Education
**Qualifications:** 5 GCSEs, BTEC National
Diploma in Building and Construction
**Career outside cricket:** Civil engineering and surveying
**Off-season:** Playing in Auckland, New Zealand
**Overseas tours:** England U18 to Canada 1991; England U19 to Pakistan 1991-92
**Overseas teams played for:** Waverley, Sydney 1992-94
**Cricketers particularly admired:** Graham Gooch, Keith Fletcher, Mark Waugh
**Other sports followed:** Golf ('play off 14')
**Relaxations:** Listening to music, socialising and golf
**Extras:** *Daily Telegraph* batting award 1988 and International Youth Tournament in
Canada batting award 1991
**Opinions on cricket:** 'A very gratifying sport, which is demanding, requires dedication
and considerable powers of concentration. Is frustrating at times when things are not
working out. Is a good character-builder, providing experience of team spirit,
comradeship, independence, socialising and the opportunity of international travel.'
**Best batting:** 123 Essex v Gloucestershire, Cheltenham 1995

69. Which Pakistan bowler celebrated his return to Test cricket with
a haul of 18 wickets in two Tests against Australia?

## 1995 Season

| | M | Inns | NO | Runs | HS | Avge | 100s | 50s | Ct | St | O | M | Runs | Wkts | Avge | Best | 5wI | 10wM |
|---|---|---|---|---|---|---|---|---|---|---|---|---|---|---|---|---|---|---|
| Test | | | | | | | | | | | | | | | | | | |
| All First | 17 | 32 | 0 | 712 | 123 | 22.25 | 2 | 1 | 25 | - | 1 | 0 | 7 | 0 | - | - | - | - |
| 1-day Int | | | | | | | | | | | | | | | | | | |
| NatWest | 2 | 2 | 0 | 65 | 55 | 32.50 | - | 1 | 1 | - | | | | | | | | |
| B & H | 5 | 4 | 1 | 99 | 35 * | 33.00 | - | - | 1 | - | | | | | | | | |
| Sunday | 17 | 17 | 3 | 239 | 38 | 17.07 | - | - | 6 | - | 2 | 0 | 19 | 0 | - | | - | - |

## Career Performances

| | M | Inns | NO | Runs | HS | Avge | 100s | 50s | Ct | St | Balls | Runs | Wkts | Avge | Best | 5wI | 10wM |
|---|---|---|---|---|---|---|---|---|---|---|---|---|---|---|---|---|---|
| Test | | | | | | | | | | | | | | | | | |
| All First | 20 | 37 | 0 | 862 | 123 | 23.29 | 2 | 2 | 28 | - | 6 | 7 | 0 | - | - | - | - |
| 1-day Int | | | | | | | | | | | | | | | | | |
| NatWest | 2 | 2 | 0 | 65 | 55 | 32.50 | - | 1 | 1 | - | | | | | | | |
| B & H | 5 | 4 | 1 | 99 | 35 * | 33.00 | - | - | 1 | - | | | | | | | |
| Sunday | 18 | 18 | 3 | 241 | 38 | 16.06 | - | - | 6 | - | 12 | 19 | 0 | - | | - | - |

# ROBINSON, M. A. Yorkshire

**Name:** Mark Andrew Robinson
**Role:** Right-hand bat, right-arm
fast-medium bowler
**Born:** 23 November 1966, Hull
**Height:** 6ft 3in **Weight:** 13st 3lbs
**Nickname:** Jessie, Coddy, Scoope
**County debut:** 1987 (Northamptonshire),
1991 (Yorkshire)
**County cap:** 1990 (Northamptonshire)
1992 (Yorkshire)
**50 wickets in season:** 1
**1st-Class 5 w. in innings:** 7
**1st-Class 10 w. in match:** 2
**1st-Class catches:** 31
**Place in bowling averages:** 73rd av. 29.89
(1994 106th av. 36.84)
**Strike rate:** 63.02 (career 68.49)
**Parents:** Joan Margarette and Malcolm
**Wife and date of marriage:**
Julia, 8 October 1994
**Family links with cricket:** Grandfather a prominent local cricketer; father was hostile bowler in back garden

**Education:** Fifth Avenue Primary; Endike Junior High; Hull Grammar School
**Qualifications:** 6 O-levels, 2 A-levels, senior coach
**Career outside cricket:** Self-employed cricket coach
**Off-season:** 'Coaching in Hull, and watching Hull City AFC'
**Overseas tours:** England U19 North to Bermuda; Yorkshire to Cape Town 1991-92 and 1992-93, to West Indies 1994
**Overseas teams played for:** East Shirley, Canterbury, New Zealand 1987-89; Canterbury, New Zealand 1989-90
**Cricketers particularly admired:** Dennis Lillee, Mike Gatting, John Emburey
**Other sports followed:** Hull City FC ('The Tigers')
**Injuries:** Troublesome right knee. Did not miss any cricket
**Relaxations:** Reading, music, 'long walks with my dog', all sports
**Extras:** Took hat-trick with first three balls of innings in Yorkshire League, playing for Hull v Doncaster. First player to win Yorkshire U19 Bowler of the Season award in two successive years. Northamptonshire Uncapped Player of the Year 1989. Endured a world record 11 innings without scoring a run during 1990 season. Took 9 for 37 v Northamptonshire at Harrogate 1993, 12 for 109 in match
**Opinions on cricket:** 'Beware the leopard in sheep's clothing.'
**Best batting:** 23 Yorkshire v Gloucestershire, Middlesborough 1995
**Best bowling:** 9-37 Yorkshire v Northamptonshire, Harrogate 1993

## 1995 Season

|  | M | Inns | NO | Runs | HS | Avge | 100s | 50s | Ct | St | O | M | Runs | Wkts | Avge | Best | 5wI | 10wM |
|---|---|---|---|---|---|---|---|---|---|---|---|---|---|---|---|---|---|---|
| Test |  |  |  |  |  |  |  |  |  |  |  |  |  |  |  |  |  |  |
| All First | 18 | 20 | 8 | 75 | 23 | 6.25 | - | - | 4 | - | 483.1 | 134 | 1375 | 46 | 29.89 | 4-46 | - | - |
| 1-day Int |  |  |  |  |  |  |  |  |  |  |  |  |  |  |  |  |  |  |
| NatWest | 4 | 1 | 1 | 0 | 0* | - | - | - | - | - | 39.5 | 3 | 142 | 5 | 28.40 | 3-21 | - |  |
| B & H | 4 | 2 | 0 | 1 | 1 | 0.50 | - | - | - | - | 37 | 13 | 68 | 5 | 13.60 | 2-15 | - |  |
| Sunday | 15 | 7 | 3 | 15 | 7 | 3.75 | - | - | 1 | - | 100.1 | 5 | 478 | 14 | 34.14 | 2-27 | - |  |

## Career Performances

|  | M | Inns | NO | Runs | HS | Avge | 100s | 50s | Ct | St | Balls | Runs | Wkts | Avge | Best | 5wI | 10wM |
|---|---|---|---|---|---|---|---|---|---|---|---|---|---|---|---|---|---|
| Test |  |  |  |  |  |  |  |  |  |  |  |  |  |  |  |  |  |
| All First | 155 | 161 | 68 | 312 | 23 | 3.35 | - | - | 31 | - | 25276 | 12059 | 369 | 32.68 | 9-37 | 7 | 2 |
| 1-day Int |  |  |  |  |  |  |  |  |  |  |  |  |  |  |  |  |  |
| NatWest | 18 | 7 | 5 | 4 | 3* | 2.00 | - | - | 2 | - | 1219 | 658 | 26 | 25.30 | 4-32 | - |  |
| B & H | 19 | 8 | 4 | 6 | 3* | 1.50 | - | - | - | 3 | 1060 | 591 | 23 | 25.69 | 3-20 | - |  |
| Sunday | 97 | 32 | 14 | 38 | 7 | 2.11 | - | - | 11 | - | 4178 | 3147 | 85 | 37.02 | 4-23 | - |  |

# ROBINSON, P. E.      Leicestershire

**Name:** Phillip Edward Robinson
**Role:** Right-hand bat, left-arm 'declaration' bowler
**Born:** 3 August 1963, Keighley, West Yorkshire
**Height:** 5ft 9in **Weight:** 13st 10lbs
**Nickname:** Roundbat, Brigadier, F.B., Skip, Robbo, Red
**County debut:** 1984 (Yorkshire), 1992 (Leicestershire)
**County cap:** 1988 (Yorkshire)
**1000 runs in a season:** 3
**1st-Class 50s:** 51
**1st-Class 100s:** 7
**1st-Class catches:** 130
**One-Day 100s:** 1
**Place in batting averages:**
(1994 40th av. 43.57)
**Parents:** Keith and Lesley
**Wife and date of marriage:** Jane, 19 September 1986
**Family links with cricket:** Father and brother played in Bradford League. Dad now an umpire
**Education:** Long Lee Primary; Hartington Middle; Greenhead Comprehensive
**Qualifications:** 2 O-levels
**Off-season:** Coaching in Leicester indoor school
**Overseas tours:** Southland CC to Tasmania 1987; Yorkshire to St Lucia and Barbados 1988; Leicestershire to Jamaica 1993, to South Africa 1994-95
**Overseas teams played for:** Southland, New Zealand 1987; Eastern Southland cricket coach 1987; Eden Roskill, Auckland 1989-90; Riverside, Wellington 1990-91
**Cricketers particularly admired:** Geoff Boycott, Richard Hadlee, Michael Holding
**Other sports followed:** Football (Manchester United), rugby league (Keighley Cougars)
**Relaxations:** War-gaming, eating out
**Extras:** Made the highest score by a Yorkshire 2nd XI player with 233 in 1983. Scored most runs by an overseas player in the Auckland Cricket League for Eden Roskill 1989-90 (1200 runs). Hit the fastest televised 50 in the Sunday League (19 balls) v Derbyshire at Chesterfield 1991. Released by Yorkshire at his own request at the end of the 1991 season. Played for Cumberland in 1992 and could play only limited-overs for Leicestershire in 1992 (apart from one match) but on full contract from 1993. Captain of Leicestershire 2nd XI. Led the team to Bain Hogg win in 1995
**Opinions on cricket:** 'Cricket should be played on uncovered pitches over three days. Alternatively, four-day games should be played Wednesday to Saturday, with the Sunday

League game after. Also, second-class cricket should be played Wednesday to Friday to allow the younger players to work with the senior players during the season.'
**Best batting:** 189 Yorkshire v Lancashire, Scarborough 1991
**Best bowling:** 1-10 Yorkshire v Somerset, Scarborough 1990

## 1995 Season

|  | M | Inns | NO | Runs | HS | Avge | 100s | 50s | Ct | St | O | M | Runs | Wkts | Avge | Best | 5wl | 10wM |
|---|---|---|---|---|---|---|---|---|---|---|---|---|---|---|---|---|---|---|
| Test |  |  |  |  |  |  |  |  |  |  |  |  |  |  |  |  |  |  |
| All First | 3 | 6 | 1 | 99 | 60 * | 19.80 | - | 1 | 5 | - |  |  |  |  |  |  |  |  |
| 1-day Int |  |  |  |  |  |  |  |  |  |  |  |  |  |  |  |  |  |  |
| NatWest | 2 | 2 | 0 | 45 | 40 | 22.50 | - | - | 2 | - |  |  |  |  |  |  |  |  |
| B & H | 4 | 4 | 1 | 85 | 54 | 28.33 | - | 1 | 3 | - |  |  |  |  |  |  |  |  |
| Sunday | 7 | 7 | 1 | 86 | 28 | 14.33 | - | - | 7 | - |  |  |  |  |  |  |  |  |

## Career Performances

|  | M | Inns | NO | Runs | HS | Avge | 100s | 50s | Ct | St | Balls | Runs | Wkts | Avge | Best | 5wl | 10wM |
|---|---|---|---|---|---|---|---|---|---|---|---|---|---|---|---|---|---|
| Test |  |  |  |  |  |  |  |  |  |  |  |  |  |  |  |  |  |
| All First | 159 | 261 | 35 | 7617 | 189 | 33.70 | 7 | 51 | 130 | - | 296 | 329 | 3 | 109.66 | 1-10 | - | - |
| 1-day Int |  |  |  |  |  |  |  |  |  |  |  |  |  |  |  |  |  |
| NatWest | 17 | 13 | 0 | 421 | 73 | 32.38 | - | 3 | 5 | - |  |  |  |  |  |  |  |
| B & H | 30 | 26 | 4 | 639 | 73 * | 29.04 | - | 4 | 12 | - |  |  |  |  |  |  |  |
| Sunday | 145 | 140 | 14 | 3111 | 104 | 24.69 | 1 | 14 | 59 | - |  |  |  |  |  |  |  |

# ROBINSON, R. T.      Nottinghamshire

**Name:** Robert Timothy Robinson
**Role:** Right-hand opening bat, right-arm medium bowler
**Born:** 21 November 1958, Sutton-in-Ashfield, Nottinghamshire
**Height:** 6ft **Weight:** 12st 7lbs
**Nickname:** Robbo, Chop
**County debut:** 1978
**County cap:** 1983
**Benefit:** 1992 (£90,040)
**Test debut:** 1984-85
**Tests:** 29
**One-Day Internationals:** 26
**1000 runs in a season:** 13
**1st-Class 50s:** 122
**1st-Class 100s:** 58
**1st-Class 200s:** 3
**1st-Class catches:** 226
**One-Day 100s:** 9

**Place in batting averages:** 17th av. 54.00
(1994 49th av. 42.53)
**Parents:** Eddy and Christine
**Wife and date of marriage:**
Patricia, 2 November 1985
**Children:** Philip Thomas; Alex James
**Family links with cricket:** Father, uncle,
cousin and brother all played local cricket
**Education:** Dunstable Grammar School;
High Pavement College, Nottingham;
Sheffield University
**Qualifications:** BA (Hons) in Accountancy
and Financial Management
**Career outside cricket:** Owns two sports
shops
**Off-season:** Working in own business. Over
35s tournament in Sharjah
**Overseas tours:** England to India and
Australia 1984-85, to West Indies 1985-86, to India and Pakistan (World Cup) 1987-
88, to New Zealand 1987-88; unofficial English XI to South Africa 1989-90
**Cricketers particularly admired:** Geoffrey Boycott
**Other sports followed:** Golf, squash
**Relaxations:** Spending time with family
**Extras:** Played for Northamptonshire 2nd XI in 1974-75 and for Nottinghamshire 2nd
XI in 1977. Had soccer trials with Portsmouth, Chelsea and QPR. One of *Wisden*'s Five
Cricketers of the Year 1985. Banned from Test cricket for joining 1989-90 tour of South
Africa, remitted in 1992. Handed over captaincy to Paul Johnson in 1995 to give more
time to business
**Best batting:** 220* Nottinghamshire v Yorkshire, Trent Bridge 1990
**Best bowling:** 1-22 Nottinghamshire v Northamptonshire, Northampton 1982

## 1995 Season

|         | M  | Inns | NO | Runs | HS  | Avge  | 100s | 50s | Ct | St | O | M | Runs | Wkts | Avge | Best | 5wI | 10wM |
|---------|----|------|----|------|-----|-------|------|-----|----|----|---|---|------|------|------|------|-----|------|
| Test    |    |      |    |      |     |       |      |     |    |    |   |   |      |      |      |      |     |      |
| All First | 18 | 32 | 0 | 1728 | 209 | 54.00 | 7 | 5 | 7 | - | | | | | | | | |
| 1-day Int |    |      |    |      |     |       |      |     |    |    |   |   |      |      |      |      |     |      |
| NatWest | 2  | 2    | 0  | 101  | 73  | 50.50 | -    | 1   | 1  | -  | | | | | | | | |
| B & H   | 6  | 5    | 1  | 225  | 84  | 56.25 | -    | 2   | 1  | -  | | | | | | | | |
| Sunday  | 16 | 16   | 0  | 488  | 82  | 30.50 | -    | 4   | 8  | -  | | | | | | | | |

## Career Performances

|        | M   | Inns | NO | Runs  | HS    | Avge  | 100s | 50s | Ct  | St | Balls | Runs | Wkts | Avge  | Best | 5wI | 10wM |
|--------|-----|------|----|-------|-------|-------|------|-----|-----|----|-------|------|------|-------|------|-----|------|
| Test   | 29  | 49   | 5  | 1601  | 175   | 36.38 | 4    | 6   | 8   | -  | 6     | 0    | 0    | -     | -    | -   | -    |
| All First | 367 | 637 | 76 | 24365 | 220 * | 43.43 | 58   | 122 | 226 | -  | 253   | 285  | 4    | 71.25 | 1-22 | -   | -    |
| 1-day Int | 26 | 26 | 0  | 597   | 83    | 22.96 | -    | 3   | 6   | -  |       |      |      |       |      |     |      |
| NatWest | 37 | 37  | 2  | 1466  | 139   | 41.88 | 2    | 7   | 15  | -  |       |      |      |       |      |     |      |
| B & H  | 67  | 65   | 9  | 2407  | 120   | 42.98 | 3    | 17  | 16  | -  |       |      |      |       |      |     |      |
| Sunday | 208 | 202  | 24 | 5726  | 119 * | 32.16 | 4    | 36  | 68  | -  |       |      |      |       |      |     |      |

# ROLLINS, A. S. Derbyshire

**Name:** Adrian Stewart Rollins
**Role:** Right-hand bat, right-arm medium bowler, occasional wicket-keeper
**Born:** 8 February 1972, Barking, Essex
**Height:** 6ft 5in **Weight:** 16st 5lbs
**Nickname:** Rollie, The Truth, Stinkmout, Full, Max, Charles Atlas
**County debut:** 1993
**County cap:** 1995
**1000 runs in a season:** 1
**1st-Class 50s:** 13
**1st-Class 100s:** 2
**1st-Class 200s:** 1
**1st-Class catches:** 39
**1st-Class stumpings:** 1
**One-day 100s:** 1
**Place in batting averages:** 100th av. 34.21 (1994 149th av. 26.22)
**Parents:** Marva
**Marital status:** Single
**Family links with cricket:** Brother Robert on Essex staff. Brother Gary at London Cricket College. Uncle plays in Essex League.
**Education:** Little Ilford Comprehensive School, Manor Park, London
**Qualifications:** 10 GCSEs, 4 A-levels, CCPR Community Sports Leaders Award, BAWLA Leaders Award, NCA coaching award
**Career outside cricket:** Fitness instructor
**Off-season:** 'Not sure. Playing in Australia or South Africa'
**Overseas tours:** London Federation of Boys Clubs to Barbados 1987
**Overseas teams played for:** Kaponga, New Zealand 1993-94
**Cricketers particularly admired:** Dominic Cork, Philip DeFreitas, Chris Adams, Lee Tatam

**Other sports followed:** 'Big basketball fan'

**Injuries:** Hamstring strain, missed two weeks

**Relaxations:** 'Weight-training and photography. A strict hip-hop, swingbeat, soul and ragga listener'

**Extras:** Made Championship debut on same day as brother. Became 500th first-class player for Derbyshire, for whom he was named Young Player of the Year 1993. Was the 100th Derbyshire player to score a hundred. Holds record for the highest score by a Derbyshire opener to carry his bat and his 200 not out against Gloucestershire was the longest innings by a Derbyshire player. He became the youngest English qualified Derbyshire double centurion. Voted Derbyshire Player of the Year for 1995

**Opinions on cricket:** 'I am happy with the current format with four-dayers and Sunday League 40 overs. Over-rates in Championship are a bit of a task with an all-seam attack.'

**Best batting:** 200* Derbyshire v Gloucestershire, Bristol 1995

**Best bowling:** 1-19 Derbyshire v Essex, Chelmsford 1995

## 1995 Season

| | M | Inns | NO | Runs | HS | Avge | 100s | 50s | Ct | St | O | M | Runs | Wkts | Avge | Best | 5wI | 10wM |
|---|---|---|---|---|---|---|---|---|---|---|---|---|---|---|---|---|---|---|
| Test | | | | | | | | | | | | | | | | | | |
| All First | 17 | 33 | 1 | 1095 | 200 * | 34.21 | 2 | 5 | 16 | - | 3 | 1 | 19 | 1 | 19.00 | 1-19 | - | - |
| 1-day Int | | | | | | | | | | | | | | | | | | |
| NatWest | 3 | 3 | 0 | 58 | 56 | 19.33 | - | 1 | 1 | - | | | | | | | | |
| B & H | 3 | 3 | 0 | 28 | 15 | 9.33 | - | - | 2 | - | | | | | | | | |
| Sunday | 15 | 14 | 1 | 271 | 126 * | 20.84 | 1 | - | 6 | - | | | | | | | | |

## Career Performances

| | M | Inns | NO | Runs | HS | Avge | 100s | 50s | Ct | St | Balls | Runs | Wkts | Avge | Best | 5wI | 10wM |
|---|---|---|---|---|---|---|---|---|---|---|---|---|---|---|---|---|---|
| Test | | | | | | | | | | | | | | | | | |
| All First | 40 | 75 | 7 | 2195 | 200 * | 32.27 | 2 | 13 | 39 | 1 | 42 | 51 | 1 | 51.00 | 1-19 | - | - |
| 1-day Int | | | | | | | | | | | | | | | | | |
| NatWest | 4 | 4 | 0 | 64 | 56 | 16.00 | - | 1 | 3 | - | | | | | | | |
| B & H | 4 | 4 | 0 | 98 | 70 | 24.50 | - | 1 | 2 | - | | | | | | | |
| Sunday | 32 | 28 | 2 | 521 | 126 * | 20.03 | 1 | 1 | 17 | - | | | | | | | |

70. Which Indian bowler celebrated his return to Test match cricket after an absence of five years with a haul of six for 59 against New Zealand?

# ROLLINS, R. J. Essex

**Name:** Robert John Rollins
**Role:** Right-hand bat, wicket-keeper
**Born:** 30 January 1974, Plaistow, London
**Height:** 5ft 9in **Weight:** 13st 4lbs
**Nickname:** Rollie
**County debut:** 1992
**County cap:** 1995
**1st-Class 50s:** 4
**1st-Class 100s:** 1
**1st-Class catches:** 59
**1st-Class stumpings:** 12
**Place in batting averages:** 161st av. 25.28
**Parents:** Marva
**Marital status:** Engaged to Joanne
**Family links with cricket:** 'Brother Adrian
plays for Derbyshire and brother Gary is
captain of the London Cricket College.
Uncle, Keith Hurst, is captain of Hainault and
Clayhill where Gary and myself still play'
**Education:** Little Ilford Comprehensive School
**Qualifications:** 6 GCSEs
**Off-season:** Playing in Natal, South Africa
**Overseas tours:** England U18 to Canada 1991; England U19 to Pakistan 1991-92, to
India 1992-93
**Overseas teams played for:** M.O.B. Pietermaritzburg, South Africa 1995-96
**Cricketers particularly admired:** Keith Hurst,Alan Knott, Keith Fletcher
**Other sports followed:** 'West Ham from the comfort of an armchair'
**Extras:** Named Essex Young Player of the Year 1992 and awarded his 2nd XI cap in
September of that year. Made Championship debut on the same day as his brother
Adrian. Both kept wicket in the same Sunday League game.
**Opinions on cricket:** 'Four-day cricket is enjoyable.'
**Best batting:** 133* Essex v Glamorgan, Swansea 1995

## 1995 Season

|          | M  | Inns | NO | Runs | HS    | Avge  | 100s | 50s | Ct | St | O | M | Runs | Wkts | Avge | Best | 5wl | 10wM |
|----------|----|------|----|------|-------|-------|------|-----|----|----|---|---|------|------|------|------|-----|------|
| Test     |    |      |    |      |       |       |      |     |    |    |   |   |      |      |      |      |     |      |
| All First| 19 | 35   | 3  | 809  | 133 * | 25.28 | 1    | 4   | 53 | 9  |   |   |      |      |      |      |     |      |
| 1-day Int|    |      |    |      |       |       |      |     |    |    |   |   |      |      |      |      |     |      |
| NatWest  | 2  | 2    | 0  | 29   | 21    | 14.50 | -    | -   | -  | 1  |   |   |      |      |      |      |     |      |
| B & H    | 3  | 1    | 0  | 0    | 0     | 0.00  | -    | -   | 3  | -  |   |   |      |      |      |      |     |      |
| Sunday   | 16 | 11   | 3  | 88   | 28 *  | 11.00 | -    | -   | 22 | -  |   |   |      |      |      |      |     |      |

## Career Performances

|  | M | Inns | NO | Runs | HS | Avge | 100s | 50s | Ct | St | Balls | Runs | Wkts | Avge | Best | 5wI | 10wM |
|---|---|---|---|---|---|---|---|---|---|---|---|---|---|---|---|---|---|
| Test |  |  |  |  |  |  |  |  |  |  |  |  |  |  |  |  |  |
| All First | 24 | 42 | 4 | 851 | 133 * | 22.39 | 1 | 4 | 59 | 12 |  |  |  |  |  |  |  |
| 1-day Int |  |  |  |  |  |  |  |  |  |  |  |  |  |  |  |  |  |
| NatWest | 2 | 2 | 0 | 29 | 21 | 14.50 | - | - | - | 1 |  |  |  |  |  |  |  |
| B & H | 3 | 1 | 0 | 0 | 0 | 0.00 | - | - | 3 | - |  |  |  |  |  |  |  |
| Sunday | 27 | 20 | 7 | 115 | 28 * | 8.84 | - | - | 33 | 4 |  |  |  |  |  |  |  |

# ROSE, G. D.                Somerset

**Name:** Graham David Rose
**Role:** Right-hand bat, right-arm
fast-medium bowler, first slip
**Born:** 12 April 1964, Tottenham
**Height:** 6ft 4in **Weight:** 15st
**Nickname:** Hagar
**County debut:** 1985 (Middlesex),
1987 (Somerset)
**County cap:** 1988 (Somerset)
**1000 runs in a season:** 1
**50 wickets in a season:** 2
**1st-Class 50s:** 30
**1st-Class 100s:** 6
**1st-Class 5 w. in innings:** 8
**1st-Class catches:** 92
**One-Day 100s:** 2
**Place in batting averages:** 122nd av. 30.84
(1994 163rd av. 24.90)
**Place in bowling averages:** 103rd av. 35.94
(1994 29th av. 25.81)
**Strike rate:** 65.53 (career 57.36)
**Parents:** William and Edna
**Wife and date of marriage:** Teresa Julie, 19 September 1987
**Children:** Georgina Charlotte, 6 December 1990
**Family links with cricket:** Father and brothers have played club cricket
**Education:** Northumberland Park School, Tottenham
**Qualifications:** 6 O-levels, 4 A-levels, NCA coaching certificate
**Off-season:** 'Looking for some form of gainful employment'
**Overseas teams played for:** Carey Park, Bunbury, Western Australia 1984-85;
Fremantle, Perth 1986-87; Paarl, Cape Town 1988-89
**Cricketers particularly admired:** Richard Hadlee, Jimmy Cook, Mushtaq Ahmed

**Other sports followed:** Football, rugby, golf
**Injuries:** Right hamstring tear, out for two weeks
**Relaxations:** Wine, music, gardening, playing golf and 'my daughter, Georgina'
**Extras:** Played for England YC v Australia YC 1983. Took 6-41 on Middlesex debut in 1985, then scored 95 on debut for Somerset in 1987. Completed double of 1000 runs and 50 wickets in first-class cricket in 1990 and scored fastest recorded centuries in NatWest Trophy (v Devon) and Sunday League (v Glamorgan)
**Opinions on cricket:** 'I feel that we play too much one-day cricket – perhaps one of the competitions could be ditched. So as to bring us into line with the international game, at least one of the B&H or NatWest competitions should be 50 overs per side.'
**Best batting:** 138 Somerset v Sussex, Taunton 1993
**Best bowling:** 6-41 Middlesex v Worcestershire, Worcester 1985

## 1995 Season

|        | M | Inns | NO | Runs | HS | Avge | 100s | 50s | Ct | St | O | M | Runs | Wkts | Avge | Best | 5wI | 10wM |
|--------|---|------|----|------|----|------|------|-----|----|----|---|---|------|------|------|------|-----|------|
| Test   |   |      |    |      |    |      |      |     |    |    |   |   |      |      |      |      |     |      |
| All First | 16 | 25 | 0 | 771 | 84 | 30.84 | - | 6 | 9 | - | 426 | 93 | 1402 | 39 | 35.94 | 5-78 | 1 | - |
| 1-day Int |   |      |    |      |    |      |      |     |    |    |   |   |      |      |      |      |     |      |
| NatWest | 1 | 1 | 0 | 30 | 30 | 30.00 | - | - | - | - | 11 | 0 | 91 | 0 | - | - | - |   |
| B & H  | 6 | 6 | 1 | 185 | 79 | 37.00 | - | 1 | - | - | 59 | 15 | 185 | 7 | 26.42 | 4-21 | - |   |
| Sunday | 13 | 13 | 1 | 365 | 60 * | 30.41 | - | 2 | 2 | - | 91.5 | 4 | 487 | 6 | 81.16 | 2-28 | - |   |

## Career Performances

|        | M | Inns | NO | Runs | HS | Avge | 100s | 50s | Ct | St | Balls | Runs | Wkts | Avge | Best | 5wI | 10wM |
|--------|---|------|----|------|----|------|------|-----|----|----|-------|------|------|------|------|-----|------|
| Test   |   |      |    |      |    |      |      |     |    |    |       |      |      |      |      |     |      |
| All First | 171 | 237 | 40 | 5910 | 138 | 30.00 | 6 | 30 | 92 | - | 22371 | 11968 | 390 | 30.68 | 6-41 | 8 | - |
| 1-day Int |   |      |    |      |    |      |      |     |    |    |       |      |      |      |      |     |      |
| NatWest | 17 | 15 | 1 | 308 | 110 | 22.00 | 1 | 1 | 3 | - | 845 | 547 | 17 | 32.17 | 3-11 | - |   |
| B & H  | 40 | 34 | 4 | 718 | 79 | 23.93 | - | 4 | 7 | - | 2232 | 1433 | 50 | 28.66 | 4-21 | - |   |
| Sunday | 135 | 118 | 19 | 2866 | 148 | 28.94 | 1 | 16 | 33 | - | 5054 | 3832 | 129 | 29.70 | 4-26 | - |   |

# ROSEBERRY, M. A.                                        Durham

**Name:** Michael Anthony Roseberry
**Role:** Right-hand bat, right-arm medium-fast bowler, county captain
**Born:** 28 November 1966, Houghton-le-Spring, Sunderland
**Height:** 6ft 2in **Weight:** 14st 7lbs
**Nickname:** Micky
**County debut:** 1985 (Middlesex), 1995 (Durham)
**County cap:** 1990 (Middlesex)
**1000 runs in a season:** 4

**1st-Class 50s:** 48
**1st-Class 100s:** 18
**1st-Class catches:** 135
**One-Day 100s:** 5
**Place in batting averages:**
165th av. 24.77 (1994 78th av. 36.56)
**Parents:** Matthew and Jean
**Wife and date of marriage:**
Helen Louise, 22 February 1991
**Children:** Jordan Louise, 29 May 1992;
Lauren Ella, 19 February 1994
**Family links with cricket:** Brother Andrew
played for Glamorgan; father is director of
Durham CCC
**Education:** Tonstall Preparatory School,
Sunderland; Durham School
**Qualifications:** 5 O-levels, 1 A-level,
advanced cricket coach
**Career outside cricket:** 'Coaching cricket.
Director in our business'
**Off-season:** Playing club cricket in Johannesburg
**Overseas tours:** England YC to West Indies 1984-85; England A to Australia 1992-93;
England XI and Lord's Taverners to Hong Kong 'on numerous occasions'; MCC to
West Africa 1993-94; Durham CCC to South Africa 1994-95
**Overseas teams played for:** Fremantle, Western Australia 1986; Melville, Perth 1988;
Alberton, Johannesburg 1994-96
**Cricketers particularly admired:** 'Desmond Haynes for the obvious and his
generosity on the golf course'
**Other sports followed:** 'Played rugby union at a good level when at school
representing Durham County at all levels except the senior side. Follow golf and very
loyal supporter of Sunderland FC'
Injuries: Broken knuckle and knee trouble, out for between four and six weeks
**Relaxations:** 'Eating out and spending time with my family which is limited during
the summer'
**Extras:** Won Lord's Taverners/MCC Cricketer of the Year 1983, Cricket Society award
for Best Young Cricketer of the Year 1984 and twice won Cricket Society award for best
all-rounder in schools cricket. Played in Durham League as a professional while still at
school. At age 16, playing for Durham School v St Bees, he hit 216 in 160 minutes. In
1992 scored 2044 runs in 1992 – joint highest in first-class cricket with Peter Bowler. In
1992 scored 2044 runs in 1992 – joint highest in first-class cricket with Peter Bowler and
was named Middlesex Player of the Year and Lucozade Player of the Year. Left
Middlesex at end of 1994 to return to his native Durham as captain for the 1995 season
**Opinions on cricket:** 'Four-day cricket is a winner, but as clubs and captains we must
improve the pitches.'
**Best batting:** 185 Middlesex v Leicestershire, Lord's 1993
**Best bowling:** 1-1 Middlesex v Sussex, Hove 1988

## 1995 Season

|  | M | Inns | NO | Runs | HS | Avge | 100s | 50s | Ct | St | O | M | Runs | Wkts | Avge | Best | 5wI | 10wM |
|---|---|---|---|---|---|---|---|---|---|---|---|---|---|---|---|---|---|---|
| Test |  |  |  |  |  |  |  |  |  |  |  |  |  |  |  |  |  |  |
| All First | 16 | 29 | 2 | 669 | 90 | 24.77 | - | 4 | 17 | - | 3.4 | 0 | 19 | 0 | - | - | - | - |
| 1-day Int |  |  |  |  |  |  |  |  |  |  |  |  |  |  |  |  |  |  |
| NatWest | 2 | 2 | 0 | 122 | 121 | 61.00 | 1 | - | 2 | - |  |  |  |  |  |  |  |  |
| B & H | 5 | 5 | 0 | 61 | 27 | 12.20 | - | - | - | - |  |  |  |  |  |  |  |  |
| Sunday | 9 | 9 | 0 | 237 | 94 | 26.33 | - | 2 | 3 | - |  |  |  |  |  |  |  |  |

## Career Performances

|  | M | Inns | NO | Runs | HS | Avge | 100s | 50s | Ct | St | Balls | Runs | Wkts | Avge | Best | 5wI | 10wM |
|---|---|---|---|---|---|---|---|---|---|---|---|---|---|---|---|---|---|
| Test |  |  |  |  |  |  |  |  |  |  |  |  |  |  |  |  |  |
| All First | 175 | 294 | 34 | 9362 | 185 | 36.00 | 18 | 48 | 135 | - | 511 | 406 | 4 | 101.50 | 1-1 | - | - |
| 1-day Int |  |  |  |  |  |  |  |  |  |  |  |  |  |  |  |  |  |
| NatWest | 15 | 15 | 0 | 580 | 121 | 38.66 | 2 | 1 | 6 | - | 36 | 42 | 1 | 42.00 | 1-22 | - |  |
| B & H | 22 | 20 | 1 | 508 | 84 | 26.73 | - | 4 | 5 | - | 6 | 2 | 0 | - | - | - |  |
| Sunday | 100 | 96 | 7 | 2752 | 119 * | 30.92 | 3 | 19 | 37 | - | 4 | 7 | 0 | - | - | - |  |

# RUSSELL, R. C.                Gloucestershire

**Name:** Robert Charles Russell
**Role:** Left-hand bat, wicket-keeper, county vice-captain
**Born:** 15 August 1963, Stroud
**Height:** 5ft 8½in **Weight:** 9st 7lbs
**Nickname:** Jack
**County debut:** 1981
**County cap:** 1985
**Benefit:** 1994
**Test debut:** 1988
**Tests:** 39
**One-Day Internationals:** 26
**1st-Class 50s:** 51
**1st-Class 100s:** 4
**1st-Class catches:** 751
**1st-Class stumpings:** 96
**One-Day 100s:** 1
**Place in batting averages:** 47th av. 44.40
(1994 93rd av. 34.65)
**Parents:** John and Jennifer
**Wife and date of marriage:** Aileen Ann, 6 March 1985
**Children:** Stepson, Marcus Anthony; Elizabeth Ann, March 1988; Victoria, 1989;

Charles David 1991
**Education:** Uplands County Primary School; Archway Comprehensive School
**Qualifications:** 7 O-levels, 2 A-levels
**Career outside cricket:** Professional artist
**Off-season:** England tour to South Africa
**Overseas tours:** England to Pakistan 1987-88, to India and West Indies 1989-90, to Australia 1990-91, to New Zealand 1991-92, to West Indies 1993-94, to Australia 1994-95, to South Africa 1995-96, to Pakistan and India (World Cup) 1995-96; England A to Australia 1992-93
**Cricketers particularly admired:** Alan Knott, Bob Taylor
**Other sports followed:** Football ('a Spurs supporter, but only on television'), snooker
**Relaxations:** Drawing, sketching, painting (oil and watercolour), watching comedy, Rory Bremner and Phil Cool especially
**Extras:** Spotted at age nine by Gloucestershire coach, Graham Wiltshire. Youngest Gloucestershire wicket-keeper (17 years 307 days) and set record for most dismissals in a match on first-class debut: 8 (7 caught, 1 stumped) for Gloucestershire v Sri Lankans at Bristol, 1981. Hat-trick of catches v Surrey at The Oval 1986. Represented England YC v West Indies YC in 1982. Was chosen as England's Man of the Test Series, England v Australia 1989 and was one of *Wisden's* Five Cricketers of the Year 1990. Appointed vice-captain to Martyn Moxon on the England A tour to Australia 1992-93. Called up as stand-by wicket-keeper for the England tour to Australia 1994-95 when Alec Stewart broke his finger for the second time on the tour. Had a three-week exhibition of his drawings in Bristol 1988 and published a book of his work entitled *A Cricketer's Art*. Co-author with Christopher Martin-Jenkins of *Sketches of a Season*, published in 1989. Commissioned by Dean of Gloucester to do a drawing of Gloucester Cathedral to raise funds for 900th Anniversary. Still turns out for his original club, Stroud CC, whenever he can. Runs six miles a day to keep fit and drinks up to 20 cups of tea a day. Broke Bob Taylor's long-standing world record for the number of dismissals in a Test match with 11 in the second Test v South Africa at Johannesburg 1995-96
**Best batting:** 128* England v Australia, Old Trafford 1989
**Best bowling:** 1-4 Gloucestershire v West Indians, Bristol 1991

## 1995 Season

|           | M  | Inns | NO | Runs | HS  | Avge   | 100s | 50s | Ct | St | O | M | Runs | Wkts | Avge | Best | 5wI | 10wM |
|-----------|----|------|----|------|-----|--------|------|-----|----|----|---|---|------|------|------|------|-----|------|
| Test      | 3  | 5    | 1  | 199  | 91  | 49.75  | -    | 1   | 9  | 1  |   |   |      |      |      |      |     |      |
| All First | 17 | 26   | 4  | 977  | 91  | 44.40  | -    | 8   | 50 | 2  |   |   |      |      |      |      |     |      |
| 1-day Int |    |      |    |      |     |        |      |     |    |    |   |   |      |      |      |      |     |      |
| NatWest   | 3  | 3    | 2  | 100  | 59 *| 100.00 | -    | 1   | 6  | 1  |   |   |      |      |      |      |     |      |
| B & H     | 6  | 6    | 5  | 147  | 42 *| 147.00 | -    | -   | 8  | -  |   |   |      |      |      |      |     |      |
| Sunday    | 12 | 10   | 4  | 280  | 76 *| 46.66  | -    | 2   | 10 | 1  |   |   |      |      |      |      |     |      |

## Career Performances

|        | M   | Inns | NO  | Runs  | HS    | Avge  | 100s | 50s | Ct  | St  | Balls | Runs | Wkts | Avge  | Best | 5wI | 10wM |
|--------|-----|------|-----|-------|-------|-------|------|-----|-----|-----|-------|------|------|-------|------|-----|------|
| Test   | 39  | 63   | 12  | 1454  | 128 * | 28.50 | 1    | 5   | 99  | 9   |       |      |      |       |      |     |      |
| All First | 318 | 462 | 102 | 10446 | 128 * | 29.01 | 4    | 51  | 751 | 96  | 38    | 53   | 1    | 53.00 | 1-4  | -   | -    |
| 1-day Int | 26 | 19  | 6   | 261   | 50    | 20.07 | -    | 1   | 26  | 5   |       |      |      |       |      |     |      |
| NatWest | 34 | 23   | 7   | 404   | 59 *  | 25.25 | -    | 1   | 43  | 8   |       |      |      |       |      |     |      |
| B & H  | 51  | 38   | 15  | 601   | 51    | 26.13 | -    | 1   | 51  | 8   |       |      |      |       |      |     |      |
| Sunday | 171 | 127  | 31  | 2285  | 108   | 23.80 | 1    | 8   | 141 | 26  |       |      |      |       |      |     |      |

# SALES, D. J.        Northamptonshire

**Name:** David John Sales
**Role:** Right-hand bat, right-arm
medium bowler
**Born:** 3 December 1977, Carshalton, Surrey
**Height:** 6ft   **Weight:** 12st 4lbs
**Nickname:** Jumble
**County debut:** 1994 (one-day)
**Parents:** John and Daphne
**Marital status:** Single
**Family links with cricket:** Father played
club cricket
**Education:** Cumnor House Prep School,
Croydon; Caterham Boys' School
**Qualifications:** 7 GCSEs, cricket coach
**Off-season:** Touring Zimbabwe with England
U19
**Overseas tours:** England U15 to South Africa
1993; England U19 to West Indies 1994-95, to
Zimbabwe 1995-96
**Cricketers particularly admired:**
Graham Gooch, Brian Lara
**Other sports followed:** Football, rugby, hockey, golf
**Relaxations:** Golf and fishing
**Extras:** Youngest batsman to score a 50 in the Sunday League. Played for England U17
against India in 1994

---

71. Who is the youngest player at 24 years and 25 days to take 200 Test wickets, who
was his 200th Test victim and how many Tests did it take him to achieve the feat?

---

## 1995 Season

| | M | Inns | NO | Runs | HS | Avge | 100s | 50s | Ct | St | O | M | Runs | Wkts | Avge | Best | 5wI | 10wM |
|---|---|---|---|---|---|---|---|---|---|---|---|---|---|---|---|---|---|---|
| Test | | | | | | | | | | | | | | | | | | |
| All First | | | | | | | | | | | | | | | | | | |
| 1-day Int | | | | | | | | | | | | | | | | | | |
| NatWest | | | | | | | | | | | | | | | | | | |
| B & H | | | | | | | | | | | | | | | | | | |
| Sunday | 4 | 3 | 1 | 40 | 27 * | 20.00 | - | - | 1 | - | | | | | | | | |

## Career Performances

| | M | Inns | NO | Runs | HS | Avge | 100s | 50s | Ct | St | Balls | | Runs | Wkts | Avge | Best | 5wI | 10wM |
|---|---|---|---|---|---|---|---|---|---|---|---|---|---|---|---|---|---|---|
| Test | | | | | | | | | | | | | | | | | | |
| All First | | | | | | | | | | | | | | | | | | |
| 1-day Int | | | | | | | | | | | | | | | | | | |
| NatWest | | | | | | | | | | | | | | | | | | |
| B & H | | | | | | | | | | | | | | | | | | |
| Sunday | 5 | 4 | 2 | 110 | 70 * | 55.00 | - | 1 | 1 | - | | | | | | | | |

# SALISBURY, I. D. K.     Sussex

**Name:** Ian David Kenneth Salisbury
**Role:** Right-hand bat, leg-break
**Born:** 21 January 1970, Northampton
**Height:** 5ft 11in **Weight:** 12st
**Nickname:** Budgie, Sals
**County debut:** 1989
**County cap:** 1991
**Test debut:** 1992
**Tests:** 7
**One-Day Internationals:** 4
**50 wickets in a season:** 3
**1st-Class 50s:** 6
**1st-Class 5 w. in innings:** 20
**1st-Class 10 w. in match:** 3
**1st-Class catches:** 111
**One-Day 5 w. in innings:** 1
**Place in batting averages:** 190th av. 22.18
(1994 222nd av. 17.42)
**Place in bowling averages:** 79th av. 31.00
(1994 45th av. 27.83)
**Strike rate:** 62.03 (career 66.65)
**Parents:** Dave and Margaret

**Wife and date of marriage:** Emma Louise, 25 September 1993
**Family links with cricket:** 'Dad is vice-president of my first club, Brixworth'
**Education:** Moulton Comprehensive, Northampton
**Qualifications:** 7 O-levels, NCA coaching certificate
**Off-season:** England A tour to Pakistan and then MCC trip to Bangladesh
**Overseas tours:** England A to Pakistan 1990-91, to Bermuda and West Indies 1991-92, to India 1994-95, to Pakistan 1995-96; England to India and Sri Lanka 1992-93, to West Indies 1993-94
**Cricketers particularly admired:** 'Any that keep performing day in, day out, for both country and county'
**Other sports followed:** Most sports
**Injuries:** Lower back, missed one game
**Relaxations:** 'Spending time with wife, Emma, meeting friends and relaxing with them and eating out – with good wine'
**Extras:** Picked to play two Tests for England against Pakistan in 1992, 'proudest moments of my career.' Originally selected for England A tour to Australia 1992-93 but was asked to stay on in India and played in the first two Tests of the series. In 1992 was named Young Player of the Year by both the Wombwell Cricket Lovers and the Cricket Writers. One of *Wisden*'s Five Cricketers of the Year 1993
**Opinions on cricket:** 'Players should be asked for their opinion on changes in the game, before authorities make the changes themselves.'
**Best batting:** 74 Sussex v Gloucestershire, Hove 1995
**Best bowling:** 7-54 Sussex v Yorkshire, Hove 1992

## 1995 Season

| | M | Inns | NO | Runs | HS | Avge | 100s | 50s | Ct | St | O | M | Runs | Wkts | Avge | Best | 5wI | 10wM |
|---|---|---|---|---|---|---|---|---|---|---|---|---|---|---|---|---|---|---|
| Test | | | | | | | | | | | | | | | | | | |
| All First | 18 | 30 | 3 | 599 | 74 | 22.18 | - | 2 | 17 | - | 558.2 | 130 | 1674 | 54 | 31.00 | 7-72 | 5 | 1 |
| 1-day Int | | | | | | | | | | | | | | | | | | |
| NatWest | 2 | 1 | 0 | 4 | 4 | 4.00 | - | - | - | - | 24 | 1 | 83 | 0 | - | - | - | - |
| B & H | 4 | 2 | 0 | 18 | 17 | 9.00 | - | - | 2 | - | 42 | 2 | 163 | 5 | 32.60 | 2-40 | - | |
| Sunday | 17 | 11 | 1 | 151 | 48 * | 15.10 | - | - | 5 | - | 98 | 2 | 478 | 20 | 23.90 | 4-39 | - | |

## Career Performances

| | M | Inns | NO | Runs | HS | Avge | 100s | 50s | Ct | St | Balls | Runs | Wkts | Avge | Best | 5wI | 10wM |
|---|---|---|---|---|---|---|---|---|---|---|---|---|---|---|---|---|---|
| Test | 7 | 13 | 1 | 205 | 50 | 17.08 | - | 1 | 3 | - | 1405 | 933 | 16 | 58.31 | 4-163 | - | - |
| All First | 142 | 181 | 45 | 2462 | 74 | 18.10 | - | 6 | 111 | - | 27127 | 14430 | 407 | 35.45 | 7-54 | 20 | 3 |
| 1-day Int | 4 | 2 | 1 | 7 | 5 | 7.00 | - | - | 1 | - | 186 | 177 | 5 | 35.40 | 3-41 | - | |
| NatWest | 14 | 9 | 3 | 33 | 14 * | 5.50 | - | - | 3 | - | 894 | 529 | 14 | 37.78 | 3-28 | - | |
| B & H | 15 | 9 | 4 | 72 | 17 * | 14.40 | - | - | 5 | - | 885 | 583 | 18 | 32.38 | 3-40 | - | |
| Sunday | 80 | 49 | 14 | 442 | 48 * | 12.62 | - | - | 23 | - | 3006 | 2446 | 76 | 32.18 | 5-30 | 1 | |

# SARGEANT, N. F.                    Surrey

**Name:** Neil Fredrick Sargeant
**Role:** Right-hand bat, wicket-keeper,
off-spin bowler
**Born:** 8 November 1965, Hammersmith
**Height:** 5ft 8in **Weight:** 11st 2lbs
**Nickname:** Sarge, Bilko, Grubby
**County debut:** 1989
**1st-Class catches:** 120
**1st-Class stumpings:** 16
**Place in batting averages:**
(1994 241st av. 15.09)
**Parents:** Barry and Christine
**Marital status:** Single
**Family links with cricket:** Brother Lee plays
for the same club side, Harrow Town CC
**Education:** Grange Primary School;
Whitmore High School
**Qualifications:** 2 O-levels, SAC cricket
coaching award, 'professional handyman'
**Career outside cricket:** Whatever pays the most
**Overseas teams played for:** Green Point, South Africa 1987-89; United, South Africa 1991
**Cricketers particularly admired:** Alan Knott, Bob Taylor, Richie Ryall, Alec
Stewart, Jack Russell, Danny Taylor
**Other sports followed:** Football, golf, horse racing
**Relaxations:** Horse racing, music
**Extras:** Played football for Tottenham Hotspur Youth Team
**Opinions on cricket:** 'I think we are heading the right way with all four-day matches. I
would also like to see 12-month contracts.'
**Best batting:** 49 Surrey v Lancashire, Old Trafford 1991
**Best bowling:** 1-88 Surrey v Gloucestershire, Guildford 1991

## 1995 Season

|          | M | Inns | NO | Runs | HS | Avge | 100s | 50s | Ct | St | O | M | Runs | Wkts | Avge | Best | 5wI | 10wM |
|----------|---|------|----|------|----|------|------|-----|----|----|---|---|------|------|------|------|-----|------|
| Test     |   |      |    |      |    |      |      |     |    |    |   |   |      |      |      |      |     |      |
| All First | 2 | 2    | 0  | 8    | 6  | 4.00 | -    |     | -  | 11 | - |   |      |      |      |      |     |      |
| 1-day Int |   |      |    |      |    |      |      |     |    |    |   |   |      |      |      |      |     |      |
| NatWest  |   |      |    |      |    |      |      |     |    |    |   |   |      |      |      |      |     |      |
| B & H    |   |      |    |      |    |      |      |     |    |    |   |   |      |      |      |      |     |      |
| Sunday   | 3 | 2    | 0  | 8    | 5  | 4.00 | -    |     | -  | 4  | - |   |      |      |      |      |     |      |

## Career Performances

| | M | Inns | NO | Runs | HS | Avge | 100s | 50s | Ct | St | Balls | Runs | Wkts | Avge | Best | 5wI | 10wM |
|---|---|---|---|---|---|---|---|---|---|---|---|---|---|---|---|---|---|
| Test | | | | | | | | | | | | | | | | | |
| All First | 52 | 67 | 11 | 786 | 49 | 14.03 | - | - | 120 | 16 | 30 | 88 | 1 | 88.00 | 1-88 | - | - |
| 1-day Int | | | | | | | | | | | | | | | | | |
| NatWest | | | | | | | | | | | | | | | | | |
| B & H | | | | | | | | | | | | | | | | | |
| Sunday | 13 | 7 | 2 | 58 | 22 | 11.60 | - | - | 10 | - | | | | | | | |

# SAVIDENT, L. Hampshire

**Name:** Lee Savident
**Role:** Right-hand bat, right-arm medium bowler
**Born:** 22 October 1976, Guernsey
**Height:** 6ft 5in **Weight:** 15st 7lbs
**County debut:** No first-team appearance
**Parents:** Nev and Sue
**Marital status:** Single
**Family links with cricket:** None
**Education:** Castel Primary School; Guernsey Grammar School; Guernsey College of Further Education
**Career outside cricket:** Student
**Off-season:** Studying at college
**Cricketers particularly admired:** Robin Smith, Graeme Hick, Allan Donald
**Other sports followed:** Football (Tottenham), basketball (Orlando Magic) and golf

**Injuries:** Knee injury, out for three weeks
**Relaxations:** Playing golf, watching TV
**Extras:** Currently holds two Hampshire U16 records. The most runs in a season (679 in 14 matches) and the highest partnership (173 with Lee Nurse against Jersey)
**Opinions on cricket:** 'Clubs should look forward and place more emphasis on coaching people at a young age, to further develop the level of ability as a country.'

# SAXELBY, M.                              Durham

**Name:** Mark Saxelby
**Role:** Left-hand bat, right-arm medium bowler
**Born:** 4 January 1969, Newark
**Height:** 6ft 4in **Weight:** 16st 7lbs
**Nickname:** Sax
**County debut:** 1989 (Nottinghamshire), 1994 (Durham)
**1000 runs in a season:** 1
**1st-Class 50s:** 17
**1st-Class 100s:** 2
**1st-Class catches:** 18
**One-day 100s:** 1
**Place in batting averages:** 226th av. 17.92 (1994 94th av. 34.43)
**Strike rate:** (career 119.27)
**Parents:** Ken and Margaret
**Marital status:** Single
**Family links with cricket:** Brother Kevin played for Notts; father played local cricket
**Education:** Nottingham High School; Nottingham University
**Qualifications:** 7 O-levels, 2 A-levels
**Career outside cricket:** Student
**Overseas teams played for:** Hutt CC, New Zealand 1989-91
**Cricketers particularly admired:** Derek Randall
**Other sports followed:** Most sports, especially rugby
**Injuries:** Back injury, missed one month
**Relaxations:** Cinema, pubs, walking
**Extras:** Released by Durham at the end of the 1995 season
**Opinions on cricket:** 'There should be 100 overs in four-day cricket, not 110. Cricketers should be paid better wages. A course should be set up so that cricketers can train as qualified PE teachers during the winter.'
**Best batting:** 181 Durham v Derbyshire, Chesterfield 1994
**Best bowling:** 3-41 Nottinghamshire v Derbyshire, Derby 1991

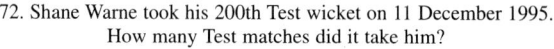

72. Shane Warne took his 200th Test wicket on 11 December 1995. How many Test matches did it take him?

**1995 Season**

| | M | Inns | NO | Runs | HS | Avge | 100s | 50s | Ct | St | O | M | Runs | Wkts | Avge | Best | 5wI | 10wM |
|---|---|---|---|---|---|---|---|---|---|---|---|---|---|---|---|---|---|---|
| Test | | | | | | | | | | | | | | | | | | |
| All First | 7 | 14 | 0 | 251 | 68 | 17.92 | - | 1 | 5 | - | 37.4 | 5 | 138 | 2 | 69.00 | 1-15 | - | - |
| 1-day Int | | | | | | | | | | | | | | | | | | |
| NatWest | 1 | 1 | 0 | 4 | 4 | 4.00 | - | - | - | - | 9 | 0 | 44 | 1 | 44.00 | 1-44 | - | |
| B & H | 5 | 4 | 1 | 102 | 80 * | 34.00 | - | 1 | - | - | 7 | 0 | 28 | 0 | - | | - | - |
| Sunday | 4 | 4 | 0 | 44 | 23 | 11.00 | - | - | - | - | 13 | 0 | 61 | 3 | 20.33 | 3-18 | - | |

**Career Performances**

| | M | Inns | NO | Runs | HS | Avge | 100s | 50s | Ct | St | Balls | Runs | Wkts | Avge | Best | 5wI | 10wM |
|---|---|---|---|---|---|---|---|---|---|---|---|---|---|---|---|---|---|
| Test | | | | | | | | | | | | | | | | | |
| All First | 60 | 104 | 7 | 2893 | 181 | 29.82 | 2 | 17 | 18 | - | 1312 | 903 | 11 | 82.09 | 3-41 | - | - |
| 1-day Int | | | | | | | | | | | | | | | | | |
| NatWest | 7 | 7 | 1 | 117 | 41 | 19.50 | - | - | 2 | - | 220 | 176 | 5 | 35.20 | 2-42 | - | |
| B & H | 10 | 8 | 1 | 151 | 80 * | 21.57 | - | 1 | - | - | 198 | 146 | 1 | 146.00 | 1-36 | - | |
| Sunday | 58 | 48 | 7 | 1118 | 100 * | 27.26 | 1 | 5 | 11 | - | 1014 | 878 | 25 | 35.12 | 4-29 | - | |

# SCHOFIELD, C. J.        Yorkshire

**Name:** Christopher John Schofield
**Role:** Right-hand bat, leg-break bowler
**Born:** 21 March 1976, Barnsley
**Height:** 5ft 7in **Weight:** 10st 3lbs
**Nickname:** Scoff, Linford, Munchkin
**County debut:** No first-team appearance
**Parents:** John and Pat
**Marital status:** Single
**Family links with cricket:** Father played local league cricket
**Education:** Kingstone School
**Qualifications:** 6 GCSEs, City and Guilds Sport and Leisure
**Off-season:** Training and relaxing
**Overseas tours:** England U19 to Sri Lanka 1993-94, to West Indies 1994-95
**Cricketers particularly admired:** Carlisle Best, Desmond Haynes, Viv Richards, Brian Lara, Richie Richardson
**Other sports followed:** Football, rugby league
**Extras:** Played Yorkshire U11 to U15, Yorkshire Cricket Association U16 and U19, Yorkshire Cricket Academy and England U19 in home series against India 1994

**Opinions on cricket:** 'Cricket needs to be made more attractive to public, e.g. televised county cricket leading to more sponsorship.'

# SCOTT, C. W.        Durham

**Name:** Christopher Wilmot Scott
**Role:** Right-hand bat, wicket-keeper
**Born:** 23 January 1964, Lincoln
**Height:** 5ft 8in **Weight:** 11st
**Nickname:** George
**County debut:** 1981 (Nottinghamshire), 1992 (Durham)
**County cap:** 1988 (Nottinghamshire)
**1st-Class 50s:** 14
**1st-Class 100s:** 2
**1st-Class catches:** 263
**1st-Class stumpings:** 17
**Place in batting averages:** 158th av. 25.91 (1994 183rd av. 22.33)
**Parents:** Kenneth and Kathleen
**Wife and date of marriage:** Jacqui, 18 March 1989
**Family links with cricket:** Father and brothers all play for Collingham, Lincoln

**Education:** Robert Pattinson Comprehensive, North Hykeham, Lincoln
**Qualifications:** 4 O-levels, intermediate and advanced cricket coach
**Career outside cricket:** Farming
**Overseas tours:** Durham to Zimbabwe 1991-92
**Overseas teams played for:** Poverty Bay, New Zealand 1983-84; Queensland University 1985-86, 1987-88; Rotorua, New Zealand 1989-90
**Cricketers particularly admired:** Ian Botham, Alan Knott, Bruce French
**Other sports followed:** Rugby union, football (Lincoln City), golf
**Relaxations:** Rugby, football, skiing, golf (occasionally), Chinese food, travel, current affairs
**Extras:** One of the youngest players to make Championship debut for Nottinghamshire – 17 years 157 days. Equalled the Nottinghamshire record for most catches in a match with ten against Derbyshire in 1988. Left Nottinghamshire at end of 1991 season to join Durham
**Opinions on cricket:** '100 overs in a day is plenty.'
**Best batting:** 108 Durham v Surrey, Darlington 1994

## 1995 Season

| | M | Inns | NO | Runs | HS | Avge | 100s | 50s | Ct | St | O | M | Runs | Wkts | Avge | Best | 5wI | 10wM |
|---|---|---|---|---|---|---|---|---|---|---|---|---|---|---|---|---|---|---|
| Test | | | | | | | | | | | | | | | | | | |
| All First | 7 | 13 | 1 | 311 | 56 | 25.91 | - | 2 | 18 | - | 3.2 | 0 | 30 | 0 | - | - | - | - |
| 1-day Int | | | | | | | | | | | | | | | | | | |
| NatWest | | | | | | | | | | | | | | | | | | |
| B & H | 4 | 4 | 0 | 8 | 6 | 2.00 | - | - | 7 | - | | | | | | | | |
| Sunday | 4 | 3 | 1 | 24 | 14 | 12.00 | - | - | 3 | - | | | | | | | | |

## Career Performances

| | M | Inns | NO | Runs | HS | Avge | 100s | 50s | Ct | St | Balls | Runs | Wkts | Avge | Best | 5wI | 10wM |
|---|---|---|---|---|---|---|---|---|---|---|---|---|---|---|---|---|---|
| Test | | | | | | | | | | | | | | | | | |
| All First | 122 | 166 | 30 | 3020 | 108 | 22.20 | 2 | 14 | 263 | 17 | 26 | 40 | 0 | - | - | - | - |
| 1-day Int | | | | | | | | | | | | | | | | | |
| NatWest | 7 | 1 | 0 | 2 | 2 | 2.00 | - | - | 7 | - | | | | | | | |
| B & H | 10 | 9 | 1 | 50 | 18 | 6.25 | - | - | 9 | - | | | | | | | |
| Sunday | 49 | 30 | 10 | 331 | 45 | 16.55 | - | - | 46 | 7 | | | | | | | |

# SEARLE, J. P.        Durham

**Name:** Jason Paul Searle
**Role:** Right-hand bat, off-spin bowler
**Born:** 16 May 1976, Bath
**Height:** 5ft 10in **Weight:** 11st 7lbs
**Nickname:** Shaggy
**County debut:** 1994
**Parents:** Paul and Chris
**Marital status:** Single
**Family links with cricket:** Father played for Chippenham and Wiltshire
**Education:** John Bentley School, Calne; Wiltshire and Swindon Building College
**Qualifications:** 6 GCSEs, bricklayer
**Career outside cricket:** Bricklayer
**Overseas tours:** England U19 to West Indies 1994-95
**Cricketers particularly admired:** Ian Botham, Robin Smith
**Other sports followed:** Football
**Relaxations:** Fishing and watching television
**Best batting:** 5* Durham v Lancashire, Stockton 1994
**Best bowling:** 2-126 Durham v Surrey, The Oval 1995

## 1995 Season

|  | M | Inns | NO | Runs | HS | Avge | 100s | 50s | Ct | St | O | M | Runs | Wkts | Avge | Best | 5wI | 10wM |
|---|---|---|---|---|---|---|---|---|---|---|---|---|---|---|---|---|---|---|
| Test |  |  |  |  |  |  |  |  |  |  |  |  |  |  |  |  |  |  |
| All First | 1 | 2 | 1 | 2 | 2 * | 2.00 | - | - | - | - | 36 | 3 | 126 | 2 | 63.00 | 2-126 | - | - |
| 1-day Int |  |  |  |  |  |  |  |  |  |  |  |  |  |  |  |  |  |  |
| NatWest |  |  |  |  |  |  |  |  |  |  |  |  |  |  |  |  |  |  |  |
| B & H | 1 | 0 | 0 | 0 | 0 | - | - | - | - | - |  |  |  |  |  |  |  |  |
| Sunday | 1 | 0 | 0 | 0 | 0 | - | - | - | - | - | 2 | 0 | 19 | 0 | - |  | - | - |

## Career Performances

|  | M | Inns | NO | Runs | HS | Avge | 100s | 50s | Ct | St | Balls | Runs | Wkts | Avge | Best | 5wI | 10wM |
|---|---|---|---|---|---|---|---|---|---|---|---|---|---|---|---|---|---|
| Test |  |  |  |  |  |  |  |  |  |  |  |  |  |  |  |  |  |
| All First | 2 | 4 | 3 | 7 | 5 * | 7.00 | - | - | - | - | 222 | 133 | 2 | 66.50 | 2-126 | - | - |
| 1-day Int |  |  |  |  |  |  |  |  |  |  |  |  |  |  |  |  |  |
| NatWest |  |  |  |  |  |  |  |  |  |  |  |  |  |  |  |  |  |  |
| B & H | 1 | 0 | 0 | 0 | 0 | - | - | - | - | - |  |  |  |  |  |  |  |
| Sunday | 1 | 0 | 0 | 0 | 0 | - | - | - | - | - | 12 | 19 | 0 | - |  | - | - |

# SHADFORD, D. J.         Lancashire

**Name:** Darren James Shadford
**Role:** Right-hand bat, right-arm medium
fast bowler
**Born:** 4 March 1975, Oldham, Lancashire
**Height:** 6ft 3in **Weight:** 14st
**Nickname:** Dead Beat, Shed Head, Amoeba
**County debut:** 1994 (one-day),
1995 (first-class )
**Parents:** Ken and Sue
**Marital status:** Single
**Family links with cricket:** Father and
brother play club cricket
**Education:** Breeze Hill High School;
Oldham College of Technology
**Qualifications:** Information Technology,
BTEC in Business and Finance. 'No O's, no
A's, no degrees, but have got First Star in
canoe training and teaching'

**Overseas teams played for:** Gold Coast
Cricket and District Club 1994-95
**Cricketers particularly admired:** Paul Thompson, Peter Sleep, Peter Seal
**Other sports followed:** Any

**Relaxations:** Listening to music. Socialising and playing other sports
**Extras:** Represented Oldham at cricket, football and athletics
**Opinions on cricket:** 'Make the balls bigger and the bats wider.'
**Best batting:** 1 Lancashire v Essex, Old Trafford 1995
**Best bowling:** 2-40 Lancashire v Surrey, The Oval 1995

## 1995 Season

|           | M | Inns | NO | Runs | HS | Avge | 100s | 50s | Ct | St | O    | M | Runs | Wkts | Avge  | Best | 5wI | 10wM |
|-----------|---|------|----|------|----|------|------|-----|----|----|------|---|------|------|-------|------|-----|------|
| Test      |   |      |    |      |    |      |      |     |    |    |      |   |      |      |       |      |     |      |
| All First | 2 | 2    | 1  | 1    | 1  | 1.00 | -    | -   | -  | -  | 29.5 | 4 | 107  | 3    | 35.66 | 2-40 | -   | -    |
| 1-day Int |   |      |    |      |    |      |      |     |    |    |      |   |      |      |       |      |     |      |
| NatWest   |   |      |    |      |    |      |      |     |    |    |      |   |      |      |       |      |     |      |
| B & H     |   |      |    |      |    |      |      |     |    |    |      |   |      |      |       |      |     |      |
| Sunday    |   |      |    |      |    |      |      |     |    |    |      |   |      |      |       |      |     |      |

## Career Performances

|           | M | Inns | NO | Runs | HS | Avge | 100s | 50s | Ct | St | Balls | Runs | Wkts | Avge  | Best | 5wI | 10wM |
|-----------|---|------|----|------|----|------|------|-----|----|----|-------|------|------|-------|------|-----|------|
| Test      |   |      |    |      |    |      |      |     |    |    |       |      |      |       |      |     |      |
| All First | 2 | 2    | 1  | 1    | 1  | 1.00 | -    | -   | -  | -  | 179   | 107  | 3    | 35.66 | 2-40 | -   | -    |
| 1-day Int |   |      |    |      |    |      |      |     |    |    |       |      |      |       |      |     |      |
| NatWest   |   |      |    |      |    |      |      |     |    |    |       |      |      |       |      |     |      |
| B & H     |   |      |    |      |    |      |      |     |    |    |       |      |      |       |      |     |      |
| Sunday    | 3 | 0    | 0  | 0    | 0  | -    | -    | -   | 1  | -  | 48    | 42   | 0    | -     |      | -   | -    |

# SHAH, O. A.                                    Middlesex

**Name:** Owais Alam Shah
**Role:** Right-hand bat, off-spin bowler
**Born:** 22 October 1978, Karachi, Pakistan
**Height:** 6ft 1in  **Weight:** 12st
**Nickname:** Robin
**County debut:** 1995 (one-day)
**Parents:** Jamshed and Mahjabeen
**Marital status:** Single
**Family links with cricket:** Father played for his college side
**Education:** Berkley's Junior School; Isleworth and Syon School
**Qualifications:** 6 GCSEs
**Off-season:** Doing a business A-level course, practising at Finchley CC, and hopefully England U19 tour to Zimbabwe
**Overseas tours:** England U19 to Zimbabwe 1995-96
**Cricketers particularly admired:** Robin Smith, Mark Waugh, Carl Hooper and Mark Ramprakash

**Other sports followed:** Table tennis, snooker and football

**Relaxations:** Listening to music, friends and television

**Extras:** Middlesex Sports Federation Award winner. Man of the Series in U17 Test series against India 1994. Played for Middlesex U13, Ken Barrington Trophy (National Champions) and Middlesex U15, county competition winners, as captain. Scored record 232 for England U15 against England U16. Man of the Series for England U17 against India U17

**Opinions on cricket:** 'It is good to see that younger players are given a chance in the Sunday League games.'

## 1995 Season

|  | M | Inns | NO | Runs | HS | Avge | 100s | 50s | Ct | St | O | M | Runs | Wkts | Avge | Best | 5wI | 10wM |
|---|---|---|---|---|---|---|---|---|---|---|---|---|---|---|---|---|---|---|
| Test |  |  |  |  |  |  |  |  |  |  |  |  |  |  |  |  |  |  |
| All First |  |  |  |  |  |  |  |  |  |  |  |  |  |  |  |  |  |  |  |
| 1-day Int |  |  |  |  |  |  |  |  |  |  |  |  |  |  |  |  |  |  |  |
| NatWest |  |  |  |  |  |  |  |  |  |  |  |  |  |  |  |  |  |  |  |
| B & H |  |  |  |  |  |  |  |  |  |  |  |  |  |  |  |  |  |  |  |
| Sunday | 5 | 5 | 1 | 86 | 64 | 21.50 | - | 1 | 1 | - |  |  |  |  |  |  |  |  |

## Career Performances

|  | M | Inns | NO | Runs | HS | Avge | 100s | 50s | Ct | St | Balls | Runs | Wkts | Avge | Best | 5wI | 10wM |
|---|---|---|---|---|---|---|---|---|---|---|---|---|---|---|---|---|---|
| Test |  |  |  |  |  |  |  |  |  |  |  |  |  |  |  |  |  |
| All First |  |  |  |  |  |  |  |  |  |  |  |  |  |  |  |  |  |  |
| 1-day Int |  |  |  |  |  |  |  |  |  |  |  |  |  |  |  |  |  |  |
| NatWest |  |  |  |  |  |  |  |  |  |  |  |  |  |  |  |  |  |  |
| B & H |  |  |  |  |  |  |  |  |  |  |  |  |  |  |  |  |  |  |
| Sunday | 5 | 5 | 1 | 86 | 64 | 21.50 | - | 1 | 1 | - |  |  |  |  |  |  |  |

**Name:** Nadeem Shahid
**Role:** Right-hand bat, leg-spin bowler
**Born:** 23 April 1969, Karachi
**Height:** 6ft **Weight:** 11st 9lbs
**Nickname:** Prince of Darkness, Nad, Jo
**County debut:** 1989 (Essex), 1995 (Surrey)
**1000 runs in a season:** 1
**1st-Class 50s:** 19
**1st-Class 100s:** 4
**1st-Class catches:** 79
**One-day 100s:** 1
**Place in batting averages:** 74th av. 39.13
(1994 178th av.23.28)
**Strike rate:** (career 67.80)
**Parents:** Ahmed and Salma
**Marital status:** Engaged
**Family links with cricket:**
Brother plays in the local Two Counties
League for Felixstowe
**Education:** Stoke High; Northgate High; Ipswich School; Plymouth Polytechnic
**Qualifications:** 6 O-levels, 1 A-level, coaching certificate
**Career outside cricket:** 'Playing golf and taking money off Darren Robinson'
**Overseas tours:** Ipswich School to Barbados (Sir Garfield Sobers Trophy) 1987;
England (South) to N Ireland (Youth World Tournament) 1988
**Overseas teams played for:** Gosnells, Perth, Western Australia 1989-91; Fairfield,
Sydney 1992-93
**Cricketers particularly admired:** Ian Botham, Abdul Qadir and Mark Waugh, Nasser
Hussain
**Other sports followed:** Golf, tennis, badminton, squash, most ball sports
**Relaxations:** 'Playing golf, eating out, going to cinema, spending time with my
fiancée, Sarah'
**Extras:** Youngest Suffolk player aged 17. Played for HMC, MCC Schools, ESCA U19,
NCA Young Cricketers (Lord's and International Youth tournament in Belfast), England
U25 and at every level for Suffolk. TSB Young Player of the Year 1987, winner of the
*Daily Telegraph* Bowling Award 1987 and 1988, Cricket Society's All-rounder of the
Year 1988 and Laidlaw Young Player of the Year for Essex 1993. Essex Society Player
of the Year 1993. Released by Essex at end of 1994 season and signed for Surrey
**Opinions on cricket:** 'The pitches in the 2nd XI competition should be greatly improved,
which is essential for producing good cricketers. All players should be treated equally.'
**Best batting:** 139 Surrey v Yorkshire, The Oval 1995
**Best bowling:** 3-91 Essex v Surrey, The Oval 1990

## 1995 Season

| | M | Inns | NO | Runs | HS | Avge | 100s | 50s | Ct | St | O | M | Runs | Wkts | Avge | Best | 5wI | 10wM |
|---|---|---|---|---|---|---|---|---|---|---|---|---|---|---|---|---|---|---|
| Test | | | | | | | | | | | | | | | | | | |
| All First | 14 | 25 | 2 | 900 | 139 | 39.13 | 2 | 5 | 15 | - | 120 | 16 | 547 | 8 | 68.37 | 2-29 | - | - |
| 1-day Int | | | | | | | | | | | | | | | | | | |
| NatWest | 2 | 1 | 0 | 11 | 11 | 11.00 | - | - | 2 | - | | | | | | | | |
| B & H | 4 | 2 | 1 | 65 | 65 * | 65.00 | - | 1 | - | - | 25 | 0 | 131 | 1 | 131.00 | 1-59 | - | |
| Sunday | 13 | 12 | 5 | 322 | 101 | 46.00 | 1 | - | 5 | - | 2 | 0 | 14 | 0 | - | | - | - |

## Career Performances

| | M | Inns | NO | Runs | HS | Avge | 100s | 50s | Ct | St | Balls | Runs | Wkts | Avge | Best | 5wI | 10wM |
|---|---|---|---|---|---|---|---|---|---|---|---|---|---|---|---|---|---|
| Test | | | | | | | | | | | | | | | | | |
| All First | 80 | 124 | 18 | 3462 | 139 | 32.66 | 4 | 19 | 79 | - | 2373 | 1628 | 35 | 46.51 | 3-91 | - | - |
| 1-day Int | | | | | | | | | | | | | | | | | |
| NatWest | 6 | 4 | 1 | 126 | 85 * | 42.00 | - | 1 | 5 | - | 18 | 0 | 1 | 0.00 | 1-0 | - | |
| B & H | 12 | 6 | 1 | 116 | 65 * | 23.20 | - | 1 | 1 | - | 150 | 131 | 1 | 131.00 | 1-59 | - | |
| Sunday | 56 | 46 | 8 | 883 | 101 | 23.23 | 1 | 1 | 19 | - | 30 | 25 | 0 | - | | - | - |

# SHAW, A. D.         Glamorgan

**Name:** Adrian David Shaw
**Role:** Right-hand bat, wicket-keeper
**Born:** 17 February 1972, Neath
**Height:** 5ft 11in **Weight:** 12st 10lbs
**Nickname:** Shawsy, Gloves, Gloveman, Teflon, Cymbals, Clangers, Eddie
**County debut:** 1992 (one-day), 1994 (first-class)
**1st-Class catches:** 9
**Parents:** David Colin and Christina
**Marital status:** Single
**Family links with cricket:** 'Grandfather has this curious obsession with former England bowler Robin Jackman?? Mum fancies Imran Khan.'
**Education:** Llangatwe Comprehensive; Neath Tertiary College, 'Wallabies, Market Tavern and very often on Saturday nights. Very enlightening!'
**Qualifications:** 9 O-levels, 3 A-levels, cricket coaching awards, 'degree from the school of life – James Williams'
**Career outside cricket:** 'Considering various options – none realistic'

**Off-season:** Playing in South Africa

**Overseas tours:** Welsh Schools to Barbados 1988; England YC to New Zealand 1990-91

**Overseas teams played for:** Welkom, Orange Free State 1995-96

**Cricketers particularly admired:** 'I admire any cricketer who has had to play a 2nd XI game at Pontymister or Melton Mowbray. Valour beyond the call of duty'

**Other sports followed:** Rugby (played for Neath RFC, Welsh Youth and Wales U21 squads), football (Leeds), rugby league (Warrington)

**Injuries:** 'Acute frustration in the lower left side of brain. No time off, eased by the odd bottle of Budweiser'

**Relaxations:** 'As in last year's edition, I am still trying in vain to bring some kind of social grace to the vast majority of Glamorgan's 2nd XI, with the notable exception of that Clifton Old Boy, James Williams – a model professional'

**Extras:** One of youngest players (18 years 7 days) to play first-class rugby for Neath. Only current county cricketer playing first-class rugby. Played for Neath against Swansea six days after playing against Zimbabwe for Glamorgan, and had the 'pleasure' of marking Scott Gibbs. Neath RFC Back of the Year 1993-94. Hopes to become the first player for a number of years to play against South Africa in two sports when Neath play them. 'Hoping to be awarded Glamorgan 2nd XI's first benefit after 10 years in the "Stiffs"!' Voted Glamorgan 2nd XI Player of the Year and Glamorgan Young Player of the Year in 1995

**Opinions on cricket:** 'Cricket is a wide, diversified and uplifting game which certainly helps raise me from the intoxication of living in a claustrophobic mining community in a very wet area of South Wales. Also, in the continual absence of Phil Tufnell from the England team there can only be one answer in my humble opinion, Stuart Phelps for England.'

**Best batting:** 14 Glamorgan v Middlesex, Lord's 1994; 14 Glamorgan v Young Australia, Neath 1995

## 1995 Season

| | M | Inns | NO | Runs | HS | Avge | 100s | 50s | Ct | St | O | M | Runs | Wkts | Avge | Best | 5wl | 10wM |
|---|---|---|---|---|---|---|---|---|---|---|---|---|---|---|---|---|---|---|
| Test | | | | | | | | | | | | | | | | | | |
| All First | 2 | 4 | 1 | 20 | 14 | 6.66 | - | - | 3 | 2 | | | | | | | | |
| 1-day Int | | | | | | | | | | | | | | | | | | |
| NatWest | | | | | | | | | | | | | | | | | | |
| B & H | | | | | | | | | | | | | | | | | | |
| Sunday | | | | | | | | | | | | | | | | | | |

73. Jack Russell set a new English record for the number of dismissals by a wicket-keeper in a Test series. How many dismissals did he claim and who's record did he beat?

## Career Performances

|          | M | Inns | NO | Runs | HS | Avge | 100s | 50s | Ct | St | Balls | Runs | Wkts | Avge | Best | 5wI | 10wM |
|----------|---|------|----|------|----|------|------|-----|----|----|-------|------|------|------|------|-----|------|
| Test     |   |      |    |      |    |      |      |     |    |    |       |      |      |      |      |     |      |
| All First | 5 | 7 | 2 | 38 | 14 | 7.60 | - | - | 9 | 2 |       |      |      |      |      |     |      |
| 1-day Int |   |      |    |      |    |      |      |     |    |    |       |      |      |      |      |     |      |
| NatWest  |   |      |    |      |    |      |      |     |    |    |       |      |      |      |      |     |      |
| B & H    |   |      |    |      |    |      |      |     |    |    |       |      |      |      |      |     |      |
| Sunday   | 2 | 0 | 0 | 0 | 0 | - | - | - | - | - |       |      |      |      |      |     |      |

# SHEERAZ, K. P.        Gloucestershire

**Name:** Kamran Pashah Sheeraz
**Role:** Right-hand bat, right-arm medium-fast bowler
**Born:** 28 December 1973, Wellington, Shropshire
**Height:** 6ft **Weight:** 12st
**County debut:** 1994
**1st-Class 5 w. innings:** 2
**1st-Class 10 w. matches:** 1
**1st-Class catches:** 4
**Place in bowling averages:** 109th av. 37.00
**Strike rate:** 56.29 (career 55.42)
**Parents:** Mohammed and Shamim
**Marital status:** Single
**Family links with cricket:** Brother, Humeran, a county youth player. Cousin, Ali, plays for Berkshire Colts
**Education:** Licensed Victuallers School, Ascot; East Berks College of Further Education; East London University
**Qualifications:** GCSE and BTEC National Diploma (Business and Finance)
**Cricketers particularly admired:** Johnny Wardle, Imran Khan, Frank Tyson, Dennis Lillee, Ray Lindwall, Richard Hadlee
**Other sports followed:** Boxing and football
**Injuries:** Damaged left shoulder, missed two weeks
**Relaxations:** Reading, music and weight-lifting
**Extras:** Toured Australia 1991-92 with Berkshire Youth XI and attended Bull Development of Excellence at Lilleshall 1992. Received Texaco (U16) outstanding bowling award (seven wickets in innings) from Ted Dexter. Represented Bedfordshire in Minor Counties Championship. Senior NABC 67kg Boxing Champion. England Amateur Boxing International

**Best batting**: 3 Gloucestershire v Glamorgan, Abergavenny 1995
**Best bowling**: 6-67 Gloucestershire v West Indies, Bristol 1995

## 1995 Season

|        | M  | Inns | NO | Runs | HS   | Avge  | 100s | 50s | Ct | St | O     | M  | Runs | Wkts | Avge  | Best | 5wI | 10wM |
|--------|----|------|----|------|------|-------|------|-----|----|----|-------|----|------|------|-------|------|-----|------|
| Test   |    |      |    |      |      |       |      |     |    |    |       |    |      |      |       |      |     |      |
| All First | 9 | 11 | 4 | 8 | 3 | 1.14 | - | - | 4 | - | 225.1 | 35 | 888 | 24 | 37.00 | 6-67 | 2 | 1 |
| 1-day Int |   |      |    |      |      |       |      |     |    |    |       |    |      |      |       |      |     |      |
| NatWest |    |      |    |      |      |       |      |     |    |    |       |    |      |      |       |      |     |      |
| B & H  |    |      |    |      |      |       |      |     |    |    |       |    |      |      |       |      |     |      |
| Sunday | 11 | 5 | 3 | 26 | 14 * | 13.00 | - | - | 1 | - | 76 | 4 | 369 | 9 | 41.00 | 2-20 | - |  |

## Career Performances

|        | M  | Inns | NO | Runs | HS   | Avge  | 100s | 50s | Ct | St | Balls | Runs | Wkts | Avge  | Best | 5wI | 10wM |
|--------|----|------|----|------|------|-------|------|-----|----|----|-------|------|------|-------|------|-----|------|
| Test   |    |      |    |      |      |       |      |     |    |    |       |      |      |       |      |     |      |
| All First | 10 | 13 | 6 | 9 | 3 | 1.28 | - | - | 4 | - | 1441 | 922 | 26 | 35.46 | 6-67 | 2 | 1 |
| 1-day Int |   |      |    |      |      |       |      |     |    |    |       |      |      |       |      |     |      |
| NatWest |    |      |    |      |      |       |      |     |    |    |       |      |      |       |      |     |      |
| B & H  |    |      |    |      |      |       |      |     |    |    |       |      |      |       |      |     |      |
| Sunday | 12 | 5 | 3 | 26 | 14 * | 13.00 | - | - | 2 | - | 492 | 399 | 9 | 44.33 | 2-20 | - |  |

# SHERIYAR, A.     Worcestershire

**Name:** Alamgir Sheriyar
**Role:** Right-hand bat, left-arm fast bowler
**Born:** 15 November 1973, Birmingham
**Height:** 6ft 1in **Weight:** 13st
**County debut:** 1993 (Leics – one-day), 1994 (Leics – first-class)
**1st-Class 5 w. innings:** 2
**1st-Class 10 w. matches:** 1
**1st-Class catches:** 5
**Place in bowling averages:** 53rd av. 27.25 (1994 103rd av. 36.36)
**Strike rate:** 39.10 (career 44.30)
**Parents:** Mohammed Zaman and Safia Sultana
**Marital status:** Single
**Education:** George Dixon Secondary School, Birmingham; Joseph Chamberlain Sixth Form College, Birmingham; Oxford Brookes University

**Qualifications:** 6 O-levels, studying for BEng (Hons) Combined Engineering
**Cricketers particularly admired:** Wasim Akram, Imran Khan
**Other sports followed:** Football, basketball
**Relaxations:** Computing, listening to different types of music and spending time with loved ones
**Extras:** Played for English Schools U17 and has also played in the Indoor National League. Became only the second player to take a hat-trick on his first-class debut. Asked to be released by Leicestershire at the end of the 1995 season and has joined Worcestershire for the 1996 season
**Opinions on cricket:** 'The rules favour the batsman too much – the bouncer rule especially. This removes one of the fast bowler's weapons.'
**Best batting**: 19 Leicestershire v West Indies, Leicester 1995
**Best bowling**: 6-30 Leicestershire v Young Australia, Leicester 1995

## 1995 Season

| | M | Inns | NO | Runs | HS | Avge | 100s | 50s | Ct | St | O | M | Runs | Wkts | Avge | Best | 5wI | 10wM |
|---|---|---|---|---|---|---|---|---|---|---|---|---|---|---|---|---|---|---|
| Test | | | | | | | | | | | | | | | | | | |
| All First | 8 | 12 | 1 | 59 | 19 | 5.36 | - | - | 3 | - | 189 | 27 | 799 | 29 | 27.55 | 6-30 | 2 | 1 |
| 1-day Int | | | | | | | | | | | | | | | | | | |
| NatWest | | | | | | | | | | | | | | | | | | |
| B & H | | | | | | | | | | | | | | | | | | |
| Sunday | | | | | | | | | | | | | | | | | | |

## Career Performances

| | M | Inns | NO | Runs | HS | Avge | 100s | 50s | Ct | St | Balls | Runs | Wkts | Avge | Best | 5wI | 10wM |
|---|---|---|---|---|---|---|---|---|---|---|---|---|---|---|---|---|---|
| Test | | | | | | | | | | | | | | | | | | |
| All First | 12 | 15 | 3 | 87 | 19 | 7.25 | - | - | 3 | - | 1722 | 1199 | 40 | 29.97 | 6-30 | 2 | 1 |
| 1-day Int | | | | | | | | | | | | | | | | | | |
| NatWest | | | | | | | | | | | | | | | | | | |
| B & H | | | | | | | | | | | | | | | | | | |
| Sunday | 3 | 1 | 1 | 0 | 0 * | - | - | - | - | - | 78 | 73 | 0 | - | | - | - | |

# SHINE, K. J.                    Somerset

**Name:** Kevin James Shine
**Role:** Right-hand bat, right-arm fast bowler
**Born:** 22 February 1969, Bracknell, Berks
**Height:** 6ft 3in **Weight:** 15st
**Nickname:** Shiney, Shoey
**County debut:** 1989 (Hampshire),
1994 (Middlesex)
**1st-Class 5 w. in innings:** 7
**1st-Class 10 w. in match:** 1
**1st-Class catches:** 11
**Place in bowling averages:**
(1994 119th av. 39.86)
**Strike rate:** (career 59.55)
**Parents:** Joe and Mary Clair
**Marital status:** Single
**Education:** Winnersh County Primary;
Maiden Erlegh Comprehensive
**Qualifications:** NCA Advanced coach,
qualified free weight training instructor
**Off-season:** Coaching
**Overseas teams played for:** Merewether, Newcastle, NSW 1990
**Cricketers particularly admired:** Malcolm Marshall, Cardigan Connor, Adi Aymes, Simon Le Tissier Sheperd ('the Middlesex physio')
**Other sports followed:** Football (Reading), basketball, golf ('the best game in the world')
**Relaxations:** 'Spending what time I have off with Nikki, relaxing in our new house'
**Injuries:** Bone spur in left ankle, 'spur taken out was the size of an acorn'. 'tried to play through 1995 season, but played in pain throughout'
**Extras:** Took 8-47 including a hat-trick against Lancashire at Old Trafford in May 1992. Has written (with Jason Harris) a weekly column for the *Reading Chronicle*. 'Told I was released four days before major surgery on left ankle.' Has joined Somerset for the 1996 season
**Opinions on cricket:** 'There are a lot of gutless people out there.'
**Best batting:** 26* Hampshire v Middlesex, Lord's 1989
**Best bowling:** 8-47 Hampshire v Lancashire, Old Trafford 1992

---

74. Which Sri Lankan bowler was repeatedly no-balled for throwing by umpire Daryll Hair in the 1995-96 series against Australia?

---

## 1995 Season

| | M | Inns | NO | Runs | HS | Avge | 100s | 50s | Ct | St | O | M | Runs | Wkts | Avge | Best | 5wI | 10wM |
|---|---|---|---|---|---|---|---|---|---|---|---|---|---|---|---|---|---|---|
| Test | | | | | | | | | | | | | | | | | | |
| All First | 2 | 1 | 0 | 6 | 6 | 6.00 | - | - | - | - | 43 | 6 | 173 | 7 | 24.71 | 4-23 | - | - |
| 1-day Int | | | | | | | | | | | | | | | | | | |
| NatWest | | | | | | | | | | | | | | | | | | |
| B & H | | | | | | | | | | | | | | | | | | |
| Sunday | | | | | | | | | | | | | | | | | | |

## Career Performances

| | M | Inns | NO | Runs | HS | Avge | 100s | 50s | Ct | St | Balls | Runs | Wkts | Avge | Best | 5wI | 10wM |
|---|---|---|---|---|---|---|---|---|---|---|---|---|---|---|---|---|---|
| Test | | | | | | | | | | | | | | | | | |
| All First | 69 | 56 | 26 | 303 | 26 * | 10.10 | - | - | 11 | - | 9231 | 5885 | 155 | 37.96 | 8-47 | 7 | 1 |
| 1-day Int | | | | | | | | | | | | | | | | | |
| NatWest | 2 | 0 | 0 | 0 | 0 | - | - | - | - | - | 129 | 92 | 3 | 30.66 | 3-31 | - | |
| B & H | 4 | 1 | 0 | 0 | 0 | 0.00 | - | - | - | - | 194 | 167 | 4 | 41.75 | 4-68 | - | |
| Sunday | 15 | 3 | 3 | 4 | 2 * | - | - | - | 1 | - | 617 | 561 | 15 | 37.40 | 2-15 | - | |

# SIDEBOTTOM, R. J.      Yorkshire

**Name:** Ryan Jay Sidebottom
**Role:** Left-hand bat, left-arm
fast-medium bowler
**Born:** 15 January 1978, Huddersfield
**Height:** 6ft 3in **Weight:** 11st 7lbs
**Nickname:** Red Pup, Gigsy, Medusa
**County debut:** No first-team appearance
**Parents:** Arnie and Gillian
**Marital status:** Single
**Family links with cricket:** Father played for
Yorkshire and England
**Education:** Almondbury Primary,
Huddersfield; King James' Grammar School,
Huddersfield
**Qualifications:** 5 GCSEs
**Off-season:** Coaching at the Yorkshire
Cricket School, running and weight training
**Overseas tours:** England U17 to Holland
1995
**Cricketers particularly admired:** Allan Donald, Darren Gough, Craig White
**Other sports followed:** Football (Huddersfield Town FC), rugby league (Leeds)
**Relaxations:** Listening to music, sleeping, watching videos

# SILVERWOOD, C. E. W.     *Yorkshire*

**Name:** Christopher Eric Wilfred Silverwood
**Role:** Right-hand bat, right-arm
fast-medium bowler
**Born:** 5 March 1975, Pontefract
**Height:** 6ft 1in **Weight:** 12st 9lbs
**Nickname:** Spoon, Silvers, Tarby
**County debut:** 1993
**1st-Class 50s:** 1
**1st-Class 5 w. innings:** 1
**1st-Class catches:** 4
**Place in batting averages:** 247th av. 15.14
(1994 265th av. 10.58)
**Place in bowling averages:** 97th av. 35.00
(1994 82nd av. 32.70)
**Strike rate:** 49.05 (career 54.28)
**Parents:** Brenda Millicent
**Marital status:** Engaged to Emma
**Education:** Gibson Lane School, Kippax;
Garforth Comprehensive

**Qualifications:** 8 GCSEs, City and Guilds in Leisure and Recreation
**Off-season:** Playing in South Africa
**Overseas teams played for:** Wellington, Cape Town 1993-94, 1995-96
**Cricketers particularly admired:** Ian Botham, Allan Donald
**Other sports followed:** Rugby league (Castleford), karate
**Injuries:** Stress fracture of back
**Relaxations:** Listening to music, watching videos,'riding my motorbike'
**Extras:** Black belt in karate. Attended the Yorkshire Cricket Academy. Represented
Yorkshire at athletics. Played for England U19 in the home series against India in 1994
**Best batting:** 50 Yorkshire v Lancashire, Old Trafford 1995
**Best bowling:** 5-62 Yorkshire v Surrey, The Oval 1995

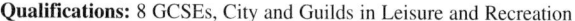

## 1995 Season

|          | M | Inns | NO | Runs | HS | Avge  | 100s | 50s | Ct | St | O     | M  | Runs | Wkts | Avge  | Best | 5wI | 10wM |
|----------|---|------|----|------|----|-------|------|-----|----|----|-------|----|------|------|-------|------|-----|------|
| Test     |   |      |    |      |    |       |      |     |    |    |       |    |      |      |       |      |     |      |
| All First| 7 | 9    | 2  | 106  | 50 | 15.14 | -    | 1   | 1  | -  | 147.1 | 23 | 630  | 18   | 35.00 | 5-62 | 1   |      |
| 1-day Int|   |      |    |      |    |       |      |     |    |    |       |    |      |      |       |      |     |      |
| NatWest  |   |      |    |      |    |       |      |     |    |    |       |    |      |      |       |      |     |      |
| B & H    |   |      |    |      |    |       |      |     |    |    |       |    |      |      |       |      |     |      |
| Sunday   | 6 | 3    | 2  | 14   | 7  | 14.00 | -    | -   | -  | -  | 38    | 7  | 182  | 10   | 18.20 | 3-31 | -   |      |

## Career Performances

| | M | Inns | NO | Runs | HS | Avge | 100s | 50s | Ct | St | Balls | Runs | Wkts | Avge | Best | 5wI | 10wM |
|---|---|---|---|---|---|---|---|---|---|---|---|---|---|---|---|---|---|
| Test | | | | | | | | | | | | | | | | | |
| All First | 17 | 25 | 5 | 233 | 50 | 11.65 | - | 1 | 4 | - | 2497 | 1588 | 46 | 34.52 | 5-62 | 1 | - |
| 1-day Int | | | | | | | | | | | | | | | | | |
| NatWest | 1 | 1 | 1 | 8 | 8 * | - | - | - | - | - | 66 | 38 | 1 | 38.00 | 1-38 | - | |
| B & H | 1 | 1 | 0 | 2 | 2 | 2.00 | - | - | - | - | 42 | 19 | 1 | 19.00 | 1-19 | - | |
| Sunday | 17 | 7 | 4 | 30 | 9 | 10.00 | - | - | 2 | - | 675 | 512 | 26 | 19.69 | 3-29 | - | |

# SIMMONS, P. V.      Leicestershire

**Name:** Philip Verant Simmons
**Role:** Right-hand bat, right-arm medium bowler, county vice-captain
**Born:** 18 April 1963, Port-of-Spain, Trinidad
**County debut:** 1994
**Test debut:** 1988
**Tests:** 22
**One-Day Internationals:** 98
**1st-Class 50s:** 41
**1st-Class 100s:** 15
**1st-Class 200s:** 2
**1st-Class 5w. in innings:** 1
**1st-Class catches:** 141
**One-Day 100s:** 5
**Place in batting averages:**
(1994 117th av. 31.76)
**Place in bowling averages:**
(1994 27th av. 25.63)
**Strike rate:** (career 75.67)
**Off-season:** Playing for West Indies
**Overseas tours:** West Indies YC to England 1982; West Indies B to Zimbabwe 1983 and 1986; West Indies to India and Pakistan (World Cup) 1987-88, to England 1988, to Sharjah and India (Nehru Cup) 1989-90, to Sharjah 1991-92, to Australia and South Africa 1992-93, to Sharjah, India (Hero Cup) and Sri Lanka 1993-94, to India 1994-95, to England 1995, to Australia 1995-95, to India and Pakistan (World Cup) 1995-96
**Overseas teams played for:** Crompton, Trinidad; Trinidad and Tobago 1983-95
**Extras:** Suffered a bad head injury on West Indies tour to England in 1988. Appointed captain of Trinidad in 1989. Scored record 261 on his debut for Leicestershire in 1994
**Best batting:** 261 Leicestershire v Northamptonshire, Leicester 1994
**Best bowling:** 5-24 Trinidad v Windward Islands, Pointe-a-Pierre 1990-91

## 1995 Season

| | M | Inns | NO | Runs | HS | Avge | 100s | 50s | Ct | St | O | M | Runs | Wkts | Avge | Best | 5wI | 10wM |
|---|---|---|---|---|---|---|---|---|---|---|---|---|---|---|---|---|---|---|
| Test | | | | | | | | | | | | | | | | | | |
| All First | 2 | 3 | 1 | 261 | 139 * | 130.50 | 2 | - | - | - | 39 | 9 | 121 | 1 | 121.00 | 1-30 | - | - |
| 1-day Int | | | | | | | | | | | | | | | | | | |
| NatWest | | | | | | | | | | | | | | | | | | |
| B & H | | | | | | | | | | | | | | | | | | |
| Sunday | | | | | | | | | | | | | | | | | | |

## Career Performances

| | M | Inns | NO | Runs | HS | Avge | 100s | 50s | Ct | St | Balls | Runs | Wkts | Avge | Best | 5wI | 10wM |
|---|---|---|---|---|---|---|---|---|---|---|---|---|---|---|---|---|---|
| Test | 22 | 41 | 2 | 919 | 110 | 23.56 | 1 | 3 | 21 | - | 396 | 158 | 2 | 79.00 | 2-34 | - | - |
| All First | 134 | 235 | 9 | 7876 | 261 | 34.84 | 15 | 41 | 141 | - | 6811 | 3178 | 90 | 35.31 | 5-24 | 1 | - |
| 1-day Int | 98 | 96 | 6 | 2810 | 122 | 31.22 | 4 | 17 | 35 | - | 2218 | 1567 | 49 | 31.97 | 4-4 | - | |
| NatWest | 4 | 4 | 0 | 84 | 33 | 21.00 | - | - | 2 | - | 234 | 189 | 5 | 37.80 | 3-31 | - | |
| B & H | 2 | 2 | 0 | 121 | 64 | 60.50 | - | 2 | 1 | - | 90 | 71 | 1 | 71.00 | 1-29 | - | |
| Sunday | 17 | 17 | 0 | 660 | 140 | 38.82 | 1 | 5 | 7 | - | 538 | 444 | 17 | 26.11 | 4-19 | - | |

# SINGH, A.     Warwickshire

**Name:** Anurag Singh
**Role:** Right-hand bat, off-spin bowler
**Born:** 9 September 1975, Kanpur, India
**Height:** 5ft 10in **Weight:** 11st
**Nickname:** Ragga, Muffin, Ragi, Ragstar
**County debut:** 1995
**1st-Class catches:** 1
**Parents:** Vijay and Rajul
**Marital status:** Single
**Education:** King Edward's School, Birmingham; Gonville and Caius College, Cambridge
**Qualifications:** 12 GCSEs, 4 A-levels
**Career outside cricket:** Student
**Off-season:** At university
**Overseas tours:** England U19 to West Indies 1994-95; Warwickshire U21 to South Africa; Warwickshire CCC to South Africa
**Cricketers particularly admired:** Brian Lara, David Gower, Dermot Reeve, Allan Donald, Mohammed Azharuddin
**Other sports followed:** Football (Wimbledon FC)
**Injuries:** Broken finger but missed no cricket

**Extras:** Broke school record for number of runs in a season (1102). *Daily Telegraph* regional award for batting (twice) and bowling (once). Tiger Smith Memorial Award for Warwickshire Most Promising Young Cricketer 1994, Coney Edmonds Trophy for Warwickshire Best U19 Cricketer 1994, Lord's Taverners Trophy for Best Young Cricketer 1994, Gray-Nicolls Len Newberry Award for ESCA U19 Best Player 1994. Scored two centuries for England U19 against India U19 in 1994. Scored one century against West Indies U20 and was Man of the Series 1994-95. Scored 128 for Warwickshire 2nd XI v Gloucestershire 2nd XI in 1994. Awarded Second XI cap in 1995
**Opinions on cricket:** 'More of the money coming into cricket should be distributed amongst the players.'
**Best batting:** 7 Warwickshire v Northamptonshire, Edgbaston 1995

## 1995 Season

|  | M | Inns | NO | Runs | HS | Avge | 100s | 50s | Ct | St | O | M | Runs | Wkts | Avge | Best | 5wI | 10wM |
|---|---|---|---|---|---|---|---|---|---|---|---|---|---|---|---|---|---|---|
| Test |  |  |  |  |  |  |  |  |  |  |  |  |  |  |  |  |  |  |
| All First | 1 | 2 | 0 | 12 | 7 | 6.00 | - | - | 1 | - |  |  |  |  |  |  |  |  |
| 1-day Int |  |  |  |  |  |  |  |  |  |  |  |  |  |  |  |  |  |  |
| NatWest |  |  |  |  |  |  |  |  |  |  |  |  |  |  |  |  |  |  |
| B & H |  |  |  |  |  |  |  |  |  |  |  |  |  |  |  |  |  |  |
| Sunday |  |  |  |  |  |  |  |  |  |  |  |  |  |  |  |  |  |  |

## Career Performances

|  | M | Inns | NO | Runs | HS | Avge | 100s | 50s | Ct | St | Balls | Runs | Wkts | Avge | Best | 5wI | 10wM |
|---|---|---|---|---|---|---|---|---|---|---|---|---|---|---|---|---|---|
| Test |  |  |  |  |  |  |  |  |  |  |  |  |  |  |  |  |  |
| All First | 1 | 2 | 0 | 12 | 7 | 6.00 | - | - | 1 | - |  |  |  |  |  |  |  |
| 1-day Int |  |  |  |  |  |  |  |  |  |  |  |  |  |  |  |  |  |
| NatWest |  |  |  |  |  |  |  |  |  |  |  |  |  |  |  |  |  |
| B & H |  |  |  |  |  |  |  |  |  |  |  |  |  |  |  |  |  |
| Sunday |  |  |  |  |  |  |  |  |  |  |  |  |  |  |  |  |  |

75. Which county cricketer was awarded the OBE in the New Year's Honours List?

# SMALL, G. C.        Warwickshire

**Name:** Gladstone Cleophas Small
**Role:** Right-hand bat, right-arm
fast-medium bowler
**Born:** 18 October 1961, St George, Barbados
**Height:** 5ft 11in **Weight:** 12st
**Nickname:** Gladys, Glad, Stoney
**County debut:** 1980
**County cap:** 1982
**Benefit:** 1992 (£129,500)
**Test debut:** 1986
**Tests:** 17
**One-Day Internationals:** 53
**50 wickets in a season:** 6
**1st-Class 50s:** 7
**1st-Class 5 w. in innings:** 29
**1st-Class 10 w. in match:** 2
**1st-Class catches:** 92
**One-Day 5 w. in innings:** 2
**Place in bowling averages:** 72nd av. 29.82
(1994 32nd av. 26.27)
**Strike rate:** 64.52 (career 58.17)
**Parents:** Chelston and Gladys
**Wife and date of marriage:** Lois, 19 September 1987
**Children:** Zak, Marcus and Zoe
**Family links with cricket:** Cousin Milton Small toured England with West Indies in 1988
**Education:** Moseley School; Hall Green Technical College, Birmingham
**Qualifications:** 2 O-levels, NCA senior coaching badge
**Career outside cricket:** Sports marketing consultant
**Off-season:** Studying Business Studies at Crewe and Alsager faculty
**Overseas tours:** England YC to New Zealand 1979-80; England to Australia 1986-87, to India and Pakistan (World Cup) 1987-88, to India and West Indies 1989-90, to Australia 1990-91, to Australia and New Zealand (World Cup) 1991-92; Warwickshire to Cape Town, to Zimbabwe, to Trinidad
**Overseas teams played for:** Balwyn, Melbourne 1982-83, 1984-85; West Torrens, Adelaide 1985-86; South Australia 1985-86
**Cricketers particularly admired:** Malcolm Marshall, Richard Hadlee, Allan Donald, Brian Lara, Robin Smith
**Other sports followed:** Golf, tennis, football (Aston Villa FC)
**Relaxations:** 'Home with family, tending my vegetable garden, wining and dining with friends'
**Extras:** Was called up for England Test squad v Pakistan at Edgbaston, July 1982, but

did not play. Bowled 18-ball over v Middlesex in August 1982, with 11 no-balls. Grandfather watched him take eight wickets in the Barbados Test v West Indies in 1989-90 on his return to the land of his birth. Was Andy Lloyd's best man

**Opinions on cricket:** 'Counties having to bowl more than over 18 overs per hour is one of the major reasons why we can't produce any bowler able to bowl fast consistently. By the time that they have reached fast bowling maturity they have long become line and length medium pacers. Please install a law to assist the bowlers.'

**Best batting:** 70 Warwickshire v Lancashire, Old Trafford 1988
**Best bowling:** 7-15 Warwickshire v Nottinghamshire, Edgbaston 1988

## 1995 Season

| | M | Inns | NO | Runs | HS | Avge | 100s | 50s | Ct | St | O | M | Runs | Wkts | Avge | Best | 5wI | 10wM |
|---|---|---|---|---|---|---|---|---|---|---|---|---|---|---|---|---|---|---|
| Test | | | | | | | | | | | | | | | | | | |
| All First | 6 | 9 | 4 | 72 | 15 | 14.40 | - | - | - | - | 182.5 | 48 | 507 | 17 | 29.82 | 5-71 | 1 | - |
| 1-day Int | | | | | | | | | | | | | | | | | | |
| NatWest | | | | | | | | | | | | | | | | | | |
| B & H | 4 | 2 | 1 | 3 | 3 | 3.00 | - | - | 1 | - | 39 | 5 | 88 | 2 | 44.00 | 2-24 | - | |
| Sunday | 4 | 3 | 2 | 17 | 9 | 17.00 | - | - | 1 | - | 32 | 4 | 126 | 4 | 31.50 | 3-23 | - | |

## Career Performances

| | M | Inns | NO | Runs | HS | Avge | 100s | 50s | Ct | St | Balls | Runs | Wkts | Avge | Best | 5wI | 10wM |
|---|---|---|---|---|---|---|---|---|---|---|---|---|---|---|---|---|---|
| Test | 17 | 24 | 7 | 263 | 59 | 15.47 | - | 1 | 9 | - | 3927 | 1871 | 55 | 34.01 | 5-48 | 2 | - |
| All First | 305 | 391 | 91 | 4341 | 70 | 14.47 | - | 7 | 92 | - | 48283 | 23698 | 830 | 28.55 | 7-15 | 29 | 2 |
| 1-day Int | 53 | 24 | 9 | 98 | 18 * | 6.53 | - | - | 7 | - | 2793 | 1942 | 58 | 33.48 | 4-31 | - | |
| NatWest | 41 | 26 | 7 | 206 | 33 | 10.84 | - | - | 6 | - | 2479 | 1283 | 44 | 29.15 | 3-22 | - | |
| B & H | 56 | 34 | 9 | 168 | 22 | 6.72 | - | - | 11 | - | 3236 | 1864 | 61 | 30.55 | 4-22 | - | |
| Sunday | 164 | 76 | 26 | 381 | 40 * | 7.62 | - | - | 35 | - | 6963 | 5150 | 204 | 25.24 | 5-29 | 2 | |

76. Who was the oldest player to play in the World Cup
and which country did he play for?

# SMITH, A. M.                                    Gloucestershire

**Name:** Andrew Michael Smith
**Role:** Right-hand bat, left-arm medium bowler
**Born:** 1 October 1967, Dewsbury, West Yorks
**Height:** 5ft 9in **Weight:** 11st 8lbs
**Nickname:** Smudge
**County debut:** 1991
**50 w. in a season:** 1
**1st-Class 50s:** 1
**1st-Class 5 w. in innings:** 1
**1st-Class catches:** 9
**Place in batting averages:** (1994 251st av. 13.50)
**Place in bowling averages:** 14th av. 21.61 (1994 75th av. 31.37)
**Strike rate:** 42.25 (career 56.88)
**Parents:** Hugh and Margaret
**Wife and date of marriage:** Sarah, 2 October 1993
**Children:** William James, 9 October 1994
**Family links with cricket:** Father and uncle both played club cricket in Yorkshire; brother plays for Ossett in the Central Yorkshire League
**Education:** Queen Elizabeth Grammar School, Wakefield; Exeter University
**Qualification:** 10 O-levels, 4 A-levels, BA (Hons) French and German
**Off-season:** England A tour to Pakistan
**Overseas tours:** Queen Elizabeth Grammar School to Holland 1985; Bradford Junior Cricket League to Barbados 1986; Exeter University to Barbados 1987; Gloucestershire to Kenya 1990, to Sri Lanka 1992-93
**Overseas teams played for:** Waimea, New Zealand 1990; WTTU, New Zealand 1991
**Cricketers particularly admired:** Richard Hadlee, Allan Lamb
**Other sports followed:** Football (Leeds United), golf, rugby
**Injuries:** Intercostal strain, out for six weeks
**Relaxations:** Crosswords, reading
**Extras:** Played for English Schools U19, NAYC and represented Combined Universities in the B&H Cup in 1988 and 1990. Persistent side strain forced him to fly home from the England A tour of Pakistan
**Opinions on cricket:** 'Dave Gilbert (ex-Australia and Gloucestershire) once said: "There is no difference in ability between English players and Australian players. The Australian players have the edge because they play less cricket and therefore they are more hungry, fresher and more fired up. They also have more time to practise and iron

out faults." The message is simple – we play too much and standards slip. Too much quantity means less quality. It's not a new idea but the message is not getting through.'

**Best batting:** 51* Gloucestershire v Warwickshire, Bristol 1992
**Best bowling:** 7-70 Gloucestershire v Essex, Cheltenham 1995

## 1995 Season

|         | M  | Inns | NO | Runs | HS  | Avge  | 100s | 50s | Ct | St | O     | M   | Runs | Wkts | Avge   | Best | 5wI | 10wM |
|---------|----|------|----|------|-----|-------|------|-----|----|----|-------|-----|------|------|--------|------|-----|------|
| Test    |    |      |    |      |     |       |      |     |    |    |       |     |      |      |        |      |     |      |
| All First | 11 | 11 | 2  | 37   | 11  | 4.11  | -    | -   | 2  | -  | 415.3 | 104 | 1275 | 59   | 21.61  | 7-70 | 4   | 1    |
| 1-day Int |    |      |    |      |     |       |      |     |    |    |       |     |      |      |        |      |     |      |
| NatWest | 3  | 1    | 1  | 0    | 0 * | -     | -    | -   | -  | -  | 27    | 2   | 110  | 1    | 110.00 | 1-28 | -   |      |
| B & H   | 6  | 2    | 1  | 1    | 1 * | 1.00  | -    | -   | -  | -  | 64.1  | 5   | 233  | 14   | 16.64  | 6-39 | 1   |      |
| Sunday  | 10 | 3    | 3  | 12   | 6 * | -     | -    | -   | -  | -  | 74.4  | 7   | 347  | 9    | 38.55  | 2-23 | -   |      |

## Career Performances

|         | M  | Inns | NO | Runs | HS   | Avge  | 100s | 50s | Ct | St | Balls | Runs | Wkts | Avge  | Best | 5wI | 10wM |
|---------|----|------|----|------|------|-------|------|-----|----|----|-------|------|------|-------|------|-----|------|
| Test    |    |      |    |      |      |       |      |     |    |    |       |      |      |       |      |     |      |
| All First | 56 | 63 | 12 | 515  | 51 * | 10.09 | -    | 1   | 9  | -  | 8874  | 4769 | 156  | 30.57 | 7-70 | 5   | 1    |
| 1-day Int |    |      |    |      |      |       |      |     |    |    |       |      |      |       |      |     |      |
| NatWest | 11 | 4    | 3  | 15   | 8 *  | 15.00 | -    | -   | 3  | -  | 607   | 379  | 9    | 42.11 | 3-45 | -   |      |
| B & H   | 22 | 16   | 8  | 69   | 15 * | 8.62  | -    | -   | 4  | -  | 1255  | 854  | 27   | 31.62 | 6-39 | 1   |      |
| Sunday  | 66 | 32   | 20 | 136  | 15 * | 11.33 | -    | -   | 10 | -  | 2535  | 2082 | 67   | 31.07 | 4-38 | -   |      |

77. Who finished 1995 on top of the Coopers and Lybrand Ratings for batting and bowling respectively?

# SMITH, A. W. Surrey

**Name:** Andrew William Smith
**Role:** Right-hand bat, right-arm off-spin bowler
**Born:** 30 May 1969, Sutton, Surrey
**Height:** 5ft 10in **Weight:** 11st
**Nickname:** Smithy, Smudge, Furball
**County debut:** 1992 (one-day), 1993 (first-class)
**1st-Class 50s:** 6
**1st-Class 100s:** 1
**1st-Class 200s:** 1
**1st-Class 5 w. in innings:** 1
**1st-Class catches:** 12
**Place in batting averages:** 197th av. 20.92 (1994 108th av. 32.75)
**Place in bowling averages:** 151st av. 64.70 (1994 139th av. 47.85)
**Strike rate:** 99.30 (career 88.25)

**Parents:** Ben and Gwen
**Marital status:** Single
**Family links with cricket:** Father played for Surrey 1960-69
**Education:** Cheam Boys Church of England School; Sutton Manor High School
**Qualifications:** 7 O-levels, senior NCA coach
**Career outside cricket:** Painter and decorator
**Off-season:** 'Working (hopefully) and gaining experience in a career outside cricket'
**Overseas teams played for:** Richmond, Adelaide 1989-91; North Perth CC, Australia 1995
**Cricketers particularly admired:** Tim May, John Emburey, Michael Slater
**Other sports followed:** Football (West Ham United), baseball (Toronto Blue Jays), American football (Washington Redskins)
**Injuries:** Tendon injury to right index finger, missed five games
**Relaxations:** 'All sports, riding my new bicycle, sleeping and tasting red wine'
**Extras:** In 1992 took catch with first touch on first-team debut in Seeboard Trophy 1992 and was named 2nd XI Bowler of the Year. In 1993 received Man of the Match award in his first NatWest game against Leicestershire and was Surrey Fielder of the Year. 'Richard Blakey almost cleared The Oval pavilion (top tier) off my bowling in the Sunday League game in August'
**Opinions on cricket:** 'Play far too much so no time to spend in the nets and work on skills.'
**Best batting:** 202* Surrey v Oxford University, The Oval 1994
**Best bowling:** 5-103 Surrey v Somerset, Bath 1994

| | M | Inns | NO | Runs | HS | Avge | 100s | 50s | Ct | St | O | M | Runs | Wkts | Avge | Best | 5wl | 10wM |
|---|---|---|---|---|---|---|---|---|---|---|---|---|---|---|---|---|---|---|
| Test | | | | | | | | | | | | | | | | | | |
| All First | 9 | 13 | 0 | 272 | 88 | 20.92 | - | 2 | 2 | - | 165.3 | 27 | 647 | 10 | 64.70 | 3-112 | - | - |
| 1-day Int | | | | | | | | | | | | | | | | | | |
| NatWest | | | | | | | | | | | | | | | | | | |
| B & H | | | | | | | | | | | | | | | | | | |
| Sunday | 9 | 7 | 1 | 129 | 42 | 21.50 | - | - | 3 | - | 48 | 1 | 282 | 7 | 40.28 | 3-36 | - | |

**Career Performances**

| | M | Inns | NO | Runs | HS | Avge | 100s | 50s | Ct | St | Balls | Runs | Wkts | Avge | Best | 5wl | 10wM |
|---|---|---|---|---|---|---|---|---|---|---|---|---|---|---|---|---|---|
| Test | | | | | | | | | | | | | | | | | |
| All First | 37 | 57 | 7 | 1356 | 202 * | 27.12 | 1 | 6 | 12 | - | 3795 | 2374 | 43 | 55.20 | 5-103 | 1 | - |
| 1-day Int | | | | | | | | | | | | | | | | | |
| NatWest | 2 | 0 | 0 | 0 | 0 | - | - | - | - | - | 120 | 56 | 3 | 18.66 | 3-25 | - | |
| B & H | 2 | 1 | 1 | 15 | 15 * | - | - | - | 1 | - | 84 | 61 | 3 | 20.33 | 2-38 | - | |
| Sunday | 31 | 24 | 6 | 496 | 58 | 27.55 | - | 2 | 15 | - | 438 | 457 | 9 | 50.77 | 3-36 | - | |

# SMITH, B. F.　　　　　　Leicestershire

**Name:** Benjamin Francis Smith
**Role:** Right-hand bat, right-arm medium bowler
**Born:** 3 April 1972, Corby
**Height:** 5ft 8in **Weight:** 10st 7lbs
**Nickname:** Smudge, Ferret, Sabba
**County debut:** 1990
**County cap:** 1995
**1st-Class 50s:** 17
**1st-Class 100s:** 2
**1st-Class catches:** 33
**One-day 100s:** 1
**Place in batting averages:** 121st av. 30.84 (1994 118th av. 31.40)
**Parents:** Janet and Keith
**Marital status:** Single
**Family links with cricket:** Both uncles played for English Schools and Leicestershire Young Amateurs. Father and grandfather played local league cricket
**Education:** Tugby Primary; Kibworth High; Robert Smyth, Market Harborough
**Qualifications:** 5 O-levels, ESB distinction

**Off-season:** Playing in Australia
**Overseas tours:** England YC to New Zealand 1990-91; Rutland Tourists to South Africa 1992
**Overseas teams played for:** Alexandria, Zimbabwe 1990; Bankstown Canterbury, Sydney 1993-96
**Cricketers particularly admired:** David Gower
**Other sports followed:** Football (Leicester City)
**Relaxations:** Eating out, going to cinema, playing golf, listening to good music
**Extras:** Played tennis for Leicestershire aged 12. Young Cricketer of the Year 1991
**Best batting:** 112 Leicestershire v Northamptonshire, Northampton 1995
**Best bowling:** 1-5 Leicestershire v Essex, Ilford 1991

## 1995 Season

|          | M  | Inns | NO | Runs | HS  | Avge  | 100s | 50s | Ct | St | O    | M | Runs | Wkts | Avge  | Best | 5wI | 10wM |
|----------|----|------|----|------|-----|-------|------|-----|----|----|------|---|------|------|-------|------|-----|------|
| Test     |    |      |    |      |     |       |      |     |    |    |      |   |      |      |       |      |     |      |
| All First| 18 | 31   | 5  | 802  | 112 | 30.84 | 1    | 6   | 8  | -  | 11.3 | 2 | 69   | 1    | 69.00 | 1-69 | -   | -    |
| 1-day Int|    |      |    |      |     |       |      |     |    |    |      |   |      |      |       |      |     |      |
| NatWest  | 1  | 1    | 0  | 27   | 27  | 27.00 | -    | -   | -  | -  |      |   |      |      |       |      |     |      |
| B & H    | 5  | 5    | 0  | 77   | 27  | 15.40 | -    | -   | 2  | -  |      |   |      |      |       |      |     |      |
| Sunday   | 14 | 13   | 2  | 479  | 115 | 43.54 | 1    | 1   | 5  | -  |      |   |      |      |       |      |     |      |

## Career Performances

|          | M  | Inns | NO | Runs | HS  |   | Avge  | 100s | 50s | Ct | St | Balls | Runs | Wkts | Avge  | Best | 5wI | 10wM |
|----------|----|------|----|------|-----|---|-------|------|-----|----|----|-------|------|------|-------|------|-----|------|
| Test     |    |      |    |      |     |   |       |      |     |    |    |       |      |      |       |      |     |      |
| All First| 75 | 117  | 17 | 2827 | 112 |   | 28.27 | 2    | 17  | 33 | -  | 225   | 190  | 2    | 95.00 | 1-5  | -   | -    |
| 1-day Int|    |      |    |      |     |   |       |      |     |    |    |       |      |      |       |      |     |      |
| NatWest  | 7  | 6    | 1  | 161  | 63  | *| 32.20 | -    | 1   | 2  | -  |       |      |      |       |      |     |      |
| B & H    | 12 | 10   | 0  | 185  | 43  |   | 18.50 | -    | -   | 5  | -  |       |      |      |       |      |     |      |
| Sunday   | 69 | 67   | 9  | 1602 | 115 |   | 27.62 | 1    | 5   | 14 | -  | 18    | 15   | 0    | -     | -    | -   | -    |

# SMITH, N. M. K.                              Warwickshire

**Name:** Neil Michael Knight Smith
**Role:** Right-hand bat, off-spin bowler
**Born:** 27 July 1967, Solihull
**Height:** 6ft **Weight:** 13st 7lbs
**Nickname:** Gurt
**County debut:** 1987
**County cap:** 1993
**1st-Class 50s:** 12
**1st-Class 100s:** 1
**1st-Class 5 w. in innings:** 12

**1st-Class catches:** 26
**One-Day 5 w. in innings:** 3
**Place in batting averages:** 158th av. 25.58
(1994 158th av. 25.58)
**Place in bowling averages:** 98th av. 35.25
(1994 93rd av. 34.55)
**Strike rate:** 70.76 (career 75.89)
**Parents:** Mike (M.J.K.) and Diana
**Wife and date of marriage:**
Rachel, 4 December 1993
**Family links with cricket:** Father captained
Warwickshire and England
**Education:** Warwick School
**Qualifications:** 3 O-levels (Maths, English,
French), cricket coach Grade 1
**Career outside cricket:** Sports teacher
**Off-season:** Training
**Overseas tours:** England to South Africa 1995-
96, to India and Pakistan (World Cup) 1995-96
**Overseas teams played for:** Phoenix, Perth, Western Australia 1988-89
**Cricketers particularly admired:** David Gower, Ian Botham, Allan Donald
**Other sports followed:** Golf, rugby and football
**Relaxations:** Sport, family and music
**Extras:** Played for England in the one-day series against South Africa and was then
selected for the squad to play in the World Cup in India and Pakistan
**Opinions on cricket:** 'Visiting teams should be given the option of batting or bowling
to try to stop doctoring of pitches by the home side.'
**Best batting:** 161 Warwickshire v Yorkshire, Headingley 1989
**Best bowling:** 7-42 Warwickshire v Lancashire, Edgbaston 1994

### 1995 Season

|         | M  | Inns | NO | Runs | HS  | Avge  | 100s | 50s | Ct | St | O   | M   | Runs | Wkts | Avge  | Best | 5wI | 10wM |
|---------|----|------|----|------|-----|-------|------|-----|----|----|-----|-----|------|------|-------|------|-----|------|
| Test    |    |      |    |      |     |       |      |     |    |    |     |     |      |      |       |      |     |      |
| All First | 18 | 23 | 2  | 486  | 75  | 23.14 | -    | 4   | 6  | -  | 460 | 105 | 1375 | 39   | 35.25 | 6-72 | 3   | -    |
| 1-day Int |    |      |    |      |     |       |      |     |    |    |     |     |      |      |       |      |     |      |
| NatWest | 5  | 5    | 1  | 105  | 65  | 26.25 | -    | 1   | 1  | -  | 46  | 4   | 150  | 8    | 18.75 | 3-36 | -   |      |
| B & H   | 5  | 3    | 1  | 13   | 10* | 6.50  | -    | -   | 1  | -  | 35  | 1   | 179  | 4    | 44.75 | 2-77 | -   |      |
| Sunday  | 17 | 16   | 0  | 504  | 71  | 31.50 | -    | 5   | 7  | -  | 78  | 3   | 386  | 18   | 21.44 | 6-33 |     |      |

78. Which year saw the introduction of coloured clothing
for Sunday League games?

## Career Performances

| | M | Inns | NO | Runs | HS | Avge | 100s | 50s | Ct | St | Balls | Runs | Wkts | Avge | Best | 5wI | 10wM |
|---|---|---|---|---|---|---|---|---|---|---|---|---|---|---|---|---|---|
| Test | | | | | | | | | | | | | | | | | |
| All First | 96 | 133 | 18 | 2816 | 161 | 24.48 | 1 | 12 | 26 | - | 15103 | 7617 | 199 | 38.27 | 7-42 | 12 | - |
| 1-day Int | | | | | | | | | | | | | | | | | |
| NatWest | 25 | 21 | 6 | 350 | 65 | 23.33 | - | 2 | 9 | - | 1138 | 666 | 32 | 20.81 | 5-17 | 1 | |
| B & H | 17 | 12 | 2 | 140 | 32 | 14.00 | - | - | 4 | - | 703 | 515 | 18 | 28.61 | 3-29 | - | |
| Sunday | 107 | 81 | 16 | 1363 | 71 | 20.96 | - | 7 | 38 | - | 3684 | 2853 | 113 | 25.24 | 6-33 | 2 | |

# SMITH, P. A. Warwickshire

**Name:** Paul Andrew Smith
**Role:** Right-hand bat, right-arm
fast-medium bowler
**Born:** 15 April 1964, Newcastle-on-Tyne
**Height:** 6ft 2in **Weight:** 12st 7lbs
**Nickname:** Smithy, Jim
**County debut:** 1982
**County cap:** 1986
**Benefit:** 1995
**1000 runs in a season:** 2
**1st-Class 50s:** 48
**1st-Class 100s:** 4
**1st-Class 5 w. in innings:** 7
**1st-Class catches:** 59
**One-Day 5 w. in innings:** 3
**Place in batting averages:**
(1994 153rd av. 25.92)
**Place in bowling averages:**
(1994 84th av. 33.00)
**Strike rate:** (career 56.06)
**Parents:** Ken and Joy
**Wife and date of marriage:** Caroline, 31 July 1987
**Children:** Oliver James, 5 February 1988; Michael Paul, 1993
**Family links with cricket:** Father played for Leicestershire. Both brothers played for
Warwickshire
**Education:** Heaton Grammar School, Newcastle
**Qualifications:** 5 O-levels, car restoration qualifications
**Overseas tours:** Warwickshire to La Manga 1989, to Trinidad and Tobago 1991, to
Cape Town 1992-93, to Zimbabwe 1993-94
**Overseas teams played for:** Florida, Johannesburg 1982-83; Belgrano, Buenos Aires
1983-84; Carlton, Melbourne 1984-85; St Augustine's, Cape Town 1992-93

**Cricketers particularly admired:** Ian Botham

**Other sports followed:** None

**Relaxations:** Classic cars, American cars, music, reading, family, working out in the gym at Edgbaston

**Extras:** Along with Andy Moles set a new world record for most consecutive opening partnerships of over 50. In 1989 scored 140 v Worcestershire, during which scored 100 out of partnership of 123 with Dermot Reeve. Took a hat-trick against Northamptonshire in 1989 and in 1990 took another against Sussex, bowling in Tim Munton's boots – two sizes too big. Warwickshire's most successful Sunday League all-rounder and has been in the winning team in two NatWest finals.

**Opinions on cricket:** 'Four-day cricket is better than three-day, but wickets around the country must improve. Coloured clothing has been good value. Umpires should decide Man of the Match awards.'

**Best batting:** 140 Warwickshire v Worcestershire, Worcester 1989

**Best bowling:** 6-91 Warwickshire v Derbyshire, Edgbaston 1992

## 1995 Season

|  | M | Inns | NO | Runs | HS | Avge | 100s | 50s | Ct | St | O | M | Runs | Wkts | Avge | Best | 5wl | 10wM |
|---|---|---|---|---|---|---|---|---|---|---|---|---|---|---|---|---|---|---|
| Test |  |  |  |  |  |  |  |  |  |  |  |  |  |  |  |  |  |  |
| All First | 3 | 5 | 0 | 124 | 57 | 24.80 | - | 1 | 1 | - | 43 | 10 | 136 | 4 | 34.00 | 2-22 | - | - |
| 1-day Int |  |  |  |  |  |  |  |  |  |  |  |  |  |  |  |  |  |  |
| NatWest | 3 | 3 | 2 | 15 | 7 | 15.00 | - | - | - | - | 21 | 1 | 114 | 2 | 57.00 | 2-47 | - |  |
| B & H | 2 | 0 | 0 | 0 | 0 | - | - | - | - | - | 11 | 1 | 49 | 2 | 24.50 | 2-49 | - |  |
| Sunday | 15 | 12 | 1 | 211 | 85 | 19.18 | - | 1 | 2 | - | 60 | 3 | 295 | 20 | 14.75 | 4-39 | - |  |

## Career Performances

|  | M | Inns | NO | Runs | HS | Avge | 100s | 50s | Ct | St | Balls | Runs | Wkts | Avge | Best | 5wl | 10wM |
|---|---|---|---|---|---|---|---|---|---|---|---|---|---|---|---|---|---|
| Test |  |  |  |  |  |  |  |  |  |  |  |  |  |  |  |  |  |
| All First | 219 | 349 | 42 | 8150 | 140 | 26.54 | 4 | 48 | 59 | - | 15755 | 10021 | 281 | 35.66 | 6-91 | 7 | - |
| 1-day Int |  |  |  |  |  |  |  |  |  |  |  |  |  |  |  |  |  |
| NatWest | 34 | 32 | 5 | 641 | 79 | 23.74 | - | 5 | 3 | - | 1429 | 1028 | 33 | 31.15 | 4-37 | - |  |
| B & H | 43 | 39 | 5 | 658 | 74 | 19.35 | - | 1 | 6 | - | 1322 | 952 | 33 | 28.84 | 3-28 | - |  |
| Sunday | 173 | 146 | 26 | 2862 | 93 * | 23.85 | - | 9 | 32 | - | 4870 | 4284 | 157 | 27.28 | 5-36 | 3 |  |

# SMITH, R. A.          Hampshire

**Name:** Robin Arnold Smith
**Role:** Right-hand bat, slip fielder
**Born:** 13 September 1963, Durban, South Africa
**Height:** 6ft **Weight:** 15st
**Nickname:** The Judge
**County debut:** 1982
**County cap:** 1985
**Test debut:** 1988
**Tests:** 57
**One-Day Internationals:** 64
**1000 runs in a season:** 9
**1st-Class 50s:** 93
**1st-Class 100s:** 48
**1st-Class 200s:** 1
**1st-Class catches:** 177
**One-Day 100s:** 20
**Place in batting averages:** 20th av. 53.19 (1994 41st av. 43.55)

**Parents:** John and Joy
**Wife and date of marriage:** Katherine, 21 September 1988
**Children:** Harrison Arnold, 4 December 1991; Margaux Elizabeth, 28 July 1994
**Family links with cricket:** Grandfather played for Natal in Currie Cup. Brother Chris played for Natal, Hampshire and England
**Education:** Northlands Boys High, Durban
**Qualifications:** Matriculation, '36 England caps'
**Career outside cricket:** Director of Masuri Helmets and Judge Tours
**Off-season:** England tour to South Africa
**Overseas tours:** England to India and West Indies 1989-90, to Australia 1990-91, to Australia and New Zealand (World Cup) 1991-92, to India and Sri Lanka 1992-93, to West Indies 1993-94, to South Africa 1995-96, to India and Pakistan (World Cup) 1995-96
**Overseas teams played for:** Natal, South Africa 1980-84; Perth, Western Australia 1984-85 (grade cricket)
**Cricketers particularly admired:** Malcolm Marshall, Brian Lara, Graeme Hick, Graham Gooch, Allan Lamb
**Other sports followed:** Soccer, athletics, rugby, golf, racing
**Relaxations:** 'Reading (Leslie Thomas in particular), trout fishing, assembling a good wine cellar, keeping fit and spending as much time as possible with my lovely wife Katherine and my children'
**Extras:** Played rugby for Natal Schools and for Romsey RFC as a full-back. Held 19

school athletics records and two South African schools records in shot put and 100-metre hurdles. One of *Wisden*'s Five Cricketers of the Year 1990. First child was born while he was on tour in Australia. Awarded benefit for 1996

**Opinions on cricket:** 'I enjoy playing cricket for Hampshire and particularly enjoy the camaraderie of the county circuit.'

**Best batting:** 209* Hampshire v Essex, Southampton 1987

**Best bowling:** 2-11 Hampshire v Surrey, Southampton 1985

## 1995 Season

|  | M | Inns | NO | Runs | HS | Avge | 100s | 50s | Ct | St | O | M | Runs | Wkts | Avge | Best | 5wI | 10wM |
|---|---|---|---|---|---|---|---|---|---|---|---|---|---|---|---|---|---|---|
| Test | 4 | 8 | 1 | 305 | 90 | 43.57 | - | 2 | - | - | | | | | | | | |
| All First | 12 | 23 | 2 | 1117 | 172 | 53.19 | 3 | 4 | 3 | - | | | | | | | | |
| 1-day Int | | | | | | | | | | | | | | | | | | |
| NatWest | 1 | 1 | 0 | 45 | 45 | 45.00 | - | - | - | - | | | | | | | | |
| B & H | 5 | 4 | 0 | 129 | 83 | 32.25 | - | 1 | 1 | - | | | | | | | | |
| Sunday | 8 | 8 | 0 | 211 | 115 | 26.37 | 1 | 1 | 2 | - | | | | | | | | |

## Career Performances

|  | M | Inns | NO | Runs | HS | Avge | 100s | 50s | Ct | St | Balls | Runs | Wkts | Avge | Best | 5wI | 10wM |
|---|---|---|---|---|---|---|---|---|---|---|---|---|---|---|---|---|---|
| Test | 57 | 105 | 15 | 3982 | 175 | 44.24 | 9 | 26 | 35 | - | 24 | 6 | 0 | - | - | - | - |
| All First | 291 | 498 | 75 | 18930 | 209 * | 44.75 | 48 | 93 | 177 | - | 924 | 693 | 12 | 57.75 | 2-11 | - | - |
| 1-day Int | 64 | 63 | 8 | 2218 | 167 * | 40.32 | 4 | 13 | 23 | - | | | | | | | |
| NatWest | 30 | 30 | 10 | 1521 | 125 * | 76.05 | 4 | 8 | 19 | - | 17 | 13 | 2 | 6.50 | 2-13 | - | |
| B & H | 43 | 40 | 8 | 1774 | 155 * | 55.43 | 4 | 8 | 19 | - | 6 | 2 | 0 | - | - | - | |
| Sunday | 126 | 120 | 14 | 4451 | 131 | 41.99 | 8 | 30 | 57 | - | 2 | 0 | 1 | 0.00 | 1-0 | - | |

79. Two sets of brothers played Test cricket in 1995. Who were they?

# SNAPE, J. N.        Northamptonshire

**Name:** Jeremy Nicholas Snape
**Role:** Right-hand bat, off-spin bowler
**Born:** 27 April 1973, Stoke-on-Trent, Staffordshire
**Height:** 5ft 8in **Weight:** 12st
**Nickname:** Snapey, Coot, Jez
**County debut:** 1992
**1st-Class 50s:** 3
**1st-Class 5 w. innings:** 1
**1st-Class catches:** 22
**Place in batting averages:** 148th av. 27.76
**Place in bowling averages:** 116th av. 39.31
**Strike rate:** 72.94 (career 77.70)
**Parents:** Keith and Barbara
**Marital status:** Single
**Family links with cricket:** Brother Jonathan plays local club cricket in North Staffs and South Cheshire League for Kidsgrove, 'Dad only umpired once as he was the only person to appeal for a caught behind – off my bowling in the U13'
**Education:** Denstone College; Durham University
**Qualifications:** 8 GCSEs, 3 A-levels, studying for BSc (Hons) Natural Science
**Career outside cricket:** 'Open to suggestions'
**Off-season:** Playing club cricket in Cape Town, South Africa
**Overseas tours:** England U18 to Canada 1991 (captain); England U19 to Pakistan 1991-92; Durham University to South Africa 1993; Northamptonshire to Cape Town 1993; Christians in Sport to Zimbabwe 1994-95; Durham Univerity to Vienna (Indoor European Championships) 1994
**Overseas teams played for:** Petone, Wellington, New Zealand 1994-95
**Cricketers particularly admired:** Allan Lamb, Carl Hooper, Anil Kumble
**Other sports followed:** Golf, rugby union, shove ha'penny, white-water rafting, Bangalore kabadi team, yarding
**Relaxations:** Good food and drink, listening to music, travelling
**Extras:** Sir Jack Hobbs award (U15 Schoolboy 1988), Gold Award winner for Combined Universities v Worcestershire 1992 (3-34) at The Parks. Player of the Tournament at European Indoor 6-a-side Championships
**Opinions on cricket:** 'Definitely in favour of four-day cricket as it induces a more disciplined approach, although I equally enjoy the challenges of one-day cricket. Counties should work harder to maximise the potential of their individual players while encouraging the teamwork essential to competition.'
**Best batting:** 87 Northamptonshire v Mashonaland Select XI, Harare 1994-95
**Best bowling:** 5-65 Northamptonshire v Durham, Northampton 1995

## 1995 Season

| | M | Inns | NO | Runs | HS | Avge | 100s | 50s | Ct | St | O | M | Runs | Wkts | Avge | Best | 5wI | 10wM |
|---|---|---|---|---|---|---|---|---|---|---|---|---|---|---|---|---|---|---|
| Test | | | | | | | | | | | | | | | | | | |
| All First | 13 | 16 | 3 | 361 | 55 | 27.76 | - | 2 | 16 | - | 231 | 53 | 747 | 19 | 39.31 | 5-65 | 1 | - |
| 1-day Int | | | | | | | | | | | | | | | | | | |
| NatWest | 4 | 3 | 1 | 35 | 21 | 17.50 | - | - | 2 | - | 24.1 | 0 | 117 | 4 | 29.25 | 2-44 | - | |
| B & H | 2 | 2 | 1 | 24 | 23 | 24.00 | - | - | - | - | 17 | 3 | 51 | 3 | 17.00 | 2-28 | - | |
| Sunday | 16 | 10 | 6 | 76 | 17 * | 19.00 | - | - | 4 | - | 76 | 2 | 381 | 10 | 38.10 | 2-25 | - | |

## Career Performances

| | M | Inns | NO | Runs | HS | Avge | 100s | 50s | Ct | St | Balls | Runs | Wkts | Avge | Best | 5wI | 10wM |
|---|---|---|---|---|---|---|---|---|---|---|---|---|---|---|---|---|---|
| Test | | | | | | | | | | | | | | | | | |
| All First | 18 | 24 | 5 | 556 | 87 | 29.26 | - | 3 | 22 | - | 2098 | 1194 | 27 | 44.22 | 5-65 | 1 | - |
| 1-day Int | | | | | | | | | | | | | | | | | |
| NatWest | 5 | 4 | 2 | 40 | 21 | 20.00 | - | - | 2 | - | 145 | 117 | 4 | 29.25 | 2-44 | - | |
| B & H | 8 | 8 | 3 | 165 | 52 | 33.00 | - | 1 | 3 | - | 492 | 320 | 10 | 32.00 | 3-35 | - | |
| Sunday | 24 | 15 | 8 | 141 | 31 * | 20.14 | - | - | 6 | - | 726 | 599 | 21 | 28.52 | 3-25 | - | |

# SOLANKI, V. S.        Worcestershire

**Name:** Vikram Singh Solanki
**Role:** Right-hand bat, off-spin bowler
**Born:** 1 April 1976, Udaipur, India
**Height:** 6ft **Weight:** 11st 7lbs
**County debut:** 1993 (one-day),
1995 (first-class)
**1st-Class catches:** 8
**Place in batting averages:** 218th av. 18.75
**Parents:** Vijay and Florabell
**Marital status:** Single
**Family links with cricket:** Father played in India
**Education:** Regis School, Wolverhampton
**Qualifications:** 9 GCSEs, 3 A-levels
**Off-season:** Playing for a club in Cape Town, South Africa
**Overseas tours:** England U18 to South Africa 1992-93, to Denmark 1993; England U19 to West Indies 1994-95
**Cricketers particularly admired:** Sachin Tendulkar, Graeme Hick, Anthony McGrath and 'anyone who has made the grade at Test level'
**Other sports followed:** 'Enjoy playing most sports'

**Relaxations:** 'Spending time with friends and family'
**Opinions on cricket:** 'Four-day cricket seems to be working. However, there may be an argument for a two-league system as this would improve the standard of the game in general and also provide players with more time to practise.'
**Best batting:** 36 Worcestershire v Northamptonshire, Northampton 1995
**Best bowling:** 1-10 Worcestershire v Northamptonshire, Northampton 1995

### 1995 Season

|  | M | Inns | NO | Runs | HS | Avge | 100s | 50s | Ct | St | O | M | Runs | Wkts | Avge | Best | 5wI | 10wM |
|---|---|---|---|---|---|---|---|---|---|---|---|---|---|---|---|---|---|---|
| Test |  |  |  |  |  |  |  |  |  |  |  |  |  |  |  |  |  |  |
| All First | 6 | 9 | 1 | 150 | 36 | 18.75 | - | - | 8 | - | 88 | 15 | 359 | 3 | 119.66 | 1-10 | - | - |
| 1-day Int |  |  |  |  |  |  |  |  |  |  |  |  |  |  |  |  |  |  |
| NatWest | 2 | 1 | 0 | 29 | 29 | 29.00 | - | - | - | - | 20 | 0 | 91 | 1 | 91.00 | 1-48 | - |  |
| B & H |  |  |  |  |  |  |  |  |  |  |  |  |  |  |  |  |  |  |
| Sunday | 9 | 6 | 2 | 33 | 12 | 8.25 | - | - | 2 | - | 3 | 0 | 32 | 0 | - |  | - | - |

### Career Performances

|  | M | Inns | NO | Runs | HS | Avge | 100s | 50s | Ct | St | Balls | Runs | Wkts | Avge | Best | 5wI | 10wM |
|---|---|---|---|---|---|---|---|---|---|---|---|---|---|---|---|---|---|
| Test |  |  |  |  |  |  |  |  |  |  |  |  |  |  |  |  |  |
| All First | 6 | 9 | 1 | 150 | 36 | 18.75 | - | - | 8 | - | 528 | 359 | 3 | 119.66 | 1-10 | - | - |
| 1-day Int |  |  |  |  |  |  |  |  |  |  |  |  |  |  |  |  |  |
| NatWest | 2 | 1 | 0 | 29 | 29 | 29.00 | - | - | - | - | 120 | 91 | 1 | 91.00 | 1-48 | - |  |
| B & H |  |  |  |  |  |  |  |  |  |  |  |  |  |  |  |  |  |
| Sunday | 10 | 7 | 2 | 55 | 22 | 11.00 | - | - | 2 | - | 18 | 32 | 0 | - |  | - | - |

# SPEAK, N. J. Lancashire

**Name:** Nicholas Jason Speak
**Role:** Right-hand opening bat, off-spin bowler
**Born:** 21 October 1966, Manchester
**Height:** 6ft **Weight:** 12st 7lbs
**Nickname:** Judge, Pod
**County debut:** 1986-87 in Jamaica
**County cap:** 1992
**1000 runs in a season:** 3
**1st-Class 50s:** 40
**1st-Class 100s:** 11
**1st-Class 200s:** 1
**1st-Class catches:** 73
**One-Day 100s:** 1
**Place in batting averages:** 109th av. 32.82 (1994 30th av. 46.57)
**Parents:** John and Irene

**Wife and date of marriage:** Michelle, 11 March 1993

**Family links with cricket:** Father and uncle were league professionals in Lancashire and Yorkshire

**Education:** Parrs Wood High School and Sixth Form College, Didsbury, Manchester

**Qualifications:** 5 O-levels, NCA coaching certificate

**Career outside cricket:** Yarra Leisure, coaching in Melbourne

**Off-season:** Playing for Hawthorne in Melbourne

**Overseas tours:** Lancashire to Jamaica 1986-87, to Zimbabwe 1989, to Perth 1990-91, to Johannesburg 1992

**Overseas teams played for:** South Canberra 1988-89; North Canberra 1991-93; Hawthorn, Melbourne 1994-96

**Cricketers particularly admired:** Mark Waugh, Shane Warne

**Other sports followed:** Most sports – Manchester City FC

**Relaxations:** Chardonnay, cold lager, Indian food, and 'constructive arguments with G.D. Lloyd', spending time at home with our new addition

**Extras:** Scored century for Australian Capital Territories v England A at Canberra 1992-93

**Opinions on cricket:** 'Tea should be ten minutes longer.'

**Best batting:** 232 Lancashire v Leicestershire, Leicester 1992

**Best bowling:** 1-0 Lancashire v Warwickshire, Old Trafford 1991

---

### 1995 Season

|  | M | Inns | NO | Runs | HS | Avge | 100s | 50s | Ct | St | O | M | Runs | Wkts | Avge | Best | 5wI | 10wM |
|---|---|---|---|---|---|---|---|---|---|---|---|---|---|---|---|---|---|---|
| Test |  |  |  |  |  |  |  |  |  |  |  |  |  |  |  |  |  |  |
| All First | 17 | 30 | 2 | 919 | 116 | 32.82 | 1 | 7 | 11 | - | 4 | 0 | 26 | 0 | - | - | - | - |
| 1-day Int |  |  |  |  |  |  |  |  |  |  |  |  |  |  |  |  |  |  |
| NatWest | 1 | 1 | 0 | 20 | 20 | 20.00 | - | - | - | - |  |  |  |  |  |  |  |  |
| B & H |  |  |  |  |  |  |  |  |  |  |  |  |  |  |  |  |  |  |  |
| Sunday | 9 | 8 | 0 | 159 | 36 | 19.87 | - | - | 1 | - |  |  |  |  |  |  |  |  |

---

80. Who is the highest run-scorer in the history of Sheffield Shield cricket?

**Career Performances**

| | M | Inns | NO | Runs | HS | Avge | 100s | 50s | Ct | St | Balls | Runs | Wkts | Avge | Best | 5wI | 10wM |
|---|---|---|---|---|---|---|---|---|---|---|---|---|---|---|---|---|---|
| Test | | | | | | | | | | | | | | | | | |
| All First | 110 | 191 | 17 | 6788 | 232 | 39.01 | 11 | 40 | 73 | - | 97 | 130 | 2 | 65.00 | 1-0 | - | - |
| 1-day Int | | | | | | | | | | | | | | | | | |
| NatWest | 6 | 6 | 0 | 136 | 60 | 22.66 | - | 1 | 2 | - | | | | | | | |
| B & H | 12 | 11 | 1 | 279 | 82 | 27.90 | - | 2 | - | - | | | | | | | |
| Sunday | 60 | 55 | 6 | 1325 | 102 * | 27.04 | 1 | 6 | 10 | - | | | | | | | |

# SPEIGHT, M. P. Sussex

**Name:** Martin Peter Speight
**Role:** Right-hand bat, reserve wicket-keeper
**Born:** 24 October 1967, Walsall
**Height:** 5ft 10in **Weight:** 12st
**Nickname:** Sprog, Hoover, Ginger
**County debut:** 1986
**County cap:** 1991
**1000 runs in a season:** 2
**1st-Class 50s:** 32
**1st-Class 100s:** 12
**1st-Class catches:** 91
**One-Day 100s:** 2
**Place in batting averages:**
(1994 98th av. 34.17)
**Parents:** Peter John and Valerie
**Marital status:** Engaged to Lisa Montague
**Education:** Hassocks Infants School; The
Windmills School, Hassocks; Hurstpierpoint
College Junior and Senior Schools; Durham University (St Chad's College)
**Qualifications:** 13 O-levels, 3 A-levels, BA (Hons) Archaeology/Ancient History
**Career outside cricket:** Artist
**Off-season:** Playing, coaching for Mana in Wellington and painting various commissions
**Overseas tours:** NCA U19 to Bermuda 1984; Hurstpierpoint to India 1986; England
YC to Sri Lanka 1986-87
**Overseas teams played for:** Karori, Wellington, New Zealand 1989-90; Wellington
CC, 1990 and 1993; Victoria University of Wellington 1990-92
**Cricketers particularly admired:** Viv Richards
**Other sports followed:** Golf, rugby, hockey
**Injuries:** ME type virus resulting in post-viral fatigue syndrome, out for six months
**Relaxations:** Most music, sports on television, painting and drawing
**Extras:** Member of Durham University UAU winning side 1987; played for Combined

Universities in B&H Cup 1987 and 1988; Sussex Most Promising Player 1989. Fastest first-class 100 in 1992 and fastest 50-overs 100 v Somerset at Taunton 1993. Painted an oil painting of the maiden first-class game at Arundel Castle between Sussex and Hampshire which was later auctioned to raise £1200 for the Sussex YC tour to India 1990-91, and of which a limited edition has also been printed and sold. Has done paintings of Hove, Southampton and The Oval for the benefits of Messrs Pigott, Parks and Greig. Member of Durham University's men's hockey team to Barbados 1988. Book of his paintings *A Cricketer's View*, a collection of 54 paintings and commentary, published in 1995

**Opinions on cricket:** 'Lunch should be one hour, tea half-an-hour.'
**Best batting:** 184 Sussex v Nottinghamshire, Eastbourne 1993
**Best bowling:** 1-2 Sussex v Middlesex, Hove 1988

### 1995 season (did nor make any first-class or one-day appearances)

### Career Performances

|          | M   | Inns | NO | Runs | HS  | Avge  | 100s | 50s | Ct | St | Balls | Runs | Wkts | Avge  | Best | 5wl | 10wM |
|----------|-----|------|----|------|-----|-------|------|-----|----|----|-------|------|------|-------|------|-----|------|
| Test     |     |      |    |      |     |       |      |     |    |    |       |      |      |       |      |     |      |
| All First| 112 | 185  | 13 | 6300 | 184 | 36.62 | 12   | 32  | 91 | -  | 21    | 32   | 2    | 16.00 | 1-2  | -   | -    |
| 1-day Int|     |      |    |      |     |       |      |     |    |    |       |      |      |       |      |     |      |
| NatWest  | 13  | 12   | 1  | 273  | 50  | 24.81 | -    | 1   | 3  | -  |       |      |      |       |      |     |      |
| B & H    | 27  | 25   | 0  | 568  | 83  | 22.72 | -    | 2   | 20 | 1  |       |      |      |       |      |     |      |
| Sunday   | 86  | 78   | 5  | 2166 | 126 | 29.67 | 2    | 11  | 25 | 1  |       |      |      |       |      |     |      |

81. Which Test-playing nation had to wait the longest before their first Test victory?/

# SPENCER, D. J.                                                    Kent

**Name:** Duncan John Spencer
**Role:** Right-hand bat, right-arm fast bowler
**Born:** 5 April 1972, Nelson, Lancashire
**Height:** 5ft 8in
**County debut:** 1993
**1st-Class catches:** 9
**Place in bowling averages:** 95th av. 34.70
**Strike rate:** 51.50 (career 54.88)
**Marital status:** Single
**Education:** Gosnells High School, Western Australia
**Overseas teams played for:** Western Australia 1993-95
**Extras:** Missed the 1995 season through injury
**Best batting:** 75 Kent v Zimbabwe, Canterbury 1993
**Best bowling:** 4-31 Kent v Leicestershire, Leicester 1994

## 1995 Season (did not make any first-class or one-day appearances)

## Career Performances

|          | M  | Inns | NO | Runs | HS   | Avge  | 100s | 50s | Ct | St | Balls | Runs | Wkts | Avge  | Best | 5wl | 10wM |
|----------|----|------|----|------|------|-------|------|-----|----|----|-------|------|------|-------|------|-----|------|
| Test     |    |      |    |      |      |       |      |     |    |    |       |      |      |       |      |     |      |
| All First| 14 | 16   | 2  | 200  | 75   | 14.28 | -    | 1   | 9  | -  | 1866  | 1257 | 34   | 36.97 | 4-31 | -   | -    |
| 1-day Int|    |      |    |      |      |       |      |     |    |    |       |      |      |       |      |     |      |
| NatWest  |    |      |    |      |      |       |      |     |    |    |       |      |      |       |      |     |      |
| B & H    |    |      |    |      |      |       |      |     |    |    |       |      |      |       |      |     |      |
| Sunday   | 10 | 6    | 2  | 60   | 17 * | 15.00 | -    | -   | 2  | -  | 388   | 268  | 8    | 33.50 | 2-16 | -   |      |

# SPIRING, K. R. Worcestershire

**Name:** Karl Reuben Spiring
**Role:** Right-hand opening bat
**Born:** 13 November 1974, Southport
**Height:** 5ft 10in  **Weight:** 12st
**County debut:** 1993 (one-day),
1994 (first-class)
**1st-Class 50s:** 2
**1st-Class catches:** 3
**Parents:** Peter and June
**Marital status:** Single
**Education:** Monmouth School; Durham
University
**Qualifications:** 9 GCSEs, 3 A-levels, NCA
Senior Coach
**Off-season:** Playing and coaching in Perth,
Australia
**Cricketers particularly admired:** Ian
Botham, Alistair Brown, Martin Speight,
Nick Holt

**Other sports followed:** Rugby, football, golf
**Injuries:** Shoulder operation, December 1994
**Relaxations:** Resting, sleeping, 'going out with the lads at Worcester and Kev, Giggsy, Atkers etc at Durham'
**Extras:** Father was a professional footballer. Rapid Cricketline 2nd XI Player of the Month June 1994. Worcestershire Uncapped Player of the Year 1994
**Opinions on cricket:** 'The rules and regs concerning who is or is not an English qualified player should be tightened up and not be allowed to be as ridiculously exposed as they were this year by Roger Twose and Andrew Symonds. Would other countries let our young players use and abuse their systems for their own good like this, when quite clearly they have no intention of playing for that country?'
**Best batting:** 56 Worcestershire v Oxford University, Worcester 1994

## 1995 Season

|          | M | Inns | NO | Runs | HS | Avge | 100s | 50s | Ct | St | O | M | Runs | Wkts | Avge | Best | 5wI | 10wM |
|----------|---|------|----|------|----|------|------|-----|----|----|---|---|------|------|------|------|-----|------|
| Test     |   |      |    |      |    |      |      |     |    |    |   |   |      |      |      |      |     |      |
| All First | 1 | 2   | 0  | 4    | 3  | 2.00 | -    | -   | 1  | -  |   |   |      |      |      |      |     |      |
| 1-day Int |   |     |    |      |    |      |      |     |    |    |   |   |      |      |      |      |     |      |
| NatWest  |   |      |    |      |    |      |      |     |    |    |   |   |      |      |      |      |     |      |
| B & H    | 4 | 4    | 0  | 87   | 35 | 21.75 | -   | -   | 1  | -  |   |   |      |      |      |      |     |      |
| Sunday   |   |      |    |      |    |      |      |     |    |    |   |   |      |      |      |      |     |      |

## Career Performances

|         | M | Inns | NO | Runs | HS | Avge | 100s | 50s | Ct | St | Balls | Runs | Wkts | Avge | Best | 5wI | 10wM |
|---------|---|------|----|------|----|------|------|-----|----|----|-------|------|------|------|------|-----|------|
| Test    |   |      |    |      |    |      |      |     |    |    |       |      |      |      |      |     |      |
| All First | 2 | 4 | 0 | 112 | 56 | 28.00 | - | 2 | 3 | - |  |  |  |  |  |  |  |
| 1-day Int |   |      |    |      |    |      |      |     |    |    |       |      |      |      |      |     |      |
| NatWest |   |      |    |      |    |      |      |     |    |    |       |      |      |      |      |     |      |
| B & H   | 4 | 4 | 0 | 87 | 35 | 21.75 | - | - | 1 | - |  |  |  |  |  |  |  |
| Sunday  | 1 | 1 | 0 | 7 | 7 | 7.00 | - | - | - | - |  |  |  |  |  |  |  |

# SRINATH, J.       Gloucestershire

**Name:** Javagal Srinath
**Role:** Right-hand bat, right-arm
fast-medium bowler
**Born:** 31 August 1969, Mysore, India
**County debut:** 1995
**Test debut:** 1990-91
**Tests:** 15
**One-day Internationals:** 77
**50 w. in a season:** 1
**1st-Class 50s:** 4
**1st-Class 5 w. in innings:** 9
**1st-Class 10 w. matches:** 2
**1st-Class catches:** 20
**One-Day 5 w. in innings:** 2
**Place in batting averages:** 245th av. 15.70
**Place in bowling averages:** 5th av. 19.09
**Strike rate:** 39.21 (career 53.15)
**Overseas tours:** India to Australia and New
Zealand (inc World Cup) 1991-92, to South
Africa and Zimbabwe 1992-93, to New Zealand 1993-94, to New Zealand (Centenary
Tournament) 1994-95, to Pakistan and Sri Lanka (World Cup) 1995-96
**Overseas teams played for:** Karnataka
**Extras:** Studied fast bowling under Dennis Lillee's guidance at Madras. Signed by
Gloucestershire when David Boon decided against playing for the county in 1995
**Best batting:** 60 India v West Indies, Bombay 1994-95
**Best bowling:** 9-76 Gloucestershire v Glamorgan, Abergavenny 1995

---

82. Who scored a Test career best of 88 to help England to victory in the
fourth Test against Australia at Adelaide in 1994-95?

## 1995 Season

| | M | Inns | NO | Runs | HS | Avge | 100s | 50s | Ct | St | O | M | Runs | Wkts | Avge | Best | 5wI | 10wM |
|---|---|---|---|---|---|---|---|---|---|---|---|---|---|---|---|---|---|---|
| Test | | | | | | | | | | | | | | | | | | |
| All First | 15 | 24 | 4 | 314 | 44 | 15.70 | - | - | 5 | - | 568.4 | 147 | 1661 | 87 | 19.09 | 9-76 | 5 | 2 |
| 1-day Int | | | | | | | | | | | | | | | | | | |
| NatWest | 3 | 2 | 1 | 11 | 11 * | 11.00 | - | - | 1 | - | 25.2 | 3 | 63 | 7 | 9.00 | 4-38 | - | |
| B & H | 6 | 6 | 1 | 12 | 6 | 2.40 | - | - | 1 | - | 64.2 | 18 | 176 | 15 | 11.73 | 4-33 | - | |
| Sunday | 6 | 4 | 1 | 13 | 11 | 4.33 | - | - | 3 | - | 43.5 | 4 | 213 | 11 | 19.36 | 3-27 | - | |

## Career Performances

| | M | Inns | NO | Runs | HS | Avge | 100s | 50s | Ct | St | Balls | Runs | Wkts | Avge | Best | 5wI | 10wM |
|---|---|---|---|---|---|---|---|---|---|---|---|---|---|---|---|---|---|
| Test | 15 | 21 | 11 | 227 | 60 | 22.70 | - | 2 | 7 | - | 3522 | 1549 | 41 | 37.78 | 4-33 | - | - |
| All First | 63 | 84 | 18 | 1110 | 60 | 15.80 | - | 2 | 15 | - | 12279 | 6033 | 231 | 26.11 | 9-76 | 9 | 2 |
| 1-day Int | 77 | 32 | 13 | 153 | 37 | 8.05 | - | - | 9 | - | 3941 | 2816 | 112 | 25.14 | 5-24 | 2 | |
| NatWest | 3 | 2 | 1 | 11 | 11 * | 11.00 | - | - | 1 | - | 152 | 63 | 7 | 9.00 | 4-38 | - | |
| B & H | 6 | 6 | 1 | 12 | 6 | 2.40 | - | - | 1 | - | 386 | 176 | 15 | 11.73 | 4-33 | - | |
| Sunday | 6 | 4 | 1 | 13 | 11 | 4.33 | - | - | 3 | - | 263 | 213 | 11 | 19.36 | 3-27 | - | |

# STANFORD, E. J.      Kent

**Name:** Edward John Stanford
**Role:** Left-hand bat, left-arm spinner
**Born:** 21 January 1971, Dartford
**Height:** 5ft 10in **Weight:** 12st
**Nickname:** Oist
**County debut:** 1995
**1st-Class catches:** 1
**Parents:** Paul and Pam
**Family links with cricket:** Father played club cricket for Dartford
**Education:** Downs Secondary School, Dartford
**Qualifications:** 'Loads'
**Career outside cricket:** 'Ex-groundsman and ex-bank clerk'
**Off-season:** Working for a courier company, watching Charlton FC, 'backing a few winners'
**Overseas tours:** Kent Schools U17 to Singapore and New Zealand 1988
**Overseas teams played for:** Petersham, Sydney 1991
**Cricketers particularly admired:** Aravinda De Silva, Matthew Walker

**Other sports followed:** Charlton FC, golf, snooker ('once beat Min Patel!')
**Relaxations:** Snooker and horse racing
**Extras:** Headed a ball for six in debut against Essex in the Bain Clarkson Championship 1993 ('Totally misjudged a top edge whilst fielding at fine leg, the ball struck me on the forehead and carried a further 20 yards to go for six!')
**Opinions on cricket:** '2nd XI fixtures should be played on better wickets and to last four days, so that players in the second team are prepared for first-class cricket.'
**Best batting:** 4 Kent v Worcestershire, Worcester 1995
**Best bowling:** 2-96 Kent v Worcestershire, Worcester 1995

## 1995 Season

|  | M | Inns | NO | Runs | HS | Avge | 100s | 50s | Ct | St | O | M | Runs | Wkts | Avge | Best | 5wI | 10wM |
|---|---|---|---|---|---|---|---|---|---|---|---|---|---|---|---|---|---|---|
| Test | | | | | | | | | | | | | | | | | | |
| All First | 2 | 2 | 1 | 4 | 4 | 4.00 | - | - | 1 | - | 77.5 | 19 | 220 | 3 | 73.33 | 2-96 | - | - |
| 1-day Int | | | | | | | | | | | | | | | | | | |
| NatWest | | | | | | | | | | | | | | | | | | |
| B & H | | | | | | | | | | | | | | | | | | |
| Sunday | | | | | | | | | | | | | | | | | | |

## Career Performances

|  | M | Inns | NO | Runs | HS | Avge | 100s | 50s | Ct | St | Balls | Runs | Wkts | Avge | Best | 5wI | 10wM |
|---|---|---|---|---|---|---|---|---|---|---|---|---|---|---|---|---|---|
| Test | | | | | | | | | | | | | | | | | |
| All First | 2 | 2 | 1 | 4 | 4 | 4.00 | - | - | 1 | - | 467 | 220 | 3 | 73.33 | 2-96 | - | - |
| 1-day Int | | | | | | | | | | | | | | | | | |
| NatWest | | | | | | | | | | | | | | | | | |
| B & H | | | | | | | | | | | | | | | | | |
| Sunday | | | | | | | | | | | | | | | | | |

# STEELE, M. V.        Northamptonshire

**Name:** Mark Vincent Steele
**Role:** Left-hand bat, right-arm fast-medium bowler
**Born:** 13 November 1976, Corby
**Height:** 6ft **Weight:** 12st 7lbs
**Nickname:** Stan
**County debut:** No first-team appearance
**Parents:** David and Carol
**Marital status:** Single
**Family links with cricket:** Father played cricket for Northants and England. Father's brother, J.F. Steele, played for Leicestershire and managed Glamorgan, father's cousin, Brian Crump, played for Northants
**Education:** Wellingborough School

**Qualifications:** 6 GCSEs
**Off-season:** Studying
**Cricketers particularly admired:**
Wayne Larkins, John Pye
**Other sports followed:** Football, table tennis
**Relaxations:** Playing football for Old
Wellingburians
**Extras:** MCC U13 Young Cricketer of the
Year 1984. Played for Midlands Schools from
U15 upwards and played for England U16 in
1993. Wellingborough scholarship in 1991.
Public School Batsman of the Year 1993

---

# STEMP, R. D. Yorkshire

**Name:** Richard David Stemp
**Role:** Right-hand bat, slow left-arm bowler
**Born:** 11 December 1967, Erdington,
Birmingham
**Height:** 6ft  **Weight:** 12st 4lbs
**Nickname:** Stempy, Sherriff, Badger
**County debut:** 1990 (Worcestershire),
1993 (Yorkshire)
**1st-Class 5 w. in innings:** 8
**1st-Class 10 w. in match:** 1
**1st-Class catches:** 36
**Place in batting averages:**
(1994 269th av. 10.11)
**Place in bowling averages:** 135th av. 45.92
(1994 62nd av. 30.46)
**Strike rate:** 103.02 (career 82.66)
**Parents:** Arnold and Rita Homer
**Marital status:** Single
**Family links with cricket:** Father played
Birmingham League cricket for Old Hill
**Education:** Britannia High School, Rowley Regis
**Qualifications:** NCA coaching award
**Off-season:** Touring Pakistan with England A

**Overseas tours:** England A to India 1994-95, to Pakistan 1995-96
**Overseas teams played for:** Pretoria Technikon 1988-89
**Cricketers particularly admired:** Ian Botham, Phil Tufnell
**Other sports followed:** Indoor cricket, American football (New England Patriots)
**Relaxations:** Ornithology, music, driving
**Extras:** Played for England indoor cricket team v Australia in ManuLife 'Test' series 1990. Moved to Yorkshire at end of 1992 season (first English non-Yorkshireman to be signed for the county). Included in England Test squad against New Zealand in 1994
**Opinions on cricket:** 'Groundsmen should prepare cricket wickets, not wickets made for corporate hospitality. Is not being given run out as much human judgement as LBW or caught behind? If we are using television to check and decide on run out, why not all decisions?'
**Best batting:** 37 Yorkshire v Essex, Chelmsford 1993
**Best bowling:** 6-37 Yorkshire v Durham, Durham University 1994

### 1995 Season

|  | M | Inns | NO | Runs | HS | Avge | 100s | 50s | Ct | St | O | M | Runs | Wkts | Avge | Best | 5wI | 10wM |
|---|---|---|---|---|---|---|---|---|---|---|---|---|---|---|---|---|---|---|
| Test |  |  |  |  |  |  |  |  |  |  |  |  |  |  |  |  |  |  |
| All First | 21 | 25 | 4 | 179 | 22 * | 8.52 | - | - | 9 | - | 721.1 | 226 | 1929 | 42 | 45.92 | 4-68 | - | - |
| 1-day Int |  |  |  |  |  |  |  |  |  |  |  |  |  |  |  |  |  |  |
| NatWest | 1 | 0 | 0 | 0 | 0 | - | - | - | - | - | 7 | 0 | 31 | 0 | - | - | - |  |
| B & H | 4 | 2 | 1 | 0 | 0 * | 0.00 | - | - | - | - | 35 | 4 | 122 | 4 | 30.50 | 2-28 | - |  |
| Sunday | 7 | 4 | 0 | 21 | 11 | 5.25 | - | - | 1 | - | 47 | 0 | 234 | 6 | 39.00 | 2-41 | - |  |

### Career Performances

|  | M | Inns | NO | Runs | HS | Avge | 100s | 50s | Ct | St | Balls | Runs | Wkts | Avge | Best | 5wI | 10wM |
|---|---|---|---|---|---|---|---|---|---|---|---|---|---|---|---|---|---|
| Test |  |  |  |  |  |  |  |  |  |  |  |  |  |  |  |  |  |
| All First | 84 | 99 | 28 | 863 | 37 | 12.15 | - | - | 36 | - | 16285 | 6721 | 197 | 34.11 | 6-37 | 8 | 1 |
| 1-day Int |  |  |  |  |  |  |  |  |  |  |  |  |  |  |  |  |  |
| NatWest | 3 | 1 | 1 | 1 | 1 * | - | - | - | 1 | - | 174 | 104 | 1 | 104.00 | 1-31 | - |  |
| B & H | 7 | 2 | 1 | 0 | 0 * | 0.00 | - | - | - | - | 390 | 236 | 4 | 59.00 | 2-28 | - |  |
| Sunday | 30 | 11 | 4 | 77 | 23 * | 11.00 | - | - | 5 | - | 1098 | 927 | 27 | 34.33 | 3-18 | - |  |

# STEPHENSON, F. D.                     Sussex

**Name:** Franklyn Dacosta Stephenson
**Role:** Right-hand bat, right-arm fast bowler
**Born:** 8 April 1959, St James, Barbados
**Height:** 6ft 3in **Weight:** 13st 7lbs
**Nickname:** Cookie
**County debut:** 1982 (Gloucestershire), 1988 (Nottinghamshire), 1992 (Sussex)
**County cap:** 1988 (Notts), 1992 (Sussex)

**1000 runs in a season:** 1
**50 wickets in a season:** 5
**1st-Class 50s:** 42
**1st-Class 100s:** 10
**1st-Class 5 w. in innings:** 43
**1st-Class 10 w. in match:** 10
**1st-Class catches:** 91
**One-Day 100s:** 1
**One-Day 5 w. in innings:** 4
**Place in batting averages:** 129th av. 30.00
(1994 143rd av. 27.85)
**Place in bowling averages:** 83rd av. 31.80
(1994 6th av. 20.07)
**Strike rate:** 61.94 (career 50.47)
**Parents:** Leonard Young and Violet Stevenson
**Wife and date of marriage:** Julia, 2 April
1981
**Children:** Ophelia, 20 October 1981;
Kathryn, 6 September 1983; Katrina, 1
November 1990
**Education:** St John Baptist Mixed School; Samuel Jackson Prescod Polytechnic
**Qualifications:** School leaving certificate
**Career outside cricket:** Owns Stevo's Bar and Restaurant and Stevo's Mini Mart in
Holders Hill. Manages Barbados PGA
**Off-season:** Playing for Orange Free State, Bloemfontein, South Africa
**Overseas tours:** West Indies U19 to England 1978; unofficial West Indies XI to South
Africa 1982-83 and 1983-84
**Overseas teams played for:** Tasmania 1981-82; Barbados 1981-82 and 1989-90;
Orange Free State 1991-96
**Cricketers particularly admired:** Sylvester Clarke, Collis King, Richard Hadlee,
Desmond Haynes, Malcolm Marshall
**Other sports followed:** All
**Injuries:** Sprained ankle, but missed no cricket
**Relaxations:** Playing golf, guitar and spending time with family
**Extras:** Played League cricket for Littleborough in the Central Lancashire League in
1979, Royton in 1980 (100 wickets and 621 runs), Rawtenstall in 1981 and 1982 (100+
wickets and 500+ runs both years). Hit 165 for Barbados in 1982, having been sent in as
night-watchman. Took ten wickets in match on debut for Tasmania. In 1988 did the
double when he scored 1018 runs and took 125 wickets in first-class cricket, being
named Britannic Assurance Player of the Year, 1988 and one of *Wisden*'s Five Cricketers
of the Year. Left Nottinghamshire at end of 1991 season and signed to play for Sussex
in 1992 when he was voted their Players' Player of the Year. Banned from Test cricket
for joining rebel West Indies tour to South Africa: ban now ended. Won second
Weatherall Award for the Best All-rounder in county cricket in 1994. Helped Orange
Free State to their sixth title in four years in 1994-95

**Opinions on cricket:** 'Too many players forget that cricket is a spectator sport.'
**Best batting:** 165 Barbados v Leeward Islands, Basseterre 1981-82
**Best bowling:** 8-47 Nottinghamshire v Essex, Trent Bridge 1989

## 1995 Season

|           | M  | Inns | NO | Runs | HS   | Avge  | 100s | 50s | Ct | St | O     | M  | Runs | Wkts | Avge  | Best | 5wI | 10wM |
|-----------|----|------|----|------|------|-------|------|-----|----|----|-------|----|------|------|-------|------|-----|------|
| Test      |    |      |    |      |      |       |      |     |    |    |       |    |      |      |       |      |     |      |
| All First | 13 | 23   | 0  | 690  | 106  | 30.00 | 1    | 3   | 4  | -  | 361.2 | 73 | 1113 | 35   | 31.80 | 5-64 | 1   | -    |
| 1-day Int |    |      |    |      |      |       |      |     |    |    |       |    |      |      |       |      |     |      |
| NatWest   | 2  | 2    | 1  | 65   | 37 * | 65.00 | -    | -   | -  | -  | 22    | 1  | 114  | 2    | 57.00 | 1-48 | -   |      |
| B & H     | 4  | 3    | 1  | 68   | 45   | 34.00 | -    | -   | -  | -  | 42.1  | 5  | 176  | 8    | 22.00 | 3-29 | -   |      |
| Sunday    | 15 | 15   | 1  | 292  | 54   | 20.85 | -    | 2   | 4  | -  | 97    | 7  | 434  | 20   | 21.70 | 5-38 | 1   |      |

## Career Performances

|           | M   | Inns | NO | Runs | HS   | Avge  | 100s | 50s | Ct | St | Balls | Runs  | Wkts | Avge  | Best | 5wI | 10wM |
|-----------|-----|------|----|------|------|-------|------|-----|----|----|-------|-------|------|-------|------|-----|------|
| Test      |     |      |    |      |      |       |      |     |    |    |       |       |      |       |      |     |      |
| All First | 207 | 324  | 34 | 8073 | 165  | 27.83 | 10   | 42  | 91 | -  | 38258 | 18278 | 758  | 24.11 | 8-47 | 43  | 10   |
| 1-day Int |     |      |    |      |      |       |      |     |    |    |       |       |      |       |      |     |      |
| NatWest   | 21  | 16   | 2  | 255  | 40   | 18.21 | -    | -   | 2  | -  | 1326  | 706   | 29   | 24.34 | 3-8  | -   |      |
| B & H     | 34  | 29   | 7  | 523  | 98 * | 23.77 | -    | 2   | 4  | -  | 2043  | 1195  | 56   | 21.33 | 5-30 | 1   |      |
| Sunday    | 126 | 107  | 15 | 1949 | 103  | 21.18 | 1    | 6   | 28 | -  | 5691  | 3970  | 192  | 20.67 | 5-23 | 3   |      |

# STEPHENSON, J. P. — Hampshire

**Name:** John Patrick Stephenson
**Role:** Right-hand opening bat, right-arm fast-medium bowler, county captain
**Born:** 14 March 1965, Stebbing, Essex
**Height:** 6ft 1in **Weight:** 12st 7lbs
**Nickname:** Stan
**County debut:** 1985 (Essex), 1995 (Hants)
**County cap:** 1989 (Essex)
**Test debut:** 1989
**Tests:** 1
**1000 runs in a season:** 5
**1st-Class 50s:** 60
**1st-Class 100s:** 19
**1st-Class 200s:** 1
**1st-Class 5 w. in innings:** 5
**1st-Class catches:** 122
**One-Day 100s:** 4
**One-Day 5 w. in innings:** 1

**Place in batting averages:** 98th av. 34.30 (1994 197th av. 20.57)
**Place in bowling averages:** 106th av. 36.35 (1994 121st av. 41.00)
**Strike rate:** 59.66 (career 61.26)
**Parents:** Pat and Eve
**Wife and date of marriage:** Fiona Maria, 24 September 1994
**Family links with cricket:** Father was member of Rugby Meteors Cricketer Cup-winning side in 1973. Three brothers played in Felsted 1st XI; Guy played for Essex 2nd XI and now plays for Teddington
**Education:** Felsted Prep School; Felsted Senior School; Durham University
**Qualifications:** 7 O-levels, 3 A-levels, BA General Arts (Dunelm)
**Off-season:** 'Undecided'
**Overseas tours:** English Schools U19 to Zimbabwe 1982-83; England A to Kenya and Zimbabwe 1989-90, to Bermuda and West Indies 1991-92
**Overseas teams played for:** Fitzroy, Melbourne 1982-83, 1987-88; Boland, South Africa 1988-89; Gold Coast Dolphins and Bond University, Australia 1990-91; St George's, Argentina 1994-95; Belgrano, Argentina 1994-95
**Cricketers particularly admired:** Brian Hardie
**Injuries:** Broken finger and pneumonia, out for three weeks
**Relaxations:** Watching cricket (*Sunday Telegraph*, *Wisden*, *The Cricketer*), reading, alternative music
**Extras:** Awarded 2nd XI cap in 1984 when leading run-scorer with Essex 2nd XI. Essex Young Player of the Year, 1985. Captained Durham University to victory in UAU Championship 1986 and captain of Combined Universities team 1987 in the first year that it was drawn from all universities. Called up to replace the injured Michael Atherton on England A tour to Bermuda and West Indies 1991-92 and was leading wicket-taker. Scored two not out centuries v Somerset at Taunton in 1992 and was on the field for the whole game (the first Essex player to achieve this). First Essex player to achieve 500 runs and 20 wickets in Sunday League season 1993. Taking over captaincy of Hampshire in 1996
**Best batting:** 202* Essex v Somerset, Bath 1990
**Best bowling:** 7-51 Hampshire v Middlesex, Lord's 1995

---

## 1995 Season

|         | M  | Inns | NO | Runs | HS  | Avge  | 100s | 50s | Ct | St | O     | M  | Runs | Wkts | Avge  | Best | 5wI | 10wM |
|---------|----|------|----|------|-----|-------|------|-----|----|----|-------|----|------|------|-------|------|-----|------|
| Test    |    |      |    |      |     |       |      |     |    |    |       |    |      |      |       |      |     |      |
| All First | 17 | 30 | 4 | 892 | 127 | 34.30 | 1 | 6 | 9 | - | 358 | 62 | 1316 | 36 | 36.55 | 7-51 | 1 | - |
| 1-day Int |    |      |    |      |     |       |      |     |    |    |       |    |      |      |       |      |     |      |
| NatWest | 1  | 1  | 0  | 34   | 34  | 34.00 | -    | -   | 1  | -  | 10    | 0  | 39   | 1    | 39.00 | 1-39 | -   |      |
| B & H   | 4  | 4  | 0  | 246  | 98  | 61.50 | -    | 3   | -  | -  | 32    | 3  | 129  | 5    | 25.80 | 2-33 | -   |      |
| Sunday  | 11 | 10 | 0  | 140  | 37  | 14.00 | -    | -   | 4  | -  | 65.3  | 2  | 398  | 8    | 49.75 | 2-56 | -   |      |

## Career Performances

|  | M | Inns | NO | Runs | HS | Avge | 100s | 50s | Ct | St | Balls | Runs | Wkts | Avge | Best | 5wI | 10wM |
|---|---|---|---|---|---|---|---|---|---|---|---|---|---|---|---|---|---|
| Test | 1 | 2 | 0 | 36 | 25 | 18.00 | - | - | - | - |  |  |  |  |  |  |  |
| All First | 205 | 354 | 36 | 11122 | 202 * | 34.97 | 19 | 60 | 122 | - | 11089 | 6193 | 181 | 34.21 | 7-51 | 5 | - |
| 1-day Int |  |  |  |  |  |  |  |  |  |  |  |  |  |  |  |  |  |
| NatWest | 18 | 17 | 1 | 627 | 90 | 39.18 | - | 7 | 7 | - | 551 | 480 | 9 | 53.33 | 3-78 | - |  |
| B & H | 33 | 28 | 3 | 1089 | 142 | 43.56 | 1 | 9 | 6 | - | 945 | 642 | 25 | 25.68 | 3-22 | - |  |
| Sunday | 121 | 106 | 13 | 2688 | 109 | 28.90 | 3 | 13 | 46 | - | 3225 | 2496 | 93 | 26.83 | 5-58 | 1 |  |

# STEWART, A. J. Surrey

**Name:** Alec James Stewart
**Role:** Right-hand bat, 'very average' bowler, wicket-keeper, county captain
**Born:** 8 April 1963, Merton
**Nickname:** Stewie
**Height:** 5ft 11in **Weight:** 12st 7lbs
**County debut:** 1981
**County cap:** 1985
**Benefit:** 1994 (£202,187)
**Test debut:** 1989-90
**Tests:** 48
**One-Day Internationals:** 64
**1000 runs in a season:** 8
**1st-Class 50s:** 94
**1st-Class 100s:** 33
**1st-Class 200s:** 1
**1st-Class catches:** 367
**1st-Class stumpings:** 13
**One-Day 100s:** 10
**Place in batting averages:** 78th av. 38.05 (1994 28th av. 46.80)
**Parents:** Michael and Sheila
**Wife and date of marriage:** Lynn, 28 September 1991
**Children:** Andrew James, 21 May 1993
**Family links with cricket:** Father played for England (1962-64), Surrey (1954 -72) and Malden Wanderers. Brother Neil captains Malden Wanderers
**Education:** Tiffin Boys School
**Qualifications:** 4 O-levels
**Off-season:** England tour to South Africa
**Overseas tours:** England to India (Nehru Cup) 1989-90, to West Indies 1989-90, to Australia 1990-91, to Australia and New Zealand (World Cup) 1991-92, to India and Sri Lanka 1992-93, to West Indies 1993-94, to Australia 1994-95; to South Africa

1995-96, to Pakistan and India (World Cup) 1996
**Overseas teams played for:** Midland Guildford, Perth, Western Australia 1981-89
**Cricketers particularly admired:** Graham Monkhouse, Geoff Boycott, Graham Gooch
**Other sports followed:** Football (Chelsea)
**Injuries:** Fractured index finger, 'out for too long'
**Relaxations:** 'Spending as much time with my family as possible'
**Extras:** Captained England in a Test match for the first time v India at Madras 1992-93 and has acted as vice-captain to both Graham Gooch and Mike Atherton. First Englishman to score a century in each innings against West Indies, at Barbados 1994
**Opinions on cricket:** 'The quality of four-day pitches must improve. Penalties for poor pitches must be used straight away.'
**Best batting:** 206* Surrey v Essex, The Oval 1989
**Best bowling:** 1-7 Surrey v Lancashire, Old Trafford 1989

## 1995 Season

|          | M  | Inns | NO | Runs | HS    | Avge  | 100s | 50s | Ct | St | O | M | Runs | Wkts | Avge | Best | 5wl | 10wM |
|----------|----|------|----|------|-------|-------|------|-----|----|----|---|---|------|------|------|------|-----|------|
| Test     | 3  | 5    | 0  | 113  | 37    | 22.60 | -    | -   | 9  | -  |   |   |      |      |      |      |     |      |
| All First| 10 | 18   | 1  | 647  | 151   | 38.05 | 2    | 2   | 23 | -  | 3 | 0 | 18   | 0    | -    | -    | -   | -    |
| 1-day Int| 3  | 3    | 0  | 98   | 74    | 32.66 | -    | 1   | 3  | -  |   |   |      |      |      |      |     |      |
| NatWest  | 1  | 0    | 0  | 0    | 0     | -     | -    | -   | 6  | -  |   |   |      |      |      |      |     |      |
| B & H    | 4  | 4    | 1  | 152  | 52    | 50.66 | -    | 1   | 6  | 1  |   |   |      |      |      |      |     |      |
| Sunday   | 5  | 5    | 1  | 114  | 44 *  | 28.50 | -    | -   | 7  | -  |   |   |      |      |      |      |     |      |

## Career Performances

|          | M   | Inns | NO | Runs  | HS     | Avge  | 100s | 50s | Ct  | St | Balls | Runs | Wkts | Avge   | Best | 5wl | 10wM |
|----------|-----|------|----|-------|--------|-------|------|-----|-----|----|-------|------|------|--------|------|-----|------|
| Test     | 48  | 87   | 6  | 3168  | 190    | 39.11 | 7    | 15  | 64  | 4  | 20    | 13   | 0    | -      | -    | -   | -    |
| All First| 284 | 471  | 55 | 16462 | 206 *  | 39.57 | 33   | 94  | 367 | 13 | 457   | 393  | 3    | 131.00 | 1-7  | -   | -    |
| 1-day Int| 64  | 59   | 4  | 1665  | 103    | 30.27 | 1    | 11  | 50  | 4  |       |      |      |        |      |     |      |
| NatWest  | 30  | 27   | 4  | 1055  | 107 *  | 45.86 | 2    | 7   | 31  | -  |       |      |      |        |      |     |      |
| B & H    | 45  | 45   | 7  | 1640  | 167 *  | 43.15 | 2    | 11  | 29  | 4  |       |      |      |        |      |     |      |
| Sunday   | 145 | 131  | 13 | 3656  | 125    | 30.98 | 5    | 22  | 108 | 8  | 4     | 8    | 0    | -      | -    | -   | -    |

83. Who won the Sheffield Shield for the first time in 1994-95?

# STREAK, H. H.             Hampshire

**Name:** Heath Hilton Streak
**Role:** Right-hand bat, right-arm fast bowler
**Born:** 16 March 1974
**Height:** 6ft 1in   **Weight:** 14st 11lbs
**Nickname:** Rhino, Streaky Bacon
**County debut:** 1995
**Test debut:** 1994-95
**Tests:** 9
**50 w. in a season:** 1
**One-day Internationals:** 16
**1st-Class 50s:** 4
**1st-Class 5 w. innings:** 3
**1st-Class catches:** 18
**Place in batting averages:** 248th av. 15.12
**Place in bowling averages:** 77th av. 30.73
**Strike rate:** 58.45 (career 59.97)
**Parents:** Denis and Sheona
**Marital status:** Single
**Family links with cricket:** Father played for
Zimbabwe (1976-85) and is on the Zimbabwe Cricket Board
**Education:** Zeps, Zimbabwe; Falcon College, Zimbabwe
**Qualifications:** 2 A-levels, learner professional hunter guide
**Career outside cricket:** Ranching
**Off-season:** Return to Zimbabwe domestic cricket season, tour to New Zealand and
the World Cup in India and Pakistan
**Overseas tours:** Zimbabwe to England 1993, to Pakistan 1993-94, to India and
Pakistan (World Cup) 1995-96
**Overseas teams played for:** Zimbabwe 1993-95; Matabeleland 1991-95
**Cricketers particularly admired:** Dennis Lillee, Malcolm Marshall, Ian Botham
**Other sports followed:** Rugby (Zimbabwe, South Africa, 'played for Zimbabwe
U19'), football (Liverpool)
**Relaxations:** Shooting, fishing, off-road dirt-biking, sport
**Extras**: Was the Man of the Series against Pakistan with 22 wickets in three Tests
**Opinions on cricket:** 'Too much is played in the English season. Only necessary to have
two limited-over competitions of 60 overs to comply with internationals. Reduce first-
class to approximately 12 games – with counties in pools, having a semi-final and final.
Present 110 overs is too many in a day: about 100 is more realistic!'
**Best batting:** 98 Matabeleland v Glamorgan, Bulawayo 1994-95
**Best bowling:** 6-90 Zimbabwe v Pakistan, Harare 1994-95

## 1995 Season

| | M | Inns | NO | Runs | HS | Avge | 100s | 50s | Ct | St | O | M | Runs | Wkts | Avge | Best | 5wI | 10wM |
|---|---|---|---|---|---|---|---|---|---|---|---|---|---|---|---|---|---|---|
| Test | | | | | | | | | | | | | | | | | | |
| All First | 19 | 28 | 3 | 378 | 69 | 15.12 | - | 1 | 6 | - | 516.2 | 114 | 1629 | 53 | 30.73 | 4-40 | - | - |
| 1-day Int | | | | | | | | | | | | | | | | | | |
| NatWest | | | | | | | | | | | | | | | | | | |
| B & H | 5 | 4 | 2 | 32 | 18 | 16.00 | - | - | 2 | - | 44 | 6 | 171 | 8 | 21.37 | 3-28 | - | |
| Sunday | 15 | 11 | 5 | 154 | 32 * | 25.66 | - | - | 1 | - | 112 | 2 | 656 | 22 | 29.81 | 4-56 | - | |

## Career Performances

| | M | Inns | NO | Runs | HS | Avge | 100s | 50s | Ct | St | Balls | Runs | Wkts | Avge | Best | 5wI | 10wM |
|---|---|---|---|---|---|---|---|---|---|---|---|---|---|---|---|---|---|
| Test | 9 | 12 | 2 | 103 | 30 * | 10.30 | - | - | 3 | - | 2182 | 886 | 43 | 20.60 | 6-90 | 3 | - |
| All First | 43 | 61 | 10 | 921 | 98 | 18.05 | - | 4 | 18 | - | 7497 | 3461 | 125 | 27.68 | 6-90 | 3 | - |
| 1-day Int | 16 | 12 | 4 | 98 | 18 * | 12.25 | - | - | 2 | - | 799 | 582 | 19 | 30.63 | 4-44 | - | |
| NatWest | | | | | | | | | | | | | | | | | |
| B & H | 5 | 4 | 2 | 32 | 18 | 16.00 | - | - | 2 | - | 264 | 171 | 8 | 21.37 | 3-28 | - | |
| Sunday | 15 | 11 | 5 | 154 | 32 * | 25.66 | - | - | 1 | - | 672 | 656 | 22 | 29.81 | 4-56 | - | |

# SUCH, P. M.    Essex

**Name:** Peter Mark Such
**Role:** Right-hand bat, off-spin bowler
**Born:** 12 June 1964, Helensburgh, Scotland
**Height:** 6ft **Weight:** 11st 7lbs
**Nickname:** Suchy
**County debut:** 1982 (Nottinghamshire),
1987 (Leicestershire), 1990 (Essex)
**County cap:** 1991 (Essex)
**Test debut:** 1993
**Tests:** 8
**50 wickets in a season:** 3
**1st-Class 50s:** 1
**1st-Class 5 w. in innings:** 27
**1st-Class 10 w. in innings:** 5
**1st-Class catches:** 81
**One-Day 5 w. in innings:** 2
**Place in batting averages:**
1993 262nd av. 10.36)
**Place in bowling averages:** 44th av. 26.80
1994 67th av. 30.82)
**Strike rate:** 58.33 (career 67.05)
**Parents:** John and Margaret

**Marital status:** Engaged
**Family links with cricket:** Father and brother both village cricketers
**Education:** Lantern Lane Primary; Harry Carlton Comprehensive, East Leake, Notts
**Qualifications:** 9 O-levels, 3 A-levels, advanced cricket coach
**Off-season:** Going to India with an England XI in September and October 1995
**Overseas tours:** England A to Australia 1992-93, to South Africa 1993-94
**Overseas teams played for:** Kempton Park, South Africa 1982-83; Bathurst, Australia 1985-86; Matabeleland, Zimbabwe 1989-92
**Cricketers particularly admired:** Bob White, Eddie Hemmings, Graham Gooch, John Childs
**Relaxations:** Gardening
**Extras:** Played for England YC v Australian YC 1983 and for TCCB XI v New Zealand 1985. Left Nottinghamshire at end of 1986 season; joined Leicestershire in 1987 and released at end of 1989; signed by Essex for 1990. Played in one-day games for England A v Sri Lanka 1991. Joint holder with J.H. Childs of the Essex Player of the Year Award 1992 and shared the award again in 1993. Took 6-67 on Test debut v Australia 1993 – best figures by England Test debutant since John Lever in India 1976-77
**Opinions on cricket:** 'Present balance of one-day and four-day cricket is about right. NatWest should be 55 overs, B&H 50 overs, Sunday League 40 overs. Over rates in Championship are too high, 102 overs per day would be better. The quality of the pitches has improved this year but needs to be maintained. The TCCB need to be very strict when monitoring the situation.'
**Best batting:** 54 Essex v Worcestershire, Chelmsford 1993
**Best bowling:** 8-93 Essex v Hampshire, Colchester 1995

## 1995 Season

|           | M  | Inns | NO | Runs | HS  | Avge | 100s | 50s | Ct | St | O     | M   | Runs | Wkts | Avge  | Best | 5wI | 10wM |
|-----------|----|------|----|------|-----|------|------|-----|----|----|-------|-----|------|------|-------|------|-----|------|
| Test      |    |      |    |      |     |      |      |     |    |    |       |     |      |      |       |      |     |      |
| All First | 18 | 30   | 8  | 214  | 32  | 9.72 | -    | -   | 11 | -  | 748.4 | 174 | 2064 | 77   | 26.80 | 8-93 | 6   | 2    |
| 1-day Int |    |      |    |      |     |      |      |     |    |    |       |     |      |      |       |      |     |      |
| NatWest   | 2  | 2    | 1  | 8    | 8 * | 8.00 | -    | -   | -  | -  | 24    | 7   | 72   | 3    | 24.00 | 2-36 | -   |      |
| B & H     | 5  | 3    | 2  | 6    | 5 * | 6.00 | -    | -   | 1  | -  | 42    | 3   | 142  | 6    | 23.66 | 3-27 | -   |      |
| Sunday    | 16 | 5    | 1  | 11   | 6   | 2.75 | -    | -   | 8  | -  | 100   | 4   | 491  | 19   | 25.84 | 3-41 | -   |      |

## Career Performances

|           | M   | Inns | NO | Runs | HS   | Avge | 100s | 50s | Ct | St | Balls | Runs  | Wkts | Avge  | Best | 5wI | 10wM |
|-----------|-----|------|----|------|------|------|------|-----|----|----|-------|-------|------|-------|------|-----|------|
| Test      | 8   | 11   | 4  | 65   | 14 * | 9.28 | -    | -   | 2  | -  | 2177  | 805   | 22   | 36.59 | 6-67 | 1   | -    |
| All First | 199 | 196  | 59 | 967  | 54   | 7.05 | -    | 1   | 81 | -  | 35941 | 15897 | 536  | 29.65 | 8-93 | 27  | 5    |
| 1-day Int |     |      |    |      |      |      |      |     |    |    |       |       |      |       |      |     |      |
| NatWest   | 12  | 5    | 3  | 14   | 8 *  | 7.00 | -    | -   | 1  | -  | 732   | 389   | 12   | 32.41 | 2-29 | -   |      |
| B & H     | 22  | 9    | 4  | 18   | 5 *  | 3.60 | -    | -   | 3  | -  | 1152  | 732   | 23   | 31.82 | 4-43 | -   |      |
| Sunday    | 82  | 30   | 14 | 116  | 19 * | 7.25 | -    | -   | 24 | -  | 3332  | 2569  | 83   | 30.95 | 5-32 | 2   |      |

# SUTCLIFFE, I. J. Leicestershire

**Name:** Iain John Sutcliffe
**Role:** Left-hand bat, leg-spin bowler
**Born:** 20 December 1974, Leeds
**Height:** 6ft 1in **Weight:** 12st
**Nickname:** Sooty, Bertie, Ripper
**County debut:** 1995
**1st-Class 50s:** 5
**1st-Class 100s:** 1
**1st-Class catches:** 11
**Place in batting averages:** 54th av. 42.35
**Parents:** John and Valerie
**Marital status:** Single
**Education:** Leeds Grammar School; Oxford
University (Queens College)
**Qualifications:** 10 GCSEs, 4 A-levels
**Off-season:** Studying, boxing
**Overseas tours:** Leeds GS to Kenya
**Cricketers particularly admired:**
Brian Lara, Graham Thorpe
**Other sports followed:** Boxing, football
**Injuries:** Broken wrist, out for six weeks
**Relaxations:** Listening to music
**Extras:** Played NCA England U14 and NCA Development Team U18/U19. Oxford boxing Blue 1994 and 1995, British Universities Light-middleweight Champion 1993. Highest partnership (283) with C. Gupte for Oxford University against a first-class county in which he scored 163 not out
**Opinions on cricket:** 'Abolish one of the one-day competitions, in order to prevent fatigue. Retain first-class status for universities as it encourages the development of youngsters wishing to combine sport with education.'
**Best batting:** 163* Oxford University v Hampshire, The Parks 1995
**Best bowling:** 1-11 Oxford University v Cambridge University, Lord's 1995

## 1995 Season

|  | M | Inns | NO | Runs | HS | Avge | 100s | 50s | Ct | St | O | M | Runs | Wkts | Avge | Best | 5wI | 10wM |
|---|---|---|---|---|---|---|---|---|---|---|---|---|---|---|---|---|---|---|
| Test |  |  |  |  |  |  |  |  |  |  |  |  |  |  |  |  |  |  |
| All First | 14 | 24 | 4 | 847 | 163 * | 42.35 | 1 | 5 | 9 | - | 12 | 1 | 51 | 1 | 51.00 | 1-11 | - | - |
| 1-day Int |  |  |  |  |  |  |  |  |  |  |  |  |  |  |  |  |  |  |
| NatWest | 1 | 1 | 0 | 68 | 68 | 68.00 | - | 1 | 1 | - |  |  |  |  |  |  |  |  |
| B & H | 3 | 3 | 0 | 70 | 39 | 23.33 | - | - | - | - |  |  |  |  |  |  |  |  |
| Sunday | 1 | 1 | 0 | 14 | 14 | 14.00 | - | - | 2 | - |  |  |  |  |  |  |  |  |

## Career Performances

|  | M | Inns | NO | Runs | HS | Avge | 100s | 50s | Ct | St | Balls | Runs | Wkts | Avge | Best | 5wI | 10wM |
|---|---|---|---|---|---|---|---|---|---|---|---|---|---|---|---|---|---|
| Test |  |  |  |  |  |  |  |  |  |  |  |  |  |  |  |  |  |
| All First | 19 | 28 | 5 | 865 | 163 * | 37.60 | 1 | 5 | 11 | - | 72 | 51 | 1 | 51.00 | 1-11 | - | - |
| 1-day Int |  |  |  |  |  |  |  |  |  |  |  |  |  |  |  |  |  |
| NatWest | 1 | 1 | 0 | 68 | 68 | 68.00 | - | 1 | 1 | - |  |  |  |  |  |  |  |
| B & H | 3 | 3 | 0 | 70 | 39 | 23.33 | - | - | - | - |  |  |  |  |  |  |  |
| Sunday | 1 | 1 | 0 | 14 | 14 | 14.00 | - | - | 2 | - |  |  |  |  |  |  |  |

# SWANN, A. J. Northamptonshire

**Name:** Alec James Swann
**Role:** Right-hand opening bat
**Born:** 26 October 1976, Northampton
**Height:** 6ft 2in **Weight:** 11st
**Nickname:** Swanny, Ron
**County debut:** No first-team appearance
**Parents:** Raymond and Mavis
**Marital status:** Single
**Family links with cricket:** Father has played
for Northumberland, Bedfordshire,
Northamptonshire 2nd XI and England
Amateurs. Brother Graeme has played for
England U14 and U15 and Northamptonshire
2nd XI
**Education:** Sponne Comprehensive,
Towcester
**Qualifications:** 9 GCSEs and 4 A-levels
**Off-season:** Playing in Australia
**Overseas teams played for:** Wallsend, NSW,
Australia 1995-96
**Cricketers particularly admired:** Mark and Steve Waugh, Robin Smith, Russell
Warren
**Other sports followed:** Football (Newcastle and Liverpool) and most other sports
except athletics
**Injuries:** Broken bone in left hand, out for six weeks
**Relaxations:** Listening to music, especially Pink Floyd, Simple Minds and INXS,
reading political thrillers, watching sports, videos and films
**Extras:** Played for England Schools U15 and U19. Opened batting for Bedfordshire
(with father in Minor Counties game). *Daily Telegraph* U15 Young Cricketer of the Year
1992. Midlands Club Cricket Conference Young Cricketer of the Year 1992
**Opinions on cricket:** '2nd XI cricket should be played over four days, club cricket

could also be played over more than one afternoon. Tea interval should be half an hour and there should be 15 minutes between innings. Batting gloves need to be reinforced, there must be some foam or plastic available that could prevent hand/finger damage.'

# SYMONDS, A.                    Gloucestershire

**Name:** Andrew Symonds
**Role:** Right-hand bat, off-spin bowler
**Born:** 9 June 1975, Birmingham
**County debut:** 1995
**1000 runs in a season:** 1
**1st-Class 50s:** 9
**1st-Class 100s:** 6
**1st-Class 200s:** 1
**1st-Class catches:** 10
**Place in batting averages:** 11th av. 55.30
**Marital status:** Single
**Off-season:** Playing in Australia
**Overseas teams played for:** Australian
Cricket Academy 1993-94; Queensland Colts
1993-94; Queensland 1994-95
**Extras:** In his first season of first-class cricket
he scored a century for Queensland against
England on their 1994-95 tour of Australia.
Born in England, he has been brought up in
Australia and is a product of the Australian Cricket Academy. Hit a world record number of sixes during his innings of 254 not out against Glamorgan in 1995. Voted the Professional Cricketers' Association Young Player of the Year. Turned down the invitation to tour with England A so that he could remain eligible to play for Australia
**Best batting:** 254* Gloucestershire v Glamorgan, Abergavenny 1995
**Best bowling:** 3-77 Queensland v New South Wales, Sydney 1994-95

## 1995 Season

|        | M  | Inns | NO | Runs | HS   | Avge  | 100s | 50s | Ct | St | O  | M | Runs | Wkts | Avge   | Best | 5wI | 10wM |
|--------|----|------|----|------|------|-------|------|-----|----|----|----|---|------|------|--------|------|-----|------|
| Test   |    |      |    |      |      |       |      |     |    |    |    |   |      |      |        |      |     |      |
| All First | 18 | 31 | 5 | 1438 | 254 * | 55.30 | 4 | 9 | 8 | - | 38 | 9 | 100 | 1 | 100.00 | 1-13 | - | - |
| 1-day Int |  |      |    |      |      |       |      |     |    |    |    |   |      |      |        |      |     |      |
| NatWest | 3 | 3 | 0 | 79 | 48 | 26.33 | - | - | - | - | 9 | 0 | 45 | 0 | - |  | - | - |
| B & H | 6 | 6 | 0 | 180 | 95 | 30.00 | - | 1 | 1 | - |  |  |  |  |  |  |  |  |
| Sunday | 15 | 15 | 2 | 391 | 69 | 30.07 | - | 1 | 6 | - | 14 | 1 | 61 | 4 | 15.25 | 3-38 | - |  |

## Career Performances

|  | M | Inns | NO | Runs | HS | Avge | 100s | 50s | Ct | St | Balls | Runs | Wkts | Avge | Best | 5wI | 10wM |
|---|---|---|---|---|---|---|---|---|---|---|---|---|---|---|---|---|---|
| Test | | | | | | | | | | | | | | | | | |
| All First | 23 | 39 | 6 | 1762 | 254 * | 53.39 | 6 | 9 | 10 | - | 522 | 298 | 5 | 59.60 | 3-77 | - | - |
| 1-day Int | | | | | | | | | | | | | | | | | |
| NatWest | 3 | 3 | 0 | 79 | 48 | 26.33 | - | - | - | - | 54 | 45 | 0 | - | | - | - |
| B & H | 6 | 6 | 0 | 180 | 95 | 30.00 | - | 1 | 1 | - | | | | | | | |
| Sunday | 15 | 15 | 2 | 391 | 69 | 30.07 | - | 1 | 6 | - | 84 | 61 | 4 | 15.25 | 3-38 | - | |

# TAYLOR, C. W. Middlesex

**Name:** Charles William Taylor
**Role:** Left-hand bat, left-arm fast-medium bowler
**Born:** 12 August 1966, Banbury, Oxfordshire
**Height:** 6ft 5in **Weight:** 14st
**Nickname:** Farmer
**County debut:** 1990
**1st-Class 5 w. in innings:** 1
**1st-Class catches:** 6
**Strike rate:** (career 61.84)
**Parents:** Richard and Ann
**Marital status:** Single
**Family links with cricket:** Brother plays for Banbury, father played village cricket for Sandford St Martin
**Education:** Spendlove Comprehensive School, Charlbury; North Oxon Technical College
**Qualifications:** 1 O-level, City & Guilds Certificate in Agriculture
**Career outside cricket:** Farmer
**Off-season:** Working on the family farm
**Overseas teams played for:** Cricketers Club, New South Wales 1988-89
**Cricketers particularly admired:** Ian Bishop, Mark Waugh, Paul Tew ('my first club captain')
**Injuries:** Knee injury, missed most of the season
**Other sports followed:** National Hunt racing, golf
**Relaxations:** Most kinds of sports
**Extras:** Returned figures of 5 for 33 in second first-class match as Middlesex gained an important win on the way to the 1990 Championship title. Retired from first-class cricket due to injury at the end of the 1995 season

**Best batting:** 28* Middlesex v Oxford University, The Parks 1993
**Best bowling:** 5-33 Middlesex v Yorkshire, Headingley 1990

## 1995 Season

| | M | Inns | NO | Runs | HS | Avge | 100s | 50s | Ct | St | O | M | Runs | Wkts | Avge | Best | 5wI | 10wM |
|---|---|---|---|---|---|---|---|---|---|---|---|---|---|---|---|---|---|---|
| Test | | | | | | | | | | | | | | | | | | |
| All First | 1 | 0 | 0 | 0 | 0 | - | - | - | - | - | 11 | 4 | 26 | 4 | 6.50 | 4-15 | - | - |
| 1-day Int | | | | | | | | | | | | | | | | | | |
| NatWest | | | | | | | | | | | | | | | | | | |
| B & H | | | | | | | | | | | | | | | | | | |
| Sunday | | | | | | | | | | | | | | | | | | |

## Career Performances

| | M | Inns | NO | Runs | HS | Avge | 100s | 50s | Ct | St | Balls | Runs | Wkts | Avge | Best | 5wI | 10wM |
|---|---|---|---|---|---|---|---|---|---|---|---|---|---|---|---|---|---|
| Test | | | | | | | | | | | | | | | | | |
| All First | 33 | 25 | 9 | 175 | 28 * | 10.93 | - | - | 6 | - | 4453 | 2421 | 72 | 33.62 | 5-33 | 1 | - |
| 1-day Int | | | | | | | | | | | | | | | | | |
| NatWest | 1 | 0 | 0 | 0 | 0 | - | - | - | - | - | 66 | 54 | 1 | 54.00 | 1-54 | - | |
| B & H | | | | | | | | | | | | | | | | | |
| Sunday | 11 | 3 | 2 | 8 | 3 * | 8.00 | - | - | 5 | - | 359 | 297 | 7 | 42.42 | 2-33 | - | |

# TAYLOR, J. P.　　　　Northamptonshire

**Name:** Jonathan Paul Taylor
**Role:** Left-hand bat, left-arm
fast-medium bowler
**Born:** 8 August 1964, Ashby-de-la-Zouch,
Leicestershire
**Height:** 6ft 2in **Weight:** 13st 7lbs
**Nickname:** Roadie, PT
**County debut:** 1988 (Derbyshire), 1991
(Northamptonshire)
**County cap:** 1992 (Northamptonshire)
**Test debut:** 1992-93
**Tests:** 2
**One-Day Internationals:** 1
**50 wickets in a season:** 3
**1st-Class 50s:** 3
**1st-Class 5 w. in innings:** 10
**1st-Class 10 w. in match:** 1
**1st-Class catches:** 35
**Place in batting averages:** 194th av. 21.82

**Place in bowling averages:** 60th av. 29.03 (1994 79th av. 31.69)
**Strike rate:** 58.33 (career 58.71)
**Parents:** Derek and Janet
**Wife and date of marriage:** Elaine Mary, 30 July 1993
**Children:** Christopher Paul, 8 July 1994
**Family links with cricket:** Father and brother played local league cricket
**Education:** Pingle School, Swadlincote, Derbyshire
**Qualifications:** 6 O-levels, NCA coaching certificate
**Off-season:** 'Coaching in Bedford as part of a new initiative devised by myself and Alan Fordham'
**Overseas tours:** Midland Club Cricket Conference to Australia 1990-91; England to India and Sri Lanka 1992-93; Northamptonshire to Natal 1993, to Zimbabwe 1995; England A to South Africa 1993-94
**Overseas teams played for:** Papakura, New Zealand 1984-85; Napier High School Old Boys, New Zealand 1985-86; North Kalgoorlie, Western Australia 1990-91; Great Boulder, Western Australia 1991-92
**Cricketers particularly admired:** Dennis Lillee, Bob Taylor, John Lever
**Other sports followed:** Soccer, rugby, basketball
**Injuries:** Groin strain
**Relaxations:** Watching videos, eating out, 'looking after hyper-active little boy, if you can call that relaxing!'
**Extras:** Spent four seasons on the staff at Derbyshire 1984-87 and played Minor Counties cricket for Staffordshire 1989-90. Won Man of the Match in the Bain Clarkson Final in 1987 for Derbyshire, after being released. Played first game at Lord's in NatWest Trophy final 1992. Called up as replacement during England A tour to South Africa 1993-94. Selected for England Indoor World Cup squad 1995
**Opinions on cricket:** 'The Sunday League should revert back to limited run-ups, but the coloured clothing and white ball should remain. More should be done by the counties to find winter employment for players staying at home.'
**Best batting:** 86 Northamptonshire v Durham, Northampton 1995
**Best bowling:** 7-23 Northamptonshire v Hampshire, Bournemouth 1992

## 1995 Season

|          | M  | Inns | NO | Runs | HS  | Avge  | 100s | 50s | Ct | St | O     | M   | Runs | Wkts | Avge  | Best | 5wl | 10wM |
|----------|----|------|----|------|-----|-------|------|-----|----|----|-------|-----|------|------|-------|------|-----|------|
| Test     |    |      |    |      |     |       |      |     |    |    |       |     |      |      |       |      |     |      |
| All First| 18 | 21   | 8  | 284  | 86  | 21.84 | -    | 2   | 6  | -  | 573.4 | 122 | 1713 | 59   | 29.03 | 7-50 | 2   | -    |
| 1-day Int|    |      |    |      |     |       |      |     |    |    |       |     |      |      |       |      |     |      |
| NatWest  | 5  | 2    | 1  | 0    | 0 * | 0.00  | -    | -   | -  | -  | 47.3  | 11  | 169  | 8    | 21.12 | 4-34 | -   |      |
| B & H    | 4  | 3    | 3  | 12   | 7 * | -     | -    | -   | 1  | -  | 28    | 5   | 107  | 3    | 35.66 | 1-15 | -   |      |
| Sunday   | 9  | 2    | 2  | 15   | 9 * | -     | -    | -   | 4  | -  | 59.1  | 1   | 275  | 6    | 45.83 | 3-23 | -   |      |

## Career Performances

|        | M  | Inns | NO | Runs | HS  | Avge  | 100s | 50s | Ct | St | Balls | Runs | Wkts | Avge  | Best | 5wI | 10wM |
|--------|----|------|----|------|-----|-------|------|-----|----|----|-------|------|------|-------|------|-----|------|
| Test   | 2  | 4    | 2  | 34   | 17* | 17.00 | -    | -   | -  | -  | 288   | 156  | 3    | 52.00 | 1-18 | -   | -    |
| All First | 99 | 101 | 43 | 739 | 86 | 12.74 | - | 3 | 35 | - | 16792 | 8671 | 286 | 30.31 | 7-23 | 10 | 1 |
| 1-day Int | 1 | 1 | 0 | 1 | 1 | 1.00 | - | - | - | - | 18 | 20 | 0 | - | - | - | |
| NatWest | 22 | 7 | 3 | 21 | 9 | 5.25 | - | - | 6 | - | 1335 | 834 | 31 | 26.90 | 4-34 | - | |
| B & H | 16 | 8 | 6 | 23 | 7* | 11.50 | - | - | 4 | - | 891 | 457 | 17 | 26.88 | 3-38 | - | |
| Sunday | 67 | 24 | 10 | 113 | 24 | 8.07 | - | - | 11 | - | 2959 | 2273 | 75 | 30.30 | 3-14 | - | |

# TAYLOR, N. R. Kent

**Name:** Neil Royston Taylor
**Role:** Right-hand bat, occasional off-spin bowler
**Born:** 21 July 1959, Farnborough, Kent
**Height:** 6ft 1in **Weight:** 15st
**Nickname:** Map
**County debut:** 1979
**County cap:** 1982
**Benefit:** 1992 (£131,000)
**1000 runs in a season:** 10
**1st-Class 50s:** 84
**1st-Class 100s:** 42
**1st-Class 200s:** 2
**1st-Class catches:** 151
**One-Day 100s:** 5
**Place in batting averages:** 58th av. 42.10 (1994 38th av. 43.70)
**Strike rate:** (career 98.43)
**Parents:** Leonard and Audrey
**Wife and date of marriage:** Jane Claire, 25 September 1982
**Children:** Amy Louise, 7 November 1985; Lauren, 21 July 1988
**Family links with cricket:** Brother Colin played for Kent U19. Father played club cricket
**Education:** Cray Valley Technical High School
**Qualifications:** 8 O-levels, 2 A-levels, advanced cricket coach
**Off-season:** Coaching
**Overseas tours:** English Schools to India 1977-78; Kent to Canada 1978, to Zimbabwe 1992-93; Fred Rumsey XI to West Indies 1988
**Overseas teams played for:** Randburg, Johannesburg 1979-85; St Stithian's College, Johannesburg (as coach) 1980-85
**Cricketers particularly admired:** Chris Tavaré, Mark Benson, Mike Gatting, Robin Smith

**Other sports followed:** Rugby union, golf
**Injuries:** Broken finger/knuckle, out for four weeks
**Relaxations:** Music and reading (mainly biographies)
**Extras:** Made 110 on debut for Kent v Sri Lankans, 1979. Won four Man of the Match awards in his first five matches and scored three successive centuries in the B&H. Played for England B v Pakistan, 1982 and twice fielded as 12th man for England – v India in 1982 and v West Indies in 1988, both matches at The Oval. Holds Kent first and second wicket record partnerships with Mark Benson (300 v Derbyshire) and Simon Hinks (366 v Middlesex). Only Kent player to score 200 and 100 in a match twice (204 and 142 v Surrey, 111 and 203* v Sussex). Has scored 13 centuries at Canterbury, beating Frank Woolley and Colin Cowdrey. Provides a weekly contribution to Radio Kent through the summer
**Best batting:** 204 Kent v Surrey, Canterbury 1990
**Best bowling:** 2-20 Kent v Somerset, Canterbury 1985

### 1995 Season

| | M | Inns | NO | Runs | HS | Avge | 100s | 50s | Ct | St | O | M | Runs | Wkts | Avge | Best | 5wI | 10wM |
|---|---|---|---|---|---|---|---|---|---|---|---|---|---|---|---|---|---|---|
| Test | | | | | | | | | | | | | | | | | | |
| All First | 7 | 12 | 2 | 421 | 127 | 42.10 | 1 | 2 | - | - | | | | | | | | |
| 1-day Int | | | | | | | | | | | | | | | | | | |
| NatWest | 2 | 2 | 0 | 88 | 86 | 44.00 | - | 1 | - | - | | | | | | | | |
| B & H | 1 | 1 | 0 | 14 | 14 | 14.00 | - | - | 1 | - | | | | | | | | |
| Sunday | 2 | 2 | 0 | 47 | 34 | 23.50 | - | - | - | - | | | | | | | | |

### Career Performances

| | M | Inns | NO | Runs | HS | Avge | 100s | 50s | Ct | St | Balls | Runs | Wkts | Avge | Best | 5wI | 10wM |
|---|---|---|---|---|---|---|---|---|---|---|---|---|---|---|---|---|---|
| Test | | | | | | | | | | | | | | | | | |
| All First | 303 | 515 | 68 | 17772 | 204 | 39.75 | 42 | 84 | 151 | - | 1575 | 891 | 16 | 55.68 | 2-20 | - | - |
| 1-day Int | | | | | | | | | | | | | | | | | |
| NatWest | 31 | 31 | 1 | 802 | 86 | 26.73 | - | 5 | 6 | - | 143 | 86 | 6 | 14.33 | 3-29 | - | |
| B & H | 51 | 48 | 2 | 1872 | 137 | 40.69 | 5 | 7 | 11 | - | 12 | 5 | 0 | - | - | - | - |
| Sunday | 147 | 141 | 14 | 3887 | 95 | 30.60 | - | 24 | 37 | - | | | | | | | |

# TERRY, V. P.          Hampshire

**Name:** Vivian Paul Terry
**Role:** Right-hand bat, right-arm medium bowler, slip and outfielder
**Born:** 14 January 1959, Osnabruck, West Germany
**Height:** 6ft **Weight:** 13st 10lbs
**County debut:** 1978
**County cap:** 1983
**Benefit:** 1994 (£143,277)

**Test debut:** 1984
**Tests:** 2
**1000 runs in a season:** 11
**1st-Class 50s:** 79
**1st-Class 100s:** 38
**1st-Class catches:** 320
**One-Day 100s:** 12
**Place in batting averages:** 124th av. 30.66
(1994 60th av. 38.96)
**Parents:** Charles Michael and Patricia Mary
**Wife and date of marriage:** Bernadette
Mary, 4 June 1986
**Children:** Siobhan Catherine, 13 September
1987; Sean Paul, 1 August 1991
**Education:** Durlston Court, Hampshire;
Millfield School
**Qualifications:** 10 O-levels, 1 A-level,
advanced cricket coach, squash coach
**Off-season:** Playing and coaching in Perth
**Overseas tours:** English Schools to India 1977-78; English Counties XI to Zimbabwe
1984-85; Bournemouth Sports to Kenya 1986
**Overseas teams played for:** Northern Districts, Sydney 1979-80; Wakatu, Nelson
1980-81; Durban Collegians 1982-84; Perth 1986-88, 1991-92
**Cricketers particularly admired:** Chris Smith, Malcolm Marshall, Gary Sobers
**Other sports followed:** Most sports – golf, rugby, football
**Relaxations:** 'My kids and watching sport'
**Opinions on cricket:** 'Heading in the right direction but still need to play less.'
**Best batting:** 190 Hampshire v Sri Lankans, Southampton 1988

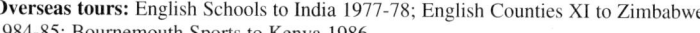

### 1995 Season

| | M | Inns | NO | Runs | HS | Avge | 100s | 50s | Ct | St | O | M | Runs | Wkts | Avge | Best | 5wI | 10wM |
|---|---|---|---|---|---|---|---|---|---|---|---|---|---|---|---|---|---|---|
| Test | | | | | | | | | | | | | | | | | | |
| All First | 20 | 35 | 2 | 1012 | 170 | 30.66 | 2 | 3 | 30 | - | | | | | | | | |
| 1-day Int | | | | | | | | | | | | | | | | | | |
| NatWest | 1 | 1 | 0 | 34 | 34 | 34.00 | - | - | 1 | - | | | | | | | | |
| B & H | 5 | 4 | 0 | 141 | 68 | 35.25 | - | 1 | 3 | - | | | | | | | | |
| Sunday | 8 | 8 | 0 | 95 | 33 | 11.87 | - | - | 3 | - | | | | | | | | |

84. Which three England players, all who played in the one-day series against South
Africa in 1995-96, were not included in the subsequent World Cup squad?

## Career Performances

| | M | Inns | NO | Runs | HS | Avge | 100s | 50s | Ct | St | Balls | Runs | Wkts | Avge | Best | 5wI | 10wM |
|---|---|---|---|---|---|---|---|---|---|---|---|---|---|---|---|---|---|
| Test | 2 | 3 | 0 | 16 | 8 | 5.33 | - | - | 2 | - | | | | | | | |
| All First | 285 | 481 | 43 | 16048 | 190 | 36.63 | 38 | 79 | 320 | - | 95 | 58 | 0 | - | - | - | - |
| 1-day Int | | | | | | | | | | | | | | | | | |
| NatWest | 39 | 37 | 4 | 1481 | 165 * | 44.87 | 4 | 9 | 16 | - | | | | | | | |
| B & H | 57 | 56 | 5 | 1874 | 134 | 36.74 | 2 | 13 | 24 | - | | | | | | | |
| Sunday | 201 | 187 | 25 | 5201 | 142 | 32.10 | 6 | 27 | 103 | - | | | | | | | |

# THOMAS, D. M. Hampshire

**Name:** David Michael Thomas
**Role:** Right-hand bat, right-arm
medium-fast bowler
**Born:** 16 November 1976, Frimley, Surrey
**Height:** 5ft 8in **Weight:** 11st 8lbs
**Nickname:** Spielberg, Swampy, Thommo
**County debut:** No first-team appearance
**Parents:** Geoff and Val
**Marital status:** Single
**Family links with cricket:** 'Both
grandfathers played to a reasonable standard
(RAF and Army). Dad plays once a year
(badly) and mum was a wicket-keeper as a girl'
**Education:** Barfield School; Lord
Wandsworth College
**Qualifications:** 9 GCSEs, 3 A-levels and
NCA coaching certificate
**Off-season:** 'Playing for West Torrens CC in
Australia and/or coaching at home'
**Overseas tours:** West of England U15 to West Indies 1992; College tour to Belgium !
**Overseas teams played for:** West Torrens, Adelaide 1994-95
**Cricketers particularly admired:** Dominic Cork, Ian Botham, Mike Atherton
**Other sports followed:** Rugby, golf, hockey, football, darts
**Injuries:** Stress fracture of back, out for six months from January to June
**Relaxations:** 'Enjoy watching *The Simpsons* or *Only Fools and Horses* in bed. Enjoy
having a drink with my mates and convincing pal Ian Nicolle it is his turn to drive.
Beating Damien Chisholm at golf'
**Extras:** Played England U15 versus South Africa. Won Hampshire Sports Achievement of
the Year for five for 81 in that series. A *Daily Telegraph* Bowling Award winner. Won
Hampshire U19 Performance of the Year award for 133 not out and five for 34 versus
Somerset

**Opinions on cricket:** 'I haven't been on the staff long enough to comment, but I think that the first team play too much.'

# THOMAS, P                                    Worcestershire

**Name:** Paul Thomas
**Role:** Right-hand bat, right-arm fast bowler
**Height:** 5ft 9in  **Weight:** 11st 8lbs
**Born:** 3 June 1971, Dudley
**Nickname:** Thommo
**County debut:** 1995
**1st-Class 5 w. in innings:** 1
**1st-Class catches:** 1
**Place in bowling averages:** 139th av 47.09
**Strike rate:** 70.03 (career 70.03)
**Parents:** Clifford and Myrtle
**Marital status:** Single
**Family links with cricket:** Father is a great fan of the game. Brothers play
**Education:** Broadway School
**Off-season:** Playing club cricket in Australia
**Extras:** Awarded Second XI cap in 1995
**Best batting:** 25 Worcestershire v Warwickshire, Edgbaston 1995
**Best bowling:** 5-70 Worcestershire v West Indies, Worcester 1995

## 1995 Season

|           | M  | Inns | NO | Runs | HS | Avge | 100s | 50s | Ct | St | O     | M  | Runs | Wkts | Avge  | Best | 5wl | 10wM |
|-----------|----|------|----|------|----|------|------|-----|----|----|-------|----|------|------|-------|------|-----|------|
| Test      |    |      |    |      |    |      |      |     |    |    |       |    |      |      |       |      |     |      |
| All First | 14 | 15   | 4  | 57   | 25 | 5.18 | -    | -   | 1  | -  | 386.4 | 67 | 1554 | 33   | 47.09 | 5-70 | 1-  |      |
| 1-day Int |    |      |    |      |    |      |      |     |    |    |       |    |      |      |       |      |     |      |
| NatWest   | 1  | 0    | 0  | 0    | 0  | -    | -    | -   | -  | -  | 10    | 2  | 30   | 2    | 15.00 | 2-30 | -   |      |
| B & H     |    |      |    |      |    |      |      |     |    |    |       |    |      |      |       |      |     |      |
| Sunday    |    |      |    |      |    |      |      |     |    |    |       |    |      |      |       |      |     |      |

## Career Performances

|           | M  | Inns | NO | Runs | HS | Avge | 100s | 50s | Ct | St | Balls | Runs | Wkts | Avge  | Best | 5wl | 10wM |
|-----------|----|------|----|------|----|------|------|-----|----|----|-------|------|------|-------|------|-----|------|
| Test      |    |      |    |      |    |      |      |     |    |    |       |      |      |       |      |     |      |
| All First | 14 | 15   | 4  | 57   | 25 | 5.18 | -    | -   | 1  | -  | 2320  | 1554 | 33   | 47.09 | 5-70 | 1   | -    |
| 1-day Int |    |      |    |      |    |      |      |     |    |    |       |      |      |       |      |     |      |
| NatWest   | 1  | 0    | 0  | 0    | 0  | -    | -    | -   | -  | -  | 60    | 30   | 2    | 15.00 | 2-30 | -   |      |
| B & H     |    |      |    |      |    |      |      |     |    |    |       |      |      |       |      |     |      |
| Sunday    |    |      |    |      |    |      |      |     |    |    |       |      |      |       |      |     |      |

# THOMAS, S. D. Glamorgan

**Name:** Stuart Darren Thomas
**Role:** Left-hand bat, right-arm
medium-fast bowler
**Born:** 25 January 1975, Morriston
**Height:** 5ft 11in **Weight:** 13st 3lbs
**Nickname:** Tomo, Dough Boy, Teddy, Ice
**County debut:** 1992
**1st-Class 50s:** 3
**1st-Class 5 w. in innings:** 4
**1st-Class catches:** 7
**Place in batting averages:** 126th av. 30.09
**Place in bowling averages:** 143rd av. 48.42
**Strike rate:** 65.03 (career 52.25)
**Parents:** Stuart and Anne
**Marital.status:** Engaged to Ceris
**Family links with cricket:** Dad played for
local 1st XI
**Education:** Craig Comprehensive;
Neath Tertiary College

**Qualifications:** 4 GCSEs, BTEC National Diploma in Sports Science, NCA coaching
certificate
**Off-season:** Playing and coaching in Bloemfontein, Orange Free State
**Overseas tours:** England U18 to South Africa 1992-93; Glamorgan to South Africa
1992-93, to Portugal 1994, to Zimbabwe 1995; England U19 to Sri Lanka 1993-94
**Cricketers particularly admired:** Steve Barwick, Steve Watkin, Phil Newport,
Courtney Walsh, Matthew Maynard
**Other sports followed:** Rugby union and league (Warrington)
**Injuries:** Rib cartilage, missed six weeks
**Relaxations:** 'Spending a lot of time horseriding with my girlfriend. Surfing off the
Gower coastline. Socialising with a few pints.'
**Extras:** Youngest player to take five wickets on debut v Derbyshire in 1992 and finished
eighth in national bowling averages. BBC Welsh Young Sports Personality 1992. Played
last U19 Test against India at Edgbaston 1994. Broke Alan Wilkins, (Glamorgan) best
Benson and Hedges bowling record on his debut in the competition with six for 20 in
1995
**Opinions on cricket:** 'Enjoy coloured clothing in Sunday League. I think that third
umpires should be used in all one-day games as there are so many close decisions made.
Happy to see the four-day game. This has showed a bigger advance of young cricketers
and gives more opportunities for the players as there is more time to play cricket.'
**Best batting:** 78 Glamorgan v Gloucestershire, Abergavenny 1995
**Best bowling:** 5-76 Glamorgan v Worcestershire, Worcester 1993

## 1995 Season

| | M | Inns | NO | Runs | HS | Avge | 100s | 50s | Ct | St | O | M | Runs | Wkts | Avge | Best | 5wI | 10wM |
|---|---|---|---|---|---|---|---|---|---|---|---|---|---|---|---|---|---|---|
| Test | | | | | | | | | | | | | | | | | | |
| All First | 11 | 15 | 4 | 331 | 78 * | 30.09 | - | 3 | 4 | - | 303.3 | 51 | 1356 | 28 | 48.42 | 5-99 | 1 | - |
| 1-day Int | | | | | | | | | | | | | | | | | | |
| NatWest | 1 | 0 | 0 | 0 | 0 | - | - | - | - | - | 9 | 1 | 36 | 0 | - | | - | - |
| B & H | 1 | 0 | 0 | 0 | 0 | - | - | - | 1 | - | 9.2 | 3 | 20 | 6 | 3.33 | 6-20 | 1 | |
| Sunday | 3 | 1 | 0 | 19 | 19 | 19.00 | - | - | - | - | 19 | 0 | 94 | 4 | 23.50 | 3-44 | - | |

## Career Performances

| | M | Inns | NO | Runs | HS | Avge | 100s | 50s | Ct | St | Balls | Runs | Wkts | Avge | Best | 5wI | 10wM |
|---|---|---|---|---|---|---|---|---|---|---|---|---|---|---|---|---|---|
| Test | | | | | | | | | | | | | | | | | |
| All First | 23 | 32 | 12 | 417 | 78 * | 20.85 | - | 3 | 7 | - | 3710 | 2533 | 71 | 35.67 | 5-76 | 4 | - |
| 1-day Int | | | | | | | | | | | | | | | | | |
| NatWest | 1 | 0 | 0 | 0 | 0 | - | - | - | - | - | 54 | 36 | 0 | - | | - | - |
| B & H | 1 | 0 | 0 | 0 | 0 | - | - | - | 1 | - | 56 | 20 | 6 | 3.33 | 6-20 | 1 | |
| Sunday | 6 | 1 | 0 | 19 | 19 | 19.00 | - | - | 1 | - | 184 | 142 | 5 | 28.40 | 3-44 | - | |

# THOMPSON, D. J.      Lancashire

**Name:** David James Thompson
**Role:** Right-hand bat, right-arm fast bowler
**Born:** 11 March 1976
**Height:** 6ft 3in
**Nickname:** Thommo
**County debut:** 1994 (Surrey)
**Marital status:** Single
**Education:** Ernest Bevin School;
Westminster College
**Qualifications:** 8 GCSEs
**Off-season:** Touring with England U19
**Overseas tours:** England U19 to
West Indies 1994-95
**Cricketers particularly admired:**
Michael Holding 'because of his sheer pace'
**Other sports followed:** Football, baseball
**Relaxations:** 'Listening to reggae music,
spending time with little cousins and family'
**Extras:** Played for Charlton FC and was
offered YTS terms, but chose cricket 'because I enjoy it much more'. Released by Surrey
at the end of the 1994 season and joined Lancashire in 1995
**Opinions on cricket:** 'I think that the rule for one bouncer is silly, because a proper

bouncer is never over head height and you can therefore bowl more than one in an over.'
**Best batting:** 22 Surrey v Oxford University, The Oval 1994
**Best bowling:** 2-37 Surrey v Oxford University, The Oval 1994

## 1995 Season (did not make any first-class or one-day appearances)

### Career Performances

|  | M | Inns | NO | Runs | HS | Avge | 100s | 50s | Ct | St | Balls | Runs | Wkts | Avge | Best | 5wI | 10wM |
|---|---|---|---|---|---|---|---|---|---|---|---|---|---|---|---|---|---|
| Test | | | | | | | | | | | | | | | | | |
| All First | 1 | 2 | 0 | 39 | 22 | 19.50 | - | - | - | - | 162 | 123 | 3 | 41.00 | 2-37 | - | - |
| 1-day Int | | | | | | | | | | | | | | | | | |
| NatWest | | | | | | | | | | | | | | | | | |
| B & H | | | | | | | | | | | | | | | | | |
| Sunday | | | | | | | | | | | | | | | | | |

# THOMPSON, J. B.     Kent

**Name:** Julian Barton Thompson
**Role:** Right-hand bat, right-arm
fast-medium bowler
**Born:** 28 October 1968, Cape Town,
South Africa
**Height:** 6ft 4in **Weight:** 13st 7lbs
**Nickname:** Thommo, Doc
**County debut:** 1994
**1st-Class catches:** 1
**Parents:** John and Joyce
**Marital status:** Single
**Family links with cricket:**
Father played club cricket
**Education:** The Judd School, Tonbridge,
Kent; Guy's Hospital Medical School,
London
**Qualifications:** MB BS
**Career outside cricket:** Doctor
**Overseas tours:**

University of London to India 1991
**Overseas teams played for:** Northern Districts, Sydney 1987-88
**Cricketers particularly admired:** Carl Hooper
**Other sports followed:** Golf, football
**Relaxations:** Golf, squash, P.G. Wodehouse, eating
**Extras:** Dismissed Brian Lara twice for a duck in Kent's game against the West Indies

in 1995 – Brian Lara's only pair in first-class cricket
**Best batting:** 40* Kent v Cambridge University, Folkestone 1995
**Best bowling:** 2-10 Kent v Cambridge University, Folkestone 1995

## 1995 Season

| | M | Inns | NO | Runs | HS | Avge | 100s | 50s | Ct | St | O | M | Runs | Wkts | Avge | Best | 5wI | 10wM |
|---|---|---|---|---|---|---|---|---|---|---|---|---|---|---|---|---|---|---|
| Test | | | | | | | | | | | | | | | | | | |
| All First | 3 | 6 | 2 | 83 | 40 * | 20.75 | - | - | 1 | - | 38 | 8 | 157 | 6 | 26.16 | 2-10 | - | - |
| 1-day Int | | | | | | | | | | | | | | | | | | |
| NatWest | | | | | | | | | | | | | | | | | | |
| B & H | | | | | | | | | | | | | | | | | | |
| Sunday | 2 | 1 | 1 | 0 | 0 * | - | - | - | 1 | - | 12 | 1 | 79 | 2 | 39.50 | 2-27 | - | |

## Career Performances

| | M | Inns | NO | Runs | HS | Avge | 100s | 50s | Ct | St | Balls | Runs | Wkts | Avge | Best | 5wI | 10wM |
|---|---|---|---|---|---|---|---|---|---|---|---|---|---|---|---|---|---|
| Test | | | | | | | | | | | | | | | | | |
| All First | 4 | 8 | 3 | 86 | 40 * | 17.20 | - | - | 1 | - | 426 | 277 | 7 | 39.57 | 2-10 | - | - |
| 1-day Int | | | | | | | | | | | | | | | | | |
| NatWest | | | | | | | | | | | | | | | | | |
| B & H | | | | | | | | | | | | | | | | | |
| Sunday | 4 | 2 | 2 | 3 | 3 * | - | - | - | 1 | - | 132 | 124 | 2 | 62.00 | 2-27 | - | |

# THORPE, G. P.     Surrey

**Name:** Graham Paul Thorpe
**Role:** Left-hand bat, occasional right-arm medium bowler
**Born:** 1 August 1969, Farnham
**Height:** 5ft 10in **Weight:** 11st 7lbs
**Nickname:** Chalky
**County debut:** 1988
**County cap:** 1991
**Test debut:** 1993
**Tests:** 21
**One-Day Internationals:** 13
**1000 runs in a season:** 6
**1st-Class 50s:** 64
**1st-Class 100s:** 18
**1st-Class 200s:** 1
**1st-Class catches:** 121
**One-Day 100s:** 5
**Place in batting averages:** 62nd av. 40.76

(1994 12th av. 54.09)
**Strike rate:** (career 86.77)
**Parents:** Geoff and Toni
**Marital status:** Married
**Family links with cricket:** Both brothers play for Farnham, father also plays cricket and mother is 'professional scorer'
**Education:** Weydon Comprehensive; Farnham Sixth Form College
**Qualifications:** 7 O-levels, PE Diploma
**Off-season:** Touring with England
**Overseas tours:** England A to Zimbabwe and Kenya 1989-90, to Pakistan 1990-91, to Bermuda and West Indies 1991-92, to Australia 1992-93; England to West Indies 1993-94, to Australia 1994-95, to South Africa 1995-96, to India and Pakistan (World Cup) 1996
**Cricketers particularly admired:** Viv Richards, Grahame Clinton, David Gower
**Other sports followed:** Football, tennis
**Extras:** Played for English Schools cricket U15 and U19 and England Schools football U18. Scored a century against Australia on his Test debut at Trent Bridge 1993
**Best batting:** 216 Surrey v Somerset, The Oval 1992
**Best bowling:** 4-40 Surrey v Australians, The Oval 1993

## 1995 Season

| | M | Inns | NO | Runs | HS | Avge | 100s | 50s | Ct | St | O | M | Runs | Wkts | Avge | Best | 5wI | 10wM |
|---|---|---|---|---|---|---|---|---|---|---|---|---|---|---|---|---|---|---|
| Test | 6 | 12 | 0 | 506 | 94 | 42.16 | - | 5 | 2 | - | | | | | | | | |
| All First | 16 | 30 | 0 | 1223 | 152 | 40.76 | 2 | 9 | 13 | - | 23 | 4 | 59 | 2 | 29.50 | 2-42 | - | - |
| 1-day Int | 3 | 3 | 0 | 61 | 28 | 20.33 | - | - | 1 | - | | | | | | | | |
| NatWest | 1 | 1 | 0 | 32 | 32 | 32.00 | - | - | 1 | - | | | | | | | | |
| B & H | 2 | 2 | 0 | 30 | 25 | 15.00 | - | - | - | - | | | | | | | | |
| Sunday | 10 | 10 | 0 | 342 | 112 | 34.20 | 1 | 3 | 1 | - | 1 | 0 | 14 | 0 | - | | - | - |

## Career Performances

| | M | Inns | NO | Runs | HS | Avge | 100s | 50s | Ct | St | Balls | Runs | Wkts | Avge | Best | 5wI | 10wM |
|---|---|---|---|---|---|---|---|---|---|---|---|---|---|---|---|---|---|
| Test | 21 | 41 | 3 | 1658 | 123 | 43.63 | 2 | 14 | 21 | - | 48 | 15 | 0 | - | - | - | - |
| All First | 167 | 282 | 36 | 10393 | 216 | 42.24 | 18 | 64 | 121 | - | 1909 | 1108 | 22 | 50.36 | 4-40 | - | - |
| 1-day Int | 13 | 13 | 0 | 353 | 89 | 27.15 | - | 2 | 6 | - | | | | | | | |
| NatWest | 18 | 17 | 4 | 690 | 145 * | 53.07 | 1 | 5 | 9 | - | 13 | 12 | 0 | - | - | - | |
| B & H | 24 | 24 | 2 | 782 | 103 | 35.54 | 1 | 5 | 9 | - | 168 | 131 | 4 | 32.75 | 3-35 | - | |
| Sunday | 95 | 88 | 12 | 2741 | 115 * | 36.06 | 3 | 21 | 31 | - | 318 | 307 | 8 | 38.37 | 3-21 | - | |

# THURSFIELD, M. J.     Hampshire

**Name:** Martin John Thursfield
**Role:** Right-hand bat, right-arm
medium-fast bowler
**Born:** 14 December 1971, South Shields
**Height:** 6ft 4in **Weight:** 14st
**Nickname:** Thursy
**County debut:** 1990
**1st-Class 5 w. in innings:** 1
**1st-Class catches:** 1
**Place in bowling averages:**
(1994 65th av. 330.82)
**Strike rate:** (career 67.30)
**Parents:** Anthony John and Maureen
**Marital status:** Single
**Family links with cricket:** Great-grandfather
played for Yorkshire, and father is a keen
club cricketer
**Education:** Boldon Comprehensive
**Qualifications:** GCSEs, NCA coaching
certificate
**Overseas tours:** England YC to New Zealand 1990-91
**Cricketers particularly admired:** Robin Smith, Malcolm Marshall, Allan Donald
**Other sports followed:** Football, golf
**Relaxations:** Playing golf, watching football and sleeping
**Extras:** Bowled two balls with broken leg in first England YC one-day International v
New Zealand 1990-91. One of the youngest golfers in the country to achieve a hole in
one, aged 10
**Best batting:** 47 Hampshire v Glamorgan, Southampton 1994
**Best bowling:** 6-130 Hampshire v Middlesex, Southampton 1994

---

### 1995 Season

| | M | Inns | NO | Runs | HS | Avge | 100s | 50s | Ct | St | O | M | Runs | Wkts | Avge | Best | 5wI | 10wM |
|---|---|---|---|---|---|---|---|---|---|---|---|---|---|---|---|---|---|---|
| Test | | | | | | | | | | | | | | | | | | |
| All First | 3 | 3 | 0 | 46 | 30 | 15.33 | - | - | - | - | 72 | 13 | 238 | 4 | 59.50 | 3-108 | - | - |
| 1-day Int | | | | | | | | | | | | | | | | | | |
| NatWest | | | | | | | | | | | | | | | | | | |
| B & H | 3 | 2 | 2 | 4 | 4 * | - | - | - | - | - | 24 | 2 | 119 | 2 | 59.50 | 2-40 | - | |
| Sunday | 6 | 3 | 1 | 12 | 7 | 6.00 | - | - | 1 | - | 44 | 3 | 224 | 3 | 74.66 | 2-26 | - | |

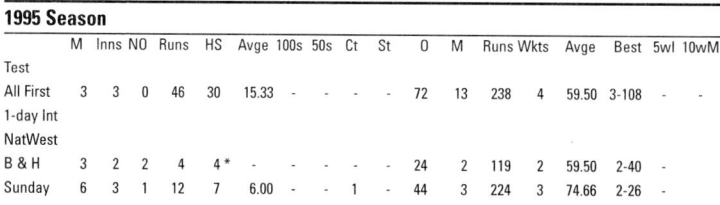

## Career Performances

|  | M | Inns | NO | Runs | HS | Avge | 100s | 50s | Ct | St | Balls | Runs | Wkts | Avge | Best | 5wI | 10wM |
|---|---|---|---|---|---|---|---|---|---|---|---|---|---|---|---|---|---|
| Test |  |  |  |  |  |  |  |  |  |  |  |  |  |  |  |  |  |
| All First | 17 | 19 | 3 | 188 | 47 | 11.75 | - | - | 1 | - | 2016 | 1070 | 30 | 35.66 | 6-130 | 1 | - |
| 1-day Int |  |  |  |  |  |  |  |  |  |  |  |  |  |  |  |  |  |
| NatWest |  |  |  |  |  |  |  |  |  |  |  |  |  |  |  |  |  |  |
| B & H | 3 | 2 | 2 | 4 | 4* | - | - | - | - | - | 144 | 119 | 2 | 59.50 | 2-40 | - |  |
| Sunday | 18 | 9 | 3 | 31 | 9 | 5.16 | - | - | 3 | - | 786 | 631 | 15 | 42.06 | 3-31 | - |  |

# TITCHARD, S. P. Lancashire

**Name:** Stephen Paul Titchard
**Role:** Right-hand bat, right-arm
medium bowler
**Born:** 17 December 1967, Warrington,
Cheshire
**Height:** 6ft 3in **Weight:** 15st
**Nickname:** Titch, Stainy, Tyrone
**County debut:** 1990
**1st-Class 50s:** 19
**1st-Class 100s:** 2
**1st-Class catches:** 39
**Place in batting averages:** 116th av. 31.68
(1994 151st av. 26.14)
**Parents:** Alan and Margaret
**Marital status:** Single
**Family links with cricket:** Father, uncle and
two brothers have played for Grappenhall 1st
XI in the Manchester Association League.
Father also represented the Army
**Education:** Lymm County High School; Priestley College
**Qualifications:** 3 O-levels, NCA Senior Coaching Award
**Career outside cricket:** Coach
**Overseas tours:** Lancashire to Tasmania and Western Australia 1990, to Western
Australia 1991, to Johannesburg 1992
**Overseas teams played for:** South Canberra, Australia 1991-92
**Cricketers particularly admired:** Graham Gooch, Malcolm Marshall
**Other sports followed:** Football (Manchester City) and rugby league (Warrington)
**Relaxations:** Snooker, golf, 'most sports'
**Extras:** Played for England U19. Made record scores for Manchester Association U18
(200*) and Cheshire Schools U19 (203*)
**Opinions on cricket:** 'In Championship games, the day should comprise of three two-

hour sessions, with an extended tea break of at least ten minutes!'
**Best batting:** 135 Lancashire v Nottinghamshire, Old Trafford 1991

## 1995 Season

| | M | Inns | NO | Runs | HS | Avge | 100s | 50s | Ct | St | O | M | Runs | Wkts | Avge | Best | 5wI | 10wM |
|---|---|---|---|---|---|---|---|---|---|---|---|---|---|---|---|---|---|---|
| Test | | | | | | | | | | | | | | | | | | |
| All First | 13 | 24 | 2 | 697 | 130 | 31.68 | 1 | 5 | 6 | - | | | | | | | | |
| 1-day Int | | | | | | | | | | | | | | | | | | |
| NatWest | 1 | 1 | 0 | 92 | 92 | 92.00 | - | 1 | 1 | - | | | | | | | | |
| B & H | | | | | | | | | | | | | | | | | | |
| Sunday | 6 | 6 | 0 | 168 | 53 | 28.00 | - | 1 | - | - | | | | | | | | |

## Career Performances

| | M | Inns | NO | Runs | HS | Avge | 100s | 50s | Ct | St | Balls | Runs | Wkts | Avge | Best | 5wI | 10wM |
|---|---|---|---|---|---|---|---|---|---|---|---|---|---|---|---|---|---|
| Test | | | | | | | | | | | | | | | | | |
| All First | 56 | 99 | 6 | 2826 | 135 | 30.38 | 2 | 19 | 39 | - | | | | | | | |
| 1-day Int | | | | | | | | | | | | | | | | | |
| NatWest | 3 | 3 | 0 | 116 | 92 | 38.66 | - | 1 | 1 | - | | | | | | | |
| B & H | 3 | 3 | 0 | 101 | 82 | 33.66 | - | 1 | 1 | - | | | | | | | |
| Sunday | 27 | 27 | 3 | 664 | 96 | 27.66 | - | 3 | 4 | - | | | | | | | |

# TOLLEY, C. M.                 Nottinghamshire

**Name:** Christopher Mark Tolley
**Role:** Right-hand bat, left-arm
medium bowler
**Born:** 30 December 1967, Kidderminster
**Height:** 5ft 9in **Weight:** 12st
**Nickname:** Treefrog, Red Dog
**County debut:** 1989 (Worcestershire)
**County cap:** 1993 (Worcestershire)
**1st-Class 50s:** 3
**1st-Class 5 w. in innings:** 1
**1st-Class catches:** 27
**Place in batting averages:**
(1994 182nd av. 22.50)
**Strike rate:** (career 75.30)
**Parents:** Ray and Liz
**Marital status:** Single
**Family links with cricket:** Father played
local league; brother Richard plays in the
Birmingham League

**Education:** Oldswinford Primary School; Redhill Comprehensive School; King Edward VI College, Stourbridge; Loughborough University
**Qualifications:** 9 O-levels, 3 A-levels, BSc (Hons)  PE Sports Science & Recreation Management. Qualified teacher status and level 2 hockey coach
**Career outside cricket:** Teaching
**Off-season:** Teaching until Christmas
**Overseas tours:** British Universities Sports Federation tour to Barbados October 1989; Worcestershire to Zimbabwe and South Africa
**Cricketers particularly admired:** Ian Botham, Richard Hadlee, Graeme Hick
**Other sports followed:** Hockey
**Injuries:** Broken thumb ('second day of pre-season'), out for one month
**Relaxations:** Food, cooking and wine
**Extras:** Played for English Schools U19 in 1986 and for the Combined Universities in B&H Cup. Asked to be released by Worcestershire at the end of the 1995 season and has joined Nottinghamshire for the 1996 season
**Best batting:** 84 Worcestershire v Derbyshire, Derby 1994
**Best bowling:** 5-55 Worcestershire v Kent, Worcester 1993

## 1995 Season

| | M | Inns | NO | Runs | HS | Avge | 100s | 50s | Ct | St | O | M | Runs | Wkts | Avge | Best | 5wI | 10wM |
|---|---|---|---|---|---|---|---|---|---|---|---|---|---|---|---|---|---|---|
| Test | | | | | | | | | | | | | | | | | | |
| All First | 3 | 5 | 0 | 62 | 24 | 12.40 | - | - | 1 | - | 4 | 0 | 23 | 0 | - | - | - | - |
| 1-day Int | | | | | | | | | | | | | | | | | | |
| NatWest | | | | | | | | | | | | | | | | | | |
| B & H | 1 | 1 | 0 | 0 | 0 | 0.00 | - | - | - | - | | | | | | | | |
| Sunday | 2 | 2 | 0 | 44 | 30 | 22.00 | - | - | 1 | - | | | | | | | | |

## Career Performances

| | M | Inns | NO | Runs | HS | Avge | 100s | 50s | Ct | St | Balls | Runs | Wkts | Avge | Best | 5wI | 10wM |
|---|---|---|---|---|---|---|---|---|---|---|---|---|---|---|---|---|---|
| Test | | | | | | | | | | | | | | | | | |
| All First | 63 | 74 | 21 | 1105 | 84 | 20.84 | - | 3 | 27 | - | 7229 | 3463 | 96 | 36.07 | 5-55 | 1 | - |
| 1-day Int | | | | | | | | | | | | | | | | | |
| NatWest | 5 | 2 | 2 | 21 | 12 * | - | - | - | - | - | 252 | 148 | 6 | 24.66 | 3-25 | - | |
| B & H | 13 | 10 | 1 | 203 | 77 | 22.55 | - | 2 | 3 | - | 654 | 397 | 6 | 66.16 | 1-12 | - | |
| Sunday | 34 | 16 | 5 | 60 | 30 | 5.45 | - | - | 8 | - | 1024 | 812 | 28 | 29.00 | 4-50 | - | |

# TREAGUS, G. R.  Hampshire

**Name:** Glyn Robert Treagus
**Role:** Right-hand bat
**Born:** 10 December 1974, Rustington, Sussex
**Height:** 5ft 11in  **Weight:** 11st 11lbs
**Nickname:** Arthur, Grommit
**County debut:** No first-team appearance
**Parents:** Bob and Annette
**Marital status:** Single
**Family links with cricket:** 'Dad was offered a place on the county staff as a fast bowler but declined'
**Education:** Oakmount; King Edward VI, Southampton; Brighton University
**Qualifications:** 9 GCSEs, 2 A-levels, certificate of Higher Education
**Off-season:** Playing in South Africa
**Overseas tours:** King Edward VI tour to South Africa 1993
**Oversaes teams played for:** Queenstown, South Africa 1995-96
**Cricketers particularly admired:** Robin Smith, Malcolm Marshall, Mike Atherton
**Other sports followed:** Hockey, tennis, golf, football
**Relaxations:** 'Clubbing, relaxing on a beach, listening to and playing music'
**Extras:** *Daily Telegraph* U19 Batting Award (National). NAYC U19 and NCA YC U19 team 1994. Development of Excellence U19 XI in 1994
**Opinions on cricket:** 'Should be floodlit cricket in England. More restriction of fielders in one-day cricket.'

85. In Test history, which pair has the highest average for an opening partnership?

# TRESCOTHICK, M. E.    Somerset

**Name:** Marcus Edward Trescothick
**Role:** Left-hand bat, right-arm swing bowler,
reserve wicket-keeper
**Born:** 25 December 1975, Keynsham, Bristol
**Height:** 6ft 3in **Weight:** 14st 7lbs
**Nickname:** Rob Turner
**County debut:** 1993
**1st-Class 50s:** 9
**1st-Class 100s:** 3
**1st-Class catches:** 31
**One-Day 100s:** 2
**Place in batting averages:** 215th av. 18.95
(1994 24th av. 48.63)
**Parents:** Martyn and Lin
**Marital status:** Single
**Family links with cricket:** Father played for
Somerset 2nd XI; uncle played club cricket
**Education:** Sir Bernard Lovell School
**Qualifications:** 7 GCSEs
**Off-season:** Training and working
**Overseas tours:** England U18 to South Africa 1992-93; England U19 to Sri Lanka
1993-94, to West Indies (captain) 1994-95
**Cricketers particularly admired:** Neil Fairbrother, Jack Russell, Mark Lathwell
**Other sports followed:** Golf, football
**Relaxations:** Playing golf, repairing and renovating cricket bats and listening to music
**Extras:** Member of England U19 squad for home series against West Indies 1993. Man
of the Series against India U19 in 1994, scoring most runs in the series. Whittingdale
Young Player of the Month, August 1994. Took a hat-trick against Young Australia in
1995. Has now scored more than 1000 runs for England U19
**Opinions on cricket:** 'There should be some sort of retainer contract.'
**Best batting:** 151 Somerset v Northamptonshire, Northampton 1995
**Best bowling:** 4-36 Somerset v Young Australia, Taunton 1995

## 1995 Season

|  | M | Inns | NO | Runs | HS | Avge | 100s | 50s | Ct | St | O | M | Runs | Wkts | Avge | Best | 5wI | 10wM |
|---|---|---|---|---|---|---|---|---|---|---|---|---|---|---|---|---|---|---|
| Test |  |  |  |  |  |  |  |  |  |  |  |  |  |  |  |  |  |  |
| All First | 12 | 22 | 0 | 417 | 151 | 18.95 | 1 | 1 | 14 | - | 33 | 6 | 143 | 5 | 28.60 | 4-36 | - | - |
| 1-day Int |  |  |  |  |  |  |  |  |  |  |  |  |  |  |  |  |  |  |
| NatWest |  |  |  |  |  |  |  |  |  |  |  |  |  |  |  |  |  |  |
| B & H | 6 | 6 | 0 | 209 | 122 | 34.83 | 1 | 1 | 5 | - |  |  |  |  |  |  |  |  |
| Sunday | 8 | 8 | 0 | 82 | 27 | 10.25 | - | - | 2 | - |  |  |  |  |  |  |  |  |

## Career Performances

|  | M | Inns | NO | Runs | HS | Avge | 100s | 50s | Ct | St | Balls | Runs | Wkts | Avge | Best | 5wl | 10wM |
|---|---|---|---|---|---|---|---|---|---|---|---|---|---|---|---|---|---|
| Test |  |  |  |  |  |  |  |  |  |  |  |  |  |  |  |  |  |
| All First | 26 | 48 | 1 | 1355 | 151 | 28.82 | 3 | 9 | 31 | - | 198 | 143 | 5 | 28.60 | 4-36 | - | - |
| 1-day Int |  |  |  |  |  |  |  |  |  |  |  |  |  |  |  |  |  |
| NatWest | 3 | 3 | 0 | 174 | 116 | 58.00 | 1 | - | 1 | - |  |  |  |  |  |  |  |
| B & H | 6 | 6 | 0 | 209 | 122 | 34.83 | 1 | 1 | 5 | - |  |  |  |  |  |  |  |
| Sunday | 23 | 23 | 0 | 484 | 74 | 21.04 | - | 2 | 7 | - |  |  |  |  |  |  |  |

# TRUMP, H. R. J. Somerset

**Name:** Harvey Russell John Trump
**Role:** Right-hand bat, off-spin bowler, gully/slip fielder
**Born:** 11 October 1968, Taunton
**Height:** 6ft 1in **Weight:** 14st
**Nickname:** Trumpy, Club Foot
**County debut:** 1988
**County cap:** 1994
**50 wickets in a season:** 1
**1st-Class 5 w. in innings:** 9
**1st-Class 10 w. in match:** 2
**1st-Class catches:** 73
**Place in batting averages:** 233rd av. 17.25 (1994 223rd av. 17.25)
**Place in bowling averages:** 129th av. 43.62 (1994 87th av. 33.57)
**Strike rate:** 89.45 (career 79.02)
**Parents:** Gerald and Jackie
**Marital status:** Single
**Family links with cricket:** Father played for Somerset 2nd XI and captained Devon
**Education:** Millfield School; Chester College of Higher Education
**Qualifications:** 7 O-levels, 2 A-levels, BA (Hons)
**Career outside cricket:** Teaching at Stamford School, Lincolnshire
**Overseas tours:** England YC to Sri Lanka 1986-87, to Australia (Youth World Cup) 1987-88
**Cricketers particularly admired:** David Graveney, John Emburey, Viv Richards
**Other sports followed:** Hockey, rugby and most other sports
**Relaxations:** Theatre, cinema, crosswords, reading
**Extras:** Played county hockey for Somerset U19. Qualified lifeguard, attaining bronze medallion life-saving award, and is preliminary teacher of disabled swimming certificate. 'He's the best fielder off his own bowling I've ever seen' – David Graveney 1991

**Best batting:** 48 Somerset v Hampshire, Taunton 1988
**Best bowling:** 7-52 Somerset v Gloucestershire, Gloucester 1992

## 1995 Season

| | M | Inns | NO | Runs | HS | Avge | 100s | 50s | Ct | St | O | M | Runs | Wkts | Avge | Best | 5wI | 10wM |
|---|---|---|---|---|---|---|---|---|---|---|---|---|---|---|---|---|---|---|
| Test | | | | | | | | | | | | | | | | | | |
| All First | 16 | 22 | 10 | 207 | 47 | 17.25 | - | - | 12 | - | 596.2 | 173 | 1745 | 40 | 43.62 | 5-85 | 1 | - |
| 1-day Int | | | | | | | | | | | | | | | | | | |
| NatWest | 1 | 1 | 1 | 10 | 10 * | - | - | - | 1 | - | 10 | 0 | 44 | 0 | - | | - | - |
| B & H | 6 | 2 | 0 | 11 | 11 | 5.50 | - | - | 1 | - | 57 | 7 | 200 | 10 | 20.00 | 3-17 | - | |
| Sunday | 15 | 6 | 5 | 21 | 6 * | 21.00 | - | - | 4 | - | 102 | 2 | 511 | 17 | 30.05 | 3-37 | - | |

## Career Performances

| | M | Inns | NO | Runs | HS | Avge | 100s | 50s | Ct | St | Balls | Runs | Wkts | Avge | Best | 5wI | 10wM |
|---|---|---|---|---|---|---|---|---|---|---|---|---|---|---|---|---|---|
| Test | | | | | | | | | | | | | | | | | |
| All First | 104 | 119 | 40 | 991 | 48 | 12.54 | - | - | 73 | - | 18888 | 9245 | 239 | 38.68 | 7-52 | 9 | 2 |
| 1-day Int | | | | | | | | | | | | | | | | | |
| NatWest | 7 | 5 | 2 | 16 | 10 * | 5.33 | - | - | 3 | - | 337 | 238 | 3 | 79.33 | 2-44 | - | |
| B & H | 13 | 6 | 1 | 14 | 11 | 2.80 | - | - | 3 | - | 660 | 397 | 14 | 28.35 | 3-17 | - | |
| Sunday | 72 | 23 | 12 | 101 | 19 | 9.18 | - | - | 25 | - | 2810 | 2133 | 55 | 38.78 | 3-19 | - | |

# TUDOR, A. J. Surrey

**Name:** Alexander Jeremy Tudor
**Role:** Right-hand bat, right-arm fast bowler
**Born:** 23 October 1977,
West Brompton, London
**Height:** 6ft 4in **Weight:** 13st 7lbs
**Nickname:** Big Al, Bambi, Tudes
**County debut:** 1995
**1st-Class 50s:** 1
**1st-Class 5 w. innings:** 1
**1st-Class catches:** 1
**Place in batting averages:** 261st av. 13.66
**Place in bowling averages:** 21st av. 22.85
**Strike rate:** 35.78 (career 35.78)
**Parents:** Daryll and Jennifer
**Marital status:** Single
**Family links with cricket:** Brother was
on the staff at The Oval
**Education:** Wandle Primary, Earlsfield; St
Mark's C of E, Fulham; City of Westminster College

**Overseas tours:** England U15 to South Africa 1992-93; England U19 to Zimbabwe 1995-96
**Cricketers particularly admired:** Curtly Ambrose, Brian Lara
**Other sports followed:** Basketball, football (QPR)
**Relaxations:** Listening to music
**Extras:** Played for London Schools at all ages from U8. Played for England U17 against India in 1994. MCC Young Cricketer. Had to return home from the England U19 tour to Zimbabwe through injury
**Best batting:** 56 Surrey v Leicestershire, Leicester 1995
**Best bowling :** 5-32 Surrey v Derbyshire, Derby 1995

## 1995 Season

|          | M | Inns | NO | Runs | HS | Avge | 100s | 50s | Ct | St | O | M | Runs | Wkts | Avge | Best | 5wI | 10wM |
|----------|---|------|----|------|----|------|------|-----|----|----|---|---|------|------|------|------|-----|------|
| Test     |   |      |    |      |    |      |      |     |    |    |   |   |      |      |      |      |     |      |
| All First | 5 | 9 | 0 | 123 | 56 | 13.66 | - | 1 | 1 | - | 83.3 | 7 | 320 | 14 | 22.85 | 5-32 | 1 | - |
| 1-day Int |   |      |    |      |    |      |      |     |    |    |   |   |      |      |      |      |     |      |
| NatWest  | 1 | 0 | 0 | 0 | 0 | - | - | - | - | - | 10 | 0 | 27 | 1 | 27.00 | 1-27 | - | |
| B & H    |   |      |    |      |    |      |      |     |    |    |   |   |      |      |      |      |     |      |
| Sunday   | 2 | 2 | 1 | 40 | 29 * | 40.00 | - | - | 2 | - | 7 | 0 | 48 | 1 | 48.00 | 1-19 | - | |

## Career Performances

|          | M | Inns | NO | Runs | HS | Avge | 100s | 50s | Ct | St | Balls | Runs | Wkts | Avge | Best | 5wI | 10wM |
|----------|---|------|----|------|----|------|------|-----|----|----|-------|------|------|------|------|-----|------|
| Test     |   |      |    |      |    |      |      |     |    |    |       |      |      |      |      |     |      |
| All First | 5 | 9 | 0 | 123 | 56 | 13.66 | - | 1 | 1 | - | 501 | 320 | 14 | 22.85 | 5-32 | 1 | - |
| 1-day Int |   |      |    |      |    |      |      |     |    |    |       |      |      |      |      |     |      |
| NatWest  | 1 | 0 | 0 | 0 | 0 | - | - | - | - | - | 60 | 27 | 1 | 27.00 | 1-27 | - | |
| B & H    |   |      |    |      |    |      |      |     |    |    |       |      |      |      |      |     |      |
| Sunday   | 2 | 2 | 1 | 40 | 29 * | 40.00 | - | - | 2 | - | 42 | 48 | 1 | 48.00 | 1-19 | - | |

86. Who was the first specialist bowler to captain the West Indies?

# TUFNELL, P. C. R. Middlesex

**Name:** Philip Clive Roderick Tufnell
**Role:** Right-hand bat, slow left-arm spinner
**Born:** 29 April 1966, Hadley Wood, Hertfordshire
**Height:** 6ft **Weight:** 12st 7lbs
**Nickname:** The Cat
**County debut:** 1986
**County cap:** 1990
**Test debut:** 1990-91
**Tests:** 22
**One-Day Internationals:** 19
**50 wickets in a season:** 5
**1st-Class 5 w. in innings:** 29
**1st-Class 10 w. in match:** 3
**1st-Class catches:** 75
**One-Day 5 w. in innings:** 1
**Place in bowling averages:** 16th av. 22.08
(1994 49th av. 28.38)
**Strike rate:** 54.98 (career 72.58)
**Parents:** Sylvia and Alan
**Marital status:** Divorced
**Education:** Highgate School; Southgate School
**Qualifications:** O-level in Art; City & Guilds Silversmithing
**Overseas tours:** England YC to West Indies 1984-85; England to Australia 1990-91, to New Zealand and Australia (World Cup) 1991-92, to India and Sri Lanka 1992-93, to West Indies 1993-94, to Australia 1994-95
**Overseas teams played for:** Queensland University, Australia
**Cricketers particularly admired:** Jason Pooley
**Other sports followed:** American football
**Relaxations:** Sleeping
**Extras:** MCC Young Cricketer of the Year 1984 and Middlesex Uncapped Bowler of the Year 1987. Was originally a seam bowler and gave up cricket for three years in his mid-teens
**Best batting:** 37 Middlesex v Yorkshire, Headingley 1990
**Best bowling:** 8-29 Middlesex v Glamorgan, Cardiff 1993

---

87. In which year did New Zealand record their first Test win in England?

## 1995 Season

| | M | Inns | NO | Runs | HS | Avge | 100s | 50s | Ct | St | O | M | Runs | Wkts | Avge | Best | 5wI | 10wM |
|---|---|---|---|---|---|---|---|---|---|---|---|---|---|---|---|---|---|---|
| Test | | | | | | | | | | | | | | | | | | |
| All First | 17 | 15 | 7 | 65 | 23 * | 8.12 | - | - | 5 | - | 678.1 | 207 | 1634 | 74 | 22.08 | 6-111 | 5 | 1 |
| 1-day Int | | | | | | | | | | | | | | | | | | |
| NatWest | 1 | 0 | 0 | 0 | 0 | - | - | - | - | - | 12 | 3 | 56 | 0 | - | | - | - |
| B & H | 2 | 0 | 0 | 0 | 0 | - | - | - | - | - | 18 | 0 | 67 | 1 | 67.00 | 1-28 | - | |
| Sunday | 6 | 4 | 2 | 7 | 5 | 3.50 | - | - | - | - | 43 | 3 | 192 | 7 | 27.42 | 3-43 | - | |

## Career Performances

| | M | Inns | NO | Runs | HS | Avge | 100s | 50s | Ct | St | Balls | Runs | Wkts | Avge | Best | 5wI | 10wM |
|---|---|---|---|---|---|---|---|---|---|---|---|---|---|---|---|---|---|
| Test | 22 | 32 | 17 | 62 | 22 * | 4.13 | - | - | 10 | - | 6378 | 2671 | 68 | 39.27 | 7-47 | 4 | 1 |
| All First | 178 | 178 | 74 | 985 | 37 | 9.47 | - | - | 75 | - | 43911 | 18563 | 605 | 30.68 | 8-29 | 29 | 3 |
| 1-day Int | 19 | 10 | 9 | 15 | 5 * | 15.00 | - | - | 3 | - | 960 | 676 | 15 | 45.06 | 3-40 | - | |
| NatWest | 6 | 1 | 0 | 8 | 8 | 8.00 | - | - | 3 | - | 426 | 257 | 8 | 32.12 | 3-29 | - | |
| B & H | 10 | 5 | 3 | 41 | 18 | 20.50 | - | - | 1 | - | 576 | 429 | 9 | 47.66 | 3-32 | - | |
| Sunday | 30 | 9 | 5 | 23 | 13 * | 5.75 | - | - | 3 | - | 1266 | 933 | 40 | 23.32 | 5-28 | 1 | |

# TURNER, R. J. — Somerset

**Name:** Robert Julian Turner
**Role:** Right-hand bat, wicket-keeper
**Born:** 25 November 1967, Worcestershire
**Height:** 6ft 2in **Weight:** 13st 9lbs
**Nickname:** Noddy, Sniper, Cymbols, Marcus
**County debut:** 1991
**County cap:** 1994
**1st-Class 50s:** 11
**1st-Class 100s:** 3
**1st-Class catches:** 157
**1st-Class stumpings:** 31
**Place in batting averages:** 120th av. 31.17
(1994 168th av. 24.40)
**Parents:** Derek Edward and Doris Lilian
**Marital status:** Single
**Family links with cricket:** Father is
chairman of Western-super-Mare CC.
Brothers Simon and Richard play for and
have both captained the club and Simon is the
current captain. Simon played for Somerset 1st XI as a wicket-keeper
**Education:** Uphill Primary School; Broadoak School, Weston-super-Mare; Millfield
School; Magdalene College, Cambridge University

**Qualifications:** BEng (Hons) in Engineering, Diploma in Computer Science
**Career outside cricket:** Maths teacher at Stanbridge Earls School, Hampshire
**Off-season:** Either teaching or playing in South Africa
**Overseas tours:** Millfield School to Barbados, 1985; Combined Universities to Barbados 1989, to Kuala Lumpur, Malaysia 1992, to Qantas, Western Australia 1993
**Overseas teams played for:** Claremont-Nedlands, Perth, Western Australia 1991-93
**Cricketers particularly admired:** Mushtaq Ahmed 'inspirational', Stuart Turner 'determination', Andy Brassington
**Other sports followed:** Golf, swimming, football ('The Villa'), rugby union
**Relaxations:** 'Reading books and magazines, playing the guitar and the piano, golf, meeting friends for beers and curry'
**Extras:** Captain of Cambridge University (Blue 1988-91) and Combined Universities 1991. Capped at end of 1994 season. Equalled Somerset record of six catches in an innings in 1995 against West Indies and eight dismissals in a match against West Indies and Durham
**Opinions on cricket:** 'Overseas players bring excitement, charisma and quality to the English game, as well as inspiring their team mates. I would be very wary of getting rid of them.'
**Best batting:** 106* Somerset v Derbyshire, Derby 1995

## 1995 Season

|           | M  | Inns | NO | Runs | HS    | Avge  | 100s | 50s | Ct | St | O | M | Runs | Wkts | Avge | Best | 5wI | 10wM |
|-----------|----|------|----|------|-------|-------|------|-----|----|----|---|---|------|------|------|------|-----|------|
| Test      |    |      |    |      |       |       |      |     |    |    |   |   |      |      |      |      |     |      |
| All First | 19 | 30   | 7  | 717  | 106 * | 31.17 | 1    | 4   | 54 | 10 |   |   |      |      |      |      |     |      |
| 1-day Int |    |      |    |      |       |       |      |     |    |    |   |   |      |      |      |      |     |      |
| NatWest   | 1  | 1    | 0  | 3    | 3     | 3.00  | -    | -   | -  | -  |   |   |      |      |      |      |     |      |
| B & H     | 6  | 4    | 2  | 67   | 37 *  | 33.50 | -    | -   | 7  | -  |   |   |      |      |      |      |     |      |
| Sunday    | 12 | 9    | 4  | 96   | 19    | 19.20 | -    | -   | 9  | 4  |   |   |      |      |      |      |     |      |

## Career Performances

|           | M  | Inns | NO | Runs | HS    | Avge  | 100s | 50s | Ct  | St | Balls | Runs | Wkts | Avge | Best | 5wI | 10wM |
|-----------|----|------|----|------|-------|-------|------|-----|-----|----|-------|------|------|------|------|-----|------|
| Test      |    |      |    |      |       |       |      |     |     |    |       |      |      |      |      |     |      |
| All First | 84 | 131  | 27 | 2694 | 106 * | 25.90 | 3    | 11  | 157 | 31 | 13    | 26   | 0    | -    | -    | -   | -    |
| 1-day Int |    |      |    |      |       |       |      |     |     |    |       |      |      |      |      |     |      |
| NatWest   | 4  | 3    | 0  | 24   | 15    | 8.00  | -    | -   | 7   | -  |       |      |      |      |      |     |      |
| B & H     | 11 | 9    | 5  | 122  | 37 *  | 30.50 | -    | -   | 11  | 1  |       |      |      |      |      |     |      |
| Sunday    | 33 | 28   | 14 | 346  | 37 *  | 24.71 | -    | -   | 30  | 6  |       |      |      |      |      |     |      |

# TWEATS, T. A. Derbyshire

**Name:** Timothy Andrew Tweats
**Role:** Right-hand bat, off-spin bowler
**Born:** 18 April 1974, Stoke-on-Trent
**Height:** 6ft 3in **Weight:** 13st
**County debut:** 1992
**1st-Class 50s:** 2
**1st-Class catches:** 8
**Place in batting averages:** 201st av. 20.53
**Parents:** Malcolm and Linda
**Marital status:** Single
**Family links with cricket:** Father and two brothers, Jon and Simon, play for the local club, Leek, for whom he played before joining Derbyshire
**Education:** Endon High School; Stoke-on-Trent Sixth Form College; Staffordshire University
**Qualifications:** 5 GCSEs, 2 A-levels
**Career outside cricket:** Student
**Overseas tours:** Kidsgrove and District Junior Cricket League to Australia 1991
**Cricketers particularly admired:** Robin Smith, Phil Tufnell
**Other sports followed:** Football
**Best batting:** 78* Derbyshire v Worcestershire, Kidderminster 1995
**Best bowling:** 1-23 Derbyshire v Surrey, Derby 1995

## 1995 Season

| | M | Inns | NO | Runs | HS | Avge | 100s | 50s | Ct | St | O | M | Runs | Wkts | Avge | Best | 5wI | 10wM |
|---|---|---|---|---|---|---|---|---|---|---|---|---|---|---|---|---|---|---|
| Test | | | | | | | | | | | | | | | | | | |
| All First | 8 | 16 | 1 | 308 | 78 * | 20.53 | - | 2 | 7 | - | 43.4 | 3 | 194 | 4 | 48.50 | 1-23 | - | - |
| 1-day Int | | | | | | | | | | | | | | | | | | |
| NatWest | 1 | 1 | 0 | 16 | 16 | 16.00 | - | - | 1 | - | | | | | | | | |
| B & H | | | | | | | | | | | | | | | | | | |
| Sunday | 9 | 5 | 1 | 60 | 19 | 15.00 | - | - | 7 | - | 4 | 0 | 27 | 0 | - | | - | - |

---

88. Who holds the record as England's leading run-scorer in first-class matches on a tour to Australia?

---

## Career Performances

|        | M | Inns | NO | Runs | HS | Avge | 100s | 50s | Ct | St | Balls | Runs | Wkts | Avge | Best | 5wI | 10wM |
|--------|---|------|----|------|----|------|------|-----|----|----|-------|------|------|------|------|-----|------|
| Test   |   |      |    |      |    |      |      |     |    |    |       |      |      |      |      |     |      |
| All First | 9 | 17 | 1 | 332 | 78 * | 20.75 | - | 2 | 8 | - | 262 | 194 | 4 | 48.50 | 1-23 | - | - |
| 1-day Int |  |      |    |      |    |      |      |     |    |    |       |      |      |      |      |     |      |
| NatWest | 1 | 1 | 0 | 16 | 16 | 16.00 | - | - | 1 | - |       |      |      |      |      |     |      |
| B & H  |   |      |    |      |    |      |      |     |    |    |       |      |      |      |      |     |      |
| Sunday | 9 | 5 | 1 | 60 | 19 | 15.00 | - | - | 7 | - | 24 | 27 | 0 | - |  | - | - |

# TWOSE, R. G.                    Warwickshire

**Name:** Roger Graham Twose
**Role:** Left-hand bat, right-arm medium bowler
**Born:** 17 April 1968, Torquay ('in a car!')
**Height:** 6ft **Weight:** 14st 7lbs
**Nickname:** Twosey, Buff, Tom Cruise
**County debut:** 1989
**County cap:** 1992
**1000 runs in a season:** 3
**1st-Class 50s:** 33
**1st-Class 100s:** 12
**1st-Class 200s:** 2
**1st-Class 5 w. in innings:** 2
**1st-Class catches:** 63
**One-Day 100s:** 3
**Place in batting averages:** 42nd av. 45.61
(1994 11th av. 54.26)
**Place in bowling averages:** 52nd av. 27.36
(1994 102nd av. 36.26)
**Strike rate:** 58.90 (career 67.83)
**Parents:** Paul and Patricia
**Marital status:** Single
**Family links with cricket:** Brother Richard plays for Devon, for whom their father played. Uncles are Roger Tolchard of Leicestershire and England and Jeff Tolchard of Leicestershire
**Education:** Wolborough Hill, Newton Abbot, Devon; King's College, Taunton
**Qualifications:** 7 O-levels, 2 A-levels, NCA coaching certificate. Currently studying for Business Management Diploma
**Off-season:** Playing for New Zealand
**Overseas teams played for:** Northern Districts, New Zealand 1989-90; Central Districts, New Zealand 1991-94
**Overseas tours:** New Zealand to India 1995-96, to India and Pakistan (World Cup) 1996

**Cricketers particularly admired:** Dermot Reeve, Mark Greatbatch
**Other sports followed:** Rugby, hockey, etc.
**Relaxations:** 'Working out with my girlfriend.'
**Extras:** 'Once took all ten wickets in an innings whilst playing in New Zealand: a feat I plan to reproduce in first-class cricket!' Warwickshire Player of the Year 1992. Parents live in New Zealand, where he has played for the past seven winters and where he now plays for and captains Central Distict. Played the first innings in the County Championship to last over 10 hours (277 v Glamorgan, 1994). Made his Test debut for New Zealand in India in 1995. No longer eligible to play for Warwickshire as an Englishman
**Best batting:** 277 Warwickshire v Glamorgan, Edgbaston 1994
**Best bowling:** 6-28 Warwickshire v Surrey, Guildford 1994

## 1995 Season

|          | M  | Inns | NO | Runs | HS   | Avge   | 100s | 50s | Ct | St | O   | M  | Runs | Wkts | Avge  | Best | 5wI | 10wM |
|----------|----|------|----|------|------|--------|------|-----|----|----|-----|----|------|------|-------|------|-----|------|
| Test     |    |      |    |      |      |        |      |     |    |    |     |    |      |      |       |      |     |      |
| All First | 19 | 30  | 4  | 1186 | 191  | 45.61  | 4    | 3   | 6  | -  | 108 | 29 | 301  | 11   | 27.36 | 3-50 | -   | -    |
| 1-day Int |    |      |    |      |      |        |      |     |    |    |     |    |      |      |       |      |     |      |
| NatWest  | 5  | 3    | 1  | 212  | 93 * | 106.00 | -    | 3   | 3  | -  | 10  | 0  | 55   | 0    | -     |      | -   | -    |
| B & H    | 5  | 4    | 1  | 206  | 90   | 68.66  | -    | 3   | 5  | -  | 6   | 0  | 43   | 1    | 43.00 | 1-23 | -   |      |
| Sunday   | 17 | 15   | 4  | 436  | 69 * | 39.63  | -    | 4   | 3  | -  | 22.5| 0  | 112  | 2    | 56.00 | 1-14 | -   |      |

## Career Performances

|          | M   | Inns | NO | Runs | HS    | Avge  | 100s | 50s | Ct | St | Balls | Runs | Wkts | Avge  | Best | 5wI | 10wM |
|----------|-----|------|----|------|-------|-------|------|-----|----|----|-------|------|------|-------|------|-----|------|
| Test     |     |      |    |      |       |       |      |     |    |    |       |      |      |       |      |     |      |
| All First | 120 | 202 | 25 | 6704 | 277 * | 37.87 | 12   | 33  | 63 | -  | 7597  | 3625 | 112  | 32.36 | 6-28 | 2   | -    |
| 1-day Int |     |      |    |      |       |       |      |     |    |    |       |      |      |       |      |     |      |
| NatWest  | 21  | 18   | 3  | 783  | 110   | 52.20 | 2    | 4   | 8  | -  | 735   | 496  | 17   | 29.17 | 3-39 | -   |      |
| B & H    | 17  | 15   | 1  | 465  | 90    | 33.21 | -    | 4   | 11 | -  | 228   | 176  | 3    | 58.66 | 1-23 | -   |      |
| Sunday   | 94  | 79   | 13 | 1880 | 100   | 28.48 | 1    | 11  | 26 | -  | 1554  | 1303 | 37   | 35.21 | 3-31 | -   |      |

89. Which three non-Test playing countries played in the World Cup for the first time in 1995-96?

# UDAL, S. D.                                    Hampshire

**Name:** Shaun David Udal
**Role:** Right-hand bat, off-spin bowler,
fields in the deep
**Born:** 18 March 1969, Farnborough
**Height:** 6ft 2in **Weight:** 13st
**Nickname:** Shaggy
**County debut:** 1989
**County cap:** 1992
**One-Day Internationals:** 10
**50 wickets in a season:** 4
**1st-Class 50s:** 9
**1st-Class 5 w. in innings:** 19
**1st-Class 10 w. in match:** 4
**1st-Class catches:** 43
**Place in batting averages:** 203rd av. 20.48
(1994 147th av. 26.30)
**Place in bowling averages:** 88th av. 33.89
(1994 39th av. 27.13)
**Strike rate:** 68.54 (career 65.58)
**Parents:** Robin and Mary
**Wife and date of marriage:** Emma Jane, 5 October 1991
**Children:** Katherine Mary, 26 August 1992, 'new arrival', 5 November 1995
**Family links with cricket:** Father played for Surrey Colts and Camberley for 42
years; brother plays for Camberley 1st XI. Grandfather played for Leicestershire and
Middlesex
**Education:** Tower Hill Infant and Junior Schools; Cove Comprehensive School
**Qualifications:** 8 CSEs, qualified print finisher
**Career outside cricket:** Director of a print finishing company
**Off-season:** Touring Pakistan with England A
**Overseas tours:** England to Australia 1994-95; England A to Pakistan 1995-96
**Overseas teams played for:** Hamilton Wickham, Newcastle, NSW 1990-91
**Cricketers particularly admired:** John Emburey, Robin Smith, Malcolm Marshall,
Peter Boot
**Other sports followed:** Football (Aldershot Town), golf
**Injuries:** Side strain, out for 10 days. Injured finger on England tour to Australia 1994-
95
**Relaxations:** 'Camberley CC. Being a bad gardener. My wife and family'
**Extras:** Has taken two hat-tricks in club cricket, scored a double hundred in a 40-over
club game and took 8-50 v Sussex in the first game of 1992 season, his seventh
Championship match. Man of the Match on NatWest debut against Berkshire 1991 and
named Hampshire Cricket Association Player of the Year 1993

**Opinions on cricket:** 'The structure must be looked at to give our top players a chance to rest and recover which is just as important as playing, but generally the game is in good health and is one I hope to enjoy for a long time to come.'
**Best batting:** 94 Hampshire v Glamorgan, Southampton 1994
**Best bowling:** 8-50 Hampshire v Sussex, Southampton 1992

## 1995 Season

| | M | Inns | NO | Runs | HS | Avge | 100s | 50s | Ct | St | O | M | Runs | Wkts | Avge | Best | 5wI | 10wM |
|---|---|---|---|---|---|---|---|---|---|---|---|---|---|---|---|---|---|---|
| Test | | | | | | | | | | | | | | | | | | |
| All First | 18 | 29 | 4 | 512 | 85 | 20.48 | - | 3 | 12 | - | 628.2 | 137 | 1864 | 55 | 33.89 | 6-65 | 5 | 1 |
| 1-day Int | 3 | 1 | 1 | 5 | 5 * | - | - | - | - | - | 27 | 0 | 129 | 0 | - | - | - | - |
| NatWest | 1 | 1 | 1 | 14 | 14 * | - | - | - | - | - | 12 | 1 | 33 | 1 | 33.00 | 1-33 | - | |
| B & H | 5 | 4 | 1 | 34 | 12 | 11.33 | - | - | - | - | 54 | 4 | 186 | 2 | 93.00 | 1-22 | - | |
| Sunday | 14 | 11 | 4 | 59 | 15 * | 8.42 | - | - | 2 | - | 95 | 2 | 537 | 9 | 59.66 | 2-31 | - | |

## Career Performances

| | M | Inns | NO | Runs | HS | Avge | 100s | 50s | Ct | St | Balls | Runs | Wkts | Avge | Best | 5wI | 10wM |
|---|---|---|---|---|---|---|---|---|---|---|---|---|---|---|---|---|---|
| Test | | | | | | | | | | | | | | | | | |
| All First | 88 | 126 | 22 | 2214 | 94 | 21.28 | - | 9 | 43 | - | 18692 | 9363 | 285 | 32.85 | 8-50 | 19 | 4 |
| 1-day Int | 10 | 6 | 4 | 35 | 11 * | 17.50 | - | - | 1 | - | 570 | 372 | 8 | 46.50 | 2-37 | - | |
| NatWest | 12 | 3 | 1 | 30 | 14 * | 15.00 | - | - | 4 | - | 792 | 433 | 15 | 28.86 | 3-39 | - | |
| B & H | 23 | 9 | 4 | 60 | 12 | 12.00 | - | - | 4 | - | 1440 | 881 | 33 | 26.69 | 4-40 | - | |
| Sunday | 80 | 46 | 15 | 355 | 44 | 11.45 | - | - | 25 | - | 3516 | 2951 | 89 | 33.15 | 4-51 | - | |

90. Who admitted to seeking psychological help before his match-winning performance in the 1995 Benson & Hedges semi-final?

# VAN TROOST, A. P. Somerset

**Name:** Adrianus Pelrus van Troost
**Role:** Right-hand bat 'specialist no 11
batsman', right-arm fast bowler
**Born:** 2 October 1972, Schiedam, Holland
**Height:** 6ft 7in **Weight:** 15st
**Nickname:** Flappie, Rooster
**County debut:** 1991
**1st-Class 5 w. in innings:** 4
**1st-Class catches:** 9
**One-Day 5 w. in innings:** 1
**Place in batting averages:** 278th av. 10.25
**Place in bowling averages:** 115th av. 39.00
(1994 114th av. 37.97)
**Strike rate:** 54.56 (career 57.58)
**Parents:** Aad and Anneke
**Marital status:** Single
**Family links with cricket:** Father plays for

Excelsior in Holland; brother plays for
Excelsior and Holland U23; grandfather
played for Excelsior and Holland
**Education:** Spieringshoek College, Schiedam
**Qualifications:** Finished Havo schooling – specialised in languages
**Career outside cricket:** Works in a bank
**Off-season:** Working in Holland
**Overseas tours:** Holland to Zimbabwe 1989, to Namibia 1990, to Dubai 1991, to
Canada, New Zealand and South Africa 1992
**Overseas teams played for:** Excelsior, Holland 1979-91; Alma Marist, Cape Town
1992-93; Griqualand West, South Africa 1994-96
**Cricketers particularly admired:** Richard Hadlee, Peter Roebuck, Roland Lefebvre,
Eric Van't Zelfde, Paul Van de Bosch
**Other sports followed:** Football, tennis and most other sports
**Injuries:** Lower back injury, missed two-thirds of the season
**Relaxations:** Playing football and travelling
**Extras:** Played for Holland at age 15 and became third Dutch national to play
professional cricket. Took 6-3 v Durham 2nd XI in 1992 season
**Opinions on cricket:** 'Too much cricket!'
**Best batting:** 35 Somerset v Lancashire, Taunton 1993
**Best bowling:** 6-48 Somerset v Essex, Taunton 1992

## 1995 Season

|  | M | Inns | NO | Runs | HS | Avge | 100s | 50s | Ct | St | O | M | Runs | Wkts | Avge | Best | 5wl | 10wM |
|---|---|---|---|---|---|---|---|---|---|---|---|---|---|---|---|---|---|---|
| Test |  |  |  |  |  |  |  |  |  |  |  |  |  |  |  |  |  |  |
| All First | 7 | 11 | 3 | 82 | 34 | 10.25 | - | - | - | - | 145.3 | 23 | 624 | 16 | 39.00 | 5-120 | 1 | - |
| 1-day Int |  |  |  |  |  |  |  |  |  |  |  |  |  |  |  |  |  |  |
| NatWest |  |  |  |  |  |  |  |  |  |  |  |  |  |  |  |  |  |  |
| B & H | 1 | 1 | 0 | 5 | 5 | 5.00 | - | - | - | - | 9 | 0 | 70 | 1 | 70.00 | 1-70 | - |  |
| Sunday | 2 | 1 | 0 | 9 | 9 | 9.00 | - | - | 1 | - | 11 | 1 | 80 | 1 | 80.00 | 1-41 | - |  |

## Career Performances

|  | M | Inns | NO | Runs | HS | Avge | 100s | 50s | Ct | St | Balls | Runs | Wkts | Avge | Best | 5wl | 10wM |
|---|---|---|---|---|---|---|---|---|---|---|---|---|---|---|---|---|---|
| Test |  |  |  |  |  |  |  |  |  |  |  |  |  |  |  |  |  |
| All First | 54 | 62 | 21 | 353 | 35 | 8.60 | - | - | 9 | - | 6622 | 4217 | 115 | 36.66 | 6-48 | 4 | - |
| 1-day Int |  |  |  |  |  |  |  |  |  |  |  |  |  |  |  |  |  |
| NatWest | 7 | 3 | 1 | 27 | 17 * | 13.50 | - | - | - | - | 366 | 274 | 12 | 22.83 | 5-22 | 1 |  |
| B & H | 3 | 3 | 1 | 19 | 9 * | 9.50 | - | - | - | - | 172 | 172 | 4 | 43.00 | 2-38 | - |  |
| Sunday | 17 | 6 | 3 | 29 | 9 * | 9.66 | - | - | 2 | - | 639 | 532 | 17 | 31.29 | 4-23 | - |  |

# VAUGHAN, M. P.     *Yorkshire*

**Name:** Michael Paul Vaughan
**Role:** Right-hand bat, off-spin bowler
**Born:** 29 October 1974, Eccles, Manchester
**Height:** 6ft 2in **Weight:** 11st 7lbs
**Nickname:** Virgil, Frankie
**County debut:** 1993
**County cap:** 1995
**1000 runs in a season:** 2
**1st-Class 50s:** 14
**1st-Class 100s:** 3
**1st-Class catches:** 21
**Place in batting averages:** 110th av. 32.73
(1994 76th av. 36.75)
**Place in bowling averages:** 120th av. 39.81
(1994 140th av. 48.42)
**Strike rate:** 74.36 (career 39.81)
**Parents:** Graham John and Dee
**Marital status:** Single
**Family links with cricket:** Dad played for Worsley CC and mother is related to the famous Tyldesley family (Lancashire and England)
**Education:** St Marks, Worsey; Dore Juniors, Sheffield; Silverdale Comprehensive, Sheffield

**Qualifications:** 4 GCSEs

**Off-season:** Yorkshire to Zimbabwe

**Overseas tours:** England U19 to India 1992-93, to Sri Lanka 1993-94; Yorkshire to West Indies 1994, to South Africa 1995, to Zimbabwe 1996; England A to India 1994-95

**Cricketers particularly admired:** Peter Hartley, Michael Slater, Alex Morris, Glenn Chapple

**Other sports followed:** Football (Sheffield Wednesday), golf, squash, tennis, snooker

**Relaxations:** Playing golf, skiing, shopping, going out with friends, following Wednesday

**Extras:** Played club cricket for Sheffield Collegiate in the Yorkshire League. *Daily Telegraph* U15 Batsman of the Year, 1990. Maurice Leyland Batting Award 1990. Rapid Cricketline Player of the Month, June 1993. The Cricket Society Most Promising Young Cricketer 1993. AA Thompson Memorial Trophy – The Roses Cricketer of the Year 1993. Whittingdale Cricketer of the Month, July 1994. Scored 1066 runs in first full season of first-class cricket in 1994. Captained England U19 in home series against India 1994. Awarded county cap at the end of the 1995 season

**Best batting:** 117 Yorkshire v Northamptonshire, Luton 1994

**Best bowling:** 4-39 Yorkshire v Oxford University, The Parks 1994

## 1995 Season

| | M | Inns | NO | Runs | HS | Avge | 100s | 50s | Ct | St | O | M | Runs | Wkts | Avge | Best | 5wI | 10wM |
|---|---|---|---|---|---|---|---|---|---|---|---|---|---|---|---|---|---|---|
| Test | | | | | | | | | | | | | | | | | | |
| All First | 21 | 39 | 1 | 1244 | 88 | 32.73 | - | 10 | 13 | - | 272.4 | 64 | 876 | 22 | 39.81 | 3-32 | - | - |
| 1-day Int | | | | | | | | | | | | | | | | | | |
| NatWest | 4 | 4 | 0 | 57 | 34 | 14.25 | - | - | - | - | | | | | | | | |
| B & H | 3 | 3 | 1 | 87 | 50 * | 43.50 | - | 1 | 1 | - | | | | | | | | |
| Sunday | 14 | 13 | 1 | 243 | 46 | 20.25 | - | - | 3 | - | 6 | 1 | 31 | 0 | - | | - | - |

## Career Performances

| | M | Inns | NO | Runs | HS | Avge | 100s | 50s | Ct | St | Balls | Runs | Wkts | Avge | Best | 5wI | 10wM |
|---|---|---|---|---|---|---|---|---|---|---|---|---|---|---|---|---|---|
| Test | | | | | | | | | | | | | | | | | |
| All First | 42 | 79 | 2 | 2478 | 117 | 32.18 | 3 | 14 | 21 | - | 3133 | 1623 | 38 | 42.71 | 4-39 | - | - |
| 1-day Int | | | | | | | | | | | | | | | | | |
| NatWest | 6 | 6 | 0 | 76 | 34 | 12.66 | - | - | - | - | | | | | | | |
| B & H | 4 | 4 | 1 | 87 | 50 * | 29.00 | - | 1 | 1 | - | 18 | 13 | 0 | - | | - | - |
| Sunday | 19 | 18 | 1 | 279 | 46 | 16.41 | - | - | 3 | - | 36 | 31 | 0 | - | | - | - |

# WAGH, M. A.                    Warwickshire

**Name:** Mark Anant Wagh

**Role:** Right-hand bat, off-spin bowler

**Born:** 20 October 1976, Birmingham

**Height:** 6ft 2in  **Weight:** 12st 7lbs
**Nickname:** Waggy
**County debut:** No first-team appearance
**Parents:** Mohan and Rita
**Marital status:** Single
**Education:** Harborne Junior School; King
Edward's School, Birmingham; Keble
College, Oxford
**Qualifications:** 12 GCSEs, 4 A-levels,
basic coaching
**Off-season:** At university
**Overseas tours:** Warwickshire U19 to South
Africa 1992
**Cricketers particularly admired:** Carl
Hooper, Brian Lara, David Gower, Daryll
Cullinan
**Other sports followed:** Hockey, snooker,
football
**Relaxations:** Snooker and going out with friends

# WALKER, A.                    Durham

**Name:** Alan Walker
**Role:** Left-hand bat, right-arm medium-fast
bowler
**Born:** 7 July 1962, Emley, near Huddersfield
**Height:** 5ft 11in **Weight:** 13st 7lbs
**Nickname:** Wacky, Walks
**County debut:** 1983 (Northants), 1994
(Durham)
**County cap:** 1987 (Northants)
**1st-Class 5 w. in innings:** 4
**1st-Class 10 w. matches:** 1
**1st-Class catches:** 39
**Place in bowling averages:** 78th av. 30.90
**Strike rate:** 55.25 (career 60.92)
**Parents:** Malcolm and Enid
**Wife and date of marriage:** Nicky, 2
October 1994
**Children:** Jessica, 3 March 1988
**Family links with cricket:** Grandfather played in local league
**Education:** Emley Junior School; Kirkburton Middle School; Shelley High School
**Qualifications:** 2 O-levels, 4 CSEs, qualified coal-face worker

**Career outside cricket:** Mining, building, coaching
**Off-season:** Landscape gardening
**Overseas tours:** NCA North U19 to Denmark; Northamptonshire to Durban
**Overseas teams played for:** Uitenhage, South Africa 1984-85 and 1987-88; Sunshine, Melbourne 1994-95
**Cricketers particularly admired:** Dennis Lillee, Richard Hadlee, Jeremy Snape 'for his ability to see the funny side of things when things are not going well'
**Other sports followed:** Football (Huddersfield Town and Emley), rugby league (Wakefield Trinity)
**Injuries:** Broken toe, out for ten days
**Relaxations:** DIY, drinking, gardening
**Extras:** Recorded best bowling and match figures by a Durham bowler in 1995 (eight for 118 and 14 for 177)
**Best batting:** 41* Northamptonshire v Warwickshire, Edgbaston 1987
**Best bowling:** 8-118 Durham v Essex, Chester-le-Street 1995

## 1995 Season

|  | M | Inns | NO | Runs | HS | Avge | 100s | 50s | Ct | St | O | M | Runs | Wkts | Avge | Best | 5wI | 10wM |
|---|---|---|---|---|---|---|---|---|---|---|---|---|---|---|---|---|---|---|
| Test |  |  |  |  |  |  |  |  |  |  |  |  |  |  |  |  |  |  |
| All First | 11 | 16 | 3 | 102 | 29 | 7.84 | - | - | 4 | - | 285.3 | 53 | 958 | 31 | 30.90 | 8-118 | 2 | 1 |
| 1-day Int |  |  |  |  |  |  |  |  |  |  |  |  |  |  |  |  |  |  |
| NatWest | 2 | 1 | 0 | 12 | 12 | 12.00 | - | - | 2 | - | 20 | 6 | 62 | 3 | 20.66 | 2-13 | - |  |
| B & H | 5 | 4 | 2 | 5 | 4 * | 2.50 | - | - | 1 | - | 40.4 | 1 | 168 | 8 | 21.00 | 4-42 | - |  |
| Sunday | 10 | 5 | 2 | 48 | 15 * | 16.00 | - | - | 1 | - | 74.3 | 1 | 386 | 9 | 42.88 | 3-23 | - |  |

## Career Performances

|  | M | Inns | NO | Runs | HS | Avge | 100s | 50s | Ct | St | Balls | Runs | Wkts | Avge | Best | 5wI | 10wM |
|---|---|---|---|---|---|---|---|---|---|---|---|---|---|---|---|---|---|
| Test |  |  |  |  |  |  |  |  |  |  |  |  |  |  |  |  |  |
| All First | 112 | 114 | 50 | 800 | 41 * | 12.50 | - | - | 43 | - | 16023 | 8276 | 263 | 31.46 | 8-118 | 4 | 1 |
| 1-day Int |  |  |  |  |  |  |  |  |  |  |  |  |  |  |  |  |  |
| NatWest | 20 | 6 | 1 | 47 | 13 | 9.40 | - | - | 5 | - | 1180 | 680 | 22 | 30.90 | 4-7 | - |  |
| B & H | 33 | 15 | 10 | 52 | 15 * | 10.40 | - | - | 7 | - | 1733 | 1259 | 39 | 32.28 | 4-42 | - |  |
| Sunday | 125 | 37 | 16 | 249 | 30 | 11.85 | - | - | 29 | - | 5163 | 4030 | 145 | 27.79 | 4-21 | - |  |

91. Of the umpires currently on the first-class list, how many have played Test cricket and who are they?

# WALKER, L.N.                                    Nottinghamshire

**Name:** Lyndsay Nicholas Walker
**Role:** Right-hand bat, wicket-keeper
**Born:** 22 June 1974, Armidale, Australia
**Height:** 6ft 1in **Weight:** 12st
**Nickname:** Max
**County debut:** 1994
**1st-Class catches:** 2
**1st-Class stumpings:** 1
**Parents:** Graham and Barbara
**Wife and date of marriage:** Laurie, 17 June 1994
**Children:** Guy, 12 September 1995
**Family links with cricket:** 'Dad and brother played a good level of grade cricket in Australia'
**Education:** New South Wales, Australia
**Qualifications:** High School Certificate, senior coaching certificate
**Career outside cricket:** 'Coaching and any aspect of building, learning car mechanics and evangelising the Lord Jesus Christ'
**Off-season:** Coaching and training at Trent Bridge
**Overseas teams played for:** Wallsend, Newcastle, Australia 1987-93; Johore,
**Opinions on cricket:** 'Twelve month contracts would be a good idea. 2nd team wickets on club grounds need to be better in general. Basically a billionaire needs to come in to revolutionise the game as in the rugby codes i.e. all grounds should have day/night cricket. Everyone in general should not be so critical of Test or first-class cricketers.'
**Best batting:** 24 Nottinghamshire v Oxford University, The Parks 1995

## 1995 Season

|          | M | Inns | NO | Runs | HS | Avge | 100s | 50s | Ct | St | O | M | Runs | Wkts | Avge | Best | 5wI | 10wM |
|----------|---|------|----|------|----|------|------|-----|----|----|---|---|------|------|------|------|-----|------|
| Test     |   |      |    |      |    |      |      |     |    |    |   |   |      |      |      |      |     |      |
| All First| 1 | 2    | 0  | 42   | 24 | 21.00| -    | -   | 2  | 1  |   |   |      |      |      |      |     |      |
| 1-day Int|   |      |    |      |    |      |      |     |    |    |   |   |      |      |      |      |     |      |
| NatWest  |   |      |    |      |    |      |      |     |    |    |   |   |      |      |      |      |     |      |
| B & H    |   |      |    |      |    |      |      |     |    |    |   |   |      |      |      |      |     |      |
| Sunday   |   |      |    |      |    |      |      |     |    |    |   |   |      |      |      |      |     |      |

## Career Performances

|  | M | Inns | NO | Runs | HS | Avge | 100s | 50s | Ct | St | Balls | Runs | Wkts | Avge | Best | 5wl | 10wM |
|---|---|---|---|---|---|---|---|---|---|---|---|---|---|---|---|---|---|
| Test |  |  |  |  |  |  |  |  |  |  |  |  |  |  |  |  |  |
| All First | 2 | 4 | 0 | 43 | 24 | 10.75 | - | - | 2 | 1 |  |  |  |  |  |  |  |
| 1-day Int |  |  |  |  |  |  |  |  |  |  |  |  |  |  |  |  |  |  |
| NatWest |  |  |  |  |  |  |  |  |  |  |  |  |  |  |  |  |  |  |
| B & H |  |  |  |  |  |  |  |  |  |  |  |  |  |  |  |  |  |  |  |
| Sunday |  |  |  |  |  |  |  |  |  |  |  |  |  |  |  |  |  |  |  |

# WALKER, M. J.          Kent

**Name:** Matthew Jonathan Walker
**Role:** Left-hand bat, right-arm medium-fast bowler
**Born:** 2 January 1974, Gravesend, Kent
**Height:** 5ft 7in **Weight:** 13st 7lbs
**Nickname:** Walkdog
**County debut:** 1992-93
**1st-Class 50s:** 1
**1st-Class 100s:** 1
**1st-Class catches:** 10
**Place in batting averages:** 268th av. 12.46
(1994 99th av. 34.14)
**Parents:** Richard and June
**Marital status:** Single
**Family links with cricket:** Grandfather played for Kent as a wicket-keeper and father was on Lord's groundstaff, having played for Middlesex and Kent 2nd XI

**Education:** Shorne Primary School; King's School, Rochester
**Qualifications:** 9 GCSEs, 2 A-levels, coaching certificates
**Career outside cricket:** 'Yet to be decided'
**Off-season:** 'Just coaching in England until Christmas, then spending two months in South Africa training and coaching'
**Overseas tours:** Kent U17 to New Zealand 1991; England U19 to Pakistan 1991-92, to India 1992-93; Kent to Zimbabwe 1992-93
**Cricketers particularly admired:** Aravinda De Silva
**Other sports followed:** Rugby, hockey, skiing, football – 'most really'
**Relaxations:** Music, watching films; 'like old pubs'
**Extras:** Captained England U15, U16 and U17 at hockey; represented Kent U18 at rugby; had football trials with Chelsea and Gillingham. Captained England U19 tour to India 1992-93 and v West Indies in 1993 home series which England U19 won 2-0 in

one-day matches and 1-0 in 'Test' series. Received Sir Jack Hobbs award for best young cricketer 1989, and *Daily Telegraph* U15 batting award 1989. Selected for Kent U21 hockey team in 1993 and 1994. Woolwich Kent League's Young Cricketer of the Year 1994

**Opinions on cricket:** 'Four-day cricket is successful, but I think the number of overs in a day should be reduced. Also lunch break should be an hour long and tea-time 35 minutes long.'

**Best batting:** 107 Kent v Surrey, The Oval 1994

## 1995 Season

|         | M | Inns | NO | Runs | HS | Avge | 100s | 50s | Ct | St | O | M | Runs | Wkts | Avge | Best | 5wI | 10wM |
|---------|---|------|----|----|-----|------|------|-----|----|----|---|---|------|------|------|------|-----|------|
| Test    |   |      |    |    |     |      |      |     |    |    |   |   |      |      |      |      |     |      |
| All First | 9 | 14 | 1 | 162 | 53 | 12.46 | - | 1 | 7 | - |   |   |      |      |      |      |     |      |
| 1-day Int |   |      |    |    |     |      |      |     |    |    |   |   |      |      |      |      |     |      |
| NatWest |   |      |    |    |     |      |      |     |    |    |   |   |      |      |      |      |     |      |
| B & H   | 5 | 4 | 1 | 137 | 69 * | 45.66 | - | 1 | 3 | - |   |   |      |      |      |      |     |      |
| Sunday  | 9 | 8 | 2 | 77 | 24 * | 12.83 | - | - | 2 | - |   |   |      |      |      |      |     |      |

## Career Performances

|         | M | Inns | NO | Runs | HS | Avge | 100s | 50s | Ct | St | Balls | Runs | Wkts | Avge | Best | 5wI | 10wM |
|---------|---|------|----|----|-----|------|------|-----|----|----|-------|------|------|------|------|-----|------|
| Test    |   |      |    |    |     |      |      |     |    |    |       |      |      |      |      |     |      |
| All First | 15 | 23 | 2 | 440 | 107 | 20.95 | 1 | 1 | 10 | - |       |      |      |      |      |     |      |
| 1-day Int |   |      |    |    |     |      |      |     |    |    |       |      |      |      |      |     |      |
| NatWest |   |      |    |    |     |      |      |     |    |    |       |      |      |      |      |     |      |
| B & H   | 5 | 4 | 1 | 137 | 69 * | 45.66 | - | 1 | 3 | - |       |      |      |      |      |     |      |
| Sunday  | 18 | 17 | 3 | 264 | 69 * | 18.85 | - | 1 | 6 | - |       |      |      |      |      |     |      |

92. Who were the respective managers of the 1995-96 England tour to South Africa, the England A tour to India and the England U19 tour to Zimbabwe?

# WALSH, C. A.                    Gloucestershire

**Name:** Courtney Andrew Walsh
**Role:** Right-hand bat, right-arm fast bowler,
county captain
**Born:** 30 October 1962, Kingston, Jamaica
**Height:** 6ft 5¹/₂in **Weight:** 14st 7lbs
**Nickname:** Mark, Walshy, Cuddy, RP
**County debut:** 1984
**County cap:** 1985
**Test debut:** 1984-85
**Tests:** 80
**One-Day Internationals:** 142
**50 wickets in a season:** 8
**100 wickets in a season:** 1
**1st-Class 50s:** 8
**1st-Class 5 w. in innings:** 75
**1st-Class 10 w. in match:** 15
**1st-Class catches:** 82
**One-Day 5 w. in innings:** 3

**Place in batting averages:** 276th av. 11.10
(1994 238th av. 15.22)
**Place in bowling averages:** 58th av. 28.82 (1994 3rd av. 17.24)
**Strike rate:** 59.12 (career 46.99)
**Parents:** Eric and Joan
**Marital status:** Single
**Education:** Excelsior High School
**Qualifications:** GCE and CXL
**Overseas tours:** West Indies YC to England 1982; West Indies B to Zimbabwe 1983-84; West Indies to England 1984, to Australia 1984-85, to Pakistan, Australia and New Zealand 1986-87, to India and Pakistan (World Cup) 1987-88, to England 1988, to Australia 1988-89, to Pakistan 1990-91, to England 1991, to Australia and South Africa 1992-93, to Sharjah, India (Hero Cup) and Sri Lanka 1993-94, to India and New Zealand 1994-95, to Australia 1995-6, to India and Pakistan (World Cup) 1996
**Overseas teams played for:** Jamaica 1981-96
**Relaxations:** Swimming, reading and listening to music
**Extras:** Took record 10-43 in Jamaican school cricket in 1979. On tour, he has the reputation as an insatiable collector of souvenirs. David Graveney, when captaining Gloucestershire, reckoned Walsh was the 'best old-ball bowler in the world'. One of *Wisden*'s Five Cricketers of the Year 1986. Took hat-trick for West Indies v Australia in 1988-89. Captain of Jamaica 1991-92 and 1993-94. Cricketers' Association Player of the Year and Wombwell Cricket Lovers' Cricketer of the Year 1993. Took over captaincy of West Indies from Richie Richardson for Test series against India and New Zealand in 1994-95

**Opinions on cricket:** 'Watch the changes.'
**Best batting:** 66 Gloucestershire v Kent, Cheltenham 1994
**Best bowling:** 9-72 Gloucestershire v Somerset, Bristol 1986

## 1995 Season

|            | M  | Inns | NO | Runs | HS | Avge  | 100s | 50s | Ct | St | O     | M  | Runs | Wkts | Avge  | Best | 5wI | 10wM |
|------------|----|------|----|------|----|-------|------|-----|----|----|-------|----|------|------|-------|------|-----|------|
| Test       | 6  | 7    | 1  | 61   | 19 | 10.16 | -    | -   | 1  | -  | 290   | 57 | 786  | 26   | 30.23 | 5-45 | 1   | -    |
| All First  | 11 | 11   | 1  | 111  | 40 | 11.10 | -    | -   | 3  | -  | 384.2 | 76 | 1124 | 39   | 28.82 | 5-45 | 1   | -    |
| 1-day Int  | 2  | 1    | 1  | 5    | 5* | -     | -    | -   | -  | -  | 15.2  | 1  | 45   | 3    | 15.00 | 3-28 | -   |      |
| NatWest    |    |      |    |      |    |       |      |     |    |    |       |    |      |      |       |      |     |      |
| B & H      |    |      |    |      |    |       |      |     |    |    |       |    |      |      |       |      |     |      |
| Sunday     |    |      |    |      |    |       |      |     |    |    |       |    |      |      |       |      |     |      |

## Career Performances

|            | M   | Inns | NO | Runs | HS  | Avge  | 100s | 50s | Ct | St | Balls | Runs  | Wkts | Avge  | Best | 5wI | 10wM |
|------------|-----|------|----|------|-----|-------|------|-----|----|----|-------|-------|------|-------|------|-----|------|
| Test       | 80  | 106  | 30 | 683  | 30* | 8.98  | -    | -   | 12 | -  | 17086 | 7534  | 301  | 25.02 | 7-37 | 11  | 2    |
| All First  | 320 | 400  | 90 | 3837 | 66  | 12.37 | -    | 8   | 82 | -  | 61326 | 29200 | 1305 | 22.37 | 9-72 | 75  | 15   |
| 1-day Int  | 142 | 50   | 21 | 251  | 30  | 8.65  | -    | -   | 20 | -  | 7476  | 4786  | 158  | 30.29 | 5-1  | 1   |      |
| NatWest    | 19  | 12   | 3  | 136  | 37  | 15.11 | -    | -   | 2  | -  | 1218  | 648   | 41   | 15.80 | 6-21 | 2   |      |
| B & H      | 21  | 13   | 4  | 87   | 28  | 9.66  | -    | -   | -  | -  | 1255  | 745   | 24   | 31.04 | 2-19 | -   |      |
| Sunday     | 100 | 64   | 10 | 493  | 35  | 9.12  | -    | -   | 20 | -  | 4090  | 2725  | 135  | 20.18 | 4-19 | -   |      |

# WALTON, T. C. — Northamptonshire

**Name:** Timothy Charles Walton
**Role:** Right-hand bat, right-arm medium bowler
**Born:** 8 November 1972, Low Lead
**Height:** 6ft **Weight:** 12st 10lbs
**Nickname:** TC, Eric Spadge
**County debut:** 1992 (one-day), 1994 (first-class)
**1st-Class 50s:** 1
**1st-Class catches:** 2
**Place in batting averages:** 230th av. 17.33
**Parents:** Alan Michael and Sally Ann
**Marital status:** single
**Family links with cricket:** Father and two brothers, Jamie and Adam, play for local village
**Education:** Leeds Grammar School; University of Northumbria, Newcastle

**Qualifications:** 7 GCSEs, 3 A-levels, studying for Sports degree
**Career outside cricket:** Student
**Overseas tours:** England U19 to Pakistan 1991-92
**Cricketers particularly admired:** Phillip DeFreitas
**Other sports followed:** Rugby union and league
**Relaxations:** Running, raving and listening to music
**Opinions on cricket:** 'Appearance should be irrelevant if the cricketer is good enough, i.e. long hair should be of no consequence. More commerciality and one-day games.'
**Best batting:** 71 Northamptonshire v Somerset, Taunton 1995
**Best bowling:** 1-46 Northamptonshire v Somerset, Taunton 1994

### 1995 Season

|  | M | Inns | NO | Runs | HS | Avge | 100s | 50s | Ct | St | O | M | Runs | Wkts | Avge | Best | 5wI | 10wM |
|---|---|---|---|---|---|---|---|---|---|---|---|---|---|---|---|---|---|---|
| Test |  |  |  |  |  |  |  |  |  |  |  |  |  |  |  |  |  |  |
| All First | 4 | 7 | 1 | 104 | 71 | 17.33 | - | 1 | - | - | 8 | 2 | 26 | 0 | - | - | - | -- |
| 1-day Int |  |  |  |  |  |  |  |  |  |  |  |  |  |  |  |  |  |  |
| NatWest |  |  |  |  |  |  |  |  |  |  |  |  |  |  |  |  |  |  |  |
| B & H | 2 | 2 | 0 | 35 | 29 | 17.50 | - | - | 1 | - | 6 | 0 | 27 | 1 | 27.00 | 1-27 | - |  |
| Sunday | 9 | 9 | 0 | 224 | 56 | 24.88 | - | 1 | 4 | - | 3 | 0 | 26 | 0 | - | - | - |  |

### Career Performances

|  | M | Inns | NO | Runs | HS | Avge | 100s | 50s | Ct | St | Balls | Runs | Wkts | Avge | Best | 5wI | 10wM |
|---|---|---|---|---|---|---|---|---|---|---|---|---|---|---|---|---|---|
| Test |  |  |  |  |  |  |  |  |  |  |  |  |  |  |  |  |  |
| All First | 6 | 9 | 1 | 120 | 71 | 15.00 | - | 1 | 2 | - | 168 | 124 | 2 | 62.00 | 1-46 | - | - |
| 1-day Int |  |  |  |  |  |  |  |  |  |  |  |  |  |  |  |  |  |
| NatWest |  |  |  |  |  |  |  |  |  |  |  |  |  |  |  |  |  |  |
| B & H | 2 | 2 | 0 | 35 | 29 | 17.50 | - | - | 1 | - | 36 | 27 | 1 | 27.00 | 1-27 | - |  |
| Sunday | 20 | 18 | 2 | 491 | 72 | 30.68 | - | 4 | 10 | - | 240 | 197 | 6 | 32.83 | 2-27 | - |  |

# WARD, D. M.                                            Surrey

**Name:** David Mark Ward
**Role:** Right-hand bat, right-arm off-spin bowler, occasional wicket-keeper
**Born:** 10 February 1961, Croydon
**Height:** 6ft 1in **Weight:** 14st
**Nickname:** Cocker, Wardy, Jaws, Gnasher, Fat Boy, Piano Man
**County debut:** 1985
**County cap:** 1990
**1000 runs in a season:** 2
**1st-Class 50s:** 31
**1st-Class 100s:** 16
**1st-Class 200s:** 3

**1st-Class catches:** 118
**1st-Class stumpings:** 3
**One-Day 100s:** 3
**Place in batting averages:** (1994 37th av. 43.85)
**Parents:** Tom and Dora
**Wife and date of marriage:** Ruth, 2 October 1993
**Family links with cricket:** 'Uncle (John Goodey) local legend with Banstead and Temple Bar CC'
**Education:** Haling Manor High School; Croydon Technical College
**Qualifications:** 2 O-levels, Advanced City & Guilds in Carpentry and Joinery
**Career outside cricket:** Mortgage expert (Home Owners Advisory Service) and carpenter
**Overseas tours:** Surrey to Barbados 1984, 1989, 1991; Lancashire to Mombasa 1990; MCC to Bahrain 1994-95
**Overseas teams played for:** Caulfield, Melbourne 1984-87; Sunshine, Melbourne 1988-89; Perth, Western Australia 1990-91; St Augustine, Cape Town 1992-93
**Cricketers particularly admired:** Robert Thompson (brother of 'Candles' Thompson) of Sturt CC, Adelaide, Geoff Howarth, Grahame Clinton
**Other sports followed:** Greyhound racing
**Extras:** In 1990 became first Surrey batsman since John Edrich to score 2000 runs in a season and shared county record stand of 413 for third wicket with Darren Bicknell v Kent at Canterbury. Hit century in 70 minutes for Surrey v Northamptonshire 1992. Awarded benefit for 1996
**Best batting:** 294* Surrey v Derbyshire, The Oval 1994
**Best bowling:** 2-66 Surrey v Gloucestershire, Guildford 1991

## 1995 Season

|           | M | Inns | NO | Runs | HS   | Avge  | 100s | 50s | Ct | St | O | M | Runs | Wkts | Avge | Best | 5wl | 10wM |
|-----------|---|------|----|------|------|-------|------|-----|----|----|---|---|------|------|------|------|-----|------|
| Test      |   |      |    |      |      |       |      |     |    |    |   |   |      |      |      |      |     |      |
| All First | 3 | 4    | 0  | 66   | 51   | 16.50 | -    | 1   | 2  | -  |   |   |      |      |      |      |     |      |
| 1-day Int |   |      |    |      |      |       |      |     |    |    |   |   |      |      |      |      |     |      |
| NatWest   |   |      |    |      |      |       |      |     |    |    |   |   |      |      |      |      |     |      |
| B & H     | 4 | 3    | 2  | 88   | 60 * | 88.00 | -    | 1   | 1  | -  |   |   |      |      |      |      |     |      |
| Sunday    | 9 | 9    | 1  | 162  | 49   | 20.25 | -    | -   | -  | -  |   |   |      |      |      |      |     |      |

## Career Performances

|  | M | Inns | NO | Runs | HS | Avge | 100s | 50s | Ct | St | Balls | Runs | Wkts | Avge | Best | 5wI | 10wM |
|---|---|---|---|---|---|---|---|---|---|---|---|---|---|---|---|---|---|
| Test |  |  |  |  |  |  |  |  |  |  |  |  |  |  |  |  |  |
| All First | 153 | 240 | 33 | 7997 | 294 * | 38.63 | 16 | 31 | 118 | 3 | 107 | 113 | 2 | 56.50 | 2-66 | - | - |
| 1-day Int |  |  |  |  |  |  |  |  |  |  |  |  |  |  |  |  |  |
| NatWest | 21 | 17 | 1 | 616 | 101 * | 38.50 | 1 | 5 | 8 | - |  |  |  |  |  |  |  |
| B & H | 34 | 30 | 6 | 673 | 73 | 28.04 | - | 4 | 12 | 2 |  |  |  |  |  |  |  |
| Sunday | 149 | 132 | 22 | 3271 | 102 * | 29.73 | 2 | 21 | 67 | 1 |  |  |  |  |  |  |  |

# WARD, T. R. Kent

**Kent**

**Name:** Trevor Robert Ward
**Role:** Right-hand bat, occasional
off-spin bowler
**Born:** 18 January 1968, Farningham, Kent
**Height:** 5ft 11in **Weight:** 13st
**Nickname:** Wardy, Chikka
**County debut:** 1986
**County cap:** 1989
**1000 runs in a season:** 4
**1st-Class 50s:** 52
**1st-Class 100s:** 20
**1st-Class 200s:** 1
**1st-Class catches:** 138
**One-Day 100s:** 6
**Place in batting averages:** 127th av. 30.06
(1994 47th av. 42.75)
**Parents:** Robert Henry and Hazel Ann
**Wife and date of marriage:** Sarah Ann,
29 September 1990
**Family links with cricket:** Father played club cricket
**Education:** Anthony Roper County Primary; Hextable Comprehensive
**Qualifications:** 7 O-levels, NCA coaching award
**Overseas tours:** NCA to Bermuda 1985; England YC to Sri Lanka 1986-87, to
Australia (Youth World Cup) 1987-88
**Overseas teams played for:** Scarborough, Perth, Western Australia 1985; Gosnells,
Perth 1993
**Cricketers particularly admired:** Ian Botham, Graham Gooch, Robin Smith
**Other sports followed:** Most sports
**Relaxations:** Fishing, watching television, golf
**Extras:** Was awarded £1000 for becoming the first player to score 400 runs in the
Benson and Hedges Cup in 1995

**Best batting:** 235* Kent v Middlesex, Canterbury 1991
**Best bowling:** 2-48 Kent v Worcestershire, Canterbury 1990

### 1995 Season

|  | M | Inns | NO | Runs | HS | Avge | 100s | 50s | Ct | St | O | M | Runs | Wkts | Avge | Best | 5wI | 10wM |
|---|---|---|---|---|---|---|---|---|---|---|---|---|---|---|---|---|---|---|
| Test |  |  |  |  |  |  |  |  |  |  |  |  |  |  |  |  |  |  |
| All First | 18 | 32 | 1 | 932 | 114 * | 30.06 | 2 | 6 | 23 | - | 3.5 | 0 | 43 | 0 | - | - | - | - |
| 1-day Int |  |  |  |  |  |  |  |  |  |  |  |  |  |  |  |  |  |  |
| NatWest | 2 | 2 | 0 | 121 | 68 | 60.50 | - | 2 | 1 | - | 3 | 0 | 14 | 0 | - |  | - | - |
| B & H | 7 | 7 | 1 | 469 | 125 | 78.16 | 2 | 3 | 2 | - |  |  |  |  |  |  |  |  |
| Sunday | 16 | 16 | 1 | 483 | 123 | 32.20 | 1 | 3 | 5 | - |  |  |  |  |  |  |  |  |

### Career Performances

|  | M | Inns | NO | Runs | HS | Avge | 100s | 50s | Ct | St | Balls | Runs | Wkts | Avge | Best | 5wI | 10wM |
|---|---|---|---|---|---|---|---|---|---|---|---|---|---|---|---|---|---|
| Test |  |  |  |  |  |  |  |  |  |  |  |  |  |  |  |  |  |
| All First | 150 | 257 | 16 | 8971 | 235 * | 37.22 | 20 | 52 | 138 | - | 987 | 580 | 6 | 96.66 | 2-48 | - | - |
| 1-day Int |  |  |  |  |  |  |  |  |  |  |  |  |  |  |  |  |  |
| NatWest | 17 | 17 | 0 | 801 | 120 | 47.11 | 1 | 7 | 2 | - | 126 | 101 | 1 | 101.00 | 1-58 | - |  |
| B & H | 31 | 31 | 3 | 1040 | 125 | 37.14 | 2 | 6 | 7 | - | 12 | 10 | 0 | - | - |  |  |
| Sunday | 110 | 109 | 4 | 3160 | 131 | 30.09 | 3 | 19 | 25 | - | 228 | 187 | 6 | 31.16 | 3-20 | - |  |

# WARNER, A. E. Derbyshire

**Name:** Allan Esmond Warner
**Role:** Right-hand bat, right-arm fast bowler, outfielder
**Born:** 12 May 1959, Birmingham
**Height:** 5ft 8in **Weight:** 10st
**Nickname:** Esis
**County debut:** 1982 (Worcestershire), 1985 (Derbyshire)
**County cap:** 1987 (Derbyshire)
**Benefit:** 1995
**1st-Class 50s:** 15
**1st-Class 5 w. in innings:** 8
**1st-Class 10 w. in match:** 1
**1st-Class catches:** 46
**One-Day 5 w. in innings:** 1
**Place in batting averages:** 217th av. 18.92
**Place in bowling averages:** 46th av. 26.92
(1994 129th av. 43.00)
**Strike rate:** 57.71 (career 63.28)

**Parents:** Edgar and Sarah
**Children:** Alvin, 6 September 1980
**Education:** Tabernacle School, St Kitts, West Indies
**Qualifications:** CSE Maths
**Cricketers particularly admired:** Malcolm Marshall, Michael Holding
**Other sports followed:** Football, boxing and athletics
**Relaxations:** Watching movies, music (soul, reggae and calypso)
**Extras:** Derbyshire Player of the Year 1993
**Best batting:** 95* Derbyshire v Kent, Canterbury 1993
**Best bowling:** 6-21 Derbyshire v Lancashire, Derby 1995

## 1995 Season

|  | M | Inns | NO | Runs | HS | Avge | 100s | 50s | Ct | St | O | M | Runs | Wkts | Avge | Best | 5wI | 10wM |
|---|---|---|---|---|---|---|---|---|---|---|---|---|---|---|---|---|---|---|
| Test |  |  |  |  |  |  |  |  |  |  |  |  |  |  |  |  |  |  |
| All First | 14 | 22 | 8 | 265 | 43 | 18.92 | - | - | 2 | - | 375.1 | 90 | 1050 | 39 | 26.92 | 6-21 | 3 | - |
| 1-day Int |  |  |  |  |  |  |  |  |  |  |  |  |  |  |  |  |  |  |
| NatWest | 1 | 1 | 0 | 0 | 0 | 0.00 | - | - | - | - | 12 | 0 | 63 | 0 | - | - | - | - |
| B & H | 3 | 1 | 1 | 2 | 2* | - | - | - | - | - | 33 | 5 | 111 | 5 | 22.20 | 2-26 | - |  |
| Sunday | 13 | 6 | 0 | 26 | 11 | 4.33 | - | - | 2 | - | 82 | 8 | 300 | 20 | 15.00 | 4-14 | - |  |

## Career Performances

|  | M | Inns | NO | Runs | HS | Avge | 100s | 50s | Ct | St | Balls | Runs | Wkts | Avge | Best | 5wI | 10wM |
|---|---|---|---|---|---|---|---|---|---|---|---|---|---|---|---|---|---|
| Test |  |  |  |  |  |  |  |  |  |  |  |  |  |  |  |  |  |
| All First | 199 | 272 | 52 | 3763 | 95* | 17.10 | - | 15 | 46 | - | 26894 | 13358 | 425 | 31.43 | 6-21 | 8 | 1 |
| 1-day Int |  |  |  |  |  |  |  |  |  |  |  |  |  |  |  |  |  |
| NatWest | 16 | 12 | 2 | 90 | 32 | 9.00 | - | - | 1 | - | 1011 | 656 | 17 | 38.58 | 4-39 | - |  |
| B & H | 50 | 29 | 12 | 213 | 35* | 12.52 | - | - | 5 | - | 2779 | 1768 | 70 | 25.25 | 4-36 | - |  |
| Sunday | 154 | 104 | 24 | 1018 | 68 | 12.72 | - | 2 | 23 | - | 6187 | 5100 | 183 | 27.86 | 5-39 | 1 |  |

# WARREN, R. J.        Northamptonshire

**Name:** Russell John Warren
**Role:** Right-hand bat, occasional off-spin bowler
**Born:** 10 September 1971, Northampton
**Height:** 6ft 2in **Weight:** 12st 4lbs
**Nickname:** Rabbit
**County debut:** 1992
**County cap:** 1995
**1st-Class 50s:** 10
**1st-Class 100s:** 1
**1st-Class catches:** 44
**1st-Class stumpings:** 1

**One-Day 100s:** 1
**Place in batting averages:** 60th av. 41.54
(1994 130th av. 29.78)
**Parents:** John and Sally
**Marital status:** Single
**Education:** Whitehills Lower School;
Kingsthorpe Middle and Upper Schools
**Qualifications:** 8 O-levels, 2 A-levels
**Overseas tours:** England YC to New
Zealand 1990-91
**Overseas teams played for:**
Lancaster Park, Christchurch, and Canterbury
B, New Zealand 1991-92
**Cricketers particularly admired:** Viv
Richards, Wayne Larkins, Graham Gooch
**Other sports followed:** Most sports,
especially golf, football, snooker
**Relaxations:** 'Playing snooker at local club
and having a relaxing nine holes of golf at

Kingsthorpe GC; keen supporter of the Cobblers and Manchester United'
**Opinions on cricket:** 'Uncovered pitches should return. This will encourage more spin
bowling and require batsmen and bowlers to be more flexible.'
**Best batting:** 154 Northamptonshire v Nottinghamshire, Northampton 1995

## 1995 Season

|  | M | Inns | NO | Runs | HS | Avge | 100s | 50s | Ct | St | O | M | Runs | Wkts | Avge | Best | 5wI | 10wM |
|---|---|---|---|---|---|---|---|---|---|---|---|---|---|---|---|---|---|---|
| Test |  |  |  |  |  |  |  |  |  |  |  |  |  |  |  |  |  |  |
| All First | 16 | 27 | 5 | 914 | 154 | 41.54 | 1 | 5 | 27 | 1 |  |  |  |  |  |  |  |  |
| 1-day Int |  |  |  |  |  |  |  |  |  |  |  |  |  |  |  |  |  |  |
| NatWest | 5 | 4 | 1 | 97 | 44 | 32.33 | - | - | 9 | - |  |  |  |  |  |  |  |  |
| B & H | 4 | 4 | 0 | 53 | 23 | 13.25 | - | - | 5 | - |  |  |  |  |  |  |  |  |
| Sunday | 15 | 12 | 2 | 186 | 44 * | 18.60 | - | - | 15 | 3 |  |  |  |  |  |  |  |  |

## Career Performances

|  | M | Inns | NO | Runs | HS | Avge | 100s | 50s | Ct | St | Balls | Runs | Wkts | Avge | Best | 5wI | 10wM |
|---|---|---|---|---|---|---|---|---|---|---|---|---|---|---|---|---|---|
| Test |  |  |  |  |  |  |  |  |  |  |  |  |  |  |  |  |  |
| All First | 35 | 57 | 9 | 1563 | 154 | 32.56 | 1 | 10 | 44 | 1 |  |  |  |  |  |  |  |
| 1-day Int |  |  |  |  |  |  |  |  |  |  |  |  |  |  |  |  |  |
| NatWest | 8 | 7 | 2 | 235 | 100 * | 47.00 | 1 | - | 10 | - |  |  |  |  |  |  |  |
| B & H | 4 | 4 | 0 | 53 | 23 | 13.25 | - | - | 5 | - |  |  |  |  |  |  |  |
| Sunday | 33 | 27 | 4 | 493 | 71 * | 21.43 | - | 3 | 24 | 4 |  |  |  |  |  |  |  |

# WASIM AKRAM                          Lancashire

**Name:** Wasim Akram
**Role:** Left-hand bat, left-arm
fast-medium bowler
**Born:** 3 June 1966, Lahore, Pakistan
**Height:** 6ft 3in **Weight:** 12st 7lbs
**County debut:** 1988
**County cap:** 1989
**Test debut:** 1984-85
**Tests:** 61
**One-Day Internationals:** 189
**50 wickets in a season:** 5
**1st-Class 50s:** 17
**1st-Class 100s:** 4
**1st-Class 5 w. in innings:** 59
**1st-Class 10 w. in match:** 14
**1st-Class catches:** 56
**One-Day 5 w. in innings:** 8
**Place in batting averages:** 188th av. 22.26

(1994 169th av. 24.40)
**Place in bowling averages:** 6th av. 19.72 (1994 16th av. 23.92)
**Strike rate:** 38.38 (career 48.13)
**Education:** Islamia College, Pakistan
**Off-season:** Playing for Pakistan
**Overseas tours:** Pakistan U23 to Sri Lanka 1984-85; Pakistan to New Zealand
1984-85, to Sri Lanka 1985-86, to India 1986-87, to England 1987, to West Indies
1987-88, to Australia 1989-90, to Australia and New Zealand (World Cup) 1991-92,
to England 1992, to New Zealand, Australia, South Africa and West Indies 1992-93,
to New Zealand 1993-94, to South Africa 1994-95, to Australia 1995-96, to India and
Sri Lanka (World Cup) 1995-96
**Overseas teams played for:** PACO 1984-86; Lahore Whites 1985-86
**Extras:** His second first-class match was playing for Pakistan on tour in New Zealand.
Imran Khan wrote of him: 'I have great faith in Wasim Akram. I think he will become a
great all-rounder, as long as he realises how much hard work is required. As a bowler he
is extremely gifted, and has it in him to be the best left-armer since Alan Davidson.' Hit
maiden Test 100 v Australia 1989-90 during stand of 191 with Imran Khan. Signed a
new four-year contract with Lancashire in 1992. Appointed captain of Pakistan 1992-93
and replaced by Salim Malik on tour to New Zealand 1993-94. Has become the second
Pakistan bowler to take over 250 Test wickets
**Best batting:** 123 Pakistan v Australia, Adelaide 1989-90
**Best bowling:** 8-30 Lancashire v Somerset, Southport 1994

## 1995 Season

| | M | Inns | NO | Runs | HS | Avge | 100s | 50s | Ct | St | O | M | Runs | Wkts | Avge | Best | 5wI | 10wM |
|---|---|---|---|---|---|---|---|---|---|---|---|---|---|---|---|---|---|---|
| Test | | | | | | | | | | | | | | | | | | |
| All First | 14 | 22 | 3 | 423 | 61 | 22.26 | - | 4 | 1 | - | 518.1 | 108 | 1598 | 81 | 19.72 | 7-52 | 7 | 3 |
| 1-day Int | | | | | | | | | | | | | | | | | | |
| NatWest | 3 | 2 | 1 | 13 | 13* | 13.00 | - | - | 2 | - | 36 | 5 | 129 | 3 | 43.00 | 2-46 | - | |
| B & H | 6 | 3 | 0 | 76 | 64 | 25.33 | - | 1 | 1 | - | 51.1 | 5 | 239 | 11 | 21.72 | 3-59 | - | |
| Sunday | 15 | 12 | 2 | 159 | 32 | 15.90 | - | - | 3 | - | 112.5 | 7 | 415 | 29 | 14.31 | 4-16 | - | |

## Career Performances

| | M | Inns | NO | Runs | HS | Avge | 100s | 50s | Ct | St | Balls | Runs | Wkts | Avge | Best | 5wI | 10wM |
|---|---|---|---|---|---|---|---|---|---|---|---|---|---|---|---|---|---|
| Test | 61 | 82 | 11 | 1398 | 123 | 19.69 | 1 | 4 | 21 | - | 14039 | 6058 | 261 | 23.21 | 7-119 | 18 | 3 |
| All First | 179 | 244 | 29 | 4679 | 123 | 21.76 | 4 | 17 | 56 | - | 35954 | 16075 | 747 | 21.51 | 8-30 | 59 | 14 |
| 1-day Int | 189 | 144 | 27 | 1680 | 86 | 14.35 | - | 2 | 33 | - | 9800 | 6174 | 273 | 22.61 | 5-15 | 5 | |
| NatWest | 17 | 14 | 3 | 192 | 50 | 17.45 | - | 1 | 5 | - | 1090 | 681 | 23 | 29.60 | 4-27 | - | |
| B & H | 28 | 21 | 4 | 454 | 64 | 26.70 | - | 2 | 2 | - | 1673 | 1088 | 54 | 20.14 | 5-10 | 2 | |
| Sunday | 91 | 73 | 19 | 1221 | 51* | 22.61 | - | 2 | 18 | - | 3922 | 2825 | 145 | 19.48 | 5-41 | 1 | |

# WATKIN, S. L.       Glamorgan

**Name:** Steven Llewellyn Watkin
**Role:** Right-hand bat, right-arm
fast-medium bowler
**Born:** 15 September 1964, Maesteg
**Height:** 6ft 3in **Weight:** 12st 8lbs
**Nickname:** Watty, Banger
**County debut:** 1986
**County cap:** 1989
**Test debut:** 1991
**Tests:** 3
**One-Day Internationals:** 4
**50 wickets in a season:** 7
**1st-Class 5 w. in innings:** 22
**1st-Class 10 w. in match:** 4
**1st-Class catches:** 42
**One-Day 5 w. in innings:** 1
**Place in batting averages:** 270th av. 12.42
**Place in bowling averages:** 49th av. 27.00
(1994 70th av. 31.03)
**Strike rate:** 54.52 (career 59.13)
**Parents:** John and Sandra
**Marital status:** Single

**Family links with cricket:** One brother plays local cricket; 'older brother a good watcher'
**Education:** Cymer Afan Comprehensive; Swansea College of Further Education; South Glamorgan Institute of Higher Education
**Qualifications:** 8 O-levels, 2 A-levels, BA (Hons) in Human Movement Studies
**Off-season:** 'Learning Welsh'
**Overseas tours:** British Colleges to West Indies 1987; England A to Kenya and Zimbabwe 1989-90, to Pakistan and Sri Lanka 1990-91, to Bermuda and West Indies 1991-92; England to West Indies 1993-94
**Overseas teams played for:** Potchefstroom University, South Africa 1987-88; Aurora, Durban, South Africa 1991-92
**Cricketers particularly admired:** Richard Hadlee, Dennis Lillee, Ian Botham
**Other sports followed:** All sports except horse racing
**Injuries:** Back ligament tear, missed two weeks
**Relaxations:** Watching television, music, DIY, motor mechanics, 'a quiet pint'
**Extras:** Joint highest wicket-taker in 1989 with 94 wickets and took most (92) in 1993. Sister Lynda has played for Great Britain at hockey. Players' Player of the Year and Glamorgan Player of the Year 1993
**Opinions on cricket:** 'Four-day should start on Wednesday and finish Saturday, with Sunday game the same except bowling off 15 yards again.'
**Best batting:** 41 Glamorgan v Worcestershire, Worcester 1992
**Best bowling:** 8-59 Glamorgan v Warwickshire, Edgbaston 1988

## 1995 Season

|           | M  | Inns | NO | Runs | HS   | Avge  | 100s | 50s | Ct | St | O     | M   | Runs | Wkts | Avge  | Best | 5wI | 10wM |
|-----------|----|------|----|------|------|-------|------|-----|----|----|-------|-----|------|------|-------|------|-----|------|
| Test      |    |      |    |      |      |       |      |     |    |    |       |     |      |      |       |      |     |      |
| All First | 16 | 23   | 9  | 174  | 30   | 12.42 | -    | -   | 8  | -  | 590.4 | 144 | 1755 | 65   | 27.00 | 7-49 | 2   | 1    |
| 1-day Int |    |      |    |      |      |       |      |     |    |    |       |     |      |      |       |      |     |      |
| NatWest   | 4  | 2    | 0  | 2    | 2    | 1.00  | -    | -   | -  | -  | 40    | 9   | 121  | 6    | 20.16 | 4-26 | -   |      |
| B & H     | 5  | 2    | 1  | 11   | 7 *  | 11.00 | -    | -   | 3  | -  | 52    | 7   | 203  | 7    | 29.00 | 3-56 | -   |      |
| Sunday    | 16 | 3    | 1  | 17   | 13 * | 8.50  | -    | -   | 2  | -  | 125.1 | 10  | 508  | 32   | 15.87 | 4-38 | -   |      |

## Career Performances

|           | M   | Inns | NO | Runs | HS   | Avge | 100s | 50s | Ct | St | Balls | Runs  | Wkts | Avge  | Best | 5wI | 10wM |
|-----------|-----|------|----|------|------|------|------|-----|----|----|-------|-------|------|-------|------|-----|------|
| Test      | 3   | 5    | 0  | 25   | 13   | 5.00 | -    | -   | 1  | -  | 534   | 305   | 11   | 27.72 | 4-65 | -   | -    |
| All First | 174 | 194  | 63 | 1235 | 41   | 9.42 | -    | -   | 42 | -  | 35184 | 17458 | 595  | 29.34 | 8-59 | 22  | 4    |
| 1-day Int | 4   | 2    | 0  | 4    | 4    | 2.00 | -    | -   | -  | -  | 221   | 193   | 7    | 27.57 | 4-49 | -   |      |
| NatWest   | 22  | 10   | 4  | 39   | 9    | 6.50 | -    | -   | 2  | -  | 1386  | 689   | 28   | 24.60 | 4-26 | -   |      |
| B & H     | 23  | 15   | 7  | 59   | 15   | 7.37 | -    | -   | 5  | -  | 1383  | 898   | 26   | 34.53 | 3-28 | -   |      |
| Sunday    | 98  | 36   | 12 | 192  | 31 * | 8.00 | -    | -   | 15 | -  | 4310  | 3134  | 125  | 25.07 | 5-23 | 1   |      |

# WATKINSON, M. Lancashire

**Name:** Michael Watkinson
**Role:** Right-hand bat, right-arm medium or off-spin bowler, county captain
**Born:** 1 August 1961, Westhoughton
**Height:** 6ft 1½in **Weight:** 13st
**Nickname:** Winker
**County debut:** 1982
**County cap:** 1987
**Test debut:** 1995
**Tests:** 3
**1000 runs in a season:** 1
**50 wickets in a season:** 7
**1st-Class 50s:** 43
**1st-Class 100s:** 9
**1st-Class 5 w. in innings:** 25
**1st-Class 10 w. in match:** 3
**1st-Class catches:** 125
**One-Day 5 w. in innings:** 2
**Place in batting averages:** 102nd av. 34.11 (1994 97th av. 34.19)
**Place in bowling averages:** 65th av. 29.38 (1994 52nd av. 28.93)
**Strike rate:** 57.47 (career 64.08)
**Parents:** Albert and Marian
**Wife and date of marriage:** Susan, 12 April 1986
**Children:** Charlotte, 24 February 1989; Liam, 27 July 1991
**Education:** Rivington and Blackrod High School, Horwich
**Qualifications:** 8 O-levels, HTC Civil Engineering
**Career outside cricket:** Draughtsman
**Off-season:** England tour to South Africa
**Overseas tours:** England to South Africa 1995-96
**Cricketers particularly admired:** Clive Lloyd, Imran Khan
**Other sports followed:** Football
**Relaxations:** Watching Bolton Wanderers
**Extras:** Played for Cheshire in Minor Counties Championship and in NatWest Trophy (v Middlesex) 1982. Man of the Match in the first Refuge Assurance Cup final 1988 and in B&H Cup final 1990. Appointed county captain for 1994 season
**Best batting:** 161 Lancashire v Essex, Old Trafford 1995
**Best bowling:** 8-30 Lancashire v Hampshire, Old Trafford 1994

## 1995 Season

| | M | Inns | NO | Runs | HS | Avge | 100s | 50s | Ct | St | O | M | Runs | Wkts | Avge | Best | 5wI | 10wM |
|---|---|---|---|---|---|---|---|---|---|---|---|---|---|---|---|---|---|---|
| Test | 3 | 4 | 1 | 156 | 82 * | 52.00 | - | 1 | 1 | - | 93 | 21 | 289 | 8 | 36.12 | 3-64 | - | - |
| All First | 18 | 29 | 3 | 887 | 161 | 34.11 | 2 | 3 | 7 | - | 622.4 | 158 | 1910 | 65 | 29.38 | 7-140 | 2 | 1 |
| 1-day Int | | | | | | | | | | | | | | | | | | |
| NatWest | 3 | 2 | 0 | 56 | 55 | 28.00 | - | 1 | 1 | - | 35 | 4 | 126 | 6 | 21.00 | 3-41 | - | |
| B & H | 7 | 5 | 2 | 42 | 34 * | 14.00 | - | - | 4 | - | 68.1 | 3 | 282 | 7 | 40.28 | 3-42 | - | |
| Sunday | 13 | 9 | 0 | 145 | 26 | 16.11 | - | - | 7 | - | 94.5 | 4 | 449 | 16 | 28.06 | 2-29 | - | |

## Career Performances

| | M | Inns | NO | Runs | HS | Avge | 100s | 50s | Ct | St | Balls | Runs | Wkts | Avge | Best | 5wI | 10wM |
|---|---|---|---|---|---|---|---|---|---|---|---|---|---|---|---|---|---|
| Test | 3 | 4 | 1 | 156 | 82 * | 52.00 | - | 1 | 1 | - | 558 | 289 | 8 | 36.12 | 3-64 | - | - |
| All First | 255 | 379 | 45 | 8984 | 161 | 26.89 | 9 | 43 | 125 | - | 40949 | 21169 | 639 | 33.12 | 8-30 | 25 | 3 |
| 1-day Int | | | | | | | | | | | | | | | | | |
| NatWest | 34 | 28 | 7 | 697 | 90 | 33.19 | - | 6 | 9 | - | 2081 | 1341 | 38 | 35.28 | 3-14 | - | |
| B & H | 62 | 44 | 12 | 665 | 76 | 20.78 | - | 3 | 15 | - | 3225 | 2236 | 69 | 32.40 | 5-49 | 1 | |
| Sunday | 186 | 143 | 36 | 2217 | 83 | 20.71 | - | 5 | 43 | - | 7356 | 5928 | 183 | 32.39 | 5-46 | 1 | |

# WAUGH, M. E.                    Essex

**Name:** Mark Edward Waugh
**Role:** Right-hand bat, right-arm
medium pace bowler
**Born:** 2 June 1965, Canterbury, New South
Wales, Australia
**Height:** 6ft 1in  **Weight:** 13st 7lbs
**Nickname:** Junior, Tugga
**County debut:** 1988
**County cap:** 1989
**Test debut:** 1990-91
**Tests:** 48
**One-Day Internationals:** 96
**1000 runs in a season:** 4
**1st-Class 50s:** 82
**1st-Class 100s:** 57
**1st-Class 200s:** 4
**1st-Class 5 w. in innings:** 2
**1st-Class catches:** 262
**One-Day 100s:** 9
**One-Day 5 w. in innings:** 1
**Place in batting averages:** 22nd av. 51.55
**Place in bowling averages:** 136th av. 46.41

**Strike rate:** 90.29 (career 71.47)
**Parents:** Rodger and Beverley
**Marital status:** Single
**Family links with cricket:** Uncle a First Grade cricketer in Sydney for Bankstown/Canterbury. Twin brother Steve plays for Australia and played for Somerset in 1988. Younger brother Dean played in Bolton League with Astley Bridge in 1989 and made debut for NSW in 1990-91
**Education:** East Hills Boys High School
**Qualifications:** Higher School Certificate, cricket coach
**Career outside cricket:** 'Own some good racehorses'
**Off-season:** Playing cricket for New South Wales and Australia
**Overseas tours:** Young Australia to Zimbabwe 1985-86; New South Wales to Zimbabwe 1987-88; Australia to West Indies 1990-91, to Sri Lanka and New Zealand 1992-93, to England 1993, to South Africa 1993-94, to New Zealand 1994-95, to West Indies 1994-95, to India and Pakistan (World Cup) 1995-96
**Overseas teams played for:** New South Wales 1985-95
**Cricketers particularly admired:** Graham Gooch, Allan Border
**Other sports followed:** All sports
**Relaxations:** Sleeping, horseracing, golf, watching sport on television
**Extras:** Steve and Mark are only twins to score centuries in the same innings of a first-class match and both to play international cricket. Chosen as New South Wales Cricketer of the Year, 1988 and Sheffield Shield Cricketer of the Year, jointly with D.Tazelaar of Queensland. First batsman to score a century on his Sunday League debut. Took English summer off in 1991 but returned to Essex for 1992 season. He is the only Australian to score 3000 runs in a calendar year. Scored a century on his Test debut. Returned to Essex for 1995 season after two-year absence
**Opinions on cricket:** 'Leg-byes should not count as runs in one-day cricket – it's bad batting to miss balls. More money for top cricketers.'
**Best batting:** 229 New South Wales v Western Australia, Perth 1990-91
**Best bowling:** 5-37 Essex v Northamptonshire, Northampton 1990

## 1995 Season

| | M | Inns | NO | Runs | HS | Avge | 100s | 50s | Ct | St | O | M | Runs | Wkts | Avge | Best | 5wI | 10wM |
|---|---|---|---|---|---|---|---|---|---|---|---|---|---|---|---|---|---|---|
| Test | | | | | | | | | | | | | | | | | | |
| All First | 16 | 29 | 2 | 1392 | 173 | 51.55 | 5 | 6 | 19 | - | 255.5 | 66 | 789 | 17 | 46.41 | 4-76 | - | - |
| 1-day Int | | | | | | | | | | | | | | | | | | |
| NatWest | 2 | 2 | 0 | 40 | 38 | 20.00 | - | - | - | - | 23 | 2 | 141 | 1 | 141.00 | 1-45 | - | |
| B & H | | | | | | | | | | | | | | | | | | |
| Sunday | 16 | 16 | 0 | 608 | 89 | 38.00 | - | 5 | 8 | - | 80.3 | 1 | 462 | 15 | 30.80 | 3-20 | - | |

## Career Performances

| | M | Inns | NO | Runs | HS | Avge | 100s | 50s | Ct | St | Balls | Runs | Wkts | Avge | Best | 5wI | 10wM |
|---|---|---|---|---|---|---|---|---|---|---|---|---|---|---|---|---|---|
| Test | 48 | 77 | 4 | 3072 | 140 | 42.08 | 8 | 18 | 62 | - | 2484 | 1172 | 34 | 34.47 | 5-40 | 1 | - |
| All First | 224 | 356 | 46 | 17260 | 229 * | 55.67 | 57 | 82 | 262 | - | 11651 | 6319 | 163 | 38.76 | 5-37 | 2 | - |
| 1-day Int | 96 | 92 | 8 | 2887 | 121 * | 34.36 | 4 | 19 | 39 | - | 1677 | 1366 | 52 | 26.26 | 5-24 | 1 | |
| NatWest | 8 | 7 | 0 | 145 | 47 | 20.71 | - | - | 1 | - | 252 | 222 | 2 | 111.00 | 1-45 | - | |
| B & H | 16 | 14 | 1 | 438 | 100 | 33.69 | 1 | 2 | 5 | - | 95 | 76 | 4 | 19.00 | 3-31 | - | |
| Sunday | 63 | 61 | 11 | 2346 | 112 * | 46.92 | 4 | 15 | 24 | - | 1297 | 1234 | 40 | 30.85 | 3-20 | - | |

# WEEKES, P. N. Middlesex

**Name:** Paul Nicholas Weekes
**Role:** Left-hand bat, off-spin bowler
**Born:** 8 July 1969, Hackney, London
**Height:** 5ft 11in **Weight:** 13st
**Nickname:** Weekesy, Twiddles
**County debut:** 1990
**County cap:** 1993
**1st-Class 50s:** 14
**1st-Class 100s:** 3
**1st-Class 5 w. in innings:** 1
**1st-Class catches:** 55
**One-day 100s:** 1
**Place in batting averages:** 97th av. 34.31
(1994 100th av. 34.10)
**Place in bowling averages:** 147th av. 52.53
(1994 89th av. 33.73)
**Strike rate:** 119.38 (career 88.17)
**Parents:** Robert and Carol
**Marital status:** 'Partner Christine'
**Children:** Cheri, 4 September 1993
**Family links with cricket:** Father played club cricket
**Education:** Homerton House Secondary School, Hackney; Hackney College
**Qualifications:** NCA cricket coach
**Career outside cricket:** Coaching for Middlesex CYT
**Overseas tours:** England A to India 1994-95
**Overseas teams played for:** Newcastle University, NSW, 1989; Sunrise, Zimbabwe 1990
**Cricketers particularly admired:** David Gower, Richie Richardson
**Other sports followed:** Boxing – 'middle and heavyweight especially'
**Relaxations:** 'Listening to music – ragga, soca. Chilling with the family'
**Extras:** Scored 50 in first innings for both 2nd and 1st teams. Took two catches whilst appearing as 12th man for England in the Second Test against West Indies at Lord's in 1995
**Opinions on cricket:** 'Lunch and tea intervals should be longer.'

**Best batting:** 143 Middlesex v Oxford University, The Parks 1995
**Best bowling:** 5-12 Middlesex v Cambridge University, Fenner's 1994

## 1995 Season

| | M | Inns | NO | Runs | HS | Avge | 100s | 50s | Ct | St | | O | M | Runs | Wkts | Avge | Best | 5wl | 10wM |
|---|---|---|---|---|---|---|---|---|---|---|---|---|---|---|---|---|---|---|---|
| Test | | | | | | | | | | | | | | | | | | | |
| All First | 20 | 31 | 2 | 995 | 143 | 34.31 | 2 | 6 | 20 | - | | 258.4 | 55 | 679 | 13 | 52.23 | 3-26 | - | - |
| 1-day Int | | | | | | | | | | | | | | | | | | | |
| NatWest | 3 | 3 | 1 | 217 | 143 * | 108.50 | 1 | 1 | 1 | - | | 34 | 2 | 157 | 4 | 39.25 | 2-55 | - | |
| B & H | 6 | 6 | 1 | 208 | 67 * | 41.60 | - | 2 | - | - | | 52 | 0 | 187 | 7 | 26.71 | 3-33 | - | |
| Sunday | 16 | 16 | 1 | 405 | 50 * | 27.00 | - | 1 | 6 | - | | 78.1 | 1 | 331 | 10 | 33.10 | 4-41 | - | |

## Career Performances

| | M | Inns | NO | Runs | HS | Avge | 100s | 50s | Ct | St | Balls | Runs | Wkts | Avge | Best | 5wl | 10wM |
|---|---|---|---|---|---|---|---|---|---|---|---|---|---|---|---|---|---|
| Test | | | | | | | | | | | | | | | | | |
| All First | 69 | 98 | 13 | 2768 | 143 | 32.56 | 3 | 14 | 55 | - | 7230 | 3391 | 82 | 41.35 | 5-12 | 1 | - |
| 1-day Int | | | | | | | | | | | | | | | | | |
| NatWest | 7 | 7 | 1 | 228 | 143 * | 38.00 | 1 | 1 | 3 | - | 450 | 293 | 8 | 36.62 | 2-36 | - | |
| B & H | 17 | 14 | 3 | 317 | 67 * | 28.81 | - | 2 | 3 | - | 726 | 469 | 15 | 31.26 | 3-32 | - | |
| Sunday | 77 | 57 | 10 | 1163 | 66 * | 24.74 | - | 3 | 30 | - | 2773 | 2340 | 81 | 28.88 | 4-37 | - | |

# WELCH, G.          Warwickshire

**Name:** Graeme Welch
**Role:** Right-hand bat, right-arm
medium-fast bowler
**Born:** 21 March 1972, Tyne and Wear
**Height:** 6ft **Weight:** 13st
**Nickname:** Pop, Red Beard, Lalas
**County debut:** 1992 (one-day),
1994 (first-class)
**1st-Class 50s:** 4
**1st-Class catches:** 6
**Place in batting averages:**
(1994 73rd av. 37.16)
**Place in bowling averages:**
(1994 132nd av. 44.09)
**Strike rate:** (career 69.23)
**Parents:** Robert and Jean
**Marital status:** Girlfriend Emma
**Family links with cricket:**
Brother Barry and father play club cricket in Durham

**Education:** Hetton Lyons Junior School; Hetton Comprehensive
**Qualifications:** 9 GCSEs, City & Guilds in Sports Leisure
**Career outside cricket:** 'Everything and anything'
**Off-season:** Playing and coaching in Northern Transvaal
**Overseas tours:** Warwickshire to Cape Town 1992 and 1993
**Overseas teams played for:** Avendale, Cape Town 1991-93
**Cricketers particularly admired:** Gladstone Small, Steve Waugh, Allan Donald, Brian Lara, Andy Moles, Mike Burns
**Other sports followed:** 'I'll try anything except golf'
**Relaxations:** 'Watching television, listening to music, going out with Emma, playing on the Megadrive with my brother Baz.'
**Extras:** Played for England YC v Australian YC 1991. Took first ever hat-trick in 2nd XI Championship v Durham 1992. Axa Equity and Law Winners Medal 1994. Britannic Assurance Winners Medal 1994. Warwickshire's most improved player in 1994
**Opinions on cricket:** 'Tea is too short and should be extended to 30 minutes. 110 overs in a day is too many and should be reduced to 100. 2nd XI wickets are a disgrace compared to 1st XI wickets. There should be more games played on county grounds. Cricketers should be better provided for in the off-season (i.e. ten-month contracts).'
**Best batting:** 84* Warwickshire v Nottinghamshire, Edgbaston 1994
**Best bowling:** 4-74 Warwickshire v Yorkshire, Scarborough 1994

## 1995 Season

|  | M | Inns | NO | Runs | HS | Avge | 100s | 50s | Ct | St | O | M | Runs | Wkts | Avge | Best | 5wI | 10wM |
|---|---|---|---|---|---|---|---|---|---|---|---|---|---|---|---|---|---|---|
| Test |  |  |  |  |  |  |  |  |  |  |  |  |  |  |  |  |  |  |
| All First | 1 | 2 | 0 | 2 | 2 | 1.00 | - | - | - | - | 17 | 1 | 80 | 2 | 40.00 | 2-80 | - | - |
| 1-day Int |  |  |  |  |  |  |  |  |  |  |  |  |  |  |  |  |  |  |
| NatWest |  |  |  |  |  |  |  |  |  |  |  |  |  |  |  |  |  |  |  |
| B & H | 4 | 3 | 1 | 36 | 27 * | 18.00 | - | - | - | - | 41 | 1 | 242 | 2 | 121.00 | 1-24 | - | - |
| Sunday | 1 | 1 | 0 | 24 | 24 | 24.00 | - | - | - | - | 3 | 0 | 19 | 0 | - | - | - | - |

## Career Performances

|  | M | Inns | NO | Runs | HS | Avge | 100s | 50s | Ct | St | Balls | Runs | Wkts | Avge | Best | 5wI | 10wM |
|---|---|---|---|---|---|---|---|---|---|---|---|---|---|---|---|---|---|
| Test |  |  |  |  |  |  |  |  |  |  |  |  |  |  |  |  |  |
| All First | 14 | 19 | 3 | 456 | 84 * | 28.50 | - | 4 | 6 | - | 1800 | 1089 | 26 | 41.88 | 4-74 | - | - |
| 1-day Int |  |  |  |  |  |  |  |  |  |  |  |  |  |  |  |  |  |
| NatWest | 2 | 1 | 1 | 0 | 0 * | - | - | - | - | - | 96 | 41 | 0 | - | - | - | - |
| B & H | 4 | 3 | 1 | 36 | 27 * | 18.00 | - | - | - | - | 246 | 242 | 2 | 121.00 | 1-24 | - |
| Sunday | 12 | 9 | 3 | 110 | 26 | 18.33 | - | - | 3 | - | 419 | 318 | 10 | 31.80 | 2-30 | - |

# WELLINGS, P. E. Middlesex

**Name:** Peter Edward Wellings
**Role:** Right-hand bat, right-arm
medium bowler
**Born:** 5 March 1970
**Height:** 6ft 1in  **Weight:** 13st 7lbs
**Nickname:** Wello
**County debut:** No first-team appearance
**Parents:** John and Sandra
**Marital status:** Single
**Family links with cricket:** 'Uncle Keith
Worrall was a keen club cricketer and always
encouraged me to play and improve'
**Education:** Smeston Comprehensive,
Wolverhampton; Wulfrew College of Further
Education; Thames Valley University
**Qualifications:** 7 O-levels, 2 A-levels, BA
(Hons) in Leisure Management, basic
coaching award
**Career outside cricket:** Sports development
**Off-season:** 'Working for my club, Ealing, doing repairs, renovation and holidaying
for five weeks in South Africa visiting friends and watching England over Christmas
and New Year'
**Overseas tours:** Harrow Chequers to South Africa 1993-94
**Overseas teams played for:** Pingrup, Western Australia 1991-92; Ongerup Green
Range, Western Australia 1991-92; Coronations, Stellenbosch, South Africa 1993-94
**Cricketers particularly admired:** Graham Gooch, Angus Fraser, Dermot Reeve,
Chris Cooper
**Other sports followed:** Rugby union (Wolverhampton RFC), football (Wolves)
**Relaxations:** 'Science fiction, sports literature, cold beer, cooking – then keeping fit'
**Opinions on cricket:** 'Everything in British cricket should be geared towards producing
a successful side, from colts to first-class. In club cricket, there should be a more focused
approach to training and fewer games – we play too much cricket.'

---

93. Dominic Cork became the 1,000th first-class victim for
which bowler on 30 August 1995?

---

# WELLS, A. P.                                          Sussex

**Name:** Alan Peter Wells
**Role:** Right-hand bat, right-arm medium
bowler, county captain
**Born:** 2 October 1961, Newhaven
**Height:** 6ft **Weight:** 'Going up'
**Nickname:** Morph, Bomber
**County debut:** 1981
**County cap:** 1986
**Benefit:** 1995
**Test debut:** 1995
**Tests:** 1
**1000 runs in a season:** 9
**1st-Class 50s:** 78
**1st-Class 100s:** 41
**1st-Class 200s:** 1
**1st-Class catches:** 191
**One-Day 100s:** 5
**Place in batting averages:** 15th av. 54.42

(1994 134th av. 29.32)
**Parents:** Ernest William Charles and Eunice Mae
**Wife and date of marriage:** Melanie Elizabeth, 26 September 1987
**Children:** Luke William Peter, 29 December 1990; Daniel Allan Christian, 24 June 1995
**Family links with cricket:** Father, Billy, played for many years for local club and had
trial for Sussex. Eldest brother Ray plays club cricket; brother Colin played for Sussex
and then joined Derbyshire
**Education:** Tideway Comprehensive, Newhaven
**Qualifications:** 5 O-levels, NCA coaching certificate
**Career outside cricket:** Family packaging business
**Overseas tours:** Unofficial England XI to South Africa 1989-90; England A to South
Africa 1993-94, to India (captain) 1994-95
**Overseas teams played for:** Border, South Africa 1981-82
**Cricketers particularly admired:** Graham Gooch
**Other sports followed:** Football (Spurs)
**Relaxations:** Good wine, cooking, spending time with family, reading books and
articles on wine
**Extras:** Played for England YC v India 1981. Banned from Test cricket for five years in
1990 for joining tour of South Africa, suspension remitted in 1992. Scored a century in
each of his first two matches as acting-captain of Sussex and won both matches. Won
top batting award for Sussex 1989-93, 'much to David Smith's annoyance'. Vice-captain
on England A tour to South Africa 1993-94 and captain for the highly successful tour to
India 1994-95. Scored a century in both innings against Kent at Hove in 1995, the first

Sussex player to do so since C.B. Fry. This was followed by a pair against Glamorgan at Swansea ('Funny old game!'). Awarded benefit for 1996

**Opinions on cricket:** 'Until groundsmen start producing the best possible pitch rather than pitches to suit their own attacks, I don't believe our game will improve. Four-day cricket may take a long time to bear its fruit, but it will only do so if played on good pitches. I think our game at international level will suffer if we don't play on good surfaces. We have to decide if county or country come first.'

**Best batting:** 253* Sussex v Yorkshire, Middlesbrough 1991
**Best bowling:** 3-67 Sussex v Worcestershire, Worcester 1987

### 1995 Season

| | M | Inns | NO | Runs | HS | Avge | 100s | 50s | Ct | St | O | M | Runs | Wkts | Avge | Best | 5wI | 10wM |
|---|---|---|---|---|---|---|---|---|---|---|---|---|---|---|---|---|---|---|
| Test | 1 | 2 | 1 | 3 | 3 * | 3.00 | - | - | - | - | | | | | | | | |
| All First | 18 | 30 | 2 | 1524 | 178 | 54.42 | 7 | 4 | 10 | - | | | | | | | | |
| 1-day Int | 1 | 1 | 0 | 15 | 15 | 15.00 | - | - | - | - | | | | | | | | |
| NatWest | 2 | 2 | 0 | 16 | 15 | 8.00 | - | - | - | - | | | | | | | | |
| B & H | 4 | 4 | 1 | 42 | 23 * | 14.00 | - | - | - | - | | | | | | | | |
| Sunday | 15 | 15 | 1 | 403 | 85 | 28.78 | - | 3 | 2 | - | | | | | | | | |

### Career Performances

| | M | Inns | NO | Runs | HS | Avge | 100s | 50s | Ct | St | Balls | Runs | Wkts | Avge | Best | 5wI | 10wM |
|---|---|---|---|---|---|---|---|---|---|---|---|---|---|---|---|---|---|
| Test | 1 | 2 | 1 | 3 | 3 * | 3.00 | - | - | - | - | | | | | | | |
| All First | 302 | 502 | 75 | 17302 | 253 * | 40.51 | 41 | 78 | 191 | - | 1045 | 765 | 10 | 76.50 | 3-67 | - | - |
| 1-day Int | 1 | 1 | 0 | 15 | 15 | 15.00 | - | - | - | - | | | | | | | |
| NatWest | 31 | 28 | 6 | 807 | 119 | 36.68 | 2 | 4 | 12 | - | 6 | 1 | 0 | - | | - | - |
| B & H | 50 | 47 | 6 | 1272 | 74 | 31.02 | - | 12 | 9 | - | 60 | 72 | 3 | 24.00 | 1-17 | - | |
| Sunday | 203 | 187 | 22 | 5157 | 127 | 31.25 | 3 | 33 | 57 | - | 62 | 69 | 4 | 17.25 | 1-0 | | |

94. Who became the first bowler in 48 years to concede over 200 runs in an innings during his side's championship game against Nottinghamshire in August 1995?

# WELLS, C. M. Derbyshire

**Name:** Colin Mark Wells
**Role:** Right-hand bat, right-arm
medium bowler
**Born:** 3 March 1960, Newhaven
**Height:** 6ft **Weight:** 13st
**Nickname:** Bomber, Dougie
**County debut:** 1979 (Sussex),
1994 (Derbyshire)
**County cap:** 1982 (Sussex)
**Benefit:** 1993 (£50,353)
**One-Day Internationals:** 2
**1000 runs in a season:** 6
**50 wickets in a season:** 2
**1st-Class 50s:** 64
**1st-Class 100s:** 23
**1st-Class 200s:** 1
**1st-Class 5 w. in innings:** 7
**1st-Class catches:** 106
**One-Day 100s:** 4

**Place in batting averages:** 87th av. 36.14 (1994 227th av. 16.83)
**Place in bowling averages:** 86th av. 32.60 (1994 99th av. 36.09)
**Strike rate:** 66.00 (career 72.25)
**Parents:** Ernest William Charles and Eunice Mae
**Wife and date of marriage:** Celia, 25 September 1982
**Children:** Jessica Louise, 2 October 1987
**Family links with cricket:** Father, Billy, had trials for Sussex and played for Sussex
Cricket Association. Elder brother Ray plays club cricket and younger brother Alan is
captain of Sussex
**Education:** Tideway Comprehensive School, Newhaven
**Qualifications:** 9 O-levels, 2 CSEs, 1 A-level, intermediate coaching certificate
**Overseas tours:** England to Sharjah 1984-85
**Overseas teams played for:** Border, South Africa 1980-81; Western Province, South
Africa 1984-85
**Other sports followed:** Football, rugby, hockey, basketball, tennis, table tennis
**Relaxations:** Sea-angling, philately, listening to music
**Extras:** Played in three John Player League matches in 1978. Was recommended to
Sussex by former Sussex player, Ian Thomson. Appointed vice-captain of Sussex in
1988 and captain in 1992. Released by Sussex at end of 1993 season and signed for
Derbyshire
**Best batting:** 203 Sussex v Hampshire, Hove 1984
**Best bowling:** 7-42 Sussex v Derbyshire, Derby 1991

## 1995 Season

| | M | Inns | NO | Runs | HS | Avge | 100s | 50s | Ct | St | O | M | Runs | Wkts | Avge | Best | 5wI | 10wM |
|---|---|---|---|---|---|---|---|---|---|---|---|---|---|---|---|---|---|---|
| Test | | | | | | | | | | | | | | | | | | |
| All First | 16 | 30 | 3 | 976 | 115 | 36.14 | 2 | 6 | 16 | - | 110 | 25 | 326 | 10 | 32.60 | 4-29 | - | - |
| 1-day Int | | | | | | | | | | | | | | | | | | |
| NatWest | 3 | 2 | 1 | 99 | 51 * | 99.00 | - | 1 | - | - | 19.2 | 4 | 61 | 1 | 61.00 | 1-0 | - | |
| B & H | 2 | 1 | 1 | 3 | 3 * | - | - | - | - | - | 15 | 1 | 40 | 1 | 40.00 | 1-18 | - | |
| Sunday | 13 | 12 | 0 | 295 | 73 | 24.58 | - | 3 | 5 | - | 48 | 2 | 236 | 8 | 29.50 | 3-31 | - | |

## Career Performances

| | M | Inns | NO | Runs | HS | Avge | 100s | 50s | Ct | St | Balls | Runs | Wkts | Avge | Best | 5wI | 10wM |
|---|---|---|---|---|---|---|---|---|---|---|---|---|---|---|---|---|---|
| Test | | | | | | | | | | | | | | | | | |
| All First | 306 | 491 | 75 | 13680 | 203 | 32.88 | 23 | 64 | 106 | - | 30273 | 14308 | 419 | 34.14 | 7-42 | 7 | - |
| 1-day Int | 2 | 2 | 0 | 22 | 17 | 11.00 | - | - | - | - | | | | | | | |
| NatWest | 35 | 28 | 4 | 532 | 76 | 22.16 | - | 2 | 8 | - | 1593 | 774 | 18 | 43.00 | 3-16 | - | |
| B & H | 55 | 53 | 7 | 1380 | 117 | 30.00 | 3 | 4 | 13 | - | 2028 | 1297 | 38 | 34.13 | 4-21 | - | |
| Sunday | 207 | 181 | 28 | 4008 | 104 * | 26.19 | 1 | 21 | 47 | - | 6966 | 4553 | 146 | 31.18 | 4-15 | - | |

# WELLS, V. J.        Leicestershire

**Name:** Vincent John Wells
**Role:** Right-hand bat, right-arm medium bowler, occasional wicket-keeper
**Born:** 6 August 1965, Dartford
**Height:** 6ft **Weight:** 13st
**Nickname:** Wellsy, Vinny, Both
**County debut:** 1987 (Kent), 1992 (Leicestershire)
**1st-Class 50s:** 19
**1st-Class 100s:** 2
**1st-Class 5 w. in innings:** 2
**1st-Class catches:** 45
**One-Day 100s:** 3
**One-day 5 w. innings:** 1
**Place in batting averages:** 142nd av. 28.43 (1994 80th av. 36.29)
**Place in bowling averages:** 24th av. 23.05 (1994 25th av. 25.07)
**Strike rate:** 44.05 (career 51.67)
**Parents:** Pat and Jack
**Wife and date of marriage:** Deborah Louise, 14 October 1989
**Children:** Harrison John, 25 January 1995

**Family links with cricket:** Brother plays league cricket in Kent
**Education:** Downs School, Dartford; Sir William Nottidge School, Whitstable
**Qualifications:** 1 O-level, 8 CSEs, coaching certificate
**Off-season:** Coaching at Leicestershire until Christmas and then playing in South Africa
**Overseas tours:** Leicestershire to Jamaica 1993, to Bloemfontein, 1994 and 1995
**Overseas teams played for:** Parnell, Auckland 1986; Avendale, Cape Town 1986-89, 1990-91
**Cricketers particularly admired:** David Gower, Robin Smith, Allan Donald
**Other sports followed:** Most sports especially football
**Injuries:** Side strain, out for three weeks
**Relaxations:** Eating out and spending time with wife and son
**Extras:** Was a schoolboy footballer with Leyton Orient. Scored 100 not out on NatWest debut v Oxfordshire. Left Kent at the end of 1991 season to join Leicestershire. Missed 1992 NatWest final owing to viral infection. Hat-trick against Durham, 1994
**Opinions on cricket:** 'The zonal Benson & Hedges games should be played straight off within the first two weeks of the season, leaving just the semi-finals and the finals to be played at a later date, then you can concentrate on four-day cricket. Over-rates are still much too high. Clubs should do more to help with winter employment or even offer longer contracts. Standard of pitches could still be better. Still dislike the fact of playing Sunday League in the middle of championship.'
**Best batting:** 167 Leicestershire v Glamorgan, Leicester 1993
**Best bowling:** 5-43 Kent v Leicestershire, Leicester 1990

## 1995 Season

| | M | Inns | NO | Runs | HS | Avge | 100s | 50s | Ct | St | O | M | Runs | Wkts | Avge | Best | 5wI | 10wM |
|---|---|---|---|---|---|---|---|---|---|---|---|---|---|---|---|---|---|---|
| Test | | | | | | | | | | | | | | | | | | |
| All First | 14 | 24 | 1 | 654 | 124 | 28.43 | 1 | 5 | 8 | - | 139.3 | 33 | 438 | 19 | 23.05 | 3-28 | - | - |
| 1-day Int | | | | | | | | | | | | | | | | | | |
| NatWest | 1 | 1 | 0 | 23 | 23 | 23.00 | - | - | - | - | | | | | | | | |
| B & H | 5 | 5 | 0 | 120 | 39 | 24.00 | - | - | 3 | - | 27 | 0 | 145 | 4 | 36.25 | 2-34 | - | |
| Sunday | 12 | 12 | 1 | 418 | 79 | 38.00 | - | 4 | 3 | - | 37 | 1 | 234 | 7 | 33.42 | 3-32 | - | |

## Career Performances

| | M | Inns | NO | Runs | HS | Avge | 100s | 50s | Ct | St | Balls | Runs | Wkts | Avge | Best | 5wI | 10wM |
|---|---|---|---|---|---|---|---|---|---|---|---|---|---|---|---|---|---|
| Test | | | | | | | | | | | | | | | | | |
| All First | 76 | 123 | 14 | 3135 | 167 | 28.76 | 2 | 19 | 45 | - | 6718 | 3361 | 130 | 25.85 | 5-43 | 2 | - |
| 1-day Int | | | | | | | | | | | | | | | | | |
| NatWest | 9 | 9 | 3 | 226 | 100 * | 37.66 | 1 | - | - | - | 353 | 222 | 8 | 27.75 | 3-38 | - | |
| B & H | 19 | 16 | 3 | 263 | 39 | 20.23 | - | - | 6 | - | 678 | 529 | 17 | 31.11 | 4-37 | - | |
| Sunday | 62 | 56 | 12 | 1288 | 101 | 29.27 | 2 | 6 | 18 | - | 2048 | 1592 | 64 | 24.87 | 5-10 | 1 | |

# WELTON, G. E. Nottinghamshire

**Name:** Guy Edward Welton
**Role:** Right-hand bat
**Born:** 4 May 1978, Grimsby
**Height:** 6ft 1in  **Weight:** 12st 7lbs
**Nickname:** Welts, Spaceman
**County debut:** No first-team appearance
**Parents:** Robert and Diana
**Marital status:** Single
**Family links with cricket:** Father Bob a
well-known cricketer and coach in the
Lincolnshire area
**Education:** Healing Comprehensive;
Grimsby College
**Qualifications:** 8 GCSEs, BTEC in Business
and Finance, qualified cricket coach
**Career outside cricket:** Football
**Off-season:** Playing football
**Overseas tours:** England U17 to Holland 1995
**Cricketers particularly admired:** David
Gower and Graeme Hick

**Other sports followed:** Football (Grimsby and West Brom)
**Relaxations:** Keeping fit, weights and listening to music
**Extras:** Has just completed a two-year YTS with Grimsby Town Football Club. Played cricket for England U14, U15 and U17. Won the Lord's Taverners Young Player Award in 1993 and MCC Young Cricketer from 1994-95. Was 12th man for England at Lord's and The Oval against West Indies in 1995
**Opinions on cricket:** 'Intervals are too short. County championship should be split into two divisions with promotion and relegation.'

95. Which minor county won the 1995 MCC Trophy final?

# WESTON, R. M. S.                                    Durham

**Name:** Robin Michael Swann Weston
**Role:** Right-hand bat, leg-break bowler
**Born:** 7 June 1975, Durham
**Height:** 6ft **Weight:** 12st 7lbs
**County debut:** 1995
**1st-Class catches:** 5
**Parents:** Michael Philip and Kathleen Mary
**Marital status:** Single
**Family links with cricket:** Father played for
Durham; brother Philip plays for
Worcestershire
**Education:** Bow School; Durham School;
Loughborough University
**Qualifications:** 10 GCSEs, 4 A-levels, basic
cricket coaching certificate
**Career outside cricket:** Student at
Loughborough
**Off-season:** Loughborough University
**Overseas tours:** England U18 to South
Africa 1992-93, to Denmark 1993; England U19 to Sri Lanka 1993-94
**Cricketers particularly admired:** Graeme Hick and Wayne Larkins
**Other sports followed:** Rugby and golf
**Relaxations:** Most sports, listening to music and socialising with friends
**Extras:** Youngest to play for Durham 1st XI, in Minor Counties competition, aged 15 in
1991. Played rugby for England U18
**Opinions on cricket:** '30 minutes for tea. Lower over-rate per hour.'
**Best batting:** 9 Durham v Gloucestershire, Bristol 1995
**Best bowling:** 1-41 Durham v Somerset, Chester-le-Street 1995

## 1995 Season

|           | M | Inns | NO | Runs | HS | Avge | 100s | 50s | Ct | St | O | M | Runs | Wkts | Avge | Best | 5wI | 10wM |
|-----------|---|------|----|------|----|------|------|-----|----|----|------|----|------|------|------|------|-----|------|
| Test      |   |      |    |      |    |      |      |     |    |    |      |    |      |      |      |      |     |      |
| All First | 3 | 6    | 0  | 15   | 9  | 2.50 | -    | -   | 5  | -  | 22.1 | 2  | 70   | 1    | 70.00| 1-41 | -   | -    |
| 1-day Int |   |      |    |      |    |      |      |     |    |    |      |    |      |      |      |      |     |      |
| NatWest   |   |      |    |      |    |      |      |     |    |    |      |    |      |      |      |      |     |      |
| B & H     |   |      |    |      |    |      |      |     |    |    |      |    |      |      |      |      |     |      |
| Sunday    |   |      |    |      |    |      |      |     |    |    |      |    |      |      |      |      |     |      |

## Career Performances

| | M | Inns | NO | Runs | HS | Avge | 100s | 50s | Ct | St | Balls | Runs | Wkts | Avge | Best | 5wI | 10wM |
|---|---|---|---|---|---|---|---|---|---|---|---|---|---|---|---|---|---|
| Test | | | | | | | | | | | | | | | | | |
| All First | 3 | 6 | 0 | 15 | 9 | 2.50 | - | - | 5 | - | 133 | 70 | 1 | 70.00 | 1-41 | - | - |
| 1-day Int | | | | | | | | | | | | | | | | | |
| NatWest | | | | | | | | | | | | | | | | | |
| B & H | | | | | | | | | | | | | | | | | |
| Sunday | | | | | | | | | | | | | | | | | |

# WESTON, W. P. C.                    Worcestershire

**Name:** William Philip Christopher Weston
**Role:** Left-hand bat, left-arm medium bowler
**Born:** 16 June 1973, Durham
**Height:** 6ft 4in  **Weight:** 13st 7lbs
**Nickname:** Junior, Sven, Captain
Mainwaring
**County debut:** 1991
**County cap:** 1995
**1000 runs in a season:** 1
**1st-Class 50s:** 19
**1st-Class 100s:** 5
**1st-Class catches:** 31
**Place in batting averages:** 92nd av. 35.50
(1994 125th av. 30.29)
**Parents:** Michael Philip and Kathleen Mary
**Marital status:** Single
**Family links with cricket:** Father played
Minor Counties cricket for Durham and
rugby for England, brother plays for Durham
CCC

**Education:** Bow School, Durham; Durham School
**Qualifications:** 9 GCSEs, 4 A-Levels, NCA Senior Coach
**Off-season:** Playing cricket in Perth, Western Australia
**Overseas tours:** England U18 to Canada; England YC to New Zealand 1990-91, to
Pakistan 1991-92 (captain)
**Overseas teams played for:** Melville, Perth 1992-95; Swanbourne, Perth 1994-96
**Cricketers particularly admired:** Graeme Hick, Phil Newport, Tom Moody, Mike
Atherton and 'many more'
**Other sports followed:** Rugby union and football (Sunderland AFC)
**Injuries:** Foot injury
**Relaxations:** Spending time with friends and family, travelling and lying on a beach

**Extras:** Scored century for England YC v Australian YC 1991. Was appointed captain of England U19 for their tour to Pakistan 1991-92 and told by Keble College, Oxford, that he would not be accepted if he decided to tour; he chose to sacrifice his place at Oxford. Downing Collge, Cambridge, offered him a place the following year, but by then he was so disillusioned with universities that he turned down the offer and decided to concentrate on his cricket. Played for Northamptonshire 2nd XI and Worcestershire 2nd XI in 1989. Cricket Society's Most Promising Young Cricketer 1992. Worcestershire Uncapped Player of the Year, 1992. Member of Whittingdale Fringe Squad 1993

**Opinions on cricket:** 'I'm happy with our game at the moment. Four-day cricket is definitely working but will further improve with better wickets (particularly at the start of the year).'

**Best batting:** 113 Worcestershire v Oxford University, Worcester 1993
**Best bowling:** 2-39 Worcestershire v Pakistanis, Worcester 1992

### 1995 Season

|         | M  | Inns | NO | Runs | HS   | Avge  | 100s | 50s | Ct | St | O    | M | Runs | Wkts | Avge | Best | 5wI | 10wM |
|---------|----|------|----|------|------|-------|------|-----|----|----|------|---|------|------|------|------|-----|------|
| Test    |    |      |    |      |      |       |      |     |    |    |      |   |      |      |      |      |     |      |
| All First | 20 | 35 | 1 | 1207 | 111 | 35.50 | 3 | 7 | 14 | - | 21.4 | 2 | 91 | 0 | - | - | - | - |
| 1-day Int |    |      |    |      |      |       |      |     |    |    |      |   |      |      |      |      |     |      |
| NatWest | 2  | 2    | 0  | 1    | 1    | 0.50  | -    | -   | -  | -  |      |   |      |      |      |      |     |      |
| B & H   | 6  | 6    | 1  | 81   | 54 * | 16.20 | -    | 1   | 1  | -  |      |   |      |      |      |      |     |      |
| Sunday  | 13 | 10   | 1  | 279  | 80   | 31.00 | -    | 2   | 5  | -  |      |   |      |      |      |      |     |      |

### Career Performances

|         | M  | Inns | NO | Runs | HS   | Avge  | 100s | 50s | Ct | St | Balls |   | Runs | Wkts | Avge   | Best | 5wI | 10wM |
|---------|----|------|----|------|------|-------|------|-----|----|----|-------|---|------|------|--------|------|-----|------|
| Test    |    |      |    |      |      |       |      |     |    |    |       |   |      |      |        |      |     |      |
| All First | 68 | 114 | 10 | 3443 | 113 | 33.10 | 5 | 19 | 31 | - | 811 | | 481 | 4 | 120.25 | 2-39 | - | - |
| 1-day Int |    |      |    |      |      |       |      |     |    |    |       |   |      |      |        |      |     |      |
| NatWest | 6  | 6    | 0  | 91   | 31   | 15.16 | -    | -   | 1  | -  |       |   |      |      |        |      |     |      |
| B & H   | 8  | 8    | 2  | 114  | 54 * | 19.00 | -    | 1   | 2  | -  |       |   |      |      |        |      |     |      |
| Sunday  | 21 | 17   | 2  | 363  | 80   | 24.20 | -    | 2   | 5  | -  | 6     |   | 2    | 1    | 2.00   | 1-2  | -   |      |

# WHARF, A. G.          Yorkshire

**Name:** Alexander George Wharf
**Role:** Right-hand bat, right-arm fast-medium bowler
**Born:** 4 June 1975, Bradford
**Height:** 6ft 4in  **Weight:** 14st 8lbs
**Nickname:** Gangster, Frank, River, Big'un
**County debut:** 1994
**Parents:** Derek and Jane

**Marital status:** Single
**Family links with cricket:** Father used to play in local league cricket
**Education:** Buttershaw Upper School
**Qualifications:** 6 GCSEs, City and Guilds in Sports Management
**Off-season:** 'Try to get a relaxing job, train very hard for 1996 season'
**Overseas teams played for:** Somerset West, Cape Town 1993-95
**Cricketers particularly admired:** Wasim Akram, Curtly Ambrose, Ian Botham, Bradley Parker, 'rubber kit and all the badgers in the game'
**Other sports followed:** Football (Manchester United)
**Relaxations:** Watching movies, eating out, sleeping. Spending time with friends outside cricket

**Opinions on cricket:** 'It's too much of a batter's game – a pitch should be 20 yards.'
**Best batting:** 46 Yorkshire v Warwickshire, Scarborough 1994
**Best bowling:** 1-78 Yorkshire v Warwickshire, Scarborough 1994

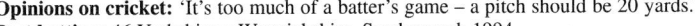

### 1995 Season (did not make any first-class or one-day appearances)

### Career Performances

|          | M | Inns | NO | Runs | HS | Avge  | 100s | 50s | Ct | St | Balls | Runs | Wkts | Avge  | Best | 5wI | 10wM |
|----------|---|------|----|------|----|-------|------|-----|----|----|-------|------|------|-------|------|-----|------|
| Test     |   |      |    |      |    |       |      |     |    |    |       |      |      |       |      |     |      |
| All First | 1 | 2    | 0  | 46   | 46 | 23.00 | -    | -   | -  | -  | 138   | 78   | 1    | 78.00 | 1-78 | -   | -    |
| 1-day Int |   |      |    |      |    |       |      |     |    |    |       |      |      |       |      |     |      |
| NatWest  |   |      |    |      |    |       |      |     |    |    |       |      |      |       |      |     |      |
| B & H    |   |      |    |      |    |       |      |     |    |    |       |      |      |       |      |     |      |
| Sunday   | 1 | 0    | 0  | 0    | 0  | -     | -    | -   | 1  | -  | 48    | 39   | 3    | 13.00 | 3-39 | -   |      |

96. Which current South African Test player holds the record for the highest score in South African first-class cricket?

# WHITAKER, J. J.　　　　　　Leicestershire

**Name:** John James Whitaker
**Role:** Right-hand bat, off-spin bowler,
county captain
**Born:** 5 May 1962, Skipton, Yorkshire
**Height:** 6ft **Weight:** 13st
**Nickname:** Jimmy
**County debut:** 1983
**County cap:** 1986
**Benefit:** 1993
**Test debut:** 1986-87
**Tests:** 1
**One-Day Internationals:** 2
**1000 runs in a season:** 9
**1st-Class 50s:** 74
**1st-Class 100s:** 30
**1st-Class 200s:** 1
**1st-Class catches:** 163
**One-Day 100s:** 6
**Place in batting averages:** 55th av. 42.20

(1994 114th av. 31.93)
**Parents:** John and Ann
**Family links with cricket:** Father is a local league player
**Education:** Malsis Hall Prep School; Uppingham School
**Qualifications:** 7 O-levels
**Off-season:** Working for Whitaker's Chocolatiers, going to South Africa and getting
fit for next season
**Overseas tours:** Uppingham to Australia 1980-81; England to Australia 1986-87, to
Sharjah 1987; England A to Zimbabwe and Kenya 1990-91; Hong Kong Sixes 1991,
1992
**Overseas teams played for:** Glenelg, Australia 1982-83; Old Scotch, Tasmania 1983-
84; Somerset West, Cape Town 1984-85
**Cricketers particularly admired:** Geoff Boycott, Dennis Amiss, Brian Davison,
Maurice Hallam
**Other sports followed:** Football (Leicester City), golf, rugby (Leicester Tigers)
**Injuries:** Ankle ligaments, out for one month
**Relaxations:** Eating out, movies, watching sport
**Extras:** One of *Wisden*'s Five Cricketers of the Year 1986. Second in batting averages
in 1986. Young Cricketer Award jointly in 1986
**Opinions on cricket:** 'Four-day game is ideal. The Sunday game in the middle is not.
The over-rate and number of overs in a day are too high. Benson & Hedges cricket
should be 50 overs, as in the World Cup. Keep pitches hard with true bounce and slightly

green to start. Do not start a four-day game on a used pitch.'
**Best batting:** 200* Leicestershire v Nottinghamshire, Leicester 1986
**Best bowling:** 1-29 Leicestershire v Somerset, Leicester 1992

### 1995 Season

|           | M  | Inns | NO | Runs | HS  | Avge  | 100s | 50s | Ct | St | O | M | Runs | Wkts | Avge | Best | 5wI | 10wM |
|-----------|----|------|----|------|-----|-------|------|-----|----|----|---|---|------|------|------|------|-----|------|
| Test      |    |      |    |      |     |       |      |     |    |    |   |   |      |      |      |      |     |      |
| All First | 15 | 25   | 0  | 1055 | 127 | 42.20 | 3    | 5   | 4  | -  |   |   |      |      |      |      |     |      |
| 1-day Int |    |      |    |      |     |       |      |     |    |    |   |   |      |      |      |      |     |      |
| NatWest   | 1  | 1    | 0  | 0    | 0   | 0.00  | -    | -   | -  | -  |   |   |      |      |      |      |     |      |
| B & H     | 5  | 5    | 0  | 214  | 88  | 42.80 | -    | 3   | -  | -  |   |   |      |      |      |      |     |      |
| Sunday    | 9  | 8    | 1  | 221  | 65* | 31.57 | -    | 1   | 4  | -  |   |   |      |      |      |      |     |      |

### Career Performances

|           | M   | Inns | NO | Runs  | HS   | Avge  | 100s | 50s | Ct  | St | Balls | Runs | Wkts | Avge   | Best | 5wI | 10wM |
|-----------|-----|------|----|-------|------|-------|------|-----|-----|----|-------|------|------|--------|------|-----|------|
| Test      | 1   | 1    | 0  | 11    | 11   | 11.00 | -    | -   | 1   | -  |       |      |      |        |      |     |      |
| All First | 276 | 442  | 46 | 14941 | 200* | 37.72 | 30   | 74  | 163 | -  | 176   | 268  | 2    | 134.00 | 1-29 | -   | -    |
| 1-day Int | 2   | 2    | 1  | 48    | 44*  | 48.00 | -    | -   | 1   |    |       |      |      |        |      |     |      |
| NatWest   | 26  | 26   | 2  | 1006  | 155  | 41.91 | 1    | 5   | 1   | -  | 24    | 9    | 0    | -      | -    | -   | -    |
| B & H     | 48  | 43   | 2  | 1232  | 100  | 30.04 | 1    | 7   | 7   | -  |       |      |      |        |      |     |      |
| Sunday    | 157 | 146  | 16 | 4433  | 132  | 34.10 | 4    | 26  | 39  | -  | 2     | 4    | 0    | -      | -    | -   | -    |

# WHITAKER, P. R. Hampshire

**Name:** Paul Robert Whitaker
**Role:** Left-hand opening bat, right-arm
off-spin bowler
**Born:** 28 June 1973, Keighley, West
Yorkshire
**Height:** 5ft 10in **Weight:** 11st 7lbs
**Nickname:** Ticket, Chicken Tikka, Finger-
lickin'
**County debut:** 1994
**1st-Class 50s:** 1
**1st-Class 100s:** 1
**1st-Class catches:** 3
**Place in batting averages:** 133rd av. 29.71
**Parents:** Robert and Maureen
**Marital status:** Single
**Family links with cricket:** Father played for
Bingley in Bradford League, and now
coaches Yorkshire U15

**Education:** 8 GCSEs, 2 A-levels
**Career outside cricket:** PE teacher
**Overseas tours:** Represented England U17, U18 and U19
**Overseas teams played for:** Bedford, Perth, Australia 1992-93; Southern Hawkes Bay, New Zealand 1993-94
**Cricketers particularly admired:** Ian Botham, Tim Tweats, Gary Streer
**Other sports followed:** Rugby league, football, horse racing
**Injuries:** Side strain, did not miss any cricket
**Relaxations:** 'A quiet meal in a restaurant drinking a bottle of Liebfraumilch 1982 wine.'
**Best batting:** 119 Hampshire v Worcestershire, Southampton 1995
**Best bowling:** 1-4 Hampshire v Essex, Colchester 1995

## 1995 Season

|          | M  | Inns | NO | Runs | HS  | Avge  | 100s | 50s | Ct | St | O  | M | Runs | Wkts | Avge  | Best | 5wI | 10wM |
|----------|----|------|----|------|-----|-------|------|-----|----|----|----|---|------|------|-------|------|-----|------|
| Test     |    |      |    |      |     |       |      |     |    |    |    |   |      |      |       |      |     |      |
| All First | 13 | 21   | 0  | 624  | 119 | 29.71 | 1    | 3   | 3  | -  | 10 | 2 | 30   | 1    | 30.00 | 1-4  | -   | -    |
| 1-day Int |    |      |    |      |     |       |      |     |    |    |    |   |      |      |       |      |     |      |
| NatWest  | 1  | 1    | 0  | 13   | 13  | 13.00 | -    | -   | -  | -  | 6  | 0 | 17   | 0    | -     |      | -   | -    |
| B & H    | 2  | 2    | 0  | 47   | 42  | 23.50 | -    | -   | -  | -  | 1  | 0 | 13   | 0    | -     |      | -   | -    |
| Sunday   | 11 | 11   | 1  | 224  | 97  | 22.40 | -    | 1   | 3  | -  | 10 | 0 | 59   | 2    | 29.50 | 2-32 | -   |      |

## Career Performances

|          | M  | Inns | NO | Runs | HS  | Avge  | 100s | 50s | Ct | St | Balls | Runs | Wkts | Avge  | Best | 5wI | 10wM |
|----------|----|------|----|------|-----|-------|------|-----|----|----|-------|------|------|-------|------|-----|------|
| Test     |    |      |    |      |     |       |      |     |    |    |       |      |      |       |      |     |      |
| All First | 15 | 24   | 0  | 758  | 119 | 31.58 | 1    | 4   | 3  | -  | 61    | 34   | 1    | 34.00 | 1-4  | -   | -    |
| 1-day Int |    |      |    |      |     |       |      |     |    |    |       |      |      |       |      |     |      |
| NatWest  | 1  | 1    | 0  | 13   | 13  | 13.00 | -    | -   | -  | -  | 36    | 17   | 0    | -     |      | -   | -    |
| B & H    | 2  | 2    | 0  | 47   | 42  | 23.50 | -    | -   | -  | -  | 6     | 13   | 0    | -     |      | -   | -    |
| Sunday   | 13 | 13   | 1  | 236  | 97  | 19.66 | -    | 1   | 6  | -  | 72    | 67   | 2    | 33.50 | 2-32 | -   |      |

# WHITE, C. Yorkshire

**Name:** Craig White
**Role:** Right-hand bat, off-spin bowler, cover fielder
**Born:** 16 December 1969, Morley, Yorkshire
**Height:** 6ft 1in **Weight:** 11st 11lbs
**Nickname:** Chalky, Bassey
**County debut:** 1990
**County cap:** 1993
**Test debut:** 1994
**Tests:** 6

**One-day Internationals:** 1
**1st-Class 50s:** 19
**1st-Class 100s:** 5
**1st-Class 5 w. in innings:** 3
**1st-Class catches:** 52
**One-day 100s:** 1
**Place in batting averages:** 119th av. 31.21
(1994 75th av. 36.83)
**Place in bowling averages:** 110th av. 37.36
(1994 10th av. 23.06)
**Strike rate:** 65.68 (career 56.20)
**Parents:** Fred Emsley and Cynthia Anne
**Wife and date of marriage:** Elizabeth Anne,
19 September 1992
**Family links with cricket:** Father played for
Pudsey St Lawrence
**Education:** Kennington Primary; Flora Hill
High School; Bendigo Senior High School
(all Victoria, Australia)
**Off-season:** England A tour to Pakistan
**Overseas tours:** Australian YC to West Indies 1989-90; England to Australia 1994-95,
to South Africa 1995-96, to India and Pakistan (World Cup)1995-96; England A to
Pakistan 1995-96
**Overseas teams played for:** Victoria, Australia 1990-94
**Cricketers particularly admired:** Graeme Hick, Mark Waugh, Brian Lara
**Other sports followed:** Leeds RFC, motorcross, golf, tennis
**Injuries:** Torn groin, out for five weeks
**Relaxations:** Playing guitar, reading, gardening and socialising
**Extras:** Recommended to Yorkshire by Victorian Cricket Academy, being eligible to
play for Yorkshire as he was born in the county. 'Fred Trueman and I are the only
Yorkshire players to debut in the 1st XI before the 2nd XI.' Had to fly home from the
World Cup in 1995-96 with a side strain and was replaced by Dermot Reeve
**Best batting:** 146 Yorkshire v Durham, Headingley 1993
**Best bowling:** 5-40 Yorkshire v Essex, Headingley 1994

---

### 1995 Season

|          | M  | Inns | NO | Runs | HS   | Avge  | 100s | 50s | Ct | St | O     | M  | Runs | Wkts | Avge  | Best | 5wl | 10wM |
|----------|----|------|----|------|------|-------|------|-----|----|----|-------|----|------|------|-------|------|-----|------|
| Test     | 2  | 4    | 0  | 26   | 23   | 6.50  | -    | -   | -  | -  | 16    | 0  | 76   | 0    | -     | -    | -   | -    |
| All First| 19 | 33   | 5  | 874  | 110  | 31.21 | 3    | 3   | 8  | -  | 273.4 | 49 | 934  | 25   | 37.36 | 4-40 | -   | -    |
| 1-day Int|    |      |    |      |      |       |      |     |    |    |       |    |      |      |       |      |     |      |
| NatWest  | 4  | 4    | 1  | 168  | 113  | 56.00 | 1    | 1   | 2  | -  | 41    | 3  | 152  | 7    | 21.71 | 3-38 | -   |      |
| B & H    | 4  | 3    | 0  | 52   | 43   | 17.33 | -    | -   | 2  | -  | 27    | 1  | 135  | 2    | 67.50 | 1-26 | -   |      |
| Sunday   | 12 | 11   | 1  | 235  | 50 * | 23.50 | -    | 1   | 4  | -  | 72    | 5  | 361  | 9    | 40.11 | 2-15 | -   |      |

**Career Performances**

| | M | Inns | NO | Runs | HS | Avge | 100s | 50s | Ct | St | Balls | Runs | Wkts | Avge | Best | 5wI | 10wM |
|---|---|---|---|---|---|---|---|---|---|---|---|---|---|---|---|---|---|
| Test | 6 | 10 | 0 | 157 | 51 | 15.70 | - | 1 | 3 | - | 565 | 334 | 8 | 41.75 | 3-18 | - | - |
| All First | 87 | 133 | 23 | 3616 | 146 | 32.87 | 5 | 19 | 52 | - | 5339 | 2900 | 95 | 30.52 | 5-40 | 3 | - |
| 1-day Int | 1 | 1 | 0 | 0 | 0 | 0.00 | - | - | - | - | 30 | 22 | 0 | - | - | - | - |
| NatWest | 11 | 9 | 2 | 353 | 113 | 50.42 | 1 | 2 | 5 | - | 473 | 303 | 11 | 27.54 | 3-38 | - | |
| B & H | 10 | 8 | 1 | 124 | 43 | 17.71 | - | - | 3 | - | 300 | 206 | 5 | 41.20 | 2-30 | - | |
| Sunday | 58 | 49 | 13 | 1101 | 63 | 30.58 | - | 4 | 21 | - | 1399 | 1106 | 33 | 33.51 | 3-25 | - | |

# WHITE, G. W. Hampshire

**Name:** Giles William White
**Role:** Right-hand bat, leg-break bowler
**Born:** 23 March 1972, Barnstaple
**Height:** 5ft 11in **Weight:** 12st
**Nickname:** Chalky, Giler
**County debut:** 1991 (Somerset),
1994 (Hampshire)
**1st-Class 50s:** 5
**1st-Class 100s:** 1
**1st-Class catches:** 27
**Place in batting averages:** 162nd av. 25.18
(1994 166th av. 24.57)
**Parents:** John and Tina
**Marital status:** Single
**Family links with cricket:** Father played
club cricket in Devon
**Education:** Millfield School; Loughborough
University
**Qualifications:** GCSEs, A-levels, BA (Hons)
**Off-season:** Playing in Cape Town, South Africa
**Overseas tours:** Millfield School to Australia 1989
**Overseas teams played for:** Waverley, Sydney 1990-91; Tigers Parrow, Cape Town
1994-95; Techs Mutual, Cape Town 1995-96
**Cricketers particularly admired:** Wayne Larkins, Brian Lara, Robin Smith, Mark
Lathwell, Paul Terry
**Other sports followed:** Rugby, football (Leeds United), tennis, golf
**Relaxations:** Painting, and sleeping
**Opinions on cricket:** 'An hour for lunch and half an hour for tea.'
**Best batting:** 104 Combined Universities v New Zealanders, Fenner's 1994
**Best bowling:** 1-30 Somerset v Sri Lanka, Taunton 1991

## 1995 Season

| | M | Inns | NO | Runs | HS | Avge | 100s | 50s | Ct | St | O | M | Runs | Wkts | Avge | Best | 5wI | 10wM |
|---|---|---|---|---|---|---|---|---|---|---|---|---|---|---|---|---|---|---|
| Test | | | | | | | | | | | | | | | | | | |
| All First | 15 | 24 | 2 | 554 | 62 | 25.18 | - | 3 | 14 | - | 4 | 1 | 22 | 0 | - | - | - | - |
| 1-day Int | | | | | | | | | | | | | | | | | | |
| NatWest | | | | | | | | | | | | | | | | | | |
| B & H | 3 | 2 | 0 | 37 | 37 | 18.50 | - | - | - | - | | | | | | | | |
| Sunday | 11 | 11 | 2 | 222 | 59 | 24.66 | - | 1 | 5 | - | | | | | | | | |

## Career Performances

| | M | Inns | NO | Runs | HS | Avge | 100s | 50s | Ct | St | Balls | Runs | Wkts | Avge | Best | 5wI | 10wM |
|---|---|---|---|---|---|---|---|---|---|---|---|---|---|---|---|---|---|
| Test | | | | | | | | | | | | | | | | | |
| All First | 27 | 45 | 3 | 1063 | 104 | 25.30 | 1 | 5 | 27 | - | 90 | 65 | 1 | 65.00 | 1-30 | - | - |
| 1-day Int | | | | | | | | | | | | | | | | | |
| NatWest | 3 | 3 | 0 | 12 | 11 | 4.00 | - | - | 2 | - | 72 | 45 | 1 | 45.00 | 1-45 | - | |
| B & H | 3 | 2 | 0 | 37 | 37 | 18.50 | - | - | - | - | | | | | | | |
| Sunday | 19 | 19 | 3 | 393 | 59 | 24.56 | - | 1 | 6 | - | | | | | | | |

# WHITTICASE, P.     Leicestershire

**Name:** Philip Whitticase
**Role:** Right-hand bat, wicket-keeper
**Born:** 15 March 1965, Wythall, Birmingham
**Height:** 5ft 8in **Weight:** 11st
**Nickname:** Jasper, Tracy, Boggy, Rat
**County debut:** 1984
**County cap:** 1987
**1st-Class 50s:** 17
**1st-Class 100s:** 1
**1st-Class catches:** 309
**1st-Class stumpings:** 14
**Parents:** Larry Gordon and Ann
**Marital status:** Single
**Family links with cricket:** Grandfather
and father played local club cricket
(both were wicket-keepers)
**Education:** Belle Vue Junior and Middle
School; Buckpool Secondary; Crestwood
Comprehensive
**Qualifications:** 5 O-levels, 4 CSEs, senior coaching certificate
**Overseas teams played for:** South Bunbury, Western Australia 1983-85
**Cricketers particularly admired:** Bob Taylor, Alan Knott, Dennis Amiss

**Other sports followed:** Football, rugby
**Relaxations:** Playing soccer, watching rugby and 'a good night out'
**Extras:** Played schoolboy football for Birmingham City. Was Derek Underwood's last first-class victim. Lost seven teeth after being struck in the mouth by a bouncer from Neil Williams in Leicestershire's game against Essex in April 1995
**Best batting:** 114* Leicestershire v Hampshire, Bournemouth 1991

### 1995 Season

| | M | Inns | NO | Runs | HS | Avge | 100s | 50s | Ct | St | O | M | Runs | Wkts | Avge | Best | 5wI | 10wM |
|---|---|---|---|---|---|---|---|---|---|---|---|---|---|---|---|---|---|---|
| Test | | | | | | | | | | | | | | | | | | |
| All First | 3 | 5 | 1 | 150 | 62* | 37.50 | - | 2 | 7 | 1 | | | | | | | | |
| 1-day Int | | | | | | | | | | | | | | | | | | |
| NatWest | | | | | | | | | | | | | | | | | | |
| B & H | 3 | 2 | 1 | 0 | 0* | 0.00 | - | - | 1 | - | | | | | | | | |
| Sunday | 1 | 0 | 0 | 0 | 0 | - | - | - | - | - | | | | | | | | |

### Career Performances

| | M | Inns | NO | Runs | HS | Avge | 100s | 50s | Ct | St | Balls | Runs | Wkts | Avge | Best | 5wI | 10wM |
|---|---|---|---|---|---|---|---|---|---|---|---|---|---|---|---|---|---|
| Test | | | | | | | | | | | | | | | | | |
| All First | 132 | 174 | 40 | 3113 | 114* | 23.23 | 1 | 17 | 309 | 14 | 5 | 7 | 0 | - | - | - | - |
| 1-day Int | | | | | | | | | | | | | | | | | |
| NatWest | 13 | 6 | 1 | 67 | 32 | 13.40 | - | - | 14 | - | | | | | | | |
| B & H | 29 | 19 | 7 | 313 | 45 | 26.08 | - | - | 29 | 4 | | | | | | | |
| Sunday | 69 | 45 | 9 | 413 | 38 | 11.47 | - | - | 56 | 4 | | | | | | | |

# WILEMAN, J. R.        Nottinghamshire

**Name:** Jonathan Ritchie Wileman
**Role:** Right-hand bat, right-arm medium bowler
**Born:** 19 August 1970, Sheffield
**Height:** 6ft 1in **Weight:** 13st
**County debut:** 1992
**1st-Class 100s:** 1
**1st-Class catches:** 9
**Place in batting averages:** 213th av. 19.16
**Parents:** Peter and Joan
**Marital status:** Engaged to Nicole
**Education:** Malvern College; Salford University
**Qualifications:** 12 0-levels, 3 A-levels, BA in Modern Languages
**Off-season:** Playing in Sydney, Australia
**Overseas teams played for:** Gordon, Sydney 1995-96
**Cricketers particularly admired:** Ian Botham, Viv Richards

**Other sports followed:** Football (Sheffield Wednesday),
skiing, tennis, baseball (Toronto Blue Jays)
**Relaxations:** 'Watching films, listening to music, being set on fire by Chris Cairns'
**Extras:** Scored 109 on first-class debut for Nottinghamshire against Cambridge University. Played for Lincolnshire and Minor Counties in 1994, did not play any first-team games for Nottinghamshire
**Opinions on cricket:** 'Required over-rate in first-class cricket is unrealistic.'
**Best batting:** 109 Nottinghamshire v Cambridge University, Trent Bridge 1992
**Best bowling:** 2-33 Nottinghamshire v Hampshire, Trent Bridge 1995

### 1995 Season

| | M | Inns | NO | Runs | HS | Avge | 100s | 50s | Ct | St | O | M | Runs | Wkts | Avge | Best | 5wI | 10wM |
|---|---|---|---|---|---|---|---|---|---|---|---|---|---|---|---|---|---|---|
| Test | | | | | | | | | | | | | | | | | | |
| All First | 8 | 16 | 4 | 230 | 43 | 19.16 | - | - | 3 | - | 95 | 36 | 217 | 4 | 54.25 | 2-33 | - | - |
| 1-day Int | | | | | | | | | | | | | | | | | | |
| NatWest | 2 | 1 | 0 | 12 | 12 | 12.00 | - | - | - | - | 8 | 0 | 55 | 2 | 27.50 | 1-9 | - | |
| B & H | 2 | 1 | 0 | 0 | 0 | 0.00 | - | - | 1 | - | 3 | 0 | 15 | 0 | - | - | - | |
| Sunday | 16 | 13 | 8 | 226 | 51 * | 45.20 | - | 1 | 9 | - | 81.2 | 0 | 476 | 17 | 28.00 | 4-21 | - | |

### Career Performances

| | M | Inns | NO | Runs | HS | Avge | 100s | 50s | Ct | St | Balls | Runs | Wkts | Avge | Best | 5wI | 10wM |
|---|---|---|---|---|---|---|---|---|---|---|---|---|---|---|---|---|---|
| Test | | | | | | | | | | | | | | | | | |
| All First | 11 | 21 | 6 | 447 | 109 | 29.80 | 1 | - | 9 | - | 570 | 217 | 4 | 54.25 | 2-33 | - | - |
| 1-day Int | | | | | | | | | | | | | | | | | |
| NatWest | 3 | 2 | 0 | 26 | 14 | 13.00 | - | - | 2 | - | 48 | 55 | 2 | 27.50 | 1-9 | - | |
| B & H | 2 | 1 | 0 | 0 | 0 | 0.00 | - | - | 1 | - | 18 | 15 | 0 | - | - | - | |
| Sunday | 16 | 13 | 8 | 226 | 51 * | 45.20 | - | 1 | 9 | - | 488 | 476 | 17 | 28.00 | 4-21 | - | |

97. In 1995 which former Test player marked his final game in county cricket with a century?

# WILLIAMS, J. R. A.                    Glamorgan

**Name:** James Robert Alexander Williams
**Role:** Right-hand opening bat
**Born:** 20 July 1973, Neath
**Height:** 5ft 11in **Weight:** 11st 7lbs
**County debut:** 1993
**Parents:** John and Beverly
**Marital status:** Single
**Family links with cricket:** Father and
grandfather played league cricket
**Education:** Clifton College Prep School;
Clifton College; Durham University
**Qualifications:** 9 GCSEs, 3 A-levels, BA
(Hons) Combined Studies in Arts, NCA
coaching award
**Off-season:** Playing in Melbourne, Australia
**Overseas tours:** Clifton College to Barbados
1987 and 1991; WCA U16 to Jersey 1989;
Scorpions to The Gambia 1991; Durham
University to South Africa 1992, to Vienna
1995

**Overseas teams played for:** East Doncaster, Melbourne 1995-96
**Cricketers particularly admired:** Michael Atherton, Courtney Walsh, Carl Hooper
**Other sports followed:** Rugby union, soccer
**Relaxations:** 'Discussing the pros and cons of being a "Jazzer" with Adrian Shaw (a
whole-hearted socialist)'
**Extras:** Represented Welsh Schools and England U19. ASW Young Player of the
Month, June 1993; Glamorgan Supporters 2nd XI Player of the Season 1993. Captain of
Durham University UAU Champions in 1995
**Best batting:** 6 Glamorgan v Australians, Neath 1993

---

**1995 Season (did not make any first-team or one-day appearances)**

---

**Career Performances**

| | M | Inns | NO | Runs | HS | Avge | 100s | 50s | Ct | St | Balls | Runs | Wkts | Avge | Best | 5wI | 10wM |
|---|---|---|---|---|---|---|---|---|---|---|---|---|---|---|---|---|---|
| Test | | | | | | | | | | | | | | | | | |
| All First | 1 | 2 | 0 | 6 | 6 | 3.00 | - | - | - | - | | | | | | | |
| 1-day Int | | | | | | | | | | | | | | | | | |
| NatWest | | | | | | | | | | | | | | | | | |
| B & H | | | | | | | | | | | | | | | | | |
| Sunday | | | | | | | | | | | | | | | | | |

**Name:** Neil FitzGerald Williams
**Role:** Right-hand bat, right-arm
fast-medium bowler
**Born:** 2 July 1962, Hope Well, St Vincent,
West Indies
**Height:** 5ft 10in **Weight:** 11st 7lbs
**Nickname:** Joe
**County debut:** 1982 (Middlesex),
1995 (Essex)
**County cap:** 1984 (Middlesex)
**Benefit:** 1994
**Test debut:** 1990
**Tests:** 1
**50 wickets in a season:** 3
**1st-Class 50s:** 13
**1st-Class 5 w. in innings:** 19
**1st-Class 10 w. in match:** 2
**1st-Class catches:** 60
**Place in bowling averages:** 100th av. 35.38
(1994 124th av. 41.84)

**Strike rate:** 53.90 (career 55.58)
**Parents:** Alexander and Aldreta
**Marital status:** Single
**Family links with cricket:** 'Uncle Joe plays first division cricket in St Vincent and the Grenadines'
**Education:** Cane End Primary School, St Vincent; Acland Burghley School, Tufnell Park
**Qualifications:** School Leaver's Certificate, 6 O-levels, 1 A-level
**Overseas tours:** English Counties to Zimbabwe 1984-85; MCC to Leeward Islands 1992
**Overseas teams played for:** St Vincent 1982-92; Windward Islands 1982-92; Tasmania 1983-84
**Cricketers particularly admired:** Viv Richards, Desmond Haynes, David Gower
**Other sports followed:** Athletics
**Relaxations:** Music, 'useful DJ', cinema
**Extras:** Was on stand-by for England in New Zealand and Pakistan 1983-84. Joined Essex for the 1995 season
**Best batting:** 77 Middlesex v Warwickshire, Edgbaston 1991
**Best bowling:** 8-75 Middlesex v Gloucestershire, Lord's 1992

**1995 Season**

| | M | Inns | NO | Runs | HS | Avge | 100s | 50s | Ct | St | O | M | Runs | Wkts | Avge | Best | 5wI | 10wM |
|---|---|---|---|---|---|---|---|---|---|---|---|---|---|---|---|---|---|---|
| Test | | | | | | | | | | | | | | | | | | |
| All First | 8 | 12 | 2 | 90 | 17 | 9.00 | - | - | 1 | - | 188.4 | 31 | 743 | 21 | 35.38 | 5-93 | 1 | - |
| 1-day Int | | | | | | | | | | | | | | | | | | |
| NatWest | | | | | | | | | | | | | | | | | | |
| B & H | 3 | 2 | 0 | 3 | 3 | 1.50 | - | - | 1 | - | 18.3 | 0 | 107 | 1 | 107.00 | 1-49 | - | |
| Sunday | 1 | 1 | 0 | 0 | 0 | 0.00 | - | - | - | - | 4 | 0 | 25 | 0 | - | - | - | |

**Career Performances**

| | M | Inns | NO | Runs | HS | Avge | 100s | 50s | Ct | St | Balls | Runs | Wkts | Avge | Best | 5wI | 10wM |
|---|---|---|---|---|---|---|---|---|---|---|---|---|---|---|---|---|---|
| Test | 1 | 1 | 0 | 38 | 38 | 38.00 | - | - | - | - | 246 | 148 | 2 | 74.00 | 2-148 | - | - |
| All First | 230 | 265 | 53 | 3999 | 77 | 18.86 | - | 13 | 60 | - | 33408 | 18103 | 601 | 30.12 | 8-75 | 19 | 2 |
| 1-day Int | | | | | | | | | | | | | | | | | |
| NatWest | 19 | 10 | 3 | 49 | 10 | 7.00 | - | - | 4 | - | 913 | 618 | 15 | 41.20 | 4-36 | - | |
| B & H | 55 | 31 | 7 | 259 | 29* | 10.79 | - | - | 7 | - | 2880 | 1812 | 56 | 32.35 | 3-16 | - | |
| Sunday | 123 | 54 | 20 | 443 | 43 | 13.02 | - | - | 31 | - | 5093 | 3789 | 135 | 28.06 | 4-39 | - | |

# WILLIAMS, R. C.      Gloucestershire

**Name:** Ricardo Cecil Williams
**Role:** Right-hand bat, right-arm
fast-medium bowler
**Born:** 7 February 1968, Camberwell, London
**Height:** 5ft 10in **Weight:** 11st
**Nickname:** Raw Deal, Tricky Ricky, Gus
**County debut:** 1991
**1st-Class catches:** 7
**Place in batting averages:**
(1994 246th av. 14.25)
**Place in bowling averages:**
(1994 83rd av. 32.92)
**Strike rate:** (career 74.02)
**Parents:** Wilfred Harry Williams and
Cecile Yvonne Jordan
**Marital status:** Single
**Education:** Haringey College; Ellerslie
Secondary School, Barbados; Haringey
Cricket College
**Qualifications:** 3 O-levels, NCA coaching award
**Overseas tours:** Haringey Cricket College to Jamaica 1988, 1989, 1990
**Overseas teams played for:** Geelong City, Victoria, Australia 1991-92

**Cricketers particularly admired:** Malcolm Marshall, Viv Richards, Richie Richardson, Jimmy Cook, Gordon Greenidge, Jack Russell, David Lawrence
**Other sports followed:** Football, tennis, volleyball, basketball, athletics, baseball
**Relaxations:** Listening to music, buying clothes, relaxing with friends, watching videos
**Extras:** Rapid Cricketline Player of the Year 1992. Released by Gloucestershire at the end of the 1995 season
**Opinions on cricket:** 'Prepare faster wickets for batsmen and bowlers to compete on in both 1st and 2nd XIs.'
**Best batting:** 44 Gloucestershire v Nottinghamshire, Worksop 1992
**Best bowling:** 4-28 Gloucestershire v Cambridge University, Bristol 1994

## 1995 Season

|          | M | Inns | NO | Runs | HS | Avge | 100s | 50s | Ct | St | O | M | Runs | Wkts | Avge | Best | 5wI | 10wM |
|----------|---|------|----|------|----|------|------|-----|----|----|---|---|------|------|------|------|-----|------|
| Test     |   |      |    |      |    |      |      |     |    |    |       |    |     |    |       |      |     |      |
| All First | 4 | 7 | 0 | 60 | 22 | 8.57 | - | - | 1 | - | 103.3 | 20 | 361 | 6 | 60.16 | 3-44 | - | - |
| 1-day Int |   |      |    |      |    |      |      |     |    |    |       |    |     |    |       |      |     |      |
| NatWest   |   |      |    |      |    |      |      |     |    |    |       |    |     |    |       |      |     |      |
| B & H     |   |      |    |      |    |      |      |     |    |    |       |    |     |    |       |      |     |      |
| Sunday    | 8 | 6 | 2 | 148 | 40 | 37.00 | - | - | 1 | - | 53 | 2 | 361 | 12 | 30.08 | 4-51 | - | |

## Career Performances

|          | M | Inns | NO | Runs | HS | Avge | 100s | 50s | Ct | St | Balls | Runs | Wkts | Avge | Best | 5wI | 10wM |
|----------|---|------|----|------|----|------|------|-----|----|----|-------|------|------|------|------|-----|------|
| Test     |   |      |    |      |    |      |      |     |    |    |       |      |      |      |      |     |      |
| All First | 26 | 41 | 6 | 453 | 44 | 12.94 | - | - | 7 | - | 3257 | 1960 | 44 | 44.54 | 4-28 | - | - |
| 1-day Int |   |      |    |      |    |      |      |     |    |    |       |      |      |      |      |     |      |
| NatWest   |   |      |    |      |    |      |      |     |    |    |       |      |      |      |      |     |      |
| B & H     |   |      |    |      |    |      |      |     |    |    |       |      |      |      |      |     |      |
| Sunday    | 32 | 25 | 7 | 296 | 40 | 16.44 | - | - | 3 | - | 1284 | 1151 | 39 | 29.51 | 4-51 | - | |

98. Prior to their victory in the series against the West Indies in 1995, when was the last time that Australia had defeated the West Indies in the Caribbean, and who was their captain?

# WILLIAMS, R. C. J.　　　　　Gloucestershire

**Name:** Richard Charles James Williams
**Role:** Left-hand bat, wicket-keeper
**Born:** 8 August 1969, Bristol
**Height:** 5ft 10in **Weight:** 11st
**Nickname:** Reg
**County debut:** 1990
**1st-Class 50s:** 4
**1st-Class catches:** 81
**1st-Class stumpings:** 13
**Place in batting averages:** 166th av. 24.77
**Parents:** Michael (deceased 1991) and Angela
**Marital status:** Single
**Family links with cricket:** Father played local club cricket
**Education:** Clifton College Preparatory School; Millfield School
**Qualifications:** PE Diploma, NCA junior coaching award
**Off-season:** Gloucestershire Gypsies tour to South Africa
**Overseas tours:** Gloucestershire to Namibia 1990, to Kenya 1991, to Sri Lanka 1992-93; Romany CC to Durban & Cape Town 1993; Gloucestershire Gypsies to Zimbabwe 1994-95, to South Africa 1995-96
**Overseas teams played for:** Manicaland, Zimbabwe 1990-91
**Cricketers particularly admired:** Andy Brassington, Jack Russell, David Gower
**Other sports followed:** Football, hockey, squash, snooker
**Relaxations:** 'Eating out, pubs and clubs, strutting my funky stuff'
**Best batting:** 90 Gloucestershire v Oxford University, Bristol 1995

## 1995 Season

|  | M | Inns | NO | Runs | HS | Avge | 100s | 50s | Ct | St | O | M | Runs | Wkts | Avge | Best | 5wI | 10wM |
|---|---|---|---|---|---|---|---|---|---|---|---|---|---|---|---|---|---|---|
| Test |  |  |  |  |  |  |  |  |  |  |  |  |  |  |  |  |  |  |
| All First | 5 | 9 | 0 | 223 | 90 | 24.77 | - | 2 | 24 | - |  |  |  |  |  |  |  |  |
| 1-day Int |  |  |  |  |  |  |  |  |  |  |  |  |  |  |  |  |  |  |
| NatWest |  |  |  |  |  |  |  |  |  |  |  |  |  |  |  |  |  |  |
| B & H |  |  |  |  |  |  |  |  |  |  |  |  |  |  |  |  |  |  |
| Sunday | 3 | 2 | 1 | 33 | 19 | 33.00 | - | - | 5 | 2 |  |  |  |  |  |  |  |  |

## Career Performances

|  | M | Inns | NO | Runs | HS | Avge | 100s | 50s | Ct | St | Balls | Runs | Wkts | Avge | Best | 5wI | 10wM |
|---|---|---|---|---|---|---|---|---|---|---|---|---|---|---|---|---|---|
| Test |  |  |  |  |  |  |  |  |  |  |  |  |  |  |  |  |  |
| All First | 30 | 36 | 8 | 507 | 90 | 18.10 | - | 4 | 81 | 13 |  |  |  |  |  |  |  |
| 1-day Int |  |  |  |  |  |  |  |  |  |  |  |  |  |  |  |  |  |
| NatWest |  |  |  |  |  |  |  |  |  |  |  |  |  |  |  |  |  |
| B & H |  |  |  |  |  |  |  |  |  |  |  |  |  |  |  |  |  |
| Sunday | 14 | 4 | 2 | 63 | 19 | 31.50 | - | - | 15 | 2 |  |  |  |  |  |  |  |

# WILLIS, S. C.                               Kent

**Name:** Simon Charles Willis
**Role:** Right-hand bat, wicket-keeper
**Born:** 19 March 1974, Greenwich, London
**Height:** 5ft 8in **Weight:** 12st
**Nickname:** Wilco, Bruce
**County debut:** 1993
**1st-Class 50s:** 2
**1st-Class catches:** 10
**Parents:** Ray and Janet
**Marital status:** Engaged
**Family links with cricket:** Father plays for
Gravesend in Kent League
**Education:** Wilmington Grammar School
**Qualifications:** 9 GCSEs, NCA Junior
Coaching Certificate
**Off-season:** Coaching youngsters at indoor
school in Canterbury
**Overseas tours:** Kent U17 to New Zealand
1990-91; Kent to Zimbabwe 1993
**Overseas teams played for:** Scarborough, Western Australia 1992-93
**Cricketers particularly admired:** Alan Knott, Viv Richards, Robin Smith, Carl
Hooper
**Other sports followed:** Golf, soccer (Arsenal FC), horse racing
**Relaxations:** 'Playing golf, listening to music and going out with my fiancée'
**Opinions on cricket:** 'I would like to see the second XI Championship changed from
three-day to four-day cricket so players can adapt quicker when playing in the first team.
I would also like the second hour in second-class cricket to finish as no-one I have talked
to is in favour of it.'
**Best batting:** 82 Kent v Cambridge University, Folkestone 1995

**1995 Season**

| | M | Inns | NO | Runs | HS | Avge | 100s | 50s | Ct | St | O | M | Runs | Wkts | Avge | Best | 5wI | 10wM |
|---|---|---|---|---|---|---|---|---|---|---|---|---|---|---|---|---|---|---|
| Test | | | | | | | | | | | | | | | | | | |
| All First | 3 | 4 | 0 | 153 | 82 | 38.25 | - | 2 | 10 | - | | | | | | | | |
| 1-day Int | | | | | | | | | | | | | | | | | | |
| NatWest | 1 | 1 | 1 | 19 | 19 * | - | - | - | 1 | - | | | | | | | | |
| B & H | 1 | 0 | 0 | 0 | 0 | - | - | - | - | - | | | | | | | | |
| Sunday | 2 | 2 | 0 | 25 | 13 | 12.50 | - | - | 3 | - | | | | | | | | |

**Career Performances**

| | M | Inns | NO | Runs | HS | Avge | 100s | 50s | Ct | St | Balls | Runs | Wkts | Avge | Best | 5wI | 10wM |
|---|---|---|---|---|---|---|---|---|---|---|---|---|---|---|---|---|---|
| Test | | | | | | | | | | | | | | | | | |
| All First | 4 | 5 | 1 | 153 | 82 | 38.25 | - | 2 | 12 | - | | | | | | | |
| 1-day Int | | | | | | | | | | | | | | | | | |
| NatWest | 1 | 1 | 1 | 19 | 19 * | - | - | - | 1 | - | | | | | | | |
| B & H | 1 | 0 | 0 | 0 | 0 | - | - | - | - | - | | | | | | | |
| Sunday | 3 | 2 | 0 | 25 | 13 | 12.50 | - | - | 6 | - | | | | | | | |

# WINDOWS, M. G. N.  Gloucestershire

**Name:** Matthew Guy Newman Windows
**Role:** Right-hand bat, left-arm bowler
**Born:** 5 April 1973, Clifton, Bristol
**Height:** 5ft 7in **Weight:** 11st 7lbs
**Nickname:** Steamy
**County debut:** 1992
**1st-Class 50s:** 8
**1st-Class 100s:** 1
**1st-Class catches:** 24
**Place in batting averages:** 198th av. 20.86
(1994 92nd av. 34.76)
**Parents:** Tony and Carolyn
**Marital status:** Single
**Family links with cricket:** Father (A.R.)
played for Gloucestershire (1960-69) and
Cambridge University
**Education:** Clifton College; Durham
University
**Qualifications:** 8 GCSEs, 3 A-levels
**Off-season:** Studying
**Overseas tours:** England U19 to Pakistan 1991-92; Durham University to South
Africa 1992

**Cricketers particularly admired:** Mike Procter, Jack Russell, Courtney Walsh
**Other sports followed:** Rugby, rackets
**Relaxations:** Listening to music, playing other sports, 'going out for a couple of quiet pints'
**Extras:** Played for Lincolnshire and in England U19 home series v Sri Lanka 1992. Public schools rackets and fives champion. 1994 Gloucestershire Young Player of the Year. Holds the record for highest individual score for Durham University (218 not out)
**Opinions on cricket:** 'We have to bowl too many overs in a day resulting in a heavy fine rate. The county circuit offers us great camaraderie.'
**Best batting:** 106 Gloucestershire v New Zealanders, Bristol 1994
**Best bowling:** 1-6 Combined Universities v West Indies, The Parks 1995

## 1995 Season

|          | M | Inns | NO | Runs | HS | Avge | 100s | 50s | Ct | St | O | M | Runs | Wkts | Avge | Best | 5wI | 10wM |
|----------|---|------|----|------|-----|-------|------|-----|----|----|-----|---|------|------|-------|------|-----|------|
| Test     |   |      |    |      |     |       |      |     |    |    |     |   |      |      |       |      |     |      |
| All First | 9 | 17   | 2  | 313  | 56  | 20.86 | -    | 2   | 11 | -  | 7.3 | 1 | 36   | 2    | 18.00 | 1-6  | -   | -    |
| 1-day Int |   |      |    |      |     |       |      |     |    |    |     |   |      |      |       |      |     |      |
| NatWest  | 2 | 2    | 0  | 9    | 9   | 4.50  | -    | -   | -  | -  |     |   |      |      |       |      |     |      |
| B & H    |   |      |    |      |     |       |      |     |    |    |     |   |      |      |       |      |     |      |
| Sunday   | 7 | 7    | 0  | 67   | 29  | 9.57  | -    | -   | 4  | -  | 8   | 0 | 49   | 0    | -     |      | -   | -    |

## Career Performances

|          | M | Inns | NO | Runs | HS  | Avge | 100s | 50s | Ct | St | Balls | Runs | Wkts | Avge | Best | 5wI | 10wM |
|----------|---|------|----|------|------|-------|------|-----|----|----|-------|------|------|-------|------|-----|------|
| Test     |   |      |    |      |      |       |      |     |    |    |       |      |      |       |      |     |      |
| All First | 23 | 43  | 2  | 1252 | 106  | 30.53 | 1    | 8   | 24 | -  | 51    | 39   | 2    | 19.50 | 1-6  | -   | -    |
| 1-day Int |   |      |    |      |      |       |      |     |    |    |       |      |      |       |      |     |      |
| NatWest  | 3 | 3    | 0  | 42   | 33   | 14.00 | -    | -   | -  | -  |       |      |      |       |      |     |      |
| B & H    | 1 | 1    | 1  | 16   | 16 * | -     | -    | -   | -  | -  |       |      |      |       |      |     |      |
| Sunday   | 23 | 23  | 1  | 459  | 72   | 20.86 | -    | 2   | 6  | -  | 48    | 49   | 0    | -     |      | -   | -    |

99. Who was dismissed from the West Indian party during the tour to England in 1995 and who replaced him?

# WOOD, J.                                    Durham

**Name:** John Wood
**Role:** Right-hand bat, right-arm
fast-medium bowler
**Born:** 22 July 1970, Wakefield
**Height:** 6ft 3in **Weight:** 16st
**Nickname:** Woody
**County debut:** 1992
**1st-Class 50s:** 2
**1st-Class 5 w. in innings:** 4
**1st-Class catches:** 6
**Place in batting averages:**
(1994 267th av. 10.21)
**Place in bowling averages:** 15th av. 21.64
(1994 85th av. 33.35)
**Strike rate:** 41.85 (career 50.19)
**Parents:** Brian and Anne
**Wife and date of marriage:** Emma Louise,
30 October 1994

**Family links with cricket:** Both father and
brother played to a good standard
**Education:** Crofton High School; Wakefield District College; Leeds Polytechnic
**Qualifications:** BTEC Diploma and HND in Electrical and Electronic Engineering,
senior coaching certificate
**Off-season:** 'Looking for work in the Durham area'
**Overseas teams played for:** Griqualand West Cricket Union, South Africa 1990-91;
TAWA, New Zealand 1993-95; Wellington, New Zealand, 1993-95
**Cricketers particularly admired:** Allan Donald, Wasim Akram, Ian Botham, Paul
Parker
**Injuries:** Stress fracture in lower spine, out for the whole season bar the first three
games
**Relaxations:** 'Local pub, good food, television, music and sorting out the house and
garden'
**Extras:** Played in the Bradford League. Made his debut for Durham (Minor Counties)
in 1991
**Opinions on cricket:** 'One year out of the game has made me realise how much I love
it.'
**Best batting:** 63* Durham v Nottinghamshire, Chester-le-Street 1993
**Best bowling:** 6-110 Durham v Essex, Stockton 1994

| | M | Inns | NO | Runs | HS | Avge | 100s | 50s | Ct | St | O | M | Runs | Wkts | Avge | Best | 5wI | 10wM |
|---|---|---|---|---|---|---|---|---|---|---|---|---|---|---|---|---|---|---|
| Test | | | | | | | | | | | | | | | | | | |
| All First | 4 | 7 | 2 | 86 | 40 * | 17.20 | - | - | - | - | 97.4 | 25 | 303 | 14 | 21.64 | 4-54 | - | - |
| 1-day Int | | | | | | | | | | | | | | | | | | |
| NatWest | | | | | | | | | | | | | | | | | | |
| B & H | 4 | 4 | 0 | 36 | 27 | 9.00 | - | - | - | - | 44 | 4 | 182 | 4 | 45.50 | 3-50 | - | |
| Sunday | | | | | | | | | | | | | | | | | | |

**Career Performances**

| | M | Inns | NO | Runs | HS | Avge | 100s | 50s | Ct | St | Balls | Runs | Wkts | Avge | Best | 5wI | 10wM |
|---|---|---|---|---|---|---|---|---|---|---|---|---|---|---|---|---|---|
| Test | | | | | | | | | | | | | | | | | |
| All First | 36 | 52 | 9 | 610 | 63 * | 14.18 | - | 2 | 6 | - | 4618 | 3073 | 92 | 33.40 | 6-110 | 4 | - |
| 1-day Int | | | | | | | | | | | | | | | | | |
| NatWest | 5 | 1 | 0 | 1 | 1 | 1.00 | - | - | - | - | 228 | 168 | 4 | 42.00 | 2-22 | - | |
| B & H | 6 | 4 | 0 | 36 | 27 | 9.00 | - | - | - | - | 348 | 224 | 5 | 44.80 | 3-50 | - | |
| Sunday | 18 | 12 | 3 | 77 | 28 | 8.55 | - | - | 2 | - | 720 | 619 | 15 | 41.26 | 2-26 | - | |

# WOOD, M. J.       Yorkshire

**Name:** Matthew James Wood
**Role:** Right-hand opening bat
**Born:** 6 April 1977, Huddersfield
**Height:** 5ft 9in   **Weight:** 11st 5lbs
**Nickname:** Chuddy, Woody
**County debut:** No first-team appearance
**Parents:** Roger and Cathryn
**Marital status:** Single
**Family links with cricket:** Father played at local club Emley
**Education:** Shelley High School; Shelley Sixth Form College
**Qualifications:** 9 GCSEs, 2 A-levels
**Off-season:** England U19 tour to Zimbabwe at Christmas
**Cricketers particularly admired:** Martyn Moxon, Michael Slater, Carl Hooper, Anthony McGrath
**Other sports followed:** Football (Liverpool FC)
**Relaxations:** Socialising, listening to music, eating
**Extras:** Played for England U17 against Sri Lanka in 1994. Yorkshire Academy 1994-95

**Opinions on cricket:** 'Second XI Championship should be four days instead of three to prepare players better for first-class cricket.'

---

# WOOD, N. T.                    Lancashire

---

**Name:** Nathan Theodore Wood
**Role:** Left-hand opening bat, right-arm off-spin bowler
**Born:** 4 October 1974, Ossett, Yorkshire
**Height:** 5ft 7in **Weight:** 10st 5lbs
**Nickname:** Ram Rod, Proff, Woderwick
**County debut:** No first-team appearance
**Parents:** Barry and Janet
**Marital status:** Single
**Family links with cricket:** Father played for Yorkshire, Lancashire, Derbyshire and England; uncle (Ron) played for Yorkshire
**Education:** Altrincham Prep School; William Hulme's Grammar School
**Qualifications:** 8 GCSEs, coaching awards
**Off-season:** 'Relaxing and maybe a bit of fitness'
**Overseas tours:** England U18 to South Africa 1992-93, to Denmark 1993; England U19 to Sri Lanka 1993-94

**Cricketers particularly admired:** 'My father', David Gower, Michael Holding, Viv Richards
**Other sports followed:** Rugby, tennis, football (Manchester United)
**Injuries:** Torn shoulder tendons, out for one game
**Relaxations:** 'House and soul music'
**Extras:** Played in Junior One-Day Internationals against Zimbabwe, India, South Africa and Sri Lanka. Played in U19 Tests against West Indies and Sri Lanka
**Opinions on cricket:** 'Some of the wickets that second XI matches are played on are a disgrace. Don't agree with the rule that allows play to continue an hour after the scheduled close of play – play too much as it is. Players fielding short leg and on the line should have to wear helmets to minimise the risk of serious injuries or even fatalities. Counties should set up extensive coaching schemes, thus nurturing young talent and providing employment for players in the winter. Would like to see a transfer system in place.'

# WREN, T. N.                                    Kent

**Name:** Timothy Neil Wren
**Role:** Right-hand bat, left-arm
medium bowler
**Born:** 26 March 1970, Folkestone
**Height:** 6ft 3in **Weight:** 14st 7lbs
**Nickname:** Bear, Balou
**County debut:** 1989 (one-day),
1990 (first-class)
**1st-Class 5 w. in innings:** 2
**1st-Class catches:** 9
**One-day 5 w. innings:** 1
**Place in bowling averages:** 89th av. 34.13
(1994 74th av. 31.35)
**Strike rate:** 53.65 (career 60.00)
**Parents:** James and Gillian
**Marital status:** Single
**Family links with cricket:** 'Brother suicidal
about his comeback!'
**Education:** Lyminge Primary; Harvey
Grammar School, Folkestone
**Qualifications:** 6 O-levels, NCA coaching certificate
**Career outside cricket:** Plumbing and central heating engineer
**Off-season:** Working as a plumber, playing golf
**Overseas teams played for:** Universals, Zimbabwe 1989-90
**Cricketers particularly admired:** Aravinda De Silva, Carl Hooper, Curtly Ambrose
**Other sports followed:** Rugby, football (Lyminge)
**Relaxations:** 'Golf, reading, eating out, walking my dog'
**Opinions on cricket:** 'Too much talk of major changes. Not too much wrong with our
cricket. Stop looking at other countries as a way to improve our cricket. Standard of pitches
is not good enough, also sides are allowed to get away with sub-standard pitches.'
**Best batting:** 23 Kent v Sussex, Hove 1995
**Best bowling:** 6-48 Kent v Somerset, Canterbury 1994

## 1995 Season

|          | M | Inns | NO | Runs | HS  | Avge  | 100s | 50s | Ct | St | O     | M  | Runs | Wkts | Avge  | Best  | 5wI | 10wM |
|----------|---|------|----|------|-----|-------|------|-----|----|----|-------|----|------|------|-------|-------|-----|------|
| Test     |   |      |    |      |     |       |      |     |    |    |       |    |      |      |       |       |     |      |
| All First | 7 | 11  | 4  | 60   | 23  | 8.57  | -    | -   | 2  | -  | 205.4 | 31 | 785  | 23   | 34.13 | 5-148 | 1   | -    |
| 1-day Int |   |      |    |      |     |       |      |     |    |    |       |    |      |      |       |       |     |      |
| NatWest  | 1 | 1    | 1  | 1    | 1*  | -     | -    | -   | -  | -  | 10    | 1  | 51   | 1    | 51.00 | 1-51  | -   |      |
| B & H    | 5 | 2    | 1  | 11   | 7   | 11.00 | -    | -   | 1  | -  | 49    | 3  | 203  | 12   | 16.91 | 6-41  | 1   |      |
| Sunday   | 6 | 3    | 3  | 10   | 4*  | -     | -    | -   | -  | -  | 38    | 1  | 178  | 5    | 35.60 | 3-20  | -   |      |

## Career Performances

| | M | Inns | NO | Runs | HS | Avge | 100s | 50s | Ct | St | Balls | Runs | Wkts | Avge | Best | 5wI | 10wM |
|---|---|---|---|---|---|---|---|---|---|---|---|---|---|---|---|---|---|
| Test | | | | | | | | | | | | | | | | | |
| All First | 22 | 28 | 10 | 115 | 23 | 6.38 | - | - | 9 | - | 3300 | 1985 | 55 | 36.09 | 6-48 | 2 | - |
| 1-day Int | | | | | | | | | | | | | | | | | |
| NatWest | 2 | 2 | 1 | 1 | 1 * | 1.00 | - | - | - | - | 120 | 92 | 1 | 92.00 | 1-51 | - | |
| B & H | 5 | 2 | 1 | 11 | 7 | 11.00 | - | - | 1 | - | 294 | 203 | 12 | 16.91 | 6-41 | 1 | |
| Sunday | 19 | 6 | 6 | 15 | 5 * | - | - | - | 4 | - | 729 | 555 | 16 | 34.68 | 3-20 | - | |

# WRIGHT, A. J.  Gloucestershire

**Name:** Anthony John Wright
**Role:** Right-hand bat, off-spin bowler
**Born:** 27 July 1962, Stevenage, Hertfordshire
**Height:** 6ft **Weight:** 14st
**Nickname:** Billy
**County debut:** 1982
**County cap:** 1987
**1000 runs in a season:** 6
**1st-Class 50s:** 62
**1st-Class 100s:** 17
**1st-Class catches:** 191
**One-Day 100s:** 2
**Place in batting averages:** 36th av. 46.60
(1994 79th av. 36.42)
**Parents:** Michael and Patricia
**Wife and date of marriage:** Rachel, 21
December 1986
**Children:** Hannah, 3 April 1988; Beth, 19
August 1992; Joseph, 29 November 1993
**Education:** Alleyn's School, Stevenage
**Qualifications:** 6 O-levels
**Off-season:** 'Working for IES Telecom, Bristol and preparing for my benefit. Also creating chances for Bobby Dawson to score for Bristol North West FC'
**Overseas tours:** Gloucestershire to Sri Lanka 1987 and 1993, to Barbados 1980, 1985, 1988, to Namibia 1990, to Kenya 1991
**Cricketers particularly admired:** Mike Gatting, Malcolm Marshall, Dermot Reeve, David Gower
**Other sports followed:** Soccer ('life-long Chelsea supporter'), rugby (Bristol RFC)
**Relaxations:** 'Celebrating any Arsenal defeat and hacking my way around a golf course'
**Extras:** Captain of Gloucestershire for 1990-93. Awarded benefit for 1996

**Opinions on cricket:** 'I feel that it is vital that the game is introduced to as many youngsters as possible. Unless kids are at private schools they are unlikely to get a chance to participate – a shocking situation! I would like to see our Test team being prepared specifically to beat the Aussies in the next series over here. I'm sick of hearing them say how poor our game is.'

**Best batting:** 193 Gloucestershire v Nottinghamshire, Bristol 1995
**Best bowling:** 1-16 Gloucestershire v Yorkshire, Harrogate 1989

## 1995 Season

| | M | Inns | NO | Runs | HS | Avge | 100s | 50s | Ct | St | O | M | Runs | Wkts | Avge | Best | 5wI | 10wM |
|---|---|---|---|---|---|---|---|---|---|---|---|---|---|---|---|---|---|---|
| Test | | | | | | | | | | | | | | | | | | |
| All First | 18 | 34 | 4 | 1401 | 193 | 46.70 | 4 | 5 | 8 | - | | | | | | | | |
| 1-day Int | | | | | | | | | | | | | | | | | | |
| NatWest | 3 | 3 | 1 | 262 | 142 * | 131.00 | 1 | 1 | 5 | - | | | | | | | | |
| B & H | 6 | 6 | 0 | 168 | 51 | 28.00 | - | 1 | 2 | - | | | | | | | | |
| Sunday | 15 | 15 | 1 | 310 | 63 | 22.14 | - | 1 | 1 | - | | | | | | | | |

## Career Performances

| | M | Inns | NO | Runs | HS | Avge | 100s | 50s | Ct | St | Balls | Runs | Wkts | Avge | Best | 5wI | 10wM |
|---|---|---|---|---|---|---|---|---|---|---|---|---|---|---|---|---|---|
| Test | | | | | | | | | | | | | | | | | |
| All First | 254 | 445 | 35 | 12264 | 193 | 29.91 | 17 | 62 | 191 | - | 74 | 68 | 1 | 68.00 | 1-16 | - | - |
| 1-day Int | | | | | | | | | | | | | | | | | |
| NatWest | 26 | 25 | 2 | 1070 | 142 * | 46.52 | 2 | 9 | 10 | - | | | | | | | |
| B & H | 39 | 36 | 0 | 1016 | 97 | 28.22 | - | 7 | 8 | - | | | | | | | |
| Sunday | 161 | 150 | 17 | 3388 | 93 | 25.47 | - | 23 | 57 | - | 26 | 22 | 0 | - | | - | - |

---

100. How many of the 1995 Warwickshire squad have played
Test cricket and who are they?

---

# WYLIE, A.         Worcestershire

**Name:** Alex Wylie
**Role:** Left-hand bat, right-arm fast bowler
**Born:** 20 February 1973, Tamworth
**Height:** 6ft 2in
**County debut:** 1993
**Education:** Bromsgrove School, Warwick College of Agriculture
**Extras:** Decided to retire from county cricket at the end of the 1995 season after struggling with a back injury since the 1993 season
**Best batting:** 7 Worcestershire v Middlesex, Worcester 1995
**Best bowling:** 1-50 Worcestershire v Nottinghamshire, Trent Bridge 1993

## 1995 Season

|  | M | Inns | NO | Runs | HS | Avge | 100s | 50s | Ct | St | O | M | Runs | Wkts | Avge | Best | 5wI | 10wM |
|---|---|---|---|---|---|---|---|---|---|---|---|---|---|---|---|---|---|---|
| Test |  |  |  |  |  |  |  |  |  |  |  |  |  |  |  |  |  |  |
| All First | 2 | 4 | 1 | 14 | 7 | 4.66 | - | - | - | - | 35 | 7 | 143 | 1 | 143.00 | 1-65 | - | - |
| 1-day Int |  |  |  |  |  |  |  |  |  |  |  |  |  |  |  |  |  |  |
| NatWest |  |  |  |  |  |  |  |  |  |  |  |  |  |  |  |  |  |  |
| B & H |  |  |  |  |  |  |  |  |  |  |  |  |  |  |  |  |  |  |
| Sunday |  |  |  |  |  |  |  |  |  |  |  |  |  |  |  |  |  |  |

## Career Performances

|  | M | Inns | NO | Runs | HS | Avge | 100s | 50s | Ct | St | Balls | Runs | Wkts | Avge | Best | 5wI | 10wM |
|---|---|---|---|---|---|---|---|---|---|---|---|---|---|---|---|---|---|
| Test |  |  |  |  |  |  |  |  |  |  |  |  |  |  |  |  |  |
| All First | 3 | 5 | 1 | 14 | 7 | 3.50 | - | - | - | - | 342 | 216 | 2 | 108.00 | 1-50 | - | - |
| 1-day Int |  |  |  |  |  |  |  |  |  |  |  |  |  |  |  |  |  |
| NatWest |  |  |  |  |  |  |  |  |  |  |  |  |  |  |  |  |  |
| B & H |  |  |  |  |  |  |  |  |  |  |  |  |  |  |  |  |  |
| Sunday |  |  |  |  |  |  |  |  |  |  |  |  |  |  |  |  |  |

# YATES, G.                    Lancashire

**Name:** Gary Yates
**Role:** Right-hand bat, off-spin bowler
**Born:** 20 September 1967, Ashton-under-Lyne
**Height:** 6ft 1in **Weight:** 12st 10lbs
**Nickname:** Yugo, Pearly, Backyard, Zippy
**County debut:** 1990
**County cap:** 1994
**1st-Class 50s:** 3
**1st-Class 100s:** 3
**1st-Class 5 w. in innings:** 2
**1st-Class catches:** 17
**Place in batting averages:** 177th av. 23.14
(1994 195th av. 20.92)
**Place in bowling averages:** 130th av. 44.90
(1994 41st av. 27.37)
**Strike rate:** 74.18 (career 84.33)
**Parents:** Alan and Patricia
**Marital status:** Single
**Family links with cricket:** Father played in Lancashire Leagues
**Education:** Manchester Grammar School
**Qualifications:** 6 O-levels, Australian Coaching Council coach
**Career outside cricket:** 'Getting more involved in family business (Digical Ltd), selling diaries, calendars and business gifts.'
**Off-season:** Playing and coaching for Hermanus, Boland, South Africa
**Overseas tours:** Lancashire to Tasmania and Western Australia 1990, to Western Australia 1991, to Johannesburg 1992, to Barbados and St Lucia 1992
**Overseas teams played for:** South Barwon, Geelong, Australia 1987-88; Johnsonville, Wellington, New Zealand 1989-90; Western Suburbs, Brisbane 1991-92; Old Selbornian, East London, South Africa 1992-93
**Cricketers particularly admired:** Michael Atherton, Ian Botham, John Emburey
**Other sports followed:** All sports, especially football (Manchester City), golf, motor rallying
**Injuries:** Finger infection, out for four weeks
**Relaxations:** Playing golf, watching football and good films, eating
**Extras:** Played for Worcestershire 2nd XI in 1987; made debut for Lancashire 2nd XI in 1988 and taken on to county staff in 1990; scored century on Championship debut v Nottinghamshire at Trent Bridge. Rapid Cricketline Player of the Month April/May 1992
**Opinions on cricket:** 'Would like to see more points awarded for rained-off games or draws. This would hopefully help to abolish contrived matches. Hope four-day cricket is here to stay.'

**Best batting:** 134* Lancashire v Northamptonshire, Old Trafford 1993
**Best bowling:** 5-34 Lancashire v Hampshire, Old Trafford 1994

## 1995 Season

|          | M  | Inns | NO | Runs | HS   | Avge  | 100s | 50s | Ct | St | O    | M  | Runs | Wkts | Avge  | Best | 5wI | 10wM |
|----------|----|------|----|------|------|-------|------|-----|----|----|------|----|------|------|-------|------|-----|------|
| Test     |    |      |    |      |      |       |      |     |    |    |      |    |      |      |       |      |     |      |
| All First| 7  | 9    | 2  | 162  | 42 * | 23.14 | -    | -   | 1  | -  | 136  | 33 | 494  | 11   | 44.90 | 4-67 | -   | -    |
| 1-day Int|    |      |    |      |      |       |      |     |    |    |      |    |      |      |       |      |     |      |
| NatWest  | 3  | 1    | 0  | 9    | 9    | 9.00  | -    | -   | -  | -  | 36   | 3  | 97   | 2    | 48.50 | 1-17 | -   |      |
| B & H    | 8  | 1    | 1  | 19   | 19 * | -     | -    | -   | 2  | -  | 62   | 1  | 264  | 10   | 26.40 | 3-42 | -   |      |
| Sunday   | 13 | 6    | 3  | 40   | 24 * | 13.33 | -    | -   | 4  | -  | 79.2 | 3  | 415  | 15   | 27.66 | 4-40 | -   |      |

## Career Performances

|          | M  | Inns | NO | Runs | HS    | Avge  | 100s | 50s | Ct | St | Balls | Runs | Wkts | Avge  | Best | 5wI | 10wM |
|----------|----|------|----|------|-------|-------|------|-----|----|----|-------|------|------|-------|------|-----|------|
| Test     |    |      |    |      |       |       |      |     |    |    |       |      |      |       |      |     |      |
| All First| 52 | 69   | 30 | 1281 | 134 * | 32.84 | 3    | 3   | 17 | -  | 8687  | 4533 | 103  | 44.00 | 5-34 | 2   | -    |
| 1-day Int|    |      |    |      |       |       |      |     |    |    |       |      |      |       |      |     |      |
| NatWest  | 5  | 2    | 1  | 16   | 9     | 16.00 | -    | -   | -  | -  | 360   | 186  | 5    | 37.20 | 2-61 | -   |      |
| B & H    | 13 | 1    | 1  | 19   | 19 *  | -     | -    | -   | 4  | -  | 630   | 426  | 15   | 28.40 | 3-42 | -   |      |
| Sunday   | 41 | 12   | 6  | 75   | 24 *  | 12.50 | -    | -   | 12 | -  | 1494  | 1268 | 43   | 29.48 | 4-34 | -   |      |

# YEABSLEY, R. S.                     Middlesex

**Name:** Richard Stuart Yeabsley
**Role:** Right-hand bat,
right-arm medium bowler
**Born:** 2 November 1973, St Albans
**Height:** 6ft 4in **Weight:** 15st
**Nickname:** Yeabo
**County debut:** 1994 (one-day)
**1st-Class 50s:** 1
**1st-Class 5 w. in innings:** 1
**1st-Class catches:** 11
**Place in bowling averages:**
(1994 38th av. 27.00)
**Strike rate:** (career 60.83)
**Parents:** Douglas and Jacqueline
**Marital status:** Single
**Family links with cricket:**
Father played for Devon for 30 years and for
Minor Counties; brother played for
Hertfordshire U19

**Education:** Haberdashers' Aske's School, Elstree, Hertfordshire; Keble College, Oxford

**Qualifications:** O-levels, A-levels, BA (Hons) in History

**Career outside cricket:** Student

**Off-season:** Studying at Oxford University

**Overseas tours:** Haberdashers' Aske's to Far East 1991-92

**Cricketers particularly admired:** Graeme Hick, Jason Harrison, Kevin Shine

**Other sports followed:** Baseball, American football, rugby

**Injuries:** 'Exams, missed three months!'

**Relaxations:** Reading, music

**Extras:** Made NatWest debut for Devon against Somerset in 1990, aged 16, and his first-class debut for Oxford University in 1993. Oxford Blue 1993 and 1994. Secretary of OUCC 1994. Played rugby for Oxford in U21 Varsity match 1992 and 1993 and toured Ireland with the full Oxford University Blues squad in 1993. Rugby Blue against Cambridge at Twickenham 1994 and 1995. Released by Middlesex at the end of the 1995 season

**Opinions on cricket:** 'Cambridge University to lose first-class status!'

**Best batting:** 52* Oxford University v Yorkshire, The Parks 1994

**Best bowling:** 6-54 Oxford University v Cambridge University, Lord's 1994

## 1995 Season

| | M | Inns | NO | Runs | HS | Avge | 100s | 50s | Ct | St | O | M | Runs | Wkts | Avge | Best | 5wI | 10wM |
|---|---|---|---|---|---|---|---|---|---|---|---|---|---|---|---|---|---|---|
| Test | | | | | | | | | | | | | | | | | | |
| All First | 3 | 4 | 0 | 13 | 4 | 3.25 | - | - | 1 | - | 85 | 16 | 277 | 8 | 34.62 | 4-34 | - | - |
| 1-day Int | | | | | | | | | | | | | | | | | | |
| NatWest | | | | | | | | | | | | | | | | | | |
| B & H | | | | | | | | | | | | | | | | | | |
| Sunday | 1 | 0 | 0 | 0 | 0 | - | - | - | 1 | - | 3 | 0 | 13 | 1 | 13.00 | 1-13 | - | |

## Career Performances

| | M | Inns | NO | Runs | HS | Avge | 100s | 50s | Ct | St | Balls | Runs | Wkts | Avge | Best | 5wI | 10wM |
|---|---|---|---|---|---|---|---|---|---|---|---|---|---|---|---|---|---|
| Test | | | | | | | | | | | | | | | | | |
| All First | 19 | 20 | 5 | 204 | 52 * | 13.60 | - | 1 | 11 | - | 2981 | 1606 | 49 | 32.77 | 6-54 | 1 | 1 |
| 1-day Int | | | | | | | | | | | | | | | | | |
| NatWest | 1 | 1 | 0 | 2 | 2 | 2.00 | - | - | - | - | 72 | 77 | 0 | - | | - | - |
| B & H | | | | | | | | | | | | | | | | | |
| Sunday | 4 | 0 | 0 | 0 | 0 | - | - | - | 1 | - | 120 | 89 | 6 | 14.83 | 5-32 | 1 | |

# THE UMPIRES

## BALDERSTONE, J. C.

**Name:** John Christopher Balderstone
**Role:** Right-hand opening bat, slow
left-arm bowler
**Born:** 16 November 1940, Huddersfield
**Height:** 6ft 1in **Weight:** 12st 10lbs
**Nickname:** Baldy
**Appointed to 1st-class list:** 1988
**Appointed to Test panel:** Stand-by
umpire in 1991
**One-Day Internationals:** 1
**Counties:** Yorkshire, Leicestershire
**County debut:** 1961 (Yorkshire),
1971 (Leicestershire)
**County cap:** 1973 (Leicestershire)
**Test debut:** 1976
**Tests:** 2
**1000 runs in a season:** 11
**1st-Class 50s:** 102
**1st-Class 100s:** 32
**1st-Class 5 w. in innings:** 5
**One-Day 100s:** 5
**1st-Class catches:** 210
**Parents:** Frank and Jenny (deceased)
**Wife and date of marriage:** Angela, January 1991
**Children:** Sally, 15 September 1970; Michael, 3 January 1973
**Education:** Paddock County School, Huddersfield
**Qualifications:** Advanced cricket coach, soccer coach
**Career outside cricket:** Professional footballer 1958-78
**Off-season:** Coaching cricket
**Overseas tours:** Leicestershire to Zimbabwe 1981, to Oman 1984
**Cricketers particularly admired:** Willie Watson, Brian Close, Fred Trueman, David
Gower, Ray Illingworth
**Other sports followed:** All sports
**Relaxations:** Golf
**Extras:** 14 One-Day Man of the Match Awards. Played a first-class cricket match and
football league game on the same day in 1975 (Leicestershire v Derbyshire, Doncaster v
Brentford).Was the first man to act as 'third umpire' in Test in England, in the second Test

against Australia at Lord's in 1993. Umpired first one-day International, England v South Africa 1994

**Opinions on cricket:** 'Our first-class game is still good, despite all the critics pushing the Australian academy players etc. We've got equally good young prospects pushing around our county cricket scene.'

**Best batting:** 181* Leicestershire v Gloucestershire, Leicester 1984

**Best bowling:** 6-25 Leicestershire v Hampshire, Southampton 1978

### First-Class Career Performances

|  | M | Inns | NO | Runs | HS | Avge | 100s | Ct | St | Runs | Wkts | Avge | Best | 5wI | 10wM |
|---|---|---|---|---|---|---|---|---|---|---|---|---|---|---|---|
| Test | 2 | 4 | 0 | 39 | 35 | 9.75 | - | - | 1 | 80 | 1 | 80.00 | 1-80 | - | - |
| All First | 390 | 619 | 61 | 19034 | 181 * | 34.11 | 32 | 210 | - | 8160 | 310 | 26.32 | 6-25 | 5 | - |

# BIRD, H. D.

**Name:** Harold Dennis Bird, MBE
**Role:** Right-hand opening bat
**Born:** 19 April 1933, Barnsley
**Height:** 5ft 10in **Weight:** 12st
**Nickname:** Dickie
**Appointed to 1st-class list:** 1969
**Appointed to Test panel:** 1972
**Appointed to International Panel:** 1994
**Tests umpired:** 64
**One-Day Internationals umpired:** 91
**Counties:** Yorkshire, Leicestershire
**County debut:** 1956 (Yorkshire), 1960 (Leicestershire)
**County cap:** 1960 (Leicestershire)
**1000 runs in a season:** 1
**1st-Class 50s:** 14
**1st-Class 100s:** 2
**1st-Class catches:** 28

**Parents:** James Harold and Ethel
**Marital status:** Single
**Education:** Burton Road Primary School; Raley School, Barnsley
**Qualifications:** MCC advanced cricket coach
**Career outside cricket:** 'Cricket is my life'
**Off-season:** After-dinner speaking and umpiring overseas
**Cricketing superstitions or habits:** Twitch of the shoulders, wears distinctive white cap
**Other sports followed:** Football
**Cricketers particularly admired:** Gary Sobers, Dennis Lillee, Viv Richards
**Cricketers particularly learnt from:** Gubby Allen, Johnny Wardle

**Players for the future:** Anthony McGrath (Yorkshire)

**Relaxations:** Listening to recordings of Barbra Streisand and Diana Ross

**Extras:** Has umpired 160 international matches to date, including three World Cup finals at Lord's (1975, 1979, 1983); also umpired at the World Cup in India in 1987. Umpired the Queen's Silver Jubilee Test, England v Australia 1977, the Centenary Test, England v Australia 1980 and the MCC Bicentenary Test, England v Rest of the World 1987. In 1982 he umpired the Women's World Cup final in Christchurch, New Zealand. During the mid-1980s he umpired several times in the various competitions staged at Sharjah, UAE. To date he has umpired 34 Cup finals all over the world, as well as the finals of other cricket events such as The Best All-rounder in the World, The Best Batsman in the World and the World Double Wicket competition. In 1977 he was voted Yorkshire Personality of the Year. He is an MCC member and author of three bestselling books, *Not Out*, *That's Out* and *From the Pavilion End*. Despite lucrative offers to join the 'Packer circus' and to visit South Africa with rebel tours, he remained loyal to the TCCB and to the established game on which he had been brought up in Yorkshire and which had given him so much in life. In June 1986 he received an MBE in the Queen's Birthday Honours List. With David Shepherd and Steve Bucknor became the first ICC officially-sponsored umpires in 1992, and was appointed to stand in Zimbabwe's first Test match (against India) in Harare. Subsequently, in Zimbabwe's second Test against New Zealand (also in Harare), he became the first umpire to officiate in 50 Test matches, having passed Frank Chester's world record of 48 Tests at Bulawayo six days earlier. Umpired all three Tests in West Indies home series against Pakistan in 1993. In 1994 he umpired Tests in New Zealand, England, Pakistan and India. Made Honorary Life Member of Yorkshire CCC in March 1994. Announced that he will retire from international duty in 1996

**Opinions on cricket:** 'The greatest game in the world. A game to be enjoyed by young and old. I have consistently advocated playing through all light unless the umpires are convinced that there is genuine physical danger to the batsman.'

**Best batting:** 181* Yorkshire v Glamorgan, Bradford 1959

## First-Class Career Performances

| | M | Inns | NO | Runs | HS | Avge | 100s | Ct | St | Runs | Wkts | Avge | Best | 5wI | 10wM |
|---|---|---|---|---|---|---|---|---|---|---|---|---|---|---|---|
| Test | | | | | | | | | | | | | | | |
| All First | 93 | 170 | 10 | 3314 | 181 * | 20.71 | 2 | 28 | - | 22 | 0 | - | - | - | - |

# BOND, J. D.

**Name:** John David Bond
**Role:** Right-hand bat
**Born:** 6 May 1932, Kearsley, Lancashire
**Nickname:** Jackie
**Appointed to 1st-class list:** 1988
**Counties:** Lancashire, Nottinghamshire
**County debut:** 1955 (Lancashire),
1974 (Nottinghamshire)
**County cap:** 1961 (Lancashire)
**1000 runs in a season:** 2
**1st-Class 50s:** 54
**1st-Class 100s:** 14
**1st-Class catches:** 222
**Education:** Bolton School
**Extras:** Captain of Lancashire 1968-1972,
during which time Lancashire won
the Gillette Cup three years in succession
(1970, 1971, 1972) and the John Player
Sunday League in 1969 and 1970. He

moved to Nottinghamshire in 1974 and was a Test selector in the same year. He was
appointed cricket manager at Lancashire CCC in 1980 and held the position until 1986
**Best batting:** 157 Lancashire v Hampshire, Old Trafford 1962

## First-Class Career Performances

|  | M | Inns | NO | Runs | HS | Avge | 100s | Ct | St | Runs | Wkts | Avge | Best | 5wl | 10wM |
|---|---|---|---|---|---|---|---|---|---|---|---|---|---|---|---|
| Test |  |  |  |  |  |  |  |  |  |  |  |  |  |  |  |
| All First | 362 | 548 | 80 | 12125 | 157 | 25.90 | 14 | 222 | - | 69 | 0 | - | - | - | - |

# BURGESS, G. I.

**Name:** Graham Iefvion Burgess
**Role:** Right-hand bat, right-arm
medium bowler
**Born:** 5 May 1943,
Glastonbury, Somerset
**Appointed to 1st-class list:** 1991
**County:** Somerset
**County debut:** 1966
**County cap:** 1968
**Testimonial:** 1977
**1st-Class 100s:** 2
**1st-Class 5 w. in innings:** 18
**1st-Class 10 w. in match:** 2
**1st-Class catches:** 120
**Education:** Millfield School
**Extras:** Played Minor Counties cricket
for Wiltshire 1981-82 and for
Cambridgeshire 1983-84

**Best batting:** 129 Somerset v Gloucestershire, Taunton 1973
**Best bowling:** 7-43 Somerset v Oxford University, The Parks 1975

## First-Class Career Performances

| | M | Inns | NO | Runs | HS | Avge | 100s | Ct | St | Runs | Wkts | Avge | Best | 5wI | 10wM |
|---|---|---|---|---|---|---|---|---|---|---|---|---|---|---|---|
| Test | | | | | | | | | | | | | | | |
| All First | 252 | 414 | 37 | 7129 | 129 | 18.90 | 2 | 120 | - | 13543 | 474 | 28.57 | 7-43 | 18 | 2 |

# CLARKSON, A.

**Name:** Anthony Clarkson
**Role:** Right-hand bat, right-arm off-spin
**Born:** 5 September 1939, Killinhall, North Yorkshire
**Height:** 6ft  **Weight:** 14st
**Appointed to 1st-class list:** 1995
**Parents:** Joe (deceased) and Clarrie
**Marital status:** Divorced, now engaged to Cheryl
**Children:** André, September 1964; Chantal, 27 May 1967; Pierre, 1 May 1969
**Family links with cricket:** Father was a league professional
**Education:** Killinghall C of E; Harrogate Grammar School; Leeds College of Building;
Bradford Polytechnic; Brunel College, Bristol

**Qualifications:** 9 O-levels, past member of highway technicians
**Career outside cricket:** Architectural, Civil Engineering and Surveying Consultant
**Off-season:** Working and relaxing
**Other sports followed:** Golf and rugby ('especially league')
**Relaxations:** Golf, DIY, gardening, winemaking and drinking
**Extras:** First English player to score a century in the Sunday League

# CONSTANT, D. J.

**Name:** David John Constant
**Role:** Left-hand bat, slow left-arm bowler
**Born:** 9 November 1941, Bradford-on-Avon, Wiltshire
**Nickname:** Connie
**Appointed to 1st-class list:** 1969
**Appointed to Test panel:** 1971
**Tests umpired:** 36
**One-Day Internationals umpired:** 29
**Counties:** Kent, Leicestershire
**County debut:** 1961 (Kent), 1965 (Leicestershire)
**1st-Class 50s:** 6
**1st-Class catches:** 33
**Extras:** County bowls player for Gloucestershire 1984-86
**Best batting:** 80 Leicestershire v Gloucestershire, Bristol 1966

## First-Class Career Performances

|  | M | Inns | NO | Runs | HS | Avge | 100s | Ct | St | Runs | Wkts | Avge | Best | 5wI | 10wM |
|---|---|---|---|---|---|---|---|---|---|---|---|---|---|---|---|
| Test |  |  |  |  |  |  |  |  |  |  |  |  |  |  |  |
| All First | 61 | 93 | 14 | 1517 | 80 | 19.20 | - | 33 | - | 36 | 1 | 36.00 | 1-28 | - | - |

# DUDLESTON, B.

**Name:** Barry Dudleston
**Role:** Right-hand opening bat, slow
left-arm bowler, occasional wicket-keeper
**Born:** 16 July 1945, Bebington, Cheshire
**Height:** 5ft 9in **Weight:** 13st
**Nickname:** Danny, Dapper
**Appointed to 1st-class list:** 1984
**Appointed to Test panel:** 1991
**Tests umpired:** 2
**One-Day Internationals umpired:** 1
**Counties:** Leicestershire, Gloucestershire
**County debut:** 1966 (Leicestershire),
1981 (Gloucestershire)
**County cap:** 1969 (Leicestershire)
**Benefit:** 1980 (£25,000)
**1000 runs in a season:** 8
**1st-Class 100s:** 32
**1st-Class 200s:** 1
**One-Day 100s:** 4
**1st-Class catches:** 234
**Parents:** Percy and Dorothy Vera

**Marital status:** Married
**Children:** Sharon Louise, 29 October 1968; Matthew Barry, 12 September 1988; Louise Wendy, 19 October 1994
**Education:** Stockport School
**Qualifications:** O-levels, junior coaching certificate, Shell marketing exams
**Career outside cricket:** Director of a sports travel company
**Off-season:** Hosting a South Africa v England supporters' tour
**Other sports followed:** Most
**Cricketers particularly admired:** Gary Sobers, Tom Graveney
**Cricketers particularly learnt from:** Vinoo Mankad
**Relaxations:** Television, bridge, wine, golf
**Extras:** Played for England U25. Suffered badly from broken fingers, breaking fingers on the same hand three times in 1978. Played for Rhodesia in the Currie Cup 1976-80. Acted as 'third umpire' in the third Test against Australia at Trent Bridge 1993
**Opinions on cricket:** 'It is still the greatest test of skill and character – beautiful to watch when played well. Am worried about the declining standards of behaviour.'
**Best batting:** 202 Leicestershire v Derbyshire, Leicester 1979
**Best bowling:** 4-6 Leicestershire v Surrey, Leicester 1972

## First-Class Career Performances

|  | M | Inns | NO | Runs | HS | Avge | 100s | Ct | St | Runs | Wkts | Avge | Best | 5wI | 10wM |
|---|---|---|---|---|---|---|---|---|---|---|---|---|---|---|---|
| Test |  |  |  |  |  |  |  |  |  |  |  |  |  |  |  |
| All First | 295 | 501 | 47 | 14747 | 202 | 32.48 | 32 | 234 | 7 | 1365 | 47 | 29.04 | 4-6 | - | - |

# HAMPSHIRE, J. H.

**Name:** John Harry Hampshire
**Role:** Right-hand bat
**Born:** 10 February 1941,
Thurnscoe, Yorkshire
**Height:** 6ft **Weight:** 13st
**Nickname:** Hamp
**Appointed to 1st-class list:** 1985
**Appointed to Test panel:** 1989
**Tests umpired:** 11
**One-Day Internationals umpired:** 5
**Counties:** Yorkshire, Derbyshire
**County debut:** 1961 (Yorkshire),
1982 (Derbyshire)
**County cap:** 1963 (Yorkshire),
1982 (Derbyshire)
**Benefit:** 1976
**Test debut:** 1969
**Tests:** 8

**1000 runs in a season:** 15
**1st-Class 50s:** 142
**1st-Class 100s:** 43
**1st-Class catches:** 445
**1st-Class 5 w. in innings:** 2
**One-Day 100s:** 7
**Parents:** Jack and Vera
**Wife and date of marriage:** Judith Ann, 5 September 1964
**Children:** Ian Christopher, 6 January 1969; Paul Wesley, 12 February 1972
**Family links with cricket:** Father (J.) and brother (A.W.) both played for Yorkshire
**Education:** Oakwood Technical High School, Rotherham
**Qualifications:** City and Guilds in Printing
**Off-season:** Coach to Zimbabwe 1992-95
**Overseas tours:** MCC to Australia and New Zealand, 1970-71
**Overseas teams played for:** Tasmania, 1966-69, 1977-79
**Cricketers particularly admired:** Peter May, Gary Sobers
**Other sports followed:** Most sports

**Relaxations:** Gardening and cooking
**Extras:** Captained Yorkshire 1979-80. Played for Tasmania 1967-69 and 1977-79. Scored a century (107) in his first Test match, against West Indies at Lord's 1969. Appointed manager/coach of the Zimbabwe Test squad for their first Test matches against India and New Zealand. Umpired four Tests in Pakistan 1989-90
**Best batting:** 183* Yorkshire v Surrey, Hove 1971
**Best bowling:** 7-52 Yorkshire v Glamorgan, Cardiff 1963

## First-Class Career Performances

|  | M | Inns | NO | Runs | HS | Avge | 100s | Ct | St | Runs | Wkts | Avge | Best | 5wl | 10wM |
|---|---|---|---|---|---|---|---|---|---|---|---|---|---|---|---|
| Test | 8 | 16 | 1 | 405 | 107 | 26.86 | 1 | 9 | - |  |  |  |  |  |  |
| All First | 577 | 924 | 112 | 28059 | 183 * | 34.55 | 43 | 445 | - | 1637 | 30 | 54.56 | 7-52 | 2 | - |

# HARRIS, J. H.

**Name:** John Henry Harris
**Role:** Left-hand bat, right-arm fast-medium bowler
**Born:** 13 February 1936, Taunton
**Appointed to 1st-class list:** 1983
**County:** Somerset
**County debut:** 1952
**1st-Class catches:** 6
**Extras:** Made his debut for Somerset aged 16 years 99 days. Played Minor Counties cricket for Suffolk (1960-62) and Devon (1975). Third year as Chairman of the First-Class Cricket Umpires Association
**Best batting:**
41 Somerset v Worcestershire, Taunton 1957
**Best bowling:**
3-29 Somerset v Worcestershire, Bristol 1959

## First-Class Career Performances

|  | M | Inns | NO | Runs | HS | Avge | 100s | Ct | St | Runs | Wkts | Avge | Best | 5wl | 10wM |
|---|---|---|---|---|---|---|---|---|---|---|---|---|---|---|---|
| Test |  |  |  |  |  |  |  |  |  |  |  |  |  |  |  |
| All First | 15 | 18 | 4 | 154 | 41 | 11.00 | - | 6 | - | 609 | 19 | 32.05 | 3.29 | - | - |

# HOLDER, J. W.

**Name:** John Wakefield Holder
**Role:** Right-hand bat, right-arm
fast bowler
**Born:** 19 March 1945,
St George, Barbados
**Height:** 6ft **Weight:** 13st 10lbs
**Nickname:** Benson
**Appointed to 1st-class list:** 1983
**Appointed to Test panel:** 1988
**Tests umpired:** 10
**One-Day Internationals umpired:** 8
**County:** Hampshire
**County debut:** 1968
**50 wickets in a season:** 1
**1st-Class 5 w. in innings:** 5
**1st-Class 10 w. in match:** 1
**1st-Class catches:** 12
**Parents:** Charles and Carnetta
**Wife:** Glenda
**Children:** Christopher 1968; Nigel 1970
**Family links with cricket:** Both sons have played for Royston in the Central Lancashire
League
**Education:** St Giles Boys School; Combermere High School, Barbados; Rochdale College
**Qualifications:** 3 O-levels, MCC advanced cricket coach
**Off-season:** Coaching part-time
**Other sports followed:** Football (Manchester United)
**Relaxations:** Keeping fit and helping coach the Rochdale Indoor Cricket Team which
plays in the National League in the winter
**Extras:** Recorded best bowling figures in Rothmans International Cavaliers cricket
matches – 6-7 for Hampshire Cavaliers at Tichborne Park in 1968. Played professional
league cricket in Yorkshire and Lancashire (1974-82). Took one first-class hat-trick,
Hampshire v Kent 1972, 'but finished with 3-100!' Umpired four Tests in Pakistan 1989-90
**Best batting:** 33 Hampshire v Sussex, Hove 1971
**Best bowling:** 7-79 Hampshire v Gloucestershire, Gloucester 1972

## First-Class Career Performances

|  | M | Inns | NO | Runs | HS | Avge | 100s | Ct | St | Runs | Wkts | Avge | Best | 5wI | 10wM |
|---|---|---|---|---|---|---|---|---|---|---|---|---|---|---|---|
| Test |  |  |  |  |  |  |  |  |  |  |  |  |  |  |  |
| All First | 47 | 49 | 14 | 374 | 33 | 10.68 | - | 12 | - | 3415 | 139 | 24.56 | 7-79 | 5 | 1 |

# HOLDER, V. A.

**Name:** Vanburn Alonza Holder
**Role:** Right-hand bat, right-arm
fast-medium bowler
**Born:** 8 October 1945,
St Michael, Barbados
**Nickname:** Van
**Appointed to 1st-class list:** 1992
**County:** Worcestershire
**County debut:** 1968
**County cap:** 1970
**Test debut:** 1969
**Tests:** 40
**1st-Class 50s:** 4
**1st-Class 100s:** 1
**1st-Class 5 w. in innings:** 38
**1st-Class 10 w. in match:** 3
**1st-Class catches:** 98
**Overseas tours:** West Indies to England
1969, 1973, to India, Sri Lanka and
Pakistan 1974-75, to Australia 1975-76, to England 1976, to India and Sri Lanka 1978-79
(as vice-captain)
**Extras:** Made his debut for Barbados in the Shell Shield competition in 1966-67
**Best batting:** 122 Barbados v Trinidad, Bridgetown 1973-74
**Best bowling:** 7-40 Worcestershire v Glamorgan, Cardiff 1974

**First-Class Career Performances**

|  | M | Inns | NO | Runs | HS | Avge | 100s | Ct | St | Runs | Wkts | Avge | Best | 5wI | 10wM |
|---|---|---|---|---|---|---|---|---|---|---|---|---|---|---|---|
| Test | 40 | 59 | 11 | 682 | 42 | 14.20 | - | 16 | - | 3627 | 109 | 33.27 | 6-28 | 3 | - |
| All First | 311 | 354 | 81 | 3559 | 122 | 13.03 | 1 | 98 | - | 23183 | 948 | 24.45 | 7-40 | 38 | 3 |

# JESTY, T. E.

**Name:** Trevor Edward Jesty
**Role:** Right-hand bat, right-arm
medium bowler
**Born:** 2 June 1948, Gosport, Hampshire
**Height:** 5ft 9in **Weight:** 11st 9lbs
**Nickname:** Jets
**Appointed to 1st-class list:** 1994

**Counties:** Hampshire, Surrey, Lancashire
**County debut:** 1966 (Hampshire),
1985 (Surrey), 1988 (Lancashire)
**County cap:** 1971 (Hampshire),
1985 (Surrey)
**Benefit:** 1982
**One-Day Internationals:** 10
**1000 runs in a season:** 10
**50 wickets in a season:** 2
**1st-Class 50s:** 110
**1st-Class 100s:** 35
**1st-Class 200s:** 2
**1st-Class 5 w. in innings:** 19
**1st-Class catches:** 265
**1st-Class stumpings:** 1
**One-Day 100s:** 7
**Parents:** Aubrey Edward and Sophia
**Wife and date of marriage:** Jacqueline, 12
September 1970
**Children:** Graeme Barry, 27 September 1972; Lorna Samantha, 7 November 1976
**Education:** Privet County Secondary Modern, Gosport
**Overseas tours:** International XI to West Indies 1982; England to Australia and New
Zealand 1982-83
**Overseas teams played for:** Border, South Africa 1973-74; Griqualand West 1974-77,
1980-81; Canterbury, New Zealand 1979-80
**Cricketers particularly admired:** Sir Garfield Sobers, Barry Richards
**Relaxations:** Watching football, gardening, golf
**Extras:** One of *Wisden*'s Five Cricketers of the Year 1982. Left Hampshire at end of 1984
when not appointed captain and offered the captaincy of Surrey for 1985 season.
**Best batting:** 248 Hampshire v Cambridge University, Fenner's 1984
**Best bowling:** 7-75 Hampshire v Worcestershire, Southampton 1976

## First-Class Career Performances

|          | M   | Inns | NO  | Runs  | HS  | Avge  | 100s | Ct  | St  | Runs  | Wkts | Avge  | Best | 5wI | 10wM |
|----------|-----|------|-----|-------|-----|-------|------|-----|-----|-------|------|-------|------|-----|------|
| Test     |     |      |     |       |     |       |      |     |     |       |      |       |      |     |      |
| All First| 490 | 777  | 107 | 21916 | 248 | 32.71 | 35   | 265 | 1   | 16075 | 585  | 27.47 | 7-75 | 19  | -    |

# JONES, A. A.

**Name:** Alan Arthur Jones
**Role:** Right-hand bat, right-arm
fast-medium bowler
**Born:** 9 December 1947, Horley, Surrey
**Height:** 6ft 3in **Weight:** 14st
**Nickname:** Jonah, Buckets
**Appointed to 1st-class list:** 1985
**Counties:** Sussex, Somerset,
Middlesex, Glamorgan
**County debut:** 1964 (Sussex),
1970 (Somerset), 1976 (Middlesex),
1980 (Glamorgan)
**County cap:** 1972 (Somerset),
1976 (Middlesex), 1980 (Glamorgan)
**50 wickets in a season:** 4
**1st-Class 5 w. in innings:** 23
**1st-Class 10 w. in match:** 3
**1st-Class catches:** 50
**Parents:** Leslie and Hazel
**Wife:** Marilyn
**Children:** Clare Michelle
**Education:** St John's College, Horsham
**Qualifications:** 5 O-levels, MCC advanced coach, NCA staff coach
**Off-season:** 'Recovering from the summer'
**Overseas teams played for:** Northern Transvaal 1971-72; Orange Free State 1976-77
**Other sports followed:** All sports
**Cricketers particularly admired:** Tom Cartwright, Brian Close
**Players for the future:** Darren Altree and Ashley Giles (Warwickshire), Jason Laney
(Hampshire)
**Other sports followed:** Golf
**Relaxations:** Reading, cooking and travel
**Extras:** Won two championship medals with Middlesex (1976 and 1977). He was the first
person to play for four counties – only one other player has done so since
**Opinions on cricket:** '110 overs in a day is too many. It should be reduced to 104 or 100.
There is one one-day competition too many. Also, if we are to continue with four-day
cricket, it should be played from Wednesday to Saturday, so that if we do continue with
the Sunday League, it is not in the middle of the four-day match. There should also be less
2nd XI cricket and more nets for younger players, with less significance on fitness and more
on skill.'
**Best batting:** 33 Middlesex v Kent, Canterbury 1978
**Best bowling:** 9-51 Somerset v Sussex, Hove 1976

## First-Class Career Performances

| | M | Inns | NO | Runs | HS | Avge | 100s | Ct | St | Runs | Wkts | Avge | Best | 5wI | 10wM |
|---|---|---|---|---|---|---|---|---|---|---|---|---|---|---|---|
| Test | | | | | | | | | | | | | | | |
| All First | 214 | 216 | 68 | 799 | 33 | 5-39 | - | 50 | - | 15414 | 549 | 28.07 | 9-51 | 23 | 3 |

# JULIAN, R.

**Name:** Raymond Julian
**Role:** Right-hand bat, wicket-keeper
**Born:** 23 August 1936,
Cosby, Leicestershire
**Height:** 5ft 11in **Weight:** 13st 3lbs
**Nickname:** Julie
**Appointed to 1st-class list:** 1972
**County:** Leicestershire
**County debut:** 1953
**County cap:** 1961
**1st-Class 50s:** 2
**1st-Class catches:** 381
**1st-Class stumpings:** 40
**Parents:** George Ernest and Doris
**Wife and date of marriage:**
Megan, 3rd April 1993
**Children:**
Peter Raymond, 1 February 1958;
John Kelvin, 13 October 1960;

David Andrew, 15 October 1963; Paul Anthony, 22 September 1967
**Family links with cricket:** Father and two brothers all played local cricket
**Education:** Wigston Secondary Modern
**Qualifications:** Cricket coach, decorator and gardener
**Career outside cricket:** As above
**Off-season:** Watching the England tour in South Africa and holidays
**Overseas tours:** MCC to West Africa, 1975
**Cricketers particularly admired:** Gary Sobers, Keith Andrew
**Players for the future:** 'All players selected on U17 and U19 tours.'
**Other sports followed:** Football, boxing, rugby
**Relaxations:** Gardening, holidays, travelling
**Extras:** Youngest player to make debut for Leicestershire (aged 15 years). Youngest wicket-keeper to play first-class cricket in 1953. Took six catches in an innings, Leicestershire v Northants, Kettering 1965. Played for the Army 1955-57. Gave eight LBW decisions in succession, Glamorgan v Sussex at Cardiff 1986. Has umpired three B&H semi-finals and one Gillette Cup semi-final. Has been stand-by umpire for two Test matches

**Opinions on cricket:** 'Good now that we have four-day games. There is too much one-day cricket and too many overs in a day.'
**Best batting:** 51 Leicestershire v Worcestershire, Worcester 1962

## First-Class Career Performances

|  | M | Inns | NO | Runs | HS | Avge | 100s | Ct | St | Runs | Wkts | Avge | Best | 5wI | 10wM |
|---|---|---|---|---|---|---|---|---|---|---|---|---|---|---|---|
| Test |  |  |  |  |  |  |  |  |  |  |  |  |  |  |  |
| All First | 192 | 288 | 23 | 2581 | 51 | 9.73 | - | 381 | 40 |  |  |  |  |  |  |

# KITCHEN, M. J.

**Name:** Mervyn John Kitchen
**Role:** Left-hand bat, right-arm medium bowler
**Born:** 1 August 1940, Nailsea, Somerset
**Appointed to 1st-class list:** 1982
**Appointed to Test panel:** 1990
**Tests umpired:** 7
**One-Day Internationals umpired:** 11
**County:** Somerset
**County debut:** 1960
**County cap:** 1966
**Testimonial:** 1973
**1000 runs in a season:** 7
**1st-Class 50s:** 68
**1st-Class 100s:** 17
**1st-Class catches:** 157
**One-Day 100s:** 1
**Education:** Blackwell Secondary Modern, Nailsea
**Extras:** Was third (replay) umpire for two Tests in 1994
**Best batting:** 189 Somerset v Pakistanis, Taunton 1967

## First-Class Career Performances

|  | M | Inns | NO | Runs | HS | Avge | 100s | Ct | St | Runs | Wkts | Avge | Best | 5wI | 10wM |
|---|---|---|---|---|---|---|---|---|---|---|---|---|---|---|---|
| Test |  |  |  |  |  |  |  |  |  |  |  |  |  |  |  |
| All First | 354 | 612 | 32 | 15230 | 189 | 26.25 | 17 | 157 | - | 109 | 2 | 54.50 | 1-4 | - | - |

# LEADBEATER, B.

**Name:** Barrie Leadbeater
**Role:** Right-hand opening bat, right-arm medium bowler, slip fielder
**Born:** 14 August 1943, Leeds
**Height:** 6ft **Weight:** 13st
**Nickname:** Leady
**Appointed to 1st-class list:** 1981
**County:** Yorkshire
**County debut:** 1966
**County cap:** 1969
**Benefit:** 1980 (joint benefit with G.A. Cope)
**1st-Class 50s:** 27
**1st-Class 100s:** 1
**1st-Class catches:** 82
**Parents:** Ronnie (deceased) and Nellie
**Wife and date of marriage:** Jacqueline, 18 September 1971
**Children:** Richard Barrie, 23 November 1972; Michael Spencer, 21 March 1976; Daniel Mark Ronnie, 19 June 1981
**Education:** Brownhill County Primary; Harehills Secondary Modern, Leeds
**Qualifications:** 2 O-levels
**Career outside cricket:** Coach, driver
**Overseas tours:** Duke of Norfolk's XI to West Indies 1970
**Overseas teams played for:** Johannesburg Municipals 1978-79
**Other sports followed:** Rugby union, most other sports
**Cricketers particularly admired:** Colin Cowdrey, Clive Rice, Richard Hadlee, Gary Sobers, Michael Holding
**Cricketers learnt from:** Brian Close, Willie Watson, Arthur Mitchell, Maurice Leyland
**Relaxations:** Family, car maintenance, DIY, music
**Extras:** Acted as 'third umpire' in the fourth Test against Australia at Headingley 1993
**Opinions on cricket:** 'Disappointed in players who lack self-control and professional pride and set bad examples to young players and public alike. Public should be regularly and properly informed during stoppages in play. Stoppages for bad light cause more frustration for public, players and, not least, umpires and a change in regulations may be needed soon if the game is to retain its support and credibility.'
**Best batting:** 140* Yorkshire v Hampshire, Portsmouth 1976

## First-Class Career Performances

| | M | Inns | NO | Runs | HS | Avge | 100s | Ct | St | Runs | Wkts | Avge | Best | 5wI | 10wM |
|---|---|---|---|---|---|---|---|---|---|---|---|---|---|---|---|
| Test | | | | | | | | | | | | | | | |
| All First | 147 | 241 | 29 | 5373 | 140 * | 25.34 | 1 | 82 | - | 5 | 1 | 5.00 | 1-1 | - | - |

# LYONS, K. J.

**Name:** Kevin James Lyons
**Role:** Right-hand opening bat, right-arm medium bowler
**Born:** 18 December 1946, Cardiff
**Appointed to 1st-class list:** 1985-91, re-appointed 1994
**County:** Glamorgan
**County debut:** 1967
**1st-Class 50s:** 8
**1st-Class catches:** 27
**Education:** Lady Mary's High School, Cardiff
**Overseas tours:**
Glamorgan to West Indies 1969-70
**Extras:** Glamorgan coach 1972-84, coach to Western Province, South Africa 1983-84, coach at Worcestershire 1992-93
**Best batting:** 92 Glamorgan v Cambridge University, Fenner's 1972

## First-Class Career Performances

|  | M | Inns | NO | Runs | HS | Avge | 100s | Ct | St | Runs | Wkts | Avge | Best | 5wI | 10wM |
|---|---|---|---|---|---|---|---|---|---|---|---|---|---|---|---|
| Test |  |  |  |  |  |  |  |  |  |  |  |  |  |  |  |
| All First | 62 | 99 | 14 | 1673 | 92 | 19.68 | - | 27 | - | 252 | 2 | 126.00 | - | - | - |

# MEYER, B. J.

**Name:** Barrie John Meyer
**Role:** Right-hand bat, wicket-keeper
**Born:** 21 August 1931, Bournemouth
**Height:** 5ft 10½in **Weight:** 12st 5lbs
**Nickname:** BJ
**Appointed to 1st-class list:** 1973
**Appointed to Test panel:** 1978
**Tests umpired:** 26
**One-Day Internationals umpired:** 23
**County:** Gloucestershire
**County debut:** 1957
**County cap:** 1958
**Benefit:** 1971
**1st-Class 50s:** 11
**1st-Class catches:** 707
**1st-Class stumpings:** 118
**Parents:** Deceased
**Wife and date of marriage:** Gillian,
4 September 1965
**Children:** Stephen Barrie; Christopher John; Adrian Michael
**Education:** Boscombe Secondary School, Bournemouth
**Career outside cricket:** Salesman
**Off-season:** Coaching and umpiring in South Africa
**Other sports followed:** Golf (handicap 9), football (was a pro footballer for Bristol Rovers, Plymouth Argyle, Newport County and Bristol City)
**Cricketers particularly learnt from:** Andy Wilson and Sonny Avery (coaches for Gloucestershire)
**Relaxations:** Golf, music, reading
**Extras:** Umpired 1979 and 1983 World Cup finals
**Best batting:** 63 (three times) Gloucestershire v Indians, Cheltenham 1959; Gloucestershire v Oxford University, Bristol 1962; Gloucestershire v Sussex, Bristol 1964

## First-Class Career Performances

|  | M | Inns | NO | Runs | HS | Avge | 100s | Ct | St | Runs | Wkts | Avge | Best | 5wI | 10wM |
|---|---|---|---|---|---|---|---|---|---|---|---|---|---|---|---|
| Test |  |  |  |  |  |  |  |  |  |  |  |  |  |  |  |
| All First | 406 | 569 | 191 | 5367 | 63 | 14.19 | - | 707 | 118 |  |  |  |  |  |  |

# PALMER, K. E.

**Name:** Kenneth Ernest Palmer
**Role:** Right-hand bat, right-arm
fast-medium bowler
**Born:** 22 April 1937, Winchester
**Height:** 5ft 10in  **Weight:** 13st
**Nickname:** Pedlar
**Appointed to 1st-class list:** 1972
**Appointed to Test panel:** 1978
**Appointed to International Panel:** 1994
**Tests umpired:** 22
**One-Day Internationals umpired:** 19
**County:** Somerset
**County debut:** 1955
**County cap:** 1958
**Testimonial:** 1968
**Test debut:** 1965
**Tests:** 1
**1000 runs in a season:** 1
**50 wickets in a season:** 6
**1st-Class 50s:** 27
**1st-Class 100s:** 2
**1st-Class 5 w. in innings:** 46
**1st-Class 10 w. in match:** 5
**1st-Class catches:** 156
**Parents:** Harry and Cecilia

**Wife and date of marriage:** Wife deceased
**Children:** Gary Vincent, 6 September 1961
**Family links with cricket:** Son played for Somerset, as did brother Roy, also a Test umpire
**Education:** Southbroom Secondary Modern, Devizes
**Overseas tours:** Commonwealth XI to Pakistan 1962; International Cavaliers to West
Indies 1963-64
**Other sports followed:** Football and squash
**Cricketers particularly admired:** Gary Sobers, Richard Hadlee, Viv Richards, David
Gower, Michael Holding, Malcolm Marshall
**Cricketers particularly learnt from:** Father and Maurice Tremlett
**Relaxations:** Car enthusiast
**Extras:** Called into Test side while coaching in South Africa 1964-65. Umpired two B&H
finals and two NatWest finals and was twice on World Cup panel in England. Won Carling
Single Wicket Competition 1961. Did the 'double' in 1961 (114 wickets, 1036 runs). With
Bill Alley holds the Somerset record for 6th wicket partnership.
**Best batting:** 125* Somerset v Northamptonshire, Northampton 1961
**Best bowling:** 9-57 Somerset v Nottinghamshire, Trent Bridge 1963

## First-Class Career Performances

|  | M | Inns | NO | Runs | HS | Avge | 100s | Ct | St | Runs | Wkts | Avge | Best | 5wl | 10wM |
|---|---|---|---|---|---|---|---|---|---|---|---|---|---|---|---|
| Test | 1 | 1 | 0 | 10 | 10 | 10.00 | - | - | - | 189 | 1 | 189.00 | 1-113 | - | - |
| All First | 314 | 481 | 105 | 7771 | 125 * | 20.66 | 2 | 156 | - | 18485 | 866 | 21.34 | 9-57 | 46 | 5 |

# PALMER, R.

**Name:** Roy Palmer
**Role:** Right-hand bat, right-arm
fast-medium bowler
**Born:** 12 July 1942, Devizes, Wiltshire
**Appointed to 1st-class list:** 1980
**Appointed to Test panel:** 1992
**Tests umpired:** 2
**One-Day Internationals umpired:** 7
**County:** Somerset
**County debut:** 1965
**50 wickets in a season:** 1
**1st-Class 50s:** 1
**1st-Class 5 w. in innings:** 4
**1st-Class catches:** 25
**Family links with cricket:** Brother of
Ken Palmer, Test umpire and former
Somerset player; nephew Gary also
played for Somerset
**Education:** Southbroom Secondary
Modern, Devizes
**Best batting:**
84 Somerset v Leicestershire, Taunton 1967
**Best bowling:** 6-45 Somerset v Middlesex, Lord's 1967

## First-Class Career Performances

|  | M | Inns | NO | Runs | HS | Avge | 100s | Ct | St | Runs | Wkts | Avge | Best | 5wl | 10wM |
|---|---|---|---|---|---|---|---|---|---|---|---|---|---|---|---|
| Test |  |  |  |  |  |  |  |  |  |  |  |  |  |  |  |
| All First | 74 | 110 | 32 | 1037 | 84 | 13.29 | - | 25 | - | 5439 | 172 | 31.62 | 6-45 | 4 | - |

# PLEWS, N. T.

**Name:** Nigel Trevor Plews
**Role:** Right-hand opening bat
**Born:** 5 September 1934, Nottingham
**Height:** 6ft 6$^{1}/_{2}$in **Weight:** 16st 8lbs
**Nickname:** Plod, Sarge
**Appointed to 1st-class list:** 1982
**Appointed to Test panel:** 1988
**Appointed to International Panel:** 1994
**Tests umpired:** 11
**One-Day Internationals umpired:** 14
**Parents:** Deceased
**Wife and date of marriage:**
Margaret, 24 September 1956
**Children:** Elaine, 1961; Douglas, 1964
**Education:** Mundella Grammar School,
Nottingham
**Qualifications:** School Certificate in
Commercial Subjects, RSA Advanced
Book-keeping

**Career outside cricket:** Nottingham City
police for 25 years (Det. Sgt in Fraud Squad for 15 years)
**Off-season:** National Grid International Panel Appointments
**Other sports followed:** Football, table tennis, swimming
**Relaxations:** Hill-walking, reading, travel, cricket administration
**Extras:** Played local league and club cricket in Nottingham. Toured as umpire with MCC
to Namibia 1991. Has now umpired in 11 Tests and 14 One-day Internationals

**Did not play first-class cricket**

# SHARP, G.

**Name:** George Sharp
**Role:** Right-hand bat, wicket-keeper
**Born:** 12 March 1950,
Hartlepool, County Durham
**Height:** 5ft 11in **Weight:** 16st
**Nickname:** Blunt, Razor, Sharpie
**Appointed to 1st-class list:** 1992
**County:** Northamptonshire
**County debut:** 1967
**County cap:** 1972
**1st-Class catches:** 565
**1st-Class stumpings:** 90
**Parents:** George and Grace
**Wife:** Audrey, 14 September 1974
**Children:** Gareth James, 27 June 1984
**Education:** Elwick Road, Hartlepool
**Qualifications:** NCA coach
**Career outside cricket:** Director of GSB
Loams Ltd, suppliers of soil and turf for sports
areas
**Off-season:** Working for GSB Loams Ltd
**Overseas tours:** England Counties XI to West Indies 1974
**Cricketers particularly admired:** Alan Knott, Bob Taylor, Keith Andrew
**Other sports followed:** Football (Newcastle and Middlesborough)
**Relaxations:** Golf
**Best batting:** 98 Northamptonshire v Yorkshire, Northampton 1983

## First-Class Career Performances

|  | M | Inns | NO | Runs | HS | Avge | 100s | Ct | St | Runs | Wkts | Avge | Best | 5wI | 10wM |
|---|---|---|---|---|---|---|---|---|---|---|---|---|---|---|---|
| Test |  |  |  |  |  |  |  |  |  |  |  |  |  |  |  |
| All First | 306 | 396 | 81 | 6254 | 98 | 19.85 | - | 565 | 90 | 70 | 1 | 70.00 | 1-47 | - | - |

# SHEPHERD, D. R.

**Name:** David Robert Shepherd
**Role:** Right-hand bat, right-arm
medium bowler
**Born:** 27 December 1940,
Bideford, Devon
**Height:** 5ft 10in **Weight:** 16st
**Nickname:** Shep
**Appointed to 1st-class list:** 1981
**Appointed to Test panel:** 1985
**Appointed to International Panel:** 1994
**Tests umpired:** 21
**One-Day Internationals umpired:** 51
**County:** Gloucestershire
**County debut:** 1965
**County cap:** 1969
**Benefit:** 1978 (joint benefit with J. Davey)
**1000 runs in a season:** 2
**1st-Class 50s:** 55
**1st-Class 100s:** 12
**1st-Class catches:** 95
**One-Day 100s:** 2
**Parents:** Herbert and Doris (both deceased)
**Marital status:** Single
**Education:** Barnstaple Grammar School; St Luke's College, Exeter
**Career outside cricket:** Teacher
**Off-season:** Assisting brother in local post office/newsagent
**Other sports followed:** Rugby, football, most ball sports
**Cricketers particularly admired:** Gary Sobers, Mike Procter
**Relaxations:** All sports, philately, television
**Extras:** Played Minor Counties cricket for Devon 1959-64. Only Gloucestershire player to score a century on his first-class debut. Umpired the MCC Bicentenary Test, England v Rest of the World, at Lord's in 1987. With Dickie Bird and Steve Bucknor was one of the first umpires officially sponsored by the ICC. Known for his superstition regarding 'Nelson' score 111, and multiples – 222, 333 etc. Was England's umpire at the 1995-96 World Cup in India and Pakistan
**Best batting:** 153 Gloucestershire v Middlesex, Bristol 1968

## First-Class Career Performances

| | M | Inns | NO | Runs | HS | Avge | 100s | Ct | St | Runs | Wkts | Avge | Best | 5wI | 10wM |
|---|---|---|---|---|---|---|---|---|---|---|---|---|---|---|---|
| Test | | | | | | | | | | | | | | | |
| All First | 282 | 476 | 40 | 10672 | 153 | 24.47 | 12 | 95 | - | 106 | 2 | 53.00 | 1-1 | - | - |

# WHITE, R. A.

**Name:** Robert Arthur White
**Role:** Left-hand bat, off-break bowler
**Born:** 6 October 1936, Fulham
**Height:** 5ft 9¹/₂in **Weight:** 12st 4lbs
**Nickname:** Knocker
**Appointed to 1st-class list:** 1982
**Counties:** Middlesex, Nottinghamshire
**County debut:** 1958 (Middlesex),
1966 (Nottinghamshire)
**County cap:** 1963 (Middlesex),
1966 (Nottinghamshire)
**Benefit:** 1974
**1000 runs in a season:** 1
**50 wickets in a season:** 2
**1st-Class 50s:** 50
**1st-Class 100s:** 5
**1st-Class 5 w. in innings:** 28
**1st-Class 10 w. in match:** 4
**1st-Class catches:** 190
**Wife:** Janice
**Children:** Robin and Vanessa
**Education:** Chiswick Grammar School
**Qualifications:** Matriculation and cricket coaching certificate
**Career outside cricket:** Fireworks salesman
**Off-season:** 'Hibernating'
**Other sports followed:** All sports – golf, football, ice-hockey and horse racing in particular
**Cricketers particularly admired:** 'Gary Sobers more than anyone else.'
**Cricketers particularly learnt from:** 'I tried to learn from everyone I encountered'
**Young players for the future:** 'All of them'
**Relaxations:** Theatre-going
**Extras:** Made independent coaching trips to South Africa 1959, 1960, 1966, 1967, 1968. Together with M.J. Smedley broke the Nottinghamshire seventh wicket record with 204 v Surrey at The Oval 1967
**Opinions on cricket:** 'The game today is not the one played yesterday.'
**Best batting:** 116* Nottinghamshire v Surrey, The Oval 1967
**Best bowling:** 7-41 Nottinghamshire v Derbyshire, Ilkeston 1971

## First-Class Career Performances

|           | M   | Inns | NO  | Runs  | HS    | Avge  | 100s | Ct  | St  | Runs  | Wkts | Avge  | Best | 5wI | 10wM |
|-----------|-----|------|-----|-------|-------|-------|------|-----|-----|-------|------|-------|------|-----|------|
| Test      |     |      |     |       |       |       |      |     |     |       |      |       |      |     |      |
| All First | 413 | 642  | 105 | 12452 | 116 * | 23.18 | 5    | 190 | -   | 21138 | 693  | 30.50 | 7-41 | 28  | 4    |

# WHITEHEAD, A. G. T.

**Name:** Alan Geoffrey Thomas Whitehead
**Role:** Left-hand bat,
slow left-arm bowler
**Born:** 28 October 1940,
Butleigh, Somerset
**Appointed to 1st-class list:** 1970
**Appointed to Test panel:** 1982
**Tests umpired:** 5
**One-Day Internationals umpired:** 12
**County:** Somerset
**County debut:** 1957
**1st-Class 5 w. in innings:** 3
**1st-Class catches:** 20
**Extras:** Acted as third (replay) umpire in the
fifth Test against Australia at Edgbaston 1993
and in two Tests in 1994
**Best batting:** 15 Somerset v Hampshire,
Southampton 1959
**Best bowling:** 6-74 Somerset v Sussex,
Eastbourne 1959

## First-Class Career Performances

|          | M  | Inns | NO | Runs | HS | Avge | 100s | Ct | St | Runs | Wkts | Avge  | Best | 5wI | 10wM |
|----------|----|------|----|------|----|------|------|----|----|------|------|-------|------|-----|------|
| Test     |    |      |    |      |    |      |      |    |    |      |      |       |      |     |      |
| All First| 38 | 49   | 25 | 137  | 15 | 5.70 | -    | 20 | -  | 2306 | 67   | 34.41 | 6-74 | 3   | -    |

# WILLEY, P.

**Name:** Peter Willey
**Role:** Right-hand bat, off-break bowler
**Born:** 6 December 1949, Sedgefield, County Durham
**Height:** 6ft 1in **Weight:** 13st 4lbs
**Nickname:** Will, 'many unprintable'
**Appointed to 1st-class list:** 1993
**Counties:** Northamptonshire, Leicestershire
**County debut:** 1966 (Northamptonshire), 1984 (Leicestershire)
**County cap:** 1971 (Northamptonshire), 1984 (Leicestershire)
**Benefit:** 1981 (£31,400)
**Test debut:** 1976
**Tests:** 26

**One-Day Internationals:** 26
**1000 runs in a season:** 10
**50 wickets in a season:** 2
**1st-Class 50s:** 101
**1st-Class 100s:** 44
**1st-Class 200s:** 1
**1st-Class 5 w. in innings:** 26
**1st-Class 10 w. in match:** 3
**1st-Class catches:** 235
**One-Day 100s:** 9
**Parents:** Oswald and Maisie
**Wife and date of marriage:** Charmaine, 23 September 1971
**Children:** Heather Jane, 11 September 1985; David, 28 February 1990
**Family links with cricket:** Father played local club cricket in County Durham
**Education:** Seaham Secondary School, County Durham
**Off-season:** 'House husband'
**Overseas tours:** England to Australia and India 1979-80, to West Indies 1980-81 and 1985-86; with unofficial England XI to South Africa 1981-82
**Overseas teams played for:** Eastern Province, South Africa 1982-85
**Cricketers particularly admired:** Malcolm Marshall
**Other sports followed:** All sports
**Relaxations:** Gardening, dog walking
**Extras:** With Wayne Larkins, received 2016 pints of beer (seven barrels) from a brewery in Northampton as a reward for their efforts in Australia with England in 1979-80. Youngest player ever to play for Northamptonshire at 16 years 180 days v Cambridge University in 1966. Banned from Test cricket for three years for joining England rebel tour of South Africa in 1982. Left Northamptonshire at end of 1983 and moved to Leicestershire as vice-captain. Appointed Leicestershire captain for 1987, but resigned after only one season. Released by Leicestershire at end of 1991 season to play for Northumberland in 1992
**Opinions on cricket:** 'I think the fun has gone out of the game for many of the players. Not enough hard work and practice is done to improve playing standards throughout the first-class game. Players of average ability are being paid silly money in the modern game, by clubs, so they may not need to try and improve their standards. Why does the English game need overseas coaches? Why do we also need team managers?'
**Best batting:** 227 Northamptonshire v Somerset, Northampton 1976
**Best bowling:** 7-37 Northamptonshire v Oxford University, The Parks 1975

## First-Class Career Performances

|  | M | Inns | NO | Runs | HS | Avge | 100s | Ct | St | Runs | Wkts | Avge | Best | 5wl | 10wM |
|---|---|---|---|---|---|---|---|---|---|---|---|---|---|---|---|
| Test | 26 | 50 | 6 | 1184 | 102 * | 26.90 | 2 | 3 | - | 456 | 7 | 65.14 | 2-73 | - | - |
| All First | 559 | 918 | 121 | 24361 | 227 | 30.56 | 44 | 235 | - | 23400 | 756 | 30.95 | 7-37 | 26 | 3 |

# ROLL OF HONOUR 1995

## BRITANNIC ASSURANCE CHAMPIONSHIP

|    |                     | P  | W  | L  | D | T | Bt | Bl | Pts |
|----|---------------------|----|----|----|---|---|----|----|-----|
| 1  | Warwickshire (1)     | 17 | 14 | 2  | 1 | 0 | 49 | 64 | 337 |
| 2  | Middlesex (4)        | 17 | 12 | 2  | 3 | 0 | 51 | 62 | 305 |
| 3  | Northants (5)        | 17 | 12 | 2  | 3 | 0 | 41 | 57 | 290 |
| 4  | Lancashire (10)      | 17 | 10 | 4  | 3 | 0 | 48 | 61 | 269 |
| 5  | Essex (6)            | 17 | 8  | 9  | 0 | 0 | 42 | 58 | 228 |
| 6  | Gloucestershire (12) | 17 | 8  | 4  | 5 | 0 | 45 | 50 | 223 |
| 7  | Leicestershire (2)   | 17 | 7  | 8  | 2 | 0 | 41 | 61 | 214 |
| 8  | Yorkshire (13)       | 17 | 7  | 8  | 2 | 0 | 39 | 55 | 206 |
| 9  | Somerset (11)        | 17 | 7  | 5  | 5 | 0 | 40 | 49 | 201 |
| 10 | Worcestershire (15)  | 17 | 6  | 7  | 4 | 0 | 29 | 57 | 182 |
| 11 | Notts (3)            | 17 | 5  | 9  | 3 | 0 | 41 | 54 | 175 |
| 12 | Surrey (7)           | 17 | 5  | 8  | 4 | 0 | 34 | 55 | 169 |
| 13 | Hampshire (13)       | 17 | 5  | 8  | 4 | 0 | 32 | 56 | 168 |
| 14 | Derbyshire (17)      | 17 | 4  | 10 | 3 | 0 | 39 | 64 | 167 |
| 15 | Sussex (8)           | 17 | 4  | 7  | 6 | 0 | 37 | 51 | 152 |
| 16 | Glamorgan (18)       | 17 | 3  | 8  | 6 | 0 | 40 | 57 | 145 |
| 17 | Durham (16)          | 17 | 4  | 13 | 0 | 0 | 20 | 53 | 137 |
| 18 | Kent (9)             | 17 | 3  | 10 | 4 | 0 | 40 | 44 | 132 |

(1994 positions in brackets)

## NATWEST TROPHY

**Winners :** Warwickshire
**Runners-up :** Northamptonshire

## BENSON & HEDGES CUP

**Winners :** Lancashire
**Runners-up :** Kent

# AXA EQUITY & LAW LEAGUE

|    |                      | P  | W  | L  | T | NR | Pts | Run Rate |
|----|----------------------|----|----|----|---|----|-----|----------|
| 1  | Kent (3)             | 17 | 12 | 4  | 0 | 1  | 50  | 93.49    |
| 2  | Warwickshire (1)     | 17 | 12 | 4  | 0 | 1  | 50  | 84.40    |
| 3  | Worcestershire (2)   | 17 | 11 | 3  | 1 | 2  | 50  | 84.22    |
| 4  | Lancashire (4)       | 17 | 11 | 5  | 0 | 1  | 46  | 82.86    |
| 5  | Essex (17)           | 17 | 10 | 6  | 1 | 0  | 42  | 90.73    |
| 6  | Glamorgan (7)        | 17 | 8  | 6  | 0 | 3  | 38  | 89.17    |
| 7  | Leicestershire (10)  | 17 | 8  | 7  | 0 | 2  | 36  | 89.47    |
| 8  | Derbyshire (8)       | 17 | 7  | 6  | 1 | 3  | 36  | 80.54    |
| 9  | Surrey (6)           | 17 | 7  | 8  | 0 | 2  | 32  | 91.79    |
| 10 | Sussex (15)          | 17 | 7  | 8  | 0 | 2  | 32  | 82.85    |
| 11 | Notts (11)           | 17 | 7  | 9  | 0 | 1  | 30  | 91.01    |
| 12 | Yorkshire (5)        | 17 | 7  | 9  | 0 | 1  | 30  | 76.20    |
| 13 | Northants (13)       | 17 | 6  | 8  | 1 | 2  | 30  | 84.94    |
| 14 | Somerset (16)        | 17 | 5  | 9  | 0 | 3  | 26  | 82.45    |
| 15 | Gloucestershire (18) | 17 | 5  | 10 | 0 | 2  | 24  | 81.41    |
| 16 | Durham (9)           | 17 | 4  | 9  | 1 | 3  | 24  | 73.48    |
| 17 | Middlesex (14)       | 17 | 4  | 11 | 0 | 2  | 20  | 76.86    |
| 18 | Hampshire (12)       | 17 | 3  | 12 | 1 | 1  | 16  | 82.89    |

(1994 positions in brackets)

# 1995 AVERAGES (all first-class matches)

**BATTING AVERAGES - Including fielding.**
**Qualifying requirements : 6 completed innings at an average of over 35.**

| Name | Matches | Inns | NO | Runs | HS | Avge | 100s | 50s | Ct | St |
|---|---|---|---|---|---|---|---|---|---|---|
| M.R.Ramprakash | 20 | 32 | 3 | 2258 | 235 | 77.86 | 10 | 7 | 14 | - |
| M.D.Moxon | 13 | 23 | 8 | 1145 | 203* | 76.33 | 3 | 8 | 6 | - |
| A.C.Gilchrist | 8 | 11 | 3 | 495 | 122 | 61.87 | 2 | 2 | 34 | 5 |
| P.A.de Silva | 16 | 30 | 0 | 1781 | 255 | 59.36 | 7 | 7 | 3 | - |
| B.C.Lara | 13 | 20 | 1 | 1126 | 179 | 59.26 | 3 | 7 | 14 | - |
| S.Chanderpaul | 15 | 25 | 8 | 1003 | 140* | 59.00 | 4 | 5 | 11 | - |
| J.L.Langer | 7 | 12 | 3 | 516 | 149 | 57.33 | 2 | 2 | 5 | - |
| K.L.T.Arthurton | 15 | 23 | 4 | 1077 | 146 | 56.68 | 3 | 6 | 8 | - |
| D.Byas | 20 | 37 | 3 | 1913 | 213 | 56.26 | 4 | 10 | 42 | - |
| A.J.Lamb | 16 | 26 | 4 | 1237 | 166 | 56.22 | 3 | 6 | 15 | - |
| A.Symonds | 18 | 31 | 5 | 1438 | 254* | 55.30 | 4 | 9 | 8 | - |
| T.M.Moody | 18 | 31 | 2 | 1600 | 168 | 55.17 | 5 | 7 | 31 | - |
| M.G.Bevan | 20 | 34 | 5 | 1598 | 153* | 55.10 | 6 | 7 | 18 | - |
| N.Hussain | 19 | 35 | 1 | 1854 | 186 | 54.52 | 6 | 10 | 34 | - |
| A.P.Wells | 18 | 30 | 2 | 1524 | 178 | 54.42 | 7 | 4 | 10 | - |
| M.W.Gatting | 16 | 22 | 1 | 1139 | 148 | 54.23 | 5 | 3 | 13 | - |
| R.T.Robinson | 18 | 32 | 0 | 1728 | 209 | 54.00 | 7 | 5 | 7 | - |
| P.D.Bowler | 19 | 33 | 3 | 1619 | 196 | 53.96 | 6 | 5 | 9 | - |
| P.C.L.Holloway | 12 | 22 | 6 | 863 | 129* | 53.93 | 2 | 6 | 3 | - |
| R.A.Smith | 12 | 23 | 2 | 1117 | 172 | 53.19 | 3 | 4 | 3 | - |
| H.Morris | 18 | 33 | 3 | 1574 | 166* | 52.46 | 6 | 8 | 5 | - |
| M.E.Waugh | 16 | 29 | 2 | 1392 | 173 | 51.55 | 5 | 6 | 19 | - |
| J.C.Pooley | 18 | 30 | 4 | 1335 | 136 | 51.34 | 5 | 6 | 25 | - |
| G.A.Gooch | 18 | 34 | 1 | 1669 | 165 | 50.57 | 7 | 6 | 12 | - |
| W.J.Cronje | 16 | 28 | 1 | 1362 | 213 | 50.44 | 4 | 7 | 13 | - |
| T.L.Penney | 19 | 27 | 3 | 1198 | 144 | 49.91 | 4 | 4 | 9 | - |
| W.G.Khan | 13 | 23 | 6 | 847 | 181 | 49.82 | 1 | 6 | 17 | - |
| G.A.Hick | 16 | 27 | 3 | 1193 | 152 | 49.70 | 4 | 5 | 22 | - |
| N.V.Knight | 13 | 23 | 5 | 887 | 174 | 49.27 | 1 | 7 | 26 | - |
| R.J.Harden | 19 | 35 | 6 | 1429 | 129* | 49.27 | 5 | 6 | 13 | - |
| P.A.Cottey | 19 | 33 | 3 | 1465 | 130 | 48.83 | 5 | 7 | 14 | - |
| J.D.Carr | 20 | 29 | 6 | 1098 | 129 | 47.73 | 4 | 3 | 39 | - |
| J.P.Crawley | 18 | 31 | 2 | 1377 | 182 | 47.48 | 3 | 10 | 21 | - |
| S.C.Ecclestone | 7 | 12 | 2 | 472 | 81 | 47.20 | - | 3 | 1 | - |
| S.L.Campbell | 16 | 26 | 0 | 1225 | 172 | 47.11 | 3 | 6 | 15 | - |
| A.J.Wright | 18 | 34 | 4 | 1401 | 193 | 46.70 | 4 | 5 | 8 | - |
| R.Q.Cake | 7 | 14 | 3 | 511 | 101 | 46.45 | 1 | 2 | 4 | - |
| M.L.Love | 7 | 13 | 2 | 510 | 181 | 46.36 | 2 | 1 | 10 | - |

| Name | Matches | Inns | NO | Runs | HS | Avge | 100s | 50s | Ct | St |
|---|---|---|---|---|---|---|---|---|---|---|
| C.L.Hooper | 15 | 25 | 2 | 1063 | 195 | 46.21 | 5 | 2 | 10 | - |
| R.T.Ponting | 7 | 12 | 2 | 460 | 103* | 46.00 | 1 | 4 | 7 | - |
| M.L.Hayden | 7 | 14 | 2 | 551 | 178 | 45.91 | 2 | 1 | 3 | - |
| R.G.Twose | 19 | 30 | 4 | 1186 | 191 | 45.61 | 4 | 3 | 6 | - |
| D.J.Cullinan | 14 | 26 | 4 | 1003 | 161 | 45.59 | 5 | 1 | 8 | - |
| M.P.Maynard | 20 | 36 | 1 | 1590 | 164 | 45.42 | 3 | 12 | 23 | - |
| C.O.Browne | 12 | 16 | 5 | 498 | 102* | 45.27 | 2 | 1 | 47 | 7 |
| K.J.Barnett | 17 | 31 | 3 | 1251 | 169 | 44.67 | 2 | 7 | 5 | - |
| R.C.Russell | 17 | 26 | 4 | 977 | 91 | 44.40 | - | 8 | 50 | 2 |
| A.J.Moles | 9 | 16 | 0 | 710 | 131 | 44.37 | 1 | 6 | 5 | - |
| G.R.Cowdrey | 13 | 22 | 1 | 930 | 137 | 44.28 | 2 | 6 | 8 | - |
| S.G.Law | 7 | 11 | 2 | 397 | 134 | 44.11 | 1 | 1 | 13 | - |
| M.A.Atherton | 18 | 31 | 1 | 1323 | 155* | 44.10 | 4 | 6 | 14 | - |
| J.C.Adams | 13 | 22 | 5 | 741 | 114* | 43.58 | 1 | 5 | 5 | - |
| J.A.Daley | 7 | 12 | 2 | 435 | 55 | 43.50 | - | 4 | 5 | - |
| I.J.Sutcliffe | 14 | 24 | 4 | 847 | 163* | 42.35 | 1 | 5 | 9 | - |
| J.J.Whitaker | 15 | 25 | 0 | 1055 | 127 | 42.20 | 3 | 5 | 4 | - |
| K.R.Brown | 19 | 27 | 4 | 970 | 147* | 42.17 | 1 | 7 | 45 | 6 |
| A.D.Brown | 16 | 29 | 4 | 1054 | 187 | 42.16 | 3 | 3 | 20 | - |
| N.R.Taylor | 7 | 12 | 2 | 421 | 127 | 42.10 | 1 | 2 | - | - |
| N.E.Briers | 15 | 27 | 2 | 1046 | 175* | 41.84 | 3 | 3 | 1 | - |
| R.J.Warren | 16 | 27 | 5 | 914 | 154 | 41.54 | 1 | 5 | 27 | 1 |
| D.P.Ostler | 18 | 26 | 2 | 983 | 208 | 40.95 | 2 | 6 | 25 | - |
| G.P.Thorpe | 16 | 30 | 0 | 1223 | 152 | 40.76 | 2 | 9 | 13 | - |
| S.J.Rhodes | 20 | 33 | 8 | 1018 | 122* | 40.72 | 1 | 7 | 51 | 7 |
| T.S.Curtis | 20 | 35 | 5 | 1221 | 169* | 40.70 | 2 | 5 | 8 | - |
| C.J.Adams | 15 | 27 | 0 | 1096 | 216 | 40.59 | 3 | 5 | 17 | - |
| S.P.James | 15 | 28 | 3 | 1011 | 230* | 40.44 | 3 | 2 | 12 | - |
| C.L.Cairns | 17 | 30 | 1 | 1171 | 115 | 40.37 | 2 | 7 | 7 | - |
| G.F.Archer | 17 | 32 | 3 | 1171 | 158 | 40.37 | 3 | 4 | 16 | - |
| M.C.J.Nicholas | 19 | 33 | 3 | 1210 | 147 | 40.33 | 4 | 4 | 5 | - |
| R.B.Richardson | 15 | 23 | 3 | 804 | 101* | 40.20 | 1 | 5 | 12 | - |
| D.J.Bicknell | 15 | 28 | 3 | 997 | 228* | 39.88 | 2 | 4 | 5 | - |
| M.T.G.Elliott | 6 | 12 | 3 | 357 | 89* | 39.66 | - | 3 | 4 | - |
| N.J.Lenham | 15 | 25 | 3 | 867 | 128 | 39.40 | 2 | 4 | 10 | - |
| N.Shahid | 14 | 25 | 2 | 900 | 139 | 39.13 | 2 | 5 | 15 | - |
| S.C.Williams | 13 | 20 | 0 | 770 | 137 | 38.50 | 3 | 3 | 13 | - |
| R.J.Bailey | 18 | 30 | 3 | 1038 | 157 | 38.44 | 4 | 2 | 21 | - |
| J.E.Morris | 19 | 35 | 1 | 1297 | 169 | 38.14 | 3 | 6 | 9 | - |
| A.J.Stewart | 10 | 18 | 1 | 647 | 151 | 38.05 | 2 | 2 | 23 | - |
| M.A.Lynch | 17 | 29 | 2 | 1026 | 114 | 38.00 | 5 | 2 | 25 | - |
| J.E.R.Gallian | 18 | 33 | 3 | 1122 | 158 | 37.40 | 2 | 4 | 18 | - |
| D.A.Leatherdale | 18 | 30 | 3 | 993 | 93 | 36.77 | - | 8 | 15 | - |
| M.A.Butcher | 18 | 34 | 1 | 1210 | 167 | 36.66 | 2 | 10 | 15 | - |

| Name | Matches | Inns | NO | Runs | HS | Avge | 100s | 50s | Ct | St |
|---|---|---|---|---|---|---|---|---|---|---|
| A.J.Hollioake | 18 | 32 | 2 | 1099 | 117* | 36.63 | 1 | 8 | 12 | - |
| A.Fordham | 16 | 29 | 1 | 1025 | 130 | 36.60 | 4 | 4 | 14 | - |
| R.C.Irani | 18 | 34 | 2 | 1165 | 108 | 36.40 | 1 | 9 | 7 | - |
| D.A.Reeve | 16 | 22 | 4 | 652 | 77* | 36.22 | - | 5 | 17 | - |
| C.M.Wells | 16 | 30 | 3 | 976 | 115 | 36.14 | 2 | 6 | 16 | - |
| K.M.Curran | 17 | 27 | 3 | 863 | 117 | 35.95 | 1 | 4 | 22 | - |
| C.W.J.Athey | 15 | 27 | 1 | 929 | 163* | 35.73 | 2 | 5 | 6 | - |
| D.J.Capel | 19 | 29 | 3 | 926 | 175 | 35.61 | 3 | 3 | 13 | - |
| G.I.Macmillan | 17 | 26 | 3 | 817 | 122 | 35.52 | 3 | 3 | 23 | - |
| W.P.C.Weston | 20 | 35 | 1 | 1207 | 111 | 35.50 | 3 | 7 | 14 | - |

## BOWLING AVERAGES
### Qualifying requirements : 10 wickets taken at an average of under 30

| Name | Overs | Mdns | Runs | Wkts | Avge | Best | 5wI | 10wM |
|---|---|---|---|---|---|---|---|---|
| A.A.Donald | 535.3 | 134 | 1431 | 89 | 16.07 | 6-56 | 6 | 1 |
| D.A.Reeve | 312 | 117 | 661 | 38 | 17.39 | 5-30 | 1 | - |
| J.Lewis | 67.4 | 12 | 209 | 12 | 17.41 | 4-34 | - | - |
| K.E.Cooper | 103 | 32 | 228 | 13 | 17.53 | 4-34 | - | - |
| J.Srinath | 568.4 | 147 | 1661 | 87 | 19.09 | 9-76 | 5 | 2 |
| Wasim Akram | 518.1 | 108 | 1598 | 81 | 19.72 | 7-52 | 7 | 3 |
| T.A.Munton | 373.5 | 111 | 952 | 48 | 19.83 | 5-37 | 3 | 1 |
| C.L.Cairns | 375.5 | 89 | 1035 | 52 | 19.90 | 8-47 | 3 | 1 |
| D.G.Cork | 586.5 | 111 | 1800 | 90 | 20.00 | 9-43 | 4 | 1 |
| R.L.Johnson | 301.4 | 79 | 812 | 40 | 20.30 | 5-48 | 2 | 1 |
| S.M.Milburn | 69 | 15 | 204 | 10 | 20.40 | 4-68 | - | - |
| A.Kumble | 899.4 | 265 | 2143 | 105 | 20.40 | 7-82 | 8 | 2 |
| K.C.G.Benjamin | 284.1 | 71 | 923 | 43 | 21.46 | 5-52 | 3 | 1 |
| A.M.Smith | 415.3 | 104 | 1275 | 59 | 21.61 | 7-70 | 4 | 1 |
| J.Wood | 97.4 | 25 | 303 | 14 | 21.64 | 4-54 | - | - |
| P.C.R.Tufnell | 678.1 | 207 | 1634 | 74 | 22.08 | 6-111 | 5 | 1 |
| A.F.Giles | 146.5 | 46 | 354 | 16 | 22.12 | 5-23 | 1 | - |
| M.S.Kasprowicz | 175.1 | 42 | 599 | 27 | 22.18 | 5-19 | 1 | - |
| S.Young | 128 | 36 | 359 | 16 | 22.43 | 3-23 | - | - |
| P.J.Newport | 548 | 148 | 1551 | 69 | 22.47 | 5-45 | 4 | - |
| A.J.Tudor | 83.3 | 7 | 320 | 14 | 22.85 | 5-32 | 1 | - |
| P.J.Hartley | 549 | 120 | 1861 | 81 | 22.97 | 9-41 | 4 | 1 |
| J.E.Emburey | 708.4 | 198 | 1701 | 74 | 22.98 | 7-82 | 5 | 2 |
| V.J.Wells | 139.3 | 33 | 438 | 19 | 23.05 | 3-28 | - | - |
| D.J.Capel | 358.2 | 70 | 1206 | 51 | 23.64 | 7-44 | 2 | - |
| M.P.Bicknell | 285 | 65 | 978 | 41 | 23.85 | 5-61 | 3 | - |
| M.C.Ilott | 582.4 | 126 | 1897 | 78 | 24.32 | 9-19 | 6 | 2 |
| P.Aldred | 108.2 | 23 | 375 | 15 | 25.00 | 3-47 | - | - |
| V.C.Drakes | 106 | 17 | 400 | 16 | 25.00 | 5-20 | 1 | - |
| J.E.Benjamin | 420.4 | 85 | 1326 | 53 | 25.01 | 5-37 | 3 | - |

| Name | Overs | Mdns | Runs | Wkts | Avge | Best | 5wI | 10wM |
|---|---|---|---|---|---|---|---|---|
| N.A.Mallender | 142.2 | 32 | 427 | 17 | 25.11 | 4-49 | - | - |
| A.J.Harris | 85.5 | 16 | 354 | 14 | 25.28 | 4-84 | - | - |
| I.D.Austin | 363.4 | 111 | 889 | 35 | 25.40 | 4-50 | - | - |
| A.R.Caddick | 183.1 | 34 | 613 | 24 | 25.54 | 8-69 | 1 | 1 |
| M.T.Brimson | 110 | 24 | 310 | 12 | 25.83 | 2-11 | - | - |
| J.H.Childs | 678.2 | 183 | 1757 | 68 | 25.83 | 6-36 | 2 | - |
| I.R.Bishop | 334.1 | 69 | 983 | 38 | 25.86 | 5-32 | 1 | - |
| D.E.Malcolm | 461.4 | 82 | 1692 | 65 | 26.03 | 6-61 | 3 | 1 |
| R.Dhanraj | 475.3 | 79 | 1596 | 61 | 26.16 | 6-50 | 4 | - |
| J.Angel | 179.4 | 38 | 709 | 27 | 26.25 | 4-31 | - | - |
| P.J.Martin | 338.5 | 96 | 922 | 35 | 26.34 | 4-51 | - | - |
| J.D.Lewry | 350.1 | 62 | 1247 | 47 | 26.53 | 6-43 | 3 | - |
| D.Gough | 414.5 | 89 | 1365 | 51 | 26.76 | 7-28 | 1 | 1 |
| P.M.Such | 748.4 | 174 | 2064 | 77 | 26.80 | 8-93 | 6 | 2 |
| A.P.Igglesden | 171.2 | 37 | 563 | 21 | 26.80 | 5-92 | 1 | - |
| A.E.Warner | 375.1 | 90 | 1050 | 39 | 26.92 | 6-21 | 3 | - |
| R.K.Illingworth | 524 | 172 | 1212 | 45 | 26.93 | 4-30 | - | - |
| M.A.Feltham | 273.1 | 72 | 783 | 29 | 27.00 | 6-41 | 1 | - |
| S.L.Watkin | 590.4 | 144 | 1755 | 65 | 27.00 | 7-49 | 2 | 1 |
| J.N.B.Bovill | 251.3 | 62 | 814 | 30 | 27.13 | 6-29 | 2 | 1 |
| D.R.Brown | 311.4 | 71 | 1011 | 37 | 27.32 | 4-24 | - | - |
| R.G.Twose | 108 | 29 | 301 | 11 | 27.36 | 3-50 | - | - |
| A.Sheriyar | 189 | 27 | 799 | 29 | 27.55 | 6-30 | 2 | 1 |
| P.W.Jarvis | 228.4 | 45 | 719 | 26 | 27.65 | 5-55 | 1 | - |
| S.R.Lampitt | 494.1 | 124 | 1524 | 55 | 27.70 | 4-34 | - | - |
| M.Prabhakar | 579.1 | 165 | 1439 | 51 | 28.21 | 7-65 | 1 | - |
| A.D.Mullally | 583.4 | 172 | 1700 | 59 | 28.81 | 6-50 | 2 | - |
| C.A.Walsh | 384.2 | 76 | 1124 | 39 | 28.82 | 5-45 | 1 | - |
| D.W.Headley | 430.5 | 101 | 1276 | 44 | 29.00 | 7-58 | 3 | - |
| J.P.Taylor | 573.4 | 122 | 1713 | 59 | 29.03 | 7-50 | 2 | - |
| D.J.Nash | 460.1 | 90 | 1512 | 52 | 29.07 | 5-35 | 2 | - |
| M.J.McCague | 424.2 | 79 | 1457 | 50 | 29.14 | 5-47 | 2 | - |
| A.R.C.Fraser | 592.1 | 156 | 1632 | 56 | 29.14 | 5-56 | 2 | - |
| P.A.J.DeFreitas | 591.1 | 128 | 1751 | 60 | 29.18 | 6-35 | 2 | - |
| M.Watkinson | 622.4 | 158 | 1910 | 65 | 29.38 | 7-140 | 2 | 1 |
| E.E.Hemmings | 177.5 | 51 | 442 | 15 | 29.46 | 4-33 | - | - |
| E.S.H.Giddins | 605.4 | 110 | 2004 | 68 | 29.47 | 6-73 | 4 | 1 |
| G.J.Parsons | 579.2 | 178 | 1570 | 53 | 29.62 | 4-46 | - | - |
| Mushtaq Ahmed | 952 | 286 | 2821 | 95 | 29.69 | 6-38 | 7 | 2 |
| C.E.L.Ambrose | 262.1 | 70 | 744 | 25 | 29.76 | 5-96 | 1 | - |
| C.G.Rackemann | 457 | 114 | 1430 | 48 | 29.79 | 6-60 | 1 | - |
| G.C.Small | 182.5 | 48 | 507 | 17 | 29.82 | 5-71 | 1 | - |
| M.A.Robinson | 483.1 | 134 | 1375 | 46 | 29.89 | 4-46 | - | - |
| P.E.McIntyre | 296.5 | 70 | 1018 | 34 | 29.94 | 5-38 | 1 | - |

# WHYTE AND MACKAY RANKINGS 1995

## BATTING

| Rank | Player | Total |
|------|--------|-------|
| 1 | M.R.Ramprakash (Middlesex) | 710 |
| 2 | N.Hussain (Essex) | 673 |
| 3 | G.A.Hick (Worcestershire) | 626 |
| 4= | M.A.Atherton (Lancashire) | 594 |
| | G.P.Thorpe (Surrey) | 594 |
| 6 | D.Byas (Yorkshire) | 584 |
| 7 | A.J.Wright (Gloucestershire) | 583 |
| 8 | G.A.Gooch (Essex) | 582 |
| 9 | R.T.Robinson (Notts) | 567 |
| 10 | M.P.Maynard (Glamorgan) | 537 |
| 11 | J.P.Crawley (Lancashire) | 529 |
| 12 | P.D.Bowler (Somerset) | 528 |
| 13 | H.Morris (Glamorgan) | 524 |
| 14 | A.Symonds (Gloucestershire) | 518 |
| 15= | R.J.Harden (Somerset) | 511 |
| | A.P.Wells (Sussex) | 511 |
| 17 | T.S.Curtis (Worcestershire) | 507 |
| 18 | K.J.Barnett (Derbyshire) | 506 |
| 19 | R.C.Russell (Gloucestershire) | 505 |
| 20 | R.A.Smith (Hampshire) | 501 |
| 21 | A.J.Lamb (Northants) | 498 |
| 22 | P.A.Cottey (Glamorgan) | 494 |
| 23 | M.P.Vaughan (Yorkshire) | 485 |
| 24 | R.C.Irani (Essex) | 473 |
| 25 | R.G.Twose (Warwickshire) | 466 |
| 26 | J.E.Morris (Durham) | 461 |
| 27 | P.J.Prichard (Essex) | 460 |
| 28 | G.F.Archer (Notts) | 458 |
| 29= | C.J.Adams (Derbyshire) | 454 |
| | M.W.Gatting (Middlesex) | 454 |
| 31= | J.E.R.Gallian (Lancashire) | 453 |
| | M.A.Butcher (Surrey) | 453 |
| 33 | T.L.Penney (Warwickshire) | 452 |
| 34 | J.C.Pooley (Middlesex) | 449 |
| 35 | R.J.Bailey (Northants) | 439 |
| 36 | T.R.Ward (Kent) | 431 |
| 37 | A.Fordham (Northants) | 430 |
| 38 | A.S.Rollins (Derbyshire) | 429 |
| 39 | D.P.Ostler (Warwickshire) | 425 |
| 40 | A.J.Hollioake (Surrey) | 421 |
| 41 | S.P.James (Glamorgan) | 420 |
| 42 | M.W.Alleyne (Gloucestershire) | 418 |
| 43 | M.C.J.Nicholas (Hampshire) | 417 |
| 44 | N.V.Knight (Warwickshire) | 414 |
| 45 | W.P.C.Weston (Worcestershire) | 413 |
| 46 | M.A.Lynch (Gloucestershire) | 410 |
| 47 | K.M.Curran (Northants) | 409 |
| 48 | A.D.Brown (Surrey) | 408 |
| 49 | R.J.Warren (Northants) | 400 |
| 50 | J.J.Whitaker (Leicestershire) | 399 |

## BOWLING

| Rank | Player | Total |
|------|--------|-------|
| 1 | D.G.Cork (Derbyshire) | 637 |
| 2 | A.R.C.Fraser (Middlesex) | 604 |
| 3 | P.J.Newport (Worcestershire) | 554 |
| 4 | M.C.Ilott (Essex) | 537 |
| 5 | P.J.Hartley (Yorkshire) | 525 |
| 6 | S.L.Watkin (Glamorgan) | 523 |
| 7 | J.E.Emburey (Middlesex) | 517 |
| 8 | P.A.J.DeFreitas (Derbyshire) | 511 |
| 9 | P.M.Such (Essex) | 503 |
| 10 | R.D.B.Croft (Glamorgan) | 499 |
| 11 | E.S.H.Giddins (Sussex) | 480 |
| 12 | A.D.Mullally (Leicestershire) | 463 |
| 13 | M.Watkinson (Lancashire) | 462 |
| 14= | P.C.R.Tufnell (Middlesex) | 458 |
| | J.P.Taylor (Northants) | 458 |
| 16 | G.J.Parsons (Leicestershire) | 454 |
| 17 | C.A.Connor (Hampshire) | 439 |
| 18 | S.R.Lampitt (Worcestershire) | 431 |
| 19 | D.E.Malcolm (Derbyshire) | 420 |
| 20 | A.M.Smith (Gloucestershire) | 418 |
| 21 | I.D.K.Salisbury (Sussex) | 405 |
| 22 | A.R.K.Pierson (Leicestershire) | 403 |
| 23 | S.J.E.Brown (Durham) | 401 |
| 24= | D.A.Reeve (Warwickshire) | 395 |
| | M.J.McCague (Kent) | 395 |
| 26 | S.D.Udal (Hampshire) | 394 |
| 27 | R.K.Illingworth (Worcestershire) | 393 |
| 28 | J.H.Childs (Essex) | 390 |
| 29 | J.E.Benjamin (Surrey) | 389 |
| 30 | D.J.Capel (Northants) | 386 |
| 31 | J.E.Hindson (Notts) | 384 |
| 32 | M.C.J.Ball (Gloucestershire) | 377 |
| 33 | D.W.Headley (Kent) | 373 |
| 34= | I.D.Austin (Lancashire) | 371 |
| | M.M.Patel (Kent) | 371 |
| 36= | T.A.Munton (Warwickshire) | 361 |
| | M.A.Robinson (Yorkshire) | 361 |
| 38 | A.E.Warner (Derbyshire) | 356 |
| 39 | D.Gough (Yorkshire) | 355 |
| 40 | H.R.J.Trump (Somerset) | 351 |
| 41 | R.A.Pick (Notts) | 346 |
| 42 | R.D.Stemp (Yorkshire) | 338 |
| 43 | P.J.Martin (Lancashire) | 334 |
| 44= | K.M.Curran (Northants) | 333 |
| | M.A.Ealham (Kent) | 333 |
| 46 | G.D.Rose (Somerset) | 332 |
| 47 | N.M.K.Smith (Warwickshire) | 322 |
| 48 | J.D.Lewry (Sussex) | 319 |
| 49 | M.P.Bicknell (Surrey) | 295 |
| 50 | G.Chapple (Lancashire) | 294 |

# INDEX OF PLAYERS BY COUNTY

*denotes not registered for 1996 season. Where a player is known to have moved in the off-season he is listed under his new county.

## DERBYSHIRE

ADAMS, C. J.
ALDRED, P.
BAIRSTOW, A.*
BARNETT, K. J.
BASE, S. J.
CASSAR, M. E.
CORK, D. G.
COTTAM, A. C.*
CULLINAN, D. J.*
DEFREITAS, P. A. J.
DESSAUR, W. A.*
GRIFFITH, F. A.
GRIFFITHS, S.
HARRIS, A. J.
HARRISON, T. W.*
JONES, D. M.
KRIKKEN, K. M.
MALCOLM, D. E.
O'GORMAN, T. J. G.
OWEN, J. E.
RICHARDSON, A.*
ROLLINS, A. S.
TWEATS, T. A.
WARNER, A. E.
WELLS, C. M.

## DURHAM

BAINBRIDGE, P.
BETTS, M. M.
BIRBECK, S. D.
BLENKIRON, D. A.
BOILING, J.
BROWN, S. J. E.
CAMPBELL, C. L.
CAMPBELL, S. L.

COLLINGWOOD, P. D.
COX, D. M.
DALEY, J. A.
HUTTON, S.
KILLEEN, N.
LARKINS, W.*
LAWRENCE, J. R. G.
LIGERTWOOD, D. G. C.
LONGLEY, J. I.
LUGSDEN, S.
MORRIS, J. E.
PRABHAKAR, M.*
PRATT, A.
ROSEBERRY, M. A.
SAXELBY, M.*
SCOTT, C. W.
SEARLE, J. P.
WALKER, A.
WESTON, R. M. S.
WOOD, J.

## ESSEX

ANDREW, S. J. W.
AYRES, D. W.
CHILDS, J. H.
COUSINS, D. M.
COWAN, A. P.
DERBYSHIRE, N. A.
GARNHAM, M. A.*
GOOCH, G. A.
GOODWIN, G. J. A.
GRAYSON, A. P.
HIBBERT, A. J. E.
HODGSON, T. P.
HUSSAIN, N.
HYAM, B. J.

ILOTT, M. C.
IRANI, R.
LEWIS, J. J. B.
PETERS, S. D.
PRICHARD, P. J.
ROBINSON, D. D. J.
ROLLINS, R. J.
SUCH, P. M.
WAUGH, M. E.*
WILLIAMS, N. F.

## GLAMORGAN

ANTHONY, H.*
BARWICK, S. R.
BUTCHER, G. P.
COSKER, D. A.
COTTEY, P. A.
CROFT, R. D. B.
DALE, A.
DALTON, A. J.
DAVIES, A. P.
EDWARDS, G.
EVANS, A. W.
GIBSON, O. D.
HEMP, D. L.
JAMES, S. P.
JONES, P. S.
KENDRICK, N. M.
LEFEBVRE, R. P.
MAYNARD, M. P.
METSON, C. P.
MORRIS, H.
PARKIN, O. T.
PHELPS, B. S.
SHAW, A. D.
THOMAS, S. D.

# INDEX OF PLAYERS BY COUNTY

# INDEX OF PLAYERS BY COUNTY

# INDEX OF PLAYERS BY COUNTY

# INDEX OF PLAYERS BY COUNTY

## YORKSHIRE

# ANSWERS TO QUIZ

1. New Zealand v Transvaal Invitation XI on 1 December 1994
2. Jason Gallian
3. Dean Jones; Durham in 1991
4. Ed Giddens
5. Henry Olanga, against Pakistan on 31 January 1995
6. Dion Nash, Stephen Fleming and Matthew Hart
7. Greg Blewett
8. John Crawley (336 runs at 67.20)
9. Peter Martin (11 wickets at 18.21)
10. Imran Khan and Wasim Akram
11. Durham
12. Adam Holllioake
13. Matthew Maynard
14. John Stephenson
15. James Whitaker
16. David Byas
17. Javagal Srinath, Gloucestershire; Anil Kumble, Northamptonshire; Manoj Prabhakar, Durham
18. Marcus Trescothik
19. Daryll Cullinan (307 runs at 51.16)
20. Rashid Latif and Basit Ali
21. Courtney Walsh
22. Angus Fraser
23. South Africa beat England
24. Jonty Rhodes
25. Arjuna Ranatunga
26. Mike Atherton
27. Brian Lara, Devon Malcolm, Tim Munton, Steve Rhodes and Kepler Wessels
28. Philip Whitticase
29. India
30. Karen Smithies
31. Bradman, D.G, Pollock, R.G, Headley, G.A. and Sutcliffe, H.
32. Warwickshire
33. John Carr, 539 runs
34. Leicestershire
35. Laurie Potter v Leicestershire
36. Stuart Law
37. Michael Atherton, Jason Gallian, John Crawley, Neil Fairbrother, Mike Watkinson and Peter Martin
38. Hansie Cronje and Gordon Parsons, David Millns and Andy Pick
39. Mark Ilott
40. Philip Defreitas and Devon Malcolm
41. David Byas
42. Old Wellingtonians
43. Ian Bishop
44. Richie Richardson, Junior Murray and Carl Hooper
45. Lee Germon
46. Dr. Julian Thompson
47. Ken and Roy Palmer
48. England defeated Ireland
49. Aravinda De Silva
50. New South Wales
51. Sussex, Worcestershire and Northamptonshire
52. Michael Atherton and Clive Lloyd (6)
53. Hampshire
54. Aravinda De Silva, Kent; Allan Lamb, Northamptonshire; Adam Holllioake, Surrey; Dermot Reeve, Warwickshire; Tom Moody, Worcestershire
55. Nigel Briers, 1971
56. Sherwin Campbell, 1225 runs
57. Dominic Cork and Andrew Symonds
58. Derek Underwood, Norman Gifford and John Emburey
59. Aravinda De Silva, 255 v Derbyshire
60. Pakistan (11 Tests)
61. Graham Kersey, Surrey
62. Mark Ramprakash, ten
63. Peter Martin and Jack Russell
64. Graham Thorpe, Nick Knight, Robin Smith
65. Devon
66. Harshad Patel, Herefordshire
67. Andrew Whittall (Cambridge) and Gregor Macmillan (Oxford)
68. Graham Gooch, 3582 runs at 58.72
69. Mushtaq Ahmed
70. Narendra Hirwani
71. Waqar Younis. He dismissed Dion Nash at Christchurch on 11 December 1995. It was his 39th Test match
72. 42
73. 27, beating Allan Knott's 24 against Australia in the 1970-71 Ashes series
74. Muttiah Muralitharan
75. Dermot Reeve
76. Nolan Clarke, Holland
77. Steve Waugh and Shane Warne
78. 1993
79. Steve and Mark Waugh (Australia), Andy and Grant Flowers (Zimbabwe)
80. Dean Jones
81. New Zealand, 26 years
82. Philip DeFreitas
83. Queensland
84. Dermot Reeve, Mike Watkinson and Mark Ramprakash
85. J.B Hobbs and H. Sutcliffe, av. of 87.81 in 25 Tests
86. Courtney Walsh
87. 1983
88. Jack Hobbs. 4, 570 runs at an average of 51.34
89. United Arab Emirates, Kenya and Holland
90. Wasim Akram
91. Five. J.C. Balderstone (2), J.H Hampshire (8), V.A. Holder (40), K.E. Palmer (1) and P. Willey (26).
92. John Barclay, John Emburey and Graham Saville.
93. John Childs
94. Min Patel (223 runs in 41 overs)
95. Cambridgeshire
96. Daryll Cullinan
97. Wayne Larkins
98. 1973, Ian Chappell.
99. Winston Benjamin was replaced by Vasbert Drakes.
100. Six. Allan Donald, Nick Knight, Tim Munton, Dermot Reeve, Gladstone Small and Roger Twose.